CASSELL'S
LATIN-ENGLISH
ENGLISH-LATIN
DICTIONARY

CASSELL'S COMPACT
LATIN-ENGLISH
ENGLISH-LATIN
DICTIONARY

ABRIDGED FROM
CASSELL'S LATIN DICTIONARY

WITH A

GEOGRAPHICAL GLOSSARY OF THE ENGLISH
NAMES OF IMPORTANT PLACES

COMPILED BY

MILLICENT INGLIS THOMAS, M.A. (Lond.)

CASSELL · LONDON

CASSELL & COMPANY LTD

35 Red Lion Square · London WC1

and at

MELBOURNE · SYDNEY · TORONTO

JOHANNESBURG

CAPE TOWN · AUCKLAND

Printed by The Chapel River Press, Ltd., Andover, Hants

F. 1161

LATIN ABBREVIATIONS

A. Aulus.

a.d. Ante diem (in dates).

A.U.C. Ab urbe condita, anno urbis conditae.

C. Caius.

C. Centum.

Cn. Cnaeus.

D. Decimus; as num. = 500.

Fl. Flavius.

G. Gaius.

HS. (Mistake for IIS., *i.e.* II et Semis) sestertius.

K. Kaeso.

Kal. Kalendae.

L. Lucius, libra.

L. As num. sign = 50.

M. Marcus.

M'. Manius.

M. As num. sign = mille.

Non. Nonae.

P. Publius.

P.R. Populus Romanus.

Prid. Pridie.

Q. Quintus.

R. Rufus.

S. Sextus.

Sp. Spurius.

S.P.Q.R. Senatus populusque Romanus.

T. Titus.

Ti. Tiberius.

X. = 10.

Most of the English abbreviations are easily understood, but note:—

> *gen.* = *generally*
> *genit.* = *genitive*
> *imper.* = *imperative*

CASSELL'S
LATIN-ENGLISH
DICTIONARY

A

A

A a, *the first letter of the Latin Alphabet.*

a, ah, *interj.* Ah!

ā, ăb, abs, *prep. with abl.* away from; *a me, a te, a se, a nobis, a vobis,* from the house of; *Zeno et qui ab eo sunt,* Zeno and his school; down from; from; on the side of; *a septentrionibus,* on the north; *a fronte, a tergo, a latere, a dextro cornu; ab novissimis,* in the rear; *a pueris,* from boyhood; by, *ab aliquo; of origin,* from, of; in relation to; from, out of; *servus a pedibus,* footman; *a manu servus,* amanuensis.

ăbactus -a -um, *partic. of abigo.*

ăbăcus, -i, *m.* counting-board; gaming-board divided into compartments; a sideboard; mosaic panelling; square slab on the top of a column.

ăbăliēnātio -ōnis, *f.* alienation of property.

ăbăliēno, 1. to separate; to alienate (*property*); to deprive; to estrange.

ăbăvus -i, *m.* a great-great-grandfather; forefather.

Abdēra -ōrum, *n. plur.* 1. town in Thrace; also **Abdēra -ae,** *f.; 2.* town in Spain. **Abdērītēs -ae** (*abl.* -a), *m.* inhabitant of Abdera.

abdĭcātĭo -ōnis, . disowning of a son; renouncing of an office.

1. abdĭco, 1. to renounce, disown; to abdicate.

2. abdīco -dixi -dictum, 3. *of augury,* to refuse assent to, disapprove of.

abdĭtē, *adv.* secretly.

abditus -a -um, *p. adj.* concealed, secret; *neut. plur., abdita rerum,* deep thoughts.

abdo -didi -ditum, 3. to put away, withdraw, remove; to hide; *of a weapon,* to drive in; *reflex.* to retire.

abdōmen -inis, *n.* the belly, gluttony.

abdūco -duxi -ductum, 3. to lead or take away; to elope with; to steal; to relieve, *a sollicitudine;* to bring down.

abĕo -ii -itum -īre, to go away; *abi,* good, very well; *abi in malam rem,* go to the devil; to come off (*e.g. from a battle*); to retire, *consulatu; of the dying,* to depart; *in auctions,* not to be knocked down to, *si res abiret a mancipe;* to digress; *of time,* to pass away; to disappear, vanish; to go over; to change into, *sic deus in flammas abiit.*

ăbĕquito, 1. to ride off.

aberrātio, -ōnis, *f.* an escape or relief from anything irksome.

ăberro, 1. to wander, lose one's way; to deviate from, *a proposito;* to free oneself from something irksome.

abhinc, *adv.* from hence. *Of space or of time; annos tres abhinc,* three years ago.

ăbhorrĕo, 2. to shrink back from, to be disinclined to, *a pace;* to be opposed to; *a fide,* to be incredible. *Pres. part., as an adjective,* unseasonable, inappropriate.

abĭcĭo -iēci -iectum, 3. to throw down, or away, *se ad pedes alicuius;* to strike to the ground; to pronounce carelessly, to break off abruptly, *versum;* to get rid of; to abandon; to dash to the ground, to deprive of all power, *senatus auctoritatem;* to dishearten; *abiecta metu filia,* desponding; *se abicere,* to degrade oneself.

abiectē, *adv.* abjectly, in a cowardly manner; meanly.

abiectĭo -ōnis, *f.* rejection; *animi,* despondency, despair.

abiectus -a -um, *p. adj. of position,* low, common; cowardly; despicable; without force, prosaic, *versus.*

abĭegnus -a -um, made of fir wood or deal.

ăbĭēs -ĕtis, *f.* the fir-tree; anything made of deal; a letter (*written on wood*); a ship; a spear.

ăbĭgo -ēgi -actum, 3. to drive away; *pecus,* to steal cattle; *uxorem,* to divorce. *Fig.,* to banish, get rid of.

ăbĭtĭo -ōnis, *f.* = *abitus* (*q.v.*).

ăbĭtus -ūs, *m.* a going away, departure; place of egress.

abiūdĭco, 1. to give sentence against any one.

abiungo -iunxi -iunctum, 3. to unharness; to estrange, detach, *abiuncto Labieno.*

1

abiūro, to abjure, deny on oath.

abj, *see under abi.*

ablātivus -a -um, ablative. *Subst.,* ablātivus -i, *m.* (*sc. casus*), ablative case.

ablēgātio -ōnis, *f.* a sending away; banishment.

ablēgo, 1. to send away, remove to a distance; *milit.,* to dislodge.

ablĭgūrio, 4. to consume in luxury.

ablŏco, 1. to let on lease.

ablūdo, 3. to be out of tune with, to be unlike.

ablŭo -lŭi -lūtum, 3. to wash.

abnĕgo, 1. to deny, refuse.

abnĕpos -ōtis, *m.* great-great-grandson.

abneptis -is, *f.* great-great-granddaughter.

abnocto, 1. to stay out all night.

abnormis -e, irregular, unconventional; *abnormis sapiens,* one of Nature's philosophers.

abnŭo -nŭi -nŭitūrus, 3. to refuse by a motion of the head *or* eye, deny.

ăbŏlĕo -ēvi -ĭtum, 2. to destroy; *viscera undis,* to cleanse; to do away with, *magistratum.*

ăbŏlesco -ēvi, *no sup.,* 3. to perish.

ăbŏlitio -ōnis, *f.* a removing, annulling, abolition; *legis,* repeal; *facti,* amnesty.

ăbolla -ae, *f.* cloak of thick woollen cloth, *worn by soldiers.*

ăbōmino = *abominor* (*q.v.*).

ăbōminor -atus sum, 1. *dep.* to deprecate an unfavourable omen; *quod abominor,* God forbid; to hate; *abominandus,* detestable; *abominatus,* detested.

ăbŏrior -ortus sum, 4. *dep. of the heavenly bodies,* to set, to disappear; *poet., of the voice,* to fail.

ăbŏriscor = *aborior* (*q.v.*).

ăbortio -ōnis, *f.* miscarriage.

ăbortīvus -a -um, prematurely born; *ovum,* addled.

abrādo -rāsi -rāsum, 3. to scrape off, *shave;* to extort.

abripio -rĭpŭi -reptum, 3. to snatch away, drag off; to rob; to drag away.

abrōdo -si -sum, 3. to gnaw off, away.

abrŏgātio -ōnis, *f.* a repealing; *legis.*

abrŏgo, 1. to repeal a law; to deprive (*of office*); *fidem,* to take way a man's credit.

abrŏtŏnum -i, *n.* and abrŏtŏnus -i, *f.* southern-wood.

abrumpo -rūpi -ruptum, 3. to break off, loosen, separate; to sever; to violate; *fas,* to destroy.

abruptio -ōnis, *f.* a tearing away; divorce.

abruptus -a -um, *p. adj.* torn off; precipitous. *Subst.,* abruptum -i, *n.* a steep ascent *or* descent; a precipice, the road to ruin.

abscēdo -cessi -cessum, 3. to go away, depart; *milit.,* to retire; to desert *one;* to desert.

abscessio -ōnis, *f.* a going away, a separation.

abscessus -ūs, *m.* a going away; withdrawal.

abscīdo -cīdi -cīsum, 3. to cut off; to separate.

abscindo -scidi -scissum, 3. to tear off, *tunicam a pectore; venas,* to open the veins; *poet., abscissa comas,* with her hair torn; to divide; to separate; to take away.

abscīsus -a -um, *p. adj.* cut off, precipitous.

abscondĭtē, *adv.* obscurely, abstrusely.

abscondo -condi (-condĭdi) -condĭtum (-consum), 3. to conceal; to lose sight of; to keep out of sight; *pass. of stars,* to set.

absens -entis, *p. adj.* absent.

absentia -ae, *f.* absence.

absĭlio, 4. to spring forth, *or* away.

absimilis -e, unlike.

absinthium -i, *n.* wormwood.

absisto -stĭti, stĭtum, 3. to go away; to desist from; *with abl.*

absŏlūtē, *adv.* completely.

absŏlūtio -ōnis, *f.* acquittal; perfection.

absŏlūtōrius -a -um, relating to acquittal.

absŏlūtus -a -um, *p. adj.* complete; unfettered.

absolvo -solvi -sŏlūtum, 3. to loosen; to acquit; to relate; to complete.

absŏnus -a -um, inharmonious.

absorbĕo -ŭi, 2. to swallow.

absque, *prep. with abl.* without.

abstēmius -a -um, temperate.

abstergĕo -tersi -tersum, 2. to wipe off.

absterrĕo -terrŭi -terrĭtum, 2, to frighten away, *hostes saxis;* to frighten from.

abstinens -entis, *p. adj.* temperate.

abstinentĕr, *adv.* abstinently.

abstinentia -ae, *f.* temperance; fasting; uprightness.

abstĭneo -tĭnŭi -tentum, 2. to keep away from.

absto, 1. to stand aloof.

abstrăho -traxi -tractum, 3. to drag away; to exclude; to restrain; to draw away from.

abstrūdo -trūsi -trūsum, 3. to hide.

abstrūsus -a -um, *p. adj.* secret; abstruse; *of character,* reserved.

absum, abfŭi, ăbesse, to be absent; to take no part in; not to help; to be wanting; to be distant; to be free from, *a culpa;* to be firmly opposed to.

absūmo -sumpsi -sumptum, 3. to take away; to consume. *Of time,* to waste; to destroy utterly; to kill.

absurdē, *adv.* harshly, discordantly; in bad taste.

absurdus -a -um, unmelodious, harsh; foolish, unreasonable; incapable.

Absyrtus -i, *m.* brother of Medea, killed by his sister on her flight from Colchis.

ăbundans -antis *p. adj.* overflowing,

abundant, *with abl.; with genit.*, lactis, abounding in, overloaded; numerous.

ăbundantĕr, *adv.* abundantly; copiously.

ăbundantĭa -ae, *f.* abundance, plenty; wealth

ăbundē, *adv.* copiously, extravagantly.

ăbundo, 1. to overflow; to grow in abundance; to abound; to be rich.

ăbūsĭo -ōnis, *f. in rhetoric,* a false use of words.

ăbusquĕ, *prep. with abl. = usque ab,* from.

ăbūsus, -ūs, *m.* using up, wasting.

ăbūtor -ūsus -sum, 3. *dep., with abl.* to use; to make full use of; to waste; to use a word wrongly.

Ăbȳdus (Abydos) -i, *f. and* Ăbȳdum -i, *n.* 1. town in Asia Minor; 2. town in Egypt.

ac, *v.* atque.

Ăcădēmĭa -ae, *f.* the Academy, *a grove near Athens where Plato taught;* the Academic school of philosophy.

Ăcădēmĭcus -a -um, belonging to the Academy at Athens; *subst.,* Ăcădēmĭci -ōrum, *m.* the Academic philosophers; *subst.,* Ăcădēmĭca -ōrum, *n.* a treatise of Cicero on the Academic philosophy.

ăcălanthis -ĭdis, *f. = acanthis, q.v.*

ăcanthis -ĭdis, *f.* the thistle finch.

ăcanthus -i, *m.* bear's foot, a plant; evergreen tree.

ăcapnŏs -ŏn, without smoke.

Ăcarnānes -um, *m.* Acarnanians; Acarnānĭa -ae, country on the west of Greece.

Acca Lārentĭa, a Roman goddess of the fields. Lārentālĭa or Accālĭa -ium, *n.* her festival at Rome in December.

accēdo -cessi -cessum, 3. to approach, to come near, *ad urbem;* to approach the city (Rome) as a candidate for a triumph; *of time,* to approach; to enter upon some work; *ad rem publicam,* to begin public life; to assent to, *ad conditiones;* to be added, to increase; *followed by* ut *and* quod, *meaning* moreover; to fall to one's share; to become like.

accĕlĕro, 1. *Trans.,* to quicken, to accelerate; *Intrans.,* to hasten.

accendo -cendi -censum, 3. to set on fire; to lighten up; to inflame; to provoke; to increase.

accensĕo -censum, 2. to reckon in addition.

1. accensus -a -um, *part. of accenseo;* *plural,* accensi -orum, those numbered with; the supernumeraries; accensus -i, *m.* a subordinate public officer.

2. accensus -a -um, *partic. of accendo.*

acceptĭo -ōnis, *f.* acceptance; frumenti, receipt.

acceptus -a -um, *p. adj.* agreeable; *with the dat.*

accerso = arcesso (q.v.).

accessĭo -ōnis, *f.* a going *or* coming to; increase; addition.

accessus -ūs, *m.* an approach to, *ad urbem;* admittance *to a person;* entrance; inclination to.

1. accĭdo -cĭdi -cīsum, 3. (a) hew *or* hack at; to ruin.

2. accĭdo -cĭdi, *no sup.* 3. to fall down, to fall to; to come to the notice of; to happen (*generally of misfortunes*); *impers.,* accidit.

accĭĕo, 2. *obs. form of accio (q.v.).*

accingo -cinxi -cinctum, 3. to gird to *or* on; to equip, to arm.

accĭo -īvi (-ĭi) -ītum, 4. to call to, fetch.

accĭpĭo -cēpi -ceptum, 3. to take, receive; *aliquid acceptum referre,* to enter on the credit side of an account book; (*subst.,* acceptum -i, what is received); to treat; to hear, orationem; *of the understanding,* to grasp; to obtain; to feel, dolorem; to learn.

accĭpĭter -tris, *m.* a hawk.

accītus -ūs, *m.* a summons.

acclāmātĭo -ōnis, *f.* a loud cry.

acclāmo, 1. to cry out at; *with acc. of person,* to name by acclamation.

acclāro, 1. to reveal (*of omens*).

acclīnis -e, leaning on; inclined to.

acclīno, 1. to lean on anything; to incline to.

acclīvis, -e, gently inclined upwards.

acclīvĭtas -ātis, *f.* acclivity.

acclīvus -a -um, *= acclivis.*

accŏla -ae, *m.* neighbour.

accŏlo -cŏlŭi -cultum, 3. to live near, locum.

accommŏdātē, *adv.* agreeably to *ad veritatem*

accommŏdātĭo -ōnis, *f.* a proportion *or* adjusting of one thing to another; courteousness, complaisance.

accommŏdātus -a -um, *p. adj.* adapted, suitable to; *with ad and the acc. or with* dat.

accommŏdo, 1. to fit, put on; to make suitable, to adjust; *se accommodare or accommodari,* to adapt oneself.

accommŏdus -a -um, fit, adapted to.

accrēdo -dĭdi -dĭtum, 3. to believe, alicui.

accresco -crēvi -crētum, 3. to grow, to increase; *trimetris accrescere iussit nomen iambeis,* ordered to be joined to.

accrētĭo -ōnis, *f.* increase.

accŭbĭtĭo (accūbātĭo) -ōnis, *f.* the act of reclining at table.

accŭbĭtus -ūs, *m. = accubitio (q.v.).*

accŭbo, 1. to lie by the side of; to recline at table; *cum aliquo,* next to; *apud aliquem,* at the house of (*as a guest*).

accumbo -cŭbŭi -cŭbĭtum, 3. to lie down, *especially at the dinner table; in sinu alicuius,* to sit next to any one at table; *apud aliquem,* at the house of (*as a guest*).

accŭmŭlātē, *adv.* abundantly.

accŭmŭlător -ōris, *m.* one who heaps together.

accŭmŭlo, 1. to heap up, to accumulate; to overwhelm; to increase.

accūrātē, *adv.* carefully, exactly.

accūrātio -ōnis, *f.* accuracy, carefulness.

accūrātus -a -um, *p. adj.*; careful, accurate.

accūro, 1. to take care of, to prepare with care.

accurro -curri *and* -cucurri -cursum, 3. to run to, to hasten up; *of things,* to occur.

accursus -ūs, *m.* a running to, concourse.

accūsābĭlis -e, blameworthy.

accūsātio -ōnis, *f.* an accusation; the indictment.

accūsātor -ōris, *m.* an accuser; an informer.

accūsātōrĭē, *adv.* after the manner of an accuser.

accūsātōrĭus -a -um, pertaining to an accuser.

accūsātrix -ĭcis, *f.* a female accuser.

accūso, 1. to accuse; *genit., of the offence, aliquem ambitus; genit., of the punishment, capitis,* on a capital charge; to blame, find fault with.

1. **ăcer** -ĕris, *n.* maple tree.

2. **ăcer** -cris -cre, sharp, cutting; *of taste,* biting; *of touch,* sharp; *of hearing,* shrill; *flammae sonitus,* crackling; *of smell,* penetrating; *of sight,* keen; *of emotions,* painful; *of the understanding,* vigorous; *of the character,* energetic; *in ferro,* brave in fight; passionate. *Subst.,* **ăcre** -is, *n.* acrimony, severity.

ăcerbē, *adv.* bitterly, harshly; with difficulty or pain, *aliquid ferre.*

ăcerbĭtas -ātis, *f.* bitterness of taste; harshness; painfulness; *in plur.,* calamities.

ăcerbo, 1. to make bitter, aggravate.

ăcerbus -a -um, bitter in taste, sour (*of unripe fruit*), unripe; harsh; rough; gloomy. *Fig.,* morose; *of speech,* bitter; *of events,* painful.

ăcernus -a -um, made of maple wood.

ăcerra -ae, *f.* casket for keeping incense.

ăcersĕcŏmēs -ae, *m.* having unshorn hair.

ăcervālis -e, that which is heaped up.

ăcervātim, *adv.* in heaps; *dicere,* to sum up.

ăcervo, 1. to heap up.

ăcervus -i, *m.* a heap.

ăcesco ăcŭi, 3. to grow sour.

ăcētum -i, *n.* vinegar; wit.

Ăchaei -ōrum, *m.* the Achaeans; Greeks in general; **Achāĭa** -ae, *f. in the north of the Peloponnese. Adj.,* **Achīvus,** Greek.

Ăchātes -ae, *m.* friend of Aeneas.

Ăchĕron -ontis, *m.* river in the lower world, *hence* the lower world itself.

Ăchillēs -is, *m., and* **Ăchillĕūs** -ĕi, *m.* Greek hero.

Achīvus -a -um = Achaeus.

ăcidus -a -um, sharp; sour; unpleasant.

ăciēs, -ēi, *f.* keenness, edge. *Of the eye,* piercing look; the pupil of the eye; the eye itself; keenness, *animi. Mīlit.,* an army drawn up in line of battle.

ăcĭnăcēs -is, *m.* a short Persian sabre.

ăcinus -i, *m. and* **ăcinum** -i, *n.* a berry.

ăcipenser -ĕris (ăcipensis -is), *m.* a fish.

Acis -idis, *m.* river in Sicily; shepherd, lover of Galatea.

ăclys -ўdis, *f.* a small javelin.

ăcŏnītum -i, *n.* monk's hood, aconite; *poet.,* poison.

acquiesco -quiēvi -quiētum, 3. to rest, repose; to die; to find comfort in; to be pleased with.

acquīro -quīsīvi -quīsītum, 3. to add to, acquire; get.

ăcrātŏphŏron -i, *n.* vessel for holding unmixed wine.

ăcrēdŭla -ae, *f.* a bird (the thrush, the owl, or the nightingale).

ăcrĭcŭlus -a -um, somewhat sharp, violent.

ăcrĭmōnĭa -ae, *f.* sharpness of taste *or* pungency of smell; energy of speech and demeanour.

Ăcrīsius, *m.* king of Argos, father of Danaē.

ăcrĭtĕr, *adv.* sharply, violently; steadfastly; painfully; with sharp insight; courageously; passionately; longingly; *in speech,* violently.

ăcrŏāmă -ătis, *n.* an entertainment at table of reading *or* music; a reader, actor, *or* singer.

ăcrŏāsis -is, *f.* an assembly of persons to listen to reading aloud.

Ăcrŏcĕraunia -ōrum, *n.* part of the Ceraunian mountains, a dangerous place.

Ăcrŏcŏrinthus -i, *f.* the citadel of Corinth.

1. **acta,** *f.* the sea-shore, the beach, the pleasures of life at the seaside.

2. **acta** -ōrum, *n.* actions; public acts, ordinances; the register *of these acts; acta diurna,* a kind of official gazette published daily in Rome.

Actaeōn -ōnis, *m.* turned into a stag by Diana, and torn to pieces by his dogs.

actio -ōnis, *f.* motion, action of the body; gesture; doing; *gratiarum,* giving of thanks; public action (of any magistrate), proposal; action in court; *actiones componere,* to draw statements of claim; a legal formula; the right to bring an action; the hearing of an action.

actito, 1. to be busy in pleading *or* acting, *used of theatres and courts of law.*

Actium -ii, *n.* 1. promontory in Acarnania; *naval battle* (31 B.C.); roadstead near Corcyra. *Adj.* **Actĭus** -a -um; *bella* the battle of Actium.

actor -ōris, *m.* a driver; an actor; one who accomplishes anything; a public speaker; the plaintiff in an action; the manager of property *or* finances.

actŭărĭŏla -ae, *f. (dim. of actuaria),* a small skiff.

actŭārĭus -a -um, easily moved, swift; *actuaria navis,* a swift-sailing vessel. *Subst.* **actŭāria -ae,** *f.*

actŭōsē, *adv.* actively, with energy.

actŭōsus -a -um, active; *of a speech,* effective.

actus -ūs, *m.* motion; putting in motion; driving of cattle; right of way for driving cattle, carts, etc.; gesture; presentation of a piece on the stage; division of a piece, an act.

actūtum, *adv.* immediately, directly.

ăcŭlĕātus -a -um, provided with prickles *or* stings; stinging; subtle.

ăcŭlĕus -i, *m. (dim. of acus),* sting; point; *in plur.,* sarcasm.

ăcūmen -ĭnis, *n.* sharp point; point (*of something witty*); sharpness of understanding; trickery.

ăcŭo -ŭi -ūtum, 3. to sharpen to a point; to whet, *gladios;* to practise; *linguam,* to make more fluent; to encourage, incite.

ăcus -ūs, *f.* needle, bodkin; *acu pingere,* to embroider.

ăcūtē, *adv.* keenly; shrilly.

ăcūtŭlus -a -um *(dim. of acutus),* somewhat subtle.

ăcūtus -a -um, *p. adj.* pointed, acute; shrill, *vox;* painful; *poet., acuta belli,* the hardships of war; *mental,* keen; *of orators,* effective.

ad, *prep. with acc.,* towards, to; *ad Dianae venire,* to the temple of Diana (*sc. uedem*); *ad me, ad te, etc.,* to my house; *of rest, near; ad judicem,* before a judge; *of aim or purpose,* for, for; *ad id,* for that object; *ad extremum,* entirely; *ad summam,* on the whole; *ad hoc,* besides; *ad verbum,* literally; at, towards.

ădactĭo -ōnis, *f.* compulsion.

ădactus -ūs, *m.* a bringing *to; dentis,* a bite.

ădaequē, *adv.* in like manner.

ădaequo, 1. to make equal with; to equalise; to compare; to come near to.

ădămantēus -a -um, hard as steel.

ădămantĭnus -a -um, made of hard steel.

ădāmas -antis, *m.* the hardest steel, adamant; *poet.,* unyielding; the diamond.

ădambŭlo, 1. to walk by *or* near anything.

ădāmo, 1. to fall in love with; to find pleasure in.

ădamussim, *v. amussis.*

ădăpĕrĭo -pĕrŭi -pertum, 4. to open fully.

ădăpertĭlis -e, that which is capable of being opened.

ădapto, 1. to fit to, adapt.

ădăquor, 1. *dep.* to fetch water.

ădauctus -ūs, *m.* an increase.

ădaugĕo -auxi, -auctum, 2. to increase; *of sacrifices,* to devote.

ădaugescō, 3. to begin to increase, *poet.*

ădbĭbo -bĭbi -bĭbĭtum, 3. to drink, drink in.

addensĕo, 2. *and* **addenso,** 1. to make thick, *or* compact.

addīco -dixi -dictum, 3. to assent to; *in augury,* to promise favourably; to award, *of the praetor (whose formula was do, dico, addico);* of an auctioneer, to knock down to a bidder; to put up for sale; to give up *or* over, to confiscate; *addictus,* bound, pledged; *se alicui,* to give oneself up to slavishly.

addictĭo -ōnis, *f.* the judge's award.

addictus -a -um, *v. addico.*

addisco -didĭci, *no sup.* 3. to learn in addition.

addĭtāmentum -i, *n.* an addition.

addo -dĭdi -dĭtum, 3. to give to, to give, to place; to inspire, to cause, produce; to add, increase; *gradum,* to hasten; to give as a respite (*of time*); *adde,* *or* *adde huc,* add to this.

addŏcĕo, 2. to teach in addition.

addŭbĭto, 1. to incline to doubt; *res addubitata,* a question undecided.

addūco -duxi -ductum, 3. to draw to oneself; to draw together, to wrinkle; to bring, *or* lead; *aliquem in ius or iudicium, or simply aliquem,* to bring to justice; *adductus,* influenced.

adductius, *adv. compar.* more severely.

adductus -a -um, *p. adj.* severe.

ădĕdo -ēdi -ēsum, 3. to nibble, to gnaw; to consume, waste away.

ădemptĭo -ōnis, *f.* a taking away.

1. ădĕo, *adv.* to that point, so far; so long; so much so, *followed by ut;* even, what is more; *with pron.,* just, *id adeo;* to such an extent, so; (*with non,* much less).

2. ădĕo, ĭi -ĭtum, 4. to go *or* come to, approach; *in ius,* to go to law; to visit; to undertake some business; *ad rempublicam,* to enter public life; to undergo, incur, *periculum; adire hereditatem,* to enter on an inheritance.

ădeps -ĭpis, *c.* the soft fat of animals.

ădeptĭo -ōnis, *f.* attainment.

ădĕquĭto, 1. to ride to; *with dat., or ad.*

ădesdum, *or ades dum,* come hither.

adf, *v. under aff . . .*

adg, *v. under agg . . .*

ădhaerĕo -haesi -haesum, 2. to stick to, adhere; to border on; to keep close to a person; *nulli fortunae ulhuerebat animus,* depended upon.

ădhaeresco -haesi -haesum, 3. to hang to, to adhere; to cling to, to remain; *ad omnium vestrum studium,* sympathise with; *o an orator,* to stop.

ădhaesio -ōnis, *f.* clinging to.

ădhaesus -ūs, *m.* an adhering.

ădhǐbĕo -ŭi -ǐtum, 2. to apply to; to seize; to join, add; to employ; *with adv.,* to treat, liberaliter.

ădhinnio, 4. to neigh after.

ădhortātǐo -ōnis, *f.* an exhortation.

ădhortātor -ōris, *m.* one who exhorts.

ădhortor, 1. *dep.* to exhort, encourage.

ădhūc. *adv.,* thus far, hitherto; still.

adiăcĕo, 2. to be adjacent. *Subst.,* adiăcĕntǐa -ǐum, *n.* the neighbourhood.

adício -ǐeci -ǐectum, 3. to throw to; to cast *a longing look upon, oculum hereditati;* to direct (*thoughts*); to apply; to add; to outbid *at an auction.*

adǐectio -ōnis, *f.* an adding to.

adǐectus -ūs, *m.* an adding to.

ădǐgo -ēgi -actum, 3. to drive to; to compel to; *aliquem ad iusiurandum,* to put a man on his oath; to fashion.

ădǐmo -ēmi -emptum, 3. to take away, *alicui pecuniam; ademptus, poet.* dead.

ădǐpātus -a -um, fatty, greasy; bombastic. *Subst.,* ădǐpāta -ōrum, *n.* pastry made with grease

ădǐpiscor -eptus, 3. *dep.* to overtake; to obtain.

ădǐtus -ūs, *m.* an approach, access; right of entrance to; opportunity of obtaining.

adǐūdǐco, 1. to adjudicate.

adǐūmentum -i, *n.* assistance.

adǐunctio -ōnis, *f.* addition to, union; connexion; *rhet.,* restriction.

adǐunctor -ōris, *m.* one who joins, connects.

adǐunctus -a -um, *p. adj.* bound to, belonging to. *Subst.,* adǐuncta -ōrum, *n.* things suitable to.

adǐungo -iunxi -iunctum, 3. to join to, bind to; to join, add; *of time, pass.,* to be near in age; to connect; to add; to give, to attribute; to bring in as a participator; to unite.

adǐūro, 1. to swear in addition; to swear.

adǐūto, 1. to be serviceable, to help.

adǐūtor -ōris, *m.* a helper; a regular assistant; deputy.

adǐūtrix -īcis, *f.* female assistant; aid; *legiones,* reserve legions.

adǐūvo -iūvi -iūtum, 1. to help, support; to be of service.

adl, *v. under all* . .

admātūro, 1. to hasten.

admētior -mensus, 4. *dep.* to measure out to.

Admētus -i, *m.* ruler of Pherae, in Thessaly, husband of Alcestis, who died for him.

admǐnǐcŭlo, 1. to support.

admǐnǐcŭlum -i, *n.* a prop, a support; help.

administer -strǐ, *m.* an attendant, an assistant.

administra -ae,. . she that helps.

administrātǐo -ōnis, *f.* the giving of help; direction, government.

administrātor -ōris, *m.* an administrator, manager.

administro, 1. to serve; to manage, administer; to steer.

admīrābilis -e, admirable; astonishing, strange.

admīrābilitas -ātis, *f.* admirableness.

admīrābiliter, *adv.* admirably, wonderfully; strangely.

admīrandus -a -um = *admirabilis,* worthy of admiration.

admīrātio -ōnis, *f.* admiration; *plur., admirationes,* outbursts of admiration; wonder, astonishment.

admīror, 1. *dep.* to admire; to be astonished at.

admiscĕo -miscŭi -mixtum (-mistum), 2. to mix with; to join; *urbes (maritimae admiscentur novis sermonibus ac disciplinis,* become familiar with.

admissārius -i, *m.* a stallion; a lascivious man.

admissǐo -ōnis, *f.* an audience, *esp. of a royal person.*

admissum -i, *m.* a crime.

admitto -misi -missum, 3. to send to; to let go; to let a horse go at full speed, to urge on, *equo admisso ;* to hurry; to give access to; to give audience to; to admit to share *in an undertaking, etc.; of entreaties, etc.* to allow to reach; *of an act,* to allow; to commit a crime.

admixtio -ōnis, *f.* a mingling.

admŏdĕrātē, *adv.* appropriately.

admŏdum, *adv.* up to the measure, up to the mark. *With numbers,* about; quite; *puer admodum,* a mere boy; *affirmative,* certainly.

admŏnĕo -ŭi -ǐtum, 2. to admonish, remind; to advise to do something; to incite.

admŏnǐtǐo -ōnis, *f.* a reminding; friendly admonition.

admŏnǐtor -ōris, *m.* one who reminds.

admŏnǐtum -i, *n.* an admonition, a calling to mind.

admŏnǐtus -ūs, *m.* a reminding; warning.

admordĕo -morsum, 2. to bite at, to gnaw; to fleece.

admōtio -ōnis, *f.* a moving to.

admŏvĕo -mōvi -mōtum, 2. to move, bring to; to direct, devote, *mentes;* to bring up, *armatos muris;* to place near; to apply; *se admovere,* to draw near.

admūgǐo, 4. to bellow after.

admurmŭrātǐo -ōnis, *f.* a murmuring.

admurmŭro, 1. to murmur at.

admūtǐlo, 1. to shear, shave; to fleece.

adn, *v. agn or ann* . . .

ădŏlĕo -ŭi, 2. *intrans.,* to smell; *trans.,* to

make to smell, to burn (of sacrifices); to light up, ulturia flammis.

ădŏlescens (ădŭlescens) **-entis**, adj. young. Subst., masc., a young man; fem., a girl.

ădŏlescentia -ae, f. youth; the young.

ădŏlescentŭlus -i, m. a very young man; ab adolescentulo, from youth upward.

1. **ădŏlesco -ŏlēvi -ultum**, 3. to grow, to grow up to maturity; to increase; of time, to advance.

2. **ădŏlesco -ēre**, 3. to blaze.

Ădōneus -ĕi, m. = Adonis (q.v.).

Ădōnis -ĭdis, and **Adōn -ōnis**, m. a beautiful youth, beloved of Venus.

ădŏpĕrio -pĕrŭi -pertum, 4. to cover; to close.

ădŏpīnor, 1. dep. to guess.

ădŏptiātio -ōnis, f. = adoptio (q.v.).

ădŏptio -ōnis, f. the adoption of a child.

ădŏptīvus -a -um, relating to adoption; of plants, grafted.

ădŏpto, 1. to choose for one's self; to take to one's aid; to adopt, sibi filium; of plants, to graft.

ădŏr -ōris, n. a species of grain, spelt.

ădōrātĭo -ōnis, f. a praying to, adoration.

ădōrĕa -ae, f. reward of valour, glory.

ădōrĕus -a -um, relating to spelt.

ădōrior -ortus, 4. dep. to rise up; to attack; to besiege with entreaties; to attempt, undertake.

ădorno, 1. to prepare, provide; to adorn.

ădōro, 1. to speak to; to address a deity, to entreat; to honour.

adp, v. under app.

adq, v. under acq.

adr, v. under arr.

adrādo -rāsi -rāsum, 3. to scrape, shave.

Adrastus -i, m. king of Argos, one of the Seven against Thebes.

Adria = Hadria (q.v.).

ads, v. under ass.

adsc, v. under asc.

adsp, v. under asp.

adst, v. under ast.

adt, v. under att.

Adŭātŭci -ōrum, m. people in Gallia Belgica.

ădūlātĭo -ōnis, f. fawning (o dogs); cringing, flattery.

ădūlātŏr -ōris, m. a base flatterer.

ădūlātōrius -a -um, flattering.

ădūlescens, etc., v. adolescens.

ădūlo, 1. to fawn.

ădūlor, 1. dep. to fawn (of dogs); to flatter, to cringe before.

ădulter -ĕri, m., **ădultĕra -ae**, f. adulterer, adulteress; poet., a gallant. Adj. adulterous.

ădultĕrīnus -a -um, adulterous; not genuine, forged.

ădultĕrium -ii, n. adultery.

ădultĕro, 1. to commit adultery; to falsify, corrupt; faciem arte (of Proteus), changes his form.

ădultus -a -um, p. adj. grown up, adult. Plur. subst., **ădulti**, adults.

ădumbrātim, adv. in outline.

ădumbrātĭo -ōnis, f. a sketch.

ădumbrātus -a -um, p. adj. sketched, imperfect; shadowy, unreal.

ădumbro, 1. to shade, to sketch.

ăduncĭtas -ātis, f. a bending inwards.

ăduncus -a -um, bent inwards crooked; naius an aquiline nose.

ădurgĕo, 2. to press to, or against; poet., to pursue closely.

ădūro -ussi -ustum, 3. to kindle, consume by burning; capillum, to singe; of frost, to nip.

ădusquĕ = usque ad; prep. with acc. as far as; adv. = usque, entirely.

ădustus -a -um, p. adj. burnt by the sun, brown.

advectīcius -a -um, foreign.

advecto, 1. to convey often.

advectus -ūs, m. a conveying, carrying.

advĕho -vexi -vectum, 3. to carry, convey to a place. Pass., advehi, to be borne to a place (on horseback, in a chariot, on a ship, etc.).

advēlo, 1. to draw a veil over; poet., to crown.

advĕna -ae, c. a stranger, foreigner; of birds, a bird of passage.

advĕnio -vēni -ventum, 4. to come to; to come, dies advenit; to happen, to come near, to break out.

adventīcius -a -um, coming from without; outward; foreign; extraordinary, accidental.

advento, 1. to approach, arrive at, ad Italiam.

adventor -ōris, m. one who arrives, a visitor.

adventus -ūs, m. an arrival.

adversārius -a -um, turned towards. Subst., **adversāria -orum**, n. journal, memorandum. [Adj., contrary; with dat. Subst., **adversārius -ii**, m. rival; **adversāria -orum**. n. the assertions of an opponent.

adversor, 1. dep. to oppose, resist; with dat., legi.

1. **adversus -a -um**, p. adj. turned towards; fronting, opposite; adversa vulnera, wounds in the front; adverso colle, on the front of the hill; venti adversi, contrary winds; ex adverso, over against; of persons, opposed, adversus alicui; of things, unpropitious; proelium, unsuccessful; res adversae, misfortune. Subst., **adversum -i**, n. misfortune.

2. **adversus, adversum**, adv., against. Prep. with acc. toward; against; of position, over against; compared with; in the presence of.

adverto (advorto) -verti (-vorti) -versum (-vorsum), 3. to turn towards; of ships, to steer; to direct; to perceive; to punish, *in aliquem;* to draw the attention of *some one.*

advespērascit -āvit, 3. (*impers.*), evening approaches.

advigilo, 1. to watch by, to guard; to be vigilant.

advŏcātio -ōnis, *f.* calling to one's aid; summoning to advise; legal advice; *concr.,* the bar.

advŏcātus -i, *m.* one who is called in as advocate or as witness.

advŏco, 1. to summon, to call. *Legal,* to consult an advocate. *Of the gods,* to ask for help.

advŏlātus, *abl.* -ū, *m.* a flying to, *poet.*

advŏlo, 1. to fly to; to hasten towards, *ad urbem.*

advolvo -volvi -vŏlūtum, 3. to roll to; *advolvi,* or *se advolvere,* to throw oneself at the feet of; *genibus alicuius.*

adversum, *adversus, adverto = adversum, adversus, adverto* (q.v.).

ădўtum, -i, *n. gen. plur.,* the shrine; *ex adyto tamquam cordis,* from the bottom of the heart.

Aeācus -i, *m.* king of Aegina; after-death judge in the infernal regions.

Aeaea -ae, *f.* island of the sorceress Circe, or of Calypso; **Aeaeus,** *surname of Circe; surname of Calypso.*

aedēs -is, *f.; originally,* a building. *Sing.,* a room, a temple. *Plur.,* a house; the family; the cells of bees.

aedicŭla -ae, *f.* (*dim. of aedes*), a small building; a small temple; a niche, shrine; *plur.,* a little house.

aedificātio -ōnis, *f.* building; the act of building; the building itself.

aedificātiuncŭla -ae, *f.* (*dim. of aedificatio*), a small building.

aedificātor ōris, *m.* builder, architect.

aedificium -i, *n.* a building.

aedifico, 1. to build, establish; *rempublicam,* to frame.

aedilicius -a -um, relating to the aediles. *Subst.,* **aedilicius** -i, *m.* one who has been aedile.

aedilis -is, *m.* an aedile.

aedilitas -ātis, *f.* the aedileship.

aeditimus -i, *m.* old form of *aedituus* (q.v.).

aeditŭens -entis, *m. = aedituus* (q.v.).

aedituus -i, *m.* the keeper of a temple.

Aedŭi (Haedŭi) -ōrum, Gallic people, *whose chief town was Bibracte.*

Aeēta -ae, *m.,* and **Aeētēs** -ae, *m.* king of Colchis, father of Medea; **Aeētias** -ădis, Medea; **Aeētine** -ēs, *f.* Medea. *Adj.* **Aeētaeus** -a -um, belonging to Colchis.

Aegaeus -a -um, Aegean. *Subst.,* **Aegaeum** -i, *n.* the Aegean Sea.

Aegātes -ium, *f.,* and **Aegātae** -ārum, *f.* islands on the west coast of Sicily.

aeger -gra -grum, sick, ill; *pedibus.* *Subst.,* **aeger** -gri, *m.* an invalid; *of*

things, unsound; *aegra municipia,* mutinous; *animi,* in mind; *of conditions,* painful; *aegris oculis,* with envious eyes.

Aegeus -ěi, *m.* king of Athens, father of Theseus. **Aegīdes** -ae, *m.* Theseus.

Aegīna -ae, *f.* island near Athens. *Adj.* **Aeginensis** -e; **Aeginenses** -ium, *m.* **Aeginētae** -ārum, *m.* natives of Aegina.

aegis -idis, *f.* the aegis, or shield; of Jupiter; of Minerva with the Medusa's head; a protection.

Aegisthus -i, *m.* murderer of Agamemnon, afterwards husband of Clytemnestra.

aegrē, *adv.* painfully; *aegre est mihi or meo animo,* I am grieved; *aegre ferre,* to be distressed; with difficulty; hardly, scarcely; unwillingly; *aegre ferre,* to take it ill that, *etc.*

aegrĕo, 2. to be sick.

aegresco, 3. to fall ill; to become worse; to be disturbed in mind.

aegrimōnia -ae, *f.* grief.

aegritūdo -inis, *f.* sickness; grief.

aegror -ōris, *m.* sickness.

aegrōtātio -ōnis, *f.* sickness.

aegrōto, 1. to be sick or ill

aegrōtus -a -um, sick, ill, *Aegyptus* -i, *m.* brother of Danaus. *f.* Egypt.

aelinos -i, *m.* a dirge.

Aemiliānus -a -um, a surname of Scipio Africanus minor.

Aemilius -a -um, *gens,* name of one of the oldest and most distinguished patrician families of Rome.

Aemōnia, *etc., v. Haemōnia.*

aemŭlātio -ōnis, *f.* a striving after, emulation; jealousy.

aemŭlātor -ōris, *m.* rival; imitator.

aemŭlātus -ūs, *m. =* aemulatio.

aemŭlor, 1. *dep.* to rival, strive to attain to; to envy, *with dat.*

aemŭlus -a -um, emulous, rivalling; zealous. *Subst.,* **aemulus** -i, *m.; alicuius,* a zealous follower. *Subst.,* **aemŭlus** i-, *m.* and **aemŭla** -ae, *f.* a rival in love.

Aemus = *Haemus* (q.v.).

Aenēas -ae, *m.* hero of Vergil's Aeneid.

ăēnĕātor -ōris, *m.* trumpeter.

ăēnĕus *and* **ăhēnĕus** -a -um, made of brass, copper, *or* bronze; of a bronze colour.

aenigma -ătis, *n.* riddle; mystery.

ăēnĭpēs (ăhēnĭpēs) -pĕdis, brazen-footed.

ăēnus (ăhēnus) -a -um, made of brass, copper, *or* bronze; firm. *Subst.,* **ăēnum** -i, *n.* a brazen vessel.

Aeōles -um, *m.* the Aeolians, one of the races of the Greeks; **Aeōlicus,** Aeolic.

Aeōlia -ae, *f.* north part of the coast of Asia Minor.

aequābilis -e, like, equal; uniform; just; *of persons,* affable.

aequābilĭtas -ātis, *f.* uniformity; equality; equanimity.

aequābilĭtĕr, *adv.* equably, uniformly, fairly.

aequaevus -a -um, of equal age.

aequālis -e, equal; level, uniform; equal in height, size, etc., with due, corresponding to, of the same age with. *Subst.*, **aequālis** -is, *c.* comrade, person of the same age.

aequālĭtas -ātis, *f.* evenness, smoothness, equality; harmony in thought, etc.; equality of age.

aequālĭtĕr, *adv.* evenly; equally; uniformly; symmetrically.

aequănĭmĭtas -ātis, *f.* impartiality; calmness.

aequātĭo -ōnis, *f.* a making equal.

aequē, *adv.* in like manner, equally; in comparison, just as, equally with, *foll. by et, atque, ac si, quam ut, etc.*; fairly, justly.

Aequi (Aequĭcŭli, Aequĭcŏli, Aequĭcŭlāni) -ōrum, *m.* people in Latium.

aequilibritas -ātis, *f.* the equal distribution of natural forces.

Aequimaelium -ii, *n.* an open space in Rome.

aequinoctĭālis -e, equinoctial.

aequinoctĭum -ii, *n.* the equinox.

aequipăro (aequipĕro), 1. to compare; to equal.

aequĭtas -ātis, *f.* uniformity, symmetry; equanimity; fairness, justice.

aequo, 1. to make level; *aequare frontem, milit.* to form a line; to make equal; to distribute equally; *sortes,* to shake up the lots; to compare, *Hannibali Philippum;* to equal.

aequor -ōris, *n.* a flat surface; *poet.,* the sea.

aequŏrĕus -a -um, belonging to the sea; *Britanni,* sea-girt; *Achilles,* a son of Thetis.

aequus -a -um, *adj.* equal; level; *ex aequo loco loqui,* to speak in the senate (Verr. cicer., aequum i, n. level ground); *aequa frons. milit.* a straight line; *of places,* advantageous; quiet, contented; *aequo animo,* patiently, with resignation; *aequa pugna,* an indecisive battle; (*adv., ex aequo,* equally); equal, impartial; propitious; *aequum est,* it is just. *Subst.,* **aequum** -i, *n.* fairness. *Plur. subst.,* **aequi**, friends.

āēr, āĕris, *m.* the atmosphere.

aerārĭa -ae, *f., v. aerarius.*

aerārium -ii, *n., v. aerarius.*

aerārĭus -a -um, *adj.* belonging to brass or copper; belonging to money; *lapis,* copper. (*Subst.,* **aerārĭus** -ii, *m.* a worker in brass; **aerārĭa** -ae, *f.* smelting-works). *Subst.,* **aerārĭus** -ii, *m. plur.,* aerarii, the citizens of the lowest

class in Rome; **aerārium** -ii, *n.* the exchequer, treasury.

aerātus -a -um, covered or fitted with brass or bronze; made of brass or bronze; provided with money.

aerĕus -a -um, made of brass or copper; covered with brass.

aerĭfĕr -fĕra -fĕrum, bearing brazen cymbals.

aerĭpēs -pĕdis, brazen footed.

āĕrĭus (āĕrĕus) -a -um, belonging to the air, airy; lofty.

aerūgo -inis, *f.* the rust of copper, verdigris; envy, avarice.

aerumna -ae, *f.* toil, hardship.

aerumnābĭlis -e, calamitous, pitiable.

aerumnōsus -a -um, full of hardship and calamity.

aes aeris, *n.* copper; the alloy of copper, brass, or bronze; something made of bronze, etc.; *aera aere repulsa,* cymbals; *aes publicum,* public inscriptions; money; copper or brass money; *aes grave,* the as; *aes meum,* my property; *aes alienum,* debt; pay; *esp.* soldiers' pay; *aes circumforaneum,* money borrowed from the moneychangers; *plur.,* aera, counters.

Aeschĭnes -is *and* -i, *m.* 1. an Athenian philosopher. 2. Athenian orator.

Aeschўlus -i, *m.* an Athenian tragic poet.

Aescŭlāpĭum -ii, *n.* a temple of Aesculapius.

Aescŭlāpĭus -ii, *m.* god of medicine.

aescŭlētum -i, *n.* an oak forest.

aescŭlĕus -a -um, relating to the winter oak.

aescŭlus -i, *f.* the winter or Italian oak.

Aeson -ōnis, *m.* father of Jason; **Aesŏnĭdes** -ae, *m.* a descendant of Aeson (Jason).

Aesōpus -i, *m.* a celebrated Greek fabulist.

aestas -ātis, *f.* summer; *ineunte or novā,* at the beginning of summer; *exactā,* at the end of.

aestĭfĕr -fĕra -fĕrum, heat-bringing.

aestĭmābĭlis -e, valuable.

aestĭmātĭo -ōnis, *f.* an appraising according to value in money; *litis,* assessment of damages; valuation; *propria aestimatio virtutis,* the absolute worth of virtue.

aestĭmātŏr -ōris, *m.* one who estimates, an appraiser.

aestĭmātus -ūs, *m.* — *aestimatio (q.v.).*

aestĭmo (aestŭmo), 1. to estimate the value of anything; *with abl. or gen., of value; tenuissime,* at a very low rate; *litem alicui or alicuius,* to assess the damages in a law-suit; to judge.

aestīva -ōrum, *n., v. aestivus.*

aestīvo, 1. to pass the summer.

aestīvus -a -um, relating to summer; *aurum,* the gold ring of the military tribunes, worn for six months. *Plur. subst.,* **aestīva** -ōrum, *n.,* a summer camp; a campaign; summer pastures.

aestuārium -ii, *n.* morass; firth, creek.

aestŭo, 1. to boil, to be hot; (*of the sea*) to rage; to be inflamed *or* excited.

aestuōsē, *adv.* hotly.

aestuōsus -a -un, *adj.* hot; agitated.

aestus -ūs, *m.* heat; *plur.*, hot days; seething and raging, *of the sea*; rage; fervour; anxiety.

aetas -ātis, *f.* age; lifetime; a generation; the age of a man; youth; old age; manhood; *aetas militaris,* the seventeenth year; *senatoria,* the twenty-fifth; the time at which a person lives; *nostra aetas,* the men of our time.

aetātŭla -ae, *f.* (*dim. of aetas*), youthful age.

aeternitas -ātis, *f.* eternity; immortality.

aeterno, 1. to immortalise.

aeternus -a -um, *adj.* eternal, immortal; everlasting; *in aeternum,* for ever.

aether -ĕris, *acc.* -ĕra, *m.* the upper air; *poet.* the lower air; the upper world.

aethĕrius (aethĕrĕus) -a -um, ethereal; heavenly; belonging to the air; belonging to the upper world.

Aethĭopes -um, *acc.* -as, *m.* inhabitants of Aethiopia.

1. **Aethra** -ae, *f.* mother of Theseus.

2. **aethra** -ae, *f.* the upper air, clear sky.

Aetna -ae, *f.* Aetna, a volcano in Sicily. *Adj.* **Aetnaeus.**

Aetŏli -ōrum, *m.* inhabitants of Aetolia, a country in the west of Greece.

aevitas -ātis, *f. old form of aetas.*

aevum -i, *n.* eternity; a generation; age; *in aevum,* for ever.

Āfer, *v. Afri.*

affābilis -e, *adj.* affable.

affābilitas -ātis, *f.* affability.

affābrē, *adv.* skilfully.

affātim, *adv.* sufficiently, enough.

affātus -ūs, *m.* address, speech.

affectātĭo -ōnis, *f.* a violent desire and striving.

affectātor -ōris, *m.* one who strives after anything.

affectĭo -ōnis, *f. active,* influence; *passive,* condition; relation; *firma corporis affectio,* good health; favourable disposition of the mind.

affecto, 1. to grasp; to aim after; to meddle with; to obtain; to strive after; to affect.

1. **affectus** -ūs, *m.* disposition; emotions; desire; affection.

2. **affectus** -a -um, *p. adj.* furnished with, *virtutibus*; disposed; disordered; near completion, *bellum affectum videmus.*

affĕro, *attŭli, allātum, afferre,* to carry, *or* bring to; to bring; *manus sibi,* to commit suicide; *alicui vim,* to offer violence to; to bring news; *mihi est allatum,* news was brought me; to bring

as an excuse *or* reason, *rationes;* to produce, cause.

afficĭo -fēci -fectum, 3. to do something to, *rhet.,* to connect; to influence; *aliquem,* to affect; *aliquem sepultura,* to bury; *aliquem capitali poena,* to punish; *passive, morbo gravi et mortifero affectus esse; beneficio affici,* to be benefited.

affīgo -fixi -fixum, 3. to fasten to, affix; to brand; *of the mind,* to imprint.

affingo -finxi -fictum, 3. to form, feign, to add to; to invent.

affinis -e, neighbouring; related by marriage; connected with, privy to. *Subst.,* **affinis** -is, *m.* brother-, sister-, father-, mother-in-law.

affinitas -ātis, *f.* neighbourhood, relationship by marriage; union.

affirmātē, *adv.* certainly.

affirmātĭo -ōnis, *f.* positive assertion.

affirmo, 1. to strengthen; to prove; to assert as true.

affixus -a -um, fixed *or* intent upon.

afflātus -ūs, *m.* a blowing *or* a breathing on; inspiration.

afflĕo -flēvi -flētum, 2. to weep at.

afflictātĭo -ōnis, *f.* bodily pain, torture.

afflicto, 1. to strike *or* beat; *aflictare se, or afflictari,* to be troubled; to damage by striking; to harass.

afflictor -ōris, *m.* a destroyer.

afflictus -a -um, *p. adj.* damaged, shattered; broken down, desponding; contemptible.

afflīgo -flixi -flictum, 3. to strike against; to dash to the ground; to ill-treat, damage; to weaken, injure; *causam sus ceptam,* to drop a lawsuit.

afflo, 1. to blow on; to blow propitiously; to bring; communicate secretly; to breathe on; to inspire.

affluens -entis, rich, abundant, full of.

affluentĕr, *adv.* abundantly.

affluentĭa -ae, *f.* abundance.

afflŭo -fluxi -fluxum, 3. to flow to; *of men,* to flock together; to come; to abound.

affor, 1. *dep.,* to accost; *esp.,* to say farewell *to the dead;* to pray to (*defective verb*).

affrĭco -frĭcŭi -frĭcātum, 1. to rub.

affulgĕo -fulsi, 2. to shine, glitter; to look favourably upon; *of hope,* to appear.

affundo -fūdi fūsum, 3. to pour into; to add; *affundere se or affundi,* to prostrate oneself.

Āfri -ōrum, *m.* the dwellers in Africa.

Āfrĭca -ae, *f.* the continent of Africa. *Adj.* **Āfrĭcānus.** *As a surname, see Cornelius. Adj.* **Āfrĭcus.**

Agămemnon -ŏnis, *m.* leader of the Greek expedition to Troy.

Agănippē -ēs, *f.* fountain in Boeotia.

ăgăso -ōnis, *m.* a horsey-boy, groom; donkey-driver; awkward servant.

Agāvē -ēs, *f.* daughter of Cadmus, mother of Pentheus, whom she killed in a Bacchic frenzy.

ăgellus -i, *m.* (*dim. of ager*), a little field.

ăgēmă -ătis, *n.* corps in the Macedonian army.

Agēnor -ŏris, *m.* father of Cadmus and Europa.

ăgens -entis (*partic. of ago*), lively, active.

ăger, agri, *m.* a field, piece of land; open country; the territory of a state.

Agēsĭlāus -i, *m.* king of Sparta.

aggĕmo, 3. to groan at, to weep at.

agger -ĕris, *m.* a mound, rampart; a funeral pile.

1. **aggĕro, 1.** to form a mound, to heap up.

2. **aggĕro -gessi -gestum, 3.** to carry to, bring to. *Fig.,* to load, heap on.

aggestus -ūs, *m.* accumulation.

agglŏmĕro, 1. *Lit.* to wind on a ball, to add.

agglūtĭno, 1. to fasten to.

aggrăvesco, 3. to grow worse (*of sickness*).

aggrăvo, 1. to make heavier; to make worse; to heighten.

aggrĕdĭo, 3. *active form of aggredior* (*q.v.*).

aggrĕdĭor -gressus sum, 3. *dep.* to approach; to attack; to begin, to undertake.

aggrĕgo, 1. to add to, join with.

agressĭo -onis, *f.* introduction to a speech.

ăgĭlis -e, quick; nimble; active.

ăgĭlĭtas -ātis, *f.* quickness, agility.

Agis -ĭdis, *m.* name of three kings of Sparta.

ăgĭtābĭlis -e, easily moved, light.

ăgĭtātĭo -ōnis, *f.* motion; management; state of motion; activity.

ăgĭtātor -ōris, *m.* a driver; a charioteer.

ăgĭtātus -ūs, *m.* = *agitatio* (*q.v.*).

ăgĭto, 1. to drive about; to hunt; to agitate, to stir up, to move hastily; to vex, harass; to ridicule; *in speech,* to treat of, discuss; to consider; to exercise; *of festivals,* to keep; to manage, observe, *imperium;* to live; to pass time.

Aglăiē -ēs, *f.* the oldest of the graces.

aglaspis -ĭdis, *m.* name of a division in the Macedonian army.

agmĕn -ĭnis, *n.* a mass in movement; a band; a large stream *of water;* an army; the army on march.

agna -ae, *f.* a female lamb.

Agnālĭa -ĭum = *Agonalia* (*q.v.*).

agnascor -nātus, 3. to be born in addition to, *of children born after their father's will.*

agnātĭo -ōnis, *f.* relationship through males only.

agnātus -i, *m.* a relation descended from a common ancestor in the male line; a child born into a family where a regular heir already exists.

agnellus -i, *m.* (*dim. of agnus*), a little lamb.

agnīnus -a -um, relating to a lamb. *Subst.,* **agnīna,** *f.* lamb's flesh.

agnitĭo -ōnis, *f.* recognition; knowledge.

agnōmen -ĭnis, *n.* surname

agnosco -nōvi -nĭtum, 3. to perceive, to recognise; to acknowledge.

agnus -i, *m.* a lamb.

ăgo, ēgi, actum, 3. to set in motion; to drive; to lead; *se agere,* to go; *animum agere,* to give up the ghost; to plunder, to drive away cattle; to construct, lay; *of plants,* to strike root; to incite; *se agere or agere,* to live; *of time,* to pass; to act, to do; *bene, male agere cum aliquo,* to treat a person well *or* badly; *of orators,* to declaim; *of actors,* to play; to express, *gratias;* to keep, observe, *pacem;* to hold a meeting, to transact; *esp., agere bellum,* to have the conduct of a war; to treat with; to bring questions *before the senate; in law, agere causam,* to plead some one's cause; *absol., agere,* to sue; *qua de re agitur,* the point at dispute; *actum est,* the transaction is finished, *so followed by de,* it is all over with. *Imperat., age, agite,* come! well! good!

agōn -ōnis, *m.* content in the public games.

Agōnālĭa -ĭum *and* **-ōrum,** *n.* festival of Janus.

ăgrārĭus -a -um, relating to land. *Subst.,* **ăgrārĭi -ōrum,** *m.* the agrarian party; **ăgrārĭa -ae,** *f.* an agrarian law.

ăgrestĭs -e, wild; savage; belonging to the country, rustic. *Subst.,* **agrestĭs -is,** *m.* countryman, rough.

1. **agrĭcŏla -ae,** *m.* tiller of the fields, farmer.

2. **Agrĭcŏla -ae,** *m.* father-in-law of Tacitus.

agrĭcultĭo -ōnis, *f.* = *agricultura* (*q.v.*).

agrĭcultor -ōris, *m.* = *agricola* (*q.v.*).

agrĭcultura -ae, *f.* agriculture.

Agrĭgentum -i, *n.* Greek town on the south coast of Sicily.

agrĭpēta -ae, *m.* a land-grabber; a settler.

Agrippa -ae, *m.* Roman family name.

Agrippīna -ae, *f.* the name of several Roman women; mother of Nero.

ah, *interj.,* ah! oh!

Ahāla -ae, *m. C. Servilius,* the master of the horse under the dictator Cincinnatus B.C. 439, who slew Sp. Maelius.

ai, ah! *interjection of grief.*

Aiax -ăcis, *m.* name of two Homeric heroes.

aiens -entis (*partic. of aio*), affirmative.

āio, *defective verb,* to say yes, to affirm; to assert.

Aius Lŏquens *or* **Aius Locūtius,** *m.*

the voice which warned the Romans of the coming of the Gauls.

āla -ae, *f.* a wing; *poet., of oars; or sails. Milit.* cavalry; squadron; wing.

ălăbaster -stri, *m., and* **ălăbastrum** -i, *n.* a perfume casket.

ălăcer -cris -cre *and (rarely)* **ălăcris** -e, *adj.* excited; quick, lively.

ălăcritas -ātis, *f.* quickness, eagerness, alacrity.

ălăpa -ae, *f.* a box on the ear; *given by a master to his slave on the manumission of the slave.*

ălārius -a -um, *and* **ălārīs** -e, belonging to the wings *of an army;* **ălāriī,** allied troops.

ālātus -a -um, winged.

ălauda -ae, *f.* a lark; name of a legion of Caesar.

Alba -ae, *f.* Alba Longa, *the oldest Latin town. Adj.* **Albānus** -a -um, Alban; **Albenses** *populi,* people of Latium. *Adj.* **Albensis** -e.

1. Albāni, *see Alba.*

2. Albāni -ōrum, *m.* the Albanians; **Albania** -ae, a country on the west of the Caspian; **Albānus** -a -um, Albanian.

albātus -a -um, clothed in white.

albĕo, 2. to be white; *albente coelo,* at daybreak.

albesco, 3. to become white; *lux albescit,* day dawns.

albico, 1. to make white; to be white.

albidus -a -um, whitish.

Albion -ōnis, *f.* old name of Britain.

Albis -is, *m.* the Elbe.

albŭlus -a -um (*dim. of albus*), whitish; **Albŭla** -ae, *f. (sc. aqua),* old name of the Tiber.

album -i, *n., v. albus.*

Albūnĕa -ae, *f.* a prophetic nymph to whom was dedicated a fountain and grotto at Tibur.

albus -a -um, *adj.* white; grey; pale; bright; making bright; *fig.,* fortunate. *Subst.,* **album** -i, *n.* white colour; white paint *or* cement; a white tablet.

Alcaeus -i, *m.* Greek lyric poet; **Alcăĭcus,** *metrum,* a metre named after him.

alcēdo -inis, *f.* the kingfisher; **alcēdōnia** -ōrum, *n. (sc. tempora);* quietness, calm.

alces -is, *f.* the elk.

Alcestis -is, *f. and* **Alcestē** -ēs, *f.* wife of Admetus, king of Pherae.

Alceus -ĕi *and* -ĕos, *m.* grandfather of Hercules; **Alcīdēs** -ae, *m.* Hercules.

Alcĭbĭădēs -is, *m.* an Athenian, pupil of Socrates.

Alcĭnŏus -i, *m.* king of the Phaeacians, the host of Odysseus.

Alcmēna -ae, *f., and* **Alcmēnē** -ēs, *f.* mother of Hercules.

alcўon, **alcўonia** = **alcedo,** *alcedonia q.v.).*

Alcўŏnē -ēs, *f.* changed with her husband into a kingfisher.

ălĕa -ae, *f.* a game with dice, hazard; chance, risk.

ālĕātor -ōris, *m.* dicer, hazard-player.

ālĕātōrius -a -um, relating to a dicer.

ălec (allec) -ēcis, *n.* a sauce prepared from fish.

Ălectō (Allecto), *acc.* '-ō, *f.* one of the three furies. *(Only in nom. and acc.)*

āles, ālitis (*genit. pl. alituum, poet.*). *Adj.* winged; *deus,* Mercury; swift. *Subst., f.* bird.

ālesco, 3. to grow up.

Alexander -dri, *m.* 1. Paris, son of Priam, king of Troy. 2. Alexander the Great, king of Macedonia. **Alexandrīa** *or* **ēa** -ae, *f.* Egyptian city, at the mouth of the Nile. *Adj.* **Alexandrĕus** -a -um. **Alexandrīnus** -a -um.

alga -ae, *f.* seaweed.

algens -tis, cold, cool.

algĕo, alsi, 2. to be cold.

algesco, alsi, 3. to become cold.

1. algidus -a -um, cold.

2. Algidus -i, *m.* mountains in Latium; **Algidum** -i, *n.* town of the Aequi. *Adj.* **Algidus** -a -um.

algor -ōris, *m.* the sensation of cold; frost.

algōsus -a -um, abounding in seaweed.

algus -ūs, *m.* = *algor (q.v.).*

ăliā, *adv.* by another way.

ăliās, *adv.* at another time; elsewhere; *alias ... alias,* at one time . . . at another time.

ălĭbī, *adv.* elsewhere, at another place; *alibi . . . alibi,* here . . . there.

ălica (hălica) -ae, *f.* spelt; drink prepared from spelt.

ălĭcŭbi, *adv.* anywhere, somewhere.

ălĭcŭla -ae, *f.* a light upper garment.

ălĭcundĕ, *adv.* from anywhere, from somewhere.

ălĭēnātĭo -ōnis, *f.* transference *or* alienation of property; *mentis,* loss of reason; enmity.

ălĭēnĭgĕna -ae, *m.* strange, foreign. *Subst.* foreigner.

ălĭēnĭgĕnus -a -um, heterogeneous.

ălĭēno, 1. to take away; *legal,* to transfer property; to remove from the mind; to estrange; *pass.,* alienari, to go out of one's mind; *alienari ab interitu,* to shun.

ălĭēnus -a -um, *adj.* that which belongs *or* relates to another; not related; foreign; *aes,* debt; *nomina,* debts contracted in the names of others. *Subst.,* **ălĭēnum** -i, *n.* another man's property. *Subst.,* **ălĭēnus** -i, *m.* a stranger; foreigner. *Of persons,* not acquainted with, strange to; unfriendly; unfavourable.

ālĭgĕr -gĕra -gĕrum, winged.

ălĭmentārĭus -a -um, relating to food.

ălĭmentum -i, *n.* food (*gen. plural*); maintenance.

ălĭmōnĭum -ii, *n.* nourishment.

ălĭō, *adv.* to another place; *alius alio,*
one in this direction, the other in that;
to another person.

ălĭōqui (**ălĭōquin**), *adv.* otherwise, in other
respects; yet, besides, moreover.

ălĭbōrsum and **ăliorsus,** *adv.* elsewhere,
in another manner.

ălĭpēs -pĕdis, having wings on the feet;
swift of foot. *Subst.,* **ălĭpēdes,** horses.

ălĭpta -ae, *m.,* and **ălĭptēs -ae,** *m.* the
anointer in the wrestling-school or the
baths; the master of the wrestling-school.

ălĭquā, *adv.* by some road; in some way.

ălĭquamdĭū, *adv.* for a moderately long
time.

ălĭquammŭltus or **aliquam multus**
-a -um, a pretty good many.

ălĭquandō, *adv.* at any time, at some
time, once; sometimes.

ălĭquantillus -a -um (*dim. of aliquan-*
tus), a very little.

ălĭquantispĕr, *adv.* a moderately long
time.

ălĭquanto, ălĭquantum. *v. aliquantus.*

ălĭquantŭlus -a -um (*dim. of aliquantus*),
little, small. *Adv.,* **ălĭquantŭlum,** a
little.

ălĭquantus -a -um, moderate, not small.
Subst., **ălĭquantum -i,** *n.* a good deal;
acc. aliquantum and abl. aliquanto,
considerably, somewhat.

ălĭquătĕnus, *adv.* in some measure.

ălĭqui, aliquae, aliquod, some, any.

ălĭquis, aliqua, aliquid, *pron. indef.*
some one, something, any one, anything;
*adj., aliquis deus; aliquid with genit.
aliquid virium.*

ălĭquō, *adv.* some or any whither.

ălĭquŏt, *numer. indef. indecl.,* some,
several.

ălĭquŏtĭēs, *adv.* several times.

ălis, alid, old form of *alius, aliud.*

ălĭtĕr, *adv.* otherwise, in another way;
alius aliter, in different ways; *in comparisons, aliter . . . atque; so aliter
. . . quam,* just as; *otherwise, else.*

ălĭŭbi, *adv.* elsewhere.

ălĭundĕ, *adv.* from some other direction;
alii aliunde coibant, from different
directions.

ălĭus -a -ud, another, other; *distribu-
tively,* one, another; *alii . . . alii,*
some . . . others; *alius alia via,* the
one in this way, the other in that; *plur.,*
the rest; *acc. plur., alia,* in other
respects; of another nature, different;
in alia omnia ire, be of a contrary opinion
(*in the senate*).

ălĭusmŏdi, of another kind.

allābor -lapsus, 3. to glide to, come to,
flow to.

allābōro, 1. to labour at.

allăcrĭmo, 1. to weep at.

allapsus -ūs, *m.* a gliding approach.

allātro, 1. to bark at; to rail at.

allaudābĭlis -e, praiseworthy.

allec, *v. alec.*

allecto, 1. to entice.

allēgātĭo -ōnis, *f.* a sending of a person
on a mission.

1 **allēgo,** 1. to send on private business
(*lego of state business*); *allegati,*
deputies; to instigate, to suborn; to
allege in excuse.

2. **allēgo -lēgi -lectum,** 3. to choose,
to elect.

allĕvāmentum -i, *n.* a means of alleviation.

allĕvātĭo -ōnis, *f.* a lifting up, alleviation.

allĕvo (**ad-lēvo**), 1. to lift up, to erect;
to alleviate, *pass., allevari,* to be cheered.

Allia (**Alia**) **-ae,** *f.* river in Latium.
Adj., **Alliensis -e.**

allicĕfăcĭo, 3. to entice.

allicĭo -lexi -lectum, 3. to allure, entice.

allīdo -līsi -līsum, 3. to strike against;
allidi, to suffer damage.

Allifae -ārum, *f.* town of the Samnites.
Adj., **Allifānus.** *Subst.,* **Allifāna**
-ōrum, earthenware drinking-vessels.

allĭgo, 1. to bind to; to bind a wound,
vulnus; to fetter; to bind by friendship or obligations; *alligatus,* implicated *in a crime.*

allĭno -lēvi -lĭtum, 3. to smear on, or
over.

allĭum -i, *n.* garlic.

Allŏbrŏges -um, *m.* the Allobroges,
Gallic people; *sing.,* **Allŏbrox.** *Adj.,*
Allŏbrŏgĭcus.

allŏquĭum -i, *n.* exhortation, consolation.

allŏquor -lŏcūtus sum, 3. to address,
encourage.

allūcĕo -luxi, 2. to shine at. or upon.

allūdo -lūsi -lūsum, 3. to jest at, to sport
with.

allŭo -ŭi, 3. to wash; *of the sea.*

allŭvĭēs -ēi, *f.* a pool caused by the overflow of a river.

allŭvĭo -ōnis, *f.* alluvial land.

almus -a -um, nourishing; fair,
gracious, kind.

alnus -i, *f.* the alder; a ship of alder-
wood.

ălo, ălŭi, altum and ălĭtum, 3. to nourish;
to rear; to keep; to increase, advance.

ălŏē -ēs, *f.* the aloe; bitterness.

Alpēs -ĭum, *f.* the Alps. *Adj.* **Alpīnus.**
Alpicus.

Alphēus -i, *m.* principal river of the
Peloponnesus.

alsĭus -a -um, frosty, cold.

altārĭa -ĭum, *n.* the slab upon the altar,
on which the fire is lighted; an altar.

altē, *adv.* on high, highly; from a
height; *spectare,* to have high aims;
deeply.

altĕr -tĕra -tĕrum, one of two, the one
the other; *consulum alter; alter . . .*

alter, the one . . . the other; the second.

altercātĭo -ōnis, *f.* a dispute, debate; *legal*, cross-examination.

altercor, 1. *dep.* to dispute, quarrel. *Legal*, to cross-examine.

alterno, 1. to do first one thing, then another. *Intrans.*, to change; to hesitate.

alternus -a -um, one after the other, by turns, alternate; *sermones*, dialogue. *Of metre*, elegiac verse.

altĕrŭter, altĕrutra, alterutrum; one of two.

Althaea -ae, *f.* mother of Meleager.

alticinctus -a -um, high girt; *hence* busy.

altilis -e, *of animals*, fattened; rich; *subst.*, altilis, *f.* a fowl.

altisŏnus -a -um, sounding from on high; sublime.

altĭtŏnans -tis, thundering from on high.

altĭtūdo -ĭnis, *f.* height; sublimity; depth; *altitudo animi*, secrecy, reserve.

altiuscŭlus -a -um (*dim. of altius*), a little too high.

altivŏlans -antis, flying high.

altor -ōris, *m.* nourisher, foster-father.

altrix -īcis, *f.* nurse, foster-mother.

altrōvorsum, *adv.* on the other side.

altus -a -um, high; shrill; high-born; *of speech*, elevated; *of character*, lofty; deep. *Subst.*, altum -i *n.* height, depth, *esp.* the deep sea.

ălūcinor, 1. *dep.* to wander in mind, dream, to talk idly.

ălumna -ae, *f.*, *v. alumnus.*

ălumnus -a -um, a nursling; pupil, disciple. *Fem.*, foster-child.

ălūta -ae, *f.* a kind of soft leather; a shoe; a purse; an ornamental patch.

alvĕārĭum -ĭi, *n.* a beehive.

alvĕātus -a -um, hollowed like a trough.

alvĕŏlus -i, *m.* (*dim. of alveus*) a little hollow, a tray, trough, bucket; a gaming board.

alvĕus -i, *m.* a hollow, an excavation; a trough; a boat; the hold of a ship; a bathing-tub; the bed of a stream; a beehive; a gaming-table.

alvus -i, *f.* the belly; the womb; the stomach; the hold of a ship; a beehive.

ămābĭlis -e, amiable, lovable.

ămābĭlĭter, *adv.* amiably; lovingly.

Amalthēa -ae, *f.* a nymph, the nurse of Jupiter in Crete, *according to others, the goat on the milk of which Jupiter was reared.*

ămandātĭo -ōnis, *f.* a sending away.

ămando, 1. to send away.

ămans -antis, *p. adj.* loving, affectionate, *amantissimus reipublicae.* *Subst.*, *c.* a lover.

ămantĕr, *adv.* lovingly.

ămănŭensis -is, *m.* secretary, clerk.

ămārăcĭnus -a -um, made of marjoram. *Subst.*, **ămārăcĭnum** -i, *n.* marjoram ointment.

ămārăcus -i, *c.*, *and* **ămārăcum** -i, *n.* marjoram.

ămārantus -i, *m.* the amaranth.

ămārĕ, *adv.* bitterly.

ămārĭtūdo -ĭnis, *f.* bitterness of taste; that which is bitter; *vocis*, harshness of voice.

ămāror -ōris, *m.* bitterness.

ămārus -a -um, bitter; pungent; unpleasant; tedious; irritable, susceptible; acrimonious, *lingua. Neut. plur.*, *ămāra* -ōrum, what is unpleasant.

Amāta -ae, *f.* wife of king Latinus.

Amāthūs -untis, *f.* city of Cyprus, *famous for the worship of Venus.*

ămātor -ōris, *m.* one who loves, a friend; lover of a woman.

ămātōrĭē, *adv.* amorously.

ămātōrĭus -a -um, loving, amorous.

ămātrix -īcis, *f.* a mistress, sweetheart.

Amāzon -ōnis, *f.*, *gen. in plur.*, **Amāzŏnes** -um, nation of female warriors; **Amāzŏnis** -idis, *f.* = Amazon. Adj., **Amāzŏnĭcus** -a -um; **Amāzŏnĭus** -a -um.

ambactus -i, *m.* a vassal.

ambāges, *abl.* -e, *f.* (*of sing. only abl.*), roundabout way, winding; circumlocution; ambiguity; prevarication.

Ambarri -ōrum, *m.* Gallic people east of the Aedui.

ambĕdo -ēdi -ēsum, 3. to eat round, consume.

Ambĭāni -ōrum, *m.* people in North Gaul.

ambĭgo, 3. to go about *or* round; to doubt, hesitate; to dispute, contend.

ambĭgŭē, *adv.* ambiguously; indecisively.

ambĭgŭĭtas -ātis, *f.* ambiguity.

ambĭgŭus -a -um, of doubtful nature; *viri*, Centaurs; uncertain, doubtful, ambiguous; untrustworthy; *res*, insecure; *aquae*, changing. *Subst.*, **ambĭgŭum** -i, *n.* uncertainty; ambiguity.

Ambĭlĭāti -ōrum, *m.* a Gallic people on the Somme.

ambĭo -ivi *and* -ĭi -ĭtum, 4. to go round; to surround; to go round canvassing; to address individuals.

Ambĭŏrix -rĭgis, *m.* prince of the Eburones in Gallia Belgica.

ambĭtĭo -ōnis, *f.* a canvassing for office in a lawful manner; desire for office; fame, display; factiousness; striving after something.

ambĭtĭōsē, *adv.* aspiringly; with a view to one's interest.

ambĭtĭōsus -a -um, twining around; *ambitiosa ornamenta*, excessive; ambitious; vain, pretentious; *amicitiae*, interested; seeking popularity; striving after anything.

ambĭtus -ūs, *m.* circuit, revolution; orbit; circumlocution; circle, edge; extent; going round to entreat; illegal canvassing; bribery; striving for.

ambō -ae -ŏ, both, two together.

Ambrācĭa -ae, *f.* town on the south of Epirus.

Ambrŏnes -um, *m.* a Keltic people defeated by Marius in the war with the Cimbri.

ambrŏsĭa -ae, *f.* ambrosia.

ambrŏsĭus -a -um, divine, immortal, ambrosial.

ambūbāiae -ārum, *f.* Syrian music women in Rome.

ambŭlātĭo -ōnis, *f.* a walk; a promenade.

ambŭlātĭuncŭla -ae, *f.* a little walk, a little promenade.

ambŭlātor -ōris, *m.* one who walks about, a lounger; pedlar.

ambŭlātōrĭus -a -um, movable.

ambŭlo, 1. (*dim. of ambĭo*), to go backwards and forwards, to walk; *bene ambula*, bon voyage; to travel over, to traverse; to go for a walk.

ambūro -ussi -ustum, 3. to burn round, to scorch. *Of cold*, to nip, numb; to injure. *Subst.*, **ambustum** -i, *n.* a burn.

ambustus -a -um, *partic. of amburo.*

āmellus -i, *m.* the purple Italian starwort.

āmens -entis, mad, senseless.

āmentĭa -ae, *f.* insanity, folly.

āmento, 1. to furnish with a strap; *hastae amentatae.*

āmentum -i, *n.* strap, thong; shoe-tie.

āmĕs -ĭtis, *m.* a forked pole, *for fowlers' nets.*

ămĕthystĭnus -a -um, amethyst-coloured; set with amethysts. *Subst.*, **ămĕthystĭna** -ōrum, *n.* dresses of that colour.

ămĕthystus -i, *f.* an amethyst.

amfractus = *anfractus (q.v.).*

ămīca -ae, *f. (v. amicus).*

ămīcē, *adv.* in a friendly manner; willingly.

ămĭcĭo -icui *and* -ixi -ictum, 4. to clothe, wrap round, *amictus toga*; to cover, conceal.

ămīcĭter = *amice (q.v.).*

ămīcĭtĭa -ae, *f.* friendship; sympathy; friends.

ămīcĭtĭes -ēi, *f.* = *amicitia (q.v.).*

ămictus -ūs, *m.* putting on of a garment; the manner of wearing the toga; a garment; covering.

ămīcŭla -ae, *f. v. amiculus.*

ămĭcŭlum -i, *n.* a mantle, cloak.

ămīcŭlus -i, *m., and* **ămīcŭla** -ae, *f.* (*dim. of amicus*), a little friend.

ămīcus -a -um, friendly, favourable to. *Subst.*, **ămīcus** -i, *m.*, a friend; *plur.*, retinue; **ămīca** -ae, *f.* a friend *or* a mistress.

āmissĭo -ōnis, *f.* a loss.

āmissus -ūs, *m.* = *amissio (q.v.).*

āmĭta -ae, *f.* a father's sister; an aunt.

āmitto -mīsi -missum, 3. to send away, to let go; to give up; to let slip; to lose; *fidem, credit.*

Ammōn (Hammon) -ōnis, *m.* a Libyan deity, *worshipped in Rome under the name of Jupiter Ammon.*

amnĭcŏla -ae, *c.* dwelling by the riverside.

amnĭcŭlus -i (*dim. of amnis*), a little river.

amnis -is, *m.* a stream, a river; a torrent; water.

āmo, 1. to love; *amare se*, to love oneself; *aliquam de re*, to feel obliged or bound to a person; *amabo te*, or *amabo*, please, be so good; *amat ianua limen*, clings to; to be accustomed.

ămoenē, *adv.* pleasantly.

ămoenĭtas -ātis, *f.* pleasantness; pleasant situation.

ămoenus -a -um, pleasant, delightful. *Subst.*, **amoena** -orum, *n.* pleasant places.

āmōlĭor, 4. *dep* to remove; *se*, to take oneself off; to get rid of. *In speech*, to pass over.

ămōmum -i, *n.* a shrub.

ămŏr -ōris, *m.* love from inclination (*caritas*, love from esteem); passion; *personif.*, the god Cupid; the object of love, darling; desire, *scribendi.*

āmōtĭo -ōnis, *f.* a removing.

āmŏvĕo -mōvi -mōtum, 2. to remove; *se amovere*, to depart; *euphemism*, to steal; to banish.

amphĭbŏlĭa -ae, *f.* ambiguity, double meaning.

Amphictyŏnes -um, *m.* the Amphictyons, a religious assembly of representatives of the Greek states.

Amphĭōn -ōnis, *m.* husband of Niobe.

amphisbaena -ae, *f.* a kind of African snake.

amphĭtheātrālis -e, belonging to the amphitheatre.

amphĭtheātrum -i, *n.* amphitheatre.

Amphĭtrītē -ēs, *f.* wife of Neptune.

amphŏra -ae, *f.* a two-handled vase, pitcher, *or* jug; a measure for liquids; measure of the tonnage of a ship.

amplē, *adv.* richly, amply; magnificently; *compar.*, **amplĭus**, more; *amplius centum cives Romani*. *Of space or time*, more, farther; further, in addition; *hoc or eo amplius*, besides, moreover.

amplector -plexus sum -plecti, 3. *dep.* to surround; to embrace; to welcome, receive; to love, esteem; to prize; to consider; to include; to touch on *in discourse.*

amplexor, 1. *dep.* to surround, embrace; to honour.

amplexus -ūs, *m.* encircling, embrace; *terrarum amplexus,* the circuit of the earth.

ampilficatio -ōnis, *f.* an enlarging, increasing; heightening; amplification.

amplificātor -ōris, *m.* one who enlarges.

amplifico, 1. to enlarge ; to increase ; to dilate upon.

amplio, 1. to enlarge, increase; to glorify; to adjourn the hearing of a case.

amplĭter, *adv.* = *ample (q.v.).*

amplitūdo, -ĭnis, *f.* breadth, size; increase; greatness; grandeur; dignity of expression.

amplus -a -um, *adj.* large, ample. (*Neut. subst.,* **amplius**); important; honourable; excellent; *amplissimi viri,* men of the highest position.

ampulla -ae, *f.* (*dim. of amphora*); flask, bottle; bombast.

ampullor 1. *dep.* to speak bombastically.

ampŭtātio -ōnis, *f.* a cutting off, pruning.

ampŭto, 1. to cut off; to prune; to amputate ; to diminish ; *amputata loqui,* to speak disconnectedly.

Amūlius -ii, *m.* king of Alba Longa.

ămurca -ae, *f.* the oil-lees.

ămussis (*acc.* **-im**), *f.* a carpenter's rule; *ad amussim,* exactly.

Amȳclae -arum, *f.* 1. town in Laconia; 2. town in Latium. *Adj.* **Amȳclaeus -a -um;** *poet.* Laconian.

ămȳgdălum -i, *n.* an almond.

Amȳmōnē -ēs, *f.* daughter of Danaus, beloved by Neptune.

Amyntās -ae, *m.* name of several Macedonian kings ; **Amyntiădēs -ae,** *m.* Philip.

ămystis -ĭdis, *f.* the emptying of a goblet at a draught.

ăn, *conj.* or, whether; or rather.

ănăbathrum -i, *n.* a raised seat.

Ānacrĕōn -ontis, *m.* a lyric poet.

ănădēma -ătis, *n.* ornament *or* fillet for the head.

ănagnostēs -ae, *m.* a reader.

ănălecta -ae, *m.* a slave whose duty it was to collect and remove crumbs after a meal.

ănăpaestus -a -um, a metrical foot, an anapaest (‿‿–).

ănăphŏră -ae, *f. in rhetoric,* the repetition of a word at the beginning of several sentences.

ănas, *ănătis, f.* a duck.

ănăticŭla -ae, *f.* (*dim. of anas*), a little duck.

ănătōcismus -i, *m.* compound interest.

Anaxăgŏras -ae, *m.* philosopher, teacher of Pericles and Euripides.

Anaximander -dri, *m.* philosopher of Miletus.

Anaximĕnēs -is, *m.* philosopher of Miletus.

anceps -cipĭtis *abl. sing.* **-cipĭti,** two-

headed, *Ianus :* *acumen montis,* two-peaked ; with two sides ; two-edged ; coming on both sides; *anceps proelium,* a battle where the enemy attack on both sides ; of two natures ; ambiguous ; undecided ; dangerous, *hic locus tam anceps.*

Anchīsēs -ae, *m.* father of Aeneas ; **Anchīsiădēs -ae,** *m.* a descendant of Anchises, *i.e.* Aeneas.

ancile -is, *n.* a shield which fell from heaven in the time of Numa.

ancilla -ae, *f.* a maid-servant.

ancillārĭŏlus -i, *m.* a lover of maid-servants.

ancillāris -e, relating to a maid-servant.

ancillor, 1. *dep.* to serve as a maid-servant.

ancillŭla -ae, *f.* (*dim. of ancilla*), a little maid-servant.

ancīsus -a -um, cut round.

Ancōn -ōnis, *f. and* **Ancōna -ae,** *f.* a town in Picenum.

ancŏra -ae, *f.* an anchor ; *tollere,* to weigh anchor.

ancŏrāle -is, *n.* a cable.

ancŏrārius -a -um, belonging to an anchor.

Ancus (Marcius), fourth king of Rome.

Ancȳra -ae, *f.* capital of Galatia, *now* Angora.

andăbătă -ae, *m.* gladiator who fought with a helmet that had no openings for the eyes.

Andēs -ium, *f.* town in the Mantuan country, *birthplace of Virgil.*

Andrŏgĕōs *or* **-gĕus -i,** *m.* son of Minos and Pasiphae, killed by the Athenians.

andrŏgȳnus -i, *m.* ; **andrŏgȳne -es,** *f.* a hermaphrodite.

Andrŏmăchē -ēs *and* **-cha -ae,** *f.* wife of Hector.

Andrŏmĕdē -ēs, *f.,* and **-da -ae,** *f.* daughter of the Aethiopian king Cepheus (*acc. sometimes* **-an**).

Andrŏnīcus -i, *m.* L. *or* T. *Livius,* the earliest of the Roman tragic poets.

ănellus -i, *m.* (*dim. of anulus*), a little ring.

ănēthum -i, *n.* dill, anise.

anfractus -ūs, *m.* a turning, bending ; *solis,* revolution ; winding ; legal intricacies ; prolixity.

angellus -i, *m.* (*dim. of angulus*), a little corner.

angīna -ae, *f.* the quinsy.

angiportum -i, *n. and* **angiportus -ūs,** *m.* a narrow street.

Anglii -ōrum, *m.* a branch of the Suevi.

ango, 3. to press together, to throttle; to distress; to torment, make anxious; *pass., angi,* to be grieved *or* troubled.

angor -ōris, *m.* throttling; distress, anguish, trouble.

anguicŏmus -a -um, having snaky hair.

anguicŏlus -i, *m.* (*dim. of anguis*), a little snake.

anguifer -fĕra -fĕrum, snake-bearing.

anguigĕna -ae, *c.* snake-born.

anguilla -ae, *f.* an eel.

anguimānus -ūs, *m.* snake-handed.

anguinĕus -a -um, pertaining to a snake, snaky.

anguinus -a -um = *anguineus* (*q.v.*).

anguipes -pĕdis, snake-footed.

anguis -is, *c.* a snake; a constellation.

Anguitĕnens -entis, *m.* the Snake-holder; the constellation Ophiuchus.

angŭlātus -a -um, angular, cornered.

angŭlus -i, *m.* a corner, angle; a bastion; a retired spot.

angustē *adv.* narrowly, in a confined manner; sparingly; in a circumscribed manner; briefly.

angustia -ae, *f., gen. pl.* **angustiae** -ārum, *f.* narrowness; *spiritus,* shortness of breath; defiles, narrow passes; obscure reasoning; *of time,* shortness; *of circumstances,* poverty; distress; narrow-mindedness.

angusticlāvius -ii, *m.* wearing a narrow stripe of purple on his tunic; *epithet of a military tribune.*

angustus -a -um, narrow; *habenae,* tightly drawn; *spiritus angustior,* short breath; *of time,* short; *of circumstances,* straitened, poor; precarious, uncertain, *res angustae; of speech,* concise; petty, subtle. *Subst.,* **angustum** -i, *n.* a narrow space; difficulty.

ānhēlātio -ōnis = *anhelitus* (*q.v.*).

ānhēlitus -ūs, *m.* short, quick breathing, panting; asthma; breath; exhalation, vapour.

ānhēlo, 1. *intransit.,* to draw a heavy breath, pant; to roar, *ignis anhelat. Transit.,* to pant for, desire eagerly.

ānhēlus -a -um, puffing, panting; causing to pant, *febris.*

ānĭcŭla -ae, *f.* (*dim. of anus*), a little old woman.

Ānĭen -ĕnis = *Anio.*

Āniensis, Aniēnus, *v. Anio.*

ānīlis -e, belonging to or like an old woman; *fabellae,* old wives' tales.

ānīlitas -ātis, *f.* old age (*of women*).

ānīlĭtĕr, *adv.* like an old woman.

ānima -ae, *f.* wind; the air as an element; the breath; the soul; the spirits of the dead; life; life-blood; a living being. (*Like animus*), the rational soul; *animam edere,* to give up the ghost; *trahere,* to drag on existence.

ānimābilis -e, animating, giving life.

ānimadversio -ōnis, *f.* perception, observation; punishment; blame.

ānimadversor -ōris, *m.* an observer.

ānimadverto (**ānimadvorto**) -verti (-vorti) -versum (-vorsum), 3. (*for animum adverto*); to take notice of, to attend to; *of the lictor,* to clear the road

for the consul; to perceive; to punish, *in iudices quosdam;* to blame.

ănimal -ālis, *n.* living being, animal.

ănimālis -e, consisting of air, airy; living.

ănimans -antis, *as adj.,* living. *Subst.,* a living being, animal.

ănimātio -ōnis, *f.* an animating; a living being.

1. **ănimātus** -a -um, alive, animated; inclined; courageous.

2. **ănimātus** -ūs, *m.* life, animation.

ănimo, 1. to animate, give life to; to endow with a particular disposition.

ănimōsē, *adv.* courageously.

ănimōsus -a -um, courageous, high-spirited, furious; *with abl.,* proud of; intent on.

ănimŭla -ae, *f.* (*dim. of anima*), a little soul; a little life.

ănimŭlus -i, *m.* (*dim. of animus*), term of endearment; *mi animule,* my life.

ănimus -i, *m.* the spiritual principle of life in man; the soul as the seat of feeling; *animi or animis pendere,* to be anxious; character, disposition; *poet.,* nature; inclination towards some one; *mi anime,* "my dear"; courage, spirit; vivacity; (*esp. in plural*), arrogance; wish, desire; the soul as the seat of the will; *habeo in animo, with infin.,* I am resolved; *so in animum habeo, est mihi in animo; ex animo,* willingly; the soul as the seat of the thoughts; consciousness; thought.

Anio -ōnis (*or* -ēnis), *m., poet.,* **Aniēnus** -i. *m.* the Anio, tributary to the Tiber. *Adj.,* **Aniensis** -e; **Aniēnus.**

Anna -ae, *f.* sister of Dido.

annālis -e, *adj.,* lasting a year; relating to a year. *Subst.,* **annālis** -is, *m. and plur.* **annāles** -ium, *m.* annals.

annecto -nexui -nexum, 3. to bind to, connect with; to connect.

annexus -ūs, *m.* a connection.

Annĭbal, *v. Hannibal.*

annĭcŭlus -a -um, one year old.

annītor -nisus *or* -nixus, 3. *dep.* to lean upon; to strive after.

anniversārius -a -um, recurring every year.

anno 1. to swim to, *or* near; to swim alongside of.

annōna -ae, *f.* yearly produce, crop; means of subsistence, *esp.* grain; price of provisions, *esp.* of corn; *esp.* high price of corn; *annona salaria,* price of salt.

annōsus -a -um, long-lived.

annōtinus -a -um, a year old, belonging to last year.

annŏto, 1. to note down.

annŭmĕro, 1. to count out, pay; to reckon with.

annŭo (*ad-nuo*) -ŭi, 3. to nod to; to assent by a nod; to promise.

annus -i, *m.* year ; *exeunte anno ; anno superiore; tempus anni,* season; *ad annum,* next year; *annos LXX natus,* seventy years old; *habere annos viginti; annus magnus,* a cycle of years; (*poet.*), time of year.

annŭus -a -um, lasting for a year; annual; *subst.,* **annŭum** -i. *n. or* **annŭa** -orum, *n.* a yearly salary, pension.

anquiro -quisīvi -quisītum, 3. to search carefully, to inquire after. *Transit.,* to investigate. *Intrans., legal,* to set an inquiry on foot.

ansa -ae, *f.* a handle, haft; *crepidae,* the eye through which a shoe-tie is passed; opportunity.

ansātus -a -um, provided with a handle; *homo,* a man with handles, *i.e.* with arms akimbo.

anser -ĕris, *m.* a goose.

Antaeus -i, *m.* a powerful giant, slain by Hercules.

antĕ, *prep. & adv.* before. *Adv., of place, ante aut post pugnare. Of time,* before. *Prep.,* before, *ante pedes; ante urbem conditam,* before the founding of the city.

anteā, *adv.,* before, formerly.

anteambŭlo -ōnis, *m.* a running footman, to clear the way.

antĕcānis, a star, the little dog.

antĕcăpio -cēpi -ceptum, 3. to seize beforehand; to anticipate, to prepare beforehand; to exite beforehand; to use beforehand; *noctem,* not to wait for.

antĕcēdens -entis, *p. adj.* preceding; *philosoph. causa,* the antecedent cause. *Subst.,* **antĕcēdens,** the antecedent cause.

antĕcēdo -cessi -cessum, 3. to go before, precede; to overtake; to excel; *with dat. and with acc.*

antĕcello -ĕre, *no perf. or sup.,* to distinguish oneself, excel.

antĕcessio -ōnis, *f.* a preceding; antecedent cause.

antĕcessus -ūs, *m.* a going before.

antĕcursor -ōris, *m.* one who runs before; *plur.,* pioneers.

antĕeo -ivi (*and gen.*) -ii, -ire, to go before, *alicui;* to go before *in time;* to excel.

antĕféro -tŭli -lātum -ferre, to carry before, to prefer ; to anticipate, consider beforehand.

antĕfixus -a -um, fastened in front. *Subst.,* **antĕfixa** -ōrum, *n.* ornaments fixed on the roofs and gutters of houses.

antĕgrĕdior -gressus -grĕdi, *dep.* to go before; *causae antegressae,* antecedent causes.

antĕhăbĕo, 2. to prefer.

antĕhāc, *adv* .before this time, formerly.

antĕlātus -a um, *v. antefero.*

antĕlūcānus -a -um, happening before daybreak.

antĕmĕrīdiānus -a -um, before noon.

antĕmitto, *ante and mitto, q.v.*

antenna (**antemna**) -ae, *f.* a sail-yard.

Antēnor -ōris, *m.* a Trojan.

antĕpagmentum -i, *n.* lining of a door or post, a jamb.

antĕpēs -pĕdis, *m.* the forefoot.

antĕpīlāni -ōrum, *m.* the soldiers who fought in front.

antĕpōno -pŏsŭi -pŏsĭtum, 3. to place before; *alicui prandium,* to place in front; to prefer, *se alicui.*

Antĕrōs -ōtis, *m.* the genius *or* avenger of slighted love.

antes -ium, *m.* rows *or* ranks.

antĕsignānus -i, *m.* plur. soldiers who fought in front of the line, skirmishers; *sing.,* a leader.

antesto (**antisto**) -stĭti, 1. to stand before; to surpass; to be prominent.

antestor, 1. *dep. legal t.t.,* to call to witness.

antĕvĕnio -vēni -ventum, 4. to come before, to get the start of; to anticipate, prevent; to excel.

antĕverto (**antĕvorto**) -verti (-vorti -versum (-vorsum), 3. *and dep.* **antĕvortor** -vorti,** to go before, to precede; to anticipate, hinder by anticipating; to prefer.

anthĭas -ae, *m.* a sea-fish.

anthŏlŏgĭca, *genit.* -ōn, *n.* anthology.

anticĭpātĭo -ōnis, *f.* a preconception, innate idea.

anticĭpo, 1. to receive before, anticipate; *viam,* to travel over before; *ludos,* to celebrate before their time; to come before.

antīcus -a -um, forward, in front.

Antīcȳra -ae,, *f.* town in Phocis, famous for its hellebore.

antĭdea, antĭdeo, antĭdhac, see *antea, anteeo, antehac.*

antĭdŏtum -i, *n.* an antidote.

Antĭgŏnē -ēs, *f. and* **Antĭgŏna** -ae, *f.* daughter of Oedipus, sister of Polynices and Eteocles, put to death for burying her brother against the command of the king of Thebes.

Antĭgŏnus -i, *m.* name of several of the successors of Alexander the Great.

Antĭŏchīa -ae, *f.* name of several towns; *adj.* **Antĭŏchensis** -e *and* **Antĭŏchīnus** -a -um.

Antĭŏchus -i, *m.* name of thirteen Syrian kings. *Subst.,* **Antĭŏchīnus.**

Antĭpătĕr -tri, *m.* name of several kings of Macedonia.

antĭquārĭus -a -um, belonging to antiquity. *Subst.,* **antĭquārĭus** -ĭi, *m. and* **antĭquārĭa** -ae, *f.* an antiquary.

antīquē, *adv.* in an ancient manner.

antīquitas -ātis, *f.* antiquity ; history of ancient times; *plur.* the ancients.

antiquitŭs, *adv.* in ancient times; from antiquity.

antiquo, 1. to leave in its former state; to reject a bill, *legem.*

antiquus -a -um, old, ancient, previous; simple, innocent; venerable; *in compar . and superl.*, more *or* most important, preferable. *Subst.*, antiqui -orum, *m.* the people of old time.

antistes -stitis, *c.* a presiding priest *or* priestess.

antistita -ae, *f.* a presiding priestess.

antisto, *v. antesto.*

antithĕton -i, *n.* antithesis.

antlia -ae, *f.* a pump.

Antōnīnus -i, *m.* name of several Roman emperors.

Antōnius -a -um, *gens,* the name of a Roman family.

antrum -i, *n.* a cave; hollow *of a tree.*

Anūbis -bidis, *m.* an Egyptian god, represented with a dog's head.

ānūlārius -a -um, belonging to a seal ring. *Subst.*, anularius -i, *m.* a ring maker.

ānūlātus -a -um, beringed, ornamented with rings.

ānūlus, annūlus -i, *m.* a ring; *anulus equestris,* the gold ring which was the sign of a knight; curtain ring; link of a fetter; ringlet of hair.

ānŭs -ūs, *f.* an old woman.

anxiē, *adv.* anxiously.

anxĭĕtas -ātis, *f.* anxiety; grief; painful accuracy.

anxĭfer -fĕra -fĕrum, causing anxiety.

anxĭtūdo -inis, *f.* anxiousness.

anxĭus -a -um, anxious, uneasy; causing anxiety.

Anxŭr -ŭris, *m. and n.,* an old town of the Volsci.

Āōn -ōnis, *m.* an old Boeotian hero.

Āŏnes, *pl.* the Boeotians.

Āornos -i, *m. and f.* lake of Avernus.

ăpăgĕ, *interj.*, away with thee! be off!

Apellēs -is, *m.* a Greek painter, friend of Alexander the Great. *Adj.* Apellēus.

Āpenninus -i, *m.* the chain of the Apennines.

ăper, *apri, m.* a wild boar.

ăpĕrio -pĕrŭi -pertum, 4. to uncover, to lay bare; to make known; *sententiam suam,* to pronounce; *refl.*, *se aperire and middle aperiri,* to reveal one's true character; to unclose; to excavate; to open up a country.

ăpertē, *adv.*, openly; without concealment.

ăpertus -a -um, *p. adj.*, open, uncovered; *caelum,* clear; *naut.*, *naves,* undecked; *milit.*, undefended; clear, manifest; *apertum est,* it is clear; *in aperto esse,* to be evident; to be practicable; *of speech,* intelligible; frank, open; free, accessible. *Subst.*, ăpertum -i, *n.* an open space.

ăpex -ĭcis, *m.* the top *or* summit; *montis;* conical cap of the Roman flamines; tiara; *so fig.,* crown; a helmet; the long mark over a vowel.

aphractus -i, *f.* a long undecked boat.

Apiacus -a -um, like parsley.

ăpiārius -ii, *m.* a bee-keeper.

ăpĭcātus -a -um, adorned with the priest's cap.

Apidānus -i, *m.* river in Thessaly.

ăpīnae -ārum, *f.* trifles.

1. ăpis -is, *f.* a bee.

2. Āpis -is, *acc.* -im. *m.* a sacred bull of the Egyptians.

ăpiscor, aptus, 3. *dep.* to attain to, reach; to grasp.

ăpĭum -ii, *n.* parsley.

ăplustrĕ -is, *n. generally plur.* aplustria -ium, *n. and* aplustra -ōrum, *n.* the carved stern of a ship, with its ornaments.

ăpŏclēti -ōrum, *m.* the supreme council of the Aetolian League.

ăpŏdўtērium -i, *n.* the dressing-room in a bath.

Āpollo -inis, *m.* Apollo, god of the sun; *ad Apollinis (sc. aedem),* to the temple of Apollo. *Adj.* Āpollĭnāris -e, sacred to Apollo; Āpollĭnĕus, pertaining to Apollo.

Āpollŏdōrus -i, *m.* a rhetorician of Pergamum, teacher of Augustus.

ăpŏlŏgus -i, *m.* a narrative, fable.

ăpŏphŏrēta -ōrum, *n.* presents given to guests.

ăpŏprŏēgmĕna -ōrum, *n. plur. in the philosophy of the Stoics,* that which is to be rejected.

ăpŏthēca -ae, *f.* store-room.

appărātē, *adv.* with much preparation, splendidly.

appărātĭo -ōnis, *f.* preparation.

1. appărātus -ūs, *m. Abstr.* a preparation. *Concr.*, preparation, equipment; pomp; *of a speech,* display.

2. appărātus -a -um, *p. adj.* ready; *of things,* sumptuous.

appārĕo -ŭi -itum, 2. to become visible, to appear; to be visible; *apparet,* it is clear, manifest; to serve, *with dat. consulibus.*

appăro, 3. to get, obtain.

appārĭtĭo -ōnis, *f.* a waiting upon, serving; *plur. apparitores,* servants.

appārĭtor -ōris, *m.* a servant; *esp.* public servant, *e.g.*, lictor.

appăro, 1. to prepare for, provide.

appellātĭo -ōnis, *f.* an addressing; speaking to. *Legal,* appeal; *tribunorum,* to the tribunes. Pronunciation, *litterarum.* Naming (= *nomen*), name, title.

appellātor -ōris, *m.* an appellant.

appellĭto, 1. to be accustomed to name.

1. appello, 1. to address, accost; to ask a person to do something; *legal,* to appeal to, *praetorem ;* to apply to for pay-

ment; to sue; to pronounce, *litteras*; to name; to mention by name.

2. appello -pŭli -pulsum, 3. to drive to, bring to; to direct the mind to, *mentem ad philosophiam. Nautical*, to bring to land; *absol.*, *huc appelle*, put in here.

appendĭcŭla -ae, *f.* (*dim. of appendix*), a little addition.

appendix -ĭcis, *f.* addition, appendix.

appendo -pendi -pensum, 3. to weigh to; *aurum alicui*, pay out.

appĕtens -entis, *p. adj.* desirous of, *gloriae*; avaricious.

appĕtentĕr, *adv.* greedily.

appĕtentia -ae, *f.* desire, longing, *laudis.*

appĕtītio -ōnis, *f.* longing for, desire; *with genit.*, *principatus.*

appĕtītus -ūs, *m.* passion, appetite, *voluptatis.*

appĕto -ĭvi and -ĭi -ĭtum, 3. to reach to; to grasp at, seize on, *solem manibus*; to desire, seek; to make for a place, to arrive at, *Europam*; to attack; to draw near, *of time.*

appingo -pinxi -pictum, 3. to paint to, *or* upon; to write in addition.

Appĭus -ĭi, *m.*, **Appĭa -ae**, *f.* a Roman praenomen. *Adj.*, **Appĭus**, Appian; *via*, the celebrated road from Rome to Capua : *Appii Forum*, *v. forum.*

Appĭānus, belonging to an Appius, Appian.

applaudo -plausi -plausum, 3. *trans.*, to strike upon, to clap. *Intrans.* to applaud.

applĭcātĭo -ōnis, *f.* inclination.

applĭcātus -a -um, *p. adj.* applied to, lying near.

applĭco -āvi -ātum and -ŭi -ĭtum, 1. to add to, to apply to, join to; *milit.*, *corpora corporibus*, to close up the ranks; *passive*, *esp. in partic. perf.*, *with dat.* lying near, situated near; to connect; *se ad and se alicui*, to attach oneself to; to turn towards; to devote oneself to. *Nautical*, to land.

applōro, 1. to lament, deplore.

appōno -pŏsŭi -pŏsĭtum, 3. to place near, to put to; to serve, put on the table; to appoint; to procure, suborn; add to, *annos alicui*; *lucro*, reckon as a gain.

apporrectus -a -um, extended near.

apporto, 1. to carry, bring to.

apposco, 3. to ask in addition.

appŏsĭtē, *adv.* appropriately, appositely.

appŏsĭtus -a -um, *p. adj.* placed near; situated, *or* lying near; fit, appropriate.

apprĕcor, 1. *dep.* to worship, pray to.

apprĕhendo -prĕhendi -prĕhensum, 3. *and poet.* **apprendo -prendi -prensum**, 3. to seize, lay hold of; to take possession of; to bring forward, allege.

apprīmē, *adv.*, above all, exceedingly.

apprīmo -pressi -pressum, 3. to press to.

apprŏbātĭo -ōnis, *f.* approbation, assent; proof.

apprŏbātor -ōris, *m.* one who approves.

apprŏbo, 1. to approve of, assent to; to prove.

apprōmitto -mĭsi -missum, 3. to promise in addition, *i.e.* to promise also in one's own name.

apprŏpĕro -āvi -ātum, -āre, to hasten, *opus.*

apprŏpinquātĭo -ōnis, *f.* approach.

apprŏpinquo, 1. to approach, *ad summam aquam*; *with dat. ianuae.*

appugno, 1. to storm, assault.

Appūlĭa, Ăpūlĭa -ae, *f.* a country in the south of Italy. *Adj.*, **Appūlĭcus -a -um**, *mare*, the Adriatic Sea; **Appūlus -a -um**, Apulian.

appulsus -ūs, *m.* a driving towards; an approach; landing.

āprĭcātĭo -ōnis, *f.* basking in the sun.

āprĭcor, 1. *dep.* to sun oneself.

āprĭcus -a -um, *adj.*, sunny; *in apricum proferre*, to bring to light; loving the sun, *flores.*

Aprīlis -e, *Aprilis mensis*, the month of April.

aptātus -a -um, fitted, appropriate.

aptē, *adv.*, fitly, appropriately.

apto, 1. to adapt to, adjust, *corpori arma*; to prepare; to make appropriate.

aptus -a -um, 1. *partic.*, fastened to; depending upon, *fortuna*; connected, allied, *omnia inter se apta*; equipped, *omnia ad bellum apta*; adorned with. *Adj.*, suitable; *with ad and the acc.*; *with dat.*

ăpŭd, *prep.*, *with acc.*, at, near, by, with; *apud aliquem sedere*, near; *apud me*, at my house; *apud se esse (fig.)*, to be in possession of one's faculties; in the presence of, *apud iudices*; *of an author*, in the works of; in the neighbourhood of, *apud Alyxiam*; at, in, *apud villam.*

Ăpŭlēĭus (Appul.) *Saturninus*, a celebrated tribune.

Ăpūlĭa, *v. Apulia.*

ăqua -ae, *f.* water; *aquam praebere*, to entertain; *aqua et ignis*, the necessaries of life; *aqua et igni interdicere alicui*, to banish; *aquam terramque poscere ab aliquo*, to demand submission from the enemy; the sea; a lake; river; rain; water in the water-clock; hence, *aquam dare*, to give time; *plur.*, *aquae*, springs, tears.

ăquaeductus -ūs, *m.* an aqueduct.

ăquālĭcŭlus -i, *m.* (*dim. of aqualis*), a small water-vessel.

ăquārĭus -a -um, belonging to water. *Subst.*, **ăquārĭus -ii**, *m.* water-carrier.

ăquātĭcus -a -um, aquatic; full of water, watery; *auster*, bringing rain.

ăquātĭlis -e, living in the water.

ăquātĭo -ōnis, *f.* a fetching of water; place whence water may be fetched.

äquätŏr -ōris, *m.* person that fetches water.

äquila -ae, *f.* eagle; eagle as the standard.

aquilifer -fĕri, *m.* standard-bearer.

äquilo -ōnis, *m.* the north wind; the north

äquilŏnālis -e, northern.

äquilŏnius -a -um, northern; belonging to Aquilo.

äquilus -a -um, dark-coloured, blackish.

Äquitāni -ōrum, *m.* inhabitants of Aquitania; Äquitānia -ae, *f.* south-west part of Gaul.

äquor, 1. *dep.* to fetch water.

äquŏsus -a -um, *adj.* full of water, watery, *Orion*; *Eurus*, rain-bringing.

äquŭla -ae, *f.* (*dim. of aqua*), a little water, a small stream.

āra -ae, *f.* an elevation of earth, stone, *&c.; ara sepulcri*, funeral pyre; an altar; a refuge; a constellation; *plur.*, *arae*, rocks.

Ärabes -um, *m.* the Arabs; Ärabs -ābis, Arabian; Ärābia -ae, *f.* the country of Arabia. *Adj.* Ärābicus. Ärābius, Ärābus.

Ärachnē -ēs, *f.* a Lydian maiden turned into a spider.

ärānĕa -ae, *f.* spider; spider's web.

ärānĕŏla -ae, *f.* (*dim.*) a little spider.

ärānĕŏlus -i, *m.* (*dim.*) a little spider.

ärānĕōsus -a -um, full of cobwebs; like a cobweb.

1. ärānĕus -i, *m.* a spider.

2. ärānĕus -a -um, relating to a spider. *Subst.*, ärānĕum -i, *n.* a cobweb.

Ärar *and* Ärăris -is, *m.* a river in Gaul.

ärātio -ōnis, *f.* ploughing, agriculture, a ploughed field.

ärātŏr -ōris, *m.* ploughman, husbandman.

ärātrum -i, *n.* plough.

Araxes -is, *m.* a river in Armenia.

arbĭtĕr -tri, *m.* a witness, spectator, hearer. *Legal*, umpire; judge; ruler.

arbĭtra -ae, *f.* a female witness.

arbĭtrātus -ūs, *m.* approval, choice, wish. arbĭtrĭum -i, *n.* the umpire's decision; judgment, choice; *arbitria funeris*, expenses of a funeral; mastery, authority.

arbĭtror, 1. *dep.* to hear, perceive; to express an opinion; to be of opinion.

arbŏr (arbos) -ŏris, *f.* a tree; *fici*, a fig tree; *infelix*, the gallows; *poet.*, *arbor*, an oar; *Pelias arbor*, the ship Argo.

arbŏrĕus -a -um, relating to trees; *cornua*, branching.

arbustum -i, *n.* plantation, vineyard planted with trees.

arbustus -a -um, full of trees.

arbŭtĕus -a -um, relating to the arbutus.

arbŭtum -i, *n.* the wild strawberry tree *or* arbutus; the fruit.

arbŭtus -i, *f.* wild strawberry *or* arbutus tree.

arca -ae, *f.* a chest, box; coffin; money coffer; a cell.

Arcādia -ae, *f.* a country of the Peloponnesus. *Adj.*, Arcădius; Arcădicus -a -um; *deus.* Pan; *juvenis*, a simpleton; Arcăs Adis. *Subst.*, Arcăs -ādis, Mercury; Arcădes -um, *m.* the Arcadians.

arcānŏ, *adv.*, secretly.

arcānus -a -um, silent; secret. *Subst.*, arcānum -i, *n.* a secret.

Arcăs -ādis, *m.* son of Jupiter and Callisto.

arcĕo -cŭi, 2. to shut in, shut up; to prohibit access to, to hinder, prevent; to protect from.

arcessītus, *abl.* -ū, *m.* calling for, summons.

arcesso (accerso) -īvi -ītum, 3. to summon; *of a thought*, to derive; *arcessitus*, strained, far-fetched.

archĕtypus -a -um, original.

Archiās -ae, *m. Aulus Licinius*, a Greek poet, defended by Cicero.

Archilŏchus -i, *m.* Greek satiric poet.

archimägīrus -i, *m.* head cook.

Archimēdēs -is, *m.* celebrated philosopher, killed on the capture of Syracuse by Marcellus.

archimimus -i, *m.* chief mime *or* buffoon.

archipirāta -ae, *m.* chief pirate.

architectōn -ōnis, *m.* master-builder.

architector, 1. *dep.* to build; to devise, provide.

architectūra -ae, *f.* architecture.

architectus -i, *m.* an architect, masterbuilder; an inventor, maker.

archōn -ontis, *m.* an archon, one of the chief magistrates of Athens.

arcitĕnens -entis, holding the bow, epithet of Apollo and Diana.

arct . . . = *art* . . . *q.v.*

Arctŏs -i, *f.* the great and little bear; north pole.

Arctōus -a -um, belonging to the north pole, northern.

ärctūrus -i, *m.* the brightest star of the constellation Boötes.

arcŭātus -a -um, bent like a bow, curved.

arcŭla -ae, *f.* (*dim. of arca*), a casket; rhetorical ornament.

arcŭo, 1. to bend *or* shape like a bow.

arcŭs -ūs, *m.* a bow; the rainbow; an arch, vault.

ardĕa -ae, *f.* a heron.

ardēlio -ōnis, *m.* a busybody.

ardens -entis, *p. adj.*, hot, glowing; glittering; *of wine*, fiery; eager; *ardentes equi*, spirited.

ardentĕr, *adv.* hotly, violently.

ardĕo, arsi, arsum, 2. to burn, glow, be on fire; *of the body*, be in pain; *ardere in proelia*, eagerly to desire fight; *in poets*, to burn with love; *of wars, &c.*, to burst out.

ardesco, arsi, 3. to take fire, kindle; to glitter; to become inflamed.

ardor -ōris, *m.* flame, heat; *the glow of the eyes,* gleam; ardour, fierceness; *pugnandi,* for fighting; the passion of love.

ardŭus -a -um, *adj.* steep. *Subst.,* **ardŭum -i,** *n.* a steep place. *Poet.,* lofty; difficult to undertake *or* reach. *Subst.,* **ardŭum -i,** *n.* what is difficult to accomplish.

ārĕa -ae, *f.* a high open space, surface; site for a house ; courtyard ; threshing-floor; the part of the circus where the games were held; sphere, scope.

ārĕfácĭo -feci -factum, 3. to make dry.

Ārēmŏrĭcus -a -um, lying on the sea; *civitates,* Gallic states on the coast of the English Channel.

ārēna -ae, *f.* sand; a sandy place ; the sea-shore; arena; the scene of any struggle.

ārēnārĭus -a -um, relating to sand, sandy. *Subst.,* **ārēnārĭa -ae,** *f.* sand pit.

ārēnōsus -a -um, sandy.

ārens, -entis, *p. adj.* dry ; dry with thirst.

ārĕo, 2. to be dry.

ārĕŏla -ae, *f. (dim. of area),* a little open space.

Ārĕŏpăgus -i, *m.* Mars' hill at Athens, upon which the court called Areopagus held its meetings; **Ārĕŏpăgītēs -ae,** *m.* a member of the court of Areopagus.

Ārēs -is, *m.* the Greek god of war.

āresco, 3. to become dry.

ārĕtălŏgus -i, *m.* a babbler about virtue.

Ārĕthūsa -ae, *f.* a fountain in the island of Ortygia; a Nereid beloved by the river Alpheus, who dived under the sea in pursuit of her. *Adj.,* **Ārĕthūsis -ĭdis;** **Ārĕthūsĭus -a -um.**

Ārĕus -a -um, relating to Mars.

Argēi -ōrum, *m.* chapels of local deities in Rome; figures of men, thrown ino the Tiber every year on the Ides of May.

argentārĭus -a -um, relating to silver; relating to money; *taberna,* a banker's stall. *Subst.,* **argentārĭus -ii,** *m.* a money-changer, banker ; **argentārĭa -ae,** *f.* a banker's office; a banker's trade; a silver mine.

argentātus -a -um, ornamented with silver; *milites,* with silvered shields; provided with money.

argentĕus -a -um, made of silver; ornamented with silver; of the colour of silver; belonging to the Silver Age.

argentum -i, *n.* silver ; *signatum,* stamped with a pattern; silver plate, silver coin, money.

Argĭlētum -i, *n.* a part of Rome where were many booksellers' shops. *Adj.,* **Argĭlētānus -a -um.**

argilla, ae, *f.* potter's clay.

Arginussae (Arginūsae) -ārum, *f.* islands on the coast of Aeolis.

Argō -ūs, *f.* the ship Argo.

Argŏnautae -ārum, *m.* the Argonauts.

Argŏs, *n.* and **Argi -ōrum,** *m.* capital of Argolis. *Adj.,* **Argēus -a -um;** **Argīvus,** Argive ; *subst.,* **Argīvi -orum,** *and poet.* **-um,** *m.* the Argives.

Argŏlis -ĭdis, 1. *Adj.* 2. *Subst.,* the district Argolis; *adj.,* **Argŏlĭcus.**

argūmentātĭo -ōnis, *f.* the bringing forward of a proof.

argūmentor, 1. *dep.* to bring forward a proof. *Transit.* to allege as a proof.

argūmentum -i, *n.* an argument, proof; subject, contents; a drama.

argŭo -ŭi -ūtum, 3. to put in clear light; to maintain, prove; to betray; to charge, convict; to censure, complain of.

Argus -i, *m.* the hundred-eyed guardian of Io.

argūtātĭo -ōnis, *f.* a rustling.

argūtē, *adv.* sagaciously, acutely.

argūtĭae -ārum, *f.* liveliness, animation; cleverness, subtlety; cunning.

argūtŭlus -a -um, somewhat acute.

argūtus -a -um, *p. adj.* expressive, lively, *oculi;* piercing; *forum,* noisy; *poeta,* melodious ; significant *(of omens);* sagacious; cunning.

argȳraspides -pidum, *m.* a picked corps in the Macedonian army, the wearers of the silver shield.

Ărĭadna -ae, *or* **Ărĭadnē -ēs,** *f.* daughter of Minos.

ărĭdŭlus -a -um *(dim. of aridus),* somewhat dry.

ărĭdus -a -um, *adj.* dry, arid; shrivelled. *Poet.,* *sonus,* a dry, crackling sound; *of living,* meagre; intellectually dry; avaricious. *Subst.,* **arĭdum -i,** *n.* dry ground.

ărĭes -ĭĕtis, *m.* a ram; a battering ram; a prop, beam.

ărĭĕtātĭo -ōnis, *f.* a butting like a ram.

ărĭĕto, 1. to butt like a ram.

Ărĭōn *or* **Ărĭo -ōnis,** *m.* a harp-player, saved from drowning by a dolphin.

ărista -ae, *f.* the point of an ear of corn; the ear itself.

Aristaeus -i, *m.* son of Apollo and Cyrene, legendary introducer of bee-keeping.

Ăristĭdēs -is, *m.* celebrated Athenian statesman.

Ăristŏphănēs -is, *m.* the great Athenian comic dramatist.

Ăristŏtĕlēs -is *and* **-i,** *m.* the celebrated Greek philosopher.

ărithmĕtĭca -ae *and* **-ē -ēs,** *f.* arithmetic.

ărithmĕtĭca -ōrum, *n.* arithmetic.

arma -ōrum, *n.* tools, implements; *arma equestria,* fittings of a horse; building tools ; implements of war ; defensive armour.

armāmenta -ōrum, *n.* implements, tackle; *esp. of a ship.*

armāmentārium -i, *n.* an armoury.

armārium -i, *n.* a cupboard, chest.

armātūra -ae, *f.* equipment, armour; *armatura levis,* light-armed troops.

1. armātus, *all. ... ...* armed troops.

2. armātus -a -um, *p. adj;.* armed, equipped.

armentālis -e, belonging to a herd.

armentum -i, *n.* cattle living in herds; *Esp. sing. collective,* a herd; *plur.,* oxen.

armifēr -fēra -fērum, bearing arms, warlike.

armigēr -gēra -gērum, bearing arms. *Subst.,* armiger -geri, *m.* an armourbearer.

armilla -ae, . a bracelet.

armillātus -a -um, adorned with a bracelet; *canes,* wearing a collar.

armilustrium -ii, *n.* a festival at which arms were consecrated.

armipōtens -entis, warlike.

armisōnus -a -um, resounding with arms.

urmo, 1. to equip, *naves;* to arm, prepare for battle; to supply arms.

armus -i, *m.* the shoulder-blade; *in animals,* the shoulder; the side of an animal.

Arnus -i, *m* the chief river of Etruria, now the Arno. *Adj.,* Arniensis -e.

āro, 1. to plough; to farm, cultivate; to furrow, wrinkle; *of ships,* to plough the sea.

Arpi -ōrum, *m.* town in Apulia. *Adj.,* Arpīnus.

Arpīnum -i, *n.* a town in Latium. *Adj.,* Arpīnās -ātis, Arpīnus,

arquatus = *arcuatus.*

arra = *arrha.*

arrectus -a -um, *p. ad.* steep.

arrēpo -repsi -reptum, 3. to creep to, to glide gently to.

Arrētium -ii, *n.* a town in Etruria, birthplace of Maecenas.

arrha -ae, *f.,* and arrhabo -ōnis. *m.* earnest money.

arrīdeo -risi -risum, 2. to laugh to; to laugh with; to laugh at; *with dat. of pers., acc. of the thing;* to be favourable; to please.

arrigo -rexi -rectum, 3. to erect; to excite; to encourage.

arripio -ripūi -reptum, 3. to seize on, snatch; *terram velis,* to sail quickly to; appropriate, take ; to comprehend quickly; *litteras Graecas; legal,* to drag before a tribunal, accuse; to satirize.

arrīsor -ōris, *m.* a flatterer.

arrōdo -rōsi -rōsum, 3. to gnaw at.

arrŏgans -antis, *p. adj.* arrogant, haughty.

arrŏgantĕr, *adv.* arrogantly, haughtily.

arrŏgantia -ae, *f.* arrogance, haughtiness.

arrŏgo, 1. *sibi aliquid,* to appropriate to oneself; to claim; to ask; to associate one person with another.

arrōsor -ōris, *m.* one who gnaws at.

Arruns (Arūns) -untis, *m.* a younger son of Tarquinius Superbus.

ars -tis. *f.* a trade, profession, art; *urbanae, jurisprudence* and *rhetoric;* art, knowledge, theory; *ex arte (dicere, scribere, &c.),* according to the rules of art; skill, cleverness, *arte laboratae vestes; plur., artes,* works of art; conduct, character; *bonae artes,* good qualities; cunning, deceit.

Artaxerxēs -is, *m.* name of three Persian kings.

artē (arctē), *adv.* narrowly, tightly, closely; fast, soundly, *dormire;* shortly; *aliquem arte colere,* stingily.

artēria -ae, *f.* the windpipe; *neut. plur., heterocl. arteria,* an artery.

arthrīticus -a -um, gouty.

articulāris -e, relating to the joints; *morbus,* gout.

articŭlātim, *adv.* limb by limb, piecemeal; properly divided, distinctly.

articŭlo, 1. to articulate, speak distinctly.

articŭlus -i, *m. (dim. of artus),* a joint; *plur.,* the limbs, *esp.,* the fingers; division of a discourse; a moment, crisis.

artifex -ficis, artist, sculptor; *artifices scenici,* actors; *artifex equus,* a trained horse; the maker, author; skilled; *passive,* skilfully wrought.

artificiōsē, *adv.* skilfully.

artificiōsus -a -um, skilful, accomplished; artificial.

artificium -i, *n.* occupation, handicraft; theory; cleverness; craft; work of art.

arto (arcto), 1. to press together to abridge.

artolăgănus -i, *m.* a cake made of meal, wine, milk, oil, lard, and pepper.

artopta -ae, *m.* baker; baker's vessel.

1. artus (arctus) -a -um, *adj.* narrow, tight, close *(subst.,* artum -i, *n.,* narrow space); fast, sound, *somnus:* oppressed by care, *animus;* meagre; difficult.

2. artus -ūs, *m. usually plur., artūs -ūum,* the joints; *dolor artuum,* gout; *poet.,* limbs.

ārula -ae, *f. (dim. of ara),* a little altar.

ărundifer -fēra -fērum, reed-bearing.

ărundinēus -a -um, reedy; *carmen,* a shepherd's song.

ărundinōsus -a -um, full of reeds.

ărundo -inis, *f.* a reed; fishing-rod; a pen: the shaft of an arrow; *poet.,* the arrow itself; a weaver's comb; a scarecrow; plaything for children.

Arverni -ōrum *m.* a Gallic people in Aquitaine.

arvīna -ae, *f.* fat, lard.

arvum -i, *n.* ploughed *or* sown field; region.

arvus -a -um, ploughed.

arx -cis, *f.* fortress, citadel; the height of heaven; temples of the gods; refuge, protection; head-quarters.

as, assis, *m.* the whole as unity, *divided into twelve unciae; haeres ex asse,* sole heir; *as a coin,* the as, *worth a little over a farthing; as a weight,* a pound.

Ascānius -ii, *m.* son of Aeneas.

ascaules -is, *m.* bagpiper.

ascendo -scendi -scensum, 3. to mount, ascend, go up.

ascensio -ōnis, *f.* an ascent; *oratorum,* lofty flight.

ascensus -ūs, *m.* a going up, ascent; the place for ascending.

ascia -ae, *f.* a carpenter's axe *or* adze.

ascio, 4. to adopt as one's own.

ascisco, ascīvi, ascītum. 3. to receive, admit; to adopt; to approve of.

1. ascītus -a -um, foreign.

2. ascītus -us, *m.* an acceptance, reception.

ascōpēra -ae, *f.* leather knapsack.

ascrībo -scripsi -scriptum, 3. to write in addition; to appoint; to enrol; to include; *with ad or in and the acc., or with the dat.;* 1. to attribute.

ascriptīcius -a -um, one who is enrolled as a member of a community.

ascriptio -ōnis, *f.* an addition in writing.

ascriptor -ōris, *m.* one who approves of.

asella -ae, *f.* (*dim. of asina*), a little she-ass.

asellus -i, *m.* (*dim. asinus*), a little ass.

Asia -ae, *f.* 1. district in Lydia. 2. The continent of Asia. 3. The peninsula of Asia Minor; the Roman province of Asia. *Adj.,* **Asiānus,** *Plur. subst.,* **Asiani** -*orum. m.* the farmers of the taxes of the province of Asia; **Asiāticus** -a -um, surname of L. Corn. Scipio; **Asis** -ĭdis, *f.* Asiatic.

asīlus -i, *m.* the gad-fly.

asina -ae, *f.* a she-ass.

asinus -i, *m.* an ass; a dolt, blockhead.

Asōpis -i, *m.* a river in Boeotia; the river-god Asopus; **Asōpĭădēs** -ae. *m.* a descendant of Asopus.

asōtus -i, *m.* a libertine.

aspărăgus -i, *m.* asparagus.

aspargo, *v. aspergo.*

Aspāsia -ae, *f.* mistress of Pericles.

aspectābilis -e, visible.

aspecto, 1. to look at earnestly, *or* with respect; *of place,* to lie towards, to face; to attend to.

aspectus -ūs, *m.* looking, sight; view; power of vision; sight, power of being seen; aspect.

aspello -puli -pulsum, 3. to drive away.

asper -ĕra -ĕrum (-pra -prum), rough; *loca,* uneven; stormy. *Subst.,* **aspĕrum** -i, *n.* a rough place; pungent, sour; harsh, grating; *litera aspera* the letter R; *morally,* rough, wild, harsh; *of animals,* fierce; *of events,* adverse; *sententia,* severe; *of speech,* harsh, bitter.

aspērē, *adv.* roughly.

1. aspergo (**aspargo**) -spersi -spersum, 3. to sprinkle; to mingle with; to bespatter; to sully, stain; to strew over.

2. aspergo (**aspargo**) -ĭnis, *f.* a sprinkling, spray.

asperitas -ātis, *f.* roughness; unevenness; sourness; harshness; fierceness, severity; calamity, difficulty.

aspernātio -ōnis, *f.* contempt.

aspernor, 1. *dep.* to despise, spurn.

aspēro, 1. to make rough; to sharpen; to excite, arouse.

aspersio -ōnis, *f.* a sprinkling.

aspicio -spexi -spectum, 3. to look at, behold, see; endure the light of day, live; *of places,* to face; to survey; to withstand, confront; to consider; to investigate; to perceive.

aspīrātio -ōnis, *f.* a breathing; exhalation; the pronunciation of the letter H, aspiration.

aspīro, 1. *Intransit.,* to breathe *or* blow upon; to assist; to approach; to climb up to; to reach to; to attain. *Transit.,* to breathe upon, blow on; to infuse.

aspis -idis, *f.* an adder, asp.

asportātio -ōnis, *f.* a carrying off.

asporto, 1. to carry off.

asprētum -i, *n.* a rough, uneven spot.

assecla (**assēcula**) -ae, *m.* follower, sycophant.

assectātio -ōnis, . respectful attendance, *e.g. of client on patron.*

assectātor -ōris, *m.* companion, follower; disciple.

assector, 1. *dep.,* to follow, attend assiduously.

assensio -ōnis, assent, applause.

assensor -ōris, *m.* one who assents *or* agrees.

assensus -ūs, *m.* assent, agreement. *Poet.,* echo.

assentātio -ōnis, *f.* a flattering assent *or* applause.

assentātiuncŭla -ae, *f.* (*dim. of assentatio*), trivial flattery.

assentātor -ōris, *m.* flatterer.

assentātōriē, *adv.* flatteringly.

assentio -sensi -sensum, 4. *and gen.* **assentior** -sensus sum, -sentīri. to assent to, agree with.

assentor, 1. *dep.* to assent constantly, to flatter.

assĕquor -cūtus sum, 3. *dep.,* to follow; come up to, attain; to gain; to comprehend.

asser -ĕris, *m.* stake, pole.

assercŭlum -i, *n.,* or **-us -i,** *m.* small stake *or* pole.

1. **assĕro -sĕvi -situm,** 3. to plant at *or* near.

2. **assĕro -sĕrŭi -sertum,** 3. to join to. *Legal,* to lay hold of a slave, *and thereby declare* him *free, aliquem in liberta-tem;* to claim as a slave, *aliquem in servitutem;* to set free from, protect; to claim.

assertio -ōnis, *f.* formal declaration as to freedom.

assertor -ōris, *m.* one who asserts that another person is free *or* a slave; libera-tor.

asservio, 4. to assist, help; *with dat.*

asservo, 1. to preserve, to watch, observe; *fig.,* to attend to.

assessio -ōnis, *f.* a sitting by the side of one (*to console*).

assessor -ōris, *m.* one who sits by the side to assist; an assistant, a judicial assessor.

assessus, *abl.* **-ū,** *m.* a sitting by the side of.

assĕvĕrantĕr, *adv.* earnestly, emphatic-ally.

assĕvĕrātio -ōnis, *f.* earnestness in action; asseveration.

assĕvēro, 1. to act with earnestness; to assert confidently.

assideo -sēdi -sessum, 2. *with dat.,* to sit near, *or* by the side of; to be next door to; to give comfort, advice, pro-tection, *&c.; iudiciis assidebat,* fre-quented. *Milit.,* to besiege.

assīdo -sēdi -sessum, 3. to sit down; to break down in a speech; *subito assedit.*

assĭdŭē, *adv.* continuously.

assĭdŭĭtas -ātis, *f.* attention of friends, clients; constancy; constant repetition.

assĭdŭo = *assidue, q.v.*

assĭdŭus -a -um, established. *Political,* **assiduus -i,** *m.* a settled *and* hence a well-to-do, taxpaying citizen; continu-ously in one place; engaged in one occupation; constant, steady; unceas-ing.

assignātio -ōnis, *f.* assignment.

assigno, 1. to assign to any one, allot; to seal.

assĭlio -silŭi, 4. to leap to, *or* on; *of water,* to dash up; to jump to.

assimilis -e, like, similar; *with dat. or gen.*

assimŭlātus -a -um, similar; pretended, simulated.

assimŭlo, 1. to make like; to compare; to imitate, pretend.

assisto, astĭti, *no sup.,* 3. to take up a position, *ad fores;* to stand by, *foribus principum;* to help.

assŏlĕo, 2. to be accustomed; *used only in the third person sing. and plur.,*

deinde quae assolent (*scribi*); *ut assolet,* as is usual.

assŏno, 1. to answer with a sound.

assuĕfăcio -fēci -factum, 3. to accustom to.

assuesco -suēvi -suētum, 3. to accus-tom; to accustom oneself; *assuevi,* I am wont; accustomed, accustomed.

assuētūdo -ĭnis, *f.* custom, use.

assuētus -a -um, *adj.* accustomed to; usual.

assŭgo -suctum, 3. to suck.

assŭla -ae, *f.* a shaving, chip.

assulto, 1. to leap violently upon; to attack.

assultus -ūs, *m.* assault.

assum (adsum), affŭi (adfŭi), adesse, to be present, to be at; *huc ades,* come here; *adesse animo* or *animis,* to attend; *also,* to be of good courage; to be at hand; to be in one's place; *rebus Romanis,* to be favourable to; to be present to witness, *or* to share in; to be present to help; to defend in the law-courts.

assūmo -sumpsi -sumptum, 3. to take to oneself; to take for one's assistance; *assumpta verba,* words borrowed from another source; to take; to claim.

assumptio -ōnis, *f.* choice, adoption.

assumptīvus -a -um, which derives a de-fence from an extraneous cause.

assŭo, 3. to sew on.

assurgo -surrexi -surrectum, 3. to rise, stand up, *assurgere alicui* (*as a sign of respect*); to appear, show itself.

assus -a -um, dried; roasted; *balnearis assa,* a sweating bath; *nutrix,* a dry-nurse.

ast = *at, q.v.*

asterno, 3. to scatter upon; to be stretched out.

astĭpŭlātor -ōris, *m.* supporter.

astĭpŭlor, 1. *dep.* to assent to.

asto -stĭti, *no sup.,* 1. to stand by, *alicui;* to assist; to stand upright.

astrĕpo -strĕpŭi -strĕpĭtum, 3. to make a noise at; to applaud.

astrictē, *adv.* concisely, briefly.

astrictus -a -um, *p. adj.,* tight, com-pressed; *limen,* shut; *frons,* wrinkled; *aquae,* frozen; *fig.* avaricious; concise.

astrĭfer -fĕra -fĕrum, starry, placed among the stars.

astringo -strinxi -strictum, 3. to tighten, compress, bind together; *of cold,* to contract; to bind, oblige; *se astringere,* to commit oneself to, to assume an obligation.

astrŏlŏgĭa -ae, *f.* astronomy.

astrŏlŏgus -i, *m.* astronomer; astrologer.

astrum -i, *n.* star, constellation.

astrŭo -struxi -structum, 3. to build near; to add to.

astu, *only acc. and abl.* **astū,** *n.* the city (*only of Athens*).

astŭpĕo, 2. to be astonished at.

asturco -ōnis, *m.* an Asturian horse.

astus -ūs, m. cleverness, cunning.
astūtē, adv. cunningly, astutely.
astūtia -ae, f. adroitness, craft.
astūtus -a -um, adroit, clever, crafty.
Astyănax -actis, m. 1. son of Hector and Andromache. 2. A tragic actor of Cicero's time.
ăsȳlum -i, n. sanctuary, place of refuge.
ăsymbŏlus -a -um, one who contributes nothing to the cost of an entertainment.
at (ast), conj., but, moreover; but at least.
ătābŭlus -i, m. the sirocco.
Ătălanta -ae and -ē -ēs, f. a maiden, famous for her speed in running. Adj., Ătălantaeus.
ătăt, attat, attatae, attattatae, etc., oh! ah! alas!
ătăvus -i, m. great-great-grandfather; atavi, plur. = ancestors.
Ătella -ae, f. city of Campania. Adj., Ătellānus; fabella, or simply Ătellāna -ae, f. a species of popular farce; Ătellānus -i, m. a player in these dramas. Adj., Ătellānius; Ătellānicus.
āter, atra, atrum, black, dark; mare, stormy; poet. = atratus, clothed in black; gloomy, sad; atri dies, in the Roman calendar, those on which the republic had suffered a great misfortune; malicious.
Ăthămās -antis, m. father of Phrixus and Helle. Adj., Ăthămanthēus.
Ăthēnae -ārum, f. Athens. Adj., Ăthēnaeus.
Ăthēniensis -e. Subst., Ăthēnienses -ium, m. the Athenians.
ăthěos and ăthěus -i, m. an atheist.
athlēta -ae, m. wrestler, athlete.
athlēticus -a -um, relating to an athlete.
Ăthōs, dat. -o, acc. -o, and -on, abl. -o, and Ăthō or Ăthōn -ōnis, m. mountain in the peninsula of Chalcidice.
Atlās -antis, m. mountain in Africa; Atlantis -idis, f. a female descendant of Atlas, or plur., Atlantides, the Pleiades and Hyades; Atlanticus mare, the Atlantic ocean; Atlantēus (finis), Libyan; Atlantiădēs -ae, m. descendant of Atlas.
ătŏmus -i, f. an atom.
atque, or ac (ac only before consonants), and, and also; and moreover, and even; so atque etiam; simul atque, as soon as.
atqui, conj. nevertheless, notwithstanding; indeed, certainly; but now, now.
ătrāmentum -i, n. any black fluid; blue vitriol, shoemaker's black.
ătrātus -a -um, clothed in black, in mourning.
Ătrĕbătes -um, m. people in Gallia Belgica.
Atreus -ĕi, m. father of Agamemnon.
ātriensis -is, m. a head slave, steward.
ātrĭŏlum -i, n. (dim. of atrium), a little atrium, or fore-court.

ātrium -ii, n. the open court in a Roman house; the hall of a temple or public building.
ătrōcitas -ātis, f. cruelty; severity, barbarity.
ătrōcitĕr, adv. severely, cruelly.
Atrŏpŏs -i, f. one of the three Parcae.
ătrox -ōcis, terrible, cruel; violent; of persons, gloomy, morose; unbending.
attactus -ūs, m. touch, contact.
attăgēn -ēnis, m. a woodcock.
Attălus -i, m. the name of several kings of Pergamos.
attāmĕn, conj., but yet.
attat = atat.
attēgia -ae, f. a hut.
attempĕrātē, adv. in a fit manner.
attempĕro, 1. to fit to, adjust to.
attendo -tendi -tentum, 3. to stretch to; attend to.
attentē, adv. attentively, carefully.
attentio -ōnis, f. attention.
attento, or attempto, 1. to strive after, to attempt; to tamper with; to attack.
attentus -a -um, adj., attentive; attentus quaesitis.
attĕnŭātē, adv. simply, without ornament.
attĕnŭātus -a -um, p. adj. made weak; of discourse, abbreviated; over-refined.
attĕnŭo, 1. to make thin; to weaken; of the voice, to make shrill; insignem, degrade.
attĕro -trīvi (-tĕrŭi) -trītum, 3. to rub against; to wear away; to weaken, ruin.
attestor, 1. dep. to bear witness to.
attexo -texŭi -textum, 3. to weave or plait on or to; to add.
Attica -ae, f. Attica, the most celebrated country of Greece, with Athens for its capital.
Atticē, adv. in the Attic or Athenian manner.
Atticus -a -um, belonging to Attica, Athenian.
Atticus, T. Pomponius, the intimate friend of Cicero.
attineo -tinŭi -tentum, 2. Transit., to hold near, keep. Intransit., to pertain to, or concern, only in 3rd person; quod ad me attinet, as far as I am concerned.
attingo -tigi -tactum, 3. to touch; to arrive at a place, Italiam; to border upon; to attack; to appropriate to oneself; to strike; to embrace; to have to do with; to reach to; attingere aliquem necessitudine, to be closely connected with; to handle, manage; to glance at cursorily; to mention.
Attis (Atthis and Atys) -idis, m. a Phrygian shepherd, beloved by Cybele.
attollo, no perf. or sup., 3. to lift up; se attollere, or attolli, to raise oneself, to erect; to elevate, excite, distinguish.
attondĕo -tondi -tonsum, 2. to shear, shave, cut; to diminish.

attonitus -a -um, *p. adj.*, struck by thunder; stunned, terrified; inspired.

attono -tonui -tonitum, 1. to strike with thunder, stun.

attorqueo, 2. to whirl.

attractio -onis, *f.* a drawing to oneself; *litterarum*, assimilation.

attraho -traxi -tractum, 3. to draw to, attract; to drag; to take with one.

attrectatus -us, *m.* a handling, touching.

attrecto, 1. to touch, handle; to touch unlawfully; to lay hands on, to appropriate.

attribuo -ui -utum, 3. to allot to; lend; to assign; to annex; to add, give, cause; *gramm.* to add as an attribute; to ascribe, impute.

attributio -onis, *f.* the assignment of a debt; *rhet.*, an attribute.

attributum -i, *n.* the predicate.

attritus -a -um, *p. adj.*, rubbed away, worn out; *frons*, shameless.

au, *interj.*, oh! ha!

auceps -cupis, *m.* a bird-catcher; *syllabarum*, a quibbling critic.

auctio -onis, *f.* an auction; that which is sold by auction; *auctionem facere, constituere*, to appoint an auction.

auctionarius -a -um, belonging to an auction; *atrium*, auction-room.

auctionor, 1. *dep.* to hold an auction.

auctito, 1. to increase very much.

aucto, 1. = *auctito*.

auctor -oris, *m.* originator, causer, doer; producer, artist; *templi*, architect; the founder of a family, ancestor; author; leader, beginner; *me auctore*, at my request; *alicui auctor esse*, to advise; the author of information; an authority; *auctor rerum Romanarum*, historian; *auctor esse*, to answer for; *auctor legis or senatus consulti*, proposer; supporter of a law; defender, protector; *of a guardian, etc.*, sanctioner.

auctoramentum -i, *n.* the pay or hire for the performance of any duty.

auctoritas -atis, *f.* validity; valid right to property arising from prescription; security, authority; example; *malorum*, the origination of a proposal or proceeding, support, aid; expression of approval or assent, resolve; the approval of the senate; authorisation, full power; might, command; influence, authority; a person in authority.

auctoro, 1. to hire for money; *refl. auctorare se*, or *pass.* to engage oneself; to bind oneself.

auctumnalis -e, autumnal.

1. **auctumnus** -i, *m.* autumn.

2. **auctumnus** -a -um, autumnal.

1. **auctus** -a -um, *p. adj.*, *only in compar.*, increased, enriched.

2. **auctus** -us, *m.* increase, growth.

aucupium -i, *n.* bird-catching; the birds caught; hunting after anything; *aucupia verborum*, cavilling, quibbling.

aucupor, 1. *dep.* to catch birds; to chase, lie in wait for; *tempestates*, to wait for finer weather.

audacia -ae, *f.* courage, daring; audacity; *boldness*, audacious deeds.

audaciter, *and* **audacter**, *adv.* boldly; rashly, impudently.

audax -acis, *adj.*, daring, bold, courageous, rash.

audens -entis, *p. adj.*, daring, bold.

audenter, *adv.* boldly.

audentia -ae, *f.* boldness, courage.

audeo, *ausus sum*, 2. to dare, venture; *audeo dicere*, I venture to assert.

audiens -entis, *Partic. of audio (q.v.). Subst.*, a hearer.

audientia -ae, *f.* hearing, listening, attention.

audio, 4. to hear. (*Perf. part.*, *as subst.*, **auditum** -i, *n.* hearsay); to listen to; *of judges*, to hear a case; to attend the lectures of a professor; to give credence to; *audio*, I believe it; *with dat.*, to obey; to be called; *bene audire*, to be well spoken of.

auditio -onis, *f.* hearing, listening; hearsay; *plur.*, *fictae auditiones*.

auditor -oris, *m.* hearer, auditor, scholar.

auditorium -i, *n.* place of audience, lecture-room, court of justice, *etc.*

auditus -us, *m.* hearing; listening.

aufero, **auferre**, **abstuli**, **ablatum**, 3. to carry away, remove; to draw away from one's aim; to rob, steal; to carry off, *i.e.* to gain, obtain; to lay aside, cease from.

Aufidus -i, *m.* river in Apulia.

aufugio -fugi, 3. to flee away.

Augeas *and* **Augias** -ae, *m.* king in Elis, *the cleansing of whose stable was one of the labours of Hercules.*

augeo, **auxi**, **auctum**, 2. to cause to grow, to fertilise; to make larger; to strengthen; *of rivers*, to cause to rise, *pass.*, *augeri* = to be swollen; to increase; to extol; to enrich, to honour.

augesco, **auxi**, 3. to begin to grow, to increase; *politically*, to increase in strength.

augmen -inis, *n.* an increase.

augur -uris, *c.* augur, soothsayer, seer.

auguralis -e, relating to an augur or augury. *Subst.*, **augurale** -is, *n.* the port of the Roman camp where the auguries were taken.

auguratio -onis, *f.* divining, soothsaying.

auguratus -us, *m.* office of an augur.

augurium -i, *n.* augury; prophecy; presentiment; the science of augury; an omen; a sign, token.

augurius -a -um, relating to an augur.

auguro, 1. to act as an augur; *pass.*, *locus auguratur*, the place is consecrated by auguries; to prophesy; to have a presentiment.

auguror, 1. *dep.* to foretell by auguries; to foretell, *alicui mortem;* to guess.

Augusta -ae, *f.* name of the wife, daughter, mother, *or* sister of the Roman Emperor.

Augustālis -e, belonging to *or* in honour of the Emperor Augustus.

augustē, *adv.* reverentially.

1. augustus -a -um, *adj.* consecrated, holy; majestic, dignified.

2. Augustus -i, *m.* surname of all Roman emperors.

3. Augustus -a -um, relating to Augustus; *mensis,* August.

aula -ae, *f.* fore-court; yard for cattle; = *atrium,* an inner court; a palace; the court; princely power; *of a bee-hive,* a cell.

aulaeum -i, *n.* usually *plur.,* curtain, tapestry; canopy; curtain of a theatre; an embroidered upper garment.

aulicus -a -um, belonging to the court, princely. *Subst.,* aulici -orum, *m.* courtiers.

Aulis -idis, *f.* a port in Boeotia, *where the Greek fleet collected before sailing to Troy.*

auloedus -i, *m.* one who sings to the flute.

aura -ae, *old genit.* aurai, air; motion of the air, wind; *plur.* aurae, the heavens; the world above; *venire superas ad auras,* the light of day; *ferre sub auras,* to make known; breath, sign, *rumoris;* the air that we breathe; smell, glitter; echo.

aurārius -a -um, golden, relating to gold. *Subst.,* auraria -ae, *f.* gold mine.

aurātus -a -um, golden, gilt.

Aurēlius, M., a Roman Emperor.

aurēolus -a -um (*dim. of aureus*), golden; splendid, beautiful.

aurĕus -a -um, golden; made of gold; beautiful; *currus,* the triumphal car; *Pactolus,* with golden sands; of the colour of gold.

aurichalchum = *orichalchum (q.v.).*

auricŏmus -a -um, golden-haired; golden-leaved.

auricŭla -ae, *f. (dim. of auris),* lobe of the ear, the ear.

aurifer -fĕra -fĕrum, gold-bearing, gold-producing *(arbor, poet.).*

aurifex -ficis, *m.* goldsmith.

auriga -ae, *c.* charioteer, driver; *esp.* in the circus; *poet.,* helmsman.

Aurigĕna -ae, *c.* begotten of gold; *of Perseus, son of Danaë.*

auriger -gĕra -gĕrum, gold-bearing; *taurus,* with gilt horns, *poet.*

aurigo, 1. to be a charioteer.

auris -is, *f.* the ear; *erigere,* to prick up the ears; *applicare,* to listen; *aures,* the mould-boards of a plough.

auriscalpium -i, *n.* an ear-pick.

aurĭtŭlus -i, *m. (dim. of auritus),* the long-eared one, *i.e.* the ass.

aurītus -a -um, long-eared; attentive.

aurŏra -ae, *f.* break of day, redness of morning. Aurora, goddess of morning; the east.

aurum -i, *n.* gold; something made of gold, gold plate; golden goblet; money; the Golden Age.

Aurunca -ae, *f.* a town in Campania.

auscultātor -ōris, *m.* a listener.

ausculto, 1. to hear attentively; to over-hear; to attend, wait at the door; to obey.

Ausŏnia, Lower Italy.

auspex -icis, *c.* one who observes the habits of birds for purposes of divination; protector, leader ; a person who witnessed the marriage contract.

auspicātō, *adv.* in a fortunate hour.

auspicātus -a -um, consecrated by auguries; auspicious.

auspicium -ii, *n.* divination by means of birds; *in auspicio esse,* to act as augur; the right to take auspices; *auspicia ponere,* to lay down a magistracy; control, protection; omen, sign.

auspico, 1. to take the auspices.

auspicor, 1. *dep.* to take the auspices.

auster -stri, *m.* the south wind; the south.

austērē, *adv.* severely, gravely, austerely.

austērus -a -um, sour, harsh in taste; strict, severe, austere; sad, melancholy, burdensome.

austrālis -e, southern.

austrīnus -a -um, southern.

ausum -i, *n.* a daring deed, undertaking.

aut, *conj. disjunct.,* or, or else, or rather; *aut . . . aut,* either . . . or.

autem, *conj. adversat.,* but, on the contrary, however, moreover; *never at the beginning of a clause.*

authepsa -ae, *f.* a cooking-stove.

autŏgrāphus -a -um, written with one's own hand.

autŏmātus (-ŏs) -a -um (-ŏn), *adj.* self-acting. *Subst.,* autŏmăton -i, *n.* an automaton.

Autŏmēdōn -ontis, *m.* charioteer of Achilles.

autumnus, *etc., v. auctumnus.*

autŭmo, 1. to say, assert.

auxiliāris -e, assisting, auxiliary; belonging to the allied troops; *auxiliares,* auxiliary *or* allied troops.

auxiliārius -a -um, auxiliary; *milit., milites,* auxiliary troops.

auxiliātor -ōris, *m.* a helper.

auxiliātus -ūs, *m.* help, assistance.

auxilior, 1. *dep.* to help ; support, *alicui.*

auxilium -i, *n.* help, aid, assistance; military power ; *auxilia,* auxiliary troops.

ăvārē, *adv.* avariciously, covetously.

ăvăritia -ae (ăvăritĭes -ei), f. avarice, covetousness.

ăvārus -a -um, covetous, greedy; with genit., pecuniae, avaricious. Subst., avarus -i, m. the avaricious man.

ăvĕho -vexi -vectum, 3. to carry off; pass. to ride off.

ăvello -velli and -vulsi (-volsi) -vulsum (-volsum), 3. to tear away; to take away with violence, separate.

ăvēna -ae, f. oats, wild oats; the shepherd's pipe; plur., iunctae avenae, the Pan-pipes.

Aventīnum -i, n. and Aventīnus -i, m. the Aventine, one of the hills of Rome. Adj., Aventīnus.

1. ăvĕo, 2. lit., to pant after; to desire.

2. ăvĕo (hăvĕo), 2. to be well; only in the imper. ave, aveto, avete, hail! farewell!

Avernus -a -um, without birds. Subst., Avernus -i, the lake Avernus, near Cumae the entrance to the infernal regions; the infernal regions themselves; adj., Avernus, Avernālis -e.

ăverrunco, 1. to avert.

ăversābilis, that from which one must turn away, horrible.

1. ăversor, 1. dep. to turn away; with acc., filium; to repel, avoid, shun.

2. ăversor -ōris, m. an embezzler.

ăversus -a -um, p. adj. turned away, backward, behind; disinclined, averse from. Plur. subst., āversa -orum, n. the back parts, urbis.

ăverto (ăvorto) -verti (-vorti) -versum (-vorsum), 3. to turn away, remove; flumina, divert ; (pass., averti, as middle, aversus ab suo itinere, turning away; active, as reflexive, prora avertit); to carry off, embezzle; to divert (thoughts, etc.); to estrange.

ăvia -ae, f. a grandmother.

ăvĭārius -a -um, relating to birds. Subst., ăvĭārium -ii, n. an aviary; haunts of wild birds in the woods.

ăvĭdē, adv. greedily.

ăvĭditas -ātis, vehement desire; cibi, for food; avarice.

ăvĭdus -a -um, greedy, laudis; covetous; (subst., a miser); ardent, eager to fight. Fig., wide, vast.

ăvis -is, f. a bird; omen.

ăvītus -a -um, relating to a grandfather, ancestral.

ăvĭus -a -um, out of the right way, untrodden. (Subst., ăvĭum -i, n. a byway, a solitary place.) Poet., remote; straying.

ăvŏcātio -ōnis, f. a calling away from.

ăvŏco, 1. to call away, or off; to withdraw; to relieve.

ăvŏlo, 1. to fly away; to hasten away.

ăvuncŭlus -i, m. (dim. of avus), a mother's brother, uncle.

ăvus -i, m. a grandfather; ancestor.

1. axis -is, m. an axle-tree; chariot, waggon; axis of the earth; the north pole; the heavens; sub axe, in the open air.

2. axis -is, m. a board, plank.

B

B b, second letter of the Latin Alphabet.

băbae, wonderful!

Băbўlon -ōnis, f. a city on the Euphrates.

Băbўlōnia -ae, f. country between the Euphrates and the Tigris.

bacca (băca) -ae, f. a berry; fruit of the olive; a pearl.

baccar (bacchar) -ăris, n. and baccaris -is, f. a plant.

baccātus -a -um, set with pearls.

Baccha -ae, f. a Bacchante.

Bacchānal -is, n. place where the festival of Bacchus was held; plur. Bacchānālia, the festival of Bacchus.

bacchātio -ōnis, f. celebration of the Bacchanalia; revelling.

Bacchēius -a -um, belonging to Bacchus.

Bacchēus -a -um, belonging to Bacchus.

Bacchis -idis, f. = Baccha.

Bacchius -a -um, belonging to Bacchus.

bacchor 1. dep. to celebrate the festival of Bacchus; to rage; to rave; to raise the Bacchic cry; of places, to be made the scene of Bacchic revels; partic. Bacchantes = Bacchae.

Bacchus -i, m. the god of wine; the vine; wine; the Bacchic cry (Io Bacche).

baccifer -fĕra -fĕrum, bearing berries.

băcillum -i, n. (dim. of baculum), a little staff; the lictor's staff.

băcŭlum -i, n. and băcŭlus -i, m. a stick, staff.

Baetis -is, m. river in Spain; Baetigĕna -ae, born on the Baetis; Baeticŏla -ae, living near the Baetis; Baeticus, relating to the Baetis; Baetici -ōrum, m. inhabitants of Baetica; Baeticātus -a -um, clothed in Baetican wool.

Baiae -ārum, f. town on the coast of Campania. Adj., Baiānus.

băiŭlo. 1. to carry a burden.

băiŭlus -i, m. a porter.

bālaena ae, f. a whale.

bălănātus -a -um, anointed with balsam, embalmed.

bălănus -i, f. rarely m., an acorn; chestnut; a date; a fruit.

bălătro -ōnis, m. a buffoon, jester.

bālātus -us, m. the bleating of sheep and goats.

balbē, adv. in a stammering manner.

balbus -a -um, stammering.

balbūtio, 4. to stammer; to speak obscurely.

Băleāres -ium, *f.* the Balearic Islands; *adj.,* Băleāris -e, Băleāricus.

bălĭnĕum *or* **balnĕum -i,** *n.* bălĭnĕa *or* **balnĕa -ōrum,** *n.* : *heteroclite pl.* **bălĭnĕae** *or* **balnĕae -ārum,** a bath, bathing place.

ballista (balista), -ae, *f.* a military engine for throwing large stones.

ballistārium -i, *n.* = *ballista (q.v.).*

balnĕae, *v. balineum.*

balnĕārius -a -um, belonging to the bath. *Subst.,* **balnĕāria -ōrum,** *n.* baths.

balnĕātor -ōris, *m.* keeper of a bath.

balnĕŏlum -i, *n.* (*dim. of balneum*), a little bath.

balnĕum, *v. balineum.*

bālo, 1. to bleat.

balsămum -i, *n.* gum of the balsam-tree; the tree itself.

baltĕus -i, *m.* (-um -i, *n.*), the girdle.

Bandūsia -ae, *f.* a fountain near Venusia.

bărăthrum -i, *n.* the abyss, the lower world.

bărăthrus -i, *m.* worthless fellow.

barba -ae, *f.* the beard; *promittere barbam,* to let the beard grow.

barbărē, *adv.* like a foreigner; barbarously.

barbăria -ae, *f. and* **barbăriēs,** *acc.* **-em,** *abl.* **-e,** *f.* a foreign country, *as opposed to Greece and Rome;* want of culture; savageness.

barbăricus -a -um, foreign, *i.e. not Greek or Roman.*

barbărus -a -um, foreign, *as opposed to Greek;* uncultivated; savage. *Subst.,* foreigner.

barbātŭlus -a -um (*dim. of barbatus*), with a slight beard.

barbātus -a -um, bearded.

barbĭgĕr -gĕra -gĕrum, wearing a beard.

barbĭtŏs -i, *m. and f.* the lyre; the song sung to the lyre.

barbŭla -ae, *f.* (*dim. of barba*), a little beard.

Barcās -ae, *m.* the founder of the family to which belonged Hannibal and Hamilcar.

bardŏcŭcullus -i, *m.* a Gallic overcoat.

1. **bardus -a -um,** *stupid, dull.*

2. **bardus -i,** *m.* a bard among the Gauls.

băris -idos, *f.* a small Egyptian skiff.

barītus, *v. barritus.*

bāro -ōnis, *m.* simpleton.

barrio -ire, to roar (*of elephants*).

barrĭtus -ūs, *m.* the roar of an elephant; the war-cry of the Germans.

barrus -i, *m.* the elephant.

bascauda -ae, *f.* a basket.

bāsiātio -ōnis, *f.* kissing, a kiss.

bāsiātor -is, *m.* a kisser.

băsilicus -a -um, *adj.* royal, kingly. *Subst.,* **băsilicus -i,** *m.* (*sc. iactus*), the best cast of the dice; **băsilica -ae,** *f.* a basilica, used as a meeting-place of merchants and for the administration of justice. **băsilicum -i,** *n.* a splendid dress.

bāsio, 1. to kiss.

băsis -is *and* **ĕos,** *f.* pedestal, base; foundation, wall; *trianguli,* base.

băsium -ii, *n.* a kiss.

Bassăreus -ei, *m.* a name of Bacchus.

Bătāvia -ae, *f.* the peninsula Batavia, Holland.

bătillum -i, *n.* a chafing-dish.

battŭo (bātuo), 3. to beat, knock.

baubor, 1. *dep.,* to bark.

bĕātē, *adv.* happily.

bĕătitas -ātis, *f.* happiness, blessedness.

bĕātĭtūdo -inis, *f.* happiness, beatitude.

bĕātus -a -um, *p. adj.* happy, blessed; prosperous. *Neut. subst.,* **bĕātum -i,** happiness.

Belgae -ārum, *m.* the Belgae, a warlike people in the North of Gaul.

bellāria -ōrum, *n.* dessert.

bellātor -ōris, *m.* warrior; *adj.* warlike.

bellātrix -īcis, *f.* a female warrior.

bellē, *adv.* finely, prettily, elegantly, neatly; *negare,* politely; *belle se habere, or esse,* to be in good health.

Bellĕrŏphōn -ontis, *m. or* **Bellĕrŏphontēs -ae,** *m.* the slayer of the Chimaera. *Adj.* **Bellĕrŏphontēus.**

bellicōsus -a -um, warlike, bellicose.

bellicus -a -um, relating to war; vigorous; warlike. *Subst.,* **bellicum -i,** *n.* the signal for the attack.

belliger -gĕra -gĕrum, warlike, fond of war.

belligĕro, 1. to wage war.

bellĭpŏtens -entis, mighty in war.

bello, 1. (**bellor,** *dep.*), to wage war; to fight.

Bellōna -ae, *f.* the goddess of war.

Bellŏvăci -ōrum, *m.* people in Gallia Belgica.

bellŭa, *v. belua.*

bellŭlus -a -um (*dim. of bellus*), pretty, elegant, beautiful.

bellum -i, *n.* (*old form,* **duellum,** a contest between two), war; *nuntiare, denuntiare, indicere,* to declare war; contest; fight.

bellus -a -um, pretty, handsome, charming, neat, agreeable.

bēlŭa -ae, *f.* any very large animal; brute, beast.

bēlŭōsus -a -um, full of monsters.

Bēlus -i, *m.* founder of Babylon; **Bēlis -idis,** *f. gen. plur.,* **Bēlides -um,** the Danaides; **Bēlĭdēs -ae,** *m.* Lynceus, son of Aegyptus.

bĕnĕ, *adv. comp. melius, superl. optime,* well, rightly, honourably; *bene facis,* excellent, I am much obliged; *bene vocas,* you are very kind (*polite refusal*). *As an exclamation,* good, excellent.

bĕnĕfăcio -fēci -factum, 3. to do well.

bĕnĕfactum -i, *n.* a good deed.

běněficentia -ae, f. kindness, liberality.

běněficiārius -a -um, relating to a favour. *Subst.*, **beneficiarii -ōrum**, *m.* privileged soldiers.

běněficium -ii, *n.* a kindness, favour, service; *aliquem beneficio afficere*, to do any one a service; *beneficium tueri*, to be mindful of a service, *beneficii causa*, *per beneficium*, as a kindness, service; a favour, distinction; *in beneficiis delatus est*, among those recommended for promotion; privilege, exemption.

běněficus -a -um, *comp.* -entior, *superl.* entissimus (beneficissimus), kind, generous, obliging.

Běněventum -i, *n.* town of the Hirpini in Samnium.

běněvŏlě, *adv.* benevolently, kindly.

běněvŏlens -entis. *Adj.*, benevolent, obliging. *Subst.*, patron.

běněvŏlentia -ae, f. good-will, benevolence.

běněvŏlus -a -um (-entior -entissimus), kind, obliging.

běnignē, *adv.* kindly, willingly; generously; *benigne*, much obliged.

běnignĭtas -ātis, f. kindness; liberality.

běnignĭter = *benigne*, q.v.

běnignus -a -um, *adj.* kindly; *dies*, fortunate; generous; abundant.

běo, 1. to make happy; to make rich.

Běrěcyntus -i, *m.* mountain of Phrygia, sacred to Cybele.

běryllus -i, c. a beryl.

bēs, bessis, *m.* two-thirds; eight ounces.

bessālis -e, containing the number 8.

Bessi -orum, *m.* people in Thrace.

bestia -ae, f. beast.

bestiārius -a -um, belonging to animals *Subst.*, **bestiārius -ii**, *m.* one who fought with wild beasts at the public shows.

bestiŏla -ae, f. (*dim. of bestia*), a small animal.

1. bēta -ae, f. a vegetable, beet.

2. bēta, *indecl.* the second letter in the Greek alphabet.

bĭbliŏpōla -ae, *m.* a bookseller.

bĭbliŏthēca -ae, f. and bĭbliŏthēcē -ēs, f. a library; the place where books are kept.

bĭbo, bĭbi, bĭbĭtum, 3. to drink; *poet.*, to drink in; *fig.*, to drink in.

Bĭbractē -is, *n.* a town in Gaul.

Bĭbrax -actis, f. fortress of the Remi.

bĭbŭlus -a -um, fond of drinking; *charta*, blotting paper. *Pass.* drinkable.

bĭceps -cĭpĭtis, two-headed. *Poet.*, *Parnassus*, double-peaked.

bĭcŏlor -ōris, of two colours.

bĭcornĭger -gĕri, *m.* two-horned.

bĭcornis -e, two-horned; *poet.*, *luna*, the new moon; *furcae bicornes*, two-pronged forks; *Rhenus*, with two mouths.

bĭcorpor -ōris, having two bodies.

bĭdens -entis, having two teeth. *Subst.*, *m.* a hoe with two crooked teeth; a sheep.

bĭdental -ālis, *n.* a place consecrated by the sacrifice of a sheep.

bĭduum -i, *n.* the space of two days; *ubi. biduum*, in the course of two days.

biennium -ii, *n.* a space of two years; *acc.*, *biennium*, for the space of two years.

bĭfer -fěra -fěrum, *of a tree*, bearing fruit twice a year.

bĭfĭdus -a -um, split into two parts.

bĭfŏris -e, having two doors or openings.

bĭformātus -a -um, *poet.*, *v. biformis*.

bĭformis -e (bĭformātus -a -um), of double form; *Janus*.

bĭfrons -frontis, with double forehead or countenance.

bĭfurcus -a -um, having two prongs or forks.

bīgae -ārum, f. and *post-Aug.* bīga -ae, f. a pair of horses.

bĭgātus -a -um, stamped with a pair of horses. *Subst.*, bīgātĭ -ōrum, *m.* silver denarii so marked.

bĭiŭgis -e, *v. biiugus*.

bĭiŭgus -a -um, yoked two together. *Subst.*, bĭiŭgi -ōrum, *m.* a pair of horses.

bĭlībra -ae, f. a mass of two pounds weight.

bĭlĭbris -e, weighing two pounds.

bĭlinguis -e, having two tongues; speaking two languages; double-tongued, treacherous.

bīlis -is, f. gall, bile; displeasure; *atra bilis*, black bile—*i.e.* melancholy, madness.

bĭlix -līcis, *only acc. sing.* bilicem, having a double thread.

bĭlustris -e, lasting ten years.

bĭmăris -e, lying on two seas; *Corinthus*.

bĭmărītus, *m.* the husband of two wives.

bĭmāter -tris, *m.* having two mothers; *epithet of Bacchus*.

bĭmembris -e, half man, half animal; *bimembres*, *subst.*, Centaurs.

bĭmestris -e, lasting two months; *porcus*, a pig two months old.

bīmŭlus -a -um (*dim. of bimus*), two years old.

bīmus -a -um, two years old; *legio*, a legion that had served for two years.

bīni -ae -a (*sing.*, bīnus -a -um), two by two; two apiece; *bini imperatores*, two consuls a year; *with substt. used only in the plur.*, two, *bina castra*; *of things that match*, *boves*, a yoke of oxen; *neut. plur. subst.*, *bis bina*, twice two.

bĭnoctium -ii, *n.* a space of two nights.

bĭnōminis -e, having two names.

bĭpalmis -e, two palms or spans long or broad.

bipartio, *or* **bipertio,** *no pref.* **-itum,** 4. to divide into two parts.

bipartītō, *adv.* in two parts, in two ways.

bipātens -entis, open in two directions.

bipēdālis -e, two feet long, broad, thick, *or* high.

bipennifer -fěra -fěrum, armed with a two-edged axe.

bipennis -e, having two wings; double-edged. *Subst.,* **bipennis -is.** *f.* a double-edged axe.

bipēs -ēdis, having two feet, biped.

birēmis -e, two-oared. *Subst.,* **birēmis -is,** *f.* a skiff with two oars; a ship with two banks of oars.

bis, *adv.* twice.

bisulcus -a -um, split into two parts; *lingua,* forked. *Subst.,* **bisulca -orum,** *n.* animals with cloven hoofs.

Bīthynia -ae, a country of Asia Minor.

bitūmen -inis, *n.* asphaltum, bitumen.

bitūminěus -a -um, bituminous.

Bitūriges -um, *m.* a people of Gaul.

bivium -ii, *n.* place where two roads meet.

bivius -a -um, having two ways.

biaesus -a -um, lisping, indistinct.

blandē, *adv.* flatteringly.

blandimentum -i, *n. usually plur.;* flattery; allurement.

blandior, 4. *dep.* to flatter, caress, coax, *with dative; sibi.* to deceive oneself; *past partic.,* **blandītus -a -um,** charming.

blanditer = *blande (q.v.).*

blanditia -ae, *f.* a caress, flattery; that which is alluring.

blanditiēs -ēi, *f.* = *blanditia (q.v.).*

blandus -a -um, flattering, caressing; enticing.

blǎtěro, 1. to chatter, babble.

blatta -ae., *f.* a cockroach.

boārius, *and* **bovārius -a -um,** relating to oxen; *forum,* the cattle market.

Boccar -āris, *m.* a king of Mauritania *at the time of the second Punic war.*

boeōtarchēs -ae, *m.* the highest magistrate of Boeotia.

Boeōtia -ae, *f.* a country in Greece.

Boii -orum, *m.* a people of Gaul.

bōlētus -i, *m.* mushroom.

bōlus -i, *m.* a throw *(classical iactus);* *of dice; of a fishing net; fig.* a good haul.

bombycīnus -a -um, silken. *Plur. subst.,* **bombȳcina -ōrum,** *n.* silken garments.

bombyx -ȳcis, *m. and f.* the silkworm.

bǒnitas -ātis, *f.* goodness, excellence; kindness, integrity.

bǒnum -i, *n.* good; plural, **bona -ōrum,** property; *esse in bonis,* to be in possession; *summum bonum,* the supreme good *(in philosoph. sense);* advantage; *cui bono,* for whose advantage.

bǒnus -a -um, *compar. melior -ius, genit.*

-ōris, superl. optǐmus, good; *nummi boni,* genuine coin; *dicta,* jests; beautiful; clever; *(subst.* **bǒni,** able men); *bono animo,* of good courage; *aetas bona,* youth; *bonae res,* good things delicacies; *bona fama,* good news; *bona venia,* with your permission; *bonae res,* good fortune; lucky *(poet.),* *dies; bona verba,* auspicious words; honest, faithful; *O bone!* my good fellow; loyal; *(often in Cic. and Sall. boni* = conservatives, the supporters of the existing system); chaste; kind; *di boni,* gracious gods!

bǒo, 1. to shout, roar; to echo.

Bǒōtēs -ae *and* **-is,** *m.* a constellation.

Bǒrěās -ae, *m.* the north wind *(Class. Lat. aquilo);* the north; *adj.,* **Bǒrěus,** northern.

bǒs, bǒvis, *c.* ox, bullock, cow; *bos Luca,* an elephant; a kind of flat fish.

Bospǒrus (Bosphorus) -i, *m.* straits between Thrace and Asia Minor; *adj.,* **Bospǒrānus;** *subst.* a dweller on the Bosphorus; **Bospǒrius** *and* **Bospǒrěus -a -um,** belonging to the Bosphorus.

Bǒviānum -i, *n.* town in Samnium *adj.,* **Bǒviānius.**

bǒvīle = *bubile (q.v.).*

Bǒvillae -ārum, *f.* town in Latium.

bǒvillus -a -um, *old form of bubulus,* relating to oxen.

brǎbeuta -ae, *m.* umpire in the public games.

brācae (braccae) -ārum, *f. pl.* breeches, trousers, hose.

brācātus (braccātus) -a -um *(bracae),* wearing breeches; foreign, barbarian, effeminate.

brāchiǒlum -i, *n. (dim. of brachium),* a small delicate arm.

brāchium -ii, *n.* the arm from the elbow to the wrist; the whole arm; the limbs of animals; an outwork connecting two points of a fortification.

bractěa -ae, *f.* a thin plate of metal, gold leaf.

bractěǒla -ae, *f. (dim. of bractea),* a little leaf of gold.

brassica -ae, *f.* cabbage.

Brennus -i, *m.* leader of the Gauls who burned Rome, 390 B.C.

brěviārius -a -um, abridged. *Subst.,* **brěviārium -i,** *n.* summary.

brěvilǒquens -entis, brief in speech.

brěvilǒquentia -ae, *f.* brevity of speech.

brěvis -e, short; shallow. *Subst.* **brěvia -ium,** *n.* shallows; *sing.,* a shoal; *brevi,* for a little time; *brevi,* in a few words.

brěvitas -ātis, *f.* shortness; *of speech,* conciseness.

brěvitěr, *adv.* shortly; briefly.

Briǎreus -ěi, *m.* a giant son of Uranus with a hundred arms and fifty heads.

Britannia -ae, *f.* Britain.

Britannicus -i, *m.* the son of Claudius and Messalina.

Brōmius -ii, *m* surname of Bacchus.

brūma -ae, *f.* the winter solstice. *Poet.*, winter.

brūmālis -e, relating to the shortest day; wintry.

Brundisium -i, *n.* a town in Calabria, a port; *adj.* Brundisinus.

Bruttii (Brūtii, Brittii) -ōrum, *m.* the inhabitants of the southern extremity of Italy; *adj.*, Bruttius.

1. **brūtus** -a -um, heavy, immovable; dull, without feeling or reason.

2. **Brūtus** -i, *m.* a cognomen of the Roman Gens Junia. *Adj.*, Brūtinus.

Bŭbastis -is, *f.* an Egyptian goddess.

bŭbīle -is, *n.* an ox-stall.

bŭbo -ōnis, *m.* the screech owl.

bŭbulcus -i, *m.* one who ploughs with oxen.

bŭbŭlus -a -um, relating to cows or oxen. *Subst.*, būbŭla -ae, *f.* beef.

bucca -ae, *f.* the cheek, *esp. when puffed out; buccas inflare*, to swell with rage; a declaimer, bawler; a parasite; a mouthful; a person with swollen cheeks (*of a trumpeter*).

buccella -ae, *f.* (*dim. of bucca*), a little mouthful.

buccina, buccinātor, *etc.*, *v. bucina, etc.*

buccŭla -ae, *f.* (*dim. of bucca*), the cheek, jaw; the beaver, the visor.

Būcĕphălās -ae, *acc.* -an, *and* -us -i, *m.* the horse of Alexander the Great.

Būcĕphăla -ae, *f. and* Būcĕphălē -ēs, *f.* town founded in its honour.

būcĕrōs -ōn, *and* būcĕrius -a -um, having ox's horns.

bucina -ae, *f.* a crooked trumpet; the shepherd's horn.

būcinātor -ōris, *m.* a trumpeter.

būcŏlicus -a -um, *and* -ŏs -ē -ŏn, relating to shepherds, rural.

būcŭla -ae, *f.* (*dom of bos*), a heifer.

būfo -ōnis, *m.* a toad.

būleutērion -ii, *n.* the place of meeting of a Greek senate.

bulla -ae, *f.* a hollow swelling, bladder, bubble; a boss, stud; *bulla aurea*, a golden ornament, an amulet.

bullātus -a -um, inflated, bombastic, transitory, furnished with a *bulla, in the sense of* a boss, knob; wearing the bulla.

bullio, 4. to well up, boil up.

būmastus -i, *f.* a kind of vine.

būris -is, *m.* the crooked hinder part of the plough.

bustŭārius -a -um, belonging to the place where corpses were burned.

bustum -i, *n.* the place where corpses were burned; a grave, sepulchre.

būthȳsia -ae, *f.* a sacrifice of oxen.

buxĭfĕr -a -um, producing the box-tree.

buxus -i, *f. and* buxum -i, *n.* the ever-green box-tree; box-wood.

Byrsa -ae, *f.* citadel of Carthage.

Byzantium -ii, *n.* a city in Thrace, now Constantinople. *Adj.*, Byzantinus, Byzantius.

C

C c, *the third letter of the Latin Alphabet, corresponding originally in sound to Greek gamma.*

căballīnus -a -um, belonging to a horse.

căballus -i, *m.* a pack-horse, nag.

căchinnātio -ōnis, *f.* a violent laughing.

1. **căchinno**, 1. to laugh aloud.

2. **căchinno** -ōnis, *m.* one who laughs heartily, a jester.

căchinnus -i, *m.* loud laughter, jeering; *poet.*

căcŏēthēs -is, *n.* incurable passion; *scribendi*, an incurable itch to write.

căcūmen -inis, *n.* the extreme point, summit, *montis*; perfection.

căcūmino, 1. to point, make pointed.

cădāver -ĕris, *n.* a dead body, carcass.

cădāvĕrōsus -a -um, like a corpse.

Cadmus -i, *m.* son of Agenor, king of Phoenicia and brother of Europa; father of Polydorus, Ino, Semele, Autonoë, and Agave; founder of Thebes in Boeotia. *Adj.*, Cadmēus, Thoban.

cădo, cĕcĭdi, cāsum, 3. to fall; *vela cadunt*, are furled; *of the sun*, *etc.*, to set; *of winds*, to be lulled; *grammat.* to come to an end; *of payments*, to fall due; *to fall to the notice of; to fall under, in unius potestatem; to be consistent with; to happen; to lose; to lose courage; to be destroyed.

cādūcĕātor -ōris, *m.* herald.

cādūcĕus -i, *m.* a herald's staff; the wand of Mercury.

cādūcĭfĕr -ĕri, he that bears the caduceus, *surname of Mercury.*

cādūcus -a -um, that which has fallen *or* is falling; ready to fall; *esp.*, destined to die; frail, transitory.

Cădurci -ōrum, *m.* a Gaulish people in Aquitania, famous for their linen manufactures; **Cădurcum**, a coverlet of Cadurcian linen.

cādus -i, *m.* wine jar; wine; *aĕneus*, a funeral urn.

caecĭgĕnus -a -um, born blind.

Caecilius -a -um, name of a celebrated plebeian gens.

caecĭtas -ātis, *f.* blindness.

caeco, 1. to make blind.

Caecŭbum -i, *n.* and **Caecŭbus** ager, a district in Latium, famed for its wine.

caecus -a -um, *adj.* active, blind; *passive*, dark; invisible, unseen;

unintelligible, unknown; blind, uncertain.

caedēs -is, *f.* a cutting down, slaughter; the persons slain.

caedo, cĕcīdi, caesum, 3. to hew, fell, cut down, beat; to kill; *testibus caedi,* to be hard pressed; *poet. caesus sanguis,* the blood of the slain.

caelāmĕn -inis, *n.* a bas-relief.

caelātor -ōris, *m.* a chaser, carver.

caelātūra -ae, *f.* the art of engraving or chasing; an engraving.

caelebs -libis, unmarried (*of the man*); *of trees, platanus,* to which no vine is trained.

caelĕs -itis, heavenly. *Subst.,* a god.

caelestis -e, heavenly; *subst.,* **caelestia -ium,** *n.* the heavenly bodies; celestial, divine; *subst.,* **caelestis -is,** *f.* a goddess; *plur., m. and f.* the gods; glorious, superhuman.

caelibātus -ūs, *m.* celibacy.

caelĭcŏla -ae, *m.* a dweller in heaven; *poet.,* a god.

caelifĕr-fĕra-fĕrum, bearing the heavens; *Atlas.*

Caelius -a -um, name of a Roman plebeian gens. *Caelius Mons,* a hill in Rome. *Adj.,* **Caeliānus.**

caelo, 1. to engrave or chase, to carve in bas-relief; *of poetry, caelatum novem Musis opus,* adorned by.

1. **caelum -i,** *n.* the burin or engraving-tool.

2. **caelum -i,** *n.* the heavens; *as the height of joy, renown, etc., esse in caelo;* air, *caelum liberum; gravitas huius caeli,* unhealthiness (*of climate*).

Caelus -i, *m.* = *Caelum* personified as a god.

caementum -i, *n.* rough stone from the quarry.

Caeneus -ĕi, *m.* a maiden changed into a boy and then into a bird.

caenōsus -a -um, muddy.

caenum -i, *n.* mud, dirt, filth.

caepa (cēpa) -ae, *f. and* **caepe (cēpe) -is,** *n.* an onion.

Caerĕ, *n. indecl., and* **Caerēs -itis** or **-ĕtis,** *f.* city of Etruria. *Adj.,* **Caerēs -itis** *and* **-ĕtis.**

caerimōnia -ae, *f.* holiness, sacredness; reverence; sacred ceremony (*gen. in plur.*).

caerŭlĕus (*poet.* **caerŭlus**) **-a -um,** dark-coloured, dark blue; **caerŭla -orum,** *n.* the sea; *of sea-gods, deus,* Neptune. *Subst.,* **caerŭleum -i,** a blue colour. *Poet.,* dark green.

Caesar -ăris, *m.* a Roman family name of the gens Julia.

caesăriēs -ĕi, *f.* a fine head of hair.

caesim, *adv.* with cutting, with the edge of the sword; *of discourse,* in short sentences.

caesius -a -um, bluish grey, *of the eyes; leo,* with grey eyes.

caespes (cespes) -itis, grass that has been cut; turf; an altar of turf.

1. **caestus -ūs,** *m.* gauntlet for boxers.

2. **caestus -i,** *m., v. cestus.*

caeterus, *etc.* . . . *v. ceterus, etc.*

Cāiēta -ae (*and* **-ē -ēs**), *f.* 1. nurse of Aeneas; 2. town on the borders of Latium and Campania.

Cāius (*poet.* **Cāius**) **-i,** *m. and* **Cāia -ae,** *f.* a common praenomen among the Romans; *usually* Gaius.

Călabri -ōrum, *m.* inhabitants of Calabria; **Călabria -ae,** *f.* the peninsula at the south-east extremity of Italy.

Cālāis, *acc.* **-in,** *abl.* **-i,** *m.* winged son of Boreas.

călămister -tri, *m. and* **călămistrum -tri,** *n.* curling-iron for the hair; excessive ornament in discourse.

călămistrātus -a -um, curled with the curling-iron.

călămitas -ātis, *f.* damage, loss, failure, misfortune; reverse in war.

călămitōsē, *adv.* unfortunately.

călămitōsus -a -um, *act.,* destructive; calamitous; *pass.,* suffering great loss, miserable.

călămus -i, *m.* a reed; pen; Pan-pipe; fishing-rod.

călăthiscus -i, *m.* (*dim. of calathus*), a small wicker basket.

călăthus -i, *m.* a wicker basket.

călātor -ōris, *m.* attendant upon priests.

calcar -āris, *n.* a spur.

calcĕāmentum -i, *n.* a covering for the foot.

calcĕārium -i, *n.* shoe money.

calcĕātus -ūs, *m.* = *calceamentum* (*q.v.*).

calcĕo, 1. to provide with shoes.

calcĕŏlus -i, *m.* (*dim. of calceus*), a half-shoe.

calcĕus -i, *m.* a shoe.

Calchās (Calcās) -antis, *acc.* **-antem** *and* **-anta,** *m.* soothsayer to the Greeks before Troy.

calcio = *calceo* (*q.v.*).

calcitro, 1. to kick; to oppose obstinately.

calco, 1. to tread, to tread upon; to trample underfoot, conquer; to insult; to stamp, compress; to visit (*a place*).

calcŭlātor -ōris, *m.* a book-keeper, accountant.

calcŭlus -i, *m.* (*dim. of 2. calx*), a little stone, pebble; *collectively,* gravel; a piece used in a Roman game; a voting pebble; a counter for reckoning, a calculation.

caidus = *calidus* (*q.v.*).

Călēdŏnes -um, *acc.* **-as,** *m.* the inhabitants of Caledonia. **Călēdŏnia -ae,** *f.* the north-west of Scotland. *Adj.,* **Călēdŏnius.**

călĕfăcio -fēci -factum 3. pass. **călĕfīo**

(calfio) -factus sum -fieri; to make warm, heat; to disturb, excite.

călĕfacto, 1. to make warm, heat.

Călendae (Kălendae) -ārum, f. the first day of the month.

călĕo -ui, 2. to be warm, to glow; to be inflamed, aroused, excited; to be in love with; to be urged on zealously; to be fresh or new.

călesco, 3. to grow hot.

căliandrum i, n. v. caliendrum.

călidus (caldus) -a -um, warm, hot; hot, passionate; speedy. Subst., călida -ae, f. warm water; călidum -i. n. warm wine and water.

căliendrum -i, n. a head-dress of Roman women.

căliga -ae, f. a stout shoe, esp. soldier's shoe.

căligātus -a -um, wearing the caliga; caligatus venire, booted and spurred. Subst. m., a common soldier.

căliginōsus -a -um, foggy, misty; dark.

1. căligo -inis, f. fog, mist, vapour; darkness; mental darkness; calamity; sadness.

2. căligo, 1. to spread a dark mist around; to be dark; to be in darkness; of the eyes, to be misty.

Călĭgŭla -ae, m. nickname of C. Caesar, the third Roman Emperor.

călix -icis, m. a goblet, a cooking vessel.

callĕo, 2. to be thick-skinned. Intransit., to be clever, experienced. Transit., to know by experience.

callĭdē, adv. cleverly; cunningly.

calliditas -ātis, f. expertness, cleverness; cunning, artifice; stratagem.

callĭdus -a -um, dexterous, skilful, cunning; a connoisseur in art; of things, cunningly devised; subtle.

Calliŏpē -ēs, f. and Calliŏpēa -ae, f. Calliope, the Muse of epic poetry.

Callirrhŏē -ēs, f. daughter of the river Achelous.

callis -is, m. and f. a narrow track, footpath.

Callistŏ ūs, f. daughter of the Arcadian king Lycaon, mother of Arcas by Jupiter, changed by Juno into a bear.

callōsus -a -um, having a hard skin, hard.

callum -i, n. and callus -i, m. the hard skin of animals; insensibility.

1. călo, 1. to call, summon.

2. călo -ōnis, m. groom, a litter-bearer; soldier's slave, camp-menial.

călor -ōris, m. warmth, heat; love.

Calpē -ēs, f. one of the pillars of Hercules, now Gibraltar.

Calpurnĭus -a -um, name of a Roman plebeian gens; Calpurnia, wife of Caesar.

caltha -ae, f. a plant, prob. the marigold.

călumnĭa -ae, f. trick, craft; false accusation; action for false recusation.

călumnĭātor -ōris, m. an intriguer, pettifogger.

călumnĭor, 1. dep. to contrive tricks, to attack with artifices.

calva -ae, f. the bald scalp of the head.

calvĕo, 2. to be bald.

calvĭtĭēs -ēi, f. baldness.

calvĭtĭum -ii, n. baldness.

calvus -a -um, bald, without hair.

1. calx -cis, f. the heel.

2. calx -cis, f. and (rarely) m. a stone, a pebble used as a counter; lime, chalk; a goal, end.

Călypsō -ūs, acc. -o, f. a nymph, who entertained Ulysses.

cămăra = camera (q.v.).

camēlla -ae, f. (dim. of camera), a kind of goblet.

cămēlus -i, m. and f. a camel.

Cămēna (Cameena) -ae, f. plur., the Muses.

cămēra -ae, f. a vaulted chamber, vault; a flat-covered boat.

Cămillus -i, m. cognomen of several members of the gens Furia, the most famous of whom, M. Furius Camillus, took Veii, and freed Rome from the Gauls.

cămīnus -i, m. a forge; fire-place; fire.

cammārus -i, m. a crab, lobster.

Campānĭa -ae, f. a district of Central Italy. Adj., Campānus, Campanian. Subst., Campāni -ōrum, m. inhabitants of Campania.

campester -tris -tre, flat; iter, march in a level country; subst., campestria -ium, n. a plain; relating to the Campus Martius and its gymnastic exercises; subst., campestre -is, n. a covering worn by wrestlers round their loins.

campus -i, m. a plain; meadow, field; poet., the sea; the Campus, or Campus Martius at Rome, the place of meeting of the comitia centuriata; the comitia.

Camulŏdūnum -i, n. a town in Britain, now Colchester.

cămur a -um, hooked, curved.

cănălis -is, m. waterpipe, channel, canal.

cănārĭus -a -um, relating to a dog; Cănārĭa, plur. Cănārĭae, the Canaries.

cancelli -ōrum, m. (dim. of cancer), a lattice, grating, or trelliswork; fori, the bar of a tribunal; bounds, limits.

cancer -cri, m. the crab, sign of the zodiac; the south, summer heat.

candĕfăcĭo -fēci -factum, 3. to make of a shining white.

candēla -ae, f. candle, taper; a rope coated with wax.

candēlābrum -i, n. candlestick.

candĕo -ui, 2. to be of a shining white, to glitter; to glow with heat.

candesco, 3. to begin to shine; to begin to glow.

candĭdātōrĭus -a -um, relating to a candidate.

candĭdātus -a -um, clothed in white. *Subst.*, candĭdātus -i, *m.* a candidate for office.

candĭdē, *adv.* in white; clearly, candidly.

candĭdŭlus -a -um (*dim. of candidus*), shining, dazzling.

candidus -a -um, shining white; (*subst.*, candidum -i, *n.* white colour); of dazzling beauty; *of the stars*, bright; *candida sententia*, an acquittal; *of time*, happy; *of writing*, clear, lucid; *of character*, straightforward.

candor -ōris, *m.* dazzling white colour; lustre; sincerity, candour.

canens -entis, *partic. of caneo and cano.*

cănĕo -ŭi, 2. to be white or hoary.

cănĕphŏros -i, *f.* basket-bearer; *plur.* cănĕphŏroe.

cănesco. 3. to become white or hoary; to become old.

cănĭcŭla -ae, *f.* (*dim. of canis*), a little dog; a violent woman; the dog-star, Sirius; the worst throw with the dice.

cănīnus -a -um, relating to a dog; *littera*, the letter R; snarling, spiteful.

cănis -is, *c.* a dog, *venaticus; cave canem*, beware of the dog; *in dice*, the worst throw.

cănistra -ōrum, *n.* a bread, fruit, or flower basket.

cănĭtĭēs, *acc.* -em, *abl.* -e, *f.* whitish-grey colour, *esp. of the hair*; grey hair; old age.

canna -ae *f.* a reed; reed-pipe; small boat.

cannăbis -is, *acc.* -im, *abl.* -i, *f.* cannăbus -i, *m.* cannăbum -i, *n.* hemp.

Cannae -ārum, *f.* in Apulia, scene of a defeat of the Romans by Hannibal. *Adj.*, Cannensis.

căno, cĕcĭni, cantum, 3. to sing. *Intransit.*, to crow; *of frogs*, to croak; to play; *canere receptui*, to sound the signal for retreat. *Transit.*, to celebrate in song; to play on a musical instrument; to prophesy.

Cănōpus -i, *m.* a city in Lower Egypt.

cănor -ōris, *m.* melody, song, sound.

cănōrus -a -um, melodious, sweetsounding. *Subst.*, cănōrum -i, *n.* harmonious sound.

Cantăbri -ōrum, *m.* people in the north of Spain.

cantāmen -ĭnis, *n.* incantation.

cantātor -ōris, *m.* a singer.

cantērius -i, *m.* a beast of burden, nag.

canthăris -idis, *f.* a beetle, the Spanish fly.

canthărus -i, *m.* a tankard; a kind of sea-fish.

canthus -i, *m.* the tire of a wheel; a wheel.

canticum -i, *n.* a scene in the Roman comedy, accompanied by music and dancing; a song.

cantĭlēna -ae, *f.* an old song, chatter.

cantĭo -ōnis, *f.* a song, an incantation.

cantĭto, 1. to sing repeatedly.

Cantĭum -ii, *n.* now Kent.

cantiuncŭla -ae, *f.* (*dim. of cantio*), flattering, enticing song.

canto -āvi -ātum, 1. to sing or play. *Intransit.*, *of the cock*, to crow; to play on an instrument. *Transit.*, to sing or play; to celebrate in singing; to praise; to recite; tell.

cantor -ōris, *m.* a singer, poet; an actor.

cantus -ūs, *m.* song, poetry; music; prophecy; incantation.

cānus -a -um, whitish-grey, grey; old, aged. *Subst.*, cani -ōrum. grey hair.

Cănŭsĭum -ii, *n.* town of Apulia.

căpācĭtas -ātis, *f.* breadth, roominess.

căpax -ācis, able to hold; broad, roomy; able to grasp, capable, fit for; *capax imperii*.

căpēdo -ĭnis, *f.* bowl used in sacrifices.

căpēduncŭla -ae, *f.* (*dim. of capedo*), a small bowl.

căpella -ae, *f.* (*dim. of capra*), a she-goat; a constellation.

Căpēna -ae, *f.* a town in Etruria. *Adj.*, Căpēnās -ātis, Căpēnus -a -um; *porta Capena*, a gate in Rome.

căper -ri, *m.* a he-goat; the smell under the armpits.

căpesso -īvi -ii -ītum, 3. to seize; to take to, *fugam*; to take in hand, *rempublicam*, to enter public life; *tuta capessere*, to adopt a safe policy; to strive to reach, to make for, *Melitam*.

căpillātus -a -um, hairy, having hair.

căpillus -i, *m.* hair of the head or of the beard; *plur.*, *compti capilli*; hair of animals.

căpio, cēpi, captum, 3. (*obsolete fut. capso*), to take, to seize; to arrive at, *portum*; to begin, *consulatum*; *of a quality*, adopt; to take possession of by force; (captus -i. *m.* (= *captivus*) a captive); *fig.* to seize; to attack; (*pass. capi*, to be injured or diseased; *oculis et auribus captus*, blind and deaf); to deceive; receive; suffer, undergo; to contain; to allow of, to comprehend.

căpis -idis, *f.* a one-handled vessel.

căpistro, 1. to fasten with a halter.

căpistrum -i, *n.* a halter.

căpital -ālis, *n. sc. facinus*, a capital crime.

căpĭtālis -e, relating to the head, relating to life; *odium*, mortal hatred; *oratio*, dangerous; chief, distinguished.

căpĭto -ōnis, *m.* a man with a large head.

Căpĭtōlium -ii, *n.* the temple of Jupiter at Rome, the Capitol; *often of the whole hill.* *Adj.*, Căpĭtōlinus. *Subst.*, Căpĭtōlini -ōrum, *m.* the superintendents of Capitoline games.

căpĭtŭlātim, *adv.* briefly, summarily.

căpĭtŭlum -i, *n. (dim. of caput)*, a little head.

Cappădōcia -ae, *f.* a district of Asia Minor.

capra -ae, *f.* a she-goat; a constellation.

căprĕa -ae, *f.* a roe, roebuck.

Capreae -ārum, *f.* small island, *now* Capri.

căprĕŏlus -i, *m.* a roebuck; *plur.,* props, supports.

căpricornus -i, *m.* a sign of the zodiac.

căprĭfĭcus -i, *m.* the wild fig-tree, and its fruit.

căprĭgĕnus -a -um, born of goats.

căprĭmulgus -i, *m.* a goat-milker *i.e.* a countryman.

căprīnus -a -um, relating to a goat.

căprĭpēs -pĕdis, goat-footed.

capsa -ae, *f.* box *or* case for books.

capsārius -i, *m.* a slave who carried to school his young master's satchel.

capsŭla -ae, *f. (dim. of capsa)*, a little chest.

captātĭo -ōnis, *f.* a catching; *verborum,* quibbling.

captātor -ōris, *m.* one who eagerly seizes; a legacy-hunter.

captĭo -ōnis, *f.* a deception; harm, loss; fallacy.

captĭōsē, *adv.* insidiously.

captĭōsus -a -um, deceitful; captious, insidious. *Subst.,* captĭōsa -ōrum, *n.* sophistries.

captiuncŭla -ae, *f. (dim. of captio)*, fallacy, quibble.

captīvĭtas -ātĭs, *f.* captivity; *urbĭum,* conquest.

captīvus -a -um, taken, captured; captive; *subst.,* captīvus -i,

capto, 1. to seize, hunt; to desire, seek; entice.

captus -ūs, *m.* a catching, taking; power of comprehension, idea.

Căpŭa -ae, *f.* chief town of Campania. *Adj.,* Căpŭānus -a -um.

căpŭlus -i, *m.* coffin; handle.

căput -ĭtĭs, *n.* the head; a person; *exactio capitum,* poll-tax; life, existence; political rights; head of cattle; the top, summit; the source; the head, chief; *of money,* capital.

Căpys -ўos, *acc.* yn, *m.* companion of Aeneas.

carbăsĕus -a -um, made of canvas, carbăsus -i, *f. plur. heterocl. gen.,* carbăsa -ōrum, fine Spanish flax; a linen garment, a sail.

carbătĭnus -a -um, of untanned leather.

carbo -ōnis, *m.* coal, charcoal; cognomen of the Paperii.

carbōnārĭus -ii, *m.* a charcoal burner.

carcer -ĕris, *m.* a prison, cell; *plur. carceres,* starting-place of a racecourse.

carchēsĭum -ii, *n.* a goblet with handles, contracted in the middle.

cardăces -um, *m.* a Persian troop.

cardĭăcus -a -um, pertaining to the stomach. *Subst.,* cardĭăcus -i, *m.* one who suffers from a disease of the stomach.

cardo -ĭnis, *m.* the hinge of a door; a pole of the heavens; *cardo duplex,* the ends of the earth's axis; *poet., quattuor cardines mundi,* the four cardinal points; a circumstance, upon which others depend.

cardŭus -i, *m.* a thistle.

cārē, *adv.* at a high price.

cārectum -i, *n.* a sedgy spot.

cārĕo -ŭi -ĭtūrus, 2. *gov. the abl.;* to be without, destitute of; to make no use of; to absent oneself from, *foro; patria,* to leave Rome; to be deprived of, to miss.

Cāria -ae, *f.* district of Asia Minor. *Subst.,* Cārĭca -ae, *f.* a kind of dried fig.

cārex -ĭcis, *f.* sedge.

cārĭēs, *acc.* -em, *abl.* -e *(other cases not found),* *f.* decay.

cărīna -ae, *f.* the keel of a ship; a ship; *plur.,* Cărīnae -ārum, *f.* a spot in Rome on the Esquiline.

cărĭōsus -a -um, rotten, decayed.

cāris -ĭdis, *f.* a kind of crab.

căristia = *Charistia (q.v.).*

cārĭtas -ātis, *f.* dearness, high price *nummorum,* scarcity of money; affection, esteem; *in plur.,* beloved objects.

carmen -ĭnis, *n.* a song, tune, *vocal or instrumental;* the screech of the owl; poetry, a poem; part of a poem; a prediction; incantation; a religious *or* legal formula.

Carmentis -is, *f., and* Carmenta -ae, *f.* a prophetess, the mother of Evander, who came with him to Latium, prophesied on the Capitoline hill, and was afterwards reverenced as a deity. *Adj.,* Carmentalis -e; *plur.,* Carmentalia -ium, *n.* the festival of Carmentis.

carnĭfex -fĭcis, *m.* the public executioner; tormentor.

carnĭfĭcĭna -ae, *f.* the hangman's office; place of torture; torture.

carnĭfĭco, 1. to slay, behead.

Carnūtes -um, *m.* people in the middle of Gaul.

1. căro, 3. to card wool.

2. căro, carnis, *f.* flesh.

carpentum -i, *n.* a two-wheeled carriage, a coach; a baggage waggon.

carpo -psi -ptum, 3. to pluck, pluck off, *flores; pensum,* to spin; *gramen,* to graze; *of bees,* to suck; to pull to pieces; to choose out; *poet.* to enjoy, *diem;* to pass over, *mare;* to carp at, calumniate; *milit.,* to harass; to weaken, *vires;* to divide.

carptim, *adv.* in pieces, in single portions; in different places; at different times.

carptor -ōris, *m.* one who carves food.

carrūca -ae, *f.* a four-wheeled carriage.

carrus -i, *m.* (carrum -i, *n.*), a four-wheeled baggage-waggon.

Carthāgo -ĭnis, *f.* the city of Carthage in N. Africa; Carthago (Nova), colony of the Carthaginians in Hispania Tarraconensis, *now* Cartagena. *Adj.*, Carthāgĭniensis -e.

cărunc̆ula -ae, *f.* (*dim. of caro*), a small piece of flesh.

cărus -a -um, high priced, dear; dear, beloved.

Căryae -ārum, *f.* in Laconia, with a temple to Artemis; Căryătĭdes, *acc.* -ĭdas, *f.* maidens who served in the temple of Artemis; *in architecture*, the figures of women in the place of pillars.

căsa -ae, *f.* a hut, cottage; barrack.

căsĕŏlus -i (*dim. of caseus*), a little cheese.

căsĕus -i, *m.* a cheese.

căsia -ae, *f.* tree with an aromatic bark.

Cassandra -ae, *f.* daughter of Priam, on whom the gift of prophecy was conferred by Apollo, with the reservation that no one should believe her.

cassē, *adv.* in vain, without result.

cassĭda -ae, *f.* a helmet.

Cassĭŏpē -ēs, *f.* mother of Andromeda.

1. cassĭs -ĭdis, *f.* a metal helmet.

2. cassĭs -is, *gen. plur.* casses -ium, *m.* a net; trap, snare; spider's web.

cassĭtĕrum -i, *n.* tin; Cassĭtĕrĭdes -um, *f.* the tin islands, the Scilly Isles.

Cassĭus -a -um, name of a Roman gens, originally patrician, afterwards plebeian.

cassus -a -um, empty, hollow; *poet., with abl. or genit.*, deprived of; worthless, useless; *in cassum*, in vain.

Castălĭa -ae, *f.* spring on Mount Parnassus, sacred to Apollo and the Muses.

castănĕa -ae, *f.* chestnut-tree; chestnut.

castē, *adv.* purely; innocently; piously.

castellānus -a -um, relating to a fortress. *Subst.*, castellāni -ōrum, *m.* garrison of a fortress.

castellātim, *adv.* in single fortresses.

castellum -i, *n.* (*dim. of castrum*), a castle, fortress; refuge.

castīgātĭo -ōnis, *f.* punishment, reproof.

castīgātor -ōris, *m.* one who reproves or punishes.

castīgātus -a -um, restrained; small, neat.

castīgo, 1. to reprove, punish; to correct; to restrain.

castĭmōnia -ae, *f.* purity.

castĭtas -ātis, *f.* chastity.

1. castor -ōris, *m.* the beaver.

2. Castor -ōris, *m.* twin-brother of Pollux and Helen. *Ecastor, mēcastor*, By Castor!

castŏrĕum -i, *n.* an aromatic secretion obtained from the beaver.

castrensis -e, pertaining to a camp.

castrum -i, *n. sing.*, a castle, fortress; *plur.*, castra -ōrum, *n.* a camp; *aestiva*, summer quarters; *hiberna*, winter quarters; *navalia*, a naval encampment; *fig., like the English* camp, *of a party, faction*; a day's march; military service; a campaign.

castus -a -um, pure, innocent; temperate, unselfish; chaste; pious.

căsŭla -ae, *f.* (*dim. of casa*), a little hut.

căsus -ūs, *m.* a falling, fall; *of a season*, end; *in grammar*, case; occasion, opportunity; accident, event; *abl. casu*, by chance; disaster; ruin; violent death.

cătădrŏmus -i, *m.* rope for rope-dancing.

Cătădūpa -ōrum, *n.* the Nile contracts, *now* cataracts of Wady Halfa.

cătăgrăphus -a -um, painted, particoloured.

cătăphractes -ae, *m.* a breast-plate of iron scales; *adj.*, cătăphractus -a -um, mail-clad.

cătăplūs -i, *m.* the arrival of a ship; a ship that is arriving.

cătăpulta -ae, *f.* engine of war, a catapult.

cătăracta (cătarr-) -ae, *f.* and cătăractes -ae, *m.* a waterfall; sluice *or* flood-gate; portcullis.

cătasta -ae, *f.* a stage upon which slaves were exposed in the market.

cătē, *adv.* skilfully, cleverly.

cătēia -ae, *f.* a kind of dart.

1. cătella -ae, *f.* (*dim. of catula*), a little bitch.

2. cătella -ae, *f.* (*dim. of catena*), a little chain.

cătellus -i, *m.* (*dim. o͡ catulus*), a little dog.

cătēna -ae, . a chain, fetter, *aliquem in catenas conciere*; restraint, *legum catenae*; series.

cătēnātus -a -um, bound; *labores*, unremitting.

căterva -ae, *f.* crowd, troop, horde; a company of actors; (*of animals*) a flock.

cătervārius -a -um, belonging to a troop.

cătervātim, *adv.* in troops, in masses.

căthedra -ae, *f.* a chair; a litter for women; a professor's chair.

Cătĭlīna -ae, *m.* a Roman, who headed a conspiracy against the state, and was killed in battle at Faesulae, B.C. 62; *adj.*, Cătĭlīnārius.

1. cătĭllus -i, *m.* (*dim. of catinus*), a small dish *or* plate.

2. Cătĭllus -i, *m.* one of the founders of Tibur.

Cătĭna -ae, *f.* and Cătănē -ēs, *f.* a town on the coast of Sicily. *Adj.*, Cătĭnensis -e,

cătĭnum -i, *and* cătīnus -i, *m.* a broad, flat fish.

Căto -ōnis, *m.* cognomen belonging to the gens Porcia. *Adj.*, Cătōnĭānus. *Subst.*,

Cătōnǐnī -orum, *m.* the party of the younger Cato. *Plur.*, **Cătōnes**, men, of the old Roman type, like Cato.

cătōnǐum -i, *n.* the lower world (*in a pun*).

catta -ae, *f.* cat *or* weasel.

Cătullus -i, *m.*, Q. *Valerius Catullus*, a celebrated Roman poet.

Cătŭlus -i, *m.* (*dim. of catus*), a young animal, *esp.* puppy.

cătus a -um, sagacious, clever; cunning.

cauda -ae, *f.* the tail of an animal.

caudex (codex) -icis, *m.* trunk of a tree.

caudǐcārius, *v. codicarius.*

Caudǐum -ii, *n.* in Samnium, near the Caudine Forks.

caulae -ārum, *f.* a hole, opening; sheepfold.

caulis -is, *m.* the stalk of a plant, *esp.* the cabbage-plant; *pennae*, a. quill.

caupo -ōnis, *m.* a small shopkeeper, *or* innkeeper.

caupōna -ae, *f.* a tavern, inn.

caupōnor, 1. *dep.* to trade in anything.

caupōnǔla -ae, . (*dim. of caupo*), a little inn.

caurus (cōrus) -i, *m.* the north-west wind.

causa (caussa) -ae, *f.* a cause, reason; excuse; pretext; plea, *causa*, on account of; *verbi causa*, for example; case; situation, condition; side, party; point in an argument, subject; lawsuit; *causam dicere*, to plead.

causārius -a -um, sickly, diseased; *subst.*, **causārii -orum**, *m. milit.* invalided.

causǐdǐcus -i, *m.* advocate, barrister, (*contemptuous*).

causor, 1. *dep.* to give as a reason, or pretext; to plead, pretend.

causǔla -ae, *f.* (*dim. of causa*), a little lawsuit; a slight occasion.

cautē, *adv.* cautiously, carefully.

cautes -is, *f.* a rough sharp rock.

cautim, *adv.* cautiously, carefully.

cautio -ōnis, *f.* caution, care. *Legal*, security, bail, bond.

cautor -ōris, *m.* one who is on his guard; one who gives bail for another.

cautus -a -um, cautious, wary, sly; *of property*, secured.

căvaedǐum -i, *n.* the open quadrangle formed by the inner walls of a house.

căvěa -ae, *f.* cavity; inclosure, den for wild animals; birdcage; a beehive; seats in a theatre.

căvěo, căvī, cautum, 2. to be on one's guard, to guard against, avoid; to take precautions; *legal*, to give security for; to get security; to provide for in writing, to order.

căverna -ae, *f.* grotto, cavern, cavity, the hold; *coeli*, the vault of heaven.

căvillātio -ōnis, *f.* jesting, irony.

căvillātor -ōris, *m.* a jester, humorist.

căvillor, 1. *dep.* to jest, satirise, make game of; to make captious objections.

căvo, 1. to hollow, excavate; *oppida cuniculis*, to undermine; *parmam gladio*, to pierce. *Partic.*, **căvātus**, hollowed out, hollow.

căvum -i, *n.* cavity, cave.

căvus -a -um, hollow, concave; *flumina*, deep-channelled; *luna, waning; empty.*

Căystrus -i, *m.* river in Lydia; *adj.*, **Căystrius -a -um.**

cě, particle joined to pronouns and adverbs—*e.g.* hisce.

Cěa -ae, *f.* and **Cěōs**, *acc.* Ceo. one of the Cyclades Islands. *Adj.*, **Cěus.**

Cecrops -ōpis, *m.* mythical founder of Athens; **Cecrōpǐdes -ae**, *m.* descendant of Cecrops; *plur.*, the Athenians; **Cecrōpis -ǐdis**, *f.* a female descendant of Cecrops; *as adj., terra*, Attica; *adj.*, **Cecrōpǐus -a -um**; *subst.*, **Cecrōpia -ae**, *f.* the citadel of Athens.

1. **cědo, cessi, cessum**, 3. to go, proceed; to turn out, to happen; to fall to the lot of; to become; to give ground, retire; to submit, yield; to be inferior to, *alicui virtute*; to give up a right.

2. **cědo** *and plur.* **cette**, here with it; give here; out with it! tell us; see here.

cědrus -i, *f.* the cedar, *or* juniper tree; cedar-wood; cedar oil.

Cělaeno -ūs, *f.* 1. daughter of Atlas, placed in the sky as one of the Pleiades; 2. one of the Harpies.

cělātor -ōris, *m.* a concealer.

cělěber -bris -bre *and* **cělěbris -e**, numerous; honoured; renowned. *Of places*, meetings, *etc.*, much frequented; often repeated, *vox celeberrima.*

cělěbrātio -ōnis, *f.* a numerous assembly; celebration.

cělěbrātor -ōris, *m.* one who extols.

cělěbrātus -a -um, *p. adj.* numerously attended; known; honoured; *of places*, much frequented; *of festivals*, solemn, festive.

cělěbrǐtas -ātis, *f.* numerous attendance, a throng; *of a festival*, celebration; a multitude; renown.

cělěbro, 1. to visit frequently, *or* in large numbers; to celebrate, solemnise; to make known; to praise, honour; to exercise.

cěler -ěris -ěre, swift, quick; hasty, rash.

Cělěres -um, *m.* the name of the bodyguard of the Roman kings.

cělěrǐpes -pědis, swift-footed.

cělěrǐtas -ātis, *f.* swiftness.

cělěrǐter, *adv.* quickly, swiftly.

cělěro, 1. *transit. or intransit.*, to hasten.

cella -ae, *f.* a room; storehouse; *cellam emere*, to buy things for the house; place for keeping birds; shrine; the cell of a beehive.

cellǔla -ae, . (*dim. of cella*), a little chamber, *or* cell.

cēlo, 1. to hide, keep secret.

cēlox -ōcis, *f.* a swift vessel, *or* yacht; *publica,* packet-boat.

celsus -a -um, high, upright; eminent; *morally,* lofty; haughty.

Celtae -ārum, *m.* the Celts. *Adj.,* Celticus.

Celtĭbēri -ōrum, *m.* race in Spain.

cēna -ae, *f.* dinner, supper; the courses at a dinner, *prima, altera, tertia*

cēnācŭlum -i, *n.* an eating-room; garret, attic.

cēnātĭo -ōnis, *f.* dining-hall.

cēnātōrius -a -um, relating to dinner. *Subst.,* cēnātōria -ōrum, *n.* clothes to dine in.

cēnātūrĭo, 4. to wish to dine.

cēnātus -a -um, *v.* ceno.

cēnĭto, 1. (*freq. of* ceno), to dine often.

cēno, 1. *intransit.,* to dine, sup. eat; *partic. perf., cenatus,* having dined, after dinner; *transit.,* to dine on, to eat.

censĕo -sŭi -sum, 2. to give an opinion; to appraise, estimate; *esp. of the censor,* to take an account of the names and property of Roman citizens; *capite censi,* the lowest class; to make a return to the censor; to vote. *Of the senate,* to resolve. order.

censor -ōris, *m.* the censor ; a severe judge, a censurer.

censōrius -a -um, relating to the censor; *tabulae,* the censor's lists; rigid, severe.

censūra -ae, *f.* the censorship.

census -ūs, *m.* the census; the censor's list, amount of property necessary for enrolment in a certain rank ; *homo sine censu,* a poor man.

centaurēum -ēi, *n. and* centaurium -ii, *n.* the plant centaury.

Centaurus -i, *m.* a centaur, a monster, half man and half horse; *adj.,* Centaurēus.

centēnārĭus -a -um, containing a hundred, relating to a hundred.

centēnus -a -um, *sing.* (*poet.*), *used collectively,* a hundred ; *plur., num. distrib.,* a hundred each.

centēsĭmus -a -um, *num. ordin.* the hundredth. *Subst.,* centēsĭma -ae, *f.* the hundredth part; a tax of one per cent. per month = 12 per cent. per annum.

centĭceps -cĭpitis, hundred-headed.

centiens *or* centiēs, *adv.* a hundred times; *HS. centies,* ten million sesterces.

centĭmānus -a -um, hundred-handed.

centĭplex, *v. centuplex.*

cento -ōnis, *m.* patchwork, a covering of rags; *in war,* coverings to ward off missiles.

centum, *indecl. number.,* a hundred ; any indefinitely large number.

centumgĕmĭnus -a -um, hundred-fold; *Briareus,* hundred-armed.

centumvir -i, *m., plur.* centumvirī

ōrum, *m.* a college of 105 magistrates.

centumvĭrālis -e, relating to the centumviri.

centuncŭlus i, *m.* (*dim. of cento*), a little patch, *or* patchwork.

centŭplex -icis, a hundred-fold.

centŭrĭa -ae, . a division of 100; a century, one of the divisions of the Roman people.

centŭrĭātim, *adv.* by centuries *or* companies.

1. centŭrĭātus -ūs, *m.* the division into companies *or* centuries.

2. centŭrĭātus -ūs, *m.* the centurion's office.

1. centŭrĭo, 1. to divide into centuries; *comitia centuriata,* the assembly in which the whole Roman people voted in their centuries.

2. centŭrĭo -ōnis, *m.* a centurion.

centŭrĭōnātus -ūs, *m.* the election of centurions.

centussis -is, *m.* a hundred asses.

cēnŭla -ae, *f.* (*dim. of cena*), a little meal.

cēnum, *v.* caenum.

Cĕos, *v.* Cea.

cēpa, *v.* caepa.

Cēpheus -ĕi, *m.* king of Aethiopia, father of Andromeda. *Adj.,* Cēphēĭus.

Cēphīsus, *or* Cēphissus -i, *m.* a river in Boeotia, and *as a river-god,* the father of Narcissus. *Adj.,* Cēphīsis -ĭdis, a river of Attica. Adj., Cēphīsĭas -ădis, *f.*

cēra -ae, *f.* wax; articles made of wax; writing-tablets coated with wax; a waxen seal; a waxen image.

Cērāmīcus -i, *m. lit.* the pottery market at Athens.

Cērārĭum -i, *n.* a fee for sealing a document.

Cērastēs -ae, *m.* the horned snake.

cĕrāsus -i, *f.* a cherry-tree; a cherry.

cĕraunĭus -a -um, *ceraunia gemma, or subst.,* cĕraunĭum -i, *n.* a kind of precious stone.

Cerbĕrŏs *and* us -i, *m.* the three-headed dog at the gates of Tartarus.

cercŏpĭthēcŏs *and* us -i, *m.* a kind of long-tailed ape.

cercūrus -i, *m.* a light vessel; a kind of sea-fish.

cerdo -ōnis, *m.* craftsman, artizan.

cĕrēbrōsus -a -um, hot-brained, hot tempered.

cĕrĕbrum -i, *n.* the brain; the understanding; anger.

Cĕrēs -ĕris, the Roman goddess of agriculture, and mother of Proserpine; grain, corn. *Adj.,* Cĕrēālis -e; *subst.,* Cĕrĕālĭa -ĭum, *n.* the festival of Ceres.

cĕrēus -a -um, waxen ; wax-coloured ; *castra,* the cells of a hive. *Subst.,* cērĕus -i, m. a wax taper; wax-coloured.

cērintha -ae, f. the wax flower.

cērinus -a -um, wax-coloured.

cerno, crēvi, crētum, 3. to separate; to distinguish; to perceive; to decide; in battle = to contend; to resolve; to accept an inheritance.

cernŭlus -a -um, falling headlong, with the face towards the ground.

cēro, 1. to cover with wax.

cērōma -ătis, n. ointment of oil and wax used by wrestlers; arena for wrestling.

cērōmáticus -a -um, anointed with the ceroma.

cerrītus -a -um, frantic, mad.

certāmen -ĭnis, n. contest; fight, rivalry.

certātim, adv. emulously, eagerly.

certātĭo -ōnis, f. a contest; emulation.

certē, adv. certainly; at least, mihi certe.

1. certō, adv. certainly; certo scio, I am sure of it.

2. certo, 1. to contend, dispute.

certus -a -um, separated; certain, definite; certum est (mihi, etc.), I am resolved; certus mori, determined to die; secure, to be depended on; true, undoubted; certum est, it is certain; certum facere aliquem, to inform.

cērŭla -ae, f. (dim. of cera), a little piece of wax.

cerva -ae, f. hind; poet., deer.

cervīcal -ālis, n. a cushion, a pillow.

cervicŭla -ae, f. (dim. of cervix), a little neck.

cervinus -a -um, relating to a stag.

cervix -īcis, f. the nape of the neck, the neck; dare cervices alicui, to submit to death.

cervus -i, m. a stag; cervi, milit., branches of trees as a palisade, to impede an enemy.

cespes, v. caespes.

cessātĭo -ōnis, f. a delaying; inactivity, idleness.

cessātor -ōris, m. one who loiters and lingers.

cessĭo -ōnis, f. a giving up, a cession.

cesso, 1. to leave off, linger; to loiter, to be idle; to be negligent; to rest; to make holiday; of land, to lie fallow.

cestrosphendŏnē -ēs, f. engine for hurling stones.

1. cestus -i, m. a girdle.

2. cestus -ūs, m. v. caestus.

cētārius -a -um, relating to sea-fish, to the tunny-fish. Subst., cētārius -ii, m. fishmonger, dealer in sea-fish; cētāria -ae, f. and cētārium -ii, n. a bay where the tunny-fish were caught.

cēte, v. cetus.

cētĕrōqui, or cētĕrōquin, adv. otherwise, else.

cētĕrus -a -um, the other, the rest; usually plur., cētĕri -ae -a; et cetera, and so on; adv., ceterum, for the rest moreover.

cētra -ae, f. a small Spanish shield.

cētrātus -a -um, armed with the cetra.

cētus -i, m. and cētos, plur. cētē, n. any large sea-fish; esp. the tunny-fish.

ceu, adv. as, like as; as if.

Cēyx -ȳcis, m. king of Trachis, changed into a kingfisher.

Chaerōnēa -ae, f. town in Boeotia, scene of a victory of Philip of Macedon over the Athenians.

Chalcis -idis, f. chief city of Euboea; adj., Chalcidicus -a -um. Adj. Chalcidensis -e.

Chaldaea -ae, f. part of Babylonia. Adj., Chaldaeus; subst., Chaldaei -ōrum, m. soothsayers; Chaldaeicus -a -um, Chaldaic.

chălȳbēius -a -um, made of steel.

Chălȳbes -um, m. people in Pontus, famous for their steel.

chălybs -ybis, m. steel; sword; horse's bit; tip of an arrow.

Chāones -um, m. people of north-western Epirus; adj., Chāŏnius -a -um, Epirote; Chāŏnia -ae, f. the district of Chaonia.

chāos, acc. chaos. abl. chao (other cases not found), n. the lower world; personified, the father of Night and Erebus; chaos.

chara -ae, f. a root, perhaps wild cabbage.

Chăristĭa (cārīstĭa) -ōrum, n. a festival celebrated in February.

Chărĭtes -um, f. the Graces.

Chăron -ontis, m. the ferryman, who took souls over the river Styx.

charta -ae, f. leaf of Egyptian papyrus; paper; letter, poem.

chartŭla -ae, f. (dim. of charta), a little paper.

Chărybdis -is, f. whirlpool in the Sicilian straits, opposite the rock Scylla.

Chatti (Catthi, Catti) -ōrum, m. a German people.

chĕlydrus -i, m. an amphibious snake.

chĕlys, acc. -ym and -yn, voc. -y, the tortoise; the lyre.

Cherrŏnēsus and Chersŏnēsus -i, f. the Thracian peninsula on the Hellespont.

chiliarchus -i, m. commander of 1,000 soldiers; among the Persians, prime minister.

Chimaera -ae, f. a monster, killed by Bellerophon.

chimaerĭfĕr -fĕra -fĕrum, producing the Chimaera.

Chios or Chius -i, f. island in the Aegean Sea; subst., Chium -i, n. Chian wine.

chirāgra -ae, f. gout in the hands.

chīrŏgrăphum -i, n. an autograph, a person's own handwriting.

Chiron, Chiro -ōnis, m. a centaur.

chīrŏnŏmos -i, c. and chīrŏnŏmōn ontis, m. a mime.

chirurgia -ae, f. surgery.

chlămўdātus -a -um, clothed in the chlamys.

chlămўs -ўdis, f., a large upper garment of wool, worn in Greece.

chŏrāgus -i, m. he who supplies the chorus.

chŏraulēs -ae, m. flute-player.

chorda -ae, f. string (of musical instrument).

chŏrea -ae, f. a dance to the sound of the dancers' voices.

chŏrŏcithăristēs -ae, m. one who accompanies a chorus on the cithara.

chŏrus -i, m. a choral dance; the chorus; crowd, troop.

Christiānus -i, m. a Christian.

Christus -i, m. Christ.

chrŏmis -is, m. a sea-fish.

chrÿsŏlithus -i, m. and f. chrysolite, or topaz.

chrÿsŏphrys, acc. -yn, f. a kind of sea-fish.

cibārius -a -um, relating to food; ordinary, common. Subst., cibāria -orum, n. food, rations, fodder.

cibātus -ūs, m. food, nourishment.

cibo, 1. to feed.

cibŏrium -ii, n. and cibōria -ae, f. seed pod of the Egyptian bean; drinking vessel.

cibus -i, m. food, nourishment, fodder; bait; sustenance.

cicāda -ae, f. a cicada.

cicātrix -icis, f. a scar, cicatrice; the marks of incisions in plants; the patch upon an old shoe.

cicer -ĕris, n. a chick-pea.

Cicĕro -ōnis, m. M. Tullius Cicero, the greatest Roman orator and writer; adj., Cicĕrōnianus.

Cicŏnes -um, m. a Thracian people.

cicōnia -ae, f. a stork.

cicur -ūris, adj. tame.

cicūta -ae, f. hemlock; poison extracted from the hemlock; a shepherd's pipe, made from the hemlock stalk.

cieo, civi, citum, 2. to move, shake; legal, herctum ciere, to divide the inheritance; to disturb, agitate; to summon to battle, aliquem ad arma; to excite, to arouse; to utter; to call by name.

Cilicia -ae, f. a country of Asia Minor.

cilium -ii, n. the eye-lid.

Cimbri -ōrum, m. a German tribe, who invaded the Roman Empire and were defeated by Marius; sing., Cimber -bri, m. a Cimbrian. Adj., Cimbricus.

cīmex -icis, m. a bug.

Cimměrii -ōrum, m. 1. Thracian people; 2. mythical people, living in the extreme west in darkness and mist. Adj., Cimmĕrius, dark.

Cīmon -ōnis, m., an Athenian general.

cinaedus -i, m. an immoral person a wanton dancer. Adj., cinaedus -a -um, bold, shameless.

1. cincinnātus -a -um, having curled hair.

2. Cincinnātus -i, m. the name of a patrician family of the gens Quinctia, to which belonged L. Quinctus Cincinnatus, a type of old Roman honesty and simplicity, consul 460 B.C., in 458 B.C. called from the plough to be dictator.

cincinnus -i, m. curled hair, a lock of hair; artificial rhetorical ornament.

Cincius -a -um, name of a Roman gens.

cinctūra -ae, f. a girdle.

cinctus -ūs, m. a girding; a girdle.

cinctūtus -a -um, girded.

cinĕfactus -a -um, changed into ashes.

cinĕrārius -ii, m. a slave who heated in hot ashes the irons for the hair-dresser.

Cingĕtŏrix -rigis, m. 1. a prince of the Treveri in Gaul; 2. a prince in Britain.

cingo, cinxi, cinctum, 3. to surround; to gird; (pass. cingi, as middle, to gird oneself; to be prepared, ready); to surround the head with a chaplet, to crown; to encircle; enclose; milit., to besiege, to fortify; to accompany; to circle round (of swans).

cingŭla -ae, f. a girdle.

cingŭlum -i, n. a girdle; a sword-belt (plur.).

cingŭlus -i, m. a zone.

ciniflo -ōnis, m. = cinerarius.

cinis -ĕris, m., rarely f., ashes.

cinnămōmum or cinnămum -i, n. cinnamon.

cippus -i, m. tombstone or small tomb; plur. milit., palisades.

circā, adv. round about. Prep. with acc., around; near to; of time, of number, about.

circāmoerium -ii, n. = pomoerium (q.v.).

Circē -ēs and -ae, acc. -am, abl. -a, f. an enchantress.

circensis -e, belonging to the circus. Subst., circenses -ium, m. the circus games.

circino, 1. to form into a circle.

circinus -i, m. pair of compasses.

circitĕr, adv. of place and time, about; near; prep. with acc., about.

circlus = circulus (q.v.).

circŭeo v. circumeo.

circŭitio and circŭmitio -ōnis, f. a going round; milit., patrol; a round-about way of speaking or acting.

circŭitus -ūs, m. circuit, revolution; rhetoric, a period; circumference extent.

circŭlātim, *adv.* in a circle.

circŭlor, 1. *dep.* to gather in groups for conversation, to enter a group, to converse.

circŭlus -i, *m.* (*dim. of circus*), circle, circular figure.

circum, *adv.* round, about, around; *Prep. with acc.*, near, in the vicinity of, around.

circumactus -a -um, *partic.* of *circumago.*

circŭmăgo -ēgi -actum, 3. to drive or turn round, *hence a technical term for the manumission of a slave, because his master took him by the right hand, and turned him round;* to drive about, distract, misload; *of time, circumagi or circumageres se,* to pass away, to be spent, *annus se circumegit.*

circumăro, 1. to plough round.

circumcaesūra -ae, *f.* the external outline of a body.

circumcido -cīdi -cīsum, 3. to cut round, trim; to diminish, cut off.

circumcircā, *adv.* all round about.

circumcīsus -a -um, *p. adj.* steep, inaccessible.

circumclūdo -clūsi -clūsum, 3. to shut in, surround.

circumcŏlo, 3. to dwell around, dwell near.

circumcurso, 1. to run round.

circumdo -dĕdi -dătum, 1. surround; *with acc. and dat., arma humeris;* to supply ; to build or place round ; to confine, limit.

circumdūco -duxi -ductum, 3. to move or drive round; to lead by a roundabout course ; to lead astray, deceive; to amplify; to take round (to prolong).

circumductus -a -um, *partic.* of *circumduco.*

circŭmĕo (circueo) -ivi or -ii -ĭtum -īre, to go, travel, or walk round in a circle; to cheat; to express by circumlocution; to surround; to go about; to visit; to canvass or solicit.

circumĕquito, 1. to ride round.

circumerro, 1. to wander round.

circumfĕro -tŭli -lātum -ferre, to carry round, bring round; to spread around; to turn in all directions, *oculos;* to spread a report; *middle, sol ut circumferatur,* revolves; to lustrate, purify, *by carrying round consecrated objects.*

circumflecto -flexi -flexum, 3. to bend round, to turn about.

circumflo, 1. to blow round.

circumflŭo -fluxi fluxum, 3. to flow round; to overflow; to abound in.

circumflŭus -a -um, *act.* flowing round; *pass.* surrounded by water.

circumfŏrānĕus -a -um, round the forum ; *aes,* money borrowed from the bankers whose shops were round the forum = debt; attending at markets.

circumfundo -fūdi -fūsum, 3. to pour around; *pass., circumfundi, or reflexive, se circumfundere,* to be poured round = to surround, *with dat.; of persons,* to flock round, to surround, to encircle, hem in; *pass.,* to be washed by.

circumgĕmo, 3. to growl round about.

circumgesto, 1. to carry round.

circumgrĕdior -gressus sum -grŏdi, to go round, travel round, esp. with hostile intent.

circumiăcĕo, 2. to lie round about, adjoin, *with dat.*

circumicio -ieci -iectum, 3. to throw round, put round ; to surround; circumiectus -a -um, surrounding, adjacent.

circumiectus -ūs, *m.* a surrounding, enclosing.

circumlăvo -āre and -ĕre, to wash round.

circumligo, 1. to bind round, bind to; to envelop.

circumlĭno, *no perf.* -lĭtum, 3. and circumlinio -linii, 4. to smear on anything; cover.

circumlŭo, 3. to wash round, flow round.

circumlustrans -antis, illuminating all round.

circumlŭvio -ōnis, *f.* formation of an island by encroachment of a river.

circummitto -mīsi -missum, 3. to send by a roundabout way, to send round; in all directions.

circummūnio, 4. to fortify round, shut in by lines of circumvallation.

circummūnītio -ōnis, *f.* circumvallation of a fortress.

circumpădānus -a -um, near the river Po.

circumplaudo, 3. to clap or applaud on all sides.

circumplector -plexus, 3. *dep.* to embrace, enclose, surround.

circumplico, 1. to fold round, wind round.

circumpōno -pŏsŭi -pŏsitum, 3. to encircle.

circumpōtātio -ōnis, *t.* drinking round in succession.

circumrētio, 4. to ensnare.

circumrōdo -rōsi, 3. to gnaw round ; to hedge, be non-committal.

circumsaepio -saeptus, 4. to hedge round, enclose.

circumscindo, 3. to tear off, strip.

circumscrībo -scripsi -scriptum, 3. to describe a circle round; to fix the boundaries of; to limit, hamper; to deceive; to defraud, embezzle, annul.

circumscriptē, *adv.* in rhetorical periods.

circumscriptio -ōnis, *f.* encircling; circumference ; outline, boundary ; *in rhetoric,* a period; deceit, swindling.

circumscriptor -ōris. *m.* a swindler.

circumscriptus -a -um, *p. adj.* concise.
circumsēco -sectum,1.to cut round about.
circumsēdĕo -sēdi -sessum, 2. to sit round; to besiege.
circumsessio -ōnis, *f.* a beleaguering.
circumsido -sēdi, 3. to besiege.
circumsilio, 4. to leap *or* jump round; to surround.
circumsisto -stĕti, *or* -stĭti, 3. to surround; press round.
circumsŏno -sŏnŭi -sŏnātum, 1. to sound around; to echo with.
circumsŏnus -a -um, sounding around.
circumspectio -ōnis, *f.* foresight, circumspection, caution.
circumspecto, 1. *Intransit.,* to look round repeatedly. *Transit.,* to look round at; to seek for; wait for.
1. circumspectus -a -um, *p. adj.* deliberate, well considered; *of persons,* cautious.
2. circumspectus -ūs, *m.* looking round; attention to; prospect.
circumspicio -spexi -spectum, 3. *Intransit.,* to look round; to consider. *Transit.,* to look round at; to consider carefully; to look for.
circumsto -stĕti, 1. to surround, encircle ; *circumstantes,* the bystanders ; to beleaguer.
circumstrĕpo -strĕpŭi -strĕpitum, 3. to roar, shout around.
circumstrŭo -struxi -structum, 3. to build round.
circumsurgens -entis, rising round.
circumtĕgo, 3. to cover all round.
circumtĕro, 3. to rub against on all sides; *poet.* to crowd round.
circumtextus -a -um, woven all round.
circumtŏno -tŏnŭi, 1. to thunder round.
circumtonsus -a -um, shorn all round; *of discourse,* artificial.
circumvādo -vāsi, 3. to attack from every side, to surround.
circumvăgus -a -um, wandering round.
circumvallo, 1. to blockade.
circumvectio -ōnis, *f.* a carrying round of merchandise ; *portorium circumvectionis,* transit dues; *solis,* circuit, revolution.
circumvector, 1. *dep.,* to ride *or* sail round; *poet.* to describe.
circumvĕho, to carry round.
circumvĕhor -vectus, 3. *dep.,* to ride *or* sail round.
circumvēlo, 1. to conceal on all sides.
circumvĕnio -vēni -ventum, 4. to surround, encircle; to beset, assail; to cheat.
circumversor, 1. *dep.,* to twist *or* turn round.
circumverto (-vorto) -verti (-vorti) -versum (-vorsum), 3. to turn, twist round; *reflex. or pass.,* to turn oneself round; *mancipium,* to manumit.
circ vestio, 4. to clothe all round, *poet.*

circumvŏlito, 1. to fly round; to rove about.
circumvŏlo, 1. to fly round.
circumvolvo -volvi -vŏlūtum, 3. to roll round.
circus -i, *m.* a circular line; *candens,* the Milky Way; circus, hippodrome.
cīris -is, *f.* a bird, into which Scylla was transformed.
cirrātus -a -um, curled, crisped.
Cirrha -ae, *f.* a city of Phocis, port of Delphi, sacred to Apollo.
cirrus -i, *m.* a lock *or* ringlet; fringe of a garment.
Cirta -ae, *f.* a town of Numidia.
cis, *prep., with acc.,* on this side.
cisalpīnus -a -um, on this side (the Roman), *i.e.* the south side of the Alps.
cisium -ii, *n.* a light two-wheeled gig.
cisrhēnānus -a -um, on this side the Rhine.
Cisseus -ĕi, *m.* father of Hecuba ; Cissēis -idis, *f.* Hecuba.
cista -ae, *f.* a chest, casket; a ballot-box.
cistella -ae, *f.* (*dim. of cista*), a little chest, *or* casket.
cisterna -ae, *f.* reservoir, cistern.
cistifer -fĕri, *m.* one who carries a box *or* chest.
cistŏphŏrus -i, *m.* an Asiatic coin.
cistŭla -ae, *f.* (*dim. of cista*), a casket.
citātim, *adv.* quickly, hastily.
citātus -a -um, *p. adj.,* quick, speedy; *citato equo or citatis equis,* at full gallop.
citĕr -tra -trum, on this side. *Compar.,* citĕrĭŏr -us, *genit.* -ōris, on this side, *Gallia; of time,* earlier. *Superl.,* citimus *or* citŭmus, very near, nearest.
Cithaerōn -ōnis, *m.* a mountain of Boeotia, scene of the Bacchic orgies.
cithăra -ae, *f.* a four-stringed instrument.
cithărista -ae, *m.* a player on the cithara.
cithăristria -ae, *f.* female player on the cithara.
cithărizo, 1. to play the cithara.
cithăroedus -i, *m.* one who sings to the cithara.
1. cĭto, *comp.* citius, *sup.* citissime, *adv.* quickly, speedily; *non cito,* not easily; *citius quam,* sooner than.
2. cĭto, 1. to put into violent motion; to summon; to shout out; to call forth, to produce.
cītrā, *adv. and prep. with acc.,* on this side; within, before.
citrĕus -a -um, belonging to the citrus tree *or* the citron tree ; *citrea,* the citron tree; *citreum,* the citron.
citrō, *adv. only with ultro ; ultro et citro,* up and down, higher and hither.
citrum -i, *n.* citrus wood.
citrus -i, *m.* the citrus, a kind of African cypress.

citus -a -um, *p.* adj., quick; *pes,* the iambus.

cīvicus -a -um, relating to a citizen, civic; *bella,* civil war; **cīvica** -ae, *f.* the civic crown.

cīvīlis -e, relating to a citizen, civic, civil ; *jurisme suroms obvious* (v. *civicus*); *ius, either* civil law *or* law of private rights; *dies,* from midnight to midnight; befitting a citizen; popular, affable; relating to public life *or* the state.

cīvīlītās -ātis, *f.* the science of politics; politeness, condescension.

cīvīlitēr, adv. like a citizen; politely.

cīvis -is, *c.* a citizen; fellow citizen; subject.

cīvitas -ātis, *f.* citizenship ; a state, commonwealth; town, city.

clādēs -is, *f.* destruction; loss, damage; *disaster, injury, defeat; cladem inferre, accipere.*

clam, adv. secretly, in secret; *esse,* to remain incognito. *Prep. with abl.*

clāmātor -ōris, *m* shouter, noisy declaimer.

clāmito, 1. to cry loudly, shout violently.

clāmo, 1. *Intransit.,* to shout, cry aloud. *Transit.,* to call to *or* upon; to proclaim aloud.

clāmor -ōris, *m.* a loud shouting, cry; shout of applause; war-cry; cry of sorrow; a sound; wail; noise.

clāmōsus -a -um, act., noisy, clamorous; *pass.,* filled with noise, *circus.*

clanculum, adv., secretly, in secret; *prep. with acc., clanculum patres.*

clandestīnus -a -um, secret; hidden.

clangor -ōris, *m.* a sound, clang, noise.

clārē, adv. clearly, brightly; aloud; distinctly; illustriously.

clārĕo, 2. to be bright, to shine; to be clear to the mind; to be distinguished.

clāresco, clāruī, 3. to become clear, bright; to sound clearly; to become evident; to become illustrious.

clārigātio -ōnis, *f.* the demand of satisfaction and declaration of war by a Fetialis.

clārīgo, to demand restitution and declare war if it were refused.

clārīsŏnus -a -um, clearly sounding.

clārītas -ātis, *f.* clearness, brilliancy; clearness to the mind; fame, celebrity.

clārītūdo -ĭnis, *f.* clearness, brilliancy; fame, celebrity.

clāro, 1. to make clear, make bright; to make plain; to make illustrious.

clārus -a -um, clear, bright, shining; *poet. of the wind,* bringing fair weather; loud; evident; illustrious; notorious.

classiārius -i, *m.* a marine.

classicŭla -ae, *f.* (*dim. of classis*), flotilla.

classicus -a -um, relating to the classes

into which the Roman citizens were distributed; relating to the army or the fleet; *bella,* naval war. *Subst.,* **classicus** -i, *m.* a citizen of the highest class; *subst.,* **classicum** -i, *n.* the signal of engagement given by a trumpet; the trumpet itself. *Subst.,* **classici** -ōrum, *m.* marines.

classis -is, *f.* a class, division; *milit.,* the forces; a land army; the fleet; *poet.,* a ship.

clātri -ōrum, *m.* and **clātra** -ōrum, *n.* a trellis *or* grating.

claudeo -ēre, 2. *and gen.* **claudo,** *clausurus,* 3. to limp, be lame.

claudīcātio -ōnis, *f.* a limping.

claudico, 1. to limp, be lame; incline (of a balance); to halt, waver.

Claudius (Clōdius) -a -um, the name of a Roman family; *Appius Claudius,* the most notorious of the decemvirs; *Appius Claudius Caecus,* censor 312 B.C., the builder of several great public works. *Adj.,* **Claudiānus, Claudiātis** -e, **Clōdiānus.**

1. **claudo,** *clausi, clausum,* 3. *and* **clūdo,** to shut close; to make inaccessible; to bring up the roar; to bring to an end; to dam up, stop, intercept; to shut up in; *milit.,* to invest; to surround; *of character, clausus,* secret, close. *Subst.,* **clausum** -i, *n.* a bolt *or* lock.

2. **claudo** = *claudeo* (q.v.).

claudus -a -um, limping, lame; defective, wavering ; *poet., carmina alterno versu,* elegiac verse.

claustrum -i, *n. gen. plur.* bolt, bar; gate, inclosure, dam, limit, boundary; custody, confinement; den, cage; pass *or* narrow place; *milit.,* key *or* critical point of a position, *fig.,* barrier.

clausŭla -ae, *f.* the end, conclusion.

clāva -ae, *f.* knotty staff *or* cudgel; the club of Hercules.

clāvārium -i, *n.* a gift of money to Roman soldiers.

clāvīcŭla -ae, *f.* (*dim. of clavis*), the tendril by which the vine clings.

1. **clāvīger** -gĕri, *m.* the club-bearer, epithet of Hercules.

2. **clāvīger** -gĕri, *m.* the key-carrier, epithet of Janus.

clāvis -is, *f.* a key; *adulterina portarum,* a false *or* skeleton key; *claves adimere uxori,* to separate from one's wife; a lock; *clavis adunca trochi,* stick for trundling a hoop.

clāvus -i, *m.* a nail; *clavus trabalis,* a spike; *annalis,* the nail which on the ides of September every year was driven into the wall of the temple of Jupiter Capitolinus at Rome; *hence fig., ex hoc die clavum anni movebis,* reckon the beginning of the year; a helm, rudder; a stripe of purple on the tunic worn broad by the senators.

Clĕanthēs -is, *m*. a Stoic philosopher, pupil of Zeno.

clēmens -entis, *adj.*, kind, merciful; *of the weather*, mild; *of water*, calm.

clēmentĕr, *adv.* gently, mercifully; *of places*, gently rising.

clēmentia -ae, *f*. mildness, mercy, clemency; mildness of weather.

Clĕōn -ōnis, *m*. a celebrated Athenian demagogue.

Clĕŏpātra -ae, *f*. queen of Egypt, the mistress of Antonius, whose forces allied with hers were overthrown by Augustus at Actium.

clĕpo, clepsi, cleptum, 3. to steal ; *se*, to conceal oneself.

clepsydra -ae, *f*. a water clock.

cliens -entis, *m*. *In Rome*, a client, dependant. *In Gaul and Germany*, a vassal; *nations*, allies.

clienta -ae, *f*. a female client.

clientēla -ae, *f*. the relation between client and patron; dependence; *(gen. in plur.)*, clients.

clientŭlus -i, *m*. *(dim. of cliens)*, a little client.

clīnāmen -inis, *n*. the inclination of a thing.

clīnātus -a -um, inclined, leaning.

Cliō -ūs, *f*. the Muse of history.

clĭpĕo *(clupeo)*, 1. to provide with a shield. *Subst.*, **clĭpĕāti -ōrum**, *m*. soldiers bearing shields.

clĭpĕus (clŭpĕus) -i, *m*. *and* **clĭpĕum (clŭpĕum) -i**, *n*. round metal shield; the disk of the sun; *(gen. clipeum)*, a medallion portrait.

Clisthĕnēs -is, *m*. an Athenian statesman.

Clītellae -ārum, *f*. a pack saddle, a pair of panniers.

clītellārius -a -um, belonging to a pack saddle.

Clīternum -i, *n*. town of the Aequi. *Adj.*, **Clīternīnus**.

Clītumnus -i, *m*. river in Umbria.

clīvosus -a -um, hilly, steep.

clīvus -i, *m*. a gentle ascent, a hill; *so clivus sacer*.

clŏāca -ae, *f*. a sewer *or* drain.

Clŏācīna -ae, *f*. the cleanser, surname of Venus.

Clōdius = *Claudius (q.v.)*.

Cloelius (Cluilius) -a -um, name of a Roman gens.

Clōthō -ūs, *f*. *(only nom. and acc.)*, one of the Parcae.

clŭĕo, 2. I am called, am named.

clūnis -is, *m. and f*. the buttocks.

Clŭpĕa (Clўpĕa) -ae, *f*. *and plur.* **Clŭpĕae -ārum**, *f*. promontory and town in Africa.

Clūsium -ii, *n*. town of Etruria. *Adj.*, **Clūsīnus**.

Clūsius -ii, *m*. the shutter, *epithet of Janus*.

ctystĕr -ēris, *m*. syringe.

Clўtaemnestra -ae, *f*. wife of Agamemnon.

Clўtiē -ēs, *f*. daughter of Oceanus, beloved by Apollo, changed into the flower heliotropium.

Cnidus (ŏs), *or* **Gnidus (-ŏs), -i**, *f*. town in Caria, famed for the worship of Venus. *Adj.*, **Cnidius -a -um**.

cŏăcervātio -ōnis, *f*. a heaping up.

cŏăcervo, 1. to heap up, accumulate.

cŏăcesco -ăcŭi, 3. to become thoroughly sour.

cŏactio -onis, *f*. a collecting.

cŏacto, 1. to compel.

cŏactor -ōris, *m*. collector of rents, money at auctions, etc. ; *coactores agminis*, the rear-guard ; one who compels.

cŏactum -i, *n*. a coverlet of thick cloth.

cŏactus -ūs, *m*. compulsion *(only in abl. sing.)*.

cŏaedifico, 1. to build on.

cŏaequo, 1. to level, make plain.

cŏagmentātio -ōnis, a connection.

cŏagmento, 1. to join together; *pacem*, to conclude.

cŏagmentum -i, *n*. a joining; a joint.

cŏăgŭlum -i, *n*. rennet; curds.

cŏălesco-ălŭi, -ălĭtum, 3. to grow together, coalesce, unite; *of plants*, to grow; to take root; *of wounds*, to be healed.

cŏangusto, 1. to limit, confine.

coarcto, *etc.* = *coarto, etc. (q.v.)*.

cŏargŭo -gŭi -gŭtum, *but* **-gŭturus**, 3. to demonstrate fully; to prove to be false; to convict; to confute; to convict of a crime.

cŏartātio -ōnis, *f*. a confining in a small space.

cŏarto, 1. to confine, draw together ; *of discourse*, to compress; *of time*, to shorten.

cŏaxo, 1. to croak *(of a frog)*.

coccinātus -a -um, clad in scarlet.

coccĭnĕus -a -um, scarlet coloured.

coccinus -a -um, scarlet coloured. *Subst.*, **coccina -orum**, *n*. scarlet clothes.

coccum -i, *n*. berry of the scarlet oak; scarlet hue; scarlet cloth *or* garments.

cochlĕa -ae, *f*. a snail; snail shell.

cochlĕar -āris, *n. and* **cochlĕārium -ii**, *n.*, *and* **cochlĕāre -is**, *n*. a spoon.

Cocles -itis, *m*. *Horatius Cocles*, the Roman who defended the bridge over the Tiber against Porsena.

coctana = *cottana (q.v.)*.

coctilis -e, baked; *muri Babylonis*, made of burnt brick.

Cōcўtŏs *and* **-ūs, -i**, *m*. river of the Lower World.

cōda = *cauda (q.v.)*.

cōdex -dicis, *m*. = *caudex*, trunk of a tree; a book, composed of wooden tablets, covered with wax; a book, document.

cōdicārius (caudicārius) -a -um, made of wooden blocks, naves.

cōdicilli -ōrum, m. (dim. of codex), small tablets; a letter: petition; codicil.

Codrus -i, m. the last king of Athens ... n. vast

cōēmo -ēmi -emptum, 3. to buy in large quantities, buy up.

cōemptio -ōnis, f. a form of marriage.

coena, &c., v. cena.

coenōsus -a -um, v. caenosus.

coenūla -ae, f., v. cenula.

coenum, v. caenum.

cōēo -ii (rarely -īvi) -itum, 4. come together, assemble; as enemies, to engage; to unite; to combine; to curdle; to be frozen.

coepio, coepi, coeptum, 3. (the perfect tenses commonly used), v. transit. and intransit., to begin, commence. Intransit., to begin, arise.

coepto, 1. to begin eagerly.

coeptum -i, n. a beginning, undertaking.

coeptus -ūs, m. a beginning, undertaking.

cōērcēo -cūi -citum, 2. to encompass, enclose ; to confine, restrain ; to keep in order ; to prune ; to check ; to punish, multā.

coērcitio -ōnis, f. a restraining; punishing.

coeruleus = caeruleus (q.v.).

coctus -ūs, m. a meeting together, assemblage.

cōgitātē, adv. carefully, thoughtfully.

cōgitātio -ōnis, f. thinking, conception; reflection, reasoning; a thought, idea; intention; plan, purpose; faculty of thought.

cōgitātus -a -um (partic. of cogito). Subst., cōgitāta -ōrum, n. thoughts, reflections, ideas.

cogito, 1. to think, reflect, consider; intend, plan; to be disposed to.

cognātio -ōnis, f. relationship; kindred, family; connexion, resemblance.

cognātus -a -um, connected by blood. Subst., cognātus -i, m., cognāta -ae, f. a relation; related, similar.

cognitio -ōnis, f. knowledge of or acquaintance with a thing or person; study of; a legal investigation; recognition; plur., an idea.

cognitor -ōris, m. a witness to the identity of a Roman citizen in a foreign country; attorney; voucher for; prosecutor.

cognitus -a -um, p. adj., known, tried, proved.

cognōmen -inis, n. a surname, family name.

cognōmentum -i, n. surname; a name.

cognōminātus -a -um, of the same meaning; verba, synonyms.

cognōminis -e having the same name.

cognōmino, 1. to give a surname to.

cognosco -gnōvi -gnitum, 3. to become acquainted with, remark; perceive; in the perf. tenses, to know; to recognise; to study; of judges, to decide.

cōgo, cōēgi, ... 0, to bring, drive, or draw to one point, to collect; to unite, gather together; to thicken; lac coactum, curdled; (subst., cōacta -ōrum, n. thick woven cloth); milit., agmen cogere, to bring up the rear; to infer, prove; to drive; to confine; to compel; partic., coactus, constrained.

cōhaerentia -ae, f. coherence, connexion.

cōhaerēo -haesi -haesum, 2. to adhere to, be closely connected with; to have coherence.

cōhaeresco -haesi, 3. to hang together.

cōhērēs -ēdis, m. a coheir.

cōhibēo -ūi -itum, 2. to hold, contain, hold together; to confine, restrain; to hinder, control.

cōhōnesto, 1. to honour or reverence.

cōhorresco -horrūi, 3. to shudder or shiver; esp., to be horrified at.

cōhors -tis, f. an enclosure for cattle; a throng; milit., a cohort; retinue of the governor of a province.

cōhortātio -ōnis, f. exhortation, encouragement.

cōhorticūla -ae, f. (dim. of cohors), a little cohort.

cōhortor, 1. dep. to encourage, exhort.

cōinquino, 1. no perf., to pollute, defile.

cōitio -ōnis, f. a meeting; party, coalition, conspiracy.

cōitus -ūs, m. a coming together, union.

cōlaphus -i, m. a box on the ear.

Colchis -idis, f. a country on the eastern shore of the Black Sea.

cōlēns -entis, p. adj., honouring, reverent.

cōliphia -ōrum, n. a nourishing food used by wrestlers.

cōlis = caulis (q.v.).

collābefacto, 1. to cause to totter.

collābefio -factus -fieri, to be made to totter or fall; igni collabefacta, melted.

collābor -lapsus sum, -labi, dep. to fall down, sink down, collapse.

collācērātus -a -um, much lacerated or torn.

collācrimātio -ōnis, f. a weeping.

collācrimo, 1. to break out into tears; with acc. to bemoan.

collactēus -i, m. -a, -ae, f. foster-brother; or sister.

collātio -ōnis, f. a bringing together; signorum, a hostile collision in the field; a contribution; comparison.

collātus -a -um, partic. of confero.

collaudātio -ōnis, f. strong, or hearty praise.

collaudo, 1. to praise very much.

collaxo, 1. to widen, extend.

collecta -ae, f. a contribution in money.

collecticius -a -um, gathered together; *exercitus*, quickly levied.

collectio -ōnis, *f.* gathering together, collection; *in rhetoric*, a brief recapitulation; *in logic*, a conclusion.

collectus -a -um, *p. adj.*, contracted, concise, concentrated.

collēga -ae, *m.* colleague; comrade.

collēgium -ii, *n.* colleagueship; a guild, corporation; a political club; a trade guild; a band, body.

collibertus -i, *m.* a fellow-freedman.

collibet, *or* **collŭbet** -bŭit *or* -bĭtum est, 2. *impers.* it pleases, is agreeable.

collīdo -līsi -līsum, 3. to strike together; *pass.* to come into hostile collision.

colligātio -ōnis, *f.* a binding together, connexion.

1 **colligo** -lēgi -lectum, 3. to bring together, collect, assemble; to contract; to gather together; to gain; *colligere se, or animum, or mentem*, to compose oneself, gain courage; *in speech*, to tell of; to think of; to reckon; to infer.

2. **colligo**, 1. to bind, fasten together; to connect; to join politically; to detain; to hinder, stop.

collinĕo, 1. to direct in a straight line.

collino -lēvi -lĭtum, 3. to besmear, daub.

collinus -a -um, hilly, situate on a hill. **Collinus** of *or* on the Quirinal hill; *porta Collina*, a gate of Rome.

colliquĕfactus -a -um, liquefied, melted.

collis -is, *m.* a hill, high ground.

collŏcātio -ōnis, *f.* a placing, *esp.* a giving in marriage; a position; *rhet.*, arrangement, order.

collŏco, 1. to place, lay, set, put; *milit.*, to station; *of time*, to pass; to erect; to arrange; to station; *milit.*, to billet; to settle in possession; *of women*, to settle in marriage; *of money*, to invest; to employ, spend; to arrange in proper order; manage.

collŏcŭplēto, 1. to enrich exceedingly.

collŏcūtio -ōnis, *f.* conversation.

collŏquium -ii, *n.* conversation, conference.

collŏquor -cūtus *or* -quūtus *sum*, -loqui, 3. *dep.* to speak with any one, to treat with; *cum aliquo; inter se.*

collūcĕo, 2. to be completely illuminated.

collūdo -lūsi -lūsum, 3. to play with, *paribus*; to act collusively.

collum -i, *n.* (**collus** -i, *m.*), the neck; *collum torquere*, to drag to prison.

collŭo -lŭi -lŭtum, 3. to wash thoroughly, rinse.

collus -i, *m.* = *collum* (*q.v.*).

collūsio -ōnis, *f.* secret understanding, *cum aliquo.*

collūsor -ōris, *m.* play-fellow; fellow-gambler.

collustro, 1. to illuminate on all sides; to survey.

collŭvio -ōnis, *and* **collŭviēs** ēi, *f.* filth; rabble.

collýbus -i, *m.* percentage charged in money-changing; the money-changer's occupation.

collýrium -ii, *n.* eye-salve.

cŏlo, *cŏlui, cultum*, 3. to cultivate, till; to dwell in, inhabit; to take care of; to cultivate, practise; to pay respect to; to worship; to honour, reverence, court.

cŏlŏcāsia -ae, *f.* and **cŏlŏcāsium** -ii, *n.* the Egyptian bean.

cŏlōna -ae, *f.* a country woman.

cŏlōnia -ae, *f.* farm, estate; colony; the colonists.

cŏlōnicus -a -um, belonging to agriculture *or* a farm; *or* to a colony, colonial.

cŏlōnus -i, *m.* farmer, agriculturist; colonist; *poet.* inhabitant.

cŏlor (**cŏlos**) -ōris, *m.* colour, tint; complexion; *fucatus*, artificial; beautiful complexion, beauty; *of oratory*, character, tone; ornament; an artful excuse.

cŏlōrātus -a -um, coloured; red.

cŏlōro, 1. to colour; to tan (*of the sun*); to give tone to style.

cŏlossēus -a -um, colossal, gigantic.

cŏlossus -i, *m.* a colossus, a statue larger than life; *esp. of Apollo at the entrance of the harbour of Rhodes.*

cŏlŭber -bri, *m.* a serpent, snake.

cŏlŭbra -ae, *f.* a female serpent, snake.

cŏlŭbrĭfer -fĕra -fĕrum, snake-bearing, snaky-haired (*Medusa*).

cŏlum -i, *n.* colander, sieve, strainer.

cŏlumba -ae, *f.* pigeon, dove.

cŏlumbīnus -a -um, relating *or* belonging to a pigeon.

cŏlumbus -i, *m.* a male dove *or* pigeon.

cŏlŭmella -ae, *f.* (*dim. of columna*), a little column.

cŏlŭmen -ĭnis, *n.* a height; *of persons*, the chief, most distinguished; a pillar.

cŏlumna -ae, *f.* pillar, column; *columnae*, the pillars in Rome round which books were exposed for sale; *columnae Herculis*, pillars of Hercules; a support, pillar of the state; a water-spout.

cŏlumnārius -a -um, belonging to a pillar. *Subst.*, **cŏlumnārii** -ōrum, *m.* rascals, thieves; **cŏlumnārium** -ii, *n.* a tax on pillars.

cŏlurnus -a -um, made of hazel wood.

cŏlus -i *and* **ūs**, *abl. colo, f.* a distaff.

cŏma -ae, *f.* hair of the head; leaves of trees; wool of sheep.

cŏmans -antis, hairy; *galea*, crested; *stella*, a comet.

cŏmātus -a -um, hairy; *silva*, in full leaf.

1. **combĭbo** -bĭbi, 3. to drink in, suck up.

2. **combĭbo** -ōnis, *m.* a boon companion.

combūro -bussi -bustum, 3. to burn up, consume entirely; *aliquem iudicio*, to ruin.

cŏmĕdo -ĕdi -ēsum (-essum) or -estum, 3. to eat up, consume entirely; se, to consume oneself in grief; to waste, squander.

cŏmes -ĭtis, c. a companion, associate; an attendant; plur. comites retinue; the body of courtiers.

cŏmētēs -æ, m. a comet.

cŏmĭcē, adv. in the manner of comedy.

cŏmĭcus -a -um, adj. relating to comedy, comic; represented in comedy. Subst. an actor in comedy; a comic poet.

cominus = comminus (q.v.).

cōmis -e, courteous, friendly, obliging.

cōmissābundus -a -um, revelling, rioting.

cōmissātio -ōnis, f. a revel.

cōmissātor -ōris, m. a reveller; comissatores coniurationis, accomplices.

cōmissor, 1. dep. to revel.

cōmĭtas -ātis, f. courtesy, friendliness.

cŏmĭtātus -ūs, m. attendance, companionship; a retinue; the court, imperial suite; convoy.

cŏmĭtĕr, adv. courteously, kindly.

cŏmĭtia, v. comitium.

cŏmĭtiālis -e, relating to the comitia.

cŏmĭtiātus -ūs, m. the assembly of the people in the comitia.

cŏmĭtium -ii, n. Sing. an enclosed place in or near the Roman forum, where the comitia were held. Plur. cŏmĭtia -ōrum, n. the assembly of the Roman people.

cŏmĭto, 1. = comitor, partic. comitatus, accompanied.

cŏmĭtor, 1. dep. to accompany, to follow.

commācŭlo, 1. to pollute.

commănĭpŭlāris -is, m. a soldier belonging to the same maniple, a comrade.

commĕātus -ūs, m. free passage, going and coming; liberty to go unhindered; milit., leave of absence, furlough; a company, caravan; supply of provisions.

commŏnĕĭtor, 1. dep. to remind, call to remembrance.

commĕmĭni -isse, to remember fully.

commĕmŏrābĭlis -e, worthy of remembrance, memorable.

commĕmŏrātio -ōnis, f. remembrance, mention, reminding.

commĕmŏro, 1. to recollect; to remind; to mention, relate.

commendābĭlis -e, praiseworthy.

commendātĭcius -a -um, relating to a recommendation; literae, a letter of introduction.

commendātio -ōnis, f. recommendation, commendation; that which recommends, excellence.

commendātrix -ĭcis, f. that which commends.

commendātus -a -um, p. adj. recommended, commended; esteemed, prized, valued.

commendo, 1. to commit to the care, keeping, or protection of any one; aliquid litteris, to commit to writing; to recommend; to set off, grace, render agreeable.

commensus, partic. of commetior.

commentārĭŏlum 1, m (dim. of commentarius), a short treatise.

commentārius -ii, m. and commentārium -ii, n. memorandum, or note-book, a diary; commentarii belli Gallici, the notes of Caesar on the Gallic war; legal, a brief.

commentātio -ōnis, f. deep reflection, meditation; practice, study of an orator; a dissertation.

commenticius -a -um, fictitious; civitas Platonis, ideal; crimen, false.

1. commentor, 1. dep. to consider thoroughly, reflect upon deeply; to study, practise; to sketch, compose, write down.

2. commentor -ōris, m. discoverer, inventor.

commentum -i, n. a fiction, contrivance; a falsehood.

commĕo, 1. to come and go, visit frequently; of letters, crebro enim illius litterae ab aliis ad nos commeant, find their way to us.

commercĭum -ii, n. trade, commerce; the right of trade; article of traffic; place of trade, commercial depot; intercourse, communication, correspondence; commercium belli, negotiations as to ransom of prisoners, truces, etc.

commercor, 1. dep. to buy together, buy up.

commĕrĕo -ŭi -ĭtum, 2. to deserve fully; to commit a fault.

commĕtior -mensus, 4. to measure; to compare.

commĕto, 1. to go frequently.

commĭgro, 1. to remove in a body, to migrate.

commĭlĭtium -ii, n. a companionship in military service; companionship, fellowship.

commĭlĭto -ōnis, m. comrade in war.

commĭnātio -ōnis, f. a threatening, threat.

commĭniscor -mentus, 3. dep. to feign, invent; perf. partic. pass., feigned, invented.

comminor, 1. dep. to threaten.

commĭnŭo -ŭi -ūtum, 3. to make small, lessen, crush to pieces; to diminish.

comminus, adv. milit. hand to hand, in close combat; close at hand; face to face.

commis, commi, cummis = gummi (q.v.).

commiscĕo -miscŭi -mixtum, or -mistum, 2. to mix together, to mix up.

commĭsĕrātio -ōnis, f. an affecting tone (of voice).

commĭsĕresco, 3. to pity.

commisĕror, . *dep.* to pity, bewail; *of a sepaker*, to excite pity.

commissio -ōnis, *f.* contest for a prize; a showy declamation.

commissum -i, *n.* an undertaking; a crime, fault; confiscation; a secret.

commissūra -ae, *f.* connection, joint, knot; thread of a discourse.

committo -misi -missum, 3. to unite, combine; to begin; to commit a crime; *with ut and the subj.*, to bring it about that; to incur a punishment, *poenam*; *perf. partic.*, forfeited; to entrust, to venture, *se urbi*.

commŏdē, *adv.* properly, appropriately; pleasantly; satisfactorily.

commŏditas -ātis, *f.* proportion, symmetry; convenience; a fit occasion; advantage; kindness.

commŏdo, 1. to make fit, adapt; to please, serve; *with acc.*, to lend, give, nomen suum alicui.

1. **commŏdum**, *adv.* at the right time, opportunely; *with cum or postquam and the indic.*, just.

2. **commŏdum** -i, *n.* convenience; *nostro commodo*, at our convenience; use, advantage; loan; *plur.*, favour, privileges.

commŏdus -a -um, proper, fit, convenient, satisfactory; *commodum est*, it pleases, is agreeable; easy, convenient; friendly, pleasant.

commŏlior, 4. *dep.* to set in motion.

commŏnĕfăcio -fēci -factum, 3. *pass.* **commŏnĕfio** -factus sum, -fieri, to remind, warn, *aliquem beneficii sui*.

commŏnĕo -ŭi -itum, 2. to remind, warn, impress upon, *animos de periculo*.

commonstro, 1. to show fully and distinctly.

commŏrātio -ōnis, *f.* a delaying, loitering, lingering.

commŏrior -mortuus, 3. *dep.* to die together with; *with dat.*, hostibus.

commŏror, 1. *dep.* to delay, linger, sojourn, remain; *rhet.* to dwell on.

commŏtio -ōnis, *f.* an emotion, excitement.

commŏtiuncŭla -ae, *f.* (*dim. of commotio*), a slight indisposition.

commŏtus -a -um, *p. adj.* tottering, unsteady; moved in mind, excited.

commŏvĕo -mōvi -mōtum, 3. to move violently, to shake; to carry about; *nummum*, to employ in commerce; to carry off; to hunt; to cause to yield; to move, influence, disturb; to call forth, produce, cause; to treat of.

commūnicātio -ōnis, *f.* a communicating, imparting.

commūnico, 1. to share, communicate; to impart, inform; to take counsel with, confer with, *cum aliquo*: to join, unite.

1. **commūnio** -īvi *or* -ii -ītum, 4. to

fortify thoroughly on all sides; to strengthen.

2. **commūnio** -ōnis, *f.* communion, mutual participation.

commūnis -e, common, general, universal, ordinary, usual, public; *loca*, public places; *of persons*, affable; *subst.*, **commūne** -is, *n.* the common property of a corporation; a state, commonwealth; *in commune*, *adv.*, for the public good; in general.

commūnitas -ātis, *f.* community, fellowship; affability.

commūnitĕr, *adv.* jointly, generally.

commurmŭror, 1. *dep.* to mutter, murmur.

commūtābilis, -e, changeable.

commūtātio -ōnis, *f.* change, alteration.

commūtātus -ūs, *m.* a change, alteration.

commūto, 2. to change, alter entirely; to exchange; *fidem suam et religionem pecuniâ*, to barter.

cōmo, compsi, comptum, 3. to place together in order, to arrange, adorn.

cōmoedia -ae, *f.* a comedy.

cōmoedus -a -um, relating to a comedy, comic. *Subst.*, **cōmoedus** -i, *m.* a comic actor.

cōmōsus -a -um, hairy.

compactio -ōnis, *f.* joining together.

compactus -a -um, *p. adj.* thick-set, compact.

compāges -is, *f.* a joining together, connexion.

compāgo -inis, *f.* = *compages* (*q.v.*).

compar -păris, like, similar. *Subst.*, **compar** -păris, *c.* companion, equal.

compărābilis -e, comparable.

compărātĕ, *adv.* in comparison, by comparison.

1. **compărātio** -ōnis, *f.* preparation.

2. **compărātio** -ōnis, *f.* comparison.

compărātīvus -a -um, containing a comparison, comparative.

comparco (comperco) -parsi, -parsum, 3. to scrape together, to save up.

compārĕo -pārŭi, 2. to appear; to be present, be in existence.

1. **compăro**, 1. to prepare, provide; to arrange, settle.

2. **compăro**, 1. to form into pairs; (for a contest) to match; to compare.

compasco -pāvi -pastum, 3. to feed *or* graze together.

compascŭus -a -um, relating to common pasturage.

compellātio -ōnis, *f.* an accosting, reprimanding.

1. **compello** -pŭli -pulsum, 3. to drive to one place, collect; to force; to compel.

2. **compello**, 1. to accost, call by name; rebuke. *Legal*, to accuse.

compendiārius -a -um, short.

compendium -ii, *n.* saving, parsimony; gain, profit; a short cut.

compensātio -ōnis, *f.* a balancing of an account, compensation.

compenso, 1. to weigh together, to balance.

compĕrendĭnātĭo -ōnis, *f.* a putting off a trial to the third day.

compĕrendĭnātĭus -ŭs, *m.* = *compĕrendĭnātĭo (q.v.).*

compĕrendĭno, 1. to remand to the third day.

compĕrĭo -pĕrī -pertum, 4. to discover, gain certain information of; *partic. perf.,* certain, undoubted; *compertus (of persons),* convicted.

compĕrĭor = *comperio.*

compĕs -pĕdis, *f.* a fetter or foot shackle, *gen. plur.*

compesco -pescŭi, 3. to restrain, check.

compĕtĭtor -ōris, *m.* a competitor.

compĕtītrīx -īcis, *f.* a female competitor.

compĕto -pĕtīvi and **-pĕtĭi -pĕtītum,** 3. to come together, to meet; to agree, coincide; to be capable of.

compīlātĭo -ōnis, *f.* a pillaging, a compilation.

compīlo, 1. to plunder, rob.

compingo -pēgi -pactum, 3. to put together, construct; *compactus,* constructed; to confine, conceal.

compĭtālĭcĭus -a -um, relating to the Compitalia.

compĭtālĭs -e, relating or belonging to cross roads. *Subst.,* **Compĭtālĭa -ium,** *n.* festival celebrated on the cross roads.

compĭtum -i, *n.* a place where two or more roads meet, a cross road.

complăcĕo -cŭi or **-cĭtus sum** 2. to please several at once; to please exceedingly.

complāno, 1. to level.

complector -plexus -plecti, 3. *dep.* to encircle, encompass; to enclose; to hold fast; to attach oneself to, esteem; to grasp, comprehend; to comprise.

complēmentum -i, *n.* a complement.

complĕo -plēvi -plētum, 2. to fill up; to fulfil; *of a sum,* to make up; to finish.

complētus -a -um, *p. adj.* perfect, complete.

complexĭo -ōnis, *f.* connexion, combination; *of discourse,* summary; *verborum,* a period.

complexus -ūs, *m.* an embrace; a loved object; an encircling, encompassing; surrounding.

complĭco -āvi -ātum (-ŭi -itum), 1. to fold together, fold up; *complicata notio,* confused, intricate.

complōrātĭo -ōnis, *f.* lamentation.

complōrātus -ūs, *m.* = *comploratio (q.v.).*

complōro, 1. to bewail or weep.

complūres, *neut.* **complūra,** and *(rarely)* **complūrĭa -ium,** *n.* very many. *Subst.,* several.

complŭvĭum -ĭi, *n.* the quadrangular roofless space in the centre of a Roman house, through which the water collected on the roofs found its way to the *impluvium* below.

compōno -pŏsŭi -pŏsĭtum, 3. to put, lay, bring together; to compare; to compose; to settle, arrange; to invent, feign; to reconcile; *ut convenito,* as we agreed.

comporto, 1. to bring together, collect.

compōs -pŏtis, having the control of, possessed of, sharing in; *mentis,* in full possession of mental faculties.

compŏsĭtē, *adv.* in good order; *composite et apte licere,* quietly.

compŏsĭtĭo -ōnis, *f.* a matching; a composing; a settlement of differences; arrangement.

compŏsĭtor -ōris, *m.* an arranger.

compŏsĭtūra -ae, *f.* a connexion, a joint.

compŏsĭtus -a -um, *p. adj.* placed together; composed, quieted; settled; *(subst.,* **compŏsĭta -orum,** *n.* the orderly condition of a state); prepared; feigned.

compōtātĭo -ōnis, *f.* a drinking party.

compōtor -ōris, *m.* drinking companion.

compōtrix -īcis, *f.* a female drinking companion.

compransor -ōris, *m.* dinner companion, boon companion.

comprĕcātĭo -ōnis, *f.* supplication of a deity.

comprĕcor, 1. *dep.* to pray to, supplicate.

comprĕhendo (comprendo) -prĕhendi (-prendi) -prĕhensum (-prensum), 3. to seize; *ignem,* to catch fire; to attack, capture; to carry off; to discover a crime; to embrace; to include; to express, tell; *aliquid numero,* to count; to comprehend, perceive.

comprĕhensĭbilis -e, comprehensible.

comprĕhensĭo -ōnis, *f.* a laying hold of; a hostile seizing; comprehending, comprehension; a period, sentence.

comprendo = *comprehendo (q.v.).*

compressē, *adv.* briefly, concisely.

compressĭo -ōnis, *f.* conciseness,
1. **compressus** a *um, partic. of comprimo.*

2. **compressus,** *abl. u. m.* pressure, embrace.

comprĭmo -pressi -pressum, 3. to squeeze together, compress; *compressis manibus sedere,* to sit with folded hands, idle; *ordines,* to close the ranks; to hold back; to suppress; to check; to subdue.

comprŏbātĭo -ōnis, *f.* approval.

comprŏbātor -ōris, *m.* one who approves.

comprŏbo, 1. to approve fully; to confirm, prove, establish.

comprōmissum -i, *n.* a mutual agreement to abide by the decision of an arbitrator.

comprōmitto -mīsi -missum, 3. to agree to refer a cause to arbitration.

1. **comptus -a -um,** *p. adj.* ornamented adorned.

2. **comptus -ūs,** *m.* a head-dress; a band, tie.

compungo - punxi -punctum, 3. *to* prick, puncture on all sides; to mark; *barbarus compunctus notis Threiciis,* tattooed.

compŭto, 1. to calculate, compute.

compŭtresco -pūtrŭi, 3. to putrefy, to become rotten.

cōnāmen -minis, *n.* an effort, endeavour.

cōnātum -i, *n.* an undertaking; *gen. in* plur.

cōnātus -ūs, *m.* an effort, undertaking, *hoc conatu desistere;* trouble, difficulty; impulse, inclination.

concaedēs -ium, *f. pl.* a barricade of trees.

concălĕfăcio (concalfăcio) -fēci -factum, 3. *and pass.* **concălĕfīo -factus sum,** to warm thoroughly.

concălesco -călŭi, 3. to become thoroughly warm; to glow with love.

concallesco -callŭi, 3. to become practised; to become callous.

Concăni -ōrum, *m.* a savage tribe in Spain, who drank horses' blood.

concăvo, 1. make hollow *or* concave.

concăvus -a -um, hollow, vaulted, arched, concave; *aqua,* welling up.

concēdo -cessi -cessum, 3. to depart, withdraw; to cease; to submit; to pass over to some one's party *or* view; to yield; *concedere naturae,* to die a natural death; *transit.,* to pardon; to yield, give up, *alicui libertatem.*

concĕlĕbro, 1. to visit a place often, *or* in large companies; to pursue eagerly, *studia;* to celebrate a festivity; to praise.

concēnātio -ōnis, *f.* a supping together.

concentio -ōnis, a singing together, harmony.

concentus -ūs, *m.* a singing together, harmony; agreement, concord.

conceptio -ōnis, *f.* conception; the drawing up of legal formulae.

conceptus -ūs, *m.* pregnancy.

concerpo -cerpsi -cerptum, 3. to tear in pieces.

concertātio -ōnis, *f.* contest, strife; dispute.

concertātor -ōris, *m.* a rival.

concertātōrius -a -um, relating to a contest in words.

concerto, 1. to strive eagerly.

concessio -ōnis, *f.* a yielding, granting.

concessus -ūs, *m.* permission.

concha -ae, *f.* mussel; mussel-shell; *poet.* pearl, the shell-fish which yielded the purple dye; *poet.* purple dye; a vessel in the shape of a shell; the horn of Triton.

conchĕus -a -um, relating to a mussel-shell; *bacca,* a pearl.

conchis -is, *f.* a kind of bean boiled with its pod.

conchȳlĭātus -a -um, purple.

conchȳlium -ii, *n.* mussel; oyster, the shell-fish which yielded a purple dye; purple dye; a purple garment.

1. **concido -idi,** 3. to fall, sink down; *of the winds,* to drop; to perish, waste away; *of persons,* to be ruined, to fail; at law, *to lose.*

2. **concido -cīdi -cīsum,** 3. to cut up, strike to the ground; to overthrow; to beat severely; to cut through; to analyse.

conciĕo -cīvi -cītum, 2. *and (in prose gen.)* **concio -īvi -ītum,** 4. to stir up; *of men,* to summon; to disturb; to produce, cause.

conciliābŭlum -i, *n.* a place of assembly, market place.

conciliātio -ōnis, *f.* a uniting; conciliating; inclination; acquiring.

conciliātor -ōris, *m.* one who prepares.

conciliātrīcŭla -ae, *f. (dīm of conciliatrix),* that which conciliates.

conciliātrix -icis, *f.* one who unites, a match-maker; that which causes.

1. **conciliātus -a -um,** *p. adj.* beloved by; inclined to.

2. **conciliātus,** *abl.* **-ū,** *m.* the union, connexion of atoms.

concilio, 1. to bring together; to unite, connect; to unite in sentiment, win over; to recommend, make acceptable; to procure, prepare, provide; to bring about, cause, *nuptias.*

concilium -ii, *n.* a union, connexion, *rerum;* assembling; an assembly; a council; *concilium Achaicum,* the Achaean League.

concinnē, *adv.* elegantly, neatly, finely, tastefully; *distribuere,* to arrange a speech artistically.

concinnitas -ātis, *f.* elegance and harmony of style.

concinnitūdo -īnis, *f.* = **concinnitas** *(q.v.).*

concinno, 1. to put *or* fit together carefully, to arrange; to produce, cause.

concinnus -a -um, well put together; pleasing on account of harmony and proportion, elegant, neat; *of discourse,* tasteful, polished; suited, fit, appropriate, pleasing.

concino -cinŭi -centum, 3. *intransit.* to sing in chorus, play instruments in concert; to join together in an utterance, to agree in saying; to agree together, harmonise. *Transit.* to celebrate; to prophesy.

1. **concio** = **concieo** *(q.v.).*

2. **concio -ōnis** = **contio** *(q.v.).*

concio, *v.* **contio.**

concipio -cēpi -ceptum, 3. to take together, hold together; to contain, hold; *of words,* to express in a certain form; to repeat words after another person; to publish, conclude; to take in, draw in, suck; to catch fire; to conceive to take, gain; to receive, incur; to commit, perpetrate; to feel; to fancy, imagine; to comprehend, grasp.

concisē, *adv.* in detached *or* minute portions; concisely.

concisio -ōnis, *f. rhet.* the breaking up of a clause into divisions.

concisus -a -um, *p. adj.* divided into short sentences, brief, concise.

concitātio -ōnis, *f.* quick movement; tumult, sedition; disturbance of the mind, passion.

concitātor -ōris, *m.* one who excites, stirs up.

concitātus -a -um, *p. adj.* quick, rapid; *quam concitatissimos equos immittere*, spur the horses to a full gallop; *concitator clamor*, louder; excited, violent, passionate.

concito, 1. to move quickly, violently, stir up, excite; to summon by the voice; *consitare astum*, to move forward the army; *se concitare in hostem*, to rush against the enemy; to incite; to cause, produce.

concitor -ōris, *m.* one who excites, stirs up.

conciuncŭla -ae = *contiuncula (q.v.).*

conclāmātio -ōnis, *f.* an exclamation, shouting together.

conclāmo, 1. to shout together; *vasa*, to give the signal for packing up baggage before a march; *with ut and the subj.*, to demand loudly; *with acc., conclamare victoriam*; *aliquem conclamare*, to bewail the death of some one; to call together.

conclāve -is, *n.* a room, a dining-room, a bedroom.

conclūdo -clūsi -clūsum, 3. to shut up, inclose ; to include, compress, confine; to bring to an end; to round off in a period; to argue, infer.

conclūsē, *adv.* with well-turned periods.

conclūsio -ōnis, *f.* a closing, a blockade; a close, conclusion ; peroration ; a period; consequence.

conclūsiuncŭla -ae, *f. (dim. of conclusio)*, a foolish inference.

concoenātio -ōnis, *f., v. concenatio.*

concŏlor -ōris, similar in colour.

concŏquo -coxi -coctum, 3. to boil together, to digest; to bear, endure; to deliberate upon.

1. **concordia -ae**, *f.* agreement, harmony, friendship, sympathy.

2. **Concordia -ae**, *f.* the goddess Concord.

concorditĕr, *adv.* harmoniously, with concord, amicably.

concordo, 1. to agree, be in union; *with dat., concordant carmina nervis.*

concors -dis, *adj.* of one mind *or* opinion, concordant, agreeing, harmonious.

concrēbresco -brŭi, 3. to increase.

concrēdo -didi -ditum, 3. to intrust, commit to.

concrĕmo, 1. to burn up, burn entirely.

concrĕpo -ŭi, 1. *intransit.* to rattle, creak, clash, grate; *si digitis concrepuerit*, at the least sign. *Transit.* to rattle, strike upon, *aera.*

concresco -crēvi -crētum, to become stiff, to congeal, curdle, harden ; to grow, collect, increase, be formed.

concrētio -ōnis, *f.* a growing together, congealing, condensing ; materiality, matter.

concrētus -a -um, *p. adj.* thickened, congealed, condensed, stiffened; *dolor*, hard, tearless.

concrŭcio, 1. to torture violently.

concŭbina -ae, *f.* a concubine.

concŭbĭtus -ūs, *m.* lying together (at table).

concŭbius -a -um, relating to sleep, *only in the phrase concubiā nocte*, at the time of men's first sleep; at dead of night.

conculco, 1. to tread, trample underfoot; to misuse, to despise.

concŭpisco -pīvi *or* **-pii -pitum**, 3. to desire eagerly, covet, to endeavour after, aim at.

concurro -curri (*rarely* **-cŭcurri**) **-cursum**, 3. to run together, come together, flock to one spot; to meet together; *concurrit dextera laevae*, of clapping the hands for applause; to happen at the same time; dash, strike together; to meet in conflict, attack, engage.

concursātio -ōnis, *f.* a running together, concourse ; going round, skirmishing of light troops.

concursātor -ōris, *m.* skirmisher.

concursio -ōnis, *f.* a running together, concourse; a figure of speech, in which the same word is frequently repeated.

concurso, 1. *Intransit.* to run about, rush hither and thither; to skirmish; to travel about; to make official visits. *Transit.*, to visit.

concursus -ūs, *m.* a running together, concourse; *facere*, to cause a tumult; *a) abstractions*, union ; *honestissimorum studiorum*, co-operation in; a striking together, meeting; a dashing together; hostile encounter; *concursus calamitatum*, attack.

concussus, *abl.* **-ū**, *m.* a shaking, concussion.

concŭtio -cussi -cussum, 3. to shake violently, agitate ; *te ipsum concute*, search, examine yourself ; to shatter, disturb, impair; to alarm, trouble; to urge, excite; to strike together.

condĕcŏro, 1. to adorn carefully.

condemnātor -ōris, *m.* an accuser.

condemno, 1. to condemn, sentence, *aliquem iniuriarum* ; to accuse ; to disapprove. *Of an accuser*, to urge *or* effect condemnation.

condenseo = *condenso (q.v.).*

condenso, 1. to make thick, press close together.

condensus -a -um, dense, thick.

condico -dixi -dictum, 3. to make arrangement with, appoint, settle.

condignus -a -um, very worthy.

condimentum -i, n. seasoning, sauce, condiment.

condio -īvi or ii -ītum, 4. to pickle, to preserve; to embalm; to season, ornament; to soften, temper, *tristitiam*.

condiscipula -ae, f. a female schoolfellow.

condiscipulus -i, m schoolfellow.

condisco -didici, 3. to learn thoroughly.

1. conditio -ōnis, preserving of fruits; a seasoning.

2. conditio -ōnis, f. state, condition, place, circumstances; a condition, stipulation; *hāc, eā, istā conditione, his conditionibus*, on these terms; marriage contract; a gallant.

conditor -ōris, m. a founder, composer, author.

conditōrium -ii, n. the place in which a corpse or its ashes are preserved.

1. conditus -a -um, *partic. of condo*.

2. conditus -a -um, *p. adj.* seasoned, savoury; ornamented.

condo -didi -ditum, 3. to put together, form, establish; to compose, write; to celebrate in song; to put in; to thrust, press in; to preserve, collect; to store up; to preserve, pickle; *of persons*, to hide; to put, place; to bury; to withdraw from sight; *condere diem*, to pass the day; to conceal.

condōcěfácio -fēci -factum, 3. to train, teach.

condōlesco -dōlŭi, 3. to suffer severely, to feel pain.

condōnātio -ōnis, f. a giving away.

condōno, 1. to give away, present; *of the praetor, alicui hereditatem*, to award the inheritance; to give up to, sacrifice to; to overlook, forgive a fault, *alicui crimen*.

condūco -duxi -ductum, 3. to bring together, collect; to unite; to hire; to farm the taxes; to undertake, contract for. *Intransit.* to profit, to serve.

conducticius -a -um, hired.

conductio -ōnis, f. a bringing together, recapitulation; hiring, farming.

conductor -ōris, m. one who hires; a contractor.

conductus -a -um, *partic. of conduco.*

condūplico, 1. to double.

condūro, 1. to harden.

cōnecto, v. connecto.

cōnesto, v. cohonesto.

confābŭlor, 1. *dep.* to talk, converse.

confarrěātio -ōnis, f. a form of marriage ceremony.

confarrěo, 1. to marry by the ceremony of *confarreatio.*

confātālis -e, determined by fate.

confectio -ōnis, f. preparation, producing, composing, completing; exaction; consumption, *escarum*; weakening.

confector -ōris, m one who prepares, finishes; a destroyer, consumer.

confercio -fersi -fertum, 4. to press close together, cram together.

confěro, contŭli, collātum, conferre, to bring together, collect; contribute; to unite, to join, connect, *vires in unum*; to place together or near; *milit.* to bring into hostile contact or collision; *signa conferre*, to engage; *conferre lites*, to contend; *of speech*, to interchange, exchange, discuss; to compare; to bring to a place; to remove, transfer; *se conferre*, to betake oneself, flee; to devote oneself, join oneself to; to postpone; to apply; *of thoughts, etc.*, to direct, use; to hand over; to impute, attribute; *confert*, it is profitable.

confertim, *adv.*, densely, thickly, compactly.

confertus -a -um, *p. adj.* closely compressed, dense; *conferti milites*, in close formation; *with abl.* full of.

confervěfácio, 3. to make very hot, to melt.

confervesco -ferbŭi, 3. to begin to boil, begin to glow.

confessio -ōnis, f. a confession, acknowledgment.

confessus -a -um, undoubted, acknowledged, certain; *ex confesso*, confessedly; *in confessum venire*, to be generally acknowledged.

confestim, *adv.* immediately, without delay.

conficiens -entis, *p. adj.* that which causes, effects; effecting, efficient.

conficio -fēci -fectum, 3. to finish, make ready, bring about, accomplish; *pretium*, settle the price; *confice cum Apella de columnis*, settle, arrange; *of time*, to complete; to procure; to produce, cause; *philosoph.* to prove; *ex quo conficitur ut, etc.*, it follows from this; to consume; to chew, eat; to digest; to waste, destroy, *patrimonium suum*; to kill; to subdue; to weaken.

confictio -ōnis, f. a fabrication, invention.

confidens -entis, *p. adj.* confident, self-reliant; shameless, impudent.

confidenter, *adv.* boldly, confidently.

confidentia -ae, f. confidence; impudence, boldness, shamelessness.

confido -fisus sum, 3. to trust, be assured, confide; *with dat., sibi; with acc. and infin.*, to believe firmly.

configo -fixi -fixum, 3. to fasten together, nail together; to pierce through, transfix with a weapon.

confindo, 3. to cleave asunder.

confingo -finxi -fictum, 3. to construct; to fabricate, feign, invent.

confinis -e, having the same boundary; adjacent, near; nearly allied, similar. *Subst.*, **confinis -is**, *m.* a neighbour.

confinium -ii, *n.* a limit, border (*of countries*); the bordering line, nearness: *confinia noctis*, twilight.

confirmatio -ōnis, *f.* an establishing, making firm; consolation, encouragement, support; verifying a fact; *rhet.* adducing of proofs.

confirmator -ōris, *m.* one who confirms, establishes.

confirmatus -a -um, *adj.* encouraged; certain, credible.

confirmo, 1. to establish, confirm, strengthen; *se confirmare*, to recover strength; *consilia*, to support; to ratify; to encourage; *erigo to si confirma*, take courage; to affirm.

confisco, 1. to lay up, preserve in a chest; to appropriate to the imperial treasury, to confiscate.

confisio -ōnis, *f.* confidence, assurance.

confiteor -fessus sum, 2. *dep.* to confess, allow, acknowledge; to reveal; *pass.*, confessed, acknowledged.

conflagro, 1. to be burnt up; *conflagrare invidiā*, to fall a victim to hatred.

conflictio -ōnis, *f.* collision, conflict.

conflicto, 1. *pass.* to combat with, contend with; *conflictari aliquā re*, to be grievously troubled, to suffer severely.

conflictus -ūs, *m.* a striking together.

confligo -flixi -flictum, 3. *transit.* to strike, bring together; to bring together to compare. *Intransit.*, to strike together; to fight, contend.

conflo, 1. to blow together, to blow up, to kindle; to excite; to melt; *falces in enses*, to forge; to coin; to unite; to rivet together, produce; to get together; invent; to brood over, meditate.

confluens -entis or **confluentes -ium**, *m.* the confluence of two rivers.

confluo -fluxi, 3. to flow together; *of a crowd*, to stream or flock together.

confodio -fodi -fossum, 3. to dig thoroughly; to stab, pierce.

conformatio -ōnis, *f.* a form, shape, forming; *vocis*, expression; *verborum*, arrangement; an idea; figure of speech.

conformo, 1. to form symmetrically, arrange.

confossus -a -um, *partic.* of confodio.

confragosus -a -um, rugged, uneven.

confremo -fremui, 3. to murmur, roar.

confrico -fricui -fricatum, 1. to rub.

confringo -fregi -fractum, 3. to break in pieces; bring to naught, *consilia*.

confugio -fugi, 3. to fly to, take refuge; to have recourse to.

confugium -ii, *n.* a place of refuge.

confulcio -fultus, 4. to prop up.

confundo -fudi -fusum, 3. to mingle, mix; to join together; to confuse, throw into disorder; to obscure; to trouble, disturb; to pour into.

confuse, *adv.* confusedly, in a disorderly manner.

confusio -ōnis, *f.* a mixture, union, connexion; confusion, disorder; *oris*, blushing.

confusus -a -um, *p. adj.* disorderly, confused; confused in appearance.

confuto, 1. to check the boiling of a liquid; to check, repress; *by speech*, to silence, overthrow.

congelo, 1. *transit.* to freeze thoroughly; to harden, thicken. *Intransit.*, to freeze; *fig.*, to become inactive.

congemino, 1. to double, redouble.

congemo -gemui, 3. *intransit.*, to sigh or groan, loudly. *Transit.*, to bewail, lament.

conger and **gonger -gri**, *m.* a sea or conger eel.

congeries -ēi, *f.* a heap, mass; a wood pile; the mass of chaos.

congero -gessi -gestum, 3. to bring together, collect; *oscula*, to add one to another; to prepare; to heap together; to build; *of birds, quo congessere palumbes*, have built their nests; *in discourse*, to bring together, comprise; to heap together; *causas in aliquem*, to ascribe, impute.

congesticius -a -um, heaped up, brought together.

congestus -ūs, *m.* a collecting, heaping together; *esp. of birds*, building nests; a heap, mass.

congiarium -ii, *n.* a donation distributed by the consuls and emperors among the people.

congius -ii, *m.* a Roman measure for liquids, containing six *sextarii*.

conglacio, 1. *intransit.*, to freeze. *Transit.*, to turn to ice.

conglobatio -ōnis, *f.* a heaping, crowding together.

conglobo, 1. to form into a ball or sphere; to press together in a mass or crowd; *maxima definitiones valent conglobatae*, accumulated.

conglomero, 1. to roll, twist, entangle together.

conglutinatio -ōnis, *f.* a sticking, cementing together; connexion, joining together.

conglutino, 1. to stick, cement together; to connect, bind closely.

congratulor, 1. *dep.* to wish joy, congratulate.

congredior -gressus, 3. *dep.* to meet, *cum aliquo*; *inter se*, to meet in combat; to engage, contend; to dispute, argue.

congregabilis -e, sociable, inclined to collect.

congregatio -ōnis, *f.* an assembling together, society, union.

congrĕgo, 1. to collect into a flock; *refl., se congregare*, or *pass., congregari*, to form into flocks; *of men*, to collect, gather together; *refl., se congregare, and pass., congregari*, to assemble; *of things*, to unite.

congressio -ōnis, *f.* a meeting; intercourse, society.

congressus -ūs, *m.* a meeting; social intercourse, conversation; combat.

congrŭens -entis, *p. adj.*, agreeing, fit, appropriate, suitable; harmonious, accordant; *clamor congruens*, unanimous.

congrŭentĕr, *adv.* agreeably, suitably.

congrŭentia -ae, *f.* agreement, symmetry, proportion.

congrŭo -ŭi, 3. to come together, meet; *of time*, to coincide; to fit, correspond with; *with cum and abl.; with dat.; with inter se.*

congrŭus -a -um = *congruens (q.v.).*

conĭcio -iēci -iectum, 3. bring together, collect; *sortem conicere*, to cast lots; to throw, *in vincula*; direct, *oculos*; to conjecture, guess; to interpret, *omen*; *se conicere*, to betake oneself, flee; to insert, *libellum in epistolam*; to thrust; *se in noctem*, to hasten away under cover of night; to introduce.

conĭectio -ōnis, *f.* a hurling, throwing; conjectural interpretation.

conĭecto, 1. to throw together; to conclude, infer, conjecture.

conĭector -ōris, *m.* an interpreter of dreams.

conĭectūra -ae, *f.* a guess, conjecture, inference; interpretation of dreams and omens; soothsaying.

conĭectūrālis -e, conjectural.

conĭectus -ūs, *m.* a throwing, casting, hurling.

cōnĭfĕr -fĕra -fĕrum, cone-bearing.

cōnĭgĕr = *conifer (q.v.).*

cōnĭtor = *connitor (q.v.).*

conĭūgālis -e, relating to marriage, conjugal.

conĭūgātio -ōnis, *f.* the etymological connection of words.

conĭūgātor -ōris, *m.* one who connects.

conĭūgiālis -e, relating to marriage, conjugal.

conĭūgium -ii, *n.* union; marriage; husband; wife.

conĭūgo, 1. *to yoke together, connect.*

conĭunctē, *adv.* conjointly, in connexion; intimately.

conĭunctim, *adv.* conjointly, in common.

conĭunctio -ōnis, *f.* uniting; connexion of ideas; a connecting particle; union; relationship.

conĭunctus -a -um, *p. adj.* connected; *with dat.* bordering on, near; contemporary with ; agreeing with, proportioned to; *of persons*, connected, allied, friendly ; *subst.*, **conĭunctum -i**, *n.* connexion.

conĭungo -iunxi -iunctum, 3. to join together, *with dat., cum and abl., inter se*, *or the abl. alone*; to unite; *noctem diei*, to travel far into the night; *conĭungere bellum*, to undertake in common; to unite in marriage, friendship, alliance, *etc.*

conĭunx = *coniux (q.v.).*

conĭūrātio -ōnis, *f.* union confirmed by an oath; conspiracy, plot; *in ea coniuratione esse*, to be implicated in; the conspirators.

conĭūrātus -a -um, united by oath, allied; *subst.*, **conĭurāti -ōrum**, *m.* conspirators.

conĭūro, 1. to swear together; to take the military oath; to unite together by oath; to plot, conspire.

conĭux (conĭunx) -iŭgis, *c.* spouse, wife; *more rarely*, husband; *pl.* a married pair; *poet.*, a betrothed virgin, bride; a concubine.

cōnīvĕo = *conniveo (q.v.).*

conl . . . = *coll . . . (q.v.).*

conm . . . = *comm . . . (q.v.).*

connecto -nexŭi -nexum, 3. to fasten, tie together, connect, unite; *of time*, *persequere connexos his funeribus dies*, close-following ; *subst.*, **connexum -i**, *n.* logical conclusion.

1. **connexus -ūs**, *m.* connexion, union.
2. **connexus -a -um**, *partic.* of *connecto.*

connitor -nīsus *or* **-nixus sum**, 3. *dep.* to lean *or* push against with violence; to climb up, *in summum iugum* ; to bring forth; to strive with all one's might.

connīvĕo -nīvi *or* **-nixi**, 2. to close the eyes, to wink, blink with the eyes; to wink at, let pass unnoticed.

connūbiālis -e, relating to marriage, connubial.

connūbium -ii, *n.* a legal Roman marriage ; *poet.* marriage *in general;* intercourse; the right of intermarriage.

cōnor, 1. *dep.* to undertake, endeavour, attempt, exert oneself, strive.

conp . . . = *comp . . . (q.v.).*

conquassātio -ōnis, *f.* a violent shaking, shattering.

conquasso, 1. to shake thoroughly, shatter.

conquĕror -questus, 3. *dep.* to bewail *or* complain loudly.

conquestio -ōnis, *f.* a loud complaint, bewailing.

conquestus, *abl.* **-ū**, *m.* a loud complaint.

conquĭesco -quĭēvi -quĭētum, 3. to rest thoroughly, take rest, repose; to rest bodily; to be still, quiet; to stop, *imbre conquiescente;* to find rest *or* recreation in.

conquīro -quīsīvi -quīsītum, 3. to seek for, to bring together.

conquisitio -ōnis, f. search, collection; conscription.

conquisitor -ōris, m. recruiting officer.

conquisitus -a -um, p. adj., chosen, precious.

conr . . . = corr . . . (q.v.).

consaepio -saepsi -saeptum, 4. to fence round; *metaph.*, consaeptum 1, *n.* an inclosure.

consalūtātio -ōnis, f. a salutation of several persons.

consalūto, 1. to hail, salute, *aliquem dictatorem.*

consānesco -sānŭi, 3. to become healthy, to get well.

consanguĭnĕus -a -um, related by blood, brotherly, sisterly. *Subst.*, consanguĭnĕus -i, m. brother; consanguĭnĕa -ae, f. sister; *plur.*, consanguĭnĕi -ōrum, m. relations.

consanguĭnĭtas -ātis, f. relationship by blood, consanguinity.

consaucio, 1. to wound severely.

conscĕlĕrātus -a -um, p. adj. wicked, depraved.

conscĕlĕro, 1. to defile with crime.

conscendo -scendi -scensum, 3. to ascend, mount, *equum ; in equos ;* to embark, *in navem; navem.*

conscensio -ōnis, f. embarkation.

conscientia -ae, f. a joint knowledge with some other person, being privy to, *coniurationis;* knowledge in oneself; conscience.

conscindo -scidi -scissum, 3. to tear in pieces; *conscissi sibilis,* hissed at.

conscio, 4. to be conscious of guilt.

conscisco -scivi *and* -scii -scitum, 3. to agree on, resolve publicly, decree; to bring *or* inflict upon oneself, inflict upon; *sibi mortem, or simply mortem,* to kill oneself.

conscius -a -um, having common knowledge with another, privy to, cognisant of ; *coniurationis,* conspirator ; conscious of guilt. *Subst.,* conscius, accomplice.

conscrībillo, 1. (*dim. of conscribo*), to scribble all over.

conscrībo -scripsi -scriptum, 3. to write together; *milit.,* to enrol, levy; *patres conscripti (for patres et conscripti),* senators; to write, compose; to prescribe; to write all over.

conscriptio -ōnis, f. a writing, composition.

conscriptus -a -um, *partic. of conscribo.*

consĕco -sĕcŭi -sectum, 1. to cut in small pieces.

consĕcrātio -ōnis, f. a consecration; execration, curse; apotheosis.

consĕcro, 1. to consecrate; to curse; to deify; to make holy; to make immortal.

consectārius -a -um, consequent. *Subst.*, consectāria -orum, n. inferences.

consectātio -ōnis, f. desire, effort, striving after.

consectātrix -īcis, f. a devoted friend.

consectio -ōnis, f. a cutting up.

consector, 1. *dep.* to pursue eagerly; to strive after, try to imitate *or* gain.

consĕnĕsco -nŭi, 3. *to become old, grow* grey; to lose one's strength, to decay; *in politics,* to lose power.

consensio -ōnis, f. agreement, harmony, consent; a plot, conspiracy.

consensus -ūs, m. agreement, unanimity, concord; *abl., consensu,* unanimously, by general consent ; a secret agreement, conspiracy.

consentānĕus -a -um, agreeing to, agreeable with, consonant with, suitable ; *impers., consentaneum est, with infin. or acc. and infin.,* it agrees, is reasonable, suitable.

consentio -sensi -sensum, 4. to agree, to assent, to resolve unanimously, *with dat. or cum and the abl.; with acc., bellum,* to resolve upon war; *with acc. and infin.* to plot, conspire, form an unlawful union ; *pres. partic.,* consentiens -entis, harmonious.

consĕpio = consaepio (q.v.).

consĕquens -quentis, p. adj. *grammat.,* appropriate, of the right construction; *philosoph.,* following logically, consequent. *Subst.,* consĕquens -quentis, *n.* a logical consequence.

consĕquentia -ae, f. a consequence, succession.

consĕquia -ae, f. = consequentia (q.v.).

consĕquor -sĕquūtus (-sĕcūtus), 3. *dep.* to follow, go after; *aliquem vestigiis,* on foot; to pursue; to follow in point of time; to follow as an effect *or* consequence, result from; to come up to, attain to, reach, obtain; to come up with, overtake; *of objects, events,* to befall, happen to; to equal; to understand, grasp.

1. consĕro -sēvi, situm, 3. to sow, plant; to cover.

2. consĕro -sĕrŭi -sertum, 3. to tie, join, twine together; *milit., manum or manus conserere,* to engage.

consertē, *adv.* connectedly.

conservans -antis, p. adj. preserving.

conservātio -ōnis, f. a preservation, keeping, laying up ; observing, observance.

conservātor -ōris, m. a preserver.

conservātrix -īcis, f. she who preserves.

conservo, 1. to keep, preserve, maintain; to observe; *iusiurandum,* to keep.

conservus -i, m. a fellow-slave, servant.

consessor -ōris, m. *in a court of justice,* an assessor; a neighbour *at a feast or spectacle.*

consessus -ūs, *m.* an assembly.
consīderātē, *adv.* thoughtfully, carefully.
consīderātio -ōnis, *f.* consideration, contemplation, thought, reflection.
consīderātus -a -um, *p. adj.* well weighed, deliberate; *of persons,* cautious.
consīdero, 1. to regard carefully, contemplate; to consider, *with secum, cum animo suo, secum in animo.*
consīdo -sēdi -sessum, 3. *neut.* to sit down; *milit.,* to take up one's position; to encamp; to stay, to land. *Of things,* to settle, subside; to cease; to fall into neglect.
consigno, 1. to seal; to authenticate.
consiliārius -a -um, relating to counsel, deliberating, *senatus. Subst.,* **consiliārius -ii,** *m.* an adviser, an assessor.
consilior, 1. *dep.* to consult, take counsel.
consilium -ii, *n.* a deliberation, consultation; council; the senate; understanding, foresight, prudence; the advice *or* counsel given; a resolution, plan; *milit.,* stratagem; advice; *capere consilium,* to form a resolution; *abl., consilio,* intentionally; *privato consilio,* in the interests of private persons.
consimilis -e, exactly similar; *with genit. or with dat.*
consipio, 3. to have possession of one's faculties.
consisto, -stiti, 3. to take one's stand, place oneself, *consistere ad mensam; milit.,* to place oneself for battle; *of dice,* to fall; to agree with, *cum Aristone;* to stand still; *milit.,* to halt; dwell in speech, *in uno nomine;* to rest, cease; to rest, fall upon; to consist; to keep one's ground, footing; to hold one's own; to be firm.
consitio -ōnis, *f.* a sowing, planting.
consitor -ōris, *m.* a sower, planter.
consitūra -ae, *f.* a sowing, planting.
consōbrīnus -i, *m.* and **consōbrīna -ae,** *f.* cousin on the mother's side; cousin; second, third cousin.
consocer -ceri, *m.* a joint father-in-law.
consociātio -ōnis, *f.* connexion, association.
consociātus -a -um, *p. adj.* united, harmonious.
consocio, 1. to unite, share, associate.
consolābilis -e, consolable.
consolātio -ōnis, *f.* consolation, encouragement, alleviation.
consolātor -ōris, *m.* a consoler.
consolātōrius -a -um, consolatory.
consolor, 1. *dep.* to console, comfort, to encourage; *of things,* to alleviate, lighten, solace.
consōno -sōnui, 1. to sound together, sound loudly; to echo; to harmonise, agree, be consonant with.
consōnus -a -um, sounding together, harmonious; accordant, suitable.
consōpio, 4. to lull to sleep, stupefy.

consors -sortis, having an equal share with, sharing in, partaking of, *with genit.; inanimate objects,* common; *poet.* brother *or* sister; *adj.* = brotherly, sisterly.
consortio -ōnis, *f.* companionship, community, partnership.
consortium -ii, *n.* community of goods; fellowship, participation in.
1. **conspectus -a -um,** *p. adj.* visible; striking, remarkable, distinguished.
2. **conspectus -ūs,** *m.* look, sight, view; *dare se alicui in conspectum,* to allow oneself to be seen by; *in conspectu alicuius esse,* to be within sight of; *e conspectu abire,* out of sight; *conspectus est in Capitolium,* the view is towards the Capitol; mental view, survey. *Pass.,* appearance.
conspergo (con-spargo), -spersi -spersum, 3. to sprinkle, moisten by sprinkling.
conspiciendus -a -um, *p. adj.* noteworthy.
conspicio -spexi -spectum, 3. to look at, view, perceive; to look at with attention; *in pass., conspici,* to attract notice, to be distinguished.
conspicor, 1. *dep.* to catch sight of, perceive.
conspicuus -a -um, visible; remarkable, striking, conspicuous.
conspīrātio -ōnis, *f.* unison, harmony, agreement, union; conspiracy, plot.
conspīrātus -a -um, sworn together, united by an oath; **conspīrāti -orum,** *m.* conspirators.
conspiro, 1. to breathe together; to blow together, sound together; to agree, harmonise in opinion and feeling, to unite; to conspire, to form a plot.
consponsor -ōris, *m.* a joint surety.
conspurco, 1. to cover with dirt, defile.
conspūto, 1. to spit upon contemptuously.
constans -antis, *p. adj.* steady, unchanging, immovable, constant; *character,* firm, resolute; consistent, harmonious, *oratio;* uniform, unanimous.
constantēr, *adv.* firmly, consistently, constantly; uniformly, harmoniously.
constantia -ae, *f.* unchangeableness; perseverance, firmness; agreement, harmony.
consternātio -ōnis, *f.* fear, dismay, confusion; a mutiny, tumult.
1. **consterno -strāvi -strātum,** 3. to strew, scatter, cover by strewing; to throw down; *constrata navis,* a decked boat; *subst.,* **constrāta -orum,** *n., pontis,* the gangway over a bridge of boats.
2. **consterno,** 1. to cause confusion, fear, to frighten; to excite to revolt.
constipo, 1. to crowd together.
constituo -stitui -stitutum, 3. to cause to stand, place, put; *milit.,* to draw up in line, place, station, arrange; to halt; to post, settle; to appoint to

an office; to found, establish; *actionem*, to begin an action; *tres legiones*, to form; to settle upon, *tempus, diem*; to agree upon, *accusatorem*; to decide, *controversiam*; to resolve.

constitūtio -ōnis, *f.* constitution, condition, disposition, nature; determining; definition or settling; *rhet.*, the point in dispute, a regulation, order.

constitūtum -i, *n.* a fixed place *or* time of meeting, rendezvous; an agreement, appointment.

constitūtus -a -um, *partic. of constituo*.

consto -stiti -stātūrus, 1. to stand still; to exist; to consist, *ex animo constamus et corpore*; to depend upon; to cost; to stand firm, remain; *milit.* to hold one's ground; *of looks, speech, etc.*, to be unaltered; to be in good order; *ratio constat*, the account is correct; to continue; to remain constant; *constare sibi or alicui rei*, to be true to; *of resolves*, to be firm; *alicui constat*, a person is resolved; *of facts, etc.*, to be certain, well known.

constrātum -i, *n.*, *v.* 1. consterno.

constringo -strinxi -strictum, 3. to bind together; to fetter; to strengthen, fortify; to restrain; to abbreviate, *sententiam*.

constructio -ōnis, *f.* building, construction, making; *rhet.* the proper connexion of words.

construo -struxi -structum, 3. to heap up together; to build up; to arrange.

constuprātor -ōris, *m.* a ravisher, defiler.

constupro, 1. to ravish, violate.

Consuālia, *v.* Consus.

consuāsor -ōris, *m.* an adviser.

consuēfacio -fēci -factum, 3. to accustom.

consuesco -suēvi -suētum, 3. to accustom to; to accustom oneself, *and often in perf., consuevi*, I am accustomed; *with infin.*, to be intimate with, *cum aliquo*.

consuētūdo -inis, *f.* custom, usage, habit; *ut est consuetudo*, as is the usual practice; *ex consuetudine*, according to custom; manner of living; manner of speaking; social intercourse, intimacy.

consuētus -a -um, *p. adj.* accustomed, customary, usual.

consul -sŭlis, *m.* a consul, *pl. consules*, the consuls; *consul designatus, consul elect; pro consule*, an officer in the place of the consul, a governor, a proconsul.

consŭlāris -e, relating to a consul, consular. *Adj.*, *aetas*, the age at which a man might be chosen consul. *Subst.*, consularis -is, *m.* an ex-consul.

consŭlārĭtěr, *adv.* in a manner worthy of a consul.

consŭlātus -ūs, *m.* the office of consul, the consulship; *abdicare se consulatu*.

consŭlo -sŭlŭi -sultum, 3. to reflect, weigh, consider, consult; *in commune*, for the common good; to come to a conclusion, to take measures; *consulere in*, to take measures against; to take counsel for some person *or* thing, to have regard for the interests of, *with dat., sibi*; *aliquid boni consulere*, to take in good part; to ask the advice of, consult.

consultātio -ōnis, *f.* a full consideration, deliberation; a case proposed for consideration; an asking for advice, inquiry.

consultē, *adv.* advisedly, after consideration.

1. consultō, *adv.* deliberately, designedly.

2. consulto, 1. to consider maturely, weigh, ponder; *in longius*, for the future; *in medium*, for the common good; *alicui*, to consult for, provide for; to consult, ask advice of, *aliquem*.

consultor -ōris, *m.* an adviser; one who asks advice, a client.

consultrix -īcis, *f.* one who consults, cares for, provides.

consultum -i, *n.* resolution, plan, decision; a decree *of the senate, senatus consultum*; the answer of an oracle.

1. consultus -a -um, *p. adj.* well considered, deliberated upon, well weighed; *of persons*, experienced; *with genit., iuris consultus (adj. or subst.)*, some one learned in the law. *Subst.*, consultus -i, *m.* a lawyer.

2. consultus -ūs, *m.* = *consultum (q.v.)*.

consum -fui -futurum -fore, to be, to happen.

consummātio -ōnis, *f.* a summing up, adding up; completion, consummation.

consummātus -a -um, *p. adj.* complete, consummate.

consummo, 1. to add together, sum up; to form a whole, complete.

consūmo -sumpsi -sumptum, 3. to take altogether, consume, to spend, employ, *omne tempus in litteris*; to kill, destroy, waste; *of time*, to spend, pass; *garrulus hunc consumet*, will be the death of him; *fame consumi*, to die of hunger.

consumptio -ōnis, *f.* a consumption, consuming, destroying.

consumptor -ōris, *m.* a consumer, destroyer.

consŭo -sŭi -sūtum, 3. to sew together.

consurgo -surrexi -surrectum, 3. to rise up, stand up; to join in an insurrection; to break out, *novum bellum*.

consurrectio -ōnis, *f.* a rising up from a seat.

Consus -i, *m.* an ancient Roman deity. Consŭālia -ium, *n.* games in honour of Consus.

consŭsurro, 1. to whisper together.

contābesco -tābŭi, 3. to waste away.

contābŭlātio -ōnis, *f.* planking, floor.

contăbŭlo, 1. to cover with boards, to plank.

contăbundus = cunctabundus (q.v.).

contactus -ūs, m. a contact, touch; contagion.

contāges -is, f. a touch, touching.

contāgĭo -ōnis, f. a touching, connexion; contagion, infection; evil example.

contāgĭum -ĭi, n. touch; infection, contagion.

contāmĭnātus -a -um, p. adj. unclean, contaminated.

contāmĭno, 1. to contaminate.

contātĭo, contātus, etc. = cunctatio, cunctatus, etc. (q.v.).

contĕgo -texi -tectum, 3. to cover; tumulo, to bury; to conceal.

contĕmĕro, 1. to pollute, defile.

contemno -tempsi -temptum, 3. to think meanly of, despise; to ridicule.

contemplātĭo -ōnis, f. attentive looking at, contemplation.

contemplātor -ōris, m. one who attentively looks at or contemplates.

contemplātus, abl. -ū, m. a looking at, contemplation.

contemplor, 1. dep. to look at attentively, regard, contemplate; to consider carefully.

contemptim, adv. contemptuously.

contemptĭo -ōnis, f. contempt, disdain.

contemptor -ōris, m. one who despises.

1. contemptus -a -um, p. adj. despised, despicable, contemptible.

2. contemptus -ūs, m. contempt, disdain.

contendo -tendi -tentum, 3. to stretch forcibly; of missiles, to shoot, cast; to strive, to strain, exert oneself; to hasten on a journey, try to reach, Bibracte ire contendit; to strive to obtain; to assert with confidence, maintain; at an auction, to bid against; to compare, contrast.

contentē, adv. eagerly, earnestly.

contentĭo -ōnis, f. the full exercise of the powers, effort, striving; combat, contest, strife; contrast, comparison; rhet., antithesis.

contentiōsus -a -um, contentions, quarrelsome.

1. contentus -a -um, p. adj. stretched, tense; eager, zealous.

2. contentus -a -um, p. adj. contented, satisfied; with abl., suis rebus.

conterminus -a -um, having the same boundary, conterminous, near. Subst., conterminum -i, n. an adjoining region, a confine.

contĕro -trīvi -trītum, 3. to rub away, to grind, pound; to destroy, wear away; conterere et contemnere, trample under foot; of time, to consume, spend.

conterrĕo -terrŭi -territum, 2. to terrify.

contestātĭo -ōnis, f. an earnest supplication, eager request.

contestor, 1. dep. to call to witness; litem, inaugurate an action by calling witnesses; virtus contesta, approved.

contexo -texŭi -textum, 3. to weave together, twine together, connect, unite; to continue; to build, construct; to devise, invent.

contextē, adv. in close connexion.

1. contextus -a -um, p. adj. interwoven, connected, united; contexta historia eorum temporum, continuous.

2. contextus -ūs, m. uniting, connexion.

conticesco -ticŭi, 3. to become silent, to be dumb, silent; to become still or quiet, to abate, cease.

contignātĭo -ōnis, f. woodwork, a flooring, joists, story.

contigno, 1. to put planks together, to floor.

contigŭus -a -um, that which touches another, contiguous, near; with dat., within reach of, contiguus missae hastae.

continens -entis, p. adj., adjacent, bordering upon; continentibus diebus, in the days immediately following; hanging together, unbroken; terra continens, the mainland; (subst., continens -entis, f. a continent); of time, continuous; temperate, continent. Rhet., subst., continens -entis, f. the main point.

continentĕr, adv. in close succession; of time, continuously, without cessation; continently, temperately.

continentĭa -ae, f. self-restraint, moderation, temperance.

contĭnĕo -tinŭi -tentum, 2. to bind together, hold fast; to keep unseparated; to connect; to surround, contain, limit; to confine; milit., to shut in; to comprehend, comprise; to maintain; to keep firm; to be silent about; to restrain, confine, risum; gradum, to check; to keep back, suos a proelio; to curb, repress.

1. contingo, 3. to wet, moisten.

2. contingo -tigi -tactum, 3. to touch; to grasp; poet. to touch, taste, cibos ore; to sprinkle; to reach to; to border on; to be related to; to concern, affect; to defile; to happen, mihi omnia.

continuātĭo -ōnis, f. an unbroken continuance; connexion, continuation; rhet., a period.

1. continŭō, adv. immediately, at once; with a negative = not necessarily; in a question = perhaps then ?

2. continŭo, 1. to connect, unite; verba, to form into a sentence; agmen latissime, to extend; to do in rapid succession, to keep on doing; to continue without interruption; diem noctemque potando, continue drinking day and night; magistratum, to prolong.

continŭus -a -um, connected with, continuous, standing next to; unseparated; successive, uninterrupted.

contio -ōnis, f. an assembly of the people or of the soldiers, a public meeting; *in contionem ascendere or escendere*, to go up to the platform to speak; a speech.

contiōnābundus -a -um, haranguing, speaking in public.

contiōnālis -e, relating to a public assembly.

contiōnārius -a -um, relating to a public assembly.

contiōnātor -ōris, m. a popular orator, demagogue.

contiōnor, 1. dep. to form an assembly; to speak in public; to speak with a loud voice.

contiuncula -ae, f. (dim. of *contio*), a small assembly; a short harangue.

contor = cunctor (q.v.).

contorqueo -torsi -tortum, 2. to twist, turn violently, contort; to direct, turn; to brandish; *verba*, to hurl forth.

contorte, adv. with compar. in distorted order, in a constrained manner, ambiguously.

contortio -ōnis, f. a swinging, twisting.

contortor -ōris, m. one who perverts.

contortŭlus -a -um (dim. of *contortus*), somewhat intricate, obscure.

contortus -a -um, intricate, confused, complicated; powerful, vigorous.

contrā, adv. opposite, over against; on the other side, on the contrary ; *of opposition*, against. Prep. with acc. opposite to, over against; in opposition to, contrary to; against; *contra ea*, on the contrary, on the other hand.

contractio -ōnis, f. a drawing together, contraction ; abbreviation, shortness ; anxiety, depression.

contractiuncula -ae, f. (dim. of *contractio*), dejection, sadness.

contractus -a -um, p. adj. drawn in, contracted, narrow; *of time*, shorter; *of circumstances*, straitened; retired, quiet.

contrādico -dixi -dictum, 3. to gainsay, speak against, contradict.

contradictio -ōnis, f. a speaking against, contradiction.

contrăho -traxi -tractum, 3. to draw together, collect, unite. *Luceriam omnes copias*; to bring together for conversation, etc.; to unite; *contrahere amicitiam*, to form friendship; to complete a business arrangement, *negotium*; to cause; *aes alienum*, to contract debt; *vela*, to furl one's sails, *fig.*, to be moderate; *of limbs*, to contract; to shorten, reduce, draw in; *of appetites*, to repress; *of courage*, etc., to lower, lessen.

contrāriē, adv. in an opposite direction or manner.

contrārius -a -um, opposite, over against; *vulnera*, wounds in front; coming from the opposite direction; *contrarius ictus*, a blow from an enemy; opposed, contrary to; injurious; *subst.*, contrarium -ii, n. the opposite; adv., *ex contrario*, against, on the other side.

contrectābilitĕr, adv. with feeling.

contrectātio -ōnis, f. a touching, handling.

contrecto, 1, to touch, feel, handle; to consider; to dishonour.

contrĕmisco (contrĕmesco) -trĕmŭi, 3. to tremble violently, to quake; to tremble before, be afraid of.

contrĕmo, 3. to tremble violently, quake.

contribŭo -tribŭi -tribūtum, 3. to contribute to in common with others; to annex, incorporate with, unite.

contristo, 1. to make sorrowful, sadden.

contrītus -a -um, p. adj. worn out, well used, common, trite.

contrōversia -ae, f. debate, dispute, controversy; *hereditatis*, about an inheritance ; *sine controversiā vicimus*, we have undoubtedly conquered; *controversia non erat quin*, there was no doubt that, etc.

contrōversiōsus -a -um, controverted, strongly disputed.

contrōversor, 1. dep. to contend, dispute, debate.

contrōversus -a -um, disputed; controverted; *act.* disputatious, fond of controversy.

contrŭcido, 1. to cut in pieces, cut down, slay.

contrūdo -trūsi -trūsum, 3. to thrust, push together; to crowd.

contŭbernālis -is, c. a messmate, comrade; supporter; mate; the husband or wife of a slave.

contŭbernium -i, n. a hut, or tent in which ten men and an officer lodged; comradeship; concubinage.

contŭĕor -tŭitus sum, 2. dep. to look at attentively; to consider, reflect upon.

contŭmācia -ae, f. stubbornness, haughtiness; firmness.

contŭmācitĕr, adv. obstinately, insolently.

contŭmax -ācis, haughty, obstinate; firm.

contŭmēlia -ae, f. insult, outrage; dishonour; damage, injury.

contŭmēliōsē, adv. insolently, abusively.

contŭmēliōsus -a -um, adj. insulting, abusive.

contŭmŭlo, 1. to heap up in a mound; to bury.

contundo -tŭdi -tūsum, 3. to bruise, crush, break to pieces; to beat; to destroy, subdue.

contŭo, contŭor, 3. = contueor (q.v.).

conturbātio -ōnis, f. disorder, perturbation.

conturbo, 1. to disturb, throw into confusion; to cause anxiety; to ruin, make bankrupt.

contus -i, *m.* a pole; a long spear *or* pike.

cōnus -i, *m.* a cone, apex of a helmet.

convălesco -vălŭi, 3. to become strong; to gain strength; to gain power; recover from a disease.

convallis -is, *f.* a valley shut in on all sides.

convăso, 1. to pack up baggage.

convecto, 1. to bring together, collect.

convector -ōris, *m.* a fellow-voyager.

convĕho -vexi -vectum, 3. to bring together.

convello -velli *and* (*rarely*) -vulsi (-volsi) -vulsum (-volsum), 3. to tear; pull away, wrench off; *milit., convellere signa,* to pluck up the standards, to decamp; to weaken, destroy

convĕna -ae, *m.f. adj.* coming together; *plur. subst.,* assembled multitude.

convĕniens -entis, *p. adj.* agreeing, unanimous; fit for, appropriate.

convĕnientĕr, *adv.* suitably to.

convĕntientia -ae, *f.* agreement, harmony.

convĕnio -vēni -ventum, 4. to come together, collect; *legal, convenire in manum* (*of the wife,* to come into the power of her husband by marriage). *Transit.,* to visit, meet, call upon; to fit; to agree with, be congenial to, harmonise, be fitting; to unite; *res convenit, or impers., convenit,* a thing is agreed upon; *bene convenit cum aliquo,* to be on good terms with.

conventicŭlum -i, *n.* (*dim. of conventus*), assembly, association; place of meeting.

conventio -ōnis, *f.* assembly ; agreement, compact.

conventum -i, *n.* covenant, agreement, compact.

conventus -ūs, *m.* a coming together, assembly; a congress of states; *conventum agere,* to hold the assizes; the union of citizens forming a corporation. *Of atoms,* union; agreement.

converro -verri -versum, 3. to sweep together, brush out; *hereditates omnium,* scrape together.

conversătio -ōnis, *f.* frequent use, frequent sojourn in a place; intercourse, conversation.

conversio -ōnis, *f.* a turning round; change ; *mensium annorumque conversiones,* periodical return ; *rhet.,* rounding off of a period; the repetition of the same word at the end of a clause.

converso, 1. to turn round frequently.

converto -verti -versum, 3. to turn round, whirl round ; *milit., signa convertere,* to wheel round; *terga or se convertere,* to flee; to change one's direction; *geograph.,* to face, be directed towards, lie towards; to revolve; to direct towards; *se in or ad aliquem,* to

attach oneself to; to devote to; to convert, pervert; to change, alter.

convestio, 4. to clothe; to cover, surround.

convexus -a -um, vaulted, arched, convex ; sloping, steep. *Subst.,* **convexum** -i, *n. and in plur.* **convexa** -orum, *n.* an arch.

conviciător -ōris, *m.* a railer, slanderer, reviler.

convicior, 1. *dep.* to rail at, revile, reproach.

convicium -ii, *n.* a loud cry, shout, clamour; violent reproach, reviling, insult.

convictio -ōnis, *f.* social intercourse, familiarity.

convictor -ōris, *m.* one who lives with another, constant associate.

convictus -ūs, *m.* a living together, constant intercourse; entertainment, feast.

convinco -vici -victum, 3. to convict of a crime *or* mistake; to prove conclusively, demonstrate.

conviso, 3. to behold attentively, examine; *poet.* (*of the sun, etc.*), to beam upon.

convitiător, *v. conviciator.*

convitior, *v. convicior.*

convitium, *v. convicium.*

conviva -ae, *c.* a guest.

convivălis -e, relating to a feast.

convivător -ōris, *m.* one who gives a feast, a host.

convivium -ii, *n.* a feast, entertainment; the guests.

convivor, 1. *dep.* feast, revel.

convŏcătio -ōnis, *f.* a calling together.

convŏco, 1. to call together, assemble.

convŏlo, 1. to fly together, come together hastily.

convolsus, *v. convulsus.*

convolvo -volvi -vŏlutum, 3. to roll round; to cover.

convŏmo, 1. to vomit all over.

convulsus -a -um, *partic. of convello.*

cŏŏlesco = *coalesco* (*q.v.*).

cŏŏpĕrio -pĕrŭi -pertum, 4. to envelop; *aliquem lapidibus,* to stone to death; *coopertus,* overwhelmed.

cŏŏptătio -ōnis, *f.* choice, election ; *censoria,* filling up of the senate by the censors.

cŏŏpto, 1. to choose, elect.

cŏŏrior -ortus sum, 4. to arise, appear; to break out, *tempestates sunt coortae;* to rise in insurrection.

cŏŏrtus -ūs, *m.* an arising, breaking forth.

Cŏos (**Cŏus**) -i, *f.,* and **Cŏs** -o, *f.* island in the Aegean Sea. *Adj.,* **Cŏus,** born at Coos. *Subst.,* **Cŏum** -i, *n.* Coan wine; **Cŏi** -orum, *m.* the inhabitants of Coos; **Cŏa** -orum, *n.* Coan garments.

cōpa -ae, *f.* hostess of a wine-shop.

cŏphinus -i, *m.* a large basket.

cōpia -ae, *f.* plenty, abundance; ability, opportunity; *plur.* supplies; troops, forces; *copia dicendi,* fullness of expression.

cōpiōsē, *adv.* abundantly; copiously.

cōpiōsus -a -um, richly provided, wealthy; copious, eloquent.

cōpis *= copiosus* (q.v.).

cōpo, cōpōna *= caupo, caupona* (q.v.).

coprea (copria) -ae, *m.* a low buffoon.

copta -ae, *f.* hard cake *or* biscuit.

cōpŭla -ae, *f.* rope, band, tie; *plur.,* **copulae,** fastenings, grapnels; connexion.

cōpŭlātio -ōnis, *f.* union, connexion.

cōpŭlātus -a -um, *p. adj.* connected, coupled; copulated.

cōpŭlo, 1. to connect, unite.

cŏqua -ae, *f.* a female cook.

cŏquo, *coxi, coctum,* 3. to cook, prepare food; to bake, burn; to ripen; to warm; to think of, meditate, contrive; to disturb.

cŏquus (cocus) -i, *m.* a cook.

cŏr, cordis, *n.* the heart; the soul, feeling; *cordi est aliquis,* is dear to; the mind, judgment; a person: the stomach.

corallium -ii, *n.* red coral.

cōram, *adv.* in presence of, in face of, before; personally. *Prep. with abl.,* in presence of.

corbis -is, *m. and f.* a wicker basket.

corbīta -ae, *f.* a slow-sailing merchant vessel.

corbŭla -ae, *f.* (*dim. of corbis*), a little basket.

corcŭlum -i, *n.* (*dim. of cor*), a little heart, *as term of endearment.*

Corcȳra -ae, *f.* island in the Ionian Sea.

cordātus -a -um, prudent, wise.

Cordŭba -ae, *f.* a town in Hispania Boetica, *now* Cordova.

Corfīnium -ii, *n.* a town of the Peligni.

Cŏrinthus -i, *f.* Corinth, a city of Greece on the Isthmus of Corinth.

Cŏriŏli -ōrum, *m.* town of the Volsci in Latium. *Adj.,* **Cŏriŏlānus -a -um.**

cŏrium -ii, *n.* hide, skin, leather; *pellis corium,* to thrash; leathern thong, strap, lash.

Cornēlius -a -um, name of a Roman gens, which included the Scipios. *Adj.,* **Cornēliānus -a -um.**

cornĕŏlus -a -um (*dim. of* 1. *corneus*), horny.

1. cornĕus -a -um, horny, made of horn; like horn, hard; horn-coloured.

2. cornĕus -a -um, belonging to the cornel-tree.

cornĭcĕn -cinis, *m.* a horn-blower.

cornĭcor, 1. *dep.* to caw like a crow.

cornīcŭla -ae, *f.* (*dim. of cornix*), a little crow.

cornĭcŭlārius -ii, *m.* a soldier who has been presented with the *corniculum,* an adjutant.

cornĭcŭlum -i, *n.* (*dim. of cornu*), a little horn.

cornĭger -gĕra -gĕrum, horned. *Subst.,* **cornĭgera -orum,** *n.* horned cattle.

cornĭpēs -pĕdis, horn-footed, hoofed.

cornix -icis, *f.* the crow.

cornu *-ūs and* **-ū,** *n.* the horn of animals; a hoof, a beak of a bird; elephant's tusk; a bow; curved trumpet, *or* horn; lantern; an oil-cruet; a funnel; top of the helmet, the ends of the sail-yards; the ends of the staff round which parchments were rolled; horns of the moon; arm of a river; end of a promontory; the corner *or* extremity of a country; wing of an army; a growth like a horn, a large wart on the head. *Cornu Copiae* (*Cornucopia*), the horn of the goat Amalthea, the sign of plenty; *cornu,* *poet. for* strength, courage; *cornua sumere,* gain courage.

cornūcōpia -ae, *v. cornu.*

cornum -i, *n.* the fruit of the cornel; the wood of the cornel-tree.

cornus -i, *and* **-ūs,** *f.* the cornel-tree; wood of the cornel-tree.

cornūtus -a -um, horned.

cŏrōlla -ae, *f.* (*dim. of corona*), a little crown.

cŏrōllārium -ii, *n.* garland of flowers; present.

cŏrōna -ae, *f.* garland, crown; *sub corona vendere,* to sell into slavery prisoners of war *who wore chaplets;* a constellation; a circle, assembly of men; (*urbem*) *corona cingere,* to invest; the halo round the sun.

cŏrōnārius -a -um, relating to a garland.

cŏrōno, 1. to wreathe, crown with a garland; to surround.

corpŏrālis -e, relating to the body.

corpŏrĕus -a -um, relating to the body, corporeal; fleshy, consisting of flesh.

corpŏro, 1. to form into a body.

corpus -pŏris, *n.* a body, substance; a person; a mass; *individua corpora,* the atoms; flesh; a corpse; *pl.* of the souls of the dead; the trunk; the framework of a ship; the "body politic"; any whole; a collection of persons; a political union.

corpuscŭlum -i, *n.* (*dim. of corpus*), corpuscle, atom.

corrādo -rāsi -rāsum, 3. to scrape together.

correctio -ōnis, *f.* improvement, amendment.

corrector -ōris, *m.* an improver, corrector.

correpo -repsi -reptum, 3. to creep *or* crawl together, to slink in; to shrink.

correptē, *adv.* shortly.

corrīdĕo, 2. to laugh together.

corrigia -ae, *f.* a shoe-string, boot-lace.

corrigo -rexi -rectum, 3. to reduce to order, set right; to correct, improve.

corripio -ripŭi -reptum, 3. to seize violently, take up ; *se corripere*, to hasten away; to plunder, carry off; to bring to trial; to blame; to overcome; to gather together; to hasten; *of time*, to shorten.

corrŏbŏro, 1. to strengthen, invigorate.

corrŏdo -rōsi -rōsum, 3. to gnaw away.

corrŏgo, 1. to bring together, collect by begging.

corrŭgo, 1. to wrinkle up.

corrumpo -rūpi -ruptum, 3. to destroy; to spoil, deteriorate; to weaken; to corrupt ; to falsify, *tabulas publicas* ; *corrumpere pecunia*, to bribe.

corruo -rui, 3. *intransit.*, to fall to the ground, sink down; to fall in battle; *of persons*, to be ruined. *Transit.*, to overthrow.

corrupte, *adv.* corruptly, incorrectly.

corruptela -ae, *f.* the means of corruption, corruption, bribery, seduction.

corruptio -ōnis, *f.* corruption.

corruptor -ōris, *m.* a corrupter, seducer, briber.

corruptrix -īcis, *f.* (*fem. of corruptor*).

corruptus -a -um, *p. adj.* spoiled, damaged, corrupted, corrupt.

cors = cohors (*q.v.*).

Corsica -ae, *f.* island in the Mediterranean Sea.

cortex -ticis, *m. and f.* bark, rind, shell; cork.

cortina -ae, *f.* a round kettle *or* cauldron; the Delphic tripod; *cortina Phoebi*, the oracle of Apollo; a circle of hearers.

cŏrŭlus = corylus (*q.v.*).

cŏrus = caurus (*q.v.*).

cŏrusco, 1. to butt with the horns. *Transit.*, to move quickly, shake. *Intransit.*, *coruscant pennis*, flutter; to shine, flash, glitter.

cŏruscus -a -um, shaking, trembling; gleaming, flashing.

corvus -i, *m.* a raven; *in cruce corvos pascere*, to be food for the crows, to be crucified.

Cŏrўbās -bantis, *m. gen. plur.*, Cŏrў-bantes -ium, *m.* priests of Cybels.

cŏrўcus -i, *m.* a sand-bag in the palaestra, which the athletes struck to exercise their strength.

cŏrўlētum -i, *n.* a hazel copse.

cŏrўlus -i, *f.* a hazel tree.

cŏrymbĭfĕr -fĕra -fĕrum, carrying bunches of ivy berries (*Bacchus*).

cŏrymbus -i, *m.* branch of flowers *or* fruit, *esp.* a cluster of ivy berries.

cŏrўphaeus -i, *m.* the leader, chief, head.

cŏrўtus -i, *m.* a quiver.

1. cōs, cōtis, *f.* any hard, flinty stone; *esp.* a whetstone.

2. Cōs, *v.* Coos.

cosmētēs -ae, *m.* the slave who had charge of his mistress's wardrobe and toilet.

cosmicos -ōn, belonging to the world. *Subst.*, a citizen of the world.

costa -ae, *f.* a rib; a side.

costum -i, *n.* an eastern aromatic plant.

cŏthurnātus -a -um, provided with a buskin, *hence* sublime, tragic.

cŏthurnus -i, *m.* a large hunting boot, reaching to the calf, and laced up the front; the thick-soled boot worn by tragic actors; tragedy; a tragic, elevated style.

cotidianus, cotidie = quotidianus, *etc.* (*q.v.*).

cottăbus -i, *m.* a game played by throwing heeltaps of wine into a brazen basin; the crack of a whip.

cottăna (cotōna, coctōna, coctăna) -ōrum, *n.* a kind of small Syrian figs.

cŏtŭla *or* cŏtўla -ae, *f.* half a sextarius.

cōturnix -īcis, *f.* a quail.

cŏvīnārius *and* cŏvinnārius -ii, *m.* one who fights from a war-chariot.

cŏvīnus (cŏvinnus) -i, *m.* a war-chariot; a travelling-chariot.

coxa -ae, *f.* the hip-bone.

coxendix -icis, *f.* the hip, the hip-bone.

cărbro -ōnis, *m.* a hornet.

crambē -ēs, *f.* cabbage; *crambe repetita*, cold cabbage warmed up, *i.e.* stale repetitions.

crăpŭla -ae, *f.* intoxication, drunken revel.

crăs, *adv.* to-morrow; in the future.

crasse, *adv.* grossly, rudely.

crassĭtūdo -ĭnis, *f.* thickness ; *aeris*, density.

1. crassus -a -um, thick, dense, solid; *aër*, misty; *toga*, coarse; *ager*, fruitful; rude, uncultivated, stupid, clumsy.

2. Crassus -i, *m.* name of a family of the gens Licinia (*q.v.*).

crastinus -a -um, relating to to-morrow; *dies crastinus. Subst.*, crastinum -i, *n.* the morrow.

crāter -ēris, *m.* = cratera (*q.v.*).

crātēra -ae, *f.* a large bowl in which wine was mixed with water ; an oil-cruet; the crater of a volcano ; a constellation.

crātis -is, *f.* a frame *or* basket made of hurdles ; a harrow ; *milit.*, fascines ; *favorum*, honeycomb; *spinae*, the joints of the backbone.

crĕātio -ōnis, *f.* choice, election.

crĕātor -ōris, *m.* the creator, founder; father.

crĕātrix -īcis, *f.* she who brings forth *or* produces.

crĕber -bra -brum, *adj. of space*, thick, crowded, close ; thick with, full of ; abounding; *with abl.*, numerous, frequent.

crēbresco (crēbesco) -brŭi (-bŭi), 3 to become frequent, increase, extend.

crēbrĭtas -ātis, *f.* closeness, frequency.

crēbro, *adv. superl.* creberrime, repeatedly, frequently.

crēdĭbĭlis -e, *adj.* credible, worthy of belief.

crēdĭbĭlĭter, *adv.* credibly.

crēdĭtor -ōris, *m.* a creditor,

crēdĭtum -i, *n.* a loan.

credo -dĭdi -dĭtum, 3. *with dat.*, to trust, trust in, rely upon; to believe; to entrust, commit; *to lend; pecunia credita,* loans; to believe something; to think, to be of the opinion; *parenthetic, credo,* I believe, I think.

crēdŭlĭtas -ātis, *f.* credulity.

crēdŭlus -a -um, *act.* believing easily, credulous, confiding, *alicui. Pass.,* easily believed.

crĕmo, 1. to burn, consume by fire.

crĕmor -ōris, *m.* the thick juice obtained from animal *or* vegetable substances, pulp, cream, *etc.*

crĕo, 1. to make, create, produce; to beget a child; to institute an office *or* magistracy; to elect a magistrate *or* priest.

crĕper -pĕra -pĕrum, dark, obscure, uncertain.

crĕpĭda -ae, *f.* a sandal.

crĕpĭdātus -a -um, wearing sandals.

crĕpīdo -ĭnis, *f.* base, foundation, pedestal.

crĕpĭtācŭlum -i, *n.* (*dim. of orepitaculum*), a little rattle.

crĕpĭtācŭlum -i, *n.* a rattle.

crĕpĭto, 1. (*freq. of crepo*), to rattle, creak, crackle, rustle, clatter.

crĕpĭtus -ūs, *m.* a rattling, creaking, rustling, clattering; *digitorum,* snapping of the fingers.

crĕpo -pŭi -pĭtum, 1. *intransit.*, to creak, rattle, rustle, crackle; *digiti crepantis signa,* a snapping of the fingers to call a servant's attention. *Transit.,* to cause to resound, rattle; to talk much of, chatter about, prate about.

crĕpundĭa -ōrum, *n.* child's playthings, rattle.

crĕpuscŭlum -i, *n.* twilight.

cresco, crēvi, crētum, 3. to grow up, spring forth, arise; *vast partic. cretus,* spring from; to grow, increase in size; *esp. of boys,* to grow up; to increase in height, number, *etc.*; *luna crescens,* waxing; to grow great, increase in fame, power, *etc.*

1. Crēta -ae, *f.* and Crētē -ēs, *f.* the Mediterranean island of Crete.

2. crēta -ae, *f.* Cretan earth, chalk, *or* a kind of fuller's earth.

crētātus -a -um, chalked; *ambitio,* the canvassing of the white-robed candidates.

crētĕus -a -um, made of chalk *or* Cretan earth.

crētĭo -ōnis, *f.* declaration of an heir accepting an inheritance.

crētŭla -ae, *f.* (*dim. o creta*), white clay for sealing.

Crĕūsa -ae, *f.* wife of Aeneas.

crībrum -i, *n.* a sieve.

crīmen -ĭnis, *n.* accusation, complaint, reproach, calumny; *esse in crimine,* to be accused; an object of reproach; the fault, crime, with which a person is charged; cause of crime.

crīmĭnātĭo -ōnis, *f.* an accusation, charge.

crīmĭnātor -ōris, *m.* an accuser.

crīmĭnor, 1. *dep,* to accuse, to calumniate; to charge with, to complain of; to reproach.

crīmĭnōsē, *adv.* reproachfully.

crīmĭnōsus -a -um, reproachful, calumnious; *criminosum est,* blameworthy.

crīnālis -e, relating to the hair. *Subst.,* crināle -is, *n.* a hair-band.

crīnis -is, *m.* the hair; the tail of a comet.

crīnītus -a -um, hairy, with long hair; *stella crinita,* a comet.

crispĭsulcans -antis, forked (*lightning*).

crispo, 1. to curl; to brandish, *hastilia manu.*

crispŭlus -a -um (*dim. of crispus*), curly-haired, curly.

crispus -a -um, curly, curly-headed; trembling, quivering.

crista -ae, *f.* the crest of a bird; the crest of a helmet.

cristātus -a -um, crested.

Crĭtĭas -ae, *m.* one of the Thirty Tyrants at Athens.

crĭtĭcus -i, *m.* a critic.

Crĭto -ōnis, *m.* disciple of Socrates.

Crĭtŏbūlus -i, *m.* disciple of Socrates.

crŏcĕus -a -um, belonging to saffron, saffron; golden, yellow.

crŏcĭnus -a -um, belonging to saffron, yellow. *Subst.,* crŏcĭnum -i, *n.* saffron-oil.

crŏcŏdīlus -i, *m.* a crocodile.

crŏcōta -ae, *f.* a saffron-coloured robe worn by women.

crŏcus -i, *m.,* crŏcum -i, *n.* saffron, yellow; *Crocus,* a young man changed into a saffron-flower.

Croesus -i, *m.* a king of Lydia famous for his wealth. *Adj.,* Croesius.

crŏtălĭa -ōrum, *n.* an earring consisting of several pendant pearls.

crŏtălistrĭa -ae, *f.* a female dancer and performer on the castanets.

crŏtălum -i, *n.* a castanet.

Crŏto (Crŏtōn) -ōnis, *c.* a town of Bruttium.

crŭcĭāmentum -i, *n.* torture, torment.

crŭcĭātus -ūs, *m.* torture, torment, execution; *quin tu abi in malam pestem malumque cruciatum,* go and be hanged!

crŭcĭo, 1. to torture, torment.

crūdēlis -e, unmerciful, cruel.

crūdēlĭtas -ātis, *f.* cruelty, inhumanity.

crūdēlĭter, *adv.* cruelly.

crūdesco -dūi, 3. to become hard, violent.

crūditas -ātis, f. overloading of the stomach, indigestion.

crūdus -a -um, raw; uncooked; unripe; undigested; suffering from indigestion; raw, not healed, *vulnera;* unprepared, rough; immature, fresh; vigorous; rough, cruel.

crŭento, 1. to make bloody, to stain with blood.

cruentus -a -um, bloody, mixed with blood; blood-red; covered, spotted with blood; wounding; bloodthirsty, cruel.

crūmēna -ae, f. a leathern pouch for money; money.

crŭor -ōris, m. the blood which flows from a wound, gore; *fig.,* murder, slaughter.

cruppellārii -ōrum, m. Gaulish gladiators, who fought in full armour.

crūs, crūris, n. the shin, shin-bone, leg; *plur.,* supports of a bridge.

crusta -ae, f. the crust, rind, shell, bark of any substance; mosaic, inlaid work on walls, bas-relief, *or* embossing on silver plate.

crustŭlum -i, n. (*dim. of crustum*), a little cake.

crustum -i, n. bread, cake.

crux, crŭcis, f. a cross; *abi in malam crucem,* go and be hanged!

crypta -ae, f. a subterranean gallery, vault, crypt, grotto.

crystallinus -a -um, crystalline, made of crystal. *Subst.,* crystallina -ōrum, n. crystal vases.

crystallus -i, f. *and (rarely)* m. (*heterocl. plur.,* crystalla), crystal; crystal drinking vessel; stone in a ring.

cŭbĭcŭlāris -e, relating to a sleeping-room.

cŭbĭcŭlārius -a -um, belonging to a sleeping-room. *Subst.,* cŭbĭcŭlārius -ii, m. a valet-de-chambre.

cŭbĭcŭlum -i, n. bedroom.

cŭbĭle, a bed (of animals), lair, den; *of bees,* hives; *fig.,* the seat of an evil.

cŭbĭtal -tālis, n. an elbow cushion.

cŭbĭtālis -e, of the length of a cubit.

cŭbĭto, 1. (*freq. of cubo*), to be accustomed to lie.

cŭbĭtum -i, n. *and* cŭbĭtus -i, m. elbow; cubit, ell.

cŭbo -ŭi -ĭtum, 1. to lie down, recline; *cubitum ire,* to go to bed; to lie in bed ill; *partic.,* cubans, sloping.

cŭcŭllus -i, m. a hood, cowl.

cŭcŭlus -i, m. the cuckoo.

cŭcŭmis -mĕris, m. a cucumber.

cŭcurbita -ae, f. a gourd; a cupping-glass.

cūdo, 3. to beat, pound; to thresh; *of metals,* to stamp, beat out, coin.

cuicuĭmŏdi, of what kind soever.

cūĭas -ātis *and* cūĭātis -is, of what country? whence?

cūĭus -a -um, 1. *interrog. pron.* to whom belonging? whose? *relat. pron.* whose.

cūĭuscēmŏdi, of whatever kind.

cūĭusdam-mŏdi, of a certain kind.

cūĭusmŏdi, of what kind?

cūĭusquēmŏdi, of every kind.

cuicĭta -ae, f. mattress, bolster, pillow.

cūlĕus (cullĕus) -i, m. a large leathern sack.

cūlex -ĭcis, m. a gnat, midge.

cūlina -ae, f. kitchen; food, fare.

cullĕus, v. *culeus.*

culmen -ĭnis, n. the top, summit; ridge of a roof. *Poet.* = *culmus,* haulm.

culmus -i, m. a stalk, haulm, *esp. of grain;* thatch.

culpa -ae, f. fault, error; by my own fault, *meā culpā, tuā culpā, etc.;* unchastity; the cause of error *or* sin.

culpātus -a -um, *p. adj.* blameworthy.

culpo, 1. to blame, accuse.

cultē, *adv.* elegantly.

cultellus -i, m. (*dim. of culter*), a little knife.

culter -tri, m. a knife; a ploughshare.

cultor -ōris, m. a cultivator, labourer; husbandman; occupier, *eius terrae;* a supporter; *bonorum* (of the optimates); a worshipper, *deorum.*

cultrix -ĭcis, f. she who tends *or* takes care of; inhabitant.

cultūra -ae, f. culture, cultivation; agriculture; mental culture; reverence, respect, *potentis amici.*

1. cultus -a -um, *p. adj.* cultivatea, adorned; polished, elegant. *Subst.,* culta -orum, n. cultivated land.

2. cultus -ūs, m. cultivation care, *corporis;* adornment, dress; mental training, education; reverence.

cŭlullus -i, m. a drinking-vessel.

1. cum, *conj.* = *quum* (*q.v.*).

2. cum, *prep. with abl.* with; together with; in relation with, in company with; provided with; at the same time with, *cum primā luce; cum eo quod ut,* or *ne,* on the condition that.

Cūmae -ārum, f. city of Campania. *Adj.* Cūmānus; Cūmaeus.

cumba = cymba (*q.v.*).

cūmĕra -ae, f. a corn-chest.

cūmĭnum -i, n. the herb cummin.

cummi, v. *gummi.*

cumprĭmis, v. *primus.*

cumque (cunque, quomque), *adverb usually in composition, e.g. quicumque, etc.*

cŭmŭlātē, *adv.* abundantly, copiously.

cŭmŭlātus -a -um, *p. adj.* heaped up, increased, enlarged; perfect.

cŭmŭlo, 1. to heap up, pile up; fill up, overload; to increase, heighten, *invidiam;* to bring to perfection.

cŭmŭlus -i, m. a heap, pile, mass; increase, surplus, summit.

cūnābŭla -ōrum, n. a cradle.

cūnae -ārum, f. a cradle; the nest of young birds; *primis cunis*, in earliest childhood.

cunctābundus -a -um, loitering, dilatory.

cunctans -antis, p. adj. lingering, slow; *ilex cunctans glebae*, tenacious.

cunctanter, adv. slowly, lingeringly

cunctātiō, -ōnis, f. a delay, hesitation.

cunctātor -ōris, m. one who delays, hesitates; surname of the dictator, *Q. Fabius Maximus*.

cunctor, 1. dep. to delay; to stay, tarry; *tardum cunctatur olivum*, drops slowly; to hesitate, be slow.

cunctus -a -um, all, the whole; plur., cuncti -ae -a.

cūneātim, adv. in shape of a wedge.

cūneātus -a -um, p. adj. pointed like a wedge.

cūneo, 1. to drive in a wedge, to wedge in.

cūneŏlus -i, m (dim. of cuneus), a little wedge.

cūneus -i, m. a wedge; *Britannia in cuneum tenuatur*, is narrowed in the shape of a wedge; compartments into which the seats of the amphitheatre were divided; *cuneis omnibus*, to all the spectators.

cūnĭcŭlōsus -a -um, full of holes and caverns.

cūnĭcŭlus -i, m. a rabbit, cony; an underground passage; *milit.*, a mine; *agere cuniculum.*

cūpa -ae, f. cask or butt.

cūpēdia -ae, f. daintiness, fondness for dainties

cūpĭdē, adv. eagerly, passionately, vehemently.

cūpĭdĭtas -ātis, f. eager desire, passionate longing; ambition; avarice; factiousness, party spirit.

cūpĭdo -ĭnis, f. (m. only in poet.), longing, desire; avarice; ambition; *honoris*, love; Cūpīdo -ĭnis, m. Cupid, the god of love; plur., Cūpīdĭnes, Cupids.

cūpĭdus -a -um, adj. with genit. desirous, eager, fond, *pecuniae*; longing for, loving; avaricious; devoted to; factious, partial.

cūpiens -entis, p. adj. desiring, eager.

cūpĭo -ivi or ii, -ītum, 3. to desire, long for, *with acc.*; *alicui*, to favour, support.

cūpĭtor -ōris, m. one who desires.

cuppēdia, v. cupedia.

cūpressētum -i, n. a cypress wood.

cūpressēus -a -um, made of cypress wood.

cūpressĭfer -fĕra -fĕrum, cypress-bearing.

cūpressus -i, f. -ūs, m. the cypress; a casket of cypress wood.

cūr, adv. why? for what reason?

cūra -ae, f. care; carefulness, solicitude, pains, trouble, attention; *ponere curam*,

to lay aside; care for something, caring, minding; adornment of the body, healing, cure; the worship of the gods; taking care of a person; the object of attention; management; business, administration; anxiety; the object of love.

cūrābĭlis -e, causing care or fear.

cūrālium -ii — corallium (q.v.).

cūrā -e, adv. carefully; *curatius legi*, between the lines.

cūrātio -ōnis, f. a taking care, attention, management; healing, cure; administration; *curatio agraria*, commission to divide land.

cūrātor -ōris, m. one who takes care; a guardian, curator.

cūrātus -a -um, p. adj. carefully prepared.

curcūlĭo -ōnis, m. a weevil, corn-worm.

Cūres -ĭum, f. town of the Sabines; the inhabitants of Cures. Adj., Cūrensis -e.

Cūrētes -um, m. the ancient inhabitants of Crete.

cūrĭa -ae, f. a curia, division of the Roman patricians; the meeting-place of a curia; the building in which the senate met; *at Athens*, the Aeropagus.

cūrĭālis -e, belonging to the same curia.

cūrĭātim, adv. by curiae.

Cūrĭātii -ōrum, m. name of an Alban gens.

cūrĭātus -a -um, relating to the curiae.

cūrĭo -ōnis, m. the priest of a curia; a herald, crier.

cūrĭōsē, adv. carefully; inquisitively.

cūrĭōsĭtas -ātis, f. curiosity.

cūrĭōsus -a -um, adj. careful; attentive, diligent; inquisitive, curious.

cūrĭs -is, f. (a Sabine word) — hasta, a lance, or javelin.

Cūrĭus -a -um, name of a plebeian gens.

cūro, 1. to care for, pay attention to; *in Sicilia frumentum emendum et ad urbem mittendum curare*, to get bought and sent; *non curare*, not to care, to decline; *cure* an invalid, or a disease; to procure a sum of money; to administer, manage, *res Romae*; to command.

curricŭlum -i, n. running; a race; a course, orbit of heavenly bodies; the chariot used in races; the race-ground.

curro, cŭcurri, cursum, 3. to run, hasten; pass. impers., *curritur*, one runs; to run in a race; *of ships*, to sail; *of time*, to pass; *of discourse*, to march easily.

currus -ūs, m. a chariot, car; the horses, the team; a plough with wheels; a ship (poet.).

cursim, adv. hastily, quickly.

cursĭto, 1. to run up and down.

curso, 1. to run hither and thither.

cursor -ōris m. a runner; one who contends in the chariot race; a messenger;

a postman; a slave who ran before a carriage; surname of *L. Papirius.*

cursus -ūs, *m.* a running, rapid motion on horseback, in a carriage, *or* ship; course, march, journey; *in cursu esse,* to travel in haste; chariot *or* horse-race; *fig.* the race for office, honour, *etc.*

curto, 1. to abridge, abbreviate.

curtus -a -um, shortened, mutilated, cut short.

cürülis -e, relating to a chariot; *sella,* the curule chair.

curvämen -inis, *n.* a curving, vaulting, arching.

curvätüra -ae, *f.* a vault, arch; *rotae,* the rim

curvo, 1. to bend, bow, curve; make to bend, move.

curvus -a -um, bent, arched, curved, crooked; *arbor,* bent with the weight of fruit; *flumen,* winding; *subst.,* **curvum** -i, *n.* what is crooked.

cuspis -idis, *f.* point, *esp.* of a spear; *of the sting of a bee;* a lance, javelin; Neptune's trident, *cuspis triplex;* a spit.

custödia -ae, *f.* a watching, guarding, custody; *milit.* keeping guard; the watch, sentinels; the station of the guard, post; custody; *custodia libera,* liberation on parole.

custödio, 4. to guard, watch, keep; to keep in sight, observe; to take care of; to keep in prison, hold captive.

custos -ödis, *c.* guardian, watchman, keeper, attendant; the guardian of a young man *or* woman; *milit.,* a sentinel, guard; an overseer; gaoler.

cüticüla -ae, *f.* (*dim. of cutis*), the skin.

cütis -is, *f.* the skin; hide, leather.

cyäthus -i, *m.* a ladle for filling goblets with wine; a measure of capacity.

cybaeus -a -um, **cybaea** -ae, *f.* a kind of transport *or* merchantman.

Cybëlë *or* **Cybebe** -ës, *f.* a Phrygian goddess, afterwards worshipped at Rome.

1. **cyclas** -ädis, *f.* a female robe of state.

2. **Cyclas** -ädis, *f.* plur. **Cyclädes** -um, *f.* islands in the Aegean Sea.

cyclicus -a -um, cyclic.

Cyclops -clöpis, *m.* a Cyclops, *plur.* **Cyclöpes** -clöpum, *m.* the Cyclopes. *Adj.,* **Cyclöpëus.**

cycnëus -a -um, belonging to the swan.

1. **cycnus** -i, *m.* the swan.

2. **Cycnus** -i, *m.* 1, king of Liguria, changed into a swan; 2, son of Neptune, changed into a swan.

cygn . . . *v. cycn* . . .

cylindrus -dri, *m.* a cylinder, a roller for levelling the ground.

Cyllënë -ës *and* -ae, *f.* mountain in Arcadia. *Subst.,* **Cyllënius** -ii, *m.* Mercury. *Adj.,* **Cyllënëus.**

cymba -ae, *f.* a small boat, skiff.

cymbälum -i, *n.* a cymbal, *usually plur.*

cymbium -ii, *n.* a small drinking-vessel.

Cynicus -i, *m.* a Cynic philosopher. *Adj.,* **Cynicus.**

cynöcëphälus -i, *m.* an ape with a head like a dog's.

Cynoscëphälae -ärum, *f.* in Thessaly where the Romans defeated the Macedonians.

Cynösüra -ae, *f.* the constellation of the Little Bear, the pole star. *Adj.,* **Cynösüris** -idis, *ursa,* the Little Bear.

Cynthus -i, *m.* mountain in Delos, the birthplace of Apollo and Diana; **Cynthius** -ii, *m.* Apollo; **Cynthia** -ae, *f.* Diana.

cypärissus = *cupressus (q.v.).*

Cyprus *and* -os -i, *f.* the island of Cyprus; *adj.,* **Cyprius;** *subst.,* **Cyprium** -i *n.* copper; **Cypria** -ae, *f.* Venus; **Cyprii** -orum, *m.* the Cypriotes.

Cyrënë -ës (-ae -arum), *f.* a city of North Africa; *adj.,* **Cyrënaeus; Cyrënaei** -orum, *m.* the Cyrenai, philosophers; **Cyrënäicus,** Cyrenaic; **Cyrënäici** -orum, the Cyrenaic philosophers; **Cyrënensis** -e, Cyrenaic.

Cyrus -i, *m.* founder of the Persian Empire; *Cyrus minor,* second son of Ochus, who fought with his brother, Artaxerxes Memnon, and was killed at Cunaxa.

Cythëra -örum, *n.* island sacred to Venus; **Cythërëa** -ae, *f.* Venus; *adj.,* **Cythërëius;** *subst.,* **Cythërëia** -ae, *f.* Venus; **Cythërëis** -idis, *f.* Venus: **Cythërïacus** -a -um, *and* **Cythërëias** -ädis, *f.* sacred to Venus.

cytisus -i, *c. and* **cytisum** -i, *n.* a kind of clover.

D

Dd, *the fourth letter of the Latin Alphabet.*

Däci -örum, *m.* Dacians, a warlike people on the Lower Danube; **Däcia** -ae, *f.* their country.

dactylicus -a -um, dactylic.

dactylöthëca -ae, *f.* a casket for rings; collection of seal rings and gems.

dactylus (-os) -i, *m.* (*lit.* a finger), a metrical foot, consisting of one long, followed by two short syllables ($-\smile\smile$), a dactyl.

1. **daedälus** -a -um, artful, full of art; artfully constructed.

2. **Daedälus** -i, *m.* a celebrated Athenian artificer, builder of the Cretan labyrinth; *adj.,* **Daedälëus** -a -um ; *iter,* the labyrinth.

dāma -ae, *f.* (*in Verg. m.*), a fallow-deer.

damma = dama (*q.v.*).

damnätio -önis, *f.* condemnation; *ambitūs,* for bribery.

damnätörius -a -um, condemnatory.

damno, 1. to condemn, declare guilty, sentence ; *with genit. of the crime, ambitus; of the punishment, damnari octupli; damnare aliquem voti or voto*, to grant a person's wish, and thereby compel him to keep his vow; *damnari voti or voto*, to attain one's wish; to blame.

damnōsē, *adv.* ruinously.

damnōsus -a -um, *adj.* causing loss or damage, detrimental.

damnum -i, *n.* loss, damage, injury ; *dare damnum*, to cause loss; *damnum naturae*, a natural defect; defeat.

Dămoclēs -is, *m.* friend of Dionysius, tyrant of Syracuse.

Dāmon -ōnis, *m.* famous for his friendship with Phintias.

Dănăē -ēs, *f.* mother of Perseus by Zeus.

Dănăus -i, *m.* father of the fifty Danaïdes, the mythical founder of Argos; *adj.*, **Dănăus** Greek, Argive ; *m.* **Dănăi** -ōrum, *m.* the Greeks; **Dănăides** -um, *f.* the daughters of Danaus.

Dănŭbius (**Dănŭvius**) -ii, *m.* the Danube (*upper*); *the lower part was called Ister.*

dăno, *v. do.*

Daphnē -ēs, *f.* daughter of the river-god Peneus, changed into a laurel tree.

Daphnis -nĭdis, *acc.* -nĭm *and* -nin, a shepherd, inventor of pastoral poetry.

daphnōn -ōnis, *m.* a grove of laurels.

daps, **dăpis**, *f.* a sacrificial feast; a meal, feast, banquet.

dapsĭlis -e, sumptuous, plentiful.

Dardănus -i, *m.* mythical ancestor of the royal family of Troy ; **Dardănus**, Trojan ; *subst.*, **Dardăni** -ōrum, *m.* the Trojans ; **Dardănius** -a -um, Trojan ; *subst.*, **Dardănia** -ae, *f.* Troy.

dătĭo -ōnis, *f.* a giving; the legal right of alienation.

dător -ōris, *m.* a giver.

Daulis -ĭdis, *f.* a city in Phocis.

Daunus -i, *m.* mythical king of Apulia, **Daunĭus** -ădis, *f.* Apulia.

dē, *prep., with abl.,* from; down from; immediately after; *diem de die proferre*, to put off from day to day ; among ; concerning, *de publico*, at the public expense ; *de improviso*, unexpectedly.

dĕa -ae, *f.* goddess.

dĕalbo, 1. to whitewash, plaster.

dĕambŭlo, 1. to take a walk.

dĕarmo, 1. to disarm.

dēbacchor, 1. *dep.* to rave, rage furiously.

dēbellātor -ōris, *m.* a conqueror.

dēbello, 1. to wage war to the end, finish a war. *Transit.,* to fight out; to conquer.

dēbĕo -ŭi -ĭtum, 2. to owe, be indebted; to remain indebted; *with infin.,* to be bound, to be pledged; to be indebted to a

person for, *alicui vitam; dēbĭtus* -a -um, bound, owed; *subst.,* **dēbĭtum** -i, *n.* a debt.

dēbĭlis -e, *adj.* weak.

dēbĭlĭtas -ātis, *f.* weakness.

dēbĭlĭtātĭo -ōnis, *f.* a weakening, weakness.

dēbĭlĭto, 1. to lame, disable; to enervate, break the force of.

dēbĭtĭo -ōnis, *f.* an owing, debt.

dēbĭtor -ōris, *m.* a debtor ; *vitae,* owing his life to.

dēbĭtum -i, *n. v. debeo.*

dēcanto, 1. to sing, repeat in singing. *Intransit.,* to leave off singing.

dēcēdo -cessi -cessum, 3. to go forth, depart; to yield to, get out of the way for, cease on account of, *calori; milit., to* evacuate; to die, *decedere de vita; of water,* to retire; *of the sun and moon,* to set; *of diseases,* to cease; to abandon an opinion, *de sententia; to sum up from* duty; *de officio,* to yield place to (*or with dat.*).

dĕcem, ten.

December -bris -bre, *abl.* -bri, *mensis December,* December; *subst.,* **December** -bris, *m.*

dĕcempĕda -ae, *f.* measuring rod ten feet in length.

dĕcempĕdātor -ōris, *m.* a land surveyor.

dĕcemplex -icis, ten-fold.

dĕcemprīmi -ōrum, *m.* the ten chief men in the senate of a *municipium.*

dĕcemscalmus -a -um, having ten tholes or rowlocks.

dĕcemvir -i, *m. gen. plur.,* **dĕcemviri** -ōrum *or* -um, a college of ten magistrates at Rome.

dĕcemvirālis -e, relating to the decemvirs.

dĕcemvirātus -ūs, *m.* office of a decemvir.

dĕcens -entis, *p. adj.,* seemly, becoming, decent; handsome, comely.

dĕcentia -ae, *f.* comeliness, decency.

dēcerno -crēvi -crētum, 3. to decide, to decree, propose; to resolve; to settle.

dēcerpo -cerpsi -cerptum, 3. to pluck off; to take away.

dēcertātĭo -ōnis, *f.* a contest.

dēcerto, 1. to contend, struggle vehemently, fight to a decision.

dēcessĭo -ōnis, *f.* a departure; diminution.

dēcessor -ōris, *m.* one who retires from an office, a predecessor.

dēcessus -ūs, *m.* departure; the retirement of a magistrate from office; death; *of water,* ebb.

dĕcet -cŭit, 2. it becomes, it fits; it is fitting, it suits.

1. **dēcĭdo** -cĭdi, 3. to fall down; to die; to sink, fall.

2. **dēcĭdo** -cĭdi -cīsum, 3. to hew off, cut off; to cut short; to decide a dispute.

dĕcĭes (-iens), *adv.* ten times.

dĕcĭma (dĕcŭma) -ae, *f.* a tenth part, tithe; a tax paid by landowners in the provinces.

dĕcĭmānus (dĕcŭmānus) -a -um, relating to the provincial tax of a tenth; *frumentum,* a tithe of corn; *subst.,* dĕcĭmānus -i, *m.* the farmer of such a tax; *milit.,* belonging to the tenth legion; to the tenth cohort; *porta,* the gate of a Roman camp farthest from the enemy; large, immense.

dĕcĭmo (dĕcŭmo), 1. to select every tenth man for punishment, to decimate.

dĕcĭmŭs (dĕcŭmus) -a -um, the tenth; *adv., decimum,* for the tenth time; large, vast, great. *Subst.,* dĕcĭmum -i, *n.* tenfold.

dĕcĭpĭo -cēpi -ceptum, 3. to cheat, deceive; *of time,* to beguile.

dĕcīsĭo -ōnis, *f.* a decision.

Dĕcĭus -a -um, name of a Roman gens, the most famous members of which, *P. Decius Mus, father and son,* devoted themselves to death in battle to save the state.

dēclāmātĭo -ōnis, *f.* loud, violent speaking, declamation.

dēclāmātōrĭus -a -um, declamatory, rhetorical.

dēclāmĭto, 1. to speak loudly, declaim; practise.

dēclāmo, 1. to speak loudly and violently; to practise speaking in public; to declaim.

dēclārātĭo -ōnis, *f.* a declaration, revealing.

dēclāro, 1. to make distinct, reveal, declare; to explain; to signify, mean.

dēclīnātĭo -ōnis, *f.* a bending away, turning aside; an avoiding; *rhet.,* a digression.

dēclīno, 1. to bend aside, turn away, *trans. and intransit.;* to avoid; *of orators, writers,* to digress.

dēclīvis -e, sloping. *Subst.,* dēclīve -is, *n.* a declivity.

dēclīvĭtas -ātis, *f.* a declivity.

dēcoctor -ōris, *m.* a spendthrift, bankrupt.

dēcollo, 1. to behead.

dēcŏlor -ōris, discoloured; deteriorated.

dēcŏlōrātĭo -ōnis, *f.* a discolouring.

dēcŏlōro, 1. to discolour.

dēcŏquo -coxi -coctum, 3. to boil; *of metals,* to melt away; to waste, squander; to become bankrupt.

dĕcor -ōris, *m.* grace, elegance; beauty.

dĕcŏrē, *adv.* properly, fitly, becomingly; beautifully.

dĕcŏro, 1. to adorn; to honour.

dĕcŏrus -a -um, fitting, becoming, decorous, beautiful. *Subst.,* dĕcōrum -i, *n.* fitness, propriety.

dēcrĕpĭtus -a -um, very old, infirm.

dēcresco -crēvi -crētum, 3. to decrease.

dēcrētum -i, *n.* resolution, decree,

senatus; philosoph., doctrine, principle.

dĕcŭmānus, *v. decimanus.*

dĕcŭmātes -ĭum, relating to tithes; *agri,* lands on which the tithe *or* land-tax was paid.

dēcumbo -cŭbŭi, 3. to lie down; to fall.

dĕcŭria -ae, *f.* a body of ten men; a class, division.

dĕcŭrĭātĭo -ōnis, *f.* a dividing into decuriae.

dĕcŭrĭātus -ūs, *m.* a dividing into decuriae.

1. dĕcŭrĭo, 1. to divide into bodies of ten.

2. dĕcŭrĭo -ōnis, *m.* the captain of a body of ten; a senator of a *municipium or colonia.*

dēcurro -curri (*more rarely* -cucurri) -cursum, 3. to run down, hasten down; to charge; to run in a race; *of ships,* to sail; to have recourse to; to finish.

dēcursĭo -ōnis, *f.* a military manœuvre, charge.

dēcursus -ūs, *m.* a running down; *milit.,* manœuvre; a charge, attack; completion of an office.

dēcurto, 1. to cut off, abridge, curtail.

dĕcus -ōris, *n.* ornament, honour, glory, grace; moral dignity, virtue; *of persons,* pride, glory; *plur.,* decora, exploits in war; renowned ancestors.

dēcusso, 1. to divide cross-wise in the shape of *X.*

dēcŭtĭo -cussi -cussum, 3. to shake down, shake off, knock off.

dēdĕcet -dĕcŭit, 2. it is unbecoming, unsuitable to, unfitting; it is unseemly; to dishonour.

dēdĕcor -ōris, *adj.,* unseemly, shameful.

dēdĕcŏro, 1. to dishonour.

dēdĕcŏrus -a -um, shameful, dishonourable.

dēdĕcus -ōris, *n.* shame, dishonour; *alicui dedecori esse,* to bring shame upon; the crime, cause of disgrace; evil, vice.

dēdĭcātĭo -ōnis, *f.* dedication.

dēdĭco, 1. to declare; to make a return of property; dedicate.

dēdignor, 1. *dep.* to disdain, scorn, reject as unworthy.

dēdisco -dĭdĭci, 3. to unlearn, forget.

dēdĭtīcĭus -a -um, relating to surrender; *plur., dediticii,* those who had surrendered unconditionally.

dēdĭtĭo -ōnis, surrender, capitulation; *in deditionem venire.*

dēdĭtus -a -um, given to, devoted to, zealous for.

dēdo -dĭdi -dĭtum, 3. to give up; to surrender; to dedicate, devote; *se,* to devote oneself; *deditā operā,* intentionally.

dēdŏcĕo, 2. to cause to unlearn.

dēdŏlĕo -dŏlŭi, 2. to make an end of grieving.

dēdūco -duxi -ductum, 3. to lead *or* bring down; *naut.*, to spread sail; to reduce; to lead away; *milit.*, to remove; to conduct, escort, accompany; to take under an escort *or* guard; to accompany a bride to the house of a bridegroom; to found a colony, *coloniam*; to bring before a court of law; to dispossess; to turn away from; to bring to; to derive one's origin; to subtract; to spin; to compose (*of writing*).

dēductio -ōnis, *f.* a leading down; the billeting of soldiers; a colonising; a deduction.

dēductor -ōris, *m.* a client *or* friend who accompanies a candidate.

dēductus -a -um, *p. adj.* fine, slender; *carmen*, light.

dĕerro, 1. to wander, lose one's way.

dēfătīgātio -ōnis, *f.* weariness.

dēfătīgo, 1. to weary, fatigue.

dēfătiscor = defetiscor (*q.v.*).

dēfectio -ōnis, *f.* desertion, rebellion; a ceasing, failure, disappearing; *defectiones solis et lunae*, eclipses; weakness.

dēfector -ōris, *m.* rebel, deserter.

1. **dēfectus -a -um**, *partic. of deficio.*

2. **dēfectus -ūs**, *m.* a failing, disappearing; eclipse.

dēfendo -fendi -fensum, 3. to repel, ward off; to defend, watch over; to maintain a proposition; to sustain a part.

dēfēnēro, 1. to plunge into debt.

dēfensio -ōnis, *f.* a defence; plea.

dēfensīto, 1. to defend frequently.

dēfenso, 1. to protect, defend.

dēfensor -ōris, *m.* one who averts, *periculi*; a defender.

dēfēro -tūli -lātum -ferre, to bring, carry down; to change, remove to a lower place; to bring from one place to another; *polit. t.t.*, *deferre sitellam*, to bring the ballot-box for voting, *i.e.* to have the vote taken; *deferre rationes*, to give in the accounts; to drive away; *ad offer*, hand over, *refer*; to report; *deferre crimen*, to bring a charge; *deferre aliquem*, to accuse; *polit.*, *ad aerarium deferre*, to register.

dēfervesco -fervi *or* -ferbŭi, 3. to cease boiling; to diminish in violence.

dēfessus, *v. defetiscor.*

dēfētiscor (dēfătiscor) -fessus, 3. *dep.* to grow weary, *gen. perf. partic.*, **dēfessus -a -um**, weary.

dēficio -fēci -fectum, 3. *intransit. or reflex.*, to rebel; *ad Poenos*, to go over to the Carthaginians; to fail, cease, become less; *of the sun or moon*, to become eclipsed; *of fire*, to go out; *of time*, to be too short for; to become weak; *animo deficere*, to lose heart; *absol.* to be disheartened. *Transit.*, to abandon, leave, fail; *pass. defici*, to be

abandoned by, to be wanting in, *defici a viribus.*

dēfigo -fixi -fixum, 3. to fix *or* fasten into; to make fast; to fix in amazement; *defixus*, motionless with astonishment, fear, *etc.*; to imprint firmly; to declare, denounce; to bind by a spell, to curse.

dēfingo -finxi -fictum, 3. to form, mould, fashion.

dēfinio, 4. to inclose within limits, to bound; to fix, define, determine; to restrain.

dēfinitē, *adv.* definitely, distinctly.

dēfinitio -ōnis, *f.* a definition; a fixing.

dēfinitivus -a -um, relating to definition, explanatory.

dēfinītus -a -um, *p. adj.* definite, distinct.

dēfio -fieri, *pass. of deficio*, to fail.

dēflāgrātio -ōnis, *f.* a burning, consuming by fire.

dēflāgro, 1. to be burnt down, to be consumed by fire; *part. pass.*, *deflagratus*, consumed; to cease burning, to abate, cool.

dēflecto -flexi -flexum, 3. *transit.*, to bend down; to turn aside; *intransit.*, to turn aside, turn away; *of speech*, to digress.

dēflĕo -flēvi -flētum, 2. to bewail, weep for; to speak with tears.

dēflōresco -flōrŭi, 3. to shed blossom, to fade; *fig.*, to lose bloom, wither.

dēflŭo -fluxi, 3. to flow down; to float; to swim down; to sail down; to fall down, descend, glide down; to be derived; to fall to the lot of; to change to; to flow away, disappear, be lost; *unus me absente defluxit*, has proved false to me; *of time*, to disappear, cease.

dēfŏdio -fōdi -fossam, 3. to dig in, to cover with earth; to bury; to dig up.

dēfōrmātio -ōnis, *f.* a deforming, disfiguring; *taniae maiestatis*, degradation.

dēformis -e, *adj.* deformed, misshapen, ugly; disgusting; disgraced, disgraceful; hateful, foul, shameful; formless, shapeless.

dēformitas -ātis, *f.* deformity, ugliness; disgrace, dishonour.

1. **dēformo**, 1. to form, fashion, delineate.

2. **dēformo**, 1. to bring out of form and shape, disarrange; *deformatus corpore*, deformed in body; to disgrace, dishonour.

dēfraudo, 1. to deceive, cheat.

dēfrēnātus -a -um, unrestrained.

dēfrico -fricŭi -fricātum, *and* **-frictum**, 1. to rub, rub hard; to satirise.

dēfringo -frēgi -fractum, 3. to break off.

dēfrŭtum -i, *n.* must *or* new wine boiled down.

dēfŭgio -fūgi, 3. to flee away. *Transit.*, to fly from, avoid, *proelium.*

défundo -fúdi -fúsum, 3. to pour down, pour out; to pour a libation.

défungor -functus sum, 3. *dep. with abl.*, to finish, perform, be relieved of an office *or* duty; *defunctus honoribus*, having filled all public offices; *vitâ defungi*, to die.

dégéněr -ěris, unworthy of one's race, not genuine; morally degenerate, ignoble.

dégěněro, 1. to fall off, degenerate. *Transit.*, to cause to degenerate; to dishonour.

dégo, dégi, 3. to pass (*time*); to live.

dégrandinat, *impers.* it ceases to hail.

dégrăvo, 1. to press down, oppress; to impede, distress; *quia vulnus degravabat*.

dégrědíor -gressus, 3. *dep.* to step, march, walk down.

dégusto, 1. to taste; (*of fire*) to lick; to graze; to make a trial of.

déhinc, *adv.* hence, henceforth; hereupon; then.

déhisco -hívi *or* hii, 3. to gape, open, split.

déhőnestámentum -i, *n.* a blemish, deformity, disgrace.

déhőnesto, 1. to dishonour, disgrace.

déhortor, 1. *dep.* to advise to the contrary, to dissuade, *aliquem*.

Dělānīra -ae, *f.* wife of Hercules, whose death she caused by sending him a garment poisoned with the blood of Nessus.

déicio, -iēci -iectum, 3. to throw, cast, hurl down; *se deicere, or pass. deici*, to rush down; *of trees*, to fell; to throw lots into an urn; *milit.*, to drive from a position, *nostros loco*; *of a ship*, to drive out of its course; *of the head, eyes, &c.* to let fall; *legal*, to eject, dispossess; to kill; *aliquem de honore*, to deprive; *uxore deiectâ*, carried off.

déiectio -ónis, *f.* a throwing down; *legal*, ejectment from property.

1. déiectus -a -um, *p. adj.* low-lying; dejected.

2. déiectus -ús, a throwing down; declivity.

déiěro (deiuro), 1. to swear solemnly.

děin, *v. deinde.*

déinceps, *adv.* one after another, successively.

déindě *and* děin, *of space*, thereupon, from that place; *of time*, thereafter, then; *in narration or order of succession*, then, next.

Délphōbus -i, *m.* son of Priam.

déiungo -iunxi -iunctum, 3. to separate, sever.

délábor -lapsus sum, 3. *dep.* to glide down, fall down, sink; *of liquids*, to flow down; to glide away, to proceed from, be derived from; to fall away, to come to; to digress; to fall into unawares, *medios in hostes*.

délámentor, 1. *dep.* to bewail, lament.

délasso, 1. to weary, tire out.

délátio -ōnis, *f.* accusation, denunciation.

délátor -ōris, *m.* accuser, informer, spy; *maiestatis*, of high treason.

délébilis -e, that can be obliterated *or* destroyed.

délectăbilis -e, *adj.* pleasant, delightful, agreeable.

délectámentum -i, *n.* delight, pleasure, amusement.

délectátio -ōnis, *f.* delight, pleasure.

délecto, 1. to delight, cause pleasure; *pass.*, to take delight in.

délectus -ús, *m.* choice, selection; *milit.*, a levy, recruiting, conscription, *delectum habere*.

délégátio -ōnis, *f.* assignment of a debt.

délégo, 1. to transfer, entrust, assign; to assign a debt; to impute, attribute.

délénimentum -i, *n.* anything that coaxes, a charm, blandishment.

délénio, 4. to soothe, coax, charm.

délénítor -ōris, *m.* one who soothes, cajoles, wins over.

déléo -lévi -létum, 2. to destroy, annihilate; *bella*, to bring to an end; to efface *or* erase.

délétrix -trícis, that which destroys.

délíběrábundus -a -um, carefully considering.

délíběrátio -ōnis, *f.* consideration, deliberation; *res habet deliberationem*, admits of.

délíběrátívus -a -um, relating to deliberation.

délíběrátor -ōris, *m.* one who deliberates.

délíběrátus -a -um, *p. adj.* decided, resolved, certain.

délíběro, 1. to consider, consult about; to ask advice, *esp. of an oracle*; to resolve, decide.

délíbo, 1. to take away a little, to taste; to enjoy; to diminish.

délíbro, 1. to peel the bark off.

délíbúo -úi -útum, 3. to besmear, anoint.

délícátě, *adv.* luxuriously.

délícátus -a -um, delightful, luxurious; soft, delicate; fastidious, dainty.

délíciae -árum, *f.* pleasure, charm, luxury; darling, sweetheart.

délíciŏlae -árum, *f.* (*dim. of deliciae*), a darling.

délíctum -i, *n.* a fault, crime.

1. délígo -légi -lectum, 3. to pick, pluck; to choose; to send away.

2. délígo, 1. to bind, fasten, bind up.

délíno (-lěvi) -lítum, 3. to wipe off.

délinquo -líqui -lictum, 3. to fail, be wanting, commit a crime.

délíquesco -lícúi, 3. to melt, dissolve; to disappear.

délírátio -ōnis, *f.* folly, dotage.

délíro, 1. to be crazy, insane, to rave.

délírus -a -um, *adj.* silly, crazy.

dēlitesco -tŭi, 3. to conceal oneself, lie hid; to take refuge.

dēlitigo, 1. to scold furiously.

Dēlius, v. *Delos.*

Dēlos -i, *f.* island of the Aegean Sea, birthplace of Apollo and Diana; *adj.*, **Dēlius -a -um.**

Delphi -ōrum, *m.* a town of Phocis, celebrated for its oracle of Apollo; *adj.*, **Delphicus.**

delphīnus -i *and* **delphin -īnis**, *m.* a dolphin.

dēlūbrum -i, *n.* temple, shrine.

dēlūdo -lūsi -lūsum, 3. to mock, cheat, deceive.

dēlumbis -e, nerveless, weak.

dēlumbo, 1. to make weak and nerveless.

dēmădesco -mădŭi, 3. to become wet.

demando, 1. to entrust.

dēmens -mentis, *adj.* insane, foolish.

dēmentĕr, *adv.* foolishly, madly.

dēmentia -ae, *f.* foolishness, insanity.

dēmentio, 4. to be mad, to rave.

dēmĕrĕo *and dep.* **dēmĕrĕor**, 2. to deserve well of, to oblige.

dēmergo -mersi -mersum, 3. to plunge into, dip under; *of ships*, to sink; to swallow.

dēmētior -mensus sum, 4. *dep.* to measure, measure out.

dēmēto -messŭi -messum, 3. to mow, cut down, *or* off, *agros.*

dēmigrātio -ōnis, *f.* emigration.

dēmigro, 1. to migrate, emigrate.

dēmĭnŭo -minŭi -minūtum, 3. to diminish; to alienate, *praedia*; *legal, capite se deminuere* or *capite deminui*, to suffer a loss of civil rights.

dēminūtio -ōnis, *f.* diminution; *legal,* right of alienation; *deminutio sui*, loss of honour; loss of civil rights.

dēmiror, 1. *dep.* to wonder at, to wonder.

dēmissē, *adv.* low, near the ground; modestly, humbly, abjectly.

dēmissio -ōnis, *f.* a sinking, lowering; dejection.

dēmissus -a -um, *p. adj.* hanging down; sunken, low-lying; feeble, weak; modest; down-cast; poor, needy.

dēmītigo, 1. to make mild, soften; *pass.*, to become mild.

dēmitto -mīsi -missum, 3. to send down, to lower, cast, cause to hang down; *se manibus*, to let oneself down by the hands; *caput*, to bend; *demittere agmen*, to lead an army to a lower position; *demittere se*, to march down; *naut., demittere antennas*, to lower sail; *navem demittere*, to sail down; to let the hair *or* beard grow long; *tunica demissa*, hanging down; to let fall; *in animo*, to lose heart; *aliquid in pectus*, to impress on one's mind; *se in causam*, to

engage in; *demitti ab aliquo*, to be descended from.

dēmiurgus -i, *m.* the highest magistrate in certain Greek states.

dēmo, dempsi, demptum, 3. to take away.

Dēmocritus -i, *m.* philosopher of Abdera.

dēmōlior, 4. *dep.* to throw down, demolish.

dēmōlītio -ōnis, *f.* demolition.

dēmonstrātio -ōnis, *f.* a pointing out; a representation, description; a laudatory style of oratory.

dēmonstrātīvus -a -um, laudatory *or* declamatory.

dēmonstrātor -ōris, *m.* one who points out *or* indicates.

dēmonstro, 1. to show, indicate, point out, describe; to express, signify.

dēmŏrior -mortŭus, 3. *dep.* to die, die off.

dēmŏror, 1. *dep. intransit.*, to delay, loiter; *transit.*, to stop, delay.

Dēmosthĕnēs -is *and* **-i**, *m.* the celebrated Athenian orator.

dēmŏvĕo -mōvi -mōtum, 2. to move away, remove; *milit., gradu aliquem*, make a person give ground; to dispossess.

dēmūgītus -a -um, filled with the noise of lowing.

dēmulcĕo -mulsi -mulsum *or* **mulctum**, 2. to stroke down, caress by stroking.

dēmum, *adv.* at length, at last.

dēmurmūro, 1. to murmur *or* mutter over.

dēmūtātio -ōnis, *f.* change, alteration; *morum*, deterioration.

dēmūto, 1. to change.

dēnārius -a -um, containing ten; *num mus* or *subst.*, *denarius -ii*, *m.* Roman silver coin.

dēnarro, 1. to narrate, tell.

dēnăto, 1. to swim down.

dēnĕgo, 1. to deny, say no; to refuse.

dēni -ae -a, *num. distrib.* ten by ten, ten at a time.

dēnicālis -e, relating to death.

dēnique, *adv.* at last, at length; in fine, in short.

dēnōmino, 1. to name.

dēnormo, 1. to make irregular.

dēnŏto, 1. to mark out, denote.

dens, dentis, *m.* a tooth; envy, slander; *dens uncus*, mattock; *dens Saturni*, the sickle.

densē, *adv.* densely, frequently.

denseo = denso (*q.v.*).

denso, *and* **densĕo**, 2. to thicken, condense, press together; *of weaving*, to make thick *with the reed*; *milit.*, to press close together.

densus -a -um, *adj.* thick, close, dense; crowded together; *of time*, uninterrupted, frequent; vehement.

dentālia -ium, *n.* ploughshare.

dentātus -a -um, provided with teeth, toothed; spiked, pronged; smoothed with a tooth.

dentiscalpium -ii, n. toothpick.

dēnūbo -nupsi -nuptum, 3. to be married, to marry (of the woman).

dēnūdo, 1. to lay bare, uncover ; to rob, plunder.

dēnuntiātio -ōnis, f. an announcement, intimation, threat; summoning of a witness; warning.

dēnuntio, 1. to intimate, threaten, denounce; bellum denuntiare, to declare war; milit., to give orders; legal, denuntiare alicui, to give notice of an action; to forewarn.

dēnŭo, adv. anew, again ; a second time; afresh.

dēŏnĕro, 1. to unload, disburden.

dēorsum, adv. downwards ; sursum deorsum, up and down, backwards and forwards.

dēpăciscor -pactus, 3. dep. to bargain for, make an agreement.

dēpango -pactum, 3. to drive into the ground, to fix in.

dēpasco -pāvi -pastum, 3. to feed off, eat down; to graze, pasture (also dep., depascor -pastus); depasta altaria poet. = food on the altars.

dēpĕciscor, v. depaciscor.

dēpecto -pexi -pexum, 3. to comb, comb down.

dēpĕcŭlātor -ōris, m. one who robs or embezzles.

dēpĕcŭlor, 1. dep. to rob, plunder.

dēpello -pŭli -pulsum, 3. to drive away; expel, remove; milit., to dislodge; naut., to drive out of one's course.

dēpendĕo, 2. to hang down, hang from, ex humeris dependet amictus; to depend upon.

dēpendo -pendi -pensum, 3. to weigh out; to pay.

dēperdo -perdidi -perditum, 3. to spoil, ruin ; deperditus fletu, exhausted ; deperditus in aliquā, desperately in love with; to lose.

dēpĕrĕo -pĕrii -pĕritūrus, 4. to perish or be ruined utterly.

dēpilo, 1. to deprive of hair, make bald.

dēpingo -pinxi -pictum, 3. to paint, depict; to picture in thought.

dēplango -planxi -planctum, 3. to bewail, lament.

dēplexus -a -um, clasping, embracing.

dēplōro, 1. intransit., to weep violently, to lament; transit., to lament, bewail; to regard as lost.

dēplŭo, 3. to rain down.

dēpōno -pŏsŭi -pŏsitum, 3. to put, lay down, put aside; comas, to cut the hair; vitulam, lay as a wager; to renounce; to deprive of an honour; to deposit, commit to the charge of; dēpŏsitus, laid out dead.

dēpŏpŭlātio -ōnis, f. a laying waste, plundering.

dēpŏpŭlātor -ōris, m. one who lays waste.

dēpŏpŭlor, 1. dep. to lay waste, ravage.

dēporto, 1. to carry away, remove; to bring home from a province; to banish for life.

dēposco -pŏposci, 3. to ask, beg, beseech; to challenge to combat.

dēprāvātē, adv. unjustly, iniquitously.

dēprāvātio -ōnis, f. a perverting, distorting; animi, depravity.

dēprāvo, 1. to pervert, distort, disfigure; to spoil, corrupt.

dēprĕcābundus -a -um, earnestly entreating.

dēprĕcātio -ōnis, f. a warding off by entreaty, deprecating; an imprecation, deorum, invoking the curse of the gods; an entreaty for forgiveness.

dēprĕcātor -ōris, m. an intercessor.

dēprĕcor, 1. dep. to pray earnestly; to beg for; to allege in excuse; aliquid ab aliquo, to beg for; to intercede; to execrate, curse; to avert by entreaty.

dēprĕhendo and dēprendo -prĕhend (-prendi) -prĕhensum (-prensum), 3. to seize, catch; to surprise, detect; to perceive, observe. Pass., deprehendi to be surprised, embarrassed.

dēprĕhensio -ōnis, f. detection.

dēpressus -a -um, p. adj. low-lying, sunk down.

dēprimo -pressi -pressum, 3. to sink down, press down; to plant or place deep in the ground, dig deep; to sink, naves; to oppress.

dēproelior, 1. to contend violently.

dēprōmo -prompsi -promptum, 3. to bring forth, produce.

dēprŏpĕro, to hasten.

dēpŭdet -pŭdŭit, 2. impers. to be shameless.

dēpŭgis = depygis (q.v.).

dēpugno, 1. to fight, struggle.

dēpulsio -ōnis, f. driving away; rhet., defence.

dēpulsor -ōris, m. one who drives away a destroyer.

dēpŭto, 1. to prune, cut off.

dēpȳgis -is, thin buttocked.

deque, v. susque deque.

dērĕlictio -ōnis, f. a deserting, forsaking.

dērĕlinquo -līqui -lictum, 3. to forsake, abandon.

dērĕpentē, adv. suddenly.

dērēpo -repsi, 3. to creep, crawl down.

dērīdĕo -rīsi -rīsum, 2. to laugh at, mock.

dērīdĭcŭlus -a -um, very ridiculous, very laughable; subst., deridiculum -i, n. ridicule, ridiculousness.

dērīgesco -rĭgŭi, 3. to grow quite stiff.

dēripio -ripŭi -reptum, 3. to tear down, snatch away.

dērīsor -ōris, m. one who mocks, derides.

dĕrīsus -ūs, *m.* mockery, derision.

dĕrīvātio -ōnis, *f.* a turning *or* drawing off of water.

dĕrīvo, 1. to turn, draw off water; to divert.

dĕrŏgātio -ōnis, *f.* the partial repeal of a law.

dērŏgo, i. tŏ modify a law**;** to diminish, take away, *fidem alicui.*

dĕrōsus -a -um, gnawed away.

dērūo -rŭi -rŭtum, 3. to cast down, over-turn.

dēruptus -a -um, broken off; steep *Subst.,* **derupta -orum,** *n.* precipices.

dĕsaevio -ii -ītum, 4. to rage violently.

descendo -scendi -scensum, 3. to step down, descend; *descendere in or ad forum, or simply descendere, in Rome* to come down into the Forum, *in order to attend the Comitia, etc.;* to lower one-self, to condescend to agree to; *of weapons,* to pierce; *of mountains,* to slope down; *of the voice,* to sink.

descensio -ōnis, *f.* a going down, de-scent.

descensus -ūs, *m.* a descending, descent.

descisco -scivi *or* **-scii -scītum,** 3. to revolt from, desert to; to withdraw, diverge from, fall off from; *a se,* to be untrue to oneself; to fall into, de-generate to.

describo -scripsi -scriptum, 3. to tran-scribe, copy; to describe, delineate; to portray; to define, explain; to mark out, arrange, classify; to impose, appoint; to divide, distribute.

descriptē, *adv.* in order, systematically.

descriptio -ōnis, *f.* a copy; a de-scription, representation; *numeri aut descriptiones,* geometric figures; a definition; fixing, limiting; distribu-tion; arrangement.

descriptus -a -um, *p. adj.* properly arranged.

dēsĕco -sĕcŭi -sectum, 1. to hew off, cut off.

dēsĕnesco -sĕnŭi, 3. to grow weaker by age.

dēsĕro -sĕrŭi -sertum, 3. to desert, for-sake; to neglect, disregard; *a mente deseri,* to lose one's head; *legal, vadi-monium,* to fail to appear.

dēsertio -ōnis, *f.* neglect.

dēsertor -ōris, *m.* a deserter; *poet.* a fugitive.

dēsertus -a -um, *p. adj.* forsaken, deserted. *Subst.,* **dēserta -ōrum,** *n.* deserts.

dēservio, 4. to serve zealously, *alicui; fig.,* to be devoted to a thing; to be a slave to.

dĕsĕs -sidis, *m.* idle, slothful, inactive.

dĕsĭdĕo -sēdi -sessum, 2. to be idle.

dĕsīdĕrābilis -e, *adj.* desirable.

dĕsīdĕrātio -ōnis, *f.* desire, longing for anything.

dĕsīdĕrium -ii, *n.* desire *or* longing, yearning, grief for absence *or* loss; object of desire; a wish.

dĕsīdĕro, 1. to long for, to wish for; to require, need; to miss; to lose.

dĕsidia -ae, *f.* idleness, inactivity.

dĕsidiōsus, agu slothfully, idly.

dĕsidiōsus -a -um, *adj.* slothful, idle; causing sloth.

dĕsīdo -sēdi *and* **-sidi,** 3. to sink down; to settle, to diminish, deteriorate.

dēsīgnātio -ōnis, *f.* a marking out, designing, describing; arrangement, order; appointment; nomination.

dēsīgnātor -ōris, *m.* umpire at the public games.

dēsīgno, 1. to mark out, trace out; to point out by signs; to sketch; to signify, allude to; to contrive; to arrange, regulate; to nominate to an office, elect; *consul designatus,* consul elect.

dēsīlio -silŭi -sultum, 4. to leap down; *ad pedes,* dismount.

dēsīno -sii -situm, 3. to leave off, cease; *poet.* to abandon; *with infin.,* to cease to. *Intransit.,* to cease, end, *in pis-cem.*

dēsipiens -entis, *p. adj.* foolish.

dēsipientia -ae, *f.* foolishness.

dēsipio -sipŭi, 3. to be foolish, to act foolishly.

dēsisto -stiti -stitum, 3. to desist, leave off, cease, *conatu.*

dēsōlo, 1. to forsake; **dēsōlātus -a -um,** forsaken, desolate.

despectio -ōnis, *f.* a looking down; con-tempt.

despecto, 1. to regard from above; to overlook; to despise.

1. **despectus -a -um,** *p. adj.* despised, despicable.

2. **despectus -ūs,** *m.* a looking down, downward view; contempt.

despērantĕr, *adv.* despairingly, hope-lessly.

despērātio -ōnis, *f.* hopelessness, despair.

desperatus -a -um, *p. adj.* desperate, hopeless.

despēro, 1. to despair, give up.

despicātio -ōnis, *f.* contempt.

1. **despicātus -a -um,** *p. adj.* despised, despicable.

2. **despicātus -ūs,** *m.* contempt.

despicientia -ae, *f.* contempt.

despicio -spexi -spectum, 3. to look down, regard from above; to despise; to look away from.

despŏlio, 1. to plunder, despoil.

despondĕo -spondi -sponsum, 2. to promise; to betroth; to give up; *de-spondere animos,* to lose courage, despond.

despūmo, 1. to skim off.

despŭo -spŭi -spūtum, 3. to spit out (*for averting evil*); to reject, abhor.

desquămo, 1. to take off the scales, to scale.

desterto -tŭi, 3. to finish snoring; *poet.* to finish dreaming.

destillo, 1. to drop down, distil.

destinātio -ōnis, *f.* determination, resolution.

destino, 1. to make fast, bind, fasten; to fix, determine; *with infin.* to resolve to do; to aim at with a missile; to fix upon, intend to buy; to betroth; to select for an office.

destitŭo -stĭtŭi -stĭtūtum, 3. to set; to set down, to place; to leave, abandon, desert.

destĭtūtus -a -um, *partic. of destituo.*

destitūtio -ōnis, *f.* a forsaking, abandoning.

destrictus -a -um, *p. adj.* sharp, severe.

destringo -strinxi -strictum, 3. to strip off; to draw the sword; to touch lightly, graze; to satirise, censure.

destrŭo -struxi -structum, 3. to pull down; to destroy.

dēsŭbito, *adv.* suddenly.

dēsūdo, 1. to sweat violently; to exert oneself.

dēsuēfăcio -fēci -factum, to disuse, make unaccustomed to.

dēsuesco -suēvi -suētum, 3. to disuse; to become unaccustomed to; unused to, *desuitus triumphis.*

dēsuētūdo -ĭnis, *f.* disuse.

dēsultor -ōris, *m.* a circus rider who leaped from one horse to another while both were at full speed; an inconstant person.

dēsultōrius -a -um, relating to a desultor.

dēsum -fŭi -esse, to be absent, away, wanting, to fail, *with dat., tibi defuit;* not to be present at.

dēsūmo -sumpsi -sumptum, 3. to choose, select.

dēsŭper, *adv.* from above, above.

dēsurgo -surrexi -surrectum, 3. to rise, stand up.

dētĕgo -texi -tectum, 3. to uncover; to detect, disclose.

dētendo (-tendi) -tensum, 3. to unstretch; *tabernacula,* to strike the tents.

dētergĕo -tersi -tersum, 2. to wipe away; to cleanse; to break off.

dētĕrior -ĭūs, *genit.* -ōris, *compar. adj. with superl. dēterrimus,* worse, inferior; *in deterius,* for the worse.

dētĕrius, *adv.* worse.

dētermĭnātio -ōnis, *f.* a boundary, end.

dētermĭno, 1. to bound, fix the limits of.

dētĕro -trīvi -trītum, 3. to rub off, rub away, wear out; to weaken.

dēterrĕo -terrŭi -territum, 2. to frighten from anything, discourage; *with acc. of thing,* to ward off; *vim a censoribus.*

dētestābĭlis -e, *adj.* abominable, horrible.

dētestātio -ōnis, *f.* execration, horror, detestation; a warding off, averting.

dētestor, 1. *dep.* to invoke the curse of a god; to execrate, abominate; to avert.

dētexo -texŭi -textum, 3. to plait; to finish (*of discourse*).

dētĭnĕo -tĭnŭi -tentum, 2. to hold away, detain; to hold fast, fetter; to occupy; to detain from; *detinere se,* to support existence.

dētondĕo -tondi -tonsum, 2. to shear, clip.

dētŏno -tŏnŭi, 1. to thunder, thunder down; to cease to thunder, cease to rage.

dētorquĕo -torsi -tortum, 2. to turn away, bend aside; to distort.

dētractio -ōnis, *f.* withdrawal; taking away of another's property.

dētracto = detrecto (*q.v.*).

dētractor -ōris, *m.* a detractor.

dētrăho -traxi -tractum, 3. to take down; to lower, humiliate; to take away, to remove; *milit.,* to detach; to subtract; to compel; to drag away; to slander.

dētrectātio -ōnis, *f.* a refusal.

dētrectātor -ōris, *m.* a detractor.

dētrecto, 1. to decline, refuse ; to depreciate.

dētrimentōsus -a -um, detrimental, hurtful.

dētrimentum -i, *n.* damage, injury; *detrimentum capere or facere,* to suffer ; *milit.,* loss, defeat; loss of money, property, *etc.*

dētrītus -a -um, *partic. of detero.*

dētrūdo -trūsi -trūsum, 3. to push away, thrust down; *milit.,* to dislodge an enemy from his position; *legal,* to eject; to force, compel; to postpone.

dētrunco, 1. to lop *or* cut off; to mutilate, behead.

dētŭrbo, 1. to drive away with violence, cast down; *milit.,* to dislodge, drive off; to deprive; *legal,* to eject, dispossess.

Deucălĭōn -ōnis, *m.* son of Prometheus, saved with his wife Pyrrha from the deluge.

dĕunx -uncis, *m.* eleven-twelfths.

dēūro -ussi -ustum, 3. to burn down; *of cold,* to destroy, nip.

dĕus -i, *m., voc. sing. deus,* a god, a deity.

dēābtor -ūti -ūsus, 3. *dep.* to misuse.

dēvasto, 1. to lay waste, devastate.

dēvĕho -vexi -vectum, 3. to carry away, convey away; *devehi,* to sail.

dēvello, -velli -vulsum, 3. to pull, pluck, tear away.

dēvēlo, 1. to unveil, uncover.

dēvĕnĕror, 1. *dep.* to venerate, worship.

dēvĕnio -vēni -ventum, 4. to arrive at, reach.

1. dēversor, 1. *dep.* to lodge as a guest *or* stranger; *apud aliquem.*

2. dēversor -ōris, *m.* guest.

dēversōrĭŏlum -i, *n.* (*dim. of deversorium*), a small lodging.

dēversōrius -a -um, relating to the accommodation of strangers. *Subst.,* **dēversōrium -ii,** *n.* inn, lodging; place of resort.

dēverticŭlum (dēvorticulum) -i, *n.* by-way, by-path; digression; inn; place of refuge, hiding place.

dēverto (dēvorto) -verti (-vorti) -versum (-vorsum), 3. *transit.,* to turn away; *pass.* (*in present tenses*), *devertor,* to turn aside from the way, betake oneself; to stay; *intransit.,* to turn aside; *of discourse,* to digress; to lodge, stay with.

dēvexus -a -um, *adj.* going aside; moving away from; *Orion devexus,* sinking; *aetas iam devexa ad otium,* inclining to; sloping downwards, steep.

dēvincio -vinxi -vinctum, 4. to bind fast, to fasten, connect; *rhet.,* to pledge.

dēvinco -vīci -victum, 3. to subjugate.

dēvinctus -a -um, *p. adj.* bound to, devoted to.

dēvītātio -ōnis, *f.* an avoiding.

dēvīto, 1. to avoid.

dēvius -a -um, out of the way; secluded; *poet.* wandering; *fig.* erroneous, unreasonable.

dēvŏco, 1. to call down; to call away, call off, recall.

dēvŏlo, 1. to fly down; to hasten down; to fly away to.

dēvolvo -volvi -vŏlūtum, 3. to roll down; (*pass.,* to roll down, fall headlong); to roll off; *pensa fusis,* to spin off; *pass., devolvi,* to fall into.

dēvŏro, 1. to swallow, devour; to consume, waste; to suppress; to bear with-out understanding; to swallow anything unpleasant, to endure.

dēvorticŭlum, *v. deverticulum.*

dēvortium -ii, *n.* a by-path.

dēvōtio -ōnis, *f.* a consecrating, devoting; a curse, enchantment, incantation; a vow.

dēvōto, 1. to consecrate, devote to death.

dēvōtus -a -um, *p. adj.* devoted; faithful, affectionate; *subst.,* **dēvōti -ōrum,** *m.* faithful followers.

dēvŏveo -vōvi -vōtum, 2. to consecrate, devote; to devote to death; to curse, execrate; to bewitch, enchant.

dextans -antis, *m.* five-sixths.

dextella -ae, *f.* (*dim. of dextra*), a little right hand.

dexter -tĕra -tĕrum, *or more freq.* **-tra -trum,** *comp.* **dextĕrior -ius,** *superl.* **dextimus -a -um.** *Adj.,* right, on the right hand; *ab dextra parte,* (*Subst.,*) **dextera** *or* **dextra -ae,** *f.* the right hand; *a dextra,* on the right hand; **dextera** *or* **dextra -orum,** *n.* what is on the right, the right side); propitious; skilful.

dextĕrē *or* **dextrē,** *adv.,* dexterously, skilfully.

dextĕritās -ātis, *f.* skilfulness, readiness.

dextrorsum *and* **dextrorsus,** *adv.* on the right hand, towards the right.

---

diădēma -ătis, *n.* diadem.

diaeta -ae, *f.* regimen, diet.

1. **diălecticē,** *adv.* dialectically.

2. **diălecticē -ēs,** *f.* art of dialectic, logic.

diălecticus -a -um, relating to discussion, dialectical; *subst.,* **dialectica -ae,** *f.* the art of dialectic; **dialectica -orum,** *n.* dialectical discussion; **dialecticus -i,** *m.* dialectician.

Diālis -e, relating to Jupiter, *flamen; or simply Dialis,* priest of Jupiter.

diălŏgus -i, *m.* philosophical dialogue.

Diāna -ae, *f.* a goddess, identified with the Greek Artemis.

diārium -ii, *n.* a day's allowance of provisions *for soldiers.*

dibăphus -a -um, double-dyed. *Subst., f.* purple-striped robe of the higher magistrates.

dica -ae, *f.* a law-suit, action *in a Greek court.*

dicācitas -ātis, *f.* pungent wit, satire.

dicātio -ōnis, *f.* settling as a citizen in another state.

dicax -ācis, *adj.* witty, ironical, sarcastic.

dichŏrēus -i, *m.* a double trochee.

dicis, *genit.* (*from root dic, to show*), *only in the phrases, dicis causā, dicis gratiā,* for form's sake, for appearance sake.

1. **dico,** 1. to consecrate, dedicate; to deify, place among the gods; to devote; *se alicui,* to devote oneself to.

2. **dico, dixi, dictum,** 3. to say, relate, tell, mention; *Hilarum dico,* I mean Hilarus; *ne dicam,* not to say; *causam,* to plead a cause; *sententiam* (*of a senator*), to vote; *foll. by ut or ne and the subj.,* to command; *dicitur,* it is said, the report is; (*intransit.*) to speak, deliver an oration; to name; to sing, describe, compose; to appoint; to fix; to say yes, affirm.

dicrŏtum -i, *n.* a vessel having two banks of oars.

dictamnum -i, *n. and* **dictamnus -i,** *f.* dittany, a plant.

dictāta -ōrum, *n.* that which is dictated by a teacher, precepts, rules.

dictātor -ōris, *m.* commander, dictator.

dictātōrius -a -um, belonging to a dictator, dictatorial.

dictātūra -ae, *f.* dictatorship.

Dictē -ēs, *f.* mountain in Crete on which Jupiter was reared; *adj.* **Dictaeus.**

dictio -ōnis, *f.* a saying, speaking, uttering; *causae,* defence; *multae,* fixing; the answer of an oracle; conversation; declamation; a speech; diction.

dictito, 1. to say often; reiterate.

dicto, 1. to repeat, dictate.

dictum -i, *n.* a word, saying, speech; *mutua dicta reddere,* to converse; a maxim; a command; watch-word, password.

Dictynna -ae, *f.* surname of Artemis.

1. **Dīdō -ūs** *or* (*gen.*) **-ōnis,** *f.* the founder of Carthage, wife of Sichaeus, *also called Elisa or Elissa.*

2. **dīdo, dĭdĭdi, dĭdĭtum,** 3. to distribute; to spread, disseminate.

dīdūco -duxi -ductum, 3. to draw apart, expand; to divide; to distribute; to scatter the enemy.

dīductio -ōnis, *f.* a separating.

dīēcŭla -ae, *f.* (*dim. of dies*), a little day; a little while.

dies -ēi, *m. and f. in sing., in plur. only masc.,* a day; *diem de die, or diem ex die,* from day to day; *in dies,* daily; *multo die,* late in the day; *exercere diem,* the day's work; a fixed day; time.

Diespiter -tris, *m.* Jupiter.

diffāmo, 1. to spread abroad an evil report, to defame.

differens -entis, *v. differo.*

differentia -ae, *f.* difference, distinction.

differitas -ātis, *f.* difference.

differo, distŭli, dīlātum, differre, *transit.,* to carry in different directions, spread abroad, scatter; *aliquem variis rumoribus,* to malign; *of time,* to delay, postpone; *se differre,* to tarry; to disperse, scatter. *Intransit.,* to differ, be different.

differtus -a -um, stuffed full, crammed.

difficilis -e, *adj.* difficult; dangerous; *of time,* critical; hard to please, morose, captious.

difficilĭtĕr, *adv.* with difficulty.

difficultas -ātis, *f.* difficulty, need, trouble, moroseness ; *nummaria,* pecuniary embarrassment.

difficultĕr, *adv.* with difficulty.

diffidens, *p. adj.* distrustful, diffident.

diffidentĕr, *adv.* diffidently.

diffidentia -ae, *f.* diffidence, distrust.

diffīdo -fīsus sum, 3. to have no confidence, to despair.

diffindo -fīdi -fissum, 3. to split, cleave; *legal, diem,* to postpone.

diffingo -finxi -fictum, 3. to form again, forge anew; *fig.,* to change.

diffĭtĕor -ēri, 2. *dep.* to deny, disavow.

diffluo -fluxi -fluxum, 3. to flow in different directions; *otio,* to give oneself up to; to melt away.

diffŭgio -fūgi, 3. to fly apart, to disperse.

diffŭgium -ii, *n.* a dispersion.

diffundo -fūdi -fūsum, 3. to pour out on all sides, pour forth; to spread, scatter; to brighten up, gladden.

diffūsē, *adv.* copiously, diffusely.

diffūsilis -e, easily extending itself, diffusive.

diffūsus -a -um, *p. adj.* spread out, extensive.

dīgamma -ātis, *n. or* **dīgammon -i,** *n. or* **dīgammos -i,** *f.* the Aeolic digamma (*F*); *in jest,* rental *or* investment book.

dīgĕro -gessi -gestum, 3. to separate, divide; to plant out; to arrange; to count.

dīgestio -ōnis, *f. rhet. fig.* distribution.

dīgestus -a -um, *v. digero.*

dīgĭtŭlus -i, *m.* (*dim. of digitus*), a little finger.

dīgĭtus -i, *m.* the finger; *tuos digitos novi,* thy skill in counting; the toe; a finger's breadth, an inch.

dīglădior, 1. *dep.* to fight for life and death, struggle fiercely; to dispute in words.

dignātio -ōnis, *f.* dignity, reputation, honour.

dignē, *adv.* worthily.

dignĭtas -ātis, *f.* worth, merit; esteem, honour; rank in the state; imposing appearance.

digno, 1. to consider worthy.

dignor, 1. *dep.* to consider worthy; to deign, *and with a neg.,* to disdain.

dignosco -nōvi, 3. to recognise as different, to distinguish.

dignus -a -um, *adj.* worthy, deserving. *With abl., laude ;* becoming, fitting; sufficient.

dīgrĕdior -gressus sum -grĕdi, 3. *dep.* to go apart, depart;] to deviate; *of discourse,* to digress.

dīgressio -ōnis, *f.* departure; a digression in discourse.

dīgressus -ūs, *m.* a separation, departure.

dĭiūdĭcātio -ōnis, *f.* an adjudication, decision.

dĭiūdĭco, 1. to decide, adjudicate; to distinguish, discern a difference.

dĭiun . . . v. disiun . . .

dīlābor -lapsus sum, 3. *dep.* to glide apart; to fall to pieces, fall down; to disappear; to be ruined; to slip away; to escape; to vanish; *of time,* to go by.

dīlăcĕro, 1, to tear in pieces.

dīlāmino, 1. to split in two.

dīlănio, 1. to tear in pieces.

dīlargior, 4. *dep.* to give liberally.

dīlātio -ōnis, *f.* a delaying, postponing.

dīlāto, 1. to spread out, extend; *litteras,* to pronounce broadly; to amplify, *orationem.*

dīlātor -ōris, *m.* a dilatory person, loiterer.

dīlātus, *v. differo.*

dīlaudo, 1. to praise highly.

1. **dīlectus -a -um,** *p. adj.* beloved, dear.

2. **dīlectus -ūs = delectus** (*q.v.*).

dīligens -entis, *p. adj.* assiduous, accurate, diligent; economical.

dīligentĕr, *adv.* carefully, diligently.

dīligentia -ae, *f.* carefulness, accuracy, diligence; frugality.

dīligo -lexi -lectum, 3. to prize, love, esteem highly; to be satisfied with.

dilŏrico, 1. to tear open.

dilūcĕo, 2. to be clear, evident.

dilūcesco -luxi, 3. to grow light, become day.

dilūcidē, *adv.* clearly, plainly.

dilūcidus -a -um, clear, lucid.

dilūcŭlum -i, *n.* dawn.

dilūdium -ii, *n.* period of rest for gladiators.

dilŭo -lŭi -lūtum, 3. to wash away, to dissolve, to dilute; to lessen, impair; to refute.

dilūtus -a -um, *v. diluo.*

dilŭviēs -ēi, *f.* a washing away, inundation.

dilŭvio, 1. to overflow.

dilŭvium -ii, *n.* a flood, deluge.

dimāno, 1. to flow in different directions, spread itself abroad.

dimensio -ōnis, *f.* a measuring.

dimētior -mensus, 4. *dep.* to measure out.

dimēto, 1. *and dep.* dimētor, 1. to measure the boundaries of.

dimicātio -ōnis, *f.* a fight, struggle ; contest.

dimico -āvi *or* -ŭi, 1. to fight, contend ; to strive.

dimidiātus -a -um, halved, divided, half.

dimidius -a -um, halved, divided in half. *Subst.,* dimidium -ii, *n.* the half ; *dimidio with compar.,* by half.

diminūtio, *v. deminutio.*

dimissio -ōnis, *f.* a sending out; dismissing, discharging.

dimitto -misi -missum, 3. to send forth, send in different directions; to send away ; *of things,* to let drop ; to adjourn a meeting, dismiss; *milit.,* to discharge; to give up, renounce.

dimŏvĕo -mōvi -mōtum, 2. separate, divide; to remove.

Dindymēnē -ēs, *f.* Cybele.

dinosco = *dignosco (q.v.).*

dinŭmĕrātio -ōnis, *f.* an enumeration.

dinŭmĕro, 1. to count up, enumerate; to count money, to pay.

dioecēsis -ĕos *and* -is, *f.* district of a magistrate.

dioecētes -ae, *m.* finance officer.

Diŏgĕnēs -is, *m.* the name of several Greek philosophers, the most notorious of whom was the Cynic philosopher of Sinope.

Diŏmēdēs -is, *m.* a hero of the Trojan war.

Diŏnȳsius -ii, *m.* 1. the Elder, Tyrant of Syracuse ; 2, his son.

Diŏnȳsus -i, *m.* the Greek name of Bacchus ; Diŏnȳsia -ōrum, *n.* the feast of Dionysus.

diōta -ae *f.* a two-handled wine-jar.

diplōma -ătis, *n.* a circular letter of introduction ; a government document conferring privileges.

Dircē -ēs, *f.* the wife of Lycus king of Thebes, bound to a bull by Amphion and Zethus, and thrown (*or* changed) into the fountain named after her.

directē, *adv.* straightforward, in a straight line; *dicere,* directly

directō, *adv.* in a straightforward way.

directus -a -um, *p. adj.* straight, direct; straightforward, simple.

diremptus -ūs, *m.* a separation.

direptio -ōnis, *f.* a plundering.

direptor -ōris, *m.* a plunderer.

diribĕo -ŭi -itum, 2. to sort the voting tickets.

diribitio -ōnis, *f.* the sorting of the voting tickets.

diribitor -ōris, *m.* the officer whose duty it was to sort the voting tickets.

dirigo -rexi -rectum, 3. to arrange in a straight line; (*pass. dirigi,* to proceed in a straight line); to arrange, direct; to aim ; *milit.,* to draw up, *aciem* ; to erect; to guide; to conduct; to direct the thoughts, attention, *etc., to something.*

dirimo -ēmi -emptum, 3. to part, divide; to interrupt, disturb ; *an alliance,* to break up.

diripio -ripŭi -reptum, 3. to tear to pieces ; to plunder, destroy ; to tear away.

diritas -ātis, *f.* disaster; cruelty.

dirumpo -rūpi -ruptum, 3. to shatter; to sever, break up; *middle, dirumpi,* to burst with envy, grief, anger, *etc.*

dirŭo -ŭi -ŭtum, 3. to pull down, destroy; *agmina vasto impetu,* to scatter; *aere dirui,* to be mulcted of one's pay; *homo diruptus dirutusque,* bankrupt.

dirus -a -um, horrible, dire; *subst.,* dirae -ārum, *f.* unlucky omens ; *so* dira -ōrum, *n.* cruel, frightful; *subst.,* dirae -ārum, *f.* curses ; Dira -ae, *f.* a Fury, *gen. plur.*

1. Dis, Ditis, *m.* name of Pluto, god of the lower world.

2. dis, ditis, *adj.* rich. *Compar. ditior;* *superl. ditissimus.*

discēdo-cessi -cessum,3.to part,separate; to depart; to march away; *ab signis,* to break the ranks; *ab armis,* to lay down arms ; to come off, *victor ;* *aequo Marte cum Volscis,* to have a drawn battle with ; to desert ; to digress (*of an orator*): *of the senate, in aliquam sententiam discedere,* to support a resolution.

disceptātio -ōnis, *f.* discussion, controversy; judicial decision, award.

disceptātor -ōris, *m.* arbitrator, judge.

disceptātrix -trīcis, *f.* one who decides.

discepto, 1. to adjudicate, determine ; to dispute, discuss ; *in uno proelio omnis fortuna reipublicae disceptat,* depends upon.

discerno -crēvi -crētum, 3. to sever,

separate; set apart; to distinguish, discern.

discerpo -cerpsi -cerptum, 3. to tear in pieces, dismember; *in discourse*, to divide.

discessio -ōnis, *f.* departure; *polit.*, voting, division in the senate; *discessionem facere*, to vote.

discessus -ūs, *m.* a parting, separation; *caeli*, lightning; a departure; *milit.*, marching off; banishment.

discidium -ii, *n.* a dividing; separation; dissension.

discido, 3. to cut in pieces.

discinctus -a -um, careless, reckless, extravagant.

discindo -scidi -scissum, 3. to cleave asunder, split; to tear open.

discingo -cinxi -cinctum, 3. to ungird; to disarm.

disciplina -ae, *f.* instruction, teaching; learning, knowledge, science; a philosophical school, a system; a rhetorical school; training, education; military training; custom, habit, order; (of a state) constitution.

discipula -ae, *f.* a female scholar.

discipulus -i, *m.* a scholar, disciple.

discludo -clusi -clusum, 3. to separate, divide; to loosen.

disco, didici, 3. to learn; *disco fidibus*, to learn to play on the lyre; *discere causam* (*legal*), to get up the facts of a case; to become acquainted with; find out.

discolor -ōris, of different colours; *miles*, black and white (*of draughts*); different from, unlike to.

disconvenio, 4. to disagree, not to harmonise.

discordia -ae, *f.* dissension, disagreement; sedition. *Personif.*, Discordia, Goddess of Discord.

discordiōsus -a -um, full of discord, mutinous.

discordo, 1. to disagree; to be mutinous; to be unlike.

discors -cordis, disagreeing, inharmonious; unlike, different.

discrepantia -ae, *f.* disagreement, difference.

discrepatio -ōnis, *f.* disagreement, disunion.

discrepito, 1. to be entirely dissimilar.

discrepo -crepui, 1. not to sound together; to be discordant; to disagree; be unlike; *impers.*, *discrepat*, there is a disagreement, people are not agreed.

discribo = describo (*q.v.*).

discrimen -inis, *n.* the dividing line; the space between; *in music*, interval; distinction, difference; turning-point; crisis, danger.

discrimino, 1. to divide.

discriptio -ōnis, *f.* a division.

discrucio, 1. to torment; *refl. or pass.* to make oneself miserable.

discumbo -cubui -cubitum, 3. to lie down; to recline at table; *impers.*, *discumbitur*, one goes to the table; to sleep, go to bed.

discupio -ivi -itum, 3. to desire vehemently.

discurro -cucurri *and* -curri -cursum, 3. to run in different directions, run to and fro; *impers.*, *totā discurritur urbe*.

discursus -ūs, *m.* a running up and down, running to and fro.

discus -i, *m.* a quoit.

discutio -cussi -cussum, 3. to strike asunder, to shatter; to disperse; to frustrate.

diserte, *adv.* clearly, eloquently.

disertus -a -um, *p. adj.* eloquent, well-expressed.

disicio -iēci -iectum, 3. to throw down, destroy; to disperse; *disiecta comas*, with dishevelled hair; to frustrate.

disiecto, 1. to cast about, scatter.

1. **disiectus** -a -um, *v. disicio.*

2. **disiectus** -ūs, *m.* a scattering, dispersing.

disiunctio -ōnis, *f.* separation; difference; disjunctive proposition.

disiunctus -a -um, *p. adj.* separated, distant; remote from; *in logic*, disjunctive; *rhet.*, disconnected.

disiungo -iunxi -iunctum, 3. to loosen, separate; to unyoke; to remove; to distinguish.

dispalor, 1. *dep.* to wander about, to stray.

dispando -pandi -pansum, 3. to extend, stretch out.

dispar -paris, unlike, unequal.

dispargo, *v. dispergo.*

disparilis -e, unlike, unequal.

disparo, 1, to separate.

dispartio = dispertio (*q.v.*).

dispello -puli -pulsum, 3. to drive in different directions; to scatter, dispel.

dispendium -i, *n.* expenditure, expense, loss; *facere*, to suffer loss.

1. **dispendo** = dispando (*q.v.*).

2. **dispendo** -pensum, 3. to weigh out.

dispensatio -ōnis, *f.* management, economical administration; office of a dispensator.

dispensator -ōris, *m.* steward, treasurer.

dispenso, 1. to put away money; to distribute; to arrange; to manage a household.

disperditio -ōnis, *f.* a total destruction, ruin.

disperdo -didi -ditum, 3. to destroy, ruin.

dispereo -ii, 4. to perish utterly.

dispergo -spersi -spersum, 3. to scatter, spread abroad; army.

disperse *and* **dispersim**, *adv.* in different places, here and there.

dispersio -ōnis, *f.* a scattering, destruction.

dispertio -īvi *and* ii -ītum, 4. to separate, distribute; *dep.,* **dispertior** -īri.

dispicio -spexi -spectum, 3. to begin to see; to catch sight of, perceive; to reflect upon, consider.

displiceo -plicui -plicitum, 2. to displease, *alicui; displicere sibi,* to be dissatisfied with oneself, to be melancholy.

displodo -plosi -plosum, 3. to spread out, dilate, burst.

dispōno -pōsŭi -pōsitum, 3. to distribute; to arrange, dispose.

dispŏsĭtē, *adv.* in proper order, methodically.

dispŏsĭtio -ōnis, . a regular arrangement in a speech.

dispŏsĭtūra -ae, *f.* arrangement, order.
1. **dispŏsĭtus** -a -um, *p. adj.* arranged.
2. **dispŏsĭtus** -ūs, *m.* arrangement.

dispŭtātio -ōnis, *f.* an arguing, argument, debate.

dispŭtātor -ōris, *m.* a debater, disputant.

dispŭto, 1. to discuss, debate, argue.

disquīro, 3. to inquire into, investigate.

disquīsĭtio -ōnis, *f.* inquiry, investigation.

dissaepio -saepsi -saeptum, 4. to hedge off, separate, divide.

dissaeptio -ōnis, *f.* partition.

dissaeptum -i, *n.* barrier, partition.

dissēmino, 1. to spread abroad, disseminate.

dissensio -ōnis, *f.* disagreement, variance; dissension, disunion; *of abstractions,* opposition.

dissensus -ūs, *m.* disunion, disagreement.

dissentānĕus -a -um, disagreeing, different.

dissentio -sensi -sensum, 4. to be of a different opinion, *inter se ;* to be at variance ; *of things,* to be opposed, different.

dissĕp . . . *n. dissaep* . . .

dissĕro -sevi -situm . . .

dissĕro -serŭi -sertum . . .

dissererat -āvit, *impers,* it clears up (*of the weather*).
1. **dissĕro** -sevi -situm, 3. to scatter seed; to plant at a distance.
2. **dissĕro** -serŭi -sertum, 3. to examine, treat of, discuss.

disserpo, 3. to creep in different directions, spread imperceptibly.

disserto, 1. to treat of, discuss, argue.

dissĭdĕo -sēdi -sessum, 2. to be drawn apart; *si toga dissidet impar,* sits unevenly; to be distant, to be separated; not to agree; to disagree; to be at variance; to be opposed.

dissĭdium ii, *n.* disagreement.

dissĭlio -silŭi -sultum, 4. to leap apart, burst asunder.

dissĭmĭlis -e, *adj.* unlike, dissimilar; *with genit.*

dissĭmĭlĭtĕr, *adv.* differently, in a different manner.

dissĭmĭlĭtūdo -inis, *f.* unlikeness, difference.

dissĭmŭlantĕr, *adv.* secretly, in a dissembling manner.

dissĭmŭlātio -ōnis, *f.* a concealing, dissembling, dissimulation.

dissĭmŭlātor -ōris, *m.* a dissembler, concealer.

dissĭmŭlo, 1. to make unlike; to conceal; to disguise, keep secret; to ignore, leave unnoticed.

dissĭpābĭlis -e, that can be scattered.

dissĭpātio -ōnis, *f.* scattering; dispersion by sale; *rhet.,* the analysis of an idea.

dissĭpātus -a -um, *p. adj.* scattered, disconnected, *oratio.*

dissĭpo, 1. to scatter, disperse; *milit.,* to rout, to destroy; to squander.

dissĭtus, *partic., v.* 1, *dissero.*

dissŏcĭābĭlis -e, *act.* that which separates, *oceanus ; pass.,* that which cannot be united, *res.*

dissŏcĭātio -ōnis, *f.* a separation, parting.

dissŏcĭo, 1. to separate, sever.

dissŏlūbĭlis -e, dissoluble, separable.

dissŏlūtē, *adv.* disconnectedly, loosely; carelessly.

dissŏlūtio -ōnis, *f.* breaking up, destruction, annihilation; *naturae,* death; abolition; refutation *of a charge;* want of energy; *rhet.,* want of connexion.

dissŏlūtus -a -um, *p. adj.* loosened; *rhet.,* disconnected, loose; lax; dissolute.

dissolvo -solvi -sŏlutum, 3. to loosen, unloose ; to melt ; to destroy ; *rhet.,* to divide; to refute a charge, *etc.*; to pay.

dissŏnus -a -um, discordant, inharmonious ; different, disagreeing.

dissors -sortis, having a different lot *or* fate; *ab omni milite dissors gloria,* not shared with.

dissuādĕo -suāsi -suāsum, 2. to advise against, oppose.

dissuāsio -ōnis, *f.* advising to the contrary.

dissuāsor -ōris, *m.* one who advises to the contrary.

dissuāvior, 1. *dep.* to kiss eagerly.

dissulto, 1. to leap apart, burst asunder.

dissŭo (*no perf.*) -sūtum, 3. to unstitch; to open wide; to loosen by degrees.

distantia -ae, *f.* difference, diversity.

distendo -tendi -tentum *and* -tensum, 3. to stretch apart, extend; to fill full; *milit.,* to divide, to distract.
1. **distentus** -a -um, *p. adj.,* distended, full.
2. **distentus** -a -um, *p. adj.,* busy, occupied.

distermino, 1. to separate by a boundary, divide, *poet.*

distichus -a -um, consisting of two rows; *subst.* **distichum** (-on) -i, *n.* a distich.

distinctē, *adv.* clearly, definitely, distinctly.

distinctio -ōnis, *f.* a separation in space; *solis lunae siderumque omnium*, different orbits; distinguishing, discriminating ; distinction, difference ; *rhet.*, a pause, division.

1. distinctus -a -um, *p. adj.*, separated, distinct.

2. distinctus -ūs, *m.* difference, distinction.

distinĕo -tinŭi -tentum, 2. to keep apart, separate, divide ; to delay, *pacem, milit.*, to prevent the union of forces; (*of thought*) to distract.

distinguo -stinxi -stinctum, 3. to separate, divide; to distinguish; to punctuate; to point out, mark out; to decorate, adorn; to vary, change.

disto (*no perf. or sup.*), 1. to be apart, separate, distant; to differ, be distinct, *inter se*; *ab aliquo*; *impers., distat*, there is a difference.

distorquĕo -torsi -tortum, 2. to twist apart, distort.

distortio -ōnis, *f.* distortion.

distortus -a -um, *p. adj.*, distorted, deformed ; *of discourse*, perverse.

distractio -ōnis, *f.* a dividing, separating; disunion, dissension.

distrăho -traxi -tractum, 3. to pull apart, tear in pieces; *acies distrahitur*, is divided; to sell by auction; *grammat.*, to leave a hiatus in a verse; to distract; to dissolve a league or union; *distrahi cum aliquo*, to fall out with some one; to bring to naught; to settle a dispute, *controversias*; to tear from something; to estrange.

distribŭo -ŭi -ūtum, 3. to distribute, divide; to arrange or divide logically.

distribūtē, *adv.* methodically, with logical arrangement.

distribūtio -ōnis, *f.* a division, distribution; logical arrangement of ideas.

distribūtus -a -um, *p. adj.*, logically arranged.

districtus -a -um, *p. adj.*, busy, occupied, engaged; severe.

distringo -strinxi -strictum, 3. to draw apart, stretch out; to engage an enemy at different points, divert, occupy.

disturbātio -ōnis, *f.* destruction.

disturbo, 1. to drive apart; throw into confusion; to destroy, raze to the ground; to frustrate, ruin.

ditesco, 3. to become rich.

dithўrambicus -a -um, dithyrambic.

dithўrambus -i, *m.* a dithyrambic poem.

ditio (dicio) -ōnis, *f.* power, sovereignty, authority.

ditior, ditissimus, *v.* 3. *dis.*

1. ditis, *v.* 2. *dis.*

2. Ditis, *v.* 1. *dis.*

dito, 1. to enrich, make wealthy; *pass., ditari*, to become rich.

1. diū, *adv.* by day; a long time, lasting for a long time ; a long time ago; *compar., diutius*, longer; too long. *Superl., diutissime.*

2. diū, *v. dius.*

diurnus -a -um, lasting for a day ; happening by day. *Subst.*, diurnum -i, *n.* journal, account-book ; diurna -orum, *v. acta.*

dius -a -um (*archaic and poet. form of divus*), *adj.*, god-like; noble; fine; *subst.*, dium -ii, *n., sub dio, and* (*archaic*) *sub diu*, in the open air.

diūtinus -a -um, lasting a long time, long.

diūtius, diūtissimē, *v.* 1. *diu.*

diūturnitas -ātis, *f.* long duration.

diūturnus -a -um, of long duration.

divărico, 1. to stretch apart, spread out.

divello -velli -vulsum (-volsum), 3. to pluck apart, separate by force; to destroy; *somnum*, interrupt; *divelli*, to tear oneself away from.

divendo (*no perf.*) -venditum, 3. to sell in separate lots.

diverbĕro, 1. to cleave, divide.

diverbium -ii, *n.* a dialogue on the stage.

diversē, *adv.* in different directions, differently.

diversitas -ātis, *f.* disagreement; diversity.

diversōrium, *v. deversorium.*

diversus -a -um, *p. adj.*, turned in different directions ; inconstant, irresolute, indecisive; isolated; turned away from; remote ; in an opposite direction ; different, opposed.

diverto (divorto) -verti (-vorti), 3. to turn away, to diverge from, differ.

dives -vitis, *compar.* divitior -ius, *genit.* -ōris, *superl.* divitissimus, rich, wealthy; *lingua*, eloquent; costly; *cultus*, rich dress.

divexo, 1. to tear asunder, destroy, plunder.

divido -vīsi -vīsum, 3. to divide; to destroy, *muros*; *polit.*, distribute, allot; *poet. imb-ūll citharā carmina*, to sing; to distinguish; to adorn.

divldŭus -a -um, divisible; divided, parted.

divīnātio -ōnis, *f.* divination.

divīnē, *adv.* by divine inspiration, prophetically, excellently.

divīnitas -ātis, *f.* divine nature, divinity; the power of divination; excellence.

divīnĭtūs, *adv.* by divine influence; by inspiration, by means of divination; admirably.

divīno, 1. to foretell, prophesy.

divīnus -a -um, *adj.* relating to a deity divine ; prophetic ; excellent. *Subst.*, divīnum -i, *n.* a sacrifice ; *subst.*, divīnus -i, *m.* a seer.

divīsio -ōnis, *f.* division; distribution.

divisor -ōris, *m.* a divider, distributor, a hired bribery agent.

1. **divīsus -a -um**, *partic. of divido*.

2. **divīsus -ūs**, *m.* division.

divitiae -ārum, *f.* riches, wealth.

divortium -ii, *n.* the point where roads, *etc.*, separate, cross-roads; the boundary line between two continents *or* countries; a divorce; separation.

divorto, *v.* diverto.

divulgātus -a -um, *p. adj.*, spread abroad, made common.

divulgo (divolgo), 1. to make public, publish, spread abroad; to make common.

divus -a -um, *adj.* belonging to the deity, divine; *diva parens. Subst.*, **divus -i**, *m.* a god; **diva -ae**, *f.* goddess; **divum -i**, *n.* the sky (*only in sub divo*, in the open air).

do, *dedi, datum, dare*, to give, offer; *of letters*, send; *dare poenas*, to suffer punishment; *vela dare ventis*, to sail; *dare alicui cervices*, to offer the neck for punishment; to lend; *id misericordiae*, to grant, give up; *dare se or pass. dari*, to give oneself up; to throw oneself, *se in viam*; *do, dico, addico*, a formula used by the praetor.

dŏcĕo, dŏcŭi, doctum, 2. to teach, instruct, *aliquem Latine*; *with double acc.*, *aliquem litteras*; *docere fabulam* (*lit.* to teach a play), to bring out, exhibit.

dochmius -ii, *m.* the dochmiac foot (⏑ – – ⏑ –).

dŏcilis -e, *adj.* teachable, docile, attentive.

dŏcilitas -ātis, *f.* teachableness, docility.

doctē, *adv.* learnedly, skilfully.

doctor -ōris, *m.* a teacher.

doctrīna -ae, *f.* teaching, instruction; knowledge, learning.

doctus -a -um, *p. adj.*, learned, instructed, well-informed, *Graecis litteris*; experienced, clever, shrewd. *Subst.*, **docti -orum**, learned men.

dŏcumen -inis, *n.* = documentum (*q.v.*).

dŏcumentum -i, *n.* example, pattern, warning, proof.

Dōdōna -ae *and* **-ē -ēs**, *f.* city of Epirus, renowned for its oracle.

dōdrans -antis, *m.* three-fourths; three-fourths of an acre; nine inches, three-fourths of a foot.

dōdrantārius -a -um, belonging to three-fourths.

dogma -ătis, *n.* a philosophical doctrine, principle, dogma.

dŏlābra -ae, *f.* an axe, hatchet.

dŏlentěr, *adv.* painfully, sorrowfully.

dŏlĕo, dŏlŭi, *fut. partic.* **dŏlitūrus**, 2. to suffer pain; to grieve, bewail; to cause pain.

dŏliŏlum -i, *n.* (*dim. of dolium*), a little cask.

dōlium -ii, *n.* a large earthenware jar *or* wooden cask.

1. **dŏlo**, 1. to hew with an axe; to work with an axe; *illud opus*, to work roughly.

2. **dŏlo**, *or* **dōlon -ōnis**, *m.* a wooden staff with an iron point; the sting of a fly; a small foresail.

Dŏlops -lopis *and plur.* **Dŏlōpes -um**, *acc.* **-as**, *m.* a people in Thessaly.

dŏlor -ōris, *m.* bodily pain; sorrow; animosity; the cause of sorrow; *thet.*, pathos.

dŏlōsē, *adv.* deceitfully, craftily.

dŏlōsus -a -um, crafty, deceitful, cunning.

dŏlus -i, *m.* deceit, guile; trick.

dŏmābilis -e, that can be tamed, tameable.

dŏmesticus -a -um, belonging to the house *or* the family, domestic; *tempus*, spent at home; (*plur.*, **dŏmestici -ōrum**, *m.* the inmates of one's house); private, domestic, native; *crudelitas*, towards citizens; *bellum*, civil war.

dŏmicilium -ii, *n.* dwelling.

dŏmina -ae, *f.* the mistress of a household, lady; mistress, queen; a sweetheart; controller.

dŏminātio -ōnis, *f.* despotism, arbitrary government; governing.

dŏminātor -ōris, *m.* ruler, governor.

dŏminātrix -īcis, *f.* a despotic mistress.

dŏminātus -ūs, *m.* absolute power; rule.

dŏminium -ii, *n.* a banquet.

dŏminor, 1. *dep.* to rule, be lord *or* master, to domineer; *in suos*.

dŏminus -i, *m.* the master of a house, lord, master; *plur.*, **domini**, master and mistress; possessor; ruler; a lover; a host.

dŏmiporta -ae, *f.* she who carries her house upon her back, the snail.

Dŏmitiānus -i, *m.* T. Flavius Domitianus, *Emperor of Rome from* A.D. 81 *to* A.D. 96.

Dŏmitius -a -um, name of a plebeian gens at Rome.

dŏmito, 1. to tame, subdue.

dŏmitor -ōris, *m.* a tamer; conqueror.

dŏmitrix -īcis, *f.* she who tames.

dŏmitus, *abl.* **-ū**, *m.* taming.

dŏmo, dŏmŭi, dŏmitum, 1. to tame, break in; to conquer, subdue; *uvas prelo*, to press.

dŏmus -ūs, *f.* a house; *domi*, at home; *domum*, home, homeward; a philosophical sect, *Socratica domus*; *domi*, at home.

dōnārium -ii, *n.* temple, shrine, altar; votive offering.

dōnātio -ōnis, *f.* gift, present, donation.

dōnātivum -i, *n.* an imperial largess.

dōněc, *conj.*, as long as, while; until.

dōno, 1. to present; to grant, bestow; to sacrifice, give up to; to remit a debt *or* obligation, *alicui aes alienum*; to forgive, pardon; to present a person with something, *cohortem donis*.

dōnum -i, *n.* gift, present ; votive offering.

dorcas -ădis, *f.* gazelle, antelope.

Dōres -um, *m.* the Dorians.

dormio -īvi *or* -ii -ītum, 4. to sleep; to rest, be inactive.

dormīto, 1. to be sleepy, to begin to sleep; *jam dormitante lucernā,* just going out; to dream, be lazy, inactive; *quandoque bonus dormitat Homerus,* nods.

dormītor -ōris, *m.* a sleeper.

dorsum -i, *n.* (**dorsus** -i, *m.*), the back, *of men or animals;* any elevation of similar form; *immane dorsum,* a rock in the sea; *of mountains,* slope.

dŏrўphŏrŏs -i, *m.* the lance-bearer, *celebrated statute by Polycletus.*

dōs, dōtis, *f.* dowry, portion; a gift, quality, endowment.

dōtālis -e, relating to a dowry.

dōtātus -a -um, *p. adj.,* richly dowered; richly endowed.

dōto, 1. to provide with a dowry, endow.

drachma -ae, *f.* a small Greek coin; *as a weight,* ⅛ of an uncia.

1. **drăco** -ōnis, *m.* a kind of snake, dragon ; a constellation so called.

2. **Drăco** -ōnis, *m.* an Athenian legislator.

drăcŏnĭgĕna -ae, *c.* dragon-born.

Drĕpănum -i, *n., and* **Drĕpăna** -ōrum, *n.* a town on the west coast of Sicily.

drŏmas -ădis, *m.* a dromedary.

drŏmos -i, *m.* the race-course of the Spartans.

Drŭides -um, *m., and* **Drŭĭdae** -ārum, *m.* the Druids.

Drūsus -i, *m.* a cognomen of the Gens Livia *and* Claudia; *subst.* **Drūsilla** -ae, *f.* female name.

Drўăs -ădis, *f.* a wood nymph, Dryad.

dŭbĭē, *adv.* doubtfully, hesitatingly; uncertainly; *haud dubie,* certainly, without doubt.

dŭbĭtābĭlis -e, doubtful, uncertain.

dŭbĭtantĕr, *adv.* doubtingly ; hesitatingly.

dŭbĭtātĭo -ōnis, *f.* doubt, uncertainty; hesitation, irresolution.

dŭbĭto, 1. to doubt, waver; be uncertain; to hesitate.

dŭbĭus -a -um, doubting, doubtful, uncertain; irresolute. *Object.,* uncertain, doubtful; dangerous, critical.

dŭcēni -ae -a, two hundred each.

dŭcentēsima -ae, *f.* the two hundredth part; *as a tax,* one-half per cent.

dŭcenti -ae -a, two hundred.

dŭcentiēs, *adv.* two hundred times.

dūco, duxi, ductum, 3. to draw; to drag behind; to draw towards oneself; *ducere remos,* to row; *colorem,* to get a darker colour; to charm, attract; to mislead; to influence; to draw in; *poet. somnos,* to sleep; to quaff, *pocula Lesbii;* to draw out, *sortes;* to extend, make,

fashion, *murum, vallum; lanas,* to spin; *poet. carmina,* to make verses; to prolong; to pass, *aetatem;* to delay, protract, *bellum;* to distort, *os;* to derive, *nomen;* to begin; to count; *aliquid parvi,* to esteem little; *with accus. and infin.,* to consider; to lead; *uxorem ducere,* to marry; to cheat; *of water,* to conduct, *aquam in urbem;* to take with one, *suas mulierculas secum;* to arrange.

ducto, 1. to lead.

ductor -ōris, *m.* a leader, commander.

ductus -ūs, *m.* drawing; *oris,* the lineaments of the face ; *muri,* building ; leading; *milit.,* command; conducting of water, *aquarum.*

dūdum, *adv.* a little while ago; *quam dudum,* as long as; *iam dudum,* now for a long time.

dŭellum, dŭellicus, dŭellātor = *bellum, bellicus, bellator, q.v.*

Dŭīlius, *C. Duilius,* consul, gained a great naval victory over the Carthaginians.

dulcĕ, *adv.* sweetly.

dulcēdo -inis, *f.* a sweet taste; sweetness, pleasantness, desire.

dulcesco, 3. to become sweet.

dulcĭcŭlus -a -um (*dim. of dulcis*), somewhat sweet.

dulcis -e, *adj.* sweet; delightful, agreeable; friendly, dear. *Subst.,* **dulcĕ** -is, *n.* what is sweet; **dulcia** -ium, *n.* sweet things.

dulcĭtĕr, *adv.* sweetly.

dulcĭtūdo -inis, *f.* sweetness.

dum, *adv., enclitic;* *nondum,* not yet; *with imperat.* then; *age dum. Conj.* while; as long as; until; *with subj., dummodo,* provided that.

dūmētum -i, *n.* a thorn bush, thicket.

dummōdo, *v. dum.*

Dumnŏrix -igis, *m.* brother of the Aeduan Divitiacus.

dūmōsus -a -um, covered with thorn bushes, bushy.

dumtaxăt = *duntaxat, q.v.*

dūmus -i, *m.* a thorn bush, bramble.

duntaxăt (*better,* **dumtaxat**), *adv.* exactly, according to the right measure, not more and not less; only, merely; at least, in so far.

dŭŏ -ae -ŏ, two.

dŭŏ-dĕcĭēs, *adv.* twelve times.

dŭŏ-dĕcim, twelve.

dŭŏ-dĕcĭmus -a -um, the twelfth.

dŭŏ-dēni -ae -a, twelve each, twelve.

dŭŏ-dĕ-quădrăgēsĭmus, thirty-eighth.

dŭŏ-dē-quădrāginta, thirty-eight.

dŭŏ-dē-quinquāgēsĭmus -a -um, the forty-eighth.

dŭŏ-dē-trīciens (-tricies), *adv.* twenty-eight times.

dŭŏ-dē-trīginta, twenty-eight.

dŭŏ-dē-vīcēni -ae -a, eighteen each.

dŭŏ-dē-vīginti, eighteen.

dŭŏ-et-vīcēsimāni -ōrum, m. soldiers of the 22nd legion.

dŭŏ-et-vīcēsimus -a -um, the twenty-second.

duplex -plicis, double, two-fold; *palmae,* both hands; twice as much; false, deceitful.

duplicārius -a -um, *miles,* a soldier who gets double rations.

duplicitĕr, *adv.* doubly.

duplico, 1. to fold in two, double up, to double; *duplicare verba,* to repeat; to increase.

duplus -a -um, twice as much, double; *subst.,* **duplum -i,** *n.* the double, *esp.* double penalty.

dūrābilis -e, lasting, durable.

dūrāmen -inis, *n.* hardness.

dūrātēus -a -um, wooden *(the Trojan horse).*

dūrē, *and* **dūritĕr,** *adv. compar. dūrius, superl. dūrissimē,* hardly; unpleasantly; *of works of art,* rudely, roughly; awkwardly; harshly, severely.

dūresco, dūrŭi, 3. to grow hard.

dūritas -ātis, *f.* harshness, unfriendliness.

dūriter = *dure (q.v.).*

dūritia -ae, *f. and* **dūritiēs -ēi,** *f.* hardness; austerity; harshness.

dūro, 1. *transit.,* to make hard; to dry up; to make hardy, inure; to render callous; to endure; *intransit.,* to become hard *or* dry; to become callous; to endure; to last, continue.

dūrus -a -um, *adj.* hard; harsh to the taste *or* to the ear; rough to the eye, rude; *of feeling,* hard, rough; strong, enduring; awkward, uncouth, shameless; hardy, austere; without taste for; stern; *weather,* severe; *of the soil,* difficult to work; *of work,* difficult; painful, adverse.

dŭumvir *and* **dŭŏvir -viri,** m. *gen. plur.,* **dŭumvirí** *or* **dŭŏvirí,** a pair of magistrates; **dŭumvirí** *navales,* a commission for looking after the fleet.

dux, dŭcis, *c.* leader, guide, conductor; a ruler, a military *or* naval commander; the emperor.

dýnastes -ae, m. ruler, prince.

Dyrrăchium -ii, *n.* later name of Epidamnus, in Illyria.

E

E **e,** *the fifth letter of the Latin Alphabet.*

ē, *prep.* = *ex (q.v.).*

ĕātĕnus = *ea tenus, adv.* so far.

ĕbĕnus -i, m. the ebony-tree, ebony.

ēbĭbo -bĭbi -bĭtum, 3. to drink up; to squander.

ēblandior, 4. *dep.* to obtain by flattery.

ēbrĭĕtas -ātis, *f.* drunkenness, revelling.

ēbrĭōsĭtas -ātis, *f.* the love of drink.

ēbrĭōsus -a -um, drink-loving.

ēbrĭus -a -um, intoxicated.

ēbullĭo, 4. to boil up; to cause to boil up; to boast of.

ēbŭlum -i, *n.* (-us -i, *m.*), the dwarf elder-tree.

ĕbur -ŏris, *n.* ivory.

ĕburnĕŏlus -a -um *(dim. of eburneus),* made of ivory.

ĕburnĕus (ĕburnus) -a -um, made of ivory, ivory; white as ivory.

Ebŭrōnes -um, *m.* a German people in Gallia Belgica.

ĕcastor, *v. Castor.*

ecce, *adv.* behold! lo! see!

ecf..., *v. eff...*

ĕchidna -ae, *f.* the viper, adder. *Echidna Lernaea,* the Lernean hydra killed by Hercules.

ĕchīnus -i, *m.* the edible sea-urchin; a brazen dish used for washing goblets.

ēchŏ -ūs, *f.* an echo; *personif.,* Echo, a wood-nymph.

ec-quando, *adv.* ever; ever, *indefinite, after nisi.*

ec-qui, ecquae *or* **ecqua, ecquod,** *pronoun interrog., adj.* any.

ec-quis, ec-quid, *pron. interrog. subst.* whether any? any one? any thing? *adj.* = *ecqui.*

ĕcŭlĕus = *equuleus (q.v.).*

ĕdācĭtas -ātis, *f.* greediness.

ĕdax -ācis, *f.* greedy; destructive.

ēdīco -dixi -dictum, 3. to make known, publish, order, appoint; to decree.

ēdictum -i, *n.* decree, edict; proclamation.

ēdisco -didici, 3. to learn thoroughly, learn by heart; *ad verbum,* word for word; to learn, study.

ēdissĕro -serŭi -sertum, 3. to explain, relate fully.

ēdisserto, 1. to explain, relate exactly.

ēdĭtĭcius -a -um, announced, proposed; *iudices,* the panel of 125 judices (jury), of which the accused could reject 75.

ēdĭtĭo -ōnis, *f.* the publishing of a book; a statement.

ēdĭtus -a -um, *p. adj.,* high, lofty; *subst.,* **ēdĭtum -i,** *n.* a lofty situation, height.

1. ĕdo, ĕdi, ĕsum, edere *or* **esse,** to eat; to consume, corrode.

2. ēdo -dĭdi -dĭtum, 3. to give out; to give birth to; *Maecenas atavis edite regibus,* descended from; to produce; to utter; to publish; to spread a report; to relate, tell; *of oracles,* to answer; to fix, *iudicium; tribus,* to nominate; to command; to cause, furnish; *of time,* to bring to an end, *vitam; partic. subst.,* **ēdita -ōrum,** *n.* commands.

ēdŏcĕo -dŏcŭi -doctum, 2. to teach, instruct thoroughly, to inform fully.

ēdŏlo, 1. to hew out with an axe, to bring into shape, complete.

ědŏmo -dŏmŭi -dŏmitum, 1. to tame thoroughly, entirely subdue.

ēdormio, 4. to have one's sleep out. *Transit.,* to sleep off.

ēdŭcātĭo -ōnis, *f.* training, education.

ēdŭcātor -ōris, *m.* one who trains or brings up; a foster-father; a tutor.

ēdŭcātrix -īcis, *f.* foster-mother, nurse.

1. **ēdŭco,** 1. to bring up, rear, educate.

2. **ēdūco -duxi -ductum,** 3. to draw out, lead out; *naut.,* to take a ship out; to bring water (*by aqueduct*); to build a wall on to a river; to raise up; *in astra,* to praise sky high; to rear a child; *of time,* to live, spend.

ēdūlis -e, eatable.

ēdūro, 1. to last, endure.

ēdūrus -a -um, very hard.

effarcio (*no perf.*) **-fertum,** 4. to stuff full.

effātum -i, *n.* an announcement, prediction; an axiom.

effectĭo -ōnis, *f.* a doing, practising; an efficient cause.

effector -ōris, *m.* one who produces, causes, originates.

effectrix -trīcis, *f.* she that causes *or* produces.

1. **effectus -a -um,** *partic.* of *efficio.*

2. **effectus -ūs,** *m.,* doing, performance; effect, consequence.

effēmĭnātē, *adv.* effeminately.

effēmĭnātus -a -um, *p. adj.,* effeminate.

effēmino, 1. to make into a woman; to make effeminate, to enervate.

efferātus -a -um, *p. adj.,* wild, savage.

effercio, *v. effarcio.*

efferĭtas -ātis, *f.* savageness.

1. **effero,** 1. to make savage.

2. **effero (ecfero), extŭli, ēlātum, efferre,** to carry out, bring out; *pedem or se efferre,* to betake oneself; *milit., efferre signa,* to march out; to bury; to bring forth; to utter, to express; to publish; *se,* to show itself ; to carry away ; to make to appear; to raise; to praise; *efferri or se efferre,* to pride oneself on; *partic., elatus,* puffed up.

effertus -a -um, *p. adj.,* stuffed full, full.

efferus -a -um, *savage.*

effervesco -ferbŭi *and* **-fervi,** 3. to boil up, effervesce; to rage; *of an orator,* to be passionate.

effervo, 3. to boil up *or* over; to swarm forth.

effētus -a -um, exhausted, effete.

efficācĭtas -ātis, *f.* efficacy, efficiency.

efficācĭtěr, *adv.* effectively, efficaciously.

efficax -ācis, *adj.* effective, efficient; *Hercules,* active.

efficiens -entis, *p. adj.,* efficient, effective; *efficiens voluptatis,* cause of.

efficienter, *adv.* efficiently, powerfully.

efficientia -ae, *f.* efficiency.

efficĭo -fēci -fectum, 3. to produce, effect, make; to build; *of land,* to bear; *of number,* to make up; (*pass., effici,* come

to); to bring together; *philosoph.,* to prove; show; to make, *Catilinam consulem;* to accomplish, complete.

effĭgĭēs -ēi, *f.* or **effĭgĭa -ae,** *f.* an image, likeness; form, shape; a shade, ghost; abstract, copy, imitation.

effingo -finxi -fictum, 3. to wipe off, wipe out; to form; to represent; to express in words; to imitate, strive to reach; to conceive.

efflāgĭtātĭo -ōnis, *f.* an urgent demand.

efflāgĭtātus -ūs, *m.* an urgent request.

efflāgĭto, 1. to demand, entreat.

efflīgo -flixi -flictum, 3. to kill, slay.

efflo, 1. *transit.,* to blow out, breathe out; *intransit.,* to breathe forth.

efflōresco -flōrŭi, 3. to blossom, flourish.

efflŭo -fluxi, 3. to flow out; to vanish; to be forgotten; *of time,* to disappear; to come to light, become known.

efflŭvĭum -ĭi, *n.* flowing out, outlet.

effŏdĭo -fōdi -fossum, 3. to dig out; to gouge out; to excavate; to dig up; to rummage.

effor, 1. *dep.* to speak out, express, speak.

effrēnātē, *adv.* unrestrainedly, violently.

effrēnātĭo -ōnis, *f.* unbridled impetuosity.

effrēnātus -a -um, *p. adj.,* unbridled; unrestrained, violent.

effrēnus -a -um, unbridled; unrestrained.

effringo -frēgi -fractum, to break open; break off.

effŭgĭo -fūgi, 3. *intransit.,* to flee, escape. *Transit.,* to escape from, avoid, flee from.

effŭgĭum -ĭi, *n.* a flight; an outlet for flight; opportunity of flight.

effulgĕo -fulsi, 2. to shine out, glitter.

effultus -a -um, resting upon, supported by.

effundo -fūdi -fūsum, 2. to pour forth, shed; to empty; to throw down; to drive forth; to loosen; to send forth; *se effundere, effundi,* to pour forth ; *fruits,* to bring forth in abundance; to spend, squander; tell, impart; *reflex. and middle,* to give oneself up to, indulge in; to use, expend, make full use of; to breathe forth.

effūsē, *adv.* far and wide; *ire,* in disorder; profusely; unrestrainedly.

effūsĭo -ōnis, *f.* a pouring forth; extravagance; exuberance of spirits.

effūsus -a -um, *p. adj.,* poured forth; let loose, *effusae comae ; effuso cursu,* at full speed; wide-spread; disorderly (*in march*), *effuso agmine;* extravagant; unrestrained.

effūtĭo, 4. to blab out, chatter.

ēgĕlĭdus -a -um, lukewarm; cool.

ĕgens -entis, *p. adj.,* poor, needy, impoverished.

ĕgēnus -a -um, needy, in need of; *with genit.*

ĕgĕo -ŭi, 2. to want, be in need, be destitute ; to be in want of ; *with abl.,* *medicina ; with genit., auxilii ;* to be without, *auctoritate ;* to desire.

Ēgĕria -ae, *f.* an Italian nymph, the instructress of Numa Pompilius.

ĕgĕro -gessi -gestum, 3. to carry, bring, get out; to carry off.

ĕgestas -ātis, *f.* extreme poverty, need; *want of.*

ēgigno, 3. to produce out of.

ĕgŏ, *pron. pers.,* I, *plur.* we; *alter ego,* my second self; *ad me,* to me, to my house; *a me,* at my expense.

ēgrĕdĭor -gressus, 3. *dep.* to go out, pass out; *egredi ex navi or simply navi,* to disembark; *egredi ex portu,* to sail away ; *in discourse,* to digress ; to ascend; *transit., urbem,* to pass beyond; to go out of, *fines.*

ēgrĕgĭē, *adv.* excellently.

ēgrĕgĭus -a -um, admirable, extraordinary, distinguished.

ēgressus -ūs, *m.* departure; disembarkation; *a passage out.*

ĕheu, ēheu, *interj.,* alas ! woe !

ei (hei), *interj.,* ah ! woe !

ĕiă and **hĕiă,** *interj.,* of joy and surprise, hallo! well then ! *eia age,* quick! come then !

ēiăcŭlor, 1. *dep.* to throw out, hurl out.

ēicio (ejicio) -iēci -iectum, 3. to throw out, cast out, eject; to utter; to drive away, *cohortes; se eicere,* to rush forth; to banish; to leave unburied; to thrust out; to hiss an actor off the stage; to disapprove of; *in pass.,* to be cast ashore, stranded; *eiectus,* a shipwrecked person.

ēiectamentum -i, *n.* that which is thrown out.

ēiectio -ōnis, *f.* banishment, exile.

ēiecto, 1. to throw, cast, eject; to vomit forth.

ēiectus -ūs, *m.* a casting out.

ēiŭlātio -ōnis, *f.* wailing, lamentation.

ēiŭlātus -ūs, *m.* wailing, lamenting.

ēiŭlo, 1. to wail, lament.

ēiūro and **ēiĕro,** 1. to refuse *or* deny on oath ; *magistratum, imperium,* to resign; to abandon, disown.

ēiusdemmŏdi or **ēiusdem mŏdi,** in the same manner.

ēiusmŏdi or **ēius mŏdi,** of this kind, such.

ēlābor -lapsus, 3. *dep.* to glide out of; to slip away, escape; to be acquitted.

ēlăbōro, 1. strive, take pains, *in litteris; transit.,* to work out, produce.

ēlāmentābĭlis -e, very lamentable.

ēlanguesco -gŭi, 3. to become weak, be relaxed.

ēlargior, 4. to give liberally.

ēlātē, *adv.* loftily, arrogantly.

ēlātĭo -ōnis, *f.* flight, soaring; elevation.

ēlātro, 1. to bark out, cry out.

ēlātus -a -um, elevated, exalted.

Ēlĕa -ae, *f.* town in Lower Italy (*Lat.*

Velia), birthplace of Parmenides and Zeno, the founders of the Eleatic school of philosophy. **Ēlĕātēs -ae,** *m.* Zeno; *adj.,* **Ēlĕātĭcus,** Eleatic.

ēlectē, *adv.* choicely.

ēlectio -ōnis, *f.* choice, selection.

Ēlectra -ae *f.* daughter of Agamemnon, wife of Pylades, sister of Orestes and Iphigenia.

ēlectrum -i, *n.* amber; an alloy of gold and silver.

1. **ēlectus -a -um,** *p. adj.,* chosen, select; *of things,* choice.

2. **ēlectus -ūs,** *m.* choosing, choice.

ēlĕgans -antis, *adj.* fine, neat, elegant; *subst., elegantes,* fine folk, fine orators; *of things,* tasteful.

ēlĕgantĕr, *adv.* neatly, elegantly.

ēlĕgantĭa -ae, *f.* taste, refinement, elegance; *of oratory,* grace, correctness.

ēlĕgi -ōrum, *m.* elegiac verses.

ēlĕgīa -ae, *f.* a poem in elegiac verse.

Ēlĕleus -ĕi, *m.* surname of Bacchus.

Ēlĕlēĭdes -um, *f.* Bacchantes.

ēlĕmentum -i, *n.* an element, first principle; *plur. elementa,* letters of the alphabet; rudiments; beginnings.

ēlenchus -i, *m.* pendant worn as earring.

ēlĕphantus -i, *c.* an elephant; ivory.

ēlĕphās (-ans) -phantis, *m.* the elephant.

Ēleusin(is) -īnis, *f.* in Attica, famous for the worship of Ceres. *Adj.,* **Ēleusīnus.**

Ēleuthĕrĭus -a -um, making free. *Subst.,* the Liberator, surname of Jupiter.

ēlĕvo, 1. to raise, elevate; to lessen; to weaken, disparage; to alleviate.

ēlĭcio -lĭcŭi (-lexi) -lĭcĭtum, 3. to allure, entice out; to invoke the presence of a god; to invite, induce; to produce, cause; to win from, gain; to search out; to awake.

ēlīdo -līsi -līsum, 3. to strike, thrust, drive out; to shatter.

ēlĭgo -lēgi -lectum, 3. to choose, select; to root out.

ēlīmino, 1. to carry over the threshold.

ēlīmo, 1. to file off, smooth, polish; to elaborate, perfect.

ēlinguis -e, speechless, without eloquence.

Ēlis -idis, *f.* territory of Western Peloponnesus, in which the Olympic games were held.

Ēlissa (Ēlisa) -ae, *f.* another name of Dido.

ēlix -icis, *m.* a deep furrow to withdraw moisture from the roots of plants.

ēlixus -a -um, boiled.

ellĕbŏrus (hellĕbŏrus) -i, *m. and gen.* **ellĕbŏrum (hellĕbŏrum) -i,** *n.* hellebore.

ēlŏco, 1. to let, let on hire.

ēlŏcūtio -ōnis, *f.* oratorical delivery, elocution.

ēlŏgĭum -ĭi, *n.* a short maxim; epitaph; clause in a will, codicil.

ēlŏquens -entis, *p. adj.,* eloquent.

ēlŏquentĭa -ae, *f.* eloquence.

ēlŏquĭum -ĭi, *n.* speech; eloquence.

ēlŏquor -lŏcūtus (-lŏquūtus) sum, 3. *dep.* to speak out, express.

Elpēnor -ŏris, *m.* one of the companions of Ulysses, changed by Circe into a hog.

ēlūcĕo -luxi, 2. to beam forth, glitter.

ēluctor, 1. *dep. intransit.*, to struggle out, burst forth; *transit.*, to surmount a difficulty.

ēlūcŭbro, 1. to compose by lamplight; *Dep. form*, **ēlūcŭbror**, 1.

ēludo -lūsi -lūsum, 3. *intransit.*, to dash forth, play (*of waves*); *transit.*, to parry a blow; to evade; to mock.

ēlūgĕo -luxi, 2. *intransit.*, to mourn for anyone during the prescribed period; *transit.*, to mourn for.

ēlumbis -e, weak in the loins; *of orators*, feeble.

ēlŭo -lŭi -lūtum, 3. to wash out, rinse, cleanse; to wash away, remove.

ēlūtus -a -um, *p. adj.*, watery, insipid.

ēlŭvies -ēm -e, *f.* flood; a sewer; a chasm, gully.

ēlŭvio -ōnis, *f.* an inundation.

Ēlўsium -ii, *n.* Elysium.

em, *interj.*, ha ! indeed !

ēmancĭpo (ēmancŭpo), 1. to release a son from the *patria potestas*; to transfer a son to the power of another; give up, transfer.

ēmāno, 1. to flow out; to arise, spring from; to spread abroad.

Ēmăthīa -ae, *f.* an old name for Macedonia; a district of Macedonia.

ēmātūresco -tūrŭi, 3. to become ripe; to be softened, *ira*.

ēmax -ācis, fond of buying.

emblēma -ătis, *n.* inlaid *or* mosaic work; raised *or* relief ornaments.

embŏlium -ii, *n.* dramatic interlude.

ēmendābilis -e, that may be amended.

ēmendāte, *adv.* correctly.

ēmendātĭo -ōnis, *f.* improvement, emendation.

ēmendātor -ōris, *m.* an amender, corrector.

ēmendātrix -īcis, *f.* she who corrects *or* amends.

ēmendātus -a -um, *p. adj.*, free from mistakes, perfect.

ēmendo, 1. to correct, improve.

ēmentĭor -ītus, 4. *dep.*, to falsify, pretend; to make false statements; *partic. perf. (pass.)*, *auspicia ementita*.

ēmĕrĕo -ŭi -ĭtum, 2. *and* **ēmĕrĕor** -ĭtus, 2. *dep.* to deserve; to deserve well of, *aliquem*; to serve; *partic.*, *emeritus*, a soldier that has served his time, a veteran; old, disused; *tempus emeritum*, ended.

ēmergo -mersi -mersum, 3. *transit.*, to cause to rise; *emergere se or emergi*, to rise, emerge; to free oneself, *ex malis. Intransit.*, to come forth, emerge; to extricate oneself; to come to light, appear.

ēmĕrĭtus -a -um (*partic. of emereo*).

ēmĕtĭca -ae, *f.* an emetic.

ēmētĭor -mensus sum, 4. *dep.* to measure out; to pass over, traverse; *partic. perf. pass.*, *toto emenso spatio;* to pass through a space of time; to bestow.

ēmēto (-messŭi) -messum, 3. to reap, mow.

ēmĭco -mĭcŭi -mĭcātum, 1. to spring out, appear quickly, dart forth; to break out; to shine forth, be distinguished; *of weapons*, to whiz forth; to rush up; to jump up.

ēmĭgro, 1. to wander forth, migrate; *e vita*, to die.

ēmĭnens -entis, *p. adj.*, prominent, projecting, lofty; illustrious, eminent. *Subst.*, **ēminentes** -ium, *m.* distinguished men.

ēmĭnentĭa -ae, *f.* prominence.

ēmĭnĕo -mĭnŭi, 2. to project, stand out; to appear, become visible; to be conspicuous, eminent.

ēmĭnŭs, *adv. milit.*, at a distance, from a distance.

ēmīror, 1. *dep.* to be astonished at.

ēmissārĭum -ii, *n.* an outlet for water.

ēmissārĭus -ii, *m.* emissary, spy.

ēmissĭo -ōnis, *f.* a sending forth; letting loose.

ēmissus -ūs, *m.* sending forth.

ēmitto -mīsi -missum, 3. to send forth; to drive away; to hurl forth; to let forth; *of a book*, to publish; to let go, let loose; *in the circus*, to start; *of slaves, aliquem manu*, to free.

ēmo, ēmi, emptum, 3. to buy, purchase; *bene*, cheap ; *male*, dear ; to bribe. *Subst.*, **emptum** -i, *n.* the contract of sale.

ēmŏdĕror, 1. *dep.* to moderate.

ēmŏdŭlor, 1. *dep.* to sing, praise in verse.

ēmŏlĭmentum = *emolumentum (q.v.)*.

ēmollĭo -īvi -ītum, 4. to soften ; to make mild; to make effeminate.

ēmŏlŭmentum -i, *n.* effort, labour, exertion; gain, advantage.

ēmŏnĕo, 2. to warn, admonish.

ēmŏrĭor -mortŭus sum -mŏri, *dep.* to die; to perish.

ēmŏvĕo -mōvi -mōtum, 2. to move out, remove; to shake, shatter.

Empĕdŏclēs -is, *m.* a philosopher of Agrigentum.

empīrĭcus -i, *m.* an unscientific physician.

empŏrĭum -ii, *n.* mart, emporium.

emptĭo -ōnis, *f.* a buying, purchasing; a purchase.

emptĭto, 1. to buy up, to buy.

emptor -ōris, *m.* buyer, purchaser.

ēmulgĕo -mulsum, 2. to milk out; *poet.* to drain out.

ēmungo -munxi -munctum, 3. to blow the nose; to cheat.

ēmūnĭo -mūnīvi *or* -mūnii -mūnītum, 4.

to fortify, make safe; prepare, make accessible.

ēn, *interj.*, lo ! behold ! see !

ēnarrābilis -e, that can be narrated.

ēnarro, 1. to tell, narrate.

ēnascor -nātus sum, 3. *dep.* to grow out of, arise from.

ēnāto, 1 to escape by swimming; to extricate oneself from a difficulty.

ēnāvātus -a -um, performed, finished.

ēnāvigo, 1. to sail away; to sail over, sail through, *undam*.

Encēlādus -i, *m.* one of the giants, slain by the lightning of Jupiter, and buried beneath Aetna.

endo, *archaic* = *in*.

Endymion -ōnis, *m.* son of Aëthlius or of Zeus and Calyce, father of Aetolus, beloved by Selene and taken to Mount Latmos in Caria, and there lulled to perpetual sleep.

ēnĕco -nĕcŭi -nectum, 1. to torment, torture.

ēnervātus -a -um, *p. adj.*, enervated, powerless, effeminate.

ēnervis -e, powerless, weak.

ēnervo, 1. to render weak, effeminate, to enervate.

ēnico = eneco (*q.v.*).

ēnim, *conj.* for; truly, certainly; *at enim, sed enim*, but then (*enim generally the second or third word in its clause*).

ēnimvēro, to be sure, certainly; but indeed.

ēnīsus, *v.* enixus and enitor.

ēnĭtĕo -ŭi, 2. to shine out, to glitter; to be conspicuous.

ēnĭtesco -tŭi, 3. to gleam, shine forth.

ēnītor -nīsus or -nixus, 3. *dep.* to struggle up, ascend, *in altiora;* to strive; to bring forth, bear; to climb.

ēnixē, *adv.* eagerly, strenuously.

ēnixus (enīsus) -a -um, *p. adj.*, strenuous, eager.

Enna = Henna (*q.v.*).

Ennius -ii, *m.* the creator of Roman epic poetry.

Ennŏsĭgaeus -i, *m.* the Earthshaker, surname of Neptune.

ēno, 1. to swim out; to escape by swimming; to fly away.

ēnōdātē, *adv.* clearly, plainly.

ēnōdātio -ōnis, *f.* explanation, exposition.

ēnōdātus -a -um, *p. adj.*, freed from knots, explained.

ēnōdis -e, without knots.

ēnōdo, 1. to take out the knots; to explain.

ēnormis -e, irregular, unusual; immense.

ēnōtesco -notŭi, 3. to become known, public.

ensĭfer -fĕra -fĕrum, sword-bearing.

ensis -is, *m.* a sword.

ēnūbo -nupsi -nuptum, 3. to marry out of one's rank *or* from one town to another.

ēnuclĕātē, *adv.* clearly, concisely.

ēnuclĕātus -a -um, *p. adj.*, of discourse, clear, unadorned.

ēnuclĕo, 1. to take out the kernel; *enucleata suffragia*, free from corrupt motives.

ēnŭmĕrātio -ōnis, *f.* enumeration; *in rhetoric, recapitulation*.

**ēnŭmĕro, 1. to reckon, enumerate, pretium*, to pay; to recapitulate.

ēnuntiātio -ōnis, *f.* enunciation, proposition.

ēnuntiātum, *n.* proposition.

ēnuntio, 1. to tell, disclose; to declare, announce; *logic*, to state a proposition.

ēnuptio -ōnis, *f.* marriage out of one's own condition.

ēnūtrio -ivi -ītum, 4. to nourish, rear.

1. **ĕo, ivi** *and* **ii, ire**, to go; *maximis itineribus*, to make forced marches; *cubitum*, to go to bed; *ad arma*, to prepare for war; *in sententiam*, to support a motion in the senate; *in alia omnia*, to oppose a motion; to move; *of liquids*, to flow; to pass away; to happen; *ire in aliquid*, to be changed to.

2. **ĕo**, *adv.* thither, to that place; so far, to such a pitch; *eo usque*, to that point; *eo magis*, the more.

ĕōdem, *adv.* to the same place, just so far.

ĕopse = eo ipso.

Ēŏs *and* **Ēōs** (*only in nom.*), *f.* dawn; *adj.* **Ēōus** *and* **Ēōus**. *Subst.*, **Ēōus -i**, *m.* **a**, the morning star, the East.

ĕpastus -a -um, eaten up.

ĕphēbus -i, *m.* a youth from his sixteenth to his twentieth year (*of Greeks*).

ĕphēmĕris -idis, *f.* journal, diary.

phēsus -i, *m.* one of the twelve Ionic towns in Asia Minor. *Adj.* **Ēphĕsius**.

ĕphippium -i, *n.* horse-cloth, saddle.

ĕphŏrus -i, *m.* the ephor, a Spartan magistrate.

ĕpicōpus -a -um, provided with oars.

Epicūrus -i, *m.* Athenian philosopher.

ĕpicus -a -um, epic.

ĕpigramma -ătis, *n.* an inscription on the base of a statue; an epigram

ĕpĭlŏgus -i, *m.* a conclusion, peroration, epilogue.

Ēpĭmētheus -ĕi *and* **-ĕos**, *m.* brother of Prometheus.

ĕpĭrēdium -ii, *n.* strap by which a horse was fastened to a vehicle, trace.

Ēpīrus -i, *f.* a country of Greece, between Macedonia, Thessaly, and the Ionian Sea, part of the present Albania.

ĕpistŏla -ae, *f.* letter, epistle.

ĕpistŏlium -ii, *n.* a little letter, note.

ĕpĭtáphius -ii, *m.* funeral oration.

ĕpĭtŏma -ae, *and* **ĕpĭtŏmē -ēs**, *f.* an abridgment, epitome.

ĕpōdes -um, *m.* a kind of salt-water fish.

ĕpops -ŏpis, *m.* the hoopoe.

ĕpos, *indecl. n.* epic poem.

ĕpōto -pōtāvi -pōtus *and* **pōtātūrus**, to drink up, drink out (*in class. Lat. only* *in partic. perf.*); *poculo epoto; poet.* to swallow up.

ĕpŭlae -ārum, *f.* food, dishes; banquet.

ĕpŭlāris -e, relating to a banquet.

ĕpŭlātĭo -ōnis, *f.* a feasting, revelling.

ĕpŭlo -ōnis, *m.* reveller, feaster.

ĕpŭlor, 1. *dep.* to feast, eat. *Intranst., unā,* together.

ĕpŭlum -i, *n.* a public banquet, entertainment.

ĕqua -ae, *f.* a mare.

ĕques -itis, *c.* horseman, horse-soldier, *and collectively,* cavalry; *equites,* the knights, a distinct order.

ĕquester -stris -stre, relating to horsemen and horsemanship, equestrian; relating to cavalry; relating to the knights. *Subst.,* **ĕquester -stris,** *m.* a knight.

ĕquidem, indeed, truly; *n a concessive sense,* of course, certainly.

ĕquīnus -a -um, relating to horses.

ĕquĭtātŭs -ūs, *m.* cavalry; the equestrian order.

ĕquĭto, 1. to ride on horseback; *of winds,* to rush.

ĕquŭlĕus -i, *m. (dim. of equus),* a young horse, colt.

ĕquŭlus -i, *m. (dim. of equus),* a colt.

ĕquus -i, *m.* a horse; *equum conscendere; vehi in equo.*

ērādo -rāsi -rāsum, 3. to scratch out, to strike off; to destroy, eradicate.

Ĕrăto -ūs, *f.* the muse of amorous poetry.

Ĕrătosthĕnēs -is, *m.* a Greek philosopher and poet.

ercisco, erctum = hercisco, herctum *(q.v.).*

Ĕrĕbus -i, *m* a god of the lower world; the lower world.

Ĕrechtheus -ĕi, *m.* mythical king of Athens, father of Orithyia; **Ĕrecthīdae -arum,** *m.* the Athenians.

ērectus -a -um, *p. adj.,* upright, erect; elevated; proud; anxious, intent; resolute, cheerful.

ērēpo -repsi -reptum, 3. to creep through; to climb.

ēreptĭo -ōnis, *f.* taking by force, seizure.

ēreptor -ōris, *m.* one who takes away by force, a robber.

ergā, *prep. with acc.* towards; in relation to (*of one's feelings*).

ergastŭlum -i, *n.* a house of correction for slaves.

ergō, *adv. with genit. preceding it,* on account of; *absol.,* consequently, accordingly, then.

ērĭcĭus -ii, *m.* a hedgehog; *milit.,* a beam thickly studded with iron spikes, chevaux-de-frise.

Ĕrĭdānus -i, *m.* poet. name of the river Padus.

ērĭgo -rexi -rectum, 3. to set up, place upright, erect; *oculos,* to raise; *of places,* to make higher; *middle,* to rise; *milit.,* to march a body of soldiers up a

height; to arouse, excite; encourage cheer; *se erigere,* to be encouraged

Ĕrĭgŏnē -ēs, *f.* the daughter of Icarus, transformed into the constellation Virgo.

Ĕrinnys (Erinys) -ўos, *f.* one of the Furies; *plur.,* **Ĕrinnyes;** scourge, curse; fury, madness.

ērĭpĭo -rĭpŭi -reptum, 3. to snatch away, pluck out, take away; *eripe te morae,* away with delay.

ērōdo (*no perf.*) **-rōsum,** 3. to gnaw away, eat into.

ērŏgātĭo -ōnis, *f.* payment, expenditure.

ērŏgo, 1. to pay from the public treasury.

errābundus -a -um, wandering.

errātĭcus -a -um, wandering, erratic.

errātĭo -ōnis, *f.* a wandering, straying.

errātum -i, *n.* a fault, error.

errātus -ūs, *m.* wandering about, straying.

1. **erro,** 1. to wander; *transit., terrae erratae,* wandered over; to lose one's way; to be mistaken.

2. **erro -ōnis,** *m.* a wanderer, vagabond.

error -ōris, *m.* a wandering about; uncertainty; error, deception; mistake.

ērŭbesco -rŭbŭi, 3. to grow red, blush; to be ashamed; **ĕrŭbescendus -a -um,** of which one should be ashamed.

ērŭcto, 1. to belch forth, vomit; to cast out.

ērŭdĭo -īvi *and* **-ii -ītum,** 4. to teach, educate.

ērŭdītē, *adv. only used in compar. and superl.* learnedly.

ērŭdītĭo -ōnis, *f.* teaching, instruction; knowledge.

ērŭdītŭlus -i, *m. (dim. of eruditus),* somewhat skilled.

ērŭdītus -a -um, *p. adj.,* learned, polished, erudite. *Subst.,* **ērŭdīti -orum,** *m.* men of education.

ērumpo -rūpi -ruptum, 3. to break through; to cause to burst forth (*reflex., se erumpere, or pass., erumpi,* to burst forth); to discharge; to vent. *Intransit.,* to burst forth; *milit.,* to rush forth; break out against; to come to light; to result.

ērŭo -rŭi -rŭtum, 3. to dig out; to dig up; to pluck away; to bring to the light of day; to destroy utterly.

ēruptĭo -ōnis, *f.* a bursting *or* breaking forth; sally, attack.

Ĕrўmanthŏs -i, *m.* a mountain in Arcadia, where Hercules slew the Erymanthian boar

Ĕrўsicthōn -thōnis, *m.* cursed by Ceres with a raging hunger.

ĕrўthīnus -a -um, a kind of red mullet.

ĕrўthraeus -a -um, reddish; *mare Erythraeum,* the Indian Ocean.

Ĕryx -rўcis, *m.* a mountain of Sicily, with a famous temple of Venus. *Adj.,* **Ĕrўcīnus.**

esca -ae, *f.* food, victuals, bait.

escārius -a -um, relating to food. *Subst.*, escāria -orum, *n.* eating utensils.

escendo -scendi -scensum, 3. to climb up, ascend.

escensio -ōnis, *f.* landing, disembarkation.

escul . . . *v.* aescul . . .

esculentus -a -um, relating to eating, edible; *subst.*, escŭlenta -orum, *n.* eatables.

Esquiliae -ārum, *f.* one of the hills on which Rome was built; *adj.*, Esquilius, Esquilīnus.

essēda -ae, *f.* = *essedum (q.v.)*.

essedārius -ii, *m.* a fighter in a warchariot.

essēdum -i, *n.* a war-chariot; a travelling chariot.

esŭrio, 4. to be hungry, desire food; to long for.

esŭritio -ōnis, *f.* hunger.

esus -a -um, *partic. of* 1. *edo.*

ĕt, *conj.* and; *et . . . et*, both . . . and; also.

ĕtĕnim, *conj.*, namely; truly, and indeed.

Ětěoclēs -is *and* -ěos, *n.* son of Oedipus.

ětēsiae -ārum, *f.* Etesian winds.

ětēsius -a -um, Etesian.

ěthŏlŏgus -i, *m.* one who mimics the peculiarities of others.

ětiam, *conj.*, as yet, still; certainly, yes, indeed; even; again; *etiam atque etiam*, again and again.

ětiam-num *and* ětiam-nunc, *adv.* yet, still, till now; *nihil etiam nunc*, nothing further.

ětiam-si, *conj.*, even if, although.

ětiam-tum *and* ětiam-tunc, *adv.*, even then, till that time, till then.

Etrūria -ae, *f.* a country in Central Italy. *Adj.*, Etruscus.

et-si, *conj.*, although, yet; and yet, notwithstanding.

eu, *interj.*, good! well done!

Euander -dri, *and* Euandrus -i, *m.* son of Hermes, who built a town on the Palatine hill. *Adj.*, Euandrius.

Euboea -ae, *f.* island in the Aegean Sea; *adj.*, Euboĭcus -a -um.

Euclīdes -is, *m.* 1. philosopher of Megara; 2. mathematician of Alexandria.

ěuge, *interj.*, well done!

euhan (euan), *interj.*, shout of the Bacchanals.

euhans (euans) -antis, shouting euhan, *of the Bacchanals.*

Euhias (Euias) -ădis, *f.* a Bacchante.

Euhius (Euius) -ii, *m.* surname of Bacchus.

euhoe, *interj.*, shout of the Bacchantes.

Euměnides -um, *f.* Eumenides, the gracious ones, *euphemistic name for the Furies.*

eunŭchus -i, *m.* a eunuch.

Euphorbus -i, *m.* a Trojan, whose soul Pythagoras believed to have descended to himself.

Euripĭdes -is *and* -i, *m.* the celebrated Athenian tragic poet.

Eurōpa -ae, *f.*, *and* Eurōpē -ēs, *f.* 1. A maiden carried off to Crete by Jupiter. 2. The continent of Europe.

eurōus -a -um, eastern.

eurus -i, *m.* a south-east wind; an east wind.

Eurydĭce -ēs, *f.* wife of Orpheus.

Eurystheūs -ěi, *m. myth.*, son of Sthenelus, king in Mycenae, who imposed on Hercules his twelve labours.

Euterpē -ēs, *f.* the muse of harmony.

Euxīnus -a -um, epithet of the Black Sea.

ēvādo -vāsi -vāsum, 3. to go out; *in transit.*, to escape, got off; to turn out, issue, become; to result; *transit.*, to climb; to pass, travel over; to escape.

ēvāgor, 1. *dep. intransit.*, to wander, stray away; *milit.*, to wheel to the right *and* left, manœuvre; *transit.*, to overstep.

ēvălesco -vălŭi, 3. to grow strong; to prevail, come into vogue; to be able.

ēvan, *v.* euhan.

ēvānesco -vānŭi, 3. to vanish, pass away.

ēvănidus -a -um, vanishing, passing away.

ēvans, *v.* euhans.

ēvasto, 1. to devastate.

ēvěho -vexi -vectum, 3. to carry out; to raise; *evehi, of ships*, to sail away; *se evehere and evehi*, to ride away.

ēvello -velli -vulsum, 3. to tear out, erase, remove; to tear away.

ēvěnio -vēni -ventum, 4. to come out; to result; *bene*, to fall to the lot of; to happen.

ēventum -i, *n.* consequence of an action; event.

ēventus -ūs, *m.* consequence, result; end catastrophe; an occurrence; fate.

ēverbero, 1. to strike violently, flap.

ēvergo, 3. to send out.

ēverricŭlum -i, *n.* fishing-net, drag-net.

ēverro -verri -versum, 3. to sweep out; to plunder.

ēversio -ōnis, *f.* an overturning; destruction, ruin.

ēversor -ōris, *m.* destroyer.

ēverto -verti -versum, 3. to throw down; to demolish, to overthrow, destroy; *aliquem* to ruin politically, to expel.

ēvestigatus -a -um, tracked out, discovered.

ēvĭdens -entis, *adj.* visible; clear, evident.

ēvĭdentěr, *adv.* visibly, manifestly.

ēvĭdentia -ae, *f.* distinctness of language.

ēvĭgilo, 1. *intransit.*, to watch, be vigilant; *transit.*, to watch through, pass watching; to elaborate carefully.

ēvĭlesco -vĭlŭi, 3. to become vile, contemptible.

4

ēvincio -vinxi -vinctum, 4. to bind, bind round.

ēvinco -vīci -victum, 3. to conquer entirely, utterly subdue; to bring it about that; *with ut and the subj.*, to prove irresistibly.

ēviscĕro, 1. to eviscerate, tear in pieces.

ēvītābilis -e, that can be avoided.

ēvīto, 1. to avoid, shun.

Ēvius, *v. Euhius.*

ēvŏcātor -ōris, *m.*, one who calls to arms.

ēvŏcātus -a -um, *subst.*, a veteran who had served his time but was liable to be called.

ēvŏco, 1. to call out; to summon; to call forth, produce.

ēvoe, *v. euhoe.*

ēvŏlo, 1. to fly out, fly away; to rush forth, hasten away; to fly up.

ēvŏlūtio -ōnis, *f.* the unrolling, *and hence*, reading of a book.

ēvolvo -volvi -vŏlūtum, 3. to roll out, roll forth; to extricate; to deprive; *of news, evolvi*, to spread; to open, unwind; *of the fates*, to spin; to read, study; to make clear, narrate; to find out; to think over.

ēvŏmo -ŭi -itum, 3. to vomit forth; cast out.

ēvulgo, 1. to publish, make known.

ēvulsio -ōnis, *f.* a plucking out.

ex (e), *prep. with abl.* from *or* out of; *ex sua persona*, in one's own name, for oneself; *of time*, since, after, immediately upon; *aliud ex alio*, one after another; *diem ex die*, day after day; from out of, of, *unus ex meis intimis;* according to, in accordance with, *ex edicto; ex mea, tua re*, for my, thy advantage. *Adv. phrases, ex industria*, designedly; *ex parte*, in part.

exācerbo, 1. to irritate, provoke.

exactio -ōnis, *f.* expulsion; exacting, collecting of debts; management; *pass.*, income.

exactor -ōris, *m.* one who expels; a collector of taxes; an inspector, superintendent.

exactus -a -um, *p. adj.*, accurate, exact.

exăcŭo -ŭi -ūtum, 3. to sharpen to a point, make sharp; to stir up, inflame.

exadversum *or* exadversus, *prep. with acc.*, opposite.

exaedificātio -ōnis, *f.* a building up.

exaedifico, 1. to build; to finish.

exaequātio -ōnis, *f.* a making equal, equality.

exaequo, 1. to make equal; to compare.

exaestŭo, 1. *intransit.*, to boil up, foam up; *transit.*, to give forth.

exaggĕrātio -ōnis, *f.* elevation, exaltation.

exaggĕro, 1. to heap up; to raise, elevate; to increase; to exalt, magnify.

exăgitātor -ōris, *m.* one who blames.

exăgito, 1. to drive anything from its position; *of animals*, to hunt; to raise;

to harass, disturb; to scold, blame; to excite.

exalbesco -bŭi, 3. to grow white, turn pale.

exāmen -inis, *n.* a swarm, *of bees;* a throng, crowd; the tongue of a balance; testing, investigation.

exāmino, 1. to weigh, to consider.

exanclo, 1. to exhaust, empty; to suffer, endure.

exănimātio -ōnis, *f.* fright, terror.

exănimis -e *and gen.* exănimus -a -um, lifeless, dead; senseless with terror.

exănimo, 1. to deprive of breath; to stun; to kill; to exhaust, weaken; to breathe out.

exantlo = *exanclo (q.v.).*

exaptus -a -um, fastened, attached.

exardesco -arsi -arsum, 3. to take fire, kindle; to become hot; *of persons*, to be violently excited; *of love*, to burn; to break out, *exarsit bellum.*

exāresco -ārŭi, 3. to dry. *Fig.*, become exhausted.

exarmo, 1. to disarm.

exăro, 1. to plough up, dig up; to plough; to write on waxen tablets.

exaspĕro, 1. *of the sea*, to make stormy; to make savage; to irritate, excite.

exauctōro, 1. to discharge; *se exauctorare*, to leave the service.

exaudio, 4. to hear plainly; to hear favourably; *aliquid*, to listen to prayers; *aliquem*, to obey.

exaugĕo, 2. to increase exceedingly.

exaugŭrātio -ōnis, *f.* a desecrating.

exaugŭro, 1. to desecrate, profane.

excaeco, 1. to make blind; to stop a river *or* channel.

excandescentia -ae, *f.* heat, irascibility.

excandesco -dŭi, 3. to become hot with passion, to glow.

excanto, 1. to charm out.

excarnifico, 1. to tear to pieces.

excăvo, 1. to hollow out, excavate.

excēdo -cessi -cessum, 3. *Intransit.*, to go out, away, from; *excedere palmā*, to resign the prize; to digress; to go beyond, exceed; to attain to; to result in, turn to; to pass beyond. *Transit.*, to leave; to pass beyond.

excellens -entis, *p. adj.*, high, excellent, remarkable.

excellentĕr, *adv.* excellently.

excellentia -ae, *f.* excellence, distinguished merit; *propter excellentiam*, pre-eminently.

excello, 1. to excel, be distinguished, be eminent.

excelsē, *adv.* loftily.

excelsitas -ātis, *f.* height; *animi*, elevation.

excelsus -a -um, *p. adj.*, lofty, elevated. *Subst.*, excelsum -i, *n.* a lofty place; distinguished, illustrious; *subst.*, excelsum -i, *n.* high dignity; *plur.*, high honours; *of the mind*, dignified, elevated.

exceptio -ōnis, *f.* an exception, restriction.

excepto, 1. to take out, catch up; *auras*, to snuff up.

excerno -crēvi -crētum, 3. to sift, sort; *haedi excreti*, separated from their mothers.

excerpo -cerpsi -cerptum, 3. to pick out; to gather out, choose; separate.

excessus -ūs, *m* death..

excētra -ae, *f.* a snake, *poet.*; a spiteful woman.

excidium -ii, *n.* destruction.

1. **excido** -cidi, 3. to fall out, fall down; to be lost; to slip out, escape; to vanish, pass away; *excidit illa metu*, swooned, fainted; he forgotten; to fail.

2. **excido** -cīdi -cīsum, 3. to cut out; to hew out; to destroy; *portas*, force open; to banish.

excieo -civi -citum, 2. *and (gen.)* **excio** -civi *and* -cii -cītum, 4. to call forth; to summon to help; to provoke; to arouse; to frighten; *of things, tumultum*, to shake.

excipio -cēpi -ceptum, 3. to take out; to except; to make a condition; to take up; to listen, overhear; to receive, *vulnera*; to undertake, *labores magnos*; to endure; to catch; to entertain; to attack; to hear; to await; to follow, succeed; to continue, prolong, *memoriam viri*; *poet.* to lie towards.

excisio -ōnis, *f.* destruction.

excitatus -a -um, *p. adj.*, vigorous, loud, *clamor*.

excito, 1. to summon; *memoriam*, to renew; to rouse; to console; to erect; to kindle; to produce; *fletum*, to provoke, cause.

exclāmātio -ōnis, *f. rhet.*, an exclamation.

exclāmo, 1. *intransit.*, to shout; *transit.*, to shout out, call aloud by name, *Ciceronem*.

exclūdo -clūsi -clūsum, 3. to shut out, exclude; *of a place*, to separate; to remove; to hinder; *of birds*, to hatch.

exclūsio -ōnis, *f.* exclusion.

excōgitātio -ōnis, *f.* a contriving.

excōgito, 1. to scheme, devise.

excolo -cōlŭi -cultum, 3. to cultivate carefully; *lanas rudes*, to spin; to adorn, refine; to serve, honour.

excŏquo -coxi -coctum, 3. to boil down; to melt down, refine; to bake.

excors -cordis, foolish.

excrēmentum -i, *n. oris*, saliva.

excresco -crēvi -crētum, 3. to grow up, spring up.

excrūcio, 1. to torture.

excubiae -ārum, *f.* a keeping watch; *poet.*, *excubiae divûm aeternae*, the everlasting fire; watchmen, guard.

excubitor -ōris, *m.* a sentinel, watchman.

excubo -bŭi -bitum, 1. *to lie, or sleep*

---

out of doors; to stand sentinel, keep watch; to be watchful.

excūdo -cūdi -cūsum, 3. to strike out; to hatch; to hammer, forge; *of bees*, to mould; to compose (*of writing*).

exculco, 1. to trample firm, tread hard.

excurro -cŭcurri *and* -curri -cursum, 3. to run out, hasten forth; *milit.*, to attack; make a sortie; to make a digression; *of places*, to project.

excursio -ōnis, *f.* a stepping forward; an attack, sally.

excursor -ōris, *m.* a scout, skirmisher.

excursus -ūs, *m.* a running forth; *milit.*, an attack, sally.

excūsābilis -e, excusable.

excūsātio -ōnis, an excuse; *plur.*, *grounds* of excuse; refusal, declining; plea, defence.

excūso, 1. to excuse; to allege in excuse, to plead; to decline; *excusari with abl.*, to be excused from.

excussus -a -um, *partic. of excutio.*

excŭtio -cussi -cussum, 3. to shake out, throw out, drive out; to remove; to tear away; *of weapons*, to shoot; to throw, to drive away; to press out; to force; to destroy, make void; to spread out; to shake violently; to search, examine; to test.

exec . . . *v.* **exsec.**

exēdo -ēdi -ēsum, 3. to eat up, consume, destroy. *Fig.*, to wear away, exhaust.

exēdra -ae, *f.* room, *or* hall for conversation *or* debate.

exēdrium -ii, *n.* sitting room.

exemplar -āris, *n.* (**exemplāre** -is, *n.*), copy, pattern, example; image, likeness.

exemplāris -e, serving as a copy. *Subst.*, **exemplāres**, copies.

exemplum -ii, *n.* a copy, manner, fashion; a pattern, original; a model; a warning, example, exemplary punishment; instance, example, proof; *ex-empli gratiâ*, for example.

exĕo -ii (-ivi) -itum, 4 *intransit.*, to go out, away, forth; to spring up, sprout forth; to rise in the air; to become known, *exit oratio*; *of time*, to come to an end, pass away; *transit.*, to pass over, beyond; to ward off.

exeq . . . *v.* **ex-seq.**

exercĕo -ŭi -itum, 2. to work thoroughly, fatigue; to exercise; to employ in work; to work hard at; to harass; to exercise, practise; *milit.*, to drill; *reflex.*, *se exercere and middle exerceri*, to practise, exercise; to employ, use; to cultivate; *of mines*, to work; to preside over, to conduct; *vectigalia*, to manage.

exercitātio -ōnis, *f.* practice, exercise.

exercitātus -a -um, *p. adj.*, busied; practised; troubled.

exercitium -ii, *n.* practice, exercise.

exercito, 1. to practise.

1. **exercitus -a -um,** *p. adj.*, trained, schooled; vexations, harassing.

2. **exercitus -ūs,** *m.* army; infantry.

exēsor -ōris, *m.* one who gnaws *or* eats away.

exhālātio -ōnis, *f.* an exhalation, vapour.

exhālo, 1. *transit.*, to exhale, emit vapour; *intransit.*, to breathe forth.

exhaurio -hausi -haustum, 4. to draw out; to take out; to take away; to empty out; to exhaust, impoverish; to complete. *mandata;* to endure.

exhērēdo, 1. to disinherit.

exhērēs -ēdis, disinherited.

exhibeo -hibŭi -hibitum, 2. to produce, bring forth; to hand over; to show, exhibit; to cause; *alicui negotium,* to cause trouble; to grant.

exhilāro, 1. to make cheerful.

exhorresco -horrŭi, 3. *intransit.,* to shudder exceedingly, be terrified; *transit.,* to tremble at.

exhortātio -ōnis, *f.* exhortation, encouragement.

exhortor, 1. *dep.* to exhort, encourage.

exigo -ēgi -actum, 3. to drive out, drive away; *otium,* to banish; to thrust; to complete, *opus; of time,* to spend; bring to an end; *exactā aetate,* at the end of life; to exact, demand; *of work,* superintend the execution of, *viam;* to measure, weigh, examine; to reflect upon.

exigŭē, *adv.* sparingly, scarcely; briefly; in a narrow spirit.

exigŭitas -ātis, *f.* smallness; paucity; shortness.

exigŭus -a -um, small, scanty; *neut.* (*subst.,* **exigŭum -i,** *n.* smallness; *spatii, of time,* short, scanty,); thin meagre; sparing; weak.

exilis -e, little, thin, meagre, poor; *of discourse,* dry; insignificant.

exilitas -ātis, *f.* thinness, meagreness, weakness.

exilitĕr, *adv.* thinly, poorly, meagrely; sparingly; uninterestingly; weakly.

eximĭē, *adv.* uncommonly, extremely.

eximius -a -um, excepted; exceptional, distinguished, excellent.

eximo -ēmi -emptum, 3. to take out, take away; *of time,* to delay, waste; *aliquid de,* to free from; *Syracusas in libertatem,* to free; to except.

exin = *exinde* (*q.v.*).

exinānio -ivi -itum, 4. to empty.

exinde (exin), *adv. of place,* from there, thereupon, next; *of time,* thereupon, after that, then.

existĭmātio -ōnis, *f.* opinion, judgment; reputation, good name, honour.

existĭmātor -ōris, *m.* one who forms an opinion, a critic.

existĭmo (exaestŭmo, existŭmo), 1. to consider, regard, esteem, deem; to think, be of opinion; to judge, decide; **existĭmantes -ium,** *m.* the critics.

exitĭābilis -e, deadly, destructive.

exitĭālis -e, destructive, fatal.

exitĭōsus -a -um, *adj.* fatal, deadly.

exitĭum -ii, *n.* destruction, ruin.

exitus -ūs, *m.* a going out, a place of going out, exit; the end; *of a tragedy,* the catastrophe; the end of life; the result, consequence.

exlex -lēgis, lawless, bound by no law.

exmŏvĕo = emoveo (*q.v.*).

exŏdium -ii, *n.* a comic afterpiece.

exŏlesco -lēvi -lētum, 3. to grow to full size; *only in perf. partic.,* exoletus, to be obsolete.

exŏlētus -a -um, *partic. of exolesco.*

exĕnĕro, 1. to unload; *plenas colos,* to spin off; to send away; to release, relieve.

exoptātus -a -um, *p. adj.,* desired, wished for.

exopto, 1. to desire eagerly.

exŏrābilis -e, *adj.* easily entreated, placable.

exordior -orsus sum, 4. *dep.* to begin to weave; to begin; **exorsa -ōrum,** *n.* the beginning.

exordium -ii, *n.* the warp of a web, the beginning; *of a speech,* the introduction.

exŏrior -ortus sum -ŏrīri, *dep.* 3. *and* 4. to rise, *of the sun, moon;* to appear, step forward; to rise from a misfortune, breathe again; to proceed from.

exornātio -ōnis, *f.* adorning, ornament.

exornātor -ōris, *m.* one who adorns.

exorno, 1. to furnish with; to ornament.

exŏro, 1. to entreat earnestly, obtain by entreaty, prevail upon; to propitiate, move.

1. **exorsus -a -um,** *partic. of exordior.*

2. **exorsus -ūs,** *m* a beginning.

exos -ossis, without bones.

exoscŭlor, 1. *dep.* to kiss frequently.

exosso, 1. to take out the bones.

exōsus -a -um, hating exceedingly.

expallesco -lŭi, 3. to become very pale.

expando -pansi -pansum *and* **-passum,** 3. to stretch out, expand; to explain.

expatro, 1. to squander.

expāvesco -pāvi, 3. to be exceedingly terrified.

expēdio -īvi *and* **-ii -ītum,** 4. to disengage, set free; to help out, bring off; *iaculum trans finem,* to throw; to settle, execute; to explain; to provide; *milit.,* to make ready, *naves;* to discover; *res expedit,* or *impers. expedit,* it is expedient, useful, advantageous.

expēdītē, *adv.* quickly; without difficulty.

expēdītio -ōnis, *f.* expedition.

expēdītus -a -um, *p. adj.,* unimpeded; lightly clad; (*subst.,* **expēdītus -i,** *m.* a light-armed foot-soldier); without obstacles; easy, quick; free; prepared; *of soldiers,* ready for fight; disentangled; settled, *negotia;* decisive, *victoria.*

expello -pŭli -pulsum, 3. to drive out, away; to thrust forth; to banish; to divorce, *ex matrimonio*.

expendo -pendi -pensum, 3. to weigh, examine, test; to pay.

expergĕfăcio -fēci -factum, 3. to wake up; to rouse, excite.

expergiscor parrectus sum, 3. *dep.*, to wake up, rise from sleep; to rouse oneself.

expĕriens entis, *p. adj.*, active, industrious, experienced in.

expĕrientia -ae, *f.* trial, experiment; experience.

expĕrimentum -i, *n.* trial, experiment.

expĕrior -pertus sum, 4. *dep.* to try, test, prove ; to measure one's strength with another ; to litigate ; to risk, hazard, make a trial of; *experiri tus*, to go to law; to experience, know by experience.

experrectus -a -um, *partic. of expergiscor*.

expers -pertis, having no part in, not sharing in, *with genit.*, *publici consilii*; wanting in, destitute of.

expertus -a -um, *p. adj.*, that which has been often tested, approved.

expetendus -a -um, *p. adj.*, to be desired, desirable.

expĕto -ĭvi -ītum, 3. *transit.*, to desire, wish, *or* long for; *intransit.*, to fall upon, befall.

expiātio -ōnis, *f.* atonement, expiation.

expilātio -ōnis, *f.* plundering.

expilātor -ōris, *m.* a robber.

expilo, 1. to plunder, rob.

expingo -pinxi -pictum, 3. to paint, describe.

expio, 1. to propitiate, appease ; to avert an omen; to purify; to atone for.

expiscor, 1. *dep.* to fish out; to search out, find out.

explānātē, *adv.* clearly, plainly.

explānātio -ōnis, *f.* explanation; interpretation; illustration.

explānātor -ōris, *m.* interpreter, expositor.

explānātus -a -um, *p. adj.*, clear, plain.

explāno, 1. to explain, expound ; to interpret; to state.

explaudo = explodo (*q.v.*).

explĕo -plēvi -plētum, 2. to fill, complete by filling; to amount to, make up; to fulfil, discharge; to satisfy, quench, appease; to make good; to fill up; to complete.

explētio -ōnis, *f.* satisfying.

explētus -a -um, *p. adj.*, perfect, complete.

explicātē, *adv.* plainly, clearly.

explicātio -ōnis, *f.* an unfolding, uncoiling ; explanation.

explicātor -ōris, *m.* an expounder, interpreter.

1. **explicātus -a -um**, *p. adj.*, ordered, arranged; plain, clear.

2. **explicātus ūs**, *m.* explanation, exposition.

explicitus -a -um, *p. adj.*, straightforward, easy.

explico -āvi -ātum, *and* -ŭi -ĭtum, 1. to unfold, unroll, disentangle; *frontem*, to unwrinkle; to shred out, extend; to provide, arrange ; to set free ; to accomplish, execute; *of a debt*, to pay off; to expound, interpret; to discover.

explōdo (explaudo) -plōsi -plōsum, 3. to hiss a player off the stage; to reject, disapprove.

explōrātē, *adv.* certainly, definitely.

explōrātio -ōnis, *f.* an investigation.

explōrātor -ōris, *m.* an explorer, scout, spy.

explōrātus -a -um, *p. adj.*, established, certain, sure.

explōro, 1. to seek out, investigate; *milit.*, to spy out, reconnoitre; to test.

explōsio -ōnis, *f.* a hissing off the stage.

expōlio -ĭvi -ītum, 4. to smooth, polish, refine.

expōlītio -ōnis, *f.* a smoothing, polishing; *of discourse*, polishing, embellishing.

expōlītus -a -um, *p. adj.*, smooth, polished; refined.

expōno -pōsŭi -pŏsitum, 3. to place out, set out; *scalas*, put up; *expositus, of places*, lying towards; to land, disembark, *milites ex navibus*; to place before one; to exhibit, explain; to leave unprotected.

exporrigo -rexi -rectum, 3. to stretch out, extend.

exportātio -ōnis, *f.* exportation.

exporto, 1. to carry out; to export; to banish.

exposco -pōposci, 3. to demand vehemently, entreat earnestly; to pray for, *victoriam a diis*.

expositio -ōnis, *f.* a statement, narration.

expositus -a -um, *p. adj.*, exposed, accessible; vulgar.

expostŭlātio -ōnis, *f.* a demand; complaint, expostulation.

expostŭlo, 1. to desire, demand earnestly; to make a complaint, to expostulate.

expostus = expositus, *v. expono*.

expōtus = epotus, *v. epoto*.

expressus -a -um, *p. adj.*, *of pronunciation*, clear, distinct ; affected ; visible.

exprimo -pressi -pressum, 3. to press out, force out; to articulate distinctly; to extort; to express, represent; to describe; to translate, *aliquid Latine*; to imitate; to raise.

exprobrātio -ōnis, *f.* reproach, upbraiding.

exprobro, 1. to reproach, lay to the charge of.

exprōmo -prompsi -promptum, 3. to bring forth, produce; to utter; to display; to pronounce, state.

expromptus -a -um, *partic. of expromo.*

expugnābilis -e, that may be besieged *or* captured.

expugnātio -ōnis, *f.* the taking of any place by storm.

expugnātor -ōris, *m.* a capturer.

expugno, 1. to take by storm, capture, overcome; to destroy, violate; *quaestiones*, thwart; to compel; to accomplish.

expulsio -ōnis, *f.* expulsion.

expulso, 1. to drive out, drive back.

expulsor -ōris, *m.* one who drives out.

expultrix -trīcis, *f.* one who expels.

expungo -punxi -punctum, 3. to strike out, blot out.

expurgo, 1. to cleanse, purify; to justify, defend.

expŭto, 1. to comprehend.

exquaero = *exquiro (q.v.).*

exquīro -quīsīvi -quīsītum, 3. to seek out; to ask, inquire; to choose, select; to search, test; to ask for; **exquīsīta** -ōrum, *n.* inquiries.

exquīsītē, *adv.* accurately, carefully, admirably.

exquīsītus -a -um, *p. adj.*, choice, exquisite; artificial, far-fetched.

exsacrifico, 1. to sacrifice.

exsaevio, 4. to rage to an end, cease to rage.

exsanguis -e, bloodless, without blood; lifeless; deathly pale; exhausted, weak; *act.*, making pale.

exsarcio -sartūm, 4. to patch up, repair.

exsātio, 1. to satisfy thoroughly, satiate.

exsātūrābilis -e, that can be satiated.

exsātūro, 1. to satisfy, satiate.

exscendo = *escendo (q.v.).*

exscensio = *escensio (q.v.).*

exscindo -scīdi -scissum, 3. to destroy utterly, raze to the ground, pull down completely.

exscrĕo, 1. to cough *or* hawk out.

exscrībo -scripsi -scriptum, 3. to copy; to note down, register.

exsculpo -sculpsi -sculptum, 3. to erase; to carve *or* scoop out.

exsĕco -sĕcŭi -sectum, 1. to cut out.

exsecrābilis -e, deserving curses; cursing, execrating; deadly.

exsecrātio -ōnis, *f.* curse.

exsecrātus -a -um, *p. adj.*, cursed, execrated.

exsecror, 1. *dep.* to curse, execrate; to swear with an imprecation.

exsectio -ōnis, *f.* a cutting out.

exsĕcūtio -ōnis, *f.* accomplishment; *exsecutio Syriae,* administration of.

exsĕquiae -ārum, *f.* a funeral procession.

exsĕquiālis -e, relating to a funeral procession.

exsĕquor -sĕcūtus sum, 3. *dep.* to follow a corpse to the grave, *poet.;* to follow; to

accomplish, execute ; to assert; to avenge, punish; to relate, describe, explain ; *laudes*, to spread abroad; to find out; to endure.

exsēro -sĕrŭi- sertum, 3. to thrust out, *linguam;* to bare; to free.

exserto, 1. to stretch out.

exsībilo, 1. to hiss an actor off the stage.

exsiccātus -a -um, *p. adj.*, dry, jejune.

exsicco, 1. to dry thoroughly; to empty *by drinking.*

exsigno, 1. to mark.

exsilio -silŭi -sultum, 4. to leap out; to spring up; *gaudio,* for joy.

exsilium -ii, *n.* banishment, exile; the place of exile.

exsisto (existo) -stiti -stitum, 3. to arise, come forth, appear; come into existence.

exsolvo -solvi -sŏlūtum, 3. to loosen, unbind; *glaciem,* to dissolve; *famem,* drive away; to free; to pay; to perform a promise.

exsomnis -e, sleepless, wakeful.

exsorbĕo -sorbŭi, 2. to suck up, suck in; to endure; to devour.

exsors -sortis, without lot; specially chosen; having no share in, deprived of.

exspātior, 1. *dep.*, to digress; to deviate from the course, *of rivers.*

exspectābilis -e, probable.

exspectātio -ōnis, *f.* a waiting for, expectation.

exspectātus -a -um, *p. adj.*, expected, wished for, welcome.

exspecto, 1. to wait for, expect; to loiter; to await; to hope for, long, dread.

exspergo -spersum, 3. to scatter.

exspēs, *adj.* (*only in nom. sing.*), without hope, hopeless.

exspīrātio -ōnis, *f.* an exhalation.

exspīro, 1. to exhale; *intransit.*, to die; to blow forth, rush forth.

exspŏlio, 1. to plunder, rob.

exspŭo -spŭi -spūtum, 3. to spit out; to cast away.

externo, 1. to frighten, terrify.

exstĭmŭlātor -ōris, *m.* an instigator.

exstĭmŭlo, 1. to goad, to excite.

extinctio -ōnis, *f.* annihilation.

exstinctor -ōris, *m.* one who extinguishes; one who destroys.

exstinguo -stinxi -stinctum, 3. to put out, extinguish; to dry up; to quench; to kill; to abolish, destroy; *middle,* *exstingui,* to die.

exstirpo, 1. to root out, extirpate.

exsto (exto), 1. to stand out, project; to be visible, appear, exist; to be extant; *exstat, impers.*

exstructio -ōnis, *f.* a building up, erection.

exstrŭo -struxi -structum, 3. to heap up, pile up.

exsūdo 1. *intransit.*, to come out in

sweat; *transit.*, to sweat out, exude; to toil through.

exsūgo -suxi -suctum, 3. to suck out, suck up.

exsul -sūlis, *c.* an exile; deprived of, *with genit.*

exsūlo (exŭlo), 1. to be banished, live in exile.

exsultātio -ōnis, *f.* a leaping up; exultation.

exsultim, *adv.* friskily.

exsulto (exulto), 1. to leap up frequently *or* violently; dash up; to rejoice exceedingly, triumph; *of orators,* to run riot; *of discourse,* to move freely.

exsŭpĕrābilis -e, that can be conquered.

exsŭpĕrantia -ae, *f.* superiority, prominence.

exsŭpĕro, 1. *intransit.*, to amount up, appear above; to be prominent, excel; to prevail; *trans.,* to project above; to exceed; to surpass, to overcome.

exsurdo, 1. to deafen; *of taste,* to make dull.

exsurgo -surrexi -surrectum, 3. to rise, stand up; to regain strength.

exsuscito, 1. to awaken from sleep; to kindle fire; to excite, arouse; *se exsuscitare,* to arouse oneself, make an effort.

exta -ōrum, *n.* the entrails of animals.

extābesco -tābŭi, 3. to waste away entirely; to vanish.

extemplo, *adv.* immediately, directly.

extempōrālis -e, extemporary.

extempŭlo = extemplo (q.v.).

extendo -tendi -tensum *and* **-tentum,** 3. to stretch out, expand, extend; *of time,* to prolong (*middle,* to last); to stretch on the ground; to increase; to exert; *itinera,* to march at great speed; *famam factis,* to spread abroad.

extento, 1. to stretch out, to extend.

extentus -a -um, *p. adj.*, extended, wide.

extĕnŭātio -ōnis, *f.* a making thin; *Rhet., a figure of speech,* lessening.

extĕnŭātus -a -um, *p. adj.*, weak, poor, slight.

extĕnŭo, 1. to reduce, diminish; *aër extenuatus,* rarefied ; *extenuari in aquas,* dissolves into; *milit.,* to extend a line *or* column; to lessen, weaken; to disparage.

exter *and* **extĕrus -a -um,** outward, foreign, strange; *compar.,* **extĕrior,** *n. superl.,* **extrēmus,** the outermost; extreme; *tempora,* extreme need; the lowest, worst; **extĭmus,** the outermost; *subst.,* **extrēmum -i,** *n.* that which is outermost; the end, *ad extremum, adv.,* to the end, entirely; *plur.,* **extrēma -orum,** *n.* the end.

extĕrebro, 1. to bore out.

extergĕo -tersi -tersum, 2. to wipe off, wipe dry; to plunder.

extĕrior, exterius, *v. exter.*

extermino, 1. to drive out, expel; to remove.

externus -a -um, external; foreign, strange. *Subst.,* **externa -ōrum,** *n.* outward appearances; **externus -i,** *m.* a foreigner, a stranger, *externi* **-ōrum,** *n.* that which is foreign *or* strange.

extĕro -trīvi -trītum, 3. to rub out, rub off.

extĕrrĕo -terrŭi -territum, 2. to terrify.

extĕrus, *v. exter.*

extĭmesco -timŭi, 3. to be terrified. *Transit.,* to dread.

extĭmus, *v. exter.*

extispex -spicis, *m.* a soothsayer who predicts from the entrails of victims.

extollo, extŭli, *and rarely* **exsustŭli,** 3. to lift up; *extollere animum,* to raise; *aliquem,* to exalt; to praise, celebrate, extol ; to adorn ; to raise to rank, power, *etc.*

extorquĕo -torsi -tortum, 2. to wrest away, wrench out; to extort; to dislocate; to torture.

extorris -e, exiled, banished.

extrā, *adv.* outside (*compar.,* exterius); except. *Prep. with acc.,* beyond ; except ; outside ; without ; *extra iocum,* joking apart.

extrāho -traxi -tractum, 3. to draw out, extract; to extricate; to destroy, root out ; to draw forth ; to bring out ; to prolong; *aliquem,* to put off; to waste.

extrānĕus -a -um, not belonging to a thing, extraneous ; foreign, strange. *Subst.,* **extrānĕus -i,** *m.* a foreigner, stranger.

extrā-ordĭnārius -a -um, extraordinary, irregular; *cupiditates,* unnatural.

extrārius -a -um, outward, external; strange, foreign.

extrēmĭtas -ātis, *f.* the end, extremity.

extrēmus -a -um, *v. exter.*

extrīco, 1. to disentangle, extricate; to procure with difficulty

extrinsĕcŭs, *adv.* from the outside; on the outside, outwardly.

extrūdo -trūsi -trūsum, 3. to push out, thrust out.

extundo -tūdi, 3. to beat out; to form by beating with a hammer; to invent, devise; to force; to drive away.

exturbo, 1. to drive away, thrust out.

exūbĕro, 1. to overflow; to abound.

exul, *v. exsul.*

exulcĕro, 1. to make sore; to make worse, aggravate; to irritate, embitter.

exŭlŭlo, 1. to howl loudly; **exŭlŭlātus -a -um,** having howled; invoked with howlings.

exundo, 1. to overflow, abound.

exŭo -ŭi -ūtum, 3. to draw out *or* off, to take out; to deprive; to strip, *hostem impedimentis;* to lay aside, take off; *hominem,* human shape; to get rid of.

exūro -ussi -ustum, 3. *trans.*, to burn out; to burn up; to parch, scorch; to heat; to inflame with love.

exustio -ōnis, *f.* conflagration.

exūviae -ārum, *f.* that which is taken off from the body; dress; spoils; *of animals*, the skin *or* slough.

F

F **f**, *the sixth letter of the Latin Alphabet.*

fāba -ae, *f.* a bean.

fābālis -e, of *or* relating to beans.

fābella -ae, *f.* (*dim. of fabula*), a little story, little narrative; a fable; a little drama.

1. **fāber** -bri, *m.* a worker; *in the army*, *fabri*, the engineers; a fish, *perhaps* the dory.

2. **fāber** -bra -brum, ingenious, skilful.

Fābius -a -um, name of a Roman gens. *Qu. Fabius Maximus Cunctator*, the opponent of Hannibal in the Second Punic war. *Adj.*, **Fabius** -a -um, Fabian. **Fābiānus** -a -um.

fabrēfăcio -fēci -factum, 3. to fashion skilfully.

fabrica -ae, *f.* the art of a *faber*; working, making; the workshop of a *faber*; *pictura et fabrica*, architecture.

fabricātio -ōnis, *f.* making, framing, construction; device.

fabricātor -ōris, *m.* a maker, artificer.

Fabricius -a -um, name of a Roman gens of which the most distinguished was *C. Fabricius*, consul 282 and 278 B.C., conqueror of Pyrrhus.

fabrico, 1. to form, make, forge out of hard materials.

fabricor, 1. *dep.* to frame, make; to fashion.

fabrīlis -e, belonging to an artificer; *neut. plur. subst.*, **fabrīlia** -ium, *n.* tools.

fābŭla -e, *f.* talk; *fabulam fieri or esse*, to be the common talk; conversation; a narrative, story, fable; a drama.

fābŭlor, 1. *dep.* to talk, converse, chatter.

fābŭlōsus -a -um, renowned in story, fabled.

făcesso, **făcessi**, 3. to perform, accomplish; to depart.

făcētē, *adv.* wittily, humorously.

făcētia -ae, *f. plur.*, wit, humour.

făcētus -a -um, fine, elegant, *orator*, *sermo*; witty.

făcies -ei, *f.* the external form *or* figure; manner, kind; beauty; face.

făcilē, *adv.* easily; indisputably; willingly, *pati*.

făcilis -e, easy; *with dat.*, suitable; *e or ex facili*, easily; favourable; facile, skilful; dexterous; willing, inclined; courteous, affable.

făcilĭtas -ātis, *f.* easiness, ease; willingness, friendliness, affability, courteousness.

făcinŏrōsus -a -um, wicked, atrocious.

făcinus -ŏris, *n.* a deed, action; a crime; a criminal.

făcio, **fēci**, **factum**, 3. *transit.*, to make, prepare, build; to produce; to compose, *orationem ;* to gain; to raise, levy, *tributum ;* to do, accomplish, execute; *alicui medicinam.* to cure; *fugam*, to take to flight, *or* to put to flight; to grant; *potestatem*, permission; to cause, bring it about; *fac sciam*, let me know; *with double acc.*, to make. *Intransit.*, to act; *iacere cum*, *or ab aliquo*, to act on the side of (*archaic fut. perf.* forms, *faxo*, etc. *The passive of facio is fio, q.v.*).

factio -ōnis, *f.* a making, doing; the right of making or doing; a political party, faction.

factiōsus -a -um, fond of power, factious.

factito, 1. to make, do frequently, be accustomed to make or do; to declare openly; to follow a trade or a profession; to celebrate usually.

factum -i, *n.* a deed, act, exploit.

factus -a -um, *p. adj.*, wrought, worked; *argentum factum*, silver plate; polished, refined.

facultas -ātis, *f.* power, ability; eloquence; opportunity, means; abundance; means, resources, *gen. plur.*

fācundē, *adv.* eloquently, fluently.

fācundia -ae, *f.* eloquence, readiness of speech.

fācundus -a -um, *adj.* eloquent, fluent.

faecŭla -ae, *f.* the crust of wine.

Faesŭlae -ārum, *f.* town in Etruria, at the foot of the Apennines, *now* Fiesole.

faex, **faecis**, *f.* the dregs *or* refuse of any liquid; the dregs, the lower orders.

fāgĭnĕus -a -um, beechen.

fāgĭnus -a -um, beechen.

fāgus -a, *f.* the beech tree.

fāla -ae, *f.* a wooden tower from which missiles were thrown into a besieged city; one of the seven wooden pillars on the barrier of the circus.

fālārica (**phălārica**) -ae, *f.* a huge spear hurled with the hand; a missile covered with tow and pitch.

falcārius -ii, *m.* a scythe *or* sickle-maker; *inter falcarios*, the street of the scythe-makers.

falcātus -a -um, furnished with scythes; scythe-shaped.

falcĭfer -fĕra -fĕrum, carrying a scythe *or* sickle.

Fălernus ăger, the Falernian country in Campania. *Adj.*, **Fălernus**. *Subst.*, **Fălernum** -i, *n.* Falernian wine.

Fălisci -ōrum, *m.* a people in Etruria.

fallācia -ae, *f.* deceit, trick, fraud.

fallāciter, *adv.* deceitfully, craftily.

fallax -lācis, *adj.* deceitful, treacherous.

fallo, fĕfelli, falsum, 3. to make to slip; to make invisible; to make ineffective, to drive away; to break *a promise, etc.*; to escape the notice of, be concealed from; to deceive; *pass., fallor as middle*; to make a mistake; *impers., me fallit*, I am mistaken.

falsē, *adv.* falsely.

falsō, *adv.* falsely, wrongly.

falsus -a -um, *p. adj.*, invented, false; *falso, adv.*, falsely, deceitful, false; *Subst.*, **falsum -i**, *n.* a lie; deceit, hypocrisy; famine.

falx, falcis, *f.* scythe, sickle, pruning-hook.

fāma -ae, *f.* talk, tradition, a report, rumour; *fama est*, there is a rumour; public opinion; reputation.

fāmātus -a -um, having an ill reputation.

fāmēlicus -a -um, hungry, famished.

fāmes -is, *f.* hunger; poverty of expression; famine.

familia -ae, *f.* household; a band of gladiators; dependants; a family; sect; *paterfamilias*, head of the household or family.

familiāris -e, belonging to the slaves of a house; relating to a family *or* household; (*res familiaris*, the household; property); intimate, friendly; *of things*, ordinary, familiar. *Subst.*, servant, friend.

familiāritas -ātis, *f.* intimacy, familiarity; familiar friends.

familiāritĕr, *adv.* confidentially, intimately.

fāmōsus -a -um, *adj.* renowned; notorious; libellous.

fāmŭla, *v. famulus.*

fāmŭlāris -e, relating to servants *or* slaves.

fāmŭlātus -ūs, *m.* service, slavery.

fāmŭlor, 1. *dep.* to be a servant.

fāmŭlus -a -um, serving, servile. *Subst.*, **fāmŭlus -i**, *m.* a servant, slave; **fāmŭla -ae**, *f.* a female slave, handmaid.

fānāticus -a -um, inspired by a deity, enthusiastic, raving.

fānum -i, *n.* a temple, a holy place.

fār, farris, *n.* spelt, meal; bread.

farciō, farsi, fartum, 4. to fill full, stuff full.

farīna -ae, *f.* meal; flour; dust *or* powder of any kind.

farrāgo -inis, *f.* mixed fodder for cattle; a medley, mixture.

farrātus -a -um, provided with grain; made of corn; *neut. plur. subst., farrata*, porridge.

fartor -ōris, *m.* a fattener of fowls.

fartum -i, *n. and* **fartus -us**, *m.* the stuffing, the inside.

fās, *n. indecl.* divine law and right, divine command; that which is lawful, right; *fas est*, it is allowed, is lawful; fate, destiny.

fascia -ae, *f.* bandage, band; a woman's girdle; a streak of cloud in the sky.

fascīcŭlus -i, *m.* (*dim. of fascis*), a little bundle or packet, *torum, a nosegay*. **fascino**, 1. to bewitch.

fascinum -i, *n. and* **fascinus -i**, *m.* an enchanting, bewitching.

fasciŏla -ae, *f.* (*dim. of fascia*), a little bandage.

fascis -is, *m.* a bundle, packet; *plur., fasces*, bundles of sticks with an axe projecting, carried by lictors before the chief Roman magistrates; *fig., dare alicui fasces*, to yield the preference to.

fāsēlus, fāsēŏlus, etc. = phaselus, etc. (q.v.).

fasti -ōrum, *m., v. fastus -a -um.*

fastīdio -ivi -ītum, 4. *intrans.*, to feel distaste; *trans.*, to dislike, loathe.

fastīdiōsē, *adv.* with loathing, dislike; daintily; contemptuously.

fastīdiōsus -a -um, *adj.* full of loathing; squeamish; sick of, disgusted with, impatient of; dainty, fastidious; contemptuous, disdainful; disgusting, loathsome.

fastīdium -ii, *n.* loathing; aversion; fastidiousness, fault-finding; haughtiness.

fastīgātē, *adv.* slantingly.

fastīgātus -a -um, *partic. of fastigo.*

fastīgium -ii, *n.* a slope, descent; height; summit; the whole of the roof; the gable end; depth; dignity, position; principal point (*in writing*).

fastīgo, 1. to sharpen to a point; to slope down, *only in partic., fastigatus.*

fastōsus -a -um, proud, haughty.

1. **fastus -ūs**, *m.* pride, haughtiness.

2. **fastus -a -um**, *plur. dies fasti, or simply fasti*, the days on which the praetor could administer justice; a list of these days; calendar; a poetical form of this calendar composed by Ovid.

fātālis -e, fated, destined by fate; fateful; deadly, fatal.

fātālitĕr, *adv.* according to fate.

fătĕor, fassus sum, 2. *dep.* to confess, admit; to discover, make known.

fātĭcănus -a -um and fātĭcĭnus -a -um, prophetic.

fātĭdĭcus -a -um, prophetic; *subst.*, soothsayer.

fātĭfĕr -fĕra -fĕrum, deadly, fatal.

fătīgātio -ōnis, *f.* fatigue.

fătīgo, 1. tire, fatigue; to harass; to worry with entreaties, *etc.*

fātĭlŏquus -a -um, announcing fate, prophetic. *Subst.*, a prophet, prophetess.

fātisco, 3. *and* **fātiscor**, 3. *dep.* to crack open, part asunder; to droop, decrease.

fătŭitas -ātis, *f.* foolishness, simplicity.

fātum -i, *n.* an utterance ; prediction ; destiny, fate ; *Fata*, the Parcae *or* Fates; *fata proferre*, to prolong life ; misfortune; a cause of calamity.

fātŭus -a -um, foolish, idiotic ; *of things*, insipid, perverse. *Subst.*, **fā-tŭus** -i, *m.* a fool, idiot.

Faunus -i, *m.* god of woods and fields.

faustē, *adv.* happily, fortunately.

faustĭtas -ātis, *f.* prosperity.

Faustŭlus -i, *m.* herdsman who saved Romulus and Remus.

faustus -a um, lucky, auspicious.

fautor -ōris, *m.* a protector, patron; an applauder.

fautrix -trīcis, *f.* a favourer, protector.

faux, faucis, *f. (usually plur.* **fauces** -ium, *f.*), the jaws, gullet, throat; chasm; entrance; a narrow pass; isthmus; straits.

făvĕo, fāvi, fautum, 2. to favour, help, protect; *with dat.*

făvilla -ae, *f.* glowing ashes, *esp.* of the dead.

făvitor -ōris, *m.* = *fautor (q.v.).*

Făvōnĭus -ii, *m.* the west wind *or* zephyr.

făvor -ōris, *m.* favour, goodwill, inclination; attention; applause, approbation.

făvōrābĭlis -e, *adj.* popular, beloved.

făvus -i, *m.* a honeycomb.

fax, făcis, *f.* a torch; a fire-brand; *faces dicendi*, fiery eloquence; *facem bello praeferre*, to kindle the flame of war; a fiery meteor, shooting star, *etc.*

faxim, faxo = fecerim, fecero, *v. facio.*

febrĭcŭla -ae, *f. (dim. of febris)*, a slight fever, feverishness.

febrĭcŭlōsus -a -um, feverish.

febris -is, *f., acc.* -em *or* -im, *abl.* -e *or* -i, fever.

februārĭus -a -um, relating to cleansing; *mensis Februarius*, February, the cleansing month.

februus -a -um, purifying ; *subst.*, **februum** -i, *n.* a **means** of religious purification; **Februa** -ōrum, *n.* the feast of purification held by the Romans at the end of February.

fēcĭālis = fetialis *(q.v.).*

fēcundĭtas -ātis, *f.* fruitfulness, fecundity; abundance.

fēcundo, 1. to fructify, fertilise.

fēcundus -a -um, *p. adj.*, fruitful, prolific; rich, abounding in; *with genit.*, abundant, full, plentiful ; making fruitful.

fel, fellis, *n.* the gall, the gall-bladder; bitterness, anger ; the venom of a serpent.

fēles (faeles) -is, *and* **fēlis (faelis)** -is, *f.* a cat.

fēlĭcĭtas -ātis, fertility, happiness, good fortune.

fēlĭcĭtĕr, *adv.* fruitfully ; happily ; auspiciously, favourably; good luck !

fēlis = feles *(q.v.).*

fēlix -īcis, fruitful, fertile; fortunate, propitious; rich; successful; bringing good luck; blessed with healing power; making joyful; making fruitful.

fēmella -ae, *f. (dim. of femina)*, a young woman, a girl.

fēmen = femur *(q.v.).*

fēmĭna -ae, *f.* a woman; *of animals*, the female.

fēmĭnĕus -a -um, relating to a woman, female, feminine; womanish, effeminate.

fēmur -ŏris *or* -ĭnis, *n.* the thigh.

fēnebris -e, relating to interest.

fēnĕrātĭo -ōnis, *f.* usury.

fēnĕrātor -ōris, *m.* money-lender, usurer.

fēnĕro (faenĕro), 1. to lend money at interest.

fēnĕror (faenĕror), 1. *dep.* to lend money at interest.

fēnestella -ae, *f. (dim. of fenestra)*, a little opening.

fēnestra -ae, *f.* a window.

fēnĕus -a -um, made of hay; *homines*, men of straw.

fēnĭcŭlārĭus -a -um, belonging to fennel.

fēnīlĭa -ium, *n. plur.* a hay-loft.

fēnĭsĕca -ae, *m.* a mower; a countryman.

fēnum (faenum, foenum) -i, *n.* hay.

fēnus (faenus) -ōris, *n.* interest of money; debt, indebtedness; capital; usury.

fēra -ae, *f. v. ferus.*

fērācĭtĕr, *adv.* fruitfully.

fērālis -e, relating to the dead, funereal ; deadly, fatal. *Subst.*, **fērālĭa** -ium, *n.* festival of the dead on the 10th of February.

fērax -ācis, fruitful, fertile.

ferbĕo = ferveo *(q.v.).*

fercŭlum *and* **fērĭcŭlum** -i, *n.* a litter, bier, tray; a course, dish.

fērē, *adv.* almost, nearly; *eădem fere horā quā veni*, about the same hour ; *with negatives*, scarcely, hardly, seldom.

fĕrentārĭus -ii, *m.* a light-armed soldier who fought with missiles.

Fĕrentīnum -i, *n.* town of the Hernici on the Via Latina.

Fēretrĭus -ii, *m.* surname of Jupiter.

fĕretrum -i, *n.* a bier for carrying a corpse to the grave.

fēriae -ārum, *f.* days of rest, holidays; rest.

fērĭātus -a -um, *p. adj.*, keeping holiday, idle, at leisure.

fērĭcŭlum = ferculum *(q.v.).*

fērīnus -a -um, relating to a wild beast, wild. *Subst.*, **fĕrīna** -ae, *f.* flesh of wild animals, game.

fĕrĭo, 4. to strike, knock, beat, hit, smite; *ferire mare*, to row ; to strike dead, slay, kill ; *foedus*, to make a treaty *(because a sow was then slain)*; to cut in pieces.

fērĭor, 1. *dep.* to keep holiday.

fērĭtas -ātis, wildness, savageness.

fermē, *adv.* almost, nearly, within

little, about, *sex millia ferme passuum*; *with negatives*, hardly, scarcely.

fermentum -i, *n.* that which causes fermentation, leaven, yeast; anger, *or* the cause of anger; a kind of beer.

fĕro, tŭli, lātum, ferre, to bear, bring, carry; *milit., arma contra aliquem; signa in aliquem*, to attack; to offer (*to the gods*); *aliquem in oculis*, to be very fond of; *prae se ferre aliquid*, to display, make public; to endure, submit to, bear; *aliquid ferre aegre, moleste, graviter molesteque*, to take it ill, be vexed at; *non ferendus*, intolerable; *conditionem ferre*, to propose terms; *aliquam*, to propose some one as a wife; *legal, suffragium*, to vote; *legem*, to propose a law; to demand, require, allow, *si ita res ferret; expensum ferre*, to set down in an account-book as paid; to spread abroad, report, speak of; *ferunt or pass. fertur, feruntur*, people say, it is reported; *fama fert*, the story goes; to give a person out to be, *si te petitorem fero*; to think over, consider; to carry off; *ferre et agere*, to plunder; to drive away, lead; *ferre se or middle ferri*, to hasten, rush, *and of things*, to flow, mount, sink; *milit., signa ferre*, to march away; *se ferre aliquem*, to act as, to profess to be, to declare oneself to be; *ferri aliquā re*, to be possessed by; *of a road, etc.*, to lead to.

fĕrōcĭa -ae, *f.* high spirit, courage; ferocity.

fĕrōcĭtas -ātis, *f.* courage, untamed spirit, fierceness.

fĕrōcĭtĕr, *adv.* courageously; roughly, fiercely.

Fĕrōnĭa -ae, *f.* an old Italian goddess.

fĕrox -ōcis, courageous, high-spirited, brave; wild, unbridled, proud.

ferrāmentum -i, *n.* any instrument *or* tool made of iron.

ferrārĭa -ae, *f. v. ferrarius.*

ferrārĭus -a -um, relating to iron; *subst.*, **ferrārĭa** -ae, *f.* iron mine.

ferrātus -a -um, furnished *or* covered with iron; *agmina*, iron-clad; of iron, iron.

ferrĕus -a -um, iron; made of iron; stern, cruel; immovable, unyielding, firm; hard, oppressive.

ferrūgĭnĕus -a -um, iron-coloured, dusky.

ferrūgĭnus = **ferrugineus** (*q.v.*).

ferrūgo -ĭnis, *f.* iron rust; the colour of iron rust, dusky.

ferrum -i, *n.* iron ore; hard-heartedness, cruelty; any iron instrument; a sword.

fertĭlis -e, fruitful, fertile; fertilising.

fertĭlĭtas -ātis, *f.* fruitfulness, fertility.

fertum -i, *n.* a kind of sacrificial cake.

fertus -a -um, fruitful (*poet.*).

fĕrŭla -ae, *f.* the herb fennel; a rod.

fĕrus -a -um, wild, untamed, unculti-

vated; savage, cruel. *Subst.*, **fera** -ae, *f.* a wild animal; **ferus** -i, *m.* a wild beast, a wild boar.

fervĕfăcĭo -fēci -factum, 3. to heat, melt.

fervens -entis, *abl.* **enti,** *p. adj.* glowing, hot; impetuous, fiery; *adv. ferventer*, *adv.* hotly, warmly.

fervĕo -bŭi -ēre *and* (*poet.*) **fervo, fervi** -ĕre, to boil, seethe, glow; to be carried on briskly; to glitter; to rage, foam, hiss; *a crowd*, to swarm forth; *of places*, to swarm with.

fervesco, 3. to become hot, begin to glow.

fervĭdus -a -um, boiling, seething; passionate, excited; glowing, hot; fiery; raging, foaming.

fervo = **ferveo** (*q.v.*).

fervor -ōris, *m.* raging heat; ardour, passion; raging, foaming.

Fescennĭa -ae, *f.*, and **Fescennĭum** -ii, *n.* a town in Etruria. *Adj.*, **Fescennīnus** -a -um, *Fescennini versus*, rude satirical verses.

fessus -a -um, weary, exhausted.

festīnantĕr, *adv.* rapidly, quickly.

festīnātĭo -ōnis, *f.* haste, speed.

festīnāto, *adv.* hastily, rapidly.

festīno, 1. *intransit.*, to hasten, hurry; *transit.*, to hasten, accelerate; *partic.*, *festinatus*, hastened.

festīnus -a -um, hastening, hasty.

festīvē, *adv.* humorously, wittily.

festīvĭtas -ātis, *f.* gaiety, pleasure; *festivitates*, embellishments (*of discourse*), cheerfulness, humour.

festīvus -a -um, pleasant, pretty; *of places*, bright, pleasant; good-humoured; lively, amusing.

festūca -ae, *f.* a stalk, straw.

festus -a -um, sacred, hallowed, festive, *dies. Subst.*, **festum** -i, *n.* a feast.

fētĭālis -is, *m.* a fetial, *plur.* **fētĭāles,** a college of heralds. *Adj.* **fētĭālis** -e, belonging to the fetiales.

fētūra -ae, *f.* the bearing of young, breeding, the young brood, offspring.

1. **fētus** (**foetus**) -a -um, pregnant; fertile (*poet.*), full of; *machina feta armis.*

2. **fētus** -ūs, *m.* the bearing, *or* hatching of young; producing; offspring; fruit, produce, shoot.

fĭber -bri, *m.* a beaver.

fĭbra -ae, *f.* a fibre, filament; entrails of an animal.

fĭbŭla -ae, *f.* buckle, brooch, clasp, iron clamp.

fictē, *adv.* falsely, fictitiously.

fictĭlis -e, earthen, made of clay. *Subst.*, **fictĭle** -is, *n. usually plur.*, earthenware.

fictor -ōris, *m.* a statuary; a feigner.

fictrix -īcis, *f.* she that forms *or* fashions.

fictus, *partic. of fingo.*

fīcŭlnus (**fīcŭlnĕus**) -a -um, relating to the fig-tree.

fīcus -i *and* -ūs, *f.* fig-tree; a fig.

fidē, *adv.* faithfully.
fidēlia -ae, *f.* earthenware pot *or* vase.
fidēlis -e, true, steadfast, faithful. (*Subst.,* **fidēles -ium,** *m.* faithful friends); *lacrimae,* genuine; durable, strong.
fidēlitas -ātis, *f.* trustworthiness, fidelity.
fidēlitēr, *adv.* faithfully, honestly, surely; properly, well.
Fīdēnae -ārum, *f. and* **Fīdēna -ae,** *f.* town in Latium.
fidens -entis, *abl.* **-enti,** *p. adj.,* confident, courageous.
fidentēr, *adv.* confidently, courageously.
fidentia -ae, *f.* confidence, courage.
1. fides -ēi, *f.* trust, confidence, reliance, belief, faith; *fidem facere,* to awake confidence; commercial credit; fidelity, honesty, credibility; *bonā fide,* in good faith, sincerely, honestly; a promise, word of honour; *fidem fallere, violare,* to break a promise; *servare,* to keep a promise, *fides publica,* a safe-conduct; faithful protection; credibility, trustworthiness, proof; certainty.
2. fides -is, *f. usually plur.* **fides -ium,** string for a musical instrument; a lyre, lute, harp.
fidicen -cinis, *m.* a player on the harp, lyre, lute.
fidicina -ae, *f.* a female player on the lute *or* harp.
fidicula -ae, *f. and gen. plur.* **fidiculae -ārum,** *f.* a little lyre *or* lute; instrument for torturing slaves.
Fidius -ii, *m. a surname of Jupiter; medius fidius,* so help me, God!
fido, fisus sum, 3. to trust, believe, confide in.
fidūcia -ae, *f.* confidence, trust, assurance; *sui,* in oneself; self-confidence, courage. *Legal,* a pledging, mortgaging, etc.
fidūciārius -a -um, entrusted.
fidus -a -um, true, faithful, sure.
figo, fixi, fixum, 3. to fix, fasten, attach, affix; to build; *vestigia,* to check one's steps; to thrust in, drive in; to transfix; *aliquem maledictis,* attack with reproaches.
figulus -i, *m.* a potter.
figura -ae, *f.* form, shape, figure; an atom; kind, nature; a figure of speech.
figūrātus -a -um, *partic. of figuro.*
figūro, 1. to mould, shape.
fīlātim, *adv.* thread by thread.
fīlia -ae, *f.* a daughter.
fīlicātus -a -um, adorned with ferns.
fīliŏla -ae, *f.* (*dim. of filia*), a little daughter.
fīliŏlus -i, *m.* (*dim. of filius*), a little son.
fīlius -ii (*voc. sing. fili*), *m.* son.
fīlix -icis, *f.* fern.
fīlum -i, *n.* a thread; a woollen fillet round the cap of the flamen; form, shape; the manner, thread of discourse.
Fimbria -ae, *m.* (*C. Flavius*), friend of

Marius, general in the Mithridatic War.
fimbriae -ārum, *f. plur.,* fringe, border, edge.
fimus -i, *m. and* **fimum -i,** *n.* dung, dirt.
findo, fidi, fissum, 3. to split, cleave, separate.
fingo, finxi, fictum, 3. to stroke; to fashion, form, mould; to imagine; to invent, devise; to feign; to arrange; *partic., fictus,* invented, feigned; *subst.,* **fictum -i,** *n.* something invented, a lie.
finiens -entis, the horizon.
finio, 4. *transit.,* to bound, enclose within limits, restrain; to define, determine, appoint; to conclude, *bellum; pass.,* to end, cease; *finiri* (*middle*), to die; *intransit.,* to die, to finish, to bring to a close.
finis -is, *m. and f.* boundary, limit, border; *plur.,* territory; term, limit; the end; *finem capere,* come to an end; death; the highest, the extremity; object, aim.
finītē, *adv.* moderately, within bounds.
finitimus (**finitūmus**) **-a -um,** neighbouring, adjacent. *Subst.,* **finitimi -ōrum,** *m.* neighbours; related to; similar.
finitor -ōris, *m.* a land surveyor.
finitūmus = finitimus (*q.v.*).
finitus -a -um, *partic. of finio.*
fio, factus sum, fieri, *pass. of facio,* to be made; to be done, to arise, *fit clamor;* to happen; *potest fieri ut fallar,* I may be deceived; to be; to become something, *consules facti sunt.*
firmāmen -inis, *n.* support, prop.
firmāmentum -i, *n.* means of support, prop.
firmātor -ōris, *m.* one who makes firm *or* establishes.
firmē, *adv.* firmly, steadfastly.
firmitas -ātis, *f.* firmness, durability; constancy.
firmitēr, *adv.* firmly, strongly.
firmitūdo -dinis, *f.* firmness, strength; constancy.
firmo, 1. to make firm, strengthen; to make secure; to encourage, animate; to prove.
firmus -a -um, firm, strong, stout; powerful, healthy; durable, lasting; valid, *acta Caesaris;* steadfast, sure; firm, to be relied upon.
fiscella -ae, *f.* (*dim. of fiscina*), a small rush *or* wicker basket.
fiscina -ae, *f.* a small basket of wickerwork.
fiscus -i, *m.* a wicker basket; moneybag, purse; the state treasury.
fissilis -e, that can be cloven *or* split.
fissio -ōnis, *f.* a splitting, dividing.
fissum -i, *n.* a split, cleft; *in augury,* a divided liver.
fistūca *or* **festūca -ae,** *f.* rammer, mallet.

fistŭla -ae, *f.* a tube, pipe; a reed; a kind of ulcer.

fistŭlātor -ōris, *m.* one who plays upon the reed-pipe.

fixus -a -um, *p. adj.*, firm, fixed, immovable.

flăbellum -i, *n.* (*dim. of flabrum*), a small fan; *fig.* o, whip.

flābrum -i, *n. gen. plur.* **flābra -ōrum**, blasts of wind, breezes.

flaccĕo, 2. to be faint, languid.

flaccesco, 3. to begin to fade, to become faint.

flaccidus -a -um, withered, flabby, languid.

1. **flaccus** -a -um, flabby, flaccid; *of men*, flap-eared.

2. **Flaccus**, *Q. Horatius, v. Horatius.*

flăgello, 1. to whip, scourge, beat.

flăgellum -i, *n.* (*dim. of flagrum*), a whip, scourge; the thong of a javelin; a young sprout. *Plur., flagella*, arms of a polypus.

flăgĭtātĭo -ōnis, *f.* an entreaty.

flăgĭtātor -ōris, *m.* one who entreats.

flăgĭtĭōsē, *adv.* basely, infamously.

flăgĭtĭōsus -a -um, disgraceful, infamous.

flăgĭtĭum -i, *n.* a disgraceful action, shameful crime, shame, disgrace, infamy; scoundrel, rascal.

flăgĭto, 1. to entreat, ask; to demand; to summon before a court of justice.

flăgrans -antis, *p. adj.*, burning, glowing with passion, ardent; *of the eyes*, glowing; glittering.

flăgrantēr, *adv.* eagerly, ardently.

flăgrantĭa -ae, *f.* glowing.

flăgro, 1. to blaze, glow; to burn; to be eager, vehement.

flăgrum -i, *n.* a scourge, whip.

1. **flāmen** -ĭnis, *m.* the priest of some particular deity.

2. **flāmen** -ĭnis, *n.* a blowing blast; the wind; *flamina tibiae*, the notes of a flute.

flāmĭnĭum - . *n.* the office of a flamen.

flamma -ae, flame, blaze; a flaming star, lightning; glitter; glow of passion, glow, raging fire, or

flammĕŏlum -i, *n.* (*dim. of flammeum*), a small bridal veil.

flammesco, 3. to become inflamed.

flammĕus -a -um, fiery, flaming; flame-coloured. *Subst.*, **flammĕum** -i, *n.* a flame-coloured bridal veil.

flammĭfer -fĕra -fĕrum, flame-bearing, fiery.

flammo, 1. *intransit.*, to flame, blaze, burn; *transit.*, to set on fire, inflame.

flammŭla -ae, *f.* (*dim. of flamma*), a little flame.

flātus -ūs, *m.* a blowing, blast; breathing; the breath, snorting, *equorum*; haughtiness, *gen. in plur.*

flāvĕo, 2. to be yellow *or* gold-coloured; *partic., flavens*, yellow, golden.

flāvesco, 3. to become yellow *or* gold-coloured.

Flāvius -a -um, name of a Roman gens, to which the Emperors Vespasian, Titus, and Domitian belonged.

flāvus -a -um, gold-coloured, yellow

flēbĭlis e, lamentable, wretched; tearful, *of persons*, weeping.

flēbĭlĭtĕr, *adv.* tearfully, dolefully.

flecto, flexi, flexum, 3. *transit.*, to bend, bow, twist, curve; *iter suum*, to diverge from one's march; to modulate, *vocem*; to change, alter; to turn, direct, *equos*; to dissuade from; to double, sail round; *of places, flectere se or middle flecti*, to turn towards; *intransit.*, to turn; go.

flĕo, flēvi, flētum, 2. *intransit.*, to weep; *of fluids*, to trickle down; *transit.*, to weep for, bewail, *iuvenem* ; *fletus*, lamented.

1. **flētus** -a -um (*partic. of fleo*).

2. **flētus** -ūs, *m.* a weeping, bewailing.

flexănĭmus -a -um, moving, affecting; affected.

flexĭbĭlis -e, flexible; pliant, tractable; changeable.

flexĭlis -e, flexible, pliant.

flexĭlŏquus -a -um, equivocal, ambiguous.

flexĭo -ōnis, *f.* bending; *vocis*, modulation of the voice; turning, winding.

flexĭpes -pĕdis, crooked-footed; *hederae*, twining.

flexŭōsus -a -um, full of windings, crooked.

flexūra -ae, *f.* a bending.

1. **flexus** -a -um, *partic. of flecto*.

2. **flexus** -ūs, *m.* a bending, turning, winding; by-path; variation; *in the circus*, the turning round of the chariots towards the goal.

flictus -ūs, *m.* a striking together, dashing against.

flīgo, 3. to bear *or* dash down.

flo, flātum, 1. *intransit.*, to blow; *transit.*, to blow from the mouth, *flammam;* to blow an instrument; to coin metals, *floccus* -i, *m.* lock of wool; a trifle; *non flocci facere*, to think nothing of.

Flōra -ae, *f.* goddess of flowers. **Flōrālĭa** -ĭum *und* iōrum, *n.* the festival of Flora.

flōrens -entis, *p. adj.*, blooming; fresh; prosperous, flourishing; *with abl.*, distinguished for.

Flōrentĭa -ae, *f.* town in Etruria *now* Florence.

flōrĕo -ŭi, 2. to bloom, flower; to prosper, be flourishing, be in high repute; to be full of; to glitter; *of wine*, to froth.

flōresco, 3. to come into flower; to begin to flourish.

flōrĕus -a -um, made of flowers; flowery.

flōrĭdŭlus -a -um (*dim. of floridus*), somewhat blooming.

flōrĭdus -a -um, flowery; blossoming;

made of flowers; rich in flowers; flourishing, *aetas*; florid.

florifer -fěra -fěrum, flower-bearing.

florilěgus -a -um, culling flowers.

flōs, flōris, *m.* a flower, blossom; the prime; the flower = the best, the pride; grace of expression; *flammae*, glitter.

floscŭlus -i, *m.* (*dim. of flos*), a little flower; pride.

fluctifrăgus -a -um, wave-breaking.

fluctŭātĭo -ōnis, *f.* fluctuation; indecision.

fluctŭo, 1. to move up and down; to heave, undulate; to rage; to be tossed about; to waver; to vacillate.

fluctŭor -ātus sum, 1. *dep.* to waver, vacillate.

fluctŭōsus -a -um, stormy.

fluctus -ūs, *m.* a streaming, flowing; a wave, billow; *fig.*, commotion.

flŭens -entis, *p. adj.*, easy, fluent; diffuse; hanging down, flabby.

flŭentěr, *adv.* in a flowing manner.

flŭentĭsŏnus -a -um, resounding with waves.

flŭentum -i, *n.* a stream.

flŭĭdus -a -um, flowing, fluid; lax, languid, dissolving.

flŭĭto, 1. to flow hither and thither; to float, be tossed about; to waver; to flutter.

flūmen -ĭnis, *n.* a stream; *flumine secundo*, downstream; a river; *of oratory, etc.*, flood, stream.

flūmĭnĕus -a -um, of a river.

flŭo, fluxi, fluxum, 3. to flow; drip with; *of clothes*, to flow down; to sink; to spread; to stream forth; to be derived from; to tend to; *of oratory*, to be diffuse; to slacken; to fall down; to disappear.

flŭto, 1. to flow, float, swim.

flŭvĭālis -e, of a river.

flŭvĭātĭlis -e, belonging to a river.

flŭvĭdus -a -um, flowing, fluid.

flŭvĭus -ĭi, *m.* stream, river.

fluxĭo -ōnis, *f.* a flowing flood.

1. **fluxus** -a -um, *p. adj.* flowing, waving, loose; uncertain, changeable; vacillating; decaying, tottering.

2. **fluxus** -ūs, *m.* a flowing, passing away.

fŏcāle -is, *n.* a wrapper for the neck.

fŏcŭlus -i, *m.* (*dim. of focus*), a small stove, brazier; a small altar.

fŏcus -i, *m.* fireplace; hearth; home; altar.

fŏdĭco, 1. to dig, pierce; *fig.*, stab.

fŏdĭo, fŏdi, fossum, 3. to dig; to dig out; to excavate; *fodientes*, miners; to pierce; to gouge out, *lumina*; to nudge.

foecundus, foecundo = fecundus, fecundo (*q.v.*).

foedē, *adv.* foully, horribly, cruelly.

foedĕrātus -a -um, confederate, allied.

foedifrăgus -a -um, treaty-breaking.

foedĭtas -ātis, *f.* foulness, hideousness, filthiness.

foedo, 1. to defile, pollute, disfigure; *agri foedati*, laid waste; to disgrace.

1. **foedus** -a -um, foul, abominable, detestable; *foedi oculi*, staring, bloodshot.

2. **foedus** -ĕris, *n.* a league; covenant, agreement.

foen . . . *v. fen* . . .

foetĭdus (faetĭdus, fētĭdus) -a -um, *adj.*, stinking, fetid.

foetor -ōris, *m.* a bad smell, stink.

foetus *v. fetus.*

fŏlĭātum -i, *n.* a salve or oil of spikenard leaves.

fŏlĭum -ĭi, *n.* a leaf.

follĭcŭlus -i, *m.* (*dim. of follis*), a little sack or bag.

follis -is, *m.* a leather bag; a pair of bellows; *of the lungs, folles spirant mendacia*; a leathern purse.

fōmentum -i, *n.* a poultice; alleviation.

fōmes -ĭtis, *m.* touchwood, tinder.

fons, fontis, *m.* spring, well, fountain; origin, source.

fontānus -a -um, relating to a spring or fountain.

fontĭcŭlus -i, *m.* (*dim. of fons*), a little fountain or spring.

for, fātus, 1. *dep.* speak, say; *fando audire*, hear by report; *partic.* **fandus** -a -um, right, lawful.

fŏrābĭlis -e, that can be bored through, vulnerable.

fŏrāmen -ĭnis, *n.* a hole, opening, eye (*of a needle*).

fŏras, *adv.* out of doors, forth, out.

forceps -cĭpis, *m. and f.* a pair of tongs, pincers.

fordux -a -um, pregnant. *Subst.*, **forda** -ae, *f.* a cow in calf.

fŏre, fŏrem, -es, *etc.*, **forem = essem**; *insin.* **fore = futurum esse**.

fŏrensis -e, relating to the market or forum; relating to the forum as a place for administration of justice, legal.

forfex -ĭcis, *c.* pair of shears or scissors.

1. **fŏris** -is, *f.* door; opening, entrance; *plur., fores*, folding-doors.

2. **fŏris**, *adv.* out of doors, outside; not at home; outside Rome; from abroad.

forma -ae, *f.* form, figure, shape; the face; beauty; character, nature, manner; figure, image; outline, sketch; a shoelast; stamp for coining.

formāmentum -i, *n.* shape, form.

formātūra -ae, *f.* formation.

Formĭae -ārum, *f.* town on the coast of Latium. *Adj.*, **Formĭānus**.

formīca -ae, *f.* an ant.

formīdābĭlis -e, fearful, formidable.

1. **formīdo**, 1. to fear, be frightened.

2. **formīdo** -ĭnis, *f.* fear, dread, terror; religious awe.

formīdŏlōsē, *adv.* fearfully, terribly.

formĭdōlōsus -a -um, exciting fear, terrible; timid.

formo, 1. to shape, fashion; to arrange, regulate; to accustom; to dispose, prepare; to build; *of actors,* to represent; to produce.

formōsē, *adv.* beautifully, gracefully,

formōsĭtās ātis, *f.* beauty.

formōsus -a -um, beautiful.

formŭla -ae, *f.* (*dim. of* forma), a rule, pattern, scheme; form of agreement; form of words.

fornācālis -e, relating to an oven.

fornācŭla -ae, *f.* (*dim. of fornax*), a little oven.

fornax -ācis, *f.* oven, furnace, kiln; *Fornax,* goddess of ovens.

fornĭcātus -a -um, arched, vaulted.

fornix -ĭcis, *m.* an arch, vault; covered way. *Milit.,* an arched sally-port.

fornus = furnus (*q.v.*).

fŏro, 1. to pierce.

fors, *abl.* forte, *f. only nom. and abl. sing.,* chance, luck; *forte,* by chance.

forsăn, *adv.* perhaps.

forsit, *adv.* perhaps.

forsĭtăn, *adv.* perhaps.

fortassĕ, *adv.* perhaps; *with numbers,* about.

fortĕ, *v. fors.*

fortĭcŭlus -a -um (*dim. of fortis*), tolerably strong, brave.

fortis -e, strong, powerful, robust, courageous, steadfast.

fortĭtĕr, *adv.* strongly, courageously.

fortĭtūdo -ĭnis, *f.* courage, steadfastness, fortitude; *plur., fortitudines,* deeds of bravery.

fortŭĭto (fortŭĭtū), *adv.* by chance, by accident.

fortŭĭtus -a -um, accidental, casual. *Subst.,* fortŭĭta -ōrum, *n.* chance occurrences.

fortūna -ae, *f. and plur.* fortūnae -ārum, *f.* chance, luck, fortune; *secunda,* good fortune; *adversa,* misfortune, condition, lot, possessions.

fortūnātē, *adv.* happily, fortunately.

fortūnātus -a -um, *p. adj.,* happy, fortunate; *insulae,* islands of the blest, Elysium; *fortunata nemora,* Elysium. *Subst.,* fortūnātus -i, *m.* a favourite of fortune, rich.

fortūno, 1. to make happy, prosper.

fŏrŭli -ārum, *m.* (*dim. of forus*), book-case.

fŏrum -i, *n.* an open square, market-place; *at Rome,* a place at the foot of the Palatine and Capitoline hills, where legal, political and commercial business was transacted; *forum attingere,* to begin to apply oneself to public business, *esp. legal; forum agere,* to hold an assize; *Apii Fŏrum,* a town of Latium.

fŏrus -i, *m.* gangway of a ship; *plur.,* row of seats in the theatre; *plur.,* cells of bees.

fossa -ae, *f.* ditch, trench; canal, bed of a river.

fossio -ōnis, *f.* digging, excavation.

fossor -ōris, *m.* digger, delver; *poet.* boor, clown.

fossūra -ae, *f.* a digging.

fŏtus, *partic. of foveo.*

fŏvĕa -ae, *f.* a pit as a trap for catching game, pitfall.

fŏvĕo, fōvi, fōtum, 2. to warm, keep warm; to bathe, foment; *poet.* to heal; to support; to stay constantly in a place, *castra; hiemem,* pass the winter in dalliance; to foster, *spem;* to cherish, pamper; to support, favour.

fractus -a -um, *p. adj.,* weak; *animus,* spiritless.

fraeno, fraenum = freno, frenum (*q.v.*).

frāga -ōrum, *n.* strawberries.

frăgĭlis -e, fragile; crackling; frail, transitory.

frăgĭlĭtas -ātis, *f.* frailty, weakness.

fragmen -ĭnis, *n.* fragment; *plur.* ruins, remains.

fragmentum -i, *n.* fragment; *plur.,* ruins.

frăgor -ōris, *m.* breaking in pieces.

frăgōsus -a -um, fragile; rough, uneven; crashing, roaring.

frăgrans -antis, *p. adj.,* sweet-scented.

frăgro, 1. to be fragrant.

frāgum, *v. fraga.*

frango, frēgi, fractum, 3. to break, dash to pieces; *gulam laqueo,* to strangle; to grind; *reflex se frangere,* to break up (*of weather, etc.*); to shorten time; to weaken; to subdue; to discourage, humble; (*frangi,* to be discouraged); to touch, move; to break, violate.

frāter -tris, *m.* a brother; *frater patruelis,* cousin.

frātercŭlus -i, *m.* (*dim. of frater*), a little brother.

frāternē, *adv.* in a brotherly manner; heartily.

frāternĭtas -ātis, *f.* brotherhood, fraternity.

frāternus -a -um, brotherly, fraternal; *hereditas,* coming from a brother; *relatus, sanguis,* friendly.

frātrĭcīda -ae, *m.* one who kills a brother.

fraudātĭo -ōnis, *f.* fraud.

fraudātor -ōris, *m.* deceiver, defrauder.

fraudo, 1. to cheat, deceive, *milites praedā;* to steal; *subst.,* fraudāta -ōrum, *n.* ill-gotten gains.

fraudŭlentus -a -um, deceitful, fraudulent.

fraus, fraudis, *f.* deceit, fraud; error; damage, loss; a crime, offence.

fraxĭnĕus -a -um, of ash-wood.

1. fraxĭnus -a -um = fraxineus.

2. fraxĭnus -i, *f.* ash-tree; a spear *or* javelin with the shaft of ash-wood.

frĕmĕbundus -a -um, growling, murmuring.

frĕmĭtus -ūs, *m.* murmuring, muttering, roar.

fremo -ŭi -ĭtum, 3. to roar, murmur, growl ; to rustle ; *transit.*, to murmur something, complain; to demand with tears *or* rage.

fremor -ōris, *m.* murmuring.

frendo, frēsum (fressum), 3. to gnash the teeth; *transit.*, to crush, grind.

frēni -ōrum, *m. v. frenum.*

frēno, 1. to bridle, curb; to restrain.

frēnum -i, *n. plur.* **frēna -ōrum,** *n.*, *and* **frēni -ōrum,** *m.* bridle, reins, bit; *frena remittere,* to give the reins to.

frēquens -entis, numerous, crowded; *of places,* full, frequented, populous; frequent, constant.

frēquentātio -ōnis, *f.* frequency, frequent use.

frēquentātus -a -um, abounding in.

frēquenter, *adv.* frequently; in large numbers.

frēquentia -ae, *f.* a large concourse ; abundance.

frēquento, 1. to collect in large numbers; to visit in large numbers; to people; to frequent; to repeat constantly.

frēsus (fressus) -a -um, *v. frendo.*

frētum -i, *n.*, and **frētus -ūs,** *m.* the sea; heat, violence; a strait, channel.

1. **frētus -a -um,** relying on; *with the abl.*

2. **frētus -ūs,** *m.* = **fretum** (*q.v.*).

frico, fricŭi, frictum, *and* **fricātum,** 1. to rub, rub down.

frīgĕo, 2. to be cold, be stiff with cold; to be inactive, to flag; to be coldy received.

frīgĕro, 1. to cool, refresh.

frīgesco, frixi, 3. to become cold; to become languid.

frīgĭdē, *adv.* coldly; languidly, feebly.

frīgĭdŭlus -a -um (*dim. of frigidus*), somewhat cold, somewhat languid.

frīgĭdus -a -um, cold, cool; inactive, remiss; *act.,* causing cold; *rumor,* chilling. *Subst., plur.,* **frīgĭda -ōrum,** *n.* cold.

frīgo, frixi, frictum, 3. to roast, parch.

frīgus -ōris, *n.* cold, coolness; cold of winter; winter; remissness; coldness in behaviour.

frio, 1. to rub, crumble.

Frisii -ōrum, *m.* the Frisians.

frĭtillus -i, *m.* a dice-box.

frīvŏlus -a -um, trifling, worthless. *Subst.,* **frīvŏla -ōrum,** *n.* wretched furniture.

frondātor -ōris, *m.* a pruner of trees.

frondĕo, 2. to be in leaf, be leafy.

frondesco, 3. to come into leaf.

frondĕus -a -um, leafy, full of leaf.

frondĭfer -fĕra -fĕrum, leaf-bearing, leafy.

frondōsus -a -um, full of leaves, leafy.

1. **frons, frondis,** *f.* a leaf, foliage ; chaplet of leaves.

2. **frons, frontis,** *f.* the forehead, brow ; *frontem contrahere,* to frown; *frontem*

explicare, to become cheerful; the outside, *tabernae;* the edge of a roll *or* volume; the front; *milit.,* the van.

frontālia -ium, *n.* frontlet of a horse.

fronto -ōnis, *m.* a man with a broad forehead. *Fronto,* a Roman surname.

fructŭārius -a -um, fruitful.

fructŭōsus -a -um, fruit-bearing, fertile.

fructus -ūs, *m.* enjoyment, enjoying ; proceeds, produce; gain, profit; *in fructu habere,* to consider profitable.

frūgālis -e, frugal, economical, excellent (*positive not used; frugi instead*).

frūgālĭtas -ātis, *f.* frugality, economy, excellence.

frūgālĭtĕr, *adv.* economically, honourably.

frūgi, *v. frux.*

frūgĭfer -fĕra -fĕrum, fruitful, fertile; profitable.

frūgĭfĕrens -entis, fruitful, fertile.

frūgĭlĕgus -a -um, collecting fruit.

frūgĭpărus -a -um, fruitful.

frūĭtus, frūĭtūrus, *v.* fruor.

frūmentārius -a -um, relating to grain *or* corn; *res,* the supply of corn. *Subst.,* **frūmentārius -ii,** *m.* corn-merchant.

frūmentātio -ōnis, *f.* a foraging.

frūmentātor -ōris, *m.* forager.

frūmentor, 1. *dep.* to forage, fetch corn.

frūmentum -i, *n.* grain, corn.

frŭor, fructus *and* **frŭĭtus sum,** 3. to enjoy, to derive advantage from; *with abl., vitā; votis,* to obtain one's wishes; to have the use of.

frustrā, in vain, without effect; *frustra esse (alicui),* to fail.

frustrātio -ōnis, *f.* failure, disappointment.

frustro, 1. *and dep.* **frustror,** 1. to cheat, deceive.

frustum -i, *n.* a piece, morsel of food.

frŭtex -ticis, *m.* a shrub, bush; blockhead.

frŭtĭcētum -i, *n.* a thicket.

frŭtĭco 1. *and* **frŭtĭcor,** 1. *dep.* to shoot out, become bushy.

frŭtĭcōsus -a -um, *adj.* bushy, full of bushes.

frux -frūgis, fruit, produce ; virtue ; *frūgi* used as *adj.,* useful, discreet, temperate.

fūcātus -a -um, painted, counterfeited.

fūco, 1. to colour, dye ; to paint, rouge.

fūcōsus -a -um, painted, counterfeited.

1. **fūcus -i,** *m.* red *or* purple colour; beeglue; rouge; deceit, pretence.

2. **fūcus -i,** *m.* a drone bee.

fŭga -ae, *f.* flight, exile, banishment; avoidance, aversion, *laboris ;* swift course.

fŭgācĭus, *adv. in compar.,* in a manner more inclined to flight.

fŭgax -ācis, ready to flee, hastening; fleeting, transitory; *with genit.,* avoiding.

fūgiens -entis, p. adj., flying from, avoiding; with genit., laboris.

fūgio, fūgi, fūgitum, 3. intransit., to flee, take to flight; to hasten away; to pass away, disappear; transit., to flee from; to avoid, shun; to decline, reject; to escape from; aliquid aliquem fugit, escapes the notice of

fugiens -entis, p. adj., flying from, avoiding.

fūgitīvus -a -um, adj., flying, fugitive; subst., a fugitive.

fūgito, 1. to fly from, avoid.

fūgo, 1. to put to flight, drive away; to drive into exile.

fulcimen -inis, n. prop, support, pillar.

fulcio, fulsi, fultum, 4. to prop up, support; to uphold; to strengthen, secure, postes.

fulcrum -i, n. a post or foot of a couch; a couch.

fulgeo, fulsi, 2. to lighten; to shine, gleam, glitter; to be distinguished.

fulgidus -a -um, shining, gleaming.

fulgo, 3. = fulgeo (q.v.).

fulgor -ōris, m. lightning; glitter, brilliancy; glory.

fulgur -ūris, n. lightning; a thunderbolt; poet., brightness, brilliancy.

fulgurālis -e, relating to lightning.

fulgurātor -ōris, m. a haruspex who interpreted the omens from lightning.

fulguro, 1. to lighten.

fūlica -ae, f. a coot (water-fowl).

fūligo -inis, f. soot; powder used for darkening the eyebrows.

fūlix -icis, f. = fulica (q.v.).

fullo -ōnis, m. a fuller.

fulmen -inis, n. a thunderbolt; crushing calamity; irresistible power.

fulminēus -a -um, relating to lightning; slaying, destructive.

fulmino, 1. to lighten, to thunder and lighten.

fultūra -ae, f. a support, stay.

Fulvius -a -um, name of a Roman gens.

fulvus -a -um, tawny, yellowish-brown.

fūmeus -a -um, smoky, full of smoke.

fūmidus -a -um, smoky, full of smoke.

fūmifer -fera -ferum, smoky.

fūmificus -a -um, causing smoke.

fūmo, 1. to smoke, steam.

fūmōsus -a -um, full of smoke, smoky, steaming.

fūmus -i, m. smoke, steam, vapour.

fūnālis -e, belonging to a rope. Subst., fūnāle -is, n. the thong of a sling; a wax-torch.

fūnambūlus -i, m. a rope-dancer.

functio -ōnis, f. a performance, performing, executing.

funda -ae, f. a sling; casting-net.

fundāmen -inis, n. foundation, base.

fundāmentum -i, n. foundation, base; basis.

fundātor -ōris, m. founder.

fundātus -a -um, firm, durable.

funditor -ōris, m. light-armed soldier, a slinger.

fundītūs, adv. from the ground; completely; at the bottom, below.

1. **fundo,** 1. to lay the foundation of, to found; to make firm.

2. **fundo, fūdi, fūsum,** 3. to pour, pour out; (middle, to pour; ingentibus procellis fusus imber); to melt, cast (metals); to sprinkle; to throw to the ground; milit., to rout, defeat; (middle, fundi, to rush away); to let loose; (middle, fundi, to spread); to discharge missiles; of persons, reflex., to rush out; to utter; of poets, to compose; to produce; to squander.

fundus -i, m. the bottom or base of anything; soil, farm, estate.

fūnebris -e, belonging to a funeral, funereal; subst., fūnebria -ium, n. funereal ceremonies; deadly, destructive, fatal.

fūnerēus -a -um, relating to a funeral, funereal; of that which causes or betokens death.

fūnero, 1. to bury with funeral rites; to kill.

fūnesto, 1. to pollute with murder.

fūnestus -a -um, filled with mourning, defiled by death; mournful, disastrous, deadly.

fungor, functus sum, 3. dep. to be busy, to perform, accomplish; with abl., dapibus, to take food; to complete.

fungus -i, m. a mushroom, fungus; a candle-snuff.

fūnicūlus -i, m. (dim. of funis), a thin rope, cord, string.

fūnis -is, m. rope, cord, line.

fūnus -ēris, n. funeral, interment; the corpse; death; destruction.

fūo, fūi, fūtūrus, etc., v. sum.

fūr, fūris, c. a thief.

fūrācitěr, adv. thievishly.

fūrax -ācis, thievish.

furca -ae, f. a two-pronged fork, pitchfork; a fork-shaped prop; an instrument of punishment; a narrow pass.

furcifer -fěra -fěrum, one who carries the furca; gallows-bird.

furcilla -ae, f. (dim. of furca), a little fork.

furcula -ae, f. (dim. of furca), a forkshaped prop; a narrow pass.

fūrentěr, adv. furiously.

furfur -ūris, m. bran, scurf on the skin.

furia -ae, f., usually plur., passion, fury; Fūria -ae, f. and plur., Fūriae -ārum, the Furies.

fūriālis -e, furious, terrible; belonging to the Furies.

fūriālitěr, adv. furiously, madly.

fūribundus -a -um, raging, furious; inspired.

fūrio, 1. infuriate; artic., furiatus, raging.

fŭrĭōsē, *adv.* furiously, madly.

fŭrĭōsus -a -um, *adj.* raging, furious; *tibia,* inspiring.

furnāria -ae, *f.* the trade of a baker.

furnus -i, *m.* an oven, a bakehouse.

fŭro, 3. to rage, rave, be mad.

1. fŭror, 1. *dep.* to steal, pilfer; to obtain by stealth; to make secret attacks.

2. fŭror -ōris, *m.* madness, insanity; inspiration, inspired rage; passionate love; delusion, frenzy; tumult, revolt.

furtim, *adv.* by stealth, secretly.

furtīvē, *adv.* secretly, furtively.

furtīvus -a -um, stolen; secret, furtive.

furtum -i, *n.* a theft; the thing stolen; anything secret; *furto, adv.* secretly; a stratagem.

fŭruncŭlus -i, *m.* (*dim. of fur*), little thief, little rascal.

furvus -a -um, dark-coloured, black.

fuscina -ae, *f.* trident.

fusco, 1. *act.* darken, blacken.

fuscus -a -um, dark-coloured, black; *the voice,* hoarse, rough.

fūsē, *adv.* at length, copiously.

fūsĭlis -e, melted, liquid.

fūsĭo -ōnis, *f.* pouring-out, outpouring.

fustis -is, *abl.* -i *and* -e, *m.* stick, cudgel, club.

fustŭārĭum -ii, *n.* beating to death with sticks, the military punishment for desertion.

1. fūsus -a -um, spread out, extended; flowing free, *crines;* diffuse.

2. fūsus -i, *m.* a spindle.

fūtĭlis -e, that cannot hold *or* contain; *glacies,* brittle; worthless, futile.

fūtĭlĭtas -ātis, *f.* worthlessness, folly.

fŭtūrus -a -um, future, about to be. *Subst.*, **fŭtūrum -i**, *n.* the future ; *plur.*, **fŭtūra -ōrum**, *n.* the future.

G

G g, *the seventh letter of the Latin Alphabet, originally represented by C.*

Găbĭi -ōrum, *m.* ancient city of Latium.

Găbīnĭus -a -um, name of a Roman gens; *adj.*, Gabinian; *lex,* a law which gave extraordinary military power to Pompeius.

Gādes *and* **Gădis -ĭum**, *f.* now Cadiz. *Adj.* **Gādītānus.**

Gāius *and* **Gāia**, *v.* Caius.

Galba -ae, *m.* cognomen of the Sulpician gens.

galbănĕus -a -um, relating to galbanum.

galbănum -i, *n.* the resinous sap of a Syrian plant.

galbănus -a -um, greenish-yellow, yellowish.

galbĕum -i, *n.* a kind of fillet *or* bandage for the arm.

galbinus -a -um, greenish-yellow; *subst.*, **galbinum -i**, *n.* greenish-yellow robe *or* garment.

gălĕa -ae, *f.* helmet.

gălĕo, 1. to put on a helmet; *partic.*, *galeatus,* armed with a helmet.

gălērĭcŭlum -i, *n.* (*dim. of galerum*), a skull-cap, wig.

gălērītus -a -um, wearing a skull-cap of fur; *galerita avis,* the crested lark.

gălērum -i, *n.* (**gălērus -i**, *m.*), skull-cap; wig.

galla -ae, *f.* the gall-nut, oak-apple.

Gallī -ōrum, *m.* the Gauls.

gallina -ae, *f.* a hen, fowl.

gallīnācĕus -a -um, relating to poultry.

gallīnārĭus -a -um, relating to poultry. *Subst.*, **gallīnārĭus -i**, *m.* one who has the care of poultry.

1. gallus -i, *m.* cock.

2. Gallus, a Gaul; *v. Galli.*

3. Galli -ōrum, *m.* priests of Cybele; *adj.*, **Gallicus -a -um**, *turba,* the priests of Isis.

gānĕa -ae, *f. and* **gānĕum -i**, *n.* a low eating-house; debauchery.

gānĕo -ōnis, *m.* a profligate person; glutton.

Gangēs -is, *m.* the river Ganges.

gannĭo, 4. to yelp, to snarl, grumble.

gannītus -ūs, *m.* a barking, yelping.

Gănўmēdēs -is, *m.* the cup-bearer of Jove.

găron = gărum (*q.v.*).

garrĭo -īvi *and* **-ii -ītum**, 4. to chatter, babble.

garrŭlĭtas -ātis, *f.* chattering.

garrŭlus -a -um, talkative, chattering; sounding.

gărum (**găron**) **-i**, *n.* fish-sauce.

Gărumna -ae, *f.* river in Gaul, now the Garonne.

gaudĕo, gāvīsus sum, 2. to rejoice, delight in.

gaudĭum -ii, *n.* joy, gladness.

gausāpa -ae, *f.*, *and* **gausāpē -is**, *n.*, *and* **gausāpum -i**, *n.*, *and* **gausāpes -is**, *m.* a woollen cloth.

gāza -ae, *f.* treasure, wealth.

gĕlāsīnus -i, *m.* a dimple.

gĕlĭdē, *adv.* coldly, feebly.

gĕlĭdus -a -um, cold, icy. *Subst.*, **gĕlĭda -ae**, *f.* ice-cold water.

gĕlo, 1. *Trans. and intransit.*, to freeze.

gĕlu, *n.*, **gĕlus -ūs**, *m.*, **gĕlum -i**, *n.* frost, icy cold; chill of age, fear, *etc.*

gĕmĕbundus -a -um, groaning, sighing.

gĕmellĭpăra -ae, *fem. adj.*, twin-bearing.

gĕmellus -a -um (*dim. of geminus*), twin, twin-born; paired, double; similar. *Subst.*, **gĕmellus -i**, *m.* a twin.

gĕmĭnātĭo -ōnis, *f.* a doubling.

gĕmĭno, 1. to double; *partic.*, **gĕmĭnātus**, doubled; to repeat, unite closely; to pair. *Intransit.*, to be doubled.

gĕmĭnus -a -um, twin ; doubled, of

double nature, *Chiron;* similar. *Subst.,*
gĕmĭni -ōrum, *m.* twins.

gĕmĭtus -ūs, *m.* sigh, groan; pain.

gemma -ae, *f.* a bud; gem; a goblet; seal-ring, seal; *gemmae,* eyes in a peacock's tail.

gemmātus -a -um, set with jewels.

gemmĭfer -fĕra -fĕrum, bearing *or* producing jewels.

gemmo, 1. to bud; to be set with jewels; to glitter like jewels.

gĕmo -ŭi -ĭtum, 3. to sigh, groan; to creak; to lament; *of the lion,* to roar; *of the turtle-dove,* to coo.

gēna -ae, *f. usually plur.,* the cheek; eyelid; socket; eyes.

Genāva -ae, *f.* town of the Allobroges, *now* Geneva.

gĕnĕălŏgus -i, *m.* a genealogist.

gĕner -ĕri, *m.* son-in-law.

gĕnĕrālis -e, belonging to a kind, generic; general.

gĕnĕrālĭter, *adv.* in general, generally.

gĕnĕrasco, 3. to be produced.

gĕnĕrātim, *adv.* according to kinds *or* classes; in general.

gĕnĕrātor -ōris, *m.* begetter, producer.

gĕnĕro, 1. to beget, produce.

gĕnĕrōsē, *adv.* nobly.

gĕnĕrōsus -a -um, of noble birth, noble; excellent, well-bred; magnanimous.

gĕnĕsis -is, *f.* the constellation which presides over one's birth.

gĕnĕtīvus (gĕnĭtīvus) -a -um, inborn, innate; *nomina,* family names; *casus,* genitive case.

gĕnĕtrix -trīcis, *f.* a mother.

gĕniālis -e, nuptial; joyful, delightful; *subst.,* **gĕniālis -is,** *m.* the marriage-bed.

gĕniālĭter, *adv.* jovially, gaily.

gĕnĭcŭlātus -a -um, full of knots.

gĕnĭcŭlum -i, *n. (dim. of genu),* the knee; knot of a plant.

gĕnista (gĕnesta) -ae, *f.* the plant broom.

gĕnĭtābĭlis -e, relating to birth, fruitful.

gĕnĭtālis -e, belonging to birth, fruitful; *dies,* birthday; **Gĕnĭtālis -is,** *f.* surname of Diana as presiding over births.

gĕnĭtālĭter, *adv.* in a fruitful manner.

gĕnĭtīvus, *v. gĕnĕtīvus.*

gĕnĭtor -ōris, *m.* father; *urbis,* producer.

gĕnĭtūra -ae, *f.* begetting, bringing forth.

gĕnius -ii, *m.* guardian spirit, genius; talent, genius.

gĕno = **gigno** *(q.v.).*

gens, gentis, *f.* a clan; species of animals; *poet.* descendant; people, tribe, nation; district.

genticus -a -um, belonging to a nation, national.

gentīlicius -a -um, belonging to a particular gens.

gentīlis -e, belonging to a gens; belonging to the same country national. *Subst.,*

gentīlis -is, *m.* clansman, person of the same gens.

gentīlitas -ātis, *f.* relationship between members of a gens.

gĕnu -ūs, *n.* the knee.

gĕnŭāle -is, *n.* knee-band, garter.

gĕnŭīnus -a -um, natural, innate.

2. gĕnŭīnus -a -um, belonging to the cheek *or* jaw. *Subst.,* **gĕnŭīnus -i,** *m.* a jaw-tooth.

1. gĕnus -ĕris, *n.* birth, descent, origin; race, stock; family, house; descendant; sex; class, kind; species; variety, sort; fashion, manner, way.

2. gĕnus -ūs = **genu** *(q.v.).*

gĕōgrăphia -ae, *f.* geography.

gĕōmetrēs -ae, *m.* a geometer.

gĕōmetrīa -ae, *f.* geometry.

gĕōmetricus -a -um, geometrical. *Subst.,* **gĕōmetrica -ōrum,** *n.* geometry.

gĕorgicus -a -um, agricultural. *Subst.,* **Gĕorgica -ōrum,** *n.* the Georgics of Vergil.

germānē, *adv.* faithfully, honestly.

Germāni -ōrum, *m.* the Germans; **Germānus,** German; **Germānia,** Germany.

germānĭtas -ātis, relationship between brothers and sisters; the connexion between colonies of the same mother-city.

1. germānus -a -um, having the same parents, brotherly, sisterly; genuine, true. *Subst.,* **germānus -i,** *m.* own brother; **germāna -ae,** *f.* own sister.

2. Germānus -a -um, *v. Germani.*

germen -inis, *n.* a bud, twig; offspring.

germino, 1. to sprout forth.

1. gĕro, gessi, gestum, 3. to carry; *se gerere,* to behave oneself, to conduct oneself; to manage *(rem), bene, or male gerere; res gestae,* exploits; to hold some public office; *bellum gerere,* to wage war; to carry, to have; to bear, produce; *amicitiam,* to entertain.

2. gĕro -ōnis, *m.* a carrier.

gerrae -ārum, *f.* wattled twigs; trifles, nonsense.

gerro -ōnis, *m.* trifler, idler.

gĕrŭlus -i, *m.* a porter.

Gēryōn (Gēryo) -ōnis, *m. and* **Cēryŏnes -ae,** *m.* a king with three bodies.

gestāmen -inis, *n.* that which is carried; a litter.

gestĭcŭlor, 1. *dep.* to make pantomimic gestures, gesticulate.

1. gestio -ōnis, *f.* management, performance.

2. gestio -īvi *and* **-ĭi -ītum, 4.** to exult, to be cheerful, lively; to be eager.

gestito, 1. to carry often.

gesto, 1. to carry, wear.

gestor -ōris, *m.* tale-bearer, gossip.

gestus -ūs, *m.* the carriage of the body; gestures of an actor *or* orator.

Gĕtae -ārum, *m.* a people of Thrace.

gibber -ĕra -ĕrum, hump-backed.

gibbus -i *m.* a hump, hunch.

Gigas -gantis, *m.* a giant. *Adj.*, **Giganteus.**

gigno, **gĕnŭi**, **gĕnĭtum**, 3. to beget, bear, bring forth; to cause.

gilvus -a -um, pale yellow.

gingīva -ae, *f.* the gum.

glăber -bra -brum, without hair, smoothskinned.

glăciālis -e, relating to ice, icy.

glăcies -ei, *f.* ice; hardness.

glăcio, 1. to freeze.

glădiātor -ōris, *m.* a gladiator; *abl.*, *gladiatoribus*, at the gladiatorial games.

glădiātōrius -a -um, gladiatorial, *ludus; familia*, troop *or* band of gladiators. *Subst.*, **glădiātōrium -ii**, *n.* pay of gladiators.

glădiātūra -ae, *f.* a combat of gladiators.

glădius -ii, *m.* sword.

glaeba = **gleba** (*q.v.*).

glaesum (**glēsum**) **-i**, *n.* amber.

glandifer -fěra -fěrum, acorn-bearing.

glans, glandis, *f.* an acorn; a bullet discharged from a sling.

glārĕa -ae, *f.* gravel.

glārĕōsus -a -um, gravelly, full of gravel.

glaucōma -ātis, *n.* a disease of the eye.

1. **glaucus -a -um**, bluish-grey.

2. **Glaucus -i**, *m.* a fisherman changed into a sea-god.

glēba (**glaeba) -ae**, *f.* clod of earth; land, soil; lump of any substance.

glēbŭla -ae, *f.* (*dim. of gleba*, a little clod), a little farm *or* estate; a small lump.

glēsum = **glaesum** (*q.v.*).

glis, glīris, *m.* a dormouse.

glisco, 3. to swell up, blaze up; to increase.

glŏbo, 1. to form into a ball; to crowd together.

glŏbōsus -a -um, spherical, globe-shaped.

glŏbus -i, *m.* a round ball, globe, sphere; crowd, mass of people.

glŏmĕrāmen -ĭnis, *n.* a round mass, globe.

glŏmĕro, 1. to wind round, make a ball; to roll into a ball; *superbos gressus*, to make a horse prance; to form into a mass.

glŏmus -ĕris, *n.* clue, skein, ball of thread.

glōria -ae, *f.* fame, renown, glory; a glorious deed; vainglory.

glōriātio -ōnis, *f.* a glorying, boasting.

glōriŏla -ae, *f.* (*dim. of gloria*), a little glory.

glōrior, 1. *dep.* to glory in, boast of, pride oneself on anything; *gloriandus*, glorious.

glōriōsē, *adv.* with glory, gloriously; vauntingly, boastingly.

glōriōsus -a -um, famous, glorious; ambitious, boastful.

glūbo, glupsi, gluptum, 2. to peel, to rob.

glūten -tĭnus, *n.* glue.

glūtĭnātor -ōris, *m.* a bookbinder.

glūtĭno, 1. to glue *or* paste together.

glūtĭo (**gluttio) -īvi** *or* **-ii -ītum**, 4. to swallow, gulp down.

glūto (**glutto) -ōnis**, *m.* a glutton.

gluttio, *v. glutio.*

Gnaeus -i, *m.* Roman name, *shortened Cn.*

gnārĭtas -ātis, *f.* knowledge.

gnārus -a -um, knowing, acquainted with, *with genit.; pass.*, known.

gnātus, gnāvus = **natus, navus** (*q.v.*).

Gnidus = **Cnidus** (*q.v.*).

Gnōsus (Gnossus) -i, *f.* ancient city of Crete; *adj.*, **Gnōsius -a -um**, Gnosian, Cretan; **Gnōsiăcus**, Gnosian; *subst.*, **Gnōsia -ae**, *f.* Ariadne.

gonger, *v. conger.*

Gorgō -gōnis . ; *plur.*, **Gorgones**, monsters, the chief of whom, Medusa, was slain by Perseus. *Adj.*, **Gorgŏnĕus**, Gorgon.

Gorgon, *v. Gorgo.*

grăbātus -i, *m.* a low couch, common bedstead.

Gracchus -i, *name of two famous tribunes.*

grăcĭlis -e, slender, slim; *of discourse*, without ornament.

grăcĭlĭtas -ātis, *f.* thinness, slenderness.

grăcŭlus -i, *m.* a jackdaw.

grădātim, *adv.* step by step, gradually.

grădātio -ōnis, *f. in rhet.*, climax.

grădior, gressus sum, grădi, *dep.*, to step, walk.

Grădīvus -i, *m.* a surname of Mars.

grădus -ūs, *m.* a step; *gradum referre*, to go back; *gradum conferre*, to come to close combat; approach; station, post; step, stair, rung of a ladder; *plur.*, the rows of seats in a theatre; *music*, gradations of sound; degree, stage; rank, position.

Graeci -ōrum, *m.* the Greeks; *sing.*, **Graecus.** *Subst.*, **Graecŭlus -i**, *m.* a little Greek.

graecor, 1. *dep.* to live in Greek fashion.

Grāii -ōrum (*and poet.-ûm*), *m.* = **Graeci**, the Greeks. *Adj.*, **Grāius -a -um.**

grāmen -ĭnis, *n.* grass, turf; plant, herb.

grāmĭnĕus -a -um, made of grass; made of cane *or* bamboo; grassy.

grammătĭca, *v. grammaticus.*

grammătĭcus -a -um, *adj.*, relating to grammar, grammatical. *Subst.*, **grammătĭcus -i**, *m.* a grammarian; **grammătĭca -ae**, *f.*, *and* **grammătĭcē -ēs**, *f.*, **grammătĭca -ōrum**, *n.* grammar, philology.

grānārium -ii, *n.* a granary; *gen. plur.*

grandaevus -a -um, very old.

grandēsco, 3. to become great.

grandifer -fěra -fěrum, producing great profit.

grandĭlŏquus -a -um, speaking grandly; boastful.

grandĭnat, *impers.* it hails.

grandĭo, 4. to make great, increase; to become great.

grandis -e, great, large; tall; old,

grandis natu; important, *res grandiores; of style,* lofty, sublime.

granditas -ātis, f. loftiness, sublimity.

grando -ĭnis, f. hail, hail-storm.

grānĭfer -fĕra -fĕrum, grain-carrying; *agmen,* ants.

grānum -i, n. a grain *or* seed.

grăphĭum -ii, n. a sharp-pointed instrument for writing on waxen tablets.

grassātor -ōris, m. an idler; nocturnal rioter.

grassor, 1. *dep.* to advance; to proceed violently, to rage; to loiter, riot.

grātē, *adv.* willingly, with pleasure; thankfully.

grātes (*acc.* **grates,** *abl.* **grātĭbus),** f. thanks, *esp. to the gods.*

grātĭa -ae, f. agreeableness, pleasantness; charm; *Gratiae,* the Graces; favour, grace; *gratiam dicendi facere,* to allow to speak; *abl., gratia,* on account of; *exempli gratiā,* for example; indulgence to; thanks; *gratias agere,* to thank; *abl. plur., gratiis or gratis,* without recompense, gratis; favour, influence; friendship; power, dignity.

grātĭfĭcātĭo -ōnis, f. complaisance, showing kindness.

grātĭfĭcor, 1. *dep.* to oblige, gratify, do a favour to; *de aliquare,* to communicate; to present to.

grātĭis, v. *gratia.*

grātĭōsus -a -um, favoured, beloved; showing favour.

grātis, v. *gratia.*

grātor, 1. *dep.* to congratulate any one, *alicui;* to rejoice.

grătuĭtō, *adv.* without payment, gratuitously.

grātuītus -a -um, gratuitous, voluntary.

grātŭlābundus -a -um, congratulating.

grātŭlātĭo -ōnis, f. congratulation; a thanksgiving festival.

grātŭlor, 1. *dep.* to manifest joy, to congratulate, *alicui;* to rejoice; to give solemn thanks to a deity.

grātus -a -um, pleasing; charming, agreeable; welcome, beloved; deserving thanks; grateful. *Subst.,* **grātus -i,** m. grateful man.

grăvantĕr, *adv.* reluctantly.

grăvātē, *adv.* with difficulty, unwillingly.

grăvēdĭnōsus -a -um, subject to cold *or* catarrh.

grăvēdo -ĭnis, f. cold, catarrh.

grăvĕŏlens -lentis, strong smelling, rank.

grăvesco, 3. to become grievous, grow worse; *nemus fetu gravescit,* is laden with fruit.

grăvĭdĭtas -ātis, f. pregnancy.

grăvĭdo, 1. to fructify.

grăvĭdus -a -um, pregnant; laden, filled, full.

grăvis -e, heavy, burdensome; *cibus,* hard to digest; *agmen,* heavy-armed; *of sound,* low, deep; weighty, impor-

tant; *of style,* dignified; grievous, painful, unpleasant; *of smell,* strong; unhealthy; troublesome, sad; laden with; pregnant; weak, ill; advanced in age, *gravis aetate.*

grăvĭtas -ātis, f. weight; consequence, importance; dignity, sublimity; authority; high price; unhealthiness; unpleasantness of smell; pregnancy; dulness, faintness.

grăvĭtĕr, *adv. of sound,* deeply; impressively; violently; in an unhealthy condition; irritably; *aliquid graviter accipere, ferre,* to be vexed with.

grăvo, 1. to load, burden; to exaggerate, increase; to oppress. *Pass., as reflex.,* to feel anything burdensome.

grĕgālis -e, belonging to a herd; belonging to the same company; of a common kind; of a private soldier; *subst., plur.,* **grĕgāles -ium,** m. companions, associates.

grĕgārĭus -a -um, belonging to the herd, common; *miles,* a private soldier.

grĕgātim, *adv.* in flocks *or* herds; in crowds.

grĕmĭum -ii, n. the lap; centre, middle.

gressus -ūs, m. a step, course, way.

grex, grĕgis, m. a herd, flock; troop, company; a philosophical sect.

grunnĭo (grundĭo) -īvi *or* **-ĭi -ītum,** 4. to grunt like a pig.

grunnītus (grundītus) -ūs, m. the grunting of a pig.

grus, grŭis, m. and (*gen.*) f. a crane.

gryllus -i, m. a cricket, grasshopper

gryps, grypis (gryphis), m. a griffin.

gŭbernācŭlum (gŭbernāclum) -i, n. rudder, helm; management, government.

gŭbernātĭo -ōnis, f. steering; direction, government.

gŭbernātor -ōris, m. helmsman, steersman, pilot; leader, governor.

gŭbernātrix -īcis, f. she that leads, governs.

gŭberno, 1. *intransit.,* to sit at the helm, to steer; *transit.,* to guide, direct, govern.

gŭbernum -i, n. = *gubernaculum (q.v.).*

gŭla -ae, f. the gullet, throat; greediness, gluttony.

gŭlōsus -a -um, greedy, dainty.

gūmĭa -ae, c. an epicure, gourmand.

gummi (cummi), n. *indecl.* gum.

gurges -ĭtis, m. a whirlpool, eddy, abyss; *poet.,* any deep water, flood, sea.

1. **gurgŭlĭo -ōnis,** f. the windpipe.

2. **gurgŭlĭo -ōnis,** n., v. *curculio.*

gurgustĭum -ĭi, n. a hut, hovel.

gustātus -ū , m. taste; the taste, flavour of anything.

gusto, 1. to taste, take a little of; to partake of, enjoy.

gustus -ūs, m. the tasting; the relish taken before a meal; flavour of anything.

gutta -ae, *f.* a drop of any liquid ; *guttae*, spots *or* marks on animals, stones.

guttur -ŭris, *n.* the windpipe, throat ; gluttony.

guttus -i, *m.* a narrow-necked jug.

Gўās -ae, *acc.* -an, *and* **Gўēs** -ae, *acc.* -en, *m.* giant with a hundred arms.

gymnăsiarchus -i, *m.* the master of a gymnasium.

gymnăsium (**gumnăsium**) -ii, *n.* a public school of gymnastics, gymnasium; a place for philosophical discussion.

gymnicus -a -um, gymnastic.

gynaecēum -i, *n.*, *and* **gynaecium** -i, *n.* the women's apartments in a Greek house.

gypso, 1. to cover with gypsum.

gypsum -i, *n.* gypsum.

gўrus -i, *m.* a circle, circular course ; *poet.* (*of time*), circuit.

H

H h, *the eighth letter of the Latin Alphabet.*

ha! *an exclamation*, ha! hold! stop! ha! ha!

hăbēna -ae, *f.* that by which anything is held ; thong, *of a sling* ; a whip ; the reins (*gen. plur.*); *immittit habenas classi*, crowds on sail ; government, guidance.

hăbĕo -ŭi -itum, 2. to have, hold; to carry, wear ; *of places*, to hold, have, contain, keep. *Tartara habent Panthoiden;* to have possession of; to inhabit; to occupy; to rule; to possess property; to maintain; *milites in castris*, to keep the soldiers in camp; to confine, to keep fast; *in animo*, to intend; to treat, behave towards; *aliquem liberalissime* ; to consider, regard ; to hold, arrange, *concilium plebis*; to utter ; *orationem in senatu*, to deliver a speech: to keep, observe, *ordines ; se habere*, or *habere*, to fare, to be situated; *graviter se habere*, to be very ill; *of things*, *res ita se habet.*

hăbĭlis -e, easily managed, handy, supple; suitable, convenient; skilful.

hăbĭlĭtas -ātis, *f.* aptitude, ability.

hăbĭtābĭlis -e, habitable.

hăbĭtātĭo -ōnis, *f.* dwelling.

hăbĭtātŏr -ōris, *m.* one who dwells *or* inhabits.

hăbĭto, 1. *transit.*, to inhabit; *in pass.*, to be inhabited; *intransit.*, to dwell, to frequent; to dwell on a subject.

hăbĭtūdo -inis, *f.* form, appearance.

1. **hăbĭtus** -a -um, *p. adj.*, formed, constituted.

2. **hăbĭtus** -ūs, *m.* condition of the body, appearance ; dress ; the nature, condition; disposition.

hāc, *adv.* here, this way, by this side.

hāctĕnus, *adv.* so far; up to this point; only so far. *Of time*, till now, hitherto.

Hadria (**Adria**) -ae, *f.* 1. town in Picenum; 2. town in the north of Italy; 3. *generally masculine*, the Adriatic Sea. *Adj.*, **Hadriăcus** (**Adriăcus**); **Hadriānus** -a -um, belonging to Hadria; **Hadriāticus**, Adriatic.

1. **Hadriānus** -a -um, *v. Hadria.*

2. **Hadriānus** -i, *n.* a Roman Emperor.

haedīnus -a -um, of *or* pertaining to a kid.

haedŭlĕa -ae, . (*dim. of haedus*), a little kid.

haedŭlus -i, *m.* (*dim. of haedus*), a little kid.

haedus -i, *m.* a kid, young goat.

Haemŏnia -ae, *f.* old name of Thessaly.

Haemus -i, *m.* mountain range in Thrace.

haerēditas = **hereditas** (*q.v.*).

haerĕo, haesi, haesum, 2. to hang to, stick to, cleave to, adhere; to remain in a place ; to be rooted to a spot; to be retarded, to cease; to be embarrassed.

haeres = **heres** (*q.v.*).

haeresco, 3. to adhere, cleave, stick.

haerĕsis -ĕos, *f.* a philosophical sect.

haesitantia -ae, *f.* a sticking fast; *linguae*, stammering.

haesĭtātĭo -ōnis, *f.* a sticking fast, stammering ; embarrassment, hesitation.

haesĭto, 1. to stick fast ; to stop ; *linguā*, to stammer; to be at a loss.

halcēdo, *v. alcedo.*

halcyon, *v. alcyon.*

Halcyŏnē, *v. Alcyone.*

hālec, *v. alec.*

hālex, *v. alec.*

hăliăĕtos *and* **hăliaĕëtos** -i, *m.* the sea-eagle, osprey.

Hălicarnassos -i, *f.* town in Caria, birth-place of Herodotus.

hālĭtus -ūs, *m.* breath, exhalation.

hallex, *v. alec.*

hālo, 1. to breathe, exhale, be fragrant. *Transit.*, to breathe forth.

hālūc . . . *v. aluc* . . .

hăma (**ăma**) -ae, *f.* bucket, *esp.* a fireman's bucket.

Hămādrўas (**Ămădrўas**) -ădis *f.* a wood-nymph, hamadryad.

hāmātus -a -um, provided with hooks, hooked; curved like a hook, crooked.

Hămilcăr -căris, *m. Hamilcar Barca*, father of Hannibal.

Hammon, *v. Ammon.*

hāmus -i, *m.* a hook; talons of a hawk.

Hannĭbăl -bălis, *m.* general of the Carthaginians in the Second Punic War.

hăra -ae, *f.* pen for animals, a pig-sty.

hărēna, *v. arena.*

hărĭŏlātĭo (**ărĭŏlātĭo**) -ōnis, *f.* soothsaying.

hăriŏlor (ărĭŏlor), 1. *dep.* to utter prophecies; to talk nonsense.

hăriŏlus (ărĭŏlus) -i, *m.* soothsayer, prophet.

1. harmŏnĭa -ae, *f.* harmony; concord.

2. Harmŏnĭa -ae, *f.* wife of Cadmus.

harpăgo -ōnis, *m.* a large hook, drag, grappling-iron; a rapacious person.

harpe -ēs, *f.* a curved sword.

Harpȳiae (*trisyll.*) -ārum, *f.* the Harpies, mythical monsters.

hărund . . . *v. arund.*

hăruspex (ăruspex) -spĭcis, *m.* soothsayer; seer, prophet.

hăruspĭcīnus -a -um, relating to the inspection of entrails. *Subst.*, hăruspĭcīna -ae, *f.* the art of the haruspex.

hăruspĭcĭum -ĭi, *n.* the inspection of entrails, divination.

Hasdrŭbăl (Asdrŭbăl) -bălis, *m.* brother of Hannibal.

hasta -ae, *f.* spear, pike, javelin; *sub hasta vendere,* to sell by auction.

hastātus -a -um, armed with a spear; *subst.,* hastāti -ōrum, *m.* the first line of the Roman army.

hastīlĕ -is, *n.* the shaft of a spear; the spear itself; a prop for vines.

hau, *interj.* (*of grief*) oh!

haud (haut), *adv.* not, not at all, by no means.

hauddum, *adv.* not at all as yet, not yet.

haudquăquam, *adv.* by no means, not at all.

haurĭo, hausi, haustum (*fut. partic.* hausurus), 4. to draw up, draw out; to tear up; to shed blood; to collect together; to take away; to drain dry, empty; to pierce, *gladio;* to squander; to accomplish; to oppress; to exhaust, weaken; to suffer; to devour, consume; to drink in.

haustrum -i, *n.* machine for drawing water.

haustus -ūs, *m.* a drawing of water; *aquae,* the right of drawing water; inhaling; drinking; a draught; a handful.

haut = haud (*q.v.*).

hăvĕo, *v. aveo.*

Hĕautontĭmōrūmĕnos -i, *m.* the Self-Tormentor, title of one of Terence's comedies.

hebdŏmăs -ădis, *f.* the seventh day of a disease.

Hebe -ēs, *f.* cup-bearer of the gods.

hĕbĕnus, *v. ebenus.*

hĕbĕo, 2. to be blunt, dull; to be dull, inactive.

hĕbĕs -ĕtis, dull; blunted, stumpy; sluggish, weak; mentally dull, stupid.

hĕbesco, 3. to become dull, blunt, dim.

hĕbĕto, 1. to make dull, blunt; to deaden, dim.

Hebraeus -a -um, Hebrew, Jewish.

Hebrus -i, *m.* chief river of Thrace.

Hĕcăbē, *v. Hecuba.*

Hĕcătē -ēs, *f. and* Hĕcăta -ae, *f.* a goddess, often identified with Diana and Luna. *Adj.,* Hĕcătēĭus.

hĕcătombē -ēs, *f.* a hecatomb, sacrifice of a hundred oxen.

Hector tŏris, *m.* son of Priam, killed by Achilles. *Adj.,* Hectŏrĕus.

Hĕcŭba -ae, *f. and* Hĕcŭbē (Hĕcăbē) ōn, *f.* wife of Priam.

hĕdĕra -ae, *f.* ivy, sacred to Bacchus.

hĕdĕrĭger -gĕra -gĕrum, ivy-bearing, ivy-crowned.

hĕdĕrōsus -a -um, ivied.

hĕdўchrum -i, *n.* a fragrant salve.

hei, *interj.,* alas! *hei mihi,* woe is me!

Hĕlĕna -ae, *f. and* Hĕlĕnē -ēs, *f.* carried off by Paris to Troy, and thus the cause of the Trojan War.

Hĕlĕnus -i, *m.* son of Priam, a soothsayer.

Hĕliădes -um, *f.* the daughters of the Sun.

hĕlĭca -ae, *f.* winding.

Hĕlĭcē -ēs, *f.* the Great Bear.

Hĕlĭcon -ōnis, *m.* a hill of Boeotia, sacred to the Muses; Hĕlĭcōnĭădes -um, *f. and* Hĕlĭcōnĭdes -um, *f.* the Muses.

Hēlĭŏpŏlis -is, *f.* 1. a town in Coele-syria, *now* Baalbek; 2. a town in Lower Egypt.

Hellē -ēs, *f.* drowned in the Hellespont, so named after her.

hellĕborus, *v. elleborus.*

Hellespontus -i, *m.* the Hellespont, Dardanelles.

hĕlops (ĕlops, ellops), -ōpis, *m.* a savoury fish, *perhaps* the sturgeon.

Hēlōtes, *v. Hilotae.*

hēllŭātĭo (hēllŭātĭo) -ōnis, *f.* gluttony.

hĕlŭo (hēllŭo) -ōnis, *m.* a glutton.

hĕlŭor (hēllŭor), 1. *dep.* to gormandise.

helvella -ae, *f.* a small pot-herb.

Helvĕtĭi -ōrum, *m.* inhabitants of the part of Gallia now called Switzerland. *Adj.,* Helvĕtĭus *and* Helvĕtĭcus.

hem, *interj.* ah! oh! well! only see! just look!

nĕmĕrŏdrŏmus -i, *m.* a special courier, express.

hēmĭcillus -i, *m.* half an ass, *term of reproach.*

hēmĭcyclĭum -ĭi, *n.* a semicircular settee for conversation.

hēmĭna -ae, *f.* a measure of capacity, *nearly half a pint.*

hendĕcăsyllăbi -ōrum, *m.* verses of eleven syllables.

Henna (Enna) -ae, *f.* an ancient city of Sicily, celebrated for a temple of Ceres.

heptĕris -is, *f.* galley with seven banks of oars.

1. hĕra (ĕra) -ae, *f.* mistress of a house; queen, female ruler.

2. Hēra -ae, *f.* the Greek goddess identified with the Roman Juno.

herba -ae, *f.* plant with stalks, grass, plant, herb; the stalk of wheat, tares.

herbidus -a -um, grassy.

herbifer -fěra -fěrum, grassy.

herbigrădus -a -um, going through the grass, *epithet of a snake.*

herbōsus -a -um, grassy.

herbūla -ae, *f.* (*dim. of herba*), a little herb

hercisco (**ercisco**), 3. to divide an inheritance.

Hercle, *an oath*, by Hercules.

herctum -i, *n.* inheritance, *only in the phrase herctum ciere*, to divide an inheritance.

Herculānĕum -i, *n.* town in Campania, destroyed by an eruption of Vesuvius.

Hercŭlēs -is *and* i, *m.* son of Jupiter and Alcmena. *Adj.*, **Hercŭlēus.**

Hercўnia silva -ae, *f.* the Hercynian forest, in Central Germany.

hěre = **heri** (*q.v.*).

hērēditārius -a -um, relating to an inheritance; inherited, hereditary.

hērēditas -ātis, *f.* inheritance.

hērēdium -ii, *n.* a patrimony.

hēres (**haeres**) -ēdis, *c.* an heir.

hěrī (**hěrě**), *adv.* yesterday; lately.

hērifŭga -ae, *m.* a fugitive, runaway.

hěrīlis -e, relating to the master *or* mistress of the house.

hermaphrŏdītus -i, *m.* an hermaphrodite.

Hermăthēna -ae, *f.* a double bust of Hermes and Athena.

Hermēs -ae, *m.* the god Hermes (Mercury); a Hermes-pillar.

Hermiŏnē -ēs, *f. and* **Hermiŏna** -ae, *f.* daughter of Menelaus and Helena.

Hērō -ūs, *f.* a priestess of Aphrodite at Sestos, beloved by Leander.

Hērŏdŏtus -i, *m.* first great Greek historian.

hērōicus -a -um, relating to the heroes, heroic.

hērōinē -ēs, *f.* a demigoddess, heroine.

hērōis -idis, *f.* a demigoddess, heroine.

hērōs -ōis, *m.* a demigod, hero.

hērōus -a -um, relating to a hero, heroic.

hěrus (**ěrus**) -i, *m.* the master of a household.

Hēsiŏdus -i, *m.* the oldest Greek poet after Homer.

Hespěris -idis, *f.* western ; *aquae*, Italian. *Subst.*, **Hespěrides** -um, *f.* the Hesperides, daughters of the Evening.

Hespěrius -a -um, western ; *terra*, Italy. *Subst.*, **Hespěria** -ae, *f.* the western land, Italy; Spain.

Hespěrus *or* -os -i, *m.* the Evening Star.

hesternus -a -um, relating to yesterday.

hesterno, *adv.* yesterday.

heu, *interj.*, oh ! alas ! woe !

heus ! *interj.* hallo ! ho there ! hark !

hexămĕtĕr -tra -trum, with six feet; *versus hexameter*, a hexameter.

hexēris -is, *f.* a galley with six banks of oars.

hiātus -ūs, *m.* a cleft, opening; the open jaws; desire after; a hiatus, the meeting of two vowels.

Hibēres -um, *or* **Hibēri** -ōrum, *m.* the Hiberians (Iberians); **Hibēria** -ae, part of Spain.

hiberna -ōrum, *n.*, *v. hibernus.*

hibernācŭlum -i, *n. plur.*, *hibernacula* tents *or* huts for winter quarters.

Hibernia -ae, *f.* Ireland.

hiberno, 1. to winter, spend the winter; *milit.*, to keep in winter quarters.

hibernus -a -um, wintry, winterly; stormy. *Subst.*, **hiberna** -ōrum, *n.* winter quarters.

1. **Hibērus** -i, *m.* river in Spain.

2. **Hibērus**, Hiberian.

hibiscum -i, *n.* marsh-mallow.

hibrida (**hybrida**) -ae, *c.* a hybrid.

1. **hic, haec, hōc**, *pron. demonstr.* this; he, she, it.

2. **hīc** *and* **heic**, *adv.* here.

hīce, haece, hōce, *pron. demonstr.* this.

hiĕmālis -e, wintry; stormy.

hiĕmo, 1. to winter ; *of soldiers*, to keep in winter quarters; to be stormy.

hiems (**hiemps**) -ĕmis, *f.* stormy weather, storm; winter; cold.

Hiĕro, *and* **Hiĕrōn** -ōnis, *m. Hiero I.*, *Hiero II*, rulers of Syracuse. *Adj.*, **Hiĕrōnicus.**

Hiĕrŏsŏlýma -ōrum, *n.* Jerusalem.

hilărē, *adv.* cheerfully, merrily.

hilăris -e, *and* **hilărus** -a -um, cheerful, merry, jovial.

hilăritas -ātis, *f.* cheerfulness, hilarity.

hilăritūdo -inis, *f.* = hilaritas (*q.v.*).

hilăro, 1. to make joyful, to cheer up.

hilărŭlus -a -um (*dim. of hilarus*), somewhat cheerful.

hilla -ae, *f.* (*dim. of hira*), *generally plur.*, the smaller intestines of all animals: a kind of sausage.

Hilōtae *and* **Ilōtae** -ārum, *m.* the Helots, slaves of the Spartans.

hilum -i, *n.* a trifle; *neque (nec) hilum*, not a whit, not in the least.

hinc, *adv.* from here, hence; from this cause; henceforth; thereupon; on this side, in this direction.

hinnio, 4. to neigh, whinny.

hinnītus -ūs, *m.* a neighing.

hinnŭlĕus (**hinnŭlus**), -i, *m.* a young hind *or* fawn.

hinnus -i, *m.* a mule.

hio, 1. *intransit.*, to open, stand open, gape ; *of discourse*, to be badly put together ; to open wide the mouth *or* jaws; long for; *transit.*, to pour forth, *carmen.*

hippăgōgi -ōrum, *f. plur.* transports for cavalry.

Hippias -ae, *m.* son of Pisistratus, tyrant of Athens.

hippŏcentaurus -i, m. a centaur.

Hippŏcrătēs -is, m. a physician of Cos (*flourishing about* 436 B.C.).

Hippŏcrēnē, -ēs, f. fountain on Mount Helicon.

Hippŏdămus -i, m. the horse-tamer-*i.e. Castor*.

hippŏdrŏmos i, m. a hippŏdrŏmŏ, or racecourse.

Hippŏlytē -ēs, f., *and* Hippŏlyta -ae, f. Queen of the Amazons.

Hippŏlytus -i, m. son of Theseus.

hippŏtŏxŏta -ae, m. a mounted archer.

hippūrus, *or* -ŏs, -i, m. *perhaps* the gold fish.

hir *and* ir, *indecl.* the hand.

hīra -ae, f. a gut, intestine.

hircīnus -a -um, relating to a he-goat.

hircŏsus -a -um, smelling like a goat.

hircŭlus -i, m. (*dim. of* hircus), a little goat.

hircus -i, m. a he-goat.

hirnĕa -ae, f. a can *or* jug.

Hīrpīnī -ōrum, m. a Samnite people.

hirquus, hirquīnus = hircus, hircīnus (*q.v.*).

hirsūtus -a -um, hairy, shaggy; rough, unadorned.

hirtus -a -um, shaggy, hairy; uncultivated.

hirūdo -ĭnis, f. a leech.

hirundinīnus -a -um, relating to swallows.

hirundo -dĭnis, f. a swallow.

hisco, 3. to open, gape; to mutter.

Hispāni -ōrum, m. the Spaniards.

Hispānia -ae, f. the Spanish peninsula.

hispidus -a -um, shaggy, hairy; *ager*, wild.

1. hister = histrio (*q.v.*).

2. Hister -tri, m. lower part of the Danube.

histŏria -ae, f. history; narrative.

histŏricus -a -um, historical. *Subst.*, histŏricus -i, m. historian.

histricus -a -um, relating to actors.

histrio -ōnis, m. an actor.

hiulcātio -ē, relating to actors.

hiulcē, *adv.* in a mouthing manner.

hiulco, 1. to cause to gape, to split.

hiulcus -a -um, gaping, cleft, open; disconnected; eager, longing.

hŏdiē, *adv.* to-day; at the present time; up to-day.

hŏdiernus -a -um, relating to to-day.

hoedus, hoedinus, *etc.* = haedus, haedinus, *etc.* (*q.v.*).

Hŏmērus -i, m. the celebrated Greek epic poet; *adj.*, Hŏmēricus.

hŏmicīda -ae, c. a murderer, murderess, homicide.

hŏmicīdium -ii, n. murder, homicide.

hŏmo -inis, m. a human being; man; *plur.*, homines, men in general, people.

hŏmoeŏmĕria -ae, f. similarity of parts.

hŏmullus -i, m. (*dim. of* homo), a little man, manikin.

hŏmuncio -ōnis, m. (*dim. of* homo), a little man, manikin.

hŏmuncŭlus -i, m. (*dim. of* homo), a little man, manikin.

hŏnestas -ātis, f. honourable reputation, respectability, *amenitas civitatis,* notabilities; worth, probity.

hŏnestē, *adv.* honourably, creditably; nobly.

hŏnesto, 1. to honour, distinguish, dignify.

hŏnestus -a -um, honourable, glorious; (*subst.* hŏnestum -i, n. morality, virtue); fine, beautiful; (*subst.,* hŏnestum -i, n. beauty); distinguished; (*subst.,* hŏnesti -ōrum, m. people of distinction)

hŏnor = honos (*q.v.*).

hŏnōrābilis -c, honourable.

hŏnōrārius -a -um, done *or* given in honour of, honorary.

hŏnōrātē, *adv.* with honour, honourably.

hŏnōrātus -a -um, *p. adj.,* honoured, distinguished, respected; placed in a high position, in office.

hŏnōrificē, *adv.,* comp. honorificentius, superl. honorificentissime, with honour, in a respectful manner.

hŏnōrificus -a -um, honourable, honouring.

hŏnōro, 1. to show honour to; dignify, honour with.

hŏnōrus -a -um, honourable.

hŏnos *and* hŏnor -ōris, m. honour, honourable distinction; *supremus honos,* the last honour = burial; a public office; title of honour; a reward, fee; a sacrifice; *poet.* beauty, ornament.

hŏra -ae, f. season; hour; *in horas,* hourly; *hora quota est?* what's o'clock? hōrae -ārum, f. a clock, dial.

Hōrae -ārum, f. the Hours, attendants on the sun-god.

Hŏrātius -a -um, name of a Roman gens; 1. *Horatius Cocles,* who defended the bridge against the army of Porsena. 2. *Q. Horatius Flaccus,* the poet.

hordēārius -a -um, relating to barley.

hordĕum (ordĕum), -i, n. barley.

hōria (ōria), -ae, f. a small fishing-boat.

hōriŏla (ōriŏla), -ae, f. (*dim. of* oria), a small fishing-boat.

hŏrizon -ontis, m. the horizon.

hornōtinus -a -um, of *or* relating to the present year.

hornus -a -um, of this year, this year's.

hōrōlŏgium -ii, n. sundial, *or* water-clock.

hŏroscŏpŏs -ŏn, m. a horoscope.

horrendus -a -um, horrible, dreadful; venerable.

horrĕo, 2. to bristle; to be rough with frost; *of hair,* to stand on end; *partic.,* horrens, prickly, rough; to shudder with cold *or* fright. *Transit.,* to shudder at.

horresco, horrŭi, 3. to bristle, be rough; to tremble, begin to shudder.

horrĕum -i, *n.* barn, storehouse, magazine.

horribilis -e, horrible, frightful, astonishing, wonderful.

horridē, *adv.* roughly, without embellishment.

horridŭlus -a -um (*dim. o horridus*), somewhat rough, projecting.

horridus -a -um, rough, shaggy; wild, savage ; without refinement ; shuddering; horrible.

horrifer -fĕra -fĕrum, causing dread, terrible.

horrificē, *adv.* with dread.

horrifico, 1. to make rough; to terrify.

horrificus -a -um, horrible, frightful.

horrisŏnus -a -um, sounding horribly.

horror -ōris, *m.* a shaking, shivering with cold; trembling; terror; religious dread.

horsum, *adv.* in this direction.

hortāmen -inis, *n.* an encouragement, exhortation.

hortāmentum -i, *n.* encouragement.

hortātio -ōnis, *f.* exhortation.

hortātor -ōris, *m.* an exhorter, encourager.

hortātus -ūs, *m.* exhortation.

Hortensius -a -um, name of a Roman gens; *Q. Hortensius Hortalus,* an orator of the time of Cicero.

hortor, 1. *dep.* to exhort, encourage; to harangue soldiers.

hortŭlus -i, *m.* (*dim. of hortus*), a little garden; *hortuli,* grounds, a small park.

hortus -i, *m.* garden.

hospes -pitis, *c.* a stranger, foreigner; a guest.

hospitālis -e, relating to a guest or host; friendly, hospitable.

hospitālitas -ātis, *f.* hospitality.

hospitālitĕr, *adv.* hospitably.

hospitium -ii, *n.,* the relation between host and guest; hospitality, friendliness; a guest-chamber.

hospitus -a -um, strange, foreign ; (*subst.,* **hospita -ae,** *f.* foreigner) ; hospitable. *Subst.,* **hospita -ae,** *f.* hostess.

hostia -ae, *f.* animal slain in sacrifice.

hosticus -a -um, relating to the enemy, hostile. *Subst.,* **hosticum -i,** *n.* the enemy's territory.

hostificus -a -um, hostile.

hostilis -e, relating to the enemy, hostile; unfriendly.

hostilitĕr, *adv.* hostilely, like an enemy.

Hostilius -ii, *m. Tullus,* third king of Rome.

hostimentum -i, *n.* compensation.

1. hostio, 4. to requite, recompense.

2. hostio, 4. to strike.

hostis -is, *c.* an enemy, a public foe.

hūc, *adv.* hither, to this place ; *huc atque illuc,* hither and thither.

hūcine, *adv.* so far ? as far as this ?

hŭi, *interj.,* of astonishment, admiration, ha ! ho ! oh !

hŭiusmŏdi *or* **hŭiuscĕmŏdi,** of this kind.

hūmānē, *adv.* humanly, like a human being; kindly, courteously.

hūmānitas -ātis, *f.* humanity, human nature; kindness, philanthropy, mildness; good breeding, culture.

hūmānitĕr, *adv.* humanly ; politely, kindly.

hūmānitŭs, *adv.* after the manner of men.

hūmānus -a -um, human, of or relating to human beings; *res humanae,* human affairs; *scelus,* against men; (*subst.,* **humanus -i,** *m.* one of the human race; **humana -ōrum,** *n.* human affairs) ; humane, kind; civilised, refined.

hūmātio -ōnis, *f.* a burying, interment.

hūmecto, 1. to wet, moisten, water.

hūmĕo, 2. to be moist, wet ; *partic. pres.,* **hūmens -entis,** moist, wet, dewy.

hūmĕrus -i, *m.* the shoulder.

hūmesco, 3. to become wet, grow moist.

hūmidŭlus -a -um (*dim. of humidus*), somewhat wet, moist.

hūmidus -a -um, *wet,* moist, humid; *mella,* liquid. *Subst.,* **hūmidum-i,** *n.* a wet place.

hūmifer -fĕra -fĕrum, containing moisture, moist, *poet.*

hūmilis -e, low; shallow; *of rank, etc.,* mean, humble, poor; (*subst.,* **humilis -is,** *m.* a person of low rank); abject, base; submissive, humble; mean.

hūmilitas -ātis, *f.* smallness, lowness ; insignificance, obscurity ; humility ; abjectness.

hūmilitĕr, *adv.* humbly, meanly.

hūmo, 1. to bury; to perform the funeral rites over a corpse (burn, *etc.*).

hūmor -ōris, *m.* moisture, liquid, fluid; *circumfluus,* the sea; the sap of plants.

hūmus -i, *f.* the ground, earth, soil; *humi,* on the ground, on the floor; land, country.

hyăcinthinus -a -um, hyacinthine, belonging to the hyacinth.

1. Hyăcinthus (-ŏs) -i, *m.* a beautiful youth, accidentally killed by Apollo.

2. hyăcinthus -i, *m.* a flower, the hyacinth (*not the flower so called by us*).

Hyădes -um, *f.* a group of seven stars.

hyaena -ae, *f.* the hyena.

hyălus -i, *m.* glass; *color hyali,* glass green.

Hydaspēs -pis, *m.* river in India.

hydra -ae, *f.* many-headed water-snake, slain by Hercules; a constellation; a monster of the lower world.

hydraulus -i, *m.* a water organ.

hydria -ae, *f.* an urn, water-jar.

hydrŏchŏus -i, *m.* the constellation Aquarius.

hydrŏpĭcus -a -um, dropsical.

hydrops -ōpis, *m.* the dropsy.

hydrus -i -m, a water-snake.

hyems, hyĕmālis, *etc.* = **hiems**, *etc.* (*q.v.*).

Hylas -ae, *m.* friend of Hercules.

Hymēn -ēnis, *m.* the god of marriage; the morning song;

Hymenaeus *or* **-ŭs -i**, *m.* the marriage song; the wedding; Hymen, the god of marriage.

Hyperborei -ōrum, *m.* the Hyperboreans; *adj.,* **Hyperborēus**, northern.

Hyperĭdes -ae, *n.* an Athenian orator.

Hyperīon -ōnis, *m.* 1. a Titan, father of the Sun; 2. the Sun god.

Hypermnestra -ae, *and* **-c, -ēs**, *f.* youngest of the Danaides, the only one who did not kill her husband (Lynceus).

hypŏdĭdascălus -i, *m.* an under-teacher.

hypomnēma -mătis, *n.* a memorandum, note.

hypŏthēca -ae, *f.* a pledge, security.

I (vowel)

I i, *the ninth letter of the Latin Alphabet.*

Iacchus -i, *m.* a name of Bacchus; wine.

iambus -i, *m.* an iambus.

ianthĭnus -a -um, violet-coloured.

Iăpĕtus -i, *m.* a giant, father of Atlas, Epimetheus, and Prometheus.

Iăpyx -pỹgis, *m.* 1. son of Daedalus; 2. a west-north-west wind; 3. a river in Apulia. **Iăpȳgia -ae**, *f.* part of Calabria.

Iāson -ŏnis, *m.* leader of the Argonauts to Colchis to fetch the golden fleece.

iaspis -ĭdis, *f.* a jasper.

Ibēr . . . *v.* **Hiber . . .**

ĭbi, *adv.* there, at that place; in that matter.

ĭbīdem, *adv.* in the same place; moreover.

ibis -is *and* **-ĭdis**, *f.* the ibis.

ĭbiscum, ibrida = **hibiscum, hibrida** (*q.v.*).

Ĭcărus -i, *m.* the son of Daedalus, drowned in the Aegean Sea, whilst flying from Crete with wings made by his father.

iccirco = **idcirco** (*q.v.*).

Icēni -ōrum, *m.* a people in Britain.

ĭco, īci, ictum, 3. to strike, smite, stab; *icere foedus*, to make a treaty; *partic., ictus*, affected, touched.

ictus -ūs, *m.* a blow, stab, thrust; *solis*, a sunbeam; assault of an enemy. In *music*, beat.

Ida -ae, *f.,* and **Ĭdē -ēs**, *f.* 1. a mountain near Troy; 2. a mountain in Crete. *Adj.,* **Idaeus**.

idcirco (iccirco), *adv.* on that account, for that reason.

īdem, ĕădem, ĭdem, the same; *sometimes* also.

identĭdem, *adv.* repeatedly, again and again.

ĭdĕō, *adv.* on that account, therefore.

idiōta (idiōtes) -ae, *m.* an ignorant, uncultivated man.

Īdŏmĕneus -ei, *m.* son of Deucalion.

**Idŏnĕă, adv. . . . **

Idŏneus -a -um, fit, appropriate; capable, suitable; *of persons,* satisfactory; worthy.

Idus -ŭum, *f.* the Ides, fifteenth day in March, May, July, October; thirteenth in the other months.

ĭgĭtur, *adv.* so, therefore, then, accordingly. *In questions,* then; *to resume an argument,* so, as I was saying.

ignārus -a -um, ignorant of, inexperienced in; *with genit., pass.,* unknown.

ignāvē *and* **ignāvĭtĕr**, *adv.* lazily, without spirit.

ignāvĭa -ae, *f.* idleness, listlessness, cowardice.

ignāvĭtĕr = **ignave** (*q.v.*).

ignāvus -a -um, idle, listless, inactive, cowardly; *subst.,* **ignāvus -i**, *m.* a coward; *of inanimate ovjects,* inert, sluggish; *nemus,* unfruitful; *act.,* causing idleness.

ignesco, 3. to kindle, catch fire, to glow with passion.

ignĕus -a -um, fiery, glowing.

ignĭcŭlus -i, *m.* (*dim. of ignis*), a little fire, little flame, spark; ardour; a beginning.

ignĭfer -fĕra -fĕrum, fire-bearing, fiery.

ignĭgĕna -ae, *m.* born of fire (*of Bacchus*).

ignĭpēs -pēdis, fiery-footed.

ignĭpŏtens -entis, ruler of fire (*of Vulcan*).

ignis -is, *m.* fire; a fire-brand; lightning; glow, heat; glitter.

ignōbĭlis -e, unknown, obscure; of low birth.

ignōbĭlĭtas -ātis, *f.* obscurity, mean birth.

ignōmĭnĭa -ae, *f.* disgrace, dishonour.

ignōmĭnĭōsus -a -um, ignominious, disgraceful.

ignōrābĭlis -e, unknown.

ignōrans -antis, ignorant.

ignōrantĭa -ae, *f.* ignorance.

ignōrātĭo -ōnis, *f.* ignorance.

ignōro, 1. to be ignorant of, not to know.

ignoscens -entis, forgiving.

ignosco -nōvi -nōtum, 3. to overlook, pardon; *with dat.*

ignōtus -a -um, unknown; ignoble, obscure; *act.,* ignorant; *subst.,* **ignōtus -i**, *m.* an unknown person.

Īlia -ae, *f.* the Trojan woman = Rhea Sylvia, mother of Romulus and Remus.

īlia -ium, *n.* the flank; the intestines of animals.

īlĭcet, let us go, you may go; it is all over, all is lost; immediately.

īlĭcētum -i, *n.* an ilex-grove.

īlĭcō = **illico** (*q.v.*).

Ilienses -ium, *m.* inhabitants of Ilium;

Ilĭăs -ădis, 1. a Trojan woman; 2. the Iliad of Homer.

Ilĭŏn or Ilĭum -ii, n. and Ilĭŏs -ii, f. Troy.

illā, adv. at that place, in that way.

illăbĕfactus -a -um, unshaken, firm.

illābor -lapsus, 3. dep. to fall, glide, fall into.

illăbŏro, 1. to work upon, labour at.

illāc, adv. there; illac facere, to stand on that side, belong to that party.

illăcessītus -a -um, unattacked, unprovoked.

illăcrĭmābĭlis -e, unwept; pitiless.

illăcrĭmo, 1. to weep, bewail; errori.

illăcrĭmor, 1. dep. to weep over, bewail; morti.

illaesus -a -um, unhurt, uninjured.

illaetābĭlis -e, sorrowful, gloomy.

illăquĕo, 1. to entrap, entangle.

illaudātus -a -um, unpraised, obscure.

illautus = illotus (q.v.).

ille, illa, illud, genit. illīus, demonstr. pron. that; he, she it; that glorious or notorious; ille Epaminondas; illa Medea.

illĕcĕbra -ae, f. an allurement, charm; an enticer, a decoy-bird.

1. illectus -a -um, unread.

2. illectus -a -um, partic. of illicio.

illĕpĭdē, adv. inelegantly.

illĕpĭdus -a -um, inelegant, unmannerly.

illĭbātus -a -um, undiminished, unimpaired.

illĭbĕrālis -e, ignoble; low, mean.

illĭbĕrālĭtas -ātis, f. stinginess, meanness.

illĭbĕrālĭtĕr, ignobly, meanly; in a sordid, niggardly manner.

1. illīc, illaec, illūc, pron. demonstr. that, yonder.

2. illīc, adv. there, at that place; in that case.

illĭcĭo -lexi -lectum, 3. to entice, decoy.

illĭcĭtātor -ōris, m. a sham bidder a tan auction.

illĭcĭtus -a -um, illicit, illegal.

illĭco (ilĭco), adv. on the spot, in that very place; immediately.

illīdo -līsi -līsum, 3. to strike, knock against; to dash to pieces.

illĭgo, 1. to bind, fasten; to connect with oneself; to attach; to impede.

illim, adv. = illinc, from there, from that place.

illĭmis -e, free from mud, clear.

illinc, adv. from that place; from that person, thence.

illĭno -lēvi -lĭtum, 3. to daub, spread over; to cover with.

illĭquĕfactus -a -um, molten, liquefied.

illĭttĕrātus -a -um, ignorant, illiterate.

illŏ, adv. to that place, thither; to that matter.

illōc, adv. thither.

illōtus (illautus) -a -um, unwashed, uncleaned, impure, not washed off.

illūc, adv. thither, to that place; to that matter, or person.

illūcesco (illūcisco) -luxi, 3. to become light, begin to shine; to appear; impers., illucescit, it grows light.

illūdo -lūsi -lūsum, 3. to play with, sport with; to mock at, laught at; illudens, in ridicule; to deceive; to destroy, disgrace.

illūmĭnātē, adv. luminously, clearly.

illūmĭno, 1. to enlighten, illuminate. Of discourse, to make clear, adorn.

illūsĭo -ōnis, f. irony.

illustris -e, light, brilliant; clear, evident; distinguished, famous, renowned; remarkable.

illustrĭus, adv. compar. and illustrissĭmē, adv. superl., more clearly, more distinctly.

illustro, 1. to enlighten, make light; to make known; to explain, illustrate; to adorn; to celebrate.

illŭvĭes -ēi, f. an inundation, flood; dirt, mud.

Ilȳrĭi -ōrum, m. people on the Adriatic Sea, in the modern Dalmatia and Albania.

Ilōtae -ārum = Hilotae (q.v.).

Ilva -ae, f. an island, now Elba.

im = eum.

imāgĭnārĭus -a -um, imaginary.

imāgĭnātĭo -ōnis, f. imagination, fancy.

imāgĭnor, 1. dep. to imagine.

imāgo -ĭnis, f. an image, portrait, bust, statue; imagines (maiorum), waxen figures, portraits of ancestors; a likeness; a shade or ghost; a dream; an echo; a metaphor, simile; the appearance, pretence; image, idea, conception.

imbēcillis, v. imbecillus.

imbēcillĭtas -ātis, f. weakness, imbecility.

imbēcillĭus, adv. compar., somewhat feebly.

imbēcillus -a -um, weak, feeble, without energy.

imbellis -e, unwarlike; cowardly; peaceful, quiet.

imber -bris, m. a shower or storm of rain; rain-cloud; water; tortus, hail.

imberbis -e and imberbus -a -um, beardless.

imbĭbo -bĭbi, 3. to drink in, conceive; to determine upon anything.

imbrex -ĭcis, c. a hollow tile, used in roofing.

imbrĭfer -fĕra -fĕrum, rain-bringing.

imbŭo -ŭi -ūtum, 3. to moisten, saturate; to fill, stain, taint; to accustom, initiate, instruct. Poet. to begin; imbue opus tuum.

imĭtābĭlis -e, that can be imitated, imitable.

imĭtāmen -ĭnis, n. an imitation, representation; image.

imĭtāmentum -i, n. an imitating, imitation.

imĭtātĭo -ōnis, f. an imitation.

imĭtātor -ōris, m. an imitator.

imĭtātrix -ĭcis, f. she that imitates.

imitor, 1. *dep.* to imitate; to resemble; *poet.* to replace by something similar; to represent, depict.

immādesco -mādŭi, *only in perf.*, 3. to become moist or wet.

immāně, *adv.* frightfully, savagely.

immānis -e, enormous, immense, monstrous; frightful, horrible, fierce; barbarity, frightfulness.

immānitas -ātis, *f.* savageness, barbarity, frightfulness.

immansuētus -a -um, untamed, wild.

immātūritas -ātis, *f.* immaturity, hence = untimely haste.

immātūrus -a -um, unripe, immature; untimely.

immědicābilis -e, that cannot be healed.

imměmor -mŏris, unmindful, forgetful; *with genit.*

imměmōrābilis -e, indescribable; uncommunicative.

imměmōrātus -a -um, not mentioned, not narrated. *Plur. subst.*, **imměmōrāta** -ōrum, *n.* new things, things not yet related.

immensitas -ātis, . immeasurableness, immensity.

immensus -a -um, immeasurable, vast, boundless. *Subst.*, **immensum** -i, *n.* space, immensity; *ad immensum*, to a vast extent; *adv.*, *immensum*, enormously.

imměrens -entis, not deserving, innocent.

immergo -mersi -mersum, 3. to dip into, immerse; *immergere se in consuetudinem alicuius*, to insinuate oneself into.

immērito, *v. immeritus*.

immēritus -a -um, *act.*, not meriting, innocent; *pass.*, undeserved, *laudes*; immērito, *adv.* undeservedly.

immersābilis -e, that cannot be sunk.

immětātus -a -um, unmeasured.

immigro, 1. to remove into.

imminěo, 2. to project over, overhang, *collis urbi imminet; luna imminente*, by the light of the moon; *of evils*, to be imminent, threaten; to be on the watch for

imminŭo -ŭi -ūtum, 3. to diminish; *verbum imminutum*, abbreviated; to our tail; to weaken; to destroy, injure.

imminūtio -ōnis, *f.* a lessening, weakening; *rhet.* figure = *litotes* (*e.g. non minime for maxime*).

immiscěo -miscŭi -mixtum or mistum, 2. to mix in, mingle with, intermix; to join with.

immiserābilis -e, unlamented, unpitied.

immisěricors -cordis, unmerciful.

immissio -ōnis, *f.* a letting grow.

immitis -e, sour, harsh; rough, cruel, stern.

immitto -mīsi -missum, 3. to send in, cause or allow to go in; *milit.*, to despatch, let go; to shoot; to sink into, let into; to conduct, convey; to engraft; to work in; *legal*, to put into possession of property;

to send, incite; to cause; to let free; *habenas classi*, to crowd on sail; to let grow.

immissus -a -um, long, uncut.

immixtus or immistus, *v. immisceo*.

immo (-imo), *adv.* yea, yes, or nay rather,

immōbilis -e, immovable; inexorable; *Ausonia*, not agitated by war.

immōděrātē, *adv.* without rule or measure; immoderately.

immōděrātio -ōnis, *f.* want of moderation, excess.

immōděrātus -a -um, without measure, endless; immoderate, unrestrained.

immōdestē, *adv.* immoderately, unbecomingly.

immōdestia -ae, *f.* intemperate conduct; insubordination.

immōdestus -a -um, intemperate, unbridled.

immōdicē, *adv.* immoderately, intemperately.

immōdicus -a -um, immoderate, excessive; unrestrained.

immōdŭlātus -a -um, inharmonious.

immoenis, *v. immunis*.

immōlātio -ōnis, *f.* a sacrificing, immolation.

immōlātor -ōris, *m.* a sacrificer.

immōlītus -a -um, built up, erected.

immōlo, 1. *orig.*, to sprinkle with sacred meal; *hence*, to sacrifice, to devote to death, slay,

immŏrior -mortŭus, 3. *dep.* to die in or upon.

immŏror, 1. *dep.* to remain, linger.

immorsus -a -um, bitten into, bitten; macerated.

immortālis -e, deathless, immortal; everlasting, imperishable; *subst.*, **immortālis -is**, *m.* an immortal.

immortālitas -ātis, *f.* immortality; everlasting renown; the highest happiness.

immortālitěr, *adv.* infinitely,

immōtus -a -um, unmoved, motionless; *dies*, calm, windless; unchanged, unbroken; steadfast.

immūglo, 4. to bellow, roar, resound in.

immulgěo, 2. to milk into.

immundus -a -um, impure, foul.

immūnio, 4. to fortify.

immūnis -e, free, exempt; tax-free; free from work, *with genit.*, *immunis operum*; contributing nothing; inactive; *manus*, stainless.

immūnitas -ātis, *f.* exemption from public offices or burdens; immunity.

immūnītus -a -um, unfortified; unpaved.

immurmŭro, 1. to murmur in or at.

immūtābilis -e, immutable, unchangeable.

immūtābilitas -ātis, *f.* immutability.

immūtātio -ōnis, *f.* change, alteration, metonymy.

1. **immūtātus -a -um,** unchanged.

2. **immūtātus -a -um,** *partic. of immuto.*

immūto, 1. to change, alter; to use allegorically; *immutata oratio,* allegory.

īmo = immo *(q.v.).*

impācātus -a -um, warlike, restless.

impallesco -palluī, 3. to grow pale over.

impar -păris, unequal, uneven ; *modi impares,* hexameter and pentameter; different; not a match for; of inferior birth.

mpărātus -a -um, unprepared ; *a pecunia,* unprovided with.

impăritĕr, *adv.* unevenly, unequal.

impartio, impartior = impertio, impertior *(q.v.).*

impastus -a -um, unfed, hungry.

impătibilis (impĕtibilis) -e, intolerable.

impătiens -entis, unable to endure, impatient; *laborum.*

impătientĕr, *adv.* impatiently, unwillingly.

impătientia -ae, *f.* impatience, inability to endure.

impăvidē, *adv.* fearlessly.

impăvidus -a -um, fearless, undaunted.

impĕdimentum -ī, *n.* a hindrance, impediment; *plur.,* heavy baggage.

impĕdio -īvī *and* **-iī -ītum,** 4. to entangle, ensure; to render a place impassable; to involve; to hinder, prevent; to surround; *equos frenis,* to bridle.

impĕdītio -ōnis, *f.* hindrance.

impĕdītus -a -um, hindered, impeded; *milit.,* hindered by baggage, not ready for battle *(opp. expeditus)* ; impassable ; encumbered ; troublesome ; embarrassed.

mpello -pŭli -pulsum, 3. to strike, strike upon; to push forward; to drive on; to incite; to throw to the ground; *milit.,* to rout ; *aliquem praecipitantem,* to complete a person's ruin.

impendĕo, 2. to overhang, *cervicibus;* to threaten, be close at hand.

impendiō, *adv.* much, very much.

impendium -ī, *n.* expense, outlay, cost; interest of money.

impendo -pendi -pensum, 3. to expend, lay out.

impĕnĕtrābilis -e, impenetrable; invincible.

impensa -ae, *f.* expense, outlay, cost.

impensē, *adv.* at great cost; urgently, eagerly.

impensus -a -um, *p. adj., of price,* considerable, great; strong, vehement.

impĕrātor -ōris, *m.* commander, leader; the commander-in-chief; the Roman emperor.

impĕrātōrius -a -um, of *or* relating to a general; imperial.

impĕrātrix -ĭcis, *f.* a female ruler *or* commander.

imperceptus -a -um, unperceived, unknown.

impercussus -a -um, not struck.

imperditus -a -um, not slain, undestroyed.

imperfectus -a -um, incomplete ; imperfect.

imperfossus -a -um, unstabbed, unpierced.

impĕriōsus -a -um, powerful, mighty; *sibi,* master of oneself; masterful, tyrannical.

impĕrītē, *adv.* unskilfully, ignorantly, clumsily.

impĕrītia -ae, *f.* want of skill and knowledge, inexperience.

impĕrito, 1. *transit.,* to command ; *intransit.,* to have power over.

impĕrītus -a -um, unskilled, ignorant; *with genit.*

impĕrium -ī, *n.* an order, command; power, mastery ; the government *or* supreme authority in a state; *in imperio esse,* to hold an office; military command; the country governed, an empire.

impĕriūrātus -a -um, that by which no one dares to swear falsely.

impermissus -a -um, forbidden.

impĕro, 1. to order, command; *with ut and the subj.;* to govern, command; to work at, *arvis;* *milit.,* to enjoin, make a requisition for ; **impĕrātum -ī,** *n.* that which has been commanded.

imperterritus -a -um, undaunted, fearless.

impertio -īvī *and* **-iī -ītum (impertior** *dep.),* 4. to impart, share, bestow ; **impertīta -ōrum,** *n.* favours, concessions.

imperturbātus -a -um, undisturbed, calm.

impervius -a -um, impassable, impervious.

impes -pĕtis, *m.* attack, force.

impĕtibilis -e = impatibilis *(q.v.).*

impĕtrābilis -e, *pass.* easy of attainment, attainable ; *act.,* that obtains easily, successful.

impĕtrātio -ōnis, *f.* an obtaining by asking.

impĕtrio, 4. to seek to obtain a good omen, to obtain by favourable omens.

impĕtro, 1. to get, obtain, accomplish, effect.

impĕtus -ūs, *m.* violent impulse, rapid motion, violence; attack, assault, charge; *impetum dare,* to attack; impulse, force; inclination.

impexus -a -um, uncombed ; rude, uncouth.

impĭē, *adv.* impiously, wickedly.

impĭĕtas -ātis, *f.* impiety; lack of reverence; treason against the emperor.

impĭger -gra -grum, diligent, active.

impĭgrē, *adv.* actively, quickly.

impĭgrĭtas -ātis, *f.* activity, quickness.

impingo -pēgi -pactum, 3. to strike, dash, push against; to press upon one, *alicui epistolam;* to drive against.

impĭus -a -um, impious, irreverent, undutiful, unpatriotic.

implācābilis -e, implacable.

implācābĭlĭus, *adv. in compar.*, more implacably.

implācātus -a -um, unappeased.

implācĭdus -a -um, rough, savage.

implecto -plexi -plexum, 3. to interweave, weave, *or* twist with.

implĕo -plēvi -plētum, 2. to fill, fill up; to satiate; to impregnate; to complete a number; to satisfy; to complete; to perform.

implexus -a -um, *partic. of impleeto*.

implĭcātĭo -ōnis, *f.* an intertwining, interweaving; embarrassment.

implĭcātus -a -um, *p. adj.*, confused, entangled.

implĭcĭtē, *adv.* confusedly.

implĭco -plĭcŭi -plĭcĭtum *and* -plĭcāvi -plĭcātum, 1. to enfold, entangle; *se dextrae,* to cling to; *implicari or implicare se,* to be engaged in; to perplex; to twine around; to surround.

implōrātĭo -ōnis, *f.* an imploring for help.

implōro, 1. to call upon with tears or entreaties; to beseech; to ask for.

implūmis -e, unfledged.

implŭo -plŭi, 3. to rain upon.

implŭvĭum -ii, *n.* a square basin in the floor of the atrium of a Roman house, in which the rain-water was received.

impŏlītē, *adv.* plainly, without ornament.

impŏlītus -a -um, rough, unrefined, inelegant; *res.*, unfinished.

impollūtus -a -um, unpolluted.

impōno -pŏsŭi -pŏsĭtum, 3. to put, lay, place in; to put, place upon; *naut., imponere in naves or simply imponere,* to embark; to put over as master; *consutem populo,* to impose; to deceive, *with dat.;* to add; *in a bad sense,* to cause, *alicui vulnus.*

importo, 1. to bring in, import; to introduce; to cause.

importūnē, *adv.* unseasonably, rudely, violently.

importūnĭtas -ātis, *f.* rudeness, incivility.

importūnus -a -um, unsuitable, illadapted; *of time,* unfavourable; *of circumstances,* burdensome; rude, churlish, savage.

importŭōsus -a -um, without harbours.

impos -pŏtis, having no power over.

impŏsĭtus -a -um, *partic. of impono.*

impŏtens -entis, weak, impotent; *(subst.,* impŏtentes -ium, the weak); having no power over; violent, unrestrained; unbridled, *laetitia.*

impŏtenter, *adv.* weakly; intemperately, passionately.

impŏtentia -ae, *f.* impotence, passionateness, intemperance.

impraesentĭārum, *adv.* in present circumstances, for the present, at present.

impransus -a -um, that has not break fasted, fasting.

imprĕcor, 1. *dep.* to invoke on, to call down upon, to imprecate.

impressĭo -ōnis, *f. in rhetoric,* emphasis, stress; *philosoph.,* impressions received through the senses; an attack, assault.

imprīmis, *adv.* especially, first of all, principally.

imprĭmo -pressi -pressum, 3. to press in or on, press into; impress, drive in; to stamp, make a mark; to impress on the mind; to seal; to inlay, cover.

imprŏbātĭo -ōnis, *f.* disapprobation, blame.

imprŏbē, *adv.* wrongly, dishonestly, wantonly, impudently.

imprŏbĭtas -ātis, *f.* wickedness, depravity.

imprŏbo, 1. to disapprove, reject.

imprŏbŭlus -a -um (*dim. of improbus*), somewhat bad, wicked.

imprŏbus -a -um, bad, poor; wicked, depraved, mischievous; bold, shameless; (*subst.,* a rogue); immense; *labor,* never-ending.

imprŏcērus -a -um, small, low of stature.

imprōmptus -a -um, not ready, not quick.

impropĕrātus -a -um, not hasty, slow.

improsper -ĕra -ĕrum, unfortunate, unsuccessful.

improspĕrē, *adv.* unsuccessfully, unluckily.

imprōvĭdē, *adv.* without forethought, improvidently.

imprōvĭdus -a -um, not foreseeing; without forethought, incautious.

imprōvīso, *adv.* suddenly, unexpectedly.

imprōvīsus -a -um, unforeseen, unexpected, sudden; *de or ex improviso,* suddenly, unexpectedly.

imprūdens -entis, not foreseeing, not expecting, not knowing; ignorant of, *legis;* unwise, rash, imprudent.

imprūdenter, *adv.* ignorantly, unawares, through ignorance; imprudently.

imprūdentĭa -ae, *f.* absence of design; ignorance of; want of foresight, imprudence, inadvertence.

impūbes -bĕris *and* impūbis -e, under age, youthful; *genae,* beardless.

impŭdens -entis, not ashamed, impudent, shameless; impudent.

impŭdenter, *adv.* shamelessly, impudently.

impŭdentĭa -ae, *f.* shamelessness, impudence.

impŭdīcĭtia -ae, *f.* unchastity.

impŭdīcus -a -um, unchaste.

impugnātĭo -ōnis, *f.* assault, attack.

impugno, 1. to attack, assault; to assail with words.

impulsĭo -ōnis, *f.* an external influence; an instigation, impulse.

impulsor -ōris, *m.* an instigator.

impulsus -ūs, *m.* an outward force, shock, pressure; instigation; an inward impulse.

impūnē, *adv.* with impunity; safely; *ferre,* to go unpunished.

impūnĭtas -ātis, *f.* impunity; freedom, licence.

impūnītě, *adv.* with impunity.

impūnītus -a -um, unpunished, exempt from punishment; unrestrained.

impūrātus -a -um, vile, infamous.

impūrē, *adv.* impurely, shamefully.

impūritas -ātis, *f.* moral impurity.

impūrus -a -um, unclean; defiled, infamous.

1. impūtātus -a -um, unpruned.

2. impūtātus -a -um, *partic. of imputo.*

impŭto, 1. to impute to, to reckon as a fault *or* merit.

imus -a -um, *superl. of inferus (q.v.).*

in, *prep. with acc.* = into, *with abl.* = in. *With the acc.; in diem,* for a short time, for the day, daily ; *in dies,* from day to day, daily; *of object,* for; *in hoc,* for this purpose; *in universum,* in general ; *in vicem, or in vices,* in turns ; towards, *amor in patriam. With abl. ; of time,* at, *in tali tempore; in eo est ut,* etc., on the point of; amongst the number of, *in quibus Catilina.*

inaccessus -a -um, inaccessible.

inăcesco -ăcŭi, 3. to become sour.

Ināchus (Ināchos) -i, *m.* a mythical king of Argos, father of Io, after whom the river Inachus in Argolis was named.

inădustus -a -um, unburnt, unsinged.

inaedifico, 1. to build in *or* upon; to block up, barricade.

inaequābilis -e, uneven ; unequal, varying.

inaequābilitěr, *adv.* unequally, variously.

inaequālis -e, unequal, uneven, unlike; making unequal ; *procellae,* disturbing the level of the sea.

inaequālitas -ātis, *f.* inequality, dissimilarity, irregularity.

inaequālitěr, *adv.* unequally, unevenly.

inaequo, 1. to make even *or* level.

inaestimābilis -e, that cannot be estimated ; priceless, inestimable; *in a bad sense,* unworthy of being valued.

inaestŭo, 1. to boil, rage in.

Inalpīnus -a -um, Alpine.

inămābilis -e, unpleasant, odious.

inămāresco, 3. to become bitter.

inambitiōsus -a -um, not ambitious, unpretentious.

inambŭlātio -ōnis, *f.* a walking up and down.

inambŭlo, 1. to walk up and down.

inămoenus -a -um, unpleasant, dismal.

inănimātus -a -um, lifeless, inanimate.

inănimus -a -um, lifeless, inanimate.

inănio -īvi (-ĭi) -ītum, 4. to empty, make void.

inānis -e, empty, void, vacant ; *navis,* unloaded ; *corpus,* soulless, dead ; **(ināne -is,** *n.* space, empty space); *esp.,* empty-handed; poor, indigent; hungry, void of ; groundless, vain ; useless;

vain, conceited ; *(subst.,* **ināne -is,** *n.* vanity, emptiness).

inānitas -ātis, *f.* emptiness, space, inanity.

inānitěr, *adv.* vainly, uselessly.

inārātus -a -um, unploughed, fallow.

inardesco -arsi, 3. to burn on; to begin to glow, to kindle; to glow.

ināresco -ārŭi, 3. to become dry.

inassuētus -a -um, unaccustomed.

inattěnŭātus, undiminished, unimpaired ; *fames,* unappeased.

inaudax -ācis, timid, fearful.

inaudio, 4. to hear; *particularly,* news, a secret.

1. inaudītus -a -um, unheard of ; unusual; without a hearing.

2. inaudītus -a -um, *partic. of inaudio.*

inaugŭrāto, *adv.* after having taken the auguries.

inaugŭro, 1. to take the auguries, to divine; to consecrate, install.

inauro, 1. to gild, cover with gold ; **inaurātus -a -um,** gilt.

inauspicāto, *adv.* without consulting the auspices.

inauspicātus -a -um, without auspices; unlucky, inauspicious.

inausus -a -um, not dared, not attempted.

incaedŭus -a -um, not cut down, unfelled.

incălesco -călŭi, 3. to glow, become warm.

incalfăcio, 3. to heat, warm.

incallidě, *adv.* not cleverly, without ingenuity.

incallidus -a -um, not clever.

incandesco -candŭi, 3. to begin to glow with heat, become very hot.

incānesco -cānŭi, 3. to become white.

incanto, 1. to consecrate with charms *or* spells.

incānus -a -um, quite grey.

incassum, *adv.* in vain, uselessly.

incastīgātus -a -um, unchastised, uncorrected.

incautě, *adv.* incautiously, carelessly.

incautus -a -um, incautious, careless, unwary ; not guarded against, unexpected, uncertain, unprotected.

incēdo -cessi -cessum, 3. to walk, go, march, enter ; *milit.,* to advance; to come on, break out; *of events,* to take place, spread abroad. *Transit.,* to walk on ; to happen to, befall.

incělebrātus -a -um, not spread abroad.

incendiārius -a -um, incendiary.

incendium -ii, *n.* a conflagration, fire; danger, destruction.

incendo -cendi -censum, 3. to kindle, set fire to, burn ; *incensi aestus,* the burning heat of fever; to kindle fire upon; to make bright, to enlighten; to incite; irritate, incense ; to excite to love ; to arouse; to increase; *incendi,* to glow, to be incensed, *amore, ira.*

incensio -ōnis, *f.* a burning, conflagration.

1. **incensus -a -um**, not enrolled by the censor, unassessed.

2. **incensus**, *partic. of incendo, or p. adj., of orators*, fiery.

inceptio -ōnis, *f.* a beginning, undertaking.

incepto, 1. to begin, undertake.

inceptor -ōris, *m.* a beginner

inceptum -i, *n.* an undertaking, beginning.

inceptus -a -um, *partic. of incipio.*

incerno -crēvi -crētum, 3. to sift upon.

incēro, 1. *no per.*, to cover with wax.

incertus -a -um, uncertain, doubtful; dim, dark; not sure (*of a blow*); disorderly; *vultus*, disturbed, undetermined, hesitating; *os*, stammering; *subst.*, **incertum -i**, *n.* uncertainty, *rerum omnium*.

incesso -cessivi, 3. to attack.

incessus -ūs, *m.* the gait, mode of walking; assault; entrance, approach.

inceste, *adv.* sinfully.

incesto, 1. to defile; dishonour.

incestum -i, *n.*, *v. incestus.*

1. **incestus -a -um**, sinful, impious; unchaste; (*subst.*, *incestus*, a sinful person); **incestum -i**, *n.* unchastity, incest.

2. **incestus -ūs**, *m.* unchastity, incest.

inchŏo, 1. to begin; to introduce; *partic. perf.*, **inchŏātus -a -um**, only begun, not finished.

1. **incido -cīdi -cāsum**, 3. to fall in or on; to fall into, to light upon; *incidere alicui or in aliquem*, to meet unexpectedly; *incidit mihi in mentem*, it comes into my mind; to happen; *with dat. pers.*, to happen to; to burst into, *castris*; *in hostem*, to attack.

2. **incido -cīdi -cīsum**, 3. to cut into, make an incision; to inscribe; to make by cutting; to prune, cut; to cut short, break off; broken off, interrupted; to take away.

incilis -e, cut; *subst.*, **incile -is**, *n.* a ditch or canal for carrying off water, for irrigation, *etc.*

incingo -cinxi -cinctum, 3. to surround.

incino, *v.* to sing.

incipio -cēpi -ceptum, 3. to begin, commence; to begin to speak; *intransit.*, to commence.

incisē and incisim, *adv.* in short, disconnected sentences.

incisio -ōnis, *f.* a clause of a sentence.

incisum -i, *n.*, a division of a sentence.

incitāmentum -i, *n.* an incitement; incentive.

incitātē, *adv.* hastily, violently.

incitātio -ōnis, *f.* an inciting, instigating; violent motion; excitement, ardour, vehemence.

incitātus -a -um, *p. adj.*, rapid, vehement, *equo incitato*, at full gallop.

incito, 1. to urge on, to hasten; (*refl.*, *se incitare, or middle incitari*, to quicken

one's pace, to hasten); to incite, urge, spur on; to inspire; to stir up; to increase; to enhance.

1. **incitus -a -um**, in rapid motion, swift.

2. **incitus -a -um**, immovable.

incīvilis -e, unjust, tyrannical; uncivil.

inclāmo, 1. to call upon loudly, to call upon for help.

inclāresco -clārŭi, 3. to become illustrious.

inclēmens -entis, unmerciful, harsh.

inclēmentēr, *adv.* harshly, unmercifully.

inclēmentia -ae, *f.* rigour, harshness.

inclīnātio -ōnis, *f.* a leaning, inclination; change of the voice; goodwill; alteration.

inclīnātus -a -um, sunk; low, deep, *vox*; fallen; inclined towards, favourable to.

inclīno, 1. to bend, bow, incline; to turn away; change for the worse; to decide; *refl.*, *se inclinare, or middle inclinari*, to bend, incline; to waver, yield; to incline in opinion; to be favourable to.

inclūdo -clūsi -clūsum, 3. to shut up, shut in; to insert; to surround; to hinder, stop.

inclūsio -ōnis, *f.* a shutting up, confinement.

inclȳtus (inclŭtus, inclitus) -a -um, celebrated, renowned.

1. **incoctus -a -um**, uncooked, raw.

2. **incoctus -a -um**, *partic. of incoquo.*

incōgitans -antis, thoughtless, heedless.

incōgitantia -ae, *f.* thoughtlessness, heedlessness.

incōgito, 1. to contrive, plan.

incognitus -a -um, unknown; *legal*, not examined; unclaimed.

incŏhibĕo, 2. to hold together.

incŏla -ae, *c.* an inhabitant, dweller.

incŏlo -cŏlŭi -cultum, 3. *transit.*, to inhabit, dwell in; *intransit.*, to dwell; **incŏlentes -ium**, *m.* the inhabitants.

incŏlŭmis -e, uninjured, safe and sound.

incŏlŭmitas -ātis, *f.* safety, preservation

incŏmitātus -a -um, unaccompanied, without retinue.

incommendātus -a -um, unrecommended; given up, abandoned.

incommŏdē, *adv.* inconveniently, unfitly, unseasonably.

incommŏditas -ātis, *f.* inconvenience, disadvantage.

incommŏdo, 1. to be unpleasant, troublesome to any one; *with dat.*

incommŏdŭlum, *v. incommodus.*

incommŏdus -a -um, inconvenient, disagreeable; *of persons*, troublesome, annoying; *subst.*, **incommŏdum -i**, *n.* disadvantage; misfortune.

incommūtābilis -e, unchangeable.

incompertus -a -um, unknown, not ascertained.

incompŏsitē, *adv.* in a disorderly manner.

incompŏsitus -a -um, disordered, irregular.

incomptus -a -um, untended, untrimmed ; *of style*, without ornament, rude.

inconcessus -a -um, not allowed, forbidden.

inconcinnus -a -um, awkward, inelegant.

inconcussus -a -um, unshaken, firm.

inconditē, *adv.* confusedly.

inconditus -a -um, disorderly, irregular; unarranged; unburied.

incongrŭens -entis, not agreeing, unsuitable.

inconsīdĕrantia -ae, *f.* thoughtlessness.

inconsīdĕrātē, *adv.* without consideration, rashly.

inconsīdĕrātus -a -um, thoughtless, unconsidered.

inconsōlābilis -e, inconsolable; *vulnus*, incurable.

inconstans -stantis, changeable, unstable.

inconstantĕr, *adv.* inconstantly, capriciously.

inconstantia -ae, *f.* changeableness, instability.

inconsultē, *adv.* unadvisedly.

inconsultus -a -um, not consulted, *inconsulto senatu*; unadvised, *poet.* ; imprudent.

inconsumptus -a -um, unconsumed, undiminished.

incontāmĭnātus -a -um, unspotted, uncontaminated.

incontentus -a -um, not stretched; *fides*, out of tune.

incontĭnens -entis, immoderate, intemperate.

incontinentĕr, *adv.* immoderately.

incontinentia -ae, *f.* intemperance.

incontrōversus -a -um, undisputed.

inconvĕniens -entis, not agreeing with, dissimilar, unsuitable.

incŏquo -coxi -coctum, 3. to boil in *or* with; to dye, colour.

incorrectus -a -um, unamended.

incorruptē, *adv.* justly, impartially.

incorruptus -a -um, *templa*, not destroyed ; unbribed, genuine, unimpaired; *virgo*, pure.

incrēbresco -crēbrŭi, 3. *and* **incrēbesco** -crēbŭi, 3. to become frequent, strong, prevalent; to increase, prevail.

incrēdĭbilis -e, incredible; extraordinary.

incrēdĭbĭlĭtĕr, *adv.* incredibly, extraordinarily.

incrēdŭlus -a -um, incredulous.

incrēmentum -i, *n.* the growth of plants *or* animals ; increase ; *poet.* = offspring.

increpĭto, 1. to call loudly to any one; *transit.*, to cry to, reproach.

increpo -ŭi (-āvi) -itum (-ātum), 1. to rustle, rattle, make a noise; to be noised abroad; to call upon; *with in and acc.*, to slander, revile; *transit.*, to cause to sound, cause to be heard; to exclaim against, chide, reproach, reprove;

to animate, excite; to throw in one's teeth, to blame for.

incresco -crēvi, 3. to grow in *or* upon: to grow.

incrētus -a -um, *partic. of incerno.*

incrŭentātus -a -um, not bloody.

incrŭentus -a -um, bloodless.

incrusto, 1. to encrust.

incŭbo -āvi -ātum *and* -ŭi -ĭtum, 1. to lie in *or* on; *of birds*, to hatch eggs, to brood; to brood over, to stay in a place.

incūdo -cūdi -cūsum, 3. to forge, fabricate.

inculco, 1. to trample in; to mix in; to impress upon; to force upon.

inculpātus -a -um, unblamed, blameless.

incultē, *adv.* roughly, rudely ; *of orators*, inelegantly.

1. **incultus** -a -um, uncultivated, untilled; (*subst.*, **inculta** -ōrum, *n.* wastes, deserts); unarranged, disordered; unpolished, unrefined.

2. **incultus** -ūs, *m.* neglect, want of cultivation.

incumbo -cŭbŭi -cŭbitum, 3. to lie upon, lean upon, bend to; *milit.*, to throw oneself upon the enemy; to press hard on, *in aliquem*, to overhang; to attack; to exert oneself, take pains with; to press heavily upon.

incūnābŭla -ōrum, *n.* swaddling-clothes; birthplace; origin, beginning.

incūrātus -a -um, uncared for, unhealed.

incūria -ae, *f.* carelessness, neglect, indifference.

incūrĭōsē, *adv.* negligently, carelessly.

incūrĭōsus -a -um, *act.*, careless, negligent; *pass.*, neglected.

incurro -curri (-cŭcurri) -cursum, 3. to run against something; to assail, attack; to make an incursion into; to inveigh against; *in oculos*, to meet the eye; *of places*, to border on; *of persons*, to stumble on; to fall into misfortune; to happen, occur.

incursio -ōnis, *f.* a running against, collision; hostile attack; an inroad, invasion.

incurso, 1. to run against, attack.

incursus -ūs, *m.* an attack, assault, incursion, influx.

incurvo, 1. to bend, curve, make crooked.

incurvus -a -um, bent, curved, crooked.

incūs -cūdis, *f.* an anvil.

incūsātĭo -ōnis, *f.* blame, accusation.

incūso, 1. to accuse, blame, reproach.

incussus, *only in abl.* -ū, *m.* a beating *or* dashing against.

incustōdītus -a -um, unwatched, unguarded; neglected; unconcealed.

incŭtĭo -cussi -cussum, 3. to strike, beat against; to throw, hurl; to inspire with, excite.

indāgātĭo -ōnis, *f.* an inquiry, investigation.

indāgātor -ōris, *m.* an investigator.

indāgātrix -trīcis, *f.* she who searches into.

1. indāgo, 1. to track; to search out, investigate.

2. indāgo -inis, *f.* a surrounding of any spot with nets *or* beaters so as to enclose the game; investigation.

indĕ, *adv.* thence, from there, from that place; from that cause; then, thereupon, from that time forth.

indēbitus -a -um, that which is not owed, not due.

indĕcens -centis, unseemly, ugly.

indĕcentĕr, *adv.* unbecomingly, indecently.

indēclīnātus -a -um, unchanged, firm.

indĕcōrē, *adv.* unbecomingly, indecorously.

indĕcōris -e, unbecoming, shameful.

indĕcŏro, 1. to disgrace, dishonour.

indĕcōrus -a -um, unbecoming; unseemly; disgraceful.

indēfensus -a -um, unprotected.

indēfessus -a -um, unwearied, untired.

indēflētus -a -um, unwept.

indēiectus -a -um, not thrown down.

indēlēbilis -e, imperishable.

indēlībātus -a -um, untouched, uninjured.

indemnātus -a -um, uncondemned.

indēplōrātus -a -um, unwept, unlamented.

indēprĕhensus (indēprensus) -a -um, unobserved.

indēsertus -a -um, not forsaken.

indestrictus -a -um, untouched, unhurt.

indētōnsus -a -um, unshorn.

indēvītātus -a -um, unavoided.

index -dicis, *c.* an informer, traitor, spy; a sign, token; the fore-finger; title *or* inscription; a touchstone.

Indi -ōrum, *m.* the inhabitants of India.

1. indīcens -entis, that does not say.

2. indīcens, *partic. of* 2. *indico.*

indicium, -ii, *n.* a discovery, disclosure; *profiteri*, to turn informer (turn king's evidence); a mark, token, evidence.

1. indīco, 1. to disclose, betray, show, indicate; *to inform against*; to value.

2. indīco -dīxi dictum, 3. to announce, proclaim, appoint ; *alicui bellum*, to declare war; to impose, *tributum.*

1. indictus -a -um, not said, unsaid; unsung; without a trial.

2. indictus -a -um, *partic. of* 2. *indico.*

indidem, *adv.* from the same place, from the same matter.

indifferens -entis, indifferent, neither good nor bad.

indigĕna -ae, *c.* native, belonging to one's own country; *and subst.,* a native.

indigĕnus, *v. indigeno.*

indigentia -ae, *f.* want, need; insatiable desire.

indigĕo -ŭi, 2. to want, need ; to require; *with genit. or abl. ; subst.,*

indigens -entis, *m.* a needy person.

1. Indiges -gĕtis, *m.* a native deity; *sing.,* Aeneas; *plur.,* descendants of Aeneas.

2. indiges -is, needy.

indīgestus -a -um, disordered, confused.

indignābundus -a -um, filled with indignation.

indignandus -a -um, deserving indignation.

indignans -antis, *p. adj.,* impatient, indignant.

indignātio -ōnis, *f.* indignation, disdain.

indignē, *adv.* disgracefully, undeservedly; impatiently, unwillingly.

indignitas -ātis, *f.* unworthiness, vileness; meanness, baseness; indignation at unworthy treatment.

indignor, 1. *dep.* to consider as unworthy, be offended, indignant at.

indignus -a -um, unworthy, not deserving ; unbecoming ; unworthy = disgraceful, shameful.

indĭgus -a -um, needy, in want of.

indīligens -entis, neglectful.

indīligentĕr, *adv.* carelessly.

indīligentia -ae, *f.* carelessness, negligence.

indĭpiscor -deptus sum, 3. *dep.* to reach, grasp, attain.

indīreptus -a -um, unpillaged.

indiscrētus -a -um, undivided, undistinguished, without difference.

indisertē, *adv.* ineloquently.

indisertus -a -um, ineloquent.

indispŏsitus -a -um, disorderly, confused.

indissŏlūbilis -e, indissoluble.

indissŏlūtus -a -um, undissolved.

indistinctus -a -um, not separated, not arranged; confused, indistinct.

indīvīdŭus -a -um, indivisible; *corpora,* atoms; *subst.,* **indīvīdŭum** -i, *n.* an atom.

indīvīsus -a -um, undivided.

indo -didi -ditum, 3. to put in *or* on; to introduce; to cause, occasion; to give, impose a name.

indŏcilis -e, unteachable, indocile; ignorant, inexperienced; untaught; artless; that cannot be learned.

indoctē, *adv.* ignorantly, in an inexperienced manner.

indoctus -a -um, untaught, unskilled.

indŏlentia -ae, *f.* freedom from pain.

indŏles -is, *f.* nature; natural disposition, talents, inclination.

indŏlesco -dŏlui, 3. to be pained, grieved at anything.

indŏmitus -a -um, untamed, unrestrained, wild; untamable, invincible.

indormio -ivi -ītum, 4. to sleep in *or* on anything; to be negligent in.

indōtātus -a -um, without a dowry, portionless ; *corpora,* without funeral honours; without the gift of eloquence.

indū, archaic form of *in.*

indūbitātē, *adv.* undoubtedly.

indūbitātus -a -um, undoubted, certain.
indūbĭto, 1. to doubt of; *with dat.*, *suis viribus.*
indūbius -a -um, not doubtful, certain.
indūciae = indutiae (*q.v.*).
indūco -dūxi -dūctum, 3. to draw over; to put on articles of clothing, arms, *etc.*; to cover; to erase writing on tablets; to revoke; to reckon in one's account-book, *pecuniam in rationem;* to lead *or* bring in; to produce on the stage; to introduce; *animum*, to resolve, to direct one's attention to; to induce.
inductĭo -ōnis, *f.* a leading *or* bringing to a place; *animi,* resolve, intention; *erroris,* misleading; induction.
1. inductus -a -um (*partic. of induco*).
2. inductus *only in abl. sing.* -ū, *m.* inducement, instigation.
indulgens -entis, *p. adj.*, kind, indulgent.
indulgentĕr, *adv.* kindly, indulgently.
indulgentĭa -ae, *f.* kindness, indulgence.
indulgĕo -dulsi -dultum, 2. *intransit.*, to be indulgent, to gratify, *sibi;* to indulge in, *novis amicitiis; ordinibus,* to set wide apart; *transit.*, to give, to grant, concede.
indŭo -dŭi -dūtum, 3. to put on, *alicui tunicam;* to clothe, surround, cover; to put on, assume; *pass. reflex. galeam indutus;* to fall into, fall on, *se hastis;* to be entangled in, *se in laqueum.*
indūpĕdĭo, indūpĕrātor = impedĭo, imperator (*q.v.*).
indūresco -dūrŭi, 3. to become hard.
indūro, 1. to harden; to steel.
industrĭa -ae, *f.* industry, diligence; *de industria, ex industria,* on purpose.
industrĭē, *adv.* diligently.
industrĭus -a -um, diligent, active.
indūtiae -ārum, *f.* truce, armistice; *indutias facere.*
Indŭtĭŏmārus -i, *m.* prince of the Treveri.
inēbrĭo, 1. to intoxicate; to saturate with.
inēdĭa -ae, *f.* fasting.
inēdĭtus -a -um, not published *or* made known.
inēlĕgans -antis, inelegant, not choice.
inēlĕgantĕr *adv.* inelegantly, tastelessly; illogically.
inēluctābilis -e, inevitable.
inēmŏrĭor -ēmŏri, 3. *dep.*, to die in *or* at.
inemptus (inemtus) -a -um, unbought.
inēnarrābilis -e, indescribable, inexpressible.
inēnarrābilitĕr, *adv.* indescribably.
inēnōdābilis -e, inextricable; *res,* inexplicable.
inĕo -ii (ivi) -ĭtum, 4. *intrans.*, to go in, enter; *of time,* to begin; *transit.*, to go in, enter; *viam,* to begin a journey; to begin, to enter upon; to undertake; *inire rationem,* to make an estimate; to consider; *consilium,* to form a plan;

gratiam ab aliquo, to earn thanks from.
ineptē, *adv.* inappropriately, absurdly.
ineptĭae -ārum, *f.* foolish behaviour, absurdity.
ineptĭo, 4. to talk nonsense.
ineptus -a -um, inappropriate, foolish, absurd; inepti -ōrum, pedants.
inermis -e, *and* inermus -a -um, unarmed, weaponless; not well versed in; *carmen,* inoffensive.
1. inerrans -antis, not wandering, fixed.
2. inerrans -antis, *partic. of inerro.*
inerro, 1. to rove *or* wander about.
iners -ertis, simple, unskilful; inactive, idle, slothful; *aqua,* stagnant; *quere-lae,* useless; making idle *or* slothful; cowardly.
inertĭa -ae, *f.* unskilfulness; slothfulness.
inērūdītus -a -um, unlearned, illiterate.
inesco, 1. to allure with a bait; to entice.
inēvectus -a -um, raised upon, borne upon.
inēvītābilis -e, inevitable, unavoidable.
inexcĭtus -a -um, unmoved, quiet.
inexcūsābilis -e, inexcusable.
inexercĭtātus -a -um, unexercised, unpractised.
inexhaustus -a -um, unexhausted, inexhaustible.
inexōrābilis -e, inexorable.
inexpēdītus -a -um, hampered.
inexperrectus -a -um, not awakened.
inexpertus -a -um, *act.*, inexperienced, unacquainted with; *pass.*, untried, unattempted; untested.
inexpĭābilis -e, inexpiable; implacable; *bellum,* obstinate.
inexplēbilis -e, insatiable.
inexplētus -a -um, unfilled, insatiable.
inexplĭcābilis -e, intricate, impracticable, difficult, inexplicable; *facilitas,* leading to no result.
inexplōrātō, *adv.* without exploring.
inexplōrātus -a -um, unexplored, uninvestigated.
inexpugnābilis -e, unconquerable, impregnable; *via,* inaccessible.
inexspectātus -a -um, unexpected.
inexstinctus -a -um, unextinguished, inextinguishable; *fames,* insatiable; *nomen,* immortal.
inexsŭpĕrābilis -e, insurmountable; unsurpassable; insuperable.
inextrĭcābilis -e, inextricable.
infabrē, *adv.* unskilfully.
infabrĭcātus -a -um, unwrought, unfashioned.
infăcētē (infĭcētē), *adv.* tastelessly, without humour.
infăcētĭae (infĭcētĭae) -ārum, *f.* coarse jests, poor wit.
infăcētus *and* infĭcētus -a -um, coarse, unpolished, without wit.
infācundus -a -um, not eloquent.

infāmia -ae, *f.* ill report, dishonour, disgrace; *movere,* to cause.

infāmis -e, disreputable, infamous; disgraceful.

infāmo, 1. to bring into ill repute, defame; *accuse,* find fault with.

infandus -a -um, unutterable, abominable.

infans -fantis, dumb, speechless; *adj.* = young, *subst.* = a little child.

infantia -ae, *f.* inability to speak; childhood.

infarcio (infercio) -farsi (-fersi) -farsum (-fersum) *and* **-fartum (-fertum),** 4. to stuff in, stuff full of.

infătŭo, 1. to make a fool of, infatuate.

infaustus -a -um, unlucky.

infector -ōris, *m.* a dyer.

1. infectus -a -um, unworked, unwrought, *aurum;* unfinished; *pro infecto habere,* to consider as having never taken place; *infectā re,* without having accomplished the business; impossible.

2. infectus, *partic. of inficio.*

infēcunditas -ātis, *f.* barrenness.

infēcundus -a -um, unfruitful, barren.

infēlicitas -ātis, *f.* unhappiness, misfortune.

infēlicitěr, *adv.* unluckily, unfortunately.

infēlix -īcis, unfruitful, barren; unlucky, unhappy; unfortunate; *infelix arbor,* the gallows.

infensē, *adv.* hostilely, acrimoniously.

infenso, 1. to treat in a hostile manner.

infensus -a -um, hostile, full of hate and bitterness, enraged; dangerous.

infer -a -um, inferi -ōrum, *v. inferus.*

infēriae -ārum, *f.* sacrifices *or* offerings in honour of the dead.

infercio, *v. infarcio.*

inferior, *v. inferus.*

inferius, *adv., v. infra.;* *neut. adj. v. inferus.*

infernē, *adv.* beneath, below.

infernus -a -um, that which is below, lower; underground; relating to the lower world; *subst.,* **inferni -ōrum,** *m.* inhabitants of the lower world; **inferna -ōrum,** *n.* infernal regions.

infěro, intŭli, illātum, inferre, to bring, carry in, to put *or* place on; to bury, inter; to give in an account, *rationes; sumptum civibus,* to put to the account of; to sacrifice, pay; *signa in hostem,* to attack, charge; *bellum alicui,* to make war on; *pedem,* to enter; to attack; *se inferre,* to betake oneself, to go; to bring forward; to cause, occasion; to conclude.

infersus *and* **infertus,** *v. infarcio.*

infěrus -a -um, *and* **infěr -a -um,** *compar.* **inferior,** *superl.* **infimus** *and* **imus -a -um, infěrus -a -um,** lower; *mare,* the Etruscan Sea; *subst.,* **inferi**

-ōrum *and* **-ûm,** *m.* the departed, the dead, the lower world); *compar.,* **inferior,** *neut.* **infěrius,** *genit.* **-iōris,** the lower; *labrum,* the under-lip; *of time,* later, younger; *superl.,* **infimus (infŭmus) -a -um,** the lowest, meanest; *imus -a -um,* the lowest, the last; *of tone,* deepest; *ab imo,* from the bottom; *neut. plur.,* **-ima -ōrum,** the lower world.

infervesco -ferbŭi, 3. to begin to boil, grow hot to be boiled down.

infestē, *adv.* in a hostile manner.

infesto, 1. to attack, harass, disquiet.

infestus -a -um, hostile, dangerous, troublesome; *milit.,* with hostile intent, prepared for battle; *hastā infestā,* with lance couched; *pass.,* made dangerous, unsafe, *mare infestum habere.*

inficētus, inficēte = infacetus, infacete (*q.v.*).

inficio -fēci -fectum, 3. to dip into anything; to tinge, dye, stain; to mix with; to imbue, instruct; to poison; to taint, corrupt.

infidēlis -e, unfaithful, untrue.

infidēlitas -tātis, *f.* unfaithfulness, faithlessness.

infidēliter, *adv.* unfaithfully.

infidus -a -um, unfaithful, untrue.

infīgo -fixi -fixum, 3. to fix, fasten to, *or* in, to thrust in; to imprint, impress; *infirum est,* it is fixed, finally resolved.

infimus -a -um, *superl. of inferus* (*q.v.*).

infindo -fidi -fissum, 3. to cut in, cleave.

infinitas -tātis, *f.* infinitely, endlessness.

infinitē, *adv.* infinitely, endlessly.

infinitio -ōnis, *f.* infinity.

infinitus -a -um, endless, unceasing; *number,* countless; boundless, immense; indefinite, general; *subst.,* **infinitum -i,** *n.* that which is boundless.

infirmātio -ōnis, *f.* a refuting; invalidating.

infirmē, *adv.* weakly, faintly.

infirmitas -tātis, *f.* weakness, infirmity; *animi,* want of spirit, instability.

infirmo, 1. to weaken; to shake; to refute; to annul.

infirmus -a -um, weak, infirm; timorous, *animo infirmo esse.*

infit, *defective verb,* he *or* she begins; he *or* she begins to speak.

infitiae, *f.* a denial; *found only in acc., infitias ire,* to deny, disown.

infitiālis -e, negative, containing a denial.

infitiātio -ōnis, *f.* a denying.

infitiātor -ōris, *m.* one who denies a debt.

infitior, 1. *dep.* to deny, not to confess.

inflammātio -ōnis, *f.* a fire, conflagration; *animorum,* inspiration.

inflammo, 1. to light up, kindle; to inflame, excite.

inflātio -ōnis, *f.* a puffing up.

inflātius, *adv. in compar.,* too pompously, haughtily.

1. **inflātus** -a -um, *p. adj.*, swelling, swollen; haughty.

2. **inflātus** -ūs, *m.* a blowing into; *primo inflatu tibicinis*, blast; inspiration.

nflecto -flexi -flexum, 3. to bend, bow, curve; *ius civile*, to warp; to modulate the voice; to alter a name; *of persons*, to change, affect.

inflētus -a -um, unwept, unlamented.

inflexio -ōnis, *f.* a bending, swaying.

inflexus -ūs, *m.* a bending, curving.

inflīgo -flixi -flictum, 3. to strike, dash against; to cause hurt or damage.

inflo, 1. to blow on or in; to play on wind instruments; to produce by blowing, *sonum*; to blow out; to puff out, *ambas buccas*; to make arrogant.

inflūo -fluxi -fluxum, 3. to flow in, stream in; to steal in.

infŏdio -fōdi -fossum, 3. to dig in, bury.

informātio -ōnis, *f.* a conception, idea.

informis -e, formless, unformed; deformed, hideous.

informo, 1. to form, fashion; to instruct; to depict; to form an idea of anything.

infortūnātus -a -um, unfortunate, miserable.

infortūnium -ii, *n.* misfortune, ill luck.

infrā, *adv.* on the under side, beneath; in the lower world; below (*in rank*); *compar.*, *inferius*, lower down. *Prepos. with acc.*; beneath, below; *of size.* less than; *of time*, later than.

infractio -ōnis, *f.* breaking; *animi*, dejection.

infractus -a -um, broken, exhausted.

infrăgilis -e, that cannot be broken, strong.

infrĕmo -frĕmŭi, 3. to roar, growl.

1. **infrēnātus** -a -um, without bridle.

2. **infrēnātus** -a -um, *partic. of infreno.*

infrendĕo, 2. to gnash with the teeth.

infrēnis -e *and* **infrēnus**, -a -um, unbridled; *Numidae*, riding without bridle.

infrēno, 1. to bridle; *currus*, to harness the horses to the chariot; to check.

infrĕquens -entis, infrequent; few in number; *of places*, scantily populated; *causa*, attended by few hearers; infrequent, occasional.

infrĕquentia -ae, *f.* fewness thinness; solitude, loneliness.

infringo -frēgi -fractum, 3. to break off, break in pieces; to destroy, enfeeble, cast down; to knock against.

infrons -frondis, leafless; *ager*, treeless.

infructŭōsus -a -um, unfruitful, unproductive, useless.

infūcātus -a -um, rouged, painted.

infŭla -ae, *f.* a band or fillet of wool, worn by priests and Vestal virgins; an ornament, badge of honour.

infŭlātus -a -um, wearing the *infula.*

infulcio -fulsi -fultum, 4. to stuff in, cram in.

infundo -fūsum, 3. to pour in or on; to administer; to present; *of people, se infundere*, to pour in, stream in; to penetrate; *infusus with dat.*, spread, lying on.

infusco, 1. to make dark; to obscure, blacken; to disfigure, corrupt, stain.

Ingaevōnes -um, a German tribe on the shores of the North Sea.

ingĕmino, 1. *transit.*, to double, redouble; *intransit.*, to become double, to increase.

ingĕmisco (ingĕmesco) -gĕmŭi, 3. to sigh or groan; *transit.*, to sigh or groan over.

ingĕmo, 3. to sigh, groan over; *with dat.*

ingĕnĕro, 1. to implant in, produce; to create.

ingĕnĕrātus -a -um, innate, natural.

ingĕniōsē, *adv.* cleverly, ingeniously.

ingĕniōsus -a -um, naturally clever, talented, able; fit for, adapted to.

ingĕnitus -a -um, *partic. of ingigno.*

ingĕnium -ii, *n.* nature, natural constitution; natural disposition, temperament, character; cleverness, talent, genius.

ingens -entis, vast, immense, enormous.

ingĕnŭē, *adv.* nobly, liberally; freely, frankly.

ingĕnŭitas -tātis, *f.* the condition of a freeman, free-birth; noble-mindedness.

ingĕnŭus -a -um, native, not foreign; free-born; noble, honourable; frank, sincere; delicate.

ingĕro -gessi -gestum, 3. to carry, throw, put, pour in or upon; to hurl at; to heap on, to utter; to press upon, force upon, *alicui nomen.*

ingigno -gĕnŭi -gĕnitum, 3. to implant by birth or nature; **ingĕnitus**, innate, inborn.

inglōrius -a -um, inglorious; undistinguished.

inglŭvies -ēi, *f.* the craw or crop of birds, the maw of animals; gluttony.

ingrātē, *adv.* unpleasantly; ungratefully.

ingrātia -ae, *f.* unthankfulness; *abl.*, *ingratiis (ingratis)*, unwillingly.

ingrātis, *v. ingratia.*

ingrātus -a -um, unpleasant, unpleasing; ungrateful; on account of; insatiable; unprofitable, thankless, *labor.*

ingrăvesco, 3. to become heavy; to become troublesome; *annona ingravescit*, becomes dearer; to be wearied.

ingrăvo, 1. to make heavy, trouble, aggravate.

ingrĕdior -gressus sum, 3. *intransit.*, to go in; to enter on, *in bellum*; to go forth, walk; *transit.*, to enter, *domum*; to begin.

ingressio -ōnis, *f.* an entering; a beginning; gait, pace.

ingressus -ūs, *m.* an entering ; an inroad; a beginning; walking, going.

ingrŭo -ŭi, 3. to break in; to attack.

inguen -guinis, *n.* the groin.

ingurgito, 1. to plunge; *se ingurgitare,* to gormandise.

industātus -a -um, untaxed, not taxed before.

inhăbilis -e, unmanageable ; useless, unfit for.

inhăbitābilis -e, uninhabitable.

inhăbito, 1. to inhabit.

inhaerĕo -haesi -haesum, 2. to stick in, cleave to; *semper alicui,* to be always in the company of.

inhaeresco -haesi -haesum, 3. to remain fast, to cleave to.

inhālo, 1. to breathe upon.

inhĭbĕo -ŭi -ĭtum, 2. to hold in, restrain; *naut., navem retro inhibere,* to back water; to practise, use.

inhĭbĭtio -ōnis, *f.* a restraining.

inhio, 1. to gape, gape with wonder; to covet, desire.

inhŏnestē, *adv.* dishonourably, disgracefully.

inhŏnesto, 1. to disgrace, dishonour.

inhŏnestus -a -um, dishonourable, shameful; ugly.

inhŏnōrātus -a -um, not honoured, private, retired; unrewarded.

inhŏnōrus -a -um, unhonoured; unsightly.

inhorrĕo -ŭi, 2. to bristle with.

inhorresco -horrŭi, 3. to bristle up; to be rough with frost; to shudder from cold, *etc.*; to shake, tremble.

inhospĭtālis -e, inhospitable.

inhospĭtālitas -tātis, *f.* want of hospitality.

inhospĭtus -a -um, inhospitable.

inhūmānē, *adv.* inhumanly.

inhūmānĭtas -tātis, *f.* cruelty ; courtesy; niggardliness.

inhūmānĭtĕr, *adv.* uncivilly, rudely.

inhūmānus -a -um, cruel, inhuman; rude; uncultivated.

inhŭmātus -a -um, unburied.

inĭbi, *adv.* therein, in that place, in that matter; almost, on the point of.

inĭcio -iēci -iectum, 3. to throw in *or* into, *se in medios hostes ;* to cause, inspire, infuse, occasion, *alicui timorem ; in conversation,* to mention, let drop; to throw *or* place on; *brachia collo,* to embrace; to throw *or* cast on; *inicere alicui manus,* to lay hands on.

iniectio -ōnis, *f.* a laying on.

iniectus -ūs, *m.* a throwing on, throwing over; an inserting.

inĭmīcē, *adv.* in an unfriendly manner.

inĭmīcĭtia -ae, *f.* enmity.

inĭmīco, 1. to make hostile, set at enmity.

inĭmīcus -a -um, unfriendly, adverse; hurtful, prejudicial; *subst.* **inĭmīcus, ri,** *m.* an enemy, foe.

inintelligens -entis, unintelligent.

inīquē, *adv.* unequally; unfairly, unjustly.

inīquĭtas -tātis, *f.* unevenness ; unfavourableness, difficulty; injustice, unreasonableness.

inīquus -a -um, uneven, unfavourable, disadvantageous ; unpropitious ; impatient, discontented ; unequal ; *sol,* too hot; unjust; hostile, adverse; *subst.,* **inīqui -orum,** *m.* enemies.

initio, 1. to initiate.

initium -ii, *n.* a beginning, commencement; *initium capere ab or ex, etc. ; ab initio,* from the beginning; *plur.,* the elements of a science, first principles; hidden rites, mysteries.

initus -ūs, *m.* an arrival, entrance; a beginning.

iniūcundē, *adv. only in compar.,* unpleasantly, in an unfriendly manner.

iniūcundĭtas -tātis, *f.* unpleasantness.

iniūcundus -a -um, unpleasant, displeasing.

iniūdĭcātus -a -um, untried, uncondemned, undecided.

iniungo -iunxi -iunctum, 3. to join to, fasten to; connect with; to cause; to inflict upon, bring upon, to impose upon, charge.

iniūrātus -a -um, unsworn, not having taken an oath.

iniūria -ae, *f.* an injury, injustice, wrong; *per iniuriam,* wrongfully; an insult; *legal,* damage, injury, affront; a possession wrongfully obtained ; revenge for an affront.

iniūriōsē, *adv.* illegally, wrongfully, injuriously.

iniūriōsus -a -um, unjust, wrongful, unlawful.

iniūrius -a -um, wrongful, unjust.

iniūrus -a -um = iniurius (q.v.).

1. **iniussus -a -um,** unbidden, spontaneous.

2. **iniussus,** *m. only in abl.* **iniussu,** without orders.

iniustē, *adv.* unjustly, unfairly.

iniustĭtia -ae, *f.* injustice, an injust proceeding.

iniustus -a -um, unjust; harsh, severe; *regna,* unjustly acquired; burdensome, oppressive ; *subst.,* **iniustum -i,** *n.* injustice.

inj-. See ini-.

inl . . . v. ill . . .

inm . . . v. imm . . .

innābilis -e, that cannot be swum in.

innascor -nātus, 3. *dep.* to be born, grow, arise in *or* upon; to be produced, arise; *partic.,* **innātus -a -um,** innate, inborn.

innăto, 1. to swim into ; to swim *or* float in *or* upon; to flow into *or* over.

innātus, *partic. of* **innascor.**

innāvĭgābĭlis -e, not navigable.

innecto -nexŭi -nexum, 3. to tie, bind,

fasten, weave together ; devise ; to implicate; to connect.

innĭtor -nixus sum, 3. *dep.* to lean upon ; *alis*, to fly.

inno, 1. to swim in *or* on, *with dat.* ; *poet.* to flow over; to sail over.

innŏcens -entis, harmless; innocent, inoffensive.

innŏcentĕr, *adv.* innocently, inoffensively.

innŏcentĭa -ae, *f.* harmlessness; innocence, disinterestedness.

innŏcŭē, *adv.* harmlessly, innocently.

innŏcŭus -a -um, *act.*, harmless; innocent; *litus*, safe; *passive*, unharmed.

innŏtesco -nŏtŭi, 3. to become known *or* noted.

innŏvo, 1. to renew; *se ad suam intemperantiam*, to return to.

innoxĭus -a -um, *act.*, harmless; innocent; *pass.*, unharmed; undeserved.

innūbĭlus -a -um, unclouded, clear.

innūbo -nupsi -nuptum, 3. to connect oneself with by marriage.

innŭba -ae, *fem. adj.*, unmarried, without a husband.

innŭmĕrābĭlis -e, innumerable.

innŭmĕrābĭlĭtas -atis, *f.* an infinite number.

innŭmĕrābĭlĭtĕr, *adv.* innumerably.

innŭmĕrālis -e, countless.

innŭmĕrus -a -um, countless.

innŭo -ŭi, 3. to give a nod to, make a sign to.

innupta -ae, *fem. adj.*, unmarried, having no husband; *subst.*, innupta -ae, *f.* a virgin.

innūtrĭo, 4. to bring up, educate with *or* among.

Ĭnō -ūs, *f.* daughter of Cadmus.

inoblītus -a -um, mindful, not forgetful.

inobrŭtus -a -um, not overwhelmed.

inobservābĭlis -e, imperceptible.

inobservantĭa -ae, *f.* negligence, inattention.

inobservātus -a -um, unobserved.

inŏdōrus -a -um, without smell.

inoffensus -a -um, without stumbling, unhindered ; *cursus honorum*, uninterrupted.

inofficiōsus -a -um, contrary to duty; disobliging.

inŏlens -entis, without smell.

inŏlesco -ŏlēvi -ŏlĭtum, 3. to grow in *or* on.

inōmĭnātus -a -um, ill-omened, unlucky.

inŏpĭa -ae, *f.* want, need; helplessness.

inŏpīnans -antis, unexpected, unawares.

inŏpīnantĕr, unexpectedly.

inŏpīnātō, *adv.* unexpectedly.

inŏpīnātus -a -um, *pass.*, unexpected; *act.*, not expecting ; *ex inopinato*, *inopinato*, unexpectedly ; *subst.*, inōpīnātum -i, *n.* an unexpected event.

inŏpīnus -a -um, unexpected.

inopportūnus -a -um, inconvenient.

inops -ŏpis, *with genit. or abl.*, *or ab and abl.*, without means; poor; wanting in; powerless, helpless.

inōrātus -a -um, not formally brought forward and heard.

inordĭnātus -a -um, disorderly, in confusion ; *subst.*, inordĭnātum -i, *n.* disorder.

inōrior, 4. *dep.*, to arise, appear.

inornātus -a -um, unadorned ; unpraised, uncelebrated.

inp . . . = *imp . . . (q.v.).*

inquam -is -it, *perf.*, inquii, *v. def.*, I say.

inquies -ētis, unquiet, restless.

inquĭēto, 1. to disquiet, disturb.

inquĭētus -a -um, unquiet, restless; *Hadria*, stormy.

inquĭlīnus -i, *m.* a tenant, lodger.

inquĭnātē, *adv.* filthily, impurely.

inquĭnātus -a -um, *p. adj.*, defiled, contaminated, sordid.

inquĭno, 1. to defile, contaminate; to corrupt.

inquīro -quīsīvi -quīsītum, 3. to seek for, search for; to investigate, inquire into; *legal*, to search for evidence against anyone.

inquīsītĭo -ōnis, *f.* a searching after; investigation.

inquīsītor -ōris, *m.* inquirer; spy; an investigator.

inr . . . *v. irr . . .*

insălūbris -e, unhealthy, unserviceable, unprofitable.

insălūtātus -a -um, ungreeted, of whom no farewell has been taken.

insānābĭlis -e, incurable.

insānē, *adv.* madly, insanely.

insānĭa -ae, *f.* madness, insanity; mad desire; poetical rapture *or* inspiration.

insānĭo -īvi *and* -ĭi -ītum, 4. to rage, be seized with frenzy; to act like a madman, to rave.

insānĭtas -ātis, *f.* insanity.

insānus -a -um, of unsound mind, insane; raging, senseless; of great size *or* violence; inspired; *act.*, making mad.

insătĭābĭlis -e, *pass.*, insatiable; *act.*, uncloying, unwearying.

insătĭābĭlĭtĕr, *adv.* insatiably.

insătŭrābĭlis -e, insatiable.

insătŭrābĭlĭtĕr, *adv.* insatiably.

inscalpo, 1. to engrave.

inscendo -scendi -scensum, 3. to ascend, go up.

insciens -entis, ignorant, unaware.

inscientĕr, *adv.* ignorantly, foolishly.

inscientĭa -ae, *f.* ignorance, inexperience.

inscītē, *adv.* clumsily, awkwardly, unskilfully.

inscītĭa -ae, *f.* clumsiness, inexperience, ignorance, *disserendi*; stupidity.

inscītus -a -um, ignorant, unskilful, absurd.

inscius -a -um, ignorant, not knowing; culpac, free from.

inscribo -scripsi -scriptum, 3. to write in or on, inscribe; librum, to give a title to a book; to impress, orationem in animo; to assign; to assume; to ascribe; deos sceleri, to charge the gods with crime; to give an inscription or title to; inscribo epistolam patri, to address; to brand.

inscriptio -ōnis, f. a writing in or upon; inscription; the title of a book.

1. **inscriptus -a -um,** unwritten.

2. **inscriptus -a -um,** partic. of inscribo.

insculpo -sculpsi -sculptum, 3. to carve in, engrave; to impress.

insēco -sēcŭi -sectum, 1. to cut into, cut to pieces.

insectātio -ōnis, f. a following, pursuit; insulting.

insectātor -ōris, m. a pursuer, persecutor.

insector, 1. dep., to follow, pursue; reproach, rail at.

insĕnesco -sĕnŭi, 3. to grow old at or among; libris.

insĕpultus -a -um, unburied; sepultura, burial without the customary solemnities.

insĕquor -sĕcūtus or -sĕquūtus sum, 3. to follow after, follow on, succeed; to pursue a subject, to pursue with hostile intent, to censure, attack.

1. **insĕro -sēvi -situm,** 3. to sow in; to implant; partic., insitus -a -um, implanted, innate; to unite.

2. **insĕro -sĕrŭi -sertum,** 3. to put, place, set in, insert; to introduce, intermingle with; se alicui rei, to meddle with; to incorporate with.

insertim, adv. by insertion.

inserto, 1. to insert, put into.

inservio, 4. to serve; to be devoted to, alicui; to take care of.

insessus, partic. of insideo and insido.

insĭbilo, 1. to hiss, pipe, whistle in.

insĭdĕo -sēdi -sessum, 2. intransit., to sit upon, with dat., or abl.; to have one's seat or place; to dwell, remain; transit., to occupy; to inhabit.

insidiae -ārum, f. an ambush; the place of ambush; a trap, treachery, deceit, plot; per insidias, ex insidiis, or insidiis, treacherously; illusion, deception.

insidiātor -ōris, m. a spy, lurker, traitor.

insidior, 1. dep., to lie in ambush against, lie in wait for, hostibus; to plot against the life of; to watch for, wait for.

insidiōsē, adv. treacherously, insidiously.

insidiōsus -a -um, deceitful, cunning, full of snares.

insīdo -sēdi -sessum, 3. to sit, settle, perch upon, floribus (of bees); sink into; to dwell; to beset a place; to sink deep.

insigne -is, n. a signal, token; the official badge of a magistracy; plur., insignia; beauties (of a brilliant passage).

insignio, 4. to put a mark upon, to impress; to distinguish; to adorn.

insignis -e, remarkable, noted; eminent, distinguished.

insignītē, adv. remarkably, extraordinarily.

insignĭter, adv. remarkably.

insignītus -a -um, marked so as to be known, noticeable, plain; striking.

insilia -ium, n. the treadle of a loom.

insilio -silŭi -sultum, 4. to leap, spring in or on.

insĭmŭlātio -ōnis, f. accusation, charge.

insĭmŭlo, 1. to charge, accuse, blame.

insincērus -a -um, tainted, putrefying.

insinŭātio -ōnis, f. rhet., the gaining the favour of the audience.

insinŭo, 1. to introduce by windings or turnings, to insinuate; se insinuare, insinuari, to penetrate, work one's way in; to gain the goodwill of.

insĭpiens -entis, foolish, stupid.

insĭpĭentĕr, adv. foolishly, stupidly.

insĭpĭentia -ae, f. foolishness, stupidity.

insisto -stĭti, 3. to stand on, set foot on; to enter on a journey, pursue, iter; to follow hard on; to persist in; to stand still; to pause; to dwell upon; to be fixed or obstinate in.

insĭtio -ōnis, f. a grafting, budding; the grafting season.

insĭtīvus -a -um, grafted, engrafted; foreign; not genuine.

insĭtor -ōris, m. a grafter.

insĭtus -a -um, partic. of 1. insero.

insŏciābilis -e, unsociable, unsocial.

insŏlābĭlĭtĕr, adv. inconsolably.

insŏlens -entis, unusual, contrary to custom; unaccustomed to; extravagant, verbum; prodigal; arrogant.

insŏlentĕr, adv. unusually, immoderately, arrogantly.

insŏlentia -ae, f. inexperience in, strangeness; affectation, novelty of diction; extravagance; arrogance.

insŏlesco, 3. to behave extravagantly; to become haughty, be elated.

insŏlĭdus -a -um, weak, soft, tender.

insŏlĭtus -a -um, act., unaccustomed to; pass., unusual, strange; uncommon.

insomnia -ae, f. sleeplessness, loss of sleep.

insomnis -e, sleepless.

1. **insomnium -ii,** n. sleeplessness.

2. **insomnium -ii,** n. a dream.

insŏno -sŏnŭi -sŏnĭtum, 1. to make a noise in, resound; transit., to make to sound.

insons -sontis, innocent, guiltless; harmless.

insŏpītus -a -um, wakeful, watchful.

inspargo = inspergo (q.v.).

inspecto, 1. to look at or in, observe, view.

insperans -antis, not hoping, not expecting.

insperatus -a -um, unhoped for, unexpected; *ex insperato*, unexpectedly.

inspergo *and* **inspargo** -spersi (-sparsi) -spersum (-sparsum), 3. to strew, sprinkle in *or* on.

inspicio -spexi -spectum, 3. to look in *or* on; to look into, read; to examine; to contemplate; to observe; to inspect; to investigate.

inspico, 1. to sharpen a point.

inspiro, 1. to breathe upon, to blow upon; to breathe into, inspire, inflame.

inspoliatus -a -um, not despoiled.

instabilis -e, *act.,* unstable, tottering, unsteady; inconstant; *pass.,* insecure.

instans -antis, *p. adj.,* present; urgent; *subst.,* **instans** -antis, *n.* the immediate present.

instanter, *adv.* urgently, earnestly.

instantia -ae, *f.* the present time.

instar, *n. indecl.,* an image, likeness, picture; *gen. with genit.,* like to, as great as, after the fashion of, *instar montis equus;* to the number of.

instauratio -onis, *f.* repetition, renewal.

instaurativus -a -um, renewed, repeated.

instauro, 1. to renew, repeat, begin anew; to restore; to repay; to prepare.

insterno -stravi -stratum, 3. to strew over, cover over; *equum,* to saddle; to spread over.

instigator -oris, *m.* an instigator.

instigatrix -tricis, *f.* she that instigates.

instigo, 1. to instigate; incite.

instillo, 1. to pour in by drops; to instil.

instimulator -oris, *m.* an instigator.

instimulo, 1. to stimulate.

instinctor -oris, *m.* an inciter.

instinctus -us, *m.* instigation.

instinguo -stinxi -stinctum, 3. to incite.

instita -ae, *f.* a seam, border, *or* flounce.

institio -onis, *f.* a standing still.

institor -oris, *m.* a broker, factor, pedlar.

instituo -ui -utum, 3. to put *or* place into; to arrange; *milit.,* draw up in order; to prepare, construct; to begin, undertake; *with infin.,* to resolve upon; to appoint, establish, *ludos;* to administer; to instruct.

institutio -onis, *f.* arrangement; method; instruction.

institutum -i, *n.* an undertaking, purpose; precept; custom, institution; *ex instituto,* according to custom, order.

insto -stiti -staturus, 1. to stand in *or* on; to be close to, follow closely, *vestigiis;* to press upon, harass; *currum,* to be zealous in building; to devote oneself eagerly to anything; to persevere; to insist; *of time,* to approach.

1. instratus -a -um, uncovered.

2. instratus, *partic. of insterno.*

instrenuus -a -um, inactive, idle.

instrepo -ui -itum, 3. to make a noise, rattle, creak.

instringo -strinxi -strictum, 3. to bind.

instructe, *adv.* with great preparation.

instructio -onis, *f.* a setting in array, drawing up in order.

instructor -oris, *m.* a preparer.

1. instructus -a -um *p. adj.,* provided with, furnished; instructed, learned.

2. instructus -us, *m.* a preparation, provision; *fig.* matter (*in a speech*).

instrumentum -i, *n.* a tool, instrument; *plur., instrumenta anilia,* dress; store, stock; means to an end.

instruo -struxi -structum, 3. to build in *or* into; to set up, build; to arrange, prepare; to equip, provide; *milit.,* to arm, to draw up in order of battle, to post; to teach.

insuavis -e, unpleasant, disagreeable, not sweet.

Insubres -ium *and* -um, *m.* a people in Cisalpine Gaul; *sing.,* **Insuber** -bris, *m.,* *adj.,* **Insuber** -bris -bre.

insudo, 1. to sweat in *or* at.

insuefactus -a -um, accustomed to, inured to.

insuesco -suevi -suetum, 3. to accustom oneself to, to become used to; *transit.,* to accustom.

1. insuetus -a -um, unaccustomed to, unused to, *laboris;* *pass.,* unusual, unwonted.

2. insuetus -a -um, *partic. of insuesco.*

insula -ae, *f.* an island; detached house, let out to several poor families; hired lodging.

insulanus -i, *m.* an islander.

insulse, *adv.* insipidly, absurdly.

insulsitas -atis, *f.* insipidity, absurdity.

insulsus -a -um, unsalted, insipid absurd, foolish.

insulto, 1. to leap at *or* on; *nemora,* dance through; to scoff at, insult.

insum -fui -esse, to be in *or* on; to be contained in, to belong to.

insumo -sumpsi -sumptum, 3. to take for any purpose, expend.

insuo -sui -sutum, 3. to sew in, sew up, sew on.

insuper, *adv.* above, over, overhead; from above; over and above, besides.

insuperabilis -e, insurmountable, impassable; unconquerable; *fatum,* inevitable.

insurgo -surrexi -surrectum, 3. to rise, raise oneself; to rise to one's full height; *insurgite remis,* put all your strength into the stroke; to increase in power; to rise up against.

insusurro, 1. to whisper, whisper in the ear.

intabesco -tabui, 3. to pine, waste, wither away; to become liquid, melt.

intactilis -e, that cannot be touched.

1. intactus -a -um, untouched; unhurt; pure, chaste; free from, *cupiditate.*

2. intactus -ūs, *m.* intangibility.

intāminātus -a -um, unstained, unspotted.

1. intectus -a -um, uncovered, unclothed, unarmed; open, frank

2. intectus -a -um, *partic. of* intego.

intĕgellus -a -um (*dim. of integer*), not seriously injured.

intĕger -gra -grum, whole, entire, undiminished; unharmed; fresh, untainted; unhurt; unmixed, pure; unexhausted, vigorous; chaste; sound, blooming, *valetudo ; integer aevi,* in the prime of life; entire, *annus ; de integro,* anew; undecided, undetermined, *rem integram relinquere ;* inexperienced; impartial, free from prejudice, *integri testes;* uncorrupted, blameless, innocent, *integer vitae scelerisque purus;* inviolate.

intĕgo -texi -tectum, 3. to cover.

integrasco, 3. to break out afresh.

integrātio -ōnis, *f.* a renewing, renewal.

integrē, *adv.* purely, correctly; uprightly, impartially; disinterestedly.

integritas -ātis, *f.* soundness, health; purity, correctness; uprightness, integrity.

integro, 1. to renew, repeat, begin afresh; to heal; to refresh.

intĕgūmentum -i, *n.* a covering; a cloak, disguise.

intellectus -ūs, *m.* perception; understanding, comprehension.

intelligens -entis, *p. adj.,* intelligent, well acquainted with anything.

intelligentĕr, *adv.* intelligently.

intelligentia -ae, *f.* a conception, idea; insight, intelligence, knowledge; taste; understanding.

intelligo (intellĕgo) -lexi -lectum, 3. to understand; to perceive, observe, feel; to form an idea; to think; to be a connoisseur; to understand a person's character.

intĕmĕrātus -a -um, unspotted, undefiled.

intĕmpĕrans -antis, extravagant, immoderate.

intĕmpĕrantĕr, *adv.* immoderately, extravagantly.

intĕmpĕrantia -ae, *f.* want of moderation, excess, intemperance; arrogance.

intĕmpĕrātē, *adv.* intemperately.

intĕmpĕrātus -a -um, intemperate, immoderate.

intĕmpĕries -ēi, *f.* inclement weather; *aquarum,* excessive fall of rain; outrageous conduct; intemperance.

intempestīvē, *adv.* unseasonably.

intempestīvus -a -um, unseasonable, untimely.

intempestus -a -um, unseasonable;

intempesta nox, the dead of night; unwholesome.

intendo -tendi -tentum, 3. to stretch out, extend; to aim; *transit.,* to direct towards; *iter in* or *ad locum,* to direct one's course towards; to direct the thoughts to; to direct with hostile intention, to excite; *intransit.* or *reflex.,* to direct one's course; to direct one's efforts; to devote oneself to, to stretch, stretch round; to exert; to intend; to raise; to try to prove.

1. intentātus -a -um, untouched, untried.

2. intentātus -a -um, *partic. of* intento.

intentē, *adv.* carefully, diligently.

intentio -ōnis, *f.* a directing, attention; stretching; *of the mind,* an effort; intention.

intento, 1. to stretch towards or against; to threaten, *arma Latinis.*

1. intentus -ūs, *m.* a stretching out.

2. intentus -a -um, anxious, intent, full of expectation; attentive to, waiting eagerly for; intent upon, zealous in; ready for battle; active, vigorous.

intĕpĕo, 2. to be lukewarm.

intĕpesco -tĕpŭi, 3. to become lukewarm, grow gradually warm.

intĕr, *prep. with acc.* between, among, amid; during, in the course of; *amare inter se,* to love one another; *inter haec,* meanwhile.

intĕrāmenta -ōrum, *n.* the woodwork of a ship.

intĕrārĕsco, 3. to become dry, to dry up, decay.

intercălāris -e, intercalary.

intercălārius -a -um, intercalary.

intercălo, 1. to insert a day or month in the calendar; to defer, put off.

intercăpēdo -inis, *f.* an interval, pause, respite.

intercēdo -cessi -cessum, 3. to go between, come between; *of places,* to stand or lie between; to intervene; to happen between; to step between; to interpose, protest against; to stand surety.

interceptio -ōnis, *f.* a taking away.

interceptor -ōris, *m.* one who takes away, an embezzler.

intercessio -ōnis, *f.* intercession, suretyship; a protest.

intercessor -ōris, *m.* surety, bail; one who protests against.

1. intercido -cīdi -cīsum, 3. to cut off, cut asunder; *pontem,* to demolish; *montem,* to cut through.

2. intercido -cidi, 3. to fall between; to happen, occur; to decay, perish.

intercino, 1. to sing between.

intercipio -cēpi -ceptum, 3. to intercept; to deprive, steal; to carry off prematurely; to cut off.

intercīsē, *adv.* confusedly, interruptedly.

interclūdo -clūsi -clūsum, 3. to block up, hinder; to cut off, separate from, *aliquem re frumentaria;* to enclose.

interclūsio -ōnis, *f.* a blocking up.

intercŏlumnium -ii, *n.* the space between two columns.

intercurro -cŭcurri *and* **-curri -cursum,** 3. to run between; to step between, intercede; to mingle with; to hasten to in the meanwhile.

intercurso, 1. to run between.

intercursus -ūs, *m.* interposition.

intercus -cŭtis, under the skin ; *aqua,* the dropsy.

interdătus -a -um, *partic. of interdo.*

interdīco -dixi -dictum, 3. to forbid, prohibit; *legal, interdicere alicui aquā et igni,* to banish; to command.

interdicto -ōnis, *f.* a forbidding, prohibition.

interdictum -i, *n.* a prohibition.

interdiū (interdius), *adv.* in the day-time, by day.

interdo -didi -dătum, 1. to distribute.

interdŭātim = *interdum (q.v.).*

interductus -ūs, *m.* interpunctuation.

interdum, *adv.* sometimes, occasionally, now and then; meanwhile.

intĕrĕā, *adv.* in the meanwhile; nevertheless.

intĕremptio -ōnis, *f.* slaughter.

intĕrĕo -ii -itum, 4. to perish, to be lost among; to be destroyed; to die.

intĕrĕquito, 1. to ride between.

interfātio -ōnis, *f.* interruption in discourse.

interfectio -ōnis, *f.* a slaying.

interfector -ōris, *m.* a murderer, slayer.

interfectrix -trīcis, *f.* a murderess.

interficio -fēci -fectum, 3. to destroy, bring to naught; to slay.

interfio -fīeri (*pass. of interficio*), to perish.

interflūo -fluxi -fluxum, 3. to flow between.

interflŭus -a -um, flowing between.

interfŏdio -fōdi -fossum, 3. to dig into, pierce.

interfor -fātus sum, 1. *dep.,* to interrupt in discourse (1*st pers. pres. not found*).

interfŭgio, 3. to flee between.

interfulgens -entis, shining among or between.

interfundo -fūdi -fūsum, 3. to pour between; *middle, interfundi,* to flow between ; *maculis interfusa genas,* stained with.

interiăcĕo, 2. to lie between or among; *with dat.*

interiectus -ūs, *m.* a putting between; *of time,* an interval.

intericio (interiăcio) -iēci -iectum, 3. to throw, put among, or between; to intermingle; **interiectus,** interposed, thrown between; *anno interiecto,* after the interval of a year.

intĕrim, *adv.* meanwhile; however.

intĕrimo -ēmi -emptum, 3. to destroy, make an end of; to kill; *se,* to commit suicide.

intĕrior, intĕrius -ōris, *compar. adj.,* **intimus -a -um,** *superl.,* inner, interior; *interior ictibus,* too close to be struck; inland; nearer, shorter (*of the race-course*); more secret, more confidential; deeper; more profound; *superl.,* **intimus -a -um,** inmost; most profound; most intimate; *subst.,* **intimus -i,** *m.* an intimate friend.

intĕritio -ōnis, *f.* destruction, ruin.

intĕritus -ūs, *m.* destruction, ruin.

interiungo -iunxi -iunctum, 3. to unite, connect.

intĕrius, *compar. adj.,* *v. interior ; compar. of intra, v. intra.*

interj. See **interi,** *e.g.* **intericio,** *etc.*

interlābor -lābi, 3. *dep.,* to glide, flow between.

interlĕgo, 3. to pluck, gather here and there.

interlino -lēvi -lĭtum, 3. to daub between; to erase, to falsify by erasure.

interlŏquor -lŏcūtus (-loquūtus) sum, 3. *dep.,* to interrupt a person speaking.

interlūcĕo -luxi, 2. to shine, gleam between ; to shine forth ; to be transparent.

interlūnium -ii, *n.* the change of the moon.

interlŭo -ŭi, 3. to flow between, wash between.

1. **interminātus -a -um,** unbounded, boundless.

2. **interminātus -a -um,** *v. interminor.*

interminor, 1. *dep.,* to threaten, forbid with threats.

intermiscĕo -miscŭi -mixtum, 2. to mix with, intermix.

intermissio -ōnis, *f.* leaving off; respite, interruption.

intermitto -mīsi -missum, 3. to place between; to leave a space between, unoccupied; to leave off for a time, interrupt, neglect ; *vento intermisso,* the wind having dropped; *of time,* to let pass; to discontinue, suspend an office; *in transit.,* to cease, leave off.

intermŏrior -mortŭus sum, 3. *dep.,* to die, perish, decay; to faint away.

intermundia -ōrum, *n.* spaces between the worlds.

intermūrālis -e, between walls.

internascor -nātus sum, 3. *dep.,* to grow between.

internĕcīnus -a -um, *v. internecivus.*

internĕcio (internicio) -ōnis, *f.* extermination, massacre.

internĕcīvus (internĕcīnus) -a -um, deadly, internecine.

internecto, 3. to bind together, to bind up.

internicio = *internecio (q.v.).*

internōdium -ii, *n.* space between two knots *or* joints.

internōsco -nōvi -nōtum, 3. to distinguish between.

internuntia, *v. internuntius.*

internuntio, 1. to send messengers between two parties.

internuntius -a -um *adj., word as subst., a* messenger, negotiator, go-between.

internus -a -um, inward, internal, civil.

intĕro -trīvi -trītum, 3. to rub, crumble into.

interpellātio -ōnis, *f.* interruption, hindrance.

interpellātor -ōris, *m.* interrupter, disturber.

interpello, 1. to interrupt a speaker; to disturb, hinder.

interpŏlo, 1. to alter, furbish, repair; to corrupt, falsify.

interpōno -pōsŭi -pōsitum, 3. to put between *or* among, interpose, to insert; to allow an interval to pass between; to introduce: to allege as a reason *or* pretext; to pledge one's word; *se interponere in aliquid,* to engage in; to falsify, *rationes.*

interpŏsitio -ōnis, *f.* introducing *(in a speech)*; insertion.

interpŏsitus, *only in abl.* **-ū,** *m.* interposition.

interpres -prĕtis, *c.* a negotiator, messenger; an expounder; *divûm,* prophet, prophetess; an interpreter.

interprĕtātio -ōnis, *f.* explanation, interpretation; translation; meaning.

interprĕtor, 1. *dep.* to explain, translate; to put an interpretation on; to understand; to decide.

interpunctio -ōnis, *f.* punctuation.

interpungo -punxi -punctum, 3. to punctuate; *partic. subst., interpuncta verborum,* divisions.

interquiesco -quiēvi -quiētum, 3. to pause between, rest in the meantime.

interregnum -i, *n.* an interregnum.

interrex -rēgis, *m.* a regent.

interritus -a -um, undaunted.

interrŏgatio -ōnis, *f.* a question; *legal,* examination of witnesses; *logic,* an argument, syllogism.

interrŏgātiuncŭla -ae, *f. (dim. of interrogatio),* a short syllogism *or* argument.

interrŏgo, 1. to ask, question; *to examine, testem;* to accuse; *subst.,* **interrŏgātum -i,** *n.* a question.

interrumpo -rūpi -ruptum, 3. to break down, break asunder; to separate; to interrupt, disturb.

interruptē, *adv.* interruptedly, disconnectedly.

intersaepio -saepsi -saeptum, 4. to hedge in, hem in, separate.

interscindo -scidi -scissum, 3. to cut *or*

hew asunder; *venas,* to open; to cut off.

intersēpio = *intersaepio (q.v.).*

1. **intersĕro -sēvi -situm,** 3. to sow *or* plant between.

2. **intersĕro -serui -sertum,** 3. to put between; *contram intersertum,* alleging.

interspirātio -ōnis, *f.* a taking breath.

1. **interstinguo -stinctus,** 3. to cover with spots *or* speckles.

2. **interstinguo,** 3. to extinguish.

interstrĕpo, 3. to roar, make a noise in the midst of.

intersum -fŭi -esse, to be between; to intervene; to be different from; to be present, take part in; *impers., interest,* it concerns, it is of importance.

intertexo -texui -textum, 3. to weave together, interweave.

intertrīmentum -i, *n.* loss by friction, loss in working gold and silver; *damage.*

interturbātio -ōnis, *f.* disturbance, disquiet.

intervallum -i, *n.* space between two palisades; an intervening space, interval, distance; difference; *of music,* an interval.

intervĕnio -vēni -ventum, 4. to come between, to intervene; to interrupt; *of events,* to happen while something else is being done.

interventor -ōris, *m.* an interrupter, a visitor.

interventus -ūs, *m.* intervention, interference.

interverto (-vorto) -verti (-vorti) -versum (-vorsum), 3. to embezzle, appropriate to one's own use; to take away, defraud of; to spend.

interviso -vīsi -vīsum, 3. to look after, inspect secretly; to visit from time to time.

intervŏlito, 1. to fly about among.

intervŏmo, 3. to pour forth among.

intestābilis -e, disqualified from being a witness *or* from making a will, dishonourable.

intestātus -a -um, intestate; *adv., intestato.*

intestinum -i, *v. intestinus.*

intestinus -a -um, inward, internal; domestic, internal, civil; subjective; *subst.,* **intestinum -i,** *n.* an intestine.

intexo -texui -textum, 3. to plait in, interweave; to interlace; to wind around, to surround.

intĭbum -i, *n. and* **intĭbus -i,** *m. f.* endive, succory.

intĭmē, *adv.* confidentially, intimately; cordially, strongly.

intĭmus, *superl. from interior (q.v.).*

intingo (intinguo) -tinxi -tinctum, 3. to dip in.

intŏlĕrābilis -e, unbearable, intolerable.

intŏlĕrandus -a -um, unbearable, unendurable.

intŏlĕrans -antis, impatient of, unable to bear; *pass.*, unbearable.

intŏlĕrantĕr, *adv.* immoderately, impatiently.

intŏlĕrantia -ae, *f.* insufferable conduct, insolence.

intŏno -tŏnŭi -tŏnătum, 1. to thunder; to clash; *transit.*, to thunder forth.

intonsus -a -um, unshorn; wooded, leafy.

intorquĕo -torsi -tortum, 2. to twist or turn round; to wind; to hurl; *ardentes oculos*, to roll; to turn, writhe; to distort, turn away.

intortus -a -um (*partic. of intorqueo*).

intrā, *adv.* within; *prepos. with acc.*, within; *of time*, within, in the space of.

intrābilis -e, accessible.

intractābilis -e, unmanageable, rough.

intractātus -a -um, not handled; unattempted.

intrĕmisco -trĕmŭi,3.to begin to tremble.

intrĕmo, 3. to tremble, quake.

intrĕpĭdē, *adv.* without trembling, intrepidly.

intrĕpĭdus -a -um, not trembling, undaunted; free from care or alarm.

intrīco, 1. to entangle, bring into confusion.

intrinsĕcŭs, *adv.* inside, inwardly, internally.

1. intrītus -a -um, not worn away; unexhausted.

2. intrītus -a -um, *partic. of intero.*

1. intrō, *adv.* within.

2. intro, 1. to go into, enter; to penetrate.

intrŏdūco -duxi -ductum, 3. to lead or conduct into; to introduce; to maintain.

introductĭo -ōnis, bringing in, introduction.

ntrŏĕo -īvi *and* -ĭi -ĭtum, 4. to go into, enter.

intrŏfĕro -tŭli -ferre, to bear, carry in.

intrŏgrĕdior -gressus sum, 3. *dep.* to enter.

intrŏĭtus -ūs, *m.* an entrance; introduction, preamble.

intrŏmitto -mĭsi -missum, 3. to send in, cause to enter.

introrsus (introrsum), *adv.* towards the inside, inwards; inwardly, internally.

intrōrumpo -rūpi -ruptum, 3. to break in, enter by force.

introspĭcĭo -spexi -spectum, 3. to look into, look within; to observe, examine.

intrōversus = *introrsus (q.v.).*

intrōvŏco, 1. to call in.

intrūdo -trūsi -trūsum, 3. to thrust in; *se*, to intrude.

intŭbum -i, *n.* intŭbus -i, *m.*, *v. intibum.*

intŭĕor -tŭĭtus sum, 2. *dep.* to look at attentively, gaze at; *in aliquem contra*, right in the face; to contemplate; to look with astonishment or admiration at.

intŭĭtus -a -um, *partic. of intueor.*

intŭmesco -tŭmŭi, 3. to swell, swell up; to swell with anger, be angry.

intŭmŭlātus -a -um, unburied.

intŭor, 3. *dep.* = *intueor (q.v.).*

inturbidus -a -um, *pass.*, undisturbed, quiet, *annus; act.*, not turbulent, *vir.*

intŭs, *adv.* within, inside, indoors; to the inside.

intūtus -a -um, unprotected, unsafe.

inŭla -ae, *f.* the plant elecampane.

inultus -a -um, unavenged; unpunished.

inumbro, 1. to shade, overshadow.

inundātĭo -ōnis, *f.* inundation, flood.

inundo, 1. *transil.*, to overflow, inundate; *intransit.*, to overflow with.

inungo -unxi -unctum, 3. to anoint, smear with ointment.

inurbānē, *adv.* inelegantly, without wit or humour.

inurbānus -a -um, rude, unpolished, boorish; *in speech*, unrefined.

inurgĕo -ursi, 2. push, thrust against.

inūro -ussi -ustum, 3. to burn in; to imprint indelibly, brand; to burn, burn up; to singe, to curl.

inŭsĭtātē, *adv.* unusually, strangely.

inŭsĭtātus -a -um, unusual, strange.

inustus -a -um, *partic. of inuro.*

inūtilis -e, useless, unserviceable, unprofitable; injurious.

inūtilitas -ātis, *f.* uselessness.

inūtilĭtĕr, *adv.* uselessly, unprofitably; injuriously.

invādo -vāsi -vāsum, 3. to go in, enter; to advance; to undertake boldly; to attack, invade; to penetrate; to fall upon, seize.

invālesco -vălŭi, 3. to become strong.

invālĕtūdo -ĭnis, *f.* indisposition.

invālidus -a -um, weak, powerless, ill.

invectĭo -ōnis, *f.* importation; invective.

invĕho -vexi -vectum, 3. to carry, bring in; to import; to introduce, bring along with; *middle*, *invehi*, to ride or travel on horseback, in a vehicle, in a ship, *equo, etc. ; flumine*, to sail on ; *se invehere and middle invehi*, to penetrate, burst into, attack; inveigh against.

invĕnĭo -vēni -ventum, 4. to light upon, meet with; to acquire, get, earn; to find out, discover; to effect, bring about; *dolor se invenit*, shows itself.

inventĭo -ōnis, *f.* invention; inventive faculty.

inventor -ōris, *m.* an inventor, finder out.

inventrix -trīcis, *f.* she that finds out.

inventum -i, *n.* an invention, discovery.

invĕnustus -a -um, inelegant; unhappy in love.

invĕrēcundus -a -um, shameless, impudent.

invergo, 3. to pour upon.

inversĭo -ōnis, *f.* irony.

inversus -a -um, *partic. of inverto.*

inverto -verti -versum, 3. to turn over,

turn about; to turn upside down, empty; to invert, change, pervert.

invesperascit, 3. *impers.* it grows dark, becomes twilight.

investigatio -ōnis, *f.* an investigation.

investigātor -ōris, *m.* an inquirer, investigator.

investigo, 1. to search out, track out.

inveterasco -āvi, 3. to become old; to grow old in; to become obsolete; to become established, to be rooted.

inveterātio -ōnis, *f.* a becoming old, an inveterate disease *or* mistake.

invetero, 1. to allow to become old; *and pass.*, **inveterāri**, to grow old; *middle*, *inveterari*, to become established, firmly rooted; **inveterātus**, old established.

invicem, *adv.* by turns, alternately; mutually, reciprocally, on both sides.

invictus -a -um, unconquered, invincible; *defensio*, unanswerable.

invidentia -ae, *f.* envying, envy.

invideo -vīdi -vīsum, 2. to look upon with the evil eye, to envy, grudge; *with dat.*

invidia -ae, *f.* envy, hatred, jealousy, ill-will, unpopularity; reproach.

invidiose, *adv.* enviously, bitterly.

invidiōsus -a -um, envious; causing envy, envied; feeling hate, hating; causing hate; hateful, detested.

invidus -a -um, envious; *subst.*, an envier.

invigilo, 1. to watch over; give great attention and care to.

inviolābilis -e, inviolable, that cannot be injured.

inviolātē, *adv.* inviolately.

inviolātus -a -um, uninjured, unhurt; inviolable.

invisitātus -a -um, not seen; unusual, strange.

inviso, -ēre -vīsi -vīsum, 3. to go to see, to visit; to perceive.

1. **invīsus** -a -um, unseen, secret.

2. **invīsus** -a -um, *pass.*, hated; *act.*, hating, hostile.

invitāmentum -i, *n.* an invitation, attraction, allurement.

invitātio -ōnis, *f.* invitation.

invitātus -ūm, an invitation.

invītē, *adv.* unwillingly, involuntarily.

invito, 1. to invite, request civilly; *invitare se*, to take one's fill; to entice.

invitus -a -um, unwilling, against one's will; *me, te, se invito*, against my, thy will, *etc.*

invius -a -um, impassable; *subst.*, invia -ōrum, *n.* impassable places.

1. **invocātus** -a -um, uncalled.

2. **invocātus** -a -um, *partic.* of *invoco.*

invoco, 1. to call in, invoke.

involātus -ūs, *m.* a flying, flight (*only in abl. sing.*).

involito, 1. to fly in; *of the hair*, to float over.

involo, 1. to fly at, attack furiously; to seize upon, take possession of.

involucrum -i, *n.* a wrapper, cover, case.

involūtus -a -um, *p. adj.*, obscure, involved.

involvo -volvi -volūtum, 3. to roll in, to roll along, to roll over (*with dat.*, to roll upon); to wrap up, cover; *se litteris*, to devote oneself to.

invulgo, 1. to publish; to give evidence.

invulnerātus -a -um, unwounded.

1. **Iō**, *interj.*, hurrah! *or of pain*, oh!

2. **Iō** -ūs *and* **Iōn** -ōnis, *f.* beloved of Jupiter, changed by Juno into a cow.

Ion -ōnis, *f.*, *v. Io.*

Iōnes -um, *m.* the Ionians.

iōta, *n. indecl.* the Greek vowel I.

Iphiānassa -ae, *f.* — *Iphigenia.*

Iphigenia -ae, *f.* daughter of Agamemnon, sacrificed by her father to appease the wrath of Diana; *or, according to another legend*, saved by Diana, and carried away, and made her priestess in Tauris.

ipse -a -um, self; *ego ipse*, I myself; *et ipse*, also, too; very, identical; *with numerals* = just, exactly; of one's own accord; alone, with oneself.

ira -ae, *f.* wrath, anger, ire, violence, rage; the cause of anger.

irācundē, *adv.* angrily, passionately.

irācundia -ae, *f.* an angry disposition, irascibility; anger.

irācundus -a -um, inclined to anger, wrathful.

irascor, 3. *dep.* to be angry.

irātē, *adv.* angrily.

irātus -a -um, angry, full of wrath.

Iris -ridis, *f.* messenger of the gods, goddess of the rainbow.

ironia -ae, *f.* irony.

Irpini — *Hirpini* (*q.v.*).

irrāsus -a -um, unshaved.

irraucesco *or* **irraucio** -rausi, 3. to become hoarse.

irrēligātus -a -um, unbound.

irrēligiōsē, *adv.* irreligiously, impiously.

irrēligiōsus -a -um, irreligious, impious.

irrēmeābilis -e, from which there is no return.

irrēparābilis -e, that cannot be restored, irreparable.

irrēpertus -a -um, not discovered.

irrēpo -repsi -reptum, 3. to creep, crawl in; insinuate oneself into.

irrēprehensus -a -um, unblamed, blameless.

irrēquiētus -a -um, restless, troubled.

irrēsectus -a -um, uncut.

irrēsolūtus -a -um, not loosed, not slackened.

irrētio, 4. to catch, entangle in a net; to ensnare.

irrētortus -a -um, not turned *or* twisted back.

irrēverentia -ae, *f.* want of respect.

irrĕvŏcābĭlis -e, irrevocable; unalterable; implacable.

irrĕvŏcātus -a -um, not called back, not to be called back.

irrīdĕo -rīsi -rīsum, 2. *intransit.*, to laugh at, jest; *transit.*, to mock, deride.

irrīdĭcŭlē, *adv.* without wit or humour.

irrĭgātĭo -ōnis, *f.* a watering, irrigation.

irrĭgo, 1. to conduct water; to diffuse; to irrigate.

irrĭgŭus -a -um, watering, irrigating; refreshing; *pass.*, watered.

irrīsĭo -ōnis, *f.* mocking, derision.

irrīsor -ōris, *m.* a laugher, mocker.

irrīsus -ūs, *m.* laughter, mockery.

irrītābĭlis -e, irritable, easily roused.

irrītāmen -ĭnis, *n.* an incitement.

irrītāmentum -i, *n.* incitement, provocation.

irrītātĭo -ōnis, *f.* provoking, irritation.

irrītātus -a -um, *partic. of irrito.*

irrīto, 1. to stimulate, incite; to irritate.

irrĭtus -a -um, void, invalid; vain, ineffectual; *of persons*, without doing anything; *subst.*, irrĭtum -i, *n.* that which is vain.

irrŏgātĭo -ōnis, *f.* the imposing of a fine *or* penalty.

irrŏgo, 1. to propose to the people a measure against anyone; to inflict.

irrōro, 1. to moisten with dew; to wet; to sprinkle upon.

irrumpo -rūpi -ruptum, 3. to break in, rush in, *in castra;* to seize upon; to seek to prevent.

irrŭo -rŭi, 3. to rush into, rush upon, *in aciem;* to take possession of; *in odium*, rush blindly into.

irruptĭo -ōnis, *f.* a bursting into, irruption.

irruptus -a -um, unbroken.

is, ĕa, ĭd, he, she, it; this *or* that person *or* thing; (*id subst.;* id *temporis*, id *aetatis*, at that age); *id est*, that is; *atque is, etc.*, and that too, and indeed.

Īsis -is *and* ĭdis, *f.* the Egyptian goddess Isis.

Īsŏcrătēs -is, *m.* a celebrated Athenian orator.

istāc, *adv.* by that way.

iste, ista, istŭd, *pron. demonstr.*, this *or* that person *or* thing; *in speeches*, the accused.

Ister = *Hister.*

Isthmus -i, *m.* an isthmus; *especially* the Isthmus of Corinth; *plur. subst.*, Isthmĭa -ōrum, *n.* the Isthmian Games.

istī, *adv.* there.

1. istic (isthic), istaec, istŏc *or* istŭc (iste *and* hic), this same, this very person *or* thing.

2. istic (isthic), there; in this affair.

istim, *adv.* from there.

istinc (isthinc), *adv.* thence.

istĭusmŏdi, of that kind, such.

istŏ, *adv.* thither, to that place.

istōc, *adv.* thither; that way; yonder.

istorsum, *adv.* in that direction.

1. istūc, *n. of* 1. *istic* (*q.v.*).

2. istūc (isthūc), *adv.* thither.

ĭtā, *adv.* so, thus, in such wise; consequently, and then; so, to such an extent; *ita . . . ut*, so . . . as, in such a manner . . . as, to the extent that; *ita plane*, certainly; *itane?* really?

Ĭtălī -ōrum *and* -ûm, *m.* the Italians. Ĭtălĭa -ae, *f.* Italy. *Adj.*, Ĭtălĭcus.

ĭtăquĕ, *adv.* and thus, and so; therefore.

item, *adv.* also, likewise; in like manner, as; and also, and even.

ĭtĕr, ĭtĭnĕris, *n.* a going, walk, way; a journey, a march; *in itinere*, on the march; a right of way; permission to march; a way, road; course; method.

ĭtĕrātĭo -ōnis, *f.* repetition, iteration.

ĭtĕro, 1. to do a second time, repeat; *pugnam*, to renew; to repeat (*words*).

ĭtĕrum, *adv.* again, a second time; secondly, *semel . . . iterum;* on the other hand.

Ĭthăca -ae, *f.* the home of Ulysses.

ĭtĭdem, *adv.* in like manner.

ĭtĭo -ōnis, *f.* a going, travelling.

Ĭtĭus portus, a port of the Morini.

ĭto, 1. to go.

ĭtus -ūs, *m.* a going, departure.

Ĭtylus -i, *m.* son of the Theban king Zethus and Aedon, killed by his own mother.

Ĭtys -tўos, *dat.* -ty, *acc.* -tyn *and* -tym, *abl.* -ty, *m.* son of Tereus and Procne, killed by his mother and served up for food to his father.

Ĭūlus -i, *m.* son of Aeneas, *also called* Ascanius.

Ixīon -ōnis, *m.* king of the Lapithae in Thessaly, father of Pirithous; for an insult to Juno he was hurled down to Tartarus, and bound to a perpetually revolving wheel.

I (consonant)

I i, *a consonant, originally written with the same sign as the vowel I.*

ĭăcĕo -cŭi -cĭtum, 2. to lie, to lie low, be flat; to lie in ruins; *of clothes*, to hang loosely; to be sunk in, *in maerore;* to be overcome, powerless; to be hopeless; to be neglected; to cease; to be low in price; *of words*, to be in common use.

ĭăcĭo, ĭēci, ĭactum, 3. to throw, cast; to scatter; to utter; to erect, *aggerem.*

ĭactans -antis, *p. adj.*, boastful.

ĭactantĕr, *adv.* boastfully.

ĭactantĭa -ae, *f.* boasting, vainglory.

ĭactātĭo -ōnis, *f. act.*, a throwing, shaking; extolling; *pass.*, being tossed about; violent emotions; applause; vainglory.

iactātor -oris, *m.* a boaster.

iactātus -ūs, *m.* a moving quickly up and down.

iactito, 1. to utter.

iacto, 1. to throw, cast; to throw away; to scatter; utter, hurl, *minas;* to throw about, toss; to drive hither and thither *(se iactare or iactari iactare, to busy oneself with);* to torment; to discuss; to boast of; *reflex., iactare se,* to boast, brag, to behave oneself in a certain way; *se magnificentissime.*

iactūra -ae, *f.* a throwing, throwing away; loss, sacrifice; expense.

iactus -ūs, *m.* a cast, throw; *intra teli iactum,* within shot; the throw of the dice.

iăcŭlābilis -e, that can be thrown.

iăcŭlātor -ōris, *m.* a thrower, a light-armed soldier.

iăcŭlātrix -icis, *f.* she that hurls, the huntress (Diana).

iăcŭlor, 1. *dep. intransit.,* to throw a javelin; to make an attack with words; *transit.,* to hurl; to shoot at; to strive after.

iăcŭlum -i, *n.* a dart, javelin; a casting-net.

iam, *adv.* now, already; moreover; *iam nunc,* just now; *iam tum,* just then; *ubi iam,* as soon as; *iam diu, iam dudum, iam pridem,* now for a long time.

iamdūdum, iamprīdem, *v. iam.*

Iānālis, *v. Ianus.*

Iānĭcŭlum -i, *n.* one of the hills of Rome.

iānĭtor -ōris, *m.* a door-keeper, porter.

iānŭa -ae, *f.* the outer door of a house; entrance, passage.

Iānŭārius -a -um, belonging to Janus; the month January.

Iānus -i, *m.* the god of the year; *presented with two faces looking in opposite directions; adj.,* **Iānālis -e.**

iĕcur, *genit.* **iĕcŏris** and **iĕcĭnŏris**, *n.,* and **iŏcur**, *genit.* **iŏcĭnĕris**, *n.* the liver; *as* the seat of the passions.

iĕcuscŭlum (iŏcuscŭlum) -i, *n. (dim. of iecur),* a little liver.

iēiūnē, *adv. of style,* dryly, without taste.

iēiūnĭtas -ātis, *f.* hungriness; *of discourse,* dryness, plainness.

iēiūnium -ii, *n.* a fast, hunger; leanness.

iēiūnus -a -um, fasting; hungry; thirsty, empty; unfruitful; scanty; *fig.,* poor, mean; weak, *oratio,* insipid.

ientācŭlum -i, *n.* a breakfast.

iento, 1. to breakfast.

iŏcātio -ōnis, *f.* a joke, jest.

iŏcor, 1. *dep.* to joke, jest; *transit.,* to say in jest.

iŏcōsē, *adv.* in jest.

iŏcōsus -a -um, humorous, merry.

iŏcŭlāris -e, laughable; *subst., n. pl.,* **iŏcŭlāria -ium**, *n.* jesta.

iŏcŭlāriter, *adv.* jestingly.

iŏcŭlātor -ōris, *m.* a joker.

iŏcŭlor, 1. *dep.* to joke, jest.

iŏcŭlus -i, 1. *(dim. of iocus),* a little joke.

iŏcur, *v. iecur.*

iŏcus -i, *m. (plur. ioci* and *ioca),* a joke, jest; a game; toying.

1. iŭba -ae, *f.* the mane of any animal; the crest of a helmet.

2. Iŭba -ae, *m., f.* king of Numidia, one of the supporters of Pompeius. 2. his son.

iŭbar -āris, *n.* light, radiance, a star.

iŭbātus -a -um, having a mane, crested.

iŭbĕo, iussi, iussum, 2. to order, command.

iūcundē (iōcundē), *adv.* pleasantly, agreeably.

iūcundĭtas (iōcundĭtas) -ātis, *f.* agreeableness, pleasure.

iūcundus (iōcundus) -a -um, pleasant, agreeable.

Iūdaea -ae, *f.* Judaea *or* Palestine; *adj.,* **Iūdaeus; subst., Iūdaei -ōrum**, *m.* the Jews; **Iūdāicus**, Jewish.

iūdex -icis, *m.* a judge.

iūdĭcātio -ōnis, *f.* a judicial investigation; a judgment, opinion.

iūdĭcātum -i, *n.* a decided case, judgment.

iūdĭcātus -ūs, *m.* the office of a judge.

iūdĭciālis -e, relating to a court of justice, judicial.

iūdĭciārius -a -um, relating to a court of justice.

iūdĭcium -ii, *n.* a trial; lawsuit; the judicial office; place of trial; the judges; judgment; opinion; *meo iudicio,* in my opinion; power of judging; reflection.

iūdĭco, 1. to judge; to determine; to esteem, value; to be of an opinion; to declare openly.

iŭgālis -e, yoked together; matrimonial; *subst.,* **iŭgāles -ium**, *m.* a team *or* yoke.

iŭgātio -ōnis, *f.* the training of vines on a trellis.

iūgĕrum -i, *n. (plur. according to the 3rd declension),* a plot of land 240 feet long by 120 broad.

iūgis -e, joined together; continuous, never-failing.

iūglans -glandis, *f.* a walnut.

iŭgo, 1. to bind together; to give in marriage.

iŭgōsus -a -um, mountainous.

iŭgŭlae -ārum, *f.* three stars which form the belt of the constellation Orion.

iŭgŭlo, 1. to cut the throat, kill; to ruin, destroy.

iŭgŭlum -i, *n. and* **iŭgŭlus -i**, *m.* the collar-bone; the hollow above the collar-bone, the throat.

iŭgum -i, *n.* a yoke; a horse's collar; a team *or* yoke; a pair, a couple; the marriage-tie; the beam of a pair of scales; the beam of a weaver's loom; ridge of a mountain; *iuga,* the rowers' benches.

Iŭgurtha -ae, *m.* king of Numidia, conquered by Marius; *adj.,* **Iŭgurthīnus.**

Iūlius -a -um, name of a Roman gens, *to which belonged Julius Caesar; mensis,* the month of July.

iūmentum -i, n. beast of burden.

iunceus -a -um, relating to rushes, made of rushes.

iuncōsus -a -um, full of rushes.

iunctim, adv. successively, both together.

iunctio -ōnis, f. a joining, connexion.

iunctūra -ae, f. a joining; a joint; *generis,* relationship.

iunctus -a -um, p. adj., yoked together, connected, united; *iunctissimus,* very intimate; well put together, *oratio.*

iuncus -i, m. a rush, bulrush.

iungo, iunxi, iunctum, 3. to join, unite, connect; to yoke; *of places, in passive,* to border on.

iūnior, v. *iuvenis.*

iūnipĕrus -i, f. the juniper tree.

Iūnius -a -um, the name of a Roman gens.

Iūno -ōnis, f. the goddess Juno, wife of Jupiter.

Iuppiter, Iŏvis, m. the supreme god among the Romans.

iūrātor -ōris, m. a sworn assessor.

iūrātus -a -um, partic. of *iuro.*

iūrĕconsultus = *iurisconsultus (q.v.).*

iūrēiūro, 1. to swear by an oath.

iūrĕpĕritus = *iurisperitus (q.v.).*

iurgium -ii, n. altercation, quarrel.

iurgo, 1. to quarrel, brawl; *transit.,* to scold.

iūrīdiciālis -e, relating to justice.

iūrisconsultus -i, m. a lawyer.

iūrisdictio -ōnis, f. judicial authority; an assize-town.

iūrispĕritus -i, m. one skilled in the law.

iūro, 1. to swear, take an oath; *transit.,* to swear; to affirm on oath; to call the gods to witness, *deos.*

iūror -ātus sum, 1. *dep.* to swear; *partic. iuratus,* sworn on oath.

1. iūs, iūris, n. broth, soup.

2. iūs, iūris, n. right, law; a court of justice; privilege; legal right, authority.

iusiūrandum, iūrisiūrandi, n. an oath.

iussum -i, n. a command, order; the prescription of a physician.

iussus, abl. -ū, m. a command, commanding.

iustē, adv. justly, rightly.

iustificus -a -um, acting justly.

iustitia -ae, f. justice, love of justice.

iustitium -ii, n. a suspension of business in the courts of law; public mourning.

iustus -a -um, just, upright; equitable, fair; justifiable; regular, proper, suitable; fitting, sufficient; *plur.,* **iusta -orum,** due forms and observances, *esp.* funeral rites.

1. iŭvĕnālis -e, youthful.

2. Iŭvĕnālis -is, m., *D. Junius,* a Roman writer of satires.

iŭvĕnālitĕr, adv. like a young man.

iŭvencus -a -um, young; *subst.,*

iŭvencus -i, m. a young bullock; a young man; **iŭvenca -ae,** f. a young cow, heifer; a young woman.

iŭvĕnesco -vēnŭi, 3. to grow up to youth; to become young again.

iŭvĕnīlis -e, youthful, juvenile.

iŭvĕnilitĕr, adv. youthful, like a youth.

iŭvĕnis -is, adj. young; *compar., iunior; subst.,* **iŭvĕnis -is,** c. a young man, young woman.

iŭvĕnor, 1. *dep.* to act like a youth.

iŭventa -ae, f. youth; the time of youth; the young; *prima iuventa,* the down on a young man's cheeks.

iŭventas -ātis, f. youth, the time of youth.

iŭventus -ūtis, f. youth; young men; *princeps iuventutis,* the first among the knights.

iŭvo, iūvi, iūtum, fut. partic., **iŭvātūrus,** 1. to help, be of service; to delight, please; *often impers., iuvat, with infin.,* it delights, it pleases.

iuxtā, adv. close to, by the side of, near; in like manner, equally; *prep. with acc.,* near to; immediately after, next to; *of time,* just before.

iuxtim, adv. near, close by.

K

K *The letter K, k, was originally a part of the Latin Alphabet, but was replaced by C. K was only used in abbreviations, as K. = Kaeso, Kal. = Kalendae.*

Kălendae = *Calendae (q.v.).*

Karthāgo = *Carthago (q.v.).*

L

L *l, the eleventh letter of the Latin Alphabet.*

lăbasco, 3. to totter, to give way.

lăbĕa -ae, f. the lip = *labia (q.v.).*

lăbēcŭla -ae, f. *(dim. of labes),* a little spot, a slight disgrace.

lăbĕfăcio -fēci -factum, 3. *pass.,* **lăbĕfīo -factus sum -fīeri,** to make to totter, shake, loosen; to weaken.

lăbĕfacto, 1. to cause to totter, shake violently; to injure, weaken, destroy.

1. lăbellum -i, n. *(dim. of 1. labrum),* a little lip.

2. lăbellum -i, n. *(dim. of 2. labrum),* a small bathing-vessel.

lābes -is, f. a falling in, sinking in; destruction; stain, blemish; dishonour, ignominy.

lăbia (lăbĕa) -ae, f. *and* **lăbium -ii,** n. a lip.

Lăbiēnus -i, m., *T.,* a legate of Julius Caesar, who deserted to Pompeius at the breaking out of the Civil War.

lăbiōsus -a -um, with large lips.

lăbium -ii, *n.* = *labia* (*q.v.*).

lābo, 1. to totter, waver, begin to sink; *memoria labat,* is uncertain.

1. **lābor, lapsus sum** 3. *dep.* to glide, fall down, slip; to run, to flow; *of time,* to pass away; to incline to, fall into; to glide down, deviate from; to stumble; to make a mistake; *ta fall out;* to be destroyed.

2. **lābor -ōris,** *m.* work, toil, effort; activity, industry; a deed, undertaking, hardship, difficulty.

lābōrifer -fēra -fērum, bearing toil and hardship.

lābōriōsē, *adv.* laboriously.

lābōriōsus -a -um, full of toil, hardship, laborious; industrious; harassed.

lābōro, 1. to work, toil, strive; to be troubled about, to care; to suffer, be oppressed with, afflicted with; *transit.,* to work out, prepare, form.

lābos -ōris, *m.* = 2. *labor* (*q.v.*).

1. **labrum -i,** *n.* a lip; the edge, rim.

2. **labrum -i,** *n.* a basin, vessel, tub.

lābrusca -ae, *f.* the wild vine.

lābruscum -i, fruit of the wild vine.

lăbўrinthēus -a -um, labyrinthine.

lăbўrinthus -i, *m.* a labyrinth.

lăc, lactis, *n.* milk, milky sap.

Lăcaena -ae, *f.* Spartan.

Lăcĕdaemon -ōnis, *f.* the city Lacedaemon *or* Sparta; *adj.,* **Lăcĕdaemŏnius.**

lăcer -cĕra -cĕrum, torn, maimed; *act.,* tearing to pieces.

lăcĕrātio -ōnis, *f.* maiming, mangling.

lăcerna -ae, *f.* a mantle worn over the tōga.

lăcernātus -a -um, clad in the lacerna.

lăcĕro, 1. to tear to pieces, mangle, lacerate; to wound deeply, destroy; to squander; to distress, torture, to rail at, attack.

lăcerta -ae, *f.* a lizard; a sea-fish.

lăcertōsus -a -um, muscular, powerful.

1. **lăcertus -i,** *m. gen. plur.* = the muscles; the muscles of the upper part of the arm.

2. **lăcertus -i,** *m.* = *lacerta* (*q.v.*).

lăcesso -īvi and -ii -ītum, 3. to provoke, stimulate, irritate; to begin, occasion, *pugnam.*

Lăchĕsis -is, *f.* one of the three Parcae that spun the thread of life.

lăchrima (lăchryma), *v. lacrima.*

lăchrimo (lăchrymo) and -or, *v. lacrimo.*

lăcinia -ae, *f.* lappet of a garment.

Lăco (Lăcōn) -ōnis, *m.* a Spartan, Lacedaemonian; *adj.,* **Lăcōnicus; Lăcōnis -idis,** *f.* Spartan.

lăcrima (lăcrŭma, lăchrima, or lăchrўma) -ae, *f.* a tear; the exudation from certain plants; *Heliadum,* amber.

lăcrimābilis (lăcrŭmābilis) -e, deplorable, lamentable.

lăcrimābundus -a -um, breaking into tears, weeping.

lăcrimo 1. *and* **lacrimor,** 1. *dep.* to weep, shed tears; *of plants,* to drip.

lăcrimōsus (lăcrŭmōsus) -a -um, tearful, shedding tears; causing tears; mournful.

lăcrimŭla -ae, *f.* (*dim. of lacrima*), a little tear.

lactĕo, 2. to suck; (*subst.,* **lactentes -ium,** *f.* unweaned animals, *as victims for a sacrifice*); to contain milk, to be full of sap.

lactĕŏlus -a -um, *adj.* (*dim. of lacteus*), milk-white.

lactesco, 3. to become milk.

lactĕus -a -um, milky; full of milk; milk-white; *via lactea,* or *orbis lacteus,* the Milky Way.

1. **lacto,** 1. to give milk.

2. **lacto,** 1. to allure, deceive.

lactūca -ae, *f.* a lettuce.

lăcūna -ae, *f.* a cavity, hollow, cavern; pond, ditch; a gap, defect, loss; *poet.* dimple.

lăcūnar -āris, *n.* a panelled ceiling.

lăcūno, 1. to work in panels.

lăcūnōsus -a -um, full of hollows *or* gaps.

lăcus -ūs, *m.* lake; water-trough; any large tank.

Lădas -ae, *m.* a Laconian athlete.

laedo, laesi, laesum, 3. to injure, damage, *zonā laedere collum;* to trouble, offend, attack.

laena -ae, *f.* an upper garment of thick cloth.

Laërtēs -ae, *m.* the father of Ulysses.

Laestrўgŏnes -um, *m. myth,* a race of cannibals in Sicily.

laetābilis -e, joyful, joyous.

laetātio -ōnis, *f.* a rejoicing, joy.

laetē, *adv.* joyfully, gladly.

laetifico, 1. to cheer, delight; to fertilise.

laetificus -a -um, cheering, joyous.

laetitia -ae, *f.* joy, delight; beauty, grace.

laetor, 1. *dep.* to rejoice, be glad.

laetus -a -um, joyful, glad; pleasing, agreeable; fortunate, propitious; fruitful; fluent.

laevē, *adv.* on the left hand, *hence* awkwardly.

laevus -a -um, *left;* left-handed, silly, unsuitable; unlucky; *in augury,* favourable, *as the Roman augurs, looking south, had the east or lucky side on their left hand; subst.,* **laeva -ae,** *f.* the left hand, the left; **laevum -i,** *n.* the left side; *plur.,* **laeva -ōrum,** places lying to the left.

lăgānum -i, *n.* a cake made of flour and oil.

lăgēna = *lagoena* (*q.v.*).

lăgēos -ēi, *f.* a Greek kind of vine.

lăgoena -ae, *f.* large jar *or* bottle with handles and a narrow neck.

lăgōis -idis, *f.* a bird, *perhaps* a heathcock *or* grouse.

lăguncŭla -ae, *f.* (*dim. of lagoena*), a little bottle *or* flask.

Lāīus -i, *m.* father of Oedipus.

lāma -ae, *f.* a bog, ditch.

lambo, lambi, lambĭtum, 3. to lick.

lāmentābĭlis -e, lamentable; mournful.

lāmentātĭo -ōnis, *f.* weeping, lamentation.

lāmentor, 1. *dep., intransit.,* to weep, wail, lament; *transit.,* to bewail, weep over.

lāmentum -i, *n.* a wailing, lamentation.

1. lāmĭa -ae, *f. gen. plur., lamiae,* vampires.

2. Lāmĭa -ae, *m.* a cognomen of the Aelian gens.

lāmĭna *and* **lamna -ae,** *f.* a plate *or* thin piece of metal *or* marble, *etc.;* the blade of a sword; a nutshell.

lampas -pădis, *acc.* **-păda,** *acc. plur.* **-pădes** *and* **-pădas,** *f.* a torch; brightness, brilliance.

Lămus -i, *m.* mythical king of the Laestrygones, founder of Formiae.

lămyrus -i, *m,* an unknown sea fish.

lāna -ae, *f.* wool; the down on leaves, *etc.*

lānātus -a -um, wool-bearing, woolly; covered with down. ; *subst.,* **lānātae -ārum,** *f.* sheep.

lancĕa -ae, *f.* a light spear *or* lance.

lancino, 1. to tear to pieces, mangle; to squander.

lānĕus -a -um, woollen; soft as wool.

Langōbardi -ōrum, *m.* a people in north Germany, on the west side of the Elbe.

languēfăcĭo, 3. to make languid *or* faint.

langŭĕo -gŭi, 2. to be faint, languid; *partic., languens,* weak, faint; to be inactive.

languesco, langŭi, 3. to become faint, to languish; to become inactive.

languĭdē, *adv.* faintly, feebly.

languĭdus -a -um, faint, languid, dull; gentle; *of wine,* mild, mellow; sluggish; *languidae voluptates,* enervating.

languor -ōris, *m.* faintness, languor, feebleness ; *aquosus,* dropsy ; listlessness, idleness.

lānĭātus -ūs, *m.* a mangling, tearing in pieces.

lānĭcĭum, *v. lanitium.*

lānĭēna -ae, *f.* a butcher's shop.

lānĭfĭcus -a -um, working in wool.

lānĭger -gĕra -gĕrum, wool-bearing; woollen; *subst.,* **lānĭger -gĕri,** *m.* a ram.

lānĭo, 1. to make, lacerate.

lānista -ae, *m.* trainer of gladiators; instigator.

lānĭtĭum -ii, *n.* wool.

lānĭus -ii, *m.* butcher.

lanterna (lāterna) -ae, *f.* a lantern, lamp.

lanternārĭus -ii, *m.* a lantern-bearer.

lānūgo -ĭnis, *f.* the down of plants; the first soft down of the beard.

Lānŭvĭum -ii, *n.* town in Latium.

lanx, lancis, *f.* plate, large flat dish; scale of a balance.

Lāŏcŏōn -ontis, *m.* priest of Neptune in Troy.

Lāŏmĕdōn -ontis, *m.* king of Troy; father of Priam.

lăpăthum -i, *n. and* **lăpăthus -i,** *f.* sorrel.

lăpĭcīdīnae -ārum, *f.* the stone quarries as a place of punishment.

lăpĭdātĭo -ōnis, *f.* a throwing of stones.

lăpĭdātor -ōris, *m.* a thrower of stones.

lăpĭdĕus -a -um, made of stone, stone.

lăpĭdo, 1. to throw stones at; *impers., lapidat,* it rains stones.

lăpĭdōsus -a -um, full of stones; as hard as stone.

lăpillus -i, *m.* (*dim. of lapis*), a little stone, pebble.

lăpis -ĭdis, *m.* a stone; *bibulus,* pumice-stone; *ardens,* a meteoric stone.

Lăpĭthēs -ae, *m., plur., Lapithae,* the Lapithae, famous for their fight with the Centaurs.

lappa -ae, *f.* a bur.

lapsĭo -ōnis, *f.* a gliding, inclination, tendency towards.

lapso, 1. to totter.

lapsus -ūs, *m.* a gradual motion, gliding; flowing of water; flight of birds; a falling; fault.

lăquĕar -āris *and* **lăquĕāre -is,** *n.* a panel in a ceiling, panelled ceiling.

lăquĕo, 1. to adorn with a panelled ceiling; *only in partic. perf., laqueatus.*

lăquĕus -i, *m.* a noose, snare, trap.

1. Lār *or* **Lars, Lartis,** *m.* Etruscan title signifying lord, found as a praenomen; *Lars Porsena.*

2. Lār, Lăris, *m., usually plur.,* **Lăres -um,** *and* **-ium,** tutelary deities among the Romans; the gods of the hearth.

lardum (lārĭdum) -i, *n.* the fat of bacon, lard.

Lārentĭa, *v. Acca.*

Lăres, *v.* 2. *Lar.*

largē, *adv.* plentifully, abundantly.

largĭfĭcus -a -um, bountiful.

largĭflŭus -a -um, flowing with full stream.

largĭor, 4. *dep.* to give abundantly; to bestow, grant.

largĭtas -ātis, *f.* liberality.

largĭtĕr, *adv.* abundantly.

largĭtĭo -ōnis, *f.* liberality, lavishing; granting, bestowing.

largītor -ōris, *m.* a liberal giver, spender.

largus -a -um, abundant, numerous ; bountiful; *with genit.,* abounding in.

lārĭdum -i, *n.* = *lardum* (*q.v.*).

Lars, *v.* 1. *Lar.*

larva -ae, *f.* a ghost; a mask.

lăsănum -i, *n.* a cooking-utensil.

lascīvē, *adv.* wantonly.

lascīvĭa -ae, *f.* playfulness, sportiveness; wantonness.

lascivio -ii -itum, 4. to sport, play, be wanton.

lascivus -a -um, playful, frolicsome; wanton.

laserpicifer -fera -ferum, producing the plant laserpitium.

lassitudo -inis, f. weariness.

lasso, 1. to tire, exhaust.

lassulus -a -um (dim. of lassus), rather tired.

lassus -a -um, weary, exhausted, languid.

late, adv. broadly, widely; longe lateque, far and wide; at length, amply.

latebra -ae, f. a concealment; lunae, eclipse of the moon; hiding-place; secret retreat.

latebrosus a -um, full of hiding-places, retired.

latens -entis, p. adj. concealed, hidden.

latenter, adv. secretly.

lateo -tui, 2. to be concealed; to live in obscurity; to be unknown; res latet aliquem, it is concealed from.

later -eris, m. a brick, tile.

lateramen -inis, n. an earthen vessel.

laterculus -i, m. (dim. of later), a brick, tile.

latericius -a -um, brick, built of brick.

laterna, v. lanterna.

laternarius, v. lanternarius.

latesco, 3. to hide oneself, be concealed.

latex -ticis, m. a fluid, liquid; water.

latibulum -i, n. a hiding-place.

laticlavius -a -um, having a broad purple stripe (a distinction of senators, etc.).

latifundium -ii, n. a large landed estate.

Latine, v. Latium.

Latinitas -atis, f. a pure Latin style, Latinity; Latin right.

1. **Latinus** -a -um, v. Latium.

2. **Latinus** -i, m., a king who received Aeneas hospitably, and gave him his daughter in marriage.

latio -onis, f. a bringing; legis, a proposing.

latito, 1. to lie hid.

latitudo -inis, f. breadth; extent, great size; broad pronunciation.

Latium -ii, n. district of Italy, in which Rome was situated; adj., **Latius**, **Latinus**; adv., **Latine**, in Latin; Latine loqui.

Latmus -i, m. a mountain in Caria, where Selene laid Endymion to sleep.

Lato -us, f. and **Latona** -ae, f. mother of Apollo and Diana.

Latobrigi -orum, m. a Gallic people, neighbours of the Helvetii.

Latona, etc., v. Lato.

lator -oris, m. the proposer of a law.

latrator -oris, m. a barker.

latratus -us, m. a barking.

1. **latro** -onis, m. to bark, bay, brawl; transit., to bark at, to shout out.

2. **latro** -onis, m. a mercenary soldier,

robber, bandit; a hunter; a piece on a draught-board.

latrocinium -ii, n. military service; highway robbery, piracy; villany; band of robbers, game of draughts.

latrocinor, 1. dep. to serve as a mercenary soldier; to practise robbery.

latrunculus -i, m. (dim. of 2. latro), a highwayman.

1. **latus** -a -um, partic. of fero.

2. **latus** -a -um, broad, wide; diffuse, rich, oratio.

3. **latus** -eris, n. the side, flank.

latusculum -i, n. (dim. of 3. latus), a little side.

laudabilis -e, praiseworthy; excellent.

laudabiliter, adv., in a praiseworthy manner.

laudandus -a -um, p. adj. laudable.

laudatio -onis, f. praise, commendation; a funeral oration.

laudator -oris, m. a praiser.

laudatrix -icis, f. a praiser.

laudatus -a -um, p. adj. praiseworthy, excellent.

laudo, 1. to praise, commend; to call happy, consider fortunate; to name, quote.

laurea -ae, f., v. laureus.

laureatus -a -um, crowned with laurel; literae, bringing tidings of victory.

laureola -ae, f. (dim. of laurea), a laurel branch, laurel crown, triumph.

laureus -a -um, relating to the laurel; subst., **laurea** -ae, f. the laurel tree; the laurel crown or branch; victory.

lauricomus -a -um, covered with laurel-trees.

lauriger -gera -gerum, crowned with laurels.

laurus -i, f. the laurel or bay-tree.

laus, **laudis**, f. praise, fame, glory, commendation.

laute, adv. splendidly, magnificently; admirably, thoroughly.

lautia -orum, n. the entertainment given to foreign ambassadors at Rome.

lautitia -ae, f. spendour, magnificence in one's manner of living.

lautumiae (latomiae) -arum, f. a stone-quarry; a prison cut out of rock at Syracuse and Rome.

lautus -a -um, p. adj., lit., washed, bathed; splendid, elegant; illustrious.

lavabrum -i, n. a bath.

lavatio -onis, f. a washing, bathing, bathing apparatus; water for bathing.

Lavinia -ae, f. wife of Aeneas.

lavo, **lavi**, **lautum**, partic. **lautus** and **lotus**, **lavere**; and **lavatum** and **lavaturus**, **lavare** to wash, bathe; to moisten, wet, bathe; to wash away.

laxamentum -i, n. a widening, extending; a relaxing, alleviation.

laxe, adv. widely, at wide intervals loosely; without restraint.

laxĭtas -ātis, *f.* wideness, roominess.

laxo, 1. to widen, enlarge; to relax; to set free from; to amuse; *annonam,* to lower the price of.

laxus -a -um, wide, spacious; loose, relaxed; *annona laxior,* a lower price of provisions.

lĕa -ae, *f.* a lioness.

lĕaena -ae, *f.* a lioness.

Lĕander *and* **Lĕandrus -i,** *m.* a youth of Abydos who swam nightly across the Hellespont to visit Hero at Sestos, till he was drowned in a storm.

lĕbes -ētis, *m.* a bronze cauldron.

lectīca -ae, *f.* palanquin *or* litter.

lecticārĭus -ii, *m.* litter-bearer.

lectĭcŭla -ae, *f.* (*dim. of lectica*), a small litter; a bier.

lectĭo -ōnis, *f.* a selecting; reading, persual; *lectio senatus,* calling over of the names of the senators.

lectisternĭum -ii, *n.* a feast offered to the gods.

lectĭto, 1. to read often, to read with attention.

lectiuncŭla -ae, *f.* (*dim. of lectio*), a short reading.

lector -ōris, *m.* a reader.

lectŭlus -i, *m.* (*dim. of lectus*), a small bed, couch.

1. lectus -a -um, *p. adj.* chosen; excellent.

2. lectus -i, *m.* a bed, couch.

Lēda -ae, *f. and* **Lēdē -ēs,** *f.* the wife of Tyndarus, who bore to Zeus Pollux and Helena, Castor and Clytemnestra.

lēgātārĭus -ii, *m.* a legatee.

lēgātĭo -ōnis, *f.* office of an ambassador, embassy, legation; the office of legatus.

lēgātor -ōris, *m.* testator.

lēgātōrĭus -a -um, relating to an ambassador *or* legatus.

lēgātum -i, *n.* legacy, bequest.

lēgātus -i, *m.* ambassador; a legate; lieutenant.

lēgĭfer -fĕra -fĕrum, law-giving.

lēgĭo -ōnis, *f.* a legion.

lēgĭōnārĭus -a -um, relating to a legion; *plur. subst.,* **lēgĭōnārii -ōrum,** *m.* legionary troops.

lēgĭtĭmē, *adv.* lawfully, legally, rightly.

lēgĭtĭmus -a -um, lawful, legal, legitimate; right, proper, appropriate.

lēgiuncŭla -ae, *f.* (*dim. of legio*), a small legion.

1. lēgo, 1. to send an ambassador; to appoint as legate; to bequeath.

2. lĕgo, lēgi, lectum, 3. to collect, to pick; *fila, of the Parcae,* to wind up, spin; *vela,* to furl the sails; to wander through a place; *of ships,* to coast along; to choose; to catch sight of, look at; to read, peruse; to read aloud, recite; *senatum legere,* to call over the senate; *as subst.* **lĕgens -entis,** *m.* a reader.

lēgŭlĕius -i, *m.* a pettifogging lawyer.

lēgūmen -ĭnis, *n.* pulse; the bean.

Lĕmannus (Lĕmānus) -i, *m.* *now* the Lake of Geneva.

lembus -i, *m.* a small, swift vessel, cutter.

Lemnĭcŏla -ae, *c.* an inhabitant of Lemnos (*of Vulcan*).

lemniscātus -a -um, adorned with ribbons.

lemniscus -i, *m.* a fillet, *or* ribbon given in token of honour.

Lemnŏs (-us) -i, *f.* island in the Aegean Sea; *adj.,* **Lemnĭus; Lemnĭăs -ădis,** *f.* a Lemnian woman.

lĕmŭres -um, *m.* shades of the dead, ghosts, spectres. **Lĕmūrĭa -ōrum,** *n.* a festival held to appease departed spirits.

Lēnaeus -a -um, Bacchic.

lēnē, *adv.* = *leniter,* gently, softly.

lēnīmen -ĭnis, *n.* a means of alleviation, mitigation.

lēnīmentum -i, *n.* a mitigation, alleviation.

lēnĭo -īvi *and* **-ii, -ītum,** 4. to alleviate, soothe, relieve.

lēnis -e, smooth, mild, gentle.

lēnĭtas -ātis, *f.* gentleness, mildness.

lēnĭtĕr, *adv.* softly, gradually, quietly.

lēnĭtūdo -ĭnis, *f.* gentleness, mildness.

lēno -ōnis, *m.* a procurer.

lēnōcĭnĭum -ii, *n.* the trade of a procurer; an enticement; finery in dress; *of discourse,* meretricious ornament.

lēnōcĭnor, 1. *dep.* to pursue the trade of a procurer; to flatter basely; to advance, increase.

lens, lentis, *f.* a lentil.

lentē, *adv.* slowly; calmly; phlegmatically.

lentesco, 3. to become pliant, sticky; to slacken.

lentiscĭfer -fĕra -fĕrum, producing the mastic-tree.

lentiscus -i, *f. and* **lentiscum -i,** *n.* the mastic-tree.

lentĭtūdo -ĭnis, *f.* slowness, sluggishness; apathy.

lento, 1. to make flexible, to bend.

lentŭlus -a -um (*dim. of lentus*), somewhat slow (in paying).

lentus -a -um, tough; pliant, flexible; sticky, tenacious; slow; (*of the sea*), unruffled; lingering; apathetic.

lēnuncŭlus -i, *m.* a small boat.

1. lĕo -ōnis, *m.* a lion.

2. *leo -ēre, to blot out.

Lĕōcŏrĭon -ii, *n.* temple at Athens.

Lĕōnĭdas -ae, *m.* king of Sparta, killed at Thermopylae.

lĕpĭdē, *adv.* pleasantly, charmingly; wittily.

lĕpĭdus -a -um, pleasant, agreeable, elegant; effeminate; humorous.

lĕpor *and* **lĕpos -ōris,** *m.* pleasantness, charm; humour.

lĕpos -ōris = *lepor* (*q.v.*).

lĕpus -ōris, *m.* rarely *f.* a hare.

lĕpuscŭlus -i *m.* (*dim. of lepus*), a little hare.

Lərna -ae, *f. and* Lernē -ēs, *f.* a marsh
in Argolis inhabited by the Lernaean
Hydra slain by Hercules; *adj.*, **Lernaeus.**
Lesbos -i, *f.* an island in the Aegean Sea,
birthplace of Alcaeus and Sappho.
lessus, *acc.* -um (*only in acc. sing.*), *m.*
lamentation for the dead.
lētālis -e, deadly, fatal.
lēthargicus -a -um, drowsy, lethargic;
subs., **lēthargicus** -i, *m.* a lethargic
person.
lēthargus -i, *m.* drowsiness, lethargy.
Lēthē -ēs, *f.* a river in the infernal regions,
the waters of which produced forgetfulness.
lēthum, *v.* letum.
lētifer -fēra -fērum, deadly, fatal.
lēto, 1. to kill, slay.
lētum -i, *n.* death; *poet.* ruin.
leucaspis -idis, *f.* having white shields.
Leucŏthēa -ae, *f. and* **Leucŏthĕē** -ēs, *f.*
name of Ino, daughter of Cadmus, after
she had been turned into a sea deity.
ēvāmen -inis, *n.* a mitigation, consolation.
lēvāmentum -i, *n.* alleviation, solace.
lēvātio -ōnis, *f.* alleviation ; diminution.
1. **lĕvātus** -a -um, *v.* 1. levo.
2. **lĕvātus (laevatus)** -a -um, *v.* 2. levo.
lēvicŭlus -a -um (*dim. of* 1. levis), somewhat vain, light-minded ; trivial.
lēvidensis -e, of thin texture ; slight, poor.
lēvipēs -pĕdis, light-footed.
1. **lĕvis** -e, light, not heavy ; rapid, swift;
gentle; trifling, insignificant; trivial;
fickle, unsteady.
2. **lēvis** -e, smooth, polished; *poet.*
beardless ; bald ; *vir,* decked out ;
slippery; *of style,* flowing, polished.
lēvisomnus -a -um, lightly sleeping.
1. **lēvitas** -ātis, *f.* lightness; fickleness;
groundlessness.
2. **lēvitas** -ātis, *f.* smoothness; polish (of
style).
lēvitĕr, *adv.* lightly, softly; slightly,
somewhat.
1. **lĕvo,** 1. to raise, lift up ; to lighten,
relieve; to console, mitigate; to refresh,
strengthen; to diminish, weaken.
2. **lēvo,** 1. to make smooth, polish.
lēvor -ōris, *m.* smoothness.
lex, lēgis, *f.* a bill; a law; *legem ferre
rogare,* to propose a bill to the people;
iubere, to accept *or* pass a bill; *antiquare,* to reject a bill; *legem ferre,* to
pass a law; a rule, principle; a formula;
a contract, agreement ; *leges pacis,*
conditions of peace.
lībāmen -inis, *n.* a libation; a sample,
specimen.
lībāmentum -i, *n.* a libation.
lībātio -ōnis, *f.* a libation.
lībella -ae, *f.* (*dim. of libra*), a small coin,
1-10th of a denarius ; *ad libellam,*
exactly; a carpenter's level.

lĭbellus -i, *m.* (*dim. of liber*), a little
book; (*pl.*, a bookseller's shop), a note-
book; a petition; a note of invitation,
programme; a placard, hand-bill; a
letter; a satire, a libel.
lĭbens *and* **lŭbens** -entis, *p. adj.* willing,
with pleasure; *me libente,* with my
goodwill; pleased, glad.
lĭbentĕr (lŭbentĕr), *adv.* willingly, with
pleasure.
Lĭbentīna (Lŭbentīna) -ae, *f.* a name of
Venus.
1. **lĭber** -ĕra -ĕrum, of free birth; free,
independent; unencumbered; *custodia,*
surveillance; *liberum est mihi, foll. by
infin.,* I am free to do; profligate, unrestrained ; *subst.,* **lĭber** -ĕri, *m.*
freedman.
2. **lĭber** -bri, *m.* the inner bark of a tree;
used as a writing material, a book,
treatise; a register, catalogue.
3. **Lĭber** -ĕri, *m.* an Italian deity, identified with the Greek Bacchus.
4. **lĭber** -ĕri, *v.* liberi -ōrum.
Lĭbĕra -ae, *f.* 1. Proserpina, 2. Ariadne.
Lĭbĕrālia -ium, *n.* festival of Liber.
lĭbĕrālis -e, relating to freedom; noble;
artes liberales, liberal arts; *sumptus,*
expenses to keep up station and appearances; kind; generous.
lĭbĕrālitas -ātis, *f.* noble disposition;
generosity.
lĭbĕrālitĕr, *adv.* nobly, becomingly ;
kindly, bountifully.
lĭbĕrātio -ōnis, *f.* a setting free; *culpae,*
a legal acquittal.
lĭbĕrātor -ōris, *m.* a liberator.
lĭbĕrē, *adv.* liberally, freely, without
restraint; spontaneously; frankly.
lĭbĕri -ērōrum *and* -ĕrum, *m.* children.
lĭbĕro, 1. to set free, liberate ; *from
slavery,* to manumit; *templa liberata,*
free from buildings which obstruct the
view.
lĭbĕrta -ae, *f. v.* libertus.
lĭbertas -ātis, *f.* freedom, liberty; In
dependence; liberty of action; licence;
frankness.
lĭbertīnus -a -um, relating to the class of
freedmen ; *subst.,* **libertīnus** -i, *m.*
a freedman; **libertīna** -ae, *f.* a freedwoman.
lĭbertus -a -um, placed in freedom;
subst., **libertus** -i, *m.* a freedman ;
liberta -ae, *f.* a freedwoman.
lĭbet (lŭbet), **-buit** *or* **-bitum est,** 3. *impers.,* it pleases, is agreeable; *mihi, tibi,
etc.*
lĭbidĭnōsē, *adv.* lustfully, wantonly.
lĭbidĭnōsus -a -um, full of desire, wanton.
lĭbido (lŭbido) -inis, *f.* violent desire,
appetite ; *ad libidinem,* according to
inclination; *ex libidine,* out of mere
caprice; wilfulness, wantonness.
Libitīna -ae, *f.* goddess of corpses; the
requisites for a funeral; death.

libo, 1. to take away from; to taste; to touch; to pour a libation; to sacrifice; to diminish.

libra -ae, *f.* a balance, pair of scales; the Roman pound of 12 oz.; a level.

librāmen -inis, *n.* balance, poise.

librāmentum -i, *n.* weight; that which gives a missile its impetus; a horizontal plane.

librāria -ae, *f.* a female who weighed out the wool to the slaves.

librāriŏlus -i, *m.* (*dim. of librarius*), a transcriber, secretary; a bookseller.

librārium -ii, *n. v. librarius.*

librārius -a -um, relating to books. *Subst.,* **librārius -ii,** *m.* a copyist ; **librārium -ii,** *n.* a bookcase.

librātor -ōris, *m.* a leveller *or* surveyor; one who hurls missiles by means of a machine.

librātus -a -um, *p. adj.,* well-poised, hurled with force.

librīlis -e, of a pound weight.

libro, 1. to poise, keep in equilibrium; to swing, hurl; keep in its place.

libum -i, *n.* a cake offered to the gods.

Liburni -ōrum, *m.* people inhabiting the modern Croatia; *subst.,* **Liburna -ae,** *f.* a light vessel of war.

Libўa -ae, *f. and* **Libўe -ēs,** *f.* Libya the northern part of Africa.

licens -centis, free, unrestrained.

licentĕr, *adv.* freely, according to one's own pleasure; unrestrainedly.

licentia -ae, *f.* freedom to do what one pleases, leave, liberty; licentiousness.

licĕo -ŭi -itum, 2. to be on sale, to be valued at.

licĕor -citus sum, 2. *dep.* to bid for, offer a price for.

licet -cŭit *or* **-citum est,** 2. *impers. and intransit.,* it is allowed, one can *or* may; granted that, allowed that.

lichen -ēnis, *m.* moss *or* lichen.

licitātio -ōnis, *f.* a bidding, bid, at a sale.

licitor, 1. *dep.* to bid for.

licitus -a -um, allowed, permitted.

licium -ii, *n.* the thrum, *or* remnant of old web to which the weaver attaches the new fabric; a thread.

lictor -ōris, *m. plur. lictores,* the lictors, the public attendants of the principal Roman magistrates.

ligāmen -inis, *n.* a string, bandage.

ligāmentum -i, *n.* a bandage.

Ligĕr -gĕris, *m.* a river, *now the* Loire.

lignārius -ii, *m.* a carpenter.

lignātio -ōnis, *f.* wood-cutting.

lignātor -ōris, *m.* a wood-cutter.

lignĕŏlus -a -um (*dim. of ligneus*), wooden.

lignĕus -a -um, wooden; dry.

lignor, 1. *dep.* to fetch wood.

lignum -i, *n.* wood, *esp.* firewood.

1. **ligo,** 1. to bind, tie; to bandage; to harness; to unite.

2. **ligo -ōnis,** *m.* a hoe.

ligŭla (lingŭla) **-ae,** *f.* (dim. of lingua), a little tongue; promontory; a shoe-strap.

Ligŭres -um, *m.* people in modern Piedmont; *sing. Ligŭr and Ligŭs.*

ligūrio (ligurrio), 4. to lick, lick up; long for.

ligūrītio (ligŭrrītio) -ōnis, *f.* daintiness.

Ligus -gŭris, *m. v. Ligures.*

ligustrum -i, *n.* privet.

lilium -ii, *n.* a lily; *milit.,* a kind of fortification consisting of low palisades.

Lilўbaeŏn (-baeum) -i, *n.* promontory and town in the west of Sicily.

lima -ae, *f.* a file; polishing, revision.

limātē, *adv.* elaborately, elegantly.

limātŭlus -a -um (*dim. of limatus*), polished, refined.

limātus -a -um, *p. adj.,* polished, refined.

limbus -i, *m.* border, hem, fringe.

limen -inis, *n.* threshold; dwelling; entrance; the starting-point of a chariot-race in the circus; border, boundary.

limes -itis, *m.* cross path *or* by-way; boundary-line; distinction difference ; a pathway; *sectus,* the zodiac.

limo, 1. to file; to sharpen, to polish ; to investigate accurately; to diminish.

limōsus -a -um, slimy, miry, muddy.

limpidus -a -um, clear, limpid.

1. **limus -a -um,** sidelong, looking sideways.

2. **limus -i,** *m.* slime, mud.

3. **limus -i,** *m.* an apron trimmed with purple, worn by a priest when offering sacrifice.

1. **linctus,** *partic. of lingo.*

2. **linctus -ūs,** *m.* a licking, taste.

linĕa (linia) -ae, *f.* a linen thread; a carpenter's plumb-line; *ad lineam,* exactly straight *or* perpendicular; a line made with a pen *or* pencil; starting-point *or* goal; line in the theatre by which the seats were separated.

linĕāmentum (liniā-) -i, *n.* line drawn with pen *or* pencil, geometrical line; feature; *pl.,* sketch, outline.

linĕus -a -um, made of linen.

lingo, linxi, linctum, 3. to lick.

lingua -ae, *f.* a tongue; speech, language; eloquence; a promontory.

linia, *v. linea.*

liniāmentum, *v. lineamentum.*

linigĕr -gĕra -gĕrum, clothed in linen.

lino, livi *and* **lēvi, litum,** 3, to smear upon, spread over; to anoint; to cover; to rub over with the blunt end of the stylus what has been written on waxen tablets; to besmear, dirty.

linquo, liqui, 3. to leave; to abandon; to depart from; *linqui,* to faint.

lintĕātus -a -um, clothed in linen.

linter -tris, *f.* a boat, skiff; a trough, tray, vat.

lintĕus -a -um, made of linen. *Subst.,*
lintĕum -i, *n.* linen cloth; a sail.
lintrĭcŭlus -i, *m.* (*dim. of linter*), a small
boat.
linum -i, *n.* flax, linen; a thread, line;
a fishing-line; a linen-cloth; a rope,
cable; a net for hunting or fishing.
lippĭo, 4. to have sore eyes, be blear-eyed.
lippĭtūdo -ĭnis, *f.* inflammation in the eyes.
lippus -a -um, blear-eyed; half-blind.
lĭquĕfăcĭo fēcĭ -factum, 3. (*pass.* **lĭquĕfĭo**
-factus sum -fĭĕri), to melt, dissolve; to
putrefy; to make weak, enervate.
lĭquĕo, lĭqui *or* **lĭcŭi, 2.** to be fluid,
liquid; to be clear, to be apparent.
lĭquesco, lĭcŭi, 3. to become fluid, to
melt; to putrefy; *fig.* to melt or waste
away; to become effeminate.
lĭquĭdŏ, *adv.,* clearly, positively.
lĭquĭdo, *v. liquidus.*
lĭquĭdus -a -um, fluid, flowing; clear,
bright; calm; clear, certain. *Subst.,*
lĭquĭdum -i, *n.* certainty; *adv., liquĭdo,*
clearly, plainly.
lĭquo, 1. to make liquid, melt; to strain,
clarify.
1. **lĭquor, 3.** *dep.* to be fluid, melt; to
pass away.
2. **lĭquor -ōris,** *m.* liquidity; a liquid.
Lĭris -is, *acc.* **em** *and* **-im,** *abl.* **-i,** *m.*
a river of Latium.
lis, lĭtis, *f.* a contention, strife; an action,
suit.
lĭtātĭo -ōnis, *f.* an auspicious offering.
lĭtĕra, lĭtĕrātor, *etc. See litt.*
lĭtĭcen -cĭnis, *m.* a trumpeter.
lĭtĭgātor -ōris, *m.* litigant.
lĭtĭgĭōsus -a -um, contentious; fond of
dispute, litigious; quarrelsome; con-
tested at law.
lĭtĭgĭum -ĭi, *n.* quarrel, contention.
lĭtĭgo, 1. to quarrel, dispute; to go to law.
lĭto, 1. *intransit.,* to bring an acceptable offering, to obtain favourable omens;
litemus Lentulo, to appease ; *of the*
victim, to give a favourable omen.
Transit., to sacrifice successfully,
lĭtŏrālis -e, relating to the shore.
lĭtŏrĕus -a -um, belonging to the shore.
lĭttĕra (lītĕra) -ae, *f.* letter of the alphabet;
handwriting ; epitaph ; a bond. *Plur.,*
litterae, that which is written; written
records ; document ; letter, espistle ;
literature.
lĭttĕrārĭus (lĭt-) -a -um, relating to reading and writing, *ludus,* an elementary
school.
lĭttĕrātē (lĭt-), *adv.* distinctly, legibly;
literally; learnedly.
lĭttĕrātor (lĭt-) -ōris, *m.* grammarian;
critic.
lĭttĕrātūra (lĭt-) -ae, *f.* that which is
written; culture, scholarship.
lĭttĕrātus (lĭt-) -a -um, inscribed with
letters; *aervus,* branded; learned, edu-
cated.

lĭttĕrŭla (lĭt-) -ae, *f.* (*dim. of littera*), a
little letter (*of the alphabet*). *Plur.,*
litterulae, a note; literature.
lĭtūra -ae, *f.* an erasure, correction; the
passage erased; *poet.* a blot.
lĭttus, etc., n. litus, q.v.
lĭtŭus (lĭtuus) -i, is, n. seashore, coast.
lĭtŭus -i, *m.* the curved staff of an augur;
a curved trumpet, clarion.
lĭvens -entis, *p. adj.* lead-coloured,
bluish-grey ; livid, black and blue ;
envious.
lĭvĕo, 2. to be of a bluish colour; to be
envious, to envy.
lĭvesco, 3. to become bluish, grow livid.
lĭvĭdŭlus -a -um (*dim. of lividus*), somewhat envious.
lĭvĭdus a -um, bluish, blue; livid,
black and blue; malicious.
Lĭvĭus -a -um, name of a Roman gens;
T. Livius Patavinus, of Padua, the
great Roman historian.
lĭvor -ōris, *m.* a bluish colour, livid spot;
malice.
lixa -ae, *m.* a sutler, camp-follower.
lŏcātĭo -ōnis, *f.* a letting out to hire, a
contract, lease.
lŏcellus -i, *m.* (*dim. of loculus*), a com-
partment in a chest.
lŏcĭto, 1. to let out to hire.
lŏco, 1. to place, lay, put, set; to give in
marriage; to let out to hire, to farm out
taxes; to give out on contract; to hire
out; to lend money at interest; *se locare,*
to yield an interest.
lŏcŭlus -i, *m.* (*dim. of locus*), a coffin;
a cast, satchel; *plur., loculi,* a coffer,
casket.
lŏcŭplēs -plētis, possessing large landed
property; rich; trusty, satisfactory.
lŏcŭplēto, 1. to enrich.
lŏcus -i, *m.* (*plur. loci,* single places;
loca, region), a place, position, rank;
milit., post; time; opportunity; *loco,*
with the genit., in the place of.
1. **lōcusta (lūcusta) -ae,** *f.* a locust, a
kind of lobster or crab.
2. **Lŏcusta -ae,** *f.* notorious for her skill
in poisoning, the accomplice of Nero.
lŏcūtĭo (lŏquūtĭo) -ōnis, *f.* a speaking,
speech ; pronunciation.
lōdix -ĭcis, *f.* a rough blanket, rug.
lŏgĕum -ĕi, *n. and* **lŏgĭum -ĭi,** *n.*
archives.
lŏgĭca -ae, *f. and* **lŏgĭcē -ēs,** *f.* logic.
lŏgĭcus -a -um, logical; *subst.,* **lŏgĭca**
-ōrum, *n.* logic.
lŏgos (-us) -i, *m.* a word; a jest.
lōlĭgo, *v. lolligo.*
lōlĭum -ĭi, *n.* darnel, tares.
lollīgo -ginis, *f.* a cuttle-fish.
lōmentum -i, *n.* an unguent.
Londīnĭum (Lundīnĭum) -ĭi, *n.* London.
longaevus -a -um, aged, old.
longē, *adv.* long; far off, at a distance;
of time, long, for a long time.

longinquitas -ātis, *f.* length; distance; *of time,* duration.

longinquus -a -um, long; distant, remote; *of time,* long, distant.

longitĕr, *adv.* far.

longitūdo -inis, *f.* length.

longiuscŭlus -a -um, somewhat long.

longŭlē, *adv.* rather far.

longŭlus -a -um (*dim. of longus*), somewhat long.

longūrius -ii, *m.* a long pole, rail.

longus -a -um, long; *navis,* a man-of-war; *versus,* the hexameter; *poet.* spacious; *of time,* tedious; *in longum,* for a long time; *of persons,* tedious; far-seeing.

lŏquācitas -ātis, *f.* talkativeness.

lŏquācĭtĕr, *adv.* loquaciously.

lŏquācŭlus -a -um (*dim. of loquax*), somewhat talkative.

lŏquax -quācis, talkative, garrulous; *ranae,* croaking; *lymphae,* babbling; *epistola,* gossiping; *vultus,* expressive.

lŏquēla (**lŏquella**) **-ae,** *f.* speech, discourse, word; language.

lŏquor, lŏcūtus (**lŏquūtus**) **sum,** 3. *dep.* *intransit.,* to speak, *of conversation* ; (*dicere, of an orator*); *cum aliquo.* *Transit.,* to say; to speak of constantly; to tell, mention.

lōrātus -a -um, bound with thongs.

lōrĕus -a -um, made of thongs.

lōrīca -ae, *f.* a leather cuirass, corselet. *Milit.,* a breastwork, parapet.

lōrīco, 1. to arm with a corselet *or* cuirass.

lōrum -i, *n.* a strap *or* thong of leather; the girdle of Venus ; a rein ; *lora dare,* to relax the reins, whip; a leathern bulla (*v. bulla*).

Lōtŏphăgi -orum, *m.* the Lotus-eaters, a people in Africa.

lōtōs (-us) -i, *f.* the Egyptian lotus ; plant used for fodder.

1. **lōtus -a -um,** *v. lavo.*

2. **lōtus -i,** . *v. lotos.*

lŭbet, lubido, *etc.* = *libet, libido, etc.* (*q.v.*).

lūbr co, 1. to make smooth *or* slippery.

lūbricus -a -um, slippery, uncertain, perilous; *poet.* smooth, slimy; fleeting; (*subst.,* **lūbricum -i,** *n.* a slippery place).

Lūcāni -orum, *m.* an Italian people in lower Italy.

Lūcānus -i, *m.,* *M. Annaeus,* poet, author of the *Pharsalia.*

lūcar -āris, *n.* money paid to actors from the treasury, salary.

lūcellum -i, *n.* (*dim. of lucrum*), a little profit.

lūcĕo, luxi, 2. to be bright, shine; *lucet,* it is light; to shine forth, be evident.

Lucĕres -um, *m.* one of the three old patrician tribes.

lūcerna -ae, *f.* a lamp.

lūcesco (**lūcisco**), **luxi,** 3. to begin to shine; appear; *lucescit,* it grows light.

lūci, *adv.* = *luce,* by day.

lūcidē, *adv.* clearly, lucidly.

lūcidus -a -um, clear, bright, lucid; *adv., lucidum fulgentes oculi,* shining white.

lūcifĕr -fĕra -fĕrum, light-bearing; bringing to light. *Subst.,* **Lūcifĕr -fĕri,** *m.* Lucifer, the morning star.

lūcifŭgus -a -um, shunning the light.

Lūcilius -a -um, name of a Roman gens.

Lūcīna -ae, *f.* the goddess of births, surname of Juno *or* of Diana.

lūcisco = *lucesco* (*q.v.*).

lūcrātīvus -a -um, profitable.

Lucrētius, *T. Lucretius Carus,* a Roman poet.

lucrifăcio -fēci -factum, 3. to gain.

Lucrīnus -i, *m.* a lake on the coast of Campania; *subst.,* **Lucrīna -ōrum,** *n.* Lucrine oysters.

lucror, 1. *dep.* to gain, profit; to win.

lucrōsus -a -um, profitable, lucrative.

lucrum -i, *n.* profit, advantage; avarice, riches.

luctāmen -ĭnis, *n.* effort, exertion.

luctātio -ōnis, *f.* wrestling; a struggle, contest; dispute.

luctātor -ōris, *m.* a wrestler.

luctificus -a -um, mournful, baleful.

luctisŏnus -a -um, sorrowfully sounding.

luctor, 1. *dep.* to wrestle; to strive.

luctŭōsē, *adv.* mournfully.

luctŭōsus -a -um, mournful, baleful.

luctus -ūs, *m.* mourning, lamentation; mourning apparel.

lucubrātio -ōnis, *f.* working by night *or* lamp-light.

lūcubro, 1. to work by night. *Transit.,* to produce by night.

lūculentē, *adv.* excellently.

lūculentĕr, *adv.* excellently, well.

lūculentus -a -um, full of light, bright; distinguished, excellent.

lūcŭlus -i, *m.* (*dim. of lucus*), a little grove.

Lūcŭmo *and syncop.,* **Lucmŏ** *or* **Lucmōn -ōnis,** *m.*; *plur.,* **Lūcŭmōnes,** the magnates of Etruria.

1. **lūcus -i,** *m.* a scared grove.

2. **lŏcus -ū,** *m.* light (*only in abl. sing.*).

lūdia -ae, *f.* actress *or* female dancer.

lūdibrium -ii, *n.* mockery, sport, jest; a laughing-stock.

lūdibundus -a -um, playful, sportive; *fig.* playing, *i.e.,* without difficulty *or* danger.

lūdicer *and* **lūdicrus -cra -crum,** serving as sport; playful, sportive; relating to the stage. *Subst.,* **lūdicrum -i,** *n.* plaything, public spectacle.

lūdificātio -ōnis, *f.* deriding, deceiving.

lūdifico, 1. to make a mock of, cheat.

lūdificor, 1. *dep.* to make game of, delude, cheat; to frustrate by cunning.

lūdimăgister -tri, *m.* schoolmaster.

lūdio -ōnis, *m.* pantomimic actor.

lūdius -ii, *m.* pantomimic actor *or* dancer; gladiator.

lūdo, lūsi, lūsum, 3. *intransit.*, to play, sport; *in numerum*, to dance; to amuse oneself; *transit.*, to play; *proelia latronum*, chess; to do for amusement, to play with; to banter; to deceive.

iūdus -i, *m.* game, sport, pastime; *ludi, publici games*; a satire; a game, a trifle; a jest; a school; *gladiatorius*, for training gladiators.

lūēla (lūella) -ae, *f.* punishment, expiation.

lūēs -is, *f.* a plague, pestilence, calamity, destruction; tempest.

Lugdūnum -i, *n.* town of *Gallia Narbonensis* (now *Lyons*). *Adj.*, **Lugdūnensis -e.**

lūgēo, luxi, luctum, 2. to mourn, be in mourning; *campi lugentes*, places of mourning (*of the lower world*). *Transit.*, to lament; to wear mourning for.

lūgubri, *adv.* mournfully.

lūgubris -e, relating to mourning, mournful. *Subst.*, **lūgubria -ium**, *n.* mourning attire.

lumbus -i, *m.* the loin.

lūmen -inis, *n.* light, lamp, taper; the eye; a window; clearness, insight; glory, ornament.

lūmināre -āris, *n.* window-shutter, window.

lūminōsus -a -um, bright, luminous.

lūna -ae, *f.* the moon; *plena*, full moon; *poet. laborans*, the moon in eclipse; *quarta luna*, the fourth day after new moon; the night; half-moon, *Luna*, the goddess of the Moon, *or* Diana.

lūnaris -e, lunar; like the moon.

lūno, 1. to bend into a crescent *or* half-moon. *Partic.*, **lūnātus**, half-moon *or* sickle-shaped.

1. **lūo**, lūi, to wash.

2. **lūo**, lūi, lūitūrus, 3. to loose; to atone for; to pay; *luere poenam or poenas*, to suffer punishment.

lūpa -ae, *f.* a she-wolf; a prostitute.

lūpātus -a -um, provided with wolf's teeth—*i.e.*, iron spikes; **lūpāti -ōrum**, *m. and* **lūpāta -ōrum**, *n.* a curb with jagged spikes.

Lūpercal -cālis, *n.* grotto on the Palatine Hill. *Plur.*, **Lūpercālia -ium**, festival of Pan *or* Lupercus.

Lūpercus -i, *m.* Italian deity, protector of flocks against wolves; a priest of Lupercus.

lūpinus -a -um, relating to a wolf, wolfish. *Subst.*, **lūpinum -i**, *n. and* **lūpinus -i**, *m.* the lupine, *used on the stage instead of coin*.

lūpus -i, *m.* a wolf; a fish, the pike; a horse's bit with jagged points; a hook.

lūridus -a -um, pale yellow, livid, lurid, ghastly.

lūror -ōris, *m.* ghastliness.

luscinia -ae, *f.* the nightingale.

luscīnus -a -um, one-eyed.

lusciōsus *and* **luscitiōsus -a -um**, dim-sighted.

luscus -a -um, blind; one-eyed.

Lūsitānin no, *f.* the country of the Lusitani.

lūsito, 1. to play, sport.

lūsor -ōris, *m.* a player; a playful writer; a mocker.

lustrālis -e, expiatory, atoning; relating to a period of five years.

lustrātio -ōnis, *f.* purification by sacrifice, expiation; a going round, wandering.

1. **lustro**, 1. to make bright, illumine.

2. **lustro**, 1. to look at, observe; to traverse, pass through; to purify; to review, muster an army; to dance round, encircle.

1. **lustrum** -i, *n.* a bog; den of a wild beast; a forest.

2. **lustrum** -i, *n.* an expiatory sacrifice; period of five years, a lustre.

lūsus -ūs, *m.* game, sport; amusement, dalliance.

lūtēolus -a -um (*dim. of luteus*), yellowish.

Lūtētia -ae, *f.* town in Gallia (now *Paris*).

1. **lūtēus -a -um**, yellow, saffron-yellow; rose-coloured.

2. **lūtēus -a -um**, of mud *or* clay; worthless; dirty.

lūto, 1. to besmear with mud *or* dirt.

lūtulentus -a -um, muddy, dirty; impure.

1. **lūtum** -i, *n.* a plant used for dyeing yellow; yellow colour.

2. **lūtum** -i, *n.* mud, dirt; clay.

lux, lūcis, *f.* light; day; *primā luce*, as soon as it was day; a heavenly body; eyesight; *fig.* publicity; help; ornament.

luxor, 1. *dep.* to riot, revel.

luxūria -ae, *f. and* **luxūriēs -ēi**, *f. of plants*, rankness, luxuriant growth; dissipation, luxury; unbridled insolence.

luxūrio, 1. *and* **luxūrior**, 1. *dep.* to be luxuriant, abundant; to be sportive; to abound in; to increase; to run riot, be dissolute.

luxūriōsē, *adv.* luxuriously.

luxūriōsus -a -um, luxuriant in growth; excessive; luxurious, prodigal.

1. **luxus -a -um**, dislocated.

2. **luxus -ūs**, *m.* luxury, revelling; splendour.

Lyaeus -i, *m.* surname of Bacchus; wine.

Lycambes -ae, *m.* a Theban attacked in verse by Archilochus.

Lycēum -i, *n. and* **Lycīum -ii**, *n.* a gymnasium at Athens.

lychnūchus -i, *m.* lamp-stand candelabrum.

lychnus -i, *m.* lamp.

Lycīum = *Lyceum* (*q.v.*).

Lycurgus -i, *m.* celebrated Spartan legislator.

lympha (limpha) -ae, *f.* clear spring *or* river water ; **Lymphae** = Nymphs of the springs.

lymphāticus -a -um, raving, frantic.

lympho, 1. to make mad ; *partic.,* **lymphātus** mad, frantic, struck with panic.

Lynceus -ĕi, *m.* one of the Argonauts, renowned for the sharpness of his sight.

lynx -cis, *c.* a lynx.

lўra -ae, *f.* the lyre; lyric poetry, song.

lўricus -a -um, relating to the lyre, lyric.

Lўsander -dri, *m.* celebrated Spartan general.

Lўsimāchus -i, *m.* one of the generals of Alexander the Great.

M

M m, *the twelfth letter of the Latin Alphabet.*

Măcĕdŏ -dōnis, *m.* a Macedonian. **Măcĕdŏnĭa -ae,** *f.* a country between Thessaly and Thrace. *Adj.,* **Măcĕdŏnicus, Măcĕdŏnĭus.**

măcellārius -a -um, relating to the provision market. *Subst.,* **măcellārĭus -ii,** *m.* provision-dealer.

măcellum -i, *n.* provision-market.

măcĕr -cra -crum, lean; *of soil,* poor.

măcĕrĭa -ae, *f.* wall enclosing a garden.

măcĕro, 1. to soak in water; to make weak, reduce; to tease, vex.

măchaera -ae, *f.* a sword, knife.

măchaerŏphŏrus -i, *m.* armed with a sabre.

măchĭna -ae, *f.* a machine, military engine; platform on which slaves were exposed for sale; a device, stratagem.

măchĭnāmentum -i, *n.* a machine, instrument.

măchĭnātĭo -ōnis, *f.* machinery; a cunning device; contrivance, machine.

măchĭnātor -ōris, *m.* a maker of machines; a contriver.

măchĭnor, 1. *dep.* to contrive, invent.

măcĭes -ēi, *f.* thinness; barrenness.

macresco, măcrŭi, 3. to become thin.

macrŏcollum -i, *n.* paper of the largest size.

mactābĭlis -e, deadly.

mactātus -ū, *m.* a slaying, killing.

macte, macti, *v. mactus.*

macto, 1. to honour, glorify; to reward; to afflict; to sacrifice; to devote.

mactus -a -um, *only* **macte, macti,** *with an abl.,* well done! bravo! *macte virtute! macte esto virtute !*

măcŭla -ae, *f.* a spot, mark; the mesh of a net; stain, blemish.

măcŭlo, 1. to make spotted, stain.

măcŭlōsus -a -um, spotted, speckled; stained, defiled.

mădĕfăcĭo -fēci -factum, 3. *pass.* **mădĕ-**

fĭo -factus sum -fĭĕri, to moisten, soak.

mădĕo -ŭi, 2. to be wet, to drip, flow; to melt (*of snow*); to be drunk; to be boiled; to be full of.

mădesco, mădŭi, 3. to become moist *or* wet.

mădĭdus -a -um, moist, wet; drunk.

mădor -ōris, *m.* moisture.

Maeander -dri, *m. and* **Maeandrŏs (-us) -dri,** *m.* river of Asia Minor, proverbial for its winding course; winding.

Maecēnās -ātis, *m. C. Cilnius,* patron of Horace and Vergil.

Maelĭus -a -um, name of a Roman gens.

maena (mēna) -ae, *f.* a kind of small seafish.

Maenădes, *v. Maenas.*

Maenăs -ădis, *f.* a bacchante.

maerĕo, 2. *intransit.,* to be sad, to grieve, lament ; *partic.,* **maerens,** sorrowful; *transit.,* to bewail.

maeror -ōris, *m.* mourning, sadness.

maestĭtĭa -ae, *f.* sadness; gloominess.

maestus -a -um, sad, melancholy; gloomy.

māga -ae, *f.* the enchantress.

măgālĭa -ium, *n.* huts, hovels.

măgĕ = *magis (q.v.).*

măgĭcus -a -um, magical.

măgis, *adv.* more; in a higher degree; more than usual; *magis quam,* rather . . . than; *quo magis . . . eo magis,* the more . . . the more. *Superl.,* **maximē (maxŭmē),** *adv.* most of all, especially; very; principally; *to form superl.,* of *adjs., maxime necessarius; quam maxime,* as much as possible.

măgister -tri, *m.* master, head, superintendent ; *equitum,* master of the horse; *elephanti,* driver; *navis,* master, captain ; *ludi,* schoolmaster ; trustee; a teacher.

măgistĕrĭum -ii, *n.* the office of a master, director; *morum,* the censorship.

măgistra -ae, *f.* a mistress, leader.

măgistrātus -ūs, *m.* magistracy, office; a magistrate.

magnănĭmĭtas -ātis, *f.* greatness of soul.

magnănĭmus -a -um, high-minded, courageous, high-spirited.

1. **magnēs -nētis,** a loadstone, magnet.

2. **Magnēs -nētis,** *v. Magnesia.*

Magnēsĭa -ae, *f.* 1. A district of Thessaly. 2. A town in Caria. 3. A town in Lydia.

Magnēs -nētis, *m.* Magnesian.

magnĭfĭcē, *compar.,* **magnĭficentĭus;** *superl.,* **magnĭficentissimē,** *adv.* splendidly, magnificently.

magnĭfĭcentĭa -ae, *f.* high-mindedness, magnanimity ; boasting, pomposity; splendour.

magnĭfĭco, 1. to prize highly.

magnĭfĭcus -a -um, *compar.,* **magnĭfĭcentĭor ;** *superl.,* **magnĭficentissimus,** magnificent, fond of display; distinguished; dignified; lofty; famous.

magnilŏquentia -ae, *f.* lofty language; boastful language.

magnilŏquus -a -um, boastful in talk.

magnitūdo -ĭnis, *f.* greatness, size, magnitude; great quantity; importance.

magnŏpĕrĕ, *and* sepărătlm **magno ĭpĕrĕ**, *adv.* greatly, exceedingly.

magnus -a -um, *compar.*, **māior -us**; *superl.*, **maximus (maxŭmus)**, great, large; long, broad; loud; important, significant; powerful; **maiores**, ancestors, forefathers.

Māgo (-ōn) -ōnis, *m.* brother of Hannibal.

1. **măgus** -i, *m.* a learned man or magician among the Persians.

2. **măgus** -a -um, magical.

Māia -ae, *f.* the daughter of Atlas, who bore Mercury to Jupiter.

māiestas -ātis, *f.* grandeur, dignity, majesty; *putria*, the paternal authority; *crimen maiestatis*, treason; honour, splendour.

māior, maiores, *v. magnus.*

Māius -i, *m.* the month of May.

māiuscŭlus -a -um (*dim. of maior*), somewhat greater.

māla -ae, *f.* the cheek-bone, jaw-bone, *both in men and animals;* the cheek.

mălăcia -ae, *f.* a calm at sea.

mălĕ, *adv.*, *compar.*, **pēius**; *superl.*, **pessĭme**, badly, ill; *male audire*, to be ill spoken of; wrongly, badly; unsuccessfully; inopportunely; wickedly; bitterly; too much, excessively; *male superbus;* to give an opposite meaning, *male gratus*, unthankful.

mălĕdĭcē, *adv.* abusively.

mălĕdĭcens -entis, *p. adj.* abusive, scurrilous.

mălĕdĭco -dixi -dictum, 3. to speak ill, slander, abuse.

mălĕdictio -ōnis, *f.* a reviling, abusing.

mălĕdictum -i, *n.* a railing accusation, abusive language.

mălĕdĭcus -a -um, abusive, scurrilous.

mălĕfăcio -fēci -factum, 3. *to* injure.

mălĕfactum -i, *n.* an ill deed, injury.

mălĕfĭcium -ii, *n.* crime, mischief; sorcery.

mălĕfĭcus -a -um, wicked, malicious.

mălĕsuādus -a -um, ill-advising, persuading to evil.

Mălĕventum -i, *n.* town in Samnium, changed to Beneventum.

mălĕvŏlens -entis, envious, malevolent; *compar.* malevolentior; *superl.*, **malevolentissimus.**

mălĕvŏlentia -ae, *f.* ill-will, hatred.

mălĕvŏlus -a -um, ill-disposed, malicious, envious. *Superl.*, *v. malevolens.* *Subst.*, **mălĕvŏli -ōrum**, *m.* ill-disposed persons.

mālĭfĕr -fĕra -fĕrum, apple-bearing.

mălignē, *adv.* maliciously, enviously; stingily.

mălignĭtas -ātis, *f.* ill-nature, spite; niggardliness.

mălignus -a -um, ill-disposed, wicked; niggardly; barren; scanty.

mălĭtia -ae, *f.* wickedness, vice; cunning, *malioa; sometimes plăyful like our "roguery."*

mălĭtiōsē, *adv.* wickedly.

mălĭtiōsus -a -um, crafty, wicked.

mallĕŏlus -i, *m.* (*dim. of malleus*), a little hammer; a hammer-shaped slip (*of a vine*); a kind of fire-dart.

mallĕus -i, *m.* a hammer, mallet; the axe used for slaying animals offered in sacrifice.

mālo, **māluī**, **malle**, to prefer; to be more favourable to.

mălŏbathron (-um) -i, *n.* a plant from which ointment was prepared; the oil of the plant.

1. **mālum** -i, *n.*, *v. malus.*

2. **mālum** -i, *n.* an apple, peach, pomegranate, *etc.*

1. **mălus** -a -um; *comp.*, **pēior -us**; *superl.*, **pessĭmus**, bad; incapable; cowardly, weak; wicked; unsuccessful; *in politics*, disloyal; *subst.*, **mălum -i**, *n.* an evil; disaster.

2. **mālus** -i, *f.* an apple-tree.

3. **mālus** -i, *m.* the mast of a ship; *in the circus*, the pole to which the awnings were fastened.

malva -ae, *f.* the mallow.

Māmers -mertis, *m.* name of Mars; **Māmertīni** -ōrum, *m.* (sons of Mars), mercenary troops who seized Messana.

māmilla -ae, *f.* (*dim. of mamma*), a breast.

mamma -ae, *f.* a breast, teat.

mammōsus -a -um, full-breasted.

mānabilis -e, flowing, penetrating.

manceps -cipis, *m.* a purchaser, contractor.

mancĭpium (mancŭpium) -ii, a formal, legal purchase of anything; a slave acquired by the process of *mancipium*.

mancĭpo (mancŭpo), 1. to transfer by formal sale; to give up to.

mancus -a -um, maimed; lame; incomplete, defective.

mandātor -ōris, *m.* one who suborns accusers *or* informers.

mandātum -i, *n.* a commission, charge, order.

mandātus, *abl.* -u, *m. only in abl. sing.*, a commission, order.

1. **mando**, 1. to commit to the charge of, entrust; *se fugae*, to take to flight; to enjoin, order.

2. **mando**, **mandi**, **mansum**, 3. to chew, masticate; to eat, consume.

mandra -ae, *f.* a stall, cattle-pen; a herd of cattle; row of pawns, *on a draught-board.*

Mandubii -ōrum, *m.* a people in Gallia Celtica.

mandūcus -i, *m.* a mask to represent a glutton.

māně, *subst. indecl. n.* the early morning. *Adv.*, in the morning.

māněo, mansi, mansum, 2. to remain, stay; to stay the night, *apud me*; to endure, last; to continue steadfast in; *in conditione*, to abide by; to wait. *Transit.*, to wait for.

mānes -ium, *m.* the shades of the departed; *poet.* the infernal regions; the punishment of the lower world; corpse, ashes, remains.

mango -ōnis, *m.* a slave-dealer.

mănica -ae, *f.* the long sleeve of the tunic; manacle.

mănicātus -a -um, having long sleeves.

mănifestě, *adv.* plainly, evidently, manifestly.

1. **mănifestō**, *adv.*, *v. manifestus.*

2. **mănifesto**, 1. to manifest, reveal.

mănifestus -a -um, visible, evident, manifest; *adv.*, *manifesto*, manifestly betraying.

Mānīlius -a -um, name of a Roman gens.

măniprětium = *manupretium (q.v.).*

mănipŭlāris (**măniplāris**) -e, belonging to a maniple. *Subst.*, **mănipŭlāris** -is, *m.* a common soldier.

mănipŭlārius -a -um, relating to a private soldier.

mănipŭlātim, *adv. milit.*, in maniples.

mănipŭlus (*poet.* **māniplus**) -i, *m.* small bundle *or* handful; a company of foot soldiers.

Manlius -a -um, name of a Roman gens.

mannus -i, *m.* a small horse of Gaulish breed; a cob.

māno, 1. *intransit.*, to flow, run; drip with anything; to come from; to spread abroad. *Transit.*, to exude, give out.

mansio -ōnis, *f.* stay, sojourn; halting-place.

mansito, 1. to stay, remain.

mansuēfácio -fēci -factum, 3. *pass.*, **mansuēfío** -factus sum -fíěri, to tame; to pacify; to civilise.

mansuesco -suēvi -suētum, 3. *Transit.*, to tame. *Intransit.*, to become tame, to become softened.

mansuētě, *adv.* gently, quietly.

mansuētūdo -ĭnĭs, *f.* tameness; clemency, gentleness.

mansuētus -a -um, *p. adj.* tame; gentle, quiet.

mantēlě (**mantĭlě**) -is, *n.* and **mantēllum** -ii, *n.* a towel, napkin.

mantēlium -ii, *n.* = *mantele (q.v.).*

mantica -ae, *f.* wallet, knapsack, saddle-bag.

Mantĭnēa -ae, *f.* a town in Arcadia, scene of the victory and death of Epaminondas.

Mantūa -ae, *f.* in north Italy, near to the birthplace of Vergil.

mānŭālis -e, adapted, fitted to the hand, relating to the hand; *saxa*, thrown by hand.

mānŭbiae -ārum, *f.* money obtained from the sale of booty; the profits of an office; plunder.

mānŭbĭālis -e, relating to booty.

mānubrium -ii, *n.* a haft, handle.

mānŭf . . . *v. manif* . . .

mānŭmissio -ōnis, *f.* the emancipation of a slave.

mānŭmitto -mīsi -missum, 3. to emancipate a slave.

mānūprětium (**mănĭprětium**) -ii, *n.* wages, pay; a reward.

mănus -ūs, *f.* the hand; *manus dare*, to surrender; the trunk of an elephant; *manus ferrea*, a grappling-iron; a band of men.

māpālia -ium, *n.* huts.

mappa -ae, *f.* a table-napkin.

Mărăthon -ōnis, *f.* a plain in Attica, where the Persian army was defeated by the Athenians. *Adj.*, **Marathōnius.**

mărăthrum -i, *n.* fennel.

Marcellus -i, *m.* the cognomen of a family of the gens *Claudia.*

marcěo, 2. to wither; to be faint, feeble.

marcesco, 3. to begin to droop, to languish, grow feeble.

marcĭdus -a -um, faded, drooping; enfeebled, heavy, besotted.

Marcius -a -um, name of a Roman gens.

Marcŏmāni and **Marcŏmanni** -ōrum, *m.* a German tribe.

marcor -ōris, *m.* rottenness, decay.

Marcus -i, *m.* a Roman praenomen.

măre -is, *n.* the sea; *superum*, the Adriatic; *inferum*, the Tuscan Sea.

margărĭta -ae, *f.* and **margărītum** -i, *n.* a pearl.

margĭno, 1.t o border.

margo -ĭnis, *m.* and *f.* a border, edge; boundary.

mărīnus -a -um, marine; *ros*, rosemary.

mărisca -ae, *f.* a large fig.

mărīta, *v. maritus.*

mărītālis -e, conjugal, matrimonial.

mărĭtĭmus (**mărĭtŭmus**) -a -um, marine, maritime; *praedo*, a private; on the sea-coast. *Subst.*, **mărĭtima** -ōrum, *n.* maritime regions.

mărīto, 1. to wed, marry, give in marriage; *of plants*, to train one on another.

mărītus -a -um, *adj.*, matrimonial, nuptial; *of plants*, tied *or* trained together. *Subst.*, **mărītus** -i, *m.* a husband; a lover; **mărīta** -ae, *f.* wife.

Mărius -a -um, *C. Marius*, seven times consul. *Adj.*, **Mărĭānus**, *Marian.*

marmor -ōris, *n.* marble; a marble statue; *plur.*, public monuments; the white foamy surface of the sea.

marmŏrěus -a -um, marble, made of marble; like marble.

Măro -ōnis, *m.* cognomen of the poet P. Vergilius.

marra -ae, *f.* hoe for rooting up weeds.

Mars, Martis, *m.* (*poet. form,* **Māvors**) Mars, the god of war; war, battle, fight. *Adj.,* **Martius, Martiālis** (*q.v.*).

Marsi 5t uni, *m.* a people of Latium Alī., **Marsicus -a -um, bellum,** the Social War.

1. **Martiālis -e,** relating to Mars; *plur. subst.* **Martiāles,** *m.* the priests of Mars.

2. **Martiālis -is,** *m. M. Valerius,* the celebrated Roman epigrammatist.

Marticŏla -ae, *c.* worshipper of Mars.

Martigĕna -ae, *c.* offspring of Mars.

Martius -a -um, relating to the god Mars, sacred to Mars; *mensis,* month of March; *Campus Martius,* the plain of Mars at Rome.

mas, māris, *m.* the male; manly, vigorous.

masculīnus -a -um, of the male sex, masculine.

masculus -a -um (*dim. of mas*), of the male sex, male; manly. *Subst.,* **masculus -i,** *m.* a male.

Māsinissa -ae, *m.* king of Numidia, ally of the Romans.

massa -ae, *f.* a lump, mass; chaos.

Massicum -i, *n.* Massic wine.

Massilia -ae, *f.* town in Gallia Narbonesis, *now* Marseilles. *Adj.,* **Massiliensis -e.**

mastīgia -ae, *m.* scoundrel.

matāra -ae, *f. and* **matāris (matĕris) -is,** *f.* a Gallic pike.

mātellio -ōnis, *m.* (*dim. of matula*), a small pot, vessel.

māter, mātris, *f.* a mother.

mātercŭla -ae, *f.* (*dim. o mater*), a little mother.

mātĕria -ae, *f. and* **mātĕries** *f. only in nom. and acc. sing.* matter, material; building materials; wood; incitement, cause; natural disposition, abilities.

mātĕrics, *f.* = *mulerta* (*q.v.*).

mātĕrio, 1. to build, construct of wood.

mātĕrior, 1. *dep.* to fell wood.

matĕris = *matara* (*q.v.*).

māternus -a -um, maternal.

mātertĕra -ae, *f.* maternal aunt.

māthēmăticus -a -um, *adj.* mathematical; *subst.,* **māthēmăticus -i,** *m.* a mathematician; an astrologer; **māthēmătica -ae,** *f.* mathematics.

mātricīda -ae, *c.* a matricide.

mātricīdium -ii, *n.* slaying of a mother by her son.

mātrimōnium -ii, *n.* marriage.

mātrimus (*the quantity of the i is doubtful*) **-a -um,** having a mother living.

1. **mātrŏna -ae,** *f.* a married woman, matron.

2. **Mātrŏna -ae,** *m.* a river *now the* Marne.

mātrōnālis -e, relating to a married woman, matronly; *feriae Matronales,* a festival of the Roman matrons.

matta -ae, *f.* a mat of rushes.

mattĕa -ae, *f.* a dainty dish.

mātūrē, *adv.,* seasonably, opportunely; in good time; early; too soon.

mātūresco, mātūrŭi, 3. to ripen; to come to maturity.

mātūritas -ātis, *f.* ripeness; maturity.

mātūro, 1. *transit.,* to ripen; to do early, betimes; to hasten. *Intransit.,* to hasten, make haste.

mātūrus -a -um, ripe, mature, perfect, seasonable; powerful; grown up; aged; developed; mature, timely; early; speedy.

Mātūta -ae, *f.* the goddess of the early morn.

mātūtīnus -a -um, early in the morning; pertaining to the morning.

Mauri -ōrum, *m.* the Moors; **Mauritānia -ae,** *f.* a district in Africa.

Maurūsia -ae, *f.* Mauritania. *Adj.,* **Maurūsius -a -um,** Mauritanian, *also post. for* African.

Mansōlus -i, *m.* king of Caria. *Adj.,* **Mausōlēus; subst.,* **Mausōlēum -i,** *n.* the tomb of Mausolus.

māvŏlo = *malo* (*q.v.*).

Māvors -vortis, *m., archaic and poet. for Mars. Adj.,* **Māvortius -a -um.**

maxilla -ae, *f.* (*dim. of mala*), the jawbone, jaw.

maximē, *superl. of magis* (*q.v.*).

maximitas -ātis, *f.* greatness, size.

1. **maximus,** *superl. of magnus* (*q.v.*).

2. **Maximus,** *v. Fabius.*

māzŏnŏmus -i, *m.* a charger, large dish.

mĕāmet, meapte, *strengthened from* **meā,** by my own, *culpa.*

mĕātus -ūs, *m.* a going, motion; a way, path, passage.

Mecastor, *v. Castor.*

meddix -īcis, *m.* a magistrate among the Oscans.

Mēdēa -ae, *f.* an enchantress, daughter of king Aeetes in Colchis; helped Jason to obtain the golden fleece.

Mēdēis -idis, *f.* magical.

mĕdens -entis, *m. subst.,* a physician.

mĕdĕor, 2. *dep.* to heal, to cure; *with dat., morbo,* to be good for; to alleviate.

Mēdi -ōrum, *m.* the Medes; *poet.* = *the Persians.*

mĕdiastīnus -i, *m.* a slave who performed menial offices, a drudge.

mĕdica -ae, *f.* lucerne, clover.

mĕdicābilis -e, curable.

mĕdicāmen -inis, *n.* drug, medicine; poison; dye, rouge.

mĕdicāmentum -i, *n.* drug, medicine, remedy; poison; dye.

1. **mĕdicātus -a -um,** *p. adj.,* healing, medicinal.

2. **mĕdicātus -ūs,** *m.* a charm.

mĕdicīna -ae, *f., v. medicinus.*
mĕdicīnus -a -um, belonging to the art of healing. *Subst.*, **mĕdicīna -ae,** *f.* the art of healing; medicine; cure.
mĕdĭco, 1. to heal, cure; to medicate, drug; to dye.
mĕdĭcor, 1. *dep.* to heal, cure.
1. **mĕdĭcus -a -um,** healing, wholesome, medicinal. *Subst.,* **mĕdĭcus -i,** *m.* doctor.
2. **Mēdĭcus,** Median, Assyrian, Persian.
mĕdĭē, *adv.* moderately.
mĕdĭētas -ātis, *f.* the middle.
mĕdĭmnum -i, *n.* and **mĕdĭmnus -i,** *m.* a bushel, a Greek measure of corn.
mĕdĭŏcris -e, moderate, middling; indifferent; calm, *animus.*
mĕdĭŏcritas -ātis, *f.* moderation, medium; inferiority.
mĕdĭŏcrĭtĕr, *adv.* moderately, tolerably; with moderation.
Mĕdĭŏlānum -i, *n.* and **-lānĭum -ii,** *n.* (now Milan). *Adj.,* **Mĕdĭŏlānensis -e.**
mĕdĭtāmentum -i, *n.* preparation.
mĕdĭtātē, *adv.* thoughtfully; designedly, thoroughly.
mĕdĭtātĭo -ōnis, *f.* contemplation; preparation; practice.
mĕdĭtātus -a -um, *partic. of meditor.*
mĕdĭterrānĕus -a -um, inland; **mĕdĭterrānĕum -i,** *n.* inland country.
mĕdĭtor, 1. *dep.* to consider, meditate; to study, intend; to practise; *partic.,* **mĕdĭtātus -a -um,** *pass.,* meditated, prepared.
mĕdĭum -ii, *n.* the middle, *v. medius.*
mĕdĭus -a -um, the middle, midst ; neutral, intermediate; ordinary; *subst.,* **mĕdĭum -ii,** *n.* the midst, the middle point, the middle.
mĕdĭus fĭdĭus, *v. Fĭdĭus.*
mĕdix, *v. meddix.*
mĕdulla -ae, *f.* marrow of bones.
Mēdus -i, *m., v. Medi.*
Mĕdūsa -ae, *f.* one of the Gorgons, slain by Perseus.
Mĕgăra -ae, *f.* a town in Sicily, and **Mĕgăra -ōrum,** *n.* a town in Megaris.
Mĕgărĭci -ōrum, philosophers of the Megaric school.
mĕgĭstānes -um, *m.* grandees, nobles.
mĕhercle, mĕhercŭle, mĕhercŭles, *an* oath, by Hercules.
mĕl, mellis, *n.* honey; sweetness, pleasantness.
mĕlanchŏlĭcus -a -um, having black bile, melancholy.
mĕlānūrus -i, *m.* a kind of sea-fish.
Mĕlĕăgĕr *and* **Mĕlĕăgrus (-ŏs) -i,** *m.* son of Oeneus and of Althaea.
mĕlĭcus -a -um, musical ; lyrical, lyric.
mĕlĭlōtos -i, *f.* a species of clover.
mĕlĭmēlum -i, *n.* a honey-apple.
mĕlĭor -us, *comp. of bonus (q.v.).*

mĕlisphyllum *and* **mĕlissŏphyllŏn -i,** *n.* balm.
Mĕlĭta -ae, *f.* and **Mĕlĭtē -ēs,** *f.* the island of Malta. *Adj.,* **Mĕlĭtensis, -e.**
mĕlĭuscŭlē, *adv.* somewhat better, pretty well (*in health*).
mĕlĭuscŭlus -a -um (*dim. of compar melior*), somewhat better in health.
mellĭfĕr -fĕra -fĕrum, producing honey.
mellītus -a -um, sweetened with honey; agreeable, delightful.
1. **mĕlos,** *n.* a tune, song, melody.
2. **Mēlos -i,** *f.* island of the Aegaean Sea. *Adj.,* **Mēlĭus.**
Melpŏmĕnē -ēs, *f.* the muse of tragic and lyric poetry.
membrāna -ae, *f.* a skin, membrane; parchment; surface of anything.
membrānŭla -ae, *f.* (*dim. of membrana*), a little membrane; parchment.
membrātim, *adv.* limb by limb; piecemeal; in short, detached sentences.
membrum -i, *n.* a limb *or* member of the body; part, portion of anything; apartment of a house ; clause in a sentence.
mĕmĭni -nisse, to remember, bear in mind; to mention.
Memnon -ŏnis, *m.* killed before Troy by Achilles.
mĕmor -ŏris, mindful, not forgetful ; thoughtful ; with a good memory ; calling to mind.
mĕmŏrābĭlis -e, *adj.* memorable.
mĕmŏrandus -a -um, memorable.
mĕmŏrātor -ŏris, *m.* a narrator.
1. **mĕmŏrātus -a -um,** *p. adj.,* celebrated, well known.
2. **mĕmŏrātus -ūs,** *m.* a mention.
mĕmŏrĭa -ae, *f.* remembrance, memory; *memoriae tradere,* to leave on record; tradition, history.
mĕmŏrĭālis -e, relating to memory.
mĕmŏrĭŏla -ae, *f.* (*dim. of memoria*), memory.
mĕmŏrĭtĕr, *adv.* by heart, from memory.
mĕmŏro, 1. to mention, call to mind, relate.
Memphis -is *and* **idos,** *f.* a city of Egypt.
Mĕnander -dri, *m.* a Greek comic poet.
menda -ae, *f., v. mendum.*
mendācĭum -ii, *n.* a lie : deception.
mendācĭuncŭlum -i, *n.* (*dim. of mendacium*), a little lie.
mendax -ācis, lying, mendacious ; counterfeit, false; *subst., mendax,* a liar.
mendīcĭtas -ātis, *f.* indigence, poverty.
mendīco, 1. *and* **mendīcor,** 1. *dep.* to beg, go begging; *transit.,* to beg for.
mendīcus -a -um, poor as a beggar, beggarly; paltry; **mendīcus -i,** *m.* a beggar.
mendōsē, *adv.* faultily, incorrectly.
mendōsus -a -um, full of faults; making a mistake.

mendum -i, *n. and* **menda** -ae, *f.* a bodily defect; an error.

Mĕnĕlāus (-ŏs) -i, *m.* husband of Helen.

mens, mentis, *f.* the mind, opinion, character; the conscience; understanding, reason, intellect, judgment; *mentis compos esse,* to be in possession of one's faculties, *cūnctis menta, insane, reflection, thought;* courage; the thoughts; plan, resolve.

mensa -ae, *f.* a table; *mensam ponere,* to bring in dinner; a course; *mensa secunda,* dessert; table of a money-changer, banker; altar.

mensārius -ii, *m.* money-changer, banker.

mensio -ōnis, *f.* a measuring.

mensis -is, *m.* a month.

mensor -ōris, *m.* a measurer.

menstrŭus -a -um, monthly; lasting for a month; *subst.,* **menstrŭum** -i, *n.* rations for a month.

mensūra -ae, *f.* a measuring; a measure; length, thickness, size, circumference, *etc.;* character, capacity.

menta (**mentha**) -ae, *f.* the herb mint.

mentiens -entis, *m., partic. of mentior, as subst.,* a fallacy.

mentio -ōnis, *f.* a speaking of, mention.

mentior, 4. *dep.* to tell a lie. *Intransit.,* to deceive; *of poets,* to feign, invent; to break one's word. *Transit.,* to say something falsely; to disappoint; to counterfeit, assume; *partic.,* **mentītus** -a -um, *as pass.,* invented, feigned.

Mentor -ōris, *m.* a celebrated artist in metal work.

mentum -i, *n.* the chin.

mĕo, 1. to go, pass.

mĕphītis -is, *f.* a noxious exhalation from the earth, malaria; *Mephitis,* the goddess who protects against malaria.

mĕrācus -a -um, pure, unmixed; undiminished.

mercābilis -e, that can be bought.

mercātor -ōris, *m.* a merchant; buyer.

mercātūra -ae, *f.* trade, traffic.

mercātus -ūs, *m.* trade, business; a market; *frequens,* a full market.

mercēdŭla -ae, *f. (dim. of mercles),* a small reward, low wages; low rent.

mercennārius (**mercēnārius**) -a -um, hired, paid; *testes,* suborned; *subst.,* **mercennārius** -ii, *m.* hireling.

merces -ēdis, *f.* hire, pay, wages; bribe; punishment; harm, loss; interest, rent, income.

mercimōnium -ii, *n.* goods, merchandise.

mercor, 1. *dep.* to carry on trade; *transit.,* to buy.

Mercŭrius -ii, *m. Mercury,* messenger of the gods; *adj.,* **Mercŭriālis** -e, *Subst.,* **Mercŭriāles** -ium, *m.* a corporation of traders at Rome.

merda -ae, *f.* dung.

mĕrenda -ae, *f.* an afternoon meal.

mĕrens -entis, *partic. of mereo.*

mĕrĕo -ŭi -ĭtum, 2. *and* **mĕrĕor** -ĭtus sum,** 2. *dep.* to earn, obtain; to serve as a soldier; to deserve.

mĕretrīcius -a -um, relating to a harlot.

mĕretrīcŭla -ae, *f. (dim. of meretrix),* a public prostitute.

mĕretrix -īcis, *f.* a public prostitute.

mergae -ārum, *f.* a two-pronged fork.

mergēs -gĭtis, *f.* a sheaf of corn.

mergo, mersi, mersum, 3. to dip, plunge into water; to sink overwhelm; to hide; *middle, mergi, of stars,* to sink.

mergus -i, *m.* a diver, gull.

mĕrīdiānus -a -um, relating to midday, meridian; southern.

mĕrīdiātio -ōnis, *f.* midday sleep, siesta.

mĕrīdies -ēi, *m.* midday, noon; the south.

mĕrīdio, 1. *and* **mĕrīdior,** 1. *dep.* to take a siesta.

1. **mĕrĭto,** 1. to earn.

2. **mĕrĭtō,** *adv.* deservedly, rightly.

mĕrītōrius -a -um, that for which hire is paid. *Subst.,* **mĕrītōria** -ōrum, *n.* lodgings.

mĕrĭtum -i, *n.* desert; reward, punishment; a good action, benefit; blame, fault; worth, importance of a thing.

mĕrĭtus -a -um, *partic. of mereo (q.v.).*

Mĕrŏpē -ēs, *f.* daughter of Atlas, wife of Sisyphus, one of the Pleiades, whose star is dimmer than the others because she married a mortal.

mĕrops -ŏpis, *f.* a bird, the bee-eater.

merso, 1. to dip in, immerse.

mĕrŭla -ae, *f.* a blackbird; a fish, the sea-carp.

mĕrum -i, *n., v. merus.*

mĕrus -a -um, pure, unmixed; naked, uncovered; mere, only, nothing but; real; *subst.,* **mĕrum** -i, *n.* wine unmixed with water.

merx, mercis, *f.* merchandise, goods, wares.

Mesŏpŏtāmia -ae, *f.* country between the Euphrates and Tigris.

Messāna -ae, *f.* town in Sicily. *Adj.,* **Messānius.**

messis -is, *f.* harvest; the gathering of honey; the crop.

messor -ōris, *m.* a reaper.

messōrius -a -um, relating to a reaper.

mēta -ae, *f.* a conical *or* pyramid-shaped figure; the pyramidal columns at the extremities of the Roman circus; the goal, end, boundary.

mĕtallum -i, *n.* a metal; a mine, quarry.

mĕtămorphōsis -is, *f.* transformation; *plur.,* **Mĕtămorphōses** -ĕōn, title of a poem by Ovid.

mĕtātor -ōris, *m.* a measurer, one who marks.

Mĕtaurus -i, *m.* river in Umbria, where Hasdrubal was slain.

Mĕtellus -i, *m.* a cognomen in the Caecilian gens.

mētĭor, mensus sum, 4. *dep.* to measure; to measure out, distribute; to traverse; to estimate.

1. **mĕto, messŭi messum** 3. to reap, gather harvest; *of bees, apes metunt flores,* to crop off, cut off; *in battle,* to hew down.

2. **mēto -āre** = *metor.*

mētor, 1. *dep.* to measure; to define the boundaries of any spot.

mĕtrēta -ae, *f.* a Greek liquid measure; a large tub.

Mētrŏpŏlis, *acc.* -**im,** *f.* town in Thessaly. *Adj.,* **Mētrŏpŏlītānus.**

metrum -i, *n.* a measure; metre.

mĕtŭendus -a -um, *p. adj.,* fearful.

mĕtŭens -entis, *p. adj.,* fearing.

mĕtŭo -ŭi -ūtum, 3. *intransit.,* to fear, be afraid; *transit.,* to fear; to shun.

mĕtus -ūs, *m.* fear, apprehension, dread; reverence; the object of fear; danger, crisis.

mĕus -a -um, *poss. pron.* my, mine, my own; *Nero meus,* my friend Nero.

mīca -ae, *f.* a crumb, morsel.

Mĭcipsa -ae, *m.* son of Masinissa, king of Numidia.

micans -antis, glittering, sparkling.

mico -ŭi, 1. to move rapidly up and down, tremble, beat like the pulse; to glitter, sparkle.

Midas (Mĭda) -ae, *m.* a king of Phrygia, whose touch turned everything to gold.

migrātio -ōnis, *f.* migration.

migro, 1. to quit a place, depart; to change. *Transit.,* to transport; to transgress.

mil . . . *v. mill . . .*

mīles -itis, *c.* a soldier.

mīlitāris -e, military. *Subst.,* **mīlitāris -is,** *m.* a soldier.

mīlitārĭtĕr, *adv.* in a military manner.

mīlitia -ae, *f.* military service, warfare; the military; *domi et militiae,* at home and abroad, at peace and in war.

mīlito, 1. to serve as a soldier.

milium -ii, *n.* millet.

millĕ, *[numeral,* a thousand; *mille passuum,* a thousand paces, a mile.

millēsimus -a -um, the thousandth.

milliārius (millĭārius) -a -um, containing a thousand. *Subst.,* **milliārium -ii,** *n.* a mile-stone.

milliēs (millĭēs, milliens), *adv.* a thousand times.

1. **Milo (-ōn) -ōnis,** *m.* a celebrated athlete.

2. **Milo -ōnis,** *m.,* **T.** *Annius Milo Papianus,* defended by Cicero.

Miltĭădēs -is *and* -**i,** *m.* celebrated Athenian general.

milŭīnus (milvīnus) -a -um, relating to a kite.

milŭus (milvus) -i, *m.* a kite, hawk; a fish, the gurnard; a star.

mīma -ae, *f.* a female mime.

Mimallōnis -idis, *f.* a Bacchante.

mīmĭcē, *adv.* like a mime *or* buffoon.

mīmicus -a -um, mimic, farcical; counterfeit.

mīmŭla -ae, *f.* (*dim. of mima*), a female mime.

mīmus -i, *m.* a mime, pantomimist; a farce.

mīna -ae, *f.* a Greek weight; a Greek silver coin.

mĭnācĭtĕr, *adv.* threateningly.

mĭnae -ārum, *f.* battlements, *poet.;* menaces.

mĭnantĕr, *adv.* threateningly.

mĭnātio -ōnis, *f.* threat, menace (*plur.*).

mĭnax -ācis, *f.* overhanging; threatening.

mĭnĕo, 2. to project, overhang.

Minerva -ae, *f.* goddess of wisdom, and patroness of all the arts; genius, skill; working in wool; *invitâ Minervâ,* without ability.

mĭniātŭlus -a -um (*dim. of miniatus*), somewhat tinged with cinnabar or red lead.

mĭniātus -a -um, *v.* minio.

mĭnĭmē, *v. parum.*

mĭnĭmus, *v. parvus.*

mĭnio, 1. to colour with cinnabar *or* red lead.

mĭnister -tri, *m. and* **mĭnistra -ae,** *f.* servant, attendant, assistant.

mĭnistĕrium -ii, *n.* service, assistance, employment, occupation ; servants ; retinue.

mĭnistra -ae, *f., v. minister.*

mĭnistrātor -ōris, *m.* servant, attendant, assistant.

mĭnistro, 1. to serve, wait upon, to wait at table, to hand, *with dat.;* to attend to, direct; *velis,* to attend to the sails; to provide.

mĭnĭtābundus -a -um, threatening, minatory.

mĭnĭtor, 1. *dep.* to threaten.

mĭnium -ii, *n.* native cinnabar, red lead, vermilion.

1. **mĭnor,** 1. *dep.* to project, hang over, to threaten, *alicui.*

2. **mĭnor -ōris,** *compar., parvus* (*q.v.*).

Mīnos -ōis, *acc.* -**ōem** *and* -**ōa,** *m.* king of Crete, judge in Tartarus.

Mīnōtaurus -i, *m.* a monster, half-bull, half-man, slain by Theseus.

mintha -ae, *f.* mint.

mĭnŭmĕ = *minime* (*q.v.*).

mĭnŭmus = *minimus* (*q.v.*).

mĭnŭo -ŭi -ūtum, 3. to make smaller; to chop up; to diminish; *minuente aestu,* at the ebbing of the tide; to reduce, limit; to confine to the point.

mĭnus, *compar. Adj., v. parvus. Adv., v. parum.*

minuscŭlus -a -um (dim. of compar. minor), somewhat less, somewhat small.

minūtal -ālis, n. a dish of mincemeat.

minūtātim, adv. in small pieces, gradually.

minūtē, adv. in small portions, meanly.

minūtia -ae, f. smallness, minuteness.

minūtus -a -um, p. adj., small, unimportant.

Minўās -ae, m. ancestor of the Minyae. Minўae -ārum, m. the Argonauts.

mīrābilis -e, wonderful, astonishing; unusual.

mīrābilĭtĕr, adv. wonderfully, extraordinarily.

mīrābundus -a -um, full of wonder.

mīrācŭlum -i, n. wonder, prodigy, miracle.

mīrandus -a -um, p. adj., wonderful, singular.

mīrātĭo -ōnis, f. wonder, astonishment.

mīrātor -ōris, m. an admirer.

mīrē, adv. wonderfully.

mīrĭfĭcē, adv. wonderfully.

mīrĭfĭcus -a -um, wonderful, astonishing.

mirmillo (murmillo) -ōnis, m. a kind of gladiator.

mīror, 1. dep. to wonder, be astonished at; to admire.

mīrus -a -um, wonderful, extraordinary.

miscellānĕa -ōrum, n. hotchpotch, the food of gladiators.

miscĕo, miscŭi, mixtum, and mistum, 2. to mix, mingle; to blend; to unite; to stir up; to confuse; to fill, domum gemitu.

mĭsellus -a -um (dim. of miser), wretched, unhappy.

Mīsēnus -i, m. trumpeter of Aeneas. Mīsēnum -i, n. promontory and town in Campania.

miser -ĕra -ĕrum, wretched, unhappy.

misĕrābilis -e, wretched, deplorable; sad, plaintive.

misĕrābilĭtĕr, adv. miserably, pitiably; in a mournful manner.

misĕrandus -a -um, deplorable.

misĕrātĭo -ōnis, f. pity, compassion.

misĕrē, adv. wretchedly.

misĕrĕo -ŭi -ĭtum, 2. and misĕrĕor -ĭtus sum, 2. dep.; to pity, commiserate. Impers., miseret.

misĕresco, 3. to pity, commiserate.

misĕria -ae, f. unhappiness, affliction.

misĕricordia -ae, f. pity, compassion, mercy.

misĕricors -cordis, compassionate, tender-hearted.

misĕritus, v. misereor.

misĕrĭtĕr, adv. wretchedly, lamentably.

misĕror, 1. dep. to pity, lament.

missīcius (-tius) -a -um, discharged from military service (late).

missile -is, v. missilis.

missilis -e, missile; ferrum, a javelin.

Subst., gen. plur., missilia -ōrum, n. missiles.

missĭo -ōnis, f. a sending off, sending away; releasing; discharge; termination.

missĭto, 1. to send repeatedly.

missor -ōris, m. an archer.

1. missus -ūs, m. a sending; a throwing, shooting; in the public races, a course, heat.

2. missus -a -um, v. mitto.

mistim (mixtim), adv. confusedly.

mistūra (mixtūra) -ae, f. mixing, mixture.

mītĕ, adv. mildly, softly, gently.

mĭtella -ae, f. (dim. of mitra), bandage for the head, head-dress.

mĭtesco, 3. to become mild; to ripen; to subside; to become tame.

Mithrĭdātēs -is, m. king in Pontus, conquered by Pompeius. Adj., Mithrĭdāticus.

mītĭfĭco, 1. to make mild, soft; cibus mitificatus, well digested.

mītĭgātĭo -ōnis, f. alleviating, appeasing.

mītĭgo, 1. to make mild, soft; to make ripe; agros, to till; to soothe, pacify; alleviate, charm.

mītis -e, mild, gentle, ripe.

mitra -ae, f. a head-dress worn by women.

mitrātus -a -um, wearing the mitra.

mitto, mīsi, missum, 3. to send, let go; to send away; funera Teucris, to prepare; to dedicate a book to a person, librum ad aliquem; to conduct; to give forth; vocem pro aliquo, to speak for; to push, throw; medic., to let blood; to release; of orators, to cease speaking, pass over; mitto illud dicere, I pass over that; in the racecourse, to start the competitors; to dismiss, discharge.

mītŭlus (mŭtŭlus, mўtŭlus, mўtĭlus), -i, m. a species of edible mussel.

mixtūra, etc. = mistura (q.v.).

mna = mina (q.v.).

Mnĕmŏnĭdes -um, f. the Muses, daughters of Mnemosyne.

Mnĕmŏsўne ēs, f. Mnemosyne, mother of the Muses.

mnēmŏsўnum -i, n. a memorial.

mōbĭlis -e, easy to be moved; not firm, not fixed; excitable, pliable; changeable; rapid.

mōbĭlĭtas -ātis, f. mobility; changeableness; rapidity.

mōbĭlĭtĕr, adv. rapidly, with quick motion.

mōbĭlĭto, 1. to put into motion.

mŏdĕrābĭlis -e, moderate.

mŏdĕrāmen -ĭnis, n. a means of guiding (e.g. a rudder); rerum, government of the State.

mŏdĕrantĕr, adv. moderately, with moderation.

mŏdĕrātē, adv. moderately with moderation.

mŏdĕrātim, *adv.* moderately, gradually.

mŏdĕrātio -ōnis, *f.* moderating, restraining ; government ; moderation ; *vocis,* articulation.

mŏdĕrātor -ōris, *m.* governor, guide, manager, ruler.

mŏdĕrātrix -īcis, *f.* she that rules.

mŏdĕrātus -a -um, moderate, temperate.

mŏdĕro, 1. to moderate, keep within bounds (*late*).

mŏdĕror, 1. *dep.* to keep within bounds; to regulate, restrain ; to direct, guide; to govern.

mŏdestē, *adv.* moderately, discreetly.

mŏdestia -ae, *f.* moderation, temperance; modesty ; respect ; good judgment; mildness.

mŏdestus -a -um, temperate ; modest, unassuming ; virtuous.

mŏdĭcē, *adv.* moderately ; tolerably; temperately.

mŏdĭcus -a -um, moderate, middling, ordinary; temperate, modest.

mŏdĭfĭco, 1. to measure, moderate.

mŏdĭus -ii, *m.* a dry measure; a peck; *pleno modio,* abundantly.

mŏdŏ, *adv.* only, alone, but ; *non modo . . . sed,* not only . . . but; now, just now, just; lately, some time ago.

mŏdŭlātē, *adv.* in good time, in time (*of music*).

mŏdŭlātor -ōris, *m.* a musician.

mŏdŭlātus -a -um, *p. adj.,* in good time, rhythmical, melodious.

mŏdŭlor, 1. *dep.* to measure regularly; *of music,* to modulate; to sing; to play.

mŏdŭlus -i, *m.* (*dim. of modus*), a measure, standard of measurement.

mŏdus -i, *m.* a measure, standard of measurement; size, quantity, length; rhythm, melody ; limit, boundary; moderation, control; order, rule; manner, mode, way, method ; *servorum modo,* after the manner of slaves; *eius modi,* in that manner, of that kind.

moecha -ae, *f.* an adulteress.

moechor, 1. *dep.* to commit adultery.

moechus -i, *m.* adulterer.

moenĕra = *munera, v. munus.*

1. moenia -ium, *n.* the walls or fortifications of a city; defence; mansion, dwelling.

2. moenia -ium, *n.* = *munia (q.v.).*

moenio = *munio (q.v.).*

moenus = *munus (q.v.).*

moerus = *murus (q.v.).*

Moesi -ōrum, *m.* a people in Moesia, the modern Servia and Bulgaria.

moerĕo, moeror, moestus = *maereo, maeror, maestus (q.v.).*

mŏla -ae, *f. sing.* a millstone, *and in pl.* a mill *for grinding corn;* coarse meal, or flour.

mŏlāris -e, relating to a mill; belonging to grinding; *subst.,* **mŏlāris -is,** *m.* a

millstone; a huge block of stone; a molar tooth, grinder.

mōles -is, *f.* a mass, a heap. *Abstract* something heavy; *opposui molem clipei,* weighty shield ; might, power; difficulty. *Concr.,* a heavy, shapeless mass; a dam, mole; a large building; *moles belli,* large military machines, preparations for war, military works; a large number; a mass of clouds, storm.

mōlestē, *adv.* unwillingly, with annoyance ; *moleste fero,* I am annoyed, I am sorry; in a disagreeable manner; affectedly.

mōlestia -ae, *f.* annoyance, dissatisfaction, disgust; *sine molestia tua,* without trouble to yourself; affectation.

mōlestus -a -um, burdensome, annoying; *of discourse,* affected, laboured.

mōlīmen -inis, *n.* a great effort, undertaking; building.

mōlīmentum -i, *n.* exertion, endeavour.

mōlior, 4. *dep. transit.,* to set in motion, remove ; *ancoras,* to weigh anchor; *fulmina dextrā,* to hurl; *habenas,* to guide; to undermine; *fidem,* to undermine credit; to cultivate the earth; to build, raise; to undertake; to cause, produce; to plot, devise; to strive after. *Reflex.,* to toil, exert oneself.

mōlītio -ōnis, *f.* a demolition; an effort, preparation.

mōlītor -ōris, *m.* builder, producer, author.

mollesco, 3. to become soft; to become effeminate.

mollicellus -a -um, (*dim. of mollis*), somewhat soft, somewhat tender.

mollĭcŭlus -a -um (*dim. of mollis*), somewhat soft or tender; somewhat effeminate.

mollio, 4. to make pliable, supple ; *lanam trahendo,* to spin; *glebas,* to loosen; to soften, to make milder; *vocem,* make womanish; to make less disagreeable, *poenam;* to tame, restrain.

mollipes -pĕdis, soft-footed, *i.e.* having a trailing walk.

mollis -e, soft, tender, pliant, yielding; *arcus,* unstrung ; *zephyri,* gentle ; graceful; *of places,* with a gentle ascent; soft to the touch; mild, *aestas;* gentle, sensitive, effeminate; pleasant; compassionate, easy; tender, moving, *illud mollissimum carmen.*

mollĭtĕr, *adv.* softly, easily, gently ; effeminately; mildly.

mollĭtia -ae, *f. and* **mollĭties -ēi,** *f.* softness, tenderness, flexibility; gentleness, mildness; effeminacy.

mollĭtūdo -inis, *f.* softness, flexibility; tenderness.

mŏlo -ŭi -ĭtum, 3. to grind in a mill; **mŏlĭtus -a -um,** ground.

Mŏlossi -ōrum, *m.* the inhabitants of Molossia, a district of Eastern Epirus;

subst., **Mŏlossus** -i, *m.* a Molossian hound.

mŏly -ўos, *n.* the herb moly

mōmen -ĭnis, *n.* motion; momentum, impulse.

mōmentum -i, *n.* movement, motion; *of time*, minute, moment; change, alteration; *impulse*; influence, cause; turning-point; importance.

Mŏna -ae, *f.* Anglesea *or* the Isle of Man.

Mŏnaeses -is, *m.* a general of the Parthians.

mŏnēdŭla -ae, *f.* a daw, jackdaw.

mŏnĕo -ŭi -ĭtum, 2. to remind; to warn; to advise, recommend; to instruct, suggest.

mŏnēris -is, *f.* a vessel having only one bank of oars.

Mŏnēta -ae, *f.* 1. the mother of the Muses; 2. a surname of Juno; 3. the mint; money; die *or* stamp.

mŏnētālis -e, *m.* relating to the mint.

mŏnīle -is, *n.* a necklace, a collar.

mŏnīmentum = *monumentum (q.v.).*

mŏnĭta -ōrum, *n.* warning; prophecies.

mŏnĭtĭo -ōnis, *f.* a reminding, warning.

mŏnĭtor -ōris, *m.* an assistant, prompter; adviser, instructor.

mŏnĭtus -ūs, *m.* a warning, admonition.

mŏnŏgrammos only in *m.* of pictures, sketched; shadowy.

mŏnŏpŏdĭum -ĭi, *n.* table with one foot.

mŏnŏpōlĭum -ĭi, *n.* a monopoly.

mons, montis, *m.* a mountain.

monstrātor -ōris, *m.* a discoverer, teacher.

monstrĭfĕr -fĕra -fĕrum, horrible, monstrous.

monstro -i, to show, teach, inform; to ordain, appoint; to denounce.

monstrum -i, *n.* a prodigy, portent; a monster; a wonder *or* marvel.

monstrŭōsē, *adv.* strangely, wonderfully, monstrously.

monstrŭōsus -a -um, strange, wonderful, monstrous.

montānus -a -um, mountainous, relating to a mountain, dwelling on mountains; *subst.*, **montānus** -i, *m.* a mountaineer; **montāna** -ōrum, *n.* mountainous districts.

montĭcŏla -ae, *c.* mountaineer.

montĭvăgus -a -um, wandering over the mountains.

montŭōsus -a -um, mountainous.

mŏnŭmentum (**mŏnĭmentum**) -i, *n.* a memorial, monument; a building; *monumenta Africani*, statues; sepulchre; annals, memoirs.

Mopsus -i, *m.* the seer of the Argonauts.

1. **mŏra** -ae, *f.* delay; *sine mora*, without delay; a pause; hindrance.

2. **mŏra** -ae, *f.* division of the Spartan army.

mŏrālis -e, moral, ethical.

mŏrātor -ōris, *m.* a loiterer; a delayer; an advocate who talked against time.

1. **mŏrātus**, *partic. of moror.*

2. **mŏrātus** -a -um, having certain manners *or* morals; characteristic.

morbĭdus -a -um, diseased, unwholesome.

morbōsus -a -um, diseased, worn out.

morbus -i, *m.* disease, sickness; *in morbo esse*, to be sick.

mordācĭtĕr, *adv.* bitingly, sharply

mordax -ācis, biting, snappish; satirical; corroding; *sollicitudines*, "eating cares"; stinging; sharp; biting in taste.

mordĕo, **mŏmordi**, **morsum**, 2. to bite, eat; sting, pain; to take fast hold of; *of rivers*, to indent, wear away; to nip, sting

mordĭcĭtus = *mordicus (q.v.).*

mordĭcus, *adv.* with the teeth, by biting.

mŏrētum -i, *n.* a rustic salad.

mŏrĭbundus -a -um, dying; mortal; *act.*, deadly.

mŏrĭgĕror, 1. *dep.* to comply with, gratify.

mŏrĭgĕrus -a -um, compliant, accommodating.

Mŏrīni -ōrum, *m.* people in Gallia Belgica.

mŏrĭor, **mortŭus sum**, **mŏrĭtūrus**, 3. *dep.* to die; to decay; *of fire*, to be extinguished; to lose strength; to perish; *adj.*, **mortŭus** -a -um, dead; *subst.*, **mortŭus** -i, *m.* a dead man.

mormyr -ўris, *f.* a sea-fish.

1. **mŏror**, 1. *dep.* to linger, loiter, delay; to stay; to detain, hinder; *nihil morari*, to care nothing for.

2. **mŏror**, 1. *dep.* to be foolish.

mŏrōsē, *adv.* peevishly.

mŏrōsĭtas -ātis, *f.* peevishness, moroseness, pedantry.

mŏrōsus -a -um, peevish, fretful.

Morphĕus -ĕi *and* -ĕos, *m.* god of dreams.

mors, mortis, *f.* death.

morsus -ūs, *m.* a bite, biting; pungency. *Fig.* attack with words; vexation.

mortālĭs -e, mortal; transitory, temporary; human. *Subst.*, **mortālis** -is, *m.* a man; *plur.*, mortals. *Subst.*, **mortālia** -ĭum, *n.* mortal affairs.

mortālĭtas -ātis, *f.* liability to death, mortality, death.

mortārĭum -ĭi, *n.* a mortar; a drug.

mortĭfĕr -fĕra -fĕrum, fatal, deadly.

mortŭus -a -um, *partic. of morior (q.v.).*

mōrum -i, *n.* a mulberry; a blackberry.

mōrus -i, *f.* a mulberry-tree.

mos, mōris, *m.* custom; quality, nature; *plur.*, manners, character, disposition, morals.

Mōsa -ae, *f.* a river, *now* the Meuse.

Mōsella -ae, *f.* a river, *now* the Moselle.

mōtĭo -ōnis *f.* movement; emotion, feeling.

mōto, 1. to move up and down, move frequently.

1. **mōtus -a -um,** *partic. of moveo.*

2. **mōtus -ūs,** *m.* a motion, movement; *terrae,* an earthquake; motion of the mind; insurrection; revolution.

mŏvĕo, mōvi, mōtum, 2. to move, set in motion, stir; *movere arma,* to take up arms; to affect; to influence; to be disturbed; to induce; *politically,* to arouse, excite; to shake; to cause; to bring to notice; to begin; to remove; to dispossess, *aliquem ex agro;* to expel.

mox, *adv.* soon, presently; then, thereupon.

mūcidus -a -um, mouldy, musty.

Mūcius -ii, *m.* name of a Roman gens. *Adj.,* **Mūciānus.**

mūcro -ōnis, *m.* sharp point *or* edge; a sword's point *or* edge; the sword; sharpness.

mūcus -i, *m.* the mucous matter of the nose.

mūgil (mūgilis) -is, *m.* a fish.

mūginor, 1. *dep.* to loiter, dally.

mūgĭo -īvi and ii -ītum, 4. to bellow as an ox, low; to roar, groan. *Subst.,* *mugientes* = oxen.

mūgītus -ūs, *m.* the lowing, bellowing of cattle; a rumbling.

mūla -ae, *f.* a she-mule.

mulcĕo, mulsi, mulsum, 2. to stroke; to charm, delight; to soothe; *vulnera,* to allay pain.

Mulcĭbĕr -ĕris and -ĕri, *m.* surname of Vulcan; fire.

mulco, 1. to thrash, handle roughly.

mulcta, mulcto = *multa, multo (q.v.).*

mulctra -ae, *f.* a milk-pail.

mulctrārium -ii, *n.* a milk-pail.

mulctrum -i, *n.* a milk-pail.

mulgĕo, mulsi, mulctum, 2. to milk.

mŭliĕbris -e, womanly, feminine; *certamen,* on account of a woman; unmanly.

mŭliĕbrĭtĕr, *adv.* after the manner of a woman, effeminately.

mŭlier -ĕris, *f.* a woman; wife, matron.

mŭliĕrārius -a -um, womanish.

mŭliercŭla -ae, *f.* (*dim. of mulier*), a little woman, *contemptuously.*

mŭliĕrōsĭtas -ātis, *f.* excessive love of women.

mŭliĕrōsus -a -um, fond of women.

mūlīnus -a -um, relating to a mule.

mūlĭo -ōnis, *m.* a mule-keeper *or* driver.

mūliōnius and (later) mūliōnicus -a -um, relating to a muleteer.

mullus -i, *m.* the red mullet.

mulsus -a -um, mixed with honey. *Subst.,* **mulsum -i,** *n.* wine sweetened with honey.

multa (mulcta) -ae, *f.* a punishment consisting in loss of property; money-fine.

multangŭlus -a -um, many-cornered.

multātīcius -a -um, relating to a fine.

multātĭo -ōnis, *f.* penalty, fine.

multēsĭmus -a -um, very small.

multicāvus -a -um, porous.

multīcia -ōrum, *n.* soft, finely-woven garments.

multĭfārĭam, *adv.* on many sides, in many places.

multĭfĭdus -a -um, cloven into many parts; *Ister,* having many branches.

multĭformis -e, having many shapes, manifold, of many kinds.

multĭfŏrus -a -um, pierced with many holes.

multĭgĕnus -a -um, of many kinds.

multĭiŭgus -a -um and multiiŭgis -e, yoked many together; manifold, of many sorts.

multĭmŏdīs, *adv.* in many ways.

multĭmŏdus -a -um, various, manifold.

multĭplex -plĭcis, having many folds; having many parts; manifold, numerous, of many different kinds; versatile.

multĭplĭcābĭlis -e, having many folds.

multĭplĭco, 1. to increase, multiply.

multĭtūdo -ĭnis, *f.* a large number, multitude; a crowd; the mob.

multĭvŏlus -a -um, having many desires.

1. **multo (mulcto),** 1. to punish; *pecuniā,* to punish with a fine.

2. **multo, multum,** *used adv.,* *v. multus.*

multus -a -um; *comp.,* **plūs, plūris;** *superl.,* **plūrĭmus -a -um,** much; *number,* many; *ne mults,* briefly, in brief; *compar.,* **plures,** several; *ad multum diem,* till late in the day; **multum,** *compar.,* **plūs,** *superl.,* **plūrĭmum,** much, a great part. *Subst.,* *ad multum diei,* till far into the day. *Adv.,* **multo,** by far; *non multo post,* not long after; **multum;** *of degree,* much, very.

mūlus -i, *m.* a mule.

Mulvius -a -um; *pons,* a bridge across the Tiber.

Mummius -a -um, name of a Roman gens, the most famous member of which was *L. Mummius Achaicus,* the destroyer of Corinth.

Munda -ae, *f.* town in Hispania Baetica, scene of a victory of Julius Caesar over the sons of Pompeius, 45 B.C.

mundānus -a -um, relating to the world, mundane. *Subst.,* **mundānus -i,** *m.* a citizen of the world.

munditia -ae, *f. and* **mundĭties -ēi,** *f.* cleanness; elegance; neatness.

mundo, 1. to cleanse, purify.

1. **mundus -a -um,** clean, neat, elegant; refined.

2. **mundus -i,** *m.* ornament; the universe; the heavens; the earth.

mūnĕro, 1. to give, present.

mūnĕror, 1. *dep.* to present.

mūnĭa -ĭum, *n.* duties, functions.

mūnĭceps -ĭpis, *c.* the citizen of a *municipium.*

mūnĭcĭpālis -e, municipal; provincial.

mūnĭcĭpĭum -ĭi, *n.* municipal town.

mūnificē, *adv.* bountifully.

mūnificentia -ae, *f.* munificence.

mūnifico, 1. to present, to give.

mūnificus -a -um, munificent, liberal.

mūnimen -inis, *n.* defence, fortification.

mūnimentum -i, *n.* fortification, defence.

mūnio (moenio) -īvi *and* -ii ītum, 4. to build; to build a wall, to fortify; to defend; to secure; to make a road.

mūnitio -ōnis, fortifying, entrenching; a fortification; a making passable, paving of roads; *munitio fluminum*, bridging over.

mūnito, 1. to pave, make passable.

mūnitor -ōris, *m.* builder of fortifications, military engineer.

mūnitus -a -um, *p. adj.*, fortified, secured.

mūnus -ĕris, *n.* an office, function, employment, duty; *reipublicae*, a public office; *officii*, the performance of a duty; a service, favour; funeral honours; a gift; a sacrifice; a public show.

mūnusculum -i, *n.* (*dim. of munus*), a small gift, little present.

mūraena = *murena* (*q.v.*).

mūrālis -e, *of or* relating to a wall, mural; *corona*, the crown given to the one who first ascended the wall of a besieged city.

1. **mūrēna (mūraena)** -ae, *f.* a sea-fish.

2. **Mūrēna** -ae, *m.* a cognomen belonging to the gens Licinia.

mūrex -icis, *m.* the purple-fish; purple dye; an edible shell-fish.

murmillo = *mirmillo* (*q.v.*).

mūria -ae, *f.* brine, pickle.

murmur -ūris, *n.* a murmur, a humming, buzzing, roaring; *of the sound of wind-instruments, cornuum*.

murmuro, 1. to murmur, make a humming, growling noise.

1. **murrha (murra)** = 1. *myrrha* (*q.v.*).

2. **murrha (murra, myrrha)** -ae, *f.* a material out of which goblets were made, *supposed to be fluor spar*; *poet.* the goblets themselves.

1. **murrhĕus (murrĕus)** = 1. *myrrheus* (*q.v.*).

2. **murrhĕus (murrĕus, myrrhĕus)** = -um, made of fluor spar.

1. **murrhinus (murrinus)** = 1. *myrrhinus* (*q.v.*).

2. **murrhinus (murrinus, myrrhinus)** -a -um, made of *or* relating to murrha.

murt . . . *v. myrt . . .*

mūrus -i, *m.* a wall; protection, defence.

mūs, mūris, *c.* a mouse.

Mūsa -ae, *f.* a muse, goddess of music, poetry, *etc.*

mūsaeus -a -um, poetical, musical.

musca -ae, *f.* a fly.

muscārium -ii, *n.* a fly-flap, fly-brush.

muscipula -ae, *f. and* **muscipulum** -i, *n.* a mouse-trap.

muscōsus -a -um, covered with moss, mossy.

musculus -i, *m.* (*dim. of mus*), a little

mouse; *milit.*, a shed, mantelet; species of whale.

muscus -i, *m.* moss.

mūsēus -a -um = *musaeus* (*q.v.*).

mūsica -ae, *f. and* **mūsicē** -ēs, *f.* music.

mūsicē -ēs, *f.* = *musica* (*q.v.*).

mūsicus -a -um, musical; poetical; *leges*, rules of music. *Subst.*, **mūsicus** -i, *m.* a musician; **mūsica -ōrum**, *n.* music.

mussito, 1. to murmur to oneself.

musso, 1. to murmur, mutter, whisper to oneself; to hum, buzz.

mustācĕum (mustācium) -i, *n. and* **mustācĕus (mustācius)** -i, *m.* a must-cake.

mustēla (mustella) -ae, *f.* (*dim. of mus*), a weasel.

mustēlīnus (mustellīnus) -a -um, relating to a weasel.

mustum -i, *n.*, *v. mustus.*

mustus -a -um, young, new, fresh. *Subst.*, **mustum** -i, *n.* new wine, must.

Mūta -ae, *f.* a nymph, whom Jupiter made dumb because of her loquacity.

mūtābilis -e, changeable, inconstant.

mūtābilitas -ātis, *f.* changeableness.

mūtātio -ōnis, change; exchange.

mūtilo, 1. to mutilate, cut off; diminish.

mūtilus -a -um, maimed, mutilated.

Mūtina -ae, *f.* now Modena.

mūtio (muttio), 4. to mutter, murmur.

mūto, 1. to move away, remove; to alter; *mutari alite*, to be changed into a bird; to dye; *vinum mutatum*, spoiled, soured; *to exchange*; *mutata verba*, used metaphorically.

mūtuātio -ōnis, *f.* a borrowing.

mūtuē, *adv.* mutually, reciprocally.

mūtuo, *adv.* mutually, reciprocally.

mūtuor, 1. *dep.* to borrow.

mūtus -a -um, dumb; silent; still, quiet, *forum*.

mūtuus -a -um, borrowed, lent; *pecuniam dare mutuam*, to lend; (*subst.*, **mūtuum** -i, *n.* a loan); mutual, reciprocal; (*subst.*, **mūtuum** -i, *n.* reciprocity).

Mȳcēnae -ārum, *f.*, *and* **Mȳcēna** -ae, *f.*, *and* **Mȳcēnē** -ēs, *f.* a city in Argolis of which Agamemnon was king; *adj.*, **Mȳcēnaeus.**

myŏparo -ōnis, *m.* a small piratica skiff.

myrīcē -ēs, *f.*, *and* **myrīca** -ae, *f.* the tamarisk.

Myrmidōnes -um, *m.* the Myrmidons, a people under the rule of Achilles.

myrmillo = *mirmillo* (*q.v.*).

1. **myrrha (murrha, murra)** -ae, *f.* the myrrh-tree; myrrh.

2. **myrrha** = 2. *murrha* (*q.v.*).

3. **Myrrha -ae**, *f.* a maiden, changed into a myrrh-tree.

1. **myrrhĕus (murrhĕus, murrĕus)** -a -um, perfumed *or* anointed with myrrh; myrrh-coloured, yellow.

1. **myrrhinus** (**murrhinus**, **murrinus**), of myrrh.

2. **myrrhinus** = 2. *murrhinus*.

myrtētum (**murtētum**) -i, *n.* a thicket of myrtle-trees.

myrtěus (**murtěus**) -a -um, relating to the myrtle; myrtle-coloured.

myrtum -i, *n.* the myrtle-berry.

myrtus -i *and* -ūs, *f.* the myrtle, myrtle-tree.

mystăgōgus -i, *m.* a priest *or* attendant who showed the temple to strangers.

mystērium -ii, *n. sing.*, a secret, secret science ; *plur.*, **mystēria** -ōrum, *n.* mysteries *or* secret rites; secrets, mysteries (*of an art*).

mystes -ae, *m.* a priest at the mysteries.

mysticus -a -um, relating to the mysteries, secret, mystic.

Mÿtilēnae -ārum, *f. and* **Mÿtilēnē** -ēs, *f.* capital of the island of Lesbos.

mÿtilus = *mitulus* (*q.v.*).

N

N **n**, *the thirteenth letter of the Latin Alphabet.*

nablium (**naulium**) -ii *and* **nablum** -i, *n.* a kind of harp *or* lyre.

nae = 1. *ne* (*q.v.*).

naenia = *nenia* (*q.v.*).

Naevius, *Cn. Naevius*, Roman dramatic and epic poet.

naevus -i, *m.* a mole on the body.

Nāīās -ădis *and* **Nāīs** -idis (-ĭdos), *acc. plur.* -idas, *f.* a water-nymph, Naiad. *Adj.*, **Nāīcus.**

nam, *conj.* for.

namque, *conj.*, more emphatic form of *nam.*

nanciscor, nactus *and* **nanctus sum**, 3. *dep.* to get, obtain, meet; to find, fall

nānus -i, *m.* a dwarf.

năpaeus -a -um, relating to the forest; *subst.*, **năpaeae** -ārum, *f.* wood-nymphs.

Narbo -ōnis, *m.* town n Gallia Narbonensis.

narcissus -i, *m.* the narcissus, daffodil. Narcissus, a youth changed into the flower.

nardus -i, *f. and* **nardum** -i, *n.* nard.

nāris -is, *f. plur.*, **nāres** -ĭum, *f.* the nostrils; the nose.

narrābilis -e, that can be narrated.

narrātio -ōnis, *f.* relating, narration.

narrātor -ōris, *m.* a narrator.

narrātus -ūs, *m.* narration, narrative.

narro, 1. to relate; to say, tell.

narthēcium -ii, *n.* a case for perfumes and medicines.

narus = *gnarus* (*q.v.*).

nascor (**gnascor**), **nātus sum**, 3. *dep.* to be born; to descend from, spring from.

Nāsīca -ae, *m.* name of a family of the Scipios.

Nāso -ōnis, *m.* cognomen of the poet *P. Ovidius.*

nassa (**naxa**) -ae, *f.* basket for catching fish; *fig.* a trap.

nasturcium (**nastrium**) -ii, *n.* a kind of cress.

nāsus -i, *m.* the nose; *aliquem naso suspendere adunco*, to turn up the nose at, ridicule.

nāsūtus -a -um, having a large nose; acute, sagacious.

nāta -ae, *f.* a daughter.

nātālicius -a -um, relating to birth. *Subst.*, **nātālicia** -ōrum, *n.* a birthday festival.

nātālis -e, relating to birth, natal. *Subst.*, **nātālis** -is, *m.* a birth-place; a birthday ; *plur.* **nātāles** -ium, *m.* birth, origin.

nătans -antis, swimming.

nătātio -ōnis, *f.* swimming.

nătātor -ōris, *m.* a swimmer.

nătes, *v. natis.*

nātio -ōnis, *f.* a being born, birth; nation, people; race.

nătis -is, *f.*, *usually plur.*, **nătes** -ium, *f.* the rump, buttocks.

nātīvus -a -um, born, come into existence by birth; innate, natural.

năto, 1. to swim; *natat uncta carina*, floats ; to stream, spread abroad ; to be insecure; to be full of, overflow; *of the eyes*, to swim, to be glassy.

nātrix -icis, *f.* a water-snake.

nātūra -ae, *f.* birth; nature; character; laws of nature; nature, possibility; *in rerum natura fuisse*, to be possible; the world, creation; an element, essence.

nātūrālis -e, natural; relating to nature.

nātūrālitĕr, *adv.* naturally.

1. **nātus** -a -um, *p. adj.*, born; born for; *pro re nata*, as things are now; *annos prope XC natus*, almost ninety years old. *Subst.*, **nātus** -i, *m.* a son; **nāta** -ae, *f.* a daughter.

2. **nātus** -ū, *m.* (*only in the abl. sing.*), birth ; *maior natu*, older ; *natu minimus*, the youngest.

nauarchus -i, *m.* captain of a ship.

nauci, *v. naucum.*

naucum -i, *n.*, *lit.*, a nutshell, *fig.*, a trifle ; *non nauci habere*, to esteem lightly.

naufrăgium -ii, *n.* a shipwreck; wreckage; *naufragium facere*, to suffer shipwreck; misfortune, ruin; *tabula ex naufragio*, literally, a plank from a shipwreck, a means of safety.

naufrăgus -a -um, that has suffered shipwreck ; *poet.* causing shipwreck, *mare.*

naulium = *nablium* (*q.v.*).

naulum -i, *n.* fare, passage-money.

naumăchia -ae, *f.* a naval battle exhibited

as a spectacle; the place in which the spectacle was exhibited.

naumăchiārius -a -um, relating to a mock sea-fight; *subst.*, **naumăchiārius -i**, *m.* one who fought in a mock sea-fight.

Naupactus (-ŏs) -i, *f.* sea-port on the Gulf of Corinth.

nausĕa (nausia) -ĕe, *f.* sea-sickness; sickness.

nauscŏ (nausio) 1. to be sea-sick; to be sick.

nausĕŏla (nausĭŏla) -ae, *f.* (*dim. of nausea*), a slight squeamishness.

nauta -ae, *m.* a sailor, mariner.

nauticus -a -um, nautical, naval; *subst.*, **nautici -ōrum**, *m.* sailors.

nŭvālis -e, *adj.*, naval, nautical; *pedes navales*, galley-slaves; *subst.*, **năvāle -is**, *n.* a station for ships; **năvālia -lum**, *n.* a dockyard; materials for ship-building.

năvarchus = *nauarchus (q.v.).*

năvē = *naviter (q.v.).*

năvicŭla -ae, *f.* (*dim. of navis*), a little ship, skiff.

năvicŭlārius -a -um, relating to small ships, boats; **năvicŭlāria -ae**, *f.* the business of a shipowner; **năvicŭlārius -ii**, *m.* a shipowner.

năvifrăgus -a -um, causing shipwreck.

năvigābilis -e, navigable.

năvigātio -ōnis, *f.* a sailing, voyage.

năviger -ğēra -ğērum, navigable.

năvigĭŏlum -i, *n.* (*dim. of navigium*), a little ship, a bark.

năvigium -ii, *n.* a sailing, navigating; a vessel.

năvigo, 1. to sail, voyage; to sail over, navigate.

năvis -is, *f.* a ship, vessel; *navis longa*, a man-of-war; *oneraria*, transport-ship; *praetoria*, flagship; *constrata*, decked.

năvita = *nauta (q.v.).*

năvitas (gnāvitas) -ātis, *f.* assiduity, zeal.

năvitĕr, *adv.* zealously, actively; entirely, quite.

năvo, 1. to do anything zealously, diligently.

năvus (gnāvus) -a -um, active, diligent.

naxa -ae, *f.* = *nassa (q.v.).*

Naxus (-ŏs) -i, *f.* an island of the Aegean Sea, the largest of the Cyclades.

1. nē (nae), *adv.* yes, verily, truly.

2. nē, *adv.* not; *ne . . . quidem*, not even; *conj.* = that not.

3. nē, *interrog. and enclitic particle.*

Nĕăpŏlis -pŏlis, *acc.* -pŏlim, *f.* 1. part of Syracuse; 2. a seaport, *now* Naples. *Adj.*, **Nĕăpŏlĭtānus.**

nĕbŭla -ae, *f.* exhalation, fog, mist; cloud, smoke.

nĕbŭlo -ōnis, *m.* a good-for-nothing fellow.

nĕbŭlōsus -a -um, misty, cloudy, dark.

nĕc *and* **nĕquĕ**, *negative particles;* and not ; *nec . . . nec*, *or* *neque . . . neque*, neither . . . nor.

necdum, *adv.* and not yet.

nĕcessāriē, *adv.* necessarily, unavoidably.

nĕcessăriō, *adv.* necessarily, unavoidably.

nĕcessārius -a -um, necessary, unavoidable; *res*, necessity; closely connected; *subst.*, **nĕcessārius -ii**, *m.*, **-a -ae**, *f.*, intimate friend, near relation.

nĕcessĕ, *adj. n. only with esse and habere*, necessary, unavoidable; *necesse habere*, to be obliged.

nĕcessĭtas -ātis, *f.* that which is inevitable, fate, poverty; friendship, relationship; *necessitates*, necessaries, necessary expenses.

nĕcessitūdo -inis, *f.* necessity, inevitableness; relationship, intimate friendship; *plur.*, intimate friends, near relations.

nĕcessum est = *necesse est*, it is necessary.

necnĕ, or not (*in indirect questions*).

nĕco, 1. to kill, slay (*usually by hunger, etc.*).

nĕcŏpīnans -antis, not expecting, unaware.

nĕcŏpīnātō, *adv.* unexpectedly.

nĕcŏpīnātus -a -um, unexpected; *ex necopinato*, unexpectedly.

nĕcŏpīnus -a -um, *pass.*, unexpected; *act.*, not expecting, careless.

nectar -ăris, *n.* nectar, the drink of the gods.

nectărĕus -a -um, sweet as nectar.

necto, nexŭi *and* **nexi, nexum, 3.** to tie, fasten, weave together; to fetter; to affix, attach.

nēcŭbi, *adv.* lest anywhere.

nēcundĕ, *adv.* lest from any quarter.

nēdum, *adv.* much less, still less, to say nothing of; *nedum his temporibus*, much less at present; much more, *nedum in bello.*

nĕfandus -a -um, impious, abominable.

nĕfāriē, *adv.* impiously, abominably.

nĕfārius -a -um, impious, abominable; *subst.*, **nĕfārius -ii**, *m.* a wicked person; **nĕfārium -ii**, *n.* an abominable action.

nĕfas, *n. indecl.*, that which is sinful, unlawful, wrong, a sin, crime; *per fas et nefas*, by fair means or foul; *as an interjection*, shocking, dreadful! *heu nefas!*

nĕfastus -a -um, forbidden, unholy; *dies nefasti*, on which no legal or public business could be transacted; unlucky, inauspicious; *of action*, forbidden, sinful.

nĕgantia -ae, *f.* a denying.

nĕgātio -ōnis, *f.* a denying.

nĕglito, 1. to persist in denying.

neglectio -ōnis, *f.* neglect.

1. **neglectus** -a -um, *p. adj.* neglected, disregarded.

2. **neglectus** -ūs, *m.* neglect, disregard.

neglĕg . . . *v. neglig* . . .

negligens -entis, *p. adj.* negligent, indifferent; *with genit., amicorum;* extravagant.

negligentĕr, *adv.* carelessly.

negligentia -ae, *f.* carelessness, negligence; neglect.

negligo (neglĕgo, neclĕgo) -lexi -lectum, 3. to neglect, disregard; to pay no heed to; to overlook.

nĕgo, 1. to say no; to deny; to refuse.

nĕgōtiālis -e, relating to business.

nĕgōtians -antis, *m.* wholesale dealer, merchant, banker.

nĕgōtiātio -ōnis, *f.* wholesale business, banker's business.

nĕgōtiātor -ōris, *m.* wholesale dealer, merchant, banker.

nĕgōtiŏlum -i, *n.* (*dim. of negotium*), a small transaction.

nĕgōtior, 1. *dep.* to carry on business; to trade.

nĕgōtiōsus -a -um, full of business, busy.

nĕgōtium -ii, *n.* absence of leisure, occupation; public business; management of a household.

Nĕmĕa -ae, *f.,* and **Nĕmĕē** -ēs, *f.* a city of Argolis; *subst.,* **Nĕmea -ōrum,** *n.* the Nemean games.

Nĕmĕsis -is *and* -ios, *f.* the goddess of justice and equity who punished pride and arrogance.

nĕmo -inis, *c.* no one, nobody; *nemo non,* every one; *non nemo,* many a one.

nĕmōrālis -e, relating to woods *or* groves, sylvan.

nĕmōrensis -e, belonging to a grove *or* wood.

nĕmōricultrix -icis, *f.* inhabitant of the woods.

nĕmōrivăgus -a -um, wandering in the woods.

nĕmōrōsus -a -um, woody; full of foliage.

nempĕ, *conj.* forsooth, certainly, to be sure, namely.

nĕmus -ŏris, *n.* a grove, forest

nēnia (naenia) -ae, *f.* a funeral song, dirge; incantation; nursery song, lullaby.

nĕo, nēvi, nētum, 2. to spin; to interweave.

nĕpa -ae, *f.* a scorpion

Nēphĕlē, -ēs, *f.* wife of Athamas, mother of Phrixus and Helle.

1. **nĕpos** -ōtis, *m. and f.* a grandson; a nephew; a descendant; a spendthrift

2. **Nĕpos** -pōtis, *m., C. Cornelius,* a Roman historian, friend of Atticus, Cicero, and Catullus

neptis -is, *f.* a grand-daughter.

Neptūnus -i, *m.* Neptune, god of the sea; *adj.,* **Neptūnius.**

nēquam, *adi. indecl.,* compar. **nēquior,** *superl.* **nēquissimus,** worthless, wicked.

nēquāquam, *adv.* by no means, in no wise.

nēquĕ = *nec (q.v.).*

nēquĕdum (necdum), *adv.* and not yet.

nēquĕo -īvi *and* -ii -ītum, 4. to be unable.

nēquiquam (nēquicquam, nēquidquam), *adv.* in vain.

nēquitĕr, *adv.* worthlessly, badly, miserably.

nēquitia -ae, *f. and* **nēquities** (*no genit. or dat.*), *f.* worthlessness, laziness, extravagance; profligacy; wickedness.

Nēreus -ĕos *and* -ĕi, *m.* a sea-god.

Nĕro -ōnis, *m. C. Claudius Nero,* fifth Roman emperor.

Nervii -ōrum, *m.* warlike people in Gallia Belgica; *adj.,* **Nervicus.**

nervōsē, *adv.* vigorously, energetically.

nervōsus -a -um, sinewy, nervous; *of discourse,* vigorous.

nervŭlus -i, *m.* (*dim. of nervus*), nerve, strength.

nervus -i, *m.* a sinew, nerve (*gen. plur.*); string of a musical instrument; a bowstring; the leather with which shields are covered; a strap *or* thong, fetters, prison, imprisonment; strength, effort; *of discourse,* vigour.

nescio -īvi *and* -ii -ītum, 4. not to know, to be ignorant of; *nescio qui, nescio quis,* somebody or other; not to recognise; not to understand, not to have learnt.

nescius -a -m, ignorant, unaware; unable to do anything; *pass.,* unknown.

Nestor -ōris, *m.* king of Pylus, the oldest of the Greek heroes before Troy.

neu = *neve (q.v.).*

neuter -tra -trum, neither of two; *nomina neutra,* neuter nouns.

neutiquam, *adv.* by no means, not at all.

neutrō, *adv.* in neither direction.

nēvĕ *or* **neu,** *adv.* and not, or not, nor (*introduces a negative clause of purpose, command, or prohibition, after a clause of a similar kind*); *sometimes repeated,* neither . . . nor.

nex, nĕcis, *f.* violent death, murder; *necem sibi consciscere,* to commit suicide; blood of the person slain (*poet.*).

nexilis -e, bound together.

nexo, 1. to bind together.

nexum -i, *n.* a formal transaction by which the debtor pledged his liberty as security for his debt.

nexus -ūs, *m.* a binding together, connecting; the obligation arising from *nexum.*

nĭ, *adv. and conj.* = *ne in sentences with the subj., ni teneant cursus; quid ni?* why not? = *si non,* if not, unless.

nĭcaeus -a -um, epithet of Jupiter.

nĭcātor -ōris, *acc. plur.* -ōras, *m.* epithet given to soldiers of the body-guard of Perseus, king of Macedonia.

nĭcētērĭum -ii, *n.* reward of victory, prize.

nĭcto, 1. *and* nictor, 1. *dep.* to wink, blink, *of lamps, etc.* to flicker, glimmer.

nīdŭlus -i, *m.* (*dim. of nidus*), a little nest.

nīdus -i, *m.* a nest.

nĭger -gra -grum, black, dark-coloured: making black, unlucky; *subst.,* nigrum -i, *n.* a black spot.

nĭgrans -antis, *p. adj.,* black, dark-coloured.

nĭgresco -grŭi, 3. to become black, grow dark.

nĭgro, 1 .to be black.

nĭgror -ōris, *m.* blackness.

nihil *and contr.* nil, *n. indecl.* nothing; nihil non, everything; non nihil, something.

nihildum, *conj.* nothing as yet.

nihilōminus, *v. nihilum.*

nihilum -i, *n.* nothing; *adv.,* in no way; nihilominus = nevertheless.

nil = nihil (*q.v.*).

nilum = nihilum (*q.v.*).

Nīlus -i, *m.* the river Nile; *adj.,* Nīliăcus; Nīligĕna -ae, *m.* born on the Nile, an Egyptian.

nimbĭfer -fĕra -fĕrum, stormy.

nimbōsus -a -um, rainy, stormy.

nimbus -i, *m.* a storm of rain, violent shower; a cloud; mist.

nimĭo, *v. nimius.*

nimīrum, *adv.* undoubtedly, doubtless; *ironically,* doubtless, forsooth.

nĭmis, *adv.* too much, excessively.

nimĭum, *v. nimius.*

nimĭus -a -um, too much, excessive; intemperate; too powerful; very large; *subst.,* excess, too much; *adv.,* nimio, by far, exceedingly; nimium, too, too much.

ningo (ninguo), ninxi (*gen. impers.*), 3. to snow; *ningit,* it snows.

ninguis -is, *f.* snow.

Nĭŏbē -ēs, *f. and* Nĭŏba -ae, *f.* daughter of Tantalus, wife of Amphion.

Nīreus -ĕi *and* -ĕos, *acc.* Nīrĕa, *m.* next to Achilles the most beautiful of all the Greek heroes at the siege of Troy.

nĭsi, *conj.* if not; *after negatives and questions,* except, unless ; *nisi quod,* except that.

1. nīsus (nixus) -ūs, *m.* a pressing or resting upon ; an ascent ; flight ; exertion, labour, effort; a giving birth.

2. nīsus -a -um, *v.* 1. *nitor.*

nĭtēdŭla -ae, *f.* field-mouse.

nĭtella = nitedula (*q.v.*).

1. nĭtens -entis, *p. adj.* shining; *taurus,* sleek ; bright, beautiful, blooming ; brilliant.

2. nĭtens -entis, *partic. of nitor*

nĭtĕo -ŭi, 2. to shine, be bright; to be brilliant; to be sleek, look bright *or* beautiful; to flourish.

nĭtesco, 3. to begin to shine.

nĭtĭdus -a -um, brilliant, shining ; *of animals, sleek,* luxuriant; elegant; *of plants,* flourishing. *Fig.* elegant, refined, cultivated.

1. nītor, nīsus *or* nixus sum, 3 *dep.* to rest, lean, support oneself upon anything; to depend upon; to confide in; to move; to give birth to; to make an effort; *of birds,* to fly; to climb; to strive.

2. nĭtor -ōris, *m.* brilliance, splendour; elegance, beauty; elegance of style.

nĭtrum -i, *n.* natural soda.

nĭvālis -e, relating to snow, snowy.

nĭvātus -a -um, cooled with snow, iced.

nĭvĕus -a -um, relating to snow, snowy.

nĭvōsus -a -um, abounding in snow, snowy.

nix, nĭvis, *f.* snow.

nīxor, 1. *dep.* to lean upon, to strive.

1. nixus =1. *nisus* (*q.v.*).

2. nixus, *v.* 1. *nitor.*

no, nāvi, nāre, to swim; to sail, float, flow, fly.

nōbĭlis -e, noticeable, well known; celebrated; notorious; of noble birth, excellent, noble.

nōbĭlĭtas -ātis, *f.* celebrity, nobility; the nobility; excellence.

nōbĭlĭter, *adv.* excellently, nobly.

nōbĭlĭto, 1. to make known; to make famous; to make notorious.

nŏcens -entis, *p. adj.* hurtful, injurious, criminal, wicked ; *subst.* nocens, a guilty person.

nŏcĕo -ŭi -ĭtum, 2. to injure, harm; *with dat.*

noctĭfer -fĕri, *m.* the Evening Star.

noctĭlūca -ae, *f.* the moon.

noctĭvăgus -a -um, wandering by night.

noctu, *adv.* by night, in the night.

noctŭa -ae, *f.* the owl.

noctŭābundus -a -um, travelling by night.

nocturnus -a -um, by night, nightly.

nŏcŭus -a -um, hurtful, injurious.

nōdo, 1. to knot, to fetter.

nōdōsus -a -um, full of knots, knotty; full of difficulties.

nōdus -i, *m.* a knot; a girdle; *anni,* the equator; bond, connexion, obligation; a difficulty.

nōlo, nōlŭi, nolle, to be unwilling, not to wish.

Nŏmas -ădis, pasturing; plur., *Nomades,* nomads.

nōmen -ĭnis, *n.* a name; *nomen dare,* to enlist; *esp.,* the gentile name of a Roman; *nomen Romanum,* the Roman power; *nomine meo,* in my name, on my behalf ; a pretext; *nomen alicuius de erre,* to give information against;

security for a debt, *nomina solvere*, to pay a debt; a debtor; *bonum nomen*, a good payer.

nōmenclātio -ōnis, *f.* a calling by name, naming.

nōmenclātor -ōris, *m.* a slave who told his master the name of his clients at his reception.

Nōmentum -i, *n.* a town fourteen miles north-east of Rome.

nōminātim, *adv.* by name, particularly.

nōminātio -ōnis, *f.* a naming, nomination.

nōminātus -a -um, *p. adj.* well known, noted.

nōminito, 1. to name, call by name.

nōmino, 1. to give a name to; to mention; to make famous, *praedicari de se et nominari volunt omnes;* to appoint; to give information against.

Nōmius (-ŏs) -ii, *m.* a name of Apollo.

nōmisma (**nŭmisma**) -mătis, *n.* a coin.

nōn, *adv.* not; *before negatives, non forms a weak affirmative, e.g., non nihil; after negatives the affirmative is emphatic, nihil non ad rationem dirigebat; non quod*, not that.

nōnae -ārum, *f.* the nones, the fifth day (*except March, May, July, and October, when it was the seventh*).

nōnāgēni -ae -a, ninety each.

nōnāgēsimus -a -um, the ninetieth.

nōnāgiēs, *adv.* ninety times.

nōnāginta, ninety.

nōnānus -a -um, belonging to the ninth legion; *subst.*, **nōnānus** -i, *m.* a soldier of the ninth legion.

nondum *adv.* not yet.

nongenti -ae -a, nine hundred.

nonnĕ, *interrog. adv.*, *asks a question to which an affirmative answer is expected.*

nonnēmo, nonnihil, *v. nemo, nihil.*

nonnullus (**non nullus**) -a -um, some, several; *subst.*, **nonnulli**, some.

nonnumquam (**non numquam**), *adv.* sometimes.

nōnus -a -um, the ninth; *subst.*, **nōna** -ae, *f.* the ninth hour.

nōnusdēcimus, nonadecima, nonumdecimum, nineteenth.

Nōricum -i, *n.* Noricum, a country between the Danube and the Alps.

norma -ae, *f.* a carpenter's square; a rule, precept, pattern.

nŏs, *plur. of ego* (*q.v.*).

noscito, 1. to get to know; to observe; to recognise again.

nosco, **nōvi**, **nōtum**, 3. to become acquainted with, *in the perfect tenses*, to know; to recognise; to investigate a case; to allow, acknowledge a reason *or* excuse; *contr. perfect tenses*, *nosti, nostis, noram, noras, nosse.*

noster -**tra** -**trum**, our, ours, *object.*, *amor noster*, love for us our, our

friend, one of us; *nostri*, our people; favourable to us, *noster Mars.*

nostras -ātis, of our country, native.

nōta -ae, *f.* a mark, token, sign; letters of the alphabet, numbers; *poet. notae*, a letter, writing; *notae librariorum*, marks of punctuation; a brand; *compunctus notis Thraeciis*, tattooed; disgrace; sort, quality; official censure of the senate; a mark of honour.

nōtābilis -e, notable, remarkable.

nōtābilitĕr, *adv.* notably.

nōtārius -ii, *m.* a rapid writer, shorthand writer.

nōtātio -ōnis, *f.* a marking; the stigma of the censor; a choice; etymology of a word; taking notice of.

nōtātus -a -um, *p. adj.* known, marked.

nōtesco, nōtŭi, 3. to become known.

nōthus -a -um, bastard; *of animals*, mongrel; spurious.

nōtio -ōnis, *f.* an idea, image, mental conception; investigation; the blame of the censor.

nōtitia -ae, *f.* fame; knowledge; an idea, conception.

nōtities -ēi, *f.* = *notitia* (*q.v.*).

nōto, 1. to mark; to mark out; *of the censor*, to place a mark against a name, to censure; to mark, denote; to express; to blame; to write; to observe; to impress.

nōtŏs = 2. *notus* (*q.v.*).

1. **nōtus** -a -um, *p. adj.* known; *noti*, friends, acquaintances; friendly; customary; distinguished; notorious.

2. **nōtus** (ŏs) -i, *m.* the south wind.

nōvācŭla -ae, *f.* a sharp knife.

nōvālis -is, *f. and* **nōvāle** -is, *n.* fallow land; a cultivated field.

nōvātrix -īcis, *f.* she that renews.

nŏvē, *adv.* newly, in an unusual manner; recently; lastly.

nŏvellus -a -um (*dim. of novus*), new, young.

nŏvem, nine.

Nŏvember -bris, *m. mensis November*, the month of November.

nŏvemdĕcim, nineteen.

nŏvendiālis -e, that which happens on the ninth day; that which lasts nine days.

Nŏvensiles dii, gods whose worship had been introduced from foreign countries.

nŏvēnus -a -um, nine each.

nŏverca -ae, *f.* a stepmother.

nŏvercālis -e, relating to a stepmother.

nŏvīcius -a -um, new, fresh.

nŏviēs, *adv.* nine times.

nŏvitas -ātis, *f.* newness ; *anni*, the spring; *novitates* = new acquaintances; novelty.

nŏvo, 1. to renew; to refresh; to alter; to invent something new.

nŏvus -a -um, *superl.*, **novissimus**, new, fresh, young ; *novae res*, novelties, revolution; *novus homo* the first of a family who held a curule office in Rome; *novae tabulae*, new account books (*that is*, a total extinction of debts); inexperienced ; novel, unusual ; *superl.*, **nŏvissimus -a -um**, the latest, last; *agmen*, the rear. *Subst.*, **nŏvum -i**, *n.* a novelty.

nox, noctis, *f.* night, *more*, by night; *multā nocte*, late at night.

noxa -ae, *f.* harm, damage ; crime, offence; punishment.

noxia -ae, *f.* a fault, offence.

noxius -a -um, hurtful, injurious; criminal, guilty.

nūbēcŭla -ae, *f.* (*dim. of nubes*), a little cloud; a troubled expression.

nūbes -is, *f.* a cloud; a cloud, *e.g. of dust, pulveris*, a great number, dense *mass*; a cloud on the countenance; veil, concealment ; miserable condition ; a phantom.

nūbĭfĕr -fĕra -fĕrum, cloud-bearing.

nūbĭgĕna -ae, *c.* born of a cloud; *of the Centaurs*, offspring of Ixion and a cloud.

nūbĭlis -e, marriageable.

nūbilus -a -um, cloudy, overcast; *plur. subst.*, **nūbĭla -ōrum**, *n.* clouds; cloud-bringing, *Auster* ; gloomy ; unfavourable.

nūbo, nupsi, nuptum, 3. to cover, veil; *of a bride*, to be married to; *subst.*, **nupta -ae**, *f.* a wife.

nŭclĕus -i, *m.* kernel of a nut, the stone of fruits.

nūdĭus = nunc dius, it is now the . . . day since; *nudius tertius*, the day before yesterday.

nūdo, 1. to make bare, strip; to uncover; *milit.*, to leave undefended; to spoil, plunder; to deprive; to expose; to reveal, *animos*.

nūdus -a -um, naked, bare, uncovered; *subsellia*, vacant; deprived of, without, *with abl. or genit.*; simple, plain; mere, only.

nūgae -ārum, *f.* trifles, nonsense; a foolish fellow.

nūgator -ōris, *m.* trifler, jester.

nūgātōrius -a -um, trifling, frivolous.

nūgax -ācis, trifling, frivolous.

nūgor, 1. *dep.* to trifle, talk nonsense.

nullus -a -um, no, none; *nullo modo, nullo pacto*, by no means; *nullus sum*, I am ruined; insignificant, poor, *nullum argumentum est*; *subst.*, **nullus = nobody**, no one; **nullum -i**, *n.* = nothing.

num, *interrog. particle*, *asking a question to which a negative answer is expected. In indirect questions*, whether.

Nūma -ae, *m.* Pompilius, second king of Rome.

Nŭmantia -ae, *f.* a town in Hispania Tarraconensis.

nūmārius = nummarius (*q.v.*).

nūmātus = nummatus (*q.v.*).

nūmen -ĭnis, *n.* a nodding; a command;

the divine will; the might of a deity, majesty, divinity; *also of deities themselves*.

nŭmĕrābilis -e, that can be counted.

nŭmĕrātus -a -um, *p. adj.* in ready money; *subst.*, **nŭmĕrātum -i**, *n.* hard cash.

nŭmĕro, 1. to count ; *per digitos*, on the fingers ; to pay money; to reckon, enumerate; to class under; to hold, consider.

nŭmĕrōsē, *adv.* rhythmically, harmoniously.

nŭmĕrōsus -a -um, numerous; populous; rhythmical, harmonious.

nŭmĕrus -i, *m.* a number; (*of the army*) company; a cipher; melody, music; dance; a metrical foot; *plur.*, *numeri*, dice; mathematics.

Nŭmĭda -ae, *m.* a Numidian.

nŭmisma = nomisma (*q.v.*).

Nŭmĭtor -ōris, *m.* grandfather of Romulus and Remus.

nummārius -a -um, belonging to money; venal.

nummātus -a -um, rich.

nummŭlus -i, *m.* (*dim. of nummus*), a little money.

nummus (nūmus) -i, *m.* money, coin; the sesterce.

numquam *and* **nunquam**, *adv.* never; *numquam non*, always; *non numquam*, sometimes.

nūmus = nummus (*q.v.*).

nunc, *adv.* now, at present, at this moment.

nunccine = nuncne ? now ?

nuncia = nuntia, *v. nuntius.*

nunciātio = nuntiatio (*q.v.*).

nuncio = nuntio (*q.v.*).

nuncius = nuntius (*q.v.*).

nuncŭpātio -ōnis, *f.* a naming; the public offering of a vow.

nuncŭpo, 1. to name, call by name; to pronounce solemnly and openly.

nundĭnae, *v. nundinus.*

nundĭnātio -ōnis, *f.* holding of a market, trade, business.

nundĭnor, 1. *dep.* to transact business; to buy; to be present in great numbers.

nundĭnus -a -um, belonging to the ninth day. *Subst.*, **nundinae -ōrum**, *f.* the market-day, held every ninth day; the market-place; trade, business; **nundĭnum -i**, *n.* the market time.

nuntiātio -ōnis, *f.* announcement made by the augur of his observations.

nuntio, 1. to announce.

nuntius -a -um, announcing, bringing news. *Subst.*, **nuntius -ii**, *m.* messenger, announcer; message; **nuntia -ae**, *f.* she that announces; **nuntium -ii**, *n.* message, news.

nūpĕr, *superl.*, **nūperrimē**, *adv.* lately, not long ago.

nupta -ae, *f.* wife, bride.

nuptiae -ārum, *f.* marriage.
nuptiālis -e, relating to a marriage.
nuptus -a -um (*partic. of nubo*), married.
nŭrus -ūs, *f.* daughter-in-law.
nusquam, *adv.* nowhere; on no occasion.
nŭto, 1. to totter, waver, nod; to falter; to be in peril.
nŭtrīcius -ii, *m.* foster-father, guardian.
nūtrīco, 1. *and* nūtrīcor, 1. *dep.* to suckle; to support, sustain.
nūtrīcŭla -ae, *f.* (*dim. of nutrix*), nurse.
nūtrimen -inis, *n.* nourishment.
nūtrimentum -i, *n.* nourishment, support, training.
nūtrio -īvi *and* -ii -ītum, 4. (nūtrior), to suckle, nourish; to tend, sustain.
nūtrix -īcis, *f.* nurse, foster-mother.
nūtus -ūs, *m.* inclination, downward tendency, gravity; nod, signal, command, assent.
nux, nŭcis, *f.* a nut; nut-tree.
nympha -ae, *f. and* nymphē -ēs, *f.* bride; *Nymphae*, the Nymphs.

O

O o, *the fourteenth letter of the Latin Alphabet.*
2. ō! *and* ŏh! *interj.* of joy, astonishment, derision, pain.
ob, *prep. with acc.* at, before; on account of; *ob eam rem*, on that account; *ob rem*, with advantage.
ŏbaerātus -a -um, *adj.* in debt; *plur. subst.*, ŏbaerāti -ōrum, *m.* debtors.
ŏbambŭlo, 1. to walk up and down.
ŏbarmo, 1. to arm against the foe.
ŏbăro, 1. to plough up.
obbrūtesco -tŭi, 3. to become brutish, stupid.
obc . . . *v. occ.* . . .
obdo -didi -ditum, 3. to place before, put against; *fores*, to shut the door.
obdormio -īvi *and* -ii -ītum, 4. to go to sleep.
obdormisco, 3. to go to sleep.
obdūco -duxi -ductum, 3. to draw over; to cover; to drink; to wrinkle, *frontem*; to lead forward, against; to pass, spend, diem.
obductio -ōnis, *f.* a covering.
obdūresco -rŭi, 3. to become hard; to become hard-hearted.
obdūro, 1. to be hard; to stand out, persist.
ŏbēdiens (ŏboediens) -entis, *p. adj.* obdient, compliant. *Subst.*, ŏbēdiens, a dependant.
ŏbēdientĕr (ŏboedientĕr), *adv.* obediently.
ŏbēdientia (ŏboedientia) -ae, *f.* obedience, compliance.

ŏbēdio (ŏboedio) -īvi *and* -ii -ītum, 4. to give ear to, listen to; to obey.
ŏbĕliscus -i, *m.* obelisk.
ŏbĕo -īvi *and* -ii -ītum, 4. to go to, go to meet, go against; to die; *of the heavenly bodies*, to set. *Transit.*, to go to, reach; to perform, accomplish; *vadimonium*, to discharge one's bail; to visit; to take part in; to surround.
ŏbĕquito, 1. to ride up to.
ŏberro, 1. to wander about.
ŏbēsus -a -um, fat, plump; swollen; coarse.
ŏbex -īcis, *m. and f.* bolt, bar, barricade; an obstacle.
obf . . . *v. off* . . .
obg . . . *v. ogg* . . .
ŏbhaerĕo, 2. to stick to, cleave to.
ŏbhaeresco-haesi-haesum,3.to adhere to.
ŏbiăcĕo -iăcŭi, 2. to lie at, against, in the way.
obicio -iēci -iectum, 3. to throw in the way of; to oppose; to expose; to cause; to place before; to offer; to hold out as an example; to reproach, upbraid.
obiectātio -ōnis, *f.* a reproach.
obiecto, 1. to put in the way, set against; to expose; *moras*, to cause delay; to reproach with anything, throw in a person's teeth.
1. obiectus -a -um, *p. adj.* lying at, near, opposite to; exposed to.
2. obiectus -ūs, *m.* a lying against, lying opposite; a putting in the way.
ŏbīrascor -īrātus sum, 3. *dep.* to be angry at.
ŏbīrātio -ōnis, *f.* a being angry, anger.
ŏbīrātus -a -um, *p. adj.* angry, wrathful.
ŏbĭtĕr, *adv.* on the way, in passing; by the way, incidentally.
ŏbĭtus -ūs, *m.* an approaching, going to; setting; destruction, death.
obiurgātio -ōnis, *f.* a blaming, reproving.
obiurgātor -ōris, *m.* a scolder, reprover.
obiurgātōrius -a -um, scolding, chiding.
obiurgo, 1. *and* obiurgor, 1. *dep.* to scold, blame.
oblanguesco -gŭi, 3. to become languid, tired.
oblātro, 1. to bark at, rail at, scold.
oblectāmen -inis, *n.* a delight, pleasure.
oblectāmentum -i, *n.* a delight, amusement, solace.
oblectātio -ōnis, *f.* a delighting.
oblecto, 1. to delight, amuse; to while away time.
oblīdo -līsi -līsum, 3. to squeeze together.
obligātio -ōnis, *f.* a being bound, legal obligation.
obligātus -a -um, *p. adj.* bound, under an obligation.
obligo, 1. to bind, fasten to; to fetter by an oath, lay under an obligation, make liable; to pledge; to make liable to punishment, make guilty; *pass.*, *obligari*, to commit an offence.

oblīmo, 1. to cover with slime; to squander.

oblīno -lēvi -lĭtum, 3. to smear, daub; to cover; to stain, defile; *aliquem versibus atris*, to satirise, lampoon.

oblīquē, *adv.* sideways, obliquely; indirectly.

oblīquo, 1. to turn sideways, slant.

oblīquus (oblīcus) -a -um, slanting, sideways; looking askance; *ab obliquo, per obliquum*, sideways, obliquely; *of discourse*, indirect.

oblītĕro, 1. to blot out.

oblītesco -tŭi, 3. to hide oneself.

oblīvio -ōnis, *f.* forgetfulness, oblivion.

oblīviōsus -a -um, oblivious, forgetful.

oblīviscor, oblītus sum, 3. *dep.* to forget, *temporum suorum ;* to lose sight of.

oblīvium -ii, *n. usually plur.*, forgetfulness.

oblongus -a -um, rather long, oblong.

oblŏquor -cūtus (-quūtus) sum, 3. *dep.* to contradict, interrupt, *alicui ;* to blame; to join in singing.

obluctor, 1. *dep.* to struggle against.

obmōlior, 4. *dep.* to build against (*as a defence*); to obstruct.

obmurmŭro, 1. to murmur against or at.

obmūtesco -mūtŭi, 3. to become dumb, *with astonishment, etc.;* to be silent; to cease.

obnātus -a -um, growing on.

obnītor -nixus (-nīsus) sum, 3. *dep.* to push against; to oppose.

obnixē, *adv.* with all one's might.

obnixus -a -um, *p. adj.* steadfast, unyielding.

obnoxiē, culpably, submissively.

obnoxius -a -um, liable to punishment, guilty, *etc.; pecuniae debitae (dat.)* indebted; obedient, dependent upon; servile; exposed to; *obnoxium est*, it is dangerous.

obnūbo -nupsi -nuptum, 3. to cover.

obnuntiātio -ōnis, *f.* the announcement of an evil omen.

obnuntio, 1. to report an unfavourable omen.

oboed . . . *v. obed . . .*

ŏbŏlĕo -ŭi, 2. to smell of anything.

ŏbŏlus -i, *m.* a Greek coin.

ŏbŏrior-ortus sum -ŏrīri, to arise, appear.

obp . . . *v. opp . . .*

obrēpo -repsi -reptum, 3. to creep to; to steal on, come on by surprise.

obreptus, surreptitious.

obrētio, 4. to catch in a net.

obrĭgesco -rĭgŭi, 3. to become frozen, to freeze.

obrŏgo, 1. to amend *or* repeal a law by another.

obrŭo -rŭi -rŭtum, *fut. partic.* **-rŭitūrus,** 3. to cover over, to bury; to overload; to overwhelm, ruin; to surpass.

obrussa -ae, *f.* the assaying of gold by fire.

obsaepio -saepsi -saeptum, 4. to fence round, enclose.

obsătūro, 1. to satisfy.

obscoenē (obscēnē), *adv.* impurely, obscenely.

obscoenĭtas (obscēnĭtas) -ātis, *f.* impurity, obscenity.

obscoenus (obscēnus) -a -um, disgusting, offensive; impure; ill-omened.

obscūrātio -ōnis, *f.* an obscuring, darkening.

obscūrē, *adv.* darkly, obscurely; secretly.

obscūrĭtas -ātis, *f.* darkness, obscurity; low birth.

obscūro, 1. to darken, obscure; *of discourse,* to make indistinct, unintelligible; *to cause to be forgotten;* to conceal.

obscūrus -a -um, dark, obscure; *ibant obscuri,* in the dark; unintelligible, indistinct; unknown; insecure; hidden; *of character,* reserved ; *subst., obscurum,* darkness.

obsecrātio -ōnis, *f.* an earnest entreaty, supplication, a public prayer.

obsecro, 1. to beseech earnestly.

obsĕcundo, 1. to be subservient to.

obsēpio = *obsaepio (q.v.).*

obsĕquens -entis, *p. adj.* compliant, obedient; *of the gods,* favourable.

obsĕquentĕr, *adv.* obediently.

obsĕquentia -ae, *f.* compliance.

obsĕquium -ii, *n.* compliance, submission.

obsĕquor -cūtus (-quūtus) sum, 3. *dep.* to comply with, gratify, obey.

1. **obsĕro,** 1. to bolt, bar, fasten.

2. **obsĕro -sevi -situm,** 3. to sow, plant; *obsĭtus,* sown with, *i.e.* full of.

observans -antis, *p. adj.* attentive, respectful.

observantia -ae, *f.* respect, attention.

observātio -ōnis, *f.* an observing, observation; accuracy, circumspection.

observātor -ōris, *m.* an observer, watcher.

observito, 1. to watch.

observo, 1. to watch, observe; to watch for; to guard; to keep a law, rule, to respect, prize.

obses -sĭdis, *c.* a hostage ; *obsides accipere, dare,* security.

obsessio -ōnis, *f.* a blockade, siege.

obsessor -ōris, *m.* one who remains a long time in a place; one who besieges.

obsĭdĕo -sēdi -sessum, 2. *intransit.,* to sit down, remain anywhere; *transit.,* to frequent a place; to besiege; to occupy; to watch for an opportunity.

obsĭdio -ōnis, *f.* a blockade, siege.

obsĭdĭōnālis -e, relating to a siege.

1. **obsĭdium -ii,** *n.* a blockade, siege.

2. **obsĭdium -ii,** *n.* the condition of a hostage.

obsīdo -sēdi -sessum, 3. to blockade, besiege.

obsignātor -ōris, *m.* one who seals.

obsigno, 1. to seal; *of a witness,* to sign and seal; to stamp, impress.

obsisto -stiti, 3. to stand in the way of; *alicui abeunti,* to oppose. *Partic.,* **obstitus -a -um** (*in the language of the augurs*) = struck with lightning.

obsitus -a -um, *partic. of,* 2. *obsero* (*q.v.*).

obsŏlěfăcio -fēci -factum, 3. to wear out; corrupt.

obsŏlesco -lēvi -lētum, 3. to fall into disuse, lose value.

obsŏlētē, *adv.* poorly, meanly.

obsŏlētus -a -um (*partic. of obsolesco*), worn out, decayed ; *verba,* obsolete ; common, everday.

obsōnium -ii, *n.* that which is eaten with bread, *e.g.* vegetables, fruit, *and esp.* fish.

obsōno, 1. *and* **obsōnor,** 1. *dep.* to buy for the kitchen.

obsorbĕo -bŭi, 2. to swallow.

obstetrix -īcis, *f.* a midwife.

obstĭnātē, *adv.* resolutely.

obstĭnātĭo -ōnis, *f.* resolution, persistence.

obstĭnātus -a -um, *p. adj.* firmly resolved, obstinate.

obstino, 1. to persist in.

obstĭpesco = *obstupesco* (*q.v.*).

obstīpus -a -um, leaning to either side; *cervix,* thrown back; *caput,* bent *or* bowed.

obsto -stĭti -stātūrus 1. to oppose, resist, hinder, *alicui;* to be inconsistent with. *Partic. subst.,* **obstantia,** *neut. plur.,* hindrances.

obstrĕpo -strĕpŭi -strĕpĭtum, 3. (*with dat.*) to make a noise, clamour against; to disturb, molest.

obstringo -strinxi -strictum, 3. to bind to, fasten to; to fetter, put under an obligation; to entangle, involve.

obstructĭo -ōnis, *f.* a hindrance, obstruction.

obstrūdo = *obtrudo* (*q.v.*).

obstrŭo -struxi -structum, 3. to build against, build before; to block up.

obstŭpĕfăcio -fēci -factum, 3. to bewilder, astound, stupefy; *pass.,* **obstŭpĕfĭo -factus -sum -fĭeri,** to be bewildered, amazed.

obstŭpesco -stŭpŭi (-stĭpŭi), 3. to become senseless, to be astounded.

obsum, obfŭi (offŭi) -esse, to hinder, be prejudicial to; *with dat.*

obsŭo -sŭi -sūtum, 3. to sew on; to close up.

obsurdesco -dŭi, 3. to become deaf, to be deaf.

obtĕgo -texi -tectum, 3. to cover, protect; to conceal.

obtempĕrātĭo -ōnis, *f.* compliance, obedience.

obtempĕro, 1. to obey, conform to.

obtendo -tendi -tentum, 3. to stretch before, spread before; to plead, allege; to conceal.

1. **obtentus -ūs,** *m,* a stretching *or* spreading before; a pretext, excuse.

2. **obtentus -a -um,** 1. *partic. of obtineo;* 2. *partic. of obtendo.*

obtĕro -trīvi -trītum, 3. to trample, crush, destroy.

obtestātĭo -ōnis, *f.* a solemn calling of God to witness; an earnest supplication.

obtestor, 1. *dep.* to call to witness; to implore, entreat in the name of the gods; to assert solemnly.

obtexto -texŭi -textum, 3. to weave on, weave over; to cover.

obticĕo, 2. to be silent.

obticesco -cŭi, 3. to become quiet.

obtĭgo = *obtego* (*q.v.*).

obtĭneo -tĭnŭi -tentum, 2. to hold with the hands; to possess, occupy; to maintain, hold firmly; *obtinuit, with ut and the subj.,* he carried his point that, *etc.;* to keep, observe, *reflex.,* to obtain, be held.

obtingo -tĭgi, 3. to happen, befall.

obtorpesco -torpŭi, to become stiff, numb, insensible.

obtorquĕo -torsi -tortum, 2. to turn towards, to turn round, wrench.

obtrectātĭo -ōnis, *f.* detraction.

obtrectātor -ōris, *m* a detractor.

obtrecto, 1. to disparage, to oppose.

obtrūdo (obstrūdo) -trūsi -trūsum, 3. to gulp down; to thrust upon one; to cover.

obtrunco, 1. to cut down, slay.

obtundo -tūdi -tūsum, 3. to make blunt, dull; to weary; *obtundere aures,* to din into a person's ears.

obturbo, 1. to disturb; to perturb; to deafen, stun.

obturgesco -tursi, 3. to swell up.

obtūro, 1. to stop up.

obtūsus -a -um, *p. adj.* blunt; darkened, dulled; insensible; powerless.

obtūtus -ūs, *m.* a looking at, gaze.

ŏbumbro, 1. to overshadow; to protect, cover; *fig.* to obscure.

ŏbuncus -a -um, bent inwards, hooked inwards.

ŏbustus -a -um, burnt, hardened in the fire.

ŏbvallo, 1. to surround with a wall.

ŏbvěnĭo -vēni -ventum, 4. to come in the way of, to meet; to occur to, happen; to fall to the lot of.

ŏbversor, 1. *dep.* to appear before, be before, show oneself.

ŏbversus -a -um (*partic. of obverto*), turned towards.

ŏbverto (-vorto) -verti (-vorti) -versum (-vorsum), 3. to turn towards; *middle, obverti,* to turn towards; *in hostem,* to oppose.

ŏbviam, *adv.* in the way, on the way; to meet, *obviam alicui ire;* to oppose.

ŏbvius -a -um, in the way, meeting; exposed to; ready at hand; affable.

ŏbvolvo -volvi -vŏlūtum, 3. to roll up, wrap up.

occaeco, 1. to make blind; to darken; to make obscure; to conceal.

occallesco -callŭi, 3. to become thick-skinned; to become unfeeling.

occăno -cănŭi, 3. to blow, sound.

occāsio -ōnis, f. opportunity, occasion; per occasionem, on a favourable opportunity.

1. occāsus -a -um, partic. of occido.

2. occāsus -ūs, m. the setting of the heavenly bodies, the west, fall, end, death.

occātio -ōnis, f. a harrowing.

occento, 1. to swing a lampoon against any one.

occidens -entis, m. the evening, the west.

occidio -ōnis, f. slaughter, extermination, utter destruction.

1. occido -cidi -cīsum, 3. to knock down; to kill; to torture, annoy.

2. occido -cidi -cāsum, 3. to fall, fall down. Of the heavenly bodies, to set; to die, perish; be ruined.

occidŭus -a -um, setting, sol; western, westerly; approaching death.

occino -cinŭi, 3. to croak.

occipio -cēpi -ceptum, 3. to begin; to enter on, magistratum.

occipitium -ii, n. the back of the head.

occiput -itis, n. the back of the head.

occisio -ōnis, f. killing, slaughter.

occisus -a -um, p. adj. ruined, unfortunate.

occlūdo -clūsi -clūsum, 3. to shut up; to restrain.

occlūsus -a -um, partic. of occludo.

occo, 1. to harrow; poet., segetem, to till.

occoepi -isse = occipio (q.v.).

occŭbo, 1. to lie down; to rest in the grave.

occulco, 1. to trample.

occŭlo -cŭlui -cultum, 3. to cover, to hide.

occultātio -ōnis, f. concealment.

occultātor -ōris, m. a concealer.

occultē, adv. secretly; dicere, obscurely.

occulto, 1. to hide.

occultus -a -um, p. adj. secret, private; ex persona, reserved, subst., occulta -ōrum, m. secrets.

occumbo -cŭbŭi -cŭbitum, 3. to fall down, sink down; to die.

occŭpātio -ōnis, f. a seizing, occupation; a business, employment.

occŭpātus -a -um, p. adj. busy, engaged.

occŭpo, 1. to occupy, seize; to fill with anything; to attack; to anticipate, to do anything first; to master; to make busy; to invest money.

occurro -curri -cursum, 3. to run to meet, hasten to meet; to attack; of things, to come in the way of; to oppose, counteract; to assist; to be present at; to come into the thoughts, to occur to any one; to happen.

occursātio -ōnis, f. attention officiousness.

occurso, 1. to go to meet, to meet; to oppose; to attack.

occursus -ūs, m. a meeting with.

Ōcĕănus -i, m. the ocean, the sea which encompasses the earth; also personified as a god. Ōcĕănĭtis -idis, f. a daughter of Oceanus.

ŏcellus -i, m. (dim. of oculus), a little eye.

ŏcior, ŏcius, adj. compar., swifter; superl. ocissimus.

ŏcius, adv. more quickly; superl. ocissimē; serius, ocius, sooner or later.

ocrĕa -ae, f. a metal greave.

ocrĕātus -a -um, wearing the ocrea.

octăphoros = octophoros (q.v.).

Octāvius -a -um, name of a Roman gens; subst., Octāviānus -i, m. name of the Emperor Augustus.

octāvus -a -um, the eighth; adv., octavum, for the eighth time; subst., octāva -ae, f. the eighth hour.

octāvusdĕcimus -a -um, eighteenth.

octiēs, adv. eight times.

octingentēsimus -a -um, the eight hundreth.

octingenti -ae -a, eight hundred.

octĭpes -pēdis, having eight feet.

octŏ, eight.

Octōber -bris -bre, m., mensis October, the month of October.

octōdĕcim, eighteen.

octōgēnārius -a -um, containing eighty, consisting of eighty.

octōgēni -ae -a, eighty each.

octōgēsimus -a -um, the eightieth.

octōgiēs, adv. eighty times.

octōginta, eighty.

octōiŭgis -e, yoked eight together.

octōni -ae -a, eight each.

octōphŏros -on, borne by four; subst., octōphŏron -i, n. litter carried by eight bearers.

octŭāgiēs, octŭāginta = octogies, octoginta (q.v.).

octŭplicātus -a -um, increased eight-fold.

octŭplus -a -um, eight fold; subst., octuplum -i, n. an eight-fold penalty.

octussis -is, m. eight asses.

ŏcŭlātus -a -um (late), having eyes.

ŏcŭlus -i, m. the eye; esse in oculis, to be visible; the spot upon a panther's skin, or a peacock's tail; bud or eye of a plant.

ŏdi, ŏdisse (no present), partic. fut., ŏsūrus ; to hate, dislike, be displeased with.

ŏdiōsē, adv. hatefully, odiously.

ŏdiōsus -a -um, hateful, irksome; orator, tedious.

ŏdium -ii, n. hatred; the object of hatred; esse odio alicui, to be hated by.

ŏdor and ŏdōs -ōris, m. a smell, odour; stench ; steam, vapour ; suspicion, inkling ; perfume ; plur., perfumery, unguents.

ŏdōrātio -ōnis, f. a smelling, smell.

1. ŏdōrātus -ūs, *m.* a smell, smelling; the sense of smell; odour.

2. ŏdōrātus -a -um, sweet-smelling.

3. ŏdōrātus -a -um, *partic. of odoror.*

ŏdōrǐfěr -fěra -fěrum, having a pleasant smell; producing perfumes.

ŏdōro, 1. to make odorous.

ŏdōror, 1. *dep.* to smell; to snuff at, nose (*as a dog*); to aim at; to track out, investigate; to have the slightest smattering of.

ŏdōrus -a -um, sweet-smelling; keen-scented.

ŏdōs = *odor* (*q.v.*).

Ŏdyssēa -ae, *f.* the Odyssey.

Oebălus -i, *m.* a king of Sparta, father of Tyndarus, grandfather of Helen.

oecŏnŏmicus -a -um, relating to domestic economy. *Subst.*, Oecŏnŏmicus -i, *m.* title of a book by Xenophon.

Oedĭpūs -pŏdis, *m.* king of Thebes, son of Laius and Jocasta, fated to kill his father and to espouse his mother.

Oenōnē -ēs, *f.* a Phrygian nymph, beloved and afterwards deserted by Paris.

oenŏphŏrum -i, *n.* a hamper for wine.

oenus = *unus* (*q.v.*).

oestrus -i, *m.* gad fly, horsefly, breeze.

oesus = *usus* (*q.v.*).

oesȳpum -i, *n.* a cosmetic.

ŏfella -ae, *f.* (*dim. of offa*), a bit, morsel.

offa -ae, *f.* a bit, morsel, pellet of flour; a piece, lump; a swelling.

offendo -fendi -fensum, 3. *intransit.*, to strike, dash against; to suffer damage; to make a mistake; to offend against a person; to suffer reverse. *Transit.*, to knock against something; to fall in with, come upon; to injure; to displease; *partic.*, offensus, injured; repulsive; *subst.*, offensum -i, *n.* something causing offence.

offensa -ae, *f.* a striking against; dislike, enmity, injury.

offensio -ōnis, *f.* a striking against; *pedis*, a stumbling; a stumbling-block; indisposition; hatred; defeat, misfortune.

offensiuncŭla -ae, *f.* (*dim. of offensio*), a slight offence, displeasure, slight failure.

offenso, 1. to strike against.

1. offensus -a -um, *partic. of offensus.*

2. offensus -ūs, *m.* a shock; offence, dislike.

offěro, obtŭli, oblātum, offerre, to carry to, present, produce, offer; to expose; to bring forward; to cause.

officīna -ae, *f.* a workshop, manufactory, laboratory.

officio -fēci -fectum, 3. to impede, hinder; to injure.

officiōsē, *adv.* obligingly, courteously.

officiōsus -a -um, courteous, kind; dutiful.

officium -ii, *n.* duty, obligation, service;

officio *fungi*, to do one's duty; allegiance; courtesy; attention, ceremony.

offīgo -fixi -fixum, 3. to fix in, fasten.

offirmātē, *adv.* firmly, obstinately.

offirmātus -a -um, firm, steadfast.

offirmo, 1. to make firm, to fasten; to make resolute.

offulgěo -fusi, 2. to shine upon, appear.

offundo -fūdi -fūsum, 3. to pour before, pour out; to spread over, to cover; *pass.*, *offundi*, to be poured out, to be spread around.

oggannio -īvi *and* -ii -ītum, 4. to yelp, growl at.

oh, *interj.* oh ! ah !

ohe, *interj.* ho ! holloa !

oi, *interj.* oh ! *an exclamation of pain.*

Oīleus -ěi *and* -ěos, *m.* king of Locris, father of Ajax (*who was also called* Ajax Oileus).

ŏlěa -ae, *f.* the olive; the olive-tree.

ŏlěăgĭněus (ŏlěăgĭnus) -a -um, relating to the olive-tree.

ŏlěārius -a -um, belonging to oil.

ŏlěaster -tri, *m.* the wild olive-tree.

ŏlens -entis, *p. adj.* smelling; fragrant; stinking.

ŏlěo, ŏlŭi, 2. to emit an odour, smell; to savour of; to be betrayed by smell.

ŏlěum -i, *n.* olive-oil, oil.

olfăcio -fēci -factum, 3. to smell; to scent out, detect.

ŏlĭdus -a -um, smelling, emitting an odour.

ŏlim, *adv.* formerly, once upon a time, in times past; at a future time; at times, often.

ŏlĭtor -ōris, *m.* kitchen-gardener.

ŏlĭtōrius -a -um, relating to culinary herbs.

ŏlīva -ae, *f.* the olive; the olive-tree; an olive-branch; a staff of olive-tree wood.

ŏlīvētum -i, *n.* olive-garden.

ŏlīvĭfěr -fěra -fěrum, olive-bearing.

ŏlīvum -i, *n.* olive-oil, oil; unguent.

olla -ae, *f.* earthenware jar *or* pot.

olle, *obsolete form of ille* (*q.v.*).

ŏlo, 3. = *olso* (*q.v.*).

ŏlor -ōris, *m.* a swan.

ŏlōrīnus -a -um, relating to a swan.

ŏlus (hŏlus) -ěris, *n.* vegetable, pot-herb.

ŏluscŭlum -i, *n.* (*dim. of olus*), a herb, vegetable.

Ŏlympĭa -ae, *f.* in Elis, where the Olympic games were celebrated.

Ŏlympus (-ŏs) -i, *m.* a mountain on the borders of Macedonia and Thessaly, supposed to be the habitation of the gods; *poet.* = heaven.

ōmāsum -i, *n.* bullock's tripe.

ōměn -inis, *n.* omen, sign, augury.

ōmentum -i, *n.* the entrails, bowels.

ōmĭnor, 1. *dep.* to augur, predict; to speak words of (*good or bad*) omen.

ōmĭnōsus -a -um, foreboding, ominous (*late*).

ŏmissus -a -um, *p. adj.* neglectful.

ŏmitto -mīsi -missum, 3. to let go, let alone, let fall; to give up: to omit; *with infin.*, to cease.

omnĭfĕr -fĕra -fĕrum, bearing everything.

omnĭgĕna -ae, *genit. plur.*, ŭm, *c.* of all sorts.

omnĭmŏdīs ĕt ŏmnĭ, in omni modo

omnĭmŏdis, *adv.* in every way, entirely.

omnīno, *adv.* altogether, entirely, wholly; in general, especially; at all; utterly

omnĭpărens -entis, all-producing.

omnĭpŏtens -entis, almighty.

omnis -e, all; each, every; the whole; *per omnia*, in every respect.

omnĭtŭens -entis, all-seeing.

omnĭvăgus -a -um, wandering everywhere.

omnĭvŏlus -a -um, all-willing.

ŏnăger *and* ŏnagrus -i, *m.* the wild ass.

ŏnĕrārĭus -a -um, relating to freight, burden. *Subst.*, ŏnĕrārĭa -ae, *f.* a merchant *or* transport ship.

ŏnĕro, 1. to load, pack, burden; to cover; to load, fill; to oppress, overwhelm; to weary; to aggravate; to put into a cask, vessel, *etc.*

ŏnĕrōsus -a -um, heavy; troublesome.

ŏnus -ĕris, *n.* a load, burden; a tax.

ŏnustus -a -um, laden, freighted; full, filled.

ŏnyx -ўchis, *m.* onyx; a shell-fish.

ŏpācĭtas -ātis, *f.* a shade.

ŏpāco, 1. to shade, overshadow.

ŏpācus -a -um, shaded, shady; dark, shadowy. *Act.*, casting a shade.

ŏpella -ae, *f.* (*dim. of opera*), a little work, service.

ŏpĕra -ae, *f.* trouble, pains, effort; *operam dare, with ut and subj.*, to do one's best to; a service; a workman; mercenaries.

ŏpĕrārĭus -a -um, relating to work. *Subst.*, ŏpĕrārĭus -ii, *m.* day-labourer, workman.

ŏpercŭlum -i, *n.* a lid, cover.

ŏpĕrīmentum -i, *n.* a cover, covering.

ŏpĕrĭo -pĕruī -pertum, 4. to bury; to cover; to conceal; to close.

ŏpĕror, 1. *dep.* to work, be occupied with; *with dat.*, to worship, sacrifice.

ŏpĕrōsē, *adv.* laboriously, carefully.

ŏpĕrōsus -a -um, painstaking, industrious; toilsome, difficult.

ŏpertum -i, *n.* a secret place; a secret.

ŏpes, *v. ops.*

Ophĭūchus -i, *m.* the snake-holder, a constellation.

ŏpĭfĕr -fĕra -fĕrum, helpful.

ŏpĭfex -ĭcis, *c.* a worker, workman, artisan.

ŏpĭfĭcīna = *officina* (*q.v.*).

ŏpĭlĭo *and* ūpĭlĭo -ōnis, *m.* a shepherd.

ŏpīmus -a -um, fruitful, fertile; well fed, fat; (*of speech*), overloaded); wealthy; sumptuous, abundant; *spolia opima*,

arms won by a general in single combat from the general of the opposing forces.

ŏpīnābĭlis -e, conjectural.

ŏpīnātĭo -ōnis, *f.* supposition, conjecture.

ŏpīnātor -ōris, *m.* one who conjectures.

1. ŏpīnātus -a -um, *p. adj.* conjectured, fancied

2. ŏpīnātus -ūs, *m.* conjecture, supposition.

ŏpīnĭo -ōnis, *f.* opinion, conjecture, imagination ; *praeter opinionem*, contrary to expectation; good opinion ; reputation; notoriety; fame, report.

ŏpīnĭōsus -a -um, full of conjectures.

ŏpīnor, 1. *dep.* to be of opinion, think, suppose.

ŏpĭpărē, *adv.* splendidly, sumptuously.

ŏpĭpărus -a -um, splendid, sumptuous.

pĭtŭlor, 1. *dep.* to help.

oppēdo, 3. to mock, insult.

oppĕrĭor -pertus *and* (*more rarely*) -pĕrītus sum, 4. *dep.* to wait; to expect.

oppĕto -īvi *and* -ii -ītum, 3. to go to meet, encounter; *mortem*, to die.

oppĭdānus -a -um, belonging to a town; provincial; *subst.*, oppĭdānī -ōrum, *m.* inhabitants of a town.

oppĭdātim, *adv.* in the towns, in all the towns.

oppĭdo, *adv.* very, exceedingly.

oppĭdŭlum -i, *n.* (*dim. of oppidum*), a little town.

oppĭdum -i, *n.* a town; a fortified wood in Britain.

oppignĕro, 1. to pledge, pawn.

oppĭlo, 1. to block up.

oppĭĕo -plēvi -plētum, 2. to fill.

oppōno -pōsŭi -pŏsĭtum (-postum), 3. to place opposite, before; to place in the way of for protection, *se alicui* ; to mortgage for; to expose; to oppose; to contrast, *virtuti vitium.*

opportūnē, *adv.* opportunely, conveniently.

opportūnĭtas -ātis, *f.* convenience, fitness, appropriateness; opportunity; an advantage.

opportūnus -a -um, opportune, suitable, favourable; serviceable, useful; liable to.

oppŏsĭtĭo -ōnis, *f.* opposing, opposition.

1. oppŏsĭtus -a -um, *p. adj.* opposed, opposite.

2. oppŏsĭtus -ūs, *m.* a setting against *or* opposite, interposition.

oppressĭo -ōnis, *f.* oppression; a forcible taking possession of.

oppressor -ōris, *m.* a suppresser.

1. oppressus -ūs, *m.* pressure.

2. oppressus -a -um, *partic. of opprimo.*

opprĭmo -pressi -pressum, 3. to press down, press together; to crush; to stifle; to extinguish; to suppress; to conceal;

to weigh down; to subdue; to hold firm; to fall upon, surprise.

opprobrium -ii, *n.* a scandal, disgrace; a taunt.

oppugnātio -ōnis, *f.* a taking by storm.

oppugnātor -ōris, *m.* one who attacks.

oppugno, 1. to attack, besiege.

ops, ōpis, *f., plur.,* **ōpes -um,** might, power; resources; troops; influence; strength; help, support.

ops . . . *v. obs.*

optābilis -e, desirable.

optandus -a -um, desirable.

optātio -ōnis, *f.* a wish.

optātō, *adv.* according to one's wish.

optātus -a -um, *p. adj.* wished for, pleasant. *Subst.,* **optātum** -i, *n.* a wish.

optimās -ātis, aristocratic. *Subst.,* **optimās -ātis,** *m.* an aristocrat; *plur.,* **optimātes -ium** *and* **-um,** *m.* the aristocratic party.

optimē, *superl. of bene (q.v.).*

optimus (optŭmus) -a -um, *superl. of bonus (q.v.).*

1. **optio** -ōnis, *f.* choice, option.
2. **optio** -ōnis, *m.* an adjutant.

optivus -a -um, chosen.

opto, 1. to choose, elect; to desire.

ŏpŭlens -entis, rich; powerful.

ŏpŭlentē *and* **ŏpŭlentĕr,** *adv.* richly, sumptuously.

ŏpŭlentia -ae, *f.* wealth; power, greatness.

ŏpŭlento, 1. to enrich.

ŏpŭlentus -a -um, rich; splendid; powerful, mighty.

1. **ŏpus** -ĕris, *n.* a work, labour; building; fortification, entrenchment; finished work; a work of art; action, business; an undertaking; trouble.
2. **ŏpus,** *n. indecl.,* **opus est** (*with abl.*) there is need, it is necessary; *opus est auctoritate tuā.*

ŏpusculum -i, *n.* (*dim. of* 1. *opus*), a little work.

1. **ōra** -ae, *f.* the border, boundary; the coast; region; *luminis orae,* the upper world; a zone, belt of the earth.
2. **ōra** -ae, *f.* a cable by which a ship was made fast to the shore.

ōrāculum (ōrāclum) -i, *n.* a place where an oracle is given; an oracle; a prophecy.

ōrātio -ōnis, *f.* eloquence; speech, utterance; a set speech; prose.

ōrātiuncŭla -ae, *f.* (*dim. of oratio*), a little speech.

ōrātor -ōris, *m.* speaker; spokesman; an orator.

ōrātōrĭe, *adv.* oratorically, like an orator.

ōrātōrius -a -um, oratorical.

ōrātrix -icis, *f.* female suppliant.

ōrātus -ūs, *m.* request, entreaty.

orbātor -ōris, *m.* one who deprives another of children *or* parents.

orbĭcŭlātus -a -um, circular, round.

orbis -is, *m.* a circle, ring, anything round; *orbis signifer,* the zodiac; *lacteus,* the Milky Way; a circular motion, winding; the rounding off of a speech; *orbis terrarum,* the circle of the world, the world; a disk; the disk of the sun *or* moon; the heavens; a shield; a wheel.

orbĭta -ae, *f.* a wheel-rut.

orbĭtas -ātis, *f.* bereavement, loss of children *or* parents.

orbo, 1. to bereave; to deprive of parents *or* children.

orbus -a -um, deprived of; bereft, destitute; *with abl., rebus omnibus;* deprived of parents *or* children, bereft; *subst.,* **orbus -i,** *m. and* **orba -ae,** *f.* an orphan.

orca -ae, *f.* a kind of whale; an earthenware pot with a large belly.

orchăs -ădis, *f.* a species of olive.

orchestra -ae, *f.* the part of a Roman theatre reserved for the senators; the senate.

orcīnus -a -um, relating to Orcus *or* the dead.

Orcus -i, *m.* Orcus, the infernal regions; the god of the lower world, Pluto; death.

ordĕum = *hordeum (q.v.).*

ordia prima = *primordia (q.v.).*

ordĭnārius -a -um, regular, ordinary.

ordĭnātim, *adv.* in order; properly.

ordĭnātio -ōnis, *f.* a setting in order, arrangement (*late*).

ordĭnātus -a -um, *p. adj.* set in order, arranged.

ordĭno, 1. to plant in rows; to arrange in rank (*of soldiers*); to settle; to appoint, classify.

ordior, orsus sum, 4. *dep.* to begin.

ordo -ĭnis, *m.* series, row, order; row of seats in a theatre; *milit.* rank, file; *politically,* rank, class; order, arrangement; *ordine,* in order; *extra ordinem,* in an unusual manner, extraordinarily.

Ŏrēăs -ădis, *f.* a mountain-nymph.

Ŏrestēs -ae *and* **-ĭs,** *m.* son of Agamemnon and Clytaemnestra, brother of Iphigenia and Electra, who killed his mother, the murderess of his father.

ŏrexis -is, *f.* desire, appetite.

orgănĭcus -a -um, musical; *subst.,* **orgănĭcus -i,** *m.* a musician.

orgănum -i, *n.* implement *or* instrument.

Orgĕtōrix -rigis, *m.* a celebrated Helvetian.

orgia -ōrum, *n.* nocturnal festivals; orgies.

ŏrĭchalcum -i, *n.* yellow copper ore; brass.

ŏrĭcilla (auricilla) -ae, *f.* an ear-lobe.

ŏrĭcŭla = *auricula (q.v.).*

ŏriens -entis, *m.* the rising sun; the east.

ŏrīgo -inis, *f.* origin, source; birth; ancestor.

Orīŏn -onis, *m.* the constellation Orion.

ŏrior, ortus sum, ŏrīrī *or* **ŏrīrī** *4 dep* to rise; to come forth; to be born; to grow; to begin.

ŏriundus -a -um, arising from, born of.

ornāmentum i, *n.* equipment, furniture; ornament; honour.

ornātē, *adv.* ornately, splendidly.

ornātrix -īcis, *f.* a tire-woman.

1. **ornātus -ūs**, *m.* dress, attire, equipment; decoration.

2. **ornātus -a -um**, *p. adj.* equipped, provided; decorated; illustrious.

orno, 1. to equip; fit out; to adorn; to honour.

ornus -i, *f.* the mountain-ash.

ōro, 1. to speak ; to argue, plead; to pray, entreat.

Ŏrōdes -is *and* **-i**, *m.* king of the Parthians, who took Crassus prisoner.

Ŏrontes -is, *m.* chief river of Syria.

Orphēus -ĕi *and* **-ĕos**, *acc.* **-ĕum** *and* **-ĕa**, *abl.* **-eo**, *m.* a celebrated minstrel of Thrace, husband of Eurydice. **Orphēus, Orphĭcus**, Orphean, Orphic.

orphus -i, *m.* a sea-fish.

orsa -ōrum, *n.* a beginning, undertaking; *poet.* speech.

1. **orsus -ūs**, *m.* a beginning.

2. **orsus -a -um**, *partic. of ordior.*

orthŏgrăphĭa -ae, *f.* orthography.

1. **ortus -ūs**, *m.* a rising of the heavenly bodies; *solis*, the east; birth; origin, source.

2. **ortus -a -um**, *partic. of orior.*

ŏryx -ȳgis, *m.* a species of wild goat *or* gazelle.

ŏrȳza -ae, *f.* rice.

1. **ōs, ōris**, *n.* the mouth ; *uno ore*, unanimously ; mouth, opening, *portus*; source; the face, *in ore hominum*, in the presence of men ; impudence ; a mask.

2. **ōs, ossis**, *n.* a bone; *dolor ossibus ingens*, in his heart.

oscen -inis, *m.* a bird from whose note auguries were taken (*e.g. the raven, owl, crow*).

oscillum -i, *n. dim. of* 1. *os*), a little mask.

oscitantĕr, *adv.* yawningly, carelessly.

oscĭtātĭo -ōnis, *f.* the opening of the mouth, a gaping.

oscĭto, 1. to yawn; to be lazy.

oscŭlābundus -a -um, kissing.

oscŭlātĭo -ōnis, *f.* a kissing.

oscŭlor, 1. *dep.* to kiss; to caress.

oscŭlum -i, *n. (dim. of* 1. *os*), a little mouth; a kiss.

Osīris -is *and* **-idis**, *m.* husband of Isis, god of Egypt.

Ossa -ae ,*m.* a mountain in Thessaly.

ossĕus -a -um (2. **os**), made of bone, like bone, bony.

ossifrăgus -i, *m. and* **ossifrăga -ae**, *f.* sea-eagle, osprey.

ostendo -tendi -tentum *and* (*later*) **-tensum** 3 to show, exhibit; to make plain, declare.

ostentātĭo -ōnis, *f.* a showing, revealing; boasting, display; pretence.

ostento, 1. to hold out, offer; to display; to show boastingly; to proffer, promise; to show off; to threaten; to reveal.

ostentum -i, *n.* a prodigy, portent.

ostentus, *dat.* **-ŭi**, *abl.* **-ū**, *m.* a display; outward show; sign, proof.

Ostia -ae, *f. and* **Ostia -ōrum**, *n.* the harbour and port of Rome; *adj.*, **Ostiensis -e.**

ostĭārĭus -a -um, belonging to a door; *subst.*, **ostĭārĭus -ii**, *m.* doorkeeper, porter ; **ostĭārĭum -ĭi**, *n.* tax upon doors.

ostĭātim, *adv.* from door to door.

ostĭum -ii, *n.* the entrance; *fluminis*, mouth; door of a house.

ostrĕa -ae, *f. and* **ostrĕum -i**, *n.* an oyster.

ostrĕōsus -a -um, abounding in oysters.

ostrĭfĕr -fĕra -fĕrum, producing oysters.

ostrīnus -a -um, purple.

ostrum -i, *n.* purple dye; a purple dress.

ōsus -a -um, *partic. of ōdi (q.v.).*

ōtĭŏlum -i, *n. (dim. of otium*), a little leisure.

ōtĭor, 1. *dep.* to be at leisure.

ōtĭōsē, *adv.* idly; leisurely, quietly.

ōtĭōsus -a -um, idle, at leisure; neutral, quiet; calm.

ōtĭum -ĭi, *n.* idleness, leisure, ease ; peace.

ŏvātĭo -ōnis, *f.* an ovation, a lesser triumph.

Ŏvĭdĭus -ii, *m.*, *P. Ovidius Naso*, the celebrated Roman poet, born at Sulmo, 43 B.C. died A.D. 17.

ŏvīle -is, *n.* a sheepfold.

ŏvillus -a -um, relating to sheep.

ŏvis -is, *f.* a sheep.

ŏvo, 1. to rejoice, exult; to celebrate an ovation.

ōvum -i, *n.* an egg.

P

P p, *the fifteenth letter of the Latin Alphabet.*

pābŭlātĭo -ōnis, *f.* foraging.

pābŭlātŏr -ōris, *m.* a forager.

pābŭlor, 1. *dep.* to forage, seek fodder.

pābŭlum -i, *n.* food; fodder.

pācālis -e, relating to peace, peaceful.

pācātus -a -um *p. adj.* pacified ;

peaceful, quiet; *subst.*, **pācātum -i**, *n.* a peaceful, friendly country.

pācĭfer -fĕra -fĕrum, peace-bringing.

pācĭfĭcātĭo -ōnis, *f.* pacification.

pācĭfĭcātŏr -ōris, *m.* one who establishes peace.

pācĭfĭcātōrĭus -a -um, establishing peace, pacificatory.

pācĭfĭco, 1. to reconcile, pacify.

pācĭfĭcor, 1. *dep.* to make peace.

pācĭfĭcus -a -um, peace-making, pacific.

pācĭscor, pactus sum, 3. *dep.* to make a bargain, contract, agreement; to stipulate; *with infin.*, to bind oneself. *Partic.*, **pactus**, agreed upon, settled.

pāco, 1. to reduce to peace, pacify; *poet.* to make fruitful.

Păcōrus -i, *m.* king of Parthia, enemy of the Romans.

pacta -ae, *f.* a bethrothed spouse.

pactĭo -ōnis, *f.* bargain, agreement, treaty.

Pactōlus -i, *m.* a river in Lydia, said to bring down golden sands.

pactŏr -ōris, *m.* one who makes a contract *or* treaty, negotiator.

pactum -i, *n.* a bargain, contract, treaty; *nullo pacto*, by no means.

pactus -a -um, *partic. of paciscor.*

Pădus -i, *m.* river in Italy, *now* the Po.

Paean -ānis, *m.* the Healer, a surname of Apollo; a hymn, paean.

paedăgōgus -i, *m.* a slave who accompanied children to and from school.

paedor -ōris, *m.* dirt, filth.

paelex = *pelex (q.v.).*

Paelĭgni -ōrum, *m.* an Italian tribe in Samnium.

paene, *adv.* nearly, almost.

paeninsŭla -ae, *f.* a peninsula.

paenŭla -ae, *f.* a species of overcoat.

paenŭlātus -a -um, clothed in the paenula.

paeōn -ōnis, *m.* a metrical foot.

Paeōnĭus -a -um, relating to the god of healing, Apollo; medicinal.

Paestum -i, *n.* a town in Lucania, famous for its roses.

paetŭlus -a -um (*dim. of paetus*), having a slight cast in the eye.

paetus -a -um, having a cast in the eyes.

pāgānus -a -um, relating to a village, rural; **pāgānus -i**, *m. subst.*, a villager, countryman.

pāgātim, *adv.* in villages, by villages.

pāgella -ae, *f.* (*dim. of pagina*), a little page.

pāgĭna -ae, *f.* a page, tablet.

pāgĭnŭla -ae, *f.* (*dim. of pagina*), a little page.

pāgŭr -i, *m.* a fish of unknown species.

pāgus -i, *m.* a village; a district, canton.

pāla -ae, *f.* a spade; the socket of a ring in which the jewel is set.

Pălaeŏpōlis, *acc.* **-pŏlim**, *f.* the older part of the town of Neapolis in Campania.

Pălaestīna -ae, *f. and* **Pălaestīnē -ēs**, *f.* Palestine.

pălaestra -ae, *f.* a gymnasium *or* wrestling school; a school of rhetoric; art.

pălaestrĭcē, *adv.* after the manner of the palaestra.

pălaestrĭcus -a -um, relating to the palaestra.

pălaestrīta -ae, *m.* the superintendent of a palaestra.

pălam, *adv.* openly, publicly. *Prep. with abl.*, in the presence of.

Pălămēdēs -is, *m.* one of the Greek heroes in the Trojan War.

Pălātĭum -ii, *n.* the Palatine Hill in Rome; a palace.

pălātum -i, *n. and* **pălātus -i**, *m.* the palate; *fig.* taste, critical judgment.

pălĕa -ae, *f.* chaff.

pălĕar -āris, *n.* the dewlap of an ox; *gen. plur.*

Pāles -is, *f.* tutelary goddess of herds and shepherds. *Adj.*, **Pălīlia -ium**, *n.* the feast of Pales.

pălimpsestos -i, *m.* a palimpsest.

Pălīnūrus -i, *m.* 1. The pilot of Aeneas; 2. a promontory on the coast of Lucania.

pălīūrus -i, *m.* a plant.

palla -ae, *f.* a long outer garment worn by Roman women, *also by* tragic actors.

pallăca -ae, *f.* a concubine.

1. **Pallăs -ădis** *and* **-ădos**, *f.* the Greek name of Minerva; *adj.*, **Pallădĭus**; *subst.*, **Pallădĭum -ii**, *n.* the image of Pallas in Troy.

2. **Pallas -antis**, *m.* son of Pandion; one of the giants.

pallens -entis, *p. adj.* pale, wan; pale yellow, pale green; making pale, *morbi.*

pallĕo -ŭi, 2. to be pale; to long for; to be yellow.

pallesco, pallŭi, 3. to turn pale, lose colour; to grow yellow.

pallĭātus -a -um, clad in a pallium, *i.e.* as a Greek.

pallĭdŭlus -a -um (*dim. of pallidus*), somewhat pale.

pallĭdus -a -um, pale, wan; causing paleness, *mors;* yellow, olive green.

pallĭŏlātus -a -um, wearing a cloak, cape, *or* hood.

pallĭŏlum -i, *n.* (*dim. of pallium*), a little Greek cloak *or* mantle; a hood.

pallĭum -i, *n.* a coverlet; a long Greek mantle.

pallor -ōris, *m.* pallor; anxiety, fright; unsightliness, unpleasant colour.

palma -ae, *f.* palm of the hand; the hand; blade of an oar; palm tree; fruit of the palm; a palm branch, broom made of palm branches; the reward of victory; a shoot, twig.

palmāris -e, deserving the palm, excellent.

palmārĭum -ii, *n.* a masterpiece.

palmātus -a -um, embroidered with palm branches.

palmes -ĭtis, *m.* shoot of a vine.

palmētum -i, *n.* a palm grove.

palmĭfĕr -fĕra -fĕrum, abounding in palm trees.

palmōsus -a -um, full of palms.

palmŭla -ae, *f. (dim. of palma),* the blade of an oar, an oar.

pālor, 1. *dep.* to wander about.

palpebra -ae, *f.* the eyelid.

palpĭto, 1. to move quickly, tremble, throb.

1. palpo, 1. *and* **palpor, 1.** *dep.* to stroke *or* touch gently, to coax.

2. palpo -ōnis, *m.* a coaxer, flatterer.

pălūdāmentum -i, *n.* military cloak.

pălūdātus -a -um, clad in the military cloak.

pălūdōsus -a -um, marshy, boggy.

pălumbes (pălumbis) -is, *m. and f.* a wood-pigeon, ring-dove.

1. pālŭs -i, *m.* a pale *or* stake.

2. pălūs -ūdis, *f.* a swamp, marsh.

pălŭster -tris -tre, marshy, boggy.

pampĭnĕus -a -um, pertaining to *or* consisting of vine-tendrils *or* leaves.

pampĭnus -i, *m. and f.* a vine-tendril, vine-leaf.

Pān, Pānos, *m.* the god of woods and shepherds.

pănăcēa -ae, *f. and* **pănăcēs -is,** *n. and* **pănax -ăcis,** *m.* a fabulous plant, panacea, heal-all.

Pănăthēnăĭcus -a -um, of *or* relating to the Athenian festival of the Panathenaea.

pānax = *panacea (q.v.).*

panchrestus -a -um, good *or* useful for everything.

pancrătĭum (-ŏn) -ĭi, *n.* a gymnastic contest.

Pandīōn -ŏnis, *m.* a king of Athens, father of Progne and Philomela.

pando, pandi, pansum *and* **passum, 3.** to stretch out, expand; *crines passi,* dishevelled hair; to throw open; *and in pass.,* to open, to fall, *pandĭtur,* lie spread out; *lac passum,* curdled.

pandus -a -um, bent, curved.

pango, panxi, panctum, *and* **pēgi** *and* **pĕpĭgi, pactum, 3.** to fasten, fix, drive in; to make; to undertake; to compose; to agree upon

pānĭcum -i, *n.* the Italian panic grass.

pānis -is, *m.* bread.

pannĭcŭlus -i, *m. (dim. of pannus),* a little rag.

Pannōnĭa -ae, *f.* part of modern Hungary, Slavonia and Bosnia.

pannōsus -a -um, ragged, tattered.

pannūcĕus (-ĭus) -a -um, wrinkled, shrivelled.

pannus -i, *m.* a piece of cloth, garment; *in sing. or plur.,* shabby clothes, rags; a rag.

Pănormus -i, *f. and* **Pănormum -i,** *n.* a town of Sicily.

pansa -ae, splay-footed.

pansus -a -um, *partic. of pando.*

panthēra -ae, *f.* a panther.

Pantheum -i, *n.* temple of Jupiter at Rome.

Panthŏus *and* **Panthus -i,** *m.* father of Euphorbus. **Panthŏīdes -ae,** *m.* a descendant of Panthus.

pantŏlābus -i, *m.* name of a parasite.

pantŏmīmus -i, *m.* a male dancer, mime.

păpae, *interj.* wonderful! indeed!

păpāver -ĕris, *n.* the poppy.

păpāvĕrĕus -a -um, of *or* relating to the poppy.

păpĭlĭo -ōnis, *m.* a butterfly.

păpĭlla -ae, *f.* a nipple, teat; the breast.

Păpĭrĭus -a -um, name of a Roman gens.

păpŭla -ae, *f.* a pimple.

păpȳrĭfĕr -fĕra -fĕrum, producing the papyrus.

păpȳrus -i, *f. and* **păpȳrum -i,** *n.* the plant papyrus; a garment made of the bark; paper made of the papyrus bark.

pār, păris, equal, like; suitable, appropriate; *par impar ludere,* to play at odd and even; *subst.,* a mate; a pair; an adversary.

părābĭlis -e, that can be easily procured.

părăsīta -ae, *f.* a toady, parasite.

părăsĭtus -i, *m.* a toady, parasite.

părătē, *adv.* with preparation, readily.

părātĭo -ōnis, *f.* a preparation.

1. părātus -a -um, *p. adj.* prepared, ready; *victoria,* easily won; inclined to; well provided, equipped; instructed.

2. părātus -us, *m.* preparation, provision, equipment.

Parca -ae, *f.* the goddess of fate. *Plur.,* *Parcae,* the three Fates.

parcē, *adv.* sparingly, economically; moderately; rarely, seldom.

parco, pĕperci, *and* **parsi, parsum, 3** to be sparing, moderate; to spare, refrain from injuring, *sibi ;* to desist from, cease; to refrain from.

parcus -a -um, sparing, thrifty; moderate; scanty, little, slight.

pardus -i, *m.* a panther, pard.

1. părens -entis, *p. adj.* obedient; *subst.,* **părentes -ium,** *m.* subjects.

2. părens -entis, *c.* a parent, *usually plur.;* author, cause, origin; *plur.* ancestors.

părentālis -e, parental; *subst.,* **părentālĭa -ĭum,** *n.* festival in honour of deceased parents.

părento, 1. to celebrate the *parentalia;* to avenge the death of a person by that of another.

pārĕo -ŭi -ĭtum, 2. to appear, become visible; to be clear; *impers. paret,* (legal), it is proved; to obey, *ducibus;* to yield; to be subject to, to serve.

părĭes -ĕtis, *m.* the wall of a house.

părĭĕtĭnae -ārum, *f.* old walls, ruins.

Părīlia = *Palilia (v. under Pales).*

părilis -e, similar, equal.
părĭo, pĕpĕri, partum, *fut. partic.*, păritūrus, 3. to bring forth; *ova*, to lay eggs; to produce; to cause, *suspicionem;* to invent, compose; to devise, obtain; *plur. subst.*, parta -ōrum, *n.* property that has been acquired.
Păris -ĭdis, *m.* son of Priam.
părĭtĕr, *adv.* in like manner, alike; at the same time as; also.
parma -ae, *f.* small round shield.
Parmĕnĭdes -is, *m.* a famous Greek philosopher of the Eleatic School.
parmātus -a -um, armed with the parma.
parmŭla -ae, *f.* (*dim. of parma*), a small round shield.
Parnāsus (ŏs) *and* Parnassus (ŏs) -i, *m.* a mountain sacred to Apollo and the Muses; *adj.*, Parnāsĭus.
1. păro, 1. to prepare, provide, equip; to obtain; to buy.
2. păro, 1. to esteem equally; to agree, arrange with.
3. păro -ōnis, *m.* a light vessel, skiff.
părŏchus -i, *m.* an officer who provided for ambassadors when on a journey; a host.
părŏpsis -ĭdis, *f.* a small dish.
Păros (-us) -i, *f.* an island in the Aegean Sea, famous for its white marble.
parra -ae, *f.* a bird of ill omen, the owl *or* the woodpecker.
parrĭcĭda -ae, *c.* a parricide; murderer of a free citizen; a traitor.
parrĭcĭdĭum -ĭi, *n.* parricide; murder of a free citizen; high treason.
pars, partis, *acc.* partim *and* partem, *f.* part, portion, piece; *pars . . . pars,* some . . . others; *parte . . . parte,* partly . . . partly; *in utramque partem* (on both sides); a party, faction; the rôle of an actor; office, duty.
parsĭmōnĭa -ae, *f.* thriftiness, parsimony.
parthĕnĭcē -ēs, *f.* the plant parthenium.
Parthĕnŏpē -ēs, *f.* old name of Neapolis.
Parthi -ōrum, *m.* a Scythian people. *Adj.*, Parthĭcus *and* Parthus.
partĭceps -cĭpis, sharing, participating in; *subst.*, a partaker, comrade.
partĭcĭpo, 1. to cause to share, share with anyone.
partĭcŭla -ae, *f.* (*dim. of pars*), a small part, particle.
partim, *adv.* partly, in part.
partĭo, 4. *and* partĭor, 4. *dep.* to divide, subdivide; to share.
partītē, *adv.* with proper divisions.
partītĭo -ōnis, *f.* a division; a distribution.
partītus -a -um, *partic. of partior.*
partŭrĭo, 4. to desire to bring forth, have the pains of labour; to bring forth, produce; *fig.* to meditate, intend; to be anxious.
partus -ūs, *m.* a bearing, a birth; the

time of bearing; that which is brought forth; *partus terrae*, the giants.
părum, *adv.* too little, not enough; *parum id facio,* I make little account of that; *compar., minus,* less; *sin minus,* but if not; *superl., minime,* in the least degree, very little, least of all; *with adjectives* = not at all; *in answers,* not at all.
părumper, *adv.* for a little while, a little space.
păruncŭlus -i, *m.* (*dim. of 3. paro*), a little skiff *or* vessel.
Pārus = *Paros* (*q.v.*).
parvĭtas -ātis, *f.* smallness.
parvŭlus -a -um (*dim. of parvus*), very small, minute; young.
parvus -a -um, *compar.* minor, *superl.* minĭmus; little, small. *Of value,* slight, unimportant; weak; *of intellect,* poor, unproductive; abject, mean; trifling, unimportant. *Compar., minor, with abl.* inferior to, dependent on; *te minor.* *Subst.,* parvum -i, *n.* a little; something little *or* slight; *adv.,* minĭmum, very little; *subst.,* parvus -i, *m.* a little boy.
pasco, pāvi, pastum, 3. to feed cattle, lead cattle to pasture; to nourish; to increase, enlarge; to feast; to feed on; to consume; pascor, pastus sum, pasci, 3. *dep.* to feed, eat, graze on. *With acc.,* to feed on.
pascŭus -a -um, fit for pasture; *subst.,* pascŭum -i, *n.* a pasture.
Pāsĭphăē -ēs, *f. and* Pāsĭphăa -ae, *f.* mother of the Minotaur.
passer -ĕris, *m.* a sparrow; a turbot *or* plaice.
passercŭlus -i, *m.* (*dim. of passer*), a little sparrow.
passim, *adv.* here and there, far and wide, in a disorderly manner; without distinction, indiscriminately.
passum -i, *n.* raisin-wine.
1. passus -a -um, *partic. of pando.*
2. passus -a -um, *partic. of patior.*
3. passus -ūs, *m.* a step, stride; a footstep, track; the pace = five feet; *mille passus*, a mile.
pastillus -i, *m.* (*dim. of panis*), a lozenge.
pastĭo -ōnis, *f.* a pasture.
pastor -ōris, *m.* a herd; a shepherd.
pastŏrālis -e, relating to a shepherd, pastoral.
pastŏrĭcĭus -a -um, relating to shepherds.
pastŏrĭus -a -um, relating to shepherds.
pastus -ūs, *m.* feeding; fodder, food; pasture.
Pătăra -ōrum, *n.* a city in Lycia, with a celebrated oracle of Apollo.
Pătăvĭum -ĭi, *n.* a town in Venetia, birthplace of the historian Livy, *now* Padua. *Adj.,* Pătăvīnus -a -um.
pătĕfăcĭo -fēci -factum, 3, *pass.,* pătĕfīo -factus sum -fĭĕri, to open, lay

open; to make accessible; to make visible; to reveal.

patĕfactĭo -ōnis, . a throwing open, disclosing.

pătella -ae, f. (dim. of patera), dish, plate.

pătens -entis, p. adj. open, accessible; exposed to.

pătentĕr, adv. openly, evidently.

pătĕo -tŭi, 2. to be open, lie open; to be accessible, to be at the service of, to be exposed to, to be visible; to be clear. Geograph. to stretch out; to spread, extend itself.

păter -tris, m. a father, sire; pater familias or familiae, the head of a household; patres, fathers, ancestors; senators.

pătĕra -ae, f. a shallow dish.

păternus -a -um, relating to a father, paternal.

pătesco, pătŭi, 3. to be opened, lie open; to be revealed, disclosed; to extend.

pătĭbilis -e, endurable; sensitive.

pătĭbŭlum -i, n. a yoke, an instrument of punishment.

pătĭens -entis, p. adj. bearing, capable of enduring, patiens laborum; patient; poet. firm.

pătĭentĕr, adv. patiently.

pătĭentĭa -ae, f. endurance; patience; faint-heartedness, subjection.

pătĭna -ae, f. a dish.

pătĭor, passus sum, 3. dep. to suffer, endure; to last, endure; to experience; to permit.

patrātŏr -ōris, m. an accomplisher (late).

patria -ae, f. fatherland, v. patrius.

patrĭcĭātus -ūs, m. the rank of a patrician.

patrĭcīda, one who murders his father.

patrĭcĭus -a -um, patrician, noble; subst., patricius, a patrician.

patrĭmōnĭum -ii, n. patrimony.

patrīmus -a -um, having a father still living.

patrĭus -a -um, paternal.

patrĭus a -um, relating to a father, paternal. Subst., pătria -ae, f. native land. Adj., pătrĭus.

patro, 1. to accomplish, execute, achieve.

patrōcĭnĭum -ii, n. protection, defence in a court of law; patrocinia = clients.

patrōcĭnor, 1. dep. to protect, defend.

Patrŏclus -i, m. friend of Achilles, slain by Hector.

patrōna -ae, f. protectress, patroness; the mistress of a freedman.

patrōnus -i, m. the protector, patron; advocate.

patruēlis -e, descended from a father's brother; cousinly.

1. **patrŭus** -i, m. paternal uncle; fig., a severe reprover.

2. **patrŭus** -a -um, of or relating to an uncle.

pătŭlus -a -um, open, standing open; wide spreading.

paucĭtas -ātis, f. fewness, scarcity.

paucŭlus -a -um (dim. of paucus), very small; in plur., very few.

paucus -a -um, plur., pauci -ae -a, few, little. Num subst., pauci -ōrum, m. a few; the oligarchs; pauca -ōrum, n. a few words.

paulātim (paullātim), adv. gradually, little by little; singly, one after another.

paulispĕr (paullispĕr), adv. a little while.

paulo (paullo), adv. a little.

paulŭlo (paullŭlo), a little.

paulŭlus (paullŭlus) -a -um (dim. of paulus), very little, very small; paulŭlum -i, n. subst., a very little; adv., a little.

paulus (paullus) -a -um, little, small subst., a little; adv., a little.

pauper -ĕris, poor, not wealthy; subst., pauper, a poor man; of things, scanty.

pauperculus -a -um (dim. of pauper), poor.

paupĕrĭes -ēi, f. poverty.

paupĕro, 1. to make poor; to deprive of anything.

paupertas -ātis, f. poverty.

pausa -ae, f. a pause, end.

Pausănĭās -ae, m. commander of the Spartans at Plataea.

pausĕa (pausĭa) and **pōsĕa** -ae, f. a species of olive.

pausillŭlum = pauxillulum, v. under pauxillulus.

pauxillŭlus -a -um (dim. of pauxillus), very small; subst., pauxillŭlum -i, n. a little.

pauxillus -a -um (dim. of paucus), small, little; subst., pauxillum -i, n. a little.

păvĕfăcĭo, 3. to frighten; only in partic., pavefactus, terrified.

păvĕo, păvi, 2. to fear, be afraid of; paveseo, 2. to fear, be afraid of.

păvĭdē, adv. in a state of terror.

păvĭdus -a -um, trembling, terrified; causing terror.

păvīmento, 1. to pave.

păvīmentum -i, n. pavement.

păvĭo, 4. to beat.

păvĭto, 1. to quake with fear; shiver with ague.

păvo -ōnis, m. a peacock.

păvŏr -ōris, m. a trembling, trepidation.

pax, pācis, f. peace; quiet; approval of the gods. Plur., paces, conditions or proposals of peace; cum pace, quietly; pace tuā, with your good leave.

peccātum -i, n. a sin, crime, fault.

peccātus -ū, m. a fault.

pecco, 1. to commit a fault, to sin; to fail, to err.

pecten -ĭnis, m. a comb; a weaver's comb; a rake; the clasping of the hands in trouble; an instrument with which the strings of the lyre were struck; a shell-fish.

pecto, pexi, pexum and **pectitum**, 3. to comb; to comb, card. *Partic.*, **pexus**, with the nap on, woolly; *tunica*, new.

pectus -ŏris, *n.* the breast, the breast-bone; the heart, soul.

pĕcu, *pl. pecua*, cattle.

pĕcŭārius -a -um, relating to cattle. *Adj.*, *res.*, the breeding of cattle. *Subst.*, **pĕcŭārius -ii**, *m.* a breeder of cattle, grazier; **pĕcŭāria -ŏrum**, *n.* herds of cattle.

pĕcūlātor -ŏris, *m.* one who embezzles the public money.

pĕcūlātus -ūs, *m.* embezzlement of the public money, peculation.

pĕcūliāris -e, belonging to one's private property; proper, special; peculiar; extraordinary.

pĕcūlio, 1. to provide with private property.

pĕcūlium -ii, *n.* property; the private property possessed by a son independent of the father.

pĕcūnia -ae, *f.* property; money, cash; *accipere pecuniam*, to allow oneself to be bribed.

pĕcūniārius -a -um, pecuniary.

pĕcūniōsus -a -um, wealthy, rich.

1. **pĕcus -ŏris**, *n.* cattle, a herd, flock.

2. **pĕcus -ŭdis**, *f.* a single head of cattle, a beast, animal.

pĕdālis -e, of the length or breadth of a foot.

pĕdārius -a -um, relating to a foot; *senatores pedarii*, senators who held no curule office; *subst.*, **pĕdārii -ōrum**, *m.*

pĕdes -itis, *m.* one who goes on foot; a foot-soldier; *collect.*, infantry.

pĕdester -tris -tre, on foot, pedestrian; *copiae*, infantry; relating to land. *Of style*, written in prose; simple, prosaic.

pĕdĕtemptim, *adv.* gradually, cautiously.

pĕdica -ae, *f.* a trap, a fetter.

pĕdisĕquus -i, and **pĕdisĕqua -ae**, *m.* lackey; *f.* a waiting-woman.

pĕditātus -ūs, *m.* infantry.

pĕdum -i, *n.* a shepherd's crook.

Pĕgăsis -idis, *f.* a water-nymph.

Pĕgăsus (-ŏs) -i, *m.* the winged horse. *Pegasides*, the Muses.

pegma -ătis, *n.* bookcase, shelf; a theatrical machine.

pĕiĕro (periĕro) and **periūro**, 1. to commit perjury.

pĕior, *comp. of malus (q.v.)*.

pĕiūrus = *periurus (q.v.)*.

pĕlăgius -a -um, relating to the sea, marine.

pĕlăgus -i, *n.* the sea, ocean. *Poet.* a flood.

pĕlămys -ȳdis, *f.* the young tunny-fish.

Pĕlasgi -ōrum and (*poet.*) **-ûm**, *m.* the oldest inhabitants of Greece; *poet.* the Greeks.

Pēlĕus -ĕi and **-ĕos**, *m.* father of Achilles; **Pēlīdēs -ae**, *m.* son of Peleus = Achilles.

pelex (pellex) and **paelex -lĭcis**, *f.* a concubine.

Pēliās -ae, *m.* king in Thessaly, half-brother of Aeson, whose son Jason he sent to fetch the golden fleece. On Jason's return Pelias, at the instigation of Medea, was slain by his own daughters.

pēlicātus (paelicātus) -us, *m.* concubinage.

Pēlīdēs, *v. Peleus*.

Pēligni = *Paeligni (q.v.)*.

Pēlion -ii, *n.* and **Pēlius -ii**, *m.* mountain in Thessaly.

pellăcia -ae, *f.* an enticing, alluring.

pellax -ācis, deceitful, seductive.

pellectio (perlectio) -ōnis, *f.* a reading through, perusing.

pellĕgo = *perlego (q.v.)*.

pellex = *pelex (q.v.)*.

pellicātus = *pelicatus (q.v.)*.

pellicio -lexi -lectum, 3. to entice, decoy.

pellĭcŭla -ae, *f. (dim. of pellis)*, a little skin or hide.

pellis -is, *f.* a hide, skin; leather; a shoe-latchet; a shoe.

pellitus -a -um, clothed in hides or skins.

pello, pĕpŭli, pulsum, 3. to strike, knock against; *fores*, to knock at the door; to make an impression upon; to impel, propel, move; to expel; to repel; to banish.

pellūcĕo = *perluceo (q.v.)*.

pellūcidŭlus = *perlucidulus (q.v.)*.

pellūcidus = *perlucidus (q.v.)*.

Pĕlŏponnēsus -i, *f.* the Peloponnesus; *adj.* **Pĕlŏponnēsius.**

Pĕlops -ŏpis, *m.* a mythical king of Phrygia, son of Tantalus, father of Atreus and Thyestes, grandfather of Agamemnon and Menelaus; when a child he was killed by his father and served up as food to the gods; he was restored to life through the agency of Hermes, and his shoulder, which had been eaten by Demeter, was replaced by an ivory one. *Subst.*, **Pĕlŏpidae -ārum**, *m.* descendants of Pelops.

pĕlōris -idis, *f.* a large species of mussel.

pelta -ae, *f.* a crescent-shaped shield.

peltastae -ārum, *m.* soldiers armed with the pelta.

peltātus -a -um, armed with the pelta.

pelvis -is, *f.* a basin.

pĕnārius (pĕnŭārius) -a -um, relating to provisions; *cella*, store-room.

Pĕnātes -ium, *m.* household deities among the Romans; the house, dwelling; *poet.* the cells of bees.

pĕnātigĕr -gĕra -gĕrum, carrying the Penates.

pendĕo, pĕpendi, 2. to hang, hang down; to be hung up; to overhang; to hover; to hang about a place; to listen attentively; to be discontinued; to be in suspense, undecided; to depend upon; to imitate.

pendo, pĕpendi, pensum, 3. to cause to hang down; to weigh; consider, judge; to value, esteem; to pay; *poenas,* suffer punishment; *intransit.,* to weigh.

pendŭlus -a -um, hanging, hanging down; undecided.

pēne = *paene* (*q.v.*).

Pēnĕlŏpa -ae, *f.* and **Pēnĕlŏpē -ēs,** *f.* the wife of Ulysses.

pĕnĕs, *prep. with acc.,* with, in possession of, in the power of; *penes se esse,* to be in one's senses.

pĕnĕtrābilis -e, that can be passed through; easily penetrating, piercing.

pĕnĕtrālis -e, penetrating; inward, internal, interior. *Subst.,* **pĕnĕtrāle** and **pĕnĕtrāl -ālis,** *n., gen. plur.,* **pĕnĕtrālia -ium,** *n.* interior of a house *or* city; shrine of a temple.

pĕnĕtro, 1. to set, place, put in; to penetrate. *Intransit.,* to enter, penetrate into.

pēnĭcillum -ae, *n.* and **pēnĭcillus -i,** *m.* (*dim. of peniculus*), painter's brush *or* pencil.

pēnĭcŭlus -i, *m.* (*dim. of penis*), a brush; a sponge.

pēnis -is, *m.* a tail.

pĕnĭtē, *adv.* inwardly, internally.

pĕnĭtūs, *adv.* internally; in the inmost part, deep within; accurately; thoroughly, entirely; far away.

penna -ae, *f.* a feather; wing; flight; *poet.,* arrow.

pennātus -a -um, feathered, winged.

pennĭgĕr -gĕra -gĕrum, feathered, winged.

pennĭpes -pĕdis, wing-footed.

pennĭpŏtens -entis, winged; *subst.,* **pennĭpŏtentes -ium,** *f.* = birds.

pennŭla -ae, *f.* (*dim. of penna*), a little wing.

pensilis -e, hanging, pendent.

pensĭo -ōnis, *f.* payment, day of payment.

pensĭto, 1. to weigh, ponder, consider; to pay.

penso, 1. to weigh; to judge; to ponder, consider; to compare; to repay, compensate; to pay for, purchase with.

pensum -i, *n.* wool weighed out to a spinner as a day's work; a day's work, task; engagement.

pensus -a -um, *p. adj.,* esteemed, valued, prized.

pentămĕter -tri, *m.* a pentameter verse.

Pentĕlĭcus mons, mountain near Athens celebrated for its marble quarries.

Penthĕūs -ĕi *and* **-ĕos,** *acc.* **-ĕum** *and* **-ĕa,** king of Thebes.

pēnūria -ae, *f.* want, need, penury.

pēnus -ūs *and* **-i,** *c.,* **pĕnum -i,** *n.,* and **pĕnus -ŏris,** *n.* provisions, victuals.

peplum -i, *n.* and **peplus -i,** *m.* the robe with which the statue of Athene was clad at the Panathenaea.

per, *prep. with acc.* through, along, over; about; *of time,* during, in the course of; by, by means of; *per se,* by oneself, without help; *per litteras,* by letter; *in oaths,* by; *oro te per deos.*

pĕra -ae, a wallet.

pĕrabsurdus -a -um, excessively absurd.

pĕraccommŏdātus -a -um, very convenient.

pĕrācer -cris -cre, very sharp.

pĕrăcerbus -a -um, very sour, harsh.

pĕractĭo -ōnis, *f.* a completion.

pĕrăcūtē, *adv.* very sharply, very acutely.

pĕrăcūtus -a -um, very sharp; piercing; sharp-witted.

pĕrădŏlescens -entis, a very young man.

pĕrădŏlescentŭlus -i, *m.* a very young man.

pĕraequē, *adv.* quite alike, quite equally.

pĕrăgĭto, 1. to drive about violently, harass.

pĕrăgo -ēgi -actum, 3. to pierce through, transfix; to drive about, harass; *agrum,* to till; to complete, accomplish; *fabulam,* to play a drama through; *legal,* to conduct a suit to the end; to go through, relate.

pĕrăgrātĭo -ōnis, *f.* a wandering through.

pĕrăgro, 1. to wander through, travel through; to penetrate, examine.

pĕrămans -antis, very loving.

pĕrămantĕr, *adv.* very lovingly.

pĕrambŭlo, 1. to walk through, trave through.

pĕrămoenus -a -um, very pleasant.

pĕramplus -a -um, very large.

pĕrangustē, *adv.* very narrowly.

pĕrangustus -a -um, very narrow.

pĕranno, 1. to live through a year.

pĕrantīquus -a -um, very old.

pĕrappŏsitus -a um, very suitable (*with dat.*).

perardŭus -a -um, very difficult.

pĕrargūtus -a -um, very clever, witty.

pĕrāro, 1. to plough through; to cover with wrinkles; to write.

pĕrattentē, *adv.* very attentively.

pĕrattentus -a -um, very attentive.

perbacchor, 1. to revel throughout *or* during.

perbĕātus -a -um, very happy.

perbellē, *adv.* very prettily, very finely.

perbĕnē, *adv.* very well.

perbĕnĕvŏlus -a -um, very well disposed to.

perbĕnignē, *adv.* very kindly.

perbĭbo -bĭbi, 3. to drink in, drink up; to take in mentally.

perblandus -a -um, very charming.

perbŏnus -a -um, very good.

perbrĕvis -e, very short.

perbrĕvĭtĕr, *adv.* very briefly.

perca -ae, *f.* a fish, the perch.

percălĕfăcio -fēci -factum, 3. to make very warm; *pass.*, **percălĕfīo -factus sum -fiĕri**, to become very warm.

percălesco -călŭi, 3. to become very warm.

percallesco -callŭi, 3. to become quite callous; to become experienced.

percārus -a -um, very costly; much beloved.

percautus -a -um, very cautious.

percĕlebro, 1. to talk of often; *in pass.* = to be in the mouths of people.

percĕlĕr -is -e, very swift.

percĕlĕritĕr, *adv.* very swiftly.

percello -cŭli -culsum, 3. to beat down, overturn, shatter; to ruin; to dispirit, daunt; to strike, push.

percenseō -censŭi, 2. to count through, reckon; to survey; to judge; to travel through.

perceptio -ōnis, *f.* a gathering together; apprehension, comprehension.

perceptus -a -um, *partic. of percipio.* *Subst.*, **percepta -ōrum**, *n.* principles, rules.

percīdo -cīdi -cīsum, 3. to beat, cut to pieces.

percio -cīvi -cītum, 4. *and* **percĭĕo**, 2. to stir up; **percitus**, aroused, excited; irritable.

percipio -cēpi -ceptum, 3. to take possession of, seize; to receive; to perceive, feel; to learn; to understand.

percitus -a -um, *partic. of percieo.*

percīvilis -e, very gracious, courteous.

1. **percōlo**, 1. to strain through a sieve.
2. **percŏlo -cŏlŭi -cultum**, 3. to adorn; to honour.

percōmis -e, very friendly, courteous.

percommŏdē, *adv.* very conveniently.

percommŏdus -a -um, very convenient, appropriate.

percontātio (percunctātio) -ōnis, *f.* an inquiry, question.

percontātor (percunctātor) -ōris, *m.* an inquirer.

percontor (percunctor), 1. *dep.* to inquire, question.

percŏquo -coxi -coctum, 3. to boil thoroughly; to heat; to ripen; to burn.

percrēbresco -brŭi, *and* **percrēbesco -bŭi**, 3. to become prevalent, be well known.

percrĕpo -crĕpŭi -crĕpĭtum, 3. to resound, ring with.

percunctor, percunctatio, *etc.* = *percontor, percontatio, etc.* (*q.v.*).

percŭpĭdus -a -um, very fond of.

percūriōsus -a -um, very inquisitive.

percūro, 1. to cure, heal thoroughly.

percurro -cŭcurri *or* **-curri -cursum**, 3. to run along *or* over; to hasten to. *Transit.*, to run through, travel through; to discuss cursorily, mention in passing.

percursātio -ōnis, *f.* a running through, travelling through.

percursio -ōnis, *f.* a rapid consideration; a rapid passing over a subject.

percurso, 1. to ramble over *or* about. *Intransit.*, to rove about.

percussio -ōnis, *f.* a striking against; a beating time, *hence* time, rhythm.

percussor -ōris, *m.* a striker; assassin.

percussus -ūs, *m.* a beating, knocking.

percŭtio -cussi -cussum, 3. to pierce, transfix; to strike; to kill; to play upon; to affect, astound, shock; to deceive; to afflict.

perdēlirus -a -um, senseless.

perdifficilis -e, very difficult.

perdifficĭlĭtĕr, *adv.* with very great difficulty.

perdignus -a -um, quite worthy of.

perdīligens -entis, very diligent.

perdīligentĕr, *adv.* very diligently.

perdisco -didici, 3. to learn thoroughly.

perdisertē, *adv.* very eloquently.

perditē, *adv.* exceedingly; in an abandoned manner.

perditor -ōris, *m.* a destroyer.

perditus -a -um, *p. adj.* wretched, ruined; immoderate; *perditus luctu*, sunk in grief; profligate.

perdiū, *adv.* for a very long time.

perdiūturnus -a -um, very tedious.

perdīvĕs -itis, very rich.

perdix -īcis, *c.* a partridge.

perdo -didi -ditum, 3. (*in pass., gen.*, **pereo, perditus, perire**),to destroy, ruin; to waste, squander; to lose.

perdŏcĕo -dŏcŭi -doctum, 2. to instruct thoroughly.

perdoctus -a -um, very learned, very skilful.

perdŏlĕo -dŏlŭi -dŏlĭtum, 2. to suffer great pain *or* grief.

perdŏlesco -dŏlŭi, 3. to suffer violent pain *or* grief.

perdŏmo -dŏmŭi -dŏmĭtum, 1. to tame thoroughly; to conquer.

perdūco -duxi -ductum, 3. to lead *or* bring to any place; to construct buildings, aqueducts, *etc., from one point to another*; to induce; to prolong; to spread over, besmear.

perductor -ōris, *m.* a pander.

perduellio -ōnis, *f.* treason.

perduellis -is, *m.* a public enemy.

perdŭim -is -it, *etc., old, pres. subj.*, perdo.

perdulcis -e, very sweet.

perdūro, 1. to endure.

pĕrĕdo -ēdi -ēsum, 3. to devour entirely; to consume.

pĕregrē, *adv.* in *or* to a foreign country, abroad; from abroad.

pĕregrīnābundus -a -um, travelling about.

pĕregrīnātio -ōnis, *f.* travelling in foreign countries.

pĕregrīnātor -ōris, *m.* one who travels about.

pĕrĕgrīnītas -ātis, f. the condition of a foreigner; foreign manners, customs.

pĕrĕgrīnor, 1. dep. to sojourn or travel in foreign countries; to stray, ramble (mentally); to be strange, foreign.

pĕrĕgrīnus -a -um, foreign, strange; inexperienced in; subst., pĕrĕgrīnus -i, m. and peregrina -ae, f.; foreigner, stranger.

pĕrēlĕgans -antis, very pretty, neat, elegant.

pĕrēlĕgantēr, adv. very prettily, elegantly.

pĕrēlŏquens -entis, very eloquent.

pĕremnis -e, relating to the crossing of a river.

pĕremptus -a -um, partic. of perimo.

pĕrendĭē, adv. the day after to morrow.

pĕrendĭnus -a -um, relating to the day after to-morrow.

pĕrennis -e, lasting throughout the year; lasting, perennial.

pĕrennĭtas -ātis, f. duration, perpetuity.

pĕrenno, 1. to last many years.

pĕrĕo, -ĭi and -īvi -ĭtum, 4. to pass away, disappear; to be lost, to perish; to pine away; to be wasted; to be ruined politically; perii ! I am undone.

pĕrĕquĭto, 1. to ride through, ride round.

pĕrerro, 1. to wander, ramble through.

pĕrērūdītus -a -um, very learned.

pĕrexĭgŭē, adv. very scantily.

pĕrexĭgŭus -a -um, very small; of time, very short.

pĕrexpĕdītus -a -um, very easy.

perfăcētē, adv. very wittily.

perfăcētus -a -um, very witty.

perfăcĭlē, adv. very easily.

perfăcĭlis -e, very easy; very courteous.

perfămĭlĭāris -e, familiar; subst., m. a very intimate friend.

perfectē, adv. perfectly, completely.

perfectĭo -ōnis, f. perfection, completion.

perfector -ōris, m. a perfecter, finisher.

perfectus -a -um, p. adj. perfect, finished.

perfĕrens -entis, p. adj. patient.

perfĕro -tŭli -lātum -ferre, to carry through, bring to a certain end; reflex., se perferre hinc, to betake oneself; to carry, bring; (pass., to reach); to bring news; to maintain, preserve; to carry through, complete; to suffer, endure.

perfĭca -ae, f. she that accomplishes.

perfĭcĭo -fēci -fectum, 3. to complete, finish; to live through; to achieve, to conduct to a close; to accomplish.

perfĭdēlis -e, very faithful.

perfĭdĭa -ae, f. faithlessness, treachery.

perfĭdĭōsē, adv. treacherously.

perfĭdĭōsus -a -um, faithless, treacherous.

perfĭdus -a -um, faithless, treacherous.

perfixus -a -um, pierced through, transfixed.

perflābĭlis -e, that can be blown through.

perflāgĭtĭōsus -a -um, very shameful.

perflo, 1. to blow through, blow over.

perfluctŭo, 1. to swarm all over.

perflŭo -fluxi -fluxum, 3. to stream through.

perfŏdĭo -fōdi -fossum, 3. to dig through, pierce through.

perfŏro, 1. to pierce through, perforate.

perfrēquens -entis, much frequented.

perfrĭco -frĭcŭi -frĭcātum and -frictum, 1. to rub over, to scratch.

perfrĭgĭdus -a -um, very cold.

perfringo -frēgi -fractum, 3. to break through, shatter; to disregard, violate; animos, to overpower.

perfrŭor -fructus sum, 3. dep. to enjoy thoroughly; to execute completely.

perfŭga -ae, m. a deserter.

perfŭgĭo -fūgi -fŭgĭtum, 3. to flee away ; take refuge ; to desert to the enemy.

perfŭgĭum -ii, n. refuge.

perfunctĭo -ōnis, f. a performing, discharging.

perfundo -fūdi -fūsum, 3. to pour over; to moisten, besprinkle; perfundi, to bathe in, swim in; to dye, stain; to imbue.

perfungor -functus sum, 3. dep. with abl., to accomplish, perform, discharge; to go through, endure; to enjoy, epulis.

perfūro, 3. to rage furiously.

Pergămum -i, n. and Pergămus (-ōs) -i, f. The citadel of Troy; gen. plur., Pergăma -ōrum, n.

pergaudĕo, 2. to rejoice exceedingly.

pergo, perrexi, perrectum, 3. to continue, proceed with, iter; pergere ad eum ire; perge porro.

pergrandis -e, very large, very great.

pergrātus -a -um, very pleasant.

pergrăvis -e, very weighty, very important.

pergrăvĭtēr, adv. very seriously.

pergŭla -ae, f. a shed or outhouse, a shop, workshop; a school.

pĕrhĭbĕo -ŭi -ĭtum, 2. to bring forward, propose; to say; to consider.

pĕrhĭlum, very little.

pĕrhŏnōrĭfĭcē, adv. very respectfully.

pĕrhŏnōrĭfĭcus -a -um, very honourable very respectful.

pĕrhorrĕo, 2. to shudder at, to dread.

pĕrhorresco -horrŭi, 3. to become rough; to be filled with dread, to shudder; to shudder at; to quake.

pĕrhorrĭdus -a -um, very dreadful.

pĕrhūmānĭtēr, adv. very civilly, very kindly.

pĕrhūmānus -a -um, very friendly, kind.

Pĕrĭclēs -is, m. a celebrated Athenian statesman.

pĕrĭclĭtātĭo -ōnis, f. a trial, experiment.

pĕrĭclĭtor, 1. dep. Intransit., to try, make a trial; to be in danger. Transit., to test, prove; to risk.

pĕrĭcŭlōsē, adv. dangerously; aegrotare.

pĕrīcŭlōsus -a -um, full of danger, perilous.

pĕrīcŭlum (contr. pĕrīclum) -i, n. a trial, proof, test; peril; periculum est, with ne and the subj., there is danger that; a trial, action; a legal record.

pĕrīdōnĕus -a -um, very fit, appropriate.

pĕrĭĕro = peiero (q.v.).

pĕrillustris -e, very evident; very distinguished.

pĕrimbēcillus -a -um, very weak.

pĕrimo -ēmi -emptum, 3. to destroy, ruin; to kill; to hinder, frustrate.

pĕrincertus -a -um, very uncertain.

pĕrincommŏdē, adv. very inconveniently.

pĕrincommŏdus -a -um, very inconvenient.

pĕrindĕ, adv. as, just as, in a like manner; foll. by ac si, atque. quasi, etc.

pĕrindignē, adv. very indignantly.

pĕrindulgens -entis, very indulgent.

pĕrinfāmis -e, very infamous.

pĕrinfirmus -a -um, very weak.

pĕringĕnīōsus -a -um, very clever.

pĕrinīquus -a -um, very unfair; very unwilling.

pĕrinsignis -e, very remarkable.

pĕrinvīsus -a -um, much hated.

pĕrinvītus -a -um, very unwilling.

Pĕrĭpătēticus -a -um, Peripatetic, belonging to the Peripatetic or Aristotelian school of philosophy; subst., Pĕrĭpătētici -ōrum, m. Peripatetic philosophers.

pĕripĕtasma -ătis, n. curtain, hanging.

pĕrīrātus -a -um, very angry.

pĕriscĕlis -ĭdis, f. garter or anklet.

pĕristrōma -ătis, n. curtain, carpet.

pĕristȳlum -i, n. peristyle.

pĕrītē, adv. skilfully, cleverly.

pĕrītĭa -ae, f. knowledge, skill.

pĕrito, 1. to perish utterly.

pĕrītus -a -um, experienced, skilful.

pĕriŭcundē, adv. very pleasantly.

pĕriŭcundus -a -um, very pleasant.

pĕriūrĭum -ii, n. perjury.

pĕriūro = peiero (q.v.).

pĕriūrus (pĕiūrus) -a -um, perjured.

perlābor -lapsus sum, 3. dep. to glide through, penetrate; reach to.

perlaetus -a -um, very joyful.

perlātē, adv. very widely, very extensively.

perlectio = pellectio (q.v.).

perlĕgo (pellĕgo) -lēgi -lectum, 3. to scan, examine accurately; to read through; call over.

perlĕvis -e, very slight.

perlĕvitĕr, adv. very slightly.

perlĭbens (perlŭbens) -entis, very willing.

perlĭbentĕr, adv. very willingly.

perlĭbĕrālis -e, well-bred.

perlĭbĕrālitĕr, adv. very liberally.

perlĭbet (perlŭbet) -bŭit, 3. it is pleasing.

perlīcĭo = pellicio (q.v.).

perlīto, 1. to sacrifice with favourable omens.

perlongē, adv. very far.

perlongus -a -um, very long.

perlŭbet, etc. = perlibet, etc. (q.v.).

perlūcĕo (pellūcĕo) -luxi, 2. to shine through; be visible; to be transparent.

perlūcĭdŭlus (pellūcĭdŭlus) -a -um (dim. of perlucidus), somewhat transparent.

perlūcĭdus (pellūcĭdus) -a -um, transparent; bright.

perluctŭōsus -a -um, very mournful.

perlŭo -lŭi -lūtum, 3. to wash, bathe.

perlustro, 1. to wander, range through; to regard, consider.

permagnus -a -um, very large; subst., permagnum -i, n. a very great thing.

permălĕ, adv. unsuccessfully.

permănantĕr, adv. by flowing through.

permănĕo -mansi -mansum, 2. to remain, stay; to last, continue.

permāno, 1. to flow through; to penetrate; to flow to; to reach.

permansĭo -ōnis, f. a remaining; abiding in an opinion.

permārīnus -a -um, relating to the sea.

permātūresco -mātūrŭi, 3. to become thoroughly ripe.

permĕdĭocris -e, very moderate.

permĕo, 1. to go through, traverse; to penetrate or reach; to pervade.

permētĭor -mensus sum, 4. dep. to measure out; to traverse.

permĕtŭens -entis = praemetuens (q.v.).

permĭnūtus -a -um, very small, very trifling.

permīrus -a -um, very wonderful.

permiscĕo -miscŭi -mixtum or mistum, 2. to mix thoroughly; to confound, confuse.

permissĭo -ōnis, f. yielding, surrender; permission.

permissus, m. permission; only in abl., permissu legis.

permitto -mīsi -missum, 3. to let go, let loose; to throw; to make use of; to surrender; to give up, sacrifice; to allow; partic. subst., permissum -i, n. permission.

permixtē, adv. confusedly.

permixtĭo -ōnis, f. a mixing, mixture.

permŏdestus -a -um, very modest, very moderate.

permŏdicus -a -um, very moderate.

permŏlestē, adv. with much difficulty.

permŏlestus -a -um, very troublesome.

permōtĭo -ōnis, f. motion, agitation.

permŏvĕo -mōvi -mōtum, 2. to move, excite, agitate mentally; to persuade; to affect.

permulcĕo -mulsi -mulsum and (rarely) -mulctum, 2. to stroke; to charm, soothe; to touch gently.

permultus -a -um, very much, very many; *subst.,* **permultum -i,** *n.* much.

permūnio -īvi -ītum, 3. to fortify completely.

permūtātio -ōnis, *f.* alteration ; an exchange.

permūto, 1. to change completely; to exchange, barter.

perna -ae, *f.* a leg of pork, a ham.

pernĕcessārius -a -um, very necessary; very intimate.

pernĕcessē, *adv.* very necessary.

pernĕgo, 1. to persist in denying.

perniciābilis -e, deadly, fatal.

perniciālis -e, deadly, fatal.

pernicies -ēi, *f.* destruction, calamity.

perniciōsē, *adv.* destructively, perniciously.

perniciōsus -a -um, calamitous, dangerous.

pernicitas -ātis, *f.* swiftness, agility.

perniciter, *adv.* swiftly, nimbly.

pernimium, *adv.* far too much.

pernix -icis, swift, nimble, active.

pernōbilis -e, very celebrated.

pernocto, 1. to pass the night.

pernosco -nōvi -nōtum, 3. to investigate thoroughly.

pernōtesco -nōtŭi, 3. to become generally well known.

pernox -nocte (*only in nom. and abl.*), lasting all night.

pernŭmĕro, 1. to count out, reckon completely.

pēro -ōnis, *m.* a boot of rough leather.

pērobscūrus -a -um, very obscure.

pērōdi -ōsus sum, to hate exceedingly; *only in partic. perf.,* **pĕrōsus -a -um,** hating.

pērōdiōsus -a -um, much hated, very troublesome.

pērofficiōsē, *adv.* very obligingly.

pērŏlĕo, 2. to emit a bad smell.

pērōnātus -a -um, wearing boots of untanned leather.

pēropportūnē, *adv.* very opportunely.

pēropportūnus -a -um, very opportune, very convenient.

pēroptātō, *adv.* according to one's desire.

pērōpus, *adv.* very necessary.

pērōrātio -ōnis, *f.* peroration.

perornātus -a -um, very ornate.

perorno, 1. to adorn greatly.

pērōro, 1. to plead a cause throughout, explain thoroughly; to end; to conclude a speech; to close a case.

pērōsus -a -um, *v. perodi.*

perpāco, 1. to tranquillize.

perparcē, *adv.* very frugally.

perparvŭlus -a -um, very little.

perparvus -a -um, very little.

perpastus -a -um, well fed.

perpauculus -a -um, very few, very little.

perpaucus -a -um, very few, very little.

perpaulŭlum (**perpaullŭlum**) **-i,** *n. dim.* a very, very little.

perpaulum (**perpaullum**), *adv.* a very little.

perpauper -ĕris, very poor.

perpello -pŭli -pulsum, 3. to drive, to urge, compel; to make a deep impression on.

perpendiculum -i, *n.* a plumb line; *ad perpendiculum,* in a straight line.

perpendo -pendi -pensum, 3. to weigh carefully, to consider.

perpĕram, *adv.* wrongly, falsely.

perpessio -ōnis, *f.* suffering, endurance.

perpĕtior -pessus, 3. *dep.* to endure, suffer steadfastly.

perpetro, 1. to complete, accomplish, effect.

perpĕtŭitas -ātis, *f.* perpetuity, continuity; *ad perpetuitatem,* for ever.

1. perpĕtŭō, *adv.* perpetually, for ever.

2. perpĕtŭo, 1. to continue, perpetuate; to pronounce in unbroken succession.

perpĕtŭus -a -um, uninterrupted, continual ; *of time,* lasting ; universal, general.

perplăcĕo, 2. to please exceedingly.

perplexē, *adv.* confusedly, obscurely.

perplexus -a -um, confused, intricate; obscure, ambiguous.

perplicātus -a -um, entangled, involved.

perpŏlio, 4. to smooth, polish thoroughly; to perfect.

perpŏlītus a -um, *p. adj.* accomplished, refined.

perpōpŭlor, 1. *dep.* to lay waste.

perporto, 1. to transport to any place.

perpōtātio -ōnis, *f.* a drinking-bout.

perpōto, 1. to continue drinking ; to drink up.

perprēmo = *perprimo* (*q.v.*).

perprimo -pressi -pressum, 3. to press hard; *cubilia,* to lie upon.

perprŏpinquus -a -um, very nearly related.

perprosper -ēra -ērum, very prosperous.

perpugnax -ācis, very pugnacious.

perpulcher -chra -chrum, very beautiful.

perpurgo, 1. to make thoroughly clean, to explain thoroughly; to refute.

perpusillus -a -um, very small.

perquam, *adv.* extremely.

perquiro -sīvi -sītum, 3. to inquire earnestly, make accurate inquiries.

perquisītē, *adv.* accurately.

perrāro, *adv.* very seldom.

perrārus -a -um, very uncommon.

perrĕconditus -a -um, very abstruse.

perrēpo -repsi -reptum, 3. to crawl through, creep over.

perrepto, 1. to crawl about, to crawl through.

perrīdĭcŭlē, *adv.* very laughably.

perrīdĭcŭlus -a -um, very laughable.

perrŏgo, 1. to ask one after another.

perrumpo -rūpi -ruptum, 3. *Intransit.,* to break through. *Transit.,* to break through; to subdue, overpower.

Persa, v. *Persae.*
Persae -ārum, m. the Persians; *sing.,*
Persa -ae, m. *and* **Perses -ae,** m.;
Persicus -i, f. the peach-tree.
persaepě, adv. very often.
persalsē, adv. very wittily.
persalsus -a -um, very witty.
persălūtātio -ōnis f. a greeting.
persălūto, 1. to greet a number in succession.
persanctē, adv. very solemnly.
persăpiens -entis, very wise.
persăpientěr, adv. very wisely.
perscientěr, adv. very discreetly.
perscindo -scidi -scissum, 3. to tear to
pieces.
perscītus -a -um, very clever, very pretty.
perscrībo -scripsi -scriptum, 3. to write
down accurately, explicitly; to note
down; to notify, announce; to assign
to in writing.
perscriptio -ōnis, f. an entering in a register *or* account book; assigning by a
written document.
perscriptor -ōris, m. one who writes down.
perscrūtor, 1. dep. to search through; to
investigate.
persěco -sěcŭi -sectum, 1. to cut off
entirely, cut through; to dissect, lay bare.
persector, 1. dep. to follow, pursue
eagerly; investigate.
persěcūtio -ōnis, f. a prosecution.
persěděo -sēdi -sessum, 2. to remain
sitting.
persěgnis -e, very sluggish.
persěnex -is, very old.
persentio -sensi -sensum, 4. to perceive
distinctly; to feel deeply.
persentisco, 3. to perceive distinctly;
to feel deeply.
Persěphŏnē -ēs, f. the Greek name of
Proserpina.
persěquor -sěcūtus *and* **sěqŭtus sum,**
-sěqui, 3. dep. to follow constantly, pursue earnestly; to search through a place;
to strive after; to busy oneself with; to
imitate; to be a follower of; to avenge;
to punish; to prosecute; to accomplish,
execute; to treat of, describe, to attain
to; to call in; to register.
1. Perses -ae *and* **Perseūs -ěi,** m.
the last king of Macedonia, defeated by
the Roman general Aemilius Paulus
(168 B.C.). *Adj.,* **Persicus.**
2. Perses -ae, m. a Persian, v. *Persae.*
Perseūs -ěi *and* **-ěos,** m. slayer of the
Medusa.
persěvērans -antis, p. adj. enduring,
persevering.
persěvērantěr, adv. perseveringly.
persěvērantia -ae, f. perseverance.
persěvēro, 1. to persist, persevere; to
continue *or* finish a journey. *Transit.,*
to proceed with; *with acc. and infin.,* to
maintain that.
persěvērus -a -um, very strict.

Persia, Persia.
Persicus, v. *Persae and Perses.*
persīděo -sēdi -sessum, 2. = *persedeo*
(q.v.).
persīdo -sēdi -sessum, 3. to settle down.
persigno, 1. to note down, record.
persimilis -e, very similar.
persimplex -icis, very simple.
persisto, 3. to remain constant, persist
in anything.
Persius -ii, m. a celebrated Roman
satirist.
persolvo -solvi -sŏlūtum, 3. to unloose;
to explain; to pay, pay off; to discharge
an obligation.
persōna -ae, f. the mask worn by actors;
the character represented; a personality,
character.
persōnātus -a -um, masked; fictitious,
not genuine.
persŏno -sŏnŭi -sŏnitum, 1. to sound
through, resound thoroughly; to shout;
to perform upon a musical instrument.
Transit., to fill with sound, cause to
resound; to cry loudly.
perspectus -a -um, p. adj. well known.
perspěcŭlor, 1. dep. to investigate.
perspergo, 3. to sprinkle, moisten.
perspicācitas -ātis, f. sharp-sightedness.
perspicax -ācis, sharp-sighted, acute.
perspicientia -ae, f. a perfect acquaintance with *or* knowledge of.
perspicio -spexi -spectum, 3. *Intransit.,*
to look into. *Transit.,* to see through,
behold; to examine; to investigate,
ascertain.
perspicŭē, adv. clearly, evidently.
perspicŭitas -ātis, f. clearness, brightness.
perspicŭus -a -um, transparent, bright;
clear, evident.
persterno -strāvi -strātum, 3. to make
quite level, pave thoroughly.
perstimŭlo, 1. to goad on violently.
persto -stiti -stātūrus, 1. to stand firm,
remain standing; to last, endure; to
persevere.
perstrěpo -ŭi, 3. to make a great noise.
perstringo -strinxi -strictum, 3. to
graze, graze against; to touch, seize;
to blame; to relate briefly.
perstŭdiōsē, adv. very eagerly, willingly.
perstŭdiōsus -a -um, very eager, fond.
persuāděo -suāsi -suāsum, 2. to convince; to persuade.
persuāsio -ōnis, f. a convincing, persuasion; a conviction, opinion.
1. persuāsus -a -um, partic. of per-
suadeo; persuasum habere, to be con-
vinced.
2. persuāsus -ūs, m. persuasion (only in
abl.).
persubtilis -e, very fine, very subtle;
very refined.
persulto, 1. *Intransit.,* to leap, skip
about a place. *Transit.,* to range
through.

pertaedet -taesum est, 2. *impers.* to be weary of.

pertendo -tendi -tensum *and* **-tentum**, 3. to continue, carry through; to go.

pertento, 1. to prove, test; to consider, to examine; to seize.

pertĕnŭis -e, very fine, very small; very slight.

pertĕrebro, 1. to bore through.

pertergĕo -tersi -tersum, 2. to wipe off, wipe up; to touch gently.

perterrēfăcio -fēci -factum, 3. to terrify exceedingly.

perterrĕo -terrŭi -terrĭtum, 2. to terrify exceedingly.

perterricrĕpus -a -um, sounding, rattling terribly.

pertexo -texŭi -textum, 3. to weave entirely; to accomplish.

pertica -ae, *f.* a long pole.

pertimĕfactus -a -um, frightened exceedingly.

pertimesco -timŭi, 3. to fear exceedingly.

pertinācia -ae, *f.* firmness, obstinacy.

pertinācĭter, *adv.* firmly, obstinately.

pertinax -ācis, tenacious; persevering; obstinate.

pertĭnĕo -tinŭi, 2. to reach to, extend to; to extend, spread; to have as an object; to relate, belong to; to attach to, to fall upon; to affect, *ad rem.*

pertingo, 3. to extend to.

pertŏlĕro, 1. to endure to the end.

pertorquĕo, 2. to twist, distort.

pertractātio -ōnis, *f.* an application to anything.

pertracto (pertrecto), 1. to handle, feel; to treat, study; to influence.

pertrăho -traxi -tractum, 3. to drag to a place; to entice to a place.

pertrecto = pertracto (*q.v.*).

pertristis -e, very sorrowful; very austere.

pertŭmultŭōsē, *adv.* in an agitated manner.

pertundo -tŭdi -tūsum (-tussum) *and* **-tunsum**, 3. to bore through, push through.

perturbātē, *adv.* confusedly.

perturbātio -ōnis, *f.* confusion, disquiet; *caeli,* stormy weather; political disturbance; emotion.

perturbātrix -īcis, *f.* she that disturbs.

perturbātus -a -um, *p. adj.* confused, disturbed.

perturbo, 1. to disturb, confuse; *condĭtiones,* to break; to alarm.

perturpis -e, very disgraceful.

pertūsus -a -um, *p. adj.* bored through, perforated.

pĕrungo -unxi -unctum, 3. to anoint thoroughly, besmear.

pĕrurbānus -a -um, very polite, refined, witty.

pĕrurgĕo -ursi, 2. to urge greatly.

pĕrūro -ussi -ustum, 3. to burn up, to inflame (*with love, etc.*); to gall, chafe; to pinch, nip with cold.

pĕrūtilis -e, very useful.

pervādo -vāsi -vāsum, 3. to go through; to pervade; to attain, to arrive at.

pervăgātus a um, *p. adj.* spread abroad, well known; common, general.

pervăgor -ātus sum, 1. *dep. Intransit.*, to wander; to be widely spread. *Transit.*, to wander through.

pervăgus -a -um, wandering everywhere.

pervălĕo -ŭi, 2. to be very strong.

pervărĭē, *adv.* very variously.

pervasto, 1. to devastate.

pervĕho -vexi -vectum, 3. to carry through, conduct through; *pass., pervehi,* to travel, sail, pass through.

pervello -velli, 3. to pluck, twitch violently; to excite; *fig.* to hurt, pain; to disparage.

pervĕnio -vēni -ventum, 4. to arrive at, reach; to attain to.

perversē, *adv.* wrongly, perversely.

perversĭtas -ātis, *f.* perversity.

perversus -a -um, *p. adj.* crooked; perverse.

pervĕrto (pervorto) -verti (-vorti) -versum(-vorsum), 3.to overturn,overthrow; to invert, pervert; to trip up, put down.

pervespĕri, *adv.* very late in the evening.

pervestĭgātio -ōnis, *f.* investigation.

pervestĭgo, 1. to track out; *fig.* to investigate.

pervĕtus -ĕris, very old.

pervĕtustus -a -um, very old.

pervĭcācia -ae, *f.* persistency; obstinacy.

pervĭcācĭter, *adv.* firmly, obstinately.

pervĭcax -ācis, firm, unyielding; obstinate.

pervĭdĕo -vīdi -vīsum, 2. to overlook, regard, behold; to review; to distinguish; to examine; to discern, to consider.

pervĭgĕo -gŭi, 2. to flourish.

pervĭgil -ĭlis, ever watchful.

pervĭgĭlātio -ōnis, *f.* a vigil.

pervĭgĭlium -ii, *n.* vigil.

pervĭgĭlo, 1. to watch, remain awake throughout the night.

pervīlis -e, very cheap.

pervinco -vīci -victum, 3. *Intransit.*, to gain a complete victory; to carry one's point. *Transit.*, to conquer completely; to surpass; to induce, prevail upon; to prove.

pervius -a -um, passable, accessible. *Subst.,* **pervĭum -ii,** *n.* a passage.

pervolgo = pervulgo (*q.v.*).

pervŏlĭto, 1. to fly through *or* round, *to* flit about.

1. pervŏlo, 1. to fly through, fly round; to fly to a place.

2. pervŏlo -vŏlŭi -velle, to wish greatly.

pervŏlūto, 1. to roll round; to unroll, read a book.

pervŏlvo -volvi -vŏlūtum, 3. to roll about; to turn over a book, to read.

pervorsē, pervorto, etc. = perverse, perverto, etc. (q.v.).

pervulgātus -a -um, p. adj. very usual; well known.

pervulgo (pervolgo), 1. to publish, make publicly known; to visit or sojourn often in a place.

pēs, pĕdis, m. the foot ; the foot of a chair, etc.; a metrical foot; a foot, as a measure of length; pedem ferre, to go; pedem referre, to go back; pedibus, on foot; pedibus vincere, in a foot-race ; pede pulsare terram, to dance; pedem conferre, to fight hand to hand; polit. (of senators), pedibus ire in sententiam alicuius, to support some one's proposal; pes secundus, fortunate arrival; pes veli, the rope or sheet attached to the lower edge of a sail; hence, pede aequo, with fair wind.

pessimus, pessime, v. malus and male.

pessŭlus -i, m. a bolt.

pessum, adv. to the ground, to the bottom, downwards; to be ruined, to perish; pessum do (or pessumdo, or pessundo) dĕdi, dătum, dăre, to let fall to the ground, to destroy, ruin.

pestĭfĕr -fĕra -fĕrum and pestĭfĕrus -a -um, pestilential; fatal, injurious.

pestĭfĕrē, adv. balefully.

pestĭlens -entis, pestilential, unhealthy; deadly.

pestĭlentĭa -ae, f. pestilence; unhealthy air, weather, place; (moral), plague, pest.

pestĭlĭtas -ātis, f. = pestilentia (q.v.).

pestĭs -is, f. plague, malaria; destruction; bane.

pĕtăsātus -a -um, wearing the petasus (q.v.) = equipped for a journey.

pĕtăsĭo (pĕtăso) -ōnis, m. a forequarter of pork.

pĕtăsuncŭlus -i, m. (dim. of petaso), a little fore-quarter of pork.

pĕtăsus -i, m. a broad-brimmed felt hat, used by travellers.

pĕtaurum -i, n. a spring-board used by tumblers and rope-dancers.

pĕtesso (pĕtisso), 3. to desire, strive after eagerly.

pĕtītĭo -ōnis, f. an attack, blow; a requesting; candidature; a legal claim; a right of claim.

pĕtītor -ōris, m. one who strives after anything; a candidate; a plaintiff.

pĕtītūrĭo, 4. to desire to become a candidate.

pĕtītus -ūs, m. an inclining towards.

pĕto -īvi and -ii -ītum, 3. to reach towards; to grasp ; to attack, aim at; to make for, hasten to; to approach; to take a certain direction; to ask, claim, request; to bring an action, to sue for; to solicit; to become a candidate for

public office, consulatum; to woo a maiden; to seek for; to seek, strive after; to fetch, derive; to bring forth.

pĕtorrītum (pĕtōrĭtum) -i, n. a Gallic carriage.

Petrōnĭus -ii, m., Petronius Arbiter, a Roman satirist under Nero.

pĕtŭlans -antis, capricious, wanton.

pĕtŭlantĕr, adv. capriciously, wantonly.

pĕtŭlantĭa -ae, f. capriciousness, wantonness.

pĕtulcus -a -um, butting with the head.

pexus -a -um, hairy, woolly; (of a garment), new.

Phaeāces -ācum, m. inhabitants of the island of Scheria. Adj., Phaeācĭus.

Phaedo or **Phaedon** -ōnis, m. disciple of Socrates and friend of Plato, who gave his name to a dialogue on the immortality of the soul.

Phaedra -ae, f. daughter of Minos, sister of Ariadne and wife of Theseus; she fell in love with her stepson Hippolytus and was, by a false accusation, the cause of his death.

Phaedrus -i, m. author of Latin fables.

Phăĕthon -ontis, m. son of Helios.

Phăĕthontĭădes -um, f. the sisters of Phaethon, who were turned into poplars.

phălangae (pălangae) -ārum, f. rollers on which heavy bodies were moved.

phălangītae -ārum, m. soldiers belonging to a phalanx.

phălanx -angis, f. a closely-serried array of soldiers; the Macedonian phalanx.

phălĕrae (fălĕrae) -ārum, a metal ornament worn as a military decoration.

phălĕrātus -a -um, adorned with the phalerae.

Phălērum -i, n. the oldest port of Athens.

phăretra -ae, f. a quiver.

phăretrātus -a -um, wearing a quiver.

pharmăceutrĭa -ae, f. a sorceress (poet.).

pharmăcŏpōla (-ēs) -ae, m. a seller of drugs, a quack.

Pharsālus (-ŏs) -i, f. a town in Thessaly, near which Pompeius was defeated by Caesar.

Phărus (-os) -i, f. island off Alexandria, where a lighthouse was built.

phăsēlus (-ŏs) -i, m. and f. kidney-bean; a light skiff.

phasma -ătis, n. a ghost, spectre.

Phēmĭus -ii, m. harp-player in Ithaca.

Phērae -ārum, f. in Thessaly, the residence of Admetus.

phĭăla -ae, f. drinking-vessel, bowl.

Phīdĭas -ae, m. celebrated sculptor of Athens.

Phīlippi -ōrum, m. city in Macedonia, where Octavianus and Antony defeated Brutus and Cassius.

Phīlippŏpŏlis -ĕos, f. town in Thrace.

Phīlippus -i, m. name of several kings of Macedon ; adj., Phīlippĭcus, orationes, the speeches of Demosthenes against Philip ; *subst.*, **Philippicae** -ārum, *f.*

philōlŏgĭa -ae, *f.* love of learning, study of letters.

philŏlŏgus -i, *m.* learned man, a scholar.

Philŏmēla -ae, *f.* daughter of Pandion, king of Athens, turned into a nightingale.

philŏsŏphia -ae, *f.* philosophy.

philŏsŏphor, 1. *dep.* to philosophise, apply oneself to philosophy.

philŏsŏphus -a -um, philosophic. *Subst.*, **philŏsŏphus** -i, *m.* a philosopher.

philtrum -i, *n.* love-potion, philtre.

philўra -ae, *f.* inner bark of the linden-tree.

phimus -i, *m.* a dice-box.

Phlĕgĕthon -ontis, *m.* a river in the infernal regions; *adj.*, **Phlĕgĕthontis**.

phōca -ae, *f. and* **phōcē** -ēs, *f.* a seal.

Phōcis -idis *and* **idos**, *f.* district in the north of Greece. *Adj.* **Phōcēus**.

Phoebē -ēs, *f.* Diana.

Phoebĭgĕna -ae, *m.* the son of Phoebus, Aesculapius.

Phoebus -i, *m.* Apollo, the Sun-god; **Phoebas** -ădis, *f.* a priestess of Phoebus.

Phoenīcē, *v.* **Phoenices**.

Phoenices -um, *m.* the Phoenicians; **Phoenĭcē** -ēs, *f. and* **Phoenīca** -ae, *f.* Phoenicia, a small strip of the coast of Syria; **Phoenissa** -ae, *f.* a Phoenician woman.

phoenīcoptĕros -i, *m.* the flamingo.

Phoenix -īcis, *m.* 1. a companion of Achilles at the Trojan War. 2. A fabulous bird.

Phorcus -i, *m.*, **Phorcȳs** -ȳos, *m.*, *and* **Phorcyn** -cȳnis, *m.* a sea-god; **Phorcȳnis** -idis, *f.* daughter of Phorcus, Medusa.

phrĕnēticus -a -um *and* **phrĕnīticus** -a -um, mad, frantic.

Phrixus -i, *m.* brother of Helle.

Phrȳges -um, *m.* the Phrygians. *Sing.*, **Phryx** -ȳgis. **Phrygia** -ae, *f.* a country in Asia Minor. *Adj.* **Phrȳgius**.

Phryx, *v. Phryges*.

Phўlăcē -ēs, *f.* city in Thessaly.

phўlarchus -i, *m.* the head of a tribe, an emir.

physĭca -ae, *f. and* **physĭcē** -ēs, *f.* physics.

physĭcē, *adv.* in the manner of the natural philosophers.

physĭcus -a -um, relating to physics, physical. *Subst.*, **physĭcus** -i, *m.* a natural philosopher; **physĭca** -ōrum, *n.* physics.

physiognōmōn -ōnis, *m.* physiognomist.

physĭŏlŏgia -ae, *f.* natural philosophy.

pĭābĭlis -e, that can be atoned for.

pĭācŭlāris -e, atoning, expiating; *subst.*, **pĭācŭlāria** -ium, *n.* expiatory sacrifices.

pĭācŭlum -i, *n.* expiatory sacrifice, sin-offering; remedy, punishment; crime, evil deed.

pĭāmen -ĭnis, *n.* means of atonement.

pīca -ae, *f.* magpie.

pĭcāria -ae, *f.* a pitch-hut.

pĭcĕa -ae, *f.* pitch-pine.

pĭceus a -um, pitchy, pitch-black.

pico, 1. to cover with pitch.

pictor -ōris, *m.* painter.

pictūra -ae, *f.* the art of painting; a picture; *pictura textilis*, embroidery.

pictūrātus -a -um, painted; *vestecs*, embroidered.

pictus -a -um, *p. adj.* ornamental, artistic; unreal, vain.

pīcus -i, *m.* woodpecker.

pĭē, *adv.* piously, dutifully.

Pĭĕris -ĭdis, *f.* a Muse. *Plur.*, **Pĭĕrĭdes**, the Muses.

pĭĕtas -ātis, *f.* dutifulness ; piety ; patriotism; justice, kindness.

pĭger -gra -grum, disinclined, lazy; tedious; *campus*, unfruitful; *pectora*, insensible. *Of waters*, sluggish.

pĭget -gŭit -gĭtum est, 2. *impers.*, it disgusts; it repents; it causes shame.

pigmentārius -ii, *m.* seller of paints and unguents.

pigmentum -i, *n.* paint, colour, pigment; *of discourse*, ornament.

pignĕro, 1. to give as a pledge, mortgage.

pignĕror, 1. *dep.* to take in pledge.

pignus -ŏris *and* -ĕris, *n.* a pledge, security; a wager; assurance, proof.

pĭgrĭtĭa -ae, *f. and* **pĭgrĭtĭes** -ēi, *f* sloth, indolence.

pĭgro, 1. to be sluggish, lazy.

pĭgror, 1. *dep.* to be slow, sluggish

1. **pīla** -ae, *f.* a mortar.

2. **pīla** -ae, *f.* a pillar; a bookstall.

3. **pĭla** -ae, *f.* a ball.

pīlānus -i, *m.*, *see pilarii*.

pīlātus -a -um, armed with the *pilum or* javelin.

pīlĕātus -a -um, wearing the *pileus or* felt cap.

pĭlentum -i, *n.* a carriage, coach.

pīlĕŏlus -i, *m. and* **pīlĕŏlum** -i, *n.* (*dim. of pileus*), a little cap, skull-cap.

pīlĕus -i, *m. and* **pīlĕum** -i, *n.* a felt cap.

pĭlōsus -a -um, covered with hair.

pīlum -i, *n.* a pestle ; javelin; *pila Horatia*, a place in Rome on the forum.

1. **pĭlus** -i, *m.* a single hair.

2. **pīlus** -i, *m.* a maniple of the *triarii* in the Roman army; *primus pilus*, the centurion of the first maniple of the *triarii*.

Pimpla -ae, *f.* in Pieria, with a mountain and spring, sacred to the Muses. **Pimplĕis** (Piplēis) -ĭdis, *f.* a Muse. *Subst.*, **Pimplēa** -ae, *f.* a Muse.

pīnă = 2. *pinna* (*q.v.*).

Pindărus -i, *m.* a celebrated lyric poet of Thebes. *Adj.*, **Pindărĭcus**.

Pindus -i, *m.* mountain in Thessaly.

pinētum -i, *n.* a pine-wood.

pinĕus -a -um, made of pine-wood *or* deal.

pingo, pinxi, pictum, 3. to paint; to embroider; to dye, colour; to decorate; *of speech,* to embellish.

pinguesco, 3. to become fat, grow fertile.

pinguis -e, fat; *of soil,* rich; besmeared; thick; stupid; *of speech,* bombastic; quiet, undisturbed. *Subst.,* **pingue -is,** *n.* fatness, fat.

pīnĭfĕr -fĕra -fĕrum, producing pines.

pīnĭgĕr -gĕra -gĕrum, producing pines.

1. **pinna -ae,** *f.* a feather; the wing; *poet.* flight; an arrow; fin of a fish; battlement.

2. **pinna (pīna) -ae,** *f.* a species of mussel.

pinnātus -a -um, feathered, winged.

pinnĭgĕr -gĕra -gĕrum, feathered, winged.

pinnīrăpus -i, *m.* a gladiator who fought against a Samnite having a crest to his helmet.

pinnŭla -ae, *f.* (*dim. of pinna* 1.), *lit.,* a small feather.

pīnōtĕres (pīnōthĕras) -ae, *m.* a small crab.

pinso, pinsi *and* **pinsŭi, pinsum, pinsitum, pistum** *and* **pīsum,** 3. to stamp, crush.

pīnus -i *and* **-ūs,** *f.* the pine, fir; something made of pine-wood; a ship, a torch.

pio, 1. to propitiate; to venerate; to purify; to atone for.

piper, pipĕris, *n.* pepper.

pīpilo, 1. to twitter, chirp.

Pīraeĕus -ĕi, *m.* **and Pīraeus -i,** *m.* the Piraeus, a port of Athens.

pīrāta -ae, *m.* pirate.

pīrāticus -a -um, piratical; *subst.,* **pīrātica -ae,** *f.* piracy.

Pīrēnē -ēs, *f.* spring in Corinth, sacred to the Muses.

pirum -i, *n.* pear.

pirus -i, *f.* pear-tree.

piscātor -ōris, *m.* fisherman.

piscātōrius -a -um, relating to fishermen and fishing.

piscĭcŭlus -i, *m.* (*dim. of piscis*), a little fish.

piscīna -ae, *f.* fish-pond; swimming-bath.

piscīnārius -ii, *m.* one fond of fish-ponds.

piscis -is, *m.* a fish.

piscor, 1. *dep.* to fish.

piscōsus -a -um, abounding in fish.

Pīsistrātus -i, *m.* tyrant at Athens.

pistor -ōris, *m.* baker.

pistrilla -ae, *f.* (*dim. of pistrina*), small mortar *or* mill.

pistrīna -ae, *f.* bakehouse.

pistrīnum -i, *n.* a mill.

pistris = *pristis* (*q.v.*).

pītŭīta -ae, *f.* phlegm, rheum.

pītŭītōsus -a -um, full of phlegm; phlegmatic.

pītysma = *pytisma* (*q.v.*).

pius -a -um, dutiful, pious; affectionate towards one's parents, patriotic; kind.

pix, picis, *f.* pitch.

plācābilis -e, easy to be appeased.

plācābilitas -ātis, *f.* placability.

plācāmen -inis, *n.* means of appeasing.

plācāmentum -i, *n.* means of appeasing.

plācātē, *adv.* calmly, composedly.

plācātio -ōnis, *f.* soothing, propitiating.

plācātus -a -um, *p. adj.,* soothed, appeased; gentle, quiet.

plăcenta -ae, *f.* a cake.

plăcĕo -ŭi -ĭtum, 2. to please, be agreeable; it pleases, it seems good, I hold (*the opinion*); *legal,* to resolve, command.

plăcidē, *adv.* quietly, composedly.

plăcidus -a -um, quiet, gentle.

plăcĭtum, *v. placitus.*

plăcitus -a -um, *adj.,* pleasant, agreeable. *Subst.,* **plăcitum -i,** *n.* that which pleases one; opinion, teaching.

plăco, 1. to soothe, appease; to reconcile.

1. **plāga -ae,** *f.* a blow, stroke.

2. **plāga -ae,** *f.* a flat surface; a district, region; *quatuor plagae,* the four zones; a net, snare.

plăgiārius -ii, *m.* kidnapper; plagiarist.

plăgōsus -a -um, fond of flogging.

plăgŭla -ae, *f.* a curtain.

planctus -ūs, *m.* beating the breast, lamentation.

plānē, *adv.* plainly, intelligibly; entirely, quite, thoroughly.

plango, planxi, planctum, 3. to beat, strike with a loud noise; to bewail.

plangor -ōris, *m.* a striking *or* beating, accompanied by noise; loud lamentation.

plangunculă -ae *f.* a little doll.

plānipēs -pĕdis, *m.* a mime who played the part of slaves, *etc.,* and wore no shoes.

plānitas -ātis, *f.* plainness, distinctness.

plānitia -ae, *f. and* **plānities -ĕi,** *f.* level surface, a plain.

planta -ae, *f.* a green twig, graft, slip; the sole of the foot.

plantāria -ium, *n.* young trees, slips.

1. **plānus -a -um,** level, flat; *filum,* thick; *fig.* plain, intelligible. *Subst.,* **plānum -i,** *n.* a plain, level ground; *de plano,* easily.

2. **plānus -i,** *m.* a vagrant, juggler.

Plătaeae -ārum, *f.* a town in Boeotia; **Plătaeenses -ium,** *m.* the inhabitants of Plataea.

plătălĕa -ae, *f.* the spoonbill.

plătănus -i, *f.* the plane-tree.

plătĕa -ae, *f.* a street.

Plăto (-ōn) -ōnis, *m.* a celebrated Greek philosopher; **Plătōnicus,** Platonic. *Plur. subst.,* **Plătōnici -ōrum,** *m.* the Platonists.

plaudo (plōdo), plausi (plōsi), plausum

(plōsum), 3. *Intransit.*, to clap. *Transit.*, to beat, clap; to strike together.

plausibilis -e, worthy of applause.

plausor -ōris, *m.* applauder at the theatre.

plaustrum (plostrum) -i, *n.* wagon, cart; Charles's Wain.

plausus -ūs, *m.* the noise made by the striking together of two bodies; the clapping of the hands, applause.

Plautus -i, *m.* T. *Maccius* (*incorrectly*, *M. Accius*), celebrated Roman comic poet.

plēbēcŭla -ae, *f.* (*dim. of plebs*), common people, mob.

plēbēius -a -um, relating *or* belonging to the plebs; plebeian. *Subst.*, **plēbēius -i**, *m.* a plebeian.

plōbēo -ēi *and* **-is**, *f.* = *plebs* (*q.v.*).

plēbicŏla -ae, *m.* friend of the common people.

plēbiscītum -i, *n.* decree of the people.

plebs, plēbis, *f.* the plebeians, the people; the lower orders, mob.

1. **plecto, plexi** *and* **plexŭi, plexum**, 3. to plait; *partic.*, **plexus -a -um**, plaited.

2. **plecto**, 3. to punish; *usually pass.*, to be punished with blows; to be blamed.

plectrum -i, *n.* short stick *or* quill with which the strings of a stringed instrument were struck. *Poet.* the lyre.

Plēiăs *and* **Pliăs -ădis**, *f.* a Pleiad ; *gen. plur.*, **Plēiădes (Pliădes)** *f.* the Pleiads, Seven Stars.

plēnē, *adv.* fully; wholly, abundantly.

plēnus -a -um, full, *with genit. or abl.; ad plenum*, completely; plump, stout; thick; pregnant; satiated; rich in; *negotiis*, occupied; numerous; complete; perfect; *pleno gradu*, at quick step; loud, *vox.*

plērumquĕ, *v. plerusque.*

plērusquĕ -răquĕ -rumquĕ, *gen. plur.*, **plēriquĕ -raequĕ -răquĕ**, very many, the majority. *Neut. plerumque*, *subst.*, the greater part, *adv.*, mostly, generally.

plico -āvi *and* **-ŭi**, 1. to fold, double up, repeat, reason

Plīnius -a -um, *i. ll. Plinius Secundus* (the Elder), author of a Natural History. 2. (the Younger), author of letters.

plōdo = *plaudo* (*q.v.*).

plōrābilis -e, lamentable.

plōrātor -ōris, *m.* wailer.

plōrātus -ūs, *m.* a weeping, lamenting; *gen. plur.*

plōro, 1. to lament, wail. *Transit.*, to weep over, deplore.

plostellum -i, *n.* (*dim. of plostrum*), a little wagon.

plostrum = *plaustrum* (*q.v.*).

ploxĕmum (ploximum, ploxinum) -i, *n.* a wagon-box.

pluit, *v. pluo.*

plūma -ae, *f.* a small, soft feather ; *plur.* = down; feather-bed, pillow; the first down on the chin.

plūmātus -a -um, covered with feathers.

plumbĕus -a -um, made of lead ; blunt; dull, stupid; burdensome.

plumbum -i, *n.* lead; *plumbum album*, tin; a bullet; a leaden-pipe.

plūmĕus -a -um, downy, covered with fine feathers.

plūmipes -pĕdis, feather-footed.

plūmōsus -a -um, feathered, downy.

plŭo, plŭi, 3. to rain; *impers., pluit.*

plūriēs, *adv.* often, frequently.

plūrĭfāriam, on many sides.

plūrĭmus, plurimum, *v. multus.*

plūs, pluris, *v. multus.*

plusculus -a -um (*dim. of plus*), somewhat more, rather many; **plusculum -i**, *n. subst.*

plŭtĕus -i, *m. and* **plŭtĕum -i**, *n.* shed, *or* mantlet ; a battlement ; a book-shelf.

Plūto (-on) -ōnis, *m.* king of the lower world, brother of Jupiter and Neptune, husband of Proserpina. *Adj.*, **Plūtōnius.**

plŭvia -ae, *f.* rain.

plŭviālis -e, *of or* relating to rain, rainy.

plŭvius -a -um, rainy, rain-bringing.

pōcillum -i, *n.* (*dim. of poculum*), a little goblet.

pōcŭlum -i, *n.* a drinking-cup, goblet; a drink, draught.

pŏdagra -ae, *f.* gout in the feet.

pŏdium -ii, *n.* balcony in the amphi-theatre, where the emperor sat.

pŏēma -ătis, *n.* a poem.

poena -ae, *f.* the fine paid for murder; punishment, penalty, compensation; *votorum*, payment of one's vows; *poenas dare*, to be punished.

Poeni -ōrum, *m.* the Phoenicians = the Carthaginians. *Adj.*, **Poenus, Pūnicus;** **Pūnicĕus** *and* **Pūnicius**, Punic, Carthaginian; purple-red.

poenio, poenior = *punio* (*q.v.*).

poenitens -entis (*partic. of poeniteo*).

poenitentia (paenitentia) -ae, *f.* repentance.

poenitĕo (paeniteo) -ŭi, 2. to feel displeasure ; to repent ; to be sorry. *Impers., poenitet aliquem alicuius rei*, *etc.*, it repents one, one is vexed, *etc.*

pŏēsis -is, *acc.* **-in**, *f.* poetry.

pŏēta -ae, *m.* poet.

pŏētica -ae, *f. and* **pŏēticē -ēs**, *f.* the art of poetry.

pŏēticē, *adv.* poetically.

pŏēticus -a -um, poetical.

pŏētria -ae, *f.* poetess.

pol! *interj.* by Pollux ! really !

pōlenta -ae, *f.* pearl-barley.

pōlio, 4. to polish, file, make smooth; to whiten; to adorn.

pōlītē, *adv.* elegantly.

pŏlītīa -ae, *acc.* **-an**, *f.* the state; the Republic (*title of a work by Plato*).

pŏlīticus -a -um, political.

pŏlītus -a -um, *p. adj.* refined, accomplished.

pollen -ĭnis, *n. and* pollis -ĭnis, *c.* fine flour, meal.

pollens -entis, *p. adj.* strong, powerful.

pollĕo, 2. to be strong, powerful, able.

pollex -ĭcis, *m.* the thumb.

pollicĕor -cĭtus sum, 2. *dep.* to offer, promise.

pollĭcĭtātĭo -ōnis, *f.* an offer, promise.

pollĭcĭtor, 1. *dep.* to promise, proffer.

pollĭcĭtum -i, *n.* that which is promised, a promise.

pollŭo -ŭi -ūtum, 3. to defile; dishonour.

pollūtus -a -um, *p. adj.* polluted; (*of women*), unchaste.

Pollux -ūcis, *m.* twin-brother of Castor.

pŏlus -i, *m.* the pole of the earth; the heavens.

Pŏlўhymnĭa -ae, *f.* one of the Muses.

Pŏlўmestŏr (Pŏlўmnestor) -ŏris, *m.* murderer of Polydorus.

Pŏlўphēmus (-ŏs) -i, *m.* the Cyclops.

pŏlўpus -i, *m.* polypus.

Pŏlyxēna -ae, *f.* daughter of Priam.

pōmārĭus -a -um, of *or* relating to fruit ; *subst.*, pōmārĭus -ii, *m.* a fruiterer; pōmārĭum -ii, *n.* orchard.

pōmērīdĭānus = *postmeridianus (q.v.).*

pōmērĭum -ii, *n.* a space left free on each side the walls of a town.

pōmĭfĕr -fĕra -fĕrum, fruit-bearing.

Pōmōna -ae, *f.* goddess of fruit-trees.

pōmōsus -a -um, full of fruit.

pompa -ae, *f.* a solemn procession; a suite, retinue; *fig.* display.

Pompēii -ōrum, *m.* town destroyed by an eruption of Vesuvius; *adj.,* Pompēiānus.

Pompēius (Pompĕius), name of a Roman gens; *Cn. Pompeius,* triumvir with Caesar and Crassus, conqueror of Mithridates and the pirates, defeated by Caesar at Pharsalia. Pompēiānus, *adj. as subst.,* a member of the Pompeian party.

Pompĭlĭus -a -um, name of a Roman gens, to which belonged *Numa Pompilius,* second king of Rome.

pompĭlus -i, *m.* the pilot-fish.

Pomptīnus, palus *and* paludes, a marshy district on the Appian road.

pōmum -i, *n.* any kind of fruit, a mulberry; a fruit-tree.

pondĕro, 1. to weigh; to consider.

pondĕrōsus -a -um, heavy, weighty ; significant.

pondo, *adv.* in weight, by weight, heavy.

pondus -ĕris, *n.* a weight; a pound weight, pound; balance; load, burden; a mass = a quantity, sum. *Fig.* weight, authority, influence.

pōnĕ, *adv.* behind, at the back. *Prep. with acc.,* behind.

pōno, pŏsŭi, pŏsĭtum, 3. to lay down, place, lay; to prepare; to stretch out;

to lay out for burial; to erect; to consecrate; to wager; *milit.,* to station men ; to publish ; to put in writing ; to bring; to place, build, rest; to hold, regard; to remark, observe; to erect; *castra,* to pitch one's camp; to found, place; to fix, settle; to put food before one; to plant, *piros;* to deposit; to invest, lend; to arrange the hair, *comas; of the winds, etc.,* to soothe; to lay aside; *arma,* to lay down; *naut.,* to throw out anchor; pŏsĭtus, *of snow, etc.,* fallen; *of places,* situated.

pons, pontis, *m.* bridge; the deck of a ship.

pontĭcŭlus -i, *m.* (*dim. of pons*), a little bridge.

Ponticus -a -um, *v. Pontus.*

pontĭfex -fĭcis, *m.* pontiff, high-priest, pontifex; pontĭfĭcālis -e, pontifical; pontĭfĭcātus, office of pontiff. *Adj.,* pontĭfĭcĭus.

pontĭfĭcālis, *v. pontifex.*

pontĭfĭcātus, *v. pontifex.*

pontĭfĭcĭus, *v. pontifex.*

ponto -ōnis, *m.* flat-bottomed boat.

1. pontus -i, *n.* the deep, depth; the deep sea; a wave of the sea.

2. Pontus -i, *m.* 1. the Black Sea; 2. a district of Asia Minor. *Adj.,* Ponticus.

pŏpa -ae, *m.* inferior priest *or* temple-servant.

pŏpānum -i, *n.* sacrificial cake.

pŏpellus -i, *m.* (*dim. of populus*), the common people, rabble.

pōpīna -ae, *f.* eating-house; food sold at an eating-house.

pōpīno -ōnis, *m.* frequenter of eating-houses, glutton.

poplĕs -ĭtis, *m.* ham, hough; knee.

Poplĭcŏla = *Publicola (q.v.).*

pŏpŭlābĭlis -e, that can be laid waste.

pŏpŭlābundus -a -um, laying waste.

pŏpŭlāris -e, belonging to the same people *or* country, native; (*subst.*, fellow-countryman; participator, partner); belonging to the people; popular; pŏpŭlāres -ium, *m.* the popular party, the democracy.

pŏpŭlārĭtas -ātis, *f.* desire to please the people.

pŏpŭlārĭtĕr, *adv.* commonly, vulgarly, in a popular manner; like a demagogue.

pŏpŭlātĭo -ōnis, *f.* a devastating, plundering.

pŏpŭlātor -ōris, *m.* devastator.

pŏpŭlĕus -a -um, relating to the poplar.

pŏpŭlĭfĕr -fĕra -fĕrum, producing poplars.

pŏpŭlĭscĭtum -i, *n.* decree of the people.

pŏpŭlo, 1. *and* pŏpŭlor, 1. *dep.* to lay waste, plunder. *Poet.* to destroy, spoil.

1. pŏpŭlus -i, *m.* the people as forming

a state; a state; a crowd, host ; the sovereign people; the democratic party.
2. **pōpŭlus** -i, *f.* the poplar-tree.
porca -ae, *f.* a sow; *poet.* a pig.
porcus -i, *m.* a pig, hog.
porgo = *porrigo* (*q.v.*).
Porphÿrio (-on) -ŏnis, *m.* one of the giants.
porrectio -ōnis, *f.* a stretching out, extension.
porrectus -a -um, *p. adj.* stretched out, extended, long; *poet. of time,* long.
porricio -rēci *and* -rexi -rectum, 3. to offer sacrifice to the gods.
1. **porrigo** -rexi -rectum, 3. to stretch out, reach out, extend; *porrigi,* to lie stretched out; *porrigere manum,* to hold up the hand in voting; *vectigalia,* to increase; to lay low; to offer to; to afford, supply.
2. **porrigo** -inis, *f.* scurf, dandruff.
porro, *adv.* forward, further; afar off; *of time,* formerly; next, further, again.
porrus -i, *m. and* **porrum** -i, *n.* a leek.
Porsēna (**Porsenna**) *and* **Porsina** (**Porsinna**) -ae, *m.* king of Etruria, who attacked Rome in order to bring back Tarquinius Superbus.
porta -ae, *f.* a gate, city-gate.
portātio -ōnis, *f.* a carrying, conveying.
portendo -tendi -tentum, 3. to indicate, predict, forbode.
portentĭfer -fĕra -fĕrum, bringing prodigies.
portentĭficus a -um, extraordinary, miraculous.
portentōsus -a -um, extraordinary, portentous.
portentum -i, *n.* a prodigy, portent; a wonderful story; a monster.
porthmeus -ĕi *and* -ĕos, *m.* a ferryman.
portĭcŭla -ae, *f.* (*dim. of porticus*), a little gallery *or* portico.
porticus -ūs, *f.* a portico, colonnade, gallery ; tribunal of the praetor ; the Stoic school.
portio -ōnis, *f.* a part, section; *pro portione, ratio,* *pro portione,* proportionally.
1. **portĭtor** -ōris, *m.* collector of customs.
2. **portĭtor** -ōris, *m.* a carrier; a boatman, ferryman.
porto, 1. to bear, convey, bring.
portōrium -ii, *n.* customs duties.
portŭla -ae, *f.* (*dim. of porta*), little gate, postern.
portŭōsus -a -um, having many harbours.
portus -ūs, *m.* harbour, port, haven.
posco, pŏposci, 3. to ask earnestly, demand; *poscimur,* we are asked for a song; to challenge to fight; to inquire, *causas;* to call; to call upon, *tua numina posco.*
pŏsĭtio -ōnis, *f.* a placing, putting.
pŏsĭtor -ōris, *m.* a founder, builder.
pŏsĭtūra -ae, *f.* position, situation.

positus -ūs, *m.* position, place; arrangement of the hair.
possessio -ōnis, *f.* possession; property.
possessor -ōris, *m.* a possessor.
possĭdĕo -sēdi -sessum, 2. to possess, have, hold; beset.
possĭdo -sēdi -sessum, 3. to take possession of, occupy,
possum, pŏtŭi, posse, to be able, I (thou,he, *etc.*) can; to avail, have influence.
post, *adv.* behind; in the rear; afterwards; *multo post,* long after. *Prep. with acc.,* behind; after; next to.
posteā, *adv.* after, afterwards; *quid postea ?* what next ?
posteāquam, *conj.* after that ; *with indic.*
postĕri, *v. posterus.*
postĕrius, *v. posterus.*
postĕritas -ātis, *f.* the future; after-ages, posterity.
postĕrus (**poster**) -a -um, *compar.,* **postĕrior** -us; *superl.,* **postrēmus** *and* **postŭmus** -a -um. *Posit.,* subsequent, next, future; *in posterum,* for the next day, *and* for the future; *subst.,* **postĕri** -ōrum, *m.* posterity. *Compar.,* **postĕrior** -us, following after, later; inferior. *Superl.,* **postrēmus** *and* **postŭmus;** *postremus,* the hindmost, last; *abl., postremo,* at last; *ad postremum,* lastly; **postŭmus,** the last, last born; posthumous.
postfĕro -ferre, to consider of less account.
postgĕnĭti -ōrum, *m.* descendants.
posthăbĕo -ŭi -ĭtum, 2. to make of less account.
posthāc, *adv.* hereafter, in future
postĭcus -a -um, hinder, back.
postĭlio -ōnis, *f.* the demand of a deity for a sacrifice.
postĭlla, *adv.* after, afterwards.
postis -is, *m.* a post, door-post. *Plur., poet.,* door, gate.
postlīmĭnium -ii, *n.* a right to return home.
postmĕrīdĭānus(**pōmĕrīdĭānus**)-a-um, belonging to the afternoon, afternoon.
postmŏdŏ *and* **postmŏdum,** *adv.* after, afterwards.
postpōno -pŏsŭi -pŏsĭtum, 3. to consider of less account, put after.
postquam, *conj.* after, after that, as soon as.
postrēmo, *v. posterus.*
postrēmum, *v. posterus.*
postrēmus, *superl. of posterus* (*q.v.*).
postrīdiē, *adv.* the day after, on the next day.
postrīdŭo = *postridie* (*q.v.*).
postscrībo -scrīpsi -scrīptum, 3. to write after.
postŭlātio -ōnis, *f.* a request, entreaty, demand; an application.
postŭlātum -i, *n.* a demand, request.

postŭlātus -ūs, *m.* legal complaint, accusation.

postŭlio = *postilio* (*q.v.*).

postŭlo, 1. to demand, entreat, request; to impeach, accuse.

postŭmus -a -um, *superl. of posterus* (*q.v.*).

pōtātio -ōnis, *f.* a drinking-bout.

pŏtĕ, *v. potis.*

pŏtens -entis, *p. adj.,* powerful in, having power over; capable of; mighty, influential; efficacious; master of; *potens irae,* able to control one's anger.

pŏtentātus -ūs, *m.* political power, supremacy.

pŏtentĕr, *adv.* powerfully, efficaciously; according to one's power.

pŏtentia -ae, *f.* power, ability; efficacy; influence; supremacy.

pŏtestas -ātis, *f.* power; might, strength, efficacy; political power, supremacy; official authority; magistracy; ability, opportunity, possibility; *potestas est,* it is possible.

pōtio -ōnis, *f.* drinking, draught, potion; philtre.

1. **pŏtior,** 4. *dep.* to get possession of, obtain; to be master of; *with abl., mari, with genit., rerum.*

2. **pŏtior,** *v. potis.*

pŏtis, pŏtĕ. *Adj., compar.,* **pŏtior** -ius; *superl.,* **pŏtissimus,** able, capable; *potis est,* he can; *neut., pote est. Compar.,* **pŏtior** -us, preferable, better. *Superl.,* **pŏtissimus,** best of all, principal. *Adv., only in compar.,* **pŏtius,** rather, more, preferably; *and superl.,* **pŏtissimum** (**pŏtissime**), chiefly, above all.

pŏtissime, potissimum, *v. potis.*

pŏtius, *v. potis.*

pōto, pōtāvi, pōtātum *and* **pōtum,** 1. to drink; to revel; to absorb; *partic.,* **pōtus** -a -um, *pass.,* drunk, drained; *act.,* having drunk, drunken.

pōtor -ōris, *m.* drinker.

pōtrix -īcis, *f.,* a female tippler.

pōtŭlentus -a -um, drinkable; *subst.,* **pōtŭlenta** -ōrum, things that can be drunk.

1. **pōtus,** *v. poto.*

2. **pōtus** -ūs, *m.* a drinking; a draught.

prae, *adv. and prep. Adv.,* before, in front. *Prep. with abl.,* before; in comparison with; on account of.

praeăcŭo (-ŭi) **-ūtum,** 3. to sharpen to a point; **praeăcŭtus** -a -um, pointed.

praealtus -a -um, very high; very deep.

praebĕo -bŭi **-bitum,** to offer, hold out; to expose; to show, give; *operam alicui,* to serve; *reflex.,* to show oneself; to supply; to cause; to allow.

praebibo -bibi, 3. to drink before, to drink to.

praebĭtor -ōris, *m.* furnisher, supplier.

praecălĭdus -a -um, very hot.

praecānus -a -um, prematurely grey.

praecăvĕo -cāvi **-cautum,** 2. *Intransit.,* to be on one's guard, to be careful. *Transit.,* to beware of.

praecēdo -cessi **-cessum,** 3. to pre ede; to surpass.

praecellens -entis, *p. adj.* excellent, distinguished.

praecello, 3. to surpass, exceed; *genti,* to have the supremacy over.

praecelsus -a -um, very high.

praecentio -ōnis, *f.* a musical prelude.

praeceps -cipitis, *adj.,* headlong, headforemost; in haste, quick; rash, hasty; *of time,* declining; *of things,* dangerour; *of places,* steep; *subst.,* **praeceps** -cipitis, *n.* a steep place, precipice; *fig.* danger. *Adv.* headlong.

praeceptio -ōnis, *f.* a preconception; a precept.

praeceptor -ōris, *m.* a teacher, preceptor.

praeceptrix -trīcis, *f.* she that teaches.

praeceptum -i, *n.* a precept, command, rule.

praecerpo -cerpsi **-cerptum,** 3. to gather before the time; *fig.,* to lessen *or* take away.

praecīdo -cīdi **-cīsum,** 3. to cut off in front, cut off; to abbreviate; *praecide,* make it short; to take away, to refuse point blank; to cut in pieces; *fig.,* to break off suddenly.

praecinctus -a -um, *partic. of praecingo.*

praecingo -cinxi **-cinctum,** 3. to gird, surround with a girdle.

praecino -cinŭi **-centum,** 3. *Intransit.,* to sing *or* play before; to sing an incantation. *Transit.,* to prophesy.

praecipes -is = *praeceps* (*q.v.*).

praecipio -cēpi **-ceptum,** 3. to take before, receive in advance; *iter,* to get the start; *praecipitur seges,* ripens too fast; to anticipate; to tell beforehand; to advise, warn; to teach.

praecipitantĕr, *adv.* headlong, headforemost.

praecipito, 1. *Transit.,* to cast down headlong; to hurry away; to hasten; to press on. *Fig.,* to cast down; to destroy, ruin. *Intransit.,* to rush down, to fall down, to sink violently; to draw to a close.

praecipŭē, *adv.* especially, particularly, principally.

praecipŭus -a -um, peculiar, especial; excellent, extraordinary; *subst.,* **praecipŭum** -i, *n.* a special right, prerogative; *plur.,* **praecipŭa** -ōrum, things (*in the Stoic philosophy*) that come next to the greatest good.

praecīsē, *adv.* briefly, in few words; absolutely, decidedly.

praecīsus -a -um, *p. adj.* steep abrupt; *rhet.,* short, broken off.

praeclārē, *adv.* very clearly; excellently.

praeclārus -a -um, very bright; noble, distinguished, excellent; *subst.*, **praeclāra -ōrum**, *n.* valuables.

praeclūdo -clūsi -clūsum, 3. to close in front, to close; deprive of access to.

praeco -ōnis, *m.* public crier, herald.

praecōgĭto, 1. to meditate, consider carefully beforehand.

praecognosco, *no perf.* **-cognĭtum**, 3. to foreknow.

praecŏlo -cŏlŭi -cultum, 3. to cultivate beforehand; to revere.

praecompŏsĭtus -a -um, composed beforehand, studied; *os*, mien.

praecōnius -a -um, belonging to a *praeco* or crier. *Subst.*, **praecōnĭum -ĭi**, *n.* the office of a public crier; a public crying; a public laudation.

praeconsūmo -consumpsi, 3. to consume beforehand.

praecontrecto, 1. to handle beforehand.

praecŏquis -e *and* **praecŏquus -a -um** = *praecox (q.v.)*.

praecordia -ōrum, *n.* the diaphragm; the stomach; the breast, heart (*as the seat of passions*).

praecorrumpo -rūpi -ruptum, 3. to corrupt, bribe beforehand.

praecox -cōcis, praecŏquis -e, *and* **praecŏquus -a -um**, premature.

praecultus -a -um, *partic.* of *praecolo*.

praecurro -cŭcurri *and* **-curri -cursum**, 3. to hasten before; to go on before; to precede; to surpass. *Partic. subst.*, **praecurrentia -ium**, *n.* antecedents.

praecursĭo -ōnis, *f.* a going before; *rhet.*, the previous preparation of the hearer.

praecursor -ōris, *m.* precursor. *Milit.*, *praecursores*, the vanguard; a spy, scout.

praecŭtĭo -cussi -cussum, 3. to shake, brandish before.

praeda -ae, *f.* booty, prey, plunder, gain.

praedābundus -a -um, plundering.

praedamno, 1. to condemn before, to give up, *spurn*.

praedatĭo -ōnis, *f.* plundering.

praedātor -ōris, *m.* plunderer; hunter; a greedy person.

praedātōrius -a -um, plundering, predatory.

praedēlasso, 1. to weary, weaken beforehand.

praedestĭno, 1. to appoint beforehand.

praediātor -ōris, *m.* dealer in estates.

praediātōrius -a -um, relating to the sale of land by auction.

praedĭcābĭlis -e, praiseworthy.

praedĭcātĭo -ōnis, *f.* public announcement; a declaration; praise.

praedĭcātor -ōris, *m.* commender, public eulogist.

1. **praedĭco**, 1. to publish; to declare, tell; to eulogise, boast.

2. **praedīco -dixi -dictum**, 3. to say beforehand, speak before; to predict; to appoint beforehand, *diem*; to warn, command.

praedictĭo -ōnis, *f.* a prophesying.

praedictum -i, *n.* a prophecy; a command; an agreement.

praediŏlum -i, *n.* (*dim.* of *praedium*), a small landed estate, little farm.

praedisco -dĭdĭci, 3. to learn before.

praedispŏsĭtus -a -um, arranged beforehand.

praedĭtus -a -um, endowed, furnished, provided with; *with abl.*

praedium -ĭi, *n.* plot of land, landed estate.

praedīvĕs -ĭtis, very rich.

1. **praedo**, 1 = *praedor (q.v.)*.

2. **praedo -ōnis**, *m.* robber, plunderer.

praedŏcĕo -doctus, 2. to instruct before.

praedŏmo -dŏmŭi, 1. to tame before.

praedor, 1. *dep. Intrans. and transit.*, to plunder, rob; to carry off as prey.

praedūco -duxi -ductum, 3. to lead, carry forward.

praedulcis -e, very sweet; very pleasant.

praedūrus -a -um, very hard, very strong.

praeēmĭnĕo (praeminĕo), 2. to surpass, excel.

praeĕo -īvi *and* **-ii -itum**, 4. to precede; to dictate any solemn form of words; to command.

praefātĭo -ōnis, *f.* a form of words, formula.

praefectūra -ae, *f.* the office of superintendent; the command of auxiliary troops; a prefecture.

1. **praefectus -a -um**, *partic.* of *praeficio*.

2. **praefectus -i**, *m.* overseer, superintendent; a civil *or* military officer; *praefectus urbis*, governor of the city (Rome).

praefĕro -tŭli -lātum -ferre, to carry before *or* in front; to bring to light, to show; to prefer, *aliquem nihi*; to carry by; to anticipate, *diem, triumphu*; *praeferri* = to hasten by, to ride by.

praefĕrox -ōcis, very bold, impetuous.

praefervĭdus -a -um, burning hot.

praefestīno, 1. to hasten exceedingly, too much; to hasten by.

praeficio -fēci -fectum, 3. to set over, appoint as superintendent.

praefĭdens -entis, very confident.

praefīgo - fixi -fixum, 3. to fix in front, fasten before; to tip, point with; to pierce through, transfix.

praefīnĭo, 4. to fix, appoint beforehand.

praeflōro, 1. to pluck the blossom prematurely; *fig.*, to diminish.

praefluo, 3. to flow past.

praefōco, 1. to choke, suffocate.

praefŏdĭo -fōdi -fossum, 3. to dig in front of; to bury previously.

praefor -fātus sum -fāri, to utter beforehand ; to mention beforehand ; to prophesy.

praefractē, sternly, resolutely.

praefractus -a -um, *p. adj.* abrupt, disconnected; stern, harsh.

praefrīgĭdus -a -um, very cold.

praefringo -frēgi -fractum, 3. to break off in front, break in pieces.

praefulcio -fulsi -fultum, 4. to support, prop up.

praefulgĕo -fulsi, 2. to gleam forth; *praefulgens*, conspicuous.

praegĕlĭdus -a -um, very cold.

praegestio, 4. to desire exceedingly.

praegnans, pregnant. *Fig.*, full of.

praegrăcĭlis -e, very slim, lank.

praegrăvis -e, very heavy; wearisome.

praegrăvo, 1. to weigh upon, oppress; to overwhelm.

praegrĕdior -gressus sum, 3. *dep.* to precede; to outstrip; to pass by.

praegressio -ōnis, *f.* a going before, precedence.

praegressus -ūs, *m.* a going on before.

praegustātor -ōris, *m.* a taster, foretaster.

praegusto, 1. to taste before.

praelăceo, 2. to lie before.

praeiūdĭcātus -a -um, *v. praeiudico.*

praeiūdĭcĭum -ii, *n.* a previous judgment, a preliminary decision *or* examination ; a premature decision ; an example, precedent.

praeiūdĭco, 1. to decide beforehand. *Partic. perf. subst.*, **praeiūdĭcātum -i**, *n.* = *praeiudicium* ; **praeiūdĭcātus**, previously decided.

praeiŭvo -iūvi, 1. to assist before.

praelābor -lapsus sum, 3. *dep.* to glide before, flow, swim before *or* along.

praelambo -lambi, 3. to lick before, taste before.

praelargus -a -um, very abundant.

praelĕgo -lēgi -lectum, 3. to sail past.

praelĭgo, 1. to bind in front; to bind up.

praelium, *etc.* = *proelium*, *etc.* (*q.v.*).

praelongus -a -um, very long.

praelūceo -luxi, 2. to carry a light before; to outshine.

praelum = *prelum* (*q.v.*).

praelustris -e, very illustrious.

praemando, 1. to order beforehand ; **praemandāta -ōrum**, *n.* a writ of arrest.

praemātūrus -a -um, too early, premature.

praemĕdĭcātus -a -um, protected by medicine *or* charms.

praemĕdĭtātio -ōnis, *f.* considering beforehand.

praemĕdĭtor, 1. *dep.* to consider beforehand ; **praemĕdĭtātus -a -um**, considered beforehand.

praemĕtŭens -entis, *p. adj.* fearing beforehand.

praemĕtŭentĕr, *adv.* anxiously.

praemĕtŭo, 3. *intrans. and trans.*, to be apprehensive ; *intransit.*, *alicui. Transit.*, to fear beforehand, *iras.*

praemitto -mīsi -missum, 3. to send on.

praemĭum -ii, *n.* advantage, profit; reward; booty.

praemoenio, *v. praemunio.*

praemŏlestia -ae, *f.* trouble beforehand.

praemŏlĭor, 4. *dep.* to prepare beforehand.

praemŏnĕo -ŭi -ĭtum, 2. to warn, advise beforehand; to foretell.

praemŏnĭtus -ūs, *m.* a prediction, premonition.

praemonstro, 1. to show, point out before; to prophesy.

praemordĕo -mordi -morsum, 2. to bite off; to pilfer.

praemŏrĭor -mortŭus sum -mŏri, 3.*dep.* to die prematurely.

praemūnio (**praemoenio**), 4. to fortify in front; to fortify, secure.

praemūnītĭo -ōnis, *f.* a fortifying beforehand; *rhet.*, a preparation by an orator of the minds of his hearers.

praenăto, 1. to swim before, flow by.

praenĭtĕo -ŭi, 2. to shine forth.

praenōmen -ĭnis, *n.* the first name (*e.g Marcus, in M. T. Cicero*).

praenosco -nōvi -nōtum, 3. to foreknow

praenōtĭo -ōnis, *f.* preconception, innate idea.

praenūbĭlus -a -um, very cloudy, very dark.

praenuncia, *etc.* = *praenuntia*, *etc.* (*q.v.*).

praenuntia, *v. praenuntius.*

praenuntio, 1. to announce, report; predict.

praenuntius -a -um, foretelling; *subst.* (*m. f. and n.*) a harbinger, sign, omen.

praeoccŭpātĭo -ōnis, *f.* a taking possession of before.

praeoccŭpo, 1. to seize before; to preoccupy; to anticipate, to surprise.

praeopto, 1. to prefer, desire more.

praepando, 3. to open wide in front, extend before.

praepărātĭo -ōnis, *f.* preparation.

praepăro, 1. to provide, prepare.

praepĕdĭo -īvi *and* **-ii -ĭtum**, 4. to shackle, fetter; to hinder, obstruct.

praependĕo -pendi, 2. *intransit.*, to hang before, hang in front.

praepĕs -pĕtis, quick in flight, swift.

praepĭlātus -a -um, having a ball *or* button in front; *missilia.*

praepinguis -e, very fat, very rich.

praepollĕo -pollŭi, 2. to be very powerful.

praepondĕro, 1. to outweigh.

praepōno -pōsŭi -pŏsĭtum, 3. to put before; to put over, set over, *aliquem militibus;* **praepŏsĭtus -i**, *m.* a commander. *Fig.*, to prefer; **praepŏsĭtum -i**, *n.* something to be preferred (*in the Stoic philosophy*).

praeporto, 1. to carry before.

praepŏsĭtĭo -ōnis, _f._ a placing before; preference; _grammat._, a preposition.

praepŏsĭtus, _partic. of praepono._

praepossum -pŏtŭi -posse, to be very powerful.

praepostĕrē, _adv._ in a reversed order perversely, absurdly.

praepostĕrus -a -um, having the last first, inverted, absurd; _of persons,_ perverse.

praepŏtens -entis, very powerful, very mighty.

praeprŏpĕrantĕr, _adv._ very hastily.

praeprŏpĕrē, _adv._ very hastily, too quickly.

praeprŏpĕrus -a -um, exceedingly quick, too quick.

praequĕror -questus sum -quĕri, to complain beforehand.

praerādĭo, 1. to outshine.

praerăpĭdus -a -um, very rapid.

praerĭgesco -rĭgŭi, 3. to grow very stiff.

praerĭpĭo -rĭpŭi -reptum, 3. to snatch away, carry off; to carry off before the time; to anticipate, forestall.

praerōdo -rōdi -rōsum, 3. to gnaw in front, bite through.

praerŏgātīvus -a -um, asked before others; _polit._, voting first; _subst._, **praerŏgātīva -ae,** _f._ the century to which the lot fell of voting first in the comitia; **praerŏgātīva -ae,** _f._ a previous choice, a sure sign, indication.

praerumpo -rūpi -ruptum, 3. to tear off in front.

praeruptus -a -um, _p. adj._ broken off; steep, overhanging ; violent ; stern ; _subst._, **praerupta -ōrum,** _n._ precipices, praes, praedis, m. surety, security.

praesaepes -is, _f._ **praesaepe -is,** _n._, and **praesaepĭum -ĭi,** _n._ an enclosure; a stall; _praesaepibus arcent,_ from the hives; _in praesaepibus,_ in low houses.

praesaepĭo -saepsi -saeptum, 4. to block up in front.

praesāgĭo, 4. to have a presentiment of; to predict.

praesāgĭtĭo -ōnis, _f._ a premonition.

praesāgĭum -ĭi, _n._ a presentiment; a prediction.

praesāgus -a -um, foreboding; predicting.

praescisco -scīvi, 3. to find out beforehand.

praescĭus -a -um, knowing beforehand.

praescrībo -scripsi -scriptum, 3. to set before in writing; to write down for imitation; to prescribe, direct beforehand.

praescriptĭo -ōnis, _f._ a writing before; a title, introduction; a precept, rule, order; limitation; a pretext; _legal,_ objection.

praescriptum -i, _n._ a prescribed limit; an order, a precept, rule.

praesĕco -sĕcŭi -sĕcātum _and_ **-sectum,** 1. to cut in front.

praesens -entis, present, in person, at hand ; _in praesens tempus,_ for the present time; immediate, momentary; _decretum, praesed instanti,_ immediately efficacious; visible; plain; urgent, resoluto; propitious, _deus. Subst.,_ **praesentĭa -ĭum,** _n._ the present.

praesensĭo -ōnis, _f._ a presentiment.

praesentĭa -ae, _f._ presence; effect; _in praesentia,_ at present.

praesentĭo -sensi -sensum, 4. to have a presentiment.

praesēpes, _etc._ = _praesaepes, etc. (q.v.)._

praesēpĭo = _praesaepio (q.v.)._

praesertim, _adv._ especially, chiefly.

praeses -sĭdis, _c._ protecting; protector, a ruler, president.

praesĭdens -entis, _m._ a president, ruler.

praesĭdĕo -sēdi -sessum, 2. _with dat.,_ to protect, guard ; to preside over, direct, govern.

praesĭdĭārĭus -a -um, serving as a protection.

praesĭdĭum -ĭi, _n._ protection, defence, _alicui esse praesidio; milit._, a guard, escort; help; post, camp, fortification; support.

praesignĭfĭco, 1. to announce beforehand.

praesignis -e, distinguished.

praesŏno -sŏnŭi, 1. to resound.

praespargo, 3. to strew before.

praestābĭlis -e, distinguished.

praestans -antis, _p. adj._ excellent, distinguished; _homo prudentiā praestans._

praestantĭa -ae, _f._ superiority, excellence.

praesterno, 3. to strew before.

praestes -stĭtis, _c._ = _praeses,_ a protecting deity.

praestĭgĭa -ae, _f._, usually _plur._, **praestĭgĭae -ārum,** _f._ deception, illusion, juggling.

praestĭtŭo -stĭtŭi -stĭtūtum, 3. to prescribe, appoint beforehand.

1. **praesto,** _adv._ at hand, here, ready; _gen. with esse,_ to be at hand, to appear, to be at one's service; _alicui,_ to appear to help one at a court of law; _fig., praesto esse,_ to serve.

2. **praesto -stĭti -stĭtum** _and_ **-stātum -stātūrus,** 1. _Intransit._, to stand before, excel; _impers._, it is better, it is preferable. _Transit._, to become surety for, be responsible for; to perform, execute; to keep; _fidem,_ to keep one's word; to show, exhibit; _se,_ to behave oneself as.

praestōlor, 1. _dep._ to wait for, expect.

praestringo -strinxi -strictum, 3. to bind up; to make blunt; to weaken, darken, _oculos._

praestrŭo -struxi -structum, 3. to build in front; to block up; to prepare.

praesŭl -sŭlis, _c._ a dancer.

praesultātor -ōris, _m._ a dancer.

praesulto, 1. to leap, spring before.

praesum -fŭi -esse, to be before; to be over, preside over; to govern; to command, *exercitui;* to take the lead in.

praesūmo -sumpsi -sumptum, 3. to take beforehand; to anticipate; to imagine ; *praesumptum habere,* to suppose, take for granted; conjecture.

praesumptus -a -um, *p. adj.* taken for granted, presumed.

praesŭo -sūtus, 3. to sew up, to conceal.

praetempto = *praetento (q.v.).*

praetendo -tendi -tentum, 3. to stretch out before, extend backwards; to place before, spread before; *praetendi, of places,* to lie before *or* in front; *fig.,* to pretend; allege in excuse for, *aliquid seditioni.*

praetento (praetempto), 1. to feel, test beforehand.

praetĕpesco -tĕpŭi, 3. to glow beforehand.

praeter, *adv.* more than, except. *Prep. with acc.,* past, by, beyond; beside, contrary to; besides, in addition to.

praetĕrăgo, 3. to drive past.

praetĕrĕă, besides, further; henceforth, hereafter.

praetĕrĕo -ĭvi *and oftener* **-ĭi -ĭtum -īre,** to go by, pass by; *of time,* to pass, elapse. *Transit.,* to go by, pass by; *praetĕritus,* past *(of time);* **praetĕrĭta -ōrum,** *n.* the past; to escape the notice of, be unknown to; *non me praeterit,* I am not unaware; to omit; to forget to do; to leave out, pass over; to outstrip; *fig.,* to surpass.

praetĕrĕquito, 1. to ride past.

praeterfĕro -tŭli -lātum -ferre, to carry past; *praeterferri,* to be carried past, to go past.

praeterflŭo, 3. to flow past.

praetergrĕdior -gressus sum, 3. *dep.* to pass by, go beyond.

praetĕritus -a -um, *partic. of praetereo.*

praeterlābor -lapsus sum, 3. *dep.* to glide by, flow by; to slip away.

praetermĕo, 1. to pass by, go by.

praetermissio -ōnis, *f.* an omission; a neglecting.

praetermitto -mīsi -missum, 3. to let pass; to neglect, omit; to overlook.

praeterquam, *adv.* except.

praetervectio -ōnis, *f.* a passing by, travelling past.

praetervĕhor -vectus sum, 3. *dep.* to ride by, sail by, be carried past. *Of soldiers,* to march past.

praetervŏlo, 1. to fly past; to slip by, escape.

praetexo -texŭi -textum, 3. to form an edge, border, fringe; to adorn; to furnish with; to fringe; to conceal; to put forward as a pretext; *subst.,* **praetexta -ae,** *f.* an upper garment, bordered with purple, *worn by magistrates at Rome;* **praetexta -ae,** *f.* a Roman national tragedy.

praetexta, *v. praetexo.*

praetextātus -a -um, clad in the *praetexta;* licentious.

praetextum -i, *n.* pretence, pretext.

praetextus -ū, *m.* outward appearance, consequence; a pretext.

praetingo -tinctus, 3. to dip in *or* moisten beforehand.

praetor -ōris, *m.* leader, chief ; *at Rome,* one of the praetors, *the Roman magistrates who administered justice.*

praetōriānus -a -um, praetorian; *plur. subst.,* **praetōriāni -ōrum,** *m.* the praetorian guard.

praetōrium, *v. praetorius.*

praetōrius -a -um, *adj.* relating to the praetor, praetorian; *cohors praetoria,* the general's body-guard; the emperor's body-guard, the praetorian guard. *Subst.,* **praetōrium -ii,** *n.* the official residence of the praetor; the place in a Roman camp, where the general's tent was; **praetōrius ii,** *m.* an ex-praetor.

praetrĕpido, 1. to tremble exceedingly, to be hasty *or* impatient.

praetūra -ae, *f.* the office of a praetor.

praeumbro, 1. to overshadow; to obscure.

praeūro -ussi -ustum, 3. to burn at the end *or* tip.

praevălens -entis, *partic. of praevaleo (q.v.).*

praevălĕo -vălŭi, 2. to be physically strong; to be very powerful; to prevail.

praevălidus -a -um, very strong, very powerful; too fertile.

praevāricātio -ōnis, *f.* a violation of duty; collusion.

praevāricātor -ōris, *m.* one who violates his duty; a double dealer.

praevāricor, 1. *dep.* to go crooked *fig.,* to play a double part.

praevārus -a -um, very perverse.

praevĕhor -vectus sum, 3. *dep.* to ride before, past.

praevĕnio -vēni -ventum, 4. to anticipate, get the start of; *morte praeventus,* overtaken by death.

praeverro, 3. to sweep before.

praeverto (praevorto) -verti (-vorti) -versum (-vorsum), 3. *and* **praevertor -verti,** 3. *dep.* to undertake before; to go before, outstrip; to anticipate; *with acc.* = to hinder; to preoccupy; to be of more importance, to surpass; to take more notice of; to make a visit to.

praevidĕo -vīdi -vīsum, 2. to see before, foresee.

praevitio, 1. to corrupt beforehand.

praevius -a -um, preceding.

praevŏlo, 1. to fly before.

pragmăticus -a -um, skilled in civil affairs ; *subst.,* **pragmăticus -i,** *m.* one who supplied orators with material for their speeches.

prandĕo, prandi, pransum, 2. to breakfast; *with acc.*, to breakfast on.

prandium -ii, *n.* a late breakfast *or* lunch.

pransus -a -um, having lunched; *(of soldiers)*, ready for action.

pratensis -e, of *or* relating to a meadow.

prătŭlum -i, *n.* *(dim. of pratum)*, a little meadow.

prātum -i, *n.* a meadow; meadow-grass.

prāvē, *adv. lit.* crookedly; wrongly.

prāvitas -ātis, *f.* crookedness, irregularity, deformity; impropriety; wickedness.

prāvus -a -um, crooked, irregular, deformed; improper, wrong.

Praxitĕles -is *and* **-i,** *m.* a sculptor of Athens.

prĕcārĭo, *adv.* by entreaty.

prĕcārĭus -a -um, asked for, obtained by entreaty; uncertain, precarious.

prĕcātĭo -ōnis, *f.* entreating, request, prayer.

preces, *v. prex.*

prĕciae (prĕtiae) -ārum, *f.* a kind of vine.

prĕcor (praecor), 1. *dep.* to beg, entreat, pray; *precari alicui,* to curse a person.

prĕhendo, prĕhendi, prĕhensum, 3. *and* **prendo, prendi, prensum,** to lay hold of, to catch, detain; to catch, detect; to reach.

prĕhenso, *and* **prenso,** 1. to lay hold of; to canvass for an office.

prēlum -i, *n.* a wine-press, olive-press.

prĕmo, pressi, pressum, 3. to press; *vestigia alicuius,* to follow in anyone's footsteps; to touch; *locum,* to frequent; to lie on; to cover; *(fig.,* to bury, wrap; to suppress); to press hard; to pursue closely; to load; to press in; to extinguish; to plant; to strike to the ground; to slander; to despise; to surpass; to rule; to draw in; to check; to prune; to shorten; to hold back.

prendo = *prehendo (q.v.).*

prensātĭo -ōnis, *f.* the canvassing for an office.

prenso = *prehenso (q.v.).*

presse, *adv.* not broadly, neatly; briefly; accurately.

pressĭo -ōnis, *f. in plur.,* props.

presso, 1. to press; *ubera,* to milk.

1. **pressus -ūs,** *m.* *p.* *adj.* slow, measured, *presso gradu;* controlled, moderate; short; accurate.

2. **pressus -ūs,** *m.* a pressing, pressure.

prestĕr -ēris, *m.* a fiery whirlwind.

prĕtiōsē, *adv.* magnificently.

prĕtiōsus -a -um, costly, precious; extravagant.

prĕtium -ii, *n.* worth, value, price; money; wages; reward; *operae pretium est,* it is worth while.

prex, prĕcis, *nom.* and *genit. sing.* obsolete; *gen. plur.*, **prĕces, prĕcum,** *f.* a request, entreaty, prayer; a curse; a wish.

Priămus -i, *m.* the last king of Troy. *Adj.,* **Priămēius.**

pridem, *adv.* long ago; formerly; *iam pridem,* long ago.

prīdĭē, *adv.* on the day before.

primaevus -a -um, youthful.

primānus -a -um, belonging to the first legion. *Subst.,* **primāni -ōrum,** *m.* soldiers of the first legion.

primārius -a -um, in the first rank, distinguished.

primigĕnia, an epithet of Fortune.

primigĕnus -a -um, original, primitive.

primipīlāris -is, *m.* the centurion of the first maniple of the *triarii.*

primipilus, the chief centurion of a legion.

primĭtiae -ārum, *f.* first-fruits.

primĭtus, *adv.* first, for the first time.

primō, *adv.* at first, in the beginning.

primor -ōris, the first; the tip, end. *Subst., primores,* the foremost *(milit.);* the most illustrious; the first in rank, most distinguished.

primordium -ii, *n.* the first beginning, origin; *gen. plur., primordia.*

primum, *adv.* first, at first; for the first time. *With ut, ubi, quam, simulac,* as soon as; *quam primum,* as soon as possible.

primus, *v. prior.*

princeps -cipis. *c. adj.* and *subst.* first; the chief; chief, leader, founder; ruler, prince; *principes, orig.* the first rank in a Roman army, afterwards the second line.

principālis -e, first, original; chief.

principātus -ūs, *m.* the first place, pre-eminence; rule, dominion; the governing principle of actions; origin.

principālis -e, original.

principium -ii, *n.* a beginning, origin; the groundwork, foundation; *plur., principia,* the elements, first principles; the tribe *or* curia which voted first; the founder. *Milit.,* **principia -ōrum,** the front ranks; the headquarters.

prior -us, *genit. -ōris, superl.,* **primus.** *Compar.,* the first of two; former; preferable; *subst.,* **priōres -um,** *m.* ancestors. *Superl.,* **primus,** the first, foremost; *in primis* and *cum primis,* especially.

priscē, *adv.* after the manner of the ancients, severely.

priscus -a -um, ancient, antique; *esp.* venerable, belonging to the good old times; former, previous; severe, stern.

pristinus -a -um, former, previous, early; just past.

pristis -is, *f.* and **pistrix -icis,** *f.* sea monster, a whale; a small, swift-sailing ship of war.

prius, *adv.* before, previously; formerly.

prīvātim, *adv.* privately, as a private person, in private life; at home.

prīvātio -ōnis, *f.* a freeing from.

prīvātus -a -um, private, of *or* relating to a private individual; *privato consilio*, without the authority of the state; *subst.*, *privatus*, a private person.

prīvīgna -ae, *f.* a stepdaughter.

prīvīgnus -i, *m.* a stepson.

prīvīlēgium -ii, *n.* a special law, private law.

prīvo, 1. to deprive of; to free from.

prīvus -a -um, single; each, every; one each; special, one's own.

1. pro, *prep. with abl.* before, in front of; for, in behalf of; in place of; as, as good as; *se pro cive gerere*, to behave as a citizen; for, as a reward; in proportion to, according to, in consideration of; *pro mea parte*, for my part; *pro eo*, just as, according as.

2. pro ! (proh !), *interj.* oh ! ah !

prŏăvītus -a -um, ancestral.

prŏăvus -i, *m.* great-grandfather; ancestor.

prŏbābilis -e, probable; acceptable.

prŏbābilitas -ātis, *f.* probability.

prŏbābilitĕr, *adv.* probably.

prŏbātio -ōnis, *f.* proving, test, trial; approval.

prŏbātor -ōris, *m.* one who approves.

prŏbātus -a -um, *p. adj.* approved, excellent; agreeable.

prŏbē, *adv.* well, rightly, excellently.

prŏbitas -ātis, *f.* uprightness, worth, modesty.

prŏbo, 1. test, prove, examine; to approve; to recommend as good, guarantee; *probari alicui*, to appear worthy of approval; to show, prove.

prŏbrōsus -a -um, shameful, disgraceful.

prŏbrum -i, *n.* a shameful, infamous deed; unchastity; disgrace; insult, libel.

prŏbus -a -um, good, excellent; upright.

prŏcācitas -ātis, *f.* shamelessness, impudence.

prŏcācitĕr, *adv.* shamelessly, impudently.

prŏcax -ācis, shameless, insolent; *auster*, blustering.

prŏcēdo -cessi -cessum, 3. to go forth, go before, proceed; *milit.*, to advance; to appear; to come forward; to make progress; to run on, continue; to be of use to; to result; to turn out well.

prŏcella -ae, *f.* a storm, tempest; onset, charge.

prŏcellōsus -a -um, stormy.

prŏcer -ĕris, *m.* an illustrious person; *usually plur.*, prŏcĕres -um, *m.* chiefs, nobles, princes.

prŏcērē, *adv.* far outstretched.

prŏcēritas -ātis, *f.* height, slenderness; length (*of a syllable*).

prŏcērus -a -um, tall, slender, long.

prōcessio -ōnis, *f.* a military advance.

prōcessus -ūs, *m.* a going forth, advance, course.

prōcido -cidi, 3. to fall forward.

prōcinctus -ūs, *m.*, a being equipped for battle, readiness for battle.

proclāmātor -ōris, *m.* a bawler.

proclāmo, 1. to call out, cry out.

prōclīno, 1. *act.* to bend, incline forwards; *proclinatā iam re*, approaching consummation.

prōclīvĕ, *adv.* downwards.

prōclīvis -e *and* prōclīvus -a -um, inclined forwards, sloping downwards, steep; inclined to, ready for, prone to; easy to do.

prōclīvitas -ātis, *f.*, a slope; *fig.*, inclination.

prōclīvus = *proclivis* (q.v.).

Procnē (Prognē) -ēs, *f.* wife of Tereus, changed into a swallow.

prōco, 1. *and* prōcor, 1. *dep.* to ask, entreat.

prōconsul -sŭlis, *m.* a proconsul.

prōconsŭlāris -e, proconsular.

prōconsŭlātus -ūs, *m.* the office *or* dignity of a proconsul.

prōcrastinātio -ōnis, *f.* procrastination.

prōcrastino, 1. to procrastinate.

prōcrĕātio -ōnis, *f.* begetting.

prōcrĕātor -ōris, *m.* a begetter.

prōcrĕātrix -īcis, *f.* one that brings forth, mother.

prōcrĕo, 1. to beget, procreate; produce, cause, make.

prōcresco, 3. to grow forth, arise; *fig.*, to increase.

Procrustes -ae, *m.* a robber in Attica, who tied his prisoners to a bed, stretching the limbs of those shorter than the bed, and cutting off the limbs of those who were taller; killed by Theseus.

prōcŭbo, 1. to lie stretched out.

prōcūdo -cūsi -cūsum, 3. to thrust forward; to forge; *fig.*, *linguam*, to form, train.

prŏcŭl, *adv.* afar off, at a distance; far from.

prōculco, 1. to tread, trample upon.

prōcumbo -cŭbŭi -cŭbĭtum, 3. to lean *or* bend forward; to fall prostrate; *fig.*, to sink, fall.

prōcūrātio -ōnis, *f.* management, administration; office of procurator; a religious act for the propitiation of a deity.

prōcūrātor -ōris, *m.* a manager, administrator, agent; *regni*, a viceroy.

prōcūrātrix -trīcis, *f.* she that governs.

prōcūro, 1. to look after, tend; to manage, administer; to offer sacrifice to avert an evil omen.

prōcurro -curri *and* -cŭcurri -cursum, 3. to run forward, charge; to project, jut out.

prōcursātio -ōnis, *f.* a running forward, charge.

prōcursātor -ōris, m. one who runs forward; *milit., procursatores,* skirmishers.

prōcurso, 1. to run forward; *milit.,* to skirmish.

prōcursus -ūs, m. a running forward; *milit.,* an advance.

prōcurvus -a -um, curved forward; winding.

prōcus -i, m. a suitor.

prōdĕo -ii -itum, 4. to go, come forth; to appear; to advance; to project; to jut out.

prōdīco -dixi -dictum, 3. to say before; to put off.

prōdictātor -ōris, m. a vice-dictator.

prōdĭgē, adv. extravagantly.

prōdĭgentia -ae, f. profusion.

prōdĭgiālĭtĕr, adv. wonderfully.

prōdĭgiōsus -a -um, unnatural, strange.

prōdĭgĭum -ii, n. portent, omen; something unnatural; a monster.

prōdĭgo -ēgi -actum, 3. to drive forth; to spend, waste.

prōdĭgus -a -um, profuse, extravagant; rich, abounding in.

prōdĭtio -ōnis, f. treachery, treason.

prōdĭtor -ōris, m. betrayer, traitor.

prōdo -didi -ditum, 3. to put forth, bring forth; to show, publish; to appoint; to relate; to reveal, to betray; to hand over, deliver; to propagate, *genus.*

prōdŏcĕo, 2. to teach, inculcate.

prōdrŏmus -i, m. a messenger, fore-runner; a wind, said to blow for eight days before the rising of the Dog-star.

prōdūco -duxi -ductum, 3. to lead forth; to entice forth; to bring before someone; to reveal; to advance; to stretch out; *in pronunciation,* to lengthen; to beget, produce; to rear, bring up; to continue; to postpone.

prōductē, adv. in a lengthened manner long *(of pronunciation).*

prōductio -ōnis, f. an extending, lengthening, *of a word or syllable, temporis,* prolonging.

prōductus -a -um, p. adj. lengthened, prolonged. *Subst.,* **prōducta -ōrum,** n. preferable things *(in the Stoic philosophy).*

proeliātor -ōris, m. a warrior, combatant.

proelior, 1. dep. to give battle, fight.

proelium -ii, n. a battle, fight.

Proetus -i, m. king in Tiryns.

prōfāno, 1. to profane, desecrate.

prōfānus -a -um, not sacred, not consecrated; common, profane; impious; uninitiated; *subst.,* **prōfānum -i,** n. that which is profane, unconsecrated.

prōfectio -ōnis, f. a departure; source, origin.

prōfecto, adv. really, indeed.

prōfĕro -tŭli -lātum -ferre, to carry forth; to deliver up; to raise a limb; to show; to publish, make known; to

reveal, to bring to light; to produce, mention; to advance; *milit., signa,* to march on; to extend; *of time,* to extend; to postpone.

prōfessio -ōnis, f. acknowledgment, declaration, profession; register of persons and property; occupation, profession.

prōfessōrius -a -um, professorial.

prōfessus -a -um, partic. of *profiteor* (q.v.).

prōfestus -a -um, not kept as a festival, common; *dies,* work-days.

prōficio -fēci -fectum, 3. to make progress, advance; to effect anything; to be of use or advantage to, to assist.

prōficiscor -fectus sum -ficisci, 3. dep. to set out, depart, go, travel, march; *fig.,* to begin with; to arise from, spring from.

prōfĭtĕor -fessus sum, 2. dep. to acknowledge openly, confess; to profess; to offer, promise; to make a return of property, etc.; *nomen profiteri* and *simply profiteri,* to announce oneself as a candidate; **prōfessus,** known, acknowledged, avowed.

prōflīgātor -ōris, m. a spendthrift, prodigal.

prōflīgātus -a -um, p. adj. cast down, ruined, wretched; profligate.

prōflīgo, 1. to overthrow, overcome; *politically,* to ruin; to abase; to bring almost to an end.

prōflo, 1. to breathe forth.

prōflŭens -entis, p. adj. flowing; *of discourse,* fluent. *Subst.,* **prōflŭens -entis,** f. running water.

prōflŭentĕr, adv. flowingly, easily.

prōflŭo -fluxi -fluxum, 3. to flow forth; to proceed.

prōflŭvium -ii, n. a flowing forth.

prōfor -fātus sum, 1. dep. to say, speak, to predict.

prōfŭgio -fūgi -fŭgitum, 3. to flee away, escape; to flee away from, *agros.*

prōfŭgus -a -um, fleeing, fugitive; wandering, banished; *subst.,* **prōfŭgus -i,** m. a fugitive, exile.

prōfundo -fūdi -fūsum, 3. to pour forth, cause to flow; to stretch at full length; *(reflex.,* se *profundere,* or *profundi,* to pour out, rush forth); to utter; to produce; to spend, sacrifice; to squander; *fig.,* to pour, expend upon.

prōfundus -a -um, deep, profound; high; dense; *subst.,* **prōfundum -i,** n. the bottomless depth; *poet.* = the sea.

prōfūsē, adv. in a disorderly manner; lavishly.

prōfūsus -a -um, p. adj. extravagant; costly.

prōgĕner -i, granddaughter's husband.

prōgĕnĕro, 1. to engender, produce.

prōgĕnies -ēi, f. descent, race; descendants.

prōgĕnĭtor -ōris, m. ancestor.

prōgigno -gĕnŭi -gĕnĭtum, 3. to engender, bring forth, bear.

prognātus -a -um, born, sprung from.

Prognē = *Procne (q.v.)*.

prōgrĕdĭor -gressus sum -grĕdi, 3. *dep.* to go out; to advance; to proceed.

prōgressĭo -ōnis, *f.* progress, increase; *rhet.*, climax.

prōgressus -ūs, *m.* advance; beginning of a speech; progress, increase.

proh ! = *pro ! (q.v.)*.

prŏhĭbĕo -bŭi -bĭtum, 2. to restrain, hinder; forbid.

prŏhĭbĭtĭo -ōnis, *f.* a hindering, prohibition.

prŏĭcĭo -iēcī -iectum, 3. to throw, cast before, throw down; to stretch forth; (*pass.*, to project); to push forth; to banish; to throw out; to throw away; *se proicere*, to lower oneself to; to abandon; to betray; to put off.

prŏiectĭo -ōnis, *f.* a throwing forward, stretching out.

1. prōiectus -ūs, *m.* a projecting, jutting out.

2. prōiectus -a -um, *p. adj.* stretching out, jutting forward, projecting; prominent; addicted to; stretched out, prostrate, lying; abject, base; cast down, *vultus*.

prōin = *proinde (q.v.)*.

prōindĕ, *adv.*, just as, in the same manner, *foll. by atque (ac)*, *ut*, *quasi*, *quam*, *tamquam*; therefore, then, hence, accordingly, *esp. in phrases of exhortation, encouragement, etc.*

prōlābor -lapsus sum -lābi, 3. *dep.* to glide forward, slip along; to come to; to slip out, escape; to fall down; to fail, to err; to go to ruin, sink.

prōlapsĭo -ōnis, *f.* a slipping, sliding.

prōlātĭo -ōnis, *f.* mentioning, *exemplorum;* an extension; a putting off.

prōlāto, 1. to extend; to put off; to prolong.

prōlecto, 1. to entice, allure.

prōles -is, *f.* offspring, descendants; *of plants*, fruit.

prōlētārĭus -ĭi, *m.* a citizen of the lowest class who served the state only by being the father of children.

prōlĭcĭo, 3. to lure forth.

prōlixē, *adv.* abundantly; willingly.

prōlixus -a -um, wide, long; willing, obliging; prosperous; fortunate.

prōlŏgus -i, *m.* prologue.

prōlŏquor -lōcūtus (-lŏquūtus) sum -lŏqui, 3. *dep.* to speak out; to prophesy.

prōlūdo -lūsi -lūsum, 3. to play beforehand, to prelude.

prōlŭo -lŭi -lūtum, 3. to wash forth *or* out; to cast up ; to wash off ; to wash.

prōlūsĭo -ōnis, *f.* prelude, preliminary exercise.

prōlŭvĭes -ēi, *f.* inundation.

prōmĕrĕo -ŭi -ĭtum, 2. *and* **prōmĕrĕor** -ĭtus sum -ēri, 2. *dep.* to deserve; *subst.*, **prōmĕrĭtum -i**, *n.* deserts, merit.

Prōmēthĕūs -ĕi *and* **ĕos**, *m.* son of Iapetus, brother of Epimetheus and father of Deucalion, stole fire from heaven, for which he was bound to a rock in the Caucasus.

prōmĭnens -entis, jutting out, projecting; *subst.*, **prōmĭnens -entis**, *n.* a projection.

prōmĭnĕo -mĭnŭi, 2. to jut out, project; *fig.*, to be prominent; extend.

prōmiscē, *adv.* = *promiscue.*

prōmiscŭē, *adv.* promiscuously, without distinction.

prōmiscus = *promiscuus (q.v.)*.

prōmiscŭus -a -um, mixed, indiscriminate, promiscuous; *in promiscuo esse*, to be common, usual, general.

prōmissĭo -ōnis, *f.* a promise.

prōmissor -ōris, *m.* a promiser, a boaster.

prōmissum -i, *n.* a promise.

prōmissus -a -um, *p. adj.* long, hanging down.

prōmitto -mīsi -missum, 3. to let go forward, send forth; to grow, to let grow; to promise; to vow.

prōmo, prompsi, promptum, 3. to bring out, produce; to bring wine out of the cellar; to bring forward, utter, mention.

prōmŏnĕo, 2. to warn.

prōmontōrium -ĭi, *n.* mountain-peak; promontory.

prōmōta -ōrum, *n.* preferable things, next in degree to the absolute good (*in the Stoic philosophy*).

prōmŏvĕo -mōvi -mōtum, 2. to move forward, push onward; cause to advance; to increase, improve; extend.

promptē, *adv.* promptly, quickly, ready; easily, freely.

1. promptus -a -um, *p. adj.* visible, manifest ; ready, at hand, prepared ; easy. *Of persons*, ready, prepared, resolute.

2. promptus -ū, *m. in promptu esse*, to be manifest, to be ready at hand, to be easy; *in promptu habere*, to have ready at hand; *in promptu ponere*, to make manifest.

prōmulgātĭo -ōnis, *f.* proclamation, promulgation.

prōmulgo, 1. to publish, promulgate.

prōmulsis -ĭdis, *f.* a relish before a meal.

prōmuntūrium = *promontorium (q.v.)*.

prōmus -i, *m.* steward, butler.

prōmūtŭus -a -um, advanced, paid beforehand.

prōnĕpos -ōtis, *m.* great-grandson.

prōneptis -is, *f.* great grand-daughter.

prōnis = *pronus (q.v.)*.

prōnūba -ae, *f.* a matron who attended on a bride.

prōnuntĭātĭo -ōnis, *f.* publication; a judgment; *in logic*, a proposition.

prōnuntiātor -ōris, *m.* a relater.

prōnuntiātum -i, *n.* in *logic*, a proposition.

prōnuntio, 1. to publish; to proclaim; to decide, pronounce a judgment; *rhet.*, to declaim, deliver.

prōnŭrus -ūs, *f.* a grandson's wife.

prōnus -a -um, inclined forward, hanging down; swiftly running; sloping; *poet.* steep; *of stars*, setting; *of time*, hastening away; inclined towards; favourable, *in aliquem.*

prōoemium -ii, *n.* introduction; beginning.

propāgātio -ōnis, *f.* an extension; planting, propagation.

propāgātor -ōris, *m.* an enlarger

1. **propāgo**, 1. to extend; to propagate, plant.

2. **propāgo** -inis, *f.* a sucker, shoot, *esp. of the vine*; offspring.

prōpălam, *adv.* publicly, in public.

prōpătŭlus -a -um, open, uncovered. *Subst.*, prōpătŭlum -i, *n.* an unroofed space.

prŏpē, *compar.*, **prŏpius**; *superl.*, **proximē**. *Adv.*, near; nearly; close to, hard by; *proxime*, just now. *Prep. with acc.*, near to; *of time*, close on.

prōpēdiem, *adv.* very soon.

prōpello -pŭli -pulsum, 3. to drive before one, drive away; to hurl down; to repulse; to compel.

prōpēmŏdŭo, *adv.* almost, nearly.

prōpēmŏdum, *adv.* almost, nearly.

prōpendĕo -pendi -pensum, 2. to hang down; *fig.*, *bona propendent*, to preponderate.

prōpensē, *adv.* readily, willingly.

prōpensio -ōnis, *f.* an inclination towards.

prōpensus -a -um, *p. adj.* inclined to, disposed to; coming near to.

prōpĕranter, *adv.* hastily, quickly.

prōpĕrantia -ae, *f.* haste, rapidity.

prōpĕrātio -ōnis, *f.* haste.

prōpĕrātō, *adv.* hastily, quickly.

prōpĕro, 1. *intransit.*, to hasten. *Transit.*, to hasten, to complete quickly.

Prōperĭtius -ii, *m.* a Roman elegiac poet.

prōpĕrus -a -um, quick, hasty.

prōpexus -a -um, combed forwards, hanging down.

prōpīnātio -ōnis, *f.* a drinking to one's health.

prōpīno, 1. to drink to anyone; to give drink to anyone.

prōpinquĭtas -ātis, *f.* nearness; relationship.

prōpinquo, 1. to come near, approach; *of time*, to draw near; *transit.*, to hasten.

prōpinquus -a -um, near; neighbouring; similar; closely connected; *subst.*, a kinsman.

prŏpĭor -us, *genit.* -ōris. *Superl.* proxi-

mus, very near, nearest; next; most recent; most like; most nearly related; near relations. *Subst.*, proximi, those standing next *or* nearest; proximum -i, *n.* the neighbourhood; next; most recent; most like; most nearly related; near relations.

prōpitius -a -um, favourable, gracious.

prōpius, *comp. of prope* (q.v.).

prōpōla -ae, *m.* retailer, huckster.

prōpolluo, 3. to pollute greatly.

prōpōno -pŏsŭi -pŏsitum, 3. to put forth, expose, display; to place before; to bring forward; to propose; to report, relate; to make known; to offer as a reward; to threaten; to intend.

Prōpontis -idis *and* -idos, *f.* now the Sea of Marmora.

prōporro, *adv.* further, moreover.

prōportio -ōnis, *f.* proportion, analogy.

prōpositio -ōnis, *f.* a setting forth, representation; a subject *or* theme.

prōpositum -i, *n.* design, plan, purpose; a subject *or* theme.

prōpraetor -ōris, *m. and* pro praetōre, propraetor.

prōprĭē, *adv.* peculiarly, exclusively for oneself; characteristically, personally; specially; accurately.

prōprĭĕtas -ātis, *f.* a property, peculiarity.

prōprītim, properly, peculiarly.

prōprĭus -a -um, one's own, special, particular, peculiar; characteristic of; exclusive; proper; permanent.

propter, *adv.* near, hard by. *Prep. with acc.* near, hard by; on account of.

proptĕrĕā, *adv.* on that account, therefore; *foll. by quia or quod.*

prōpŭdĭum -ii, *n.* villain, rascal.

prōpugnācŭlum -i, *n.* fortification, fortress, defence.

prōpugnātio -ōnis, *f.* defence, defending.

prōpugnātor -ōris, *m.* defender, combatant, soldier; marine.

prōpugno, *intransit.*, to fight in defence, *pro vallo*; propugnantes, defenders.

prōpulso, 1. to repel, ward off.

prōpȳlaeon -i, *n.* gateway, entrance; *plur.*, Prōpȳlaea -ōrum, *n* entrance to the Parthenon at Athens.

prōquaestōre, proquaestor.

prōquam, *conj.* according as.

prōra -ae, *f.* prow, bow of a ship; *poet.* a ship.

prōrēpo -repsi -reptum, 3. to creep forward.

prōrĭpĭo -rĭpŭi -reptum, 3. to snatch, drag forth; *se proripere*, to rush forward, hurry.

prōrŏgātio -ōnis, *f.* prolongation of a term of office; deferring of a fixed time, prorogation.

prōrŏgo, 1. to propose an extension, to prolong; to put off.

prorsum, *adv.* forwards ; wholly, at all.

prorsūs, *adv.* turned forwards, forwards; utterly, entirely; in a word, to sum up.

prōrumpo -rūpi -ruptum, 3. *transit.* to cause to break forth, send forth; *prorupta audacia*, unbridled; *intransit.*, to burst forth; break out.

prōrŭo -rŭi -rŭtum, 3. *intransit.*, to rush forth ; *transit.*, to overthrow, destroy.

prōsāpia -ae, *f.* a family, race, stock.

proscaenium (proscēnium) -ii, *n.* stage.

proscindo -scĭdi -scissum, 3. to rend; to plough up; to censure.

proscrībo -scripsi -scriptum, 3. to publish; to advertise; to confiscate; to proscribe, outlaw.

proscriptio -ōnis, *f.* an advertisement of sale; a proscription.

proscriptūrio, 4. to desire to declare anyone an outlaw.

prōsĕco -sĕcŭi -sectum, 1. to cut off in front, cut off.

prōsectum -i, *n.* the entrails of a victim.

prōsēmĭno, 1. to sow; *fig.*, to disseminate.

prōsĕquor -cūtus (-quūtus) sum -sĕqui, 3. *dep.* to follow, accompany; to honour *or* present with ; *of a discourse*, to continue; to attack, pursue.

Proserpĭna -ae, *f.* the daughter of Ceres and Jupiter, queen of the lower world.

prōsĕucha -ae, *f.* a place of prayer for the Jews.

prōsĭlio -ŭi (-īvi *or* -ĭi), 4. to leap forth.

prōsŏcer -ĕri, *m.* a wife's grandfather.

prospecto, 1. to look forward, look forth upon; to look towards, be situate towards; *fig.*, to look for, expect.

prospectus -ūs, *m.* view, prospect; *in prospectu*, within sight.

prospĕcŭlor, 1. *dep.* to look out to a distance ; to explore ; *transit.*, to wait for.

prosper (prospĕrus) -a -um, fortunate, lucky, prosperous ; *subst.*, **prospĕra -ōrum**, *n.* good fortune; *transit.*, propitious.

prospĕrē, *adv.* prosperously, favourably.

prospergo -spersi -sparsum, 3. to besprinkle.

prospĕritas -ātis, *f.* prosperity.

prospĕro, 1. to cause to succeed.

prospĕrus = prosper (q.v.).

prospĭcientia -ae, *f.* foresight, precaution.

prospĭcio -spexi -spectum, 3. *intransit.*, to look forward into the distance; to be upon the watch; to take precaution; *transit.*, to see, behold; *of places*, to be situate towards ; *fig.*, to foresee ; provide.

prosterno -strāvi -strātum, 3. to cast down; to overthrow, ruin; **prostrātus**, lying on the ground.

prostĭtŭo -stĭtŭi -stĭtūtum, 3. to prostitute.

prosto -stĭti, 1. to stand before; to project; to be exposed for sale; to prostitute oneself.

prōsŭbigo, 3. to dig up, throw up.

prōsum, prōfŭi, prōdesse, to be lawful, advantageous to; *with dat.*

Prōtăgŏras -ae, *m.* a Greek philosopher of Abdera, contemporary with Socrates, banished from Attica on a charge of atheism.

prōtĕgo -texi -tectum, 3. to cover, protect.

prōtēlum -i, *n.* yoke of oxen; a series, succession.

prōtendo -tendi -tentum *and* -tensum, 3. to stretch forward, stretch out.

prōtĕnūs (prōtĭnūs), *adv.* forward, further, continuously; constantly; immediately, at the beginning.

prōtĕro -trīvi -trītum, 3. to trample under foot; to rout, defeat; to despise; to drive away.

prōterrĕo -terrŭi -territum, 2. to frighten away.

prōtervē, *adv.* boldly, shamelessly.

prōtervitas -ātis, *f.* boldness, impudence.

prōtervus -a -um, violent; bold, impudent.

Prōtĕūs -ĕi *and* -ĕos, *m.* a god of the sea, who had the power of changing himself into different shapes.

prōtĭnam (prōtĕnam), *adv.* immediately (*early Lat.*).

prōtĭnus = protenus (q.v.).

prōtrăho -traxi -tractum, 3. to draw, drag forth; to reveal; to compel; *of time*, to protract, defer.

prōtrūdo -trūsi -trūsum, 3. to push forward; to put off.

prōturbo, 1. to drive forward, repel; *silvas*, to throw down.

prŏŭt, *adv.* according as.

prōvectus -a -um, advanced in age, grown old.

prōvĕho -vexi -vectum, 3. to carry forward, to lead forward; to carry away, lead on; to advance, raise. Pass., *provehi*, *in a middle sense*, to go forward, ride, drive, sail to a place; *fig.*, to go too far.

prōvĕnio -vēni -ventum, 4. to come forth ; *in scenam*, to appear upon the stage; to come up, grow; to result; prosper.

prōventus -ūs, *m.* product, crop; the result; success.

prōverbium -ii, *n.* a proverb.

prōvĭdens -entis, *p. adj.* provident, prudent.

prōvĭdentĕr, *adv.* with forethought.

prōvĭdentia -ae, *f.* foresight, foreknowledge; forethought.

prōvĭdĕo -vīdi -vīsum, 2. to look forward to, see at a distance; to foresee; to take precautions for or against, to make preparation for, care for.

prōvidus -a -um, foreseeing; providing for; cautious.

prōvincia -ae, f. employment, office. *Polit.,* the sphere assigned to a magistrate; the government of a province, the province itself.

prōvinciālis -e, relating to a province. *Subst.,* **prōvinciāles -ium,** m. provincials.

prōvīsio -ōnis, f. foreknowledge; foresight; provision.

1. **prōvīso, 3.** to go or come forth to see.

2. **prōvīso,** adv. with forethought.

prōvīsor -ōris, m. one who foresees; a provider.

prōvīsus -ūs, m. a looking before, into the distance; foreseeing; provision.

prōvīvo -vīxi, 3. to continue to live.

prōvocātio -ōnis, f. an appeal to a higher court.

prōvocātor -ōris, m. one who challenges to fight, a kind of gladiator.

prōvoco, 1. to call forth, call out; to rouse; to challenge; to appeal to a higher tribunal.

prōvolo, 1. to fly forth; hasten forth.

prōvolvo -volvi -volūtum, 3. to roll forward, roll along; to fall down before; *reflex.,* to abase oneself.

prōvomo, 3. to vomit forth.

proxime, *superl. of prope* (q.v.).

proximitas -ātis, f. nearness; proximity; similarity.

proximo, adv. very lately.

proximus, *superl. of propior* (q.v.).

prūdens -entis, foreseeing. *Adj.,* skilled, experienced; discreet, judicious.

prūdenter, adv. prudently, wisely.

prūdentia -ae, f. knowledge; prudence, discretion.

prūina -ae, f. hoar-frost, rime.

prūinōsus -a -um, covered with hoar-frost.

prūna -ae, f. a live coal.

prūnicius -a -um, of plum-tree wood.

prūnum -i, n. a plum.

prūnus -i, f. plum-tree.

prūrīgo -inis, f. the itch.

prūrio, 4. to itch.

prytanēum -i, n. the town-hall in Greek cities.

prytănis, acc. **-in,** m. a chief magistrate in Greek states.

psallo, psalli, 3. to play on, sing to a stringed instrument.

psaltērium -ii, n. a stringed instrument.

psaltria -ae, f. female player on the cithara.

psĕcăs -ădis, f. female slave who anointed her mistress's hair.

Pseudŏlus -i, m. The Liar (a comedy by Plautus).

pseudothyrum -i, n. a secret door; secret manner.

psithius (psythius) -a -um, psithian, a kind of Greek vine; *subst.,* **psithia -ae,** f.

psittăcus -i, m. a parrot.

psychŏmantīum -ii, n. the place where the souls of the dead were invoked.

psythius = psithius (q.v.).

-pte, enclit., self, own.

ptisănārium -ii, n. decoction of crushed barley or rice.

pūbens -entis, of plants, luxuriant.

pūber -ĕris = 2. pubes (q.v.).

pūbertas -ātis, f. age of maturity.

1. **pūbes -is,** f. signs of puberty, hair on the chin; the youth.

2. **pubes -ĕris,** adult; ripe; *subst.,* **pūbĕres -um,** m. the adult population.

pūbesco -bui, 3. to grow up, arrive at maturity.

publicānus -a -um, relating to the farming of the public taxes; *subst.,* **publicānus -i,** m. a farmer of the Roman taxes.

publicātio -ōnis, f. a confiscation.

publice, adv. publicly; in the name or at the command of the state; for the state; at the cost of the state; generally, all together.

publicitus, adv. at the public expense, in the public service; publicly (early Lat.).

publico, 1. to confiscate; to make public, publish.

Publicŏla -ae, m. (also Poplicola and Poplicula), P. Valerius Publicola, the first consul of the Roman republic.

publicus -a -um, belonging to the people, public; of or belonging to the commonwealth; universal, common, general. *Subst.,* **publicum -i,** n. the property of the state, public territory; the treasury; (plur., societates publicorum, companies of the farmers of the taxes); the public stores; publicity, an open place.

pūdendus -a -um, shameful, disgraceful.

pūdens -entis, p. adj. modest.

pūdenter, adv. modestly, bashfully.

pūdĕo -ui (puditum est), 2. to be ashamed; to cause shame; *partic. subst., pudentes,* modest persons. *Impers.,* I (you, he, etc.) am ashamed, with acc. of the pers. and genit. of thing.

pūdibundus -a -um, modest, bashful.

pūdice, adv. modestly, virtuously.

pūdicitia -ae, f. modesty, virtue.

pūdicus -a -um, modest, virtuous.

pūdor -ōris, m. the feeling of shame, modesty; chastity; a disgrace.

pūella -ae, f. a girl, maiden.

pūellāris -e, girlish, maidenly.

pūellŭla -ae, f. (dim. of puella), little girl.

pūellus -i, m. (dim. of puer), little boy.

pūer -i, m. a child; boy; a puero, from boyhood.

pūerilis -e, youthful, boyish; childish.

pūerilitĕr, adv. like a boy; childishly.

pūeritia -ae, f. boyhood.

pūerpĕrium -ii, n. childbirth.

pŭerpĕrus -a -um, relating to childbirth.

pŭertia = *pueritia* (q.v.).

pŭĕrŭlus -i, m. (*dim. of puer*), little boy, young slave.

pūga (pȳga) -ae, f. buttocks.

pŭgil -ilis, m. boxer, pugilist.

pŭgĭlātĭo -ōnis, f. boxing.

pŭgĭllāris -e, that can be grasped with the fist; *subst.*, **pŭgĭllāres -ium**, m. writing-tablets.

pŭgillus -i, m. (*dim. of pugnus*), a handful.

pŭgĭo -ōnis, m. a dagger.

pŭgĭuncŭlus -i, m. (*dim. of pugio*), a little dagger.

pugna -ae, f. a fight; athletic games; contest.

pugnācĭtas -ātis, f. pugnacity.

pugnācĭtĕr, pugnaciously.

pugnātor -ōris, m. combatant, soldier.

pugnax -ācis, combative, martial; contentious.

pugno, 1. to fight, give battle; to contend; to contradict; to strive, exert oneself.

pugnus -i, m. the fist.

pulchellus -a -um, (*dim. of pulcher*), very pretty.

pulcher -chra -chrum *and* pulcer -cra -crum, beautiful, lovely; excellent, fine; lucky, happy.

pulchrē (pulcrē), adv. beautifully, admirably, nobly; bravo! well done!

pulchrĭtūdo (pulcrĭtūdo) -ĭnis, f. beauty, excellence.

pūlex -ĭcis, m. a flea.

pullārĭus -ii, m. feeder of the sacred chickens.

pullātus -a -um, clad in dirty *or* black garments (*of mourners*).

pullŭlo, 1. to shoot up, sprout out.

1. pullus -i, m. a young animal; a young cock; *term of endearment*, darling.

2. pullus -a -um, dark-coloured, blackish, greyish-black; gloomy; *subst.*, **pullum -i**, n. a dark-coloured garment.

pulmentārĭum -ii, n. a relish.

pulmentum -i, n. a relish; food.

pulmo -ōnis, m. the lung; *usually plur.*

pulpa -ae, f. flesh.

pulpāmentum -i, n. flesh; relish.

pulpĭtum -i, n. a platform, stage.

puls, pultis, f. porridge, pulse.

pulsātĭo -ōnis, f. a knocking, beating.

pulso, 1 to strike, beat, knock; *foros*, to knock at; to move, affect; to alarm; to drive away.

pulsus -ūs, m. a beating, striking, blow, stroke; influence, impulse.

pulto, 1. to knock, beat, strike.

pulvĕrĕus -a -um, full of dust, dusty; raising dust.

pulvĕrŭlentus -a -um, full of dust, dusty; won by hard work.

pulvillus -i, m. (*dim. of pulvinus*), a little pillow.

pulvīnar -āris, n. couch covered with cushions placed for the images of the gods at the Lectisternium (q.v.); a cushioned seat; a state coach; marriage-couch.

pulvīnārĭum -ii, n. cushioned seat for the gods.

pulvīnus -i, m. pillow, cushion.

pulvis -ĕris, m. *and rarely* f. dust; *poet.* arena; scene of action; *sine pulvere palmae*, without effort; the earth.

pūmex -ĭcis, m. pumice-stone, *etc.*; any porous stone.

pūmĭcĕus -a -um, made of pumice-stone.

pūmĭco, 1. to polish with pumice-stone.

pūmĭlĭo -ōnis, c. dwarf.

punctim, adv. by stabbing, by thrusting.

punctum -i, n. a little hole; point; a short clause, section; a vote; approval, applause; a mathematical point, the smallest quantity; *ad punctum temporis*, in a moment.

pungo, pŭpŭgi, punctum, 3. to prick, puncture, stab; to penetrate, enter; to touch, move; *fig.*, to sting, annoy.

Pūnĭcĕus, v. *Poeni*.

Pūnĭcus, Punĭce, v. *Poeni*.

pūnĭo (poenĭo) -īvi *and* -ĭi -ītum -īre, *and dep.* pūnĭor (poenĭor) -ītus sum -īri, to punish; to avenge.

pūnītor -ōris, m. punisher, avenger.

pūpa -ae, f. a little girl; a doll.

pūpilla -ae, f. (*dim. of pupa*), an orphan girl, minor; the pupil of the eye.

pūpillāris -e, relating to a ward.

pūpillus -i, m. (*dim. of populus*), an orphan ward.

puppis -is, f. the poop *or* stern of a vessel; the whole ship.

pūpŭla -ae, f. (*dim. of pupa*), the pupil of the eye.

pūpŭlus -i, m. (*dim. of pupus*), a little boy.

pūpus -i, m. a boy, child.

pūrē *and poet.* pūrĭtĕr, adv. purely; brightly; clearly, naturally; uprightly; finely, perfectly.

purgāmen -ĭnis, n. filth, sweepings; a means of expiation.

purgāmentum -i, n. sweepings, rubbish.

purgātĭo -ōnis, f. a cleansing; purging; justification.

purgo, 1. to cleanse; to purge, purify; to excuse, justify; to make good.

pūrĭtĕr = *pure* (q.v.).

purpŭra -ae, f. the purple-fish, the purple dye, purple; purple cloth.

purpŭrasco, 3. to become purple *or* dark.

purpŭrātus -a -um, clad in purple.

purpŭrĕus -a -um, purple, blackish, dark-red; clad in purple; bright, beautiful.

pūrus -a -um, clean, pure; *terra*, cleared of stones, stubble, *etc.*, *of the air, sun, etc.*, bright, clear; simple, plain; *argentum*, without reliefs; unmixed; clear (profit); spotless; holy, upright;

free from crime; *discourse*, faultless; unconsecrated ; undefiled ; purifying ; natural, simple ; *legal*, without conditions.

pūs, pūris, *n.* corrupt matter; *fig.*, gall, venom.

pūsillus -a -um, tiny, puny *Subst.*, **pūsillum -i**, *n.* a trifle; very insignificant; petty, mean.

pūsio -ōnis, *m.* a little boy

pūtā, for example, for instance.

pūtāmen -inis, *n.* a cutting, paring, shell.

pūteal -ālis, *n.* stone curb round the mouth of a well or round a sacred place.

pūteālis -e, relating to a well.

pūteārius -ii, *m.* well-sinker.

pūtĕo, 2. to stink.

pūter -tris -tre *and* **putris -e**, rotten, stinking; loose, soft, crumbling.

pūtesco (pūtisco) -tŭi, 3. to decay.

pūtĕus -i, *m.* pit, trench; well, spring.

pūtĭdĕ, *adv.* affectedly, disgustingly.

pūtidus -a -um, rotten, putrid; *cerebrum*, addled; nauseous, pedantic.

1. **pūto**, 1. to cleanse; to prune trees.

2. **pūto**, 1. to reckon value at; to consider, believe, suppose; *putare deos*, to believe in the gods; to count over; to weigh, reflect.

pūtor -ōris, *m.* bad smell.

putrĕfācĭo -fēci -factum, 3. *pass.*, **putrĕfĭo -factus sum -fĭĕri**, to make rotten, *and pass.*, to become rotten; to soften.

putresco -trŭi, 3. to become rotten.

putridus -a -um, rotten, decayed; flabby.

pycta (-es) -ae, *m.* boxer, pugilist (*late*).

pȳga = *puga (q.v.)*.

pȳgargus -i, *m.* a species of antelope.

Pygmaei -ōrum, *m.* Pygmies, a race of dwarfs.

Pygmălĭōn -ōnis, *m.* a sculptor who fell in love with a beautiful statue.

Pȳlădēs -ae *and* **-is**, *m.* the faithful friend of Orestes.

pȳlae ārum, *f.* passes between mountains.

pȳra -ae, *f.* funeral pyre. **Pyra -ae**, *f.* on Mount Oeta, where Hercules burnt himself.

pȳrămis -ĭdis, *f.* pyramid.

Pȳrămus -i, *m.* lover of Thisbe.

Pȳrēnē -ēs, *f. Pyrenaei Montes*, the Pyrenees.

Pȳrĭphlĕgĕthōn -ontis, *m.* river in the lower world; *gen.* Phlegethon.

pȳrōpus -i, *m.* bronze.

Pyrrha -ae, *f.* daughter of Epimetheus, wife of Deucalion.

Pyrrhus -i, *m.* 1. son of Achilles; 2. king in Epirus, enemy of the Romans.

Pȳthăgŏras -ae, *m.* Greek philosopher of Samos. *Adj.*, **Pȳthăgŏrēus.**

Pȳtho -ūs, *f.* the old name of part of Phocis where the town of Delphi lay.

Adj., **Pȳthĭcus, Pȳthĭus** ; *subst.*, **Pȳthia -ae**, *f.* the priestess who delivered the oracles at Delphi; **Pȳthia -ōrum**, *n.* the Pythian games.

Pȳthōn -ōnis, *m.* a great snake killed by Apollo, near Delphi.

pȳtisma -ātis, *m.* the wine which spurted through the lips (*in tasting*).

pȳtisso, 1. to spit out wine (*in tasting*).

pyxis -ĭdis, *f.* a little box, casket.

Q

Q q, *the sixteenth letter of the Roman Alphabet; see Table of Abbreviations.*

quā, *adv.* where ; (*qua ... qua*, partly ... partly ; both ... as well as); in so far as.

quācumque, *adv.* wherever, by all means.

quādamtĕnŭs, *adv.* to a certain point, so far.

quadra, *v. quadrus.*

quadrāgēni -ae -e, *num. distrib.* forty each.

quadrāgēsimus -a -um, fortieth; *subst.*, **quadrāgēsima -ae**, *f.* the fortieth part.

quadrāgiēs, *adv.* forty times.

quadrāginta, forty.

quadrans -antis, *m.* a quarter; the fourth part of an as.

quadrantārius -a -um, pertaining to a quarter.

quadrātus -a -um, square ; *subst.*, **quadrātum -i**, *n.* a square.

quadrĭdŭum (quatrĭdŭum, quatrĭdŭum) -i, *n.* a space of four days.

quadriennium -ii, *n.* a period of four years.

quadrĭfāriam, *adv.* fourfold, in four parts.

quadrĭfidus -a -um, split into four portions.

quadrĭgae -arum, *f.* a team of four horses abreast.

quadrĭgārĭus -ii, *m.* the driver of four horses.

quadrĭgātus -a -um, stamped with the figure of a quadriga.

quadrĭgŭlae -ārum, *f.* (*dim. of quadriga*), a little team of four horses.

quadrĭjŭgis -e, yoked four together.

quadrĭjŭgus -a -um, yoked four together; *subst.*, **quadrĭjŭgi -ōrum**, *m.* a team of four horses.

quadrīmus -a -um, four years old.

quadringēnārius -a -um, of four hundred each.

quadringēni -ae -a, four hundred each.

quadringentēni -ae -a, four hundred each.

quadringentēsimus -a -um, the four hundredth.

quadringenti -ae -a, four hundred.

quadringentiēs, four hundred times.

quadripartītō, in four parts.

quadripartītus (quadrĭpertītus) -a -um, divided into four parts, fourfold.

quadrĭrēmis -e, with four banks of oars; *subst.*, **quadrĭrēmis -is**, *f.* a ship with four banks of oars.

quadrĭvĭum -ii, *n.* a place where four roads meet.

quadro, 1. to make square; to join properly; to be square; to fit exactly; correspond with; *of accounts*, to agree.

quadrum, *v. quadrus.*

quadrŭpēdans -antis, going on four feet, galloping; *subst.*, a horse.

quadrŭpēs -pēdis, four-footed; *subst.*, **quadrŭpēs -pēdis**, a quadruped.

quadruplātōr -ōris, *m.* an informer who received a fourth part of the penalty.

quadruplex -plĭcis, fourfold, quadruple.

quadruplor, 1. *dep.* to be an informer.

quadruplus -a -um, fourfold. *Subst.*, **quadruplum -i**, *n.* four times as much.

quadrus -a -um, square. *Subst.*, **quadra -ae**, *f.* a square; **quadrum -i**, *n.* a square.

quaerito, 1. to seek eagerly; to inquire eagerly.

quaero, quaesivi, quaesitum, 3. to seek, search for; to seek to obtain; to prepare; to miss, want; to investigate; to ask, to inquire; to win, gain; to demand, make necessary; *subst.*, **quaesitum -i**, *n.* a question; *plur.*, **quaesita -ōrum**, *n.* gains, acquisition.

quaesĭtĭo -ōnis, *f.* an interrogation by torture.

quaesĭtor -ōris, *m.* an investigator, inquirer.

quaesitum, *v. quaero.*

quaesitus -a -um, *p. adj.* sought out, uncommon; unnatural, affected.

quaeso -īvi, 3. to seek for; to beg, entreat.

quaestĭcŭlus -i, *m.* (*dim. of quaestus*) a slight profit.

quaestio -ōnis, *a.* seeking, searching; questioning; inquiry; subject of inquiry; subject of debate; the main point, the issue; a public judicial inquiry; *quaestiones perpetuae*, courts for the investigation of crime.

quaestĭuncŭla -ae, *f.* (*dim. of quaestio*), a little question.

quaestor -ōris, *m.* the quaestor, *plur.*, the quaestors, magistrates in Rome.

quaestōrius -a -um, belonging or relating to a quaestor. *Subst.*, **quaestōrium -ii**, *n.* the quaestor's tent in camp. *Subst.*, **quaestōrius -ii**, *m.* one who had been quaestor.

quaestŭōsus -a -um, profitable; eager after profit; rich.

quaestūra -ae, *f.* quaestorship.

quaestus -ūs, *m* profit, advantage.

quālĭbĕt (quālŭbĕt), *adv.* wherever you like, everywhere; in any way you please.

quālis -e, *interrog.*, of what sort, what kind of; *rel.*, *with talis*, as; *without talis*, of such a kind, such as.

quāliscumquĕ(-cunquĕ), quālĕcumquĕ; *rel.*, of whatever kind; *indef.*, any, any whatever.

quālislĭbĕt, quālĕlĭbĕt, of what sort you will.

quālĭtas -ātis, *f.* a quality, property.

quālĭtĕr, *adv.* as, just as.

quālus -i, *m. and* **quālum -i**, *n.* a wicker-basket.

quam, how, in what way; how much; *in comparisons, with tam*; *quam saepissime*, as often as possible; *with comparatives*, than, as; after that, that, *postero die quam*; *to express degree*, how, how great, how little.

quamdĭū, so long as, as long as, until.

quamlĭbĕt, *adv.* as you please; howsoever, ever so much.

quamobrem (quam ob rem), on which account, wherefore, why.

quamprīmum, *adv.* as soon as possible.

quamquam, *conj.* although.

quamvīs, *adv.* as you will; ever so much; exceedingly. *Conj.*, however much, although.

quānam, where indeed.

quandō, *adv. and conj. Adv. interrog.* when; *indef.* at any time, ever. *Conj.*, since.

quandōcumquĕ, *adv.* whenever.

quandōquĕ, *adv. rel.*, whenever, as often as; *indef.*, at some time or other.

quandōquĭdem, *conj.* since, because.

quanto, *adv.* by how much.

quantŏpĕrĕ (quanto ŏpĕrĕ), *adv.* with what care, how much.

quantŭlus -a -um (*dim. of quantus*), how little, how unimportant.

quantŭluscumquĕ -ācumquĕ -umcumquĕ, however small.

quantum, *v. quantus.*

quantumvīs, *adv.* as much as you please, ever so much; *conj.* although.

quantus -a -um, of what size, how great; *rel.*, as great as; *of time*, how long, so long as; *neut. subst.*, *quantum*; *quantum in me est*, as far as in me lies; *in quantum*, in so far; *quantum*, *adv.*, as far as. *Interrog.* = how great? *neut. subst.*, *genit. quanti*, at what a price? how dear? *quantum*, *adv.*, how much; how little !

quantuscumquĕ-ācumquĕ -umcumquĕ how great soever; as much soever as.

quantuslĭbet -tālĭbet -tumlĭbet, however great, however much.

quantusvis -āvis -umvis, how great *or* how much soever.

quāpropter, wherefore.

quārĕ, *adv.* whereby; wherefore.

quartădĕcŭmāni -ōrum, *m.* soldiers of the fourteenth legion.

quartāna, *v. quartanus.*

quartānus -a -um, relating to the fourth. *Subst.,* **quartāna -ae,** *f.* a quartan fever; **quartāni -ōrum,** *m.* soldiers of the fourth legion.

quartārius -ii, *m.* the fourth part of a sextarius.

quartō, adv. for the fourth time.

quartum, v. quartus.

quartus -a -um, the fourth. *Subst.,* **quartus -i,** *m.* the fourth book; **quarta -ae,** *f.* the fourth hour. *Adv.,* **quartum,** for the fourth time.

quartusdĕcĭmus -a -um, *f.* the fourteenth.

quăsi, *adv.* as if; *often ironical,* as if, just as if; as, like as; as it were, a sort of; almost, all but.

quăsillus -i, *m. and* **quăsillum -i,** *n.* (*dim. of qualis*), a little wicker-basket.

quassātio -ōnis, *f.* a shaking.

quasso, 1. to shake violently; to shatter. *Intransit.,* to shake (*poet.*).

quassus -a -um, *partic. of quatio.*

quătĕnŭs, *adv.* how far; in so far as; *of time,* how long.

quătĕr, *adv. numer.,* four times.

quăterni -ae -a, *num. distrib.* four each.

quătio, quassi, quassum, 3. to shake; to brandish ; to convulse, *risu* ; to strike, hit, beat; to shatter; *quassae naves,* leaky, shattered; to agitate; to harass.

quărĭdŭum = *quadriduum (q.v.).*

quătŭor (quattŭor), *adj. num.* four.

quătŭordĕcim, *adj. num.* fourteen.

quătŭorvirātus -ūs, *m.* the office of the *quatuorviri.*

quătŭorviri -ōrum, *m.* a college of four magistrates.

-quĕ (*an enclitic conj.*), and; *que . . . que,* both . . . and, and . . . and.

queis, quis = *quibus,* dat. and abl. plur. of *qui.*

quēmadmŏdum (quem ad mŏdum), in what manner, how. *Interrog. or rel., with sic, ita, etc.,* as, just as.

quĕō, quivi and quii, quĭtum, quĭre, to be able (to be in a position to do).

quercētum -i, *n.* an oak-wood.

quercĕus -a -um, oaken.

quercus -ūs, *f.* the oak; *poet.* that which is made of oak; an acorn.

quĕrēla (quĕrella) -ae, *f.* a complaint; wailing.

quĕribundus -a -um, complaining, plaintive.

quĕrimōnia -ae, *f.* complaining, complaint.

quĕritor, 1. *dep.* to complain excessively.

quernĕus -a -um, relating to the oak, oaken.

quernus = *quereus (q.v.).*

quĕror, questus sum, 3. *dep.* to complain, bewail; to complain of.

querquĕtŭlānus -a -um, belonging to an oak-wood.

querquĕtum = *quercetum (q.v.).*

quĕrŭlus -a -um, complaining, plaintive; querulous.

questus -ūs, *m.* complaint, lament.

1. **qui, quae, quŏd,** *pron. rel.,* who which, that; *interrog.,* who? which? what? *indef. adj., aliq., some, some one,* any one.

2. **qui,** *rel.,* wherewith, wherefrom; *interrog.,* in what manner? how then?

quiă, *conj.* because.

quĭcumquĕ, quaecumquĕ, quodcumquĕ, whoever, whichever, whatever.

quĭdam, quaedam, quoddam, *and subst.,* **quiddam,** a certain person or thing; *plur.,* some.

quĭdem, *conj.* Indeed, even ; *ne . . quidem,* not even.

quĭdni ? why not ?

quĭes -ētis, *f.* rest ; repose, quiet; a place of rest; sleep; *ire ad quietem,* to go to sleep; night, silence; peace, neutrality; calm.

quĭesco -ēvi -ētum, 3. to rest, repose; to lie down; to sleep; to keep quiet; to be silent; *in politics,* to be inactive; to be at peace; to be neutral; to calm, *aequora;* *of the soil,* to remain fallow; to remain undisturbed; to rest; to leave off doing something.

quĭētē, *adv.* quietly, peaceably.

quĭētus -a -um, quiet, peaceful; resting, sleeping, inactive; *of places,* at peace; neutral ; retired ; peaceful, mild ; deliberate, slow.

quĭlibet, quaelibet, quodlibet, *and subst.,* **quidlibet,** any you will, any one, anything ; *subst.,* **quidlibet,** anything and everything ; *contemptuous,* the first that comes, any.

quin, that not, so that not, without; *after verbs of doubting,* that, but that; *to add emphasis,* rather, yea rather.

quīnam, quaenam, quodnam, *pron. interrog.,* who, which, what then ?

Quinctĭus (Quintĭus) -a -um, name of a Roman gens.

quincunx -cuncis, five-twelfths.

quindĕciēs, *adv.* fifteen times.

quindĕcim, *num.* fifteen.

quindĕcimprimi -ōrum, *m.* the fifteen chief senators of a municipium.

quindĕcimvir -i, *m. and* **quindĕcimviri -ōrum and (gen.) -ūm,** a college of fifteen magistrates.

quindĕcimvirālis -e, relating to the quindecimviri.

quingēni -ae -a, *num. distrib.* five hundred each.

quingentēsimus -a -um, the five hundredth.

quingenti -ae -a, *num.* five hundred.

quingentiēs, *adv.* five hundred times.

quīni -ae -a, *num. distrib.* five each.

quinīdēni -ae -a, *num. distrib.* fifteen each.

quīnīvīcēni -ae -a, *num. distrib.* twenty-five each.

quinquāgēni -ae -a, *num. distrib.* fifty each.

quinquāgēsimus -a -um, *num.* the fiftieth; *subst.*, quinquāgēsima -ae, *f.* a fiftieth part.

quinquāginta, *num.* fifty.

quinquātrus -ŭum, *f. and* quinquātria -ium, *n.* a festival of Minerva.

quīnquĕ, *num.* five.

quinquennālis -e, quinquennial; lasting five years.

quinquennis -e, five years old; *poet.* celebrated every five years.

quinquennium -ii, *n.* a period of five years.

quinquĕpertītus (quinquĕpartītus) -a -um, divided into five portions, fivefold.

quinquĕprīmi -ōrum, *m.* the five chief senators in a municipium.

quinquĕrēmis -e, having five banks of oars ; *subst.*, quinquĕrēmis -is, *f.* a quinquereme.

quinquĕvir -i, *m.*, *plur.* quinqueviri, a commission of five persons.

quinquĕvīrātus -ūs, *m.* the office of a quinquevir.

quinquiēs, *adv.* five times.

quinquiplico, 1 to make fivefold.

quintādĕcimāni -ōrum, *m.* the soldiers of the fifteenth legion.

quintānus -a -um, relating to the fifth. *Subst.*, quintāna -ae, *f.* road in a Roman camp dividing the fifth maniple from the sixth ; quintāni -ōrum, *m.* soldiers of the fifth legion.

Quintīlis (Quinctīlis) -is, *m.* the fifth month, afterwards Iulius (*July*).

Quintilius Vārus, friend of Horace and Vergil.

1. quintus -a -um, the fifth; *quintum*, *quinto*, for the fifth time.

2. Quintus, *fem.* Quinta, a common Roman praenomen, *the masc. usually* abbreviated Q.

quintusdĕcimus -a -um, the fifteenth.

quippĕ, *conj.* certainly, indeed, to be sure; *ironically*, forsooth.

quippini (quippĕni), *adv.* why not ?

Quirīnus -i, *m.* the name of Romulus after his apotheosis. *Adj.*, Quirīnālis -e; *sub.*, Quirīnālia -ium, *n.* festival in honour of Romulus.

1. Quiris, *v.* Quirites.

2. quiris -is, *f.* a spear. uirītātio -ōnis, *f.* a shriek, scream.

Quirītes -ium *and* -um, *m.* the inhabitants of the Sabine town Cures; *Quirites was used of the citizens of Rome considered in their civic character, Romani of them in their political and military character; sing.*, Quiris -ītis, *m.* a Roman citizen.

quirīto, 1. *and* quirītor -āri, 1. *dep.* to utter a cry of distress.

1. quis, quae, quid, *pron. interrog.* ,who ? what ? *adv.*, *quid !* what! how ! why ? *quidni !* why not?

2. quis, quae, quid, *pron. indef.*, anyone, anything.

3. quīs, = *quibus, from* qui.

quisnam, quidnam, *pron. interrog.*, who then ? what then ?

quispiam, quaepiam, quodpiam *and* *subst.*, quidpiam *or* quippiam, any, anyone, anything, someone, something ; many a one.

quisquam, quaequam, quidquam(quicquam), any person, anyone, anything (*in negative sentences or questions*) ; *nec* quisquam . . . and no one . . .

quisquĕ, quaequĕ, quidquĕ *and* *adj.*, quodquĕ, each, every.

quisquiliae -ārum, *f.* rubbish, offscourings.

quisquis, quaeque, quidquid (quicquid), *and adj.* quodquod, whoever, whichever, whatever.

quīvis, quaevis, quidvis *and adj.*, quodvis, whoever, whatever you will, anyone, anything whatever.

quīviscumquĕ, quaeviscumquĕ, quodviscumquĕ, who *or* whatsoever you will.

quō, *adv. indef.*, any whither; anyhow; *rel.*, whither; how far; to what end; wherefore; *quominus*, that not, *after verbs of hindering.*

quŏăd, *adv.* how far, as far as; *quoad eius facere possum. Of time*, as long as.

quŏcircā, *conj.* therefore, on that account.

quŏcumquĕ, *adv.* whithersoever.

quod, *conj.*, because; as to that, *quod scribis*; although; *quod si*, but if.

quŏdammŏdo, *adv.* in a certain way, in a certain measure.

quŏlĭbĕt, *adv.* whithersoever you please.

quŏminus, *v. quo.*

quōmŏdŏ, *adv.* in what manner, how.

quōmŏdŏcumquĕ, *adv.* howsoever.

quŏmŏdŏnam, *adv.* how then ?

quŏnam, whither then ?

quondam, *adv.* at a certain time; once; *of past time*, once; of the future, at some future time, sometime.

quŏniam, *conj.* since, whereas.

quŏquam, *adv.* to any place, any whither.

1. quŏquĕ, *adv.* also.

2. quŏquĕ, *from quisque; also* = *et quo.*

quŏquŏ, whithersoever.

quŏquŏversus (quŏquŏvorsus) *ana* quŏquŏversum (quŏquŏvorsum), *adv.* in every direction.

quorsum (quorsŭs), *adv.* whither, to what place ? to what purpose ? to what end ?

quŏt, *adj. plur. indecl.* how many ; *interrog.*, how many ? all, every; *quot annis*, yearly.

quŏtannis, v. quot.

quotcumquĕ, as many as.

quŏtēni -ae -a, how many each.

quŏtīdiānus (cŏtīdiānus, cottīdiānus) -a -um, every day, daily; everyday, ordinary.

quŏtīdiē (cŏtīdie, cottīdie), adv. daily, every day.

quŏtiēs (quŏtiens), adv. interrog., how often? Rel., in correlation, as often . . . so often; toties . . . quoties.

quŏtiescumquĕ, adv. how often soever.

quotquŏt, num. indecl. however many.

quŏtus -a -um, how many? quotusquis-que, how many, ironically = how few.

quŏtuscumquĕ -ācumquĕ -umcumquĕ, how great or how small soever.

quŏtusquisque, v. quotus.

quŏtusquĕ, adv. how long? how far?

quum (cum), conj. when; whenever; since; quum . . . tum, both . . . and, although.

R

R r, the seventeenth etter of the Latin Alphabet.

răbĭdē, adv. madly, savagely.

răbĭdus -a -um, raging mad; savage.

răbĭes -em -e, f. madness; fury, rage.

răbĭo, 3. to be mad (late).

răbĭōsē, adv. madly, furiously.

răbĭōsŭius -a -um (dim. of rabiosus), somewhat raging.

răbĭōsus -a -um, raging, mad; savage.

Răbīrius -a -um, name of a Roman gens.

răbŭla -ae, m. a bawling advocate, pettifogger.

răcēmĭfer -fĕra -fĕrum, bearing berries.

răcēmus -i, m. the stalk of a cluster of grapes; a cluster of grapes; the juice of the grape.

rădĭātus -a -um, beaming.

rādīcĭtus, adv. with the root; utterly.

rādīcŭla -ae, f. (dim. of radix), a little root.

rădĭo, 1. and **rădĭor**, 1. dep. to gleam, radiate.

rădĭus -ii, m. a staff, rod; the spoke of a wheel; the staff that mathematicians used for drawing figures on the abacus; a shuttle; the sting of a fish; radii, the spurs of birds; a kind of long olive; the radius of a circle; a ray of light.

rādix -īcis, f. a root; the foot of a mountain; origin, source; a radish.

rādo, rāsi, rāsum, 3. to scrape, shave; to make smooth by scraping, etc.; to graze, touch; to erase.

rallum -i, n. a scraper for cleaning a ploughshare.

rāmāle -is, n. usually plur., twigs, brushwood.

rāmentum -i, n. a shaving, chip; a morsel.

rāmĕus -a -um, relating to branches.

rāmex -īcis, m. a rupture.

Ramnes -ium, m. and **Ramnenses** -ium, m. one of the three tribes into which the early Roman citizens were divided.

rāmōsus -a -um, full of boughs, branching.

rāmŭlus -i, m. (dim. of ramus), a little branch, twig.

rāmus -i, m. branch, twig.

rāna -ae, f. a frog.

rancens -entis, putrid.

rancĭdŭlus -a -um (dim. of rancidus) somewhat putrid; loathsome.

rancĭdus -a -um, stinking, rank; disgusting.

rānuncŭlus -i, m. (dim. of rana), a little frog, a tadpole.

răpācĭtas -ātis, f. greediness.

răpax -ācis, furious, violent; grasping; greedy of plunder. Subst., a robber.

răpĭdē, adv. hurriedly, rapidly.

răpĭdĭtas -ātis, f. rapidity.

răpĭdus -a -um, seizing; violent; devouring; of motion, hurried, rapid.

răpīna -ae, f. robbery, plundering; booty.

răpĭo -răpŭi -raptum, 3. to snatch; to hurry away; (reflex., as rapere, to hasten away); to overpower; to hasten through; to enjoy or use in haste; to hasten, nuptias; to carry off; to carry off as plunder, to seize, rob; to carry off prematurely, of death or disease; to lead astray. Subst., **rapta** -ae, f. she that is carried off; **ruptum** -i, n. that which is carried off, plunder, booty.

raptim, adv. violently, hastily.

raptĭo -ōnis, f. a carrying off, abduction.

rapto, 1. to carry away in haste, hurry away; to rob, plunder, to drag along.

raptor -ōris, m. a robber, plunderer, abductor.

raptus -ūs, m. a tearing off; a carrying off.

rāpŭlum -i, n. (dim. of rapum), a little turnip.

rāpum -i, n. a turnip.

rārē, adv. sparsely; rarely, seldom.

rārēfăcĭo -fēci -factum, 3. to make thin, rarefy.

rāresco, 3. to become thin, to lose density; to expand; to diminish.

rārĭtas -ātis, f. want of density, thinness, distance apart; fewness.

rārō, adv. seldom, rarely.

rārus -a -um, loose in texture, wide apart, thin; scattered, scanty; dispersed; few in number; rare, extraordinary.

rāsĭlis -e, scraped, polished.

rastrum -i, n. plur., gen. **rastri** -ōrum, m. a hoe, rake, mattock.

rătĭo -ōnis, f. a reckoning, account; rationem ducere, to compute; rationem *referre*, give in an account; a register, list; a sum, number; business transaction, affair ; *meae rationes*, my interest; a reference to; respect, consideration; plan; method, nature, kind, way; *rationes belli gerendi*, principles; the faculty of reason; *ratio est*, it seems reasonable; reason, motive; reasonableness; tendency; theory, system, knowledge; a view, opinion.

rătĭŏcĭnātĭo -ōnis, *f.* a reasoning, argument.

rătĭŏcĭnātĭvus -a -um, argumentative.

rătĭŏcĭnātor -ōris, *m.* calculator, accountant.

rătĭŏcĭnor, 1. *dep.* to calculate; to argue, infer.

rătĭōnālis -e, reasonable, rational (*late*).

rătĭōnārĭum -ii, *n.* a statistical account.

rătĭs -is, *f.* a raft; a bridge of boats; *poet.* a ship, boat.

rătĭuncŭla -ae, *f.* (*dim. of ratio*), a little reckoning, account ; an insufficient reason.

rătus -a -um, *p. adj.* calculated; *pro rata*, in proportion; fixed, settled; valid; *ratum facere*, to ratify.

raucĭsŏnus -a -um, hoarse.

raucus -a -um, hoarse ; *palumbes*, cooing; *poet.* hoarse, deep.

Raudĭus -a -um, *Raudii Campi*, a plain in Upper Italy, where Marius defeated the Cimbri.

raudus (**rōdus, rūdus**) -ĕris, *n.* a piece of brass used as a coin.

rauduscŭlum -i, *n.* (*dim. of raudus*), a small sum of money.

Raurĭci -ōrum, *m.* Celtic people in Gaul.

Răvenna -ae, *f.* a town in Gallia Cispadana, near the Adriatic, made a naval station by Augustus.

rāvus -a -um, grey, greyish.

1. **rĕa**, *v. reus.*

2. **Rĕa** = *Rhea* (*q.v.*).

rĕapsĕ, *adv.* indeed, really.

rĕbellātĭo = *rebellio* (*q.v.*).

rĕbellātrix -ĭcis, *f.* renewing war.

rĕbellĭo -ōnis, *f.* a renewal of war by a conquered people; a revolt.

rĕbellis -e, renewing a war, insurgent.

rĕbello, 1. to renew a war.

rĕbŏo, 1. to echo, resound.

rĕcalcĭtro, 1. *of a horse*, to kick backwards; *fig.*, to deny access.

rĕcălĕfăcĭo = *recalfacio* (*q.v.*).

rĕcălĕo, 2. to be warm again.

rĕcălesco -călŭi, 3. to become warm again.

rĕcalfăcĭo (**rĕcălĕfăcĭo**) -fēci -factum, 3. to make warm again.

rĕcandesco -candŭi, 3. to grow white; to begin to glow.

rĕcanto, 1. *intransit.*, to resound, echo; *transit.*, to recall; to charm away.

rĕcēdo -cessi -cessum, 3. to go back, retreat, retire; to recede in the distance;

to go away, depart; to separate from; to disappear; to abandon; to renounce.

rĕcello, 3. to spring back, bend back.

rĕcens -entis, new, fresh, young, recent; *with ab and the abl.*, fresh from, soon after ; fresh, vigorous. *Adv.*, lately, recently.

rĕcensĕo -censŭi -censĭtum *and* -censum, 2. to review, muster; to pass through; to go over in words, recount.

rĕcensĭo -ōnis, *f.* a reviewing, mustering.

rĕcensus -ūs, *m.* a reviewing, mustering.

rĕceptācŭlum -i, *n.* a magazine, reservoir, receptacle; shelter, retreat.

rĕcepto, 1. to draw back, *hastam ;* to receive back ; *reflex., se receptare*, to retire.

rĕceptor -ōris, *m.* one who receives *or* harbours.

rĕceptrix -trīcis, *f.* a receiver (*of stolen goods*).

rĕceptus -ūs, *m.* a drawing back; retractation; a retreat; recourse to.

rĕcessus -ūs, *m.* a receding, retreating; a recess; a place of retreat.

rĕcĭdīvus -a -um, returning, repeated.

1. **rĕcĭdo** -cĭdi -cāsūrus, 3. to fall back; to relapse; to fall to; to fall upon; to happen; to become.

2. **rĕcīdo** -cīdi -cīsum, 3. to cut off, cut away; to abbreviate.

rĕcingo, *no. perf.*, -cinctum, 3. to ungird.

rĕcĭno, 3. to resound, echo; *transit.*, to re-echo.

rĕcĭpĭo -cēpi -ceptum, 3. to draw back, fetch back; *milit.*, to cause to retreat; *se recipere*, to withdraw, retreat; to have recourse to; to retain a portion; to seize from the enemy; to take back, receive; to recover; to accept; to conquer; to admit, allow; *fabulas*, to believe; to undertake, *officium ;* to guarantee ; **rĕceptum** -i, *n.* an engagement, guarantee; *of the praetor, recipere nomen*, to receive an accusation against anyone.

rĕcĭprōco, 1. *transit. and intrans.*, to move backwards and forwards; *animam*, to breathe.

rĕcĭprŏcus -a -um, returning; *mare*, ebbing.

rĕcīsus -a -um, *partic.*, *of recido*.

rĕcĭtātĭo -ōnis, *f.* a reading aloud.

rĕcĭtātor -ōris, *m.* a reader aloud; a reciter.

rĕcĭto, 1. to read, read aloud; to recite.

rĕclāmātĭo -ōnis, *f.* loud disapprobation.

rĕclāmĭto, 1. to cry out against loudly.

rĕclāmo, 1. to contradict loudly; *poet.* to re-echo, resound.

rĕclīnis -e, leaning backwards, reclining.

rĕclīno, 1. to bend back, cause to lean back; **rĕclīnātus** -a -um, bent back, reclined.

rĕclūdo -clūsi -clūsum, 3. to open; to reveal ; to cultivate; *ensem* to draw from the scabbard; to pierce; *fata*, to relax the decrees of fate.

rĕcōgĭto, 1. to consider, deliberate upon.

rĕcōgnĭtĭo -ōnis, *f.* recollection; investigation.

rĕcōgnōsco -nōvi -nĭtum, 3. to recognise; to recall; to investigate; to examine critically.

rĕcollĭgo -lēgi -lectum, 3. to collect again; *se*, to regain courage.

rĕcŏlo -cŏlŭi -cultum, 3. to cultivate again; to resume; to repair; to honour again; to reflect upon again; to recollect.

rĕcompōno (*no perf.*) **-pŏsĭtum**, 3. to re-arrange.

rĕconcĭlĭātĭo -ōnis, *f.* a restoration; reconciliation.

rĕconcĭlĭātŏr -ōris, *m.* a restorer.

rĕconcĭlĭo, 1. to restore, repair; to reconcile; to re-establish.

rĕconcinno, 1. to restore, renovate.

rĕcondĭtus -a -um, *p. adj.* far removed, concealed; profound; mysterious.

rĕcondo -dĭdi -dĭtum, 3. to put back; to lay aside; to lay up in store; to conceal; to thrust, *etc.*; to devour.

rĕconflo, 1. to rekindle.

rĕcŏquo -coxi -coctum, 3. to boil again; to forge again.

rĕcordātĭo -ōnis, *f.* a recollection, remembrance.

rĕcordor, 1. *dep.* to remember, recollect; to ponder over.

rĕcrĕo, 1. to create again; to revive; *reflex.*, to recover.

rĕcrĕpo, 1. to echo, resound.

rĕcresco -crēvi -cretum, 3. to grow again.

rĕcrūdesco -crūdŭi, 3. to become raw again; *of wounds*, to open afresh; to break out again.

rectā, *adv.* straightway, right on.

rectē, *adv.* in a straight line; properly, duly, suitably; favourably, safely.

rectĭo -ōnis, *f.* a ruling, governing.

rector -ōris, *m.* a ruler, guide, leader; *navis*, steersman.

rectus -a -um, *p. adj.* straight, upright; in a horizontal direction; *fig.*, right, correct; natural, straightforward; honest, upright.

rĕcŭbo, 1. to lie back, recline.

rĕcumbo -cŭbŭi, 3. to lie backwards, recline; to sink down.

rĕcŭpĕrātĭo -ōnis, *f.* a recovery.

rĕcŭpĕrātŏr -ōris, *m.* one who recovers; *recuperatores*, magistrates appointed by the praetor to decide causes speedily.

rĕcŭpĕrātōrĭus -a -um, relating to the *recuperatores*.

rĕcŭpĕro, 1. to regain.

rĕcūro, 1. to restore, refresh.

rĕcurro -curri -cursum, 3. to run back, hasten back; to return to.

rĕcurso, 1. to hasten back, return.

rĕcursus -ūs, *m.* a return, retreat.

rĕcurvo, 1. to bend *or* curve back.

rĕcurvus -a -um, bent *or* curved backwards.

rĕcūsātĭo -ōnis, *f.* a refusal; a protest.

rĕcūso, 1. to refuse, reject; *legal*, to object, plead in defence.

rĕcŭtĭo -cussi -cussum, 3. to cause to rebound.

rēda (**rhēda**) *and* **raeda -ae**, *f.* a travelling carriage.

rĕdămo, 2. to return love for love.

rĕdardesco, 3. to break out again (*into flames*).

rĕdargŭo -gŭi -gūtum, 3. disprove, contradict.

rēdārĭus -ii, *m.* driver of a *reda*.

reddo -dĭdi -dĭtum, 3. to give back, restore; to repay; to translate; to imitate; to answer; to resemble; to render; to give what is due; *vota*, to fulfil; *of sacrificing*, to offer; to communicate; to give, grant; *reddere ius*, to administer justice; to give forth; *sonum*, to sing *or* play; narrate.

rĕdemptĭo -ōnis, *f.* a buying up; bribing; a farming of taxes; ransoming.

rĕdempto, 1. to ransom, redeem.

rĕdemptor -ōris, *m.* a buyer, contractor farmer (*of taxes*).

rĕdemptūra -ae, *f.* a contracting, farming (*of taxes, etc.*).

rĕdĕo -ii (-īvi) -ĭtum, 4. to go back, return; *redire ad se*, to return to one's senses; *res redit*, the matter comes up again; to return to the previous subject; *of income*, to come in; to come to, fall to; *of things, bona in tabulas publicas redierunt*, have been registered in.

rĕdhālo, 1. to breathe out again.

rĕdhĭbĕo -ŭi -ĭtum, 2. to give back, return.

rĕdĭgo -ēgi -actum, 3. to drive back, bring back, lead back; to bring to; to collect; to confiscate; to reduce to a condition; *ad certum*, to make certain; to reduce, lessen.

rĕdĭmĭcŭlum -i, *n.* a lappet *or* fillet, frontlet, necklace.

rĕdĭmĭo -ii -ītum, 4. to bind round, wreathe round, crown.

rĕdĭmo -ēmi -emptum (-emtum), 3. to buy back; to buy; to farm, hire; to contract for; to ransom; to deliver; to avert; *litem*, to compromise.

rĕdintĕgro, 1. to restore, repair, *proelium*.

rĕdĭtĭo -ōnis, *f.* a going back, return.

rĕdĭtus -ūs, *m.* a coming back, going back, return; income.

rĕdĭvia = *reduvia* (*q.v.*).

rĕdĭvīvus -a -um, renewed; renovated; *subst.*, **rĕdĭvīvum -i**, *n. and* **rĕdĭvīva -ōrum**, *n.* old building materials used again.

rĕdŏlĕo -ŭi, 2. to emit an odour.

rĕdŏmĭtus -a -um, tamed again, subdued again.

rĕdŏno, 1. to give back; to pardon.

rĕdormĭo, 4. to sleep again.

rĕdūco -duxi -ductum, 3. to bring back, lead back; to draw back; to extend (a fortification); to rescue; to keep back from; to escort; to restore (an exile); *milit.*, to withdraw; to re-introduce; to reduce to a certain condition.

rĕductĭo -ōnis, *f.* a bringing back.

rĕductor -ōris, *m.* one who brings back.

rĕductus -a -um, *p. adj.* withdrawn, retired; rĕducta -ōrum, *n. (of the Stoics),* things which though not evils were to be regarded as inferior.

rĕduncus -a -um, bent, curved.

rĕdundantĭa -ae, *f.* an overflowing; redundancy.

rĕdundo, 1. to overflow, to abound.

rĕdŭvĭa (rĕdīvia) -ae, *f.* a hangnail, whitlow.

rĕdux -dŭcis, restoring (*epithet of Jupiter*); *pass.*, brought back.

rĕfectĭo -ōnis, *f.* repairing, restoration (*late*).

rĕfello -felli, 3. to refute, disprove.

rĕfercĭo -fersi -fertum, 4. to stuff quite full; to crowd together.

rĕfĕrĭo, 4. to strike back, strike again; to reflect.

rĕfĕro, retŭli (rettŭli), rĕlātum, rĕferre, to carry back, bring back; to restore, give back; to cause to echo; (*pass.* = to echo, to resound); to restore to a condition; to bring again before a court of justice; to refer to, to judge by; *referri*, to retreat, yield; to requite; *gratiam* to return thanks; to repeat, renew; to represent, recall; to present, deliver; to pay off; to offer as a sacrifice; to confer upon; to report, relate; to apply to, refer to; *referre ad senatum,* to bring a question before the senate; to register, record; to write in an account-book.

rĕfert, rĕtŭlit, rĕferre, *impers.,* it matters, it concerns, is one's interest; *with meā, tuā, nostrā, vestrā.*

rĕfertus -a -um, *p. adj.* stuffed, crammed, full.

rĕfervĕo, 2. to boil over.

rĕfervesco, 3. to boil up, bubble up.

rĕficĭo -fēci -fectum, 3. to make again, to prepare again; to choose again; to re-establish, restore; to build again; to repair; to kindle again; to fill up, complete; to cure; to revive; to get back again.

rĕfīgo -fixi -fixum, 3. to pluck off, unfasten; to repeal; to pack up.

rĕfingo, 3. to form anew.

rĕflagĭto, 1. to ask back.

rĕflātus -ū, *m.* a blowing against; a contrary wind.

rĕflecto -flexi -flexum, 3. to turn back, bend back; *pass.,* to turn back, divert.

rĕflo, 1. *intransit.,* to blow against; *transit.,* to breathe out.

rĕflŭo -fluxi -fluxum, 3. to flow back, to overflow.

rĕflŭus -a -um, flowing back.

rĕfŏdĭo -fōdi -fossum, 3. to dig out, dig up (*late*).

rĕformātor -ōris, *m.* one who forms again.

rĕformīdātĭo -ōnis, *f.* excessive dread, terror.

rĕformīdo, 1. to dread, fear, shun.

rĕformo, 1. to form again, mould anew.

rĕfŏvĕo -fōvi -fōtum, 2. to warm again, restore, refresh.

rĕfrāgor, 1. *dep.* to oppose, thwart.

rĕfrēno, 1. to rein in; to restrain.

rĕfrico -fricŭi -fricātum, 1. to rub again, gall; *vulnera,* to tear open; to excite again, renew, *dolorem.*

rĕfrīgĕrātĭo -ōnis, *f.* a cooling, coolness.

rĕfrīgĕro, 1. to make cool; *refrigerari (in middle sense),* to grow cool; *pass.,* to be cold, exhausted.

rĕfrīgesco -frixi, 3. to become cool; to lose zeal, to flag.

rĕfringo -frēgi -fractum, 3. to break up, break open; to destroy.

rĕfŭgĭo -fūgi -fūgitum, 3. to take to flight, escape; to avoid; *of places,* to recede from; to have recourse to; *transit.,* to fly from, avoid, shun.

rĕfŭgĭum -ĭi, *n.* a place of refuge.

rĕfŭgus -a -um, flying, fugitive, receding; *refugi,* fugitives.

rĕfulgĕo -fulsi, 2. to gleam *or* glitter back.

rĕfundo -fūdi -fūsum, 3. to pour back; to cause to flow forth; *refundi,* to overflow.

rĕfūtātĭo -ōnis, *f.* a refutation.

rĕfūtātus, *abl.* -ū = *refutatio* (*q.v.*).

rĕfūto, 1. to drive back; to resist, repel; to disprove.

rēgālis -e, royal, regal; kingly.

rēgālĭter, *adv.* royally, regally; tyrannically.

rĕgĕlo, 1. to thaw, warm.

rĕgĕro -gessi -gestum, 3. to carry back; to throw back, retort.

rēgĭa, *v. regius.*

rēgĭē, *adv.* royally; tyrannically.

rēgĭficus -a -um, royal, splendid.

rēgigno, 3. to bring forth again, beget again.

Rēgillus -i, *m.* a lake in Latium, scene of a victory of the Romans over the Latins, 496 B.C. *Adj.,* Rēgillensis -e.

rĕgĭmen -ĭnis, *n.* guiding, leading; guidance; direction; *poet.* the rudder; a ruler.

rēgīna -ae, *f.* a queen.

rĕgĭo -ōnis, *f.* a direction, line; a boundary line, boundary; geographical position; a region, country, district;

province ; quarter, district of Rome ; *fig.*, sphere.

rēgiōnātim, *adv.* according to districts.

Rēgium -ii, *n.* in S. Italy, now Reggio.

rēgius -a -um, royal, kingly; *morbus*, jaundice. *Subst.*, **rēgii** -ōrum, *m.* the troops of the king; **rēgia** -ae, *f.* the palace.

reglūtino] to unglue, separate.

regnātor -ōris, *m.* ruler, governor, king.

regnātrix -īcis, *f.* ruling.

regno, 1. *intransit.*, to be a king, reign; to be master; *transit.*, to rule (*poet.*).

regnum -i, *n.* royal power or authority, monarchy, the throne; tyranny; a kingdom.

rēgo, rexi, rectum, 3. to guide, direct; *legal*, *regere fines*, to mark out boundaries; to rule, govern; to set right, *errantem*.

regrĕdior -gressus sum, 3. to retreat, step back.

regressus -ūs, *m.* a going back, return; *milit.*, retreat, refuge, recourse.

rēgŭla -ae, *f.* rule, bar, staff, stick ; pattern.

1. **rēgŭlus** -i, *m.* (*dim. of rex*), a petty king, prince.

2. **Rēgŭlus**, surname of the gens Atilia, the most famous member of which was the consul *M. Atilius Regulus*, famous for his devoted return into captivity in the First Punic War.

rĕgusto, 1. to taste again *or* repeatedly.

rēicio -iēci -iectum, 3. to throw back; to cast behind; *reicere or reici*, to sink back; to place behind; to drive back; cause to echo; to repulse; to spurn; *legal*, to challenge *the judices or jury*; to refer to; to bring a matter before the senate; to put off.

rēiectānĕus -a -um, to be rejected; *subst.*, **rēiectānĕa** -orum, *in the Stoic philosophy*, things which, though not evil, are to be rejected.

rēiectio -ōnis, *f.* a throwing out, throwing up; rejection.

rēiecto, 1. to cast back, throw back.

rēicio, *v. rēicio*.

rēlābor -lapsus sum, 3. *dep.* to slide, glide, flow, fall back.

rēlanguesco -langŭi, 3. to become faint, languid; to be made effeminate; to abate.

rēlātio -ōnis, *f.* a carrying back, bringing back; a motion, proposal; relation, reference.

rēlātor -ōris, *m.* a mover, proposer in the senate.

rēlātus -ūs, *m.* a narrative, recital; a proposal, report.

rēlaxātio -ōnis, *f.* a relaxation.

rēlaxo, 1. to loosen, enlarge; to ease, to open; *fig.*, to alleviate; *relaxari =* to slacken; to enliven, cheer up.

rēlēgātio -ōnis, *f.* banishment.

1. **rēlēgo**, 1. to send away; to banish; to reject.

2. **rēlĕgo** -lēgi -lectum, 3. to collect again; to traverse again; to read over again; to talk over.

rēlentesco, 3. to become feeble again.

rēlĕvo, 1. to lift again; to lighten; to relieve, diminish; to alleviate, refresh.

rīliotio ōniɔ, *f.* a lasting, deacribing.

rĕlicŭus *and* **rĕlicus** = *reliquus (q.v.)*.

rēligātio -ōnis, *f.* a tying up, training.

rēligio (relligio) -ōnis, *f.* conscientiousness, scrupulousness ; conscientious scruples, respect for conscience; religious feeling; superstition; that which is sacred; *in a bad sense*, sin, curse; religious obligation; holiness; worship of the gods; *religiones*, religious observances; an object of worship.

rēligiōsē (relligiōsē), *adv.* conscientiously; piously, religiously.

rēligiōsus (relligiōsus) -a -um, conscientious; *dies*, a day of evil omen; religious, pious ; sacred ; superstitious.

rēligo, 1. to fasten behind; to moor; to unfasten.

rēlino -lēvi -litum, 3. to unseal.

rēlinquo -līqui -lictum, 3. to leave behind, leave; to leave over, to let remain; to desert; to neglect; to pass over, not to notice; to leave unpunished.

reliquiae (relliquiae) -ārum, *f.* remains, relics, remnant.

rĕliquus (rĕlicuus) -a -um, that which is remaining, left; *subst.*, *plur.*, **rēliqui** -ōrum, *m.* the rest; **rēliquum** -i, *n.* *and* **rēliqua** -ōrum, *n.* the rest, the remainder; *reliquum facere*, to leave remaining; *subst.*, **rĕliquum** -i, *n. and plur.* **rēliqua** -ōrum, *n.* what is outstanding, remaining.

relligio, relligiosus, *etc.*, *v. religio, etc.*

relliquiae = *reliquiae (q.v.)*.

rēlūcĕo -luxi, 2. to glitter, shine.

rēlūcesco -luxi, 3. to become bright again.

rōluotor, 1. *dep.* to strive against.

rēmānĕo -mansi -mansum, 2. to remain behind, remain; to abide, continue.

rēmāno, 1. to flow back.

rēmansio -ōnis, *f.* a remaining in one place.

rēmĕdium -ii, *n.* a cure, remedy; means of relief.

rēmĕo, 1. to go back, return.

rēmētior -mensus sum, 4. to measure over again; *astra rite*, to observe carefully; to go back; *pass.*, *iter remensum est*, has been traversed.

rēmex -igis, *m.* a rower.

Rēmi (Rhēmi) -ōrum, *m.* a people of N. Gaul, between the Matrona (*Marne*) and the Axona (*Aisne*), whence modern Rheims.

rēmigātio -ōnis, *f.* a rowing.

rēmĭgĭum -ii, *n.* rowing; the oars; the oarsmen.

rēmĭgo, 1. to row.

rēmĭgro, 1. to wander back, return.

rēmĭnĭscor, 3. *dep.* to remember.

rēmiscĕo (*no perf.*) -mistum (-mixtum), 2. to mix, mingle.

rēmissē, *adv.* loosely; gently.

rēmissĭo -ōnis, *f.* sending back; a letting down ; a lowering ; sinking, *vocis* ; interrupting ceasing; relaxation; tranquillity.

rēmissus -a -um, *p. adj.* relaxed, languid; negligent; less severe; gentle; cheerful.

rēmitto -mīsi -missum, 3. to send back, send ; to throw back ; to give back; to cause, produce; to relax; *habenas,* to loosen; to make liquid (again); to free; to relieve, release; *se remittere,* to leave off work; to give free scope to; to grant; to renounce, remit.

rēmōlĭor, 4. *dep.* to push back, move back.

rēmollesco, 3. to become soft again; to be moved by; to become effeminate.

rēmollĭo, 4. to make soft again; *fig.,* to weaken.

rēmŏrāmen -inis, *n.* a delay.

rēmordĕo (*no perf.*) -morsum, 2. to bite again; *fig.,* to annoy.

rēmŏror, 1. *dep.* to remain behind, linger; *transit.,* to delay, hinder.

rēmōtē, *adv.* afar off.

rēmōtĭo -ōnis, *f.* a putting away, removing.

rēmōtus -a -um, *p. adj.* distant, remote; *fig.,* removed from ; free from ; disinclined to; *subst.,* rēmōta -ōrum, *of the Stoics,* things to be rejected.

rēmŏvĕo -mōvi -mōtum, 2. to move back, remove.

rēmūgĭo, 4. to bellow again, bellow back; to resound, echo.

rēmulcĕo -mulsi -mulsum, 2. to stroke back.

rēmulcum -i, *n.* a tow-rope.

rēmūnĕrātĭo -ōnis, *f.* a recompense.

rēmūnĕror, 1. *dep.* to repay, reward.

rēmurmŭro, 1. to murmur against, murmur back.

1. rēmus -i, *m.* an oar.

2. Rēmus -i, *m.* the twin brother of Romulus, first king of Rome, who slew Remus in a dispute respecting the foundation of the city.

rēnarro, 1. to relate again.

rēnascor -nātus sum, 3. *dep.* to be born again, grow again.

rēnāvĭgo, 1. to sail back.

rēnĕo, 2. to unravel.

rēnes -um, *m.* the kidneys.

rēnĭdĕo, 2. to shine, glitter, shimmer; to be joyful; to laugh scornfully.

rēnĭdesco, 3. to glitter.

rēnĭtor, 3. *dep.* to oppose.

1. rēno, 1. to swim back.

2. rēno (rhēno) -ōnis, *m.* an animal, *perhaps* the reindeer.

rēnōdo, 1. to unbind, untie.

rēnŏvāmen -inis, *n.* a renewal.

rēnŏvātĭo -ōnis, *f.* renewal, renovation; *renovatio singulorum annorum,* compound interest.

rēnŏvo, 1. to renew, renovate, restore.

rēnŭmĕro, 1. to count over, pay back.

rēnuntĭātĭo, -ōnis, *f.* a proclamation, declaration.

rēnuntĭo (rēnuncĭo), 1 to bring back word, report, announce; to renounce.

rēnŭo -ŭi, 3. to refuse, deny, disapprove, reject.

rēnūto, 1. to refuse, deny.

rēnūtus, *abl.* -ū, *m.* denial, refusal (*late*).

rĕor, rătus sum, 2. *dep.* to think, suppose, judge.

rĕpāgŭla -ōrum, *n.* the barrier in a circus *or* racecourse to keep in the horses; bars *or* bolts; restraints.

rĕpandus -a -um, bent backwards, turned up.

rĕpărābĭlis -e, that can be restored.

rĕparco (rĕperco), 3. to spare, refrain from.

rĕpăro, 1. to repair, renew; to fill up, complete; to barter for.

rĕpastĭnātĭo -ōnis, *f.* a digging up again.

repello, rĕppŭli (reppŭli) -pulsum, 3. to drive away; to banish, repel; *aliquem a spe,* deprive of hope; to repulse ; *criminationes,* to refute ; to spurn.

rĕpendo -pendi -pensum, 3. to weigh against; to ransom; to repay.

rĕpens -entis, sudden, unexpected.

rĕpentē, *adv.* suddenly, unexpectedly.

rĕpentīnus -a -um, sudden, unexpected; *adv.,* rĕpentino, suddenly.

rĕpercussus -ūs, *m.* a rebounding, reverberation, echo, reflection.

rĕpercŭtĭo -cussi -cussum, 3. to strike back, drive back, cause to rebound (*of sound, etc.*); *pass., repercuti,* to bound back, *and repercussus,* bounding back; to re-echo; to be reflected.

rĕpĕrĭo, rĕpĕri (reppĕri) -pertum, 4. to find, meet again; to reveal, ascertain; to acquire; to discover, invent; *pass.,* to be found out = to appear.

rĕpertor -ōris, *m.* discoverer, inventor.

rĕpertus -a -um, *partic. of reperio.*

rĕpĕtentĭa -ae, *f.* a recollection, remembrance.

rĕpĕtītĭo -ōnis, *f.* repetition.

rĕpĕtītor -ōris, *m.* one who demands back again.

rĕpĕto -īvi *and* -ii -ītum, 3. to strive after again; to attack again; to return to; to ask for; to demand back; *res repetere,* to demand satisfaction of an enemy; (*pecuniae*) *repetundae,* extortion; to fetch back; to renew, begin again; to recall, remember; to repeat by words or writing; to trace back; to regain, recover; to reckon again.

repĕtundae, v. *repeto*.

replĕo -plēvi -plētum, 2. to fill again, fill up; to satisfy; replētus, full.

replētus -a -um, *partic. of repleo* (q.v.).

replĭcātĭo -ōnis, f. a rolling again, rolling round.

replĭco, 1. to unroll; *fig.*, to unfold, turn over.

rēpo, repsi, reptum, 3. to creep, crawl.

rēpōno -pŏsŭi -pŏsĭtum (-postum), 3. to put behind; to lay by; to lay aside; to give up; to bury; to restore; put in the place of; to answer again; to requite; to place in *or* on; to place.

rēporto, I. to bring back, carry back.

rēposco, 3. to demand back; to claim.

rēpŏsĭtus (rēpostus) -a -um, remote, distant.

rēpostor -ōris, m. a restorer.

rēpōtĭa -ōrum, n. revelling the day after an entertainment.

repraesentātĭo -ōnis, f. a lively description; payment in cash.

repraesento, 1. to represent, show; to express, imitate; to perform immediately; to pay ready money.

reprĕhendo -prĕhendi -prĕhensum, 3. *and* reprendo -prendi -prensum, 3. to catch, hold fast, detain; to blame; to refute.

reprĕhensĭo -ōnis, f. a holding back; a check in speaking; blame, reputation.

reprĕhenso, 1. to hold back eagerly, to hold fast.

reprĕhensor -ōris, m. a censurer, reformer.

repressor -ōris, m. a restrainer.

reprĭmo -pressi -pressum, 3. to restrain, hinder; to check.

reprōmissĭo -ōnis, f. a counter-promise.

reprōmitto -mīsi -missum, 3. to promise in return.

reptātĭo -ōnis, f. a creeping, crawling.

repto, 1. to creep, crawl.

rēpŭdĭātĭo -ōnis, f. a refusal.

rēpŭdĭo, 1. to refuse, disdain; to divorce.

rēpŭdĭum -ĭi, n. divorce.

rēpŭĕrasco, 3. to become a boy again, to frolic like a child.

rēpugnans, p. adj. contrary, opposed; subst., rēpugnantĭa -ĭum, n. contradictory things.

rēpugnantĕr, adv. unwillingly.

rēpugnantĭa -ae, f. resistance; *fig.*, discordance.

rēpugno, 1. to oppose, resist; to be repugnant to, to be inconsistent with.

rēpulsa -ae, f. rejection; denial, refusal.

rēpulso, 1. to beat back; to repel again and again.

1. rēpulsus -a -um, p. adj. removed.

2. rēpulsus -ūs, m. a striking back, the reflection of light, echoing (only abl. sing.).

rēpungo, 3. to prick again, goad again.

rēpurgo, 1. to cleanse again; to purge out.

rēpŭtātĭo -ōnis, f. a consideration, pondering (late).

rēpŭto, 1. to reckon, count; to think over, consider.

rēquĭes -ētis, f. rest, repose; a resting-place.

rēquĭesco -quĭēvi -quĭētum, 3. to rest, repose; to sleep; find rest.

rēquĭētus -a -um, p. adj. rested, refreshed; ager, fallow.

rēquīro -quīsīvi -quīsītum, 3. to seek, search for again; to miss, feel the want of; to desire, consider necessary; to ask for; to investigate.

rēquīsītum -i, n. need, necessity.

rēs, rēi, f. thing, object, matter, affair, circumstance; pro re, according to circumstances; the thing itself, the reality; et re vera, and in truth; property, wealth; advantage, benefit; ex re mea, to my advantage; ob eam (hanc) rem, on this account, on that account; a matter of business, an affair; a lawsuit, action; res publica, the republic, the state, commonwealth, government.

rēsaevĭo, 4. to rage again (poet.).

rēsălūtātĭo -ōnis, f. a greeting in return.

rēsălūto, 1. to salute again, return a greeting to.

rēsānesco -sānŭi, 3. to become sound again, to heal again.

rēsarcĭo -sarsi -sartum, 4. to patch again, repair; to restore.

rescindo -scĭdi -scissum, 3. to tear off again, cut away; pontem, to break away; luctus, to renew; to open; to repeal a law.

rescisco -scīvi and -scĭi -scītum, 3. to find out, ascertain.

rescrībo -scripsi -scriptum, 3. to write again, to write anew; to answer in writing; rescriptum -i, n. an imperial rescript; to pay, repay; to transfer.

rēsĕco -sĕcŭi -sectum, 1. to cut off, remove.

rēsēmĭno, 1. to beget, produce again.

rēsĕquor -sĕcūtus (-sĕquūtus), 3. dep. to follow, pursue.

rēsĕro, 1. to open; to reveal.

rēservo, 1. to keep back, reserve; to retain, preserve.

rēses -ĭdis, remaining; motionless.

rēsĭdĕo -sēdi -sessum, 2. to abide, stay; to celebrate a festival.

rēsīdo -sēdi -sessum, 3. to sit down; to settle; to remain; to sink down; to grow quiet; to be weary, exhausted.

rēsĭdŭus -a -um, remaining, outstanding; subst., rēsĭdŭum -i, n. the remainder.

rēsigno, 1. to unseal; open; to annul,

destroy; to release; to enter from one account-book into another; to give back.

rĕsilio -silŭi -sultum, 4. to leap back; to rebound; to diminish.

rĕsīmus -a -um, bent backwards, turned up.

rēsīna -ae, *f.* resin.

rēsīnātus -a -um, flavoured with resin; smeared with resin.

rĕsĭpio, 3. to have a flavour of anything.

rĕsĭpisco -sipīvi *and* **-sipii**, 3. to recover one's senses (*from fainting, etc.*); to become rational again.

rĕsisto -stiti, 3. to remain standing; to continue; to halt; to recover a footing; to resist.

rĕsŏlūtus -a -um, *p. adj.* relaxed, effeminate.

rĕsolvo -solvi -sŏlūtum, 3. to unbind, loosen, open; to melt; to dissipate; to end; to dissolve, weaken; to destroy; to free; to reveal; to pay.

rĕsŏnābilis -e, resounding, echoing.

rĕsŏno -sŏnāvi, 1. to resound, echo; to re-echo, repeat; to fill with sound.

rĕsŏnus -a -um, resounding, echoing.

rĕsorbĕo, 2. to swallow, absorb again.

respecto, 1. to look eagerly back, look about for ; to have regard for ; to expect.

respectus -ūs, *m.* a looking back, looking around one; regard, consideration towards; a place of refuge, retreat.

respergo -spersi -spersum, 3. to besprinkle, sprinkle over.

respersio -ōnis, *f.* a sprinkling over.

respicio -spexi -spectum, 3. *transit. and intransit.*, to look behind, to look back; to look back upon; to observe; reflect upon; to have respect to; to provide for; to be mindful of, consider; to hope, expect.

respīrāmen -inis, *n.* the windpipe.

respīrātio -ōnis, *f.* a taking breath, respiration.

respīro, 1. to blow back, blow in a contrary direction; to take breath, breathe out; to be relieved from fear, *etc.*; to abate, decline; violence.

resplendĕo -ŭi, 2. to glitter back, be bright.

respondĕo -spondi -sponsum, 2. to promise in return; to answer; to give decisions; to give an echo; to appear, be present; to take one's place; to correspond to; to agree with; to requite; to lie over against; to be punctual in paying, *ad tempus*; to balance.

responsio -ōnis, *f.* a reply, answer.

responsĭto, 1. to give an answer, opinion (*of legal advisers*).

responso, 1. to answer, reply; to re-echo.

responsum -i, *n.* an answer; the opinion of a lawyer.

respublica, *v. res*.

respŭo -ŭi, 3. to spit out, to reject; to refuse, disapprove of.

restagno, 1. to overflow; *of places*, to be overflowed.

restauro, 1. to restore, rebuild.

restinctio -ōnis, *f.* a slaking, quenching.

restinguo -stinxi -stinctum, 3. to quench; to subdue, control; to put an end to.

restio -ōnis, *m.* a rope-maker.

restĭpŭlātio -ōnis, *f.* a counter-engagement.

restĭpŭlor, 1. to promise in return.

restis -is, *acc.* **-im** *and* **-em**, *abl.* **-e**, *f.* a rope, cord.

restĭto, 1. to remain behind, loiter.

restĭtŭo -ŭi -ūtum, 3. to replace, restore; *se aiicui*, to become friends again.

restĭtūtio -ōnis, *f.* a restoration; a pardoning.

restĭtūtor -ōris, *m.* a restorer.

resto -stiti, 1. to remain behind, stand still; to resist; to remain over; to await.

restrictē, *adv.* sparingly; accurately, strictly.

restrictus -a -um, *p. adj.* close, tight; stingy; strict, severe.

restringo -strinxi -strictum, 3. to bind back, bind fast; to draw back, restrain.

rĕsulto, 1. to rebound; to echo, resound.

rĕsūmo -sumpsi -sumptum, 3. to take again, take back; to renew, repeat; to obtain again.

rĕsŭpīno, 1. to bend backwards; to break open; *resupinari*, to bend back.

rĕsŭpīnus -a -um, bent backwards; lying on one's back; throwing back the head.

rĕsurgo -surrexi -surrectum, 3. to rise again, appear again; to reappear.

rĕsuscĭto, 1. to revive.

rĕsūtus -a -um, ripped open.

rĕtardātio -ōnis, *f.* a retarding, delay.

rĕtardo, 1. to delay, impede; to prevent.

rēte -is, *n.* a net.

rētĕgo -text -tectum, 3. to uncover, reveal; *poet.* to illuminate.

rĕtendo -tendi -tensum *and* **-tentum**, 3. to slacken, unbend.

rĕtentio -ōnis, *f.* a keeping back; a withholding.

1. **rĕtento**, 1. to hold firmly back, hold fast; to maintain.

2. **rĕtento (rĕtempto)**, 1. to attempt again.

rĕtentus -a -um. 1. *Partic. of retendo*. 2. *Partic. of retineo*.

rĕtexo -texŭi -textum, 3. to unravel to annul, reverse; to retract; to revise; to weave again; *poet.* to renew.

rētĭārius -ii, *m.* a gladiator who used a net.

rĕtĭcentia -ae, *f.* a keeping silent, silence.

rĕtĭcĕo -cŭi, 2. *intransit.*, to be silent, keep silence; *transit.*, to keep secret.

rētĭcŭlus -i, *m. and* rētĭcŭlum -i, *n.* (*dim. of rete*), a little net; a bag of net-work.

rŏtīnācŭlum -i, *n.* a rope, cable, cord.

rĕtĭnens -entis, *p. adj.* tenacious of any-thing.

rĕtĭnentĭa -ae, *f.* recollection.

rĕtĭnĕo -tĭnŭi -tentum, ? to hold fast, delay, detain; to keep, preserve.

rĕtĭnnĭo, 4. to resound, to ring again.

rĕtŏno, 1. to thunder back, to resound.

rĕtorquĕo -torsi -tortum, 2. to twist back, turn back; to change, *mentem.*

rĕtorrĭdus -a -um, parched up, dried up.

retractātĭo -ōnis, *f.* refusal, denial.

retracto (-retrecto), 1. to handle again, undertake anew; to use again; to re-new; to think of again; to draw back; to retract; to refuse.

rĕtractus -a -um, *p adj.* distant, remote.

retrăho -trāxi -tractum, 3. to draw back; to bring back; to keep back, prevent; to hold back; *se,* to withdraw oneself; to draw forth again; to draw towards.

retrĭbŭo -trĭbŭi -trĭbūtum, 3. to give again; to give back, restore.

retrō, *adv.* backwards, back; formerly; *retro ponere,* to postpone; again, on the contrary.

retrŏăgo -ēgi -actum, 3. to drive back, lead back, turn back (*late*).

retrorsum *and* retrorsŭs, *adv.* (= *retro-versum* [-vorsum] *and* retroversus [-vorsus]), backwards, behind; in re-turn, in reversed order.

retrorsus = *retrorsum* (*q.v.*).

retrŏversus -a -um, turned backwards, back.

retrŭgus, *partic.* remote, obscure.

rĕtundo, rĕtŭdi (rettŭdi) -tūsum (-tun-sum), 3. to beat back, to drive back; to check; to blunt.

rĕtūsus (rĕtunsus) -a -um, *p. adj.* dull, blunt.

rĕus -i, *m. and* rĕa -ae, *f.* an accused person, prisoner, defendant; one bound by or answerable for a thing; *plur., rei,* the parties to a suit.

rĕvălesco -vălŭi, 3. to be restored to health.

rĕvĕho -vexi -vectum, 3. to carry, bring back; *revehi,* to drive back, ride back, sail back.

rĕvello -velli -vulsum, 3. to tear, pluck away; to destroy, banish; to open.

rĕvēlo, 1. to unveil, lay bare.

rĕvĕnĭo -vēni -ventum, 4. to come back. rĕvĕra, *adv.* indeed, in truth.

rĕvĕrendus -a -um, *p. adj.* venerable.

rĕvĕrens -entis, *p. adj.* respectful.

rĕvĕrentĕr, *adv.* reverently.

rĕvĕrentĭa -ae, *f.* reverence, respect.

rĕvĕrĕor -vĕrĭtus sum, 2. *dep.* to revere, respect, to fear.

rĕversĭo (rĕvorsĭo) -ōnis, *f.* a turning back; a return recurrence.

rĕverto (rĕvorto) -verti (-vorti) -versum (-vorsum) -ĕre *and* rĕvertor (rĕvortor) -versus (-vorsus) sum -verti (-vorti), *dep.* to turn back, return; *reverti,* to turn to.

rĕvincĭo -vinxi -vinctum, 4. to tie back, tie behind; bind fast.

rĕvinco -vīci -victum, 3. to conquer, to convict.

rĕvĭresco -virŭi, 3. to grow green again, to revive.

rĕvīso -vīsi -vīsum, 3. to look back at, revisit.

rĕvīvisco -vixi, 3. to come to life again, revive.

rĕvŏcābĭlis -e, that can be revoked or called back.

rĕvŏcāmen -ĭnis, *n.* a calling back, re-call.

rĕvŏcātĭo -ōnis, *f.* a calling back, a with-drawal.

rĕvŏco, 1. to call again; to summon again; to encore; to invite back or again; *pedem,* to turn away; *se re-vocare,* to recover oneself, collect oneself; to confine; to recall, revoke; to apply to; to bring to; to judge according to.

rĕvŏlo, 1. to fly back.

rĕvŏlūbĭlis -e, that can be rolled back.

rĕvolvo -volvi -vŏlūtum, 3. to roll back, unroll; to traverse again; *revolu-tus equo,* falling down from; *revoluta dies,* returning; to unroll or open a book; to read again; to think of again; to tell again; *pass.,* to be reduced to; *middle, revolvi,* to return to, to come to (something bad).

rĕvŏmo -vŏmŭi, 3. to vomit up, disgorge.

rĕvorsĭo = *reversio* (*q.v.*).

rex, rēgis, *m.* ruler, prince; tyrant; chief, leader.

Rhădămanthus (-ŏs) -i, *m.* brother of Minos, judge in the lower world.

Rhaeti (*better* Raeti), a people between the Alps and the Danube.

Rhamnes = *Ramnes* (*q.v.*).

Rhamnus -untis, *f.* in Attica, where Nemesis was worshipped.

1 Rhea (Rēa) -ae, *f.* Rhea Silvia, mother of Romulus and Remus.

2. Rhĕa -ae, *f.* old name of Cybele.

rhēda = *reda* (*q.v.*).

rhēdārĭus = *redarius* (*q.v.*).

Rhēgĭum = *Regium* (*q.v.*).

Rhēmi = *Remi* (*q.v.*).

Rhēnus -i, *m.* the Rhine.

Rhēsus -i, *m.* a king who came to the help of Troy.

rhētor -ŏris, *m.* teacher of rhetoric, rhetorician; an orator.

rhētŏrĭca, *v. rhetoricus.*

1. rhētŏrĭcē, *v. rhetoricus.*

2. rhētŏrĭcē, *adv.* rhetorically.

rhētŏrĭcus -a -um, rhetorical; *subst.,* rhētŏrĭca -ae, *f.* rhētŏrĭcē -ēs, *f.* rhetoric.

rhīnŏcĕrōs -ōtis, *m.* rhinoceros.

Rhŏdānus -i, _m._ a river, _now_ the Rhone.

Rhŏdŏpē -ēs, _f._ a mountain in Thrace.

Rhŏdus (-ŏs) -i, _f._ Rhodes, an island in the Carpathian Sea, off the coast of Asia Minor, famous for its trade, its school of rhetoric, and its colossus; _adj._ Rhŏdius -a -um, Rhodian; _plur. subst._, Rhŏdii -ōrum, _m._ the Rhodians.

rhombus (-ŏs) -i, _m._ magician's circle; the turbot.

rhompaea -ae, _f._ a long missile weapon.

rhythmicus -i,|_m._ one who teaches rhythm.

rhythmus -i, _m._ rhythm, time.

rhŷtium -ii, _n._ a drinking-horn.

ricinium -ii, _n._ a small veil.

rictum = _rictus (q.v.)._

rictus -ūs, _m. and_ rictum -i, _n._ the opening of the mouth, the open mouth.

rīdĕo, rīsi, rīsum, 2. to laugh; to smile; to look cheerful; to please; _transit._, to laugh at; to ridicule.

rīdiculē, _adv._ jokingly, humorously; absurdly.

rīdiculus, droll, humorous; ridiculous. _Subst._, rīdiculus -i, _m._ a jester; rīdiculum -i, _n._ joke, jest.

rīgens -entis, _p. adj._ stiff, unbending.

rīgĕo, 2. to be stiff, to stiffen; _of hair_, to stand on end.

rīgesco, rīgui, 3. to become stiff; _of hair_, to stand on end.

rīgĭdē, _adv._ stiffly; _fig._, severely.

rīgidus -a -um, stiff, unbending; in-flexible; rough; savage.

rīgo, 1. to conduct water to any place; to wet, moisten.

Rīgŏdūlum -i, _n._ a town in the country of the Treveri.

rigor -ōris, _m._ stiffness, hardness; severity; rudeness; numbness.

rĭgŭus -a -um, _act._, watering, irrigating; _pass._, well-watered.

rīma -ae, _f._ a crack, fissure.

rīmor, 1. _dep._ to cleave; to turn up, _terram_; to root up; to search, examine.

rīmōsus -a -um, full of cracks, fissures.

ringor, 3. _dep._ to show the teeth; _fig._, to snarl, be angry at.

rīpa -ae, _f._ bank of a river.

rīpŭla -ae, _f._ (_dim. of ripa_), a little bank.

riscus -i, _m._ a box, chest.

rīsor -ōris, _m._ laugher, mocker.

rīsus -ūs, _m._ laughter; ridicule; object of laughter.

rītē, _adv._ with suitable religious cere-monies; duly, rightly; _poet._ fortu-nately.

rītus -ūs, _m._ religious ceremony, rite; a custom; _abl._, _ritu_, after the manner of.

rīvālis -e, relating to a brook _or_ canal; _subst._, a rival.

rīvālitas -ātis, _f._ rivalry (_in love_).

rīvŭlus -i, _m._ (_dim. of rivus_), small brook, rivulet.

rīvus -i, _m._ a stream; a brook; _fig._, course, _fortunae._

rixa -ae, _f._ quarrel, strife.

rixor, 1. _dep._ to quarrel, brawl.

1. rōbīgo (rūbīgo) -inis, _f._ rust.

2. Rōbīgo (Rūbīgo) -inis, _f. and_ Rōbī-gus (Rūbīgus) -i, _m._ the deity invoked by the Romans to preserve their grain from mildew. Rōbīgālia -ium, _n._ the festival of the deity Robigo, celebrated annually on the 25th of April.

rōbŏr = _robur (q.v.)._

rōbŏrĕus -a -um, oaken.

rōbŏro, 1. to strengthen, make firm.

rōbur (rōbus, _archaic_) -ŏris, _n._ hard wood; oak; strength; firmness; _robur iuventae_, constancy; _concr._, the pith of anything; _of soldiers_, the flower of the army.

rōbustus -a -um, of oak, oaken; strong, robust.

rōdo, rōsi, rōsum, 3. to gnaw; to cal-umniate: to eat away, consume.

rōdusculum = _raudusculum (q.v.)._

rŏgālis -e, relating to a funeral pile.

rŏgātĭo -ōnis, _f._ asking; a question; a proposal, bill laid before the people; a request, entreaty.

rŏgātiuncŭla -ae, _f._ (_dim. of rogatio_), a little question; an unimportant pro-posal _or_ bill.

rŏgātor -ōris, _m._ proposer of a bill; a polling clerk.

rŏgātus, _abl._ -ū, _m._ request, entreaty.

rŏgĭto, 1. to ask frequently.

rŏgo, 1. to ask, inquire, question; _rogare populum or legem_, to propose a bill; to entreat, request; to invite.

rŏgus -i, _m._ a funeral pile.

Rōma -ae, _f._ Rome, the chief city of Latium and the Roman empire, founded 753 _or_ 754 B.C. Rōmānus, _adj._

Rōmŭlus -i, _m._ son of Ilia _or_ Rhea Silvia and Mars, twin brother of Remus, the founder of Rome, worshipped after his death under the name of Quirinus.

rōrārii -ōrum, _m._ light-armed troops, skirmishers.

rōridus -a -um, bedewed.

rōrĭfĕr -fĕra -fĕrum, dew-bringing.

rōro, 1. _intransit._, to drop _or_ distil dew; to drip, be moist; _transit._, to bedew; to moisten; to drip, let fall in drops.

rōs, rōris, _m._ dew. _Poet._, _rores pluvii_, rain-clouds.

rŏsa -ae, _f._ a rose.

rŏsārium -i, _n._ a rose-garden.

rŏscidus -a -um, dewy; _mella_, dripping like dew; _poet._ watered.

Roscius -a -um, name of a Roman gens.

rŏsētum -i, _n._ a garden of roses.

rŏsĕus -a -um, made of roses, full of roses; rosy.

rōsidus = _roscidus (q.v.)._

rosmārīnus, rosemary.

rostra -ōrum, _n._, _v._ rostrum.

rostrātus -a -um, beaked ; curved ; _columna rostrata_, the pillar adorned with ships' prows, erected in the forum.

rostrum -i, n. beak; snout; the prow of a ship; rostra -ōrum, n. the speaker's platform in the forum.

rōta -ae, f. a wheel; the sun's disk; course in a circus.

rōto, 1. to cause to turn like a wheel, to swing round; to brandish; middle, rotari, to revolve; intransit., to turn or wheel round.

rŏtundē, adv. roundly ; elegantly, smoothly.

rŏtundo, 1. to round, make round.

rŏtundus -a -um, round, circular, spherical; complete; of style, smooth, well-turned.

rŭbĕfăcĭo -fēci -factum, 3. to redden, make red.

rubellus -a -um (dim. of ruber), reddish.

rūbens -entis, p. adj. red, reddish ; blushing.

rūbĕo, 2. to be red; to blush.

rūber -bra -brum, red, ruddy.

rūbesco -būi, 3. to become red.

1. rūbēta -ae, f. a species of toad.

2. rūbēta -ōrum, n. bramble-bushes.

rūbĕus -a -um, made of bramble.

Rūbĭco -ōnis, m. a small river in Italy.

rŭbĭcundus -a -um, red, reddish.

rŭbīgo = robigo (q.v.).

rŭbor -ōris, m. redness; red paint, rouge ; purple ; a blush ; modesty ; disgrace.

rŭbrīca -ae, f. red earth, red ochre; a law written in red, the rubric.

rŭbus -i, m. a bramble-bush; a black-berry.

ructo, 1. and ructor, 1. dep. to belch.

ructor = ructo (q.v.).

ructus -ūs, m. belching.

rūdens -entis, m. a strong rope, cable.

rūdīmentum -i, n. an attempt, essay.

1. rūdis -e, rough, uncultivated ; un-skilled ; lana, unspun ; poet. young, fresh.

2. rūdis -is, f. a small stick ; a ladle ; (in fencing exercise) a foil.

rūdo, rūdīvi, 3. to bellow, roar.

rūdusculum = raudusculum (q.v.).

rūfus -a -um, red, ruddy.

rūga -ae, f. a wrinkle; a crease, fold.

rūgōsus -a -um, wrinkled.

rūīna -ae, f. a fall; ruin, disaster; ruins of a building.

rūīnōsus -a -um, going to ruin.

rūmen -ĭnis, n. the gullet.

Rūmīna -ae, f. a Roman goddess, whose temple stood near the fig-tree under which, according to the legend, the she-wolf had suckled Romulus and Remus.

rūmĭnātĭo -ōnis, f. a chewing the cud; repetition; ruminating upon.

rūmĭno, 1. and rūmĭnor, 1. dep. to chew the cud.

rūmor -ōris, m. a dull noise; murmur,

confused cry; a report, rumour; general opinion.

rumpo, rūpi, ruptum, 3. to break, burst, tear asunder; milit., to break through; to force open; to utter; to destroy, annul; to interrupt.

rūmuscŭlus -i, m. (dim. of rumor), idle talk, gossip.

rūna -ae, f. a dart or javelin.

runco, 1. to weed, thin out.

rŭo, rŭi, rŭtum, but partic. fut., rŭĭtūrus, 3. to run, to rush, to hasten; to fall down; to be ruined; to snatch up; to collect together; to cast up from below; to cast down.

rūpes -is, f. a rock, cliff.

ruptor -ōris, m. a breaker, violator.

rūrĭcŏla -ae, c. inhabiting, cultivating the country; subst., rūrĭcŏla -ae, m. a countryman.

rūrĭgĕna -ae, m. born in the country, rustic; subst., rūrĭgĕnae -ārum, c. the countryfolk.

rursūs and rursum, adv. backward, back; on the contrary; again, afresh.

rūs, rūris, n. the country, a villa, farm; acc., rus, to the country ; locative, ruri, in the country.

russus -a -um, red, russet.

rustĭcānus -a -um, relating to the country, rustic.

rustĭcātĭo -ōnis, f. a living in the country; agriculture.

rustĭcē, adv. in a countrified manner; awkwardly.

rustĭcĭtas -ātis, f. awkwardness; timid-ity.

rustĭcor, 1. dep. to live in the country.

rustĭcus -a -um, rural, rustic; simple, homely ; awkward, boorish ; subst., rustĭcus -i, m. a countryman; a boor; rustĭca -ae, f. a country-girl.

rūta -ae, f. the herb rue; bitterness, unpleasantness.

rŭtĭlo, 1. to glitter like gold; to dye red.

rŭtĭlus -a -um, red, golden.

rŭtrum -i, n. spade, shovel.

rŭtŭla -ae, f. (dim. of ruta), a little bit of rue.

Rŭtŭli -ōrum and (poet.) -ūm, m. an ancient people of Latium.

S

S s, the eighteenth letter of the Latin Alphabet.

Sāba -ae, f. district in Arabia Felix, famous for its perfumes.

Sabbāta -ōrum, n. the Sabbath. Adj., Sabbātārius.

Săbelli -ōrum, m. (dim. of Sabini), poetic name of the Sabines.

Săbīni -ōrum, m. ancient people of Italy neighbours of the Latins.

săbŭlum -i, *n.* graver, sand.

săburra -ae, *f.* sand used as ballast.

sacco, 1. to strain *or* filter.

saccŭlus -i, *m.* (*dim. of saccus*), small bag.

saccus -i, *m.* a sack, bag, a purse.

săcellum -i, *n.* (*dim. of sacrum*), a small shrine.

săcer -cra -crum, holy, consecrated; accursed, horrible ; *subst.,* sacrum -i, *n.* a holy thing; festival, sacrifice; a secret, mystery.

săcerdos -ōtis, *c.* priest, priestess.

săcerdōtium -ii, *n.* priesthood.

sacrāmentum -i, *n.* that which binds a person; money deposited by the parties in a suit; a civil suit; the military oath.

sacrārium -ii, *n.* the sacristy of a temple; a chapel, temple.

sacrātus -a -um, *p. adj.* sacred, holy, consecrated.

sacricŏla -ae, *c.* a sacrificing priest *or* priestess.

sacrifĕr -fĕra -fĕrum, carrying sacred things.

sacrificālis (sacrificiālis) -e, relating to the sacrifices.

sacrificātio -ōnis, *f.* a sacrificing.

sacrificium -ii, *n.* a sacrifice.

sacrifico, 1. *and* sacrificor, 1. *dep.* to offer sacrifice; *transit.,* to sacrifice.

sacrificŭlus -i, *m.* (*dim. of sacrificus*), a sacrificing priest.

sacrificus -a -um, sacrificing; relating to a sacrifice.

sacrilĕgium -ii, *n.* robbery of a temple, sacrilege.

sacrilĕgus -a -um, sacrilegious; irreligious, impious; *subst.,* a temple-robber.

sacro, 1. to dedicate, consecrate; to give, allot; to immortalise.

sacrōsanctus -a -um, sacred, inviolable.

sacrum, *v. sacer.*

saeclum = *saeculum* (*q.v.*).

saeculāris (sēculāris) -e, relating to a *saeculum* or age.

saeculum (sēcŭlum, saeclum, sēclum) -i, *n.* race; a generation, age; the age, the times; spirit of the age; a century.

saepĕ, *adv. comp.* saepius, *superl.* saepissime, often, frequently; *saepenumero,* repeatedly.

saepes (sēpes) -is, *f.* a hedge, fence.

saepia = *sepia* (*q.v.*).

saepimentum (sēpimentum) -i, *n.* an enclosure.

saepio (sēpio), saepsi, saeptum, 4. to surround with a hedge, to enclose; to beset, to occupy; to guard, protect.

saepta -ōrum, *n., v. saeptum.*

saeptum (septum) -i, *n.* an enclosure, barrier; saepta -ōrum, *n.* the enclosure where the Romans voted at the comitia.

saet . . . *v. set* . . .

saetiger *and* saetōsus = *setiger, setosus* (*q.v.*).

saevē, *adv.* cruelly, ferociously.

saevidicus -a -um, angrily spoken.

saevio -ii -ītum, 4. to rage, be fierce, furious.

saevitĕr = *saeve* (*q.v.*).

saevitia -ae, *f.* ferocity; cruelty; *annonae,* high price of provisions.

saevum = *sebum* (*q.v.*).

saevus -a -um, violent, fierce; savage; terrible.

sāga -ae, *f.* prophetess, fortune-teller.

sāgācitas -ātis, *f.* keenness; sagacity, shrewdness.

sāgācitĕr, *adv.* sharply, keenly; sagaciously, shrewdly.

sāgātus -a -um, clothed with a sagum.

sāgax -ācis, having keen senses; keen-scented; of quick hearing; clever.

sāgina -ae, *f.* feasting, nourishment, food, fodder.

sāgino, 1. to fatten, feed up, cram.

sāgio, 4. to perceive quickly, feel keenly (*intransit.*).

săgitta -ae, *f.* arrow.

săgittārius -a -um, relating to arrows; *subst.,* săgittārius -ii, *m.* an archer.

săgittifĕr -fĕra -fĕrum, carrying arrows; armed with arrows.

Săgittipŏtens -entis, *m.* the constellation Sagittarius.

sagmen -inis, *n.* bunch of sacred herbs borne by Roman ambassadors.

sāgŭlum -i, *n.* (*dim. of sagum*), a small military cloak.

sāgum -i, *n.* mantle of coarse wool worn by slaves, also the plaid of the Celts; a military cloak.

Săguntum -i, *n. and* Săguntus (-ŏs) -i, *f.* a town in Spain; *adj.* Săguntīnus. Săgūntini -ūm, *m.* people of Saguntum.

sāgus -a -um, prophetical, soothsaying; presaging, *aves.*

săl, sălis, *m. and n., and plur.,* săles, *m.* salt; wit; the salt sea.

sălāco -ōnis, *m.* swaggerer, boaster.

Sălămis -minis, *acc.* -mina, *f.* 1. island and town in the Saronic Gulf; 2. town in Cyprus, built by Teucer. *Adj.,* Sălāminius.

sălăputtium (sălăpūtium) -ii, *n.* a manikin.

sălārius -a -um, relating to salt; *subst.,* sălārium -ii, *n.* money given to soldiers for salt; wages, salary.

sălax -ācis, lustful; exciting lust.

sălebra -ae, *f.* a rough, uneven road; *fig.,* roughness, ruggedness.

sălebrōsus -a -um, rugged, rough.

Sălliāris, *v. Salii.*

Sălliātus -ūs, *m.* the office of a priest of Mars.

sălictum -i, *n.* plantation of willows.

sălignus -a -um, made of willow-wood.

Sălii -ōrum, *m.* the Salii, a college of priests of Mars. Sălliāris -e, relating to the Salii; magnificent.

sălillum -i, n. (dim. of salinum), a little salt-cellar.

sălīnae -ārum, f. salt-works, brine-pits.

sălīnum -i, n. a salt-cellar.

sălio, sălŭi, saltum, 4. to spring, leap; subst., sălientes -ium, m. fountains.

sălĭunca -ae, f. wild or Celtic nard.

săliva -ae, f. saliva; appetite; taste.

sălix -ĭcis, f. a willow.

Sallustius (Sălustius) -ii, m. a Roman name. C. Sallustius Crispus, the celebrated Latin historian; adj., Sallustiānus.

Salmōnēus -ĕi and -ĕos, m. son of Aeolus, brother of Sisyphus, king in Elis, founder of the town Salmone; he imitated the thunder and lightning of Zeus, who on that account struck him with a thunderbolt.

salpa -ae, f. a kind of stock-fish.

salsāmentārius -a -um, relating to salt-fish; subst., salsāmentārius -ii, m. dealer in salt-fish.

salsāmentum -i, n. brine, salted fish.

salsē, adv. wittily, humorously.

salsus -a -um, p. adj. salted, salt; sharp; witty, satirical.

saltātio -ōnis, f. dancing, pantomimic dance.

saltātor -ōris, m. a (pantomimic) dancer.

saltātōrius -a -um, relating to dancing.

saltātrix -īcis, f. a dancing-girl.

saltātus -ūs, m. a dancing, dance.

saltem, adv. at least, at all events.

salto, 1. to dance with pantomimic gestures.

saltuōsus -a -um, wooded.

1. saltus -ūs, m. spring, leap.

2. saltus -ūs, m. pass through a mountain or forest, a ravine; mountain pasture, cattle-run.

sălūbris -e, and sălūber -bris -bre, healthy; wholesome; sound, useful; vigorous, corpora.

sălūbritas -ātis, f. wholesomeness, salubrity; soundness, health.

sălūbrĭtĕr, adv. healthfully; advantageously.

sălum -i, n. open sea, roadstead; poet. the sea.

sălūs -ūtis, f. health; welfare, good fortune; deliverance; safety; salutation, greeting.

sălūtāris -e, healthful, beneficial, wholesome, advantageous; sălūtāria -ium, n. remedies, medicines.

sălūtārĭtĕr, adv. beneficially.

sălūtātio -ōnis, f. greeting, salutation, a call, visit of ceremony.

sălūtātor -ōris, m. a visitor, caller.

sălūtātrix -īcis, f. greeting, saluting; paying a visit.

sălūtĭfĕr -fĕra -fĕrum, health-bringing, salubrious.

sălūto, 1. to greet, salute; to call upon.

salvē, v. salveo.

salvĕo, 2. to be well in health; salve salvete, Good day!

salvus -a -um, safe, unhurt, well.

sambūca -ae, f. a species of harp.

sambūcistria -ae, f. woman that plays on the sambuca.

Samnis, Samnites a Samnium

Samnium -ii, n. a mountainous region of central Italy; adj., Samnis -ītis, Samnite; Samnītes -ium, m. the Samnites.

Sămŏs (-us) -i, f. an island in the Aegean Sea; Sămius, Samian; Sămii -ōrum, m. Samians.

Sămōthrācē (Sămōthrēcē) -ēs, f. and Sămōthrāca -ae, f. and Sămōthrācia -ae, f. an island of the Aegean Sea; Sămōthrāces -um, m. the inhabitants. Adj. Sămōthrācius.

sānābĭlis -e, curable.

sānātio -ōnis, f. a healing.

sancio, sanxi, sanctum, 4. to make sacred by a religious act; to make irrevocable; to sanction, render valid; to lay under a penalty.

sanctē, adv. piously, conscientiously.

sanctĭmōnia -ae, f. sanctity; purity.

sanctĭo -ōnis, f. the clause in a law which recites the penalty; in treaties, a clause.

sanctĭtas -ātis, f. inviolability, sanctity; piety.

sanctĭtūdo -ĭnis, f. = sanctitas (q.v.).

sanctor -ōris, m. an ordainer.

sanctus -a -um, p. adj. sacred, inviolable; venerable, holy; divine; pious, virtuous.

sandăpila -ae, f. a kind of bier used by poor persons.

sandix -dĭcis, c. vermilion.

sānē, adv. soberly, sensibly; really, indeed; to be sure; certainly; exceedingly; with imperatives, then.

sanguĭnārius -a -um, bloody, blood-thirsty.

sanguĭnĕus -a -um, of blood, bloody; blood-red; bloodthirsty.

sanguĭnŏlentus (sanguĭnŭlentus) -a -um, stained with blood, bloody; wounding; blood-red.

sanguis (sanguen) -ĭnis, m. blood; vigour, force; murder; blood-relationship, race; a descendant, progeny.

sănies, no genit. or dat., f. diseased blood; venom, poison.

sānĭtas -ātis, f. health; reasonableness, sanity; soundness, purity.

sanna -ae, f. a mocking grimace.

sannio -ōnis, m. a buffoon.

sāno, 1. to heal, cure; to restore, repair.

Santōnes -um, m. and Santōni -ōrum, m. people in Aquitanian Gaul.

sānus -a -um, sound, healthy; sane; of discourse, sound.

săpa -ae, f. must or new wine.

săperda -ae, _m._ a kind of herring.

săpiens -entis, _p. adj._ wise, sensible, prudent, judicious; _subst._, a sensible, judicious person; a wise man.

săpientĕr, _adv._ wisely, discreetly, judiciously.

săpientia -ae, _f._ good sense, prudence; wisdom; _plur._, rules of wisdom.

săpio -ii, 3. to taste, have a flavour _or_ taste; to smell something; to discern, understand, to be sensible, wise.

săpor -ōris, _m._ the taste of a thing; elegance in discourse; a delicacy, a titbit; scent; _sapores,_ pleasant odours; _fig.,_ good taste.

Sapphicus -a -um, _v. Sappho._

Sapphō -ūs, _f._ a lyrical poetess of Mytilene in Lesbos, who threw herself into the sea on account of her unrequited love for Phaon. _Adj.,_ **Sapphicus.**

sarcĭna -ae, _f._ bundle, pack; _fig.,_ burden.

sarcĭnārĭus -a -um, pertaining to baggage.

sarcĭnŭla -ae, _f._ (_dim. of sarcina_), a little bundle.

sarcĭo, sarsi, sartum, 4. to patch, repair, restore.

sarcŏphăgus -i, _m._ coffin, sarcophagus.

sarcŭlum -i, _n._ a light hoe.

1. **Sardi,** _v. Sardis._

2. **Sardi -ōrum,** _m._ the Sardinians. _Adj.,_ **Sardōnius. Sardĭnia -ae,** _f._ the island; **Sardĭniensis -e,** Sardinian.

Sardīs -ium, _acc._ -is, _f._ old capital of Lydia; **Sardi,** Sardians, Lydians. _Adj._ **Sardĭānus.**

sardŏnyx -nychis, _m. and f._ sardonyx.

sargus -i, _m._ a salt-water fish.

sărisa (sărissa) -ae, _f._ the Macedonian pike.

sărisŏphŏrus (sarissŏphŏrus) -i, _m._ a Macedonian pikeman.

Sarmăta -ae, _m._ a Sarmatian; _plur.,_ **Sarmătae,** the Sarmatians, a nation in modern Poland and adjoining countries. **Sarmătia -ae,** _f._ Sarmatia; _adj._ **Sarmăticus,** _adv._ **Sarmătĭcē, Sarmătis -idis,** _f._ Sarmatian.

sarmen -inis, _n._ = _sarmentum (q.v.)._

sarmentōsus -a -um, full of twigs.

sarmentum -i, _n._ twigs, brushwood.

Sarpēdōn -ŏnis, _m._ 1. son of Jupiter, king of Lycia, who came to the help of the Trojans, and was slain by Patroclus. 2. Promontory in Cilicia.

sarrācum -i, _n._ = _serracum (q.v.)._

sartāgo -inis, _f._ frying-pan.

sartus -a -um, _partic. of sarcio (q.v.)._

săt = _satis,_ enough, sufficient.

sătellēs -itis, _c._ a guard, attendant (_plur.,_ escort); companion; accomplice.

sătias -ātis, _f._ abundance ; satiety, loathing.

sătĭĕtas -ātis, _f._ abundance ; satiety, loathing.

sătĭnĕ, satin' = _satisne, v. satis._

1. **sătĭo,** 1. to satisfy, satiate; appease; sate; to cloy, disgust.

2. **sătĭo -ōnis,** _f._ a sowing; planting; _plur.,_ **sătĭōnes,** the sown fields.

sătĭra (sătūra) -ae, _f._ satire.

sătis, _compar.,_ **sătĭus,** enough, sufficient; _adj._ enough ; _adv._ (_often satine ro satin'_ = _satisne_) _de hoc satis,_ enough of this; _legal, satis accipere,_ to take bail, security; _compar., satius,_ more advantageous.

sătisdătio -ōnis, _f._ a giving bail _or_ security.

sătisdo -dĕdi -dătum, 1. to give bail _or_ security.

sătisfăcĭo -fēci -factum, 3. to satisfy, give satisfaction; pay a creditor; to make amends, _alicui._

sătisfactĭo -ōnis, _f._ satisfaction, excuse, apology.

sătĭus, _comp. of satis (q.v.)._

sător -ōris, _m._ a sower, planter; father, producer.

sătrăpes -ae _and_ **-is,** _m._, **sătrăpa -ae,** _m._, _and_ **sătraps -āpis,** _m._ the governor of a Persian province, satrap.

sătur -tūra -tūrum, full, satiated ; satisfied ; fertile ; _of colours,_ deeply dyed, dark; _fig.,_ copious.

sătūra -ae, _f._ a mixture, medley; _per saturam,_ indiscriminately. _Hence,_ _satira (q.v.)._

sătūrēia -ae, _f._ the herb savory ; _heteroclite plur.,_ **sătūrēia -ōrum,** _n._

sătūritas -ātis, _f._ abundance.

Sāturnālĭa, _etc.,_ _v. Saturnus._

Sāturnus -i, _m._ an old Latin god; the planet Saturn; _adj.,_ **Sāturnālis -e;** _subst. plur.,_ **Sāturnālia -ium,** _n._ the festival beginning with the 17th of December ; _adj.,_ **Sāturnālĭcĭus,** relating to the Saturnalia.

sătūro, 1. to satisfy, satiate; glut, appease.

1. **sătus -a -um,** _partic. of 1. sero (q.v.)._

2. **sătus -ūs,** _m._ sowing, planting ; seed; origin, race.

Sătyrus -i, _m._ a Satyr.

sauciātĭo -ōnis, _f._ a wounding.

saucio, 1. to wound, hurt; to let blood.

saucĭus -a -um, wounded, injured ; attacked by illness; drunken; troubled.

Saurŏmătēs -ae, _m._ a Sarmatian; _plur.,_ **Saurŏmătae,** the Sarmatians.

sāvĭŏlum -i, _n._ (_dim. of savium_), a little kiss.

sāvĭor, 1. _dep._ to kiss.

sāvium -i, _n._ a kiss.

saxētum -i, _n._ a rocky place.

saxĕus -a -um, rocky, stony.

saxifĭcus -a -um, turning into stone.

saxifrăgus -a -um, stone-breaking.

saxōsus -a -um, rocky, stony, flowing between rocks. _Subst.,_ **saxōsa -ōrum,** _n._ rocky places.

saxŭlum -i, n. (*dim. of saxum*), a little rock.

saxum -i, n. a rock *or* large stone.

scăbellum -i, n. (*dim. of scamnum*), footstool; musical instrument played with the foot.

scăber -bra -brum, rough, scurvy; untidy.

scăbies -em -e, f. roughness; the itch; itching desire.

scăbiōsus -a -um, rough, mangy.

scăbo, scăbi, 3. to scratch, rub.

Scaea porta -ae, f. west gate of Troy.

scaena (**scēna**) -ae, f. the stage, the scene; publicity, the world; parade, outward show; deception, fraud.

scaenālis -e, theatrical.

scaenicus -a -um, scenic, theatrical; **scaenicus** -i, m. a stage-hero, an actor.

Scaevŏla -ae, m. (*dim. of scaevus*), a surname of the gens *Mucia*.

scaevus -a -um, left, on the left hand; awkward.

scālae -ārum, f. a flight of stairs, ladder.

Scaldis -is, m. river in Gallia Belgica, *now* the Scheldt.

scalmus -i, m. a rowlock.

scalpellum -i, n. (*dim. of scalprum*), *and* **scalpellus** -i, m. lancet, scalpel.

scalpo, scalpsi, scalptum, 3. to scrape, scratch, tear; to engrave; *fig.*, to tickle.

scalprum -i, n. a sharp instrument; a cobbler's awl; a chisel; a penknife.

scalptūra -ae, f. cutting, engraving; a carving, sculpture.

Scămander -dri, m. river in Troas.

scammōnia (**scămōnia**) *and* **scammōnĕa** -ae, f. scammony (*a plant*).

scamnum -i, n. a prop, bench, stool, step.

scando, scandi, scansum, 3. to climb, *in aggerem*; to rise.

scăpha -ae, f. a small boat, skiff.

scăphium -ii, n. a drinking-vessel.

scăpŭlae -ārum, f. the shoulder-blades.

scăpus -i, m. a weaver's beam.

scărus -i, m. salt-water fish.

scătebra -ae, f. a bubbling up of water.

scătĕo, 2, *and* (*archaic*) **scăto,** 3. to gush forth, bubble out; to abound.

scătŭrīgo (**scătŭrrīgo**) -inis, f. a spring of bubbling water.

scaurus -a -um, having swollen ankles. *Scaurus,* a Roman surname.

scĕlĕrātē, adv. impiously, wickedly.

scĕlĕrātus -a -um, p. adj. polluted; impious, accursed; wretched, noxious; (*subst.*, **scĕlĕrāti** -ōrum, m. villains); unlucky, calamitous.

scĕlĕro, 1. to pollute.

scĕlĕrōsus -a -um, wicked, accursed.

scĕlestē, adv. wickedly.

scĕlestus -a -um, wicked, infamous.

scĕlus -ĕris, n. impiety, wickedness; a crime; a villain.

scēna = scaena (q.v.).

scēnālis = scaenalis (q.v.).

scēnicus = scaenicus (q.v.).

sceptrĭfĕr -fĕra -fĕrum, sceptre-bearing.

sceptrĭgĕr = sceptrifer (q.v.).

sceptrum -i, n. a sceptre; dominion.

sceptŭchus -i, m. the wand-bearer, an official in Eastern courts.

schĕda (**schĭda**) *and* **scĭdo** -ae, f. a leaf of paper.

schēma -ae, f. *and* **schēma** -ătis, n. shape, form, fashion.

schĭda = scheda (q.v.).

Schoenēus -ĕi *and* **ĕos**, m. a king of Boeotia, father of Atalanta.

schoenŏbătes -ae, m. rope-walker.

schŏla (**scŏla**) -ae, f. debate, dissertation; a school; a gallery of works of art; a sect.

schŏlasticus -a -um, relating to a school; rhetorical; **schŏlastica** -ōrum, n. rhetorical exercises; **schŏlasticus** -i, m. a student of rhetoric; a teacher of rhetoric.

scĭda = schida (q.v.).

sciens -entis, adj. knowing something; knowingly; versed in, acquainted with, *with genit.*

scientĕr, adv. skilfully, expertly.

scientia -ae, f. knowledge of, acquaintance with; theory, science.

scīlĭcĕt, adv. actually, just think! naturally, of course; *ironically*, of course, forsooth; to wit, namely.

scilla (**squilla**) -ae, f. a sea-leek, squill; small sea-crab.

scin' = scisne, *from scio.*

scindo, scĭdi, scissum, 3. to tear, rend, break; to part, separate; to break off, interrupt; to destroy.

scintilla -ae, f. a spark; *fig.*, a spark, glimmer.

scintillo, 1. to sparkle, glitter.

scintillŭla -ae, f. (*dim. of scintilla*), a little spark.

scio -ivi *and* -ii -ītum, 4. to know, to have knowledge of, to experience; to perceive; have learned; *scire Latine,* to understand Latin.

Scĭpĭădas *and* **Scĭpĭădes**, v. 2. *Scipio.*

1. **scipio** -ōnis, m. a staff, wand.

2. **Scĭpĭo** -ōnis, m. family name of the gens *Cornelia;* **Scĭpĭădas** (-es) -ae, m. one of the Scipios.

Scīron -ōnis, m. a noted robber killed by Theseus.

scirpĕus (**sirpĕus**) -a -um, made of rushes; *subst.*, **scirpea**, basket-work of rushes.

scirpĭcŭlus (**sirpĭcŭlus**) -a -um, made of rushes; *subst.*, **scirpĭcŭlus** -i, m. a rush-basket.

scirpus (**sirpus**) -i, m. a rush, bulrush.

sciscitor, 1. *dep.* to investigate, ask; to consult, *deos.*

scisco, scīvi, scītum, 3. to investigate, inquire; to assent to; to resolve; to vote for.

scissus -a -um, *p. adj.* torn, rent; harsh, grating.

scitē, *adv.* cleverly, elegantly.

scītor, 1. to inquire; to consult.

scītum -i, *n.* decree, statute.

1. scītus -a -um, *p. adj.* clever, shrewd, skilful; *with genit.*, acquainted with.

2. scītus -ū (*only in abl.*), *m.* a statute.

scōbis -is, *f.* cuttings, shavings, sawdust.

scōla, *etc.* = *schola, etc.* (*q.v.*).

scomber -bri, *m.* a mackerel.

scōpa -ae, *f.* a sprig; *plur.*, **scōpae -ārum**, a broom.

scōpŭlōsus -a -um, rocky.

scōpŭlus -i, *m.* rock, crag, cliff.

scorpio -ōnis, *m. and* **scorpius (-ŏs) -i**, *m.* a scorpion; military engine for throwing missiles; a prickly plant.

scortātor -ōris, *m.* a fornicator.

scortěus -a -um, leathern ; *subst.*, **scortěa -ae**, *f.* a leathern garment.

scortĭlum -i, *m.* (*dim. of scortum*).

scortum -i, *n.* skin, hide, a prostitute.

scrěātus -ūs, *m.* a coughing, hemming.

scrība -ae, *m.* clerk *or* secretary.

scrĭblīta -ae, *f.* a kind of tart.

scrībo, scripsi, scriptum, 3. to engrave, draw lines; to draw; to write; to write about, describe; to enrol soldiers, *etc.*

Scrībōnius -a -um, name of a Roman gens.

scrīnium -ii, *n.* a case, *or* box for books.

scriptio -ōnis, *f.* writing, the art of writing.

scriptito, 1. to write frequently; to compose.

scriptor -ōris, *m.* a writer, secretary; author, composer.

scriptŭla -ōrum, *n.* (*dim. of scriptum*), lines on a draught-board.

scriptum -i, *n.* line on a draught-board; a writing; written decree.

scriptūra -ae, *f.* a writing; written composition ; rent paid for public pastures.

scrōbis -is, *c.* a ditch; a grave.

scrōfa -ae, *f.* a breeding sow.

scrūpěus -a -um, rugged, rough.

scrūpōsus -a -um, rough, rugged.

scrūpŭlōsē, *adv.* accurately.

scrūpŭlōsus -a -um, rough, rugged; *fig.* (*late*) accurate.

scrūpŭlum, a scruple, $\frac{1}{24}$ of an ounce.

scrūpŭlus -i, *m.* (*dim. of scrupus*), a small stone; *fig.*, uneasiness, scruple.

scrūpus -i, *m.* a sharp stone ; *fig.*, anxiety.

scrūta -ōrum, *n.* trash.

scrūtātor -ōris, *m.* one who searches, examines.

scrūtor, 1. *dep.* to examine, inspect; to search into, find out.

sculpo, sculpsi, sculptum, 3. to carve, hew.

sculptilis -e, carved, hewn, cut.

sculptūra -ae, *f.* a carving in wood, marble, *etc.*; sculpture.

scurra -ae, *m.* a dandy; a jester, parasite.

scurrīlis -e, mocking, jeering.

scurrīlitas -ātis, *f.* buffoonery.

scurror, 1. *dep.* to play the buffoon.

scūtāle -is, *n.* the thong of a sling.

scūtātus -a -um, armed with a shield.

scŭtella -ae, *f.* (*dim. of scutra*), a little dish *or* salver.

scūtica (scỹtica) -ae, *f.* a whip, lash.

1. scŭtŭla -ae, *f.* roller for moving heavy weights.

2. scŭtŭla -ae, -f. a small tray *or* dish; a diamond *or* lozenge-shaped figure.

scūtŭlum -i, *n.* (*dim. of scutum*), little shield.

scūtum -i, *n.* a quadrangular shield.

Scylla -ae, *f.* rock at the entrance to the straights between Sicily and Italy, personified as the daughter of Phorcus, changed by Circe into a monster.

scymnus -i, *m.* a young animal, whelp.

scỹphus -i, *m.* drinking-cup, goblet.

Scỹriās, of Scyros.

Scỹrŏn = *Sciron* (*q.v.*).

Scỹrus (-ŏs) -i, *f.* an island in the Aegean Sea, near Euboea.

scỹtăla -ae, *f. and* **scỹtăle -es**, *f.* a roller.

Scỹthes (Scỹtha) -ae, *m.* a Scythian. *Plur., Scythae.*

1. sē, *inseparable particle* = without, *e.g. securus.*

2. sē, *acc. and abl. of sui* (*q.v.*).

sēbum (sēvum) *and* **saevum -i**, *n.* tallow, suet, fat.

sēcēdo -cessi -cessum, 3. to withdraw; to be distant.

sēcerno -crēvi -crētum, 3. to separate, *se a bonis*; to distinguish; to reject.

sēcessio -ōnis, *f.* a withdrawal, secession.

sēcessus -ūs, *m.* migration (*of birds*); retirement, retreat; place of retirement; a recess; a bay running far into the land.

sēclūdo -clūsi -clūsum, 3. to shut away, to separate; *curas*, to banish.

sēcius, *v. secus.*

sēclūsus -a -um, *partic. of secludo.*

sĕco, sĕcŭi, sectum, but sĕcātūrus, 1. to cut, cut off, cut in pieces; to wound, injure, hurt ; to cut through, traverse ; to satirise ; to divide ; to decide ; to pursue.

sēcrētō, *adv.* separately.

sēcrētus -a -um, *perf. pass. part. of* **secerno**, separate, apart, remote, solitary, secret; *subst.*, **sēcrētum -i**, *n.* retirement, solitude, a solitary place; a secret, mystery.

secta -ae, *f.* a mode of life ; conduct ; political method, party; a philosophical school, sect.

sectātor -ōris, *m.* follower, hanger on; a member of a sect; *plur.*, retinue; clients.

sectĭlis -e, cut, cleft; that can be cut; *pavimenta*, mosaic.

sectio -ōnis, *f.* a cutting up; the buying

of confiscated property ; *concr.* = property of this kind put up to auction.

1. **sector** -**ōris**, *m.* a cutter; buyer of confiscated *or* other public property.

2. **sector**, 1. *dep.* to follow eagerly, continually; to accompany constantly; to hunt, pursue; to strive after; to try to find out.

sectūra -**ae**, *f.* a cutting; *aerariae secturae*, copper-mines.

sēcŭbĭtus -**ūs**, *m.* a sleeping alone.

sēcŭbo -**ŭi**, 1. to sleep alone ; to live a solitary life.

sēcŭlāris = *saecularis (q.v.)*.

sēcŭlum = *saeculum (q.v.)*.

sēcum = *cum se, v. se and cum.*

sĕcundāni -**ōrum**, *m.* soldiers of the second legion.

sĕcundārĭus -**a** -**um**, belonging to the second rank, of second-rate quality; *subst.*, **sĕcundārĭum** -**ii**, *n.* secondary matter of discussion.

1. **sĕcundŏ**, *adv.* in the second place; for the second time.

2. **sĕcundo**, 1. to make favourable, to favour.

sĕcundum, *adv.*, afterwards, behind ; secondly; *prep. with acc.*, after, along, near to; next to; according to; *legal*, to the advantage of.

sĕcundus -**a** -**um**, following ; second ; *fig.*, second in rank, next; inferior ; *(subst.*, **sĕcundae** -**ārum**, *f.* the second role; **sĕcunda** -**ae**, *f.* the second hour); following easily *or* willingly; *of wind or tide*, favourable; *secundo flumine*, with the stream ; *subst.*, **sĕcundum** -**i**, *n.* prosperity.

sēcūrē, *adv.* composedly, unconcernedly, securely *(late)*.

sēcūrĭfĕr -**fĕra** -**fĕrum**, carrying an axe.

sēcūrĭgĕr -**gĕra** -**gĕrum**, carrying an axe.

sēcūris -**is**, *acc.* -**im**, *abl.* -**i**, an axe, hatchet; supreme power.

sēcūrĭtas -**ātis**, *f.* freedom from care ; peace of mind; carelessness; security.

sēcūrus -**a** -**um**, free from care; fearless, tranquil; untroubled, *quies;* negligent; safe, secure.

1. **sĕcus**, *n. indecl.* = *sexus*, sex.

2. **sĕcus**, *adv.* otherwise, not so; *non (haud) secus*, just as; *compar.*, **sēquĭus** (**sēcĭus**) *and* **sectĭus** (**sētĭus**), otherwise, not so; less well, badly.

sĕcūtor -**ōris**, *m.* a gladiator armed with a sword and shield who fought with a *retiarius*.

sĕd, *conj.* but, yet ; *sed etiam*, but also, nay rather ; *non modo, sed etiam*, not only . . . but also.

sēdātē, *adv.* quietly, tranquilly.

sēdātĭo -**ōnis**, *f.* an allaying, soothing.

sēdātus -**a** -**um**, *p. adj.* quiet, composed.

sēdĕcim *and* **sexdĕcim**, sixteen.

sēdēcŭla -**ae**, *f. (dim. of sedes)*, a low seat *or* stool.

sĕdĕo, **sēdi**, 2. to sit; to settle; to sit in council, sit in judgment; to settle, sink down; *of food*, to be digested; to stay; to be idle; *milit.*, to remain encamped, to remain inactive; to be fixed; to remain unchanged.

sēdēs -**is**, *f.* seat; stool, chair, throne; *proprie sedes tenere*, the first rank ; abode, home; a temple; *scelerutorum*, the infernal regions; the grave; dwelling place of the soul, the body; place, foundation, *montes moliri sede suâ*.

sēdīle -**is**, *n.* a seat; *plur.*, *sēdilia*, row of seats; benches for rowers.

sēdĭtĭo -**ōnis**, *f.* dissension ; quarrel; revolt; tumult.

sēdĭtĭōsē, *adv.* seditiously.

sēdĭtĭōsus -**a** -**um**, seditious, turbulent, restless.

sēdo, 1. to settle, soothe, put an end to, *bellum*.

sēdūco -**duxi** -**ductum**, 3. to take *or* lead apart; *poet.*, to separate.

sēductĭo -**ōnis**, *f.* a drawing aside.

sēductus -**a** -**um**, *p. adj.* remote, distant, far from.

sēdŭlē = *sedulo (q.v.)*.

sēdŭlĭtas -**ātis**, *f.* assiduity, zeal.

sēdŭlŏ, *adv.* zealously; purposely.

sēdŭlus -**a** -**um**, busy; earnest.

Sēdūni -**ōrum**, *m.* a Helvetian people.

sĕgĕs -**ĕtis**, *f.* a cornfield; standing corn, crop.

segmentātus -**a** -**um**, ornamented with a purple *or* gold border.

segmentum -**i**, *n.* a cutting, shred; a zone *or* region.

segnē, *adv.*, *v. segniter*.

segnĭpēs -**pĕdis**, slow-footed.

segnis -**e**, slow, dilatory ; *bellum*, sluggishly prosecuted.

segnĭtas -**ātis**, *f.* sluggishness, tardiness.

segnĭtĕr *and* **segnē**, sluggishly, slowly.

segnĭtĭa -**ae** *f. and* **segnĭtĭēs** -**ēm** -**ē**, *f.* sluggishness, slowness.

Segontĭāci -**ōrum**, *m.* people in the south of Britain.

sēgrĕgo, 1. to separate from the flock; to remove.

Sēgūsĭāvi (**Sēgūsĭāni**) -**ōrum**, *m.* people in Gallia Lugdunensis.

Sēiānus, a Roman cognomen.

sēiūgātus -**a** -**um**, disjointed, separated.

sēiūgēs -**ĭum**, *m.* chariot drawn by six horses abreast.

sēiunctim, *adv.* separately.

sēiunctĭo -**ōnis**, *f.* a separation.

sēiungo -**iunxi** -**iunctum**, 3. to separate; to distinguish.

sēlectĭo -**ōnis**, *f.* selection.

Sēleucus -**i**, *m. Nicator*, a famous general of Alexander the Great, afterwards king of Syria.

sēlībra -**ae**, *f.* half a pound.

sēlĭgo -**lēgi** -**lectum**, 3. to choose.

sella -ae, f. seat, stool; a bench; a throne; a sedan-chair.

sellisternium -ii, n. a religious banquet in honour of goddesses.

sellŭla -ae, f. (dim. of sella), a little sedan-chair.

sellŭlārius -a -um, relating to a seat; subst., sellŭlārius -ii, m. a handicraftsman.

sēmĕl, adv. numer., once, a single time.

Sĕmēla -ae, f. and Sĕmēlē -ēs, f. daughter of Cadmus, mother of Bacchus by Jupiter; she asked Jupiter to appear to her in his person as a god, and was consumed by the blaze of his majesty.

sēmen -ĭnis, n. seed ; the race ; descendant, child; origin, author.

sēmentĭfĕr -fĕra -fĕrum, seed-bearing, fruitful.

sēmentis -is, acc. -em and -im, f. a sowing ; sementes, the young growing corn.

sēmentīvus -a -um, relating to seed or seed-time.

sēmestris (sēmenstris) -e, of six months.

sēmēsus -a -um, half-eaten, half-consumed.

sēmiambustus -a -um, half-burnt.

sēmiānĭmis -e and sēmiānĭmus -a -um, half-alive, half-dead.

sēmiăpertus -a -um, half-open.

sēmĭbos -bŏvis, m. half-ox.

sēmĭcăper -pri, m. half-goat.

sēmĭcircŭlus -i, m. a semicircle.

sēmĭcrĕmātus -a -um, half-burnt.

sēmĭcrĕmus, half-burnt.

sēmĭcŭbĭtālis -e, half a cubit in length.

sēmĭdĕus -a -um, half-divine; subst., demigod, demigoddess.

sēmĭdoctus -a -um, half-taught.

sēmĭermis (sēmermis) -e and sēmĭermus (sēmermus) -a -um, half-equipped.

sēmĭēsus = semesus (q.v.).

sēmĭfactus -a -um, half done.

sēmĭfĕr -fĕra -fĕrum, half-man and half-animal; half-savage.

sēmĭgermānus -a -um, half-German.

sēmĭgrăvis -e, half-intoxicated.

sēmĭgro, 1. to go away.

sēmĭhians -antis, half-open.

sēmĭhŏmo -hŏminis, m. half a man; half-wild.

sēmĭhōra -ae, f. half an hour.

sēmĭlăcer -cĕra -cĕrum, half-mangled.

sēmĭlautus -a -um, half-washed.

sēmĭlīber -bĕra -bĕrum, half-free.

sēmĭlixa -ae, m. half a sutler.

sēmĭmārinus -a -um, half in the sea.

sēmĭmas -măris, m. hermaphrodite.

sēmĭmortŭus -a -um, half-dead.

sēmĭnārius -a -um, relating to seed; subst., sēmĭnārium -ii, n. a plantation, nursery.

sēmĭnātor -ōris, m. producer, author.

sēminex -nĕcis, half-dead.

sēmino, 1. to sow, to beget, produce.

sēminūdus -a -um, half-naked; nearly defenceless.

sēmipāgānus -i, m. half a rustic.

sēmiplēnus -a -um, half-full.

sēmipūtātus -a -um, half-pruned.

sēmirāsus -a -um, half-shaven, half-shorn.

sēmirĕductus -a -um, half bent back.

sēmirĕfectus -a -um, half-repaired.

sēmirŭtus -a -um, half-ruined.

sēmis -issis, m. sometimes indecl., the half of anything; 6 per cent. per annum.

sēmisĕpultus -a -um, half-buried.

sēmisomnus -a -um, half-asleep, drowsy.

sēmisŭpīnus, -a -um, half-inclined backwards.

sēmĭta -ae, f. footpath.

sēmĭtactus -a -um, half-touched.

sēmĭtārius -a -um, frequenting lanes or by-paths.

sēmĭtectus -a -um, half-covered.

sēmĭustŭlātus = semustulatus (q.v.).

sēmĭustus (sēmustus) -a -um, half-burnt.

sēmĭvir -viri, m. half-man; Chiron, the centaur.

sēmĭvīvus -a -um, almost dead; voces, faint.

Semnones -um, m. a German people.

sēmŏdĭus -ii, m. a half-modius.

sēmŏtus -a -um, p. adj. remote, distant; different from.

sēmŏvĕo -mōvi -mōtum, 2. to separate; to exclude.

sempĕr, adv. always, at all times.

sempĭternus -a -um, everlasting.

sēmuncia -ae, f. half an uncia.

sēmunciārius -a -um, relating to half an ounce.

sēmustŭlātus (sēmĭustŭlātus) and sēmustilātus (sēmĭustilātus) -a -um, half-burnt.

sēnācŭlum -i, n. a senate-house.

sēnārĭŏlus -i, m. (dim. of senarius), little trifling senarius.

sēnārius -a -um, composed of six; subst., sēnārius -ii, m. a verse of six feet.

sēnātor -ōris, m. senator.

sēnātōrius -a -um, senatorial.

sēnātus -i, and -ūs, m. the Roman senate; a meeting, assembly of the senate ; frequens, a full house ; datur alicui senatus, obtains an audience of the senate ; senatus consultum, a formal resolution of the senate.

sēnātusconsultum, v. senatus.

Sĕnĕca -ae, m. L. Annaeus Seneca, the tutor of Nero.

sĕnecta, v. 1, senectus.

1. sĕnectus -a -um, old, aged; subst., sĕnecta -ae, f. old age; the slough of a serpent.

2. sĕnectus -ūtis, f. age, old age; the slough of a serpent.

sěněo, 2. to be old.

sěnesco, sěnŭi, 3. to become old; to lose strength; to decay; to wane, lose power.

sěnex, sěnis, *compar.*, sěnior, *neut. sěnius, genit. sěnĭōris*, old, aged; *subst.*, an old man; *f.* an old woman.

sēni -ae -a, six each.

sěnīlis -e, relating to an old man, senile.

sěniō -ōnis, *m.* the number six upon dice.

sěnior, *compar. of senex (q.v.)*.

sěnium -ii, *n.* old age; decay; moroseness; vexation, sadness.

Sěnōnes -um, *m.* a Gallic tribe.

sensa -ōrum, *n.* thoughts.

sensǐfěr -fěra -fěrum, causing sensation.

sensǐlis -e, endowed with sensation.

sensim, *adv.* gradually, by degrees.

sensus -ūs, *m.* perception, observation; consciousness; a sense; emotion, feeling; meaning; *plur.*, senses.

sententia -ae, *f.* opinion, meaning, purpose; *meā sententiā*, in my opinion; vote of senators; decision; meaning of a word; the purport of a speech; sentence; a maxim.

sententiǒla -ae, *f. (dim. of sententia)*, a short sentence, maxim.

sententiōsē, *adv.* sententiously.

sententiōsus -a -um, pithy, sententious.

sentǐna -ae, *f.* bilge-water; rabble, dregs of the population.

Sentīnum -i, *n.* town in Umbria.

sentio, sensi, sensum, 4. to feel, perceive; to experience, learn; to observe; to judge, think; to vote.

sentis -is, *c.* thorn-bush, briar.

sentisco, 3. to perceive.

sentus -a -um, thorny, rough.

sěorsum (sěorsus) *and* sěvorsus, apart from; *seorsus corpore*, without a body.

sěpǎrātē, *adv.* apart, particularly.

sěpǎrātim, *adv.* apart, separately, differently.

sěpǎrātio -ōnis, *f.* separation.

sěpǎrātus -a -um, *p. adj.* separated, distinct.

sěpǎro, 1. to disjoin, separate.

sěpělio -pēlivi *and* -pělii -pultum, 4. to bury; to destroy; *sepultus*, immersed in anything.

sēpes = *saepes (q.v.)*.

sēpia -ae, *f.* the cuttle-fish.

sēpimentum = *saepimentum (q.v.)*

sēpio = *saepio (q.v.)*.

sēpōno -pŏsŭi -pŏsĭtum, 3. to lay on one side, place apart; to keep back, reserve; to separate; to distinguish; to banish.

sēpǒsitus -a -um, *p. adj.* remote; choice, select.

1. seps, sěpis, *c.* a species of venomous lizard; an insect.

2. seps = *saepes (q.v.)*.

sepsē = *se ipse*.

septa, *v. saeptum*.

septem, seven.

September -bris -bre, *abl.* -bri, belonging to September; September.

septemděcim, seventeen.

septemflŭus -a -um, with seven mouths, *Nilus*.

septemgěmǐnus -a -um, with seven mouths, *Nilus*.

septemplex -plicis, sevenfold.

septemtrio (septemptrio, septentrio) -ōnis, *m.*, *gen. plur.*, *septemtriones*, the Great Bear; the north.

septemtrǐōnālis -e, northern; *subst.*, septemtrǐōnālia -ium, *m.* the northern regions.

septemvir -viri, *m.*, *plur.*, septemviri -ōrum *and* -ūm, *m.* a college or guild of seven persons.

septemvirālis -e, relating to the septemviri.

septemvirātus -ūs, *m.* office of a septemvir.

septēnārius -a -um, containing the number seven; *plur. subst.*, septēnāriī, *m.* verses containing seven feet.

septenděcim = *septemdecim (q.v.)*.

septēni -ae -a, seven each.

septentrio = *septemtrio (q.v.)*.

septentrǐōnālis = *septemtrionalis (q.v.)*.

septiēs (septiens), *adv.* seven times.

septǐmānus (septūmānus) -a -um, relating to the number seven; *subst.*, septǐmāni -ōrum, *m.* soldiers of the seventh legion.

septǐmus (septūmus) -a -um, the seventh; *adv.*, septǐmum, for the seventh time.

septingentēsimus -a -um, the seven hundredth.

septingenti -ae -a, seven hundred.

septūāgēsimus -a -um, the seventieth.

septūāginta, seventy.

septum = *saeptum (q.v.)*.

septunx -uncis, *m.* seven-twelfths.

sepulch . . , *v. sepulc* . . .

sěpulcrālis (sěpulchrālis) -e, belonging to a tomb, sepulchral.

sěpulcrētum -i, *n.* a burial-place.

sěpulcrum (sěpulchrum) -i, *n.* place of burial; sepulchre; the tomb.

sěpultūra -ae, *f.* a burying, burial; the burning of a body.

Sěquāna -ae, *m.* river of Gaul, *now* the Seine.

Sěquāni -ōrum, *m.* a Gallic people.

sěquax -ācis, following easily *or* quickly; *fumus*, penetrating; pliable.

sěquester -tra -trum *and* sěquester -tris -tre, mediating; *subst.*, sěquester -tri *or* -tris, *m.* a go-between *or* agent; a stake-holder.

sěquius = *secius*, *compar. of secus (q.v.)*.

sěquor, sěcūtus sum, sěqui, 3. *dep.* to follow, accompany; to pursue; to fall to the share of; to follow a person's

example, opinion, *amicum;* to agree to,
leges ; to strive after, *amicitiam.*

sēra -ae, *f.* a bar *or* bolt for fastening doors.

Sĕrāpis (Sărāpis) -pis *and* -pĭdis, *m.*
deity of the Egyptians, in later times
worshipped at Greece and at Rome.

sĕrēnĭtas -ātis, *f.* clearness, serenity,
fair weather.

sĕrēno, 1. to make clear. bright.

sĕrēnus -a -um, clear, bright, fair ;
bringing fair weather; cheerful, serene;
subst., sĕrēnum -i, *n.* fair weather.

Sēres -um, *m.* people in eastern Asia,
famous for their silken stuffs, the Chinese;
adj., Sēricus; *subst.,* Sērica -ōrum,
n. silken garments.

sĕresco, 3. to become dry.

sēria -ae, *f.* a large earthen jar.

sēricātus -a -um, clothed in silken garments.

Sēricus, *v. Seres.*

sēries, *genit. and dat. not found, f.* a
row, chain, series ; line of descent,
lineage.

sērio, *v.* 1. sērius.

Sērĭphus (-ŏs) -i, *f.* island in the Aegean
Sea; *adj.,* Sērĭphius.

1. sērius -a -um, serious, earnest; *subst.,*
sērium -ii, *n.* seriousness; *abl. serio,*
in earnest, seriously.

2. sērius, *compar. adv., v. sero under*
serus.

sermo -ōnis, *m.* conversation, discourse;
discussion, dialogue; spoken words,
utterance ; report, rumour ; language,
style, expression.

sermōcĭnor, 1. *dep.* to converse, discuss
with anyone; to hold a learned discussion.

sermuncŭlus -i, *m.* (*dim. of sermo*),
rumour, tittle-tattle.

1. sĕro, sēvi, sătum, 3. to sow, plant
(*Subst.,* săta -ōrum, *n.* the sown fields,
standing corn); to beget, bring forth;
partic. perf., sătus, sprung from, born
of; *fig.,* to spread abroad, cause; *men-*
tionem, to make mention of.

2. sĕro, sĕrŭi, sertum, 3. to join together, weave together; *partic., perf.,*
sertus, *loricae,* linked; *fig.,* to connect,
combine.

3. sĕro, *v. serus.*

serpens -entis, *c.* a snake, serpent.

serpentĭgĕna -ae, *c.* offspring of a serpent.

serpentĭpēs -pĕdis, snake-footed.

serpĕrastra -ōrum, *n.* bandages *or*
knee-splints.

serpillum = *serpyllum (q.v.).*

serpo, serpsi, serptum, 3. to creep,
crawl; to spread abroad, increase.

serpyllum (serpillum) *and* serpullum
-i, *n.* wild thyme.

serra -ae, *f.* a saw.

serrācum (sarrācum) -i, *n.* a kind
of wagon.

serrātus -a -um, serrated ; *subst.,*

serrāti -ōrum, silver denarii notched on
the edge.

serrŭla -ae, *f.* (*dim. of serra*), a little
saw.

serta, *v. sertum.*

Sertōrius -ii, *m.* Q., celebrated Roman
general, who, on Sulla gaining the upper
hand in Rome, fled to Spain, and re-
sisted there bravely and successfully till
he was killed.

sertum -i, *n., gen. plur.,* serta -ōrum,
n., and serta -ae, *f.* a garland of flowers.

1. sērum -i, *n.* whey.

2. sērum, *v. serus.*

sērus -a -um, late; aged; lasting a long
time; too late; *subst.,* sērum -i, *n.*
serum diei, late in the day, evening;
sero, adv. = late.

serva, *v. servus.*

servābĭlis -e, that can be saved.

servans -antis, *p. adj. only in superl.,*
observing.

servātor -ōris, *m.* a preserver.

servātrix -īcis, *f.* she that preserves.

servīlis -e, relating to a slave, servile.

servīlĭtĕr, *adv.* servilely.

Servīlius -a -um, name of a Roman
gens.

servĭo -īvi *and* -ii -ītum, 4. to serve,
alicui; of buildings, etc., to be subject to
certain burdens; to be useful, serviceable
for; to assist, gratify, *alicui;* to devote
one's attention to; to adapt oneself to.

servĭtĭum -ii, *n.* slavery, servitude, subjection.

servĭtūdo -ĭnis, *f.* slavery, servitude.

servĭtus -ūtis, *f.* slavery, servitude; subjection; *of houses, lands, etc.,* liability
to certain burdens.

Servĭus -ii, *n.* Roman praenomen.

servo, 1. to keep, preserve, deliver; to
pay heed to; to preserve, reserve; to
watch; *sidera,* to observe; to take precautions; detain; *limen,* stay at home;
to dwell, inhabit.

servŭlus (servŏlus) -i, *m.* (*dim. of ser-*
vus), a young slave.

servus -i, *m. and* serva -ae, *f.* a slave,
servant; *adj.,* servus -a -um, servile,
slavish.

sĕsĕlis -is, *f.* a plant, hartwort.

sesqui, *adv. num.* half as much again.

sesquialter *and* sesqualter -altĕra
-altĕrum, one and a half.

sesquĭmōdius -ii, *m.* a modius and a half.

sesquĭoctāvus -a -um, containing nine-
eighths of anything.

sesquĭpĕdālis -e, a foot and a half
long.

sesquĭpĕdānĕus = *sesquipedalis (q.v.).*

sesquĭpēs -pĕdis, *m.* a foot and a half.

sesquĭplāga -ae, *f.* a blow and a half.

sesquĭplex -plicis, taken one and a half
times.

sesquĭtertĭus -a -um, containing four-
thirds of anything.

sessilis -e, fit for sitting upon ; *of plants,* low, dwarf, spreading.

sessio -ōnis, *f.* the act of sitting; a sitting idle, loitering; a session.

sessito, 1. to sit much, always.

sessiuncŭla -ae, *f.* (*dim. of sessio*), a little company for conversation.

sessor -ōris, *m.* a sitter; inhabitant

sestertius -ii, *m.* a sesterce; a silver coin = 2½ asses.

Sestus (Sestŏs) -i, *f.* town on the Helles pont.

set = *sed* (*q.v.*).

sēta (saeta) -ae, *f.* a bristle, stiff hair; part of an angler's line.

sētĭgĕr (saetĭgĕr) -gĕra -gĕrum, having bristle, bristly; *subst.,* **sētĭgĕr -gĕri,** *m.* a boar.

sētōsus (saetōsus) -a -um, bristly.

seu = *sive* (*q.v.*).

sēvērē, *adv.* seriously, severely.

sēvēritas -ātis, *f.* seriousness, strictness.

sēvērĭtūdo -inis, *f.* = *severitas* (*q.v.*).

sēvērus -a -um, grave, stern, severe ; *of wine,* harsh; hard, cruel.

sēvŏco, 1. to call aside, call away; to separate.

sēvum = *sebum* (*q.v.*).

sex, *numer.* six.

scxāgēnārĭus -a -um, containing the number sixty; sixty years old.

sexāgēni -ae -a, sixty each.

sexāgēsimus -a -um, the sixtieth.

sexāgiēs (sexāgiens), *adv.* sixty times.

sexāginta, *num.* sixty.

sexangŭlus -a -um, hexagonal.

sexcēnārĭus -a -um, consisting of six hundred.

sexcēni (sēceni) -ae -a, six hundred each.

sexcentēni = *sexceni* (*q.v.*).

sexcentēsimus -a -um, the six hundredth.

sexcenti -ae -a, six hundred; countless.

sexcentiēs (sexcentiens), *adv.* six hundred times.

sexdĕcim = *sedecim* (*q.v.*).

sexennis -e, six years old.

sexennium -ii, *n.* a period of six years.

sexiēs (sexiens), *adv.* six times.

sexprimi -ōrum, *m.* the six highest magistrates in colonies and municipia.

sextādĕcĭmāni -ōrum, *m.* soldiers of the 16th legion.

sextans -antis, *m.* a sixth part.

sextārĭus -ii, *m.* the sixth part of a measure.

Sextĭlis -is, *m.* the month of August.

Sextĭus (Sestĭus) -a -um, name of a Roman gens.

sextŭla -ae, *f.* 1-72nd of an as.

sextus -a -um, the sixth; *adv.,* **sextum,** for the sixth time; *Sextus,* a Roman name.

sextusdĕcimus -a -um, sixteenth.

sexus -ūs, *m.* a sex.

si, *conj.* if, in case that; *si minus,* if not; *quod si,* and if, but if; if only, provided that.

sībilo, 1. to hiss; to hiss at.

1. **sībilus -i,** *m.* (*plur.,* **sibili,** *and poet.* **sibila**), hissing, rustling.

2. **sībilus -a -um,** hissing.

Sibylla -ae, *f.* a Sibyl.

Sibyllīnus -a -um, relating to the Sibyl, Sibylline.

sic, si, thus, in this manner; as follows; *in wishes,* so; so = on condition that; to such a degree, *often foll. by ut.*

sīca -ae, *f.* dagger; assassination, murder.

Sicāni -ōrum, *m.* a people of Sicily.

sīcārĭus -ii, *m.* an assassin, murderer.

siccē, *adv.* dryly ; *dicere,* plainly, vigorously.

siccĭnē (sīcinē or sīcin'), *adv.* is it thus ?

siccĭtas -ātis, *f.* dryness; drought; sound health; *fig.,* plainness, simplicity.

sicco, 1. to dry; to drain dry, to drink up, empty; to milk; *intransit.,* **siccat,** it dries up.

siccus -a -um, dry; tearless; thirsty; temperate; fasting; bright, cloudless; in sound health; *fig.,* cold, impassive; *of discourse,* plain, simple; *subst.,* **siccum -i,** *n.* the dry land.

Sicilia -ae, *f.* the island of Sicily. *Adj.,* **Siciliensis -e,** Sicilian.

sīcŭbi, *adv.* if anywhere.

Sicŭli -ōrum, *m.* the Sicilians; *sing.,* **Sicŭlus -i,** *m.*

sīcunde, *adv.* if from anywhere.

sīcut and sīcutĭ, *adv.* as, just as; just as if; as for example.

Sicyŏn -ōnis, *m. and f.* a city of Peloponnesus; *adj.,* **Sicyōnĭus** Sicyonian; *subst.,* **Sicyōnĭa -ōrum,** *n.* a kind of soft shoes from Sicyon.

sīdĕrĕus -a -um, belonging to the stars, starry; solar; gleaming, glittering.

sīdo, sīdi and sēdi, sessum, 3. to sit down, settle, alight; to sink down; to remain lying *or* fixed; *naut.,* to be stranded; to disappear.

Sidon -onis, *f.* a city of Phoenicia ; **Sidonii -ōrum,** *m.* the Sidonians *or* Tyrians; *adj.* **Sidonicus and Sidonius.**

sīdus -ĕris, *n.* constellation, *sometimes a single star;* the time of year, *e.g. hiberno sidere,* in winter; climate; weather; *plur.,* the heavens.

Sigambri = *Sugambri* (*q.v.*).

Sigēum -i, *n.* promontory and port in Troas.

sigilla -ōrum, *n.* (*dim. of signum*), small figures, images; a seal.

Sigillāria -ōrum, *abl.* **-iis and -ibus,** *n.* a festival in Rome, at which little figures were exchanged as presents.

sigillātus -a -um, ornamented with small figures.

sigillum, *sing. of sigilla.*

sigma -ătis, *n.* a semicircular dining-couch.

signātor -ōris, *m.* witness to a will, *etc.*

signĭfĕr -fĕra -fĕrum, adorned with, figures; *subst.*, signĭfĕr -fĕri, *m.* standard-bearer.

significans -antis, *p. adj.* distinct, clear.

significantĕr, *adv.* plainly, clearly.

significantia -ae, *f.* energy, distinctness (*late*).

significātio -ōnis, *f.* sign, indication; approbation, applause; emphasis; the meaning of a word.

significo, 1. to give a sign, to indicate; *of words*, to mean.

signo, 1. to mark, designate; to seal; to coin; to adorn; to express; to observe.

signum -i, *n.* a sign, mark, token ; *milit.*, a standard; *signa inferre*, to attack ; legion, company ; the signal, command ; a watchword ; a figure, statue ; seal, signet.

silānus -i, *m.* a fountain.

silens, *v. sileo.*

silentium -ii, *n.* silence, stillness, quietness; perfectness in taking the auspices; obscurity; repose, inactivity.

Silēnus -i, *m.* the tutor and attendant of Bacchus, represented with a bald head, as always drunk, and riding on an ass.

sĭlĕo -ŭi, 2. to be still, silent; *with acc.*, to be silent about; to rest, to be inactive; *partic.*, silens, silent; *subst.*, silentes, the silent = the dead *or* the Pythagoreans; silenda -ōrum, *n.* secrets, mysteries; silens, quiet, still.

sĭler -ĕris, *n.* the brook-willow.

sĭlesco, 3. to become silent, grow still.

sĭlex -ĭcis, *m.* (*rarely f.*), flint, granite.

silicernium -ĭi, *n.* a funeral feast.

silicŭla -ae, *f.* (*dim. of siliqua*), a little pod *or* husk.

siligo -ĭnis, *f.* a very white wheat; wheaten flour.

siliqua -ae, *f.* a husk, pod, shell; *plur.*, pulse.

Sillius -a -um, name of a Roman gens.

sillȳbus = *sittybus* (*q.v.*).

Silūres -um, a people in Britain.

silūrus -i, *m.* a species of river-fish.

silus -a -um, snub-nosed.

silva (sylva) -ae, *f.* a wood, forest.

Silvānus -i, *m.* god of forests.

silvesco, 3. *of a vine*, to run wild.

silvester -tris -tre *an.' gen.* silvestris -e, belonging to a wood *or* forest; wooded; growing wild; *subst.*, silvestria -ium, *n.* woody places.

Silvia, *v.* 1. *Rhea.*

silvĭcŏla -ae, *c.* an inhabitant of the woods.

silvĭcultrix -trĭcis, *f.* inhabiting the woods.

silvĭfrăgus -a -um, shattering the woods.

silvōsus -a -um, well wooded.

sīmĭa -ae, *f. and* sīmius -i, *m.* an ape, monkey.

sĭmĭla -ae, *f.* the finest wheaten flour.

sĭmĭlāgo = *simila* (*q.v.*).

sĭmĭlis -e, like, resembling, similar ; *with genit. or dat; subst.*, simile -is, *n.* a resemblance.

sĭmĭlĭter, *adv.* in like manner, similarly.

similĭtūdo -ĭnis, *f.* likeness, resemblance; *veri similitudo*, probability ; a metaphor, simile; comparison; uniformity.

sĭmĭlo = *simulo* (*q.v.*).

sīmĭŏlus -i, *m.* (*dim. of simius*), a little ape.

sĭmĭtu, *adv., old form of simul* (*q.v.*).

Sĭmŏis -mŏentis, *m.* a small stream in Troas.

Sĭmōnĭdes -is, *m.* a lyric poet of Cos.

simplex -ĭcis, simple, unmixed ; single, one ; plain, not complicated ; natural; upright.

simplĭcĭtas -ātis, *f.* simplicity; honesty, candour.

simplĭcĭtĕr, *adv.* plainly, straightforwardly; simply, candidly, honestly.

simplum -i, *n.* that which is single.

simpŭlum -i, *n.* a ladle.

simpŭvĭum -ĭi, *n.* a sacrificial vessel.

sĭmŭl (*archaic* sĕmŭl), *adv.* at once, at the same time as; *simulatque* (*simulac*), as soon as.

sĭmŭlācrum -i, *n.* image, likeness ; doll; reflection; vision; shade, ghost; recollection; imitation.

sĭmŭlāmen -ĭnis, *n.* an imitation.

sĭmŭlans -antis, *p. adj. only in compar.* imitating.

sĭmŭlātĕ, *adv.* in appearance, not sincerely.

sĭmŭlātĭo -ōnis, *f.* pretence.

sĭmŭlātor -ōris, *m.* an imitator; hypocrite.

sĭmŭlo, 1. to present, represent ; to imitate ; to simulate, feign ; *partic.* sĭmŭlātus -a -um, feigned.

sĭmultas -ātis, *f.* rivalry, jealousy, feud.

sīmŭlus -a -um (*dim. of simus*), somewhat snub-nosed.

sīmus -a -um, flat-nosed, snub-nosed.

sĭn, *conj.* but if, if however; *sin minus*, but if not.

sĭnāpi, *indecl. n. and* sĭnāpis -is, *acc.* -im, mustard.

sincērē, *adv.* honestly, frankly.

sincērĭtas -ātis, *f.* purity, clearness, integrity.

sincērus -a -um, pure, genuine; upright; sound, healthy; uninjured; mere.

sinciput -pĭtis, *n.* half a head; the smoked chap of a pig.

sindon -ōnis, *f.* muslin.

sĭnĕ, *prep. with abl.*, without.

singillātim (singŭlātim), *adv.* singly, one by one.

singŭlāris -e, single, individual; *grammat.*, singular; distinguished, unique, extraordinary.

singŭlārĭter, *adv.* singly; particularly, extraordinarily.

singŭlātim = singillatim (q.v.).

singŭli, v. singulus.

singultim, adv. in sobs; stammeringly.

singultio, 4. to hiccough; to throb.

singulto, 1. to hiccough, to sob; transit., to sob out, gasp out.

singultus -ūs, m. weeping, sobbing; croaking; gurgling.

vingŭlus -a -um, gen. plur., singŭli -ae -a, single, one alone; one each.

sinister -tra -trum, left, on the left hand; awkward, wrong, perverse; adverse; of augury, favourable; compar., sinistĕrior; subst., sinistra -ae, f. the left hand.

sinistrē, adv. unfavourably.

sinistrorsus (sinistrorsum), adv. on the left hand.

sino sivi, situm, 3. to place, to set down (only partic. situs); to permit, allow.

Sinōpa -ae, f. and Sinōpē -ēs, f. town on the Black Sea. Sinōpis -idis, f. a kind of red ochre, found near Sinope.

Sīnum, v. 1. sinus.

sinŭo, 1. to bend, curve.

sinŭōsus -a -um, full of windings, sinuous; fig., diffuse.

1. sĭnus -i, m. and sīnum -i, n. a large bowl.

2. sĭnus -ūs, m. a bending, curve, fold; the hanging fold of the toga, the bosom, lap; a bay, gulf.

sĭpārĭum -ii, n. a drop-scene at a theatre; a curtain to exclude the sun.

sīpho (sīpo) -ōnis, m. a siphon.

sĭquando, adv. if ever.

sĭquidem, conj. if indeed; since.

Sīrēn -ēnis, f., usually plur., Sīrēnes -um, f. the Sirens, birds with the faces of women, who by their song lured mariners to destruction.

sīrĭus -ii, m. the dogstar.

sirpĕa and sirpia, v. scirpeus.

sirpĭcŭlus = scirpiculus (q.v.).

sirpus = scirpus (q.v.).

sīs, 1. subj. of sum. 2 = si vis, v. 1. volo.

sisto, stĭti and stĕti, stătum, 3. to cause to stand, put, place; legal, sistere aliquem, to cause to appear before a court of justice; to erect; to stop; to establish; intrans., to stand; to appear in court; to halt; to stand firm; partic., stătus -a -um, fixed, determined.

sistrum -i, n. a rattle used in the worship of Isis.

sĭsymbrĭum -ii, n. an aromatic herb sacred to Venus.

Sĭsyphus (-os) -i, m. condemned in the lower world to roll uphill a great stone which constantly fell back.

sĭtella -ae, f. (dim. of situla), an urn, used for drawing lots.

Sīthon -ŏnis, m. king in the Thracian Chersonese.

sĭtĭcŭlōsus -a -um, very dry, parched.

sĭtĭens, v. sitio.

sĭtĭentĕr, adv. thirstily, eagerly.

sĭtĭo -ivi and -ii -ītum, 4. to thirst, be thirsty; to be dry; to suffer from heat; to be eager; to thirst after; partic., sĭtĭens, thirsting, eager.

sĭtis -is, f. thirst; dryness, drought, eager desire.

sĭtĭtor -ōris, m. one who thirsts.

sĭttӯbus -i, m. a strip of parchment on which the title of a book was written.

sĭtŭla -ae, f. and sĭtŭlus -i, m. a small urn.

1. sĭtus -a -um, v. sino.

2. sĭtus -ūs, m. site, situation; a region of the earth, zone, quarter; rust, mould; filthiness of the body; rusting, dulness.

sīvĕ and seu, conj. or if; sive . . . sive, seu . . . seu, whether . . . or.

smăragdus -i, m. and f. an emerald.

smīlax -ācis, f. bindweed; Smilax, a maiden changed into the plant.

Smintheŭs -ĕi, m. surname of Apollo.

1. smyrna -ae, f. myrrh.

2. Smyrna -ae, f. famous trading town in Ionia. Adj., Smyrnaeus.

smyrrhiza = myrrha (q.v.).

sōbŏles, sōbŏlesco = suboles, subolesco (q.v.).

sōbrĭē, adv. moderately, frugally, soberly.

sōbrīna -ae, f. cousin on the mother's side.

sōbrīnus -i, m. cousin on the mother's side.

sōbrĭus -a -um, sober, not intoxicated; moderate, frugal; fig., sober-minded, prudent.

soccātus -a -um, wearing the soccus.

soccus -i, m. low shoe worn by comic actors.

sŏcer -ĕri, m. father-in-law; plur., soceri, the father- and mother-in-law.

sŏcĕra = socrus (q.v.).

sŏcĭa -ae, f., v. socius.

sŏcĭābĭlis -e, sociable, easily united.

sŏcĭālis -e, social, sociable, conjugal; allied.

sŏcĭālĭtĕr, adv. sociably.

sŏcĭĕtās -ātis, f. society, companionship, fellowship, association; commercial partnership; alliance between states.

sŏcĭo, 1. to combine, associate, share.

sŏcĭus -a -um, taking part, sharing in; subst., sŏcĭus -ii, m. and socia -ae, f. an ally; a partner, companion.

sōcordĭa -ae, f. stupidity, weakness of intellect; carelessness, inactivity.

sōcordĭtĕr, adv. lazily, carelessly.

sōcors -ōrdis, weak-minded, stupid; negligent.

socra = socrus (q.v.).

Sōcrătēs -is, m. the famous Athenian philosopher, contemporary of Zenophon and Alcibiades, put to death on a charge of impiety and of corrupting the youth by his teaching. Adj., Sōcrătĭcus.

Plur. subst., **Sŏcrătĭcĭ -ōrum**, *m.* followers of Socrates.

socrus -ūs, *f.* mother-in-law.

sŏdălĭcĭus -a -um, relating to companionship; *subst.*, **sŏdălĭcĭum -ĭi,** *n.* comradeship, intimacy; a secret society.

sŏdālis -e, relating to comradeship; *subst.*, **sŏdālis -is,** *m.* comrade, mate, friend; attendant on; a boon-companion; a member of a club.

sŏdālĭtas -ātis, *f.* companionship; a club, association.

sŏdes, pray, if you please.

sōl, sōlis, *m.* the sun; *Sol,* the sun-god; *plur., soles* = sunny days.

sōlācĭum = *solatium (q.v.).*

sōlāmen -ĭnis, *n.* a means of consolation, comfort.

sōlāris -e, relating to the sun, solar.

sōlārĭum -ĭi, *n.* sundial; a terrace exposed to the sun.

sōlātĭŏlum -ĭ, *n.* (*dim. of solatium*), a small consolation.

sōlātĭum (sōlācĭum) -ĭi, *n.* a consolation, relief ; a means of help ; compensation.

sōlātor -ōris, *m.* a comforter.

soldurĭi -ōrum, *m.* retainers, vassals.

soldus = *solidus (q.v.).*

sŏlĕa -ae, *f.* a sandal; a shoe for animals; a fish, the sole.

sŏlĕātus -a -um, wearing sandals.

sōlennis = *sollemnis (q.v.).*

sŏlĕo, sŏlĭtus sum, 2. to be accustomed; *ut solet,* as is the custom.

sōlers, sŏlertia = *sollers, sollertia (q.v.).*

sŏlĭdē, *adv.* firmly, densely, solidly; certainly.

sŏlĭdĭtas -ātis, *f.* solidity.

sŏlĭdo, 1. to make dense, solid; to make firm; to join together.

sŏlĭdus -a -um, dense, firm, solid; whole, complete; enduring, substantial; *subst.*, **sŏlĭdum -ĭ,** *n.* the whole sum.

sŏlistĭmum (sollistŭmum) and sollistŭmum trĭpudĭum, the good omen afforded when the sacred chickens ate so eagerly that the food fell out of their beaks.

sōlĭtārĭus -a -um, solitary, lonely; single by itself.

sōlĭtūdo -ĭnis, *f.* solitude, loneliness; want.

sŏlĭtus -a -um, *p. adj.* usual, customary; *subst.*, **sŏlĭtum -ĭ,** *n.* custom.

sŏlĭum -ĭi, *n.* a chair of state, throne; regal power; a bathing-tub of stone *or* wood; a stone coffin.

sŏlĭvāgus -a -um, solitary, single.

sollemnis (sōlemnis, sōlennis) -e, yearly, annual ; solemn, festive, religious; usual, customary; *subst.*, **sollemne -is,** *n.* a solemn rite; a custom.

sollemnĭter (sōlemnĭter, sōlennĭter), *adv.* solemnly; according to custom.

sollers (sōlers) -ertis, clever, skilful; *of things,* ingenious, intelligent.

sollertĕr (sōlertĕr), *adv.* skilfully, adroitly.

sollertĭa (sōlertĭa) -ae, *f.* cleverness, skilfulness, ingenuity.

sollĭcĭtātĭo -ōnis, *f.* instigation, solicitation.

sollĭcĭtē, *adv.* anxiously, carefully (*late*).

sollĭcĭto, 1. to shake, stir, agitate; to weaken; *fig.*, to disturb, trouble; to vex, annoy; to incite; to persuade.

sollĭcĭtūdo -ĭnis, *f.* uneasiness, anxiety, solicitude.

sollĭcĭtus -a -um, stirred up, agitated; uneasy, solicitous; *of animals,* watchful; *act.*, disquieting, causing trouble.

sollĭferrĕum (sōlĭferrĕum) -ĭ, *n.* a javelin entirely of iron.

sollus -a -um = *totus (q.v.).*

1. **sōlo,** 1. to make solitary.

2. **Solo** = *Solon (q.v.).*

Sŏlon (Sŏlo) -ōnis, *m.* one of the Seven Wise Men of Greece, a famous Athenian legislator, living about 600 B.C.

sōlor, 1. *dep.* to comfort; soothe, relieve; to compensate.

solstĭtĭālis -e, relating to the summer solstice; *dies,* the longest day; relating to summer; solar

solstĭtĭum -ĭi, *n.* a solstice; the summer solstice; summer.

1. **sŏlum -ĭ,** the bottom *or* lowest part of anything; floor of a room; the sole of a foot; soil, earth, land; country; *fig.*, ground, foundation.

2. **sōlum,** *adv.* alone, only.

sōlus -a -um, alone, only, sole; solitary, desert.

sōlūtē, *adv.* without impediment, freely; easily; carelessly.

sōlūtĭo -ōnis, *f.* a loosening; payment; dissolution; explanation.

sōlūtus -a -um, *p. adj.* loosened, free; unbound, independent; unhindered; unencumbered; fluent; loose, not carefully constructed, *verba;* unrestrained, dissolute; lazy; negligent.

solvo, solvi, sŏlūtum, 3. to loosen, unbind; to release; to open; *ancoram,* to weigh anchor; to pay a debt; to fulfil an engagement; to break up ; to melt, dissolve; to separate; to relax, *membra ;* to terminate ; (*pass., hiems solvitur,* disappears); to violate; to banish; to solve, explain.

Sŏlўmi -ōrum, *m.* the earliest inhabitants of Lycia, from whom, according to some, the Jews were descended, whence the name Hierosolyma, Jerusalem; *adj.* **Sŏlўmus -a -um,** belonging to Jerusalem *or* the Jews.

somnĭcŭlōsus -a -um, sleepy.

somnĭfer -fĕra -fĕrum, sleep-causing; narcotic.

somnĭo, 1. to dream; to imagine foolishly.

somnĭum -ĭi, *n.* a dream.

somnus -i, *m.* sleep; *somnum tenere,* to keep oneself from sleeping; inactivity.

sŏnābilis -e, sounding, resounding.

sŏnans -antis, *p. adj.* sounding ; *of words,* sonorous.

sŏnĭpēs -pēdis, sounding with the feet; *subst., m.* the horse.

sŏnĭtus -ūs, *m.* a sound, noise.

sŏnīvius -a -um, sounding; *sonivium tripudium,* the noise of the food falling from the beaks of the sacred chickens.

sŏno, sŏnŭi, sŏnĭtum, 1. *intransit.,* to sound, resound, make a noise; to re-echo; *transit.,* to produce a sound; to shout, sing; to celebrate.

sŏnor -ōris, *m.* sound, noise, din.

sŏnōrus -a -um, ringing, loud, sonorous.

sons, sontis, guilty; *subst., sontes,* the guilty.

sonticus -a -um, dangerous; *causa,* a serious, important excuse.

sŏnus -i, *m.* a noise, sound, din; a word; voice, speech; tone.

sŏphia -ae, *f.* wisdom.

sŏphista -ae, *m.* and **sŏphistes** -ac, *m.* a sophist; a quibbler.

Sŏphŏclēs -is, *m., voc.* Sophocle, the famous Greek tragic poet; *adj.,* **Sŏphoclēus.**

1. **sŏphōs** (-us) -i, *m.* wise; *subst.,* a wise man.

2. **sŏphōs**, *adv.* bravo, well done.

sōpio -ivi *and* -ii -itum, 4. to put to sleep; to stun; *pass., sopiri,* to slumber, rest.

sōpor -ōris, *m.* deep sleep; sleepiness, laziness; a sleeping draught.

sŏpōrātus -a -um, *p. adj.* sleeping; stupefying.

sŏpōrĭfĕr -fĕra -fĕrum, causing deep sleep.

sŏpōro, 1. to put to sleep.

sŏpōrus -a -um, sleep-bringing.

Sōracte (Sauracte) -is, *n.* a mountain near Rome.

sorbĕo, sorbŭi, 2. to suck up; to swallow; *fig.,* to swallow, put up with.

sorbilo (sorbillo), 1. (*dim. of sorbeo*), to suck in, sip.

sorbĭtio -ōnis, *f.* a draught, potion.

sorbum -i, *n.* the fruit of the *sorbus.*

sorbus -i, *f.* the service-tree.

sordĕo, sordŭi, 2. to be dirty, filthy; to be mean, sordid in appearance; to be contemptible.

sordes -is, *f. plur.,* sordes -ium, *f.* dirt, filth; dirty garments; meanness, baseness; stinginess.

sordesco, sordŭi, 3. to become dirty.

sordidātus -a -um, wearing dirty clothes; clad in mourning.

sordidē, *adv.* meanly, in a low station; vulgarly; stingily.

sordĭdŭlus -a -um (*dim. of sordidus*), somewhat dirty.

sordidus -a -um, dirty, filthy; in soiled or dirty clothes, as a sign of mourning;

poor, mean, humble; vile, disgraceful; stingy.

sŏrex -icis, *m.* a shrew-mouse.

sŏror, a sister.

sŏrōricīda -ae, *m.* one who murders a sister.

sŏrōrius -a -um, sisterly.

sors, sortis, *f.* a lot; an oracular response, prophecy; lot, fate, fortune, destiny; money, capital.

sorticŭla -ae, *f.* (*dim. of sors*), a little lot *or* ticket.

sortĭlĕgus -a -um, prophetic, oracular; *subst.,* **sortĭlĕgus** -i, *m.* soothsayer.

sortior, 4. *dep.* to cast lots; to decide by lot, *provincium;* to choose; to share, divide; to gain by lot; to obtain; **sortītus** -a -um, *pass.,* gained by lot.

sortītio -ōnis, *f.* a casting lots.

sortīto, *adv.* by lot.

1. **sortītus** -ūs, *m.* a casting of lots.

2. **sortītus** -a -um, *partic. of sortior.*

sospes -itis, safe, unhurt; lucky, favourable.

Sospīta -ae, *f.* the Saviour.

sospito, 1. to keep safe, preserve.

sōtēr -ēris, *acc.* -ēra, *m.* a saviour.

sōtēria -ōrum, *n.* presents given in celebration of a recovery from sickness.

spādix -icis, chestnut-coloured.

spădo -ōnis, *m.* a eunuch.

spargo, sparsi, sparsum, 3. to scatter, sprinkle; to sow; to throw; to disperse; to circulate a report; to distribute; to dissipate property; to tear in pieces, *corpora;* to moisten; to speckle, *alas coloribus.*

sparsio -ōnis, *f.* a sprinkling of perfumed waters in the theatre.

sparsus -a -um, *p. adj.* spread out, scattered; spotted.

Sparta -ae, *f.* and **Spartē** -ēs, *f.* Sparta, the capital of Laconia; *adj.,* **Spartānus;** *subst.,* **Spartiātes** -ae, *m.* a Spartan.

Spartăcus -i, *m.* a gladiator, head of the Gladiatorial War.

spartum (-on) -i, *n.* esparto grass.

spărŭlus -i, *m.* (*dim. of sparus*), a kind of fish, a bream.

spărus -i, *m.* and **spărum** -i, *n.* a hunting-spear.

spătha -ae, *f.* a broad two-edged sword.

spătior, 1. *dep.* to walk about, to take a walk; to spread out.

spătiōsē, *adv.* widely, extensively; *of time,* long.

spătiōsus -a -um, spacious, large; *of time,* long.

spătium -ii, *n.* space, distance, breadth; interval ; circumference, size ; tract, extent; a walk; a place for walking in; space of time; leisure, opportunity.

spĕciālis -e, individual, particular, special.

spĕcies -ēi, *f.* sight, view, look; appearance, *speciem ridentis praebere* ;

form, figure; beauty; spendour; model,
ideal; idea, notion; a dream, phantom;
appearance, show ; a statue, representation; a kind, species.

spĕcillum -i, *n.* a surgeon's probe.

spĕcimen -ĭnis, *n.* mark, token, sample;
a pattern, ideal.

spĕcĭōsē, *adv.* beautifully, showily.

spĕcĭōsus -a -um, beautiful, handsome;
dazzling; imposing, plausible.

spectābĭlis -e, visible; notable.

spectācŭlum -i, *n.* a sight, spectacle; the
stage, the seats; the theatre.

spectātĭo -ōnis, *f.* a looking at, beholding;
inspection of money.

spectātor -ōris, *m.* spectator, observer;
inspector; *formarum*, connoisseur.

spectātrix -īcis, *f.* a female spectator,
observer.

spectātus -a -um, *p. adj.* proved, approved, tried; excellent, renowned.

spectĭo -ōnis, *f.* the right of observing the
auspices.

specto, 1. to contemplate, observe; look
on at; to test, to examine; *of places,* to
look towards, be situate towards; to bear
in mind, strive after; to incline to.

spectrum -i, *n.* the appearance of anything, spectre.

1. **spĕcŭla** -ae, *f.* a watch-tower.

2. **spēcŭla** -ae, *f.* (*dim. of spes*), a little
hope.

spĕcŭlābundus -a -um, watching, on the
watch.

spĕcŭlāris -e, relating to a mirror;
subst., **spĕcŭlāria** -ium *and* -ōrum, *n.*
window-panes made of talc.

spĕcŭlātor -ōris, *m.* scout, spy; observer,
investigator.

spĕcŭlātōrius -a -um, relating to a
scout ; *subst.,* *speculatoriae,* spy-
boats.

spĕcŭlātrix -īcis, *f.* observer, watcher.

spĕcŭlor, 1. *dep.* to spy, to look about;
transit., to spy out, watch, explore.

spĕcŭlum -i, *n.* a mirror; *fig.,* image,
copy.

spĕcus -ūs, *m. f. and n.* a cave; a covered
watercourse; a hole, hollow.

spēlaeum -i, *n.* cave, grotto, hole, den.

spēlunca -ae, *f.* a cave, grotto.

sperno, sprēvi, sprētum, 3. to separate,
remove; to reject, scorn.

spēro, 1. to look for, to expect; to hope,
hope for; to forebode, fear; *subst.,*
spērāta -ōrum, *n.* one's hopes.

spēs -ēi, *f.* hope; that which is hoped for;
spe potitur, realises his hope; expectation of, fear of, foreboding.

sphaera -ae, *f.* a globe, sphere; orbit.

sphaeristērium -ii, *n.* a place for playing ball.

Sphinx, Sphingis, *f.* a female monster at
Thebes, who proposed riddles to all the
passers-by, and destroyed them if they
could not answer the riddles.

spīca -ae, *f.,* **spīcus** -i, *m., and* **spīcum,**
-i, *n.,* a spike; an ear of corn.

spīcĕus -a -um, consisting of ears of
corn.

spīcifer -fĕra -fĕrum, wearing *or* carrying ears of corn.

spīcātus -a -um, having spikes *or* ears.

spīcŭlum -i, *n.* sharp point, sting ;
poet., spear, javelin.

spīcum, spicus = *spica* (*q.v.*).

spīna -ae, *f.* a thorn; spine of the hedge-
hog, *etc.;* the backbone; a fish-bone;
spinae = cares, anxieties, difficulties.

spīnētum -i, *n.* a thornbush (*only in
plur.*).

spīnĕus -a -um, made of thorns, thorny.

spīnĭger -gĕra -gĕrum, thorn-bearing,
poet.

spīnōsus -a -um, thorny, prickly; *of
discourse,* obscure; full of anxiety.

spīnus -i, *m.* the blackthorn.

spīra -ae, *f.* anything coiled, twisted; the
winding of a snake; base of a column;
string for fastening a hat under the chin.

spīrābĭlis -e, that may be breathed;
vital ; fitted for breathing.

spīrācŭlum -i, *n.* air-hole, breathing-
place.

spīrāmen -ĭnis, *n.* a breathing-hole, air-
hole.

spīrāmentum -i, *n.* a breathing-hole, air-
hole; breathing; a short pause.

spīrĭtus -ūs, *m.* a breath of air; breath;
angustior, short breath; life; a sigh;
hissing of a snake ; the voice ; the
spirit, soul; pride, courage; opinion,
feeling; irritation; inspiration.

spīro, 1. *intransit.,* to blow, breathe ;
poet. = to rush, to foam, roar; to live,
be alive; to be inspired; *transit.,* to
breathe, exhale.

spissē, *adv.* densely, closely; slowly.

spissesco, 3. to become thick, thicken.

spisso, 1. to make thick, thicken.

spissus -a -um, close, dense, thick ;
theatrum, full; slow, difficult.

splendĕo, 2. to glitter, be bright; to be
illustrious.

splendesco -dŭi, 3. to become bright.

splendĭdē, *adv.* splendidly, magnificently; clearly.

splendĭdus -a -um, shining, brilliant;
well-sounding; fine, illustrious; clear.

splendor -ōris, *m.* brilliance, lustre;
splendour ; honour, distinction ; clearness.

splēnĭātus -a -um, plastered.

splēnĭum -ii, *n.* an adhesive plaster.

Spŏlētium -ii, *n.* town of Umbria;
adj., Spŏlētinus.

spŏliārium -ii, *n.* the place in the amphitheatre where the slain gladiators were
stripped of their arms and clothing; a
den of robbers.

spŏliātĭo -ōnis, *f.* a plundering.

spŏliātor -ōris, *m.* a plunderer.

spŏliātrix -īcis, f. plundering, she that plunders.

spŏliātus -a -um, p. adj. plundered.

spŏlĭo, 1. to strip, despoil; to plunder.

spŏlĭum -ii, n. the skin or hide stripped from an animal; plur., arms taken from an enemy, booty.

sponda -ae, f. bedstead; a body, a bier.

spondaulĭum (spondaulĭum) -ii, n. a sacrificial hymn, accompanied on the flute.

spondĕo, spŏpondi, sponsum, 2. to pledge oneself, promise solemnly; to be a security; to promise, betroth a daughter; sponsus -i, m. bridegroom, and sponsa -ae, f. bride.

spondēus (spondīus) -i, m. a spondee.

spondўlus -i, m. a kind of mussel.

spongĭa (spongĕa) -ae, f. a sponge; an open-worked cuirass.

spons, spontis, f. free-will; only in genit. and abl., of oneself; without assistance.

sponsa, v. spondeo.

sponsālis -e, relating to a betrothal; subst., sponsālĭa -um or -ōrum, n. a betrothal; betrothal feast.

spousĭo -ōnis, f. a solemn promise, engagement; pledge, guarantee.

sponsor -ōris, m. a surety, bail, guarantee.

sponsum -i, n. that which is guaranteed, a covenant.

1. sponsus -a -um, v. spondeo.

2. sponsus -ūs, m. an engagement.

spontāneus -a -um, voluntary.

spontĕ, spontis, v. spons.

sporta, f. a basket, hamper.

sportella -ae, f. (dim. of sporta), a little basket.

sportŭla -ae, f. (dim. of sporta), a little basket; a gift.

sprētĭo -ōnis, f. a despising.

sprētor -ōris, m. a despiser.

spūma -ae, f. foam, froth, scum.

spūmesco, 3. to begin to foam.

spūmeus -a -um, foaming, frothy.

spūmĭfer -fĕra -fĕrum, foaming.

spūmĭger -gĕra gĕrum, foaming.

spūmo, 1. to foam, froth; to, cover with foam.

spūmōsus -a -um, foaming.

spŭo, spŭi, spūtum, 3. to spit out.

spurcē, adv. filthily; basely.

spurcitĭa -ae, f. and spurcitĭes -ēi, f. dirt, filth.

spurco, 1. to defile, pollute.

spurcus -a -um, filthy, impure; base, mean, low.

spūtātor -ōris, m. a spitter.

spūto, 1. to spit, spit out.

spūtum -i, n. spittle.

squālĕo, 2. to be rough, stiff; to be thickly covered with; to be dirty; to mourn; to be untilled.

squālĭdē, adv. in a slovenly manner.

squālĭdus -a -um, rough, stiff; unpolished; dirty; in mourning attire; waste, desert.

squālor -ōris, m. roughness; filthiness, squalor; dirty clothing as a sign of mourning.

squālus -i, m. a kind of salt-water fish.

squāma -ae, f. a scale; scale armour; a fish

squāmeus -a -um, scaly.

squāmĭfer -fĕra -fĕrum, scaly.

squāmĭger -gĕra -gĕrum, scale-bearing, scaly; subst., squāmĭgĕri -ōrum, m. fishes.

squāmōsus -a -um, scaly.

st! interj. hush! hist!

stābĭlīmen -ĭnis, n. a stay, support.

stābĭlīmentum = stabilimen (q.v.).

stābĭlĭo, 4. to make firm; to establish.

stābĭlis -e, firm, steadfast; subst., stābĭlĭa -ĭum, n. things that are stable.

stābĭlĭtas -ātis, f. firmness, steadfastness; durability.

stābĭlĭtĕr, adv. firmly, durably.

stābŭlo, 1. to have a stall or abode, to stall.

stābŭlor, 1. dep. to be stabled, abide.

stābŭlum -i, n. habitation; den, lair; stable; tavern, pot-house.

stacta -ae, f. and stactē -ēs, f. oil of myrrh.

stădĭum -ii, n. a Greek measure of length; a race-course; fig., contest, emulation.

Stăgīra -ōrum, n. town in Macedonia, birthplace of Aristotle. Stăgīrītes -ae, m. the Stagirite, i.e., Aristotle.

stagno, 1. intransit., to overflow; of places, to be overflowed; transit., to overflow.

stagnum -i, n. standing water, pond, marsh, swamp; (poet.), a sluggish stream of water; an artificial lake.

stāmen -ĭnis, n. the wrap, the thread; stamina ducere or torquere, to spin the string of a lyre; cloth woven of thread; the fillet worn by priests.

stāmĭneus -a -um, full of threads.

stannum -i, n. tin.

Stāta mater = Vesta.

stătārĭus -a -um, steady, stationary; stataria comoedia, a quiet kind of comedy; subst., stătārĭi -ōrum, m. actors in the comoedia stataria.

stătēra -ae, f. a steelyard, a balance.

stătim, adv. firmly, steadfastly; immediately.

stătĭo -ōnis, f. a standing, standing still; a place of abode; of soldiers, post, watch, guard, quarters; resting-place; roadstead, anchorage; the proper place (of things).

Stătĭus -ii, m. Caecilius Statius, Roman comic poet.

stātīvus -a -um, standing still; subst., stātīva -ōrum, n. permanent camp.

1. **stător -ōris,** *m.* a magistrate's attendant.

2. **Stător -ōris,** *m.* a surname of Jupiter.

stătŭa -ae, *f.* a statue, image.

stătŭārius -a -um, relating to statues; *subst.,* **stătŭāria -ae,** *f.* the art of casting statues; **stătŭārius -ii,** *m.* a statuary.

stătūmen -inis, *n.* support, prop; *plur.,* ribs of a ship.

stătŭo -ŭi -ūtum 3. to cause to stand, to place, set up; to build; *tabernacula,* to pitch ; to consider, believe ; to resolve, decide.

stătūra -ae, *f.* stature.

1. **stătus,** *v. sisto.*

2. **stătus -ūs,** *m.* a standing position; posture, position; condition; stability, prosperity; state of the case.

stella -ae, *f.* star, planet; *stella comans,* a comet.

stellans -antis, starry, bright, shining.

stellātus -a -um, set with stars, starry; *ensis,* bright, studded with.

stellĭfĕr -fĕra -fĕrum, starry.

stellĭgĕr -gĕra -gĕrum, starry.

stellio (stēlio) -ōnis, *m.* a lizard with spots on its back.

stemma -ătis, *n.* a crown, chaplet; a genealogical tree.

Stentor -ōris, *m.* one of the Greeks before Troy, famed for his loud voice.

stercŏro, 1. to dung, manure.

stercus -ŏris, *n.* dung, manure.

stĕrilis -e, barren, unfruitful ; vain ; *amor,* unrequited ; *poet.* making unfruitful.

stĕrilitas -ātis, *f.* unfruitfulness, barrenness.

sternax -ācis, throwing to the ground; *equus,* throwing his rider.

sterno, strāvi, strātum, 3. to stretch out, spread out; to lay down, throw down; *se sternere,* to lie down; (**strātus -a -um,** stretched out, prostrate;) *poet. ventos,* to calm; *fig.,* to overthrow; to make smooth, level; to pave; to cover; to saddle a horse

sternūmentum -i, *n.* a sneezing, sneeze.

sternŭo -ŭi, 3. *intransit.,* to sneeze ; *of a light,* to sputter; *transit.,* to give by sneezing: *omen.*

sterquilinium -ii, *n.* a dung-pit.

sterto, 3. to snore.

Sthĕnĕlus -i, *m.* leader of the Argives against Troy.

stĭbādium -ii, *n.* a semicircular sofa.

stĭbium -ii, *n.* (**stibi** *and* **stimmi -is,** *n.*), antimony.

stigma -ătis, *n.* a mark *or* brand put upon slaves; *fig.,* stigma.

stigmătias -ae, *m.* a branded slave.

stilla -ae, *f.* (*dim. of stiria*), a drop.

stillicidium -ii, *n.* a dripping moisture.

stillo, 1. *intransit.,* to drip, drop ; *transit.,* to drop, let drop.

stilus -i, *m.* a stake, pale; the pointed iron *or* bone instrument with which the Romans wrote on their waxen tablets; written composition, mode of writing, style.

stĭmŭlātio -ōnis, *f.* a spurring on.

stĭmŭlo, 1. to goad, prick; to vex, annoy; to incite, stimulate.

stĭmŭlus -i, *m. milit.,* stimuli, pointed stakes to repel the advance of troops ; a goad; *fig.,* a sting, torment; incentive, stimulus.

stinguo, 3. to extinguish.

stĭpātio -ōnis, *f.* a crowd of attendants, retinue.

stĭpātor -ōris, *m.* attendant, follower; *plur.,* retinue.

stĭpendiārius -a -um, liable to taxes, tributary; *vectigal,* a yearly contribution ; *subst.,* **stĭpendiārii -ōrum,** *m.* tributaries. *Of soldiers,* mercenary.

stĭpendium -ii, *n.* a tax, tribute, contribution; punishment; pay of a soldier; military service; campaign.

stĭpes -itis, *m.* a log, trunk of a tree; a stake, post; blockhead.

stipo, 1. to press closely together, compress; to crowd a place; to press round, accompany.

stips, stĭpis, *f.* an offering, gift, alms.

stĭpŭla -ae, *f.* the stalk, haulm; *plur.* = straw; a reed-pipe.

stĭpŭlātio -ōnis, *f.* a verbal agreement, stipulation.

stĭpŭlātiuncŭla -ae, *f.* (*dim. of stipulatio*), an unimportant engagement *or* stipulation.

stĭpŭlātor -ōris, *m.* one who stipulates for.

stĭpŭlor, 1. *dep.* to demand, stipulate for.

stīria -ae, *f.* an icicle.

stirpĭtŭs, *adv.* root and branch, thoroughly.

stirps (stirpes, stirpis), stirpis, *f.* the stock *or* stem of a tree; the trunk; a branch ; a plant, stalk, root ; *of men,* family, race, offspring ; foundation, origin.

stīva -ae, *f.* a plough-handle.

stlātārius -a -um, brought by sea, *and therefore,* costly.

stloppus -i, *m.* the noise of a slap on the inflated cheeks.

sto, stĕti, stătum, stătūrus, stāre, to stand; to remain standing; *milit.,* to be stationed ; *of ships,* to be at anchor; to stand upright ; *with abl.,* to be loaded with; to support; to rest upon; to cost ; *milit.,* to stand, hold one's ground; to remain; to be fixed; to be resolved; *stat per aliquem,* foll. *by quominus and subj.,* it is owing to some one that not.

Stŏĭcē, *adv.* like a Stoic, stoically.

Stŏĭcus -a -um, Stoic; *subst.*, **Stŏĭcus -i**, *m.* a Stoic philosopher; **Stŏĭca -ōrum**, *n.* the Stoic philosophy.

stŏla -ae, *f.* a long outer garment.

stŏlātus -a -um, clad in a stola.

stŏlĭdē, *adv.* stupidly, foolishly.

stŏlĭdus -a -um, stupid, obtuse; indolent.

stŏmăchor, 1. *dep.* to be angry, irritated.

stŏmăchōsē, *adv.* peevishly, angrily.

stŏmăchōsus -a -um, irritable, angry.

stŏmăchus -i, *m.* the gullet; the stomach; *stomachus bonus*, a good digestion = good humour ; taste, liking ; dislike, vexation, anger.

stŏrĕa (stŏria) -e, *f.* a rush mat.

strābo -ōnis, *m.* a squintor ; *fig.* an envious person.

străges -is, *f.* overthrow, downfall; dying away through illness; a defeat, massacre, a fallen mass.

strāgŭlum, *v. stragulus.*

strāgŭlus -a -um, covering ; *subst.*, **strāgŭlum -i**, *n.* a covering, carpet, mattress.

strāmen -ĭnis, *n.* a straw, litter.

strāmentārius -a -um, relating to straw.

strāmentum -i, *n.* the stalk of corn, straw, litter; a saddle, housing *(for mules)*.

strāmĭnĕus -a -um, made of straw.

strangŭlo, 1. to choke, strangle; *fig.*, to torture.

strătēgēma -ătis, *n.* a piece of generalship, a stratagem.

strātum -i, *n.* a covering; rug, bed, blanket; a horse-cloth, saddle; a pavement.

strātus -a -um, *partic. of sterno.*

strēna -ae, *f.* a new year's gift.

strēnŭē, *adv.* briskly, promptly, strenuously.

strēnŭĭtās -ātis, *f.* promptness, activity.

strēnŭus -a -um, brisk, prompt, strenuous, vigorous; turbulent, restless.

strĕpĭto, 1. to make a loud noise, to rustle, rattle, clatter.

strĕpĭtus -ūs, *m.* clattering, crashing, creaking, rumbling; *poet.*, a measured regular sound.

strĕpo ŭi ĭtum, 3. to creak, rattle, clash, rumble, clatter; *of places*, to resound.

strictim, *adv.* closely; *fig.*, superficially, briefly, summarily.

strictūra -ae, *f.* a bar of iron.

strictus -a -um, *p. adj.* drawn together; close, tight; brief, concise; *of character*, severe, strict.

strīdĕo (strīdo), strīdi -ēre *and* **-ĕre**, to make a harsh noise, to creak, grate, hiss, *etc.*, *of bees*, to hum.

strīdor -ōris, *m.* a creaking, grating, hissing, whistling noise, *etc.*

strīdŭlus -a -um, creaking, hissing, whistling, grating.

strĭges -um, *f.*, *v. strix.*

strĭgĭlis -is, *abl.* **-i**, *genit. plur.* **-ium**, *f.* a scraper used by bathers.

strĭgōsus -a -um, lean, thin ; *of an orator*, dry.

stringo, strinxi, strictum, 3. to draw tight together, to bind together; to strip off, pluck, prune; to draw a weapon from its sheath; to graze, to wound slightly; *fig.*, to touch, affect.

stringor -ōris, *m.* a drawing together.

strix, strĭgis, *f.* a screech-owl.

strŏpha -ae, *f. and* **strŏphē -ēs**, *f.* a trick, artifice.

Strŏphădes -um, *f.* two islands, abode of the Harpies.

strŏphĭum -ĭi, *n.* a stomacher ; a chaplet.

structĭlis -e, used in building.

structor -ōris, *m.* a builder, mason, carpenter ; a slave who arranged the table.

structūra -ae, *f.* a building, constructing; *concr.* a building; an arrangement, *of words.*

strŭes -is, *f.* a heap; a dense mass.

strūma -ae, *f.* a scrofulous tumour.

strūmōsus -a -um, afflicted with struma.

strŭo, struxi, structum, 3. to join together, pile up; to build; to devise, contrive; to arrange; to load with.

Strȳmo (-on) -ōnis *and* **-ŏnos**, *m.* one of the most important rivers of Thrace.

stŭdĕo -ŭi, 2. to be eager, take pains about anything, to be busy with, aim at; *with dat.*, *praeturae*; to support, favour, *alicui.*

stŭdĭōsē, *adv.* eagerly, diligently; intentionally.

stŭdĭōsus -a -um, zealous, diligent, fond of; favourable to; studious; *subst.* **stŭdĭōsi -ōrum**, *m.* students.

stŭdĭum -ĭi, *n.* zeal, eagerness, fondness, desire ; inclination ; attachment to, devotion to ; application to learning, study.

stultē, *adv.* foolishly, sillily.

stultĭtĭa -ae, *f.* folly, stupidity.

stultus -a -um, foolish, fatuous; *subst.*, **stultus -i**, *m.* a simpleton, fool.

stŭpa = *stuppa (q.v.).*

stŭpĕfăcĭo -fēci -factum, 3. *(pass.,* **stŭpĕfĭo -factus sum -fĭĕri**), to benumb, stun, stupefy; **stŭpĕfăctus**, astounded.

stŭpĕo -ŭi, 2. to be struck senseless, to be stunned ; *partic.*, *stupens*, stunned, stupefied ; to be astonished, amazed ; *of things*, to stand still, to rest.

stŭpesco, 3. to begin to be amazed.

stŭpĭdĭtas -ātis, *f.* dullness, stupidity.

stŭpĭdus -a -um, senseless, stunned; stupid, dull.

stŭpor -ōris, *m.* senselessness, insensibility; astonishment; stupidity.

stuppa (stūpa) -ae, *f.* tow, oakum.

stuppĕus (stūpĕus) - -um, made of tow *or* oakum.

stŭpro, 1. to defile,

stuprum -i, *n.* pollution, violation.

sturnus -i, *m.* a starling.

Stỹgiālis, Stygius, *v. Styx.*

Stymphālus (-os) -i, *m. and* Stymphālum -i, *n.* a lake in Arcadia, the abode of birds of prey.

Styx, Stỹgis *and* Stỹgos, *acc.* Stỹgem *and* Stỹga, *f.* a river in the infernal regions. Stỹgiālis -e, Stygian. Stỹgius -a -um, Stygian, infernal.

suādĕo, suāsi, suāsum, 2. *intransit.*, to advise, give advice, persuade; *transit.*, to advise, recommend something, recommend to.

suāsio -ōnis, *f.* advice; the advocacy of a proposed law; eloquence of the persuasive kind.

suāsor -ōris, *m.* adviser, counsellor; one who advocates a proposed law.

suāsōrius -a -um, relating to persuasion; *subst.*, suāsōria -ae, *f.* persuasive discourse *or* eloquence.

suāsus -ūs, *m.* exhorting, persuasion.

suāvĕ, *adv.* sweetly, pleasantly.

suāvĕŏlens -entis, *and* suāvĕ ŏlens -entis, sweet-smelling.

suāvĭdĭcus -a -um, sweetly speaking.

suāvillum (sāvillum) -i, *n.* a kind of sweet cake.

suāvĭlŏquens -entis, agreeable.

suāvĭlŏquentĭa -ae, *f.* agreeable manner of speaking.

suāvĭlŏquus = *suaviloquens* (*q.v.*).

suāvĭŏlum = *saviolum* (*q.v.*).

suāvĭor = *savior* (*q.v.*).

suāvis -e, pleasant, agreeable.

suāvĭtas -ātis, *f.* agreeableness, pleasantness.

suāvĭtĕr, *adv.* agreeably, pleasantly.

suāvĭtūdo = *suavitas* (*q.v.*).

suāvĭum = *savium* (*q.v.*).

sŭb, *prep. with abl. and acc. With abl. of place*, under ; at the foot of ; *of time*, at, *sub luce. With acc., of place, to express motion;* under, very near to, *sub montem succedunt milites; of time*, about, towards ; *sub noctem*, about night, towards night.

sŭbabsurdē, *adv.* somewhat absurdly.

sŭbabsurdus -a -um, somewhat absurd.

sŭbaccūso, 1. to accuse, blame.

sŭbactio -ōnis, *f.* a preparing; preparation, discipline.

sŭbactus, *part. of subigo* (*q.v.*).

sŭbagrestis -e somewhat rustic.

sŭbāmārus -a -um, somewhat bitter.

sŭbarrŏgantĕr, *adv.* somewhat arrogantly.

sŭbausculto, 1. to listen secretly.

subcăvus -a -um, somewhat hollow.

subcentŭrio = *succenturio* (*q.v.*).

subcingo = *succingo* (*q.v.*).

subcontŭmēliōsē, *adv.* somewhat insolently.

subcresco = *succresco* (*q.v.*).

bcrispus -a -um, somewhat curled.

subcumbo = *succumbo* (*q.v.*).

subdifficilis -e, somewhat difficult.

subdiffīdo, 3. to be somewhat mistrustful.

subditīvus -a -um, not genuine, false.

subdo -didi -ditum, 3. to put, set under; (*partic., subditus, of places*, lying near;) to subdue; to substitute: to counterfeit.

subdŏcĕo 2. to assist in teaching.

subdŏlē *adv.* somewhat slyly.

subdŏlus -a -um, somewhat sly.

subdŭbito 1. to doubt *or* hesitate a little, be undecided.

subdūco -duxi -ductum, 3. to draw from under, to withdraw, take away; to steal; *se subducere*, to withdraw secretly ; *subducere rationem*, to balance an account, cast up; to lift up; to haul up a ship.

subductio -ōnis, *f.* the drawing up of a ship on dry land; a reckoning, computing.

subdūrus -a -um, somewhat hard.

sŭbēdo -ēdi -ēsum, 3. to eat under, wear away.

sŭbĕo -ii -itum -īre, to go under, come under, pass under, dive under, crawl under; to approach to; to advance to, climb to; to approach secretly *or* gradually, to steal into; to submit to, to take upon oneself; to undertake; to come upon one, happen to ; *of thoughts*, to occur; to follow.

sŭber -ĕris, *n.* the cork-tree.

subf . . . *v. suff.* . . .

subg . . . *v. sugg.* . . .

sŭbhorrĭdus -a -um, somewhat rough.

subiăcĕo -iăcŭi, 2. (*late*) to lie under; to be subject to; to be connected with.

subicio -iēci -iectum, 3. to throw, place, put under; *milit.*, to advance near; to present; to subdue; to expose; to have sold by auction; to subordinate; to append; to whisper to, to suggest; to raise, lift ; to haul from under ; to substitute ; to forge, counterfeit ; to suborn.

subiectē, *adv. only in superl.*, submissively.

subiectio -ōnis, *f.* a laying under, placing under; a counterfeiting, forging.

subiecto, 1. to place under; to throw up from below.

subiector -ōris, *m.* a forger.

subiectus -a -um, *p. adj. with dat.* lying near, adjacent; subject to; exposed to; *subst.*, subiecti -ōrum, *m.* subjects, dependents.

sŭbigo -ēgi -actum, 3. to drive under *or* to a place; to force, compel; to work through, to work thoroughly; to plough, cultivate; to tame; to train, inure; to subdue.

sŭbimpŭdens -entis, somewhat impudent.

sŭbĭnānis -e, somewhat vain.

sŭbindĕ, *adv.* immediately after; repeatedly, from time to time.

sŭbinsulsus -a -um, somewhat insipid.

sŭbinvĭdĕo, 2. to envy somewhat; **sŭbin-vīsus,** somewhat hated.

sŭbinvīto, 1. to invite secretly.

sŭbīrascor -īrasci, *dep.* to be a little angry.

sŭbīrātus -a -um, somewhat angry.

sŭbĭtārius -a -um, sudden, hasty

subĭto, *adv.* suddenly, unexpectedly; *dicere,* to speak extempore.

sŭbĭtus -a -um, *p. adj.* sudden, unexpected; *subst.,* **sŭbĭtum** -i, *n.* a sudden occurrence, unexpected chance.

sublungo -iunxi -iunctum, 3. to unite to; to yoke; to subdue.

sublābor -lapsus sum -lābi, 3. *dep.* to glide in, slide in, to glide away.

sublātē, *adv.* highly; sublimely; haughtily.

sublātio -ōnis, *f.* a lifting up, elevation.

sublātus -a -um, *p. adj.* raised aloft, haughty.

sublĕgo -lēgi -lectum, 3. to gather below, pick up; to carry off; to choose in the place of another.

sublĕvātio -ōnis, *f.* a relieving, assuaging.

sublĕvo, 1. to lift up, hold up; to diminish; to relieve by consoling; to support, *causam.*

sublĭca -ae, *f.* a pile, palisade.

sublĭcius -a -um, resting upon piles.

sublĭgācŭlum -i, *n.* a cloth worn round the loins.

sublĭgo, 1. to bind below, bind on.

sublīmē, *adv., v. sublimis.*

sublīmis -e (**sublīmus** -a -um), high; exalted; in the air, aloft; sublime; *subst.,* **sublīmě** -is, *n.* height; *adv.* **sublīme,** on high, aloft.

sublīmitas -ātis, *f.* loftiness; height; sublimity.

sublīmĭter, *adv.* aloft, on high.

sublīmus, *v. sublimis.*

sublīno -lēvi -lĭtum, 3. to lay on colour as a ground; to line, overlay; *os alicui,* to deceive.

sublūcĕo -luxi, 2. to gleam forth, glimmer.

sublŭo, *no perf.* -lūtum, 3. to wash from below; to flow beneath, flow at the foot of.

sublustris -e, having a glimmering light.

submergo -mersi -mersum, 3. to plunge under, to sink; *pass., submergi* = to dive *or* plunge under, to be drowned.

submĭnistro, 1. to aid, give, supply.

submissē (**summissē**), *adv.* softly, calmly; humbly.

submissim (**summissim**), *adv.* gently, quietly.

submissio (**summissio**) -ōnis, *f.* sinking, lowering.

submissus (**summissus**) -a -um, *p. adj.* lowered, low; *the voice,* low, soft, gentle; *of discourse,* quiet, mild; unpretentious; mean, abject; humble.

submitto (**summitto**) -mīsi -missum, 3. to lower; *in pass., submitti,* to slope down; (*fig.,* cause to sink; *se,* to abase oneself; to diminish; to give over; to subject to; to slacken); to place under; (*fig.,* to submit); to send up from below, to raise; to cause to spring up; to produce; to let grow; to rear; to send secretly.

submŏlĕstē (**summŏlestē**), *adv.* with some vexation.

submŏlestus (**summŏlestus**) -a -um, somewhat vexatious.

submŏnĕo (**summŏnĕo**) -mŏnŭi, 2. to remind secretly.

submŏrōsus (**summŏrōsus**) -a -um, somewhat morose.

submŏtor (**summŏtor**) -ōris, *m.* one who clears a space in a crowd.

submŏvĕo (**summŏvĕo**) -mōvi -mōtum, 2. to remove, cause to withdraw; *of the lictor,* to clear away, to keep off *the people;* to expel; to drive away, force back; *pass. partic., submotus,* remote; to force from, compel to give up.

submūto (**summūto**), 1. to exchange.

subnascor -nātus sum, 3. *dep.* to grow up under.

subnecto, *no perf.* -nexum, 3. to bind, tie; to join together.

subnĕgo, 1. to deny a little, partly deny.

subnixus (**subnīsus**) -a -um, propped under; supported by, resting upon; *fig.,* trusting, depending upon.

subnŏto, 1. (*late*) to mark beneath, write underneath; to notice secretly.

subnŭba -ae, *f.* a rival (*poet.*).

subnūbĭlus -a -um, somewhat cloudy.

subo, 1. to be in heat.

sŭbobscoenus (**sŭbobscēnus**) -a -um, somewhat obscene.

sŭbobscūrus -a -um, somewhat obscure.

sŭbŏdiōsus -a -um, somewhat unpleasant.

sŭboffendo, 3. to give some offence.

sŭbŏlĕo, 2. to detect (*impers.*).

sŭbŏles (**sŏbŏles**) -is, *gent. plur.* -um, a sprout, offshoot; race, offspring.

sŭbŏlesco, 3. to grow up.

sŭbŏrior, 4. *dep.* to arise, come forth.

sŭborno, 1. to furnish, equip; to incite secretly.

sŭbortus -ūs, *m.* a coming forth, arising.

subp . . . v. supp . . . .

subrādo (**surrādo**) -rāsi -rasum, 3. to scrape below.

subrancidus (**surrancidus**) -a -um, somewhat putrid.

subraucus (**surraucus**) -a -um, somewhat hoarse.

subrectus (**surrectus**), *v. subrigo.*

subrēmigo (**surrēmigo**), 1. to row underneath, row along.

subrēpo (**surrēpo**) -repsi -reptum, 3. to creep to, approach imperceptibly.

subrīdĕo (**surrīdĕo**) -rīsi -rīsum, 2. to smile.

subrīdĭcŭlē (**surrīdĭcŭlē**), *adv.* somewhat laughably.

subrigo (surrigo) *and contr.* surgo, subrexi (surrexi), subrectum (surrectum), 3. to raise on high, lift up; *partic.*, *subrectus*, rising up; surgo, *transit.*, to raise, lift; *intransit.*, to rise, stand up; to come forward; to arise, appear, *dies*; to grow up, spring up, be built.

subriguus (surriguus) -a -um, watered.

subringor (surringor), 3. *dep.* to make a somewhat wry face.

subripio = *surripio* (*q.v.*).

subrogo (surrogo), 1. to cause a person to be chosen as substitute for another.

subrostrani (surrostrani) -orum, *m.* idlers.

subrubeo (surrubeo), 2. to be somewhat red; *part.*, *subrubens* = reddish.

subrubicundus (surrubicundus) -a -um, reddish.

subruo (surruo) -rui -rutum, 3. to dig under, destroy.

subrusticus (surrusticus) -a -um, somewhat clownish.

subscribo -scripsi -scriptum, 3. to write under; to sign a document; to support; to prosecute; to make a note of.

subscriptio -onis, *f.* inscription ; the signing of a document; register.

subscriptor -oris, *m.* the signer of an indictment, a joint-accuser.

subsecivus = *subsicivus* (*q.v.*).

subseco -secui -sectum, 1. to cut away below.

subsellium -ii, *n.* a low bench *or* form; *subsellia* = *iudicia*, courts.

subsequor -secutus (-sequutus) sum, 3. *dep.* to follow, follow after; imitate any-one.

subservio, 4. to serve, comply with.

subsicivus (subsecivus) -a -um, cut off; *subst.*, subsecivum -i, *n.* a remainder *or* small parcel of land; *of time*, spare; *tempora*, leisure hours.

subsidiarius -a -um, reserve; *subst.*, subsidiarii -orum, *m.* reserve troops.

subsidior, 1. *dep.* to serve as a reserve.

subsidium -ii, *n. milit.*, a reserve, auxiliary forces; help, succour; *subsidio esse*, to be a help to; a place of refuge.

subsido -sedi *and* -sidi -sessum, 3. to sit down ; settle down, sink down ; lurk in ambush; to abate; to stay, remain, settle.

subsignanus -a -um, serving beneath the standard.

subsigno, 1. sign, subscribe; to register; to pledge.

subsilio (sussilio) -silui, 4. to leap up.

subsisto -stiti, 3. *transit.*, to withstand; *intransit.*, to stand still, halt ; to cease ; to remain, abide; to continue; to oppose, hold out; *fig.*, to support.

subsortior -sortitus sum, 4. *dep.* to choose by lot, to substitute.

subsortitio -onis, *f.* the choosing of a judicial substitute by lot.

substantia -ae, *f.* substance, essence (*late*), property, means of subsistence.

substerno -stravi -stratum, 3. to spread beneath, lay under; to cover; *fig.*, to offer, give up.

substituo -ui -utum, 3. to put under; substitute.

substo, 1. to stand firm.

substrictus -a -um, *p. adj.* narrow, tight, small.

substringo -strinxi -strictum, 3. to draw together, to tie beneath, bind up.

substructio -onis, *f.* base, foundation.

substruo -struxi -structum, 3. to lay a foundation.

subsultim, *adv.* springing up.

subsulto (sussulto), 1. to spring up, leap.

subsum -fui -esse, to be under; to be behind; to be near at hand; *fig.*, to be subjected to; to exist, to be in question.

subsutus -a -um, sewed beneath; edged below.

subtemen (subtegmen) -inis, *n.* the weft *or* woof in weaving; thread, yarn.

subter, *adv. and prep.*, beneath, below.

subterfugio -fugi, 3. *transit.*, to escape by stealth, evade.

subterlabor -lapsus sum, 3. *dep.* to glide, flow under; to escape.

subterraneus -a -um, subterranean.

subtexo -texui -textum, 3. to weave beneath; to draw together under; to cover, darken; to weave on to; to join to; *in speech*, to connect, subjoin.

subtilis -e, finely woven; fine, slender; accurate; *of expression*, plain, simple, unadorned; *of the senses*, fine, acute.

subtilitas -atis, *f.* thinness, fineness, minuteness; accuracy, subtlety; plainness, simplicity.

subtiliter, *adv.* finely, minutely; accurately; plainly, simply.

subtimeo, 2. to be a little afraid.

subtraho -traxi -tractum, 3. to draw away secretly; remove.

subtristis -e, somewhat sad.

subturpiculus -a -um, somewhat disgraceful.

subturpis -e, somewhat disgraceful.

subtus, *adv.* below, underneath.

subucula -ae, *f.* an inner tunic, shirt.

subula -ae, *f.* a shoemaker's awl.

subulcus -i, *m.* a swineherd.

Subura -ae, *f.* a street in the noisiest quarter of Rome.

suburbanitas -atis, *f.* nearness to the city.

suburbanus -a -um, near the city, suburban; *subst.*, suburbanum -i, *n.* an estate near Rome; suburbani -orum, *m.* inhabitants of the suburbs.

suburbium -ii, *n.* a suburb.

suburgeo, 2. to drive close to.

sŭbūro (*no perf.*) -ustum, 3. to singe.
Sŭburra = *Subura* (*q.v.*).
subvectio -ōnis, *f.* a carrying, transport.
subvecto, 1. to carry, convey.
subvectus = *subvectio* (*q.v.*).
subvĕho -vexi -vectum, 3. to bring up
stream, convey.
subvĕnĭo *(sub* -veniunt, 3. to come up
to aid, to assist, to remedy an evil.
subvĕrĕor, 2. to be a little anxious.
subversor -ōris, *m.* an overthrower.
subvĕrto (subvorto) -verti (-vorti)
-versum (-vorsum), 3. to overthrow; to
ruin, destroy.
subvexus -a -um, sloping upward.
subvŏlo, 1. to fly up, fly forth.
subvolvo, 3. to roll up.
succăvus = *subcavus* (*q.v.*).
succēdo -cessi -cessum, 3. to go under;
to ascend, mount; to submit to; approach; to march forward, advance; to
take the place of, *defatigatis*; to follow,
succeed to; to prosper, succeed; *suc-
cedit*, it is successful.
succendo -cendi -censum, 3. to kindle,
set on fire from below; to inflame.
succenseo = *suscenseo* (*q.v.*).
1. succentŭrĭo, 1. to receive in a century as a substitute; to substitute.
2. succentŭrĭo -ōnis, *f.* an under-
centurion.
successio -ōnis, *f.* a succeeding, succession.
successor -ōris, *m.* a successor.
successus -ūs, *m.* an advance, approach;
happy issue.
succĭdĭa -ae, *f.* a flitch of bacon.
1. succĭdo -cĭdi, 3. to fall under, sink.
2. succĭdo -cīdi -cīsum, 3. to cut off, cut
down.
succĭdŭus -a -um, falling, sinking.
succinctus -a -um, *p. adj.* ready,
equipped; short.
succingo -cinxi -cinctum, 3. to gird up,
tuck up the clothes in the girdle; *partic.*,
succinctus -a -um, with the clothes
tucked up; to surround; arm, prepare,
provide; *partic.*, succinctus -a -um,
armed with.
succĭno, 3. to sing to, to accompany; to
agree, chime in with.
succlāmātĭo -ōnis, *f.* a shouting, acclamation.
succlāmo (subclāmo), 1. to shout at,
call out.
succollo, 1. to take upon the shoulders.
succontŭmēllōsē = *subcontumeliose*
(*q.v.*).
succresco (subcresco) -crēvi -crētum,
3. to grow beneath, grow up, increase.
succrispus = *subcrispus* (*q.v.*).
succumbo -cŭbŭi -cŭbĭtum, 3. to lie
down under, sink down; *fig.*, to yield.
succŭro -curri -cursum, 3. to run or
go under; to come into the thoughts of;
to hasten to help; to help, succour.

successus -ūs, *m.* a shaking.
succŭtĭo -curri -cussum, 3. to shake up
fling aloft.
sūcĭdus -a -um, juicy, full of sap.
sūcĭnum -i, *n.* amber.
sūcĭnus -a -um, of amber.
sūco ῥόνίς, *m.* a rucker *(applied to a
sucker).*
sŭcus (succus) -i, *m.* juice, sap; taste;
vigour; any thick fluid; a draught,
potion.
sūdārĭum -ii, *n.* a handkerchief.
sūdātōrĭus -a -um, producing perspiration; *subst.*, sūdātōrĭum -ii, *n.* a
sweating-room.
sūdātrix -īcis, *f. toga*, causing perspiration.
sūdis -is, *f.* a stake, pile.
sūdo, 1. to sweat, perspire; to drip; to
toil; *transit.*, to sweat out, to exude.
sūdor -ōris, *m.* sweat, perspiration;
fatigue, effort.
sūdus -a -um, dry, without moisture;
bright, cloudless; *subst.*, sūdum -i, *n.*
bright weather.
Suēbi -ōrum, *m.* a German nation. Suēbĭa
-ae, *f.* the country of the Suebi.
sŭēo, 2. to be accustomed.
suesco, suēvi, suētum, 3. to become accustomed, inured to; *suevi*, I am accustomed.
Suessĭōnes -um, *m.* a Gallic people.
Suētōnĭus -ii, *m.*, *C. Suetonius Tranquillus*, author of the Lives of the Caesars.
suētus -a -um, *p. adj.* accustomed to;
usual.
Suēvi = *Suebi* (*q.v.*).
sūfes (suffes) -ētis, *m.* the highest
magistrate in Carthage.
suffarcĭno, 1. to stuff full, cram.
suffarrānĕus -a -um, carrying corn.
suffĕro, sufferre, to carry under, put
under; to support; *se sufferre*, stand
upright; to bear, endure.
suffertus -a -um, stuffed full, crammed
full.
suffes = *sufes* (*q.v.*).
sufficio -fēci -fectum, 3. to put under;
to imbue, suffuse; to add; to choose as
a substitute; *suffectus consul*, a consul
chosen in the place of another; to supply; to give; *intransit.*, to be sufficient;
with infin., to be able.
suffīgo -fixi -fixum, 3. to fasten, fix
beneath; *aliquem cruci*.
suffimen = *suffimentum* (*q.v.*).
suffimentum -i, *n.* incense.
suffĭo -ivi *and* -ii -ītum; *intransit.*, to
burn incense; *transit.*, to fumigate,
perfume; to warm.
sufflāmen -inis, *n.* a drag, clog; obstacle.
sufflo, 1. *intransit.*, to blow upon; *transit.*,
to puff up, inflate.
suffōco, 1. to strangle, choke, suffocate.

suffŏdio -fōdi -fossum, 3. to pierce, undermine; to stab from below.

suffrāgātio -ōnis, f. favourable vote, support.

suffrāgātor -ōris, m. a political supporter.

suffrāgātōrius -a -um, relating to the support of a candidate.

suffrāgium -ii, n. a voting tablet, a ballot; vote, support; franchise.

suffrāgor, 1. dep. to vote in anyone's favour; to approve, support.

suffringo -frēgi -fractum, 3. to break underneath, break in pieces.

suffŭgio -fūgi -fŭgitum, 3. to fly to any place; transit., to evade.

suffŭgium -ii, n. a place of refuge; a resort, remedy.

suffulcio -fulsi -fultum, 4. to underprop.

suffundo -fūdi -fūsum, 3. to pour beneath, suffuse ; to bedew, colour, fill with; to pour out, pour into.

Sŭgambri (**Sўgambri, Sĭgambri**) -ōrum, m. a German tribe.

suggĕro -gessi -gestum, 3. to carry, put, place under; to add, subjoin; to place next; to put upon secretly; to furnish, supply; to give opportunity for.

suggestum -i, n. a heap, height, elevation; a platform.

suggestus -ūs, m. an elevation, height; a platform.

suggill . . . v. sugill . . .

suggrandis -e, somewhat large.

suggrĕdior -gressus sum, 3. dep. to approach, to attack.

sŭgillātio -ōnis, f. a mocking, insulting.

sŭgillo, 1. to beat black and blue; to insult.

sūgo, sūxi, suctum, 3. to such; fig., to suck in, imbibe.

sŭi (genit.), of himself, herself, itself, themselves; dat., sibi, to himself, etc.

sŭillus -a -um, relating to swine, swinish.

sulco, 1. to furrow, plough, cut through; to sail over.

sulcus -i, m. a furrow; a long, narrow trench.

sulfur (sulphur) -ūris, n. sulphur.

sulfŭrātio -ōnis, f. a vein of sulphur in the earth.

sulfŭrātus -a -um, containing sulphur, sulphureous; subst., **sulfŭrāta** -ōrum, brimstone matches; veins of sulphur.

sulfŭrĕus -a -um, sulphureous.

Sulla (Sylla) -ae, m. the name of a family in the gens Cornelia, e.g. L. Cornelius Sulla, the dictator; adj., **Sullānus** (**Syllānus**); subst., **Sullāni**, partisans of Sulla. **sullātūrio**, 4. to wish to imitate Sulla.

Sulmo -ōnis, m. birthplace of Ovid; adj., **Sulmōnensis** -e.

sulphur = sulfur (q.v.).

Sulpicius -a -um, name of a Roman gens.

sultis = si vultis, v. volo.

sum, fŭi, esse, to be, to exist.

sūmen -inis, n. the udder of a sow; a sow, pig.

summa -ae, f. the highest, the highest place; the main thing, most important point; the whole; belli, supreme command; the sum total; a sum of money; a quantity; ad summam, adv. in a word, in short.

summātim, adv. summarily, briefly.

summātus -ūs, m. the chief authority.

summē, adv. in the highest degree, extremely.

summergo = submergo (q.v.).

sumministro = subministro (q.v.).

summissē = submisse (q.v.).

summissim = submissim (q.v.).

summissio = submissio (q.v.).

summissus = submissus (q.v.).

summitto = submitto (q.v.).

summŏlestē = submoleste (q.v.).

summŏlestus = submolestus (q.v.).

summŏnĕo = submoneo (q.v.).

summŏpĕre, adv. very much, exceedingly.

summŏrōsus = submorosus (q.v.).

summōtor = submotor (q.v.).

summŏvĕo = submoveo (q.v.).

summŭla -ae, f. (dim. of summa), a little sum.

summus -a -um, superl. of superus (q.v.).

summūto = submuto (q.v.).

sūmo, sumpsi, sumptum, 3. to take, lay hold of; pecuniam mutuam, to borrow; to put on; to buy; to hire; to employ; supplicium, to punish; to choose; to begin; to mention, assert; to assume; to take upon oneself.

sumptio -ōnis, f. an assumption.

sumptŭārius -a -um, relating to expense, sumptuary; lex.

sumptŭōsē, adv. in a costly manner, sumptuously.

sumptŭōsus -a -um, expensive, sumptuous; extravagant.

sumptus -ūs, m. cost, expense.

Sūnĭŏn (-ium) -ii, n. a promontory in Attica.

sŭo, sŭi, sūtum, 3. to sew, join together.

sŭopte, v. suus.

sŭŏvĕtaurilia (**sōlĭtaurīlia**) -ium, n. a purificatory sacrifice of a pig, a sheep, and a bull.

sŭpellex -lectilis, abl. -lectile and -lectili, f. household furniture; ornament, equipment.

1. **sŭper** -a -um, v. superus.

2. **sŭper,** adv. over, above, on the top of; from above; besides; super quam, moreover ; thereupon ; more ; prep. with abl. and acc. over, above.

sŭpĕrā, adv. over ; prep. with acc., over.

sŭpĕrābilis -e, that can be ascended; that can be conquered.

sŭpĕraddo -addĭdi -addĭtum, 3. to add over and above.

sŭpĕrans -antis, *p. adj.*, prevailing.

sŭpĕrātor -ōris, *m.* a conqueror.

sŭperbē, *adv.* proudly, haughtily.

sŭperbia ae, *f.* pride, haughtiness ; lofty spirit, honourable pride.

sŭperbĭfĭcus -a -um, making proud.

sŭperbio, 4. to be proud, to pride oneself on; to be splendid.

sŭperbus -a -um, proud, haughty; distinguished; magnificent.

sŭperciliōsus -a -um, severe, gloomy.

sŭpercĭlĭum -ii, *n.* the eyebrow; ridge, summit; pride, arrogance.

sŭpĕrēmĭnĕo, 2. to project over, overtop.

sŭperfĭcies -ēi, *f.* the top, surface.

sŭperfixus -a -um, fixed on the top.

sŭperflŭo -fluxi, 3. to flow over, overflow; to be superfluous.

sŭperfundo -fūdi -fūsum, 3. to pour over, pour upon; *superfundi*, to overflow; to spread about, throw about ; *hostes superfusi*, rushing in numbers.

sŭpergrĕdĭor -gressus sum -grĕdi, 3. *dep.* to go over or beyond, overstep; *fig.*, to surpass.

sŭpĕri, *v.* superus.

sŭpĕrimmĭnĕo, 2. to overhang.

sŭpĕrimpendens -entis, overhanging.

sŭpĕrimplĕo, 2. to fill quite full.

sŭpĕrimpōno (*no perf.*) **-pŏsĭtum**, 3. to lay over, place upon.

sŭpĕrincĭdens -entis, falling from above.

sŭpĕrincŭbans -antis, lying over or upon.

sŭpĕrincumbo -cŭbŭi, 3. to lie on, lie over.

sŭpĕrindŭo -ŭi -ūtum, 3. to put on over (*late*).

sŭpĕringĕro (*no perf.*) **-gestum**, 3. to throw upon, heap upon.

sŭpĕrinĭcio -iēci -iectum, 3. to throw over.

sŭpĕrinsterno -strāvi -strūtum, 3. to spread over.

sŭpĕrior -ōris, *comp. of* sŭpĕrus (*q.v.*).

sŭpĕriăcio -iēci iectum (**-iactum**), 3. to throw over, throw upon; to flow over; to exceed, go beyond.

sŭperlābor, 3. *dep.* to glide, slide over.

sŭperlātĭo -ōnis, *f. rhet.* exaggeration, hyperbole.

sŭperlātus -a -um, *p. adj.* exaggerated.

sŭpernē, *adv.* upwards; from above; above.

sŭpernus -a -um, above, over; *Tusculum*, lying high.

sŭpĕro, 1. *intransit.*, to be above ; to overtop, project ; *milit.*, to have the upper hand, to conquer; to be superior, overcome; to be remaining; to be in abundance; to survive; to overflow with; *transit.*, to rise above, ascend, *montes*; to

sail by, to round; to penetrate to; to surpass; to conquer.

sŭpĕrobrŭo -ŭi -ŭtum, 3. to cover over.

sŭperpendens -entis, overhanging.

sŭperpōno -pŏsŭi -pŏsĭtum, 3. to lay, place over, or upon; to set over.

sŭperscando (**sŭperscendo**), 3. to climb up, climb over.

sŭperscrībo -scripsi -scriptum, 3. to write over or upon.

sŭpersĕdĕo -sēdi -sessum, 3. to sit above, sit upon; to omit, leave off.

sŭperstagno, 1. to spread out into a lake.

sŭpersterno -strāvi -strātum, 3. to strew, spread over.

sŭperstes -stĭtis, standing near, present, witnessing ; surviving, *with dat. or gen.*

sŭperstĭtĭo -ōnis, *f.* superstition: a binding oath; *plur* = religious observances or ceremonies.

sŭperstĭtĭōsē, *adv.* superstitiously.

sŭperstĭtĭōsus -a -um, superstitious.

sŭpersto, 1. to stand over or upon.

sŭperstrŭo -struxi -structum, 3. to build over or upon.

sŭpersum -fŭi -esse, to be over and above; to be left, remain ; *quod superest*, the rest, as for the rest ; to survive, *alicui*; to abound.

sŭpertĕgo -texi -tectum, 3. to cover over.

sŭpĕrurgĕo, 2. to press from above.

sŭpĕrus (*rarely* **sŭpĕr**) **-a -um** (*from adv.* super), compar., **sŭpĕrior**; superl., **sŭprēmus** and **summus**; **sŭpĕrus -a -um**, upper, higher ; *mare superum*, the upper sea, *i.e.*, the Adriatic Sea; *subst.*, **sŭpĕri -ōrum**, *m.* the gods above; men on the earth. Compar., **sŭpĕrior -ōris**, higher, upper; *in writing*, *scriptura superior*, preceding; earlier, prior ; *milit.*, *discessit superior*, gained the advantage. *Superl.*, **sŭprēmus -a -um**, the highest; the last; *adv.*, *suprēmum*, for the last time; *subst.*, **suprēma -ōrum**, *n.*, death ; funeral rites ; **summus**, the highest; *subst.*, **summum -i**, *n.* the highest point.

sŭpervācānĕus -a -um, superfluous, useless.

sŭpervācŭus -a -um, superfluous, useless.

sŭpervādo, 3. to go over, surmount.

sŭpervĕhor -vectus sum, 3. *dep.* to ride, pass over, sail by.

sŭpervĕnĭo -vēni -ventum, 4. to come over; to come up; to come upon unexpectedly.

sŭperventus -ūs, *m.* a coming up, arrival.

sŭpervīvo -vixi, 3. to survive (*late*).

sŭpervolito, 1. to fly over.

sŭpervolo, 1. to fly over, fly above.

sŭpīno, 1. to bend, stretch backwards, to throw back.

sŭpīnus -a -um, bent backwards, lying

on the back; going backwards, returning; sloping, outstretched; careless, negligent, supine; arrogant.

suppar -păris, almost equal, nearly contemporary with.

suppărum (**sipărum** *and* **siphărum**) -i, *n. and* **suppărus** (**siphărus**) -i, *m.* a linen garment; a topsail.

suppěditătĭo -ōnis, *f.* abundant provision, superfluity.

suppědito, 1. to abound, be in store; to suffice; *transit.*, to provide, supply; *with dat.*, to stand by.

suppernātus -a -um, lamed in the hip.

suppětiae -ārum, *f.* help, assistance, *only in nom. and acc.*

suppětior, 1. *dep.* to come to help.

suppěto -īvi *and* -ĭi -ĭtum, 3. to be in store, be in hand; to suffice, correspond with.

supplanto, 1. to throw down a person by tripping up his heels.

supplaudo = **supplodo** (*q.v.*).

supplēmentum -i, *n.* supplement; *milit.*, recruiting of troops, reinforcements.

supplěo -plēvi -plētum, 2. to fill up, complete; to make good, repair; *milit.*, to recruit.

supplex -ĭcis, supplicating, suppliant.

supplicātĭo -ōnis, *f.* a solemn public thanksgiving *or* fast on some public misfortune.

supplicĭter, *adv.* suppliantly, humbly.

supplicĭum -ii, *n.* prayer; punishment; torture.

supplico, 1. to beseech humbly, *alicui*; to pray to the gods.

supplōdo (**supplaudo**) -plōsi -plōsum, 3. to stamp.

supplōsĭo -ōnis, *f.* a stamping.

suppoenĭtet, 2. *impers.* to repent somewhat.

suppōno -pŏsŭi -pŏsĭtum (*syncop. partic.*, **suppostus**), 3. to put, place, lay under; *aliquem tumulo*, to bury; to subject, *se criminibus*; to add, annex; to esteem less; to substitute; to counterfeit, forge.

supporto, 1. to bring, convey to.

supposĭtīcĭus -a -um, substituted; not genuine.

suppostus, *v.* **suppono**.

suppressĭo -ōnis, *f.* embezzlement.

suppressus -a -um, *p. adj.* low, subdued; *vox.*

supprĭmo -pressi -pressum, 3. to press down, press under; *navem*, to sink; to restrain; to conceal; *pecuniam*, to embezzle.

suppŭdet, 2. *impers.* to be somewhat ashamed.

suppŭto, 1. to cut, prune beneath; to count up.

suprā, *adv. and prep.*; *adv.*, *of place*, above, over, on the top; *of time*, before, previously; *of degree*, more, beyond;

supra quam, more than; *prep. with acc.*, above, over; *supra caput esse*, to be a burden; *of time*, before; above, beyond, *supra vires;* besides.

suprēmus, *etc.*, *v.* **superus**.

sūra -ae, *f.* the calf of the leg.

surcŭlus -i, *m.* young shoot, sucker.

surdaster -tra -trum, somewhat deaf, hard of hearing.

surdĭtas -ātis, *f.* deafness.

surdus -a -um, deaf; *pass.*, not heard, silent.

Surēna -ae, *m.* a grand vizier among the Parathians.

surgo = **subrigo** (*q.v.*).

surpŭit, **surpere**, **surpite**, *contr. for* **surripŭit**, *etc.*, *v.* **surripio**.

surr, *v. under* **subr**.

surripio -ripŭi -reptum, 3. to take away secretly, to steal.

surrōgo = **subrogo** (*q.v.*).

sursum, *adv.* upwards, on high; above.

sūs, **sŭis**, *c.* a sow, pig; a kind of fish.

suscensěo -censŭi -censum, 2. to be angry with, to be enraged.

susceptĭo -ōnis, *f.* an undertaking.

suscĭpĭo -cēpi -ceptum, 3. to carry; to take upon oneself; to undertake, begin; to suffer, submit to; to receive, catch up; to beget a child; to receive as true; to admit of; to answer; *fig.*, to support, defend.

suscĭto, 1. to lift up; to raise on high; to rouse up, awake; to stir up; to arouse; to bring about.

suspecto, 1. to look at, regard, suspect.

1. **suspectus** -a -um, *p. adj.* suspected.

2. **suspectus** -ūs, *m.* a looking upwards; height; *fig.*, honour, respect.

suspendĭum -ii, *n.* a hanging of oneself.

suspendo -pendi -pensum, 3. to hang up; (**suspensus**, hanging up); to consecrate; to raise up; to cause to waver; to vault; to support prop up; to check, break off; to leave undecided.

suspensus -a -um, *p. adj.* hovering, suspended; *fig.*, dependent upon; uncertain, wavering; anxious, restless.

suspĭcax -ācis, suspicious.

1. **suspĭcĭo** -spexi -spectum, 3. to look upwards; *transit.*, to regard, contemplate; to esteem, respect; to suspect.

2. **suspĭcĭo** -ōnis, *f.* mistrust, suspicion; a notion, idea.

suspĭcĭōsē, *adv.* suspiciously.

suspĭcĭōsus -a -um, cherishing suspicion, suspicious; exciting suspicion, suspicious.

suspĭcor, 1. *dep.* to suspect; to conjecture, surmise.

suspīrātĭo -ōnis, *f.* a drawing a deep breath (*late*).

suspīrātŭs -ūs, *m.* a sigh.

suspīrĭtus -ūs, *m.* a sigh.

suspīrĭum -ii, *n.* a sigh.

suspiro, 1. to breathe deeply, to sigh; *transit.*, to sigh forth, long for.

susque deque, *adv.* up and down.

sustentāculum -i, *n.* prop, support.

sustentātio -ōnis, *f.* delay; keeping in suspense.

sustento, 1. to support, sustain ; to strengthen, maintain, to bear, to hold out; to put off, hinder.

sustinĕo -tinŭi -tentum, 2. to support, sustain; to carry; to restrain; *se*, to refrain from; *milit.*, to stand one's ground; to support, maintain; to delay; to preserve, *dignitatem*.

sustollo, 3. to lift up, elevate; to carry off.

sustringo = *substringo (q.v.).*

sūsurrator -ōris, *m.* a murmurer.

sŭsurro, 1. to murmur, whisper ; *of bees*, to hum.

1. **sŭsurrus -i**, *m.* a murmuring, whispering, humming.

2. **sŭsurrus -a -um**, whispering.

sūtilis -e, stitched together, fastened together.

sūtor -ōris, *m.* a shoe-maker, cobbler.

sūtōrius -a -um, relating to a shoe-maker.

sūtrīnus -a -um, relating to a shoe-maker.

Sūtrium -ii, *n.* a town in Etruria.

sūtūra -ae, *f.* a seam.

sŭus -a -um, *pron. poss.*, his, her, its, own ; *strengthened by* **-pte** *or* **-met**, **suāpte manu** ; *subst.*, **sui**, his men, countrymen, *etc.* ; **sŭum -i**, *n.* one's own property.

Sўbāris -is, *f.* a Greek town in Lucania, famous for its luxury.

Sўchaeus -i, *m.* husband of Dido.

sўcŏphanta -ae, *f.* an informer, trickster.

Sylla = *Sulla (q.v.).*

syllăba -ae, *f.* syllable ; *syllabae*, verses.

syllăbātim, *adv.* syllable by syllable.

syllĭbus = *sittybus (q.v.).*

syllŏgismus -i, *m.* syllogism.

symbŏla -ae, *f.* contribution of money to a common feast.

symphōnia -ae, *f.* musical performance.

symphōniăcus -a -um, relating to a concert.

Symplēgădes -um, *f.* the Symplegades, rocks in the entrance to the Euxine, which, according to the fable, dashed against one another till they were fixed after the passage of the Argo between them.

syngrăpha -ae, *f.* a bond, agreement to pay.

synthēsinus -a -um, of a dressing-gown.

synthĕsis -is, *f.* set of dishes; a suit of clothes; dressing-gown.

Sўphax -phăcis, *m.* king of Numidia at the time of the Second Punic War.

Sўrācūsae -ārum, *f.* the chief town of Sicily. *Adj.*, **Sўrācūsānus**.

Sўri (Sūri) -ōrum, *m.* the Syrians.

Sўria -ae, *f.* a country in Asia.

syrma -ătis, *n.* a long robe worn by tragic actors; tragedy.

Sўrŏphoenix -īcis, *m.* a Syrophoenician

Sўrtis -is *and* **-idos**, *f.* a sandbank, *esp.*, on the coast of Northern Africa.

Sўrus -a -um, *v.* Syri.

T

T t, *the nineteenth letter of the Latin Alphabet.*

tăbella -ae, *f.* (*dim. of tabula*), a small flat board *or* tablet; a picture; votingticket; *plur.*, a letter, note; record, register *etc*

tăbellārius -a -um, relating to letters or voting; *subst.*, **tăbellārius -ii**, *m.* lettercarrier.

tābĕo, 2. to waste away; to drip with.

tăberna -ae, *f.* a booth, hut; a stall, shop.

tăbernāculum -i, *n.* hut, tent.

tăbernārius -ii, *m.* shopkeeper.

tăbernŭla -ae, *f.* (*dim. of taberna*), a little shop, small tavern.

tābes -is, *f.* wasting away ; melting ; pestilence; corruption.

tābesco, tābŭi, 3. to melt, waste away; to perish; to pine away.

tābidŭlus -a -um (*dim. of tabidus*), wasting, consuming.

tābidus -a -um, decaying, pining away, dissolving; *act.*, consuming.

tābificus -a -um, melting, causing to waste away.

tăbŭla -ae, *f.* a board, plank; a bench; draught-board; picture; tablet for writing; a vote; map; a register, record; *tabulae*, account-book, public records; money-changer's table.

tăbŭlārius -ii, *m.* a keeper of records.

tăbŭlārium -ii, *n.* archives.

tăbŭlātio -ōnis, *f.* a flooring, story.

tăbŭlātum -i, *n.* a flooring, story; a row of vines.

tābum -i, *n.* (= *tabes*), pestilence; clotted blood, matter.

tăcĕo, tăcŭi, tăcĭtum, 2. to be silent, still, quiet; to pass over in silence.

tăcĭtē, *adv.* silently; secretly.

tăcĭturnĭtas -ātis, *f.* silence.

tăcĭturnus -a -um, silent, still, quiet.

1. **tăcĭtus -a -um**, *p. adj.* that which is unmentioned; (*subst.*, **tăcĭtum -i**, *n.* a secret); implied, tacit; secret, concealed; not speaking, silent.

2. **Tăcĭtus -i**, *m.*, *Cornelius*, the celebrated historian, born between A.D. 50 and 60.

tactilis -e, that can be touched.

tactio -ōnis, f. the sense of touch.

tactus -ūs, m. a touch, touching, handling ; influence, effect ; the sense of touch.

taeda -ae, f. the pine-tree ; plur., pinewood; a board of pine; a torch of pinewood.

taedet, taedŭit and taesum est, 2. impers. to be disgusted with.

taedifĕr -fĕra -fĕrum, torch-bearing.

taedium -ii, n. disgust, weariness.

Taenărus (-os) -i, c. and Taenărum (-on) -i, n. and Taenăra -ōrum, n. promontory in Laconia, whence there was supposed to be a descent into Tartarus; Taenărius, Spartan.

taenia -ae, f. a fillet, the ribbon of a chaplet.

taeter = teter (q.v.).

tăgax -ācis, thievish.

Tăgus -i, m. a river in Lusitania, celebrated for its golden sands.

tālāria, v. talaris.

tālāris -e, relating to the ankles; subst., tālāria -ium, n. winged sandals.

tālārius -a -um, relating to the ankles.

tālĕa -ae, f. a bar, rod, stick.

tālentum -i, a Greek weight; a sum of money.

tālio -ōnis, f. retaliation or recompense.

tālis -e, of such a kind, such.

tālitrum -i, n. a snap of the finger, fillip.

talpa -ae, f. a mole.

Talthўbius (Talthūbius) -ii, m. a herald of Agamemnon.

tālus -i, m. the ankle, ankle-bone; the heel; a die.

tam, adv. so far, to such a degree; so much.

tămărix -īcis, f. the tamarisk.

tamdiū, adv. so long.

tămen, adv. however, yet, nevertheless; still.

tămĕn-etsi, conj. although.

Tămĕsis -is, m. and Tămĕsa -ae, m. now the Thames.

tămetsi, conj. although, nevertheless; however.

tamquam (tanquam), adv. as, just as, as if, as though.

Tănăis -is, m. a river, now the Don.

tandem, adv. at length, at last. In interrogations, pray, then.

tango, tĕtigi, tactum, 3. to touch; to border on; to reach a place; to strike; de caelo tactus, struck by lightning; to sprinkle, to take ; to taste, eat ; to move, affect; to mention; to cheat; to prepare.

Tantălus (-os) -i, m. a king of Phrygia, father of Pelops and Niobe, who set his own child as food before the gods, and was punished in Hades by being placed near fruits and water, which drew back

whenever he attempted to satisfy his everlasting hunger and thirst.

tantillus -a -um = tantulus, so small.

tantispĕr, adv. so long, foll. by dum; meanwhile.

tantŏpĕrĕ, or tanto ŏpĕrĕ, adv. so greatly, so much.

tantŭlus -a -um (dim. of tantus), so small; subst., tantŭlum -i, n. such a trifle.

tantum, v. tantus.

tantummŏdo, adv. only.

tantundem, v. tantusdem.

tantus -a -um, correl. adjectival pron. of such size, so great, foll. by quantus, etc.; tantum, adv. so much; only; tantum non, all but; non tantum . . . sed etiam, not only . . . but also.

tantusdem, tandădem, tantumdem and tantundem, just so much, just so great.

tăpĕtĕ -is, n. and tăpētum -i, n. drapery, tapestry.

Taprŏbănĕ -ēs, f. now Ceylon.

tardĕ, adv. slowly; late, not in time.

tardesco, 3. to become slow.

tardigrădus -a -um, slowly stepping.

tardipēs -pĕdis, slow footed ; deus, limping.

tardĭtas -ātis, f. slowness; inactivity; dullness, stupidity.

tardo, 1. to loiter; to be slow; transit., to hinder, retard.

tardus -a -um, slow, tardy; coming late; lasting a long time, lingering; poet. making slow; dull, stupid; measured, deliberate.

Tărentum -i, n. and Tărentus -i, f. a wealthy town on the coast of Magna Graecia; adj. Tărentīnus.

Tarpēius -a -um, name of a Roman family; mons Tarpeius, a peak of the Capitoline Hill, from which criminals were thrown.

Tarquinius, name of two kings of Rome, Tarquinius Priscus and the last king of Rome, Tarquinius Superbus.

Tarrăcina -ae, f. and Tarrăcīnae, f. a town in Latium.

Tarrăco -ōnis, f. a town in Spain. Adj., Tarrăcōnensis -e.

Tartărus (-ŏs) -i, m., plur. Tartăra -ōrum, n. the infernal regions ; adj., Tartărĕus.

Tartessus (-os) -i, f. town in Hispania Baetica.

Tātius -ii, m. king of the Sabines.

taurĕus -a -um, relating to an ox ; subst., taurĕa -ae, f. a whip of bull's hide.

Tauri -ōrum, m. people near the Crimea. Adj., Tauricus.

tauriformis -e, shaped like a bull.

Taurini -ōrum m. people in Gallia Cisalpina.

taurīnus -a -um, relating to a bull.

Taurŏpŏlos, f. surname of Artemis.

1. **taurus -i,** *m.* a bull.
2. **Taurus -i,** *m.* mountain-range in Asia.

taxātio -ōnis, *,* . a rating, valuing.

taxillus -i, *m.* a small die.

taxo, 1. to touch, handle; to reproach; to estimate,

taxus -i, *f.* a yew-tree.

1. **tē,** *acc. and abl. sing. of tu.*

2. **tē,** *pronominal suffix added to tu.*

Tĕātes -um, *m.* people in Apulia.

techna -ae, *f.* cunning trick, artifice.

tectē, *adv. with compar.* **tectius,** cautiously; secretly.

tector -ōris, *m.* a plasterer.

tectōrius -a -um, relating to the plastering, stuccoing of walls; **tectōrium -ii,** *n.* plaster, stucco.

tectum -i, *n.* a roof; shelter, dwelling.

tectus -a -um, *p. adj.* covered; *fig.,* reserved, cautious; secret; obscure.

tēges -ĕtis, *f.* mat, rug, covering.

tēgĕticŭla -ae, *f.* (*dim. of teges*), a little mat or rug.

tĕgimen (tĕgŭmen) *and* **tegmen -inis,** *n.* covering; shield.

tĕgimentum (tĕgŭmentum) *and* **tegmentum -i,** *n.* covering.

tegmen = *tegimen* (*q.v.*).

tĕgo, texi, tectum, 3. to cover; to bury; to conceal; to protect.

tēgŭla -ae, *f.* a roofing-tile; *plur., tegulae,* roof.

tĕgŭmentum = *tegimentum* (*q.v.*).

tĕgŭmen = *tegimen* (*q.v.*).

tēla -ae, *f.* a web, that which is woven; a device; the warp; the loom.

Tēlĕmăchus -i, *m.* son of Ulysses and Penelope.

tellūs -ūris, *f.* the earth; soil; *poet.,* land, district, country.

tēlum -i, *n.* a missile, dart, javelin, spear; sword, dagger, *etc.,* weapon; the beams of the sun.

Tēmĕnos, a place at Syracuse, where was a grave sacred to Apollo.

tĕmĕrārius -a -um, by chance, casual; thoughtless, rash.

tĕmĕrē, *adv.* by chance, accidentally, casually.

tĕmĕritas -ātis, *f.* chance, accident; rashness, temerity; an unfounded opinion.

tĕmĕro, 1. to defile, dishonour.

tēmētum -i, *n.* any intoxicating drink, wine.

temno, tempsi, 3. to despise, contemn.

tēmo -ōnis, *m.* a pole; a plough-beam; a waggon; Charles's Wain.

Tempē, *neut. plur.* a valley in Thessaly, famous for its beauty, through which the river Peneus flowed.

tempĕrāmentum -i, *n.* a right proportion of things mixed together; a mean, moderation.

tempĕrans -antis, *p. adj.* moderate, temperate, self-denying.

tempĕrantĕr, *adv.* temperately, moderately.

tempĕrantia -ae, *f.* temperance, moderation.

tempĕrātē, *adv.* moderately, temperately.

tempĕrātio -ōnis, *f.* temperateness, proper mixture of ingredients, organisation; the organising principle.

tempĕrātor -ōris, *m.* one who arranges *or* governs.

tempĕrātus -a -um, *p. adj.* properly arranged; ordered, moderate; mild, temperate.

tempĕri, *adv.* at the right time, in time.

tempĕries -ēi, *f.* a proper mixture, organisation, tempering.

tempero, 1. *intransit.,* to be temperate; *with dat.,* to control, use with moderation; *with ab and abl.,* to refrain from; to spare, *with dat.;* *transit.,* to distribute *or* mix properly, to temper; to regulate; to rule; to temper, make mild.

tempestas -ātis, *f.* period of time, season; weather; storm, tempest; *fig.,* attack, fury.

tempestīvē, *adv.* at the right time, seasonably.

tempestīvitas -ātis, *f.* the fit time, proper season.

tempestīvō = *tempestive* (*q.v.*).

tempestīvus -a -um, opportune, seasonable, appropriate; early; *of fruit,* in season, ripe; *of persons,* ripe, mature.

templum -i, *n.* a part cut off; a space marked out by the augur for taking auspices; a place from which one can survey; a height; any clear, open space; sanctuary; temple; the tribunals; *of the curia, because consecrated by an augur,* e.g. *curia templum publici consilii.*

tempŏrālis -e, temporary.

tempŏrārius -a -um, temporary; seasonable.

tempŏrī = *temperi* (*q.v.*).

tempus -ŏris, division, section, period of time; *ex tempore,* without preparation; time; occasion, opportunity; *plur.,* the times; tense of a verb; the temple on the forehead.

tēmŭlentus -a -um, intoxicated.

tĕnācitas -ātis, *f.* tenacity; frugality.

tĕnācitĕr, *adv.* firmly, tenaciously.

tĕnax -ācis, tenacious; frugal, stingy; holding firmly together; *gramen,* matted; resolute, steadfast; obstinate.

tendĭcŭla -ae, *f.* a noose, snare.

tendo, tĕtendi, tentum *and* **tensum,** 3. to stretch, extend; *transit.,* to string, *barbiton;* to direct, shoot; to present, give; *intransit.,* to pitch one's tent, encamp; to direct one's course to, march towards; to extend to; to have recourse to; to be inclined, strive after; to contend against; *foll. by infin.,* to try, attempt.

tĕnebrae -ārum, *f.* darkness; *poet.* blindness; a dark place; obscurity.

tĕnebricōsus -a -um, dark, obscure.

tĕnebricus -a -um, dark, gloomy, *poet.*

tĕnebrōsus -a -um, dark, gloomy.

Tĕnĕdus (-ŏs) -i, *f.* an island near Troy.

tĕnĕo, tĕnŭi, tentum, 2. to hold; *rem manu tenere*, to have at one's fingers' ends; to understand, know; to reach a place, arrive at, land on; to direct; to direct one's course; *of ships*, to sail to; to have, possess; to occupy, garrison; to hold fast; to defend, keep; *memoriā tenere*, to remember; to catch, detect; *of passions*, to possess, master; to charm, amuse; to bind; to hold fast, preserve; to keep; to observe, remain true to; to keep in, hold back; to restrain, suppress; to detain; to contain, comprise; *intransit.*, to last, endure.

tĕner -ĕra -ĕrum, tender, delicate, soft, youthful; *subst.*, *in teneris*, in childhood; effeminate.

tĕnĕrasco, 3. to grow tender, delicate, soft.

tĕnĕrē, *adv.* tenderly, delicately, softly.

tĕnĕritas -ātis, *f.* tenderness, softness.

tĕnĕritūdo = *teneritas* (*q.v.*).

tĕnor -ōris, *m.* course; duration, tenor, career ; *adv.*, *uno tenore*, in an uninterrupted course, uniformly.

tensa -ae, *f.* a car on which the images of the gods were carried at the Circensian games.

tensus -a -um, *partic. of tendo* (*q.v.*).

tentābundus (temptābundus) -a -um, trying, attempting.

tentāmen (temptāmen) -inis, *n.* a trial, attempt.

tentāmentum (temptāmentum) -i, *n.* a trial, attempt, test.

tentātio (temptātio) -ōnis, *f.* an attack; a trial, test.

tentātor (temptātor) -ōris, *m.* a tempter.

tentīgo -inis, *f.* lust.

tento (tempto), 1. to touch, feel, handle; *venas*, to feel the pulse; to try, prove, to attempt; to attack; to tempt, excite, disturb.

tentōrium -ĭi, *n.* a tent.

tentus -a -um, *partic. of tendo and teneo.*

tĕnŭicŭlus -a -um (*dim. of tenuis*), very poor, mean, miserable.

tĕnŭis -e, thin, fine, slender ; small, narrow ; shallow ; bright, clear ; plain, simple ; subtle ; weak, unimportant, slight ; poor, needy ; *of position*, low, mean ; *subst.*, *tenuiores*, persons of lower rank.

tĕnŭitas -ātis, *f.* thinness, fineness; simplicity, plainness; poverty.

tĕnŭĭter, *adv.* thinly; plainly, simply; sparingly; lightly.

tĕnŭo, 1. to make thin, fine; to contract; to weaken, diminish.

tĕnus, *prep. with abl. and genit.*, up to as far as ; *verbo tenus*, in name, nominally.

Tĕōs -i, *f.* a town on the coast of Ionia, birthplace of Anacreon.

tĕpĕfăcio -fēci -factum, 3. *pass.*, tĕpĕfīo -factus sum -fĭĕri, to warm, heat.

tĕpĕo, 2. to be lukewarm, tepid; *partic.*, *tepens*, warm.

tĕpesco, tĕpŭi, 3. to grow warm; to grow cool.

tĕpĭdē, *adv.* lukewarmly.

tĕpĭdus -a -um, lukewarm, tepid.

tĕpor -ōris, *m.* lukewarmness.

tĕr, *adv. num,* three times, thrice.

terdĕcĭēs (terdĕciens), *adv.* thirteen times.

tĕrĕbinthus -i, *f.* the terebinth-tree.

tĕrĕbra -ae, *f.* a gimlet, borer.

tĕrĕbro, 1. to pierce, perforate.

tĕrĕdo -inis, *f.* a worm that gnaws wood.

Tĕrentius -a -um, the name of a Roman gens; *P. Terentius Afer*, the celebrated Roman comic dramatist.

tĕrēs -ĕtis, *abl.* -ĕti, rounded, polished; graceful; refined.

Tĕreus -ĕi *and* -ĕos, *m.* king in Thrace, husband of Procne, sister of Philomela, father of Itys, changed into a hoopoe.

tergĕminus = *trigeminus* (*q.v.*).

tergĕo *and* tergo, tersi, tersum -ĕre *and* ĕre, to wipe, wipe off, clean; *specula*, to polish.

tergiversātio -ōnis, *f.* reluctance, delay.

tergiversor, 1. *dep.* to shuffle, find excuses, to delay.

tergo = *tergeo* (*q.v.*).

tergum -i, the back ; *terga dare*, to turn one's back, flee ; *a tergo*, from behind.

tergus -ŏris, *n.* the back; body of an animal ; skin, leather.

termes -itis, *m.* a branch cut off a tree.

Terminālia -ium *and* -iōrum, *n.* Festival of Terminus.

terminātio -ōnis, *f.* a limiting, bounding; a fixing; determining.

termino, 1. to bound, limit; to restrain; to define, determine; to close, end, terminate.

terminus -i, *m.* a boundary-mark, boundary; limit, object; end, conclusion; Terminus, the god of boundaries.

terni -ae -a, three each; three together.

tĕro, trīvi, trītum, 3. to rub; to smooth, adorn; to turn (*at a lathe*); to thresh out *corn;* to rub, bruise, grind; to wear away; to visit, frequent; *fig.*, to tire, exhaust; to pass away *time.*

Terpsichŏrē -ēs, *f.* the muse of dancing; muse, poetry.

terra -ae, *f.* the earth, land, ground, soil; a particular country, land, region ; *plur.*, *terrae*, the world; *orbis terrarum*, the world.

Terracĭna = *Tarracina (q.v.)*.

terrēnus -a -um, earthy, earthen; belonging to the earth, terrestrial; *subst.* **terrēnum -i**, *n.* land, ground.

terrĕo, terrŭi, terrĭtum, 2. to frighten, terrify; to scare away; to deter.

terrester -tris -tre, *gen.*, **terrestris -e**, terrestrial; earthly.

terrĕus -a -um, made of earth, earthly.

terribĭlis -e, terrible, dreadful.

terrĭcŭla -ae, *f. and* **terrĭcŭlum -i**, *n.* something that causes fright.

terrĭfĭco, 1. to frighten, terrify.

terrĭfĭcus -a -um, frightful, terrible.

terrĭgĕna -ae, *c.* sprung from the earth.

territo, 1. to frighten, terrify.

territōrium -ii, *n.* the land belonging to a town, district, territory.

terror -ōris, *m.* fright, fear, panic; that which causes terror.

tersus -a -um, *p. adj.* wiped, clean, neat; free from mistakes.

tertĭădĕcĭmāni -ōrum, *m.* soldiers of the thirteenth legion.

tertĭānus -a -um, belonging to the third; belonging to the third legion; *subst.* **tertĭāna -ae**, *f.* a tertian fever; *subst.* **tertĭāni -ōrum**, *m.* soldiers of the third legion.

tertĭō, *adv.* for the third time; thirdly.

tertĭum, *adv.* for the third time.

tertĭus -a -um, the third; *tertius e nobis*, one of us three.

tertĭusdĕcĭmus -a -um, the thirteenth.

tĕruncĭus -ii, *m.* three-twelfths; the fourth part of an as; the fourth part of an inheritance.

tesca (tesqua) -ōrum, *n.* wastes, deserts.

tessella -ae, *f. (dim. of tessera)*, a small cube of marble.

tessellātus -a -um, set with small cubes; *pavimentum*, mosaic.

tessĕra -ae, *f.* a cube of wood, stone, *or* other substance; a piece of mosaic for paving; a die, *tesseras iacere*; a token; a square tablet.

tessĕrārĭus -ii, *m.* the officer who received the watchword.

tessĕrŭla -ae, *f. (dim. of tessera)*, a little cube of stone; a ticket.

testa -ae, *f.* pitcher, urn; a brick, a tile; shell.

testāmentārĭus -a -um, relating to a will, testamentary; *subst.*, **testāmentārĭus -ii**, *m.* a forger of wills.

testāmentum -i, *n.* a last will, testament.

testātĭo -ōnis, *f.* a calling to witness; a bearing witness.

testātor -ōris, *m.* a testator.

testātus -a -um, *p. adj.* attested, proved.

testĭfĭcātĭo -ōnis, *f.* testifying; evidence, proof.

testĭfĭcor, 1. *dep.* to call to witness; to testify; to publish.

testĭmōnium -ii, *n.* evidence, testimony; a proof.

testis -is, *c.* a witness; spectator.

testor, 1. *dep.* to bear witness, to declare, testify; to call to witness; to make a will.

testūdĭnĕus -a -um, made of tortoiseshell.

testūdo -ĭnis, *f.* tortoise; shell of the tortoise; the lyre; a formation in which soldiers charged, holding their shields over their heads.

testŭla -ae, *f. (dim. of testa)*, a potsherd, an Athenian voting-ticket.

testum -i, *n. and abl.* testū, earthen pot.

tēter (taeter) -tra -trum, foul, offensive; disgraceful, abominable.

Tēthys -ўos, *acc.* -thyn, *f.* a marine goddess, wife of Oceanus.

tetrachmum -i, *genit. plur.* -ōrum *and* -ūm, *n.* a Greek coin of four drachmae.

tetrāchordos -on, having four notes.

tetrădrachmum = *tetrachmum (q.v.)*.

tetrarches *and* **tĕtrarcha -ae**, *m.* ruler over one-fourth of a country, a tetrarch.

tetrarchĭa -ae, *f.* tetrarchy.

tētrē (taetrē), *adv.* foully, hideously, offensively.

tētrĭcus -a -um, harsh, gloomy, forbidding.

Teucer -cri, *m. and* **Teucrus -i**, *m.* 1. *(Teucer and Teucrus)* son of Telamon, king of Salamis, brother of Ajax, who after his return from Troy, sailed away to Cyprus. 2. *(Teucrus)*, son of Scamander, first king of Troy. *Adj.*, **Teucrus, Teucrĭus.** *Subst.*, **Teucri -ōrum**, *m.* the Trojans.

Teucrĭus, Teucrus, *v. Teucer*.

Teutŏni -ōrum, *m. and* **Teutŏnes -um**, *m.* collective name of the German peoples. *Adj.*, **Teutŏnĭcus.**

texo, texŭi, textum, 3. to weave, plait, build; to compose.

textĭlis -e, woven, textile; plaited; *subst.*, **textĭle -is**, *n.* a piece of cloth.

textor -ōris, *m.* a weaver.

textrīnus -a -um, relating to weaving. *Subst.*, **textrīnum -i**, *n.* weaving.

textrix -īcis, *f.* a female weaver.

textum -i, *n.* that which is woven, a web; a fabric; *fig.*, texture, style.

textūra -ae, *f.* a web, texture; a putting together, connexion.

textus -ūs, *m.* a web, texture, structure; *of discourse*, connexion *(late)*.

thălămus -i, *m.* a living-room; dwelling; a bedroom; a marriage-bed; marriage.

thalassĭnus -a -um, sea-green.

Thălēa = *Thalia (q.v.)*.

Thălēs -lis *and* **-lētis**, *m.* a philosopher of Miletus.

Thălīa -ae, *f.* the Muse of comic poetry.

thallus -i, *m.* a green branch.

Thămÿras -ae, *m. and* **Thămÿris -ĭdis**, *m.* a Thracian poet.

9

Thapsus (-os), -i, *f.* 1. peninsula and town in Sicily; 2. town in Africa, where Caesar conquered the Pompeians.

theātrālis -e, relating to a theatre, theatrical.

theātrum -i, *n.* a theatre.

Thēbae -ārum, *f.* 1. a city of Upper Egypt; 2. a city of Boeotia. **Thēbāis** -idis *and* -idos, *f.* belonging to Thebes in Egypt or to Thebes in Boeotia. **Thēbānus**, belonging to Thebes in Boeotia.

thēca -ae, *f.* case, covering.

thēma -ātis, *n.* theme, subject.

Thēmis -idis, *f.* goddess of justice, also regarded as the goddess of prophecy.

Thēmistoclēs -is *and* -i, *m.* the celebrated general of the Athenians in the Persian War.

Theocritus -i, *m.* famous Greek poet.

Thēogónia -ae, *f.* the Theogony, a poem by Hesiod.

theōlōgus -i, *m.* a theologian.

Theōphrastus -i, *m.* a celebrated Greek philosopher.

Thērāmēnēs -ae, *m.* one of the thirty tyrants at Athens.

thermae -ārum, *f.* warm baths.

Thermōpȳlae -ārum, *f.* a pass where a small body of Spartans fell fighting against the whole Persian army.

thermūlae -ārum *f.* (*dim. of thermae*), warm baths.

Thersītes -ae, *m.* one of the Greeks before Troy.

thēsaurus -i, *m.* a treasury, store; a treasure; a storehouse.

Thēseus -ĕi *and* -ĕos, *m.* king of Athens, conqueror of the Minotaur.

thēsis -is, *f.* a proposition, thesis.

thesmophōria -ōrum, *n.* the great Greek festival in honour of Demeter.

Thespis -is, *m.* founder of the Greek drama.

Thessālia -ae, *f.* Thessaly.

Thessālōnīca -ae, *f.* and **Thessālōnīcē** -ēs, *f.* a town in Macedonia.

Thessālus -a -um, Thessalian.

Thētis -idis, *f.* a sea-nymph, mother of Achilles.

thiāsus -i, *m.* dance in honour of Bacchus.

Thisbē -ēs, *f.* a maiden, beloved by Pyramus.

thŏlus -i, *m.* a cupola, dome.

thōrax -ācis, *m.* the breast, chest, a breast-plate.

Thrāces -um, *acc.* -es *and* -as, *m.* inhabitants of Thrace; *sing.* **Thrāx** -ācis, *m.*; **Thrācia** -ae, *f.* the country of Thrace. *Adj.*, **Thrācius** (**Thrēcius**), *poet.* **Thrēicius**.

Thrāsȳmennus = *Trasumenus.*

Thrax, *v. Thraces.*

Threx = *Thrax, v. Thraces.*

Thūcȳdīdēs -is, *m.* an Athenian general and historian.

Thūlē (**Thȳlē**) -ēs, *f.* island in the extreme north of Europe.

thunnus (**thynnus**) -i, *m.* a tunny-fish.

Thūrii -ōrum, *m. and* **Thūriae** -ārum, *f.* town on the Tarentine Gulf.

thūs = *tus* (*q.v.*).

thȳa -ae, *f. and* **thȳia** -ae, *n.* Greek name of the citrus-tree; *adj.*, **thȳius.**

Thybris = *Tiberis* (*q.v.*).

Thyēne -ēs, *f.* a nymph, nurse of Jupiter.

Thyestes -ae *and* -is, *m.* brother of Atreus.

Thyiās (*dissyll.*) -ādis, *f.* a Bacchante.

thȳius, *v. thya.*

Thȳlē = *Thule* (*q.v.*).

thymbra -ae, *f.* the herb savory.

thȳmum -i, *n. and* **thȳmus** -i, *m.* the herb thyme.

Thȳni -ōrum, *m.* a Thracian people. **Thȳnia** -ae, *f.* the northern part of Bithynia.

Thȳnus, Bithynian.

thynnus = *thunnus* (*q.v.*).

Thȳōnē -ēs, *f.* mother of Bacchus. **Thȳōnēus** -ĕi, *m.* a nymph, nurse of Jupiter.

thyrsigĕr-**gĕra**-**gĕrum**, bearing a thyrsus.

thyrsus -i, *m.* the stem of a plant; a wand, carried by Bacchus and his attendants.

tiāra -ae, *f. and* **tiāras** -ae, *m.* a turban.

Tiberis -is, *acc.* -im, *abl.* -i, *m. and poet.*, **Thybris** -idis, *acc.* -in *or* -im, *m.* the river Tiber. *Adj.*, **Tiberinus.**

Tiberius -ii, *m.* the second emperor of Rome.

tibia -ae, *f.* the shin-bone, tibia; a pipe, flute.

tibicen -inis, *m.* a flute-player.

tibicina -ae, *f.* a female flute-player.

tibicinium -ii, *n.* playing on the flute.

Tibris = *Tiberis* (*q.v.*).

Tibullus -i, *m.*, *Albius*, a Roman poet.

Tibūr -ūris, *abl.* -ūre, *loc.*, **ūri**, *n.* an old town in Latium, *now* Tivoli.

Ticinus -i, *m.* tributary of the Padus.

tigillum -i, *n.* (*dim. o stignum*), a small beam.

tignārius -a -um, relating to beams.

tignum -i, *n.* beam of wood.

Tigrānes -is, *m.* king in Great Armenia.

Tigrānōcerta -ae, *f. and* **Tigrānōcerta** -ōrum, *n.* chief town of Armenia.

tigris -idis *and* -is, *c.* a tiger.

tilia -ae, *f.* a linden *or* lime-tree.

timĕfactus -a -um, frightened, alarmed.

timendus -a -um, fearful, dread.

timens -entis, *p. adj.* fearing, fearful.

timĕo -ŭi, 2. to be afraid, dread.

timidē, *adv.* timidly, fearfully.

timiditas -ātis, *f.* fearfulness, timidity.

timidus -a -um, fearful, timid.

timor -ōris, *m.* fear, dread ; super stition.

tinctilis -e, in which something is dipped.

tinĕa (tinia) -ae, f. a moth, bookworm.

tingo (tinguo), tinxi, tinctum, 3. to wet, moisten; to dye; fig., to tinge, imbue.

tinnio -ivi and **-ii -itum**, 4. to ring, tinkle; to sing, to scream; to chink; of money = to pay.

tinnītus -ūs, m. a ringing tinkling

tinnulus -a -um, ringing, tinkling.

tintinnābŭlum -i, n. a bell.

tintinno (tintino), 1. to ring, tinkle

tinus -i, f. a shrub.

Tiphÿs, acc. **-phyn**, voc. **-phy**, m. the helmsman of the Argo.

Tirēsiās -ae, m. the blind soothsayer of Thebes.

Tiridātes -ae, m. name of several kings in Armenia.

tiro (tÿro) -ōnis, m. a young soldier, a recruit; a beginner, learner.

tirōcinium -ii, n. military inexperience; recruits.

tiruncŭlus -i, m. (dim. of tiro), a young beginner.

Tiryns, acc. **-ryntha**, f. town where Hercules was brought up.

Tisiphŏnē -ēs, f. one of the Furies.

Tissaphernes -ae, m. a Persian satrap.

Titan -ānis, m. and **Titānus -i**, m. plur., Titanes and Titani, who warred against Jupiter, and were cast down into Tartarus.

Tithōnus -i, m. the husband of Aurora.

Tities -ium, m. and **Titienses -ium**, m. one of the three tribes of the Romans.

titillātio -ōnis, f. a tickling.

titillātus -ūs, m. = titillatio (q.v.).

titillo, 1. to tickle.

titŭbantĕr, adv. hesitatingly.

titŭbantia -ae, f. a wavering, staggering.

titŭbātio -ōnis, f. a staggering; fig., uncertainty.

titŭbo, 1. to totter, stagger; to stammer; to blunder; fig., to hesitate.

titŭlus -i, m. inscription, label, title, glory, honour; pretence, reason.

Tityos -yi, m. son of Jupiter, punished in Tartarus.

tōcullio -ōnis, m. usurer.

tōfus (tōphus) -i, m. tufa.

tōga -ae, f. the white woollen upper garment worn by the Romans in time of peace.

tōgātŭlus -i, m. (dim. of togatus), a client.

tōgātus -a -um, wearing the toga, as a sign of a Roman citizen; **tōgāta -ae**, f. (fabula), the national drama of the Romans.

tōgŭla -ae, f. (dim. of toga), a little toga.

tŏlĕrābilis -e, bearable, tolerable.

tŏlĕrābilitĕr, adv. patiently.

tŏlĕrandus -a -um, endurable.

tŏlĕrans -antis, p. adj. enduring, patient.

tŏlĕrantĕr, adv. patiently.

tŏlĕrantia -ae, f. enduring, supporting.

tŏlĕrātio -ōnis, f. capacity for endurance.

tŏlĕro, 1. to bear, endure; to support, sustain.

tollēno -ōnis, m. a swing-beam.

tollo, sustŭli, sublātum, 3. to lift up, raise, elevate, soften unawares, to weigh anchor; to extol, magnify; amicum, to comfort; to bring up a child; to take away, carry off, to destroy, get rid of; fig., to remove; to annul, legem.

tŏlūtārius -a -um, trotting.

tōmācŭlum (tōmaclum) -i, n. a kind of sausage.

tōmentum -i, n. stuffing of a pillow, etc.

Tŏmi -ōrum, m. and **Tŏmis -idis**, f. on the Black Sea, the place of exile of Ovid.

tōmus -i, m. a cutting, shred.

tondĕo, tŏtondi, tonsum, 2. to shave, shear, clip; to mow, cut down; to browse upon.

tŏnitrus -ūs, m. and **tŏnitrŭum -i**, n. thunder.

tŏno -ŭi, 1. to sound, resound; to thunder.

tonsa -ae, f. an oar.

tonsillae -ārum, f. the tonsils.

tonsor -ōris, m. a barber.

tonsōrius -a -um, for clipping, cutting.

tonstrīcŭla -ae, f. (dim. of tonstrix), little female barber.

tonstrīna -ae, f. a barber's shop.

tonstrix -icis, f. a female barber.

tonsūra -ae, f. a shearing, shaving.

tŏphus = tofus (q.v.).

tŏpia -ōrum, n. ornamental gardening; adj., **tŏpiārius**; subst. **tŏpiārius -ii**, m. a landscape gardener; **tŏpiāria -ae**, f. the art of landscape gardening; **tŏpiārium -ii**, n. landscape gardening.

tŏral -ālis, n. valance of a couch.

tŏreuma -ătis, n. carved or embossed work.

tormentum -i, n. an instrument for twisting, winding, pressing; a windlass, pulley, instrument of torture, the rack; torture; a military engine; missile.

tormina -um, n. the colic.

torminōsus -a -um, suffering from the colic.

torno, 1. to turn in a lathe, make round.

tornus -i, m. a lathe.

tŏrōsus -a -um, muscular, fleshy.

torpēdo -inis, f. torpor, sluggishness; the fish called the torpedo.

torpĕo, 2. to be stiff, inert, numb; to be mentally benumbed.

torpesco -pŭi, 3. to become stiff.

torpidus -a -um, stiff, numb.

torpor -ōris, m. stiffness, numbness, stupefaction; duliness, inertness.

torquātus -a -um, wearing a twisted collar or necklace; **Torquātus**, surname of T. Manlius.

torquĕo, torsi, **tortum**, 2. to twist, bend, wind; to spin; *fig.*, to guide, turn; to roll; to whirl; to turn up; to throw round oneself; to distort, sprain; to torment.

torquis (torques) -is, *m.* a twisted collar *or* necklace; a chaplet.

tŏrrens -entis, *p. adj.* burning, hot, parched ; *of water*, boiling ; *subst.*, torrens -entis, *m.* a torrent.

torrĕo, torrŭi, tostum, 2. to burn, parch; *tosti crines*, singed.

torresco, 3. to become parched, be dried up.

torridus -a -um, *pass.*, parched, burnt; dry ; meagre ; nipped with cold; *act.*, burning, hot.

torris -is, *m.* a firebrand.

tortĕ, *adv.* crookedly, awry.

tortilis -e, twisted, twined.

torto, 1. to torture.

tortor -ōris, *m.* a torturer, executioner.

tortŭōsus -a -um, tortuous; perplexed, involved.

1. tortus -a -um, *p. adj.* twisted, crooked.

2. tortus -ūs, *m.* a winding, curve.

tŏrus -i, *m.* any round swelling, protuberance ; a knot ; muscle ; a bed, cushion, couch; a bier; a mound.

torvitas -ātis, *f.* savageness, wildness.

torvus -a -um, savage, gloomy, grim.

tŏt, *num. indecl.*, so many ; *with quot*, as.

tōtidem, *num. indecl.*, just as many.

tōtiens = *toties* (*q.v.*).

tōtĭēs, *adv.* so often, so many times ; just as many times.

tōtus -a -um, *genit.* tōtīus, *dat.* tōti, the whole, all, entire; complete, full; *subst.*, tōtum -i, *n.* the whole.

toxĭcon (-um) -i, *n.* poison for arrows.

trābālis -e, relating to beams of wood; *clavus*, a spike.

trābĕa -ae, *f.* a white robe, *worn by kings, knights, etc.*

trābĕātus -a -um, clad in the *trabea*.

trabs, trābis, *f.* a beam of wood; trunk of a tree; roof, house.

tractābilis -e, that can be handled, manageable; yielding, tractable.

tractātio -ōnis, *f.* a handling, management.

tractātor -ōris, *m.* a shampooer.

tractātrix -īcis, *f.* a female shampooer.

tractātus -ūs, *m.* a handling, management; treatment.

tractim, *adv.* gradually, by degrees ; slowly.

tracto, 1. to drag along, haul; to touch; to handle, treat, manage; to act, play; to treat, behave oneself towards; to discuss, handle a subject.

tractum -i, *n.* a flock of wool when carded *or* combed out.

1. tractus -a -um, *p. adj.* drawn from, proceeding from; fluent, flowing.

2. tractus -ūs, *m.* drawing, draught,

course; the extent, position, *castrorum;* a tract of country, district; *fig.*, course, motion; *of time*, course; delay.

trādĭtĭo -ōnis, *f.* a transferring, surrender ; *of a teacher*, instruction ; *of a writer*, relation.

trādĭtor -ōris, *m.* a traitor.

trādo -dĭdi -dĭtum, 3. to give up, hand over; to consign to; to entrust; to give in marriage; to give over to the enemy, deliver up ; *se*, to devote oneself to some thing *or* person; to recommend ; to hand down to posterity ; to hand down in writing, relate.

trādūco (transdūco) -duxi -ductum, 3. to carry over, lead over, bring over *or* across ; (*fig.*, to transpose, change ; to alter, bring over) ; *of time*, to pass, spend ; to direct ; to lead, conduct through ; to lead by, lead past; to show, let be seen; to expose to ridicule.

trāductĭo -ōnis, *f.* a leading on ; *fig.*, transferring from a patrician family to a plebeian ; a bringing to public disgrace ; a figure of speech, metonymy; *temporis*, passage, lapse of time.

trāductor -ōris, *m.* a transferrer.

trādux -ŭcis, *m.* a vine-layer.

trăgĭcē, *adv.* tragically, after the manner of a tragedy.

trăgĭcus -a -um, tragic; lofty, sublime; fearful, terrible; *subst.*, trăgĭcus -i, *m.* a tragic poet.

trăgoedĭa -ae, *f.* a tragedy ; a tragic scene; tragic pathos.

trăgoedus -i, *m.* a tragic actor.

trăgŭla -ae, *f.* a species of javelin.

trăgus -i, *m.* a kind of fish.

trăhĕa (trăha) -ae, *f.* a sledge, drag.

trăho, traxi, tractum, 3. to draw, drag along, *aliquem pedibus* ; to lead, draw away; to bring upon; to ascribe, refer to; to attract; *poet.* to assume ; to receive, gain ; to take ; to draw together; *vela*, to furl; to drag off, plunder, to borrow, derive ; to squander; to reflect on; to lengthen; to spin out; to put off.

trāiectĭo -ōnis, *f.* a crossing over; passage; transposition; hyperbole.

trāiectus -ūs, *m.* a passing over, passage.

trāĭcĭo -iēci -iectum, 3. to throw over *or* across, convey over; to lead over *or* around ; to transport, *etc.* ; to hurl beyond, *murum iaculo*; to stab, transfix; to break through; *reflex.*, to cross over, go over.

trālātĭcĭus = *translaticius* (*q.v.*).

trālātĭo = *translatio* (*q.v.*).

trālātus *v. transfero*.

trālūcĕo = *transluceo* (*q.v.*).

trāma -ae, *f.* the woof *in weaving*.

trāmĕo = *transmeo* (*q.v.*).

trāmes -ĭtis, *m.* a by-way, cross-road; *poet.* way, path.

trāmigro = *transmigro* (*q.v.*).

trāmitto = transmitto (q.v.).

trānāto (transnāto), 1. to swim across.

trāno (transno), 1. to swim across; to pass through.

tranquillē, adv. quietly, tranquilly.

tranquillitas -ātis, f. calmness, tranquillity; rest, peace.

1. **tranquillō**, adv. quietly.

2. **tranquillō**, 1. to make tranquil.

tranquillus -a -um, tranquil, calm, peaceful; subst., **tranquillum** -i, n. a calm, quiet.

trans, prep. with acc. on the other side of; across.

transābeo -ii -itum, 4. to go through, penetrate.

transactor -ōris, m. manager.

transādigo -ēgi -actum, 3. to drive through, thrust through; to pierce, penetrate.

transalpīnus -a -um, beyond the Alps, transalpine.

transcendo(transscendo) -scendi -scensum, 3. to climb over, pass over; fig., to transgress.

transcrībo(transscrībo) -scripsi -scriptum, 3. to copy, transcribe; to transfer, assign.

transcurro -cŭcurri and -curri -cursum, 3. to hasten over; fig., to pass over; to hasten through; to travel past; of time, to pass by.

transcursus -ūs, m. a hastening through; a brief mention (late).

transdānŭvĭānus -a -um, beyond the Danube.

transdo = trado (q.v.).

transdūco = traduco (q.v.).

transenna -ae, f. a lattice.

transeo -ii -itum, 4. intransit., to go over to, go to, to pass by; to go over as a deserter; to be transformed into; of discourse, to make a transition; to go through, to penetrate; of time, to pass; transit., to go over; to overtake; to touch lightly on; of time, to pass, spend.

transfĕro (trāfĕro), transtŭli, translātum and trālātum, transferre, 3. to carry over or across, transport, convey; to write down; to transpose; sermonem alio, turn to another subject; to put off; to change to; to translate; to use figuratively.

transfīgo -fixi -fixum, 3. to pierce through, transfix.

transfiguro, 1. to transform (late).

transfŏdio -fōdi -fossum, 3. to stab through, transfix.

transformis -e, changed, transformed.

transformo, 1. to change, transform.

transfrĕto, 1. to cross the sea (late).

transfŭga -ae, c. a deserter.

transfŭgio -fūgi -fūgitum, 3. to desert to the enemy.

transfŭgium -ii, n. a deserting.

transfundo -fūdi -fūsum, 3. to pour from one vessel into another; to transfer.

transfūsio -ōnis, f. a pouring out, pouring off.

transgrĕdior -gressus sum, 3. dep. intransit. to go across or over; to advance; transit. to pass over, pass through; to surpass.

transgressio -ōnis, f. a going over, passage; transposition of words.

transgressus -ūs, m. a going over, passage.

transĭgo -ēgi -actum, 3. to stab, pierce through; to pass time; to finish, accomplish; to settle a difference; to put an end to.

transilio (transsilio) -ŭi and (rarely) -ii and -ivi, 4. to leap across; to hasten over; to pass over; to transgress.

transitio -ōnis, f. a going across, passing over; infection, contagion; a passage.

transitōrius -a -um, having a passage through.

transitus -ūs, m. a passing over or across, transit; transition; a passing by.

transiectio, etc. = traiectio, etc. (q.v.).

translāticius (trālāticius) -a -um, handed down as customary, prescriptive; common, usual.

translātio (trālātio) -ōnis, f. a transferring; a grafting of plants; a metaphor.

translātīvus -a -um, relating to a transference.

translātor -ōris, m. a transferrer.

translūceo (trālūceo), 2. to shine through.

transmărīnus -a -um, foreign.

transmĕo (trāmĕo), 1. to go over, through.

transmigro, 1. to migrate.

transmissio -ōnis, f. a passage.

transmissus -ūs, m. a passage.

transmitto (trāmitto) -misi -missum, 3. to send across, transmit; to give over; to entrust; to yield; to devote; to let through; to lead from one point to another; to pass through or over; to hurl over; to leave unnoticed, not to mind.

transmontāni -ōrum, m. dwellers beyond the mountains.

transmŏvĕo -mōvi -mōtum, 2. to remove; to transfer.

transmūto, 1. to change, transmute.

transnăto = tranato (q.v.).

transnōmino, 1. to change the name.

transpădānus -a -um, beyond the Po, transpadane.

transpectus -ūs, m. a looking through, seeing through.

transpicio (transspicio), 3. to look through, see through.

transpōno -pŏsŭi -pŏsitum, 3. to put over, transfer; to put across.

transportātio -ōnis, f. a migration.

transporto, 1. to convey, transport.

transrhēnānus -a -um, beyond the Rhine.

transs ... *v. trans* ...

transtiběrīnus -a -um, beyond the Tiber.

transtrum -i, *n.* a cross-bench on which rowers sat; a cross-beam.

transulto (transsulto), 1. to spring across.

transŭo (transsŭo) -sŭi -sūtum, 3. to sew through, pierce through.

transvectio (trăvectio) -ōnis, *f.* a carrying over or across; the riding of a Roman knight past the censor at the periodical muster.

transvěho (trăvěho) -vexi -vectum, 3. to carry over, transport; to carry through or by; to bear along in triumph; *transvehi*, to ride, sail, pass over; *of time*, to pass.

transverběro, 1. to pierce through, transfix.

transversārius -a -um, lying across, transverse.

transversus (trăversus *and* **transvorsus) -a -um**, *p. adj.* transverse, oblique, athwart; *transverso ambulare foro*, across the forum; *transverso itinere*, in an oblique direction; *transversum digitum*, a finger's breadth; *subst.*, **transversum -i**, *n.* a cross-direction; *de* or *ex transverso*, unexpectedly. *Adv.*, *transversum* and *plur.*, *transversa*, across, sideways.

transvŏlito, 1. to fly across.

transvŏlo (trăvŏlo), 1. to fly over or across; to hasten over, across; to fly through or to; to fly past; to hasten past.

trăpētus -i, *m.* **trăpētum -i**, *n.*, *and plur.*, **trăpētes -um**, *m.* an oil-press.

Trăsŭmēnus (Trăsūmennus, Trăsĭmēnus, Trăsўmēnus) -i, *m.* the Trasimene lake, where Hannibal conquered the Romans.

trav ... *v. transv* ...

trăvio, 1. to go through, penetrate.

Trěbia -ae, *m.* river in Cisalpine Gaul, where Hannibal conquered the Romans.

trěcēni -ae -a, three hundred each.

trěcentēsimus -a -um, the three-hundredth.

trěcenti -ae -a, three hundred.

trěcentiēs (trěcentiens), *adv.* three hundred times.

trěchědipnum -i, *n.* a light garment worn by parasites at table.

trěděcim, thirteen.

trěmēbundus (trěmĭbundus) -a -um, trembling.

trěmēfăcio -fēci -factum, 3. to cause to tremble.

trěmendus -a -um, fearful, terrible.

trěmesco (trěmisco), 3. to tremble, quake; *transit.*, to tremble at.

trěmĭbundus = *tremebundus* (*q.v.*).

trěmisco = *tremesco* (*q.v.*).

trěmo -ŭi, 3. to tremble, quake; *transit.*, to tremble, quake at.

trěmor -ōris, *m.* a trembling, tremor.

trěmŭlus -a -um, trembling, tremulous; *act.*, causing trembling.

trěpidantěr, *adv.* anxiously, with trepidation.

trěpidātio -ōnis, *f.* agitation, anxiety.

trěpidē, *adv.* tremblingly, anxiously.

trěpido, 1. to be in anxious, confused motion, be agitated ; *circa signa*, give way in front ; *trepidant flammae*, flicker.

trěpidus -a -um, anxious, alarmed, restless; *unda*, boiling, bubbling.

trēs, trĭa, three.

tressis -is, *m.* three asses.

tresvĭri = *triumviri* (*q.v.*).

Trēvěri (Trēvĭri) -ōrum, *m.* a powerful German nation.

triangŭlus -a -um, three-cornered, triangular; *subst.*, **triangŭlum -i**, *n.* a triangle.

triārii -ōrum, *m.* the Roman soldiers who were drawn up in the third rank.

tribŭārius -a -um, relating to a tribe.

tribŭla = *tribulum* (*q.v.*).

tribūlis -is, *m.* a fellow-tribesman.

tribŭlo, 1. to press.

tribŭlum, 1, *n.* threshing machine.

tribŭlus -i, *m.* a thorny plant.

tribūnal -ālis, *n.* the tribunal; a raised platform for magistrates ; the magistrates.

tribūnātus -ūs, *m.* tribuneship.

tribūnicius -a -um, relating to a tribune; *subst.*, **tribūnicius -ii**, *m.* a person who has been tribune.

tribūnus -i, *m.* a tribune; *tribuni aerarii*, paymasters.

tribŭo -ŭi -ūtum, 3. to allot, give ; to show; to give up, yield to; to attribute to.

tribus -ūs, *f.* a tribe.

tribūtārius -a -um, relating to tribute.

tribūtim, *adv.* tribe by tribe.

tribūtio -ōnis, *f.* a distribution.

tribūtum -i, *n.* tax, tribute; gift.

1. **tribūtus -a -um**, arranged according to tribes.

2. **tribūtus**, *v. tribuo.*

trīcae -ārum, *f.* trifles, nonsense ; vexations.

trīcēnārius -a -um, containing the number thirty.

trīcēni -ae -a, thirty each.

trĭceps -cĭpitis, three-headed.

trīcēsimus -a -um, thirtieth.

trĭchila -ae, *f.* a summer-house, arbour.

trĭciēs (trĭciens), *adv.* thirty times.

trĭclīnium -ii, *n.* a dining-couch ; dining-room.

trĭcor, 1. *dep.* to make difficulties, to shuffle, trifle.

trĭcorpor -pŏris, having three bodies.

tricuspis -ĭdis, having three points.

tridens -entis, having three teeth *or* prongs ; *subst.*, **tridens -entis,** *m.* a trident.

tridentifer -fĕri, *m.* the trident-bearer.

tridentiger -gĕri, *m.* the trident-bearer.

trĭdŭum -i, *n.* a space of three days.

triennia -ium, *n.* a festival celebrated every three years.

triennium -ii, *n.* a space of three years.

triens -entis, *m.* a third part, one-third.

trientăbŭlum -i, *n.* the equivalent in land for the third part of a sum of money.

triērarchus -i, *m.* the commander of a trireme.

triēris -e, having three banks of oars; *subst.*, **triēris -is,** *f.* a trireme.

triētēricus -a -um, recurring every three years, triennial.

triētēris -idis, *f.* a space of three years; a triennial festival.

trĭfārĭam, *adv.* in a threefold manner = in three places, on three sides.

trifaux -faucis, having three throats.

trifidus -a -um, split in three parts, three-forked.

trifilis -e, having three hairs.

triformis -e, having three forms; three-fold.

trigĕminus (tergĕminus) -a -um, three-fold.

trĭginta, *num.* thirty.

trigōn -ōnis, *m.* a ball for playing; a game at ball.

trigōnālis -e, three-cornered.

trilibris -e, of three pounds' weight.

trilinguis -e, having three tongues.

trilix -icis, having three threads.

trimestris, 3. three monthly.

trimĕtĕr = *trimetrus (q.v.).*

trimetros (-us) -a -um, containing three *metra, i.e.,* three double feet; *subst.*, **trimetros (-us),** *and* **trimĕtĕr -tri,** a trimeter.

trĭmus -a -um, three years old.

Trinacria -ae, *f.* the oldest name of Sicily.

trini -ae -a, three each.

Trinobantes -um, *m.* people in the east of Britain.

trinōdis -e, having three knots.

trĭōnes -um, *m.* the ploughing oxen; the constellations known as the Great Bear and Little Bear.

tripartīto (*and gen.*) **tripertītō,** *adv.* in three parts.

tripartītus (*and gen.*) **tripertītus -a -um,** threefold, triple.

tripectŏrus -a -um, having three breasts.

tripĕdālis -e, of three feet in measure.

tripĕdānĕus = *tripedalis (q.v.).*

tripert . . . *v. tripart . . .*

tripēs -pĕdis, having three feet.

triplex -plicis, threefold, triple; *subst.*, **triplices -um,** *m.* a writing tablet with three leaves.

triplus -a -um, threefold, triple.

trĭpŭdio, 1. to dance.

trĭpŭdium -ii, *n.* a religious dance; a favourable omen when the sacred chickens ate so fast that the food fell out of their beaks.

tripūs -pŏdis, *m.* a tripod.

triquetrus -a -um, three-cornered.

trirēmis -e, having three banks of oars; *subst.*, **trirēmis -is,** *f.* a trireme.

triscurria -ōrum, *n.* gross buffooneries.

tristĕ, *adv.* sadly, sorrowfully, mourn-fully; harshly.

tristi = *trivisti, v. tero.*

tristĭcŭlus -a -um (*dim. of tristis*), some-what sorrowful.

tristificus -a -um, causing sadness.

tristimōnia -ae, *f.* sadness, melancholy.

tristis -e, sad, melancholy ; gloomy ; disastrous; surly; harsh.

tristitia -ae, *f.* sadness, melancholy ; ill-humour; sternness.

trisulcus -a -um, threefold; three-forked.

trīticĕus (trīticĕĭus) -a -um, of wheat, wheaten.

trīticum -i, *n.* wheat.

Trītōn -ōnis, *m.* son of Neptune, a deity of the sea.

trītūra -ae, *f.* threshing.

1. trītus -a -um, *p. adj.* much trodden, much frequented ; *of discourse,* common, trite.

2. trītus -ūs, *m.* a rubbing.

triumphālis -e, triumphal ; *subst.*, **triumphālia -ium,** *n.* decorations of a triumphing general.

triumpho, 1. *intransit.,* to have a tri-umph ; to gain a victory ; to exult ; *transit.,* to triumph over.

triumphus -i, *m., old form,* **triumpus -i,** *m. lit.,* a solemn dance; a triumphal procession, a triumph; victory.

triumvir -viri, *m.* a triumvir; *plur.,* *triumviri,* commissioners.

triumvirālis -e, relating to a triumvir.

triumvirātus -ūs, *m.* the office of a trium-vir.

Trivia, Diana.

triviālis -e, ordinary, trivial.

trivium -ii, *n.* a place where three roads meet; a public place.

trivius -a -um, honoured at three cross-roads.

Trōas -ădis *and* **-ădos,** *v. Tros.*

trŏchaeus -i, *m.* a trochee, a metrical foot.

trochlĕa (troclĕa) -ae, *f.* set of blocks and pulleys for raising weights.

trŏchus -i, *m.* a boy's hoop.

Trōes, *v. Tros.*

Trōglŏdȳtae -ārum, *m.* cave-dwellers in Aethiopia.

Trōia, Troianus, *v. Tros.*

Trōïădes, *v. Tros.*

Trōicus, *v. Tros.*

Trōïlus (-ŏs) -i, *m.* son of Priam.

Trōïŭgĕna -ae, *c.* born in Troy, Trojan.

trŏpaeum -i, *n.* trophy, monument of victory.

trŏpis -is, *f.* the lees of wine.

trŏpus -i, *m.* a trope, figure of speech (*late*).

Trōs, Trōis, *m.* son of Erichthonius, after whom Troy was named; **Troia -ae**, *f.* the town of Troy; *adjs.* **Trōius, Trō-iānus, Trōicus**; **Trōs, Trōis**, *m.* a Trojan; plur., **Trōes -um**; **Trōäs -adis** *or* **-ădos**, *adj. fem.*, Trojan; *subst.*, a Trojan woman; **Trōiädes -um**, *f.* Trojan women.

trossŭli -ōrum, *m.* name given to the Roman knights; dandies.

trŭcīdātio -ōnis, *f.* a slaughtering, massacre.

trŭcīdo, 1. to cut to pieces, massacre; to destroy.

trŭcŭlentĕr, *adv.* fiercely.

trŭcŭlentia -ae, *f.* severity of climate.

trŭcŭlentus -a -um, savage, cruel; unfriendly; *of the sea*, disturbed.

trŭdis -is, *f.* a sharp stake.

trŭdo, trūsi, trūsum, 3. to push, press; to put forth buds; to force.

trulla -ae, *f.* a ladle; a basin.

trunco, 1. to shorten, mutilate.

1. **truncus -i**, *m.* the trunk of a tree; the stem; the trunk of the body.

2. **truncus -a -um**, maimed, mutilated.

truso, 1. to push violently.

trutina -ae, *f.* a pair of scales.

trutinor, 1. *dep.* to weigh.

trux, trucis, savage grim; threatening.

tu, *pron. pers.* thou.

tuba -ae, *f.* war-trumpet.

1. **tuber -eris**, *n.* a swelling, hump; a truffle.

2. **tuber -eris**, *m.* a kind of tree.

tŭbĭcen -ĭnis, *m.* a trumpeter.

tŭbĭlustrium -ii, *n.* a feast of trumpets.

tŭbŭlus -i, *m.* (*dim. of tubus*), a little pipe.

tŭbus -i, *m.* a pipe.

tuccētum -i, *n.* a kind of sausage.

tŭdĭto, 1. to strike violently, strike often.

tŭĕo, 2. = *tueor* (*q.v.*).

tŭĕor, tŭĭtus *and* **tūtus sum, tŭĕri**, 2. *dep.* to look at, regard, see; to care for, protect; to support, maintain.

tŭgŭrium -ii, *n.* a peasant's hut, cottage.

tŭĭtio -ōnis, *f.* a protecting, preserving.

Tulliŏla -ae, *f.* (*dim. of Tullia*), the pet name of Tullia, Cicero's daughter.

Tullius -a -um, the name of a Roman family; *adj.*, **Tulliānus**; *subst.*, **Tul-liānum -i**, *n.* part of a Roman state prison.

tum, *adv. of time*, then, at that time; then, thereupon; afterwards, in the next place; *quum* (*cum*) ... *tum*, both ... and especially; not only ... but also.

tŭmĕfăcio -fēci -factum, 3. *pass.*,

tŭmĕfio -factus sum -fiĕri, to cause to swell; to puff up with pride.

tŭmĕo, 2. to swell, be swollen; to glow with passion *or* pride.

tŭmesco, tŭmŭi, 3. to begin to swell, to swell; to begin to break out; *tumescunt bella.*

tŭmidus -a -um, swollen, puffed up, tumid; raging with passion *or* excitement; puffed up with pride; pompous.

tŭmor -ōris, *m.* a swelling, tumour; anger; pride; commotion.

tŭmŭlo, 1. to bury.

tŭmŭlōsus -a -um, hilly.

tŭmultŭārius -a -um, hastily brought together, suddenly levied; sudden, disorderly.

tŭmultŭātio -ōnis, *f.* a confusion, tumult.

tŭmultŭor, 1. *dep. and* **tŭmultŭo**, 1. to be confused, in an uproar.

tŭmultŭōsĕ, *adv.* confusedly, tumultuously.

tŭmultŭōsus -a -um, alarmed, turbulent; causing alarm.

tŭmultus -ūs, *m.* noise, confusion, tumult; insurrection; excitement.

tŭmŭlus -i, *m.* a mound of earth, hill.

tunc, *adv.* then; at that time.

tundo, tŭdŭdi, tunsum *and* **tūsum**, 3. to beat, strike repeatedly; to deafen, importune.

tŭnica -ae, *f.* a tunic; a skin, covering, peel.

tŭnicātus -a -um, clothed in a tunic.

tŭnicŭla (tŭnicla) -ae, *f.* (*dim. of tunica*), a little tunic.

tŭor = *tueor* (*q.v.*).

turba -ae, *f.* tumult, disturbance; a crowd; the mob.

turbāmentum -i, *n.* a means of disturbance.

turbātĕ, *adv.* confusedly.

turbātio -ōnis, *f.* disturbance, confusion.

turbātor -ōris, *m.* a disturber, troubler.

turbātus -a -um, *p. adj.* disturbed; restless, troubled; angered.

turben -inis, *n.* a whirlwind.

turbĭdĕ, *adv.* in disorder.

turbidus -a -um, confused, wild; turbid, disquieted; angry; agitated, *res*; causing disturbance.

turbĭnĕus -a -um, shaped like a top.

1. **turbo**, 1. to disturb, throw into disorder; to cause disorder; to become bankrupt; to alarm; to stir up.

2. **turbo -inis**, *m.* an eddy; a whirlwind, hurricane, storm; a top, a plaything; a reel, spindle.

turbŭlentĕ *and* **turbŭlentĕr**, *adv.* turbulently, tumultuously.

turbŭlentus -a -um, stormy, boisterous; restless; confusing.

turda, *v. turdus.*

turdus -i, *m. and* **turda -ae**, *f.* a thrush.

tūrĕus -a -um, relating to incense.

turgĕo, 2. to be swollen; *of discourse*, to be pompous, turgid.

turgesco, 3. to begin to swell, swell up; to be excited with passion.

turgĭdŭlus -a -um (*dim. of turgidus*), somewhat swollen.

turgĭdus -a -um, swollen, turgid.

turĭbŭlum -i, *n.* a censer for burning incense.

tūricrĕmus -a -um, burning with incense.

tūrĭfer -fĕra -fĕrum, producing incense.

tūrĭlĕgus -a -um, collecting incense.

turma -ae, *f.* troop of cavalry; a squadron.

turmālis -e, relating to a troop *or* squadron.

turmātim, *adv.* troop by troop, in troops.

Turnus -i, *m.* king of the Rutuli, killed by Aeneas.

turpĭcŭlus -a -um (*dim. of turpis*), somewhat ugly *or* deformed.

turpĭfĭcātus -a -um, corrupted.

turpis -e, ugly, filthy; disgraceful, dishonourable. *Subst.*, **turpe -is**, *n.* a disgrace.

turpĭtĕr, *adv.* foully, in an ugly manner; scandalously, dishonourably.

turpĭtūdo -ĭnis, *f.* ugliness, unsightliness; baseness, dishonour.

turpo, 1. to make ugly, defile; to dishonour.

turrĭcŭla -ae, *f.* (*dim. of turris*), a little tower, turret; a dice-box.

turrĭgĕr -gĕra -gĕrum, tower-bearing.

turris -is, *f.* a tower; a dovecot.

turrītus -a -um, furnished with towers; *poet.* towering high.

turtur -ŭris, *m.* a turtle-dove.

tūs (thūs), tūris, *n.* incense, frankincense.

Tusci -ōrum, *m.* the Tuscans, Etruscans. **Tuscŭlānus**, Tusculan.

Tuscŭlum -i, *n.* an old town in Latium.

tussio, 4. to have a cough, to cough.

tussis -is, *acc. -im*, *f.* a cough.

tūtāmen -ĭnis, *n.* defence, protection.

tūtāmentum -i, *n.* defence, protection.

tūtē, *strengthened form of tu.*

tūtō, *adv.* safely, securely.

tūtēla -ae, *f.* protection, guard, charge; guardianship; care, management.

tūtō, *adv.* safely, securely.

1. **tūtor -ōris**, *m.* a protector; a guardian.

2. **tūto**, 1. *and* **tūtor**, 1. *dep.* to protect, watch, keep; to ward off.

tūtus -a -um, *p. adj.* safe, secure; cautious; *subst.*, **tūtum -i**, *n.* a safe place, safety.

tŭus -a -um, *pron. poss.* thy, thine.

Tỹbris = Tiberis (*q.v.*).

Tỹbur = Tibur (*q.v.*).

Tỹdĕus -ĕi *and* **-ĕos**, *m.* father of Diomedes.

tympănum -i, *n.* a tambourine, kettledrum; drum *or* wheel for raising weights.

Tyndărĕus -ĕi, *m.* king of Sparta, husband of Leda and father of Castor and Pollux, Helen and Clytemnestra.

Tỹphōĕus -ĕos, *m.* a giant.

1. **Tỹphōn -ōnis**, *m.* another name of Typhoeus.

tỹpus -i, *m.* a figure on a wall.

tỹrannĭcē, *adv.* tyrannically.

tỹrannĭcĭda -ae, *c.* a tyrannicide.

tỹrannĭcus -a -um, tyrannical.

tỹrannis -ĭdis, *f.* tyranny.

tỹrannoctŏnus -i, *m.* slayer of a tyrant.

tỹrannus -i, *m.* lord, master; a usurper, despot.

Tỹrĭanthĭna -ōrum, *n.* violet-coloured garments.

Tỹrĭus, Tyrian.

tỹrŏtărĭchum -i, *m.* a dish of cheese and salt-fish.

Tyrrhēni -ōrum, *m.* the Etruscans, the people who inhabited the country north of Latium. **Tyrrhēnia -ae**, *f.* Etruria.

Tỹrus (-os) -i, *f.* a city of Phoenicia.

U

U u, *originally written* V, *v, the twentieth letter of the Latin Alphabet.*

1. **ūber -ĕris**, *n.* udder, teat, breast; abundance, fertility.

2. **ūber -ĕris**, rich, fertile, abundant; full, copious.

ūbĕrius, *superl.*, **ūberrĭmē**, *adv.* more abundantly; more at length, *disputare.*

ūbertas -ātis, *f.* fertility, abundance.

ūbertim, *adv.* abundantly.

ŭbi, where.

ŭbicumquĕ (ŭbicunquĕ), *adv.* wherever, wheresoever; *indef.*, anywhere, everywhere.

Ubĭi -ōrum, *m.* a German people who, in Caesar's time, dwelt on the east bank of the Rhine near Cologne.

ŭbiquăquĕ (*sc. parte*), wherever.

ŭbiquĕ, *adv.* wherever, everywhere.

ŭbĭvis, *wherever you will, anywhere, everywhere.*

ūdo -ōnis, *m.* a fur shoe *or* sock.

ūdus -a -um, wet, moist; soft, yielding.

ulcĕro, 1. to make sore, to ulcerate; *tecur*, to wound the heart.

ulcĕrōsus -a -um, ulcerated.

ulciscor, ultus sum, ulcisci, 3. *dep.* to avenge; to take vengeance on, to punish.

ulcus -ĕris, *n.* a sore, ulcer.

ūlīgo -ĭnis, *f.* moisture of the soil.

Ŭlixes -is, *m. Latin name for Odysseus,* son of Laertes, husband of Penelope, father of Telemachus, king of Ithaca, famed for his cunning and for his wanderings after the siege of Troy.

ullus -a -um, any. *Subst.*, *m.* anyone (= *quisquam*).

ulmus -i, *f.* the elm.

ulna -ae, f. the elbow; an ell.

ultĕrior, compar. adj.; posit., only in the adverbial forms ultra, ultro. Compar., ultĕrior, on the other side, beyond; distance, farther. Superl., ultimus, the most distant, farthest, last; the last, final; subst., ultimum -i, n. the greatest; the worst; ultimum bonorum, the highest good; adv., ad ultimum, utterly, entirely.

ultĕrius, neut. of ulterior.

ultimus, v. ulterior.

ultio -ōnis, f. an avenging, revenge.

ultor -ōris, m. avenger, punisher.

ultrā, adv. on the other side of; beyond, further; of time, longer; compar., ulterius, further; prep. with acc., beyond.

ultrix -īcis, f. avenging.

ultrō, adv. on the other side, beyond; besides, moreover; of one's own accord.

ŭlŭla -ae, f. a screech-owl.

ŭlŭlātus -ūs, m. wailing, shrieking.

ŭlŭlo, 1. to howl, yell; of places, to resound with howling.

ulva -ae, f. sedge.

Ŭlysses = Ulixes (q.v.).

umbella -ae, f. (dim. of umbra), a parasol.

umbilicus -i, m. the navel; the middle of anything; the end of a roller on which a MS. was rolled.

umbo -ōnis, m. the boss of a shield; a shield; the elbow.

umbra -ae, f. a shade, shadow; protection; an uninvited guest; any shady place; a ghost.

umbrācŭlum -i, n. a shady place, arbour; a parasol.

umbrāticus -a -um, belonging to the shade (late).

umbrātilis -e, retired, contemplative; of discourse, in the manner of the schools.

Umbri -ōrum, m. a people in Italy between the Padus, the Tiber, and the Adriatic Sea. Umbria -ae, f. Umbria.

umbrĭfer -fĕra -fĕrum, shady.

umbro, 1. to shade, overshadow.

umbrōsus -a -um, shady, salix.

ŭmecto = humecto (q.v.).

ŭmĕrus = humerus (q.v.).

ŭmesco, umidus = humesco, humidus (q.v.).

ŭmor = humor (q.v.).

umquam (unquam), adv. at any time, ever.

ŭnā, adv. at the same time, together.

ūnănĭmans = ūnanimus (q.v.).

ūnănĭmitas -atis, f. unanimity.

ūnănĭmus -a -um, agreeing, unanimous.

uncia -ae, f. an ounce, the twelfth part of any whole.

unciārius -a -um, relating to a twelfth part.

unciātim, adv. little by little.

uncīnātus -a -um, hooked.

unciŏla -ae, f. (dim. of uncia), a little ounce, a little twelfth part.

unctio -ōnis, f. an anointing; ointment.

unctor -ōris, m. an anointer.

unctōrium -ii, n. anointing-room in the bath.

unctūra -ae, f. anointing of the dead.

unctus -a -um, p. adj. smeared, anointed; rich, copious; subst., unctum -i, n. a sumptuous repast.

1. uncus -i, m. a hook.

2. uncus -a -um, hooked, curved.

unda -ae, f. a wave of the sea; storm, surge; moisture; water.

undĕ, adv. whence, from where; from what origin; legal, unde petitur = the defendant.

undĕciēs (undĕciens), adv. eleven times.

undĕcim, eleven.

undĕcĭmus -a -um, the eleventh.

undĕcumque (undĕcunque), adv. whencesoever.

undēni -ae -a, eleven each.

undēnōnāginta, eighty-nine.

undēoctōgintā, seventy-nine.

undēquadrāgintā, thirty-nine.

undēquinquāgēsimus -a -um, the forty-ninth.

undēquinquāgintā, forty-nine.

undēsexāgintā, fifty-nine.

undētrīcēsimus -a -um, the twenty-ninth.

undētrigintā, twenty-nine.

undēvīcēsimus (undēvīgēsimus), the nineteenth.

undēviginti, nineteen.

undĭquĕ, adv. on all sides, from everywhere, everywhere; in every respect.

undisŏnus -a -um, resounding with waves.

undo, 1. to rise in waves, surge; to wave, to undulate.

undōsus -a -um, surging, billowy.

ūnetvīcēsĭmāni -ōrum, m. soldiers of the twenty-first legion.

ūnetvīcēsimus -a -um, the twenty-first.

ungo (unguo), unxi, unctum, 3. to anoint, smear, salve.

unguen -inis, n. a fatty substance, salve.

unguentārius -a -um, relating to salve or ointment; subst., unguentārius -ii, m. dealer in unguents.

unguentātus -a -um, anointed.

unguentum -i, n. ointment, unguent.

unguicŭlus -i, m. (dim. of unguis), the finger-nail, the toe-nail.

unguis -is, m. a finger or toe-nail; de tenero ungui, from childhood; ad (in) unguem, to a hair, perfectly.

ungŭla -ae, f. a hoof, claw, talon.

unguo = ungo (q.v.).

ūnĭcē, adv. singly, especially.

ūnĭcŏlor -ōris, of one colour.

ūnĭcus -a -um, only, sole; singular, unique.

ūnĭformis -e, having one form, simple.

ūnĭgĕna -ae, born at one birth, of the same race; only-begotten.

ūnĭmănus -a -um, having but one hand.

1. **ūnio**, 4. to unite.

2. **ūnio -ōnis**, m. a single large pearl.

ūnĭtas -ātis, f. unity, agreement (late).

ūnĭtĕr, adv. in one, together.

ūnĭusmŏdi, adv. of one kind.

ūnĭversālis -e, general (late).

ūnĭversā, adv. in general.

ūnĭversĭtas -ātis, f. the whole; the world; rerum, the universe.

ūnĭversus (archaic, **unĭversus**) -a -um, whole, entire; plur., **ūnĭversi -ae -a**, all together; relating to the whole, general; pugna, a general engagement; in universum, in general, generally; subst., **universum -i**, n. the whole; the whole world, the universe.

ūnus -a -um, one; ad unum omnes, all to a man; only one, alone; uno tempore, at the same time; indefinite, a, an, one.

ŭpĭlio (ŏpĭlio) -ōnis, m. a shepherd.

Ŭrănĭa -ae, f. and **Ŭrănĭē -ēs**, f. the Muse of Astronomy.

urbānē, adv. politely, wittily, elegantly.

urbānĭtas -ātis, f. city life; the city manner; politeness, refinement; elegance; fine wit.

urbānus -a -um, belonging to a city (esp. to Rome), urban; refined, elegant; humorous; subst., a wit; subst., **urbāni -ōrum**, m. the inhabitants of the city, the townsfolk.

urbĭcus -a -um, civic, urban.

urbs -bis, f. the city.

urcĕŏlus -i, m. (dim. of urceus), a small jug or pitcher.

urcĕus -i, m. earthenware jug, pitcher.

ūrēdo -ĭnis, f. blight upon plants.

urgĕo (urgŭeo), ursi, 2. to push, drive, urge; to press upon, burden, bear hard upon; to apply oneself to diligently.

ūrīnātor -ōris, m. a diver.

ūrīnor, 1. dep. to dive.

Ŭrĭos -ii, m. giver of a favourable wind (of Jupiter).

urna -ae, f. pitcher for drawing water; a jug, urn.

urnŭla -ae, f. (dim. of urna), a little pitcher.

ūro, ussi, ustum, 3. to burn; to parch; to pinch, chafe; to disturb, harass.

ursa -ae, f. a female bear; poet. = bear generally.

ursus -i, m. a bear.

urtīca -ae, f. a nettle.

ūrus -i, m. a kind of wild ox.

Ŭsĭpĕtes -um, m. and **Ŭsĭpĭi -ōrum**, m. a German tribe conquered by Caesar.

ūsĭtātē, adv. in the usual manner.

ūsĭtātus -a -um, p. adj. usual, accustomed.

uspĭam, adv. anywhere.

usquam, adv. anywhere; in any case; in any direction.

usquĕ, adv. at every point, through and through; continuously; usque Romam,

as far as Rome; of time; always, constantly; with prep., usque a Romulo, from the time of Romulus.

usquĕquāquĕ, everywhere.

ustil . . . v. ustul . . .

ustor -ōris, m. a burner of corpses.

ustŭlo (ustĭlo), 1. (rarely), to singe.

1. **ūsūcăpĭo -cēpi -captum**, 3. to acquire ownership by length of possession.

2. **ūsūcăpĭo -ōnis**, f. ownership acquired by length of possession or prescription.

ūsūra -ae, f. the use, enjoyment of anything; interest for money borrowed.

ūsurpātĭo -ōnis, f. a using, use; itineris, undertaking of.

ūsurpo, 1. to use, to bring into use; to lay claim to; to take possession of; to usurp; to perceive, to notice; to use, to mention.

ūsus -ūs, m. use, using, application, practice; social intercourse, familiarity; usefulness; usui and ex usu esse, to be useful, of use; occasion, need; usus est, it is necessary; usu venit, it happens.

ūsusfructus -ūs, use of property belonging to another.

ūt (orig. **ŭtī**), adv. and conj. Adv., as; as if; in exclamations, how! how much! how? ut valet? when, as soon as, ut haec audivit; since. Conj., with the subj., that, so that; in final clauses, in order that, that; in consecutive clauses, that, so that; with verbs of fearing — that not; timeo ut sustineo.

utcumquĕ (utcunquĕ), adv. in what manner soever, however; whenever.

ūtens -entis, p. adj. using, possessing.

ūtensĭlĭa -ĭum, n. necessaries, utensils.

1. **ūter, ūtris**, m. the skin of an animal used as a bag or bottle.

2. **ūter, utra, utrum**, which of two, which; indefinite, one of the two.

ūtercumquĕ (-cunquĕ), utrācumquĕ, utrumcumquĕ, whichever of the two, whichever.

ūterlĭbĕt, utrălĭbĕt, utrumlĭbĕt, whichever of the two you please, either of the two.

ūterquĕ, utrăquĕ, utrumquĕ, each of two, both.

ūtĕrus -i, m. and **ūtĕrum -i**, n. belly, paunch; the womb; birth; the inside of a ship, etc.

ūtervīs, utrāvīs, utrumvīs, either of the two.

ūtĭ = ut (q.v.).

ūtĭbĭlis -e, that can be used, useful.

Ūtĭca -ae, f. a town in Africa, north of Carthage, where the senatorial party made the last stand against Caesar, and where M. Porcius Cato the younger killed himself. Adj., **Ūtĭcensis -e**.

ūtĭlis -e, useful, serviceable, advantageous.

ūtilitas -ātis, f. usefulness, utility, advantage.

ūtilitĕr, adv. usefully, profitably.

ŭtinam, adv. would that! oh that!

ŭtĭquĕ, adv. at any rate, at least.

ūtor, ūsus sum, ūti, 3. dep. (with abl.), to use, enjoy; to associate with; to possess; to have occasion for.

ŭtpŏtĕ, adv. seeing that, since.

ūtrārius -ii, m. a water-carrier.

ūtrĭcŭlārius -ii, m. a bagpiper.

utrimquĕ (utrinquĕ), adv. from both sides, on both sides.

utrŏ, adv. to which side, whither.

utrŏbĭquĕ (utrūbĭquĕ), adv. on both sides.

utrŏquĕ, adv. to both sides; in both directions.

utrŭbĭque = utrōbique (q.v.).

utrum, adv. whether; in direct questions, foll. by an, annon; in indirect questions, with an, necne.

ŭtut, adv. however.

ūva -ae, f. a cluster, bunch; a bunch of grapes.

ūvens -entis, moist, wet.

ūvesco, 3. to become moist, be wet.

ūvĭdŭlus -a -um (dim. of uvidus), somewhat moist, wet.

ūvĭdus -a -um, moist, damp, humid.

uxor -ōris, f. a wife, spouse; uxorem ducere, to marry a wife.

uxōrius -a -um, relating to a wife; too devoted to one's wife.

V

V v, the twenty-first letter of the Latin Alphabet.

văcātĭo -ōnis, f. a freedom from, immunity, exemption, a being without; vacatio (militiae), furlough.

vacca -ae, f. a cow.

vaccīnium -ii, n. whortleberry.

văcēfĭo, v. vacuefacio.

văcerrōsus -a -um, mad, crazy.

văcillātĭo -ōnis, f. a rocking, reeling motion.

văcillo, 1. to totter, stagger, hesitate.

văcīvē, adv. idly, at leisure.

văcīvus -a -um, empty.

văco, 1. to be empty, free from, without anything; with abl., terra vacat humore; of property, to be vacant; to be idle, at leisure; impers., vacat, there is time for.

văcŭĕfăcĭo -fēci -factum, 3. pass., vacŭĕfĭo (văcēfĭo) -factus sum -fĭĕri, to make empty; in pass., to be empty.

văcŭĭtas -ātis, f. emptiness, freedom, immunity from, a being without anything; vacancy of a public office.

văcŭo, 1. to make empty.

văcŭus -a -um, empty, exempt, without;

(subst., văcŭum -i, n. an empty place); vacant, without a master; of women, free, unmarried; at leisure, idle.

vădĭmōnium -ii, n. bail, security.

vădo, 3. to go, walk, hasten.

vădor, 1. dep. to bind over by bail.

vădōsus -a -um, full of shallows, shallow.

vădum -i, n. a shallow, shoal, ford; poet. water, river, sea.

vae, interj. alas! woe!

vaecors = vecors (q.v.).

vaesanus = vesanus (q.v.).

văfer, vafra, vafrum, cunning, subtle, crafty.

vafrē, adv. cunningly, craftily.

văgē, adv. scattered far and wide.

vāgīna -ae, f. sheath of a sword, scabbard; the husk of grain.

vāgĭo -īvi and -ii -ītum, 4. to cry, whimper like a child.

vāgītus -ūs, m. crying of young children.

1. văgo, 1. and văgor, 1. dep. to wander about, ramble; to cruise.

2. văgor = vagitus (q.v.).

văgus -a -um, wandering, unsettled; fickle; diffuse, aimless.

văh (văhă), interj. ah! oh!

valdē, adv. very, very much, exceedingly.

vălēdĭco, 3., v. valeo.

vălens -entis, p. adj. strong, powerful; well, healthy; energetic, effective.

vălentĕr, adv. strongly, powerfully.

vălĕo -ŭi -ĭtum, 2. to be strong; to be well, healthy; vale, valeas, good-bye; valere iubere, or dicere, to say good-bye; to avail; to be strong, prevail; to be worth; of words, to mean.

Vălērius -a -um, name of a Roman gens.

vălesco, 3. to grow strong.

vălētūdĭnārius -a -um, sickly.

vălētūdo -ĭnis, f. state of health, health; ill-health; good health.

vălĭdē, adv. strongly, powerfully, mightily.

vălĭdus -a -um, strong, powerful, valida urbs; healthy; mighty, influential.

vallāris -e, relating to the vallum.

valles (vallis) -is, f. a vale, valley.

vallo, 1. to surround with a vallum; to fortify, protect.

vallum -i, n. a stockade; a fortification.

vallus -i, m. a post, stake; a stockade.

valvae -ārum, f. folding-doors.

valvātus -a -um, provided with folding-doors.

Vandăli -ōrum, m. the Vandals, in the time of Tacitus a tribe in North Germany, who, in the fifth century, invaded the south of Europe, and settled in Spain and Africa.

vănesco, 3. to pass away, disappear.

Vangĭōnes -um, m. a German people on the Rhine.

vānĭlŏquentĭa -ae, f. idle talking, vaunting.

vānĭlŏquus -a -um, lying; boasting.

vănĭtas -ātis, *f.* emptiness, unreality; fruitlessness; lying, boasting.

vannus -i, *f.* a winnowing-fan.

vānus -a -um, empty, void; vain, lying, groundless; fickle, boastful.

văpĭdē, *adv.* poorly, badly.

văpĭdus -a -um, spoiled, flat, vapid.

văpor (văpōs) -ōris, *m.* vapour, steam; warmth.

văpōrārĭum -ii, *n.* a flue for conveying hot air.

văpōrātĭo -ōnis, *f.* exhalation, vapour.

văpōro, 1. *intransit.,* to steam, reek; *transit.,* to fumigate, heat, to warm.

vappa -ae, *f.* spoiled, flat wine; worthless fellow.

văpŭlo -āvi -ātūrus, 1. to get a flogging, to be whipped; to be conquered; to be attacked by words.

Vargunteius -i, *m., Lucius,* accomplice of Catiline.

vărĭantĭa -ae, *f.* difference, variation.

vărĭātĭo -ōnis, *f.* difference, variation.

vărĭco, 1. to stand with feet apart.

vărĭcōsus -a -um, having varicose veins.

vărĭcus -a -um, straddling.

vărĭē, *adv.* with various colours; variously, in different ways.

vărĭĕtas -ātis, *f.* variety, difference; manysidedness; fickleness.

vărĭo, 1. *transit.,* to vary, to change, alter; to colour, spot; to give a different account of; to cause to waver; (*pass.,* variari,* to waver, to vary); *intransit.,* to be different, to vary; to change.

1. **vărĭus -a -um,** manifold, variegated, various; changeable; *of success,* varying, uncertain; mansided; fickle.

2. **Vărĭus -a -um,** name of a Roman gens.

vărix -ĭcis, *c.* a varicose vein.

Varro -ōnis, *m.* surname in the gens Terentia.

1. **vărus -a -um,** bent outwards; bandy-legged; different.

2. **Vărus -i,** *m.* name of several Roman families.

1. **vās, vădis,** *m.* bail, surety.

2. **vās, vāsis,** *n.* (*plur.,* **vāsa -ōrum**), a vessel, vase, utensil; *plur.,* war materials, baggage.

vāsārĭum -ii, *n.* money given to the governor of a province for his outfit; the hire of an oil-press.

vascŭlārĭus -ii, *m.* a maker of metal vessels, goldsmith.

vascŭlum -i, *n.* (*dim. of* 2. *vas*), small vessel *or* dish.

vastātĭo -ōnis, *f.* a devastating, laying waste.

vastātor -ōris, *m.* devastator; *ferarum,* a hunter.

vastē, *adv.* widely, extensively; rudely, roughly, *loqui.*

vastĭfĭcus -a -um, laying waste, devastating, *poet.*

vastĭtas -ātis, *f.* an empty space, waste, emptiness; desolation; vastness.

vasto, 1. to empty; to devastate; to plunder; *fig.,* to prey upon.

vastus -a -um, empty, desolate; devastated; enormous, horrible; rude, unrefined.

vātes -is, *c.* a prophet, prophetess, seer; bard, poet.

Vătĭcānus -a -um, mons, collis, the Vatican Hill on the west side of the Tiber.

vātĭcĭnātĭo -ōnis, *f.* a soothsayer, prophesying.

vātĭcĭnātor -ōris, *m.* soothsayer, prophet.

vātĭcĭnor, 1. *dep.* to prophesy; to talk nonsense, to rave.

vātĭcĭnus -a, -um- prophetic.

vătĭlum (bătĭlum) -i, *n.* a chafing-dish.

Vătĭnĭus -a -um, name of a Roman family.

vătĭs = *vates* (*q.v.*).

-vĕ, *enclitic,* or, or perhaps.

vēcordĭa (vaecordĭa) -ae, *f.* foolishness, madness.

vēcors (vaecors) -cordis, silly, foolish, insane.

vectātĭo -ōnis, *f.* a riding, driving, sailing, *etc.*

vectĭgal -ālis, *ab -āli,* *n.* a tax, duty; *portorium,* dues on merchandise; private income, revenue.

vectĭgālis -e, relating to taxes; bringing in income.

vectĭo -ōnis, *f.* a carrying, conveyance.

vectis -is, *m.* a crowbar; a bar, bolt.

vecto, 1. to carry, convey; *pass.,* to ride (*equis*), to be driven.

vector -ōris, *m.* one who carries; one who is carried; a passenger.

vectōrĭus -a -um, relating to carrying; *navigia,* transports.

vectūra -ae, *f.* a conveying.

vĕgĕtus -a -um, lively, active.

vĕgrandis -e, small, tiny.

vĕhĕmens -entis, violent, impetuous; strong, powerful, vigorous.

vĕhĕmentĕr, *adv.* vehemently, violently; powerfully, exceedingly.

vĕhĭcŭlum -i, *n.* vehicle; a boat; waggon, carriage.

vĕho, vexi, vectum, to carry, convey; (*pass., vehi,* to ride, drive; to advance); *intransit.,* to be borne, to ride, *only partic. pres. and gerund.*

Veii -ōrum, *m.* an old town in Etruria, destroyed by Camillus.

vĕl, or; *doubled,* either . . . or.

vēlāmen -ĭnis, *n.* covering, garment.

vēlāmentum -i, *n.* a covering; *velamenta,* olive-branches wound round with wool, carried by suppliants.

vēlārĭum -ii, *n.* the awning spread over a theatre.

vēlāti -ōrum, *m., milit.,* the reserve.

vēles -ĭtis, *m., plur., velites,* light-armed infantry, skirmishers.

vēlĭfĕr -fĕra -fĕrum, carrying sail.

vēlĭfĭcātĭo -ōnis, f. a sailing.

vēlĭfĭco, 1. to sail; *transit., partic.*, vē-lĭfĭcātus, sailed through (*poet.*).

vēlĭfĭcor, 1. *dep.* to spread the sails, sail; *fig.*, be zealous for.

Veliocasses -ium, *m.* and Veliocassi -ōrum, *m.* a Gallic people.

vēlĭtāris -e, relating to the velites *or* light-armed troops.

vēlĭvŏlans = velivolus (*q.v.*).

vēlĭvŏlus -a -um, flying with sails; *of the sea*, traversed by sails.

vellĭco, 1. to pluck, twitch; to taunt, criticise.

vello, vulsi (volsi) *and* velli, vulsum (volsum), 3. to pluck, pull, twitch; to pluck off, pluck out; *milit.*, vallum, to pull up the palisade, tear down the rampart; *signa*, to take the standards out of the ground, to march away.

vellus -ĕris, *n.* a fleece; *poet.*, any hide.

vēlo, 1. to cover, veil; to crown, adorn; to conceal.

vēlōcĭtas -ātis, f. quickness, velocity.

vēlōcĭter, *adv.* quickly, swiftly.

vēlox -ōcis, swift, fleet.

1. vēlum -i, *n.* a covering, curtain; a sail (*gen. plur.*); vela dare, to sail away.

vēlŭt (vēlŭtī), *adv.* as, even as, just as; *velut si*, or simply velut, as if, just as if.

vēna -ae, f. a blood-vessel, vein; an artery; *plur.* = the pulse; a watercourse; a vein of metal; the inmost, vital part; disposition, natural inclination.

vēnābŭlum -i, *n.* hunting-spear.

Vēnāfrum -i, *n.* a very old town of the Samnites in Campania.

vēnālĭcĭus -a -um, relating to sale; *subst.*, vēnālĭcĭa -ium, *n.* import and export wares; *subst.*, vēnālĭcĭus -ii, *m.* a slave-dealer.

vēnālis -e, on sale, to be sold; that can be bribed, venal; *subst.*, venales, slaves put up for sale.

vēnātĭcus -a -um, relating to the chase, canis.

vēnātĭo -ōnis, f. the chase, hunting; game.

vēnātor -ōris, *m.* hunter, sportsman.

vēnātōrĭus -a -um, relating to the chase.

vēnātrix -īcis, f. a huntress.

vēnātus -ūs, *m.* the chase, hunting.

vendax -ācis, fond of selling.

vendĭbĭlis -e, on sale, saleable; pleasant, acceptable.

vendĭtātĭo -ōnis, f. a putting up for sale; a vaunting display.

vendĭtātor -ōris, *m.* a boaster.

vendĭtĭo -ōnis, f. a selling, sale.

vendĭto, 1. to try to sell; to recommend.

vendĭtor -ōris, *m.* a seller, vendor.

vendo -dĭdi -dĭtum, 3. to sell, vend; *male*, cheap; *fig.*, to cry up, recommend; (*the passive is veneo*).

vĕnēfĭcĭum -ii, *n.* a poisoning; poison; sorcery.

vĕnēfĭcus -a -um, poisonous, magical; *subst.*, vĕnēfĭcus -i, *m.* poisoner, enchanter.

vĕnēnārĭus -ii, *m.*, a poisoner.

vĕnēnātus -a -um, poisonous, poisoned; enchanted.

vĕnēnĭfĕr -fĕra -fĕrum, poisonous.

vĕnēno, 1. to poison.

vĕnēnum -i, *n.* poison; (*fig.* = ruin, destruction, bane); a magic draught; dye; rouge.

vēnĕo (vaenĕo), vēnii, vēnitum, 4. to go to sale, to be sold (*pass. of vendo*); to be let to the highest bidder.

vĕnĕrābĭlis -e, venerable, reverend.

vĕnĕrābundus -a -um, reverent, respectful.

vĕnĕrandus -a -um, *p. adj.* worthy of reverence.

vĕnĕrātĭo -ōnis, f. reverence, respect; *pass.*, venerable character.

vĕnĕrātor -ōris, *m.* a venerator.

vĕnĕro = veneror (*q.v.*).

vĕnĕror, 1. *dep.* to reverence, honour; to ask reverently; *partic.*, veneratus, *pass.* honoured (*poet.*).

Vĕnĕti -ōrum, *m.* 1. people on the northwest coast of the Adriatic; Vĕnĕtĭa -ae, f. the land of the Veneti. 2. a people in Gallia Lugdunensis.

vĕnĕtus -a -um, bluish, sea-coloured.

vĕnĭa -ae, f. grace, indulgence, favour; pardon.

vĕnĭo, vēni, ventum, 4. to come; *of time*, to happen, arrive.

vennūcŭla (vennuncŭla) -uva -ae, f. a kind of grape.

vēnor, 1. *dep.* to hunt, chase; *fig.*, to strive after.

vĕnōsus -a -um, dry, meagre.

venter -tris, *m.* the belly; the womb.

ventĭlo, 1. to fan, brandish in the air; to winnow grain; to excite, provoke.

ventĭto, 1. to come often, be wont to come.

ventōsus -a -um, full of wind, windy; swift *or* light as the wind; *fig.*, empty, vain; changeable.

ventrĭcŭlus -i, *m.* (*dim. of venter*), the belly; the stomach.

ventŭlus -i, *m.* (*dim. of ventus*), a gentle breeze.

ventus -i, *m.* wind; favour of the people.

vĕnŭcŭla = vennucula (*q.v.*).

vēnundo -dĕdi -dătum, 1. to sell; *captivos sub corona*.

1. vĕnus -ĕris, f. beauty, charm; love; Vēnus, the goddess of love and beauty; the Venus throw, the highest throw of the dice.

2. vēnus -ūs *and* -i, *m. only in dat. and acc.*, sale; *venum dare*, to sell; *venum ire*, to be sold.

Vĕnŭsĭa -ae, f. birthplace of Horace.

vĕnustas -ātis, f. beauty, charm; grace, wit.

vĕnustē, adv. beautifully, charmingly.

vĕnustus -a -um, charming, graceful; attractive.

vēpallĭdus -a -um, very pale.

vēprēcŭla -ae, f. (dim. of vepres), a thorn bush.

vepres -is, m. a thorn-bush, briar.

vēr, vēris, n. spring ; primo vere, in the beginning of spring; ver sacrum, an offering of the firstlings.

vērātrum -i, n. hellebore.

vērax -ācis, truthful, veracious.

verbēnae -ārum, f. sacred boughs, carried by the Fetiales.

verbēnātus -a -um, crowned with sacred boughs.

verber -ĕris, n. in sing. only in genit. and abl. a blow, stroke, lash; plur., verbera, a flogging, whipping; a cudgel, or a whip, scourge; the thong of a sling.

verbērātĭo -ōnis, f. punishment.

1. verbĕro, 1. to beat, strike; to scourge; fig., to attack, assail.

2. verbĕro -ōnis, m. a rascal.

verbōsē, adv. diffusely, verbosely.

verbōsus -a -um, copious, diffuse.

verbum -i, n. a word, expression; a verb; plur., talk, discourse; uno verbo, in a word, briefly ; ad verbum, word for word; verba dare alicui, to cheat, deceive.

Vercingĕtŏrix -ĭgis, m. a chief of the Gauls.

vērē, adv. truly, rightly.

vērēcundē, adv. modestly, shyly.

vērēcundia -ae, f. modesty, shame, shyness; awe, respect.

vērēcundor, 1. dep. to be ashamed, shy.

vērēcundus -a -um, feeling shame, modest, shy; translatio, not forced, natural.

vērēdus -i, m. a swift horse, hunter.

vĕrendus -a -um, p. adj. venerable, reverend.

vĕreor -ĭtus sum, 2. dep. to stand in awe of; to fear; to revere; to be afraid.

Vergĭlĭus -ii, m. P. Vergilius Maro, the great Roman poet, author of the Aeneid, the Georgics, and the Eclogues.

Verginĭus -a, name of a Roman family. L. Verginius slew his daughter to deliver her from the decemvir Appius Claudius.

vergo, versi, 3. intransit., to bend, to be inclined; to approach; of places, to be situated towards ; of time, to come to an end ; transit., to bend, incline; to pour in.

vergobrĕtus, the highest magistrate of the Aedui.

vērīdĭcus -a -um, truthful.

vērīlŏquium -ii, n. etymology.

vērīsĭmĭlis -e, probable, likely.

vērīsĭmĭlĭtūdo -ĭnis, f. probability.

vērĭtas -ātis, f. truth; reality; truthfulness, honesty.

vermĭcŭlus -i, m. (dim. of vermis), a little worm.

vermĭno, 1. to have worms; to have pain in the limbs.

vermĭnis in, m. a worm.

verna -ae, c. a slave born in the house; a native.

vernācŭlus -a -um, relating to a slave born in the house; (subst., vernācŭlus -i, m. a jester, buffoon) ; native, i.e., Roman.

vernīlis -e, slavish, mean, abject; pert.

vernīlĭter, adv. like a house-slave.

verno, 1. to flourish, grow green.

vernŭla -ae, c. (dim. of verna), a slave born in the house.

vernus -a -um, spring-like, vernal.

vērō, adv. in truth, really, indeed ; certainly; but indeed; in a climax, even, indeed.

Vērōna -ae, f. in North Italy, birthplace of Catullus.

1. verres -is, m. a boar.

2. Verres -is, m., C. Cornelius, praetor in Sicily, prosecuted on a charge of extortion.

verrīnus -a -um, relating to a boar.

verro, verri, versum, 3. to brush ; to sweep the ground; to sweep along; to sweep together, collect together; to clean.

verrūca -ae, f. a wart, excrescence.

verrunco, 1. to turn out; bene verruncare, to turn out well.

versābĭlis -e, movable, changeable.

versābundus -a -um, revolving.

versātĭlis -e, revolving; versatile.

versĭcŏlor -ōris, of various colours.

versĭcŭlus -i, m. (dim. of versus), a little line; little verse.

versĭfĭcātĭo -ōnis, f. versification.

versĭfĭcātor -ōris, m. versifier.

versĭfĭco, 1. to versify.

verso (vorso), 1. to turn about often, to turn hither and thither; lumina suprema, cast a last look; sortem urnā, shake (reflex. and middle, to turn oneself round) ; to move hither and thither ; oves, to pasture ; (middle, versari, to stay, live, dwell; to be engaged in, be occupied with) ; to direct, turn hither and thither; to change; to explain, to twist; to influence; to meditate upon; to disturb; to turn round and round, to turn up.

versum = 1. versus.

versūra -ae, f. a turning; borrowing of money to pay a debt.

1. versus (vorsus), versum (vorsum). Adv., towards, in the direction of. Prep. with acc., towards.

2. versus, partic. (1) of verro (q.v.), (2) of verto (q.v.).

3. versus (vorsus) -ūs, m. a row, line; a furrow; a verse.

versūtē, *adv.* craftily, adroitly.

versūtia -ae, *f.* cunning, craftiness.

versūtilóquus -a -um, slyly speaking.

versūtus -a -um, *fig.,* dexterous, cunning.

vertāgus = *vertragus (q.v.).*

vertex (vortex) -icis, *m.* a whirl; a whirlpool of water; a whirlwind; the crown of the head; the head; the pole of the heavens; any height; *a vertice,* from above.

verticōsus (vorticōsus) -a -um, full of whirlpools.

vertīgo -inis, *f.* a turning round, revolution; giddiness.

verto (vorto), verti (vorti), versum (vorsum), 3. to turn; *milit., in fugam,* to put to flight, rout; *terga,* to flee; *of money, etc.,* to devote, turn to; to construe as, impute; to alter, change; to translate; *vertere solum,* to go into exile; to roll; to move about; *of time,* to roll round; *anno vertente,* in the course of a year; to turn round *or* over; to empty; to overthrow; *middle, verti,* to move in a certain sphere; *versus with in or ad,* turned, lying towards.

vertrāgus -i, *m.* and **vertrāha** -ae, *f.* a greyhound.

Vertumnus (Vortumnus) -i, *m.* the god of exchange.

vēru -ūs, *n.* a spit; a javelin.

1. **vērum,** *adv.* in truth, really; but, nevertheless.

2. **vērum,** *v. verus.*

vēruntāmen (vērumtāmen), *conj.* but yet, notwithstanding.

vērus -a -um, true, genuine; right, fitting, reasonable; truthful; *subst.,* **vērum** -i, *n.* the truth.

vērūtum -i, *n.* a javelin.

vērūtus -a -um, armed with a javelin.

vervex -ēcis, *m.* a wether; a sheepish, silly person.

vēsānia -ae, *f.* insanity.

vēsāniens -entis, raging.

vēsānus (vaesānus), -a -um, mad, insane; fierce, furious.

vescor, 3. *dep. gen. with abl.,* to eat, feed on; to use, enjoy.

vescus -a -um, *act.* = devouring, consuming; *pass.,* wasted, thin.

vēsica -ae, *f.* the bladder; anything made from a bladder, a purse, a lantern, *etc.;* bombast.

vēsicūla -ae, *f. (dim. of vesica),* a blister.

vespa -ae, *f.* a wasp.

Vespāsiānus -i, *m.,* T. *Flavius Vespasianus,* a Roman emperor.

vesper -ēris *or* -ěri, *m.* the evening star; the evening; *vespere and vesperi,* in the evening.

vespěra -ae, *f.* the evening.

vespěrasco, 3. to become evening.

vespěrě, vesperi, *v. vesper.*

vespertīnus -a -um, relating to evening; western.

vespillo -ōnis, *m.* a corpse-bearer.

Vesta -ae, *f.* daughter of Saturn and Ops, goddess of the hearth and domestic life; the hearth; *adj.,* **Vestālis; subst., Vestālis** -is, *f.* a Vestal virgin.

vester (voster) -tra -trum, your, yours.

vestibūlum -i, *n.* courtyard; the entrance to a place; *fig.,* a beginning.

vestīgium -ii, *n.* the sole of the foot; a foot-step; a trace; a mark, sign; a position, station; a moment; *adv., e vestigio,* immediately, on the spot.

vestīgo, 1. to track, investigate.

vestimentum -i, *n.* clothing, garment.

vestio -ivi *and* -ii -ītum, 4. to cover with a garment, clothe; to adorn.

vestis -is, *f.* a covering; a garment, clothing; a carpet, tapestry.

vestītus -ūs, *m.* clothes, apparel; *vestītum mutare,* to go into mourning.

Vēsūvius -ii, *m.* the celebrated volcano in Campania.

větěrānus -a -um, old; *of soldiers,* veteran.

větěrasco -āvi, 3. to become old.

větěrātor -ōris, *m.* one who has grown old in *or* become experienced in anything; subtle, tricky.

větěrātōriē, *adv.* cunningly.

větěrātōrius -a -um, cunning.

větěrīnus -a -um, of *or* relating to draught; *subst.,* **větěrīnae** -ārum, *f.* draught-animals.

věternus -i, *m.* age; lethargy, sleepiness.

větĭtum -i, *n.* that which is forbidden; a prohibition.

věto (vǒto), větŭi (vǒtŭi), větĭtum (vǒtĭtum), not to allow to happen, to forbid, prevent.

větŭlus -a -um *(dim. of vetus),* somewhat old, oldish. *Subst.,* **větŭlus** -i, *m.* an old man; **větŭla** -ae, *f.* an old woman.

větus -ěris, *abl. sing.* -ěre, *compar.,* **větěrior** *(classical compar.,* **větustior),** *superl.,* **věterrimus,** old, ancient; *with genit.* = grown grey in; *subst.,* **větěres** -um, *m.* ancestors.

větustas -ātis, *f.* age; antiquity; length of time.

větustus -a -um, old, ancient; old-fashioned.

vexāmen -inis, *n.* a shaking.

vexātio -ōnis, *f.* annoyance, hardship; ill-treatment.

vexātor -ōris, *m.* one who annoys, disturbs.

vexillārius -ii, *m.* a standard-bearer; *plur.,* **vexillārii** -ōrum, *m.* a special corps of veterans, a reserve corps; a detachment.

vexillum -i, *n. (dim. of velum),* a flag, standard.

vexo, 1. to shake, shatter; to harass, annoy, vex.

via -ae, *f.* a way; highway, road;

militaris, main road; *dare alicui viam*, to give place; a street in a town; a passage ; the gullet, the windpipe ; a cleft; a stripe in a garment; march, journey; means, way, method; manner; *viā*, methodically.

viāticus -a -um, relating to a journey; *subst.*, **viāticum** -i, *n.* money for a journey.

viātor -ōris, *m.* a traveller; a runner *or* messenger.

vibix (vibex) -icis, *f.* a weal.

vibro, 1. *trans.*, to cause to vibrate, brandish, shake ; to curl, frizzle; *intrans.*, to shake, vibrate; to quiver; to flash, glitter.

viburnum -i, *n.* a tree.

vicānus -a -um, dwelling in a village; *subst.*, **vicāni** -ōrum, *m.* villagers.

vicārius -a -um, substituted, vicarious; *subst.*, **vicārius** -ii, *m.* a substitute; successor.

vicātim, *adv.* from street to street; in villages.

vice, vicem, *v. vicis.*

vicēni -ae -a, twenty each.

vices, *v. vicis.*

vicēsima, *v. vicesimus.*

vicēsimāni -ōrum, *m.* soldiers of the twentieth legion.

vicēsimārius -a -um, relating to the twentieth part.

vicēsimus (vigēsimus) -a -um, the twentieth ; *subst.*, **vicēsima** -ae, *f.* the twentieth part.

vicia -ae, *f.* a vetch.

viciēs (viciens), *adv.* twenty times.

Vicilinus -i, *m.* the watchful one.

vicīnālis -e, neighbouring, near.

vicīnia -ae, *f.* neighbourhood, nearness; similarity.

vicīnitas -ātis, *f.* neighbourhood, nearness; likeness, affinity.

vicīnus -a -um, near, neighbouring ; *fig.*, similar ; *subst.*, **vicīnus** -i, *m.*, **vicīna** -ae, *f.* a neighbour ; **vicīnum** -i, *n.* the neighbourhood, vicinity.

vicis (*genit.*, *nom. not found*), change, alternation, vicissitude; (*per vices*, alternately ; *in vicem, invicem*, by turns); recompense ; fate, destiny ; office, duty ; *adv.*, **vicem, vice**, instead of, like, as.

vicissātim = *vicissim* (*q.v.*).

vicissim, *adv.* in turn ; on the other hand.

vicissitūdo -inis, *f.* change, vicissitude.

victima -ae, *f.* a victim.

victimārius -ii, *m.* an assistant at a sacrifice.

victito, 1. to feed upon.

victor -ōris, *m.* conqueror, victor ; victorious.

victōria -ae, *f.* victory, conquest. **Victōria**, the goddess of Victory.

victōriātus -i, *m.*, *genit. plur.* victoria-

tum, a silver coin stamped with a figure of Victory.

victōriōla -ae, *f.* (*dim. of Victoria*), a small statue of Victory.

victrix -icis, *f.* she that conquers.

victus -ūs, *m.* manner of life, way of living ; support, food.

viculus -i, *m.* (*dim. of vicus*), a little village, a hamlet.

vīcus -i, *m.* a quarter *or* district of a town, a street; a village, an estate.

vidēlicět, *adv.* clearly, evidently; *ironically*, forsooth, to be sure; namely.

viden' = *videsne?* v. *video.*

vidĕo, **vīdi**, **vīsum**, 2. to see ; to be awake; to perceive, observe; to look at, behold; see to; *in pass.*, to seem, appear, *videtur* (*alicui*), it seems good, it is the opinion of.

viduitas -ātis, *f.* widowhood.

viduo, 1. to deprive of; *partic.*, **viduāta** -ae, *f.* widowed.

viduus -a -um, deprived of, bereaved of, destitute of, *with genit. or abl.*; **vidua** -ae, *f.* a widow.

Vienna -ae, *f.* town in Gallia Narbonensis, *now* Vienne.

viētus -a -um, shrivelled, withered.

vigĕo, 2. to be vigorous, thrive, to be active; to be prosperous.

vigesco, 3. to become vigorous.

vigēsimus = *vicesimus* (*q.v.*).

vigil -ilis, wakeful, watchful ; *subst.*, a watchman.

vigilans -antis, *p. adj.* watchful, vigilant.

vigilantĕr, *adv.* wakefully, vigilantly.

vigilantia -ae, *f.* vigilance, wakefulness.

vigilax -ācis, watchful, wakeful.

vigilia -ae, *f.* wakefulness, sleeplessness; watch, guard; a watch (division of the night); sentinels; vigilance, care.

vigilo, 1. *intransit.*, to be awake, watch; to be vigilant ; *transit.*, to watch through; to provide for.

viginti, *num.* twenty.

vigintivirātus -ūs, *m.* the office of the *vigintiviri.*

vigintiviri -ōrum, *m.* a commission of twenty, appointed by Caesar for the division of lands in Campania.

vigor -ōris, *m.* vigour, force, energy.

vilicus = *villicus* (*q.v.*).

vīlis -e, cheap ; worthless ; abundant, common.

vīlitas -ātis, *f.* cheapness, low price ; worthlessness.

villa -ae, *f.* a country-house, an estate, country seat, farm.

villico, 1. to manage an estate.

villicus -a -um, belonging to a country-seat ; *subst.*, **villicus** -i, *m.* a bailiff, steward.

villōsus -a -um, shaggy, hairy.

villŭla -ae, *f.* (*dim. of villa*), a small country-house, little farm.

villum -i, *n.* (*dim. of vinum*), a little drop of wine.

villus -i, *m.* shaggy hair.

vimen -inis, *n.*, an osier, twig.

vimentum = *vimen* (*q.v.*).

viminālis -e, relating to osiers.

viminĕus -a -um, made of osiers, wicker.

vin' = *visne, from volo*.

vinācĕus -a -um, belonging to wine; *subst.*, **vinācĕus** -i, *m.* a grape-stone.

vinālia -ium, *n.* the wine festival.

vinārius -a -um, relating to wine; *adj.*, *vas*, a wine-cask; *subst.*, **vinārius** -ii, *m.* a vintner; **vinārium ii**, *n.* a wine-jar.

vincio, vinxi, vinctum, 4. to bind, to tie round; to fetter; to pledge; to limit, restrain; to strengthen, protect; to embrace closely.

vinco, vīci, victum, 3. to conquer, subdue; *at an auction*, to outbid; to get the mastery over; to control; to surpass; to prove victoriously; *vicisti*, you are right.

vinculum (**vinclum**) -i, *n.* a band, cord, noose; *vincula*, bonds, fetters, imprisonment.

Vindēlici -ōrum, *m.* a German people.

vindēmia -ae, *f.* the vintage; grapes, wine.

vindēmiātor -ōris, *m.* a vintager.

vindēmiŏla -ae, *f.* (*dim. of vindemia*), a little vintage.

vindex -icis, *c.* a surety, protector, vindicator; an avenger.

vindicātio -ōnis, *f.* a defending, avenging.

vindiciae -ārum, *f.* a laying claim to a thing in presence of the praetor.

vindico, 1. to lay claim to, assume, appropriate; to liberate; to preserve; to avenge, take vengeance on.

vindicta -ae, *f.* a manumission staff; deliverance; vengeance, punishment.

vīnĕa, *v. vineus*.

vīnētum -i, *n.* a vineyard.

vīnĕus -a -um, belonging to wine; *subst.*, **vīnĕa** -ae, *f.* a vineyard; *milit.*, a mantlet.

vīnitor -ōris, *m.* a vinedresser.

vīnŏlentia -ae, *f.* wine-drinking, intoxication.

vīnŏlentus -a -um, mixed with wine; intoxicated.

vīnōsus -a -um, drinking much wine.

vīnum -i, *n.* wine.

viŏla -ae, *f.* a violet; the colour violet.

viŏlābilis -e, that can be injured.

viŏlārium -ii, *n.* a bed of violets.

viŏlātio -ōnis, *f.* an injury, violation.

viŏlātor -ōris, *m.* injurer, violator.

viŏlens -entis, vehement, furious.

viŏlentĕr, *adv.* violently, impetuously.

viŏlentia -ae, *f.* violence, impetuosity.

viŏlentus -a -um, violent, impetuous.

viŏlo, 1. to violate, injure; to plunder; to lay waste; to dishonour.

vīpĕra -ae, *f.* a viper, snake, serpent.

vīpĕrĕus -a -um, of a viper or a snake; having snakes.

vīpĕrīnus -a -um, relating to a viper or snake.

vir, viri, *m.* a man, male person; a husband; a man of character, courage.

virāgo -inis, *f.* female warrior, heroine.

virectum (**virētum**) -i, *n.* greensward, turf.

virens, *p. adj.* green; blooming, youthful.

virĕo, 2. to be green; to be fresh, youthful.

vires -ium, *f., v. vis.*

viresco, 3. to grow green.

virētum = *virectum* (*q.v.*).

virga -ae, *f.* a thin green twig, bough; a slip for planting; a rod; magic wand; *plur.*, the fasces.

virgātus -a -um, made of twigs or osiers; striped.

virgētum -i, *n.* an osier-bed, thicket of brushwood.

virgĕus -a -um, made of twigs or rods.

Virgilius = *Vergilius* (*q.v.*).

virginālis -e, of a virgin, maidenly.

virginārius = *virginalis* (*q.v.*).

virgineus -a -um, of a virgin, maidenly.

virginitas -ātis, *f.* virginity.

Virginius = *Verginius* (*q.v.*).

virgo -inis, *f.* a maiden, virgin.

virgŭla -ae, *f.* (*dim. of virga*), a little twig, little bough; a rod, staff.

virgultum -i, *n.* a thicket, a slip for planting.

virguncŭla -ae, *f.* (*dim. of virgo*), a little girl.

Viriāthus (**Viriātus**) -i, *m.* a Lusitanian who commanded his countrymen against the Romans.

viridārium (**viridiārium**) -ii, *n.* a pleasure garden.

viridis -e, green, fresh, young; *subst.*, **viride** -is, *n.* the colour green; *plur.*, **viridia** -ium, *n.* green trees or herbs.

viriditas -ātis, *f.* greenness; the freshness, bloom of youth.

virido, 1. *intransit.*, to be green; *transit.*, to make green.

Viridŏmārus (**Virdŏmārus**) -i, *m.* a Gallic leader.

virilis -e, manly, male, virile.

virilitas -ātis, *f.* manhood; virility.

virilitĕr, *adv.* courageously, vigorously.

viritim, *adv.* man by man, individually; singly.

Viromandŭi (**Vĕromandi**) -ōrum, *m.* people in Gallia Belgica.

virōsus -a -um, stinking, fetid.

virtus -ūtis, *f.* manly excellence; capacity, worth, virtue; valour, courage.

virus -i, *n.* slime, poison; a harsh, bitter taste.

vis, *plur.*, **vires** -ium, *f.* force, power, strength; *per vim*, by force; a large number or quantity; (*plur.*, **vires**, troops forces) ; power, influence ; nature, essence; the meaning of a word.

viscātus -a -um, smeared with birdlime.

viscěra, v. viscus.

viscěrātio -ōnis, f. a public distribution of meat.

visco, 1. to make sticky.

viscum -i, n. mistletoe; birdlime.

viscus -ěris, n. usually plur., **viscěra** -um, n. entrails, viscera; the flesh; the inmost part of anything.

visendus -a -um, p. adj. worthy to be seen.

visio -ōnis, f. a seeing, view; an appearance; idea.

visito, 1. to see often, to visit.

viso -si -sum, 3. to look at carefully, contemplate; to come to see, see after; to visit.

visum -i, n. an appearance, vision; a dream.

visus -ūs, m. a sight, vision, look; appearance.

vita -ae, f. life.

vitābilis -e, that may or ought to be shunned.

vitābundus -a -um, trying to avoid, shunning.

vitālis -e, relating to life, vital; subst., **vitālia** -ium, n. vital parts.

vitālitěr, adv. vitally.

vitātio -ōnis, f. an avoiding.

Vitellius -ii, m., Aulus, a Roman emperor.

vitellus -i, m. (dim. of vitulus), the yolk of an egg.

viteus -a -um, relating to a vine.

viticŭla -ae, f. (dim. of vitis), a little vine.

vitifer -fěra -fěrum, vine-bearing.

vitigěnus -a -um, produced from the vine.

vitio, 1. to injure, corrupt, spoil; to defile; to forge; vitiare diem, to declare a day unfit for holding the census.

vitiosě, adv. faultily, defectively ; wrongly; against the auguries.

vitiositas -ātis, f. wickedness.

vitiosus -a -um, faulty, corrupt; wicked, depraved.

vitis -is, f. a vine; the centurion's staff.

vitisător -ōris, m. one who plants vines.

vitium -ii, n. a fault, defect, blemish; dross; a defect in the auguries; a crime, vice.

vito, 1. to avoid; to escape.

vitrěus -a -um, made of glass; transparent, glittering.

vitricus -i, m. a stepfather.

vitrum -i, n. glass; woad.

vitta -ae, f. a ribbon, band, fillet.

vittātus -a -um, decorated with a fillet.

vitŭla -ae, f. a calf, heifer.

vitŭlinus -a -um, relating to a calf; assum, roast veal.

vitŭlus -i, m. a bull-calf; applied to the young of other animals.

vitŭpěrābilis -e, blameable.

vitŭpěrātio -ōnis, f. a blaming, scolding; blameable conduct.

vitŭpěrātor -ōris, m. a blamer.

vivārium -ii, n. a park, preserve, fishpond.

vivātus -a -um, lively, vivid.

vivax -ācis, long-lived, lasting; vigorous, vivacious.

vivesco (vivisco), vixi, 3. to begin to live; to be vigorous.

vividus -a -um, animated ; lifelike, sigma; vigorous.

viviradix -icis, f. a cutting which has a root.

vivisco = vivesco (q.v.).

vivo, vixi, victum, 3. to live, be alive; to last, continue ; to live on anything, lacte.

vivus -a -um, alive, living; lifelike, lasting, natural, lively; flumen, running water; ros, fresh.

vix, adv. with effort, scarcely; vixdum, hardly.

vixdum, v. vix.

vocābŭlum -i, n. name, appellation.

vocālis -e, uttering sounds, vocal, singing; subst., **vocālis** -is, f. a vowel.

vocāmen -inis, n. name, appellation.

vocātio -ōnis, f. a summoning before a court of law; invitation to dinner.

vocātor -ōris, m. an inviter.

vocātus -ūs, m. a calling, invocation; invitation.

vocifěrātio -ōnis, f. a loud shouting.

vocifěrātus -ūs, m. = vociferatio (q.v.).

vocifěro, 1. = vociferor.

vocifěror, 1. dep. to cry loudly, vociferate.

vocito, 1. to be accustomed to name; to call repeatedly.

voco, 1. to call, summon; to invoke; to invite; to provoke; to call, name; to bring, place in any state; in dubium, to call in question.

vocŭla -ae, f. (dim. of vox), a low, weak voice; a petty speech.

volaema, v. volemum.

Volaterrae -ārum, f. an old town in Etruria.

volāticus -a -um, winged; flying; fig., inconstant.

volātilis -e, winged; swift; transitory.

volātus -ūs, m. a flying, flight.

volēmum pirum, gen. plur., a kind of pear.

volens -entis, p. adj. willing, voluntary; favourable, inclined to.

volgo, volgus = vulgo, vulgus (q.v.).

volito, 1. to fly about, to fly to and fro, to flutter; to hover about.

volněro = vulnero (q.v.).

1. **volo, volŭi, velle,** to be willing, to

wish; to think, mean ; *polit.*, to will, ordain.

2. **vŏlo**, 1. to fly ; **volantes -ium**, *f.* birds.

3. **vŏlo -ōnis**, *m.* a volunteer.

Volsci (Vulsci) -ōrum, *m.* a people in Latium, on both banks of the Liris.

volsella -ae, *f.* a pair of pincers.

Volsinii (Vulsinii) -ōrum, *m.* a town in Etruria.

volsus -a -um, *v. vello.*

Voltumna -ae, *f.* an Etruscan goddess.

voltur = *vultur (q.v.).*

Volturnus = *Vulturnus (q.v.).*

voltus = *vultus (q.v.).*

vŏlūbilis -e, rolling, revolving, turning round ; changeable : *of discourse*, fluent.

vŏlūbilitas -ātis, *f.* revolution; vicissitude, inconstancy; fluency.

vŏlūbĭliter, *adv.* fluently.

vŏlŭcer, **vŏlŭcris**, **vŏlŭcre**, flying, winged ; swift ; fleeting, transitory ; *subst.*, **volucris -is**, *f.* a bird.

vŏlŭcris -is, *f. v. volucer.*

vŏlūmen -ĭnis, *n.* a book, roll, writing; a wreath, fold, eddy.

vŏluntārius -a -um, voluntary; *plur. subst.*, **vŏluntārii -ōrum**, *m.* volunteers.

vŏluntas -ātis, *f.* will, wish, inclination; *voluntate*, willingly; good disposition in purpose; a last will, testament; meaning of words.

vŏlup (vŏlŭpĕ), *adv.* agreeably.

vŏluptārius -a -um, relating to pleasure; devoted to pleasure, sensual; capable of pleasure.

vŏluptas -ātis, *f.* pleasure, delight ; *voluptates*, public shows.

vŏluptŭōsus -a -um, delightful *(late).*

vŏlūtābrum -i, *n.* a place where pigs roll, slough.

vŏlūtābundus -a -um, rolling, wallowing.

vŏlūtātio -ōnis, *f.* a rolling about, wallowing; disquiet; vicissitude.

vŏlūto, 1. to roll round, tumble about; *volutans*, *reflex.*, rolling oneself ; to spread abroad; echo back; to consider; to busy, occupy.

volva -ae, *f.* a sow's paunch.

volvo, **volvi**, **vŏlūtum**, 3. to roll, revolve, twist round; *(reflex., or middle*, to roll round, eddy ; to roll along) ; to read, *libros* ; *of time*, to make to roll round ; *(middle*, to roll round) ; to reflect on, ponder over.

vōmer -ĕris, *m.* a ploughshare.

vŏmica -ae, *f.* an ulcer, boil; *fig.*, a plague, curse.

vōmis -ĕris, *m.* = *vomer (q.v.).*

vŏmĭtio -ōnis, *f.* a vomiting.

vŏmĭto, 1. to vomit.

vŏmĭtus -ūs, *m.* a vomiting.

vŏmo -ŭi -ĭtum, 1. *intransit.*, to vomit; *transit.*, to give forth.

vŏrāgĭnōsus -a -um, full of chasms.

vŏrāgo -ĭnis, *f.* a pit, chasm; *in water*, an abyss, whirlpool.

vŏrax -ācis, gluttonous.

vŏro, 1. devour, consume; to squander.

vors . . . *v. vers . . .*

vort . . . *v. vert . . .*

vōs, ye, *plural of tu.*

vōtīvus -a -um, votive, vowed.

vōtum -i, *n.* a vow; a prayer; a desire.

vŏvĕo, **vōvi**, **vōtum**, 2. to vow ; to wish.

vox, **vōcis**, *f.* the voice; pronunciation; sound ; a word, utterance, discourse ; a command ; a formula, sentence ; accent, tone.

Vulcānus (Volcānus) -i, *m.* Vulcan, the god of fire, son of Jupiter and Juno, husband of Venus, who made the weapons, thunderbolts, *etc.*, of the gods; *subst.*, **Vulcānālia -ōrum**, *n.* the festival of Vulcan.

vulgāris -e, common, ordinary, usual, vulgar.

vulgāriter, *adv.* commonly, vulgarly.

vulgātus -a -um, *p. adj.* common ; generally known.

vulgīvăgus -a -um, wandering, vagrant.

1. **vulgo (volgo)**, 1. to make common to all, to communicate; to publish a book; to make generally known.

2. **vulgō (volgō)**, *adv.* generally, in public, openly.

vulgus (volgus) -i, *n.*, *rarely m.*, the people, the public; a mass, crowd; the mob.

vulnĕrātio -ōnis, *f.* wounding.

vulnĕro (volnĕro), 1. to wound, injure.

vulnĭfĭcus (volnĭfĭcus) -a -um, inflicting wounds.

vulnus (volnus) -ĕris, *n.* a wound; injury, loss; a blow.

vulpēcŭla -ae, *f.* (*dim. of vulpes*), little fox.

vulpes (volpes) -is, *f.* a fox.

Vulsci = *Volsci (q.v.).*

vulsus -a -um, *p. adj.* having the hairs plucked out, smooth.

vulticŭlus -i, *m.* (*dim. of vultus*), a (mere) look.

vultŭōsus -a -um, grimacing, affected.

1. **vultur (voltur) -ŭris**, *m.* a vulture.

2. **Vultur (Voltur) -ŭris**, *m.* mountain in Apulia.

vultŭrīnus (voltŭrīnus) -a -um, relating to a vulture.

vultŭrius (voltŭrius) -i, *m.* a vulture.

Vulturnum (Volturnum) -i, *n.* town in Campania on the river Volturnus.

1. **Vulturnus (Volturnus) -i**, *m.* river in Campania.

2. **vulturnus (volturnus) -i**, *m.* a south-east wind.

vultus (voltus) -ūs, *m.* the countenance, expression, mien.

X

X x, *the twenty-second letter of the Latin Alphabet.*

Xanthippē -ēs, *f.* the shrewish wife of Socrates.

xěnium -ii, *n.* a gift, present.

Xěnō -ōnis, *m.* an Epicurean philosopher.

Xěnŏphōn -ontis, *m.* pupil of Socrates, historian and general.

Xerxēs -is, *m.* the king of the Persians, who invaded Greece and was defeated at Salamis.

xystus -i, *m. and* **xystum -i,** *n.* an open colonnade, a promenade.

Y

Y y, *a letter borrowed from the Greek to represent the Greek upsilon (v).*

Z

Z z, *represents the Greek zeta (Z, ζ).*

Zăcynthus (-ŏs) -i, *f.* an island in the Ionian Sea.

Zăma -ae, *f.* a town in Numidia, scene of the victory of Scipio over Hannibal.

Zanclē -ēs, *f.* old name of the town of Messana.

zēlŏtўpia -ae, *f.* jealousy.

zēlŏtўpus -a -um, jealous.

Zēnō (-ōn) -ōnis, *m.* a Greek philosopher.

zěphўrus -i, *m.* a warm west wind, zephyr.

Zētēs -ae, *m.* son of Boreas; one of the Argonauts.

zm . . . v. sm . . .

zōdiăcus -i, *m.* the zodiac, *poet.*

zōna -ae, *f.* a girdle ; *zonae,* terrestrial zones.

zōnārius -ii, *m.* girdle-maker.

zōnŭla -ae, *f. (dim. of zona),* a little girdle.

SIGNS AND ABBREVIATIONS PECULIAR TO THE ENGLISH-LATIN SECTION

I.—(a) Brackets ( ) enclosing the first syllable of a compound verb denote that both the simple and compound forms of the verb are in use, as (de)currĕre.

(b) Brackets enclosing a single letter denote that the word was written sometimes with and sometimes without that letter, e.g. ex(s)pectare = exspectare and expectare.

(c) Brackets enclosing a whole word denote that the word may be inserted or omitted according to the context. Thus for " tide," aestus (maritimus) implies that aestus alone may sometimes serve.

II.—* prefixed to a word denotes that it is of modern or very late Latin origin. † appended to a word denotes that it is only used, in the Classical period, by poets.

III.—

alqs	= aliquis	alqm	= aliquem
alqd	= aliquid	alqam	= aliquam
alcis	= alicuius	alqo	= aliquo
alci	= alicui	alqā	= aliquā

Many words may be strengthened by combination, e.g. cruciatus et tormentum; integer atque inviolatus.

CASSELL'S
ENGLISH-LATIN
DICTIONARY

A

A an, *adj. generally not translated;* unus; quidam; is.

abaft, aft, *adv.* a puppi, a tergo.

abandon, *v.tr.* relinquĕre, deserĕre, re desistĕre; — *hope,* spem omittĕre. **abandoned,** *adj.,* nefarius. **abandonment,** *n.* relictio.

abase, *v.tr.* (de)minuĕre; frangĕre (*e.g.* animum). **abasement,** *n.* deminutio.

abash, *v.tr.* percellĕre, perturbare.

abate, *v.tr.* (de)minuĕre ; *a charge,* remittĕre; *v.intr.* (de)minui; defervescĕre (*e.g.* ira, *etc.*). **abatement,** *n.* deminutio.

abbreviate, *v.tr.* praecidĕre; contrahĕre. **abbreviation,** *n.* compendium, contractio; *see* EPITOME.

abdicate, *v.tr.* (magistratu) se abdicare. **abdication,** *n.* abdicatio.

abduction, *n.* furtum; raptus.

aberration, *n.* error; *mental* —, mentis error.

abet, *v.tr.* instigare; auxilio alci esse. **abettor,** *n.* socius; particeps conscius (*adj.*).

abeyance, *n. to be in* , in dubio esse; *to leave in* —, rem integram relinquĕre.

abhor, *v.tr.* odisse, alqm odio habēre. **abhorrence,** *n.* odium. **abhorrent,** *adj.* ab alqā re abhorrens, alienus.

abide, v.intr. (com)morari, versari; *last,* durare. **abiding,** *adj.* diuturnus.

abject, *adj.* abiectus, humilis.

ability, *n.* vires, -ium; *mental,* facultas, ingenium.

abjure, *v.tr.* abiurare; recusare.

ablative, *n.* (casus) ablativus.

able, *adj.* potens; habilis; sagax; *to be* —, posse. **able-bodied,** *adj.* validus.

ablution, *n.* ablutio.

abnegation, *n.* temperantia.

abnormal, *adj.* enormis; novus, inusitatus, singularis; maximus; infrequens. *Adv.* praeter morem.

aboard, *adv. to go* —, (navem) conscendĕre.

abode, *n., see* HOUSE.

abolish, *v.tr.* abolēre, tollĕre; *legal,* abrogare. **abolition,** *n.* dissolutio ;

legal, abrogatio ; — *of debts,* tabulae novae.

abominable, *adj.* foedus. **abominate,** *v.tr., see* ABHOR.

aboriginal, *adj.* priscus. **aborigines,** *n.* indigenae.

abortive, *adj.* abortivus ; *fig.* irritus. *Adv.* ad irritum.

abound, *v.intr.* abundare, suppeditare. **abundance,** *n.* abundantia, copia. **abundant,** *adj.* affluens. *Adv.* abunde.

about, *adv. of place,* circa, circum ; *of time or number,* circiter ; *prep. with acc.* circa circum ; *of respect,* de *with abl.*

above, *adv. of place,* super, supra ; *of degree, more than,* plus *or* amplius ; *prep. super,* supra.

abreast, *adv.* pariter ; *two horses* —, equi biiuges.

abridge, *see* ABBREVIATE.

abroad, *adv.* foras (*of motion*) ; foris (*of rest*) ; *to travel* —, preregrinari.

abrogate, *see* ABOLISH.

abrupt, *adj. steep,* abruptus ; *fig.* incompositus ; *sudden,* subitus. *Adv.* abrupte; incomposite; subito.

abscess, *n.* ulcus, fistula.

abscond, *v.intr.* se in occultum abdĕre.

absence, *n.* absentia ; *in my* —, me absente ; — *of mind,* oblivio. **absent,** *adj.* absens ; *to be* , abesse. *v.tr., (myself,* *see* removēre.

absolute, *adj.* perfectus, absolutus; simplex; *power,* summum imperium ; — *ruler,* imperator. **absolutely,** *adv.* omnino; per se.

absolution, *n.* venia. **absolve,** *v.tr.* solvĕre ; *legal,* (ab)solvĕre.

absorb, *v.tr.* exhaurire ; *fig.* occupatissimus esse.

abstain, *v.intr.* abstinēre. **abstinence,** *n.* abstinentia ; *days of* —, ieiunium. **abstinent,** *adj.* abstinens.

abstract, *adj.* quod nullo sensu percipi potest. *v.tr.* abstrahĕre ; sevocare; *see* STEAL. *n.* epitome. **abstractly,** *adv.* subtiliter. **abstracted,** *adj.* sui oblitus. **abstraction,** *n.* oblivio.

abstruse, *adj.* obscurus. **abstruseness,** *n.* obscuritas. *Adv.* obscure.

absurd, *adj.* ineptus; ridiculus. *Adv.* inepte ; ridicule. **absurdity**, *n.* insulsitas ; *joke*, ridiculum ; *an act*, res inepta.

abundance, abundant(ly), *see* ABOUND.

abuse, *n. wrong use*, immoderatio ; *language*, maledictum. *v.tr. misuse*, abuti; *to rail at*, maledicĕre. **abusive**, *adj.* maledicus, contumeliosus. *Adv.* contumeliose.

abut, *v.tr.* adiacĕre, attingĕre.

abyss, *n.* profundum ; gurges ; locus praeceps; *fig.* exitium.

academy, *n. the Platonic school*, Academia ; collegium. **academical**, *adj.* academicus.

accede, *v.intr.* accedĕre ; *see* AGREE.

accelerate, *v.tr.* accelerare.

accent, *n.* vox, accentus; apex, -icis, *m.* (*mark over a vowel*).

accept, *v.tr.* accipĕre; recipĕre. **acceptable**, *adj.* iucundus, gratus. *Adv.* iucunde, grate. **acceptation**, significatio.

access, *n.* aditus, accesus ; = *addition*, accessio. **accessible**, *adj.* facilis aditu. **accession**, *n.* = *increase.* accessio ; — *to the throne*, initium regnandi.

accident, *n.* casus; calamitas. **accidental**, *adj.* fortuitus. *Adv.* forte, casu.

acclaim, acclamation, *n.* acclamatio. **acclaim**, *v.tr.* acclamare.

accommodate, *v.tr.* accommodare. **accommodating**, *adj.* facilis. **accommodation**, *n.*, *see* AGREEMENT ; hospitium.

accompany, *v.tr.* comitem se alci adiungĕre, comitari; stipare (*of a crowd*); *accompanied by*, cum. **accompaniment**, *n.* comitatus, stipatio.

accomplice, *n.* criminis conscius.

accomplish, *v.tr.* conficĕre, perficĕre. **accomplished**, *adj.* (per)politus, doctus. **accomplishment**, *n.* confectio; = *the end*, finis, exitus; (*of the mind*), ars.

accord, *n.* concentus, concordia ; *of one's own* —, sponte, ultro. *v.intr.* concinĕre; cum alqo congruĕre. **accordance**, *see* ACCORD. *In — with*, ex. **accordant**, *adj.* congruens; unanimus. **according** to, ex, ad, secundum. **accordingly**, *adv.* itaque.

accost, *v.tr.* alloqui, salutare, compellare.

account, *v.tr.* habĕre, aestimare; *to — to anyone*, rationem alci reddĕre. *n. reckoning*, ratio ; — *book*, tabula ; *on my* —, meā de causā ; *on — of*, propter; *narrative*, narratio; **accountable**, *see* RESPONSIBLE. **accountant**, *n.* scriba, *m.*

accredited, *adj.* probatus.

accretion. *n.* accessio, cumulus.

accumulate *v.tr.* (co)acervare, exaggerare. **accumulation**, *n.* cumulus.

accurate, *adj.* accuratus, emendatus. *Adv.* accurate. **accuracy**, *n.* diligentia.

accuse, *v.tr.* compellare, citare, reum facĕre, in iudicium adducĕre ; *the accused*, reus. **accusation**, *n.* accusatio, crimen. **accusative**, accusativus (casus). **accuser**, *n.* qui alqm accusat (*public*), petitor (*in private case*); *informer*, index.

accustom, *v.tr.* assuefacĕre; *be accustomed*, consuescĕre. **accustomed**, *adj.* assuetus.

ace, *n. the best throw*, Venus (iactus), Venereus, basilicus.

ache, *n.* dolor. *v.intr.* dolēre.

achieve, *v.tr.* facĕre, conficĕre; *to gain*, consequi. **achievement**, *n. the doing*, confectio; *a deed*, facinus.

acid, *adj.* acerbus, acer; *fig.* morosus. **acidity**, *n.* acerbitas.

acknowledge, *v.tr.* a(d)gnoscĕre; *to — a child*, suscipĕre ; confitēri (*to confess*); — *a payment*, (in), acceptum referre. **acknowledged**, *adj.* cognitus. **acknowledgment**, *n.* approbatio; confessio; *see* RECEIPT.

acme, *n. use* summus.

acorn, *n.* glans.

acquaint, *v.tr.*, *see* INFORM. **acquaintance**, *n. with a thing*, scientia; *with a person*, usus or familiaritas ; *with literature*, eruditio ; *a person*, amicus. **acquainted**, *adj.* notus ; — *with*, alci familiaris ; — *with anything*, peritus, doctus.

acquiesce, *v.intr.* acquiescĕre, aequo animo ferre. **acquiescence**, *n.* assensus.

acquire, *v.tr.*, *see* GAIN. **acquirement, acquisition**, *n.* res adepta; *knowledge*, cognitio ; *the process*, comparatio. **acquisitive**, *adj.* aptus ad impetrandum.

acquit, *v.tr.*, *see* ABSOLVE. **acquittal**, *n.* absolutio.

acrid, *adj.* acerbus.

acrimonious, *adj.* mordax. *Adv.* mordaciter. **acrimony**, *n.* acerbitas.

across, *prep.* trans.

acrostic, *n.* = *riddle*, aenigma.

act, *v.intr. to do*, agĕre, facĕre. *v.tr.* partes agĕre ; *to — a play*, fabulam agĕre ; *to feign*, simulare ; *n. of a play*, actus ; — *of Parliament*, Senatusconsultum; *achievements*, res gestae. **action**, *n. deed*, factum ; *in battle*, res gesta ; *the battle itself*, praelium ; *gesture*, gestus; *legal*, lis; *to bring an — against*, actionem in alqm instituĕre. **actionable**, *adj.* quod contra leges est. **actor**, *n.* histrio, actor; *comic* —, comoedus ; *tragic* —, tragoedus (*only men acted*). **active**, *adj.* celer ; impiger. *Adv.* acriter. **activity**, *n.* celeritas ; impigritas. **actual**, *adj.* verus. *Adv.* re verā. **actuate**, *v.tr.* impellĕre.

acumen, *n.* ingenii acies, acumen.

acute, *adj.* acutus, gravis; *of intellect*, acutus, sagax. *Adv.* acute, graviter. **acuteness**, *n.* sagacitas, subtilitas.

adage, n. proverbium.

adamant, n. adamas. **adamantine**, adj. adamantinus ; fig. validissimus.

adapt, v.tr. accommodare, aptare. **adapted**, adj. aptus, or idoneus. **adaptation**, n. accommodatio.

add, v.tr. addĕre; to — up, computare. **addition**, n. adjunctio, accessio ; in arith. additio. **additional**, adj. novus, additus.

adder, n. vipera.

addict, v.tr. alci rei se dare. **addicted**, adj. deditus, studiosus.

address, v.tr. alloqui ; alci li(t)teras inscribĕre; n. alloquium; public, contio, oratio; of a letter, inscriptio.

adduce, v.tr. adducĕre, proferro; witnesses, citare.

adept, adj. callidus, peritus.

adequate, adj. proprius, aptus, idoneus. Adv. apte.

adhere, v.intr. haerēre, adhaerēre; to — together, cohaerēre ; — to a party, favēre. **adherence**, **adhesion**, n. amor, studium. **adherent**, n. discipulus ; his — s, sui. **adhesive**, adj. tenax.

adieu ! vale ! pl. valete; to bid —, alqm valēre iubēre.

adjacent, adj. adiacens, finitimus; to be —, adiacēre; contingĕre.

adjective, n. nomen, adiectivum.

adjoin, see ADJACENT.

adjourn, v.tr. differre; — the day of trial, diem prodicĕre. **adjournment**, n. dilatio.

adjudge, v.tr. adiudicare; decernĕre.

adjunct, n. accessio ; aliquid additum.

adjure, v.tr. to entreat, obtestari. **adjuration**, n. obtestatio.

adjust, v.tr., see ARRANGE and ADAPT. **adjustment**, n. accommodatio.

administer, v.tr. administrare, gerĕre ; to — an oath, iusiurandum deferre ; — justice, ius dicĕre. **administration**, n. administratio, procuratio.

admiral, n. praefectus classis.

admire, v.tr. (ad)mirari, **admiration**, n. (ad)miratio. **admirable**, adj. (ad)mirabilis. Adv. mirum in modum, (ad)mirabiliter, eximie.

admit, v.tr. admittĕre, aditum dare ; concedĕre ; fatēri (some excuse), pati. **admission**, n. aditus, adeundi copia; concessio. **admissible**, accipiendus, aequus.

admonish, v.tr. (ad)monēre, (ad)hortari. **admonition**, n. (ad)hortatio.

ado, n. with much —, vix, aegro.

adolescence, n. adulescentia (adol.).

adopt, v.tr. adoptare, a(d)sciscĕre ; accipĕre ; — a resolution, constituĕre. **adoption**, n. adoptio.

adore, v.tr. venerari colĕre ; diligĕre, amare. **adorable** adj. sanctus. **adoration**, n. cultus.

adorn, v.tr. (ex)ornare. **adornment** n. ornamentum.

adrift, adj. fluctibus iactatus.

adroit, adj. callidus, habilis. Adv. callide.

adulation, n. adulatio.

adult, adj. adultus. n. pubes.

adulterate, v.tr. corrumpĕre, vitiare.

adumbrate, v.tr. adumbrare. **adumbration**, n. adumbratio.

advance, v.intr. progredi, procedĕre; in years, aetate provehi. v.tr. augēre; to — anyone's interests, alci consulĕre; an opinion, sententiam dicĕre. n. progressus, iter. **advance-guard**, n. primum agmen. **advancement**, n. gradus.

advantage, n. commodum, fructus, utilitas; (pl. bona, — s); of a position, loci opportunitas ; to be of —, usui esse, prodesse. **advantageous**, adj. utilis. Adv. utiliter.

advent, lit. adventus. **adventitious**, adj. externus.

adventure, n. facinus, n. audax inceptum. v.tr. audēre. **adventurer**, n. a mere —, fraudator. **adventurous**, adj. audax. Adv. audacter.

adverb, n. adverbium.

adversary, n. adversarius.

adverse, adj. adversus, contrarius. Adv. contra. **adversity**, n. res adversae.

advert to, v.tr. animadvertĕre.

advertise, v.tr. nuntiare; pronuntiare. **advertisement**, n. indicium.

advice, n. consilium ; by my —, me auctore. **advise**, v.tr. consilium dare, monēre. Adv. consulte. **adviser**, n. suasor.

advocate, n. legal, patronus, procurator ; to be an —, caus(s)as dicĕre, agĕre; in foro versari. v.tr. defendĕre.

aerial, adj. aërius, aetherius.

afar, adv. procul, longe, eminus; to be —, procul abesse.

affable, adj. mansuetus, commodus. **affability**, n. mores commodi, comitas.

affair, n. res, opus, negotium.

affect, v.tr. (com)movēre, afficĕre; to — constancy, etc., constantiam, etc., simulare. **affectation**, n. simulatio. **affected**, mollis, ineptus ; of things, simulatus. Adv. inepte, moleste.

affection, n. love, amor, studium, pietas (dutiful). **affectionate**, adj. amans, pius. Adv. amanter.

affiance, v.tr., see BETROTH.

affidavit, n. testimonium per tabulas datum.

affinity, propinquitas, necessitudo; similarity, cognatio.

affirm, v.tr. aio, affirmare. **affirmation**, n. affirmatio; legal, confirmatio. **affirmative**, adj. — answer, affirmatio. Adv. to reply —, aio.

affix, v.tr. (af)figĕre.

afflict, v.tr. commovēre dolore alqm

afficĕre ; (ex)cruciare. **affliction**, *n.* dolor ; — *of body*, morbus. **afflicting**, *adj.* tristis.

affluence, *n.* abundantia, copia.

afford, *v.tr. to supply*, praebĕre, potestatem facĕre (*to* — *an opportunity*) ; *to yield*, reddĕre ; *to have the means*, posse.

affranchise, *see* FREE, *v.tr.*

affray, *n.* rixa, pugna.

affright, *see* FRIGHTEN.

affront, *v.tr.* offendĕre, laedĕre. *n.* iniuria. **affronting**, *adj.* contumeliosus.

afield, *adv.* in agros (*of motion*), in agris (*of rest*).

afloat, *adj. & adv. to be* —, navi vehi.

afoot, *adv.* pedibus (*e.g.* pedibus ire).

aforesaid, *adj.* quem *or* quod supra scripsi.

afraid, *adj.* pavidus, (per)territus ; *to be* —, timēre.

afresh, *adv., see* AGAIN.

after, *prep.* post (*with accus*) ; *abl. abs.* (Aeginā relictā, — *leaving Ægina*) ; *according to*, secundum. *conj.* postquam, ut, ubi. *adv. also* **afterwards**, post, postea ; dein(de), inde ; deinceps; *three years* —, post tres annos.

afternoon, *n. in the* —, post meridiem.

again, *adv.* iterum, rursum; *to rise* —, resurgĕre ; *in a speech*, ad hoc.

against, *prep. with accus.* contra; adversus, in ; — *one's will*, alqo invito.

age, *n.* aetas; *of the name* —, aequalis (*contemporaries*) ; saeculum, tempus (*or in pl.*); *to be of* —, sui potens esse; *old* —, senectus. **aged**, *adj.* aetate provectior; — *man*, senex.

agent, *n.* actor, procurator.

aggrandize, *v.tr.* amplificare, augēre. **aggrandizement**, *n.* amplificatio.

aggravate, *v.tr.* augēre ; *exasperate*, lacessĕre, incitare.

aggregate, *n.* summa. **aggregation**, *n.* congregatio.

aggression, *n.* impetus, incursio, oppugnatio ; iniuria. **aggressive**, *adj.* infensus. *Adv.* infense. **aggressor**, qui iniuriam facit.

aghast, *adj* (ex)territus; *to stand* —, stupēre.

agile, *adj.* velox. **agility**, *n.* velocitas.

agitate, *v.tr.* agitare, quatĕre, (com)movēre. **agitation**, *n.* agitatio, iactatio (*as of the sea*); — *of mind*, animi per turbatio. **agitator**, *n.* turbator; *to be an* —, rebus novis studēre.

ago, *adv.* abhinc; *long* —, iam pridem.

agony, *n.* dotor ; aegritudo. **agonize**, *v.intr.* (ex)cruciari. *v.tr.* (ex)cruciare, torquēre.

agrarian, *adj.* agrarius.

agree, *v.* concinĕre, congruĕre; idem sentire ; *to* — *upon terms*, conditiones accipĕre. **agreement**, *n.* consensio, concordia ; *a compact* pactum. **agree-**

able, *adj.* gratus, dulcis ; — *to*, aptus, *with dat.*

agriculture, *n.* agri cultura. **agriculturist**, *n.* agricola, *m.*

aground, *adv.* in litore.

ague, *n.* febris intermittens.

ah ! ah ! aha ! *interj.* eu, euge.

ahead, *adv.* ante ; *to run* —, praecurrĕre.

aid, *n.* auxilium, opem (*no nom. sing.*). *v.tr.* auxilium afferre, (ad)iuvare.

ailing, *adj.* aeger.

aim, *n.* meta (*goal*) ; scopos (*mark*) ; *fig.* propositum. *v.tr.* telum dirigĕre, telo petĕre alqm; (animo) intendĕre.

air, *n.* caelum ; aër, aether, aura (*breeze*) ; *appearance*, vultus, facies ; *to have an* —, se gerĕre (*e.g.* honeste); *a tune*, modus, cantus. *v.tr.* aëri exponĕre. **airy**, *adj.* aërius, aetherius, aëri expositus.

aisle, *n.* ala (*side*), spatium medium (*mid*).

akin, *adj.* propinquus, a(d)gnatus, cognatus.

alabaster, *n.* alabastrites.

alack ! alack-a-day ! *interj.* eheu, vae mihi.

alacrity, *n.* pernicitas; alacritas.

alarm, *n.* strepitus ; tumultus ; *to sound the* —, classicum canĕre ; *fear*, terror, trepidatio; *v.tr.* terrēre.

alas ! *see* ALACK.

album, *n.* liber.

alcove, *n.* zotheca.

alder, *n.* alnus, *f. adj.* alneus.

alert, *adj.* vigil, alacer.

alias, *n.* nomen alienum.

alien, *adj.* alienus. *n.* alieni gena, advena. **alienate**, *v.tr.* (ab)alienare. **alienation**, *n.* (ab)alienatio.

alight, *v.intr.* descendĕre.

alike, *adv.* pariter, eodem modo. *adj.* similis.

alive, *adj.* vivus; *to be* —, vivĕre.

all, *adj. every*, omnis ; *the whole*, totus, solidus ; — *together*, cunctus ; *at* —, omnino; *not at* —, minime.

allay, *v.tr.* lenire, mitigare.

allege, *v.tr., see* ASSERT. **allegation**, *n.* affirmatio; *a charge*, accusatio.

allegiance, *n.* fides ; *to swear* —, in verba alcis iurare.

allegory, *n.* allegoria.

alleviate, *v.tr., see* ALLAY. **alleviation**, *n.* levatio, levamen(tum).

alley, *n.* ambulatio; angiportus.

allot, *v.tr. by lot*, sortiri, sorte legĕre. **allotting**, *n.* sortitio ; *to assign*, (at)tribuĕre. **allotment**, *n.* assignatio ; *ground*, ager.

allow, *v.tr.* sinĕre, pati, permittĕre ; concedĕre ; *to give*, dare. **allowable**, *adj.* concessus. **allowance**, *n.* concessio; *to make* — *or*, condonare ; *money*, pecunia.

alloy, *n.* corruptio; *without —,* sincerus, purus. *v.tr.* vitiare.

allude to, *v.tr.* significare. **allusion,** *n.* significatio.

allure, *v.tr.* allicĕre; inescare *(by a bait).* **alluring,** *adj.* dulcis. **allurement,** *n.* invitamentum, incitamentum.

ally, *n.* socius, foederatus. *v.tr.* foedus inire ; *to — oneself,* se (con)iungĕre. **alliance,** *n.* societas, foedus.

almanack, *n.* fasti ephemeris.

almighty, *adj.* omnipotens.

almond, *n.* amygdala ; *— tree,* amygdalus.

almost, *adv.* prope, paene, fere.

alms, *n.* stips, is *(nom. not used),* beneficium. **almoner,** *n.* qui largitionibus praeest.

aloe, *n.* aloē, -es, *f.*

aloft, *adv.* sublime.

alone, *adj.* solus. *See* ONLY.

along, *adv.* porro ; *prep.* secundum, praeter; *— with,* una cum.

aloof, *adv.* procul.

aloud, *adv.* clarā voce.

already, *adv.* iam.

also, *conj.* etiam, quoque, item.

altar, *n.* ara, altaria, -ium.

alter, *v.tr.* (com)mutare. *v.intr.* converti. **alterable,** *adj.* mutabilis; *adv.* mutabiliter. **altering, alteration,** *n.* (com)mutatio; vicissitudo.

altercation, *n.* iurgium.

alternate, *v.tr.* alternare. *v.intr.* variari ; *adj.* alternus ; *adv.* in vicem, vicissim. **alternation,** *n.* (per)mutatio, vicissitudo. **alternative,** *adj., see* ALTERNATE.

although, *conj.* tametsi, quanquam (quamq.), etsi; licet, quamvis.

altitude, *n.* altitudo.

altogether, *adv.* eodem tempore ; *all together,* cuncti, universi ; *wholly,* prorsus.

always, *adv.* semper ; *I — do it,* hoc facĕre soleo.

amalgamate, *v.tr.* (com)miscĕre. **amalgamation,** *n.* coniunctio.

amanuensis, *n.* a manu servus.

amass, *v.tr.* accumulare.

amaze, *v.tr.* obstupefacĕre. **amazed,** *adj.* obstupefactus ; *to be —,* stupĕre. **amazing,** *adj.* mirus. *Adv.* mirum in modum. **amazement,** *n.* stupor.

amazon, *n.* Amazon ; *fig.* mulier bellicosa.

ambassador, *n.* legatus.

amber, *n.* electrum, sucinum.

ambiguous, *adj.* anceps, ambiguus. *Adv.* ambigue. **ambiguity,** *n.* ambiguitas.

ambition, *n.* studium honorum. **ambitious,** *adj.* laudis et honoris cupidus; *adv.* cupide, *or* avid.

ambrosia, *n.* ambrosia. **ambrosial,** *adj.* ambrosius.

ambush, *n.* insidiae.

ameliorate, *v.tr.* corrigĕre ; *to — your condition,* augĕre opes.

amen ! *interj.* ita fiat !

amenable, *adj.* obediens; docilis.

amend, *v.tr.* emendare, corrigĕre. **amendment,** *n.* emendatio **amends,** *n.* expiatio; *to make — for,* expiare.

amethyst, *n.* amethystus.

amiable, *adj.* suavis, dulcis, iucundus. *Adv.* iucunde. **amiability,** *n.* suavitas.

amicable, *adj. see* FRIENDLY.

amidst, *prep.* in medio; inter.

amiss, *adv.* male; *to take —,* aegre ferre.

ammunition, *n.* apparatus belli, arma, -orum, tela, -orum.

amnesty, *n.* venia, impunitas.

among, *prep.* inter ; in *(with abl.) ; from —,* ex, de.

amorous, *adj.* amans ; *in bad sense,* libidinosus. *Adv.* maximo cum amore, libidinose. **amorousness,** *n.* amor, libido.

amount, *n.* summa; *whole —,* solidum. *v.intr.* *what does it — to,* quae summa est ? *it —s to the same thing,* idem *or* par est, nihil interest utrum.

amphibious, *adj.* animal cuius et in terrā et in aquā vita est.

amphitheatre, *n.* amphitheatrum.

ample, *adj.* amplus. *Adv.* ample, abunde. **amplitude,** *n.* amplituao.

amplify, *v.tr.* amplificare.

amputate, *v.tr.* praecidĕre. **amputation,** *n. by the verb.*

amuse, *v.tr.* delectare. **amusing,** *adj.* iucundus. *Adv.* iucunde. **amusement,** *n.* delectatio, oblectamentum.

anachronism, *n.* error de temporibus factus.

analogy, *n.* analogia, similitudo. **analogous,** *adj.* analogus, similis.

analysis, *n.* explicatio, expositio. **analyse,** *v.tr.* explicare; quasi in membra discerpĕre.

anapaest, *n.* anapaestus.

anarchy, *n.* turba et confusio.

anathema, *n.* *to put under —,* aquā et igni interdicĕre alci.

anatomy, *n.* anatomia. **anatomical,** *adj.* anatomicus. **anatomize,** *v.tr.* incidĕro corpus mortui. **anatomist,** *n.* qui incidit, *etc.*

ancestor, *n.* auctor gentis. **ancestors, ancestry,** *n.* priores, maiores, patres. **ancestral,** *adj.* avitus.

anchor, *n.* ancora ; *to cast —,* ancoram iacĕre ; *to raise —,* ancoras tollĕre. *v.tr.* navem ad ancoras deligare. **anchorage,** *n.* statio.

ancient, *adj.* antiquus, vetus, priscus, obsoletus ; *the —s,* veteres, antiqui, maiores.

and, *conj.* et, que *(enclit.),* atque, ac; *and so,* itaque; *and not,* neque, nec, et non.

anecdote, *n.* fabula, fabella.

anemone, *n.* anemone, -es, *f.*

anew, *adv.* denuo, ab integro.

anger, *n.* ira, iracundia ; *outbreaks of* —, iracundiae. *v.tr.* lacessĕre. **angry**, *adj.* iratus. *Adv.* irate, iracunde.

angle, *n.* angulus ; *for fishing*, hamus. **angler**, *n.* piscator.

anguish, *n.* cruciatus, dolor.

angular, *adj.* angularis.

animadvert, *v.tr.* animadvertĕre ; in alqm animadvertĕre ; *to criticize*, iudicare.

animal, *n.* animal, belua, pecus, pecudis, *f.* (*a head of cattle*) ; fera (*wild* —). *adj.* (*e.g. animal pleasures*, corporis voluptates).

animate, *v.tr.* animare ; *fig.* incitare ; *courage*, animum erigĕre. **animated**, *adj.* animatus ; *lively*, alacer. **animation**, *n.* alacritas, vehementia.

animosity, *n.* odium, invidia.

ankle, ankle-bone, *n.* talus. **anklet**, *n.* periscelis.

annals, *n.* annales, -ium, *m.*

annex, *v.tr.* addĕre ; subicĕre. **annexation**, *n.* adiunctio.

annihilate, *v.tr.* delēre, ex(s)tinguĕre. **annihilation**, *n.* ex(s)tinctio, excidium.

anniversary, *n.* sacra, -orum.

annotate, *v.tr.* annotare. **annotation**, *n.* annotatio.

announce, *v.tr.* (re)nuntiare. **announcement**, *n.* (re)nuntiatio.

annoy, *v.tr.* vexare ; *fatigare*. **annoyance**, *n.* molestia, cruciatus ; onus.

annual, *adj.* annuus, anniversarius. *Adv.* quotannis. **annuity**, *n.* annua pecunia.

annul, *v.tr.* legem tollĕre, abrogare ; *a contract*, (dis)solvĕre.

anodyne, *n.* quod dolorem mitigat.

anoint, *v.tr.* unguĕre. **anointing**, *n.* unctio.

anon, *adv.* brevi (tempore), mox.

anonymous, *adj.* sine nomine.

another, *pron.* alius ; *one* —, alius alium, inter se (*of two*) alter alterum.

answer, *n.* responsum ; *to a charge*, defensio. *v.tr.* respondēre ; *of an oracle*, responsum dare ; *succeed*, bene evenire. **answerable**, *adj.* *to anyone*, qui alci rationem reddit.

ant, *n.* formica. **anthill**, formicarum cuniculus.

antagonist, *n.* adversarius ; iste (*legal*).

antecedent, *adj.* antecedens, prior ; praeterita, *pl.* (*past events*).

antechamber, *n.* vestibulum.

antediluvian, *adj.* priscus, antiquus ; obsoletus.

antelope, *n.*, *see* DEER.

anterior, *adj.* prior, superior.

anthem, *n.* cantus, -ūs.

anthropoid, *adj.* homini similis.

anticipate, *v.tr.* anticipare (*to do*

before) ; ex(s)pectare. **anticipation**, *n.* ex(s)pectatio, spes.

antics, *n.* ludi, ioca, -orum.

antidote, *n.* remedium.

antipathy, *n.* rerum discordia, odium.

antipodes, *n.* *fig.* by *adj.* adversus, contrarius.

antiquary, antiquarian, *n.* rerum antiquarum studiosus. **antiquated**, *adj.* obsoletus. **antique**, *adj.* antiquus. **antiquity**, *n.* antiquitas.

antithesis, *n.* contrarium.

antler, *n.* cornu.

anvil, *n.* incus, -ūdis, *f.*

anxiety, *n.* pavor, sol(l)icitudo. **anxious**, *adj.* sol(l)icitus ; *to be* —, angi. *Adv.* sol(l)icite.

any, *pron.* quisquam (*in neg. sentences and questions*) ; quilibet, quivis (*any you please*) ; *etc. adj.* ullus, quivis ; — *one*, aliquis ; — *where*, alicubi.

apace, *adv.* celeriter.

apart, *adv.* by *prefix* se- (*e.g.* secernĕre). **apartment**, *n.*, *see* ROOM.

apathy, *n.* socordia. **apathetic**, *adj.* hebes.

ape, *n.* simia. *v.tr.*, *see* IMITATE.

aperture, *n.*, *see* OPENING.

apex, *n.* apex.

aphorism, *n.* sententia, dictum.

apiary, *n.* alvearium, mellarium.

apiece, *adv.* by *distrib.* numeral.

apologist, *n.* defensor. **apology**, *n.* defensio ; excusatio. **apologize**, *v.intr.* alqd excusare. **apologetical**, *adj.* qui se excusat, *etc.*

apophthegm, *n.* dictum.

apostrophize, *v.tr.*, *see* ADDRESS.

apothecary, *n.* medicus.

appal, *v.tr.* terrēre ; *see* FRIGHTEN.

apparatus, *n.* apparatus, -ūs.

apparel, *n.* vestis, vestimentum.

apparent, *adj.* manifestus ; *to make* —, aperire ; *opp. to real*, simulatus. *Adv.* manifeste. **apparition**, *n.* simulacrum, species.

appeal, *v.intr.* legal, alqm appellare, ad alqm provocare ; *to refer to*, alqm testari. *n.* appellatio, provocatio ; *entreaty*, preces. **appealing**, *adj.* supplex.

appear, *v.intr.* apparēre, conspici ; *to be present*, adesse ; *in court*, in iudicium venire ; *to seem*, videri. **appearance**, *n.* adventus ; species ; *personal* —, corporis habitus.

appease, *v.tr.* placare ; (re)conciliare ; *hunger*, famem depellĕre.

appellant, *n.* qui provocat.

append, *v.tr.* addĕre. **appendage**, -ant, *n.* appendix, alqd additum. **appendix**, *n.* appendix, quaedam libro addita.

appertain, *v.tr.*, *see* BELONG.

appetite, fames ; *to have no* —, cibum fastidire.

applaud, *v.tr.* (ap)plandĕre. **applause,** *n.* (ap)plausus.

apple, *n.* malum; — *tree*, malus, .

apply, *v.tr.* applicare. *v.intr.* se convertĕre, adire, appellare. **appliance,** *n.* apparatus. **application,** *n.* appellatio, petitio; *putting to, admonitio, aaminotio (n.)*; diligentia; *of a word*, significatio. **applicable,** *adj.* utilis ; *to be — to anything*, ad alqd pertinēre.

appoint, *v.tr.* constituĕre, eligĕre. **appointment,** *n.* — *of consuls*, consules designare ; *an office*, munus.

apportion, *v.tr.* distribuĕre, disponĕre.

apposite, *adj.* accommodatus. *Adv.* accommodate.

appraise, *v.tr.* aestimare.

appreciate, *v.tr.* aestimare ; agnoscĕre.

apprehend, *v.tr.* apprehendĕre; *mentally*, comprehendĕre, intellegĕre. **apprehension,** *n.* mental, comprehensio ; *fear*, timor. **apprehensive,** *adj., see* TIMID.

apprentice, *n.* alci addictus. *v.tr.* alci addicĕre.

approach, *v.intr.* accedĕre, appropinquare. *n.* adventus, aditus.

appropriate, *v.intr.* *to give*, dedicare ; *to claim*, vindicare. *adj.* idoneus. *Adv.* accommodate. **appropriation,** *n.* legal, assignatio, additio.

approve, *v.tr.* (com)probare ; *legal*, sancire. **approved,** *adj.* probatus.

approver, *n. legal*, index. **approval,** *n. see* APPROBATION. **approbation,** *n.* (com)probatio; *with your —*, pace tuā.

approximate, *v.tr. & adj., see* APPROACH, NEAR.

April, *n.* Aprilis (mensis).

apron, *n.* subligaculum.

apt, *adj., see* APPROPRIATE ; habilis ; — *to learn*, docilis. *Adv.* convenienter.

aptitude, *n.* facultas.

aquatic, **aqueous,** *adj.* aquatilis.

aqueduct, *n.* aquae ductus ; *to form an — or the city*, aquam in urbem ducĕre.

aquiline, *adj.* aduncus.

arable, *adj.* arabilis.

arbiter, *n.* arbiter, disceptator.

arbitrate, *v.tr.* diiudicare. **arbitration,** *n.* arbitrium. **arbitrary,** *adj.* inconstans ; *proud*, superbus. *Adv.* superbe. **arbitrariness,** *n.* superbia.

arbour, *n.* umbraculum.

arc, *n.* arcus. **arcade,** *n.* porticus.

arch, *n.* arcus, fornix. *v.tr.* arcuare, conformicare. *v.intr.* arcuari. *adj.* petulans; subtilis.

archaeology, *n.* rerum antiquarum scientia. **archaism,** *n.* verbum obsoletum.

archer, *n.* sagittarius.

architect, *n.* architectus. **architecture,** *n.* architectura.

archives, *n.* tabulae publicae.

arctic, *adj.* septentrionalis.

---

ardent, *adj.* ardens, acer. *Adv.* acriter, ardenter.

ardour, *n.* ardor, fervor.

arduous, *adj.* arduus, difficilis.

area, *n.* superficies.

arena, *n.* arena.

argue, *v.tr.* (disputare ; *arguĕre* **argument,** argumentum; sententia.

arid, *adj.* aridus, siccus.

aright, *adv.* recte, bene. *See* RIGHT.

arise, *v.intr.* emergĕre, exoriri.

aristocrat, *n.* unus e nobilibus *or* patriciis. **aristocracy,** *n.* optimates, -(i)um, nobiles.

arithmetic, *n.* arithmetice, -es, *f.,* *or* arithmetica, -ae. **arithmetical,** *adj.* arithmeticus. **arithmetician,** *n.* arithmeticus.

ark, *n.* arca.

arm, *n. lit.* brachium (*lower*); lacertus (*upper*). *v.tr.* armare. *v.intr.* arma capĕre, armari, *adj.* armatus. **armistice,** *n.* indutiae. **armour,** *n.* arma, -orum, *pl. : — bearer,* armiger. **armourer,** *n.* faber armorum. **armpit,** *n.* ala. **armoury,** *n.* armamentarium. **arms,** *n.* arma, -orum, tela, -orum. **army,** *n.* exercitus, milites, -um, agmen; acies.

aromatic, *adj.* odoratus.

around, *adv.* circa, circum. *prep.* circa, circum *with accus.*

arouse, *v.tr.* excitare.

arraign, *v.tr., see* ACCUSE.

arrange, *v.tr.* ordinare, disponĕre ; (aciem) instruĕre. **arrangement,** *n.* compositio ; ratio ; *good —,* res bene disposita, etc.

arrant, *adj. by superl. or* summus.

array, *n.* vestis ; *battle —,* acies. *v.tr.* vestire, ornare.

arrears, *n.* reliqua -orum.

arrest, *v.tr.* comprehendĕre ; in custodiam dare.

arrive, *v.intr.* advenire. **arrival,** *n.* adventus.

arrogant, *adj.* arrogans, superbus. **arrogance,** *n.* superbia. *Adv.* arroganter, superbe. **arrogate,** *v.tr.* sibi arrogare.

arrow, *n.* sagitta.

arsenal, *n.* armamentarium ; *nava —,* navalia, -ium.

arsenic, *n.* arsenicum.

art, *n.* ars, artificium; *mental,* scientia, *an —,* ars, disciplina ; *fine —s,* artes ingenuae; *by — or craft,* per dolum et frandem. **artful,** *adj.* callidus. *Adv.* callide. **artfulness,** *n.* dolus. **artificer,** *n.* artifex ; auctor. **artificial,** *adj.* artificiosus. *Adv.* arte. **artisan,** *n.* faber. **artist,** *n.* poeta, pictor, *etc.* **artistic,** *adj.* artium studiosus. **artistically,** *adv.* summa arte. **artless,** *adj.* simplex. *Adv.* simpliciter. **artlessness,** *n.* simplicitas.

article, *n.* res; condicio (*e.g.* pacis), lex.
articulate, *v.tr.* pronuntiare. *adj.* clarus. *Adv.* clare. **articulation**, *n.* pronuntiatio.
artillery, *n.* tormenta -orum.
as, *adv. and conj.* et — et (= — *well as*); — *quickly as possible*, quam celerrime; — *far as I know*, quod sciam; *like*, instar, tanquam; *time*, ubi, ut, cum; *as if*, tanquam si.
ascend, *v.tr.* a(d)scendĕre. **ascension**, *n.* a(d)scensus. **ascent**, *n.* locus editus; a(d)scensus.
ascendancy, *n.* praestantia.
ascendant, *n. by adj.* summus; *to be in the —*, praestare.
ascertain, *v.tr.* explorare.
ascetic, *n.* qui cibo abstinet.
ascribe, *v.tr.* a(d)scribĕre, tribuĕre.
ash, *n.* fraxinus. *Adj.* fraxineus.
ashamed, *adj.* pudore affectus; *to be —*, pudet (alqm).
ashes, *n.* cinis, favilla. **ashy**, *adj.* cinereus.
ashore, *adv. of rest*, in litore; *of motion*, in litus; *to go —*, (e nave) exire; *to put men —*, exponĕre.
aside, *adv.* seorsum; *to go —*, secedĕre; *to lay —*, seponĕre.
ask, *v.tr.* rogare, quaerĕre, petĕre, poscĕre.
askance, *adv.* oblique; *to look — at*, limis oculis a(d)spicĕre.
aslant, *adv.* oblique, ex transverso.
asleep, *adj.* dormiens.
asp, *n.* aspis, vipera.
aspect, *n.* conspectus; *condition*, status.
asperity, *n.* asperitas, acerbitas.
asperse, *v.tr.* a(d)spergĕre. **aspersion**, *n.* a(d)spersio; *fig.* calumnia; *to cast an —*, calumniari.
aspirate, *n.* a(d)spiratio. *v.tr.* a(d)spirare.
aspire, *v.intr.* a(d)spirare, contendĕre, operam dare ut. **aspiration**, *n.* appetitio.
ass, *n.* asinus. **ass-driver**, *n.* asinarius.
assail, *v.tr.* oppugnare. **assailant**, *n.* qui alqm adoritur. **assault**, *n.* impetus, incursus; *of a town*, oppugnatio; *to commit an —*, vim afferre.
assassin, *n.* sicarius. **assassination**, *n.* caedes facta; *to accuse of —*, accusare inter sicarios. **assassinate**, *v.tr.* ex insidiis interficĕre.
assay, *v.tr., see* ATTEMPT.
assemble, *v.tr.* cogĕre, convocare. *v.intr.* cogi, convenire. **assembly**, *n.* convocatio; conventus, contio.
assent, *n.* assensus. *v.intr.* assentire; *to nod —*, annuĕre.
assert, *v.tr.* affirmare, dicĕre; *to — your right*, ius tenēre. **assertion**, *n.* sententia; affirmatio; defensio.
assess, *v.tr.* censēre; *to be — ed at anything*, alqd conferre. **assessment**, *n.*

aestimatio, vectigal. **assessor**, *n.* assessor; — *of taxes*, censor. **assets**, *n.* bona, -orum.
assiduous, *adj.* impiger, diligens. *Adv.* impigre, diligenter. **assiduity**, *n.* assiduitas.
assign, *v.tr.* attribuĕre. **assignation**, *n.* attributio; *appointment*, constitutum.
assimilate, *v.tr.* similem facĕre; *digest*, concoquĕre. **assimilation**, *n.* aequalitas; concoctio.
assist, *v.tr.* auxilio esse, subvenire. **assistance**, *n.* auxilium. **assistant**, *n.* adiutor; *colleague*, collega, *m.*
associate, *v.tr.* foedus facĕre, se coniungĕre. *v.intr.* foedere coniungi, esse cum alqo; *n.* socius, conscius. **association**, *n.* societas, collegium.
assort, *v.tr.* digerĕre. **assortment**, *n.* apparatus; numerus.
assuage, *v.tr.* mitigare. **assuagement**, *n.* mitigatio.
assume, *v.tr.* sibi arrogare, sumĕre; *to take for granted*, ponĕre. **assumption**, *n.* usurpatio; *arrogance*, superbia.
assure, *v.tr.* (pro certo) affirmare; *be assured*, crede mihi. **assurance**, *n.* certain, certus. *Adv.* certo.
assured, *adj. fearless*, securus; *certain*, certus. *Adv.* certo.
astern, *adv.* in *or* a puppe.
astonish, *v.tr.* perturbare. **astonished**, *adj.* attonitus. **astonishing**, *adj.* mirabilis, mirus. *Adv.* mirabiliter. **astonishment**, *n.* stupor, (ad)miratio.
astound, *v.tr., see* ASTONISH.
astray, *adv.* vage; *to be —*, vagari.
astrologer, *n.* astrolŏgus. **astrology**, *n.* astrologia.
astronomer, *n.* astrolŏgus.
astute, *adj.* callidus.
asunder, *adv.* seorsum.
asylum, *n.* asylum.
at, *prep.* ad, apud, iuxta, in; *old locative*, Romae; *of time, abl.* eodem tempore.
atheist, *n.* qui Deum esse negat.
athlete, *n.* athleta, *m.*
athwart, *adv.* in obliquum.
atmosphere, *n.* caelum. **atmospheric**, *adj. genit.*, caeli.
atom, *n.* atŏmus.
atone, *v.tr.* expiare, poenas dare. **atonement**, *n.* placatio, poena.
atrocious, *adj.* nefandus, atrox. *Adv.* atrociter. **atrocity**, *n.* immanitas; res atrox.
attach, *v.tr.* figĕre, affigĕre; conciliare. **attachment**, *n.* studium, amor.
attack, *n.* impetus, incursio, oppugnatio; *v.tr.* petĕre, aggredi, oppugnare; *to be —ed by a disease*, morbo corripi.
attain, *v.tr.* consequi, pervenire ad. **attainable**, *adj.* facilis. **attainment**, *n.* adeptio; *—s*, doctrina. **attainder**, *n.* accusatio.
attempt, *n.* conatus. *v.tr.* tentare.

attend, *v.tr.* comitari; alci apparēre; ministrare; *lectures, etc.,* alqm audire; *pay attention to,* curare. **attendance,** *n.* ministerium; *a great —,* frequentia. **attendant,** *n.* comes; minister. **attention,** *n.* anim attentio; diligentia, studium. **attentive,** *adj.* diligens, dofentus ; *to be ,* animo aequal. atbesse, attente, intente.

attenuate, *v.tr.* attenuare. **attenuation,** *n.* extenuatio.

attest, *v.tr.* testari. **attestation,** *n.* testificatio; testimonium.

attire, *v.tr.* restire. *n.* vestis.

attitude, *n.* corporis habitus; *(mentis)* ratio.

attract, *v.tr.* attrahēre. **attraction,** *n.* vis attrahendi; oblectamentum. **attractive,** *adj.* iucundus, suavis. *Adv.* iucunde, suaviter.

attribute, *n.* nota, insigne; proprium, natura. *v.tr.* attribuēre.

attune, *v.tr.* efficēre ut concinat.

auburn, *adj.* flavus.

auction, *n.* auctio; *to sell by —,* auctionari. **auctioneer,** *n.* magister auctionis, praeco.

audacious, *adj.* procax, impudens. *Adv.* impudenter. **audacity,** *n.* procacitas, impudentia.

audience, *n.* admissio; *hearers,* auditores. **audible,** *adj.* quod audiri potest. *Adv.* clarā voce. **audit,** *v.tr.* rationem ducēre.

augment, *v.tr.* augēre. **augmentation,** *n.* amplificatio.

augur, *n.* augur. *v.tr.* augurari. **augury,** *n.* augurium; omen.

August, *n.* Augustus, Sextilis (mensis).

august, *adj.* illustris.

aunt, *n.* amita, matertera.

auspice, *n.* auspicium. **auspicious,** *adj.* secundus. *Adv.* prospere.

austere, *adj.* severus, tristis. *Adv.* severe. **austerity,** *n.* severitas.

authentic, *adj.* verus, sincerus. *Adv.* certo auctore. **authenticity,** *n.* fides.

author, *n.* auctor; sculptor. **authoritative,** *adj.* imperiosus. *Adv.* arroganter.

authority, *n.* auctoritas, gravitas; dominatio; *the —s,* magistratus. **authorize,** *v.tr.* mandare, permittēre.

autocrat, *n.* dominus.

autumn, *n.* autumnus. **autumnal,** *adj.* autumnalis.

auxiliary, *n.* civitas foederata; *pl.* auxilia *(milites)* ; subsidia, -orum. *adj.* auxiliaris.

avail, *v.intr.* valēre, obtinēre.

avarice, *n.* cupiditas. **avaricious,** *adj.* habendi cupidus, avarus. *Adv.* avare.

avaunt ! *interj.* abi ! apage !

avenge, *v.tr.* ulcisci. **avenger,** *n.* ultor.

avenue, *n. approach,* aditus ; *shady walk,* xystus.

aver, *v.tr., see* ASSERT.

avert, *v.tr.* avertēre. **aversion,** *n.* fuga, odium. **averse,** *adj.* aversus.

avoid, *v.tr.* vitare. **avoiding,** *n.* fuga.

avow, *v.tr.* confiteri. **avowal,** *n.* confessio. **avowed,** *adj.* apertus. *Adv.* aperte.

await, *v.tr.* ex(s)pectare.

awake, *v.tr.* (e somno) excitare. *v.intr.* expergisci. *adj.* vigilans ; *to be —,* vigilare. **awakening,** *n. by verb* AWAKE.

award, *v.tr.* adiudicare. *n.* iudicium, arbitrium.

aware, *adj.* gnarus ; *to be —,* scire, novisse.

away, *adv.* procul ; *— with !* aufer ! *— you !* apage te !

awe, *n.* veneratio, religio. *v.tr.* terrēre.

awful, *adj.* verecundus, venerabilis venerandus, terrible, dirus. *Adv.* terribly, atrociter.

awhile, *adv.* aliquamdiu ; *— ago,* paul(l)o ante.

awkward, *adj.* rusticus, inscitus. *Adv.* inscite, rustice. **awkwardness,** *n.* inscitia.

awl, *n.* subula.

awning, *n.* velum.

awry, *adj.* obliquus ; *fig.* perversus. *adv.* oblique, perverse.

axe, *n.* securis, dolabra.

axiom, *n.* axioma, pronuntiatum.

axis, axle, *n.* axis, *m.*

ay, *adv.* ita, sane.

azure, *adj.* caeruleus.

B

baa, *v.intr.* balare. *n.* balatus.

babble, *v.* garrire. **babbling,** *n.* loquacitas. **babbler,** *n.* loquax.

babe, baby, *n.* infans.

baboon, *n.* simia (= ape).

bachelor, *n.* caelebs.

back, *n.* tergum, dorsum; *to lie on the —,* supinum cubare ; *of the head,* occipitium. *Adv.* **backwards,** retro, retrorsum. *Adj.* posterior. *v.tr.* retro movēre; *to support,* favēre.

backbite, *v.tr.* maledicēre.

bad, *adj.* malus ; *— road,* iter difficile; *in — health,* aeger ; *(moral)* malus, turpis. *Adv.* male, turpiter. **badness,** *n.* *(moral)* turpitas.

badge, *n.* signum, nota.

badger, *n.* meles. *v.tr.* vexare.

baffle, *v.tr.* eludēre, spem fallēre.

bag, *n.* saccus.

baggage, *n.* sarcinae, impedimenta, -orum.

bail, *n.* vadimonium ; *to give —,* vadimonium facēre ; *one who gives —,* sponsor, vas.

bailiff, *n. on an estate*, villicus; *officer*, apparitor.

bait, *n. for fish*, esca; *fig.* illecebra; *for horses*, cibus. *v.tr.* escam (hamo) imponěre ; cibum praebēre ; *(bulls, etc.)*, lacessěre.

bake, *v.tr.* coquěre, torrēre. **baking**, *n.* coctura ; *bakehouse*, pistrina ; *baker*, pistor.

balance, *n. (scales)* libra; *fig.* aequalitas; *in book-keeping*, reliquum. *v.tr.* librare; *fig.* perpenděre. *v.intr. of accounts*, constare.

balcony, *n.* solarium.

bald, *adj.* calvus ; *fig.* inornatus. **baldness**, *n.* calvitium.

bale, *n.* fascis, -is, *m.* **baleful**, *adj.* exitiosus. **bale out**, *v.tr.* exhaurire.

balk, *n. a beam*, tignum, trabs. *v.tr.* impedimento esse.

ball, *n.* pila ; *eye —*, pupilla ; *dance*, saltatio.

ballad, *n.* carmen.

ballast, *n.* saburra.

ballet, *n.* pantomimus ; *— dancer*, pantomimus.

ballot, *n. to vote by —*, suffragia ferre ; *— box*, cista.

balm, *n.* balsamum; *fig.* solatium.

balustrade, *n.* cancelli, -orum.

bamboo, *n.* arundo Indica.

ban, *n.* aquae et ignis interdictio.

band, *n. fillet*, vitta; *(of metal)* armilla; *persons*, turba, grex. *v.tr.* (con)sociare.

bandage, *n.* fascia. *v.tr.* deligare.

bandit, *n.* latro.

bandy, *v.tr. words*, altercari. **bandy-legged**, *adj.* varus.

bane, *n.* venenum ; *pestis.* **baneful**, *adj.* exitiosus.

bang, *n.* percussio; sonitus.

banish, *v.tr.* aquā et igni interdicěre, (ex)pellěre. **banishment**, *n.* interdictio aquae et ignis, ex(s)ilium.

bank, *n. of a river*, ripa ; *of oars*, transtrum ; *earth*, agger ; *a money-changer's table*, argentaria. **banker**, *n.* argentarius. **bankrupt**, *n.* decoctor; *to become —*, decoquěre.

banner, *n.* vexillum; *see* FLAG.

banquet, *n.* epulae, convivium.

banter, *n.* irriso, ludibrium ; *in —*, per ludibrium. *v.tr.* alqm ludibrio habēre.

bar, *n. metal, etc.*, later, -eris, *m.*; *bolt*, claustrum ; *a stake*, sudes ; *partition*, cancelli ; *to practise at the —*, caus(s)as agěre ; *(advocates)*, patroni. *v.tr. to bolt*, occluděre ; *fig.* impedimento esse; *to except*, excipěre.

barbarous, **barbaric**, *adj.* barbarus (*foreign*), saevus. *Adv.* barbare, crudeliter. **barbarity**, *n.* crudelitas.

barbed, *adj.* hamatus.

barber, *n.* tonsor ; *a —'s shop*, tonstrina.

bard, *n.* vates, -is, *m. and f.*

bare, *adj.* nudus ; *mere*, merus ; *plain*, simplex. *Adv. scarcely*, vix ; *simpliciter*. **bareness**, *n. by adj.* BARE. **barefaced**, impudens. **barefoot**, pedibus nudis.

bargain, *n.* res, pactum ; *to make good —*, bene eměre. *v.intr.* pacisci.

bark, *n.* cortex. *v.tr.* delibrare.

bark, *v.intr.* latrare. *n.* latratus.

barley, *n.* hordeum. *adj.* hordeaceus.

barn, *n.* horreum.

barracks, *n.* castra, -orum.

barrel, *n.* dolium.

barren, *adj.* sterilis. **barrenness**, *n.* sterilitas.

barricade, *n.* munimentum. *v.tr.* obstruěre.

barrier, *n.* limes, fines; murus.

barrister, *n., see* ADVOCATE.

barrow, *n.* ferculum (*a stand for carrying*).

barter, *v.tr.* permutare merces. *n.* permutatio mercium.

base, *adj.* perditus, turpis ; *— coin*, nummi adulterini. *Adv.* turpiter. **baseness**, *n.* turpitudo, dedecus.

base, *n.* basis, fundamentum; *radices (montis)*.

bashful, *adj.* pudens. *Adv.* pudenter. **bashfulness**, *n.* pudor.

basin, *n.* pelvis.

basis, *n., see* BASE, *n.*

bask, *v. intr.* apricari.

basket, *n.* corbis, sporta. **basketwork**, opus vimineum.

bas-relief, *n.* opus caelatum.

bastard, *n.* nothus.

bastinado, *n.* ictus.

bat, *n. an animal*, vespertilio.

bat, *n. for games*, clava.

batch, *n.* numerus.

bate, *v.tr.* (im)minuěre. *v.intr.* (im)minui.

bath, *n.* balineum, balneum ; *pl.* balneae. (*hot*). **bathe**, *v.tr.* lavare ; *bathing-rooms*, balnearia ; *— for cold, hot baths, etc.*, frigidarium, tepidarium, calidarium, sudatorium. *v.intr.* lavari.

battalion, *n.* cohors (*cavalry*), legio.

batter, *v.tr.* verberare; pulsare.

battering-ram, *n.* aries-ětis, *m.*

battery, *n.* agger (*mound*), tormenta, -orum (*weapons*).

battle, *n.* praelium, certamen. **battle-array**, *n.* acies. **battle-axe**, *n.* bipennis; securis. **battle-cry**, *n.* clamor. **battle-field**, *n.* locus pugnae.

battlement, *n.* pinna.

bawl, *v.tr.* vociferari.

bay, *n. laurel*, laurus ; *gulf*, sinus ; *to stand at —*, adversus alqm se defenděre. *v.intr.* latrare.

bayonet, *n.* gladius ; *with fixed —s*, constrictis gladiis.

be, *v.intr.* esse, ex(s)istěre.

beach, *n.* litus, -ōris, *n.*

beacon, n. (*lighthouse*), pharus; ignis.

bead, n. globulus.

beak, n. rostrum.

beaker, n. poculum, calix.

beam, n. lignum, trabs; *of a* —, trabalis; *of light*, radius ; *of a balance*, iugum. *v.intr.* fulgēre. beaming, n. fulgor. *adj.* hilaris.

beam, n. faba.

bear, n. ursus, ursa (*constellation*), Arctos, Ursa ; *the Great* —, Ursa Major ; *the Lesser* —, Ursa Minor ; (*the two*, Septentriones, -um). *v.tr.* ferre, portare ; — (*to endure*), pati ; *to give birth to*, parēre. bearer, n. baiulus; nuntius (*of news*); tabellarius (*of letters*). bearing, n. portatio, gestatio; *of children*, partus.

beard, n. barba, *v.tr.* alqm provocare.

beast, n. iumentum (*of burden*), belua, — *wild* —, fera. beastly, adj. immundus. beastliness, n. spurcitia.

beat, *v.tr.* ferire, pulsare; *to be beaten*, vapulare ; *to overcome*, superare. *v.intr.* palpitare. beating, n. verbera, -um.

beau, n. homo bellus *or* elegans.

beautiful, adj. pulcher, formosus, bellus, amoenus. *Adv.* pulchre, amoene, belle. beautify, *v.tr.* (ex)ornare. beauty, n. pulchritudo, forma, amoenitas (*of places*).

beaver, n. castor, fiber.

becalmed, adj. ventis destitutus.

because, conj. quod, quia, quoniam ; — *of*, *prep.*, propter, ob *with accus.*

beck, n. nod, nutus; *to be at any one's* — *or call*, ad nutum alcis esse, beckon, *v.tr.* digito innuēre.

become, *v.intr.* fiēri. *v.tr. to suit*, alqm convenit.

bed, n. lectus ; *to make a* —, lectum sternēre ; *to go to* —, cubitum ire ; — *of a river*, alveus. — chamber, n. cubiculum. bedding, n. lodix, stragulum. — post, n. fulcrum lecti.

bedaub, *v.tr.* (ob)linēre.

bedeck, *v.tr.* (ex)ornare.

bedew, *v.tr.* inrorare. bedewed, adj. roscidus; *to be* —, humescēre.

bedizen, *v.tr.* (ex)ornare.

bee, n. apis ; — *hive*, alvus, alveus ; *a swarm of* —, examen apium ; *queen* —, rex apium.

beech, n. fagus, *f.*; *of* —, faginus.

beef, n. (caro) bubula.

beetle, n. scarabaeus. *v.intr.* imminēre.

befall, *v.intr.* accidēre, contingēre.

befit, *v.tr.* aptus esse ; *it* —*s thee*, te decet.

before, adv. prius, citius, ante; prior; *rather*, potius ; *the* — *mentioned*, qui supra dictus est. *prep. in presence of*, coram. *conj.* antequam. beforehand, *adv.* antea; *to be* —, praevenire.

befoul, *v.tr.* inquinare.

befriend, *v.tr.* (ad)iuvare, favēre.

beg, *v.intr.* mendicare. *v.tr.* orare. beggar, n. mendicus. beggarly, adj. miser, vilis. beggary, n. paupertas. begging, n. mendicitas.

beget, *v.tr.* gignēre.

begin, *v.intr.* incipēre *v.tr.* incipēre, ordiri, beginning, n. initium; *speech*, exordium ; *of a science*, elementa. beginner, n. author, auctor; *novice*, tiro, rudis.

begone ! *interj.* abi ! apage te !

begrime, *v.tr.* inquinare, maculare.

begrudge, *v.tr.* invidēre.

beguile, *v.tr.* decipēre, fallēre.

behalf, n. *on* — *of*, pro.

behave, *v.tr.* se gerēre. behaviour, n. mores, -um

behead, *v.tr.* caput alcis praecidēre.

behind, adv. pone, a tergo, *prep.* pone, post, *with acc.* behindhand, *adv.* parum (= *too little*); sero.

behold, *v.tr.* intueri, spectare. behold! *interj.* en ! ecce ! beholden, *to be* —, debēre.

behove, *v.tr. impers.* decet; oportet.

being, n. natura atque vis ; condicio, res.

belated, adj. serus.

belch, *v.intr.* ructare. *v.tr.* evomēre.

beleaguer, *v.tr.* obsidēre.

belfry, n. turris.

belie, *v.tr.* criminari, calumniari.

belief, n. opinio ; persuasio, fides. believe, *v.tr.* credēre, arbitrari, sentire; *I firmly* —, mihi persuasum est. believer, n. qui credit.

bell, n. tintinnabulum, aes.

belle, n. (puella) pulchra.

bellow, *v.intr.* mugire.

bellows, n. follis, -is, *m.*

belly, n. venter ; alvus, abdomen ; *of a ship*, alveus.

belong, *v. intr.* — *to*, alci *or* alcis esse.

below, adv. subter, infra. *prep.* sub.

belt, n. cingulum, zona.

bemoan, *v.tr.* deplorare.

bench, n. scamnum ; *for work*, mensa ; *of rowers*, transtrum ; *of judges*, consessus.

bend, *v.tr.* (in)flectēre ; *to* — *one's mind to*, animadvertēre. *v.intr.* flecti. bending, n. flexus. bent, n. animi inclinatio, voluntas.

beneath, *see* BELOW.

benediction, n. *to give*, bonis ominibus prosequi.

benefit, n. beneficium. *v.tr.* (ad)iuvare, usui esse. beneficial, adj. utilis, salutaris. *Adv.* utiliter, salubriter. beneficent, adj. benignus. *Adv.* benigne. beneficence, n. benignitas. benefactor, n. beneficus (adj).

benevolent, adj. benevolus. benevolence, n. benevolentia.

benighted, adj., *see* IGNORANT.

benign, adj. benignus. Adv. benigne. **benignity,** n. benignitas.

benumb, v.tr. obstupefacĕre ; to be —ed, torpēre.

bequeath, v.tr. legare. **bequest,** n. legatum.

bereave, v.tr. orbare. **bereaved,** adj. orbus. **bereavement,** n. orbitas.

berry, n. bao(c)a, acinus.

beseech, v.tr. obtestari, orare.

beset, v.tr. premĕre, obsidēre.

beshrew, v.tr.; — me, di(i) me perdant.

beside, prep. prope, iuxta ; except, praeter ; this is — the point, nihil ad rem: —oneself, sui impotens.

besides, adv. praeterea, ad hoc. prep. praeter.

besiege, v.tr. obsidēre. **besieger,** n. obsessor, obsidens.

besmear, v.tr. (ob)linĕre.

bespatter, v.tr. a(d)spergĕre.

bespeak, v.tr. imperare.

best, adj. optimus; see GOOD.

bestir, v.tr. (se) (com)movēre, incitare.

bestow, v.tr., see GIVE.

bet, n. pignus.

betake oneself, v.intr. se conferre, ire.

betimes, adv. mox, brevi.

betoken, v.tr. signare.

betray, v.tr. prodĕre. **betrayal,** n. proditio, perfidia, delatio. **betrayal,** n. proditor.

betroth, v.tr. (de)spondēre. **betrothal,** n. sponsalia, -ium.

better, adj. melior, praestantior; I am getting —, convalesco. adv. melius.

between, prep. inter with acc.

beverage, n. potio.

bevy, n. grex, grĕgis, m.

bewail, v.tr. deplorare.

beware, v.tr. cavēre.

bewilder, v.tr. (con)turbare.

bewitch, v.tr. fascinare; fig. capĕre.

beyond, adv. ultra, supra. prep. trans.

bias, n. inclinatio animi. v.tr. apud alqm plus quam aequum est valēre.

bibulous, adj. † bibulus.

bid, v.tr. iubēre ; invite, invitare ; at a sale, licēri ; — welcome, salvēre iubēre. **bidding,** n., see COMMAND ; at a sale, licitatio. **bidder,** n. illicitator.

bide, v.tr. manēre.

biennial, adj. biennis.

bier, n. feretrum.

big, adj. magnus, grandis.

bigot, n. superstitiosus. **bigotry,** n. nimia et superstitiosa religio.

bile, n. bilis.

bilge-water, n. sentina.

bill, n. tool, falx; of a bird, rostrum.

bill, n. proposed law, rogatio; to bring forward a —, roga'ionem ferre ; to adopt a —, accipĕre ; to refuse a —, antiquare; to carry a - -, perferre.

billet, n. — doux, epistula amatoria. v.tr. milites per domos disponĕre.

billow, n. fluctus. **billowy,** adj. fluctuosus.

bind, v.tr. alligare, revincire; restrain, coërcēre; to — together, colligare; fig. sacramento a(d)stringĕre ; to — books, glutinare ; to — over, vadari. **bindweed,** n. convolvulus.

biography, n. vitae alcis descriptio. **biographer,** n. qui alcis res gestas enarrat.

biped, n. bipes, -ĕdis, adj.

birch, n. betula.

bird, n. avis, volucris ; — cage, n. cavea; — catcher, n. auceps; lime, n. viscus.

birth, n. ortus ; of noble —, nobili genere. **birthday,** n. dies natalis. **birthright,** n. patrimonium.

biscuit, n. panis.

bishop, n. episcopus.

bit, n. of a horse, frenum; see PIECE.

bitch, n. canis (femina).

bite, v.tr. mordēre. n., morsus. **biting,** adj. mordens.

bitter, adj. amarus, acerbus. Adv. amare. **bitterness,** n. acerbitas.

bivouac, v.intr. in armis excubare. n. excubiae.

black, adj. niger ; dressed in —, sordidatus; negro, Aethiops.

blackberry, n. rubus.

blackbird, n. merula.

blackguard, n. sceleratus.

blacksmith, n. faber.

bladder, n. vesica.

blade, n. grass, herba ; oar, palma ; knife, lamina.

blame, n. reprehensio. v.tr. culpare. **blameable, blameworthy,** adj. reprehensione dignus. **blameless,** adj. integer, sanctus. **blamelessness,** n. vitae integritas.

bland, adj. blandus, mitis. Adv. blande. **blandness,** n. lenitas. **blandishment,** n. blanditiae.

blank, adj. vacuus.

blanket, n. lodix.

blasphemous, adj. impius erga Deum.

blast, n. venti impetus. v.tr., see BLIGHT; igne diruĕre.

blaze, n. flamma, ardor. v.intr. ardēre.

bleach, v.tr. candidum reddĕre. v.intr. become white, albescĕre.

bleak, adj., see COLD.

blear-eyed, adj. lippus.

bleat, v.intr. balare. n. balatus.

bleed, v.intr. sanguinem fundĕre. v.tr. to — a person, alci sanguinem mittēre.

blemish, n. macula, labes. v.tr. (com)-maculare.

blend, v.tr. (com)miscēre.

bless, v.tr. bonis omnibus prosequi. **blessed,** adj. beatus. Adv. beate. **blessedness,** n. felicitas.

blight, n. robigo. v.tr. robigine afficĕre.

blind, adj. caecus, oculis captus ; fig.

occaecatus, stultus. *Adv. by* caecus; *rashly*, temere. *v.tr.* oculis privare.

blindfold, *adj.* oculis opertis. **blindness**, *n.* caecitas; *fig.* stultitia.

blink, *v.intr.* con(n)īvēre.

bliss, *n.* summa felicitas.

blister, *n.* pustula. *v.tr.* pustulare.

blithe, *adj.* laetus. *Adv.* laete. **blitheness**, *n.* laetitia.

bloated, *adj.* turgidus; *fig.* tumidus.

block, *n.* truncus, caudex. *v.tr.* claudēre. **blockade**, *n.* obsidio. *v.tr.* obsidēre. **blockhead**, *n.* stolidus.

blood, *n.* sanguis, cruor. **bloodless**, *adj.* exsanguis, incruentus. **blood-relation**, *n.* consanguineus. **bloodshed**, *n.* caedes. **bloodshot**, *adj.* sanguine suffusus. **bloodthirsty**, *adj.* sanguinarius. **blood-vessel**, *n.* arteria, vena. **bloody**, *adj.* cruentus.

bloom, *n.* flos. *v.intr.* florēre, vigēre. **blooming**, *adj.* florens.

blossom, *v.intr.*, *see* BLOOM.

blot, *n.* litura; macula. *v.tr. to dry ink*, abstergēre; *fig.* (com)maculare.

blow, *n.* plaga, verbera, -um; *fig.* casus. *v.intr.* flare. *v.tr.* tibiā canēre.

blubber, *n.* adeps balaenarum.

bludgeon, *n.* fustis, -is, *m.*

blue, *adj.* caeruleus, lividus.

blunder, *m.* error, erratum. *v.intr.* errare.

blunt, *adj.* hebes; obtusus. *Adv.* rustice. *v.tr.* hebetare; *fig.* obtundēre. **bluntness**, *n. adj.* hebes; *fig.* rusticitas.

blur, *n.* macula. *v.tr.* obscurare.

blush, *n.* rubor. *v.intr.* erubescēre.

bluster, *v.intr.* tumultum facēre, saevire.

boar, *n.* verres; *a wild —*, aper.

board, *n.* axis, tabula; *food*, victus; *— a ship*, navem conscendēre.

boast, *v.intr.* gloriari, se iactare. **boaster**, *n.* iactator. **boasting**, *n.* iactatio. **boastful**, *adj.* gloriosus. *Adv.* gloriose.

boat, *n.* scapha; *— man*, nauta, *m.*

body, *n.* corpus, *a — guard*, cohors praetoria; *company*, societas; *of cavalry*, ala. **bodily**, *adj.* corporeus.

bog, *n.* palus. **boggy**, *adj.* paluster.

boil, *v.tr.* coquēre. *v.intr.* fervēre, aestuare; *fig.* aestuare.

boil, *n.* vomica.

boisterous, *adj.* turbidus; *of the sea*, agitatus.

bold, *adj.* audax; *to be —*, audēre. *Adv.* audacter, bolluisse, *n.* audacia.

bolster, *n.* culcita, pulvinus.

bolt, *n.* obex, claustrum. *v.tr.* claudēre, occludēre.

bombard, *v.tr.* urbem tormentis verberare.

bombast, *n.* inflata oratio. **bombastic**, *adj.* inflatus.

bond, *n.* vinculum, ligamentum, compes;

fig. societas; *surety*, syngrapha.

bondage, *n.* servitus.

bone, *n.* os, ossis, *n.* **bony**, *adj.* osseus.

book, *n.* liber. **bookseller**, *n.* bibliopola.

boon, *n.* beneficium. *Adj.* iucundus.

boorish, *adj.* inurbanus. *Adv.* inurbane.

boot, *n.* calceamentum.

boot, *n. gain*, commodum, *ω —*, ultro. **bootless**, *adj.* inutilis. *Adv.* frustrā.

booty, *n.* praeda.

border, *n. of a river*, margo, ripa, ora; *of a country*, fines, -ium. *v.tr.* cingēre. *v.intr.* attingēre; *finitimus esse.*

bore, *v.tr.* perterebrare; *to weary*, defatigare, *n. homo importunus.*

born, *v.intr. to be —*, nasci.

borrow, *v.tr.* mutuari.

bosom, *n.* sinus; *fig.* pectus. **bosom friend**, amicus coniunctissimus.

boss, *n.* umbo.

botany, *n.* herbaria (ars). **botanical**, *adj.* herbarius. **botanize**, *v.intr.* herbas colligēre.

both, *adj.* ambo. *pron.* uterque. *conj.* et — et, cum — tum.

bother, *n.* incommodum. *v.tr.* defatigare.

bottle, *n.* ampulla. *v.tr.* vinum, *etc.*, diffundēre.

bottom, *n.* fundus; *to drain to the —*, faece tenus potare; *fig. to go to the —*, perire. **bottomless**, *adj.* immensae altitudinis.

bough, *n.* ramus.

bounce, *v.intr.* resilire.

bound, *n.* limes, fines. *v.tr.* definire. *n. and v.intr.*, *see* LEAP. **bounden**, *adj. — duty*, officium. **boundless**, adj. infinitus.

bounty, *n.* liberalitas. **bountiful**, *adj.* liberalis. *Adv.* liberaliter.

bout, *n. drinking —*, comissatio.

bow, *v.tr.* flectēre, demittēre. *v.intr.* recti, se dēmittēre; *n. corporis inclinatio*; *weapon*, arcus; *of a ship*, prora.

bowman, *n.* sagittarius. **bowstring**, *n.* nervus.

bowels, *n.* intestina, viscera; *fig.* viscera.

bower, *n.* umbraculum.

bowl, *v.tr.* volvēre. *n.* poculum; *ball*, pila.

box, *v.intr.* pugnis certare. *n. on the ear*, alapa. **boxer**, *n.* pugil.

box, *n. (tree)*, buxus, *f.*, buxum (*box-wood*); *of —*, buxeus; *small chest*, cista, armarium; *ballot —*, cista.

boy, *n.* puer. **boyhood**, *n.* aetas puerilis. **boyish**, *adj.* puerilis. *Adv.* pueriliter.

brace, *v.tr.* alligare; *fig.* (animum) erigēre; *of air*, salūbre. *n.* of a ship, funis quo antenna vertitur; *pair*, par; *braces*, fascia.

bracelet, *n.* armilla.

brackish, *adj.* amarus.

brag, *v.intr.* se iactare, gloriari.

braid, *v.tr.* nectĕre. *n.* gradus (*of hair*).

brain, *n.* cerebrum.

bramble, *n.* rubus.

bran, *n.* furfur.

branch, *n.* ramus; *fig.* familia.

brand, *n.* fax; *mark*, nota; *to* —, notam inurĕre.

brandish, *v.tr.* vibrare, iactare.

brasier, foculus; *worker in brass*, faber qui vasa ex orichalco facit.

brass, *n.* orichalcum, aes; *of brass*, a(h)eneus.

bravado, *n.* iactatio, ostentatio.

brave, *adj.* fortis. *Adv.* fortiter. **bravery**, *n.* fortitudo.

bravo! *interj.* euge! factum bene! laudo!

brawl, *v.intr.* altercari. *n.* iurgium.

brawny, *adj.* robustus.

brazen, *adj.* a(h)eneus; *fig.* impudens. *v.tr.* confirmare.

breach, *n.* via patefacta; *to make a* —, muros perfringĕre; *fig.* — *of treaty*, foedus ruptum.

bread, *n.* panis, *m.*; victus (*nourishment*).

breadth, *n.* latitudo.

break, *v.tr.* frangĕre; *a treaty*, foedus violare; *to* — *a promise*, fidem fallĕre. *v.intr.* frangi; *to* — *out*, erumpĕre; *of a war*, oriri. *n.* intervallum; — *of day*, prima lux. **breaker**, *n.* fluctus.

breakfast, *n.* prandium. *v.intr.* prandĕre.

breakwater, *n.* moles, -is, *f.*

breast, *n.* pectus, animus (*fig.*). **breastplate**, *n.* thorax. **breastwork**, *n.* pluteus.

breath, *n.* spiritus, anima; *to take* —, se colligĕre. **breathless**, *adj.* exanimatus. **breathe**, *v.intr.* spirare; *to* — *upon*, afflare; *to* — *out*, exhalare.

breeches, *n.* bracae; *wearing* —, bracatus.

breed, *v.tr.* gignĕre, parĕre; *rear*, alĕre. *n.* genus. **breeding**, *n.* cultus.

breeze, *n.* aura.

brew, coquĕre. *v.intr.* (*fig.*) imminĕre. **brewing**, *n.* coctura.

bribe, *n.* largitio. *v.tr.* corrumpĕre. **briber**, *n.* corruptor.

brick, *n.* later, laterculus.

bride, *n.* sponsa. **bridegroom**, sponsus. **bridal**, *adj.* nuptialis; — *procession*, pompa.

bridge, *n.* pons, *m.*

bridle, *n.* frenum. *v.tr.* (in)frenare; *fig.* coërcĕre.

brief, *adj.* brevis; *in* —, ne longus sim. *Adv.* breviter. **brevity**, *n.* brevitas.

brier, *n.* frutex. **briery**, *adj.* fruticosus.

brigade, *n.*, *see* TROOP.

brigand, *n.* latro.

bright, *adj.* clarus, candidus; *to be* —,

clarēre; *sky*, serenus. *Adv.* clare.

brightness, *n.* candor, fulgor; *weather*, serenitas. **brighten**, *v.tr.* illustrare; *fig.* oblectare.

brilliant, *adj.* splendidus. *Adv.* splendide. **brilliancy**, *n.* splendor.

brim, *n.* ora, margo, labrum.

brine, *n.* aqua salsa.

bring, *v.tr.* afferre, advehĕre; *to* — *forth*, parĕre, (fructus) edĕre; *to* — *about*, efficĕre ut.

brink, *n.* margo, ripa.

brisk, *adj.* alacer, acer. *Adv.* acriter. **briskness**, *n.* alacritas.

bristle, *n.* seta. *v.intr.* horrēre. **bristly**, *adj.* setosus.

brittle, *adj.* fragilis.

broach, *v.tr.* aperire, divulgare.

broad, *adj.* latus. *Adv.* late. **breadth**, *n.* latitudo; *of mind*, humanitas.

brogue, *n.* barbara locutio.

broil, *v.tr.* torrēre. *v.intr.* torrēri.

bronze, *adj.* a(h)eneus.

brooch, *n.* gemma.

brood, *v.intr.* ova incubare; *fig.* incubare, meditari. *n.* foetus. **brooding**, *n.* incubatio; *fig.* meditatio.

brook, *n.* rivulus. *v.tr.* ferre.

broom, *n.* *plant*, genista; *besom*, scopae.

brother, *n.* frater. **brotherhood**, *n.* societas. **brotherly**, *adj.* fraternus.

brow, *eyebrow*, *n.* supercilium; *the forehead*, frons; *of a hill*, summus collis.

brown, *n.* fuscus, fulvus.

browse, *v.intr.* depascĕre.

bruise, *v.tr.* contundĕre. *n.* contusio.

bruit, *v.tr.* divulgare.

brunt, *n.* impetus, -ūs.

brush, *n.* penicillus. *v.tr.* verrĕre, tergĕre. **brushwood**, *n.* virgultum.

brute, *n.* belua, animal. **brutish**, **brutal**, *adj.* ferus, crudelis. *Adv.* atrociter. **brutalize**, *v.tr.* crudelem reddĕre. **brutality**, *n.* crudelitas.

bubble, *n.* bulla. *v.intr.* bullare; *fig.* effervescĕre.

buccaneer, *n.* pirata, *m.*

bucket, *n.* situla, situlus.

buckle, *n.* fibula. *v.tr.* fibulā nectĕre.

buckler, *n.* scutum, clipeus.

bud, *n.* gemma; calyx. *v.intr.* gemmare.

budge, *v.intr.* loco cedĕre.

budget, *n.* saccus; *of accounts*, ratio pecuniae publicae.

buff, *adj.* luteus.

buffalo, *n.* bos.

buffet, *n.* alapa, colaphus; *sideboard*, abacus. *v.tr.* pugnis caedĕre.

buffoon, *n.* scurra. **buffoonery**, *n.* lascivia.

bug, *n.* cimex. **bugbear**, *n.* quod terret, monstrum.

bugle, *n.* cornu.

build, *v.tr.* aedificare, condĕre. **building**,

n. aedificatio, aedificium. **builder,** n. architectus; *fig.* auctor.

bulb, n. bulbus.

bulk, n. moles. **bulky,** adj. ingens.

bull, n. bos, taurus. **bullock,** n. iuvencus.

bullet, n. glans plumbea, lapis, missile.

bullion, n. aurum, argentum.

bulrush, n. scirpus.

bulwark, n. propugnaculum.

bump, n. tumor ; impetus. *v.tr.* offendĕre. *v.intr.* — against, in alqd incidĕre.

bumper, n. calix plenus.

bunch, n. berries, racemus ; *grapes,* uva.

bundle, n. fascis, sarcina. *v.tr.* colligĕre.

bungling, *adj.,* see AWKWARD.

buoy, *v.tr.* sustinĕre. **buoyant,** *adj.* lĕvis ; *fig.* hilaris. **buoyancy,** n. lĕvitas, hilaritas.

burden, n. onus; *beast of —,* iumentum. *v.tr.* onerare. **burdensome,** adj. gravis.

burgess, n. civis, m. *and* f.

burglar, n. fur, latro. **burglary,** n. furtum.

burlesque, n. alqd in ridiculum versum.

burn, *v.tr.* incendĕre. *v.intr.* (de)flagrare, incendi ; *fig.* ardēre. n. *a wound,* ambustum.

burnish, *v.tr.* polire.

burrow, n. cuniculus. *v.tr.* cuniculos facĕre.

burst, *v.tr.* (di)rumpĕre. *v.intr.* (di)rumpi; *to* — *open,* effringĕre.

bury, *v.tr.* sepelire, efferre ; *fig.* opprimĕre. **burial,** n. sepultura. **burial-ground,** n. sepulc(h)rum.

bush, n. frutex, sentis. **bushy,** adj. fruticosus.

bushel, n. modius, medimnus.

business, n. mercatura, negotia, -orum.

buskin, n. cothurnus.

bust, n. effigies.

bustle, n. festinatio. *v.intr.* festinare.

busy, adj. occupatus, negotiosus. *Adv.* industrie. *v.tr. to be busied with,* alqd agĕre. **busybody,** n. homo importunus.

but, *conj.* autem, vero, at; — *yet,* sed, vero, atqui. *prep., see* EXCEPT. *adv. only,* modo, tantum.

butcher, n. lanius. *v.tr.* caedere; *fig.* trucidare. **butchery,** n. caedes.

butler, n. cellarius.

butt, n. *to make a* — *of,* ludibrio habĕre ; sinum (*wine-cask*). *v.tr.* cornu ferire.

butterfly, n. papilio.

button, n. fibula. *v.tr.* fibulā nectĕre.

buttress, *v.tr.* fulcire.

buxom, adj. hilaris.

buy, *v.tr.* (co)emĕre. **buyer,** n emptor.

buzz, v. susurrare. **buzzing,** n. susurrus.

by, *prep. place,* ad, apud, iuxta, prope ;

to go —, praeterire; *to stand* —, adesse; — *night,* nocte ; — *moonlight,* ad lunam ; — *this time,* iam ; *of means,* per *with acc.*; *an agent,* a(b); *according to,* secundum *or* ad; — *the authority of,* iussu *or* ex auctoritate ; — *chance,* forte ; — *heart,* memoriter ; *one —one,* singillatim. **by-way,** n. trames.

byword, n. *to become a* — contemptui esse.

C

cabbage, n. brassica, caulis.

cabin, n. casa ; *of a ship,* cubiculum.

cabinet, n. conclave, cista, armarium.

cable, n tunis.

cackle, v. strepĕre. n. strepitus.

cadaverous, adj. exsanguis.

cadet, n. tiro.

cage, n. cavea.

cajolery, n. blanditiae.

cake, n. placenta. *v.intr.* concrescĕre.

calamity, n. calamitas, res adversae. **calamitous,** adj. tristis. *Adv.* calamitose.

calculate, *v.tr.* computare. **calculation,** n. ratio. **calculated,** adj. accommodatus.

caldron, n. a(h)enum, cortina.

calendar, n. ephemeris, fasti.

calf, n. vitulus ; — *of the leg,* sura.

call, n. vox ; salutatio. *v.tr.* clamare; vocare ; *to* — *together,* convocare. *v.intr. to* — *visit,* visĕre. **caller,** n. = visitor, salutator.

callous, callosus ; durus. *Adv.* dure.

calm, n. quies, tranquillitas; *at sea,* malacia. *Adj.* tranquillus. *Adv.* tranquille. *v.tr.* sedare.

calumny, n. crimen. **calumniate,** *v.tr.* calumniari. **calumniator,** n. obtrectator.

camel, n. camelus.

camp, n. castra, -orum.

campaign, n. stipendium.

can, n., *see* JUG. *v.intr.* posse.

canal, n canalis, is, m., fossa.

cancel, *v.tr.* delēre.

candid, adj. sincerus, simplex. *Adv.* candide. **candour,** n. sinceritas.

candidate, n. candidatus.

candle, n. candela, lumen. **candlestick,** n. candelabrum.

cane, n. arundo, calamus ; ferula; baculum. *v.tr.* verberare.

canine, adj. caninus.

canker, *v.tr.* corrumpĕre.

cannibal, n. qui hominibus vescitur.

cannon, n. tormentum.

canoe, n. cymba.

canopy, n. aulaeum.

canton, n. pagus.

canvas, n. carbasus (*a sail*).

canvass, *for office*, ambire. *n.* ambitio, ambitus.
cap, *n.* pileus; — *for women*, mitra.
capable, *adj.* aptus ; capax. **capability**, *n.* facultas, ingenium.
capacious, *adj.* capax.
caparison, *n.* phalerae.
capital, *n.* urbs potentissima ; *of a pillar*, capitulum ; *money*, sors, caput. *adj.* — *punishment*, poena capitalis.
capitalist, *n.* dives.
capitulate, *v.intr.*, *see* SURRENDER.
caprice, *n.* voluntas. **capricious**, *adj.* inconstans. *Adv.* ad libidinem.
captain, *n.* centurio ; *of a ship*, praefectus navis.
captious, *adj.* iracundus. *Adv.* iracunde. **captiousness**, *n.* iracundia.
captivate, *v.tr.* capĕre.
captive, *n.* captivus. **captivity**, *n.* captivitas ; vincula (*pl.*). **capture**, *v.tr.* capĕre.
car, *n.* vehiculum.
caravan, *n.* comitatus, -ūs.
carbuncle, *n.* carbunculus.
carcase, *n.* cadaver, -ĕris, *n.*
card, *n.* charta. *v.tr.* pectĕre.
care, *n.* cura, diligentia ; *anxiety*, sol(l)icitudo. *v.intr.* *to take — of*, curare ; *what do I — ?* quid mihi est ? **careful**, *adj.* diligens, accuratus. *Adv.* diligenter, accurate. **careless**, *adj.* securus, imprudens. **carelessness**, *n.* securitas, imprudentia.
career, *n.* curriculum, cursus. *v.intr.* currĕre.
caress, *n.* blanditiae. *v.tr.* permulcēre. **caressing**, *adj.* blandus.
cargo, *n.* onus, -ĕris, *n.*
carmine, *n.* coccum; *of —*, coccineus.
carnage, *n.* caedes, -is, *f.*
carnal, *adj.* libidinosus. *Adv.* libidinose.
carnival, *n.* Saturnalia, -ium.
carnivorous, *adj.* qui carne vescitur.
carousal, *n.* convivium. **carouse**, *v.intr.* comissare.
carp, *v.intr.* *to — at*, carpĕre.
carpenter, *n.* faber (lignarius).
carpet, *n.* tapete, tapetum.
carrion, *n.* cadaver.
carry, *v.tr.* potare, ferre, vehĕre, gerĕre; — *a point*, consequi. **carriage**, *n.* vectura, gestatio ; *vehicle*, vehiculum ; *gait*, incessus. **carrier**, *n.* *letter —*, tabellarius.
cart, *n.* plaustrum. *v.tr.* plastro vehĕre. **cart-load**, *n.* onus.
carve, *v.tr.* caelare, sculpĕre ; *of meat*, secare ; **carver**, *n.* *of meat*, carptor ; *art*, sculptor. **carving**, *n.* *act*, caelatura. sculptura ; *object*, caelatura, signum, effigies.
cascade, *n.* aquae ex alto desilientes.
case, *n.* theca ; casus, res ; *judicial —*, cau(s)sa.
casement, *n.* fenestra.

cash, *n.* pecunia. *v.tr.* praesenti pecuniā solvĕre. **cashier**, *n.* custos pecuniarum. *v.tr.* *to discharge*, alqm dimittĕre.
cask, *n.* dolium. **casket**, *n.* cistula.
casque, *n.* galea.
cast, *v.tr.* iacĕre, mittĕre ; *to found*, fundĕre ; *to be — down*, affligi ; *to — off*, exuĕre ; *to — out*, (ex)pellĕre. *n.* iactus ; *dice*, alea ; *image*, imago. **castaway**, *n.* perditus ; *by shipwreck*, naufragus.
caste, *n.* societas, sodalitas.
castigation, *n.* supplicium.
castle, *n.* arx, castellum.
casual, *adj.* fortuitus. *Adv.* forte, casu. **casualty**, *n.* fortuita, -orum. **casuistry**, *n.* sophisma, quaestio de moribus. **casuist**, *n.* sophistes.
cat, *n.* feles (felis), -is.
catacomb, *n.* puticuli.
catalogue, *n.* librorum index.
catapult, *n.* catapulta.
cataract, *n.* *in the eye*, glaucoma ; *see* CASCADE.
catarrh, *n.* gravedo.
catastrophe, *n.* casus durus.
catch, *v.tr.* capĕre, excipĕre, deprehendĕre ; *a disease*, morbum contrahĕre. *n.* lucrum. **catching**, *adj.* pestilens.
category, *n.* genus, numerus. **categorical**, *adj.* simplex.
cater, *v.intr.* obsonare.
caterpillar, *n.* eruca.
Catholic, * homo Catholicus (*Eccl.*). **Catholicism**, *n.* * fides Catholica(*Eccl.*).
cattle, *n.* pecus, -oris, armenta, -orum.
caul, *n.* omentum.
cauldron, *n.* a(h)enum.
cause, *n.* caus(s)a, auctor (*a person*); *v.tr.* efficĕre ut, (com)movēre. **causal**, *adj.* quod efficit ut. **causeless**, *adj.* vanus. *Adv.* sine caus(s)ā.
causeway, *n.* viae.
caustic, *adj.* acerbus. **cauterize**, *v.tr.* adurĕre.
caution, *n.* prudentia. *v.tr.* monēre. **cautious**, *adj.* prudens. *Adv.* prudenter.
cavalcade, *n.* equites.
cavalier, *n.* eques. *Adv.* arroganter.
cavalry, *n.* equitatus, equites, -um.
cave, *n.* caverna, specus. **cavity**, *n.*, *see* HOLE.
cavil, *v.intr.*, *see* CARP.
caw, *v.intr.* crocire, crocitare.
cease, *v.intr.* intermittĕre, desistĕre. **ceaseless**, *adj.* perpetuus, continuus. *Adv.* perpetue.
cedar, *n.* cedrus, *f.*
cede, *v.tr.* cedĕre, concedĕre.
ceiling, *n.* laquear.
celebrate, *v.tr.* celebrare, agĕre. **celebrated**, *adj.* clarus, illustris. **celebration**, *n.* celebratio. **celebrity**, *n.* goria, laus; *person*, vir insignis.
celerity, *n.* celeritas.

celestial, *adj.* caelestis, divinus ; *fig.* praestans.

cell, *n.* cella, cubiculum.

cellar, *n. a wine* —, apotheca.

cement, *n.* gluten. *v.tr.* conglutinare.

cemetery, *n.* sepulc(h)ra, -orum.

censor, *n.* censor. **censorious,** *adj.* severus. *Adv.* severe.

censure, *v.tr.* reprehendere. *n.* reprehensio.

census, *n.* census.

cent, *n. per* —, centesimae, = 12 *per* — *per annum.*

centaur, *n.* centaurus.

centenary, *n.* festum saeculare.

centre, *n.* media pars ; medius (*e.g.* media urbs).

century, *n.* centum anni, saeculum.

ceremonial, ceremony, *n.* ritus. **ceremonious,** *adj.* urbanus. *Adv.* urbane.

certain, *adj.* certus, stabilis ; *a certain person,* quidam. *Adv.* certe, profecto. **certainty, certitude,** *n.* fides. **certificate,** *n.* testimonium.

cerulean, *adj.* caeruleus.

chafe, *v.tr.* calefacere. *v.intr.* irasci, commoveri.

chaff, *n.* palea.

chagrin, *n.* maeror, dolor.

chain, *n.* catena, vinculum ; series. *v.tr.* vincire.

chair, *n.* sella. **chairman,** *n.* qui conventui praeest.

chaise, *n.* carpentum.

chalice, *n.* calix, calathus.

chalk, *n.* creta.

challenge, *n.* provocatio. *v.tr.* pro vocare.

chamber, *n.* cubiculum. **chambermaid,** *n.* serva.

champ, *v.tr.* mandere, mordere.

champion, *n.* propugnator.

chance, *n.* casus, fors ; *by* —, forte, casu. *v.intr.* accidere.

Chancellor of the Exchequer, *n.* aerarii tribunus.

chandler, *n.* candelarum propola.

change, *v.tr.* (com)mutare. *v.intr.* (com)mutari. *n.* (com)mutatio, vicissitudo. **changeable,** *adj.* mutabilis, inconstans. *Adv* mutabiliter, inconstanter. **changeableness,** *n.* mutabilitas. **changeling,** *n.* puer subditus.

channel, *n.* fossa, canalis, *m.*

chant, *v.tr.* canere, cantare.

chaos, *n.* chaos (*only in abl.* chao) ; perturbatio. **chaotic,** *adj.* perturbatus.

chapter, *n. of a book,* caput.

character, *n. a sign,* nota ; — *of a person,* natura, mores, -um ; *reputation,* fama. **characteristic,** *adj.* proprius. *Adv.* suo more. *n.* proprietas. **characterize,** *v.tr.* designare.

charcoal, *n.* carbo.

charge, *n.* munus, officium ; *price,* pretium ; mandatum ; hortatio cura ; (*accusation*) crimen ; *attack,* impetus ; *v.tr.* iubere, imperare ; (ad)hortari ; *of price,* indicare ; accusare ; impetum facere. **chargeable,** *adj.* obnoxius.

charger, *n.* lanx ; equus (ecus).

chariot, *n.* currus, -us. **charioteer,** *n.* auriga.

charity, *n.* amor, benignitas ; liberalitas ; alms, stips. **charitable,** *adj.* benignus, liberalis. *Adv.* benigne, liberaliter.

charm, *n.* carmen ; blanditiae ; amoenitas. *v.tr.* fascinare, incantare ; capere. **charming,** *adj.* venustus. **charmer,** *n.* magus ; *mistress,* deliciae.

chart, *n.* tabula. **charter,** *n.* privilegium.

chary, *adj.* parcus.

chase, *v.tr.* venari, *see* **pursue.** *n.* venatio.

chasm, *n.* hiatus.

chaste, *adj.* castus. **chastity,** *n.* castitas.

chastise, *v.tr.* castigare. **chastisement,** *n.* castigatio.

chatter, *v.intr.* garrire. *n.* garrulitas. **chattering,** *adj.* garrulus.

cheap, *adj.* vilis, parvi pretii.

cheat, *n.* fraus, dolus ; fraudator. *v.tr.* fallere, decipere.

check, *n.* impedimentum. *v.tr.* obstare, impedimento esse.

cheek, *n.* gena.

cheer, *n.* hilaritas ; hospitium. **cheerful,** hilaris. *Adv.* hilariter. **cheerless,** *adj.* tristis.

cheese, *n.* caseus.

cheque, *n.* perscriptio.

cherish, *v.tr.* curare, colere.

cherry, *n. tree,* cerasus ; *fruit,* cerasum.

chess, *n.* lusus latrunculorum.

chest, *n.* pectus ; *receptacle,* arca, cista.

chestnut, *n.* castanea.

chew, *v.tr.* mandere.

chicanery, *n.* dolus.

chicken, *n.* pullus.

chide, *v.tr.* obiurgare. **chiding,** *n.* obiurgatio.

chief, *n.* caput, princeps. *Adj.* primus, praecipuus. *Adv.* praecipue.

child, *n.* filius, filia, liberi (*children*). **child-birth,** partus. **childhood,** *n.* aetas puerilis. **childlike,** *adj.* puerilis. **childish,** *adj.* ineptus. *Adv.* pueriliter. **childless,** *adj.* (liberis) orbus.

chill, *adj.* frigidus. *n.* frigus. *v.tr.* refrigerare ; *fig.* reprimere.

chime, *n.* concentus. *v.intr.* concinere.

chimney, *n.* compluvium (*an opening in the roof*).

chin, *n.* mentum.

china, *n.* murrha ; *adj.* murrhinus.

chink, *n.* rima.

chip, *n.* assula, scobis.

chirp, *v.* pipilare.

chisel, *n.* scalprum, caelum. *v.tr.* sculpere.

chivalry, *n.* ordo equester ; summa comi-

tas. **chivalrous**, *adj.* fortis et urbanus.
choice, *n.* delectus, electio. *adj.* praecipuus. **choose**, *v.tr.* eligĕre, deligĕre.
choir, *n.* chorus.
choke, *v.tr.* suffocare. *v.intr.* suffocari.
choler, *n.*, *see* ANGER. **cholera**, *n.*
pestis.
chop, *v.tr.* abscidĕre. *v.intr.* se vertĕre.
n. offa.
chord, *n.* nervus, fides, -ium.
chorus, *n.* chorus; *leader*, choragus.
chough, *n.* corvus.
Christ, * Christus.
chronic, *adj.* longinquus, diuturnus.
chronicle, *v.tr.* in annales referre, *n.*
annales, -ium, *m.*, fasti. **chronicler**,
n. annalium scriptor. **chronology**, *n.*
annorum ratio. **chronological**, *adj.*—
errors, temporum aetatumque errores.
Adv. servato temporum ordine.
church, *n.* ecclesia.
churl, *n.* rusticus; sordidus. **churlish**,
adj. inurbanus. *Adv.* rustice. **churlish-
ness**, *n.* rusticitas.
churn, *n.* labrum.
cicatrice, *n.* cicatrix.
cider, *n.* vinum ex malis confectum.
cipher, *n.* nota, lit(t)era secretior; *see*
NUMBER. *v.intr.* computare.
circle, *n.* orbis, circulus; *to describe a*
—, circulum ducĕre; *assembly*, corona.
circuit, *n.* circuitus, ambitus, orbis.
circular, *adj.* rotundus. *n.* lit(t)erae
circum alqos dimissae. **circulation**, *n.*
circuitas. **circulate**, *v.tr.* circumagĕre.
v.intr. circumagi; in usum venire.
circumference, *n.* orbis, circuitus.
circumlocution, *n.* circuitio.
circumnavigate, *v.tr.* circumvehi navi.
circumscribe, *v.tr.* circumscribĕre.
circumspect, *adj.* prudens. *Adv.* prudenter. **circumspection**, *n.* prudentia.
circumstance, *n.* res, caus(s)a; hoc,
id, *etc.*; *under these* —*s*, quae cum ita
sint. **circumstantial**, *adj.* — *evidence*,
testimonium a rebus collectum. *Adv.*
accurate.
circumvallation, *n.* circummunitio.
circumvent, *v.tr.* circumvenire.
cistern, *n.* cisterna, puteus.
citadel, *n.* arx, castellum.
cite, *v.tr.* memorare; *before a court*,
citare.
citizen, *n.* civis. **citizenship**, *n.* civitas. **city**, *n.* urbs, oppidum, municipium.
citron, *n.* malum citrum.
civic, *adj.* civilis, civicus.
civil, *adj.* civilis ; — *rights*, ius civile;
— *war*, bellum civile *or* intestinum ;
polite, urbanus. *Adv.* urbane. **civili-
zation**, *n.* cultus, humanitas. **civilize**,
v.tr. expolire, ad humanitatem effin-
gere.
clad, *adj.* vestitus.

claim, *n.* petitio; ius, *n.* *v.tr.* petĕre,
poscĕre. **claimant**, *n.* petitor.
clammy, *adj.* lentus.
clamour, *n.* clamor, voces, -um, . *v.intr.*
(con)clamare.
clan, *n.* gens, tribus, *f.*
clandestine, *adj.* furtivus. *Adv.* clam,
furtim.
clang, *n.* sonus, sonitus. *v.intr.* (re)-
sonare.
clank, *n.* crepitus, -ūs. *v.tr.* crepare.
clap, *n.* strepitus, plausus. *v.tr.* ap-
plaud, (ap)plaudĕre.
clarify, *v.tr.* deliquare.
clash, *v.tr.* pulsare. *v.intr.* concurrĕre;
inter se (re)pugnare; sonare. *n.* concursus; sonus.
clasp, *n.* fibula. *v.tr.* fibulā coniungĕre;
see EMBRACE, GRASP.
class, *n.* classis, ordo, *m.*, genus. **classic**,
adj. optimus. **classify**, *v.tr.* in genera
describĕre.
clatter, *n.* crepitus, sonus. *v.intr.*
sonare.
clause, *n.* pars, caput.
claw, *n.* unguis. *v.tr.* lacerare.
clay, *n.* argilla; *of* —, argillaceus.
clean, *adj.* purus. *v.tr.* purgare. *Adv.*
= *quite*, prorsus. **cleanliness**, *n.* munditia.
clear, *adj.* clarus, lucidus; *it is* —, apparet. *Adv.* perspicue, lucide. *v.tr.*
acquit, absolvĕre. *v.intr.* *it* —*s up*,
tempestas fit serena. **clearness**, *n.*
claritas; serenitas (*of weather*). **clear-
sighted**, *adj.* sagax.
cleave, *v.intr.*, *see* ADHERE. *v.tr.*
scindĕre. **cleaver**, *n.* cultellus. **cleft**,
n. fissura, rima.
clemency, *n.* clementia, mansuetudo.
clement, *adj.* clemens, mansuetus.
clench, *v.tr.* manum comprimĕre.
clerk, *n.* scriba, *m.* librarius.
clever, *adj.* habilis, peritus alcis rei.
Adv. perite. **cleverness**, *n.* peritia.
client, *n.* cliens. **clientship**, *n.* clientēla.
cliff, *n.* scopulus, saxum.
climate, *n.* caelum, aër.
climax, *n.* gradatio.
climb, *v.tr.* a(d)scendĕre, scandĕre.
clinch, *v.tr.* clavulo figĕre.
cling, *v.intr.* adhaerēre; amplecti.
clink, *v.intr.* tinnire. *n.* tinnitus.
clip, *v.tr.* praecidĕre, circumcidĕre.
cloak, *n.* pallium, sagum, paenula. *v.tr.*
tegĕre.
clod, *n.* glaeba (gleb).
clog, *n.* impedimentum. *v.tr.* impedire.
cloister, *n.* porticus.
close, *v.tr.* claudĕre, occludĕre ; finire.
n. saeptum; finis, *m. and f.* *Adj.* taciturnus ; (*near*) propinquus, finitimus,
densus. *Adv.* tecte; solide. **closeness**,
n. taciturnitas; propinquitas; soliditas.
closet, *n.* cubiculum.

clot, *n.* — *of blood*, sanguis concretus. *v.tr.* congelare.

cloth, *n.* textum, pannus. clothes, *n.* vestimenta. clothe, *v.tr.* vestire, induĕre.

cloud, *n.* nubes, *f.* *v.tr.* obscurare. *v.intr.* nubibus obducĕre. cloudy, *adj.* nubilus. cloudless, *adj.* serenus clover, *n.* trifolium.

clown, *n.* agrestis. clownish, *adj.* agrestis. *Adv.* rustice.

cloy, *v.tr.* satiare.

club, *n.* clava ; *society*, sodalitas. *v.tr.* conferre. club-footed, *adj.* scaurus.

cluck, *v.intr.* singultire.

ciue, *n.* glomus ; *fig.* indicium.

clump, *n.* glaeba.

clumsy, *adj.* agrestis, ineptus. *Adv.* laeve, rustice. clumsiness, *n.* rusticitas, inscitia.

cluster, *n.* uva, racemus. *v.intr.* (frequentes) convenire.

clutch, *v.tr.* comprehendĕre.

coach, *n.* carpentum, raeda. coachman, *n.* raedarius, auriga.

coadjutor, *n.* socius, collega.

coagulate, *v.intr.* coire, coagulari.

coal, *n.* carbo.

coalesce, *v.intr.* coalescĕre. coalition, *n.* coniunctio.

coarse, *adj.* crassus; *rude*, inurbanus. *Adv.* crasse, inurbane. coarseness, *n.* crassitudo; inhumanitas.

coast, *n.* litus, ora. *Adj.* maritimus. *v.tr.* praetervehi.

coat, *n.* toga, tunica; *hide*, vellus, pellis. *v.tr.* induĕro.

coax, *v.tr.* permulcĕre.

cobble, *v.tr.* sarcire. cobbler, *n.* sutor.

cock, *v.tr.* crigĕre.

cock, *n.* gallus. cockcrow, *n.* cantus. cockroach, cockchafer, scarabaeus.

code, *n.* leges. codify, *v.tr.* leges describĕre.

coemption, *n.* coëmptio.

coequal, *adj.* aequalis.

coerce, *v.tr.* coërcēre coercion, *n.* necessitas coercive, *adj.* validus or qui cohibet.

coexistent, *adj.* quod eodem tempore est.

coffer, *n.* cista.

coffin, *n.* arca, sarcophagus.

cog, *n.* dens, *m.*

cogent, *adj.* validus. cogency, *n.* persuasio.

cogitate, *v.intr.* cogitare. cogitation, *n.* cogitatio. cognizance, *n.* cognitio. cognizant, *adj.* conscius.

coheir, *n.* coheres.

cohere, *v.intr.* cohaerēre. coherent, *adj.* cohaerens, sibi congruens. *Adv.* sibi constanter.

cohort, *n.* cohors.

coin, *n.* nummus. *v.tr.* cudĕre. coinage, *n.* res nummaria.

coincide, *v.intr.* eodem tempore fieri, coincidence, *n.* fors, casus.

cold, *adj.* frigidus ; *in* — *blood*, consulto ; *fig.* superbus. *Adv.* frigide ; superbe. *n.* *or* coldness, *n.* frigus. cold-blooded, *adj.*, *see* CRUEL.

collapse, *v.intr.* collabi, concidĕre. collar, *m.* torquis ; *dog* —, armilla ; *horse* —, iugum. *v.tr.* prehendĕre. collar-bone, *n.* iugulum.

collation, *n.* collatio ; *meal*, cena. collate, *v.tr.* conferre.

colleague, *n.* collega, *m.*

collect, *v.tr.* conferre, congerĕre ; — *oneself*, se colligĕre ; — *taxes*, exigĕre. *v.intr.* convenire. collection, *n.* collatio; thesaurus.

college, *n.* collegium, societas; *building*, schola.

collocation, *n.* collocatio.

colloquy, *n.* colloquium. colloquial, *adj.* — *speech*, sermo communis.

collusion, *n.* collusio.

colonel, *n.* tribunus militum, praefectus.

colony, *n.* colonia. colonist, *n.* colonus. colonial, *adj.* *gen.* *of colonia.* colonize, *v.tr.* coloniam constituĕre.

colonnade, *n.* columnarum ordo, porticus.

colossal, *adj.* vastus, ingens.

colour, *n.* color; *paint*, pigmentum. *v.tr.* inficĕre. *v.intr.*, *see* BLUSH.

colt, *n.* pullus equinus.

column, *n.* columna ; *in printing*, pagina ; *army*, agmen ; *in two* —*s*, bipartito.

comb, *n.* pecten ; *(of a cock)* crista, iuba, *v.tr.* pectĕre.

combat, *n.* pugna, certamen, proelium. *v.intr.*, *see* FIGHT.

combine, *v.tr.* (con)iungĕre. combination, *n.* (con)iunctio, societas.

combustion, *n.* exustio. combustible, *adj.* quod comburi potest.

come, *v.intr.* (per)venire, advenire; *near*, appropinquare ; — *together*, convenire ; coming, *n.* adventus.

comedy, *n.* comoedia. comic, *adj.* comicus, ridiculus, facetus. *Adv.* facete.

comely, *adj.* venustus, pulcher. comeliness, *n.* venustas, pulchritudo.

comet, *n.* cometes, -ae, *m.*

comfort, *v.tr.* consolari. *n.* solatium, consolatio ; *ease*, copia ; *comforts*, commoda, -ōrum. comfortable, *adj.* gratus, iucundus. *Adv.* grate, iucunde. comfortless, *adj.* sine spe ; incommodus. comforter, *n.* consolator.

command, *v.tr.* iubēre, imperare. *n.* imperium ; *order*, iussum ; *of the senate*, decretum. commander, *n.* dux, imperator; *of a fleet*, praefectus classis.

commemorate, *v.tr.* celebrare. commemoration, *n.* celebratio.

commence, *v.intr.* incipĕre.

commend, *v.tr.* commendare; laudare. commendation, *n.* commendatio, laus, *f.* **commendable,** *adj.* laudabilis. *Adv.* laudabiliter. **commendatory,** *adj.* commendaticius.

comment, *v.tr.* interpretari, commentari. *n. and* **commentary,** *n.* interpretatio. **commentator,** *n.* interpres.

commerce, *n.* commercium, negotia, -orum. **commercial,** *adj.* ad commercium pertinens.

commiserate, *v.tr.* **commiseration,** *n., see* PITY.

commissariat, *n.* res frumentaria.

commission, *n.* mandatum; munus, *n.; in the army,* ordines ducĕre. **commissioner,** *n.* procurator.

commit, *v.tr.* entrust, dare, committĕre; facĕre; — *murder,* occidĕre.

committee, *n.* consilium.

commodious, *adj.* commodus. *Adv.* commode. **commodity,** *an article,* res, merx.

common, *adj.* communis, publicus; — *wealth,* res publica; *ordinary,* plebeius, cot(t)idianus; *the* —*s,* plebs. *Adv.* communiter, *n.* ager publicus. **commonplace,** tritum.

commotion, *n.* tumultus, motus.

commune, *v.intr.* colloqui. **communicate,** *v.tr., see* SHARE, TELL. **communication,** *n.* communicatio, colloquium. **communicative,** *adj.* loquax.

communion, *n.* societas. **community,** *n. the state,* civitas, respublica.

commute, *v.tr.* (per) mutare, remittĕre.

compact, *n.* pactum, conventum. *Adj.* confertus. *Adv.* presse.

companion, *n.* comes, *m. and f.,* socius, sodatis, *m.* **companionable,** *adj.* affabilis. **company,** *n.* societas.

compare, *v.tr.* comparare, conferre. **comparable,** *adj.* comparabilis. **comparison,** *n.* comparatio. **comparative,** *adj.* comparativus. *Adv.* comparate.

compass, *n. extent,* ambitus. *v.tr.* circumdare; *go round,* circumire; *see* ATTAIN.

compassion, *n.* misericordia. **compassionate,** *adj.* misericors. *Adv.* cum misericordiā.

compatible, *adj., see* ACCORDANCE.

compatriot, *n.* civis, *m. and f.*

compel, *v.tr.* cogĕre. **compulsory,** *adj.* per vim. **compulsion,** *n.* vis, necessitas; *by* —, vi, per vim.

compendious, *adj.* brevis. **compendium,** *n.* epitome, -ēs.

compensate, *v.tr.* compensare; — *a loss,* damnum restituĕre. **compensation,** *n.* compensatio.

compete, *v.intr.* competĕre. **competent,** *adj., see* ABLE. *Adv.* satis. **competency,** *n.* divitiae. **competition,** *n.* aemulatio. **competitor,** *n.* aemulus, competitor.

compile, *v.tr.* in unum conferre.

complacent, *adj., see* COMPLAISANT;

libens; qui sibi placet. **complacency,** *n.* amor sui.

complain, *v.intr.* (con)queri. **complaint,** *n.* questus, querela; morbus.

complaisant, *adj.* indulgens.

complete, *v.tr.* complēre, conficĕre. *Adj.* perfectus. *Adv.* perfecte. **completion,** *n.* confectio, finis. **complement,** *n.* complementum.

complex, *adj.* multiplex. **complexity,** *n.* implicatio. **complexion,** *n.* color.

complicate, *v.tr.* implicare. **complicated,** *adj.* difficilis, impeditus. **complication,** *n.* difficultas.

compliment, *n.* laus. *v.tr.* laudare. **complimentary,** *adj.* honorificus.

comply, *v.intr.* obsequi; *to — with requests,* precibus indulgēre. **compliance,** *n.* indulgentia. **compliant,** *adj., see* COMPLAISANT.

components, *n.* partes, -ium, *f.*

compose, *v.tr.* (con)scribĕre; *music,* modos facĕre; *see* ARRANGE. **composed,** *adj.* tranquillus. *Adv.* tranquille. **composer,** *n.* scriptor. **composition,** *n.* compositio; *a writing,* scriptum. **composure,** *n.* tranquillitas.

compound, *v.tr.* componĕre; *to be* —*ed of,* ex alqā re constare. *Adj.* compositus, multiplex, *n.* res admixta; *enclosure,* saeptum.

comprehend, *v.tr.* continēre, comprehendĕre. **comprehensible,** *adj.* perspicuus. *Adv.* plane, perspicue. **comprehension,** *n.* comprehensio, intellegentia. **comprehensive,** *adj.* late patens. *Adv.* prorsus.

compress, *v.tr.* comprimĕre. **compression,** *n.* compressio, compressus.

compromise, *v.tr.* compromittĕre. *n.* compromissum.

compulsion, *n., see* COMPEL.

compunction, *n.* poenitentia.

compute, *v.tr.* oemputare.

comrade, *n.* socius. **comradeship,** *n.* contubernium.

concave, *adj.* concavus.

conceal, *v.tr.* celare.

concede, *v.tr.* concedĕre. **concession,** *n.* concessio, concessus.

conceit, *n.* arrogantia. **conceited,** *adj.* arrogans. *Adv.* arroganter.

conceive, *v.tr.* concipĕre; *fig.* cogitare.

concentrate, *v.tr.* contrahĕre.

conception, *n.* conceptio, conceptus; *fig.* notio, opinio.

concern, *n.* res, negotium, cura; *fig.* sol(l)icitudo. *v.tr.* pertinēre ad; *it* —*s, interest.* **concerning,** *prep.* de, *abl.*

conciliate, *v.tr.* conciliare. **conciliation,** *n.* conciliatio. **conciliatory,** *adj.* blandus.

concise, *adj.* brevis. *Adv.* breviter. **conciseness,** *n.* brevitas.

conclave, *n., see* ASSEMBLY.

conclude, *v.tr.* finire, conficĕre; *decide,* constituĕre. **conclusion,** *n.* finis; conclusio. **conclusive,** *adj.* gravis. *Adv.* graviter.

concoct, *v.tr.* miscēre ; *fig.* fingĕre. **concoction,** *n.* potus.

concomitant (*adj.*) **-ly,** *adv.* cum *with* abl,

concord, *n.* concordia. **concordant,** *adj.* concors. *Adv.* congruenter.

concourse, *n.* concursus, concursio.

concrete, *adj.* concretus, solidus.

concur, *v.intr.* consentire. **concurrence,** *n.* consensus. **concurrent,** *adj.,* **-ly,** *adv.* una, simul.

concussion, *n.* concussio, concursus.

condemn, *v.tr.* damnare, condemnare ; — *to death,* capitis damnare ; *disapprove,* improbare. **condemnation,** *n.* damnatio; reprehensio. **condemnable,** *adj.* reprehensione dignus. **condemnatory,** *adj.* damnatorius.

condense, *v.tr.* densare, spissare. *v.intr.* concrescĕre.

condescend, *v.intr.* comiter se gerĕre. **condescending,** *adj.* comis. *Adv.* comiter. **condescension,** *n.* comitas.

condign, *adj.* meritus; acerbus.

condiment, *n.* condimentum.

condition, *n.* condicio, res (*state*) ; pactum ; *under the* —, eā lege. *v.tr.* circumscribĕre. **conditional,** *adj.* incertus. *Adv.* eo pacto ut, *etc.* **conditioned,** *adj.* affectus; *well, ill* —, bene, male moratus.

condole, *v.intr.* casum alcis dolēre.

conduce, *v.intr.* facĕre *or* efficĕre ut. **conducive,** *adj.* utilis, *dat., or* ad.

conduct, *v.tr.* ducĕre ; deducĕre ; *manage,* gerĕre ; — *oneself,* se gerĕre. *n.* mores, -um ; *management,* administratio. **conductor,** *n.* dux. **conduit,** *n.* aquaeductus.

cone, *n.* conus.

confectionery, *n.* dulcia, -ium.

confederacy, *n.* societas, confoederatio, n. socii. **confederate,** *adj.* foederatus.

confer, *v.intr.* deliberare. *v.tr., see* GIVE. **conference,** *n.* consilium, colloquium.

confess, *v.tr.* confiteri. **confessedly,** *adv.* sine dubio. **confession,** *n.* confessio.

confide, *v.tr.* committĕre, credĕre. *v.intr.* — *in,* (con)fidĕre. **confidant,** *n.* conscius. **confidence,** *n.* fides, fiducia. **confident,** *adj.* confidens ; *see* CERTAIN. *Adv.* (con)fidenter. **confidential,** *adj.* fidus; *see* SECRET. *Adv., see* SECRETLY. **confiding,** *adj.* credulus.

confine, *n.* finis, terminus. *v.tr., see* RESTRAIN, IMPRISON. **confinement,** *n.* custodia.

confirm, *v.tr.* confirmare, sancire.

confiscate, *v.tr.* publicare. **confiscation,** *n.* publicatio.

conflagration, *n.* incendium, ignis, *m.*

conflict, *n.* certamen, pugna; dissensio. *v.intr.* concurrĕre; pugnare; dissentire.

confluence, *n.* confluens.

conform, *v.tr.* accommodare, *v.intr.* obtemperare. **conformable,** *adj.* accommodatus, congruus. *Adv.* congruenter. **conformation,** *n.* forma. **conformity,** *n.* consensus.

confound, *v.tr.* percutĕre ; evertĕre ; *an exclamation,* — *it,* di perdant.

confront, *v.tr.* adversus alqm stare.

confuse, *v.tr.* (per)turbare. **confusion,** *n.* perturbatio.

confute, *v.tr.* redarguĕre.

congeal, *v.tr.* (con)gelare. *v.intr.* frigēre.

congenial, *adv.* congruens ; iucundus.

congratulate, *v.tr.* gratulari. **congratulation,** *n.* gratulatio. **congratulatory,** *adj.* gratulabundus.

congregate, *v.tr.* cogĕre. *v.intr.* convenire. **congregation,** *n.* coetus.

congress, *n.* conventus.

conjecture, *n.* coniectura, opinio. *v.tr.* conicere. **conjectural,** *adj.* quod coniecturā prospici potest. *Adv.* coniecturā.

conjugal, *adj.* coniugalis.

conjugate, *v.tr.* declinare. **conjugation,** *n.* declinatio.

conjure, *v.tr.* obtestari ; adiurare ; *to* — *up,* animas elicĕre. *v.intr.* praestigias agĕre.

connect, *v.tr.* (con)iungĕre. **connected,** *adj.* = *coherent,* continens. *Adv.* continenter. **connexion,** *n.* coniunctio, societas; *by marriage,* affinis.

connive, (*at*), *v.intr.* co(n)nivēre. **connivance,** *n.* indulgentia.

connoisseur, *n.* peritus, homo doctus.

conquer, *v.tr.* vincĕre, superare. **conqueror,** *n.* victor. **conquest,** *n.* victoria, occupatio.

consanguinity, *n.* sanguinis coniunctio.

conscience, *n.* conscientia, fides. **conscientious,** *adj.* religiosus, sanctus. *Adv.* religiose, sancte. **conscientiousness,** *n.* religio, sanctitas.

conscious, *adj.* conscius, gnarus. *Adv.* *use adj.* (*I did it* —, gnarus feci).

conscription, *n.* delectus.

consecrate, *v.tr.* (con)secrare, (de)dicare. **consecrated,** *adj.* sacratus, sacer. **consecration,** *n.* dedicatio.

consecutive, *adj.* continuus. *Adv.* continenter.

consent, *v.intr., see* AGREE. *n.* consensus; *see* AGREEMENT.

consequent, *adj.* consequens. *Adv., see* THEREFORE. **consequence,** *n.* exitus, eventus; *to be of* —, multum valēre.

conserve, *v.tr., see* KEEP. **conservation,** *n.* conservatio. **conservative,** *adj.* optimatibus addictus.

consider, *v.tr.* contemplari ; ducĕre, existimare. **considerable,** *adj.* magnus, gravis ; aliquantum *with* genit. *Adv.*

aliquanto. **considerate**, *adj.* alci consulens, benignus. *Adv.* benigne. **considerateness**, *n.* benignitas. **consideration**. *n.* contemplatio; iudicium; *with* —, consulto.

consign, *v.tr.* deferre, mandare.

consist, *v.intr.* constare, consistĕre. **consistent**, *adj.* congruens ; constans. *Adv.* congruenter, constanter. **consistence**, **consistency**, *n. thickness*, crassitudo; constantia.

console, *v.tr.* consolari. **consolation**, *n.* solatium, consolatio. **consoler**, *n.* consolator.

consonant, *n.* consonans. *adj.* congruus.

consort, *n.* comes, socius ; coniu(n)x. *v.intr.* familiariter uti.

conspicuous, *adj.* clarus, manifestus ; insignis. *Adv.* clare, manifeste.

conspire, *v.intr.* coniurare. **conspiracy**, *n.* coniuratio. **conspirator**, *n.* coniuratus.

constable, *n.* apparitor.

constant, *adj.* continuus, perpetuus ; fidelis. *Adv.* perpetuo, continuo, fideliter. **constancy**, *n.* constantia; perseverantia; fides, fidelitas.

constellation, *n.* sidus, stella.

consternation, *n.*, *see* BUILD, MAKE. **construction**, *n.* aedificatio ; interpretatio ; *to put a good — on*, in bonam partem accipĕre.

constitute, *v.tr.* constituĕre. **constituent**, *adj.* pars *or* res. **constitution**, *n.* habitus ; *a good —*, corpus bene constitutum ; *of a state*, reipublicae ratio. **constitutional**, *adj.* innatus ; legitimus. *Adv.* e naturā; legitime.

constrain, *v.tr.* vi cogĕre. **constraint**, *n.* vis, constrained, *adj.* invitus ; (oratio) difficilis.

construct, *v.tr.*, *see* BUILD, MAKE. **construction**, *n.* aedificatio ; interpretatio ; *to put a good — on*, in bonam partem accipĕre.

construe, *v.tr.*, *see* INTERPRET.

consult, *v.tr.* consulĕre.

consume, *v.tr.* edĕre. **consumption**, *n.* consumptio ; *disease*, tabes.

consummate, *v.tr.* conficĕre. *Adj.* summus, perfectus, *or by superl. Adv.* summe, perfecte. **consummation**, *n.* perfectio.

contact, *n.* (con)tactus. **contagion**, *n.* contagio. **contagious**, *adj.* pestilens.

contain, *v.tr.* continĕre, comprehendĕre ; *to — oneself*, se cohibēre.

contaminate, *v.tr.* polluĕre. **contamination**, *n.* macula, labes.

contemplate, *v.tr.* contemplari. **contemplation**, *n.* contemplatio. **contemplative**, *adj.* in contemplatione versatus.

contemporaneous, *adj.* quod eodem tempore est *or* fit. *Adv.* uno tempore, simul. **contemporary**, *n.* aequalis.

contempt, *n.* contemptus. **contemptible**, *adj.* contemnendus, turpis. *Adv.* turpiter.

contend, *v.intr.* certare, pugnare ; *fig.* resistĕre. **contention**, *n.*, *see* QUARREL. **contentious**, *adj.* aemulus. *Adv.* summā vi.

content, *v.tr.* satisfacĕre. *Adj.* contentus. *Adv.* tranquille. **contentment**, *n.* tranquillitas animi. **contents**, *n.* scripta, -orum.

conterminous, *adj.* alci loco confinis.

contest, *n.* certamen. *v.intr.* contendĕre.

context, *n.* argumentum.

contiguous, *adj.* propinquus; *see* CONTERMINOUS. **contiguity**, *n.* propinquitas.

continence, *n.* continentia. **continent**, *n.* continens. **continental**, *adj.* by *genit. of* continens.

contingent, *adj.* fortuitus. *n.* auxilia, -orum. **contingency**, *n.* casus.

continual, *adj.* continuus, perpetuus. *Adv.* continenter, perpetuo. **continuance**, *n.* perpetuitas. **continuation**, *n.*, *see* CONTINUANCE ; *the latter part*, reliqua pars. **continue**, *v.tr.* producĕre ; *renovare*. *v.intr.* perseverare ; *last*, durare, stare. **continuity**, *n.* perpetuitas.

contort, *v.tr.* distorquēre. **contortion**, *n.* distortio.

contraband, *n.* merces vetitae.

contract, *n.* pactum, locatio. *v.tr.* contrahĕre ; *agree to do*, alqd faciendum conducĕre. *v.intr.* se contrahĕre. **contraction**, *n.* contractio ; *in writing*, compendium. **contractor**, *n.* conductor, redemptor.

contradict, *v.tr.* contra dicĕre ; *fig.* discrepare. **contradiction**, *n.* quod contra dictum est ; diversitas. **contradictory**, *adj.* contrarius. *Adv.* contrarie.

contrary, *adj.* adversus, contrarius; *on the —*, contra; *in answers* immo (vero); *— to*, praeter, contra.

contrast, *n.* diversitas, dissimilitudo. *v.tr.* comparare, conferre.

contravene, *v.tr.* violare.

contribute, *v.tr.* conferre, dare; prodesse. **contribution**, *n.* pecunia. **contributor**, *n.* qui dat; scriptor.

contrite, *adj.*, *see* SORROWFUL. **contrition**, *n.* poenitentia.

contrive, *v.tr.* fingĕre ; *— to do*, facĕre *or* efficĕre ut. **contrivance**, *n.* inventio; inventum.

control, *n. self —*, temperatio. *v.tr.* coercēre; *oneself*, sibi temperare.

controversy, *n.* controversia. **controversial**, *adj.* controversus. *Adv.* per disputationem. **controvert**, *v.tr.* refutare. **controvertible**, *adj.* dubius.

contumacy, *n.* contumacia. **contumacious**, *adj.* contumax, pertinax. *Adv.* contumaciter.

contumely, *n.* contumelia. **contumelious**, *adj.* contumeliosus. *Adv.* contumeliose.

convalescent, adj. use verb conválescĕre.
convene, v.tr. convocare, convenient, adj. commodus. Adv. commode. convenience, n. commoditas, occasio. convention, n. conventus, -ūs ; custom, mos. conventional, adj. a majoribus traditus. Adv. ex usu.

conversation, n. sermo, colloquium. converse, v.intr. colloqui. Adj., see CONTRARY convorsans, adj. ...ibus.
convert, v.tr., see CHANGE ; be —ed, sententiam mutare. n. qui adductus est ad. conversion, n. (com)mutatio.
convex, adj. convexus.
convey, v.tr., see CARRY ; legal, (con)cedĕre. conveyance, n., see CARRIAGE.
convict, v.tr condemnare; convincĕre. n. damnatus. conviction, n. damnatio; sententia.
convince, v.tr. persuadēre. convincing, adj. gravis. Adv. graviter.
convivial, adj. hilaris. conviviality, n. hilaritas.
convoke, v.tr. convocare.
convoy, n. praesidium, v.tr. comitari.
convulse, v.tr. percutĕre ; the state, civitatem quassare. convulsion, n. convulsio.
cook, n. coquus. v.tr. coquĕre.
cool, adj. frigidus ; fig. tranquillus, superbus, fortis, impudens ; n. frigus ; v.tr. refrigerare. v.intr. frigescĕre, frigēre ; fig. animum remittĕre. coolness, n. frigus ; fig. superbia. Adv. frigide, tranquille.
co-operate, v.intr. una agĕre. co-operation, n. auxilium. co-partner, co-operator, n. socius.
cope, v.intr. — with, certare cum.
coping, n. corona, fastigium.
copious, adj. copiosus. Adv. copiose. copiousness, n. copia.
copper, n. aes. Adj. a(h)eneus.
coppice, copse, n. virgultum.
copy, n. exemplum. v.tr. imitari.
coquette, n. quae viros pellicit.
cord, n. restis, v.s. colligare, cordon, n. militus.
cordial, adj. amicus. Adv. amice. cordiality, n. amicitia.
core, n. nucleus, granum, semen.
cork, n. cortex. v.tr. obturare.
corn, n. frumentum.
corner, n. angulus.
cornet, n. cornu.
corporal, n. decurio. Adj. by genit. of corpus. corporal punishment, n. verbera, -um.
corporation, n. municipium, collegium.
corps, n. manus, ala equitum, agmen.
corpse, n. cadaver, -ĕris, m.
corpulent, adj. obēsus.
correct, v.tr. corrigĕre, emendare ; tollĕre. Adj. honestus; of style, emendatus, purus; true rerus. Adv. recte, etc.

correspond, v.intr. agree, respondēre, convenire ; by letter, lit(t)eras dare et accipĕre. correspondent, n. qui per lit(t)eras communicat. correspondence, n. per lit(t)eras. corresponding, adj. par. Adv. pariter.

duration, n. confirmatio.
corrode, v.tr. erodĕre. corrosive, adj. qui (quae, quod) erodit.
corrupt, adj. perditus, turpis. Adv. perdite, turpiter. v.tr. corrumpĕre. v.intr. corrumpi.
corrupter, n. corruptor. corruptible, adj. quod corrumpi potest. corruption, n. corruptio. corrupting, adj. perniciosus.
corsair, n. pirata, m.
corselet, n. thorax, lorica.
cortege, n. comitatus, -ūs.
coruscation. n. fulguratio, fulgor, splendor.
cosmetic, n. fucus.
cost, n. sumptus, impensa. v.tr. alqd (con)stat (with genit. or abl. of price).
costly, adj. sumptuosus, pretiosus. costiness, n. caritas.
costume, n. habitus, ornatus.
cottage, n. casa. cottager, n. rusticus.
couch, n. lectus. v.tr. of spears, hastas dirigĕre.
cough, n. tussis. v.intr. tussire.
council, n. concilium. council chamber, n. curia. councillor, n. senator.
counsel, n. deliberatio ; consilium. v.tr., see ADVISE.
count, v.tr. computare ; — upon, alci confidĕre. counter, n. mensa ; for reckoning, calculus. countless, adj. innumerabilis.
countenance, n. vultus, os. v.tr. alci favēre.
counter, adv. contra. counteract, v.tr. resistĕre. counterbalance, par esse.
counterfeit, v.tr. simulare. Adj. simulatus. counterpane, n. lodix. counterpart, n. res simillima. counterpoise, n. re. (ad)aequare.
country, n. rus; in the —, ruri ; native land, patria ; of what — ? cuias ? region, terra. country house, n. villa. countryman, n. homo rusticus. country town, n. municipium.
couple, n. par, bini. v.tr. (con)iungĕre.
courage, n. animus, fortitudo, virtus. courageous, adj. fortis. Adv., fortiter.
courier, n. nuntius.
course, n. (de)cursus ; — of water, lapsus ; — of the stars, motus ; — of nature, naturae lex ; plan, ratio, consilium ; — at dinner, ferculum ; manner of life, mores, -um. of course, adv. necessario, plane.
court, n. area ; royal —, aula ; — of justice, forum, tribunal. v.tr. petĕre.

courtier, *n.* nobilis. **courteous,** *adj.* comis. *Adv.* urbane, comiter. **courtesy, courteousness,** *n.* urbanitas, comitas.

cousin, *n.* (con)sobrinus, patruelis.

covenant, *n.* pactum. *v.tr.* pacisci.

cover, *n. of a bed, etc.,* lodix; *under —of,* tectus ; *fig.* per speciem. *v.tr.* operire.

covert, *n.* latebra, perfugium ; virgultum. *Adj.* tectus.

covet, *v.tr.* appetěre. **covetous,** *adj.* avarus. *Adv.* avare. **covetousness,** *n.* avaritia.

cow, *n.* vacca. **cowherd,** *n.* armentarius. **cow-hide,** *n.* corium vaccae.

coward, *n.* homo ignavus. **cowardly,** *adj.* ignavus. *Adv.* ignave. **cowardliness,** *n.* ignavia.

cower, *v.intr.* perterritus esse.

cowl, *n.* cucullus.

coxcomb, *n.* homo ineptus.

coy, *adj.* verecundus. **coyness,** *n.* pudor.

cozen, *v.tr., see* CHEAT.

crab, *n.* cancer. **crabbed,** *adj.* morosus; difficilis. *Adv.* morose.

crack, *n.* crepitus ; *fissure,* rima. *v.intr.* crepare, (dif)findi. *v.tr.* rumpěre ; *a whip,* sonitum flagello eděre.

cradle, *n.* cunabula, -orum. *v.tr.* in cunabulis poněre.

craft, *n.* dolus ; *skill,* ars ; *see* SHIP. **crafty,** *adj.* dolosus. *Adv.* dolose. **craftsman,** *n.* opera.

crag, *n., see* ROCK.

cram, *v.tr.* farcire ; comp1ěre ; *crowd,* stipare.

cramp, *v.tr. to be —ed,* circumscribi.

crane, *n.* grus; *machine,* troclea.

crank, *n.* uncus.

cranny, *n.* rima.

crash, *n.* fragor. *v.tr.* crepare. *v.n.* sonare.

crate, *n.* crates, -is, *f.*

crater, *n.* crater, -ēris, *m.*

crave, *v.tr., see* BEG, NEED. **craving,** *n.* desiderium.

crawl, *v.* repěre, serpěre.

crazy, *adj.* mente captus; *see* MAD.

creak, *v.* (con)crepare. **creaking,** *n.* crepitus.

cream, *n.* flos lactis.

crease, *n.* ruga. *v.tr.* rugare.

create, *v.tr.* (pro)creare, facěre ; *fig. appoint,* creare. **creation,** *n. since the — of the world,* post mundum conditum.

creator, *n.* fabricator, auctor. **creature,** *n.* animal.

credit, *v.tr. believe,* creděre ; *put to one's account,* alci in acceptum conferre. *n.* fides; *do — to,* decori esse. **credible,** *adj.* fide dignus. *Adv.* credibiliter. **credibility,** fides. **credentials,** *n.* auctoritas. **creditable,** *adj.* honestus. *Adv.* honeste. **creditor,** *n.* creditor. **credulous,** *adj.* credulus. *Adv.* nimiā cum

credulitate. **credulity,** *n.* credulitas.

creed, *n.* fides; doctrina.

creek, *n.* sinus, -ūs.

creep, *v.intr., see* CRAWL.

crescent, *n.* luna crescens. *Adj.* lunatus.

crest, *n.* crista, iuba. **crested,** *adj.* cristatus. **crestfallen,** *adj.* fractus, demissus.

crevice, *n., see* CRACK.

crew, *n.* nautae; *fig.* coetus.

crib, *n. for animals,* praesepe ; *see* CRADLE.

crime, *n.* facinus, scelus. **criminate,** *v.tr.* criminari. **crimination,** *n.* criminatio. **criminal,** *adj.* sceleratus.

crimson, *adj.* coccineus. *n.* coccum. *v.intr.* erubescěre.

cringe, *v.intr.* adulari.

cripple, *n.* claudus.

crisis, *n.* discrimen, momentum.

crisp, *adj.* crispus; *brittle,* fragilis.

criterion, *n.* discrimen. **critic,** *n.* criticus, sapiens. **criticism,** *n.* iudicium. **criticize,** *v.tr.* iudicare. **critical,** *adj.* callidus. *Adv.* callide, sapienter.

croak, *v.intr.* crocire (*birds*).

crockery, *n.* (vasa) fictilia.

crocodile, *n.* crocodilus.

crocus, *n.* crocus.

crone, *n.* vetula, anus, -ūs, *f.*

crook, *n.* pedum. *v.tr., see* CURVE. **crooked,** *adj.* curvatus; *bad,* pravus. *Adv.* oblique; prave. **crookedness,** *n.* pravitas.

crop, *n. of corn, etc.,* messis, fruges, -um ; *of birds,* ingluvies. *v.tr.* praeciděre, tonděre.

cross, *n.* crux ; *fig.* mala, -orum. *adj.* transversus. *v.tr.* transversum poněre ; *go across,* locum transire ; *thwart,* obsistěre. **cross-purpose,** *by adj.* contrarius. **crosswise,** *adv.* in transversum. **crossing,** *n.* transitus.

crouch, *v.intr.,* se demittěre.

crow, *n.* cornix. *v.intr.* caněre.

crowd, *n.* turba, multitudo. *v.tr.* stipare, *v.intr.* congregari.

crown, *n.* corona; *top,* summus. *v.tr.* coronare; cingere.

crucify, *v.tr.* cruci affigěre. **crucifixion,** *n.* crucis supplicium.

crude, *adj.* crudus; *fig.* rudis. *Adv.* inculte.

cruel, *adj.* crudelis. *Adv.* crudeliter. **cruelty,** *n.* crudelitas, saevitia.

cruise, *v.intr.* (per)vagari.

crumb, *n.* panis mollia (-ium) ; *small piece,* mica, micula. **crumble,** *v.tr.* friare, conterěre. *v.intr.* friari, *etc.*

crumple, *v.tr.* rugare. *v.intr.* rugari.

crush, *v.tr.* compriměre. *fig.* affligěre. *n. crowd,* turba.

crust, *n.* crusta. **crusty,** *adj.* crustosus.

crutch, *n.* baculum.

cry, *v.tr.* (con)clamare clamitare *see*

WEEP, *n.* clamor ; lacrimae vagitus.
crier, *n.* praeco.
crystal, *n.* crystallus.
cub, *n.* catulus. *v.tr.* fetus edĕre.
cube, *n.* cubus.
cubit, *n.* cubitum.
cuckoo, *n.* cuculus.
cucumber, *n.* cucumis, -ĕris, *m.*
cud, *n. to chew the* —, ruminari.
cudgel, *n.* fustis. *v.tr.* ferire.
cue, *n.* signum ; *to give a* , signum
dare.
cuff, *n. blow,* alapa, colaphus ; *sleeve,*
manica extrema. *v.tr.* verberare.
cuirass, *n.* thorax.
culinary, *adj.* coquinarius.
culmination, *n.* fastigium. **culminate,**
v.intr. in (summo) fastigio esse.
culpable, *adj.* culpā dignus, turpis.
culprit, *n., see* CRIMINAL.
cultivate, *v.tr.* colĕre ; *fig.* expolire ;
practise, studĕre. **cultivation, culture,**
n. cultus ; humanitas. **cultivator,** *n.*
agricola, *m.,* cultor ; *fig. by verb.*
cumber, *v.tr.* impedire. **cumbrous,** *adj.*
gravis, incommodus.
cunning, *adj.* dolosus; *skilful,* peritus.
Adv. callide, per dolum ; perite. *n.*
calliditas, dolus; *skill,* ars, so(l)lertia.
cup, *n.* poculum, cyathus. *v.tr.* san-
quinem detrahĕre. **cup-bearer,** *n.* minister *or* servus. **cupboard,** *n.* armarium.
cupidity, *n.* cupiditas.
curb, *n.* frenum. *v.tr.* coercĕre, prohibĕre.
curd, *n.* lac concretum. **curdle,** *v.tr.*
coagulare. *v.intr.* coire.
cure, *n.* curatio, medicina. *v.tr.* sanare.
curiosity, *n.* noscendi studium ; res
nova *or* rara. **curious,** *adj.* curiosus;
strange, insolitus. *Adv.* anxie, *or*
adj.
curl, *v.tr.* crispare. *v.intr.* crispari. *n.*
cirrus. **curling-irons,** *n.* calamister.
curly, *adj* crispus.
current, *adj. this,* hic ; *common,* usu
raeqdus *Adv* vulgo. *n.* flumen.
curry, *v.tr.* conficĕre ; *favour,* blandiri.
currycomb, *n.* strigilis.
curse, *n.* exsecratio, maledictum ; *fig.*
pestis. *v.tr.* exsecrari.
cursory, *adj.* rapidus. *Adv.* breviter.
curt, *adj.* brevis. *Adv.* breviter.
curtail, *v.tr.* praecidĕre.
curtain, *n.* velum, aulaeum.
curve, *n.* (in)flexio, sinus. *v.tr.* (in)-
flectĕre. *v.intr.* flecti.
cushion, *n.* pulvinar.
custard, *n.* placenta ex ovis facta.
custody, *n.* custodia, vincula, -orum.
custom, *n.* consuetudo, mos, usus ;
duty, vectigal, portorium. **customer,**
n. emptor. **customary,** *adj.* usitatus,
communis ; *to be* —, solēre. *Adv.* ex
consuetudine, vulgo.

cut, *v.tr.* secare ; *with a scythe,* (de)-
metĕre ; *the throat,* iugulare ; *on a*
gem, scalpĕre ; *the hair,* tondĕre ; *to*
— *down,* excidĕre. *n. by verbi, short* —,
via brevissima. **cutting,** *adj.* acerbus.
Adv. acerbe. *n. of a plant,* propago,
cullery, *n.* cultri (pl.). **cut-throat,** *n.*
sicarius.
cyclops, *n.* cyclops.
cygnet, *n.* pullus cycnorum.
cylinder, *n.* cylindrus.
cymbal, *n.* cymbalum.
cynic, *n.* cynicus ; homo acerbus.
cynical, *adj.* acerbus. *Adv.* acerbe.
cypress, *n.* cupressus, *f.*

D

dabble, *v.tr.* a(d)spergĕre. *v.intr.* in
aquā ludĕre; *fig.* leviter attingĕre.
daffodil, *n.* narcissus.
dagger, *n.* pugio, sica.
dainty, *adj.* fastidiosus ; elegans. *n.*
cibus delicatus. **daintiness,** *n.* venustas.
dairy, *n.* cella.
dale, *n.* (con)vallis.
dally, *v.intr.* nugari. **dalliance,** *n.* nugae,
blanditiae.
dam, *n.* mater.
dam, *n.* agger, moles. *v.tr.* flumen
coercĕre.
damage, *n.* damnum. *v.tr.* nocēre.
damages, *n. pl.,* imponsa.
dame, *n.* mulier, matrona, domina.
damn, *v.tr.* damnare.
damp, *adj.* humidus. *v.tr.* humectare ;
fig. deprimĕre.
damsel, *n.* puella, virgo.
dance, *n.* saltatio. *v.intr.* saltare. **dancer,**
n. saltator, *m.* saltatrix, *f.*
dandy, *n.* homo elegans.
danger, *n.* periculum. **dangerous,** *adj.*
periculosus. *Adv.* periculose.
dangle, *v.intr.* (de)pendĕre.
dank, *adj.* humidus.
dapper, *adj.* pernix, nitidus.
dapple, *adj* maculosus.
dare, *v.tr.* audēre. **daring,** *adj.* audax.
Adv. audacter. *n.* audacia.
dark, *adj.* obscurus ; *in colour,* fuscus.
Adv. obscure. **darkness,** *n.* obscuritas.
dark red, *adj.* ex rubro subniger. **darken,**
v.tr. obscurare. *v.intr.* obscurari ; *it* —*s,*
vesperascit.
darling, *n.* deliciae.
darn, *v.tr.* sarcire.
dart, *n.* iaculum. *v.tr.* iaculari. *v.intr.*
se conicĕre.
dash, *v.tr.* offendĕre ; spem reprimĕre.
v.intr., see DART. *n.* impetus ; *see*
DISPLAY.
dastard, *n.* homo ignavus.
date, *n. (fruit),* palmula. **data,** *n.*

concessa, -orum. **date,** *n.* dies. *v.tr.* diem a(d)scribĕre. **dative,** *n.* dativus.

daub, *v.tr.* (ob)linĕre, (per)ungĕre.

daughter, *n.* filia ; — *in-law,* nurus.

daunt, *v.tr.,* *see* FRIGHTEN. **dauntless,** *adj.* impavidus. *Adv.* impavide.

dawdle, *v.intr.* cessare. **dawdler,** *n.* cessator.

dawn, *n.* diluculum. **it dawns,** *v.* (di)lucescit.

day, *n.* dies, lux; *at break of* —, primā luce ; — *breaks,* (il)lucescit ; *good* — ! salve (salvete) ; *the* — *before, after,* pridie, postridie. **daybreak,** *n.* diluculum. **daily,** *adj.* cot(t)īdianus (quot-). *adv.* cot(t)idie.

dazzle, *v.tr.* caecare; *fig.* obstupefacĕre ; *to be* —d, stupēre.

dead, *adj.* mortuus. **deaden,** *v.tr.* hebetare. **deadly,** *adj.* mortifer; *fig.* gravis.

death, *n.* mors, exitus.

deaf, *adj.* surdus, auribus captus. **deafen,** *v.tr.* exsurdare.

deal, *v.tr.* distribuĕre. *v.intr.* — *with, see* TREAT. **dealer,** *n.* mercator, negotiator, institor, propola. **dealing,** *n.* commercium, negotium, usus.

dear, *adj.* carus, magni pretii; *how* — ? quanti ? *so* —, tanti ; *beloved,* carus. *Adv.* care, magno pretio ; *maxime or* adj. **dearness,** *n.* magnum pretium.

dearth, *n.* inopia, fames.

debar, *v.tr.* excludĕre, prohibĕre.

debase, *v.tr.* corrumpĕre. **debasement,** *n.* ignominia.

debate, *n.* contentio. *v.intr.* disputare.

debauch, *v.tr.* corrumpĕre, vitiare. *n.* comissatio. **debauchery,** *n.* stuprum, mores dissoluti.

debenture, *n.* syngrapha.

debility, *n.* infirmitas.

debt, *n.* debitum, aes alienum. **debtor,** *n.* qui debet. **debit,** *v.tr.* alci expensum ferre.

decade, *n.* decem anni.

decamp, *v.intr.* discedĕre.

decant, *v.tr.* diffundĕre. **decanter,** *n.* lagena.

decapitate, *v.tr.* caput praecidĕre.

decay, *n.* deminutio, tabes. *v.intr.* (de)minui, senescĕre, tabescĕre ; *decayed tooth,* dens exesus.

decease, *n.* obitus; *see* DEATH.

deceit, *n.* fraus, dolus. **deceive,** *v.tr.* fallĕre. **deceiver,** *n.* fraudator. **deceitful,** *adj.* fallax. *Adv.* fraudulenter, per dolum.

December, *n.* (mensis) December.

decent, *adj.* quod decet, decōrus. *Adv.* decōre. **decency,** *n.* modestia, decōrum.

deception, *n.* fraus, dolus.

decide, *v.tr.* statuĕre, constituĕre. **decided,** *adj.* certus; *I am* —, certum est mihi ; *resolute,* firmus. *Adv.* certo, constanter ; *in answers,* certe, sane. **decision,** *n.* iudicium, sententia con-

stantia. **decisive,** *adj.* ultimus, maximi momenti.

deciduous, *adj.* deciduus.

decimate, *v.tr.* decimare ; *fig., see* DESTROY.

decipher, *v.tr.* explicare.

deck, *n.* constratum navis. *v.tr., see* ADORN.

declaim, *v.tr.* declamare. **declamation,** *n.* declamatio. **declaimer,** *n.* declamator.

declare, *v.tr.* dicĕre, praedicĕre, asseverare. **declaration,** *n.* praedicatio, dictum ; *of war,* belli denuntiatio.

decline, *v.tr.* recusare, negare ; *gram.* declinare. *v.intr.* (de)minui, decrescĕre ; *the day* —s, vesperascit. *n.* (de)minutio; *disease,* phthisis.

declivity, *n.* declivitas, acclivitas.

decoction, *n.* decoctum.

decompose, *v.tr.* (dis)solvĕre. *v.intr.* dissolvi, tabescĕre. **decomposition,** *n.* (dis)solutio, tabes.

decorate, *v.tr.* (ex)ornare. **decoration,** *n.* ornatus. **decorous,** *adj.* decōrus. *Adv.* decōre. **decorum,** *n.* decōrum.

decoy, *v.tr.* allicĕre. *n.* illex.

decrease, *v.tr.* (de)minuĕre. *v.intr.* (de)minui. *n.* deminutio.

decree, *v.tr.* decernĕre, edicĕre ; alci placet ut; *see* DETERMINE. *n.* decretum, senatusconsultum.

decrepit, *adj.* senectute confectus.

decry, *v.tr.* vituperare.

dedicate, *v.tr.* (de)dicare, consecrare.

deduce, *v.tr.* (de)ducĕre; *logic,* concludĕre. **deduct,** *v.tr.* detrahĕre. **deduction,** *n.* deminutio; *logic,* conclusio.

deed, *n.* facinus; —*s,* facta; *document,* tabula, syngrapha.

deep, *adj.* altus, profundus; *fig.* summus. *Adv.* alte, profunde; penitus, graviter. *n.* altum. **deepen,** *v.tr.* altius fodĕre; *increase,* augēre. *v.intr.* *grow darker,* obscurari. **depth,** *n.* altitudo; *fig. of character,* summo ingenio, *etc.,* praeditus; *of night,* mediā nocte.

deer, *n.* cervus, dama.

deface, *v.tr.* deformare, foedare.

defame, *v.tr.* calumniari.

default, *n.* culpa, peccatum; *lack,* defectus ; *legal,* go by —, vadimonium deserĕre. **defaulter,** *n.* qui vadimonium deserit.

defeat, *n.* clades. *v.tr., see* CONQUER.

defect, *n.* quod deest ; *of character,* vitia, -orum. **defective,** *adj.* imperfectus ; *to be* —, deficĕre, deesse. *Adv.* vitiose. **defection,** *n.* defectio. **deficiency,** *n.* inopia.

defend, *v.tr.* defendĕre ; *legal,* caus(s)am dicĕre. **defendant,** *n.* reus. **defence,** *n.* praesidium ; *legal,* patrocinium. **defenceless,** *adj.* inermis. **defensible,** *adj.* quod defendi potest. **defensive,** *adj.; — weapons,* arma, -orum.

defer, *v.tr.* differre, prorogare ; alci cedĕre. **deference**, *n.* observantia. **deferential**, *adj.* submissus. *Adv.* submisse.

deficient, *adj.*, *see* DEFECTIVE.

defile, *n.* angustiae, -ium. *v.tr.* maculare, violare. **defilement**, *n.* labes.

define, *v.tr.* (de)finire, circumscribĕre. **definition**, *n.* (de)finitio. **definite**, *adj.* certus. *Adv.* certe, certo.

deflect, *v.intr.* declinare, errare.

deform, *v.tr.* deformare. **deformed**, *adj.* distortus. **deformity**, *n.* deformitas.

defraud, *v.tr.* fraudare. **defrauder**, *n.* fraudator.

defray, *v.tr.* solvĕre.

defunct, *adj.* mortuus.

defy, *v.tr.* provocare. **defiance**, *n.* provocatio, contumacia.

degenerate, *v.intr.* mores mutare. **degenerate**, *adj.* degener.

degrade, *v.tr.* in ordinem cogĕre (*of soldiers*) ; deicĕre. **degrading**, *adj.* indecōrus. **degradation**, *n.* ignominia.

degree, *n.* gradus ; *by* —*s*, paul(l)atim.

deify, *v.tr.* inter deos referre. **deified**, *adj.* divus. **deification**, *n.* consecratio.

deign, *v.intr.* dignari, velle *with infin.*

dejected, *adj.* maestus, tristis. *Adv.* maeste. **dejection**, *n.* tristitia.

delay, *v.tr.* (re)morari; *prolong*, ducĕre ; *postpone*, differre. *v.intr.* (com)morari. *n.* mora.

delegate, *n.* legatus, nuntius. *v.tr.* legare; committĕre, mandare.

deleterious, *adj.* perniciosus. *Adv.* perniciose.

deliberate, *v.intr.* deliberare, consulĕre. *Adj.* lentus ; prudens. *Adv.* lente ; prudenter. **deliberative**, *adj.* — *assembly*, consilium, senatus. **deliberation**, *n.* deliberatio; *see* SLOWNESS.

delicate, *adj.* tener, mollis; infirmus ; exquisitus. *Adv.* infirme. **delicacy**, *n.* mollitia ; *of taste, style*, humanitas ; infirmitas ; *tact*, prudentia ; venustas, elegantia; cibus delicatus.

delicious, *adj.* dulcis. *Adv.* suaviter.

delight, *n.* voluptas. *v.tr.* oblectare, *v.intr.* oblectari. **delightful**, *adj.* iucundus. *Adv.* iucunde. **delightfulness**, *n.* suavitas.

delineate, *v.tr.* designare, depingĕre. **delineation**, *n.* adumbratio, descriptio.

delinquent, *n.* maleficus. **delinquency**, *n.*, delictum, scelus.

delirium, *n.* delirium. **delirious**, *adj.* delirus; *to be* —, mente alienari.

deliver, *v.tr.*, *see* FREE; *see* SPEAK; — *up*, prodĕre. **deliverer**, *n.* liberator. **delivery**, *n.* liberatio; actio; traditio.

dell, *n.* (con)vallis.

delude, *v.tr.*, *see* DECEIVE. **delusion**, *n.* fallacia ; error. **delusive**, *adj.* fallax. *Adv.* fallaciter.

deluge, *n.* eluvio. *v.tr.* inundare.

delve, *v.tr.* fodĕre.

demagogue, *n.* novarum rerum auctor.

demand, *v.tr.* (de)poscĕre. *n.* postulatio, preces, -um.

demarcation, *n.* limes.

demean, *v.tr.* se gerĕre ; *descendĕre ad alqd.* **demeanour**, *n.* mores, -um.

demerit, *n.* culpa.

demigod, *n.* heros.

demise, *n.* obitus. *v.tr. by will*, legare.

democracy, *n.* ratio popularis. **democratical**, *adj.* popularis. **democrat**, *n.* popularium fautor.

demolish, *v.tr.* evertĕre. **demolition**, *n.* eversio.

demonstrate, *v.tr.* demonstrare, probare. **demonstration**, *n.* demonstratio; *proof*, argumentum ; *meeting*, coitio. **demonstrable**, *adj.* quod doceri potest. **demonstrative**, *adj.* vehemens. *Adv.* vehementer.

demoralize, *v.tr.* mores corrumpĕre. **demoralization**, *n.* mores corrupti.

demur, *v.intr. legal*, contra dicĕre.

demure, *adj.* verecundus.

den, *n.* caverna, latibulum.

denizen, *n.* incola, *m. & f.*

denominate, *v.tr. & n.*, *see* NAME. **denominator**, *n.* index.

denote, *v.tr.* designare. **denotation**, *n.* designatio.

denounce, *v.tr.* denuntiare ; accusare. **denunciation**, *n.* denuntiatio; delatio, accusatio. **denouncer**, *n.* accusator, delator.

dense, *adj.* confertus. *Adv.* solide, confertim. **density**, *n.* soliditas.

dent, *n.* nota, iniuria. *v.tr.* alci rei iniuriam afferre.

deny, *v.tr.* (de)negare, recusare; *to* — *oneself*, sibi temperare. **denial**, *n.* negatio, recusatio.

depart, *v.intr.* abire, abscedĕre, egredi. **departure**, *n.* abitus, discessus.

department, *n.* munus, provincia; *district, region*.

depend, *v.intr.* pendēre ; *alci (con)fidĕre ; — upon it, nihil urget*. **dependent**, *adj.* *il n.* use verb. **dependence**, *n.* dicio; fiducia.

deplete, *v.tr.* (de)pingĕre, describĕre.

deplore, *v.tr.* deplorare. **deplorable**, *adj.*, *see* MISERABLE.

deponent, *n. legal*, testis ; *gram.* (verbum) deponens.

depopulate, *v.tr.* (de)vastare, (de)populari. **depopulation**, *n.* populatio, vastatio.

deport, *v.tr.* se gerĕre. **deportment**, *n.* gestus; mores, -um.

depose, *v.tr.* loco suo movēre ; *as a witness*, testari. **deposition**, *n.* use verb; testimonium.

deposit, *v.tr.* (de)ponĕre. *n.* quod depositum est; *pledge*, pignus.

deprave, *v.tr.* corrumpĕre. **deprava-**

tion, n. corruptio. **depravity,** n. turpitudo.

deprecate, v.tr. deprecari. **deprecation,** n. deprecatio.

depreciate, v.tr. minuĕre, elevare. **depreciation,** n. obtrectatio.

depredation, n. latrocinium. **depredator,** n. latro.

depress, v.tr. deprimĕre, animum affligĕre. **depression,** n. tristitia.

deprived, v.tr. privare, orbare. **deprived,** adj. orbus (orbatus); — of use of limbs, membris captus. **deprivation,** n. spoliatio.

depth, n., see DEEP.

depute, v.tr. legare, allegare. **deputy,** n., see AGENT. **deputation,** n. legati.

derange, v.tr. perturbare. **deranged,** adj. insanus. **derangement,** n. perturbatio; insania.

deride, v.tr. irridēre. **derider,** n. irrisor. **derision,** n. irrisio. **derisive,** adj. by verb.

derive, v.tr. (de)ducĕre.

derogate from, v.tr. derogare, obtrectare. **derogatory,** adj. to be —, dedecori esse.

descend, v.intr. descendĕre ; fig. tradi ; —ed from, ortus ab alqo. **descendant,** n. prognatus; pl. posteri. **descent,** n. going down, use verb ; of a hill, declivitas ; origin, genus.

describe, v.tr. describĕre, enarrare. **description,** n. descriptio, (e)narratio.

desecrate, v.tr. profanare, polluĕre, violare. **desecration,** n. polluta sacra, -orum.

desert, n. meritum.

desert, n. solitudo, loca deserta. v.tr. deserĕre, prodĕre. v.intr. transfugĕre. **deserter,** n. transfuga.

deserve, v.tr. (com)merēri, dignus esse re. **deserving,** adj. dignus. Adv. merito.

design, n. and v.tr., see SKETCH ; see PURPOSE. **designing,** adj. prudens, fraudulentus. Adv. consulto.

designate, v.tr. designare, nominare. **designation,** n. designatio, nominatio.

desire, n. cupiditas, desiderium. v.tr. appetĕre, cupĕre. **desirable,** adj. optabilis. **desirous,** adj. cupidus. Adv. cupide.

desist, v.intr. desistĕre re (ab re).

desk, n. mensa, scrinium.

desolate, adj. desertus; spe destitutus. v.tr. vastare.

despair, n. desperatio. v.intr. desperare. **despairing,** adj., see DESPERATE.

despatch, dispatch, v.tr. conficĕre; maturare ; send off, (di)mittĕre. n. confectio; missio; caedes. **despatches,** n.pl. lit(t)erae publice missae.

desperate, adj. exspes, desperatus; periculosus; sceleratus. Adv. desperanter. **desperation,** n. desperatio.

despise, v.tr. contemnĕre. **despicable,** adj. turpis. Adv. turpiter.

despite, n. odium. prep. contra.

despond, v.intr. desperare, spe delectus esse. **despondency,** n., see DESPAIR.

despot, n. tyrannus. **despotism,** n. tyrannis, dominatio. **despotical,** adj. superbus. Adv. superbe, crudeliter.

dessert, n. mensa secunda.

destine, v.tr. destinare. **destined,** adj. constitutus. **destination,** n. finis ; locus quem petimus. **destiny,** n. fatum, sors.

destitute, adj. inops ; privatus, sine with abl. **destitution,** n. inopia.

destroy, v.tr. perdĕre, delēre. **destroyer,** n. qui alqd perdit. **destructible,** adj. fragilis. **destructibility,** n. fragilitas. **destruction,** n. excidium. **destructive,** adj. perniciosus. Adv. perniciose.

desuetude, n. oblivio.

desultory, adj. inconstans. Adv. parum diligenter.

detach, v.tr. disiungĕre.

details, n. singula. **detail,** v.tr. res explicare.

detain, v.tr. (de)tinēre. **detention,** n. mora; custodia.

detect, v.tr. deprehendĕre, invenire. **detection,** n. deprehensio.

deter, v.tr. deterrēre.

deteriorate, v.tr. corrumpĕre. v.intr. in peius mutari. **deterioration,** n. deterior condicio.

determine, v.tr. settle, constituĕre; decide to, constituĕre. **determination,** n. arbitrium, sententia; consilium. **determined,** adj. constans.

detest, v.tr. detestari. **detestable,** adj. detestabilis. Adv. foede. **detestation,** n. odium.

dethrone, v.tr. regi imperium abrogare.

detract, v.tr. minuĕre. **detraction,** n. obtrectatio.

detriment, n. detrimentum. **detrimental,** adj. perniciosus. Adv. perniciose.

deuce, n. go to the —, abi in malam rem.

devastate, v.tr. (per)vastare. **devastation,** n. vastatio.

develop, v.tr. (resources) excolĕre. v.intr. crescĕre. **development,** n. anctus, progressus.

deviate, v.intr. deflectĕre. **deviation,** n. digressio. **devious,** adj. devius.

device, n. consilium; motto, dictum.

devil, n. go to the — ! abi in malam partem !

devise, v.tr. fingĕre; see BEQUEATH.

devoid, adj. vacuus ; — of care, securus.

devolve, v.tr. deferre. v.intr. transmitti.

devote, v.tr. (de)vovēre, (con)secrare ;

fig. destinare ; *to — oneself to*, se alci dedĕre. **devoted**, *adj.* studiosus. *Adv.* studiose, *or by superl.* **devotion**, *n.* studium, amor; *religious*, pietas erga Deum. **devotions**, *n.* preces, -um.

devout, *adj.* pius erga Deum. *Adv.* pie.

dew, *n.* ros; *the — falls*, rorat. **dewy**, *adj.* roscidus.

dexterity, *n.* sol(l)ertia. **dexterous**, *adj.* sol(l)ers. *Adv.* sol(l)erter.

diadem, *n.* diadema.

diagonal, *adj.* diagonalis.

diagram, *n.* descriptio, forma (geometrica).

dial, *n.* solarium.

dialect, *n.* lingua; *to speak in the Doric —*, Dorice loqui.

dialectics, *n.* dialectica, -orum. disserendi ratio.

dialogue, *n.* dialogus, sermones ; *conversation*, sermo.

diameter, *n.* linea media.

diamond, *n.* adamas.

diaphragm, *n.* praecordia, -ium, *pl.*

diary, *n.* ephemeris, adversaria, -orum.

dice, die, *n.* talus, tessera; *a — box*, fritillus. *v.intr.* talos *or* tesseras facĕre. **dicer**, *n.* aleator.

dictate, *v.tr.* dictare ; *see* ORDER. **dictation**, *n.*, *see* SWAY; quod dictatum est. **dictator**, *n.* dictator. **dictatorial**, *adj.* imperiosus. **dictatorship**, *n.* dictatura.

diction, *n.* dicendi genus.

die, *v.intr.* mori.

diet, *n.* victus ; *assembly*, conventus. *v.tr.* victum alci imponĕre.

differ, *v.intr.* discrepare, differre. **different**, *adj.* discrepans, dissimilis. *Adv.* aliter. **difference**, *n.* varietas, dissensio.

difficult, *adj.* difficilis, impeditus. **difficulty**, *n.* difficultas ; *pecuniary*, pecuniae inopia; *with —*, vix.

diffidence, *n.* diffidentia. **diffident**, *adj.* timidus. *Adv.* modeste.

diffuse, *v.tr.* (di)vulgare. *adj.* verbosus. *Adv.* diffuse, copiose. **diffusion**, *n.* propagatio, *or by adj.*

dig, *v.tr.* fodĕre ; *to — up*, effodĕre. **digger**, *n.* fossor.

digest, *v.tr.* concoquĕre. *n.* digesta, -orum. **digestible**, *adj.* facilis ad concoquendum.

dignity, *n.* honestas, gravitas, auctoritas, dignitas. **dignify**, *v.tr.* amplificare, augĕre. **dignified**, *adj.* gravis ; *in a — way*, summã gravitate.

digress, *v.intr.* digredi. **digressive**, *adj.* a proposito digredi. **digression**, *n.* digressio.

dike, *n.* moles, agger.

dilapidation, *n.* injuria, detrimentum.

dilate, *v.tr.* dilatare; *fig.* latius dicĕre.

dilatory, *adj.* lentus. **dilatoriness**, *n.* cunctatio.

dilemma, *n.* complexio; *the horns of a —*, res in angustias deductae.

diligence, *n.* diligentia. *Adv.* diligenter. **diligent**, *adj.* diligens.

dilute, *v.tr.* diluĕre.

dim, *v.tr.* obscurare. *Adj.* obscurus. **dimness**, *n.* obscuritas.

dimension, *n.* dimensio.

diminish, *v.tr.* (im)minuĕre. *v.intr.* (im)minui.

din, *n.* strepitus. *v.tr.* aures obtundĕre.

dine, *v.tr.* prandĕre, cenare. **dining-room**, *n.* conclave. **dinner**, *n.* prandium, cena.

dingy, *adj.* sordidus.

dint, *n.* *by — of*, *by abl.*

dip, *v.tr.* mergĕre. *v.intr.* (im)mergi ; *see* INCLINE; *to — into*, librum strictim attingĕre. *n.* declivitas.

diploma, *n.* diploma. **diplomacy**, *n.* legatio; astutia. **diplomat**, *n.* legatus. **diplomatic**, *adj.* astutus.

dire, *adj.* atrox.

direct, *v.tr.* administrare, dirigĕre ; *viam* monstrare ; epistolam inscribĕre. *Adv.*, *see* DIRECTLY. *Adj.* (di)rectus. **direction**, *n.* cura, administratio; *see* ORDER ; iter. **directly**, *adv.* recta viã ; statim. **director**, *n.* magister, praefectus.

dirge, *n.* nenia.

dirt, *n.* sordes. **dirty**, *adj.* sordidus ; *fig.* turpis. *Adv.* sordide. *v.tr.* maculare.

disable, *v.tr.* infirmare.

disabuse, *v.tr.* dedocēre.

disadvantage, *n.* incommodum. **disadvantageous**, *adj.* incommodus. *Adv.* incommode.

disaffect, *v.tr.* (ab)alienare. **disaffected**, *adj.* (ab)alienatus. **disaffection**, *n.* animus alienus.

disagree, *v.intr.* dissentire. **disagreeable**, *adj.* injucundus. *Adv.* moleste. **disagreement**, *n.* dissidium.

disallow, *v.tr.* improbare, vetare.

disappear, *v.intr.* abire, evanescĕre. **disappearance**, *n.* exitus.

disappoint, *v.tr.* frustrari, spem fallĕre; **disappointment**, *n.* (*I have met with a —*, spes me fefellit).

disapprove, *v.tr.* condemnare. **disapproval**, *n.* improbatio.

disarm, *v.tr.* armis exuĕre.

disarrange, *v.tr.* perturbare. **disarrangement**, *n.* perturbatio.

disaster, *n.* clades ; incommodum. **disastrous**, *adj.* gravis, tristis. *Adv.* graviter.

disavow, *v.tr.* abnuĕre. **disavowal**, *n.* infitiatio.

disband, *v.tr.* dimittĕre.

disbelieve, *v.tr.* non credĕre. **disbelief**, *n.* use verb.

disburden, *v.tr.* liberare.

disburse *v.tr. see* PAY

discern, *v.tr.* discernĕre. **discernible**, *adj.* conspicuus. **discerning**, *adj.* prudens. **discernment**, *n.* distinctio; *insight*, intelligentia.

discharge, *v.tr.* missum facĕre, (di)mittĕre; *unload* (navem) exonerare; *pay*, solvĕre; *perform*. fungi; *acquit*, absolvere. *v.intr. of rivers*, effundi. *n.* (di)missio; solutio; functio.

disciple, *n.* discipulus.

discipline, *n.* disciplina. *v.tr.* coercēre.

disclaim, *v.tr.* repudiare.

disclose, *v.tr.* detegĕre, aperire. **disclosure**, *n.* indicium.

discolour, *v.tr.* decolorare.

discomfit, *v.tr.* fundĕre ; *fig.* repellĕre. **discomfiture**, *n.* clades.

discomfort, *n.* incommodum.

disconcerted, *adj.* perturbatus.

disconsolate, *adj.* spe destitutus. *Adv.* maeste.

discontent, *n.* taedium. **discontented**, *adj.* non contentus; *to be* —, moleste ferre.

discontinue, *v.tr.* intermittĕre, omittĕre.

discord, *n. fig.* discordia. **discordant**, *adj. music*, absonus ; discors. *Adv.* non congruenter.

discount, *n.* deductio ; *to pay without* —, solidum solvere.

discountenance, *v.tr.* improbare.

discourage, *v.tr.* animum infringĕre, affligĕre ; *to be discouraged*, de alqā re desperare ; *to — anything*, dissuadēre. **discouragement**, *n.* quod animum affligit.

discourse, *n.* sermo; *a speech*, contio. *v.intr.* colloqui; contionari, orationem facĕre.

discourteous, *adj.* inurbanus. *Adv.* inurbane. **discourtesy**, *n.* inurbanitas.

discover, *v.tr.* invenire. **discoverer**, *n.* inventor, auctor. **discovery**, *n.* inventio, investigatio ; *thing discovered*, inventum.

discredit, *n.* dedecus. *v.tr.* fidem minuĕre. **discreditable**, *adj.* turpis.

discreet, *adj.* prudens, gravis. *Adv.* prudenter, graviter. **discretion**, *n.* prudentia.

discriminate, *v.tr.* discernĕre. **discrimination**, *n.* discrimen.

discursive, *adj.* inconstans, vagus. *Adv.* varie, inconstanter. **discursiveness**, *n.* error.

discuss, *v.tr.* disputare. **discussion**, *n.* disputatio.

disdain, *v.tr.* spernĕre. *n.* fastigium. **disdainful**, *adj.* arrogans.

disease, *n.* morbus. **diseased**, *adj.* aeger.

disembark, *v.tr.* exponĕre. *intr.* (e nave) egredi. **disembarkation**, *n.* egressus.

disembarrass, *v.tr.* expedire.

disembodied, *adj.* corporis sui expers.

disengage, *v.tr.* liberare. **disengaged**, *adj.* otiosus.

disentangle, *v.tr.* expedire, explicare.

disfavour, *n.* odium ; *to fall into* —, alci in odium venire.

disfigure, *v.tr.* deformare.

disfranchise, *v.tr.* civitatem adimĕre.

disgorge, *v.tr.* eicĕre; *give up*, reddĕre.

disgrace, *n.* turpitudo; *mark of* —, nota; *shameful act*, dedecus. *v.tr.* dedecori esse. **disgraceful**, *adj.* turpis, infamis. *Adv.* turpiter.

disguise, *n.* vestis mutata; *mask*, persona ; *appearance*, simulatio, persona. *v.tr.* vestum mutare; *fig.* (dis)simulare.

disgust, *n.* fastidium, taedium. **disgusting**, *adj.* teter. *Adv.* tetre.

dish, *n.* patina, lanx. *v.tr.* — *up*, apponĕre.

dishearten, *v.tr.* animum frangĕre.

dishonest, *adj.* malus, inhonestus. *Adv.* male, fraudulenter. **dishonesty**, *n.* improbitas.

dishonour, *v.tr.* dedecorare, polluĕre. *n.* ignominia.

disinclination, *n.* declinatio, animus aversus. **disinclined**, *adj.* alienus.

disinherit, *v.tr.* exheredare.

disinter, *v.tr.* effodĕre, eruĕre.

disinterested, *adj.* suae utilitatis immemor. *Adv.* liberaliter. **disinterestedness**, *n.* liberalitas.

disjoin, *v.tr.* disiungĕre, seiungĕre.

disjoint, *v.tr.* *cut up*, scindĕre, (dis)secare. **disjointed**, *adj.* haud bene compositus. *Adv.* incomposite.

disk, *n.* discus, orbis, m.

dislike, *v.tr.* improbare, fastidire.

dislocate, *v.tr.* luxare (*only in past part.*).

dislodge, *v.tr.* (de)pellĕre, expellĕre.

disloyal, *adj.* perfidus. *Adv.* perfide. **disloyalty**, *n.* perfidia ; *to show* — perfide agĕre.

dismal, *adj.* maestus, miser. *Adv.* maeste.

dismantle, *v.tr.* nudare.

dismast, *v.tr.* malis privare.

dismay, *n.* terror. *v.tr.* terrēre alqm.

dismember, *v.tr.*, *see* DISJOINT.

dismiss, *v.tr.* (di)mittĕre. **dismissal**, *n.* (di)missio; *see* DISCHARGE.

dismount, *v.intr.* desilire ex equo.

disobey, *v.tr.* non parēre. **disobedient**, *adj.* non parens. *Adv.* non oboedienter. **disobedience**, *n.* contumacia.

disoblige, *v.tr.* alci morem non gerĕre.

disorder, *n.* perturbatio. *v.tr.* perturbare, miscēre. **disordered**, *adj. body*, aeger ; *mind*, alienatus. **disorderly**, *adj.* (con)turbatus ; *conduct*, corruptus.

disorganise, *v.tr.* (dis)solvĕre. **disorganisation**, *n.* dissolutio.

disown, *v.tr.* detrectare; infitiari.

disparage, *v.tr.* parvi facĕre, obtrectare.

disparagement, *n.* obtrectatio. **disparaging,** *adj.* invidiosus.

disparity, *n.* dissimilitudo.

dispassionate, *adj.* placidus. *Adv.* tranquille.

dispatch, *v.tr., see* DESPATCH.

dispel, *v.tr.* discutĕre, dissipare.

dispense, *v.tr.* distribuĕre ; — *with,* (di)mittĕre. **dispensation,** *n.* venia.

disperse, *v.tr.* dissipare, fugare. *v.intr.* effundi. **dispersion,** *n.* dissipatio, fuga.

dispirit, *v.tr.* animum frangĕre.

displace, *v.tr.* transferre.

display, *v.tr.* ostendĕre. *n.* ostentatio.

displease, *v.tr.* displicĕre. **displeasure,** *n.* ira ; *without —,* aequo animo.

dispose, *v.tr.* statuĕre ; *see* SELL ; *see* FINISH. **disposal,** *n.* arbitrium ; *to be at the — of anyone,* penes alqm. **disposed,** *adj.* inclinatus. **disposition,** *n.* mores, -um.

dispossess, *v.tr.* depellĕre.

disproportion, *n.* inaequalitas. **disproportionate,** *adj.* impar. *Adv.* dissimiliter.

disprove, *v.tr.* redarguĕre. **disproof,** *n.* refutatio.

dispute, *v.tr.* contendĕre ; *quarrel,* rixari. *n.* disputatio ; rixa.

disqualify, *v.tr.* impedire.

disquiet, *n.* perturbatio. **disquieted,** *adj.* inquietus.

disregard, *n.* neglegentia. *v.tr.* parvi facĕre.

disrespect, *n.* contemptio. **disrespectful,** *adj.* insolens.

dissatisfy, *v.tr.* displicĕre. **dissatisfied,** *adj.* tristis. **dissatisfaction,** *n.* molestia.

dissect, *v.tr.* (dis)secare.

dissemble, *v.tr.* (dis)simulare. **dissembler,** *n.* dissimulator.

disseminate, *v.tr.* spargĕre. **dissemination,** *n. use verb or* rumor (*e.g.* rumor percrebuit).

dissension, *n.* discordia.

dissent, *v.intr.* dissentire. **dissentient,** *or* **dissenter,** qui dissentit.

dissever, *v.tr.* seiungĕre, secernĕre.

dissimilar, *adj.* dissimilis. **dissimilitude,** *n.* dissimilitudo. **dissimulation,** *n.* dissimulatio.

dissipate, *v.tr.* dissipare. **dissipated,** *adj.* effusus, pravus. **dissipation,** *n.* licentia.

dissolve, *v.tr.* liquefacĕre ; (dis)solvĕre. **dissolute,** *see* DISSIPATED. **dissolution,** *n.* dissolutio. **dissoluteness,** *n.* mores pravi, *etc.*

dissonant, *adj.* absŏnus. **dissonance,** *n.* vox absŏna.

dissuade, *v.tr.* dissuadĕre. **dissuasion,** *n.* dissuasio.

distaff, *n.* colus, .

distance, *n.* spatium, intervallum; *at a long —* intervallo interiecto. *v.tr.*

superare. **distant,** *adj.* remotus; *be —,* abesse ab. *Adv.* procul.

distaste, *n.* taedium. **distasteful,** *adj.* molestus. *Adv.* moleste.

distemper, *n., see* DISEASE.

distend, *v.tr.* refercire (*stuff full*).

distil, *v.tr.* (de)coquĕre ; stillare, **distiller,** in qui alqd (dis)coquit.

distinct, *adj.* separate, disiunctus ; *clear,* distinctus, clarus. *Adv.* separatim, clare. **distinction,** *n.* distinctio; *rank, etc.,* honor ; *mark of —,* insigne. **distinctive,** *adj.* proprius. *Adv.,* proprie. **distinctiveness,** *n.* perspicuitas. **distinguish,** *v.tr.* ; *— between,* (inter) diiudicare ; *honour,* ornare ; *— oneself,* gloriam adipisci. **distinguished,** *adj.* insignis.

distort, *v.tr.* detorquĕre.

distract, *v.tr.* distrahĕre ; perturbare. **distracted,** *adj.* perturbatus. *Adv. by adj.* amens. **distraction,** *n.* impedimentum ; animi conturbatio ; neglegentia.

distrain, *v.tr.* bona vendĕre.

distress, *v.tr.* angĕre, vexare. *n.* anxietas ; *poverty,* res angustae ; *to be in —,* laborare, in periculo versari ; **distressed,** *adj.* sol(l)icitus. **distressing,** *adj.* gravis. *Adv.* graviter.

distribute, *v.tr.* distribuĕre. **distribution,** *n.* distributio, assignatio (*of land*).

district, *n.* ager, regio, terra.

distrust, *n.* diffidentia, suspicio. **distrustful,** *adj.* suspiciosus, diffidens. *Adv.* diffidenter, suspiciose.

disturb, *v.tr.* perturbare. **disturbance,** *n.* tumultus. **disturber,** *n.* turbator.

disunion, *n.* dissensio, discordia. **disunite,** *v.tr.* disiungĕre.

ditch, *n.* fossa. **ditcher,** *n.* fossor.

ditty, *n.* carmen, cantus.

diurnal, *adj.* cot(t)idianus, diurnus.

dive, *v.intr.* urinari, se (de)mergĕre. **diver,** *n.* urinator.

diverge, *v.intr.* discedĕre ; *roads, in* diversas partes ferri ; *fig.* discrepare, dissentire. **divergence,** *n.* declinatio ; dissensio.

diverse, *adj.* dissimilis. *Adv.* dissimiliter. **diversion,** *n.* delectatio, oblectamentum. **diversify,** *v.tr.* variare, distinguĕre. **diversity,** *n.* diversitas, dissensio. **divert,** *v.tr. a river,* avertĕre; avocare ; *flectĕre ; to amuse,* delectare. **diverting,** *adj.* iucundus.

divest, *v.tr.* exuĕre.

divide, *v.tr.* dividĕre, distribuĕre. *v.intr.* discedere ; in contrarias sententias distrahi. **dividend,** *n.* usura, foenus.

divine, *adj.* divinus, caelestis; *by — inspiration,* divinitus ; *fig.* eximius,

division, *n.* partitio ; *of an army,* legio ; *part,* pars. **divisible,** *adj.* quod dividi potest.

Adv. divine, divinitus, eximie. *n.* sacerdos. *v.tr.* divinare, vaticinari ; *fig.* praecipĕre. **divination,** divinatio, augaratio. **diviner,** *n.* vaticinator, vates. **divinity,** *n.* natura divina.

divorce, *n.* divortium. *v.tr.* divortium facĕre.

divulge, *v.tr.* (di)vulgare.

dizzy, *adj.* vertiginosus ; — *height,* immensa altitudo. **dizziness,** *n.* vertigo.

do, *v.tr.* facĕre, agĕre, gerĕre, administrare ; *to — again,* reficĕre, redintegrare. **doer,** *n.* auctor.

docile, *adj.* docilis. *Adv.* dociliter. **docility,** *n.* docilitas.

dock, *n.* navalia, -ium. *v.tr. cut short,* praecidĕre.

doctor, *n.* medicus. *v.tr.* mederi.

doctrine, *n.* doctrina, praeceptum.

document, *n.* lit(t)erae, tabulae.

dodge, *v.tr.* illudĕre. *n.* dolus.

doff, *v.tr.* exuĕre.

dog, *n.* canis ; *to go to the —s,* pessum ire. *v.tr.* indagare. **dogged,** *adj.* morosus; constans. *Adv.* morose, constanter. **doggedness,** *n.* morositas; perseverantia.

doggerel, *n.* versus inculti.

doings, *n., see* ACTION.

dole, *n.* stips, *see* ALMS. *v.tr.* distribuĕre. **doleful,** *adj.* tristis. *Adv.* maeste. **dolefulness,** *n.* tristitia.

dolphin, *n.* delphīnus.

dolt, *n.* stipes, caudex ; homo rusticus, stultus.

domain, *n.* ager, possessio.

dome, *n.* tholus (= *cupola*).

domestic, *adj.* domesticus, familaris ; intestinus. *n.* servus, minister. **domesticate,** *v.tr., see* TAME.

dominion, *n.* postestas, imperium, dicio, regnum. **dominate,** *v.tr.* dominari. **dominant,** *adj.* summus. **domination,** *n.* dominatio. **domineering,** *adj.* superbus. **domineer,** *v.intr.* dominari.

donation, *n.* donum; *see* GIFT.

doom, *n.* fatum, sors ; iudicium. *v.tr.* damnare.

door, *n.* ostium, ianua, limen (= *threshold*). **doorpost,** *n.* postis, *m.* **doorkeeper,** *n.* ianitor.

dormant, *adj.* mortuus.

dormouse, *n.* glis, gliris, *m.*

dose, *n.* potio ; medicamentum. *v.tr.* medicamentum dare.

dot, *n.* punctum. *v.tr.* pungĕre.

dote, *v.intr.* delirare ; — *on,* perdite amare. **dotage,** *n.* senectus. **dotard,** *n.* senex, stultus.

double, *adj.* duplex ; geminus (*of pairs*). *v.tr.* duplicare ; *sail round,* circumvehi ; — *turn,* se flectĕre. *Adv.* bis. **double-dyed,** *adj., a — villain,* homo scleratissimus. **double sense,** *n.* ambiguitas ; *of —,* anceps. **double-**

tongued, *adj.* bilinguis. **doublet,** *n.* tunica.

doubt, *n.* dubitatio, dubium. *v.intr.* dubitare, dubius esse, in dubio esse. **doubtful,** *adj.* dubius, incertus. *Adv.* dubitanter, ambigue. **doubtless,** *adj.* sine dubio.

dough, *n.* farina.

doughty, *adj.* fortis.

dove, *n.* columba. **dovecot,** *n.* columbarium. **dovetail,** *v.tr.* securiculā compingĕre.

dower, *n.* dos. **dowerless,** *adj.* indotatus.

down, *prep.* de, *with abl.; — the stream,* secundo flumine. *n.* campus paul(l)o editus. **downcast,** *adj.* tristis. **downfall,** *n.* exitium. **downpour,** *n.* imber. **downright,** *adj.* totus, *or* summus ; *straightforward,* simplex. *Adv.* omnino. **downwards,** *adv.* desuper.

down, *n.* *plumage,* plumae ; lanugo. **downy,** *adj.* plumosus.

doze, *v.intr.* semisomnus esse.

dozen, duodecim.

drab, *adj.* ravus; *see* BROWN.

drag, *v.tr.* trahĕre. *n.* sufflamen.

dragon, *n.* draco, serpens.

dragoon, *n.* eques. *v.tr.* dominari.

drain, *n.* fossa, cloaca. *v.tr.* siccare.

drake, *n.* anas mas.

dram, *n.* drachma.

drama, *n.* fabula. **dramatic,** *adj.* scaenicus.

draper, *n.* qui pannos vendit. **drapery,** *n.* (*hangings*), tapete; vestitus.

draught, *n.* *drink,* haustus ; *of air,* spiritus.

draw, *v.tr.* trahĕre ; *a sword,* gladium stringĕre ; — *a carriage,* currum ducĕre; — *out,* educĕre ; — *wine, etc.,* ex dolio promĕre ; *to portray,* delineare, (de)pingĕre ; — *aside,* sevocare ; — *down,* deducĕre ; — *tight,* a(d)stringĕre ; — *up,* scribĕre. *v.intr.* — *near,* accedĕre; — *back,* recedĕre, se recipĕre. **drawbridge,** *n.* use pons, *m.* **drawer,** *n.* (*of water*), aquarius; *chest,* armarium; **drawing,** *n.* pictura.

drawl, *v.intr.* in dicendo lentus esse.

dray, *n.* vehiculum, plaustrum.

dread, *n., see* FEAR.

dream, *n.* somnium ; *in a —,* per somnum. *v.intr.* somniare ; — *of,* vidēre per somnum. **dreamy,** *adj.* somniculosus.

dreary, *adj.* tristis, maestus. *Adv.* misere, maeste. **dreariness,** *n.* tristitia.

dregs, *n.* faex; *fig.* faex populi.

drench, *v.tr.* madefacĕre.

dress, *n.* vestis, ornatus ; *to adopt the — of the Romans,* Romano habitu uti. *v.tr.* vestire, vestem induĕre. *v.intr.* vestiri. **dressed,** *adj.* indutus ; — *in black,* sordidatus ; — *white,* albatus. **dressing-gown,** *n.* vestis. **dressing-**

room, *n.* cubiculum. **dressing-table**, *n.* mensa.

dresser, *n.* mensa ; — *of wool*, lanarius.

drift, *v.intr.* (de)ferri. *n. tendency*, consilium, ratio ; *what is the* — ? quo spectat oratio ?

drill, *v.tr. to bore*, terebrare; *exercise*, exercēre ; terebra ; armatilibulo.

drink, *n.* potio. *v.tr.* bibĕre, haurire (*drink up*) ; — *to*, salutem propinare. **drinker**, *n.* potor, potator. **drinking-bout**, *n.* comissatio.

drip, *v.intr.* stillare.

drive, *v.tr.* agĕre, pellĕre; — *forward*, propellĕre ; — *from*, abigĕre, (ex)pellĕre ; — *hither and thither*, agitare ; *necessity* —*s*, necessitas urget, *v.intr.* (in) curru vehi ; — *at*, petĕre ; *of rain*, in alqm ferri, gestatio ; *approach*, aditus. **driver**, *n.* raedarius, auriga ; *of animals*, agitator; *donkey* —, asinarius.

drivel, *v.intr. fig.* ineptire ; delirare. *n.* ineptiae.

drizzle, *v.intr.* leniter pluĕre ; *it* —*s*, rorat.

droll, *adj.* lepidus, iocularis. *Adv.* lepide. **drollery**, *n.* lepor, iocus.

drone, *n.* fucus. **droning**, *n.* bombus.

droop, *v.tr.* demittĕre. *v.intr.* demitti; languescĕre; *fail*, affligi.

drop, *n.* gutta, stilla. *v.tr.* (de)stillare; *see* FALL. *v.tr.* demittĕre ; *cease*, dimittĕre.

dropsy, *n.* hydrops. **dropsical**, *adj.* hydropicus.

dross, *n. fig.* faex, sentina.

drought, *n.* siccitas.

drove, *n.* grex, armenta, -orum. **drover**, *n.* pecuarius, bubulcus.

drown, *v.tr.* (de)mergĕre in aquam ; *overspread*, inundare.

drowsy, *adj.* dormitans, somno gravis.

drudge, *n.* servus. *v.intr.* servire. **drudgery**, *n.* officium servile.

drug, *n.* medicamentum ; *poisonous*, venenum. *v.tr.* medicamentum dare.

drum, *n.* tympanum.

drunk, *adj.* ebrius. **drunkenness**, *n.* ebriositas. **drunkard**, *n.* ebriosus.

dry, *adj.* siccus, aridus, sitiens (*thirsty*); *fig.* exilis, aridus. *Adv.* sicce, ieiune *v.tr.* (ex)siccare ; — *tears*, abstergĕre lacrimas. *v.intr.* siccari. **dryness**, *n.* ariditas; ieiunitas.

dubious, *see* DOUBTFUL.

duck, *n.* anas. *v.tr.* (sub)mergĕre; *the head*, caput demittĕre. *v.intr.* se (sub)mergĕre.

ductile, *adj.* ductilis ; *fig.* facilis. **ductility**, *n.* facilitas.

dudgeon, *n.* ira.

due, *adj.* debitus; idoneus, dignus. *n.* debitum ; *harbour*—*s*, portorium.

duel, *n.* certamen.

dulcimer, *n.* sambuca.

---

dull, *v.tr.* hebetare ; obscurare. *adj.* hebes ; *fig.* obtusus, tardus ; aridus. *Adv.* tarde, ieiune, *etc.* **dullness**, *n.* (ingenii) tarditas; inertia.

dumb, *adj.* mutus ; *become* —, obmutescĕre. **dumbfounder**, *v.tr.* obstupefacĕre, dumbness, *n.* usu adj. *or verb.*

dun, *adj.* fuscus. *v.tr.* flagitare.

dunce, *n.* stipes, -itis, *m.*

dung, *n.* stercus. **dunghill**, *n.* sterquilinium.

dungeon, *n.* carcer, -ēris, *m.*

dupe, *n.* homo credulus. *v.tr.*, *see* DECEIVE.

duplicate, *n.* exemplum.

duplicity, *n.* fraus.

durable, *adj.* firmus. *Adv.* firme. **durability**, *n.* firmitas. **duration**, *n.* temporis spatium; *long* —, diuturnitas; *short* —, brevitas. **during**, *prep.* per, inter ; *abl. abs.* (*e.g.* Augusto imperatore).

dusk, *n.* crepusculum ; *at* —, primo vespere. **dusky**, *adj.* fuscus.

dust, *n.* pulvis. *v.tr.* detergĕre. **duster**, *n.* peniculus. **dusty**, *adj.* pulverulentus.

duty, *n.* officium, munus; *tax*, vectigal. **dutiful**, **duteous**, *adj.* pius, obediens. *Adv.* pie, obedienter. **dutifulness**, *n.* pietas, obedientia.

dwarf, *n.* nanus. **dwarfish**, *adj.* pusillus.

dwell, *v.intr.* habitare. **dwelling**, *n.* domicilium, sedes.

dwindle, *v.intr.* (de)minui.

dye, *v.tr.* tingĕre ; inficĕre. *n.* color. **dyer**, *n.* infector.

dyspepsia, *n.* cruditas.

E

each, *adj. and pron.* quisque, uterque (*of two*) ; — *other*, alii alios, *or* inter se ; *one each*, singuli, *see* EVERY.

eager, *adj.* cupidus, studiosus; acer. *Adv.* cupide, studiose, acriter. **eagerness**, *n.* cupiditas, studium, ardor.

eagle, *n.* aquila.

ear, *n.* auris ; *o corn*, spica, arista.

earrings, *n.* inaures, -ium, *f.*

early, *adj.* matutinus (*in the morning*), maturus ; *too* —, immaturus ; *from* — *youth*, a puero. *Adv.* mane, primā luce.

earn, *v.tr.* merēri. **earnings**, *n.* quaestus.

earnest, *adj.* gravis. *Adv.* serio, graviter. **earnestness**, *n.* diligentia; gravitas.

earth, *n.* terra, solum; *the globe*, orbis terrarum, tellus. **earthen**, *adj.* terrenus. **earthenware**, *n.* fictilia -ium. **earthly**,

adj. terrestris ; — *goods,* res externae ; — *happiness,* voluptas (humana).
earthquake, *n.* terrae motus. **earth-work,** *n.* agger.
ease, tranquillitas, otium ; *to be at* —, quiescēre ; *at* —, tranquillo animo ; *readiness,* facilitas. *v.tr.* exonerare, expedire. **easiness,** *n.* facilitas. **easy,** *adj.* facilis, expeditus ; — *circumstances,* res secundae ; *of temper,* facilis ; *of manners,* comis. *Adv.* facile, nullo negotio ; indulgenter ; comiter.
east, *n.* oriens, orientis solis partes, -ium. **eastward, eastern, easterly,** *adj.* in orientem spectans ; *(as adverb)* ad orientem versus ; — *nations,* Asiatici.
eat, *v.tr.* edēre, vesci ; *to* — *away* (e)rodēre. *v.intr. to* — *well* = *taste,* iucunde sapēre. **eatable,** *adj.* esculentus. **eatables,** *n.* cibus, cibi, esca; victus (*living, victuals*). **eating-house,** *n.* popina.
eavesdropper, *n.* qui alqd subauscultat.
ebb, *n.* aestūs decessus. *v.intr.* recedēre; — *and flow,* affluēre et remeare.
ebony, *n.* (h)ebĕnus, *f.*
ebullition, *n. use* effervescĕre; *fig.* aestus.
eccentric, *adj.* inusitatus. **eccentricity,** *n.* quod inusitatum est, *etc.*
ecclesiastical, *adj.* * ecclesiasticus.
echo, *n.* imago vocis ; *to give an* —, vocem reddĕre.
eclat, *n.* laus, splendor.
eclipse, *n.* obscuratio (solis. *etc.*). *v.tr.* obscurare; *fig.* alqm superare.
economy, *n.* rei familiaris administratio; *political* —, rei publicae administratio; *frugality,* parsimonia. **economical,** *adj.* parcus. *Adv.* parce. **economist,** *n.* qui rem suam bene administrat.
ecstasy, *n.* secessus mentis et animi a corpore, furor ; summa voluptas. **ecstatic,** *adj.* mente incitatus. *Adv.* per furorem.
eddy, *n.* vertex, vorago.
edge, *n.* acies, labrum (*of a cup, etc.*); margo, ora.
edible, *adj.* esculentus.
edict, *n.* decretum, consultum, iussum.
edify, *v.tr.* erudire, docēre. **edifying,** *adj.* ad bonos mores docendos aptus.
edit, *v.tr.* librum edēre. **editor,** *n.* editor. **edition,** *n.* editio.
educate, *v.tr.* docēre, educare. **education,** *n.* educatio, disciplina ; *of good* —, homo (e)doctus ; *without* —, humanitatis expers. **educator,** *n.* magister, praeceptor. **educational,** *adj.* ad disciplinam, *etc.*, pertinens.
eel, *n.* anguilla.
efface, *v.tr.* delēre, (e)radēre.
effect, *n.* effectus, eventus; *to have great* —, multum valēre; *without* —, frustra; *to this* —, his verbis; *in* —, re (verā); —*s,* res, rerum. *v.tr.* efficĕre. **effective, effectual,** *adj.* valens, *or by verb*

qui, *etc.*, efficit. *Adv.* efficienter, prospere. **efficacy,** *n.* efficientia.
effeminate, *adj.* mollis. *Adv.* molliter. **effeminacy,** *n.* mollitia.
effervesce, *v.intr.* effervescĕre.
effete, *adj.* effetus, obsoletus.
effigy, *n.* effigies, imago.
effort, *n.* labor, conatus ; *to make an* —, operam dare.
effrontery, *n.* impudentia, os.
effulgence, *n.* splendor, fulgor.
egg, *n.* ovum. **egg-shell,** *n.* ovi putamen.
egoism, *n.* sui ostentatio ; sui amor. **egoist,** *n.* qui sibi soli studet. **egoistical,** *adj. use n.*
egregious, *adj.* maximus, summus. *Adv.* maxime.
egress, *n.* egressus, exitus.
eider-down, *n.* plumae mollissimae.
eight, *adj.* octo ; octoni (*eight each*). **eighteen,** *adj.* duodeviginti. **eighteenth,** *adj.* duodevicesimus. **eighty,** *adj.* octoginta, octogeni (— *each*). **eightieth,** *adj.* octogesimus.
either, *pron.* alteruter, utervis, uterlibet; *not* —, neuter. *conj. either ... or,* aut ... aut, vel ... vel, sive (seu) ... sive (seu).
ejaculate, *v.tr.* voces interruptas mittĕre. **ejaculation,** *n.* voces interruptae.
eject, *v.tr.* eicĕre. **ejection,** *n.* expulsio; *legal,* deiectio.
eke, *v.tr. to* — *out,* parcĕre.
elaborate, *v.tr.* perficĕre. *adj.* exquisitus. *Adv.* exquisite. **elaboration,** *n. use the verb.*
elapse, *v.intr.* transire.
elastic, *adj.* qui (quae, quod) produci potest.
elated, *adj.* elatus. **elation,** *n.* gaudium, superbia.
elbow, *n.* cubitum.
elder, *adj.* (natu) maior. **elderly,** *adj.* aetate provectus.
elect, *v.tr.* creare. *adj.* designatus. **election,** *n.* electio; *political,* comitia, -orum. **elective,** *adj.* suffragiis creatus. **elector,** *n.* qui ius suffragii habet, suffragator.
elegant, *adj.* elegans, nitidus. *Adv.* eleganter, nitide. **elegance,** *n.* elegantia, urbanitas.
elegy, *n.* elegia.
element, *n.* elementum, natura ; —*s,* principia rerum. **elementary,** *adj.* primus.
elephant, *n.* elephantus (elephas).
elevate, *v.tr.* (at)tollĕre, extollĕre. **elevated,** *adj.* editus, altus. **elevation,** *n. fig.* elatio ; *rising ground,* locus superior.
eleven, *adj.* undecim ; — *each,* undēni; — *times,* undecie(n)s. **eleventh,** *adj.* undecimus.
elicit, *v.tr.* elicĕre, evocare.

eligible, *adj.* dignus.

elk, *n.* alces, -is, *f.*

ell, *n.* ulna, cubitum.

elm, *n.* ulmus, *f.*; *of an* —, ulmeus.

elocution, *n.* (e)locutio, pronuntiatio.

elongate, *v.tr., see* LENGTHEN.

elope, *v.intr.* effugĕre. **elopement,** *n.* fuga.

eloquence, *n.* facundia. **eloquent,** *adj.* facundus. *Adv.* facunde.

else, *adj.* alius. *adv.* praeterea. *prep., e.g. nothing* —, praeter hoc nihil; *otherwise,* aliter; — *where,* alibi.

elucidate, *v.tr., see* EXPLAIN.

elude, *v.intr.* effugĕre, (e)vitare. **elusive,** *adj.* fallax. *Adv.* fallaciter.

Elysium, *n.* Elysium. **Elysian,** *adj.* Elysius.

emaciate, *v.tr.* attenuare. **emaciated,** *adj.* macrotus. **emaciation,** *n.* macies.

emanate, *v.intr.* emanare.

emancipate, *v.tr.* liberare; *slaves, etc.,* manumittĕre. **emancipation,** *n.* liberatio ; *of slaves,* manumissio. **emancipator,** *n.* liberator.

embalm, *v.tr.* condire.

embank, *v.tr.* flumen coërcēre. **embankment,** *n.* agger, moles.

embark, *v.tr.* imponĕre in navem. *v.intr.* conscendĕre (navem).

embarrass, *v.tr.* (con)turbare; impedire. **embarrassed,** *adj.* impeditus. **embarrassing,** *adj.* difficilis. **embarrassment,** *n.* perturbatio ; *pecuniary* —, angustiae.

embassy, *n. office,* legatio ; *persons,* legatio, legati.

embellish, *v.tr.* (ad)ornare. **embellishment,** *n.* decus.

embers, *n.* cinis, favilla.

embezzle, *v.tr.* avertĕre, retinēre ac supprimĕre. **embezzlement,** *n.* peculatus. **embezzler,** *n.* pecuniae aversor.

embitter, *v.tr.* exacerbare. **embittered,** *adj.* infestus.

emblem, *n.* imago, signum. **emblematic,** *adj.* aliqd significans.

embody, *v.tr.* adiungĕre, inserĕre ; *to exclude ;* — *in a society,* in societatem a(d)scribĕre.

embolden, *v.tr.* confirmare.

emboss, *v.tr.* caelare. **embossed,** *adj.* caelatus.

embrace, *v.tr.* amplecti; *contain,* comprehendĕre ; — *an opinion,* sententiae assentiri. *n.* amplexus.

embroider, *v.tr.* (acu) pingĕre. **embroidery,** *n.* ars acu pingendi ; *a piece of* —, opus acu pictum.

embroil, *v.tr.* implicare, conturbare.

embryo, *n.* partus, ūs.

emendation, *n.* emendatio (et correctio).

emerald, *n.* smaragdus; *of* —, smaragdinus.

emerge, *v.intr.* emergĕre. **emergency,** *n.* discrimen.

---

emigrant, *n.* extorris, advena. **emigrate,** *v.intr.* (e)migrare. **emigration,** *n.* (e)migratio.

eminent, *adj.* insignis, clarus. *Adv.* egregie, ex omnibus optimus. **eminence,** *n.* locus editus, clivus; *moral* —, praestantia; *of rank,* amplissimus gradus.

emissary, *n.* emissarius.

emit, *v.tr.* (e)mittĕre.

emolument, *n.* emolumentum, lucrum.

emotion, *n.* animi motus.

emperor, *n.* imperator, princeps. **empress,** *n.* domina.

emphasis, *n.* vis ; *with* —, cum vi. **emphatic,** *adj.* gravis, vehemens. *Adv.* graviter, vehementer.

empire, *n.* imperium, potestas, regnum.

empirical, *adj.* in usu tantum et experimentis positus.

employ, *v.tr.* occupare, occupatum tenēre ; uti; *to spend in,* consumĕre. **employment,** *n.* usus, occupatio ; *business,* negotium, studium. **employer,** *n.* qui operas conducit.

empower, *v.tr.* potestatem facĕre, mandare ; *to be empowered,* mandata habēre.

empty, *adj.* inanis, vacuus; *fig.* inanis, omnium rerum rudis (*e.g. of learning*). *v.tr.* vacuefacĕre, exhaurire ; — *itself (of a river),* se effundĕre. **emptiness,** *n.* inanitas, vacuitas ; *fig.* inanitas, vanitas.

empyrean, *n.* caelum.

emulate, *v.tr.* aemulari. **emulation,** *n.* certamen, aemulatio. **emulator,** *n.* aemulus. **emulous,** *adj.* aemulus. *Adv.* certatim.

enable, *v.tr.* facultatem dare.

enact, *v.tr.* sancire, iubēre; constituĕre. **enactment,** *n.* lex, plebiscitum, senatus-consultum.

enamoured, *adj., see* LOVE.

encamp, *v.intr.* castra ponĕre.

enchant, *v.tr.* (ef)fascinare, incantare; *fig.* capere, permulcēre. **enchantment,** *n.* (ef)fascinatio, carmen.

encircle, *v.tr., see* ENCLOSE.

enclose, *v.tr.* includĕre, cingĕre. **enclosure,** *n.* inclusio; *place,* saeptum.

encomium, *n.* laus, laudatio.

encompass, *v.tr., see* ENCLOSE.

encore, *v.tr.* revocare. **encore !** *interj.* revoco.

encounter, *n.* concursus. *v.tr.* inter se concurrĕre; incidĕre in, convenire.

encourage, *v.tr.* cohortari, (con)firmare. **encouragement,** *n.* confirmatio, cohortatio.

encroach, *v.intr.* invadĕre. **encroachment,** *n.* violatio.

encumber, *v.tr.* onerare, impedire. **encumbrance,** *n.* onus, impedimentum.

end, *n.* finis, exitus ; consilium, propositum ; *at the* —, in extremo. *v.intr.* finem habēre. *v.tr.* finire. **ending**

n. finis, terminatio, exitus. **endless,** *adj.* perpetuus, aeternus. *Adv.* perpetuo. **endlessness,** *n.* perpetuitas.

endanger, *v.tr.* in discrimen adducĕre.

endearments, *n.* blanditiae.

endeavour, *n.* conatus, studium ; ambitio. *v.intr.* (e)niti, operam dare ut, studĕre, conari (*with infin.*).

endorse, *v.tr.* syngrapham inscribĕre.

endow, *v.tr.* donare. **endowed,** *adj.* praeditus.

endure, *v.tr., see* ENDOW.

endure, *v.tr.* ferre, pati. **endurance,** *n.* toleratio. **endurable,** *adj.* tolerabilis ; *to make* —, mitigare. **enduring,** *adj.* perpetuus.

enemy, *n.* hostis, inimicus (*private*).

energy, *n.* vis, vigor, virtus. **energetic,** *adj.* acer, impiger. *Adv.* acriter.

enervate, *v.tr.* enervare, frangĕre. **enervation,** *n.* debilitatio.

enfeeble, *v.tr., see* ENERVATE.

enforce, *v.tr. an argument,* confirmare; vim praebĕre.

enfranchise, *v.tr.* civitatem dare. **enfranchisement,** *n.* civitas.

engage, *v.tr. to fight with,* confligĕre cum alqo ; *to bind,* obligare ; *to hire,* conducĕre; *undertake,* spondĕre, suscipĕre. **engaged,** *adj.* occupatus; *in marriage,* sponsus. **engagement,** *battle,* pugna, proelium; *pledge,* sponsio; *to keep an* —, fidem servare. **engaging,** *adj.* suavis. *Adv.* suaviter.

engender, *v.tr.* gignĕre; *see* CAUSE.

engine, *n.* machina, tormentum.

engrave, *v.tr.* scalpĕre. **engraving,** *n.* scalptura. **engraver,** *n.* scalptor.

engross, *v.tr.* occupare.

engulf, *v.tr.* (de)vorare.

enhance, *v.tr.* augĕre. **enhancement,** *n.* amplificatio.

enigma, *n.* aenigma, ambages. **enigmatical,** *adj.* obscurus. *Adv.* ambigue, per ambages.

enjoin, *v.tr., see* COMMAND.

enjoy, *v.tr.* frui, gaudĕre. **enjoyment,** *n.* gaudium, fructus.

enlarge, *v.tr.* amplificare, augĕre. **enlargement,** *n.* amplificatio.

enlighten, *v.tr.* illustrare; docĕre. **enlightenment,** *n.* humanitas.

enlist, *v.tr.* milites conscribĕre. *v.intr.* nomen dare.

enliven, *v.tr.* alqm (ex)hilarare.

enmity, *n.* inimicitia.

ennoble, *v.tr.* nobilium ordini a(d)scribĕre; (*in Roman sense*) transitio fit a plebe ad patricios ; *fig.* illustrare.

ennui, *n.* taedium.

enormous, *adj.* ingens, immanis. *Adv.* praeter modum, *or by superl. of adj.* **enormity,** *n.* res atrox, scelus.

enough, *adj.* satis; *more than* — satis superque.

enquire, *v.tr., see* ASK. **enquiry,** *n., see* QUESTION; *legal,* quaestio.

enrage, *v.tr.* exasperare, lacessĕre.

enrapture, *v.tr.* oblectare, capĕre.

enrich, *v.tr.* locupletare.

enroll, *v.tr.* inscribĕre, consignare.

ensign, *n.* signum, vexillum ; *officer,* signifer, vexillarius.

enslave, *v.tr.* in servitutem redigĕre. **enslaved,** *adj. to be* —, (in)servire.

ensnare, *v.tr.* laqueo capĕre; *fig.* capĕre.

entail, *v.tr.* terram heredi ita addicĕre ut nunquam alienari possit ; *fig., see* CAUSE.

entanglement, *n.* implicatio.

enter, *v.intr.* introire, ingredi; — *upon,* suscipĕre ; — *public life,* ad rempublicam accedĕre. *v.tr.* — *accounts,* in tabulas referre. **entrance,** *n. act of* — ingressio; aditus, ianua, limen. **entry,** — *in accounts,* nomen (referre).

enterprise, *n.* inceptum, conatus. **enterprising,** *adj.* acer, audax.

entertain, *v.tr.* habĕre ; *to amuse,* delectare ; (*hospitality*) hospitio accipĕre. **entertainer,** *n.* hospes. **entertainment,** *n.* hospitium ; *banquet,* epulae ; *see* AMUSEMENT. **entertaining,** *adj., see* AMUSING.

enthusiasm, *n.* ardor, furor divinus. **enthusiast,** *n. religious* —, homo fanaticus; alci deditus. **enthusiastic,** *adj.* ardens. *Adv.* ardenter.

entice, *v.tr.* allicĕre, pellicĕre. **enticement,** *n.* illecebrae. **enticing,** *adj.* blandus. *Adv.* blande.

entire, *adj.* totus, solidus. *Adv.* omnino. **entireness, entirety,** *n. by* totus.

entitle, *v.tr.* inscribĕre (*a writing*) ; ius faciendi dare; *I am entitled to,* facĕre possum.

entomb, *v.tr.* humare.

entrails, *n.* intestina, -orum, viscera, -um.

entreat, *v.tr.* precari, orare, petĕre.

entrust, *v.tr.* (con)credĕre, mandare.

entwine, *v.tr.* innectĕre.

enumerate, *v.tr.* numerare.

enunciate, *v.tr.* edicĕre, enuntiare. **enunciation,** *n.* enuntiatio.

envelop, *v.tr.* involvĕre, obducĕre. **envelope,** *n.* involucrum.

envenom, *v.tr.* veneno imbuĕre ; *fig.* exacerbare. **envenomed,** *adj., see* SPITEFUL.

environ, *v.tr.* circumdare. **environs,** *n.* quae circum alqm locum sunt.

envoy, *n.* legatus.

envy, *n.* invidia. *v.tr.* invidĕre. **enviable,** *adj.* fortunatus, beatus. **envious,** *adj.* invidus, malignus. *Adv.* cum invidiā, maligne.

ephemeral, *adj.* unius diei, brevis.

epic, *adj.* — *poem,* epos (*nom. and accus. sing. only*).

Epicurean, *n.* Epicūrēus; homo luxuriosus.

epidemic, *adj. and n.* morbus, pestilentia.

epigram, *n.* epigramma. epigrammatic, *adj.* salsus.

epilepsy, *n.* morbus comitialis.

epilogue, *n.* epilŏgus.

episode, *n.* excursus.

epistle, *n.* epistula. epistolary, *adj.* per litt(v)eras.

epitaph, *n.* titulus, elogium.

epitome, *n.* epitome.

epoch, *n.* aetas, saeculum.

equal, *adj.* aequus, similis. *Adv.* aeque, pariter. *n.* par. *v.tr.* (ad)aequare.

equality, *n.* aequalitas. equable, *adj.* aequus, constans. *Adv.* aequo animo, aequaliter. equability, *n.* aequus animus. equalize, *v.tr.* (ex)aequare.

equanimity, *n.* aequus animus.

equestrian, *adj.* equester. *n.* eques.

equidistant, *adj.* pari intervallo.

equilateral, *adj.* aequis lateribus.

equilibrium, *n.* aequilibrium.

equinox, *n.* aequinoctium. equinoctial, *adj.* aequinoctialis.

equip, *v.tr.* armare, ornare. equipment, *n.* arma, -orum, armatura.

equipoise, *n., see* EQUILIBRIUM.

equitable, *adj.* aequus, iustus. equity, *n.* aequitas.

equivalent, *adj., see* EQUAL.

equivocal, *adj.* ambiguus. equivocation, *n.* ambiguitas. equivocate, *v.intr.* tergiversari.

eradicate, *v.tr.* ex(s)tirpare. eradication, *n.* excidium.

erase, *v.tr.* delēre. erasure, *n.* litura.

ere, *adv.* priusquam, antequam.

erect, *adj.* (e)rectus. *v.tr.* erigĕre; aedificare. erection, *n.* aedificatio; *building,* aedificium.

err, *v.intr.* errare, peccare. error, *n.* error, erratum; peccatum. erratic, *adj.* inconstans, erroneus. erroneous, *adj.* falsus. *Adv.* falso. erroneousness, *n., see* ERROR.

errand, *n.* mandatum.

erst, *adv.* quondam, olim.

erudite, *adj.* doctus. erudition, *n.* doctrina.

eruption, *n.* eruptio.

escape, *v.tr. and intr.* fugĕre, evadĕre. *n.* fuga.

escarpment, *n.* vallum.

eschew, *v.tr.* vitare.

escort, *n.* comitatus; *under someone's* —, aliquo comitante. *v.tr.* comitari.

esoteric, *adj.* arcanus, occultus.

especial, *adj.* praecipuus, maximus. *Adv.* praesertim, maxime.

esplanade, *n.* ambulatio.

espouse, *v.tr., see* MARRY.

essay, *v.tr.* conari. *n.* experimentum, conatus; *treatise,* libellus. essayist, *n.* scriptor.

essence, *n.* natura, vis. essential, *adj.*

versus, praecipuus; necessarius. *Adv.* vere, praecipue, necessario.

establish, *v.tr.* statuere, constituĕre; confirmare. establishment, *n.* constitutio; *household,* familia.

estate, *n.* *condition,* status, res, sors; *property,* res, praedium, ager.

esteem, *n.* aestimatio; observantia. *v.tr.* aestimare, putare; *to be esteemed,* magni haberi. estimable, *adj.* dignus, bonus.

estimate, *n.* aestimatio, iudicium. *v.tr.* aestimare, censēre. estimation, *n., see* ESTEEM.

estrange, *v.tr.* (ab)alienare. estrangement, *n.* alienatio.

estuary, *n.* aestuarium.

eternal, *adj.* aeternus, perpetuus; *enmity,* odium inexplabile. *Adv.* in aeternum, perpetuo. eternity, *n.* aeternitas.

ether, *n.* aether. ethereal, *adj.* aetherius.

ethics, *n.* de moribus, ethice. ethical, *adj.* de moribus.

etiquette, *n.* mos, usus.

eulogy, *n.* laudatio, laus. eulogist, *n.* laudator. eulogize, *v.tr.* laudare.

euphemism, *n.,* euphemistic, *adj.* ut bona de his loquar.

euphony, *n.* sonus dulcis.

evacuate, *v.tr.* (de)relinquĕre, discedĕre.

evade, *v.tr.* fugere; effugĕre. evasion, *n.* ambages, tergiversatio. evasive, *adj.* ambiguus. *Adv.* ambigue.

evaporate, *v.tr.* (e)vaporare, exhalare. *v.intr.* (e)vaporari, exhalari. evaporation, *n.* (e)vaporatio, exhalatio.

even, *adj.* aequus, planus; *numbers,* par. *Adv.* aequaliter, pariter. evenness, *n.* aequalitas; *of temper,* aequus animus.

even, *adv.* etiam, vel, ipse; *not* —, ne ... quidem; — *now,* iam nunc.

evening, *n.* vesper; *towards* —, ad (sub) vesperum; *in the* —, vesperi; *the* — *before,* pridie vesperi; *good* — I salve; *adj.* vespertinus; — *star,* Hesperus, Vesper.

event, *n.* eventus; res gesta), eventful, *adj.* memorabilis, maximi momenti.

ever, *adv.* always, semper; umquam; *if* —, si quando; *for* —, in aeternum. everlasting, *adj., see* ETERNAL.

every, *adj.* quisque, omnis; — *one, each separately,* unusquisque; — *day,* singulis diebus; — *one,* nemo non; — *where,* ubique.

evict, *v.tr.* (ex)pellĕre, detrudĕre.

evident, *adj.* manifestus; *it is* —, constat, certum est. *Adv.* manifeste. evidence, *n.* *legal,* testimonium; argumentum, *or by verb* probare.

evil, *adj.* malus, maleficus. *n.* malum. evil-doer, *n.* maleficus. evil-speaking, *adj.* maledicus.

evince, *v.tr.* ostendĕre, probare.

evoke, *v.tr.* evocare, excitare.

evolve, *v.tr.* evolvĕre, explicare. **evolution,** *n. of soldiers,* decursus ; *rerum* progressio.

ewe, *n.* ovis femina.

ewer, *n.* urceus, hydria, urna.

exact, *adj.* exactus, accuratus. *v.tr.* exigĕre, extorquĕre. *Adv.* accurate ; — *so,* ita plane. **exacting,** *adj.* rapax, exaction, *n.* exactio. **exactitude, exactness,** *n.* diligentia.

exaggerate, *v.tr.* verbis exaggerare, verbis augĕre. **exaggeration,** *n.* amplificatio.

exalt, *v.tr.* augĕre, extollĕre. **exaltation,** *n.* dignitatis accessio. **exalted,** *adj.* altus ; *of — position,* gradu amplissimo.

examine, *v.tr.* explorare, (per)scrutari. **examination,** *n.* scrutatio, inquisitio. **examiner,** *n.* investigator.

example, *n.* exemplum.

exasperate, *v.tr.* exasperare.

excavate, *v.tr.* effodĕre. **excavation,** *n.* cavum.

exceed, *v.tr.* transgredi, transire fines. **excess,** *n.* licentia. **excessive,** *adj.* nimius, immoderatus. *Adv.* nimis, immoderate.

excel, *v.tr.* excellĕre, (ex)superare, praestare. **excellent,** *adj.* egregius, optimus. *Adv.* excellenter, optime. **excellence,** *n.* praestantia.

except, *v.tr.* excipĕre, excludĕre ; *not one excepted,* ad unum omnes. *prep.* praeter, nisi *after a neg.* **exception,** *n.* exceptio. **exceptional,** *adj.* rarus. *Adv.* praeter modum.

exchange, *v.tr.* (per)mutare ; *of money,* collybus ; *place of —,* forum, mensa publica.

exchequer, *n.* aerarium, fiscus.

excite, *v.tr.* excitare, (com)movĕre. **excitable,** *adj.* fervidus. **excited,** *adj.* commotus. **excitement,** *n.* commotio.

exclaim, *v.tr.* exclamare.

exclude, *v.tr.* excludĕre. **exclusion,** *n.* exclusio, *or verb.* **exclusive,** *adj.* (*property*) proprius. *Adv.* by *adj.* proprius. **exclusiveness,** *n.* rari aditus esse.

excrescence, *n.* tuber.

excruciating, *adj.* acerbissimus.

exculpate, *v.tr.* excusare. **exculpation,** *n.* excusatio, purgatio.

excursion, *n.* iter.

excuse, *v.tr. ask pardon,* veniam petĕre, rogare ; *grant pardon,* veniam dare ; ignoscĕre. *n.* excusatio; venia. **excusable,** *adj.* cui ignosci potest.

execrate, *v.tr.* exsecrari, detestari. **execrable,** *adj., see* ABOMINABLE.

execute, *v.tr.* persequi ; — *a command,* (imperium) officĕre ; *punishment,* poenam capĕre, necare. **execution,** *n.* effectio, *or by verb ;* supplicium. **executive,** *n. power,* administratio.

exegesis, *n.* interpretatio.

exemplary, *adj., see* EXCELLENT ; — *punishment,* exemplum severitatis.

exempt, *v.tr.* excipĕre. *adj.* immunis, solutus ; (*a soldier*), emeritus. **exemption,** *n.* immunitas.

exercise, *n.* exercĕre, facĕre. *n.* exercitatio; thema; *task,* pensum.

exert, *v.tr.* contendĕre ; — *yourself,* (con)niti. **exertion,** *n.* contentio, conatus, -ūs.

exhale, *v.tr.* exhalare. **exhalation,** *n.* exhalatio.

exhaust, *v.tr.* exhaurire. **exhausted,** *adj., see* WEARY. **exhaustion,** *n., see* FATIGUE.

exhibit, *v.tr.* proponĕre, praebĕre. **exhibition,** *n. by verb; show,* spectaculum, ludi.

exhilarate, *v.tr.* (ex)hilarare. **exhilaration,** *n.* hilaritas, gaudium.

exhort, *v.tr.* hortari.

exigence, *n.* necessitas, angustiae.

exile, *n.* ex(s)ilium ; *person,* exsul. *v.tr.* eicĕre, (ex)pellĕre.

exist, *v.intr.* ex(s)istĕre, esse. **existence,** *n. use* esse.

exit, *n.* exitus; *way out,* exitus, ianua.

exonerate, *v.tr., see* EXCULPATE.

exorbitant, *adj.* immoderatus. *Adv.* immoderate.

exordium, *n.* exordium.

exotic, *adj.* peregrinus, externus.

expand, *v.tr., see* SPREAD. **expanse,** *n.* spatium.

expatiate, *v.tr.* pluribus (verbis) dicĕre.

expatriate, *v.tr., see* BANISH.

expect, *v.tr.* ex(s)pectare ; sperare. **expectant,** *adj. use* spes. **expectation,** *n.* spes.

expectorate, *v.tr.* exscreare, exspuĕre.

expedient, *adj.* utilis ; *it is —,* expedit. *n.* ratio. **expediency,** *n.* utilitas.

expedite, *v.tr.* expedire. **expedition,** *n. speed,* celeritas; *military —,* expeditio. **expeditious,** *adj.* celer. *Adv.* celeriter.

expel, *v.tr.* (ex)pellĕre. **expulsion,** *n.* exactio, expulsio.

expend, *v.tr.* expendĕre. **expense,** *n.* inpensa. **expensive,** *adj.* sumptuosus, carus. *Adv.* sumptuose, pretiose. **expenditure,** *n.* sumptus.

experience, *n.* usus, experientia ; *I write from —,* expertus scribo quod scribo. *v.tr.* experiri, experientiā discĕre. **experienced,** *adj.* (usu) peritus, exercitatus. **experiment,** *n.* experimentum.

expert, *adj. & n.* aptus, peritus. **expertness,** *n.* sol(l)ertia.

expiate, *v.tr.* luĕre, poenas dare. **expiation,** *n.* satisfactio, piaculum. **expiatory,** *adj.* piacularis.

expire, *v.intr., see* DIE. **expiration,** *n. by abl. abs* (*e.g.* anno exeunte).

explain, *v.tr.* explicare, interpretari.

explanation, n. explicatio, interpretatio. **explanatory,** adj. use verb.
explicit, adj. definitus. Adv. definite.
explode, v.intr. (di)rumpi. v.tr. (di)rumpĕre. **explosion,** n. †fragor.
export, v.tr. exportare. **exportation,** n. exportatio. **exports,** n. merces (quae exportantur)
expose, v.tr. exponĕre ; — to anything, opponĕre ; to lay open, detegĕre ; nudare. **exposition,** n. expositio. **exposure,** n. by verb.
expound, v.tr., see EXPLAIN.
express, v.tr. exprimĕre, verbis consequi ; — oneself, dicĕre. adj., see EXACT ; quick, celer. Adv. his ipsis verbis. **expression,** n. verbum, dictum ; of the features, etc., vultus. **expressive,** adj. significans, gravis. Adv. significanter, diserte.
expunge, v.tr. delēre.
expurgate, v.tr. (ex)purgare. **expurgation,** n. (ex)purgatio.
exquisite, adj. exquisitus, venustus. Adv. exquisite, venuste.
extant, adj., to be —, exstare.
extemporary, adj. subitus ; power of — speaking, ex tempore dicendi facultas.
extend, v.tr. extendĕre, augēre. v.intr. patēre, extendi, etc. **extension,** n. porrectio (e.g. digitorum), prolatio. **extensive,** adj. magnus, latus. Adv. late.
extent, n. ambitus, spatium.
extenuate, v.tr. attenuare ; levare. **extenuation,** n. levatio.
exterior, adj., see EXTERNAL. n. facies, forma.
exterminate, v.tr. ad unum interficĕre, ex(s)tirpare.
external, adj. externus, exterior. Adv. extrinsecus.
extinct, adj. exstinctus, obsoletus.
extinguish, v.tr. ex(s)tinguĕre, delēre.
extirpate, v.tr. ex(s)tirpare.
extol, v.tr. augēre, extollĕre.
extort, v.tr. exprimĕre, extorquēre. **extortion,** n. res repetundae. **extortionate,** adj. rapax, avarus. Adv. avare. **extortioner,** n. immodici fenoris exactor.
extra, adv. praeterea.
extract, v.tr. extrahĕre ; to make an extract, excerpĕre ; to press out, exprimĕre. n. excerptio ; — of a plant, etc., quod expressum est. **extraction,** n. origin, n. origo, genus.
extraneous, adj., see EXTERNAL.
extraordinary, adj. insolitus, mirus. Adv. extra ordinem.
extravagant, adj. prodigus ; immoderatus. Adv. prodige, immoderate. **extravagance,** n. sumptus ; immoderatio.
extreme, adj. extremus, ultimus, summus ; to go to —s, modum excedĕre. Adv. summe, quam maxime, or by superl. (e. : — good, optimus). **extremity,** n.

extremus, with n.; top, vertex ; distress, etc., extrema, -orum, pl.
extricate, v.tr., see RELEASE.
exuberant, adj. luxuriosus, laetus ; of style, redundans. Adv. ubertim. **exuberance,** n. ubertas.
exude, v.intr. (ex)sudare.
exult, v.intr. exsultare, laetari. **exultant,** adj. laetus. Adv. laete. **exultation,** n. laetatio.
eye, n. oculus. v.tr. a(d)spicĕre. **eyeball,** n. pupula. **eyebrow,** n. supercilium. **eyelash,** n. pili pupillas tegentes. **eyelid,** n. palpebra (usu. pl.). **eyesight,** n. acies, oculus. **eyesore,** n. res foeda. **eyewitness,** n. testis.

F

fable, n. fabula. **fabulous,** adj. fabulosus, fictus.
fabric, n. fabrica ; of weavers, textum, textile ; structure, aedificium. **fabricate,** v.tr. fabricari. **fabricator,** n. artifex ; auctor.
face, n. facies, vultus ; os, oris ; — to —, coram. v.tr. and intr. ad alqd spectare ; encounter, obviam ire ; — about, signa convertĕre. **facial,** adj. quod ad faciem pertinet.
facetious, adj. iocosus, facetus. Adv. iocose, facete. **facetiousness,** n. lepos, facetiae.
facilitate, v.tr. expedire. **facility,** n. facilitas ; with —, facile, nullo negotio.
facing, prep. contra.
facsimile, n. descriptio imagoque.
fact, n. res, factum.
faction, n. factio. **factious,** adj. factiosus. Adv. seditiose. **factiousness,** n. factio.
factitious, adj., see FALSE.
factory, n. fabrica, officina.
faculty, n. ingenium ; sol(l)ertia, facultas.
fade, v.intr. evanescĕre. **faded,** adj., marcidus. **fading,** n. coloris mutatio. Adj. caducus.
fagot, n. fascis, sarmenta, -orum.
fail, v.intr. of duty, delinquĕre ; to fall short, deesse, deficĕre ; be bankrupt, foro cedĕre ; without —, certo, omnino. **failing,** n. peccatum, delictum. **failure,** n. defectio.
fain, adv. libenter (lub-), volens.
faint, adj. languidus. v.intr. swoon, †collabi ; be weary, languēre. **fainthearted,** adj. timidus. **faintness,** n. languor.
fair, adj. beautiful, pulcher, venustus; weather, serenus ; morally, aequus. Adv. aeque. n. mercatus. **fairness,** n. pulchritudo, venustas ; serenitas ; aequitas.

fairy, n. nympha; dryas; faunus.
faith, n. fidelitas, pietas; *belief,* fides ; *to have — in,* alci credĕre. **faithful,** *adj.* fidelis. *Adv.* fideliter. **faithfulness,** n. fidelitas, fides. **faithless,** *adj.* perfidus. *Adv.* perfide. **faithlessness,** n. perfidia, infidelitas.
fall, *v.intr.* cadĕre; *to — away, desert,* deficĕre; *to — out, disagree,* dissentire ; *to sink,* delabi ; *at the feet of,* se ad pedes alcis proicĕre. n. casus, lapsus; ruina, excidium; *lessening,* deminutio.
fallacy, n. fallacia, vitium. **fallacious,** *adj.* fallax. *Adv.* fallaciter, falso.
fallow, *adj. the field lies —,* ager cessat. **fallow soil,** n. novalia.
false, *adj.* falsus, suppositus *(forged)*; fallax, mendax; *treacherous,* perfidus. *Adv.* falso, fallaciter, perfide. **falsehood,** n. mendacium. **falseness,** n. fallacia, dolus. **falsify,** *v.tr.* vitiare, corrumpĕre. **falsification,** n. *use verb.*
falter, *v.intr.* haesitare, titubare. *Adv.* timide, titubanter.
fame, n. laus, gloria. **famous,** *adj.* (prae)clarus. *Adv.* (prae)clare, bene. (= *well*).
familiar, *adj.* familiaris ; *acquainted with,* sciens, peritus ; *— with a language,* linguam intellegĕre. *Adv.* familiariter. **familiarity,** n. familiaritas.
family, n. familia, domus; *clan,* gens; *of good —,* nobilis. *adj.* privatus.
famine, n. fames. **famish,** *v.tr.* fame conficĕre. *v.intr.* fame mori.
fan, n. *agricultural,* vannus; *of a lady,* flabellum.
fanatic, *adj.* fanaticus.
fancy, n. opinio (falsa) ; cogitatio ; *a mere —,* somnium ; *according to —,* ex libidine. *v.tr.* opinari, fingĕre. **fanciful,** *adj. imaginative,* summo ingenio praeditus; morosus *(captious)*. *Adv.* morose.
fang, n. dens. **fanged,** *adj.* dentatus. **fangless,** *adj.* sine dentibus.
far, *adv.* procul, longe *(from afar),* eminus ; *to be —,* procul abesse ; *— be it !* di meliora (dent); *so —,* hactenus. **farther,** *adv.* longius, ultra.
farce, n. mimus, fabula Atellana. **farcical,** *adj.* mimicus, ridiculus. *Adv.* ridicule.
fare, *v.intr.* se habĕre; *to — well,* bene valēre ; laute vivēre. n. victus ; *for journey,* vectura. **farewell !** *interj.* vale ! valete !
farm, n. ager, fundus; *belonging to a —,* agrarius. *v.tr.* arare, colĕre ; *to let out on contract,* (e)locare. **farmer,** n. agricola, arator ; *of the revenues,* publicanus. **farming,** n. agricultura ; conductio.
farrago, n. farrago.
farrier, n. faber ferrarius.
farrow, n. fetus. *v.tr.* fetum edĕre.

farthing, n. quadrans; *I do not care a — for,* haud flocci facio.
fascinate, *v.tr.* tenēre, capĕre *(fig.)*. **fascination,** n. *fig.* blanditiae.
fashion, n. mos, habitus ; *to be in the — (of things),* moris esse, *v.tr., see* MAKE. **fashionable,** *adj.* elegans. *Adv.* eleganter.
fast, *adj.* celer, agilis, rapidus; *fixed,* firmus; *to hold —,* tenēre ; *to stick —,* adhaerēre; *to make —,* firmare. *Adv.* celeriter. *v.intr.* cibo abstinēre. n. ieiunium. **fasten,** *v.tr.* (af)figĕre ; *see* TIE, BIND ; *— together,* coniungĕre. **fastening,** n. vinculum, claustra, -orum. **faster!** *interj.* propera !
fastidious, *adj.* fastidiosus, mollis. *Adv.* fastidiose, molliter.
fat, *adj.* opimus, pinguis, adipatus *(greasy).* n. adeps. **fatten,** *v.tr.* saginare, farcire. **fatted,** *adj.* saginatus. **fatty,** *adj.* pinguis.
fate, n. fatum, necessitas, sors ; *the —s,* Parcae. **fated,** *adj.* † fatalis, funestus. *Adv.* fataliter *(by fate)*; funeste.
fatality, n. *power of fate,* fatum ; *accident,* casus.
father, n. pater, parens ; *— and mother,* parentes. *v.tr. — upon,* alci tribuĕre. **fatherhood,** n. *by* pater. **father-in-law,** n. socer. **fatherless,** *adj.* orbus. **fatherly,** *adj.* paternus.
fathom, n. ulna. *v.tr.* explorare.
fatigue, n. lassitudo. *v.tr.* (de)fatigare. **fatigued,** *adj.* defessus.
fatuous, *adj.* ineptus. *Adv.* inepte, stulte.
fault, n. vitium, culpa ; *find — with,* accusare, reprehendĕre. **faultless,** *adj.* innocens. *Adv.* innocenter, emendate. **faultlessness,** n. innocentia. **faulty,** *adj.* mendosus. *Adv.* mendose, vitiose.
favour, *v.intr.* favēre, indulgēre, propitius esse *(generally of the gods)* ; studēre ; suffragari. n. goodwill, favor, studium; *by your —,* pace tuā; *benefit,* beneficium, gratia. **favourable,** *adj.* propitius *(of the gods),* amicus ; commodus; *of wind or tide,* secundus. *Adv.* amice, benigne. **favourer,** n. fautor. **favourite,** n. deliciae (= *pet*). *adj.* gratus. **favouritism,** n. gratia.
fawn, n. hinnuleus. *v.tr. — on, fig.* adulari. **fawning,** n. adulatio. *Adv.* blande.
fealty, n. fides, fidelitas.
fear, n. metus, timor, pavor. *v.tr.* metuĕre, timēre, verēri. **fearful,** *adj.* timidus, pavidus ; *dreadful,* dirus. *Adv.* timide, pavide. **fearless,** *adj.* metu vacuus, impavidus. *Adv.* sine metu, impavide. **fearlessness,** n., *see* COURAGE.
feasible, *adj.* quod fieri potest. **feasibility,** n. potestas, facultas faciendi.

feast, n. dies festus; *a meal,* convivium, epulae. v.intr. epulari.

feat, n. facinus, n., factum.

feather, n. penna (pinna).

feature, n. lineamentum, *the —s,* vultus.

February, n. (mensis) Februarius.

fecund, adj. fecundus. **fecundity,** n. fecunditas.

federate, federal, adj. foederatus.

fee, n. merces, honos (honor).

feeble, adj. infirmus, invalidus ; *of sight, etc.,* hebes. Adv. infirme. **feebleness,** n. imbecillitas, infirmitas.

feed, v.tr. cibum praebēre, pabulum dare *(oxen, etc.),* pascēre *(to pasture)* ; fig. alēre. v.intr., *see* EAT, GRAZE.

feeder, n. qui alit; *eater,* qui edit.

feel, v.tr. tangĕre, tentare ; *mentally,* sentire, percipĕre ; — *joy,* laetari ; — *pain,* dolēre. v.intr. esse videri *or* esse. **feeler,** n. crinis, corniculum. **feeling,** n. sensus, animus. adj. humanus, misericors.

feign, v.tr. fingĕre, simulare, dissimulare. **feigned,** adj. fictus, simulatus. Adv. ficte, simulate. **feint,** n., *see* PRETENCE.

felicitate, v.tr. gratulari. **felicitation,** n. gratulatio. **felicity, felicitousness,** n. vita beata; *appropriateness,* proprietas. **felicitous,** adj. beatus ; aptus. Adv. beate, apte.

fell, v.tr. caedĕre ; *knock down,* (con)sternĕre.

fell, adj. crudelis, saevus.

fellow, n. associate, socius, comes ; *a bad —,* homo dissolutus. **fellow-citizen,** n. civis. **fellow-countryman,** n. civis. **fellow-feeling,** n. societas. **fellow-heir,** n. coheres. **fellow-servant,** n. conservus. **fellow-soldier,** n. commilito. **fellowship,** n. societas ; collegium, *a corporation.*

felon, n., reus; *see* CRIMINAL.

female, adj. muliebris, femineus. n. femina, mulier. **feminine,** adj. (gram.) femininus.

fen, n. palus. **fenny,** adj. paluster.

fence, n. saepes. v.tr. saepire; armis uti. **fencer,** n. gladiator. **fencing,** n. ars gladii, ars gladiatoria; — *master,* lanista.

ferment, n. fermentum ; fig. fervor. v.tr. * fermentare. v.intr. fervēre.

fern, n. filix.

ferocious, adj. ferox.

ferret, n. viverra.

ferruginous, adj. ferrugineus ; ferratus.

ferry, n. traiectus ; — *boat,* scapha ; — *-man,* portitor. v.tr. transmittĕre.

fertile, adj. fecundus. **fertility,** n. fecunditas.

ferule, n. ferula *(reed or staff).*

fervent, fervid, adj. fervidus ; fig.

ardens. Adv. ardenter. **fervency, fervour,** n. fervor.

festival, n. dies festus, dies sol(l)emnia.

festive, adj. hilaris, festus. Adv. hilariter, festive. **festivity,** n., *see* FESTIVAL ; *mirth,* hilaritas.

festoon, n. serta, -orum.

fetch, v.tr. afferre, arcessĕre.

fetid, adj. putidus. **fetidness,** n. foetor.

fetter, n. compes, vinculum ; fig. vincula, -orum. v.tr. vincula inicĕre ; fig. impedire.

feud, n. simultas; inimicitia.

fever, n. febris. **feverish,** adj. febriculosus; fig. (com)motus.

few, adj. pauci, rari ; *very —,* perpauci.

fiat, n., *see* COMMAND.

fib, n. mendaciunculum.

fibre, n. fibra. **fibrous,** adj. *by the* genit. fibrae.

fickle, adj. inconstans, lēvis. **fickleness,** n. inconstantia, levitas.

fiction, n. res ficta, fabula, commentum. **fictitious,** adj. commenticius.

fiddle, n. fides, -ium, pl. **fiddler,** n. fidicen.

fidelity, n. fidelitas.

fidget, v.tr. vexare ; *see* DISTURB. v.intr. quiescĕre non posse. **fidgety,** adj. inquietus.

field, n. campus ; ager, arvum ; seges *(a sowed field)* ; *relating to —,* agrarius.

fiendish, adj. nefandus, crudelis. Adv. nefande. **fiendishness,** n. (summa) ferocitas.

fierce, adj. ferox. Adv. ferociter. **fierceness,** n. ferocitas, saevitia.

fiery, adj. igneus, ardens.

fife, n. tibia. **fifer,** n. tibicen.

fifteen, adj. quindecim; — *apiece,* quini deni ; — *times,* quindecie(n)s. **fifteenth,** adj. quintus decimus. **fifth,** adj. quintus. **fifty,** adj. quinquaginta; — *apiece,* quinquageni. **fiftieth,** adj. quinquagesimus.

fig, n. ficus.

fight, n. pugna, certamen ; *with the fist,* pugilatus. v.intr. (de)pugnare, dimicare. **fighter,** n. pugnator, gladiator.

figment, n., *see* FICTION.

figure, n. forma, facies ; *a beautiful —,* dignitas corporis ; *rhetorical —s,* ornamenta ; *a cipher,* lit(t)era. v.tr. *see* IMAGINE. **figurative,** adj. translatus. Adv. per translationem. **figured,** adj. sigillatus.

filament, n. fibra.

file, n. lima, scobina ; *soldiers,* ordo. v.tr. limare. **filings,** n. scobis.

filial, adj. pius (erga parentes). Adv. pie.

fill, v.tr. implēre, refercire *(to stuff)* ; fig. (e.g. an office) fungi.

filet, n. vitta, infula *(of priests).*

film, n. membrana.

filter, *n.* colum. *v.tr.* (per)colare.

filth, *n.*, *see* DIRT ; *fig.* impuritas. **filthy**, *adj.*, *see* DIRT ; impurus. *Adv.*, *see* DIRTY ; impure. **filthiness**, *n.* squalor.

fin, *n.* pinna.

final, *adj.* ultimus, extremus. *Adv.* ad extremum, denique.

finances, *n.* res familiaris ; *o a state*, vectigalia, -ium.

find, *v.tr.* invenire, reperire ; *to — out*, excogitare, experiri ; cognoscere.

fine, *adj.* bellus, elegans ; *the — arts*, artes liberales ; *very — !* belle ! pulchre ! *thin*, tenuis, subtilis ; *of weather*, serenus. — *Adv.* belle, eleganter, tenuiter. *n. in —*, denique ; *penalty*, multa. *v.tr.* multare. **fineness**, *n.* elegantia; tenuitas, subtilitas ; serenitas. **finery**, *n.* munditia. **finesse**, *n.* artificium. *v.intr.* artificiis uti.

finger, *n.* digitus. *v.tr.* tangĕre.

finish, *v.tr.* finire, perficĕre. *n.* perfectio. **finished**, *adj.* limatus (*polished*), perfectus. **finisher**, *n.* perfector. **finishing**, *adj.*, *see* FINAL.

finite, *adj.* finitus, circumscriptus. *Adv.* finite.

fir, *n.* abies, -ĕtis, *f.*, pinus.

fire, *n.* ignis, *m.*, flamma, focus (*fireside*) ; *conflagration*, incendium ; *fig.* ignis, ardor. *v.tr.* incendĕre. *v.intr.* incendi. **fire-brand**, *n.* torris, *m.*, fax. **fireescape**, *n.* scalae. **fireplace**, **fireside**, *n.* caminus, focus. **firewood**, *n.* lignum (*usu. pl.*).

firm, *adj.* firmus, solidus ; *fig.* constans. *Adv.* firme, constanter. **firmness**, *n.* firmitas (*lit.*), constantia.

first, *adj.* primus, prior (*of two*), princeps (= *chief*). *Adv.* primum, primo. **first-born**, *n.* natu maior (*of two*), maximus. **first-fruits**, *n.* primitiae. **firstling**, *n.* primus genitus.

fish, *n.* piscis, *m.* *v.intr.* piscari ; *fig.* — *for*, captare. **fish-bone**, *n.* spina piscis. **fisher**, *n.* piscator. **fish-hook**, *n.* hamus. **fishmonger**, *n.* qui pisces venditat. **fishing**, *n.* piscatus ; — *line*, linum ; *a — net*, rete. **fishy**, *adj.* *by gen.* piscium.

fissure, *n.* fissura, rima.

fist, *n.* pugnus. **fisticuffs**, *n.* pugilatus.

fit, *adj.* aptus, idoneus. *Adv.* apte, commode. *v.intr.* aptus esse, convenire ad. *v.tr.* aptare, accommodare. *n. of illness*, impetus, accessio ; *of anger, etc.*, impetus ; *by —s and starts*, modo . . . modo.

five, *adj.* quinque ; quini (*five each*) ; quinquennium, *a period of — years*, *also* lustrum ; — *times*, quinquie(n)s ; — *fold*, quincuplex. **fifth**, *adj.* quintus. **fives**, *n. use* pila.

fix, *v.tr.* (af)figĕre. **fixed**, *adj.* certus. *Adv.* intentis oculis. **fixture**, *n.* res

quae moveri non potest. **fixedness**, *n.* constantia.

flabby, **flaccid**, *adj.* marcidus, fluidus.

flag, *n.* signum, vexillum ; — *ship*, navis praetoria. *v.intr.* languescĕre, frigĕre (*of conversation, etc.*). **flagstaff**, *n.* *use* vexillum.

flag, *n.* = *flat stone*, quadratum saxum. *v.tr.* quadratis saxis sternĕre.

flagitious, *adj.* flagitiosus. *Adv.* flagitiose.

flagon, *n.* lagĕna, ampulla.

flagrant, *adj.* impudens, apertus. *Adv.* impudenter, aperte. **flagrancy**, *n.* impudentia.

flail, *n.* pertica.

flake, *n. of snow*, *use in pl.* nives.

flambeau, *n.* fax, taeda.

flame, *n.* flamma, ignis. *v.intr.* ardĕre. **flame-coloured**, *adj.* flammeus. **flaming**, *adj.* flammeus ; — *eyes*, oculi ardentes.

flank, *n.* latus.

flap, *n.* lacinia. *v.tr.* alis plaudĕre. *v.intr.* fluitare.

flare, *v.intr.* fulgĕre.

flash, *n.* fulgur. *v.intr.* fulgĕre, (e)micare; *the eyes —*, oculi scintillant.

flask, *n.* ampulla.

flat, *adj.* planus, pronus (*on the ground*) ; — *nose*, nasus simus ; *of wine, etc.* vapidus ; *insipid*, insulsus. *Adv.* *fig.* plane.

flatter, *v.tr.* adulari. **flatterer**, *n.* adulator. **flattering**, *adj.* blandus, gratus. *Adv.* per blanditias. **flattery**, *n.* adulatio, blandimentum.

flaunt, *v.intr.* se ostentare. *v.tr.* *to display*, iactare.

flavour, *n.* sapor. *v.tr.* condire.

flaw, *n.* vitium. **flawless**, *adj.* sine culpā. *Adv.* emendate.

flax, *n.* linum. **flaxen**, *adj.* lineus ; *colour*, flavus.

flay, *v.tr.* pellem detrahĕre.

flea, *n.* pulex.

fledged, *adj.†* plumatus ; *to be —*, pennas habēre.

flee, *v.intr.* fugam petĕre, terga vertĕre (*of soldiers*) ; — *from*, fugĕre ab. *v.tr.* alqm fugĕre. **flight**, *n.* fuga.

fleece, *n.* vellus. *v.tr.* tondĕre ; *rob*, spoliare. **fleecy**, *adj.* † laniger.

fleet, *adj.* pernix. *n.* classis. **fleeting**, *adj.* fugax. **fleetness**, *n.* velocitas.

flesh, *n.* caro, viscera (*pl.*).

flexible, *adj.* lentus ; facilis. **flexibility**, *n.* facilitas.

flicker, *v.intr.* coruscare, vibrare, trepidare.

flight, *n.* fuga ; *to put to —*, fugare ; *way of flying*, lapsus ; *of stairs*, scalae.

flighty, *adj.* levis. **flightiness**, *n.* levitas.

flimsy, *adj.* tenuis. **flimsiness**, *n.* tenuitas.

flinch, *v.intr.* (re)cedĕre.

fling, *v.tr.* mittĕre, iaculari.

flint, *n.* silex; *heart of* —, silicens.

flippant, *adj.* lascivus, petulans. **flippancy,** *n.* petulantia.

flirt, *v.intr.* alqm specie amoris illicĕre. *n.* amator inconstans.

flit, *v.intr.* volitare.

flitch, *n.* succidia.

float, *v.intr.* innare, pendĕre (*in air*).

flock, *n.* grex, pecus, *v.intr.* concurrĕre; — *together*, concurrĕre.

flog, *v.tr.* verberare; *be* — *ged*, vapulare. **flogging,** *n.* verbera, -um.

flood, *n.* aestūs commutatio; *the* — (*tide*) *rises*, aestus crescit; *overflow*, diluvies; *fig.* vis (*e.g.* lacrimarum). *v.tr.* inundare.

floor, *n.* solum, coaxatio; *area* (*barn-floor*); tabulatum, contignatio (*story*).

floral, *adj.* floreus.

florid, *adj.* rubicundus; *fig.* floridus.

flounce, *n.* instita, segmenta, -orum (*pl.*). **flounced,** *adj.* segmentatus.

flounder, *v.intr.* volutari; *fig.* titubare.

flour, *n.* farina.

flourish, *v.intr.* florēre. *v.tr.*, *see* BRANDISH.

flout, *v.tr.* ludificari, deridēre.

flow, *v.intr.* fluĕre; *into the sea*, effundi; — *between*, interfluĕre; — *past*, praeterfluĕre; — *together*, confluĕre. *n.* fluxio, lapsus; *fig.* copia (*e.g.* verborum); *of the tide*, accessus. **flowing,** *adj.* fluens; — *speech*, (pro)fluens. *Adv.* (pro)fluenter.

flower, *n.* flos; *goddess of* —*s*, Flora; *best part of*, flos, robur. *v.intr.* florēre, (ef)florescĕre.

fluctuate, *v.intr.* fluctuare, incertus esse, dubitare. **fluctuation,** *n.* dubitatio.

fluency, *n.* facundia. **fluent,** *adj.* volubilis. *Adv.* volubiliter.

fluid, *n.* humor, aqua. *adj.* fluens.

flurry, *n.* *and v.tr.*; *see* EXCITE.

flush, *n.* rubor. *v.intr.* erubescĕre.

fluster, *v.tr.* agitare, commovēre.

flute, *n.* tibia *or* tibiae. **flute-player,** tibicen. **fluted,** *adj.* striatus.

flutter, *v.intr.* volitare. *v.tr.* commovēre. *n.* trepidatio.

fly, *n.* musca. *v.intr.* volare, volitare. **flying,** *adj.* volucer.

foal, *n.* pullus equi, pullus equinus. *v.tr.* parĕre.

foam, *n.* spuma. *v.intr.* spumare. **foamy,** *adj.* spumans.

fodder, *n.* pabulum, pastus.

foe, *n.* hostis; inimicus (*private* —).

fog, *n.* nebula, caligo. **foggy,** *adj.* nebulosus.

foible, *n.* vitium.

foil, *n.* rudis. *v.tr.* ad irritum redigĕre.

foist, *v.tr.* — *on*, supponĕre.

fold, *n.* sinus, ruga (*wrinkle*). *v.tr.*

(com)plĭcare; *with* —*ed hands*, compressis manibus. *As suffix*, plex, *e.g.* triplex. **folding-doors,** *n.* valvae.

fold, *n. for sheep*, ovile; *for cattle*, stabulum.

foliage, *n.* frons, *pl.* frondes.

folk, *n.*, *see* PEOPLE.

follow, *v.tr.* (con)sequi, prosequi, comitari (*to accompany*); *to* — *after or succeed*, succedĕre; *hence it* —*s*, sequitur, ex quo efficitur *following*, sequens, secutus; proximus, secundus. **follower,** *n.* discipulus; —*s of Socrates*, Socratici.

folly, *n.*, *see under* FOOL.

foment, *v.tr.* fovēre; excitare. **fomenter,** *n.* concitator.

fond, *adj.* foolish, stultus; loving, amans; — *of literature*, lit(t)erarum studiosus. *Adv.* stulte, amanter. **fondness,** *n.* stultitia; studium, amor.

fondle, *v.tr.* blandiri, amplexari. **fondling,** *n.* blanditiae.

food, *n.* cibus, alimentum; *a food-shop*, popina; *of animals*, pabulum.

fool, *n.* homo stultus. *v.tr.* ludĕre. **foolery,** *n.* ineptiae, nugae. **foolhardy,** *adj.* temerarius. **foolish,** *adj.* stultus, ineptus, insulsus. *Adv.* stulte, inepte. **folly,** *n.* stultitia, amentia, dementia.

foot, *n.* pes; *to go on* —, pedibus ire; *foot of the mountain*, infimus mons; *a measure*, pes; *half a* — *semipedalis* (*versification*) pes. *adj.* pedester; — *soldier*, pedes. **footing,** *n.* status. **footpad,** *n.* latro. **footpath,** *n.* semita, trames. **footprint,** *n.* vestigium. **footstool,** *n.* scabellum.

fop, *n.* homo ineptus. **foppery,** *n.* ineptiae.

for, *prep. in behalf of*, *in return for*, pro; — *this reason*, propter hoc; *of time*, — *the next day*, in posterum diem; *love* —, amor alcis; — *the present*, in praesens. *conj.* nam(que), enim (*enclit.*).

forage, *n.* pabulum. *v.tr.* pabulari. **forager,** *n.* pabulator. **foraging,** *n.* pabulatio.

forbear, *v.tr.* se tenēre; patientiā uti, pati ac ferre. **forbearance,** patientia. **forbearing,** *adj.* temperatus.

forbid, *v.tr.* vetare, interdicĕre; *it is* —*den*, vetitum est, non licet.

force, *n.* vis, momentum; *to use* — vim adhibēre. *v.tr.*, *see* COMPEL. **forcible,** *adj.* per vim; *morally*, gravis, vehemens. *Adv.* vi, per vim, graviter.

ford, *n.* vadum.

fore, *adv.* ante, antea. **forearm,** *n.* bracchium. *v.tr.* to be —*ed*, praecavēre. **forebode,** *v.intr.* *and tr.* portendĕre; praesentire. **foreboding,** *n.* praesensio. **forecast,** *v.tr.* (animo)

praevidēre, providēre. **forefather,** *n.*
proävus ; *pl.* maiores, patres. **fore-
finger,** *n.* digitus index. **forego,** *v.tr.*
(con)cedēre. **forehead,** *n.* frons. **foreknowledge,** *n. by* providēre. **fore-
man,** *n.* procurator. **foremost,** *adj.*
primus. **forerunner,** *n.* praenuntius.
foresee, *v.tr.* praevidēre, prospicēre.
foresight, *n.* providentia. **forestall,**
v.tr. praevenire. **foretell,** *v.tr.* praedicēre. **forethought,** *n.* providentia ;
by —, consulto. **forewarn,** *v.tr.* prae-
monēre.

foreign, *adj.* externus, barbarus, alienus.
foreigner, *n.* peregrinus, advena.
forensic, *adj.* forensis.
forest, *n.* silva.
forfeit, *v.tr.* amittēre, multari. *n.*
multa, damnum.
forge, *v.tr.* tundēre, procudēre, fabricari;
to falsify, corrumpēre; *money,* cudēre.
forger, *n.* subiector (*of wills, etc.*).
forgery, *n.* sublectio.
forget, *v.tr.* oblivisci ; *I have forgotten,* e memoriā excessit ; *to be forgotten,* e memoriā excidēre. **forgetful**
adj. immemor. **forgetfulness,** *n.*
oblivio.
forgive, *v.tr.* ignoscēre, veniam dare.
forgiveness, *n.* venia. **forgiving,** *adj.*
facilis, clemens.
fork, *n.* furca, furcilla (*for making hay*).
forked, *adj.* bifurcus.
forlorn, *adj.* spe deiectus.
form, *n.* forma, facies; *of a fine* —, formosus ; *human* —, species humana ;
bench, scamnum. *v.tr.* fingēre, fabricari ; — *troops,* instruēre ; *plans, etc.,*
(consilia) inire ; — *friendship,* amicitiam coniungēre. *v.intr. of troops,*
se explicare. **formal,** *adj.* dicis caus(s)ā;
artificial, compositus, frigidus ; (*of
manners*), urbanus. *Adv.* rite, composite, urbane. **formality,** *n.,* see
CEREMONY. **formation,** *n.* conformatio, forma. **formless,** *adj.* informis,
rudis. **formula,** *n.* formula, verba,
-orum.
former, *adj.* prior, pristinus, superior
(*e.g.* annus) ; *the* —, *the latter,* hic
... ille, *or* ille ... hic. *Adv.* antea,
olim.
formidable, *adj.* metuendus, horrendus.
Adv. formidulose.
forsake, *v.tr.* deserēre.
forsooth ! *interj.* scilicet (*ironical*), sane.
forswear, *v.tr.* adiurare ; *to swear
falsely,* periurare.
fort, *n.* arx, castellum. **fortification,**
n. munitiones, opera, -um. **fortify,**
v.tr. (com)munire.
forth, *adv. of place,* foras; *in composi
tion,* e, ex, *and* pro (*e.g. to bring* —,
effere; *to go* —, exire); *of time,* inde.
forthcoming, *adj. by ut.* **forthwith,**
adv. extemplo, statim.

fortitude, *n.* fortitudo, virtus.
fortune, *n.* fortuna, fors, casus; *wealth,*
divitiae, bona, -orum. **fortune-teller,**
n. sortilegus ; *female* —, saga. *Adv.*
forte. **fortunate,** *adj.* felix, secundus,
— *condition,* res secundae. *Adv.* feliciter, prospere.
forty, *adj.* quadraginta, quadrageni
(— *each*), quadragesie(n)s (— *times*).
forum, *n.* forum.
forward, *adv.* porro; *to go* —, pergēre.
v.tr. send on, perferendum curare ;
help, (ad)iuvare. *Adj. early,* praecox;
rude, protervus.
foster, *v.tr.* curare, nutrire. **foster-
child,** *n.* alumnus. **foster-father,** *n.*
nutricius.
foul, *adj.* putidus, foedus, turpis (*morally*), immundus (*dirty*). **foul play,** *n.*
dolus malus. *Adv.* putide, foede, turpiter.
foulness, *n.* foeditas.
found, *v.tr.* condēre, instituēre. **foundation,** *n.* fundamenta, -orum, sedes.
founder, *n.* conditor, auctor. *v.intr.*
submergi.
fount, *or* **fountain,** *n.* fons, caput (*the
spring*).
four, *adj.* quat(t)uor, quaterni (— *each*);
a period of — *years,* quadrien-
nium ; — *times,* quater. **fourteen,** *adj.*
quat(t)uordecim. **fourteenth,** *adj.*
quartus decimus. **fourth,** *adj.* quartus.
n. quadrans.
fowl, *n.* avis, volucris; *hen,* gallina.
fowler, *n.* auceps. **fowling,** *n.* aucupium.
fox, *n.* vulpes; *fig.* homo callidus.
fraction, *n.* pars. **fractious,** *adj.* morosus.
Adv. morose. **fractiousness,** *n.* morositas. **fracture,** *v.tr.* frangēre.
fragile, *adj.* fragilis. **fragility,** *n.* fragilitas. **fragment,** *n.* fragmentum.
fragmentary, *adj.* fractus.
fragrance, *n.* odor suavis. **fragrant,**
adj. suavis.
frail, *adj.* infirmus. **frailty,** *n.* infirmitas.
frame, *n.* forma; *body,* corpus; — *of
mind,* animus. *v.tr.* in formā includēre;
compose, componēre. **framework,** *n.*
compages.
France, *n.* Gallia. **French,** *adj.* Gallicus.
franchise, *n.* civitas, ius, suffragium.
frank, *adj.* sincerus, simplex. *Adv.*
sincere. **frankness,** *n.* sinceritas.
frankincense, *n.* t(h)us, *genit.* t(h)uris.
frantic, *adj.* insanus, demens. *Adv.*
insane.
fraternal, *adj.* fraternus. *Adv.* fraterne.
fraternity, *n.* fraternitas ; *society,*
sodalitas, collegium. **fraternize,** *v.intr.*
amicitiā inter se coniungi.
fratricide, *n. murder,* parricidium
fraternum ; *murderer,* fratricida, *m.*
fraud, *n.* fraus, dolus. **fraudulent,** *adj.*

fraudulentus, dolosus. *Adv.* dolose, fraudulenter.

fraught, *adj.* repletus, oneratus.

fray, *n.* pugna.

free, *adj.* liber, solutus ; vacuus ; immunis ; *from care,* securus ; *without cost,* gratuitus ; *generous,* largus ... liberare, solvere, manumittère (*of a slave*). **free agent,** *n.* qui sui iuris est. **freebooter,** *n.* latro. **free-born,** *adj.* ingenuus. **freedman,** *n.* libertus, libertinus. **freedom,** *n.* libertas ; *from business,* otium ; *from taxes,* immunitas ; *from punishment,* impunitas ; *moral* —, arbitrium (liberum) ; *license,* licentia. **free-hearted,** *adj.,* see GENEROUS. **freehold,** *n.* praedium liberum. **freeholder,** *n.* possessor. **freeman,** *n.* civis. **free speech,** *n.* sermo liberior. **free-will,** *n.* voluntas ; *to have* —, sponte suâ agère.

freeze, *v.tr.* glaciare, urère. *v.intr.* gelare ; *it* —*s,* gelat ; *to feel cold,* frigère. **frozen,** *adj. to be* —, rigère.

freight, *n.* onus. *v.tr.* onerare. **freighted,** *adj.* onustus.

frenzy, *n.* furor.

frequent, *adj.* creber (*thickly filled*), multus, celeber. *Adv.* frequenter, crebro, saepe. *v.tr.* frequentare. **frequency,** *n.* frequentia, crebritas. **frequented,** *adj.* frequens, celeber, tritus.

fresh, *adj. cool,* frigidus ; recens, novus ; integer, viridis ; *complexion,* nitidus color. *Adv. use* frigidus ; nove, integre. **freshen,** *v.tr.* recreare, reficère. **freshness,** *n.* viriditas ; *the* — *of a book,* liber novus.

fret, *v.tr. rub,* terère ; *wear away,* atterère ; *fig.* sol(l)icitare. *v.intr.* aegre ferre, dolère. *n.* molestia (*or pl.*). **fretful,** *adj.* morosus. *Adv.* morose. **fretfulness,** *n.* morositas.

friction, *n.* tritus.

friend, *n.* amicus, sodalis, necessarius, familiaris ; *my* — *!* O bone ! **friendless,** *adj.* sine amicis. **friendly,** *adj.* amicus, comis. *Adv.* comiter, amice. **friendliness,** *n.* comitas. **friendship,** *n.* amicitia, necessitudo.

frieze, *n. cloth.* gausapa.

fright, *n.* terror, pavor ; *to take* —, pavescère. **frighten,** *v.tr.* (ex)terrère. **frightful** *adj.* terribilis, immanis. *Adv.* terribilem in modum, immaniter. **frightened,** *adj.* territus, trepidus.

frigid, *adj.* frigidus.

frill, *n.* segmenta, -orum (*flounce*).

fringe, *n.* fimbriae, limbus.

frisk, *v.intr.* salire. **frisky,** *adj.* lascivus. *Adv.* lascive. **friskiness,** *n.* lascivia.

fritter, *v.tr. time,* tempus (con)terère ; *property,* dissipare. *n.* laganum.

frivolous, *adj.* levis. *Adv.* maximâ cum levitate. **frivolity,** *n.* levitas.

fro, *adv., e.g. to and* —, huc (et) illuc.

frock, *n.,* see GOWN.

frog, *n.* rana ; *a small* —, ranunculus.

frolic, *n.* ludus et iocus. *v.tr.* ludère. **frolicsome,** *adj.* hilaris, lascivus.

from, *prep.* a, ab ; *out of,* e, ex ; *per* ... ab urbe condita, *from the foundation of the city* ; *cause or source,* a, de, *or* ex, *e.g.* discère a patre, perire a peste ; a metu, *from fear* ; ex irâ, *from anger.*

front, *n.* frons ; *in* — *of the camp,* pro castris ; *to attack in* —, hostes adversos aggredi. *adj.* prior. *v.tr.* a(d)spectare ; *to oppose,* adversari. **frontage,** *n.* frons. **frontispiece,** *n.* libri prima tabula. **fronting,** *adj.* adversus. **frontier,** *n.* continium.

frost, *n.* frigus, gelu, pruina. **frosty,** *adj.* frigidus.

froth, *n.* spuma. *v.intr.* spumare.

froward, *adj.* contumax, pervicax. *Adv.* contumaciter. **frowardness,** *n.* contumacia, pervicacia.

frown, *n.* frontis contractio. *v.intr.* frontem contrahère.

frugal, *adj.* parcus. *Adv.* parce, frugaliter. **frugality,** *n.* parsimonia, frugalitas.

fruit, *n.* fructus, fruges, -um, fetus, pomum. **fruitful,** *adj.* fecundus, fertilis, pomifer. *Adv.* fecunde, utiliter (*profitably*). **fruitfulness,** *n.* fertilitas, ubertas. **fruition,** *n.* fructus. **fruitless,** *adj.* inutilis, sterilis. *Adv.* frustra, re infectâ. **fruit-tree,** *n.* pomum, pomus, *f.*

frustrate, *v.tr.* ad irritum redigère, frustrari ; *to be frustrated,* irritus fieri ; — *a hope,* spem fallère. **frustration,** *n.* frustratio.

fry, *n. of fish,* examen ; *of men, common* —, plebs. *v.tr.* frigère. **frying-pan,** *n.* sartago.

fudge ! *interj.* gerrae ! nugae !

fuel, *n.* lignum (*or pl.*).

fugitive, *adj.* fugiens, fugax. *n.* fugitivus, extorris.

full, *adj.* plenus, completus, frequens (*e.g.* senatus). *Adv.* plene. **full grown,** *adj.* adultus, pubes. **full moon,** *n.* luna plena. **fullness,** *n.* copia. **fulfil,** *v.tr.* conficère, efficère, fungi (— *an office*).

fuller, *n.* fullo ; —*'s earth,* creta fullonica.

fulminate, *v.tr.* minas iactare. **fulmination,** *n.* minae.

fulsome, *adj.* — *flattery,* nimia adulatio. *Adv.* putide. **fulsomeness,** *n.* nimia adulatio.

fumble, *v.intr.,* see FEEL.

fume, *n.* fumus, vapor. *v.intr.* (ex)aestuare.

fun, *n.* iocus, ludus. **funny,** *adj.* ridiculus. *Adv.* ridicule.

function, *n.* munus, officium, magistratus.

fund, *n.* pecunia. **fundamental,** *adj.*

primus, principalis. *Adv.* funditus, penitus. **fundamentals,** *n.* elementa, -orum, principia, -orum.

funeral, *n.* funus, exsequiae. *adj.* funebris ; — *pile,* rogus, pyra. **funereal,** *adj.* funebris, lugubris.

fungus, *n.* fungus.

funnel, *n.* infu(n)dibulum, cornu.

fur, *n.* pellis. **furry,** *adj.* vellosus. **furrier,** *n.* pellio.

furbelow, *n.* instita.

furbish, *v.tr.* interpolare, expolire.

furl, *v.tr.* vela legere.

furlong, *n.* stadium.

furlough, *n.* commeatus.

furnace, *n.* fornax.

furnish, *v.tr.* instruere, orare; *supply,* praebere. **furnished,** *adj.* instructus.

furniture, *n.* supellex, apparatus.

furrow, *n.* sulcus. *v.tr.* sulcos facere.

further, *adj.* ulterior. *Adv.* ulterius, amplius; *besides, moreover,* praeterea, huc accedit quod. *v.tr.* (ad)iuvare. **furtherance,** *n.* auxilium. **furtherer,** *n.* adiutor. **furthest,** *adj.* ultimus.

furtive, *adj.* furtivus. *Adv.* furtim.

fury, *n.* furor, rabies ; *a* —, Furia, Erinnys. **furious,** *adj.* rabidus, furens. *Adv.* rabide, furiose.

fuse, *v.tr.* liquefacere. **fusible,** *adj.* fusilis.

fuss, *n.* tumultus, -ūs. *v.intr.* tumultuari. **fussy,** *adj.* curiosus.

fusty, *adj.,* *see* MOULDY.

futile, *adj.* inanis, vanus. **futility,** *n.* futilitas, inanitas.

future, *adj.* futurus, posterus. *n.* futura, -orum. **futurity,** *n.* tempus futurum.

G

gabble, *v.intr.* garrire. *n.* garrulitas.

gable, *n.* fastigium.

gad, *v.intr.* vagari.

gadfly, *n.* oestrus.

gag, *v.tr.* os obvolvere et praeligare. *n.* (*e.g.* linteum in os iniectum).

gage, *n.* pignus, -ōris, *n.*

gain, *n.* lucrum, quaestus, commodum, fructus. *v.tr.* lucrari, capere ; — *a battle,* vincere ; — *a lawsuit,* caus(s)am vincere ; — *a prize,* praemium auferre ; — *over,* conciliare.

gainsay, *v.tr.,* *see* CONTRADICT.

gait, *n.* incessus.

gala, *n.,* *see* FESTIVAL.

galaxy, *n.* orbis *or* circulus lacteus.

gale, *n.* ventus magnus.

gall, *n.* fel, bilis. *v.tr.* rub, terere; *fig.* mordere. **galling,** *adj.* mordax.

gallant, *adj.* fortis ; amori deditus. amatorius. *Adv.* fortiter. *n.* iuvenis fortis ; amator. **gallantry,** *n.* virtus ; amores, -um.

gallery, *n.* porticus, *f.* pinacotheca (*picture* —), superior locus (*as in a theatre*).

galley, *n.* navis actuaria; navis longa, biremis, triremis.

gallon, *n.* congius.

gallop, *n.* gradus citatus; *at a* —, equo admisso. *v.intr.* equo admisso vehi *or* currere.

gallows, *n.* crux.

gamble, *v.intr.* ludere ; — *with dice,* tesseris *or* talis ludere. **gambler,** *n.* aleator. **gambling,** *n.* alea.

gambol, *v.intr.* ludere, lascivire.

game, *n.* ludus ; — *of chance,* alea ; *animal,* ferae, *on table,* caro ferina; *to make* — *of,* ludibrio habere. **gamester,** *n.* alveus.

gaming, *see* GAMBLE. **gaming-table,** *n.* alveus.

gammon, *n.* — *of bacon,* perna.

gammon, *interj.* nonsense ! gerrae nugas !

gander, *n.* anser (mas *or* masculus).

gang, *n.* caterva, operae. **gangway,** *n.* forus.

gangrene, *n.* ossium caries.

gaol, *n.* carcer, vincula, -orum. **gaoler,** *n.* custos.

gap, *n.* lacuna, hiatus. **gape,** *v.intr.* hiare.

garbage, *n.* quisquiliae.

garble, *v.tr.* corrumpere.

garden, *n.* hortus; *small* —, hortulus. *v.intr.* hortum colere. **garden-stuff,** *n.* olus. **gardening,** *n.* hortorum cultus. **gardener,** *n.* qui hortum colit.

garish, *adj.* clarus, splendidus; *gay,* nitidus.

garland, *n.* sertum.

garlic, *n.* a(l)lium.

garment, *n.* vestis.

garner, *n.* horreum. *v.tr.* condere.

garnish, *v.tr.* (ex)ornare, instruere.

garret, *n.* cenaculum; *to live in a* —, sub tegulis habitare.

garrison, *n.* praesidium. *v.tr.* urbi praesidium imponere.

garrulity, *n.* loquacitas. **garrulous,** *adj.* loquax. *Adv.* loquaciter.

gasconade, *n.* iactatio.

gash, *n.* vulnus. *v.tr.* vulnerare.

gasp, *v.intr.* anhelare. *n.* anhelitus.

gastric, *adj.* ad stomachum pertinens.

gastronomy, *n.* quae ad gulam pertinent.

gate, *n.* ianua, porta. **gate-keeper,** *n.* ianitor. **gate-post,** *n.* postis.

gather, *v.tr.* legere, colligere ; — *flowers,* flores carpere ; — *grapes,* vindemiare; *conjecture,* conicere. *v.intr.* convenire; *of a sore,* suppurare. **gathering,** *n.* coetus; *a sore,* suppuratio.

gaudy, *adj.* magnificus. *Adv.* magnificenter.

gauge, *v.tr.* metiri.

gaunt, *adj.* exilis.

gauntlet, *n.* manicae; *to run the* —, per militum ordines currens virgis caedi.

gauze, n. vestis coa.

gay, adj. hilaris (hilarus), laetus ; of colour, etc., splendidus, nitidus. Adv. hilare, laete. **gaiety**, n. hilaritas, laetitia.

gaze (at), v.intr. intueri contemplari. n. obtutus, conspectus. **gazing-stock**, n. spectaculum.

gear, n. ornatus, supellex.

gem, n. gemma, † lapis.

gender, n. genus. **genealogy**, n. origo, stirps.

general, n. dux, imperator ; the —'s tent, praetorium ; to be —, exercitui praeesse. adj. generalis, communis, vulgaris ; — good, omnium salus ; in —, in universum. Adv. usually, fere, vulgo, plerumque. **generality**, n. vulgus. **generalization**, n. quod de omnibus rebus dictum est. **generalship**, n. ductus; under the — of Caesar, Caesare duce.

generate, v.tr. cause, facere, efficere. **generation**, n. saeculum, aetas.

generous, adj. nobilis, eximius; liberalis. Adv. bene, eximie, liberaliter. **generosity**, n. liberalitas; benignitas.

genesis, n., see ORIGIN.

genial, adj. comis, genialis (e.g. hiem(p)s). Adv. comiter, genialiter. **geniality**, n. comitas.

genitive, n. (casus) genitivus (Gramm.).

genius, n. ability, ingenium, indoles.

genteel, adj. elegans, urbanus. Adv. eleganter, urbane. **gentility**, n. elegantia, urbanitas.

gentle, adj. well-born, nobilis, nobili loco ortus; in disposition, mildis; mollis, lenis. Adv. leniter, molliter. **gentleman**, n. hom. nobilis : well-bred, homo urbanus. **gentlemanly**, adj. urbanus. **gentleness**, n. nobilitas, mansuetudo; lenitas. **gentry**, n. nobilitas, optimates, -(i)um. **gentlewoman**, n., see LADY.

genuflexion, n., see KNEEL.

genuine, adj. sincerus Adv. reapse, sincere, vere. **genuineness**, n. auctoritas, fides.

geometry, n. geometria. **geometrical**, adj. geometricus. **geometer**, or **geometrician**, n. geometres, -ae, m.

germ, n. fig. semen. **germinate**, v.intr. germinare. **germination**, n. germinatio. **germane**, adj. affinis.

Germany, n. Germania. **German**, adj. Germanicus.

gesture, n. gestus (mode of carrying the body) ; see GESTICULATION. **gesticulate**, v.intr. se iactare. **gesticulation**, n. iactatio, motus.

get, v.tr. capere, adipisci; — anything done, alqd faciendum curare; — up, surgere.

ghastly, adj. exsanguis, pallidus. **ghastliness**, n. pallor; see HORROR.

ghost, n. breath, spiritus anima ; spirits of the dead, lemures, manes, (pl.); umbra.

ghoul, n. larva teterrima.

giant, n. homo ingentis magnitudinis; gigas. **gigantic**, adj. immanis magnitudinis.

gibbet, n., see GALLOWS.

gibe, n. ludibrium. v.tr. ludibrio habere.

giddy, adj. vertiginosus; fig. levis, inconstans. Adv. inconstanter. **giddiness**, n. vertigo; animus levis.

gift, n. donum; see GIVE.

giggle, v.intr. cachinnare.

gild, v.tr. inaurare.

gill, n. a measure, hemina.

gills, n. branchiae.

gimlet, n. terebra.

gin, n. — trap, laqueus, tendicula.

gingerly, adv. pedetentim, sensim.

giraffe, n. camelopardalis.

gird, v.tr. (suc)cingere ; — yourself, (suc)cingi. **girder**, n. trabs. **girdle**, n. zona, cestus, balteus.

girl, n. puella, virgo. **girlish**, adj. puellaris. Adv. more puellarum.

girth, n. ambitus, circuitus.

give, v.tr. dare, reddere, tradere; to — up for lost, desperare de alqo. **gift**, n. donum, praemium ; to make a —; donum dare. **gifted**, adj. praeditus; a — man, vir summi ingenii. **giver**, n. qui donum dat.

gizzard, n. ingluvies, guttur.

glad, adj. laetus ; — at, gaudere. Adv. laete. **gladden**, v.tr. (ex)hilarare. **gladness**, n. laetitia.

glade, n. silva.

gladiator, n. gladiator. **gladiatorial**, adj. gladiatorius ; a trainer of —s, lanista.

glance, n. oculorum coniectus. v.intr. — at, oculos conicere in alqd.

glare, v.intr. fulgere ; — at, intentis oculis tueri. n. fulgor ; intenti (ut aiunt) oculi.

glass, n. vitrum **glazier**, n. qui fenestris vitrum imponit. **glassy**, adj. vitreus

gleam, n. fulgor: fig. aura; — of hope, specula. v.intr. fulgere.

glee, n. hilaritas. **gleeful**, adj. hilaris. Adv. hilariter.

glen, n. (con)vallis.

glib, adj. loquax. Adv. oquaciter. **glibness**, n. loquacitas.

glide, v. (pro)labi.

glimmer, v.intr. sublucere.

glimpse, n., see SIGHT, n.

glisten, **glitter**, v.intr. micare, candere, fulgere. **glistening**, **glittering**, adj. lucidus, candidus, fulgens.

gloat, v.intr. — over, se a(d)spectu alcis rei delectare.

globe, n. globus; orbis terrarum. **globular**, adj. globosus.

gloom, n. obscuritas, tenebrae ; fig.

tristitia. **gloomy,** *adj.* obscurus, tristis. *Adv.* obscure, maeste.

glory, *n.* gloria, honos, decus, *n. v.intr.* gloriari. **glorify,** *v.tr.* laudibus ornare, celebrare. **glorious,** *adj.* (prae)clarus, illustris. *Adv.* (prae)clare.

gloss, *n.* nitor; *explanation,* interpretatio. *v.tr. — over,* extenuare. **glossary,** *n.* glossarium. **glossy,** *adj.* nitidus.

glove, *n.* manicae *(sleeves).*

glow, *n.* ardor, aestus. *v.intr.* candēre, ardēre ; *to begin to —,* (ex)ardescēre, incandescēre. **glowing,** *adj.* candens, fervidus. **glow-worm,** *n.* cicindēla.

glue, *n.* gluten. *v.tr.* (con)glutinare. **glutinous,** *adj.* glutinosus, lentus.

glut, *v.tr. lit.* explēre ; *fig. — the market,* vilitatem annonae efficĕre. *n.* satietas.

glutton, *n.* homo vorax. **gluttonous,** *adj.* vorax. *Adv.* avide.

gnarled, *adj., see* KNOTTY.

gnash, *v.tr.* dentibus (in)frendēre. **gnashing,** *n.* stridor dentium.

gnat, *n.* culex.

gnaw, *v.tr.* (ar)rodĕre ; *fig.* mordēre. **gnawing,** *adj.* mordax.

go, *v.intr.* ire, gradi, ingredi, vadĕre, ambulare *(to — forth)* ; procedĕre, *to — out,* exire, egredi ; *— in,* inire ; *— over, transire; — on board,* (navem) conscendĕre ; *— down,* descendĕre ; *— up,* a(d)scendĕre ; *— through,* transire. *In imper.* abi ! apage sis ! *to — after,* petĕre. **go-between,** *n.* conciliator, interpres.

goad, *n.* stimulus. *v.tr.* stimulare, incitare.

goal, *n.* meta, calx.

goat, *n.* capra, capella. **he-goat,** *n.* caper, hircus.

gobble, *v.tr.* (de)vorare.

goblet, *n.* scyphus; *see* CUP.

God, *n.* Deus, numen *(the supreme will); the —s,* di(i), † caelestes, superi; *of the house,* lares, penates ; *by the —s,* per deos. **goddess,** *n.* dea. **Godhead,** *n.* numen. **godless,** *adj.* impius. **godlessness,** *n.* impietas erga deos. **godlike,** *adj.* divinus. **godly,** *adj.* pius erga deos. **godliness,** *n.* pietas erga deos.

gold, *n.* aurum. **gold-leaf,** *n.* bractea, auri lamina. **goldsmith,** *n.* aurifex. **golden,** *adj.* aureus, ex auro factus.

good, *adj.* bonus, probus, secundus; *(res prosperae = — circumstances)* ; utilis, honestus *(hoonourable),* benignus *(kind). interj. — bye,* vale. *n.* bonum ; *the highest —,* summum bonum ; *possessions,* bona ; *wares,* merx. **good breeding,** *n.* humanitas. **good-fellowship,** *n.* comitas. **good-for-nothing,** *adj.* nequam. **good-humour,** *n.* comitas, facilitas. **good-humoured,** *adj.* comis, facilis, benignus. *Adv.* comiter, benigne. **good-looking,** *adj.* pulcher.

goodly, *adj., see* GOOD-LOOKING. **good-nature,** *n. see* GOOD-HUMOUR. **goodness,** *n.* bonitas ; *moral —,* probitas, virtus; *kindness,* benignitas.

goose, *n.* anser, *m.*

gore, *n.* cruor. *v.tr.* transfigĕre. **gory,** *adj.* cruentus.

gorge, *n. a pass,* angustiae, saltus. *v.tr.* (ex)satiare ; *— oneself,* exsatiari.

gorgeous, *adj.* splendidus, magnificus. *Adv.* splendide, magnifice. **gorgeousness,** *n.* splendor, magnificentia.

gormandize, *v.intr.* hel(l)uari.

gossamer, *n.* aranea *(spider's web).*

gossip, *n.* sermo, rumor; *person,* homo garrulus ; *friend,* familiaris. *v.intr.* sermonem cum alqo conferre.

gourd, *n.* cucurbita.

gout, *n.* arthrītis ; *— in the hands,* chiragra ; *— in the feet,* podagra. **gouty,** *adj.* arthriticus.

govern, *v.tr.* gubernare, administrare, curare; moderari, temperare. **government,** *n.* administratio ; *power,* imperium, regnum. **governor,** *n.* gubernator; *state —,* praefectus.

gown, *n.* toga, vestis; *lawyer's —,* toga forensis ; *the manly —,* toga virīlis ; *a woman's —,* palla, stola.

grace, *n. favour,* gratia, favor, indulgentia ; *by the grace of God,* Deo favente ; *the —s,* Gratiae ; *with a good, bad —,* cum bonā, malā gratia; *gracefulness,* elegantia; *lepos (— in words). v.tr.* (ad)ornare. **graceful,** *adj.* venustus, elegans. *Adv.* venuste, eleganter. **graceless,** *adj.* improbus. *Adv.* improbe. **gracious,** *adj.* propitius; *see* KIND.

grade, *n. step,* gradus. **gradual,** *adj.,* **gradually,** *adv.* gradatim, sensim.

graft, *n.* surculus. *v.tr.* surculum arbori inserĕre.

grain, *n. seed, etc.,* granum; *corn,* frumentum.

graminivorous, *adj.* (animal) quod herbis pascitur.

grammar, *n.* grammatica, grammatice. **grammatical,** *adj.* grammaticus. *Adv.* grammatice. **grammarian,** *n.* grammaticus.

granary, *n.* horreum.

grand, *adj.* grandis, magnificus. *Adv.* magnifice. **grandeur,** *n.* amplitudo. **grandees,** *n.* optimates. **grandiloquent,** *adj.* grandiloquus. *Adv.* tumide. **grandiloquence,** *n.* oratio tumida. **granddaughter,** *n.* neptis. **grandfather,** *n.* avus. **grandmother,** *n.* avia. **grandson,** *n.* nepos. **great-granddaughter,** *n.* proneptis. **great-grandfather,** *n.* proăvus. **great-grandmother,** *n.* proăvia. **great-grandson,** *n.* pronĕpos.

grange, *n.* villa.

granite, *n.* lapis, saxum.

grant, n. beneficium, donum. v.tr. concedĕre; this —ed, hoc dato; —ed that, or that not, ut sit, ne sit.

grape, n. acinus, uva (bunch of grapes).

graphic, adj. expressus. Adv. clare.

grapple, v.tr. cum alqo luctari. grappling-iron, n. ferrea, harpago.

grasp, v.tr. (ap)prehendĕre (manu), manum amplecti, fig. concipĕre ; see COMPREHEND ; at, (ap)petĕre. n. complexus ; manu, captus. grasping, adj. avarus.

grass, n. herba. grassy, adj. herbidus.

grasshopper, n. gryllus.

grate, n. focus, caminus.

grate, v.tr. conterĕre. grating, n. cancelli.

grateful, adj. pleasant, (per)gratus, iucundus ; thankful, gratus. Adv. grate. gratitude, n. gratus animus.

gratify, v.tr. gratificari, delectare. gratification, n. delectatio. gratifying, adj. gratus. gratis, adv. grat(i)is, sine mercede. gratuitous, adj. gratuitus. Adv., see GRATIS. gratuity, n., see GIFT.

grave, adj. gravis, severus. gravity, n. gravitas. gravitate, v.intr. (in medium) niti.

grave, n. sepulc(h)rum, tumulus.

gravel, n. glarea.

gravy, n. ius, sucus.

gray (grey), adj. canus, ravus (of the sea, the eyes), glaucus. grayness (greyness), n. canities.

graze, v.tr. pascĕre. v.intr. pasci. grazier, n. pecuarius.

graze, v.tr. touch, stringĕre, radĕre.

grease, n. adeps, lardum. v.tr. ung(u)ĕre, oblinĕre. greasy, adj. unctus, pinguis.

great, adj. magnus, grandis, immanis ; too —, nimius. Adv. magnopere, valde, vehementer (e.g. veh. commotus) ; so —, tantus ; how —, quantus ; how soever, quantuscunque ; twice as —, duplo maior; as — as, tantus, followed by quantus. greatcoat, n. pallium, lacerna, paenula. greatness, n. magnitudo, amplitudo ; — of mind, gravitas, magnanimitas.

greaves, n. ocreae.

Greece, n. Graecia. Greek, adj. Graecus.

greedy, adj. cupidus. Adv. cupide. greediness, n. cupiditas.

green, adj. viridis, virens, glaucus ; fresh, recens, rivus, crudus (not ripe). n. viriditas, color viridis; grassy spaces, campus. greens, n. olera, -um. greenness, n. viriditas.

greet, v.tr. (con)salutare. greeting, n. (con)salutatio.

gregarious, adj. qui congregari solent.

gridiron, n. craticula.

grief, n. aegritudo, dolor, maeror, luctus. grieve, v.tr. dolore afficĕre. v.intr. dolēre. grievance, n. iniuria queri-

monia (= complaint). grievous, adj. gravis, molestus. Adv. moleste, graviter.

grievousness, n. molestia, gravitas.

grill, v.tr., see ROAST.

grim, adj. † torvus, saevus. Adv. saeve, ferociter. grimness, n. ferocia.

grimace, n. os distortum; to make —s, os (dis)torquēre.

grimy, adj., see DIRTY.

grin, n. rictus. v.intr. rictu ridēre.

grind, v.tr. molĕre, dte terĕ, dentibus frendĕre. grinder, n. qui molit; teeth, dens geninus. grindstone, n. cos.

grip, v.tr., see SEIZE. n. manus. gripe, v.tr. torminibus afficĕre.

grisly, adj. foedus, teter.

grist, n. farina.

groan, v.intr. gemĕre. n. gemitus.

groin, n. inguen.

groom, n. agaso. v.tr. curare.

grope, v.intr. errare; (iter) explorare. Adv. pedetemptim (pedetenti-).

gross, adj. crassus, densus; too great, nimius ; turpis. Adv. nimium, turpiter. n. 144, duodecies duodecim; in the —, in universum. grossness, n. crassitudo; nimia magnitudo; turpitudo.

grotesque, adj. immanis, mirus. grotesqueness, n. mira species.

grotto, n. antrum.

ground, n. humus, solum, terra; on the —, humi ; reason, fundamentum, caus(s)a. v.intr. of a ship, sidēre. groundless, adj. vanus, fictus. Adv. sine caus(s)ā. groundlessness, n. vanitas. groundwork n. fundamentum ; principium.

group, n. caterva, v.tr. disponĕre. grouping, n. dispositio.

grove, n. lucus, nemus.

grovel, v.intr. humi iacēre. grovelling, adj. abiectus, servilis. Adv. humiliter, turpiter.

grow, v.intr. crescĕre, augeri ; — up, adolescĕre. v.tr. colĕre. grower, n. cultor. grown-up, adj. adultus. growth, n. auctus.

growl, n. fremitus. v.intr. fremĕre.

grub, n. vermiculus. v.tr. — up, eruĕre.

grudge, n. simultas, invidia. v.tr. invidēre.

gruff, adj. raucus. Adv. raucā voce. gruffness, n. rauca vox.

grumble, v.intr. murmurare.

grunt, n. grunnitus. v.intr. grunnire.

guarantee, n. surety, sponsio, vadimonium, fides ; guarantor, vas, sponsor. v.tr. fidem dare.

guard, n. custodia, praesidium, vigiliae; to keep —, excubare ; custodes. v.tr. custodire. guardian, n. defensor, custos ; of a ward, tutor, curator. guardianship, n. custodia, tutela. guarded, adj. cautus. Adv. caute.

guerdon, n. praemium, merces.

guess, *v.tr.* conicĕre, suspicari. *n.* coniectura.

guest, *n.* hospes.

guide, *n.* dux. *v.tr.* ducĕre; moderari. **guidance,** *n.* ductus, consilium.

guild, *n.* collegium.

guile, *n.* dolus. **guileful,** *adj.* dolosus. *Adv.* dolose. **guileless,** *adj.* simplex, sincerus. *Adv.* simpliciter, sincere. **guilelessness,** *n.* simplicitas.

guilt, *n.* vitium, culpa, delictum. **guilty,** *adj.* sons, sceleratus. *Adv.* scelerate. **guiltless,** *adj.* innocens, insons.

guise, *n.* mos, habitus.

gulf, *n.* sinus, gurges, vorago (*whirlpool*).

gull, *v.tr.* decipĕre. **gullible,** *adj.* credulus.

gullet, *n.* gula, guttur.

gully, *n.* alveus (*bed of a stream*).

gulp, *n.* haustus. *v.tr.* haurire.

gum, *n.* gingiva ; *of plants,* gummi. *v.tr.* glutinare.

gurgle, *v.intr.* murmurare.

gush, *v.intr.* — *out,* effundi *or* se effundĕre.

gust, *n.* venti impetus, procella. **gusty,** *adj.* turbidus.

gut, *n.* intestinum. *v.tr. fig.* exinanire.

gutter, *n.* canalis, cloaca.

guttural, *adj.* (sonus) **gravis.**

gymnasium, *n.* gymnasium, palaestra. **gymnastic,** *adj.* gymnicus, palaestricus. **gymnastics,** *n.* ars gymnastica, palaestra.

gypsum, *n.* gypsum.

H

ha ! *interj.* ha !

habiliment, *n.* vestis, vestitus.

habit, *n.* consuetudo, mos, usus ; *of body,* habitus. **habitable,** *adj.* habitabilis. **habitation,** *n.* domicilium, sedes. **habitual,** *adj.* usitatus ; — *drunkard,* ebriosus. *Adv.* de *or* ex more. **habituate,** *v.tr.* assuefacĕre.

hack, *v.tr.* caedĕre. **hackneyed,** *adj.* tritus.

haft, *n.* manubrium, capulus.

hag, *n.* anus; *an old —,* vetula. **haggard,** *adj.* morbo *or* maerore confectus.

haggle, *v.tr.* pretium facĕre. *See* QUARREL.

hail, *n.* grando. *v.intr.* it —s, grandinat.

hail, *v.tr.* salutare. *interj.* salve ! ave !

hair, *n.* pilus, pili (*pl.*), capilli (*gen. pl.*); seta (*bristle*), crinis, coma (*of the head*), caesaries (*flowing* —); *to a* —, rem acu tetigisti ; *false* —, alieni capilli: *a* — *band,* vitta. **hair-cloth,** *n.* cilicium. **hairdresser,** *n.* tonsor. **hairpin,** *n.* crinale. **hair-splitting,** *n.* disserendi spinae. **hairy,** *adj.* capillatus.

halcyon, *n.* (h)alcedo, (h)alcyon. *adj.* serenus ; — *days,* dies sereni et tranquilli.

hale, *adj.* sanus, validus, robustus.

hale, *v.tr.* rapĕre, trahĕre.

half, *adj.* dimidius. *n.* dimidium, semis (*heir to* — *an estate,* heres ex semisse). *adv.* semi *as prefix, e.g.* **half-asleep,** *adj.* semisomnus. **half-brother,** *n.* eodem patre, eâdem matre natus. **half-circle,** *n.* semicirculus. **half-hour,** *n.* semihora. **half-moon,** *n.* luna dimidiata. **half-open,** *adj.* semiapertus. **half-ounce,** *n.* semuncia. **half-pound,** *n.* selibra. **half-sister,** *n.* eodem patre *or* eâdem matre nata. **halve,** *v.tr.* in aequas partes dividĕre. **halved,** *adj.* bipartitus. **halves !** *interj.* in commune !

hall, *n.* atrium, vestibulum.

halloo, *n.* clamor. *v.intr.* clamare. **halloo !** *interj.* heus ! ohe !

hallow, *v.tr.* consecrare. **hallowed,** *adj.* sacer, sanctus.

hallucination, *n.* error.

halm, *n.* culmus, calamus.

halt, *adj.* claudus. *v.intr.* claudicare ; *to stop,* consistĕre ; *to hesitate,* dubitare. *n. use verb.* **halter,** *n.* capistrum ; *to put on a* —, capistrare ; laqueus (*noose*).

ham, *n.* poples; *salted* —, perna. **hamstring,** *n.* poplitis nervus. *v.tr.* poplitis nervum secare.

hamlet, *n.* viculus, parvus vicus.

hammer, *n.* malleus. *v.tr.* malleo (con)tundĕre; — *out,* ducĕre.

hamper, *n.* corbis; *see* BASKET.

hamper, *v.tr.* impedire.

hand, *n.* manus, palma ; *to give the* —, dextram porrigĕre ; *to lay* —s *on a person,* alci manus afferre ; *to be at* —, adesse ; *on the one* —, *on the other,* et . . . et; *of a clock, etc.,* index; *workman,* opera, usu. *in pl. v.tr.* dare, tradĕre ; — *down,* tradĕre, prodĕre ; — *round,* circumferre. **hand-breadth,** *n.* palmus. **handcuff,** *n.* —s manicae. *v.tr.* manicas alci iniicĕre. **handful,** *n.* pugillus ; *fig.* exigua manus, pauci. **handicraft,** *n.* artificium ; —*sman,* artifex. **handiwork,** *n.* opus, opificium. **handkerchief,** *n.* suadarium. **handle,** *n.* capulus, manubrium (*of a sword, etc.*), ansa (*of a cup, etc.*). *v.tr.* tractare ; *fig.* tractare. **handling,** *n.* tractatio. **handy,** *adj.* habilis (*skilful*); promptus (*ready*).

handsome, *adj.* bellus, pulcher; liberalis. *Adv.* belle, liberaliter. **handsomeness,** *n.* pulchritudo.

hang, *v.intr.* pendĕre (ab, de, ex). *v.tr.* suspendĕre; — *the head,* caput demittĕre. **hangdog,** *n.* verbero, furcifer. **hanger,** *n.* gladius. **hanger-on,** *n.* assec(u)la, *m.* **hanging,** *n.* suspendium. *adj.* pendens. **hangman,** *n.* carnifex.

hanker, *v.tr. to — after,* desiderare.

haphazard, *adv. at —,* temere. **hapless,** *adj.* infelix. **haply,** *adv.* forte.

happen, *v.intr.* fieri, accidĕre, contingĕre, evenire. **happy,** *adj.* felix; beatus; *of language*, aptus. Adv. feliciter, fortunate, *etc.* **happiness,** *n.* felicitas.

harangue, *n.* contio. *v.intr.* contionari.

harass, *v.tr.* fatigare, sol(l)icitare; *military term,* carpĕre, premĕre.

harbinger, *n.* praenuntius, antecursor.

harbour, *n.* portus ; — *toll or dues,* portorium. *v.tr. receive,* (hospitio) excipĕre; *fig.* colĕre.

hard, *adj.* durus, solidus, crudus (*unripe*); *feelings,* asper, acerbus; *difficult,* difficilis. *adv. strenuously,* summâ vi, aulxe; *to go — with,* alqd aegre ferre. **harden,** *v.tr.* durum facĕre. *v.intr.* oburescĕre. **hardened,** *adj.* inveteratus. **hard-hearted,** *adj.* durus, ferreus. **hardihood,** *n.* audacia. **hardly,** *adv. scarcely,* vix, aegre ; *cruelly,* aspere, acerbe. **hardness,** *n.* duritia ; *fig.* crudelitas, saevitia. **hardship,** *n.* labor; molestia, aerumna. **hardy,** *adj.* durus, robustus; *fig.* strenuus. *Adv.* duriter. **hardiness,** *n.* robur.

hardware, ferramenta, -orum.

hare, *n.* lepus, lepŏris, *m.*

hark ! *interj.* heus !

harlequin, *n.* sannio, *m.*

harm, *n.* damnum, detrimentum; calamitas. *v.tr.* nocĕre, laedĕre. **harmful,** *adj.* nocens. **harmless,** *adj.* innoxius. *Adv. by* adj. **harmlessness,** *n.* innocentia.

harmony, *n.* concentus, concordia. **harmonious,** *adj.* consonus ; *fig.* concors. *Adv.* consonanter, concorditer. **harmonize,** *v.tr.* concordes facĕre; componĕre, (re)conciliare. *v.intr.* concinĕre.

harness, *n.* ornamenta equi. *v.tr.* equum ornare, equum ad currum iungĕre.

harp, *n.* lyra. **harper,** *n.* fidicen.

harpy, *n.* harpyia; *fig.* homo rapax.

harrow, *n. m.,* rastrum. *v.tr.* occare ; *fig.* (ex)cruciare. **harrowing,** *adj.* terribilis.

harry, *v.tr.* vexare, cruciare.

harsh, *adj.* asper, crudelis, saevus ; *in taste,* acer ; *in sound,* dissonus, raucus. *Adv.* crudeliter, acriter. **harshness,** *n.* asperitas, crudelitas, acerbitas.

hart, *n.* cervus.

harvest, *n.* messis; fructus. *v.tr.* messem facĕre. **harvester,** *n.* messor.

hassock, *n.* scabellum.

haste, *n.* festinatio, celeritas, trepidatio. **hasten,** *v.intr.* properare ; festinare. *v.tr.* accelerare, properare, festinare. **hasty,** *adj.* citus, festinans, praeceps ; *irritable,* vehemens or acer. *Adv.* propere, raptim, vehementer. **hastiness,** *n.,* see HASTE; iracundia.

hat, *n.* petăsus; pileus (*cap*).

hatch, *v.tr.* parĕre ; *fig.* machinari. **hatches,** *n.* clat(h)ri, claustra, -orum.

hatchet, *n.* securis, dolabra.

hate, hatred, *n.* odium, invidia, inimicitia. *v.tr.* odisse ; *to be hated by,* odio alci esse. **hateful,** *adj.* invisus. *Adv.* invidiose.

haughty, *adj.* superbus. *Adv.* superbe. **haughtiness,** *n.* superbia.

haul, *v.tr.* trahĕre, ducĕre, subducĕre. *n.* tractus.

haulm, *n.,* see STALK.

haunch, *n.* clunis, *m.* and .

haunt, *v.tr.* frequentare ; *of spirits,* agitare. *n.* locus quem alqs frequentare solet ; *of animals,* latibulum. **haunted,** *adj. — house,* domus ab umbris frequentata.

have, *v.tr.* habēre, tenēre ; gestare (*to carry*) ; *to hold by the hand,* manuducĕre ; possidēre, *to possess* ; *to — an illness,* morbo affectus esse ; *to — favourable wind,* uti vento secundo.

haven, *n.* portus; refugium.

havoc, *n.* (de)populatio; eversio (*of a town*); caedes (*slaughter*).

haw, *v.intr.* balbutire (*also trans.*); balbus esse.

hawk, *v.tr. sell,* venditare.

hawk, *n.* accipiter. **hawk-eyed,** *adj.* lynceus.

hay, *n.* faenum. **haycock, hayrick,** *n.* faeni acervus. **hay-fork,** *n.* furca.

hazard, *n.* sors (*lot*), casus, fortuna, periculum (*risk*), alea (*i.e. gambling*); *at —,* temere, forte. *v.tr.* audĕre or tentare. **hazardous,** *adj.* periculosus, anceps. *Adv.* periculose.

haze, *n.* nebula, caligo. **hazy,** *adj.* nebulosus; *fig.* dubius.

hazel, *n.* corylus, *f.*

he, *pron.* ille, is, iste; ipse (*he himself, himself*).

head, *n.* caput ; cacumen (*the top*); vertex (*top of the —*) ; bulla (bulla clavi, — *of a nail*) ; occiput (*hinder part of the —*) ; biceps (*adj. with two —s*); praeceps (*adj. — foremost*); *life,* caput alcis agitur (*it costs his —*); *chief,* princeps; *understanding,* mens, animus, ingenium; caput (*of a discourse*); — *of the table,* lectus summus. *adj.* summus or maximus (*chief, original*). *v.tr.* alqm ducĕre, alci rei praeesse. **headache,** *n.* capitis dolor. **headband,** *n.* vitta. **headland,** *n.* promontorium. **headlong,** *adj.* imprudens ; temerarius ; demens, praeceps. *Adv.* temere, or *by* adj. praeceps. **head-quarters,** *n.* praetorium. **headship,** *n.* principatus. **headstrong,** *adj.* pertinax, contumax, pervicax. **head-wind,** *n.* ventus adversus. **heady,** *adj.* vehemens ; *intoxicating,* fervidus.

heal, *v.tr.* sanare, mederi. **healing,** *adj.* saluber, salutaris. *n.* sanatio. **health,** *n.* sanitas; bona valetudo, salus; bene te! bene tibi! (*your good — !*). **healthful, healthy,** *adj.* sanus, salvus, integer; saluber *or* salubris (*of a place*); mens sana (*sound mind*). *Adv.* salubriter.

heap, *n.* acervus, agger (*mound*). *v.tr.* coacervare, aggerare; cumulare.

hear, *v.tr. and intr.* audire ; — *badly,* surdus esse (*never male audire*); alci aures dare (*to lend an attentive ear*); (*to learn*) cognoscere ; percipĕre (*to — distinctly*); accipĕre (*to learn from hearsay*). **hearer,** *n.* auditor. **hearing,** *n.* auditus; *trial,* interrogatio. **hearsay** *n.* rumor.

hearken, *v.intr., see* HEAR.

heart, *n.* cor, pectus ; *of a country, interior ; morally,* animus ; mens (*mind, disposition*) ; bonitas (*good —*); animus fractus (*a broken —*) ; ex animo (*from the —*); I have at —, cordi est ; *to take to —,* (com)moveri ; *as endearing term* — my dear, meum cor *or* anime mi, meum corculum; *courage,* animus ; *by —,* memoriter ; *to know by —,* memoriā tenēre; *to learn by —,* ediscĕre. **heartache,** *n.* dolor. **heart-break,** *n.* dolor. **heart-breaking,** *adj.* maestus. **heart-rending,** *adj.* maestus. **heart-broken,** *adj.* animo fractus. **heart-burning,** *n. fig.* odium occultum, dolor. **heartfelt,** *adj.* verus, sincerus. **heartless,** *adj.* crudelis, saevus. *Adv.* crudeliter, saeve. **heartlessness,** *n.* crudelitas, saevitia. **heart-sick,** *adj.* animo aeger. **heart-whole,** *adj.* nondum amore captus. **hearty,** *adj.* vigens, robustus ; *cordial,* benignus, amicus ; *to receive a welcome,* summo studio excipi. *Adv.* firme, benigne, amice. **heartiness,** *n.* ardor ; studium amicitia.

hearth, *n.* focus.

heat, *n.* calor; ardor, aestus; *fig.* ardor, vis ; violentia, ira ; *course at a race,* cursus. *v.tr.* (per)calefacĕre ; (*fig.*), accendĕre. **heated,** *adj., see* HOT.

heath, *n.* loca (-orum) deserta *or* inculta.

heathen, *the* —, barbarae gentes.

heave, *v.tr.* (at)tollĕre ; *a sigh,* gemitum dare. *v.intr.* fluctuare (*waves, etc.*); anhelare (*of the breast*).

heaven, *n.* caelum ; *by* — *!* medius fidius ! *may* — *fulfil your wishes !* di(i) tibi dent ; *for* —*'s sake !* per deos immortales ! — *forbid,* di meliora. **heavenborn,** *adj.* caelestis. **heavenly,** *adj.* caelestis. **heavenward,** *adv.* in *or* ad caelum.

heavy, *adj.* gravis; *fig.* gravis, molestus; *of air,* caelum crassum ; *soil,* solum spissum ; *rain,* imber magnus. *Adv.* graviter, aegre; vasto corpore (— *built*); magnopere. **heavy-armed,** *adj.* the —

troops, gravior armatus. **heaviness,** *n.* gravitas, pondus; molestia; crassitudo (*air*) ; — *of mind,* tristitia.

Hebrew, *adj.* Hebraeus *or* Hebraicus.

hecatomb, *n.* hecatombe.

hectic, *adj.* febriculosus.

hector, *v.intr.* se iactare. **hectoring,** *adj.* gloriosus.

hedge, *n.* saepes. *v.tr.* saepire. **hedge-hog,** *n.* echinus.

heed, *v.tr. take care,* curare, observare ; parēre. *n.* cura ; *take —,* (prae)-cavēre. **heedful,** *adj.* cautus ; obediens. *Adv.* caute, obedienter. **heedless,** *neglegens;* rash, temerarius. *Adv.* temere. **heedlessness,** *n.* temeritas.

heel, *n.* calx. *v.intr. of a ship,* labare.

heft, *n.* manubrium.

heifer, *n.* iuvenca.

height, *n.* altitudo, proceritas; *fig.* altitudo, sublimitas, *or by* summus (*e.g.* summa gloria); *place,* locus superior. **heighten,** *v.tr.* altius efferre; *to raise, to increase,* augēre ; *to enlarge,* amplificare, (ex)ornare; *to raise the price,* pretium efferre.

heinous, *adj.* foedus, impius; nefarius, sceleratus. *Adv.* foede, nefarie, scelerate.

heir, *n.* heres; *sole —,* heres ex asse. **heiress,** *n.* heres, *f.* **heirloom,** *n.* alqd paternum. **heirship,** *n.* hereditas.

hell, *n.* inferi, Tartarus(os) *or pl.* Tartara. **hellish,** *adj.* infernus; nefandus.

hellebore, *n.* (h)elleborus, veratrum.

Hellenic, *adj.* Graecus.

helm, *n.* gubernaculum. **helmsman,** *n.* gubernator.

helmet, *n.* cassis; galea.

help, *n.* auxilium (*pl.* auxilia, = *auxiliaries*) subsidium (*pl. — the reserves*); ops, *f.* (*only* opis, opem, ope *in use, power to assist*) ; praesidium. *v.tr.* (ad)iuvare, subvenire, succurrĕre ; I can't —, *etc.,* fieri non potest quin. **helper,** *n.* adiutor. **helpful,** *adj.* utilis. *Adv.* utiliter. **helping,** *adj.* auxiliaris. **helpless,** *adj.* inermis, inops. **helplessness,** *n.* inopia. **helpmeet,** *n.* socius, consors.

helter-skelter, *adj.* praeceps. *Adv.* raptim.

hem, *n.* limbus, instita (*fringe or border*). *v.tr.* suĕre (*sew*); *fig.* — *in,* obsidēre.

hem, *v.intr. to* — *and haw,* haesitare, dubitare; *interj.* (e)hem ! *See* HAW.

hemp, *n.* cannabis. **hempen,** *adj.* cannabinus.

hen, *n.* gallina. **hen-coop,** *n.* cavea. **hen-house,** *n.* gallinarium. **hen-pecked,** *adj.* (maritus) cui uxor imperat.

hence, *adv.* hinc ; *as interj.,* apage, procul ; paucis diebus, *a few days —,* *or* post paucos dies. **henceforth, henceforward,** *adv.* dehinc, posthac.

her, *see* SHE. *adj.* eius, illius, suus.

herald, *n.* caduceator, (legatus) fetialis; *crier*, praeco ; *forerunner*, praenuntius. *v.tr.* nuntiare.

herb, *n.* herba ; *kitchen-stuff*, olus. herbage, *n.* herba *or* herbae. **herbalist**, *n.* herbarius.

herculean *adj.* fortissimus.

herd, *n.* grex, armentum ; *of people*, multitudo ; *the common* —, vulgus. *v.tr.* pascĕre. *v.intr.* congregari. **herdsman**, *n.* pastor, armentarius.

here, *adv.* hic ; *hoc loco* ; *from* —, hinc. **hereafter**, *adv.* posthac, aliquando. **herein**, *adv.* in hac re. **hereupon**, *adv.* hic ; ad haec.

hereditary, *adj.* hereditarius, paternus. **heritage**, *n.* hereditas.

hero, *n.* heros ; *brave man*, vir fortis *or* fortissimus ; — *of the drama*, persona prima. **heroic**, *adj.* heroicus, praestans; *brave*, fortis. *Adv.* fortiter. **heroine**, *n.* *brave woman*, femina fortissima. **heroism**, *n.* virtus, animi magnitudo.

heron, *n.* ardea.

hers, *pron.* suus; eius, illius.

herself, *pron.* (ea) ipsa, se, *etc.*

hesitate, *v.intr.* dubitare, cunctor ; haesitare. **hesitation**, *n.* dubitatio; haesitatio.

heterogeneous, *adj.* diversus et dissimilis. **heterogeneousness**, *n.* natura diversa et dissimilis.

hew, *v.tr.* caedĕre. **hewer**, *n.* qui ligna caedit. **hewn**, *adj.* quadratus (*e.g.* saxum).

hexameter, *n.* hexameter.

hiatus, *n.* hiatus ; *there is an* — (*in MS.*), alqd deest.

hibernal, *adj.* hibernus. **hibernate**, *v.intr.* hibernare; per hiemem dormire.

hiccough, hiccup, *n.* singultus.

hide, *n.* corium, pellis. *v.tr.* abdĕre, condĕre, celare. **hidden**, *adj.* abditus, *etc.*; *to lie* —, latēre. **hiding-place**, *n.* latibulum.

hideous, *adj.* foedus, deformis. *Adv.* foede. **hideousness**, *n.* foeditas.

hierarchy, *n.* of priests, sacerdotium

higgledy-piggledy, *adv.* confuse.

high, *adj.* altus, (ex)celsus, editus, elatus, arduus, procērus, sublimis ; acutus (*sharp*, *clear*) ; *most* —, summus, supremus; *a* — *price*, pretium magnum; *to bid* —*er* (*at an auction*), contra liceri; *bad*, *of meat*, *etc.*, rancidus. *adv.* alte. **high-born**, *adj.* nobili loco ortus. **high-bred**, *adj.* generosus. **high day**, *n.* dies festus. **high-flown**, *adj.* tumidus ; *to use* — *words*, ampullari. **high-handed**, *adj.* superbus. **high-heeled**, *adj.* — *boot*, cothurnus (*of tragedy*). **highlands**, *adj.* loca mont-(u)osa, -orum. **highlander**, *n.* homo montanus. **highly**, *adv.* magni (*e.g.* magni aestimare, *to value* —); magnopere. **high-minded**, *adj.* magnanimus.

high-mindedness, *n.* magnanimitas. **high priced**, *adj.* carus. **high-priest**, *n.* Pontifex Maximus. **high-spirited**, *adj.* fortis, animosus. **high tide**, *n.* plurimus aestus. **highway**, *n.* via. **highwayman**, *n.* latro.

hilarity, *n.* hilaritas.

hill, *n.* collis, clivus; *locus superior*; *up* —, acclivis, *adj.* ; *down* —, declivis. **hillock**, *n.* tumulus. **hilly**, *adj.* mont(u)osus.

hilt, *n.* capulus.

hind, *n.* *female stag*, cerva.

hind, *n.* *servant*, servus ; *peasant*, agricola.

hind, *adj.* aversus; *that is behind*, posterior. **hindermost**, *adj.* postremus ; ultimus.

hinder, *v.tr.* impedire, prohibēre. **hinderer**, *n.* turbator, interpellator (*e.g.* sermonis); interventor. **hindrance**, *n.* impedimentum; *delay*, mora ; *difficulty*, difficultas.

hinge, *n.* cardo. *v.intr.* in alqâ re versari.

hint, *n.* significatio; *a* — *is sufficient*, rem ostendisse satis est. *v.intr.* alqd alci subicĕre.

hip, *n.* coxendix.

hire, *n.* conductio ; *wages*, merces. *v.tr.* conducĕre ; *to* — *oneself out*, se locare. **hireling**, *n.* mercenarius. *adj.* venalis. **hirer**, *n.* conductor.

his, *adj.* suus (*in reference to the subject*); eius, illius.

hiss, *v.intr.* sibilare. *v.tr.* *to* — *off* (*a bad actor*), explodĕre. *n.* sibilus.

hist ! *interj.* st !

historian, *n.* rerum gestarum scriptor. **historic**, *adj.* historicus ; — *writings*, libri ad historiam pertinentes. *Adv.* historice. **history**, *n.* historia, annales.

histrionic, *adj.* scaenicus ; — *art*, ars ludicra.

hit, *v.tr.* ferire, percutĕre ; tangĕre ; — *upon*, offendĕre, incurrĕre. *n.* ictus, plaga ; *a lucky* —, fortuna secunda ; *a* —, bon bobot.

hitch, *n.* impedimentum.

hither, *adv.* *of place*, huc ; — *and thither*, huc illuc. **hitherto**, *adv.* adhuc, ad hoc tempus.

hive, *n.* alvus *or* alveus. *v.tr.* in alveum congerĕre.

ho ! *interj.* heus !

hoar, *adj.* canus. **hoar-frost**, *n.* pruina. **hoary**, *adj.* canus.

hoard, *n.* copia. *v.tr.* coacervare.

hoarse, *adj.* raucus ; *a little* —, subraucus. *Adv.* raucâ voce. **hoarseness**, *n.* rauca vox.

hoax, *n.* ludificatio. *v.tr.* ludificari.

hobble, *v.tr.* claudicare.

hobby, *n.* voluptas, studium.

hobgoblin, *n.* larva.

hobnob, *v.intr.* alqo familiariter uti.

hock, *n.* poples.

hockey, *n.* pila ; *to play* —, pilis ludĕre.

hoe, *n.* ligo ; *a rake, harrow,* rastrum ; *weeding-hook,* sarculum. *v.tr.* sarrire.

hog, *n.* sus, porcus. **hoggish**, *adj.* suillus; *fig.,* see GLUTTONOUS.

hogshead, *n.* dolium (*cask*).

hoist, *v.tr.* sublevare, tollĕre ; — *sails,* velva dare.

hold, *n. grasp,* manus ; *to take* —, prehendĕre ; *of a ship,* alveus. *v.tr.* tenēre ; habēre, possidēre ; — *an office,* gerĕre ; *to contain,* continēre ; agĕre, habēre (*an election*) ; — *a festival,* celebrare. *v.intr. to hold good,* certus esse ; — *on,* — *one's course,* cursum tenēre.

hole, *n.* cavum, foramen ; rima (*chink*), lacuna (*a pit*) ; *to bore a* —, pertundĕre.

hollow, *adj.* (con)cavus ; *hollowed out,* exesus ; vanus (*empty*) ; simulatus (*counterfeit*). *n.* cavum, foramen ; *valley,* vallis. *v.tr.* (ex)cavare.

holy, *adj.* sacer; sanctus. *Adv.* sancte. **holiness**, *n.* sanctitas, religio.

homage, *n.* cultus, observantia.

home, *n.* domus, domicilium ; *at* —, domi ; *is not at* —, est foris. *adj.* domesticus, familiaris. **homeless**, *adj.* profugus. **homely**, *adj.* simplex. **homeliness**, *n.* simplicitas.

homicide, *n.* caedes ; *murderer,* homicida.

homœopathy, *n.* ea medendi ratio quae similia morbis adhibet remedia.

homogeneous, *adj.* eiusdem generis. **homogeneity**, *n.* natura similis.

homologous, *adj. by* par, similis.

honest, *adj.* bonus, probus; fidus; simplex ; incorruptus. *Adv.* probe, sine fraude ; sine fuco et fallaciis; simpliciter. **honesty**, *n.* probitas; sinceritas; fides ; simplicitas ; *to show* —, fidem adhibēre.

honey, *n.* mel. **honeycomb**, *n.* favus. **honeyed, honied**, *adj.* mellitus; *fig.* dulcis.

honorary, *adj.* honorarius. **honorarium**, *n.,* see FEE.

honour, *n.* dignitas, honos (honor) ; *moral quality,* honestas, honos; *reputation,* existimatio ; *chastity,* pudor ; *mark of respect,* honos ; *v.tr.* honorare, celebrare ; *esteem,* colĕre. **honourable**, *adj.* honoratus, honestus ; *proper,* decōrus ; laude dignus. *Adv.* honeste; cum laude; egregie; *most* —, summo cum honore; *to die* —, bene mori.

hood, *n.* mitra; reticulum. **hoodwink**, *v.tr.* illudĕre, fallĕre.

hoof, *n.* ungula ; *cloven* —, ungula bisulca.

hook, *n.* hamus, uncus; *by* — *or by*

crook, quocunque modo; *a sickle,* falx, *v.tr. to* — *a fish,* hamo pisces capĕre ; *to* — *on,* alci rei suspendĕre. **hooked**, *adj.* aduncus; *having* —*s,* hamatus.

hoop, *n.* circulus; trochus.

hoopoe, *n.* upupa, epops.

hoot, *v.intr.* (*of owls*), canĕre; (*of men*), vociferari ; — *off the stage,* alqm explodĕre. **hooting**, *n.* cantus, carmen (*of owls*), clamor (*of men*).

hop, *v.intr.* (*of birds*), salire; (*of men*), altero pede salire.

hope, *n.* spes; opinio ; ex(s)pectatio; *I have no* — *in,* despero de alqā re. *v.tr.* sperare. **hopeful**, *adj.* spe animoque impletus ; *very* —, eximiā spe. *Adv.* cum magnā spe. **hopeless**, *adj.* spe deiectus ; *one who must be given up,* desperatus. *Adv.* sine spe. **hopelessness**, *n.* desperatio; res desperatae (*of affairs*).

horde, *n.* grex ; caterva (*of people*) ; vagus *with noun* (e.g. — *of Gaetulians,* Gaetuli vagi).

horizon, *n. the sun passes the* —, sol emergit supra terram ; *a clear* —, caelum vacuum ; *limits our* —, a(d)spectum nostrum definit. **horizontal**, *adj.* aequus, libratus. *Adv.* ad libram.

horn, *n.* cornu ; *of the moon,* cornua lunae; *drinking-cup,* poculum ; *musical instrument,* cornu ; *to blow the* —, cornu *or* buccinam inflare. **horned**, *adj.* corniger. **horny**, *adj.* corneus.

hornet, *n.* crabro.

horoscope, *n.* horoscopus ; *to cast a* —, sidera natalicia notare.

horrible, horrid, *adj.* horrendus, foedus. *Adv.* nefarie, foede. **horribleness**, *n.* foeditas, *better adj. with n.* **horrify**, *v.tr.* (ex)terrēre ; *to be horrified,* obstupescĕre. **horror**, *n.* horror, pavor; *hatred,* odium; *a perfect* —, monstrum portentum.

horse, *n.* equus (ecus); *fleet* —, veredus; *cavalry,* equites, -um, equitatus; *to ride on* —, equo vehi, equitare; *to fight on* —, ex equo pugnare. **horsebreaker**, *n.* equorum domitor. **horse-cloth**, *n.* stratum. **horse-dealer**, *n.* qui equos vendit. **horse-flesh**, *n.* caro equina. **horse-fly**, *n.* tabanus. **horsehair**, *n.* pilus equinus. **horseman**, *n.* eques. **horsemanship**, *n.* equitandi ars. **horse-race**, *n.* curriculum equorum. **horse-shoe**, *n.* solea. **horse-soldier**, *n.* eques.

hortatory, *adj.* monens.

horticulture, *n.* hortorum cultura.

hospitality, *n.* hospitium. **hospitable**, *adj.* hospitalis. *Adv.* hospitaliter.

host, *n.* hospes; caupo (*tavern-keeper*), **hostess**, *n.* hospita.

host, *n.* multitudo; *army,* exercitus.

hostage, *n.* obses, -idis, *m.*

hostel(ry), n. caupona. **hostler,** n. stabularius.

hostile, adj. inimicus, infestus. Adv. inimice, infeste. **hostility,** n. inimicitia; hostilities, bellum.

hot, adj. calidus, fervidus, fervens, candens; to be —, fervēre, aestuare; to make —, calefacĕre. Adv. calide, fervide, ferventer. **hot-headed,** adj. iracundus, imprudens.

hotel, n. deversorium, caupona.

hound, n. canis (venaticus). v.tr. to — on, instigare.

hour, n. hora; what — is it? quota hora est? from — to —, in horas. **hourglass,** n. horologium. **hourly,** adj. singulis horis.

house, n. domus, aedes, domicilium; villa (country —). **house-servants,** n. familia. v.tr. to store, condĕre. **household,** n. domus, familia. adj. domesticus; — gods, lares, penates. **householder,** n. paterfamilias. **housekeeper,** n. quae res domesticas dispensat. housekeeping, n. cura rei domesticae. **housemaid,** n. ancilla. **housewife,** n. hera. **housewifery,** n. diligentia.

hovel, n. tugurium, gurgustium.

hover, v.intr. circum volitare.

how, adv. quomodo? quemadmodum? (to express surprise), quid? (— many?) quot? (— few?) quotusquisque; (— often?) quotie(n)s? (— great?) quantus? (— much?) quanti? (in exclamations), quam. **howbeit,** adv. (at)tamen. **however,** adv. quamvis. conj. autem, (at)tamen.

howl, v.intr. ululare; of the wind, fremĕre; at funerals, eiulare; to weep aloud, plorare. n. ululatus; eiulatus, ploratus.

hubbub, n. tumultus, -ūs.

huckster, n. caupo, institor. v.intr. cauponam exercēre.

huddle, n. turba; huddled, conferti.

hue, n. color.

huff, n. be in a —, irasci.

hug, v.tr. amplecti. n. complexus.

huge, adj. immanis, vastus; ingens. Adv. valde, magnopere. **hugeness,** n. magnitudo, moles.

hulk, n. alveus navis.

hum, v.intr. fremĕre, murmurare; to buzz, bombum facĕre; sing softly, secum canĕre. n. fremitus; murmur, bombus, comprobatio (applause). Interj. hem!

human, adj. humanus; (— vices and errors, hominum vitia et errores). Adv. humano modo. **humane,** adj. clemens. Adv. clementer. **humaneness,** n. clementia. **humanity,** n. natura humana; mankind, hominum genus, gens humana; kind feelings, misericordia. **humanize,** v.tr. humanum reddĕre. **humankind,** n. genus humanum.

humble, adj. humilis; demissus; modestus; suppliant, supplex. Adv. demisse, submisse, modeste; to request humbly, supplicibus verbis orare. v.tr. infringĕre; to — oneself, submisse se gerĕre. **humbling, humiliating,** adj. use n. dedecus. **humiliation,** n. dedecus. **humility,** n. animus submissus; of origin, humilitas; modestia.

humbug, n. nugae. v.tr. illudĕre, alci verba dare.

humdrum, adj. iners, segnis (sluggish).

humid, adj. humidus. **humidity,** n. humor.

humour, n. (fluid), humor; temper, (animi) affectio; disposition, ingenium, animus; inclination, voluntas; to be in good-, bene affectus esse; ill-, natura difficilis; I am in the —, libet mihi facĕre; (wit) lepos; facetiae. v.tr. obtemperare; indulgēre. **humorist,** n. homo facetus.

hump, n. tuber; gibber. **humpbacked,** adj. gibber.

hunch, n., see HUMP.

hundred, adj. centum; — each, centeni, -ae, -a; — years old, centenarius; a — times, centie(n)s; a — thousand, centum mil(l)ia. **hundredfold,** adj. to bear fruit a —, cum centesimo efferre.

hunger, n. fames, inedia. v.intr. esurire. **hungry,** adj. esuriens, ieiunus. Adv. avide.

hunt, v.tr. venari; — after, (con)sectari. n. venatio, venatus. **hunter,** n. venator. **huntress,** n. venatrix.

hurdle, n. crates, -is.

hurl, v.tr. iacĕre, conicĕre. **hurling,** n. coniectus.

hurly-burly, n. tumultus.

hurrah, see HUZZA.

hurricane, n. tempestas, procella.

hurry, v.tr. accelerare; incitare, excitare, urgēre. v.intr. festinare, properare; whither are you —ing? quo te agis? n. festinatio, trepidatio. **hurried,** adj. citatus, praeceps. Adv. festinanter, propere.

hurt, v.tr. laedĕre, nocēre; fig. laedĕre; to be —, alqd aegre ferre. n. vulnus; damnum. adj. saucius (wounded); fig. tristis. **hurtful,** adj. nocens, noxius, damnosus. Adv. perniciose. **hurtfulness,** n. pernicies.

husband, n. maritus, vir, coniu(n)x. v.tr. rem familiarem curare, parcēre. **husbandman,** n. agricola, m. arator. **husbandry,** n. res rustica, res rusticae; agricultura; economy, frugalitas.

hush, interj. st! tace, pl. tacēte. v.tr. ex(s)tinguĕre; to — up a rumour, rumorem opprimĕre.

husk, n. folliculus. **husky,** adj. (sub)raucus.

hustings, n. suggestus, comitium.

hustle, v.intr. premĕre.

hut, *n.* casa, tugurium.

hutch, *n.* cavea (= *cage*).

huzza, *interj.* eia! eie! evoē! io! io! *n.* clamor et gaudium. *v.intr.* conclamare.

hyacinth, *n.* hyacinthus (hyacinthos) (*not our kind*).

Hymen, *n.* Hymen *or* Hymenaeus. Hymeneal, *adj* nuptialis.

hymn, *n.* (*of triumph*), paean, *m.* *v.tr.* cantu alcis laudes prosequi.

hyperbolical, *adj.* veritatis modum excedens.

hypercritical, *adj.* severus. *Adv.* nimiā cum severitate.

hypochondria, *n.* atra bilis. hypochondriacal, *adj.* melancholicus.

hypocrisy, *n.* (dis)simulatio, fraus.

hypocrite, *n.* (dis)simulator. hypocritical, *adj.* simulatus, fictus. *Adv.* simulate, ficte.

hypothesis, *n.* opinio, sententia (*opinion*), coniectura; *on this* —, quo posito.

I

I, *pron.* ego, egomet.

iambic, *adj.* iambeus. *n.* iambus.

ice, *n.* glacies, gelu. iceberg, *n.* glaciei moles. icy, *adj.* glacialis, frigidus; *fig.* superbus. *Adv.* superbe.

idea, *n.* notio; opinio; *mental picture*, imago; ex(s)pectatio; informatio; species, idea ; *to form a correct* —, recte sentire. ideal, *adj.* optimus, summus; pulcherrimus. ideal, *n.* optimum; effigies, imago, species, forma; *pattern, model*, exemplar.

identical, *adj.* eiusdem generis (*of the same kind*); idem ; *to be* —, nihil differre. identify, *v.tr.* agnoscēre. identity, *n.* idem; *e.g.* reum ipsum eundem esse confirmat.

ides, *n.* idus, -uum.

idiom, *n.* proprietas ; quae Latinae linguae propria sunt; loquendi ratio ; *genius of a language*, idiōma. idiomatic, *adj.* proprius. *Adv.* proprie.

idiot, *n.* (homo) stultus. idiocy, *n.* stultitia.

idle, *adj.* otiosus, piger ; *useless*, inutilis, irritus ; *unprofitable*, lēvis, vilis. *Adv.* ignave, frustra. *v.intr.* nihil agĕre. idleness, *n.* otium ; desidia.

idler, *n.* homo deses; cessator.

idol, *n.* *fig.* amores, deliciae. idolator, *n.* deorum fictorum cultor. idolatry, *n.* deorum fictorum cultus.

idyll, *n.* bucolica, -orum (*of a poem*).

if, *conj.* si; quod si *is often used; but* —, sin, sin autem; *but* — *not*, si non, sin aliter ; — *only*, dummodo ; *even* —, etiamsi, quamvis ; *whether* . . .

or —, sive (seu) . . . sive (seu) ; *as* —, quasi, tamquam, velut si.

ignite, *v.tr.* incendĕre. *v.intr.* exardescĕre, incendi. igneous, *adj.* igneus.

ignoble, *adj.* ignobilis ; obscuro loco natus ; humilis (*persons and things*); abiectus, turpis. *Adv.* humiliter, turpiter.

ignominy, *n.*, ignominia, dedecus. ignominious, *adj.* ignominiosus, turpis. *Adv.* turpiter.

ignoramus, *n.* homo inscius alcis rei. ignorance, *n.* inscientia ; ignoratio. ignorant, *adj.* insciens, inscitus; *unawares*, imprudens; *unskilful*, ignarus; *inexperienced*, imperitus ; rudis ; indoctus ; *to be* —, nescire, ignorare. *Adv. by adj. or* imprudenter, inscienter, imperite, indocte. ignore, *v.tr.* praeterire.

Iliad, *n.* Ilias.

ill, *adj.* aeger, morbidus ; *to be* —, aegrotare ; *in gen.* malus ; *of an* — *reputation*, male audire. *Adv.* male, misere ; *it goes* — *with me*, male mecum agitur. *n.* malum, incommodum. ill-advised, *adj.* inconsultus. ill-affected, *adj.* infestus ; *disloyal*, infidelis. ill-bred, *adj.* inurbanus. ill-breeding, *n.* mores inurbani. ill-fated, *adj.* infelix. ill-favoured, *adj.* *see* UGLY. ill-gotten, *adj.* male partus. ill-health, *n.* valetudo infirma. ill-matched, *adj.* impar. ill-mannered, *adj.*, *see* ILL-BRED. ill-nature, *n.* malignitas. ill-natured, *adj.* malignus. illness, *n.* morbus. ill-omened, *adj.* dirus, inauspicatus. ill-temper, *n.* malignitas, iracundia.

illegal, *adj.* legi contrarius. *Adv.* contra legem *or* leges.

illegible, *adj.* quod legi non potest.

illegitimate, *adj.* incerto patre natus ; *unlawful*, non legitimus, contra leges. *Adv.* non legitime, contra leges.

illiberal, *adj.* parcus, malignus. illiberality, *n.* parsimonia (parc.), malignitas.

illicit, *adj.* vetitus; nefas, *n. indecl.* (*impious*); — *means*, artes malae.

illimitable, *adj.* infinitus.

illiterate, *adj.* indoctus ; *to be* —, nescire lit(t)eras. *Adv.* indocte.

illume, illumine, illuminate, *v.tr.* collustrare, illustrare, illuminare ; *the mind*, colĕre, docēre ; *with pictures*, varie pingĕre. illumination, *n.* picture, pictura, tabula.

illusion, *n.* error, somnium, opinio vana. illusive, illusory, *adj.* vanus, falsus.

illustrate, *v.tr.* illustrare ; *a book*, picturis ornare ; *to explain*, illustrare. illustration, *n.* explicatio ; *of a book*, pictura, tabula ; *example*, exemplum. illustrious, *adj.* (prae)clarus, insignis.

image, *n.* imago, simulacrum; *statue*, statua; *a conception*, imago, species; *in rhetoric*, figura. **imaginary**, *adj.* fictus, inanis. **imagination**, *n.* cogitatio *(the faculty of thinking)*; *the faculty of understanding*, mens; *see* FANCY. **imaginative**, *adj. use* imagines concipere; ingeniosus; *adv.* ingeniose. **imagine**, *v.tr. and intr.* animo concipěre, fingěre ; *v. nt opinor*

imbecile, *adj.* fatuus, stultus. **imbecility**, *n.* stultitia.

imbibe, *v.tr.* bibere, imbibere.

imbue, *v.tr. to dye*, inficěre *(also fig.).*

imitable, *adj.* imitabilis. **imitate**, *v.tr.* imitari; aemulari; (per)sequi. **imitation**, *n.* imitatio; aemulatio; *the thing imitated*; effigies, imago, simulacrum. **imitative**, *adj.* qui facile imitatur

immaculate, *adj.* purus, incorruptus, integer; castus. *Adv.* pure, incorrupte, caste.

immaterial, *adj. (e.g. spirits)*, corpore vacans; *unimportant*, *by* nullius momenti, lĕvis.

immature, *adj.* immaturus, crudus.

immeasurable, *adj.* immensus; infinitus, vastus. *Adv.* in *or* ad immensum.

immediate, *adj.* ipse, proximus; *an cause*, caus(s)a proxima; *without delay*, praesens. *Adv. use adj.*; *without delay*, statim, confestim, extemplo.

immemorial, *adj. it is an — custom*, ex antiquis temporibus inveteravit.

immense, *adj.* ingens, vastus. *Adv.* ad *or* in immensum; *very much*, maxime, valde. **immensity**, *n.* vastitas.

immerge, *v.tr.* (im)mergēre, demergēre. **immersion**, *n. by the verb.*

immigrate, *v.intr.* (im)migrare. **immigrant**, *n.* advena. **immigration**, *n.* adventus.

imminent, *adj.* praesens; *by* subesse, imminēre.

immobility, *n.* immobilitas, *or by adj.*; *see* IMMOVABLE.

immoderate, *adj.* immodicus | intemperans; impotens *(e.g. joy*, laetitia); effrenatus. *Adv.* immoderate; *to drink —*, vino se obruere. **immoderation**, *n.* intemperantia.

immodest, *adj.* arrogans; impudicus. *Adv.* arroganter, impudice. **immodesty**, *n.* arrogantia; insolentia; impudicitia.

immolate, *v.tr.* immolare. **immolation**, *n.* immolatio.

immoral, *adj.* perditus; turpis; nequam, corruptus. *Adv.* turpiter, prave. **immorality**, *n.* mores corrupti; turpitudo.

immortal, *adj.* immortalis, aeternus. **immortality**, *n.* immortalitas, aeternitas.

immovable, *adj.* immobilis, stabilis. *Adv. use adj.* **immovableness**, *n.* immobilitas.

immunity, *n.* vacatio, immunitas.

immure, *v.tr.* muro saepire, cingěre.

immutability, *n.* immutabilitas; constantia. **immutable**, *adj.* immutabilis; contans; ratus *(e.g. cursus lunae).* *Adv.* constanter, perpetuo.

impair, *v.tr.* deminuěre, infringěre.

impale, *v.tr.* (hastā *or* palo) transfigěre.

impalpable, *adj.* quod tangi non potest.

impart, *v.tr.* impertire; communicare, participem facěre alqm; dare.

impartial, *adj.* aequus; *to be —*, neutri parti favēre. *Adv.* aequo animo, sine irā et studio. **impartiality**, *n.* animus studio et irā vacuus; aequitas.

impassable, *adj.* invius, impeditus.

impassioned, *adj.* ardens, vehemens.

impatience, *n.* festinatio. **impatient**, *adj.* ardens, impatiens morae, acer; *to be — at a thing*, alqd aegre ferre. *Adv.* ardenter, acriter, iracunde.

impeach, *v.tr.* accusare. **impeacher**, *n.* accusator, *n.* impeachment, *n.* accusatio.

impede, *v.tr.* impedire. **impediment**, *n.* impedimentum; *stammer*, haesitantia linguae.

impel, *v.tr.* impellěre, urgēre; incitare.

impend, *v.intr.* impenděre, imminēre.

impenetrable, *adj.* impenetrabilis; impervius; impeditus; caliginosus *(of darkness)*; *fig.* ambiguus.

impenitence, **impenitency**, *n.* animus obstinatus. **impenitent**, *adj.* obstinatus. *Adv.* obstinate.

imperative, *adj. with* imperare, *or by* necessarius.

imperfect, *adj.* imperfectus; inchoatus; *faulty*, mendosus; *rough*, rudis; *defective*, mancus; *tempus imperfectum (gram.). Adv.* imperfecte, mendose. **imperfection**, **imperfectness**, *n.* vitium, culpa.

imperial, *genit.* imperatoris; *adj.* imperatorius. **imperious**, *adj.* imperiosus; superbus. *Adv.* imperiose, superbe.

imperil, *v.tr.* in discrimen adducěre.

imperishable, *adj.* immortalis.

impersonate, *v.tr.* partes alcis agěre.

impertinence, *n.* insolentia. **impertinent**, *adj.* insolens; *not to the point*, quod nihil ad rem est. *Adv.* insolenter.

imperturbable, *adj.* stabilis, gravis. *Adv.* constanter, graviter.

impervious, *adj.* impervius.

impetuous, *adj.* violentus, vehemens, acer. *Adv.* magno impetu; acriter. **impetuosity**, *n.* violentia; impetus. **impetus**, *n.* impetus, vis.

impiety, *n.* impietas erga Deum; nefas, scelus. **impious**, *adj.* impius; nefarius; nefandus *(of a deed). Adv.* impie, nefarie.

implacable, *adj.* implacabilis; inexorabilis. *Adv.* atrociter, saeve.

implant, *v.tr.* inserěre, poněre.

implement, *n.* instrumentum, ferramentum.

implicate, *v.tr.* implicare, illaqueare.

implicated, *adj.* implicatus, *etc.*, conscius. **implication**, *n.* implicatio. **implicit**, *adj.* tacitus ; *complete*, totus, omnis. *Adv.* tacite, prorsus.

implore, *v.tr.* implorare, petĕre ; exposcĕre ; exorare ; supplicare ; obsecrare ; orare.

imply, *v.tr.* in se habēre ; *to be implied in*, alci rei inesse.

impolite, *adj.* inurbanus. *Adv.* inurbane. **impoliteness**, *n.* rusticitas.

impolitic, *adj.* imprudens.

import, *v.tr.* invehĕre, importare ; *signify*, significare. *n.* quod importatur ; significatio. **import-duty**, *n.* portorium. **importance**, *n.* auctoritas, pondus, vis ; *to be of no* —, nullo esse numero ; *of high position*, auctoritas. **important**, *adj.* gravis ; *to be* —, magni momenti esse. **importation**, *n.* invectio. **importunate**, *adj.* molestus. **importune**, *v.tr.* molestus esse, (ef)flagitare. **importunity**, *n.* (ef)flagitatio.

impose, *v.tr.* imponĕre ; — *a punishment*, multam alci irrogare ; — *upon ; see* CHEAT. **imposing**, *adj.* speciosus ; magnificus. **imposition**, *n.* irrogatio (*e.g.* multae) ; fraus (*deception*). **impost**, *n.* vectigal. **impostor**, *n.* fraudator. **imposture**, *n.* fraus, fallacia.

impossibility, *n.* usu. fieri non posse, *etc.* **impossible**, *adj.* quod effici non potest ; *it is* — *for me to, etc.*, fieri non potest ut, *etc. ; adv.* by nullo pacto or plane non.

impotence, *n.* infirmitas corporis, or animi. **impotent**, *adj.* impotens.

impound, *v.tr.* pignus capĕre ; includĕre (*e.g. cattle*).

impoverish, *v.tr.* in egestatem reducĕre. **impoverishment**, *n.* egestas, paupertas.

impracticable, *adj.* quod fieri non potest.

imprecate, *v.tr.* (im)precari, ex(s)ecrari. **imprecation**, *n.* ex(s)ecratio.

impregnable, *adj.* inexpugnabilis ; *fig.* stabilis.

impress, *v.tr.* imprimĕre ; *fig.* inurĕre, inculcare. **impression**, *n.* impressio ; *the copy*, exemplum ; *to take or make an* —, exprimĕre ; *on the mind*, animi motus ; *to make an* — *on anyone*, alqm movēre. **impressive**, *adj.* gravis. *Adv.* graviter. **impressiveness**, *n.* gravitas.

imprint, *v.tr.* imprimĕre.

imprison, *v.tr.* in custodiam dare, tradĕre. **imprisonment**, *n.* custodia, vincula, -orum.

improbable, *adj.* non verisimilis. *Adv.* non verisimiliter.

improbity, *n.* improbitas.

impromptu, *adv.* ex tempore.

improper, *adj.* indecōrus ; improprius ;

unsuitable, alienus ; *it is* — *to, etc.*, indecorum est. *Adv.* indecore. **impropriety**, *n.* quod indecorum est.

improve, *v.tr.* melius facĕre ; excolĕre. *v.intr.* melior fieri, se colligĕre (*morally*), convalescĕre (*in health*). **improvement**, *n.* correctio, emendatio ; — *of circumstances*, amplificatio rei familiaris ; disciplina.

improvidence, *n.* temeritas, imprudentia. **improvident**, *adj.* improvidus, incautus ; imprudens ; neglegens (neglig-). *Adv.* improvide, imprudenter.

imprudence, *n.* imprudentia, temeritas. **imprudent**, *adj.* imprudens, temerarius. *Adv.* imprudenter, temere.

impudence, *n.* impudentia, os impudens. **impudent**, *adj.* impudens, procax, improbus. *Adv.* impudenter, confidenter.

impugn, *v.tr.* impugnare ; oppugnare ; negare ; improbare (*e.g. a will*, testamentum) ; repugnare (*e.g.* opinioni).

impulse, *n.* impulsio, impulsus (*better by verbs*, *e.g.* agĕre, pellĕre, *etc.*) ; *motive*, impulsus, caus(s)a ; *from one's own* —, sponte or suā sponte ; per se ; — *from without*, stimulus.

impunity, *n. with* —, impunitus, inultus, impune.

impure, *adj.* impurus ; obscenus ; contaminatus (*e.g.* sanguine) ; foedus, turpis. *Adv.* impure, foede, turpiter. **impurity**, *n.* impuritas, foeditas, turpitudo.

imputation, *n. charge*, crimen, culpa. **impute**, *v.tr.* assignare ; a(d)scribĕre.

in, *prep. of place, by old locative* ; in *with abl.* ; *abl.* (*e.g.* eo loco) ; in *with accus.* (*to place* — *a ship*, in navem imponĕre) ; apud *with accus.* (— *Cicero*, apud Ciceronem) ; — *the hands of*, penes alqm ; — *the beginning*, ab initio.

inability, *n.* infirmitas, inopia, or non posse.

inaccessibility, *n. by* **inaccessible**, *adj.* inaccessus ; invius ; impeditus ; *of persons*, rari aditūs. *Adv.* — *situated*, quo non aditus est.

inaccuracy, *n.* indiligentia, pravitas, or *use* falsus. **inaccurate**, *adj.* indiligens. *Adv.* indiligenter.

inaction, inactivity, *n.* segnities, inertia, ignavia ; desidia ; *leisure*, otium, desidia ; *rest*, quies. **inactive**, *adj.* ignavus, segnis, iners. *Adv.* ignave, segniter, quiete.

inadequacy, *n. by* **inadequate**, *adj.* alienus ab, non sufficiens, non satis idoneus, impar. *Adv.* parum, haud satis.

inadmissibility, *n. by* **inadmissible**, *adj.* quod admitti non potest.

inadvertence, *n.* neglegentia ; incuria. **inadvertent**, *adj.* neglegens. *Adv.* neglegenter ; *unintentionally*, sine consilio.

inalienable, *adj.* quod abalienari non potest.

inane, *adj.* inanis.

inanition, inanity, *n.* inanitas.

inapplicable, *adj.* non pertinēre ad; non valēre.

inapposite, *adj.* quod non aptum est.

inappreciable, *adj. or by* minimus.

inappropriate, *adj.* non idoneus.

inaptitude, *n.* inutilitas.

inarticulate, *adj.* non satis distinctus. *Adv.* parum distincte.

inattention, *n.* neglegentia, indiligentia. **inattentive,** *adj.* non attentus.

inaudible, *adj.* quod audiri non potest.

inaugural, *adj. to deliver an discourse,* oratione munus auspicari. **inaugurate,** *v.tr.* inaugurare, auspicare, dedicare *(altars, temples, etc.)* ; *see* BEGIN. **inauguration,** *n.* dedicatio.

inauspicious, *adj.* infelix, laevus, nefastus ; *an — day,* dies ater. *Adv.* infeliciter, inauspicato.

incantation, *n.* carmen.

incapability, *n.* inscitia, *but better* non posse. **incapable,** *adj.* indocilis; *dull,* hebes. **incapacitate,** *v.tr.* inutilem reddēre. **incapacity,** *n., see* INCAPABILITY.

incarcerate, *v.tr.* (in carcerem) inicēre. **incarceration,** *n.* custodia, vincula, -orum, *n.*

incarnate, *adj.* corpore indutus.

incautious, *adj.* imprudens. *Adv.* imprudenter, temere.

incendiarism, *n.* incendium. **incendiary,** *n.* incendiarius, incendii auctor.

incense, *n.* tus, turis ; *of* —, † tureus.

incense, *v.tr.* incendēre *(rouse, irritate).*

incentive, *adj.* quod instigat. *n.* impulsus, stimulus ; *means of inciting,* irritamentum.

inception, *n.* initium. **inceptive,** *adj.* incipiens.

incessant, *adj.* assiduus, continuus. *Adv.* assidue, continuo.

inch, *n.* digitus, uncia.

inchoate, *adj.* inchoatus.

incident, *adj.* quod ad alqd pertinet. *n.* eventus, res. **incidental,** *adj.* fortuitus, forte oblatus. *Adv.* forte.

incisive, *adj.* mordens, asper. **incisor,** *n.* dentes qui secant.

incite, *v.tr.* incitare, permovēre ; stimulare ; accendēre ; impellēre. **incitement,** *n.* impulsus.

incivility, *n.* inurbanitas.

inclemency, *n.* inhumanitas, crudelitas ; *of weather,* gravis *with* n. (*e.g.* tempestas gravis). **inclement,** *adj.* inclemens, servus; gravis, asper.

inclination, *n.* inclinatio ; *in geom.* fastigium ; declivitas *(from the top),* acclivitas *(from the bottom)* ; *fig.* ad alqd voluntas ; *to have an — for anything,* alci rei studēre. **incline,** *v.intr.* *to slope,* proclivis *or* declivis esse; *fig.*

to lean, inclinari, (se) inclinare. *v.tr.* inclinare, demittēre *(e.g.* caput). **inclined,** *adj.* inclinatus: pronus.

inclose, *v.tr.* saepire (sep-).

include, *v.tr.* comprehendēre, complecti, a(d)scribēre ; *to — among the accused,* in reos referre. **inclusive, included,** *adj. that matter* —, additā eā re ; *by* cum *or* in.

incognito, *adv.* dissimulato nomine.

incoherence, incoherency, *n. by circumloc. with* **incoherent,** *adj.* interruptus, dissipatus, sibi non constans. *Adv.* interrupte; *to speak incoherently,* haud cohaerentia dicēre.

income, *n.* vectigal *(public and private),* reditus, fructus, pecunia ; *to make an* —, quaestum facēre.

incommode, *v.tr.* incommodum alci afferre. **incommodious,** *adj.* incommodus; molestus.

incomparable, *adj.* maximus; divinus; eximius, egregius. *Adv.* sine exemplo, egregie, praestanter.

incompatibility, *n.* repugnantia, diversitas ; — *of temper,* importunitas. **incompatible,** *adj.* alienus, contrarius; *to be* —, abhorrēre ab.

incompetence, incompetency, *n.* inscitia. **incompetent,** *adj. legally,* faciendi potestatem non habēre; inscitus, inhabilis. *Adv.* inscite.

incomplete, *adj.* imperfectus. *Adv.* imperfecte. **incompleteness,** *n.* quod imperfectum est.

incomprehensibility, *n. by* **incomprehensible,** *adj.* quod comprehendi non potest.

inconceivable, *adj.* quod intellegi non potest ; incredibilis. *Adv.* incredibiliter, mirum in modum.

inconclusive, *adj.* (argumentum) quo nihil efficitur.

incongruity, *n.* repugnantia. **incongruous,** *adj.* alienus ab, incongruens. *Adv.* non apte.

inconsequent, *adj., see* INCOHERENT.

inconsiderable, *adj.* levis ; mediocris ; exiguus ; parvus ; *not* —, nonnullus. **inconsiderate,** *adj.* inconsideratus ; alci non consulens. *Adv.* inconsiderate; nullius ratione habitā.

inconsistency, *n.* discrepantia, inconstantia. **inconsistent,** *adj.* inconstans, contrarius. *Adv.* inconstanter.

inconsolable, *adj.* qui nullo solatio levari potest.

inconspicuous, *adj.* quod vix sentiri. *Adv.* sensim.

inconstancy, *n.* inconstantia; varietas; infidelitas; levitas; mutabilitas (mentis). **inconstant,** *adj.* inconstans ; varius ; infidelis ; infirmus ; lēvis ; mutabilis ; mobilis.

incontestable, *adj.* quod refutari non potest.

incontinent, *adj.* incontinens. *Adv.* incontinenter; *immediately,* statim.

incontrovertible, *adj.* quod refutari non potest.

inconvenience, inconveniency, *n.* incommoditas ; molestia ; *to cause* —, molestus esse. **inconvenient,** *adj.* inopportunus, incommodus. *Adv.* incommode.

inconvertible, *adj.* immutabilis.

incorporate, *v.tr.,* *see* UNITE.

incorrect, *adj.* non iustus ; vitiosus ; falsus ; *the account is* —, ratio non convenit. *Adv.* perperam ; vitiose ; falso. **incorrectness,** *n. by adj.* INCORRECT. **incorrigibility,** *n.* pravitas. **incorrigible,** *adj.* qui corrigi non potest ; saucy, improbus.

ncorrupt, *adj.* incorruptus ; *fig.* integer, innocens. *Adv.* integre. **incorruptibility,** *n.* quod corrumpi non potest; *fig.* integritas.

increase, *v.intr.* (ac)crescĕre, augeri, ingravescĕre (*in bad sense*), increbrescĕre. *v.tr.* augēre, amplificare. *n.* amplificatio, auctus.

incredible, *adj.* incredibilis. *Adv.* incredibiliter. **incredulous,** *adj.* qui non facile adduci potest ut credat, incredulus.

increment, *n.* incrementum.

incriminate, *v.tr.* suspectum reddĕre ; — *oneself,* se scelere alligare.

inculcate, *v.tr.* docēre.

incumbency, *n.* officium; munus. **incumbent,** *adj. anything is* — *upon me,* debeo alqd facĕre ; *it is* — *upon me, you, etc.,* meum, tuum est.

incur, *v.tr.* incidĕre in alqd ; contrahĕre; suscipĕre ; *to* — *disgrace,* dedecus in se admittĕre.

incurability, *n. by* **incurable,** *adj.* insanabilis; *hopeless,* desperatus.

indebted, *adj. to be* — *to,* alci pecuniam debēre ; alci obnoxius esse.

indecency, *n.* turpitudo, obscenitas. **indecent,** *adj.* indecōrus ; turpis. *Adv.* indecore, turpiter.

indecision, *n.* dubitatio. **indecisive,** *adj.* dubius, anceps. *Adv. by adj. ;* *see* INDEFINITE.

indecorous, *adj.* indecōrus. **indecorum,** *n.* deformitas ; vitium ; *bu the adj.* turpis, *also by* dedecet.

indeed, *adv.* quidem *or* enim (*enclit.*), profecto, vero, re verā ; sane; *I* —, equidem ; scilicet, videlicet = *of course* (*ironical*) ; *surely,* immo vero ; *then* —, tum vero.

indefatigable, *adj.* assiduus, impiger; indefessus. *Adv.* assidue, impigre. **indefatigability,** *n.* assiduitas, diligentia, impigritas.

indefensible, *adj.* quod defendi non potest : (locus) qui teneri non potest.

indefinable, *adj.* quod definiri non potest;

an — *sense of danger,* nescio quid periculi. **indefinite,** *adj.* incertus ; dubius, anceps ; ambiguus ; *pronomen indefinitum* (*gram.*). *Adv.* ambigue, incerte *or* incerto.

indelibility, *n. by adj.* **indelible,** *adj.* quod deleri non potest; perpetuus.

indelicate, *adj.* inurbanus, impudicus. *Adv.* inurbane, impudice. **indelicacy,** *n. by adj.*

indemnification, *n.* damni restitutio; compensatio. **indemnify,** *v.tr.* damnum alci restituĕre, pensare. **indemnity,** *n. see* INDEMNIFICATION ; *act of* —, lex oblivionis.

indent, *v.tr.* alqd incidĕre.

independence, *n.* libertas, arbitrium liberum (*i.e. liberty of judgment*). **independent,** *adj.* liber, solutus ; sui iuris (*of age*) ; sui potens. *Adv.* libere, solute, suo arbitrio (*at one's own will*).

indescribable, *adj.* incredibilis ; mirus; infandus; *by* nescio quid. *Adv.* incredibiliter, mirum in modum.

indestructible, *adj.* quod dirui non potest, perennis, perpetuus.

indeterminate, *adj.* incertus. *Adv.* dubitanter.

index, *n.* index ; *of a dial,* gnomon, *or* horarum index.

Indian, *adj.* Indianus, Indicus.

indicate, *v.tr.* indicare, indicio esse ; significare ; nuntiare ; *to denounce,* deferre. **indication,** *n.* indicium, vestigium, signum. **indicative,** *adj.* indicans ; modus indicativus (*gram.*). **indicatory,** *adj.* significans.

indict, *v.tr.* accusare, postulare. **indictment,** *n. bill of* —, libellus, accusatio. **indictable,** *adj.* accusabilis.

indifference, *n.* lēvitas, vilitas (*insignificance*) ; carelessness, neglegentia, contemptio ; *calmness,* aequus animus ; *coldness,* lentitudo ; *hardness,* animus durus ; *impartiality,* aequitas. **indifferent,** *adj.* nec bonus nec malus ; medius ; *trifling,* lēvis, vilis ; *careless,* remissus, dissolutus ; *slow,* lentus ; *hard-hearted,* durus ; *it is* — *to me whether, etc.,* nihil meā interest ; *to remain* —, aequo animo ferre ; *pretty fair,* satis bonus. *Adv. without distinction,* promiscue ; neglegenter ; *coolly,* lente ; *hard-heartedly,* duriter ; aequo animo ; mediocriter.

indigence, *n.* inopia ; egestas, mendicitas. **indigent,** *adj.* inops, egens.

indigenous, *adj.* indigĕna, *or* illā terrā natus ; *the* — *inhabitants,* indigĕnae ; *animals, vegetables, etc.,* indigĕna.

indigested, *adj.* crudus. **indigestible,** *adj.* difficilis ad concoquendum, gravis.

indigestion, *n.* cruditas.

indignant, *adj.* iratus, acundus. *Adv.*

iracunde. **indignation**, n. indignatio,
iracundia. **indignity**, n. ignominia.
indirect, adj. devius ; fig., by circumloc.; there are direct and — causes,
caus(s)arum aliae sunt adiuvantes, aliae
proximae ; gram. obliquus. Adv.
obscure, clam, or by per voum acc., per
per occultum.
indiscernible, adj. quod cerni non potest.
indiscoverable, adj. quod inveniri non
potest.
indiscreet, adj., see IMPROVIDENT, IM-
MODEST. **indiscretion**, n. see IMPRO-
VIDENCE, IMMODESTY.
indiscriminate, adj. promiscuus. Adv.
promiscue.
indispensable, adj. necessarius; it is —,
necesse est. Adv. necessario.
indispose, v.tr. inutile reddere. **indis-
posed**, adj. to be, feel —, leviter aegrotare ; unwilling, aversus ab.
indisputable, adj. certus, manifestus.
Adv. certo, sine dubio; by far, longe,
with adj.
indissoluble, adj. indissolubilis ; everlasting, aeternus.
indistinct, adj. parum clarus; obscurus;
an — voice, vox obtusa, (weak). Adv.
minus clare, obscure. **indistinguish-
able**, adj. quod discerni non potest.
indite, v.tr. scribere.
individual, adj. proprius, singularis,
singuli. Adv. viritim, in singulos, n.
an —, homo. **individuality**, n. natura
alcis propria.
indivisibility, n. by adj. **indivisible**,
adj. quod dividi non potest.
indocile, adj. indocilis. **indocility**, n.
ingenium indocile.
indolence, n. ignavia, desidia, indolent, adj. ignavus, piger. Adv. ignave,
segniter.
indomitable, adj. quod vinci non potest,
invictus.
indoor, adj. umbratilis. **indoors**, adv.
domi.
indubitable, adj. non dubius ; certus,
Adv., see CERTAIN.
induce, v.tr. inducere ; impellere ad.
inducement, n. caus(s)a, impulsus, incitamentum. **induct**, v.tr. inaugurare.
induction, n. in logic, inductio.
indulgence, n. indulgentia, venia. **indulge**, v.tr. indulgere, veniam dare, se
dedere. v.intr. nimis sibi indulgere.
indulgent, adj. indulgens, benignus,
facilis. Adv. indulgenter, benigne.
industry, n. industria, labor. **industrious**, adj. industrius, acer, diligens. Adv.
acriter, diligenter.
indweller, n. incola. **indwelling**, adj.
qui intus est, insitus; natural, innatus.
inebriated, adj. ebrius.
ineffable, adj. incredibilis, inauditus.
Adv. supra quam enarrari potest.
ineffective, **inefficient**, adj. invalidus ;

inutilis. Adv. frustra, nequi(c)quam.
ineffectiveness, **inefficiency**, n. use
adj.
inelegance or **inelegancy**, n. by sine elegantia. **inelegant**, adj. invenustus, inelegans ; illepidus. Adv. ineleganter, ille-
pide, inurbane.
ineligible, adj. qui non eligendus est,
inopportunus.
inept, adj. ineptus.
inequality, n. inaequalitas, dissimilitudo. **inequitable**, adj. iniquus; iniustus. Adv. inique, iniuste.
inert, adj. iners, tardus. Adv. tarde.
inertness, n. inertia.
inestimable, adj. inaestimabilis; mirus;
eximius, singularis Adv. eximie, excellenter, mire.
inevitable, adj. quod vitari non potest,
necessarius. Adv. necessario.
inexact, adj. haud accuratus (things),
indiligens (persons). **inexactness**, n. indiligentia.
inexcusable, adj. quod excusari non
potest. Adv. use adj.
inexhaustible, adj. quod exhauriri non
potest, infinitus.
inexorable, adj. nexorabilis ; durus.
Adv. use adj.
inexpedient, adj. inutilis, inopportunus.
inexperience, n. imperitia; inscientia.
inexperienced, adj. imperitus, ignarus,
rudis. **inexpert**, adj., see INEXPERI-
ENCED.
inexpiable, adj. inexpiabilis.
inexplicable, adj. inexplicabilis. Adv.
use adj.
inexpressible, adj. inauditus, inenarra-
bilis.
inextinguishable, adj. quod ex(s)tingui
non potest.
inextricable, adj. inexplicabilis. Adv.
use adj.
infallibility, n. e.g. (of a remedy) certum remedium. **infallible**, adj. certus,
qui errare non potest ; to be —, quasi
errore carere. Adv. certo.
infamous, adj. turpis, foedus. Adv.
turpiter, foede. **infamy**, n. turpitudo,
ignominia.
infant, n. infans, filiolus, filiola. **infan-
ticide**, n. infantium caedes.
infantry, n. pedites, -um.
infatuate, v.tr. infatuare ; pellicere.
infatuated, adj. amens, demens. **infatu-
ation**, n. amentia, dementia, furor.
infect, v.tr. inficere. **infection**, n.
contagio, contactus. **infectious**, adj. by
contagio morbi ; — disease, pestilentia.
infelicitous, adj. infelix. **infelicity**, n.
malum.
infer, v.tr. concludere, colligere. **inference**, n. coniectura; conclusio.
inferior, adj. inferior, minor. **inferiority**, n. in number, paucitas.

infernal, *adj.* infernus ; — *regions,* inferi, † Orcus.

infertility, *n.* sterilitas.

infest, *v.tr.* infestum reddĕre ; infestare ; vexare. **infested,** *adj.* infestus.

infidelity, *n.* perfidia.

infinite, *adj.* infinitus, immensus. *Adv.* infinite, ad *or* in infinitum. **infinitesimal,** *adj.* minimus. **infinitude, infinity,** *n.* infinitas, infinitum tempus ; magna copia *(great quantity).*

infirm, *adj.* infirmus, invalidus. **infirmity,** *n.* infirmitas, debilitas; *complaint,* morbus.

inflame, *v.tr.* accendĕre, inflammare ; *fig.* incitare, incendĕre ; *to be inflamed, angry,* inflammari, ardĕre. **inflammable,** *adj.* facilis ad exardescendum. **inflammation,** *n.* inflammatio. **inflammatory,** *adj.* inflammans ; *fig.* seditiosus.

inflate, *v.tr.* inflare; spiritu distendĕre *(e.g. a bladder) ; to become inflated,* se inflare. **inflated,** *adj.* inflatus ; *of speech,* turgidus. **inflation,** *n.* inflatio; *conceit,* superbia inanis.

inflect, *v.tr. to bend,* (in)flectĕre ; *(grammat.)* declinare. **inflection,** *n.* flexus; *(grammat.)* declinatio. **inflexibility,** *n.* pertinacia. **inflexible,** *adj.* rigidus ; pertinax. *Adv.* pertinaciter, perseveranter.

inflict, *v.tr.* alci alqd afferre ; alqm alqâre afficĕre ; — *punishment,* poenam capĕre. **infliction,** *n.* malum.

inflorescence, *n.* flos.

influence, *n.* vis ; effectus, auctoritas, gratia ; amplitudo *(through office) ; divine* —, afflatus divinus ; *to have* —, *with a person,* multum auctoritate posse ; *to have no* —, nihil valēre. *v.tr.* movēre, persuadēre. **influential,** *adj.* potens ; gravis, magna auctoritate ; *an* — *person,* qui multum valet. **influx,** *n. by* influĕre.

inform, *v.tr. lit.* alci alqd nuntiare ; certiorem facĕre alqm ; docēre ; — *against,* accusare nomen alcis. **informality,** *n.* vitium *(in an election, etc.); without formality,* amice. **informant,** *n.* auctor alcis rei. **information,** *n.* nuntius; *written* —, lit(t)erae; *to receive* —, nuntium accipĕre, certior fieri, accipĕre, audire ; *accusation,* delatio, indicium. **informer,** *n.* delator, index.

infraction, *n. (e.g. of a treaty,* violatum foedus). **infrangible,** *adj.* quod frangi non potest.

infrequency, *n.* raritas. **infrequent,** *adj.* rarus.

infringe, *v.tr.* frangĕre, violare. **infringement,** *n.* immunitio ; violatio ; — *of the law,* delictum. **infringer,** *n.* qui non (ob)servat.

infuriate, *v.tr.* exasperare.

infuse, *v.tr.* infundĕre. **infusion** *n.* infusio *(the act)* ; decoctum.

ingenious, *adj.* subtilis; callidus, artificiosus ; ingenio summo ; argutus *(e.g.* sententia). *Adv.* subtiliter, callide, artificiose; argute. **ingenuity,** *n. (of persons),* acumen ; prudentia; sagacitas; ars, sol(l)ertia, machinatio. **ingenuous,** *adj.* l'ber; apertus. *Adv.* libere, aperte. **ingenuousness,** *n.* libertas.

ingle-nook, *n. in the* —, domi.

inglorious, *adj.* inglorius, turpis *(e.g. deed).* *Adv.* sine gloriâ; turpiter.

ingraft, *v.tr.* inserĕre ; *ingrafted,* insitus.

ingrained, *adj.* insitus; inveteratus.

ingratiate, *v.tr.* favorem quaerĕre; gratiosus esse alci. **ingratitude,** *n.* animus ingratus.

ingredient, *n.* pars ; —*s,* elementa ; *(the following* —*s,* haec).

ingress, *n.* ingressus, -ûs.

inhabit, *v.tr.* habitare ; (in)colĕre, tenĕre ; *densely inhabited,* frequens. **inhabitable,** *adj.* habitabilis. **inhabitant,** *n.* incŏla ; *tenant,* inquilinus ; *citizen,* civis ; *colonist,* colŏnus; *of a town,* oppidanus.

inhale, *v.tr.* spiritu (spirando) ducĕre, haurire.

inharmonious, *adj.* discors, absonus, dissonus; *on bad terms,* discrepans. *Adv.* haud consonanter, haud congruenter.

inherent, *adj.* insitus, innatus, proprius. *Adv.* naturâ, in *or* per se.

inherit, *v.tr.* and *intr.* hereditatem accipĕre ; *to succeed to,* hereditatem adire ; *to* — *everything,* heres ex asse esse. **inheritance,** *n.* hereditas. **inherited,** *adj.* patrius, paternus.

inhibit, *v.tr.* interdicĕre. **inhibition,** *n.* interdictum.

inhospitable, *adj.* † inhospitalis; inhumanus. **inhospitality,** *n. by* inhospitalis.

inhuman, *adj.* inhumanus, *unfeeling; monstrous,* immanis; *unfeeling,* ferus. *Adv.* inhumane, crudeliter, saeve. **inhumanity,** *n.* inhumanitas, immanitas, crudelitas.

inimical, *adj.* inimicus.

inimitability, *n. by* **inimitable,** *adj.* non imitabilis. *Adv. by adj.*

iniquitous, *adj.* iniustus, iniquus. *Adv.* iniuste, inique. **iniquity,** *n.* iniustitia, iniquitas.

initial, *adj. by* initio positus *or* primus. *n.* prima lit(t)era. **initiate,** *v.tr.* initiare ; coepisse. **initiation,** *n. by* initiare ; initium. **initiative,** *to take the* —, initium capere.

injudicious, *adj.* nullius consilii; imprudens, stultus; inconsultus; temerarius. *Adv.* inconsulte, temere. **injudiciousness,** *n.* imprudentia, stultitia, *or by adj.*

injunction, *n.* interdictum.

injure, *v.tr.* laedĕre, vulnerare, *fig.* alci nocĕre; violare; *the storm —s the ship,* tempestas afflictat navem. **injury,** *n. as act,* vulneratio, sauciatio; *without — to duty,* salvo officio; iniuria, detrimentum, damnum, vulnus (*wound*). **injurious,** *adj.* noxius, iniuriosus, damnosus, gravis, malus; *— words,* verba contumeliosa. *Adv.* iniuriose, damnose, graviter, male.

injustice, *n.* iniustitia; *an —,* iniuria.

ink, *n.* atramentum. **inky,** *adj.* atramento foedatus.

inkling, *n.* susurrus.

inland, *adj.* mediterraneus.

inlay, *v.tr.* inserĕre, variare, distinguĕre.

inlet, *n.* aditus; aestuarium (*of the sea*).

inmate, *n.* deversor, inquilinus; *of a country,* incola.

inmost, innermost, *adj.* intimus; *the — part,* intima pars; intima, -orum; viscera, -um, *pl.*

inn, *n.* deversori(ol)um, hospitium, caupona. **innkeeper,** *n.* caupo.

innate, *adj.* innatus, insitus; proprius.

inner, *adj.* interior; intestinus; domesticus. *Adv.* intus; *within,* interius.

innocence, *n.* innocentia; integritas; *simplicity,* simplicitas. **innocent,** *adj.* innocens; *guiltless,* insons; integer. *Adv.* integre, caste. *n.* idiot, (homo) stultissimus. **innocuous,** *adj.* innocuus; *to be —,* nihil nocēre.

innovate, *v.tr.* novare, mutare. **innovation,** *n.* renovatio; res nova. **innovator,** *n.* novitatis cupidus.

innumerable, *adj.* innumerabilis; *endless,* infinitus; *an indefinite number,* sescenti.

inobservance, *n.* neglegentia.

inodorous, *adj.* odore carens.

inoffensive, *adj.* quod nihil habet offensionis; simplex. *Adv.* simpliciter. **inoffensiveness,** *n. by adj.* INOFFENSIVE.

inopportune, *adj.* inopportunus. *Adv.* haud opportune.

inordinate, *adj.* immoderatus, nimius, incredibilis. *Adv.* praeter modum, immoderate, nimis.

inorganic, *adj. e.g. — bodies,* corpora nullā cohaerentia naturā.

inquire, *v.intr.* quaerĕre; sciscitare; percontari; cognoscĕre; investigare. **inquiry,** *n.* investigatio; percontatio; *legal,* cognitio; quaestio; inquisitio; *to institute an —,* quaestionem habēre *or* instituĕre. **inquisition,** *n. see* INQUIRY. **inquisitive,** *adj.* audiendi studiosus, curiosus. *Adv.* curiose. **inquisitiveness,** *n.* cupiditas cognoscendi. **inquisitor,** *n.* quaesitor.

inroad, *n.* irruptio, incursio.

insalubrious, *adj.* insaluber; gravis; *air or climate,* gravitas caeli. **insalubrity,** *n. — of a place,* pestilens loci

natura; *— of the air,* pestilentia *or* gravitas caeli.

insane, *adj.* insanus, demens, furiosus; stultus. *Adv.* dementer, insane, furiose, stulte, inepte. **insanity,** *n.* insania, furor, dementia, stultitia.

insatiable, *adj.* insatiabilis; *an — desire,* aviditas. *Adv. by adj.*

inscribe, *v.tr.* inscrībĕre. **inscription,** *n.* inscriptio, index; titulus; epigramma.

inscrutability, *n.* obscuritas, *or by* **inscrutable,** *adj.* obscurus.

insect, *n.* insectum.

insecure, *adj.* non *with* tutus; infestus, incertus, lubricus (*of footing*). *Adv.* non *with* tuto *or* firmiter.

insensible, *adj.* sensūs expers; *fig.* lentus. *Adv.* sensim, pedetemptim. **insensibility,** *n.* torpor; animus durus, lentitudo.

inseparability, *n. by* **inseparable,** *adj.* indissolubilis; *indivisible,* individuus; *an — friend,* amicus fidissimus. *Adv. use adj.* INSEPARABLE.

insert, *v.tr.* inserĕre, includĕre, interponĕre; addĕre; adscrībĕre; *in the ground, plant,* defigĕre. **insertion,** *n. by verb* INSERT; *parenthesis,* interpositio.

inside, *n.* pars interior. *Adv.* intus. *Prep.* in *with abl.,* intra *with accus.*

insidious, *adj.* fallax, dolosus. *Adv.* fallaciter, dolose. **insidiousness,** *n.* fallacia, dolus.

insight, *n.* intellegentia; *knowledge,* sapientia; iudicium, consilium; *man of deep —,* vir prudentissimus.

insignia, *n.* fasces, -ium, insignia, -ium.

insignificant, *adj.* parvus, exiguus; *unimportant,* lēvis, nullius momenti. **insignificance,** *n.* exiguitas; nullius *or* parvi momenti.

insincere, *adj.* falsus, simulatus, dolosus. *Adv.* falso, simulate. **insincerity,** *n.* fucus, fraus, dolus.

insinuate, *v.tr. and intr.* se insinuare, arrepĕre; *to suggest,* significare. **insinuation,** *n.* blanditiae; significatio. **insinuating,** *adj.* blandus. *Adv.* blande.

insipid, *adj.* nihil sapiens, insulsus; ineptus; *not seasoned,* non conditus. *Adv.* insulse, absurde, inepte. **insipidity,** *n. by* INSIPID; *fig., see* ABSURDITY.

insist, *v.intr.* exigĕre, postulare.

insolence, *n.* insolentia; superbia, audacia. **insolent,** *adj.* insolens, audax. *Adv.* insolenter, audaciter.

insoluble, *adj.* quod liquefieri non potest; *fig.* inexplicabilis, difficilis.

insolvent, *adj.* qui non est ad solvendum. **insolvency,** *n.* non solvendo esse, *or* foro cedĕre.

insomuch, *adv.* sic, ita, adeo.

inspect, *v.tr.* visĕre, invisĕre; inspicĕre; intueri. **inspection,** *n. a looking on* *by verbs.* **inspector,** *n.* custos, censor. **inspectorship,** *n.* custodis munus, cura.

inspiration, *n. inhaling,* spiritus ; *by divine* —, divinitus; *counsel,* consilium.

inspire, *v.tr.* inspirare ; *to* — *with, instil,* alci inicĕre ; *to excite,* incitare.

inspired, *adj.* mente incitatus; *frenzied,* furens.

instability, *n.* inconstantia. **instable,** *adj.* inconstans.

install, *v.tr.* inaugurare. **installation,** *n. by* inaugurare. **instalment,** *n. prima* (secunda, *etc.*) pars.

instance, *n.* (*at the* — *of these men,* his petentibus, or his auctoribus); *example,* exemplum ; *for* —, exempli caus(s)ā *or* gratiā. *v.tr.* referre, dicĕre. **instant,** *adj.* urgent, acer, gravis ; *immediate,* praesens. *n.* punctum temporis ; momentum temporis ; *to the* —, ad tempus ; *the, this very* —, by ipse (*e.g. at the very* —, ipso tempore). *Adv. immediately,* statim, extemplo; *urgently,* acriter. **instantaneous,** *adj.* brevissimus ; fugax ; subitus (*e.g.* consilia). *Adv.* e vestigio; *immediately,* extemplo.

instate, *v.tr. to* — *in an office,* muneri alqm praeficĕre; apponĕre.

instead, *prep.* loco alcis *or* pro (*with abl.*); — *of taking to flight,* omissā fugā.

instep, *n.* pes superior.

instigate, *v.tr.* incitare. **instigation,** *n.* impulsus ; *at your* —, te auctore. **instigator,** *n.* auctor, concitator, suasor.

instil, *v.tr. to fill with,* implēre; imbuĕre.

instinct, *n.* natura ; *desire,* appetitus. *Adj.* — *with anything,* alqā re imbutus. **instinctive,** *adj.* naturalis, duce naturā suā. *Adv.* naturā (duce), naturaliter.

institute, *v.tr.* condĕre ; instituĕre ; *to erect,* constituĕre. **institution,** *n.* initium (*beginning*), or *verb* ; *custom,* lex, mos; *society,* societas, collegium.

instruct, *v.tr.* erudire ; docēre ; *see* ORDER ; *to be instructed,* discĕre ; *order,* praescribĕre. **instructed,** *adj.* eruditus ; doctus. **instruction,** *n. the act of teaching,* institutio ; eruditio ; *education in school,* disciplina ; *doctrina* ; praeceptum ; mandatum. **instructive,** *adj.* utilis. *Adv.* utiliter. **instructor,** *n.* magister, praeceptor.

instrument, *n.* utensilia, -ium, *n.* (*household*) *tools* ; instrumentum ; *means,* minister (*fig.*); *in law,* lit(t)erae, tabulae. **instrumental,** *adj.* utilis (*useful*) ; *convenient,* commodus, aptus ; *you were* — *in hindering,* per te stetit quominus, *etc., or* te auctore; — *music,* cantus tibiarum nervorumque. **instrumentality,** *n.* opera, ministerium.

insubordination, *n.* disciplina nulla ; seditio. **insubordinate,** *adj.* seditiosus, turbulentus. *Adv.* seditiose, turbulente(r).

insufferable, *adj.* intolerabilis.

insufficient, *adj.* haud satis. *Adv.* haud satis, parum. **insufficiency,** *n.* inopia, paupertas.

insult, *n.* iniuria, contumelia, maledictum ; *disgrace,* dedecus. *v.tr.* maledicĕre, contumeliam imponĕre. **insulting,** *adj.* contumeliosus, maledicus ; — *words,* voces contumeliosae. *Adv.* contumeliose.

insuperable, *adj.* in(ex)superabilis, quod superari non potest ; *invincible,* invictus.

insupportable, *adj., see* INTOLERABLE.

insurgent, *adj. and n.* seditiosus. **insurrection,** *n.* seditio, motus.

intact, *adj.* intactus ; integer, salvus, incolumis.

intangible, *n.* quod sentire non possumus.

integral, *adj.* pars ad totum necessaria. **integrity,** *n.* (*e.g.* — *of the empire*), *adj.* regnum integrum; *incorruptness,* integritas, probitas.

integument, *n.* cutis, teg(u)men, (in)teg(u)mentum.

intellect, *n.* mens, ingenium, animus, intellegentia. **intellectual,** *adj. by genit. of* mens, *etc.* **intelligence,** *n.* perspicacitas, sol(l)ertia; *see* INTELLECT ; *news,* nuntius ; *see* NEWS. **intelligent,** *adj.* mente praeditus, sanus ; intellegens, sapiens, prudens. *Adv.* intellegenter, sapienter, prudenter. **intelligible,** *adj.* quod facile intellegi potest; explicatus ; perspicuus; planus. *Adv.* perspicue, plane, aperte.

intemperance, *n.* intemperantia, immoderatio ; *in drink,* ebrietas. **intemperate,** *adj.* intemperans, immoderatus ; *in drink,* ebriosus, temulentus; *angry,* iracundus. *Adv.* intemperanter, immoderate.

intend, *v.tr. and intr.* propositum habēre; *to think of,* cogitare; *to be about to,* velle, in animo habēre. **intense,** *adj.* magnus, acer, summus. *Adv.* magnopĕre, acriter, summe. **intensify,** *v.tr.* maiorem reddĕre, augēre. **intensity,** *n.* vis, *f.,* gravitas ; — *of cold,* rigor. **intent,** *adj.* studiosus, intentus ; *to be* — *upon,* incumbĕre ad, studēre *n. to all* —*s and purposes,* omnino. **intention,** *n.* consilium, propositum. **intentional,** *adj.* quod consulto fit.

inter, *v.tr.* sepelire. **interment,** *n.* sepultura.

intercalary, *adj.* intercalaris.

intercede, *v.intr.* (de)precari *or* rogare *or* supplicare pro alqo. **intercession,** *n.* deprecatio. **intercessor,** *n.* deprecator.

intercept, *v.tr.* intercipĕre; *to cut off,* intercludĕre.

interchange, *v.tr. by* (com)mutare. *n.* (com)mutatio. **interchangeable,** *adj.*

quae inter se (com)mutari possunt. *Adv.* invicem.
intercourse, *n.* conversatio, usus, commercium; *habitual* —, consuetudo.
interdict, *v.tr.* interdicĕre. *n.* interdictum.
interest, *v.tr.* delectare; capĕre; *to* — *anyone,* alci placēre; tenēre (*e.g.* audientium animos); *anything* — *I me,* alqd meā interest ; *I feel an* — *in anything,* alqd mihi curae. *n.* studium ; delectatio ; *to have an* — *in, by interest or refert* ; *advantage,* commodum ; bonum, usus ; *the common* —, res *or* caus(s)a communis ; *it is to my* —, expedit mihi ; — *on capital,* usura *or* usurae, faenus (fe-); *to lend out money on* —, pecuniam faenorari. **interested,** *adj.* attentus, erectus ; studiosus (*hmd of*). **interesting,** *adj.* by alqm tenēre, iucundus.
interfere, *v.intr.* intercedĕre, intervenire, se immiscēre ; *to hinder,* prohibēre. **interference,** *n.* by verb. *or* by inter cessio.
interim, *n.* spatium, temporis intervallum; *ad* —, interim.
interior, *adj.* interior, internus. *n.* pars interior.
interject, *v.tr.* interponĕre, intericĕre. **interjection,** *n.* (*in grammar*) interiectio.
interlace, *v.tr.* implicare, intexĕre.
interline, *v.tr.* interscribĕre.
interlocutory, *adj.* in sermone.
intermarriage, *n.* connubium.
intermeddle, *v.intr.* se interponĕre, se admiscēre. **intermediate,** *adj.* medius.
interminable, *adj.* infinitus. *Adv.* infinite.
intermingle, *v.tr.* (inter)miscēre.
intermission, *n.* intermissio. **intermit,** *v.tr.* intermittĕre. **intermittent,** *adj. med.* febris intermittens. *Adv.* intervallo interposito, nonnumquam.
intermix, *v.tr., see* INTERMINGLE. *v.intr.* intermiscēri.
internal, *see* INNER. *Adv.* intus, penitus.
international, *adj.* — *law,* ius gentium.
internecine, *adj.* internecivus.
interpellation, *n.* interpellatio.
interpolate, *v.tr.* addĕre, inserĕre ; *to falsify,* corrumpĕre. **interpolation,** *n. use verb.*
interpose, *v.tr.* interponĕre, interiicĕre. *v.intr.* se interponĕre in rem. **interposition,** *n. use abl., abs.* (*e.g.* mari interiecto); *by the* — *of the sea* ; *by my* —, me auctore).
interpret, *v.tr.* interpretari; explanare ; *as an insult,* in contumeliam convertĕre; *to* — *differently,* aliter accipĕre. **interpretation,** *n.* interpretatio, explanatio. **interpreter,** *n.* interpres.
interregnum, *n.* interregnum. **interrex,** *n.* interrex.

interrogate, *v.tr. and intr.* quaerĕre, exquirĕre. **interrogation,** *n.* interrogatio, percontatio ; *question,* (inter)rogatum. **interrogative,** *adj. use verb.* **interrogator,** *n.* qui interrogat.
interrupt, *v.tr.* interrumpĕre ; interpellare ; intermittĕre ; *to cut short,* incidĕre **interrupted,** *adj.* interruptus, intermissus. *Adv.* interrupte. **interruption,** *n.* interpellatio ; interfatio ; intermissio.
intersect, *v.tr.* secare ; *to divide,* scindĕre ; *thus,* **X,** decussare ; *by ditches,* fossis concidĕre. **intersection,** *n.* sectio (*the act*); *the* — (**X**) *of two lines,* decussatio.
intersperse, *v.tr.* immiscēre.
interstice, *n.* rima, foramen.
intertwine, *v.tr., see* ENTWINE.
interval, *n.* intervallum ; — *of time,* tempus interiectum ; *to leave an* —, spatium relinquĕre ; *in the* —, interim ; *at* —s, aliquando.
intervene, *v.intr.* to be between, interiacēre ; *to come between,* intercedĕre. **intervention,** *n.* interventus.
interview, *n.* congressio, congressus ; conventus ; *conversation,* colloquium, sermo.
interweave, *v.tr.* intexĕre.
intestate, *n. adj.* intestatus.
intestine, *adj.* intestinus. *n.* viscera, exta (*both pl.*).
intimacy, *n.* familiaritas, necessitudo. **intimate,** *adj.* familiaris, intimus. *Adv.* familiariter. *v.tr.* indicare, docēre, nuntiare. **intimation,** *n.* significatio, nuntius.
intimidate, *v.tr.* timorem alci inicĕre, afferre. **intimidated,** *adj.* timefactus. **intimidation,** *n.* minae.
into, *prep.* in *with accus.*
intolerable, *adj.* intolerabilis, vix tolerabilis; *you are* — *to me,* odiosus mihi es. *Adv.* intoleranter. **intolerance,** *n.* intolerantia, superbia. intolerant, *adj.* difficilis ; superbus ; *in religion,* erga alqos parum indulgens.
intone, *v.tr.* to — *prayers,* preces canĕre.
intoxicate, *v.tr.* ebrium reddĕre. **intoxicated,** *adj.* ebrius. **intoxicating,** *adj.* qui alqm ebrium reddit. **intoxication,** *n.* ebrietas.
intractable, *adj.* difficilis. **intractability,** *n. by adj.*
intransitive, *adj.* intransitivus.
intrench, *v.tr.* vallare, vallo *or* fossā cingĕre. **intrenchment,** *n.* vallum, opera, -um.
intrepid, *adj.* intrepidus. **intrepidity,** *n.* animus impavidus ; fortitudo.
intricacy, *n.* implicatio; *the* — *of the road,* iter impeditum. **intricate,** *adj.* contortus, impeditus.
intrigue, *n.* dolus ; artificia, -iorum ;

fraus. *v.tr.* fallacias fabricari. **intriguing**, *adj.* callidus, fraudulentus.

intrinsic(al), *adj.* verus, *or* per se, *or* ipse. *Adv.* re verā, per se, vere.

introduce, *v.tr. lit.* invehĕre, importare ; *to* — *anyone*, introducĕre ; *by letter*, commendare ; *to induct*, inaugurare ; *to have been introduced*, usu receptus esse; *to* — *many changes*, multa mutare. **introduction**, *n.* invectio (*of goods, etc.*); inductio (*letting go in*) ; — *of persons*, introductio ; — *to a book, etc.*, proemium, exordium. **introductory**, *adj. by v.*, *to make* — *remarks*, praefari.

introspect, *v.tr.*, **introspection**, *n.* ipsum se inspicĕre.

intrude, *v.intr.* se intrudĕre. **intruder**, *n. by* importunus, molestus. **intrusion**, *n.* importunitas. *Adv.* moleste, importune.

intrust, *v.tr.* committĕre, tradĕre.

intuition, *n.* cognitio, perceptio. **intuitive**, *adj.* perspicuus. *Adv.* perspicue.

inundation, *n. by verb*, inundare, *or by* magnae aquae.

inure, *v.tr.* assuefacĕre.

invade, *v.tr.* irruptionem *or* incursionem facĕre in, invadĕre. **invader**, *n.* hostis. **invasion**, *n.* incursio.

invalid, *adj. in law*, irritus; *fruitless*, vanus; *of arguments*, infirmus, vitiosus; *to rescind, to annul*, rescindĕre, *n.* aeger — *ill*. **invalidate**, *v.tr.* irritum facĕre, tollĕre, rescindĕre.

invective, *n.* convicium, maledictum, verba *with adj., e.g.* acerba. **inveigh**, *v.intr.* in alqm invehi.

inveigle, *v.tr., see* MISLEAD.

invent, *v.tr.* reperire; (*in the mind*), excogitare ; comminisci (*gen. something bad*). **invention**, *n.* inventio, excogitatio ; *alqd inventum* ; *fiction*, fabula, mendacium (*lie*). **inventive**, *adj.* ingeniosus ; sol(l)ers ; — *faculty*, inventio, excogitatio. **inventor**, *n.* inventor. **inventory**, *n.* index.

inverse, *adj.* inversus, conversus. *Adv.* retro, permutato ordine. **inversion**, *n.* conversio ; — *of words*, inversio verborum. **invert**, *v.tr.* (con)vertĕre ; invertĕre ; *to turn everything topsy-turvy*, omnia miscēre.

invest, *v.tr., see* CLOTHE ; *with an office*, magistratum alci dare; *money*, collocare, ponĕre ; *to besiege*, circumsedĕre, obsidĕre. **investment**, *n. with an office*, inauguratio, *or by verb*; *of money, by verb* INVEST; *siege*, obsessio.

investigate, *v.tr.* exquirĕre, investigare, cognoscĕre. **investigation**, *n.* investigatio, percontatio, quaestio. **investigator**, *n.* investigator, quaesitor.

inveterate, *adj.* inveteratus, confirmatus. *Adv.* penitus.

invidious, *adj.* nvidiosus, malignus.

Adv. maligne, invidiose. **invidiousness**, *n.* invidia, malignitas.

invigorate, *v.tr.* corroborare ; *to become invigorated*, se corroborare, se recreare. **invigorating**, *adj.* aptus ad reficiendum. **invigoration**, *n.* confirmatio animi ; *of the body, use verb*.

invincible, *adj.* invictus, inexpugnabilis. *Adv.* quod superari non potest.

inviolability, *n.* sanctitas, religio. **inviolable**, *adj.* inviolabilis ; sanctus. *Adv.* inviolate. **inviolate**, *adj.* integer, inviolatus, incorruptus ; *safe*, incolumis.

invisibility, *n. by* invisible, *adj.* caecus *or by circumloc.*; *to be* —, sub oculos non cadĕre. *Adv.* quod cerni non potest.

invitation, *n.* invitatio ; *at your* —, vocatus a te. **invite**, *v.tr.* invitare ; vocare. **inviting**, *adj.* blandus, dulcis.

invocation, *n.* imploratio; testatio.

invoice, *n.* (mercium) libellus *or* index.

invoke, *v.tr.* invocare, implorare; *to* — *God as a witness*, Deum testari.

involuntary, *adj.* invitus et coactus. *Adv.* invite, *or by adj.* **involuntariness**, *n.* necessitas.

involve, *v.tr.* involvĕre; implicare, illaqueare ; *to be involved in debt*, aere alieno oppressus esse.

invulnerable, *adj.* invulnerabilis.

inward, *adj.* interior. *Adv.* introrsum, intus; *bent* —, incurvus.

inweave, *v.tr.* intexĕre.

inwrought, *adj. by* intextus.

irascible, *adj.* iracundus. *Adv.* iracunde. **irascibility**, *n.* iracundia. **ire**, *n., see* ANGER. **ireful**, *adj., see* ANGRY.

irks, *v.tr. impers.*; *it* —, piget, taedet. **irksome**, *adj.* gravis, molestus. *Adv.* graviter, moleste. **irksomeness**, *n.* taedium, molestia.

iron, *n.* ferrum; *to put in* —*s*, in vincula conicĕre. *Adj.* ferreus ; —*ware*, ferramentum. **ironmongery**, *n.* ferramenta, -orum.

ironical, *adj.* alqd per ironiam dictum. *Adv.* per ironiam. **irony**, *n.* ironia (*Greek*), dissimulatio.

irradiate, *v.tr.* luce suā collustrare, illustrare.

irrational, *adj. without reason*, rationis expers, brutus; *foolish*, amens, caecus. *Adv.* insane, stulte.

irreclaimable, *adj.* quod emendari non potest.

irreconcilable, *adj.* inexorabilis ; (res) inter se repugnantes, contrariae. *Adv. by adj.*

irrecoverable, *adj.* irreparabilis ; irrevocabilis. *Adv. by adj.*

irrefragable, *adj.* certus, gravis, (argumentum) quod refelli non potest. *Adv. by adj.*

irrefutable, *adj., see* IRREFRAGABLE.

irregular, *adj.* enormis, inusitatus, in

aequalis (*unequal*) ; *of an election*, vitiosus ; — *conduct*, licentia. incomposite, inaequaliter ; *of conduct*, dissolute ; *of an election*, vitio. **irregularity**, *n.* inaequalitas ; — *of conduct*, licentia; *in an election*, vitium.

irrelevant, *adj.* alienus ; *it is* —, nihil ad rem.

irreligion, *n.* impietas erga Deum or Deos. **irreligious**, *adj.* impius erga Deum or Deos. *Adv.* impie.

irremediable, *adj. see* INCURABLE.

irremovable, *adj.* immobilis.

irreparable, *adj. see* IRREVOCABLE.

irreproachable, *adj.* innocens ; probus.

irresistible, *adj.* cui nullà vi resisti potest.

irresolute, *adj.* dubius ; incertus ; in constans. *Adv.* dubitanter. **irresolution**, *n.* dubitatio.

irrespective, *adj.* nullâ ratione (alcis rei) habitâ.

irresponsible, *adj.* cui nulla ratio reddenda est. **irresponsibility**, *n. use adj.*

irretrievable, *adj. see* IRRECOVERABLE.

irreverence, *n.* impietas erga Deum or Deos. **irreverent**, *adj.* impius erga Deum or Deos. *Adv.* impie.

irrevocable, *adj.* irrevocabilis, irreparabilis, immutabilis. *Adv.* in perpetuum.

irrigate, *v.tr.* irrigare. **irrigation**, *n.* irrigatio.

irritable, *adj.* stomachosus, iracundus. *Adv.* stomachose, iracunde. **irritate**, *v.tr. a wound*, inflammare; *fig.* irritare. **irritation**, *n.* ira, stomachus.

irruption, *n.* by irrumpere ; *of the enemy*, incursio.

island, *n.* insula. **islander**, *n.* insulae incola. **isle**, *n. see* ISLAND. **islet**, *n.* parva insula.

isolate, *v.tr.* secernere, separare. **isolated**, *adj.* remotus, solus. **isolation**, *n.* solitudo.

issue, *n. act of flowing*, by verb ; (*the* — *of an order, money*), by verb ; *result*, exitus, eventus ; *offspring*, filius, filia; *progenies*, stirps. *v.intr. to flow out*, effluere, emanare; *to go out*, evadere; *to rush out* (*e.g. troops*), erumpere ; *to end*, finire, terminari. *v.tr.* (*money*), promere ; *a new coinage*, distribuere ; (*an order, a book*), edere; *to be issued*, exire ; *to* — *an order*, edicere, edictum proponere.

isthmus, *n.* isthmus (isthmos).

it, *pers. pron.* by hic, haec, hoc, *or* is, ea, id.

Italian, *adj.* Italicus.

itch, *n. disease*, scabies. *v.intr.* prurire, *fig.* gestire.

item, *n.* —*s of expenditure*, rationes sumptuariae; res.

iterate, *v.tr.* iterare. **iteration**, *n. use verb.*

---

itinerant, *n. and adj.* viator. **itinerary**, *n.* itineris descriptio.

ivory, *n.* ebor. *Adj.* eburneus.

ivy, *n.* hedera.

J

jabber, *v.intr.* blaterare, garrire. **jabbering**, *n.* clamor.

jackass, *n.* asinus. **jackdaw**, *n.* monedula, *perhaps* graculus.

jacket, *n.* vestis or vestimentum.

jade, *n. poor horse*, caballus ; *of a woman* mulier importuna. **jaded**, *adj.* (de)fessus.

jag, *v.tr.* incidere. **jagged**, *adj.* serratus; — *rocks*, saxa praerupta.

jail, *n. see* PRISON.

jamb, *n.* (*in architecture*) postis, *m.*

jangle, *v. see* QUARREL.

janitor, *n.* ianitor; *fem.* ianitrix.

January, *n.* Ianuarius (mensis).

jar, *v. intr.* stridere, dissonare, discrepare. *n. quarrel*, rixa, iurgium. **jarring**, *adj.* dissonus, discors.

jar, *n. a vessel*, olla, cadus, dolium (*cask*); urceus; hydria; amphora.

jargon, *n.* sermo barbarus.

jasper, *n.* iaspis.

jaundice, *n.* morbus regius or arquatus. **jaundiced**, *adj. fig.* invidus.

jaunt, *n.* iter; *to take a* —, excurrere.

javelin, *n.* pilum, iaculum.

jaw, *n.* maxilla ; *jaws*, fauces, -ium. **jaw-bone**, *n.* maxilla.

jealous, *adj.* aemulus; invidus; *to be* —, aemulari, invidere. *Adv. use adj.* **jealousy**, *n.* aemulatio.

jeer, *v.tr. and intr.* in ludibrium vertere; ludificare; illudere. *n.* ludificatio, ludibrium. **jeerer**, *n.* cavillator.

jejune, *adj.* ieiunus, aridus. *Adv.* ieiune.

jeopardize, *v.tr.* in aleam dare, in discrimen adducere. **jeopardy**, *n. see* DANGER.

jerk, *v.tr. n.* quatere. *n.* impetus.

jerkin, *n. see* JACKET; vestis.

jest, *v.intr.* iocari, ioculari. *n.* iocus, ludus ; facetiae ; *in* —, per iocum ; *for* —, per ridiculum. **jester**, *n.* qui iocatur; buffoon, scurra.

jet, *n. of water*, aqua saliens.

jetsam, *n.* res naufragio eiectae.

jetty, *n.* moles, -is.

Jew, *n.* Iudaeus. **Judaism**, *n.* doctrina Iudaica. **Jewish**, *adj.* Iudaicus, Iudaeus.

jewel, *n.* gemma. **jewelled**, *adj.* gemmatus. **jeweller**, *n.* qui gemmas vendit.

jig, *n. and v.tr. see* DANCE.

jilt, *v.tr.* repudiare.

jingle, *v.intr.* tinnire. *n. or* **jingling,** *n.* tinnitus.

job, *n.* opus ; *office,* munus parvum ; *trickery,* fraus. **jobber,** *n.* operarius ; *cheat,* fraudator.

jockey, *n.* agaso (*groom*). *v.tr.* (*to cheat*), circumvenire.

jocose, jocular, *adj.* iocosus, ridiculus; facetus, salsus. *Adv.* iocose, facete, salse. **jocoseness, jocularity, jocundity,** *n.* facetiae.

jog, *v.tr. see* PUSH. *v.intr.* lente progredi.

oin, *v.tr.* (con)iungĕre ; nectĕre, con-(n)ectĕre; conglutinare; *to tie together,* colligare ; — *battle,* proelium *or* pugnam committĕre. *v.intr. in partnership, etc.,* se (con)iungĕre, societatem inire *or* coire cum alqo ; *to take part in,* particeps esse. **joiner,** *n.* faber ; **joint,** *n.* commissura ; artus, articulus; vertebrae. *Adj.* communis. *Adv.* una, simul. coniuncte, communiter. **jointheir,** *n.* coheres.

joist, *n.* tignum transversarium.

joke, *see* JEST.

jolly, *adj.* hilaris, lascivus. **jollity,** *n.* hilaritas, lascivia.

jolt, *v.tr.* iactare, quassare. *v.intr.* iactari, quassari. *n.* iactatio, quassatio.

jostle, *v.intr.* alqm offendĕre.

jot, *n. not a —,* nihil; *not to care a —,* non flocci. *v.tr. to — down,* scribĕre.

journal, *n.* ephemĕris, *f.; newspaper,* acta (diurna), -orum.

journey, *n.* iter, *n.* via (*road*); peregrinatio ; *a march,* iter. *v.intr.* iter facĕre, peregrinari.

journeyman, *n. in a trade,* opifex.

Jove, *n.* Iuppiter; *genit.* Iovis; *by —* l mehercle l

jovial, *adj.* hilaris. *Adv.* hilariter. **joviality,** *n.* hilaritas.

joy, *n.* gaudium, laetitia ; *pleasure,* voluptas ; *delight,* delectatio. **joyous, joyful,** *adj.* laetus, hilaris; *pleasing,* iucundus, dulcis. *Adv.* laete, hilariter, iucunde. **joyless,** *see* SAD. **joyousness, joyfulness,** *n. see* JOY.

jubilant, gaudio ex(s)ultare; ex(s)ultans.

judge, *n.* iudex, assessor; qui iudicat ; *mediator, umpire,* disceptator; censor; *see* CRITIC. *v.intr.* iudicare ; *to have an opinion*) ; *to give a formal judgment,* censĕre. *v.tr.* iudicare; *to — between,* diiudicare. **judgment,** *n.* iudicium ; *to give —,* ius dicĕre, agĕre ; *as a faculty,* sapientia, prudentia ; *to show —,* iudicium habĕre ; *determination,* arbitrium, sententia (*opinion*) ; *estimation,* existimatio ; *in my —,* meo iudicio; — *seat,* tribunal, iudicium; *to bring before the —,* in iudicium vocare. **judicial,** *adj.* iudicialis ; *of the forum,* forensis. *fig.* aequus. *Adv.* iure, lege. **judicious,**

adj. sapiens, prudens. *Adv.* sapienter, prudenter. **judiciousness,** *n.* prudentia, sapientia, consilium.

jug, *n.* urceus, urceolus, amphora.

juggle, *v.intr. lit.* praestigias agĕre ; *fig. see* DECEIVE. *n.* praestigiae; *deception,* deceptio (*the act*) ; fallacia ; simulatio, dissimulatio. **jugglery, juggling,** *n.* ars, dolus. **juggler,** *n. lit.* praestigiator; *see* DECEIVER.

juice, *n.* sucus. **juicy,** *adj.* suci plenus.

July, *n.* Iulius (mensis) ; *during the Republic,* Quinctilis (mensis).

jumble, *v.tr.* (per)miscĕre; *to make a regular —,* omnia miscĕre. *v.intr.* (per)misceri. *n.* mistura ; farrago ; *of words,* sartago; colluvies, varietas.

jump, *v.intr.* salire; *up,* exsilire; *with joy,* ex(s)ultare gaudio; *upon or into,* insilire in alqd; *over,* transilire; *down from,* desilire ex, *etc. n.* leap, saltus. **jumper,** *n.* qui salit.

junction, *n.* coniunctio. **juncture,** *n. of affairs,* tempora, -um.

June, *n.* (mensis) Iunius.

jungle, *n.* silva.

junior, *adj. and n.* iunior aetate ; *the —* (natu) minor.

juniper, *n.* iuniperus, *f.*

jurisconsult, *n.* iuris *or* iure consultus. **jurisdiction,** *n.* iurisdictio, ius. **jurisprudence,** *n.* iuris civilis prudentia. **jurist,** *n. see* JURISCONSULT. **juror,** *n. as judge,* iudex. **jury,** *n.* iudices, -um.

just, *adj.* iustus, aequus. *Adv. — now,* in praesentia ; *only — lately,* modo, proxime. *Adj.* recens ; *comparison, — as,* aeque, perinde, pariter ; non secus . . . ac ; *— as much . . . as,* non magis . . . quam ; *— now,* modo ; *— then,* tum maxime; *not —, not exactly,* haud ita; *in answers, — so,* inquam, ita plane *or* prorsus; *sub lucem, — before daybreak.* *Adv.* iuste, iure, legitime, merito. **justice,** *n.* iustitia, aequitas; *right, law,* ius; *to see — done,* ius dare *or* reddĕre; *in —, iure.* **justifiable,** *adj.* iustus; *lawful,* legitimus; recte ac iure factum. *Adv.* recte ac iure. **justification,** *n.* excusatio, satisfactio. **justify,** *v.tr.* purgare (*to prove one's innocence*); *to excuse,* excusare ; culpâ liberare.

jut, *v.intr. — out,* exstare, eminēre ; *of land,* excurrĕre.

juvenile, *adj.* puerilis, *or genit.* adolescentis *or* adolescentium, iuvenitis.

K

keel, *n.* carina.

keen, *adj.* acer, acerbus, acutus, sagax. *Adv.* acriter, acute, sagaciter. **keenness,** *n.* acerbitas, sagacitas.

keep, *v.tr.* servare, tenēre; *to store up,* condĕre ; *to preserve,* conservare ; *to support,* alĕre ; *to observe,* observare ; *to — faith,* fidem servare ; *to — a secret,* occultum tenēre; *to — apart,* distinēre. *v.intr.* contineri, firmus esse; *to — to,* retinēre ; *to — in,* claudĕre, cohibēre ; *to — off,* arcēre, defendĕre ; *to — from (se)* abstinēre ; *to — up,* conservare, tueri ; *to — up with,* subsequi. *n.* arx. **keeper,** *n.* custos, curator. **keeping,** *n.* custodia, tutela. **keepsake,** *n.* donum.

keg, *n.* dolium.

ken, *n.* conspectus, -ūs.

kennel, *n.* stabulum canis; *hounds,* canes.

kerb, *n.* crepido (viae).

kerchief, *n.* *see* HANDKERCHIEF.

kernel, *n.* nucleus; *fig.* medulla.

kettle, *n.* cortina; lebes. **kettledrum,** *n.* tympanum.

key, *n.* clavis.

kick, *v.intr. and tr.* calcitrare, calcĭbus caedĕre; *n.* pedis ictus.

kid, *n.* haedus, haedulus.

kidnap, *v.tr.* *see* STEAL. **kidnapper,** *n.* plagiarius; *see* THIEF.

kidney, *n.* renes, -um. **kidney-bean,** *n.* phasēlus.

kill, *v.tr.* occīdĕre, caedĕre ; interficĕre ; necare, enecare; trucidare (*to murder*); *to — oneself,* se interficĕre, mortem sibi consciscĕre ; mactare (*to slay victims for sacrifice*).

kiln, *n.* fornax.

kin, *n.* *see* RELATION. **kind,** *n.* genus, *n.* species ; modus (*esp.* eiusdem modi, *ois.*) ; *of the same —,* eiusdem generis ; *every — of danger,* omnia pericula. *Adj.* benignus, facilis; indulgens; liberalis; clemens; propitius (*of the gods*) ; *Adv.* benigne, liberaliter, *etc.* **kindness,** *n.* benignitas, clementia, facilitas ; *a benefit,* beneficium. **kindred,** *n.* **kinsman,** *n.* *see* RELATIVE.

kindle, *v.tr.* accendĕre ; incendĕre ; *fig.* accendĕre, incitare. *v.intr.* (ex)ardescĕre; *fig.* ardēre.

king, *n.* rex, regis, *m.* **kingdom,** *n.* regnum. **kingfisher,** *n.* (h)alcēdo, later (h)alcyon. **kingly,** *adj.* regius, regalis. **kingship,** *n.* regia potestas, regnum.

kiss, *v.tr.* osculari; *each other,* osculari inter se. *n.* osculum.

kitchen, *n.* culina. *Adj.* culinarius. **kitchen-garden,** *n.* hortus olitorius.

kitten, *n.* *see* CAT.

knapsack, *n.* pera, mantica, sarcina (*of soldiers*).

knave, *n.* furcifer (*colloquial*), homo sceleratus. **knavery,** *n.* nequitia, dolus. **knavish,** *adj.* nequam, perfidus; lascivus. *Adv.* perfide.

knead, *v.tr.* (con)depsĕre; *fig.* subigĕre.

knee, *n.* genu ; *to bend the —,* genua flectĕre, curvare. **kneel,** *v.intr.* genibus niti; (in genu) procumbĕre.

knife, *n.* culter; *a small —,* cultellus.

knight, *n.* eques. **knighthood,** *n.* ordo equester; locus equester.

knit, *v.tr.* texĕre; *to — the brow,* frontem contrahĕre.

knob, *n.* bulla (*of a door, etc.*); nodus (*in plants*).

knock, *v.tr. and intr.* pulsare (*e.g.* fores, ostium); tundĕre; *to — against,* offendĕre ; *to — down,* sternĕre ; *—ed up,* fatigatus, defessus. *n.* pulsatio (*e.g.* forium). **knock-kneed,** *adj.* varus.

knot, *n.* nodus; difficultas; *a group,* circulus. *v.tr.* nodare, nectĕre ; *see* TIE. **knotty,** *adj.* nodosus; *fig.* difficilis; *a — point,* nodus.

know, *v.tr.* scire, novisse, cognoscere ; accipere ; *I don't —,* nescio, ignoro ; *you must —,* scito, scitote; *to recognise,* agnoscere. **knowing,** *adj.* sciens, prudens ; clever, callidus. *Adv.* consulto; de industriā. **knowledge,** *n.* scientia, notitia, cognitio ; ars ; doctrina, disciplina ; *— about the past,* memoria praeteritorum. **known,** *adj.* notus; *it is —,* constat, certum est ; *to make —,* declarare.

knuckle, *n.* articulus (digiti).

L

label, *n.* scheda. *v.tr.* titulum inscribĕre.

laborious, *adj.* laboriosus ; diligens. *Adv.* laboriose, diligenter.

labour, *n.* labor, opus, opera, pensum; *— by night,* lucubratio ; *in childbirth,* partus. *v.intr.* laborare ; *— under a delusion,* decipi; *to strive,* (e)niti; *of childbirth,* parturire. **laboured,** *adj.* affectatus. **labourer,** *n.* qui opus facit, opera ; *hireling,* mercenarius ; *skilled —s,* artifices.

labyrinth, *n.* labyrinthus. **labyrinthine,** *adj.* inexplicabilis.

lace, *n.* texta reticulata, -orum. *v.tr.* nectĕre.

lacerate, *v.tr.* lacerare (*fig.* acerbissimo dolore afficĕre animum). **laceration,** *n.* laceratio.

lachrymose, *adj.* lacrimabundus.

lack, *n.* defectio, inopia, penuria (*of necessaries*). *v.tr.* egēre, indigēre, denĕre ; *nothing,* nihil deesse. **lack-a-day!** *interj.* ah ! o! proh! **lacklustre,** *adj.* decolor.

laconic, *adj.* brief, brevis. *Adv.* breviter, paucis (verbis).

lacteal, *adj.* † lacteus.

lad, *n.* puer.

ladder, *n.* scalae ; *the step of a —,* scalarum gradus.

lade, *v.tr.* onerare ; *— anyone,* onus alci imponĕre. **laden,** *adj.* oneratus ; *with* *debt*, aere alieno obrutus. **lading**, *n.* onus.

ladle, *n.* cochlear ; cyathus. *v.tr.* haurire.

lady, *n.* domina, matrona, materfamilias. **ladylike**, *adj.* honestus, quod matronâ dignum est. **lady's maid**, *n.* famula.

lag, *v.intr.* morari. **lagging**, *n.* mora. **laggard**, *n.* cessator.

lagoon, *n.* lacuna.

lair, *n.* latibulum, cubile.

lamb, *n.* agnus, agna ; *small* —, *lamb-kin*, agnellus ; *as meat*, (caro) agnina. *v.tr.* agnum edĕre.

lambent, *adj. use* † lambĕre.

lame, *adj.* claudus, debilis (*feeble*) ; — *in speech*, in oratione claudicat ; — *excuse*, excusatio vana. *v.tr.* alqm claudum reddĕre. *Adv. by adj. or v.* (*e.g. to walk* —, claudicare). **lameness**, *n.* claudicatio.

ament, *n. or* **lamentation**, lamentum (*usu. pl.*), lamentatio, fletus, gemitus, questus (*dirge*). *v.tr.* lamentari, deflĕre. *v.intr.* lamentari, flēre, (de)plorare. **lamentable**, *adj.* deflendus, flebilis. *Adv.* miserabiliter. **lamented**, *adj. past part. of v.*

lamp, *n.* lucerna, lychnus. **lamp-black**, *n.* fuligo.

lampoon, *n.* libellus famosus. *v.tr.* libellum ad infamiam alcis edĕre.

lance, *n.* lancea, hasta. *v.tr. med.* incidĕre. **lancet**, *n.* scalpellum.

land, *n.* terra ; *to gain the* —, terram capĕre ; *cultivated* —, *field*, arvum ; *estate*, fundus, regio ; *in the* — *of the Etruscans*, in Etruscorum finibus. *Adj.* terrestris, terrenus. *v.intr.* e nave *or* navem egredi. *v.tr.* in terram exponĕre ; *to* — *a fish*, piscem capĕre. **landed**, *adj.* — *property*, ager, possessio (*usu. in pl.*) ; — *proprietor*, agrorum possessor. **landing**, *n.* e(x)scensio, egressus ; — *place*, aditus. **landlord**, *n.* agrorum possessor, caupo (" *mine host* "). **landmark**, *n.* lapis. **landscape**, *n.* regio, terra. **landslip**, *n.* terrae lapsus.

lane, *n.* angiportum (*narrow street*) ; *country lane*, via.

language, *n.* vox, oratio, lingua ; *the* — *of common life*, sermo cot(t)idianus.

languid, *adj.* languidus, defessus ; *to be* —, languĕre ; *fig.* iners, frigidus. *Adv.* languide. **languidness**, *or* **languor**, *n.* languor. **languish**, *v.intr.* languĕre, languescĕre ; *to pine away*, tabescĕre.

lank, **lanky**, *adj.* prolixus, procērus, tenuis. **lankness**, *n.* proceritas, tenuitas.

lantern, *n.* laterna (lanterna).

lap, *n.* gremium (*bosom*), sinus, (*fold of the gown*); *of a racecourse*, spatium. *v.tr.* ligur(r)ire, lingĕre ; *to touch*, lambĕre. **lap-dog**, *n.* catellus.

apidary, *n.* sculptor.

lapse, *n.* lapsus ; *after the* — *of a year*, interiecto anno. *v.intr.* labi ; errare ; *of property*, reverti (ad dominum).

lard, *n.* adeps, lar(i)dum. **larder**, *n.* cella penaria, carnarium.

large, *adj.* magnus, grandis, amplus ; *assembly*, celeber conventus. *Adv.* magnopere. **large-hearted**, *adj.* magnanimus ; benignus. **large-heartedness**, *n.* magnanimitas ; benignitas. **largeness**, *n.* magnitudo. **largess**, *n.* largitio.

lark, *n.* alauda.

larynx, *n.* gutter, -ōris, *n.*

lash, *n.* lorum (*usu. pl.*), flagellum ; *a blow*, verber. *v.tr.* flagellare, virgis caedĕre ; *to bind*, alligare.

lassitude, *n.* lassitudo, languor.

last, *n. let the shoemaker stick to his* —, ne ultra crepidam sutor.

last, *adj.* ultimus, extremus, postremus, proximus, summus (*highest*), novissimus (*latest*) ; *to the* —, ad ultimum. *n. by* extremus ; *at* —, (tum) demum, denique, *or* postremum. *v.intr.* durare. **lasting**, *adj.* firmus, diuturnus, perennis. **lastly**, *adv.* postremo, denique, quod superest.

latch, *n.* pessulus (*bolt*).

late, *adj.* serus ; tardus (*slow*) ; *the* —, defunctus, mortuus ; — *in the day*, multo die ; — *at night*, multâ nocte. **lately**, *adv.* nuper, modo. **lateness**, *n. use adj.*

latent, *adj.* occultus, abdĭtus, recondĭtus.

lateral, *adj.* lateralis, a latere. *Adv.* a latere.

lath, *n.* asser, -eris, *m.*, asserculus.

lathe, *n.* tornus ; *to work at the* — tornare.

Latin, *adj.* Latinus ; *the* — *tongue*, lingua Latina ; *to translate into* —, Latine reddĕre. **latinity**, *n.* latinitas.

latitude, *n.* latitudo; *liberty*, licentia.

latter, *adj.* posterior ; *the former*, *the* —, hic . . . ille. *Adv. see* LATELY.

lattice, *n.* cancelli, clathri.

laud, *n.* laus. *v.tr.* alqm laudare, extollĕre. **laudable**, *adj.* laudabilis, laude dignus. *Adv.* laudabiliter. **laudatory**, *adj.* honorificus.

laugh, **laughing**, *or* **laughter**, *n.* risus ; *immoderate* —, cachinnatio ; *a* — *stock*, ludibrium. *v.intr.* ridĕre ; *to* — *at*, alqm deridĕre ; *to burst into* —, cachinnari. **laughable**, *adj.* ridiculus. *Adv.* ridicule. **laughter**, *n. see* LAUGH.

launch, *v.tr.* navem deducĕre ; *to* — *out*, in aequor efferri.

laurel, *n.* laurus ; *adj.* laureus ; *fig.* gloria ; *decorated with* —, laureatus. **laurelled**, *adj.* laureatus.

lava, *n.* massa ardens, saxa liquefacta, *pl.*

lave, *v.tr.* lavare, abluĕre. **lavatory**, *n.* bal(i)neum (*bath*). **laver**, *n.* pelvis.

lavish, *adj.* prodigus, profusus ; *a* — *giver*, largitor. *Adv.* prodige, profuse.

v.tr. largiri. **lavishness,** *n.* largitas.

law, *n.* lex, regula (*rule*), norma (*standard*) ; edictum ; *body of* —s, ius ; *divine* —, fas. **law-breaker,** *n.* legis violator. **lawful,** *adj.* legitimus; legalis. *Adv.* legitime, per leges. **lawfulness,** *n.* ius adji. **lawgiver,** *n.* see LEGISLATOR. **lawless,** *adj.* effrenatus. *Adv.* effrenate. contra legem. **lawlessness,** *n.* licentia. **lawsuit,** *n.* lis. **lawyer,** *n.* iurisconsultus.

lawn, *n.* sindon ; see LINEN ; grass, herba.

lax, *adj.* laxus, fluxus ; *fig.* (dis)solutus, neglegens. *Adv. fig.* (dis)solute, laxe, neglegenter. **laxness, laxity,** *n.* neglegentia; dissolutio, or adj.

lay, *n.* see SONG.

lay, *v.tr.* ponĕre; *fig.* — *the foundations,* fundamenta iacĕre ; — *an ambush,* insidias collocare ; — *siege,* obsidĕre ; — *a wager,* sponsione provocare ; — *hands on,* manus alci inferre ; — *waste,* vastare ; — *eggs,* (ova) parĕre ; — *before,* proponĕre ; — *down,* (de)ponĕre; — *down an office,* se abdicare; — *down arms,* ab armis discedĕre ; — *up,* condĕre.

lazy, *adj.* piger, ignavus. *Adv.* pigre, ignave. **laziness,** *n.* ignavia.

lead, *v.tr.* ducĕre, agĕre ; praeesse (*to command*); — *the way,* praeire; *fig.* — *a life,* vitam agĕre; *the road* —s, via fert; *the matter* — *s to, etc.,* res spectat; — *away,* abducĕre ; — *a colony,* coloniam deducĕre. *n. or* **leadership,** ductus; *under your* —, te duce. **leader,** *n.* dux, princeps. **leading,** *adj.* princeps.

lead, *n.* plumbum. **leaden,** *adj.* plumbeus.

leaf, *n.* folium, frons; *of paper,* pagina, charta ; *of metal, wood, etc.,* bractea, lamina. **leafless,** *adj.* foliis nudatus. **leafy,** *adj.* † frondosus.

league, *n.* foedus, pactum, societas. *v.tr.* foedus cum alqo inire; consociare.

league, *n.* tria mil111a passuum.

leak, *n.* rima ; *to spring a* —, rimas agĕre. **leakage,** *n.* rima. **leaky,** *adj.* rimosus.

lean, *adj.* macer; strigosus (*of horses, etc.*). *v.intr.* niti; — *on,* (in)niti; *ad alqd acclinare* (*to* — *towards*); *to* — *backward,* se reclinare ; *to* — *to* (*in opinion*), sententiae favēre. **leaning,** *adj.* — *on,* innixus. **leanness,** *n.* macies.

leap, *u.* saltus ; *by* — *s,* per saltus. *v.intr.* salire ; — *down,* desilire ; — *forward,* prosilire ; — *for joy,* ex(s)ultare; — *over,* tran(s)silire. **leaping,** *n.* saltus. **leap-year,** *n.* annus intercalaris.

learn, *v.tr.* discĕre, ediscĕre (*by heart*); cognoscĕre (*esp. by inquiry*). **learned,**

adj. doctus. *Adv.* docte. **learner,** *n.* discipulus. **learning,** *n.* doctrina.

lease, *n.* conductio. *v.tr., to hire on* —, conducĕre; *to let on* —, locare.

leash, *n.* lorum; *of hounds,* tres canes.

least, *adj.* minimus. *Adv.* minime ; *at* —, saltem ; *not in the* —, nihil omnino.

leather, *n.* corium (*the hide*) ; aluta (*tanned*). *Adj.* scorteus.

leave, *n.* concessio, permissio, potestas, venia ; *to give* —, potestatem facĕre; *with your* —, pace tuā; *I have* —, mihi licet.

leave, *n.* *departure, by verb, to take* —, salvēre alqm iubēre. *v.tr.* (de)relinquĕre, deserĕre, destituĕre ; — *property,* legare; *to depart from,* proficisci, egredi; — *off,* desistĕre ; — *out,* omittĕre.

leavings, *n.* quae reliqua sunt.

leaven, *n.* fermentum. *v.tr.* fermentare.

lecture, *n.* schola, oratio, sermo. *v.tr and intr.* scholam habēre; *fig. see* REPROVE. **lecturer,** *n.* qui scholas habet. **lecture-room,** *n.* schola.

ledge, *n.* proiectura ; *of rocks,* dorsum.

ledger, *n.* codex accepti et expensi.

lee, *n.* (*of a ship*), navis latus a vento tutum.

leek, *n.* porrum *and* porrus.

leer, *v.intr.* oculis limis intueri, **leering,** *adj.* limus. *Adv.* limis oculis.

lees, *n.* faex, dregs; *so* faex populi.

left, *adj.* rel(l)iquus; *to be* —, restare.

left, *adj.* sinister, laevus; — *hand,* sinistra; *on the* —, a sinistrā.

leg, *n.* crus; *of mutton,* caro ovilla ; — *of a table,* pes mensae. **leggings,** *n.* ocreae

legacy, *n.* legatum.

legal, *adj.* legitimus, quod ex lege fit. *Adv.* legitime, lege. **legality,** *n.* quod ex lege fit. **legalize,** *v.tr.* legibus constituĕre.

legate, *n.* legatus, nuntius. **legation,** *n.* legatio.

legend, *n.* on coin, inscriptio, titulus ; fable, fabula. **legendary,** *adj.* fictus, fabulosus.

legible, *adj.* quod facile legi potest.

legion, *n.* legio. **legionary,** *n. and adj.* legionarius.

legislate, *v.intr.* leges dare, constituĕre. **legislation,** *n.* legis (legum) datio, legis latio. **legislator,** *n.* legis *or* legum lator. **legislative,** *adj.* — *body,* senatus. **legislature,** *n.* comitia, -orum, senatus.

leisure, *n.* otium ; *to be at* —, vacare, cessare; *at* —, otiosus, vacuus. **leisurely,** *adj.* lentus, otiosus. *Adv.* otiose.

lend, *v.tr.* mutuum dare; — *on interest,* fenerari; *fig.* praebere.

length, *n.* longitudo; *tallness,* proceritas; — *in time,* diuturnitas; *in* —, per longitudinem *at* — tandem. **lengthwise,**

adv. in longitudinem. **lengthy,** *adj.*
verbosus, longus. **lengthen,** *v.tr.* producĕre; — *the war,* bellum prorogare.
lenient, *adj.* mitis, clemens. *Adv.* clementer. **leniency,** *n.* clementia.
lentil, *n.* lens, lenticula.
leopard, *n.* leopardus (*very late*).
less, *adj.* minor. *Adv.* minus. **lessen,**
v.tr. (de)minuĕre. **lessening,** *n.* deminutio.
lessee, *n.* conductor.
lesson, *n.* discenda; *to take* —*s of anyone,* audire magistrum ; *fig.* praeceptum.
lest, *conj.* ne *with subj.*
let, *v.intr.* — *us go,* eamus ; *to* — *go,*
dimittĕre ; — *down,* demittĕre ; — *in,*
admittĕre ; — *off,* absolvĕre ; — *slip,*
omittĕre ; — *that pass,* ut ista omitta-
mus; *to allow,* sinere, pati, permittĕre;
— *not,* cave ne; *to let (house, etc.),* see
LEASE.
lethal, *adj.* mortifer, exitialis.
lethargic, *adj.* veternosus, torpidus.
lethargy, *n.* torpor, veturnus.
letter, *n.* lit(t)era; *to the* —, ad verbum;
the — *of the law,* verba legis; *epistle,*
lit(t)erae, epistula (epistola) ; *by* —,
per lit(t)eras. **letter-carrier,** *n.* tabellarius. **letters,** *n.* = *learning,* doctrina, lit(t)erae ; *a man of* —, homo
doctus. **lettered,** *adj.* lit(t)eratus.
lettuce, *n.* lactuca.
levee, *n.* salutatio.
level, *adj.* aequus, planus, libratus
(*balanced*). *n.* aequum, planities. *v.tr.*
aequare; *to destroy,* diruĕre.
lever, *n.* vectis, -is, *m.*
leveret, *n.* lepusculus.
levity, *n.* inconstantia, lĕvitas; iocus.
levy, *v.tr.* milites conscribĕre ; —
tribute, tributum imponĕre. *n.* delectus ; *to make a* —, delectum habĕre.
lewd, *adj.* impurus. *Adv.* impure.
liable, *adj.* obnoxius. **liability,** *n.* use
adj.
libation, *n.* libatio; *to make a* —, libare.
libel, *n.* libellus famosus, calumnia. *v.tr.*
calumniari. **libellous,** *adj.* famosus.
liberal, *adj.* liberalis, largus ; *too* —,
prodigus. *Adv.* liberaliter, large, profuse; *to give* —, largiri. **liberality,** *n.*
liberalitas, munificentia.
liberate, *v.tr.* liberare; *a slave,* manumittĕre. **liberator,** *n.* liberator, vindex.
liberation, *n.* liberatio ; *of a slave,*
manumissio.
libertine, *n.* homo dissolutus. **libertin-
ism,** *n.* mores dissoluti.
liberty, *n.* libertas ; *too much* —, licentia ; *leave,* potestas ; *at* —, liber ;
you are at — *to do it,* nihil impedit quominus facias.
library, *n.* bibliotheca.
license, *n.* potestas ; *liberty,* licentia.

v.tr. privilegio munire ; *see* PERMIT.
licentious, *adj.* dissolutus. *Adv.* dissolute. **licentiousness,** *n.* libido, libidines.
lick, *v.tr.* lingĕre, lambĕre.
lid, *n.* operculum.
lie, *n.* mendacium, falsum. *v.intr.* men-
tiri. **liar,** *n.* (homo) mendax.
lie, *v.intr.* iacĕre ; *cubare (in bed, etc.);*
positus esse; *to* — *between,* interiacĕre;
— *in wait,* alci insidiari; — *down,* procumbĕre.
lief, *adj. e.g. I had as* —, malim.
liege, *adj.* imperio alcis subiectus.
lieu, *n. in* — *of,* pro, loco. **lieutenant,**
n. legatus.
life, *n.* vita, anima ; *in my* —, dum
vivo ; *mode of* —, victus ; *prime of* —,
bona aetas; *to lead a* —, vitam agĕre;
fig. see VIGOUR ; *in oratory,* sucus.
life-blood, *n.* sanguis. **life-guards,**
n. milites *or* cohortes praetoriani. **lifeless,** *adj.* exanimus; frigidus, exsanguis.
Adv. fig. languide, frigide. **lifetime,**
n. aetas. **lively,** *adj.,* **liveliness,** *n.,*
livelihood, *n., see* LIVE.
lift, *v.tr.* (at)tollĕre, (sub)levare; — *upright,* erigĕre ; —*ed up,* levatus, *with
pride, etc.,* elatus.
ligament, *n.* ligamentum.
light, *n.* lumen, lux; *to bring to* —, in
lucem proferre ; *lamp,* lumen, lucerna,
candela, *taper or torch* ; *to study by*
—, lucubrare. *adj.* clarus, illustris, luminosus, candidus. *v.tr. to set light to,*
accendĕre; *to fill with light,* illustrare.
lighten, *v.intr.* fulgĕre, fulgurare (*usu.
impers.* fulget, fulgurat). *v.tr. see*
LIGHT. **lighthouse,** *n.* pharus (pharos).
lightning, *n.* fulmen, fulgur.
light, *adj. not heavy,* lĕvis ; *slight,*
parvus ; — *clad or armed,* expeditus,
nudus; *nimble,* pernix; — *hearted,* hilaris, curis vacuus; *trivial,* nihil negotii;
— *-minded,* lĕvis, vanus. *Adv.* leviter,
temere, inconsulte (inconsulto). **lighten,**
v.tr. exonerare, iacturam facĕre (*of a
ship*). **lightness,** *n.* lĕvitas.
like, *adj.* similis, par; *instar (indecl.,
n.) ; that is* — *him,* hoc dignum est
illo. *Adv.* similiter. *v.tr.* amare, diligĕre ; *I do not* — *that,* hoc displicet
mihi ; *if you* —, si tibi placet. **like-
minded,** *adj.* congruens. **likely,** *adj.* veri
similis, probabilis. **likelihood,** *n.* veri
similitudo, probabilitas. **liken,** *v.tr.* comparare. **likeness,** *n.* similitudo, *or by
adj.;* effigies, imago; *painted* —, picta
imago. **liking,** *n.* amor, voluptas ;
libido ; *to one's* —, gratus, iucundus.
likewise, *adv.* item, itidem.
lily, *n.* lilium.
limb, *n.* membrum, artus, -uum.
lime *or* **limestone,** *n.* calx; *quick-* —,
calx viva; *bird-* —, viscum. *v.tr. to
smear with bird-* —, visco illinĕre.

lime-kiln, *n.* (fornax) calcaria. **limed**, *adj.* viscatus.

lime-tree, *n.* tilia.

limit, *n.* terminus, finis. *v.tr.* finire, terminare. **limitation**, *or* **limiting**, *n.* determinatio, definitio. **limited**, *adj.* short, brevis, **limitless** *adj.* immensus, infinitus.

limp, *adj.* languidus, flaccidus. **limpness**, *n.* languor.

limp, *v.intr.* claudicare.

limpet, *n.* lepas.

limpid, *adj.* limpidus, pellucidus.

linden-tree, *n.* tilia.

line, *n.* linea ; *to draw a* —, lineam ducĕre ; *boundary* —, finis ; (*in poetry*), versus ; acies (*in battle*), agmen (*on the march*) ; *front* —, prima acies, hastati ; *the second* —, principes ; *the third* —, triarii ; *soldier of the* —, (miles) legionarius ; *rope*, funis ; *carpenter's* —, amussis, linea ; *a fishing* —, linea ; *a plumb* —, perpendiculum. *v.tr.* *to fill*, complĕre. **lineal**, *adj.* (*e.g. a* — *descendant*, unus e posteris alcis). **lineage**, *n.* stirps, genus. **lineament**, *n. generally pl.*, lineamenta.

linen, *n.* linum ; linteum, lintea, -orum ; *clad in* —, linteatus.

linger, *v.intr.* cessare, morari. **lingerer**, *n.* cessator. **lingering**, *n.* cessatio, mora. *Adj.* tardus, lentus. *Adv.* tarde, lente.

linguist, *n.* homo multarum linguarum sciens.

liniment, *n.* unguentum.

link, *n.* torch, fax, taeda ; *bond*, vinculum, familiaritas, affinitas (*by marriage*), necessitudo ; *of a chain*, annulus. *v.tr.* coniungĕre.

lint, *n.* linamentum.

lintel, *n.* limen (superum *or* superius).

lion, *n.* leo ; *of a* —, leoninus. **lion-hearted**, *adj.* magnanimus. **lioness**, *n.* leaena.

lip, *n.* labrum. **lip-salve**, *n.* unguentum.

liquid, *adj.* liquidus, fluens ; *to grow* —, liquescĕre. *n.* liquor, sucus. **liquidate**, *v.tr. see* PAY. **liquefy**, *v.tr.* liquefacĕre. **liquor**, *n. see* LIQUID.

lisp, *v.intr.* balbutire (*to stammer*).

list, *n.* tabula, index.

listen, *v.intr. see* HEAR. **listener**, *n.* auscultator, auditor.

listless, *adj.* socors, languidus. *Adv.* languide. **listlessness**, *n.* torpor, desidia.

literal, *adj. a* — *translator*, ad verbum interpres. *Adv.* (lit(t)eratim, ad verbum. **literary**, *adj.* lit(t)eratus, lit(t)erarum studiosus. **literature**, *n.* lit(t)erae, lit(t)erarum monumenta, -orum.

lithe, *adj.* mollis, flexibilis.

litigate, *v.tr. and intr.* litigare, lites sequi. **litigant**, *n.* qui cum alqo litigat.

litigation, *n.* lis. **litigious**, *adj.* litigiosus.

litter, *n.* lectica ; fetus, suboles (*a brood*) ; — *for cattle*, stramentum ; *confusion*, turbae ; *to make a* —, res turbare. *v.tr.* parĕre, fetum edĕre, *to bring forth* ; *see* DIRTY.

little, *adj.* parvus, exiguus ; *often by diminutives* ; *a little gain*, paul(l)um lucri ; *a* — *pride*, alqd superbiae ; *a* — *time*, tempus breve ; *for a* —, parumper, paul(l)isper ; *in a* —, brevi ; *a* — *after*, paul(l)o post ; *by* — *and* —, paul(l)isper, gradatim ; *a* — *before sunset*, sub occasum solis ; *how* —, quantulus ; *so* —, tantulus. *Adv.* paul(l)um, aliquantulum, parum (*too* —). *n.* aliquantum, nonnihil. **littleness**, *n.* parvitas, exiguitas. **less**, *adj.* minor. **least**, *adj.* minimus. *at least*, *adv.* saltem.

live, *v.intr.* vivĕre, in vitâ esse ; *as I* — *!* ita vivam ! — *for a thing*, deditus esse rei ; *to* — *on anything*, vivĕre re ; *to* — *at or in a place*, locum incolĕre, locum habitare. *Adj. or* **living**, *adj.* vivus. **livelihood**, *n.* victus (*provisions*). **livelong**, *adj.* totus. **lively**, *adj.* strenuus, acer ; hilaris ; *of places*, celeber. **liveliness**, *n.* alacritas, hilaritas.

liver, *n.* iecur.

livid, *adj.* lividus ; *a* — *colour*, livor.

lizard, *n.* lacerta, stellio.

lo ! *interj.* en, ecce.

load, *n.* onus ; — *on the mind*, tristitia, molestia. *v.tr.* onerare, gravare ; *of firearms*, arma parare. **loaded**, *adj.* onustus, oneratus.

loaf, *n.* panis, -is, *m.*

loam, *n.* lutum. **loamy**, *adj.* lutosus.

loan, *n.* res mutuata ; pecunia mutua.

loath, *adj.* invitus ; *I am* —, piget me. **loathe**, *v.tr.* fastidire, abhorrēre. **loathing**, *n.* fastidium, odium, taedium. **loathsome** *adj.* taeter, foedus. **loathsomeness**, *n.* foeditas.

lobby, *n.* vestibulum.

lobster, *n.* cancer (= crab).

local, *adj. by the genitive* loci, regionis, *etc.* **locality**, *n.* locus, loci natura, situs.

loch, *n.* lacus.

lock, *n.* claustra, -orum. *v.tr.* obserēre ; *to* — *in*, claustro includĕre ; *to* — *up*, concludĕre. **locker**, *n.* armarium. **lock-jaw**, *n.* tetanus.

lock, *n. of hair*, cirrus ; *of wool*, floccus.

locomotion, *n.* motus.

locust, *n.* locusta.

lodge, *n.* casa. *v.intr.* deversari apud alqm. *v.tr.* — *a complaint*, alqm deferre. **lodger**, *n.* deversor (*at an inn*), inquilinus. **lodgings**, *n.* cenaculum meritorium, *or by* domus. **lodging-house**, *n.* insula.

loft, *n.* caenaculum. **lofty**, *adj.* altus,

(ex)celsus, editus ; *fig.* sublimis ; *of speech*, grandis. *Adv.* alte, excelse, superbe. **loftiness,** *n.* altitudo.

log, *n.* lignum (ligna, *pl. firewood*) ; stipes. **logbook,** *n.* tabulae. **logger-head,** *n. to be at —s, see* QUARREL.

logic, *n.* logica, -orum, *or* dialectica. **logical,** *adj.* — *questions*, dialectica, -orum ; — *conclusion*, consequentia, -ium. *Adv.* dialectice, quod ex concessis consequitur. **logician,** *n.* dialecticus.

loin, *n.* lumbus.

loiter, *v.intr.* cessare.

loll, *v.intr. and tr.* recumbĕre, recubare.

lonely, lonesome, lone, *adj.* solus, solitarius. **loneliness,** *n.* solitudo.

long, *adj.* longus, procērus (*tall*), promissus (*hanging down*) ; — *hair*, capillus promissus ; *six feet —*, longus pedes sex ; *time*, diuturnus ; *during a — while*, diu ; *slow*, tardus, lentus. *Adv.* diu ; — *ago*, pridem, iampridem; *how —*, quandiu. *v.intr. and tr. to — for*, cupĕre, desiderare. **longevity,** *n. see* OLD. **longing,** *n.* desiderium. *Adj.* cupidus. *Adv.* cupide, avide.

look, *n. to direct a —,* oculos convertĕre; *appearance*, vultus; species. *v.tr.* a(d)-spicĕre, ĭntueri. *v.intr.* videri ; *see* SEEM; *to — about*, circumspicĕre ; *to — for, see* SEEK ; *to look towards*, spectare ad ; *to — up*, suspicĕre ; *to — up to*, verēri. **looking-glass,** *n.* speculum.

loom, *n.* tela.

loop, *n.* laqueus (*noose*). *v.tr.* annectĕre. **loophole,** *n.* foramen, fenestra.

loose, *adj.* laxus ; *with — hair*, passis crinibus ; *of soil*, rarus ; *of teeth*, mobilis ; (*carcere, etc.*) liberatus ; *of morals*, (dis)solutus. *Adv.* laxe, (dis)solute. *v.tr.* (re)laxare. **looseness,** *n. use adj.* LOOSE.

lop, *v.tr.* tondĕre, praecidĕre. **lopsided,** *adj.* uno latere grandis.

loquacious, *adj.* loquax, garrulus. *Adv.* loquaciter. **loquacity,** *n.* loquacitas, garrulitas.

lord, *n.* dominus. **lordly,** *adj.* illustris, nobilis; superbus. **lordliness,** *n.* superbia, arrogantia. **lordship,** *n.* imperium, dominatus.

lore, *n.* eruditio, doctrina.

lose, *v.tr.* amittĕre, perdĕre; *having lost a member*, captus (*e.g.* oculo); *to be bereaved*, orbari re; *to — hope*, spe excidĕre; *to — a battle*, vinci ; *to — patience*, patientiam rumpĕre ; *to be lost*, amitti, perire; *to give up for lost*, desperare de re ; *to be lost in thought*, in cogitatione defixus esse ; *I am lost*, perii. **loser,** *n.* qui damno afficitur. **losing,** *n.* amissio. **loss,** *n.* damnum; *the — of a battle*, pugna adversa ; *I am at a —*, dubius sum.

lot, *n.* sors ; *by —*, sorte ; *casting of —s*, sortitio. **lottery,** *n.* sors, alea (*game of dice*).

loth, *adj. see* LOATH.

loud, *adj.* clarus, magnus ; — *voice*, vox clara, vox magna. *Adv.* clare, clarā voce. **loudness,** *n.* magnitudo, vox clara.

lounge, *v.intr.* nihil agĕre, desidĕre. **lounger,** *n.* homo deses, ambulator.

lout, *n.* homo rusticus.

love, *n.* amor, caritas, pietas, studium; *the god of —*, Cupido, Amor ; *the goddess of —*, Venus ; *my — !* mea voluptas ! meum cor ! deliciae meae. *v.tr.* amare, diligĕre, studēre alci. **loves,** *n.* amores. **loved,** *adj.* carus. **loving,** *adj.* alcis amans, studiosus. *Adv.* amanter. **loving-kindness,** *n.* misericordia. **lovely,** *adj.* bellus, amoenus ; *worthy of love*, amabilis. **loveliness,** *n.* venustas, amoenitas. **lover,** *n.* amator; *a — of literature*, lit(t)erarum studiosus.

low, *adj.* humilis, demissus ; *of voice*, suppressus ; *of price*, vilis ; *condition*, humilis, obscurus ; *lower*, inferior ; (*origin*) ; *of — birth*, humili loco ortus; *the lowest class*, faex, vulgus, plebs ; *turpis* (*base*). *Adv.* humiliter ; *to speak —*, submisse. **lowly,** *adj. see* LOW ; *humble*, modestus. **lowliness,** *n.* humilitas ; modestia. **lowness,** *n.* humilitas ; obscuritas ; *of price*, vilitas ; *voice*, vox gravis ; *of mind*, turpitudo. **low-born,** *adj.* obscuro loco natus. **low-lands,** *n.* loca (-orum) plana. **low-spirited,** *adj.* tristis. **lower,** *adj.* inferior ; *the — world*, apud inferos, † Tartara, -orum, *pl. v.tr.* demittĕre; *to — the voice*, submittĕre. **lowering,** *adj. see* DARK, THREATENING.

low, *v.tr.* mugire. **lowing,** *n.* mugitus.

loyal, *adj.* fidelis. *Adv.* fideliter. **loyalty,** *n.* fides, fidelitas.

lubber, *n.* **lubberly,** *adj. see* LOUT.

lubricate, *v.tr.* ung(u)ĕre.

lucid, *adj.* lucidus. *Adv.* (dī)lucide. **lucidness, lucidity,** *n.* perspicuitas, *better use adj. or adv.*

Lucifer, *n. morning star*, Lucifer.

luck, *n.* fortuna, fors, sors, casus ; *good —*, res secundae ; *bad —*, res adversae. **lucky,** *adj.* felix, fortunatus. *Adv.* feliciter, auspicato.

lucre, *n.* lucrum (*gain*). **lucrative,** *adj.* lucrosus.

ludicrous, *adj.* (de)ridiculus, ridendus. *Adv.* (per)ridicule.

lug, *v.tr.* trahĕre, vehĕre. **luggage,** *n.* impedimenta, -orum ; vasa, -orum ; sarcinae (*the knapsacks, etc., of soldiers*).

lugubrious, *adj.* flebilis, maestus, tristis. *Adv.* flebiliter, maeste.

lukewarm, *adj.* tepidus ; *indifferent*, lentus, neglegens (neglig-). *Adv.* lan-

guide, lente. **lukewarmness,** *n.* tepor
(*lit.*), languor, *or by adj.*
lull, *v.tr.* sedare ; *to — to sleep,* sopire.
v.intr. the wind —s, venti vis cadit.
n. use verb. **lullaby,** *n.* cantus.
lumber, *n.* scruta, -orum.
luminous, *adj.* luminosus, lucidus. *Adv.*
(di)lucide, perspicue, aperte, **luminary,**
n. sol, lumn; *fig.* lumen.
lump, *n.* massa, gleba (gleba). **lumpish,**
adj. hebes. **lumpy,** *adj.* glebosus.
lunar, *adj.* lunaris. **lunatic,** *adj. see*
MAD, MADMAN.
lunch, *n.* prandium.
lung, *n.* pulmo ; *—s,* pulmones.
lurch, *n. to leave in the —,* deserère.
v.intr. see ROLL.
lure, *n.* illecebra. *v.tr.* allicère, pellicère.
lurid, *adj.* luridus (*ghastly*).
lurk, *v.intr.* latère, latitare.
luscious, *adj.* (prae)dulcis. **lusciousness,** *n.* dulcedo.
lust, *n.* libido, cupiditas. *v.tr.* concupiscère (*to desire earnestly*). **lusty,**
adj. validus; robustus; *to be —,* vigère.
Adv. valide. **lustiness,** *n.* vigor, robur.
lustration, *n.* lustratio. **lustral,** *adj.*
lustralis.
lustre, *n.* nitor, fulgor, splendor; *space
of five years,* lustrum. **lustrous,** *adj.*
splendidus, clarus.
lute, *n.* lyra, cithara.
luxuriant, *adj.* laetus, luxuriosus. *Adv.*
laete. **luxuriate,** *v.intr.* luxuriare.
luxurious, *adj.* sumptuosus, mollis.
Adv. luxuriose, molliter. **luxury,** *n.*
luxus, luxuria.
lynx, *n.* lynx. **lynx-eyed,** *adj.* lynceus.
lyre, *n.* lyra, cithara. **lyrical,** *adj.*
lyricus.

M

mace, *n.* fasces, -ium. **mace-bearer,**
n. lictor.
macerate, *v.tr.* macerare. **maceration,**
n. maceratio.
machination, *n.* dolus ; *to make —s,*
consilia (con)coquère. **machine,** *n.*
machina. **machinery,** *n.* machinamenta, -orum, machinae.
mackerel, *n.* scomber.
mad, *adj.* insanus, demens. *Adv.* insane,
dementer. **madden,** *v.tr.* mentem
alienare ; *fig.* exacerbare, incendère.
madman, *n.* homo insanus. **madness,**
n. insania, dementia, furor, rabies (*esp.
of animals*).
madam, *n.* domina.
magazine, *n. store, granary,* horreum,
receptaculum, armamentarium (*for arms*);
pamphlet, acta, -orum.
maggot, *n.* vermis, vermiculus. **maggoty,** *adj.* verminosus.

magic, *n.* ars magica. *Adj.* magicus ;
mirus.
magistracy, *n.* magistratus. **magistrate,**
n. magistratus. **magisterial,** *adj.* ad
magistratum pertinens.
magnanimity, *n. see* GENEROSITY.
magnanimous, *adj. see* GENEROUS.
magnet, *n.* (lapis) magnes. **magnetic,**
magnetical, *adj.* magnesius ; mira
quaedam vis (*fig.*).
magnificent, *adj.* magnificus, splendidus;
lautus. *Adv.* magnifice, splendide,
sumptuose. **magnificence,** *n.* magnificentia, splendor. **magnifier,** *n.*
laudator. **magnify,** *v.tr.* augère ; amplificare; (*verbis*) exaggerare (*to make much
of*). **magniloquence,** *n.* magniloquentia.
magnitude, *n.* magnitudo, amplitudo,
spatium (*extent*).
magpie, *n.* pica.
maid, *n. see* GIRL ; *servant,* ancilla,
famula. **maiden, maidenly,** *adj.* virgineus, virginalis. **maidenhood,** *n.*
virginitas. **maid-servant,** *n. see* MAID.
mail, *n. armour,* lorica, thorax ; *letters,*
lit(t)erae. **mailed,** *adj.* loricatus.
maim, *n.* mutilare, truncare. **maimed,**
adj mancus, truncus.
main, *adj.* primus, princeps ; (*greater
part*), pars prima; caput (*chief point*);
— point, summa. res magni momenti ;
— object, finis. *Adv.* praecipue. *n.
the sea,* altum ; *see* OCEAN. **mainland,**
n. terra (continens).
maintain, *v.tr.* sustinère ; (con)servare ;
tueri ; alère ; retinère ; *to — an
argument,* confirmare. **maintainer,** *n.*
(con)servator, *or by verbs.* **maintenance,** *n.* victus (*food*), alimenta, -orum.
maize, *n.* far.
majestic, *adj.* augustus, magnificus. *Adv.*
auguste. **majesty,** *n.* maiestas; dignitas, numen.
major, *adj. e.g. the — part,* maior pars;
in music (*the — mode*), modus maior
n. military, centurio, praefectus ; *in
law,* suae potestatis. sui potens. **majority,**
n. maior pars, plures (= *several*), plurimi ; *the — of historical writers,*
plures auctores ; *to have the — of votes,*
vincère.
make, *v.tr.* facère ; *accomplish,* conficère, efficère, perficère ; fingère (*to
invent*) ; facère, instituère, *to appoint*;
creare, *to elect*; *to — friendship,* conciliare ; *to — money, see* GAIN ; *to
— land,* capère ; *to — a bed,* lectum
sternère ; *to — verses,* facère, scribère;
to — amends, satisfacère ; *to — arrangements,* comparare. *n. of the body,*
corporis figura. **maker,** *n.* qui facit,
etc., or auctor. **making,** *n.* factio,
fabricatio, *or verb.*
maladjustment, *n.* incompositus (*e.g.
the — of parts,* partes incompositae).

12

maladministration, *n.* prava rerum administratio.

malady, *n. see* ILLNESS.

malapropos, *adv.* intempestive.

malaria, *n.* aër pestilens, caelum grave et pestilens.

malcontent, *n.* rerum mutationis cupidus.

male, *adj.* virilis, mas, masculinus.

malediction, *n.* ex(s)ecratio, dirae, -arum.

malefactor, *n.* homo maleficus. **malevolent**, *adj. see* MALICE, MALICIOUS.

malformation, *n.* quod informe est.

malice, *n.* malignitas, invidia. **malicious**, *adj.* malitiosus, malevolus; *saucy*, procax. *Adv.* malitiose. **maliciousness**, *n. see* MALICE. **malign**, *v.tr. see* SLANDER. **malignant**, *adj. see* MALICIOUS. **maligner**, *n.* obtrectator. **malignity**, *n.* malevolentia; *of disease*, vis morbi. **malpractice**, *n. see* MISDEED. **maltreat**, *v.tr.* male tractare; *see* INJURE. **maltreatment**, *n. see* INJURY.

mallet, *n.* fistuca; malleus (*hammer*).

mallow, *n.* malva.

mammal, *n.* animal.

mammon, *n.* divitiae, opes, -um.

man, *n.* homo (*in gen.*), vir (*esp.*); *men*, (*collective*), homines, mortales, -ium; *a young* —, adulescens (adol-); *quite a young* —, adulescentulus (adol-), iuvenis; *there are men who, etc.*, sunt qui, *etc.*; *this* —, hic; — *by* —, *every* —, viritim; *to the very last* —, ad unum omnes; *his men*, sui; *our men*, nostri; *in chess*, miles; *in draughts*, calculus; *merchant-*, navis (*mercatoria*); — *-of-war*, navis longa. *v.tr.* navem militibus complēre. **manhood**, *n. to reach* —, togam virilem sumēre. **mankind**, *n.* homines, genus humanum. **manly**, *adj.* virilis; fortis. **manliness**, *n.* virtus. **mannikin**, *n.* homunculus. **manslaughter**, *n.* hominis caedes.

manacle, *n.* manica. *v.tr.* vincire catenis.

manage, *v.tr.* tractare, administrare, perfungi (*duties of an office*), gerēre (*to hold a public office*). **manageable**, *adj.* habilis, *or by verbs*; *fig.* docilis, facilis. **management**, *n.* administratio, tractatio, cura; dispensatio (*of a steward*). **manager**, *n.* negotiorum (pro)curator; magister (*director*).

mandate, *n.* edictum; mandatum.

mandible, *n.* maxilla.

mandrake, **mandragora**, *n.* mandrágoras.

mane, *n.* iuba, coma; *with a* —, iubatus, comatus.

manes, *n.* Manes, -ium, *m.*

mange, *n.* scabies.

manger, *n.* praesaepe, praesaepium (praesep-).

mangle, *v.tr. fig.* (di)laniare. **mangled**, *adj.* mutilus.

mania, *n.* insania. **maniac**, *n.* homo insanus; *see* MAD.

manifest, *adj.* apertus, manifestus; *it is* —, apparet; *to make* —, aperire. *Adv.* aperte, palam. *v.tr.* aperire, patefacēre; divulgare. **manifestation**, *n.* demonstratio, indicium. **manifesto**, *n. of the government*, edictum.

manifold, *adj.* multiplex, multiformis; (— *learning*, varietas doctrinarum).

maniple, *n.* manipulus. **manipulate**, *v.tr.* tractare. **manipulation**, *n.* tractatio.

manliness, *n.* **manly**, *adj. see* MAN.

manner, *n.* ratio, modus, mos, via; dicendi genus, — *of expressing*; ritus (*established by custom*); *in like* —, eodem *or* pari modo; *in my* —, meo more; *in this* —, hoc modo. **manners**, *n. pl.* mores; urbanitas (*courteous* —); *without* —, rudis, inurbanus. **mannerly**, *adj.* urbanus, humanus. *Adv.* urbane, humane, humaniter.

manoeuvre, *n. military*, decursus; *see* TRICK. *v.intr.* decurrēre; *see* TRICK.

manor, *n.* fundus, praedium.

mansion, *n.* aedes, -ium.

mantelet, *n.* vinea, testudo. **mantle**, *n.* amiculum, palla (*for women*), pallium, sagulum (*soldier's*). **mantelpiece**, *n.* by mensa (*table*), tabula (*shelf*).

manual, *adj.* — *labour*, opera. *n. small book*, libellus.

manufactory, *n.* officina. **manufacture**, *n.* artis opus, opera fabrilis; *the article* — *d*, opus. *v.tr* fabricare. **manufacturer**, *n.* opifex, fabricator, artifex, textor (*a weaver*).

manumission, *n.* missio, manumissio (*of a slave*). **manumit**. *v.tr.* manumittēre.

manure, *n.* stercus, fimus. *v.tr.* stercorare.

manuscript, *n.* liber.

many, *n.* multi, haud pauci; *a good* —, complures, plerique; *as* — *as*, quot . . . tot; — *times*, saepe, saepenumero, crebro, iterum atque iterum, (*again and again*), etiam atque etiam; *how* — *times*, quotie(n)s; *so* — *times*, totie(n)s. **many-coloured**, *adj.* variis coloribus distinctus.

map, *n.* tabula.

maple, *n.* acer; *of* —, acernus.

mar, *v.tr.* corrumpēre.

marauder, *n.* praedator. **marauding**, *adj.* praedatorius.

marble, *n.* marmor; *statue*, signum marmoreum. *Adj.* marmorius.

March, *n.* (mensis) Martius.

march, *v.intr.* ambulare, incedēre; *to* — *out*, proficisci; *to be on the* —, iter facēre; *to be marching quicker*, accelerare iter; *to* — *in the rear*, agmen claudēre. *v.tr.* ducēre; — *back*, reducĕre ; — *across*, tra(ns)ducĕre. *n. military*, iter ; *to change the route*, iter (com)mutare ; *the troops on the —*, agmen ; (*command*) procedite ! *a day's journey*, iter ; *to make forced* —es, magnis itineribus contendĕre. **marches**, *n*. fines, -ium.

mare, *n.* equa.

margin, *n.* margo. **marginal**, *adj.* in margine scriptus.

marine, *adj.* marinus. *n.* nauta. **mariner**, *n.* nauta. **maritime**, *adj.* maritimus.

mark, *n.* nota, signum, vestigium ; *it is the — of a wise man*, est sapientis ; *thing aimed at*, scopus. *v.tr.* (de)signare, notare ; *to notice*, observare ; — *out*, *lit.* metiri , *fig.* designare. **marked**, *adj.* illustric ; *in a bad sense*, infamis. **marksman**, *n.* homo iaculandi peritus.

market, *n.* macellum (*provision —*), forum (— *-place*) ; *cattle —*, forum boarium ; *to find a —*, vendi. *v.intr.* nundinari. **marketable**, *adj.* venalis. **market-day**, *n.* nundinae. **market-garden**, *n.* hortus. **market-place**, *n.* forum. **marketing**, *n. to go —*, nundinari.

marriage, *n.* coniugium, matrimonium, nuptiae, con(n)ubium. **marriage contract**, *n.* sponsalia, -ium, pactio nuptialis ; *the document*, tabulae legitimae. **marriage feast**, *n.* nuptiae. **marriage settlement**, *n.* dos. **marriageable**, *adj.* pubes, nubilis, adultus. **marry**, *v.tr. dispose of (of females only)*, (in matrimonium) collocare ; *to — a woman*, ducĕre in matrimonium, *or simply* ducĕre; *to — a man*, nubĕre alci. **marrying**, *n.* nuptiae.

marrow, *n.* medulla ; *the essence, the best part*, medulla, flos.

marry ! *interj.* mehercle.

marsh, *n.* palus. **marshy**, *adj.* paluster.

marshal, *n. use* dux *for field —* ; *of procession, etc.*, ductor pompae. *v.tr.* instruĕre.

martial, *adj.* militaris, bellicosus.

martyr, *n. to become a — for*, pro alqâ re mortem occumbĕre. *v.tr.* alqm pro alqâ re interficĕre.

marvel, *n.* miraculum, portentum. **marvellous**, *adj.* (per)mirus, immanis. *Adv.* mirum in modum, mirifice.

masculine, *adj.* masculus, masculinus.

mask, *n.* persōna, larva ; *fig.* simulatio. *v.tr.* personam alci aptare ; *fig.* tegĕre, occultare.

mason, *n.* structor (*builder*), caementarius. **masonry**, *n.* structura.

masquerader, *n.* homo personatus.

mass, *n.* moles, summa (*the whole*) ; — *of people*, multitudo. *v.tr.* colligĕre, (ac)cumulare. **massive**, *adj.* solidus, magnus, gravis; *fig.* gravis.

massacre, *n.* caedes. *v.tr.* caedĕre.

mast, *n. on ships*, malus.

master, *n.* dominus ; pater familias ; possessor ; *lord, ruler*, dominus, princeps ; *to be —*, imperare, praeesse; *of apprentices*, magister; *teacher*, magister; *skilled*, a — *in anything* artifex (*with the genit.*); — *over oneself*, sui compos; — *of the ceremonies at court*, magister officiorum. *v.tr.* domare, vincĕre, superare; *passions*, continĕre; *to — a thing*, intellegĕre, discĕre. **masterful**, *adj.* superbus. *Adv.* superbe. **masterfulness**, *n.* insolentia, superbia. **masterly**, *adj.* summâ arte. **mastery**, *n.* victoria; *see* POWER.

masticate, *n.* manducare, mandĕre.

mat, *n.* storea, *or* storia, tegus. *v.tr.* — *together*, implicare.

match, *n. a — for . . .*, par alci ; alqd sustinēre ; *contest*, certamen. *v.tr.* — *oneself with*, cum alqo in certamen descendĕre; *to suit*, adaequare. *v.intr. to be like*, alci rei similis esse. **matchless**, *adj.* singularis, egregius. **matchmaker**, *n.* nuptiarum conciliator.

mate, *n. mess —*, convictor, socius, coniu(n)x (*husband or wife*). *v.tr. in chess*, alqm vincĕre.

material, *adj. not spiritual*, corporeus; — *point*, res ; — *gain*, lucrum. *Adv.* valde (*greatly*), re(vera) (*really*). *n.* materia (materies), res ; —s *for war*, belli apparatus.

maternal, *adj.* maternus. **maternity**, *n. use* mater, matres.

mathematical, *adj.* mathematicus, accuratus. *Adv. by adj.* **mathematician**, *n.* mathematicus, *or* mathematicarum artium peritus. **mathematics**, *n.* mathematica.

matricide, *n.* matricidium (*the crime*); matricida (*the person*).

matrimony, *n.* matrimonium. **matrimonial**, *adj. see* CONJUGAL.

matron, *n.* matrona ; custos. **matronly**, *adj.* matronalis.

matter, *n.* pus (*from a wound*); corpus, res corporeae ; (*philosophical*), rerum natura ; (*thing treated of*), res propositum ; *that has nothing to do with the —*, hoc nihil est ad rem ; *to come to the —*, ad rem ipsam venire ; — *material*, materia, *etc.* ; *event*, res, res gesta; *affair*, res ; *negotium* (*business*), caus(s)a (*in a war*); *how do* —s *stand ?* quo loco res est ? *the — is settled*, indicata res est; *what's the — ?* quid accidit ? *what's the — with her ?* quid tristis est ? quo morbo laborat ? (*in illness*); *a small —*, paul(l)ulum. **it matters**, *v.imp.* interest, refert.

matting, *n. see* MAT.

mattress, *n.* stragulum.

mature, *adj.* maturus ; *of judgment*, sapiens. *Adv.* mature (*soon*), sapienter.

v.tr. ripen, maturare, coquĕre ; *fig.* parare. *v.intr.* maturescĕre. **matureness, maturity,** *n. to bring to* —, ad maturitatem perducĕre.

matutinal, *adj.* matutinus.

maudin, *adj. see* DRUNK, SILLY.

maul, *v.tr.* laedĕre (*injure*).

maunder, *v.intr.* nugari.

mausoleum, *n.* mausoleum.

maw, *n.* ingluvies, venter.

mawkish, *adj.* putidus. *Adv.* putide.

maxim, *n.* dogma, decretum, praeceptum, institutum, sententia, regula.

maximum, *n.* quod maximum est.

May, *n.* (mensis) Maius. **May-day,** *n.* Kalendae Maiae.

may, *verb,* posse ; licet, *impers.;* — *be, see* PERHAPS.

mayor, *b.* urbis praefectus. **mayoralty,** *n.* urbis praefectura.

maze, *n.* labyrinthus.

mead, meadow, *n.* pratum; *adj.* pratensis.

meagre, *adj. fig.* ieiunus, exilis, aridus. *Adv.* ieiune, exiliter. **meagreness,** *n. see* LEANNESS; ieiunitas, exilitas.

meal, *n.* farina.

meal, *n.* cibus; *the morning* —, prandium; *chief meal,* cena. *To take a* —, edĕre, *etc.*

mean, *adj.* illiberalis, sordidus, turpis ; humilis. *Adv.* illiberaliter, sordide, abiecte, turpiter. **meanness,** *n.* illiberalitas, improbitas; *of rank,* humilitas.

mean, *or* **medium,** *n.* res media, modus. **means,** *n.* via, consilium, facultas, auxilium; *ways and* —, via atque ratio; *to try all* —, omnia experiri; *by fair* —, recte; *by foul* —, foede, turpiter ; *by all* —, omnino ; *by no* —, haudquaquam ; *resources,* opes, facultates, divitiae ; *by* — *of ladders,* scalis; per Caeciliam agĕre, *to carry on by* — *of Caecilia.*

mean, *v.tr* velle, cogitare ; *to signify,* significare, designare ; *I* — *Hilarus,* Hilarum dico ; *what does he mean?* quid sibi vult? meaning, *n.* (*yes, that is my* —, sic hoc mihi videtur) ; *see* PURPOSE ; *signification,* significatio, vis, *force.*

meander, *v.intr.* flexuoso cursu fluĕre.

measurable, *adj.* quod metiri possumus. **measurableness,** *n. by adj.* **measure,** *n.,* mensura; *modus (proportion, limit),* moderatio; *with full* —, pleno modio; *according to the* — *of,* pro modo; *beyond* —, praeter modum; (*exceedingly*), *with superl.; in a certain* —, quodam modo; *plan,* consilium ; *in music,* modi, numeri. *v.tr.* (di)metiri. *v.intr.* magnitudine esse (*e.g.* quinque pedum). **measured,** *adj. see* MODERATE. **measurer,** *n.* qui metitur. **measureless,** *adj.* infinitus. **measurement,** *n.* mensio; mensura. **measuring-rod,** *n.* decempĕda.

meat, *n.* caro.

mechanic, *n.* faber, opifex. **mechanical,** *adj.* mechanicus. *Adv.* sine mente ac ratione. **mechanism,** *n.* machinatio.

medal, *n.* numisma.

meddle, *v.intr. see* INTERFERE. **meddler,** *n.* homo importunus, molestus. **meddling,** *adj. see* INQUISITIVE.

mediate, *v.intr.* RECONCILE. **mediation,** *n.* (*e.g.* me deprecatore, *by my* —). **mediator,** *n.* qui se interponit, arbiter, deprecator.

medical, — *properties, by* vis medendi. **medicament, medicine,** *n.* medicina, remedium; *medical science,* medicina, ars medendi; *to practise* —, medicinam exercĕre. **medicinal,** *adj.* salutaris. *Adv.* remedio.

mediocre, *adj.* mediocris.

meditate, *v.intr.* cogitare, meditari. **meditation,** *n.* cogitatio, meditatio. **meditative,** *adj. by adv.* attento animo.

medium, *n. fig.* media consilia, -orum; *see* MEANS.

medley, *n.* farrago, colluvio rerum.

meek, *adj.* demissus, modestus. *Adv.* modeste, verecunde. **meekness,** *n.* animus demissus, modestia.

meet, *adj. see* FIT, PROPER, USEFUL.

meet, *v.tr.* occurrĕre, obviam venire ; obviam ire; *to go to* —, obviam ire ; *v.intr.* convenire ; confinĕre (*in large numbers*), concurrĕre. **meeting,** *n.* assembly, conventus, concursus; *a large* —, celeber conventus, celebritas, frequentia.

melancholy, melancholic, *adj.* tristis, maestus. *n.* atra bilis; tristitia, maestitia.

melee, *n.* concursus, pugna, praelium.

mellow, *adj. of fruit,* mitis, mollis ; *of wine,* lenis, mollis ; *ripe,* maturus ; *fig.* sapiens, sagax. *v.tr.* coquĕre. *v.intr.* maturescĕre.

melodious, *adj.* canōrus, numerosus. *Adv.* numerose. **melodiousness,** *n. use adj.* **melody,** *n.* modus. melos, cantus; *of the voice,* vocis modulatio.

melt, *v.tr.* liquidum facĕre, liquefacĕre, dissolvĕre; *fig.* mentem ad misericordiam revocare. *v.intr.* liquescĕre, dissolvi, tabescĕre (*of snow, etc.*), desiderio; *fig. to* — *into tears,* in lacrimas effundi. **melting,** *adj.* mollis et delicatus (*of sounds); see* PITEOUS.

member, *n.* membrum, artus ; *see* LIMB ; *fig.* pars ; *a* — *of a senate,* senator ; — *of a community,* civis ; — *of a society,* socius, sodalis.

membrane, *n.* membrana.

memoir, *n. private,* dicta factaque alcis; *historical* —, commentarii. **memorable,** *adj.* memoriā dignus, memorabilis; insignis. **memorandum,** *n. list of goods,* index ; *a sign whereby to remember,* nota ; — *-book,* adversaria, -orum. **memorial,** *n.* monumentum. **memoirs,**

n. commentarii. **memory,** *n.* memoria, recordatio ; *to keep in* —, memoriā tenēre; *from* —, ex memoriā, memoriter; *to commit to* —, ediscēre; *to hand down to* —, memoriae tradēre.

menace, *v. and n., and* **menacing,** *adj. and adv., see* THREATEN, THREAT, THREATENING.

menagerie, *n.* vivarium, *or* ferae saeptis inclusae.

mend, *v.tr.* reficēre, reparare, (re)sarcire *(to patch up)* ; *fig.* emendare ; — *one's pace* gradum addēre. *v.intr.* physically, convalescēre ; *to improve,* melius ire.

mendacious, *adj.* mendax. *Adv.* falso. **mendacity,** *n.* mendacium.

mendicancy, mendicity, *n.* mendicitas, egestas. **mendicant,** *adj.* mendicus.

menial, *adj.* servilis. *n. see* SERVANT.

mensuration, *n.* ars metiendi.

mental, *adj. by* animi, ingenii ; — *gifts,* animi facultates ; ingenium *(natural talent) Adv.* mente.

mention, *n.* commemoratio, mentio. *v.tr.* (com)memorare; mentionem facēre; *not to* — *that, etc.,* ut omittam quod, *etc.* ; *above-* —*ed,* de quo (quā) supra commemoravimus ; *as we have* —*ed above,* ut supra dictum est.

mentor, *n. see* ADVISER.

mercantile, *adj. by* genit. mercatoris *or* mercatorum ; *or by* mercatura *(e.g.* mercaturas facēre, *to be engaged in* — *transactions).* **mercenary,** *adj.* mercenarius *(for hire),* avarus, venalis. **mercer,** *n.* tabernarius. **merchandise,** *n.* merx, res venales. **merchant,** *n.* mercator. **merchantman,** *n.* navis mercatoria, *or simply* oneraria.

mercurial, *adj. fig.* mobilis, lēvis. **mercury,** *n. the god,* Mercurius ; *metal,* argentum vivum.

mercy, *n.* misericordia, venia. **merciful,** *adj.* misericors, mitis. *Adv.* clementer. **merciless,** *adj.* inclemens, saevus. *Adv.* inclementer, (dure), saeve **mercilessness,** *n.* inclementia, crudelitas.

mere, *adj.* merus *(not mixed),* solus, unus ; *also by* ipse. *Adv.* solum, tantum.

meretricious, *adj. of style,* fucatus.

merge, *v.tr. see* DIP, MIX.

meridian, *adj.* meridianus.

merit, *n.* dignitas, virtus; praestantia; *according to* —, pro merito. *v.tr. see* DESERVE. **merited,** *adj.* meritus. **meritorious,** *adj.* laude dignus. *Adv.* bene, optime.

merle, *n.* merula.

merriment, *n.* hilaritas, lascivia. **merry,** *adj.* hilaris, lascivus *Adv.* hilariter. **merry-making,** *n.* voluptas.

mesh, *n.* macula. **meshy,** *adj.* reticulatus.

mess, *n. common meal,* convivium.

v.intr. cenare (coen-). **messmate,** *n.* convīva, sodalis.

mess, *n. dirt,* illuvies ; *fig.* perturbatio rerum.

message, *n.* nuntius, legatio. **messenger,** *n.* nuntius; tabellarius.

metal, *n.* metallum

metamorphose, *v.tr.* mutare in alqd. **metamorphosis,** *n.* metamorphosis *(only as title of Ovid's poem) ; use* verb.

metaphor, *n. and adj.* translatio, verba translata. **metaphoric,** *adj.* translatus. *Adv. by* translatis verbis *(e.g. to speak).*

metaphysics, *n. where possible use* philosophia.

mete, *v.tr. see* MEASURE.

meteor, *n.* fax (caelestis). **meteorolite, meteorite,** *n.* lapis qui caelo decidit.

method, *n.* ratio, modus. **methodic, methodical,** *adj. with* ratio. *Adv.* ratione et via.

metonymy, *n.* immutatio.

metope, *n.* metopa, intertignium.

metre, *n.* metrum. **metrical,** *adj.* metricus.

metropolis, *n.* caput.

mettle, *n.* audacia ; *man of* —, homo acer. **mettlesome,** *adj.* audax.

mew, *v.intr. perhaps* vagire.

mews, *see* STABLE.

miasma, *n.* noxius terrae halitus.

midday, *n.* meridies ; *at* —, meridie. **midland,** *adj.* mediterraneus. **midnight,** *n.* media nox ; *at* —, mediā nocte. **midst,** *prep.* in, inter, in medio. **midsummer,** *n.* summa aestas. **midway,** *adv.* medius. **midwife,** *n.* obstetrix. **midwinter,** *n.* bruma.

middle, *adj. and n.* medius. **middling,** *adj.* mediocris.

mien, *n.* habitus, vultus.

might, *n.* vis, robur ; *with all one's* —, omni vi. **mighty,** *adj.* potens, validus. *Adv.* magnopere, summā vi.

migrate, *v.intr.* abire, migrare. **migration,** *n.* mutatio loci. **migratory,** *adj. by* (de)migrare ; — *bird,* advena volucris.

mild, *adj.* mollis, mitis, lenis ; *temperatus (climate),* tepidus *(warm);* levis *(light, e.g. punishment) ; of disposition,* clemens, indulgens, placidus. *Adv.* leniter, clementer. **mildness,** *n.* lenitas, clementia, indulgentia.

mildew, *n.* robigo (rub-), mucor, situs, uredo.

mile, *n.* mille passus *pl.* millia passuum. **milestone,** *n.* mil(l)iarium, lapis.

militant, *adj. by* pugnare, *etc.* ; **military,** *adj.* militaris, bellicus ; — *service,* militia ; — *preparations,* apparatus belli ; — *skill,* rei militaris peritia, usus belli. *n. the* —, milites, *or*

collect, miles, copiae. **militate**, *v.intr.*
to — against, alci adversari.

milk, *n.* lac; *goat's- —*, lac caprinum;
new —, lac recens. *v.tr.* mulgēre.

milker, *n.* qui mulget. **milking**, *n.*
mulctus. **milk-pail**, *n.* mulctrum.

milk-sop, *n.* homo effeminatus et mollis.

milk-white, *adj.* lacteus. **milky**, *adj.*
lacteus (*full of milk*), lacteus (*like milk*).
Milky Way, *n.* orbis lacteus.

mill, *n.* mola (*— -stone*), pistrinum.
v.tr. see GRIND. **millstone**, *n.*
mola.

millennial, *adj.* mille annorum. **millen-
nium**, *n.* mille annorum spatium.

millet, *n.* milium.

million, *n.* decies centena mil(l)ia ;
a — times, decies centies millie(n)s ;
sescenties (*colloquial*). **millionaire**, *n.*
vir magnis opibus praeditus.

mimic, *adj.* mimicus ; fictus. *n.* artis
mimicae peritus, mimus. *v.tr.* imitari.
mimicry, *n.* ars mimica.

minaret, *n.* turricula.

mince, *v.tr.* concidēre; *not to — matters*, sine fuco ac fallaciis dicēre. *v.intr.*
mollius incedēre. **mincemeat**, *n.* minu-
tal. **mincing**, *adj.* putidus. *Adv.*
putide.

mind, *n.* animus, mens ; ingenium
(*natural abilities*) ; *a philosophical —*,
sapientia ; *inclination*, studium, cupiditas ; *to have no — to*, abhorrēre ; *to
keep in —*, cogitare in animo, deliberare
alqd ; secum meditari. *v.tr. to attend
to*, animum advertēre (advert-) *or* alqd
animadvertēre ; *— your own business*,
res tuas cura ; *to obey*, parēre. **mindful**, *adj.* diligens; memor.

mine, *possess. pron.* meus, mea, meum.

mine, *n.* metallum, *or pl.* metalla ; *in
fortification*, cuniculus. *v.tr.* milit.
by cuniculos agēre. **miner**, *n.* metalli-
cus. **mineral**, *n.* metallum. *Adj. —
waters*, aquae salubres.

mingle, *v.tr. and intr., see* MIX.

miniature, *n.* tabella *or* pictura.

minimum, *n.* minimum, pars minima.

minion, *n.* minister, servus.

minister, *n. of a state*, principis socius et
administer omnium consiliorum. *v.intr.
see* SERVE. **ministry**, *n.* administratio.

minor, *adj. see* SMALL. *n.* nondum
adulta aetate. **minority**, *n.* aetas nondum adulta ; *smaller number*, pars *or*
numerus minor.

minotaur, *n.* minotaurus.

minstrel, *n.* citharaedus.

mint, *n. in botany*, ment(h)a.

mint, *n. where money is coined*, monēta.
v.tr. see COIN.

minus, *prep.* sine *with abl.*

minute, *adj. see* SMALL; *fig.* minutus,
accuratus. *Adv.* diligenter. *n. of time*,
see MOMENT. **minutes**, *n.* scriptum,
acta, -orum (*of the Senate*). **minute-

ness, *n.* exiguitas; diligentia. **minutiae**,
n. by omnia.

miracle, *n.* res mira, miraculum. **miraculous**, *adj.* mirabilis; *in a — manner*, mirum in modum.

mirage, *n.* species oculis oblata.

mire, miriness, *n.* lutum. **miry**, *adj.*
lutosus.

mirror, *n.* speculum.

mirth, *n.* laetitia, lusus. **mirthful**, *adj.*
laetus, iocosus. *Adv.* laete, iocose.

misadventure, *n.* casus (adversus), incommodum.

misanthrope, *n.* qui genus humanum
odit. **misanthropic, misanthropical**,
adj. hominibus inimicus. **misan-
thropy**, *n.* animus hominibus inimicus.

misapplication, *n.* usus perversus.
misapply, *v.tr.* abuti, male interpretari
(*misinterpret*).

misapprehend, *v.tr. see* MISUNDER-
STAND. **misapprehension**, *n. see* MIS-
UNDERSTANDING.

misbehave, *v.intr.* indecōre se gerēre.
misbehaviour, *n.* error, culpa.

miscalculate, *v.tr.* male computare, *or*
ratio me fefellit; *fig.* decipi. **miscalcu-
lation**, *n.* rationes falsae; error.

miscarriage, *n. failure*, res ad irritum
cadit. **miscarry**, *v.intr.* praeter spem
evenire, ad irritum cadēre.

miscellaneous, *adj. — kinds*, varia et
diversa genera. **miscellany**, *n.* liber
de diversis rebus scriptus.

mischance, *n. see* MISFORTUNE.

mischief, *n.* incommodum, maleficium.
mischief-maker, *n.* mali auctor. **mischievous**, *adj. harmful*, noxius ; *full
of tricks*, lascivus. *Adv.* calamitose,
lascive. **mischievousness**, *n.* (*e.g. who
does not see the — of the thing?* quis
non intelligit rem nocēre ?); lascivia.

misconceive, *v.tr. and intr.* perperam ac-
cipēre. **misconception**, *n.* opinio falsa.

misconduct, *n. see* MISBEHAVIOUR.

misconstrue, *v.tr. see* MISINTERPRET.

miscreant, *n.* homo illiberalis, turpis.

misdeed, *n.* facinus, scelus, peccatum.

misdemeanour, *n.* mores pravi ; *in
law*, peculatus, scelus.

misdirect, *v.tr.* epistulam perperam in-
scribēre ; *a passenger*, a rectā viā ab-
ducēre; *fig.* inducēre in errorem.

miser, *n.* homo avarus. **miserable**,
adj. miser, infelix ; calamitosus ;
worthless, turpis, vilis ; *— food*, tenuis
victus ; *to live in — circumstances*,
tenuiter vivēre. *Adv.* misere, infeliciter,
calamitose, turpiter. **miserliness**, *n.*
avaritia. **miserly**, *adj.* avarus, parcus.
misery, *n.* res miserae, calamitas,
tristitia, egestas (*poverty*).

misfortune, *n.* malum, *and pl.* mala,
calamitas, res adversae ; *he had the —
to, etc.*, accidit ei ut, *etc.*

misgive, *v.intr. see* DOUBT. **misgiving**, *n.* metus, timor.

misgovern, *v.tr.* male rem gerère. **misgovernment**, *n.* mala administratio.

misguidance, *n.* error.

mishap, *n. see* ACCIDENT.

misinform, *v.tr. by* alqm falsa docēre.

misinterpret, *v.tr.* falso explicare, peram interpretari. **misinterpretation**, *n.* interpretatio perperam facta.

misjudge, *v.tr.* male iudicare.

mislay, *v.tr. see* LOSE.

mislead, *v.tr.* in errorem inducēre ; *to be misled*, errare. **misleading**, *adj.* falsus.

mismanage, *v.tr. see* MISGOVERN.

misogamist, **misogynist**, *n.* qui mulieres odit.

misplace, *v.tr.* (in) alieno loco collocare; *to — confidence, etc.*, alqā re falli.

mispronounce, *n.* male pronuntiare.

misreckoning, *n.* falsae rationes.

misrepresent, *v.tr. fig.* alqd narrando depravare. **misrepresentation**, *n. use verb.*

misrule, *n. see* MISGOVERN.

miss, *n.* error. *v.tr.* carēre, desiderare; *the right way*, de-errare; *to omit*, praetermittēre. *v.intr. see* FAIL. **missing**, *adj. to be —*, deesse, desiderari. **missile**, *n.* iaculum. *Adj.* missilis.

misshapen, *adj.* deformis.

mission, *n. sending out*, missio.

misspend, *v.tr.* perdēre.

misstatement, *n.* quod falsum est; mendacium.

mist, *n.* nebula. **misty**, *adj.* nebulosus; *fig.* obscurus.

mistake, *v.tr. you — me for another*, me alium esse putas ; *see* MISUNDERSTAND. *v.intr. to be —n*, errare. *n.* error, erratum ; *a — in writing*, mendum. *Adv.* per errorem.

mistress, *n.* domina; *governess*, magistra.

misunderstand, *v.tr.* non recte intellegēre. **misunderstanding**, *n.* error.

misuse, *n.* usus perversus. *v.tr.* perverse (ab)uti.

mite, *n. a — of a thing*, res minima.

mitigate, *v.tr.* lenire. **mitigation**, *n.* levatio, (al)levamentum ; *or by verbs.*

mix, *v.tr.* temperare ; admiscēre ; *see* CONFUSE ; *to associate oneself*, permisceri. **mixed**, *adj.* (per)mixtus, promiscuus. **mixture**, *n.* mistura ; temperatio; farrago; varietas.

mnemonics, *n.* ars *or* disciplina memoriae.

moan, *v.intr.* gemēre. *n.* gemitus.

moat, *n.* fossa.

mob, *n.* vulgus ; turba ; faex populi *(the dregs)*. *v.tr. see* SURROUND. *v.intr.* concurrēre.

mobile, *adj.* mobilis. **mobility**, *n.* mobilitas; *fickleness*, lēvitas.

mock, *v.tr. see* IMITATE ; *to deride*, deridēre; ludibrio habēre; *to disappoint*, ludificari. *v.intr. to — at*, in ludibrium vertēre. *Adj.* falsus. **mocker**, *n.* derisor.

mockery, *n.* ludibrium, ludificatio ; *counterfeit*, fallacia, falsa imago.

mode, *n.* ratio, modus, via, mos, consuetudo (*custom*); *of dress*, habitus.

model, *n.* exemplum. *v.tr.* fingēre ; formare. *Adj.* optimus.

moderate, *adj.* modestus, temperans, mediocris, sobrius. *Adv.* modeste, temperate. *v.tr.* moderari (*to — limit*) ; coēcēre. **moderation**, **moderateness**, *n.* modus, temperantia, modestia; abstinentia.

modern, *adj.* recens, novus, qui nunc est ; hic, haec, hoc, — *the present, e.g.* haec *or* nostra aetas ; — *times*, haec tempora.

modest, *adj.* modicus (*slight*), modestus (*moderate*), pudens, demissus. *Adv.* modice, modeste, pudenter. **modesty**, *n.* modestia, pudor, verecundia.

modicum, *n.* paul(l)ulum.

modification, *n., with this —, that, etc.*, eam eo ut, *etc.* **modify**, *v.tr.* immutare, temperare.

modulate, *v.tr.* vocem *or* cantum modulari. **modulation**, *n.* flexio (vocis).

moiety, *n. see* HALF.

moist, *adj.* humidus, **moisten**, *v.tr.* conspergēre, (ir)rigare (*to — water*). **moisture**, *n.* humor.

molar, *adj.* (*e.g. tooth*) dens genuinus.

mole, *n. mound*, moles, agger. **molecule**, *n. see* PARTICLE.

mole, *n. mark on the body*, naevus.

mole, *n.* talpa. **mole-hill**, *n. fig. to make mountains out of —s*, difficilia ex facillimis redigēre.

molest, *v.tr.* sol(l)icitare, vexare. **molestation**, *n.* molestia.

mollify, *v.tr.* (e)mollire, lenire.

molten, *adj.* liquefactus.

moment, *n.* punctum *or* vestigium temporis ; *in a —*, statim ; *of great —*, magni momenti. **momentary**, *adj.* brevissimus ; *see* INSTANTANEOUS. **momentous**, *adj.* magni momenti. **momentousness**, *n. see* IMPORTANCE. **momentum**, *n.* vis quā alqd movetur.

monarch, *n.* rex, princeps, imperator. **monarchical**, *adj. government, use* rex (*e.g.* regi parent). **monarchist**, *n.* defensor imperii regii. **monarchy**, *n.* principatus.

monetary, *adj.* quod ad pecuniam pertinet, pecuniarius. **money**, *n.* pecunia, argentum ; *ready —*, pecunia praesens. **money-bag**, *n. see* PURSE. **money-making**, *n.* quaestus. **money-market**, *n.* res nummaria. **moneyed**, *adj.* dives.

mongrel, *n.* nothus. *n.* (h)ibrida.

monition, *n.* monitum. **monitor**, *n.* monitor.

monkey, *n.* simia.

monopolize, *v.tr.* vindicare.

monosyllable, *n. only in pl.* monosyllaba.

monotheist, *n.* qui unum modo Deum esse credit.

monotonous, *adj. e.g.* oratio omni varietate carens.

monsoon, *n.* ventus qui (certo tempore) flare consuevit.

monster, *n.* monstrum, belua. **monstrosity,** *n. see* MONSTER. **monstrous,** *adj.* deformis, immanis. *Adv.* praeter naturam.

month, *n.* mensis. **monthly,** *adj.* singulis mensibus.

monument, *n.* monumentum. **monumental,** *adj. fig.* gravis.

mood, *n. of mind,* animus ; modus (*gram.*). **moody,** *adj. see* PEEVISH.

moon, *n.* luna. **moonlight,** *n.* lunae lumen. *Adj.* lunā illustris.

moor, *n.*, **moorland,** *n.* loca(-orum) palustria.

moor, *v.tr.* navem ad terram religare.

moorings, *n. use verb.*

moot point, *n. it is a* —, incertum est an.

mop, *n.* pēniculus. *v.tr.* peniculo detergēre.

mope, *v.intr.* maestus esse. **moping,** *adj.* tristis, maestus.

moral, *adj.* — *philosophy,* de moribus ; *upright,* honestus. *Adv.* honeste. *n. teaching of a story,* res ad quam fabula spectat. **morals,** *n.* mores, -um; *ethics,* de moribus. **moralist,** *n.* qui de moribus praecipit. **morality,** *n.* mores, -um. **moralize,** *v.intr.* de moribus praecipĕre.

morass, *n.* palus.

morbid, *adj.* aeger. *Adv.* maeste.

more, *adj.* plures (*neut.* plura); plus, *n.* (*e.g.* — *money,* plus pecuniae) ; *adv.* (*often rendered by a comparative*) ; plus (*e.g.* plus amrae) ; — *than six hours,* amplius sex horis; magis; potius (*rather*) ; *what is* —, et quod plus est ; *still* —, plus etiam ; *the* — . . . *the* — . . . , eo . . . quo, tanto . . . quanto.

moreover, *adv.* praeterea, ad hoc, accedit quod.

moribund, *adj.* moribundus.

morn, **morning,** *n.* mane (*indcl.*) ; *in the* —, mane ; *early in the* —, primā luce; *until* —, ad lucem; *this* —, hodie mane ; *yesterday* —, hesterno mane ; *good* — *! salve! salvete! Adj.* matutinus. **morning star,** *n.* Lucifer.

morose, *adj.* morosus, acerbus. *Adv.* morose, acerbe. **moroseness,** *n.* morositas, acerbitas.

morrow, *n.* dies posterus. *Adv. to-* —, cras ; *'or to-* —, in crastinum diem ; *the day after to-* —, perendie.

morsel, *n.* offa, pars exigua.

mortal, *adj.* mortalis, humanus, cadūcus; —*s,* homines, mortales ; *deadly,* mortifer ; — *enemy,* homo infensissimus. *Adv. to be mortally wounded,* morti-

ferum vulnus accipĕre. **mortality** *n.* *there was a great* —, plurimi morte absumpti sunt.

mortar, *n.* = *a vessel,* pila, mortarium.

mortar, *n.* = *cement,* mortarium.

mortgage, *n.* hypotheca, pignus. *v.tr.* pignori dare.

mortification, *n. fig. see* VEXATION.

mortify, *v.intr.* by putrescĕre. *v.tr. see* HUMBLE.

mosaic, *adj.* tessellatus. *n.* opus tessellatum.

mosquito, *n.* culex.

moss, *n.* muscus. **mossy,** *adj.* muscosus.

most, *adj.* maximus, plurimus ; — *people,* plerique. *Adv.* maxime, valde ; *see* VERY. **mostly,** *adv.* plerumque, saepe.

mote, *n. see* PARTICLE.

moth, *n.* tinea.

mother, *n.* mater. **mother-country,** *n.* terra patria. **mother-in-law,** *n.* socrus. **motherless,** *adj.* matre orbus. **motherly,** *adj.* maternus. **mothertongue,** *n.* patrius sermo.

motion, *n.* motus ; *to be in* —, movēri ; *proposal,* rogatio. *v.tr.* significare.

motionless, *adj.* immotus.

motive, *n.* caus(s)a, ratio.

motley, *adj.* coloris maculosi.

motto, *n.* dictum.

mould, *n.* = *shape,* forma.

mould, *n.* = *soil,* terra. **moulder,** *v. intr.* putrescĕre. **mouldiness,**' *n.* mucor.

mouldy, *adj.* mucidus.

moult, *v.intr.* plumas ponĕre.

mound, *n.* tumulus, agger.

mount, *v.intr. see* RISE ; *on horseback,* conscendĕre (equum). *v.tr.* —*ed,* equo vectus ; *to ascend,* scandĕre, conscendĕre.

mountain, *n.* mons. **mountaineer,** *n.* homo montanus. **mountainous,** *adj.* montuosus.

mourn, *v.intr.* maerēre, lugēre. *v.tr. see* LAMENT. **mournful,** *adj.* tristis. *Adv.* maeste. **mournfulness,** *n.* tristitia.

mourning, *n.* maeror, luctus; — *dress,* vestis lugubris, squalor.

mouse, *n.* mus. **mouse-hole,** *n.* cavum muris.

mouth, *n.* os ; *with open* —, hians.

move, *v.tr.* (com)movēre, agitare (*up and down*). *v.intr.* se (com)movēre. **movable,** *adj.* mobilis, agilis. **movement,** *n.* motus.

mow, *v.tr.* demetĕre. **mower,** *n.* faenisex (fen-).

much, *adj. and adv.* multus; copia, vis; — *more,* multo magis.

muck, *n. see* DIRT. **muck-heap,** *n.* sterquilinum.

mud, *n.* lutum, caenum. **muddy,** *adj.* lutosus.

muddle, *n.* turba, confusio. *v.tr.* miscēre, turbare.

muff, *n.* manica (= *a long sleeve*).

muffle, *v.tr.* velare, obvolvěre. **muffler,** *n.* tegumentum.

muggy, *adj.* humidus, calidus.

mulberry, *n.* morum; — -*tree*, morus, *f.*

mulct, *v.tr.* multare.

mule, *n.* mulus, mula.

mull, *v.tr.* *ad vina*, *bonum fervidum.*

mullet, *n.* mullus.

multifarious, *adj.* multiplex, varius. *Adv.* multis modis.

multiform, *adj.* multiformis.

multiplication, *n.* multiplicatio. **multiply,** *v.tr.* multiplicare. *v.intr.* augeri.

multitude, *n.* multitudo, vis, vulgus, frequentia. **multitudinous,** *adj.* creber, numerosus.

mummer, *n.* qui partes agit. **mummery,** *n.* partes, -ium.

munch, *v.tr.* manducare.

mundane, — *affairs,* res humanae. *fig. worldly,* alcis rei (*e.g.* divitiarum), studiosus.

municipality, *n.* municipium.

munificence, *n.* liberalitas. **munificent,** *adj.* liberalis. *Adv.* liberaliter.

munition, *n.* apparatus belli.

mural, *adj.* muralis.

murder, *n.* caedes, nex ; *to commit to* —, caedem facěre. *v.tr.* caeděre, necare. **murderer,** *n.* homicida ; sicarius.

murmur, *n.* murmur, fremitus, susurrus ; *to bear without a* —, aequo animo ferre ; *complaint,* querela. *v.intr.* murmurare ; *to* — (*approbation or disapproval*), admurmurare ; *to complain,* queri.

muscle, *n. in the arm,* lacertus. **muscular,** *adj.* lacertosus; *see* STRONG.

muse, *n.* Musa.

mushroom, *n.* boletus.

music, *n.* ars musica, musica, -orum ; *with instruments,* cantus, concentus. **musical,** *adj.* musicus ; *understanding music,* artis musicae peritus; *melodious,* canorus. *Adv. by adjs.;* numerose. **musician,** *n.* fidicen, tibicen cornicen.

muslin, *n.* sindon.

mussel, *n.* mitulus.

must, *by gerundive, we* — *die,* moriendum est ; *by* oportet ; *by* debēre ; *by* opus est; *by* necesse est.

must, *n.* mustum.

mustard, *n.* sinapi.

muster, *v.tr.* recensēre, colligēre ; *to* — *courage,* animum erigěre. *v.intr.* congregari.

musty, *adj.* mucidus.

mutable, *adj.* (com)mutabilis. **mutability,** *n.* mutabilitas.

mute, *adj.* mutus.

mutilate, *v.tr.* mutilare, truncare. **mutilated,** *adj.* mutilatus, truncatus. **mutilation,** *n. by verb.*

mutiny, *n.* seditio, motus. *v.intr.* seditionem facěre. **mutineer,** *n.* homo seditiosus. **mutinous,** *adj.* seditiosus. *Adv.* seditiose.

mutter, *v.intr. and tr.* mussari.

mutton, *n.* caro ovilla.

mutual, *adj.* mutuus. *Adv.* mutuo.

my, *pron.* meus.

myriad, *n. indefinitely large number,* sescenti.

myrmidon, *n.* satelles.

myrrh, *n.* murra (myrrha) ; *of* — murrinus.

myrtle, *n.* myrtus (mur-).

myself, *pron. see* I, SELF.

mysterious, *adj.* arcanus. **mystery,** *n. in a religious sense,* mysteria, -orum ; *a secret,* res occulta. **mystic,** *adj.* mysticus. **mystification,** *n.* ludus. **mystify,** *v.tr.* alqm fraudare.

myth, *n.* fabula. **mythical,** *adj.* †fabulosus. **mythology,** *n.* fabulae. **mythological,** *adj.* quod ad fabulas pertinet.

N

naiad, *n.* naias.

nail, *n.* unguis ; *iron or wooden* —, *etc.,* clavus. *v.tr.* (clavis) affigěre ; —*ed,* fixus.

naïve, *adj. perhaps* simplex. *Adv.* simpliciter; *perhaps* sine fuco ac fallaciis.

naked, *adj.* nudus. *Adv.* aperte (*openly*). **nakedness,** *n.* nudatum corpus ; *fig. of style,* ieiunitas.

name, *n.* nomen, vocabulum, appellatio, cognomen (*family name*) ; *in the* — *of the state,* publice ; *in* — *only,* verbo non re ; *to have a* —, magnum nomen habēre. *v.tr.* nominare, nomen dare, appellare. **nameless,** *adj.* nominis expers.

namely, *adv. by apposition ; by rel. and est; dico or* inquam, = *I mean.*

namesake, *n.* eodem nomine appellatus.

nap, *n.* somnus brevis. *v.tr.* pau(l)um conquiescěre.

napkin, *n.* mappa.

narcissus, *n.* narcissus.

narcotic, *adj.* somnifer, somnificus. *n.* medicamentum.

nard, *n.* nardus.

narrate, *v.tr.* (e)narrare, exponěre. **narration, narrative,** *n.* narratio, historia (*story*). *Adj. by* narrare, *etc.* **narrator,** *n.* narrator; auctor.

narrow, *adj.* angustus, contractus ; *to have a* — *escape,* aegre periculum effugēre. *Adv.* aegre, vix ; *by* haud multum abest. *v.tr.* contrahěre. *v.intr.* cogi. *n. or* **narrows,** aditus, angustiae; fauces, -ium, *jaws, lit and fig.* **narrowness,** *n.* angustiae ; — *of mind,* animus angustus et parvus.

nasal, *adj.* narium (*gen. of* nares, *nose*).
nasty, *adj.* amarus, iniucundus, gravis; *foul*, foedus, obscenus. *Adv.* graviter, foede, obscene. **nastiness**, *n. of taste*, amaritas; *of smell*, gravitas; foeditas.
natal, *adj.* natalis, natalicius.
nation, *n.* populus, gens, natio. **national**, *adj.* domesticus, popularis. **nationality**, *n. by* populus, gens, *etc.*
native, *adj.* indigěna, *or* in eā terrā natus; — *land*, patria. *n., the* —*s*, indigenae.
natural, *adj.* naturalis; nativus; innatus *or* insitus, sincerus, verus ; filius non legitimus, *a* — *son ; to die a* — *death*, naturae conceděre ; — *philosophy*, physica, -orum ; — *gift*, ingenium, indoles. *Adv.* secundum naturam, naturaliter ; *unaffectedly*, simpliciter; *clearly*, manifesto. **naturalization**, *n., by* **naturalize**, *v.tr., to* — *someone*, alci civitatem dare ; *to be* —*d*, civis esse ; *an animal or plant*, importare. **nature**, *n.* natura; ingenium, indoles; *by* —, naturā.
naught, *n.* nihil ; *to set at* —, parvi facěre.
naughty, *adj.* improbus.
nausea, *n.* nausea, fastidium. **nauseous**, *adj. see* DISGUSTING.
nautical, **naval**, *adj.* navalis, nauticus.
navigable, *adj.* navigabilis. **navigate**, *v.tr.* navigare. **navigation**, *n.* navigatio, ars navalis. **navigator**, *n.* nauta.
navy, *n.* classis.
nay, *adv.* im(m)o (vero).
near, *adv.* prope. *prep.* ad, prope. *Adj.* propinquus ; —*er*, propior ; —*est*, proximus. **nearly**, *adv.* prope, fere. **nearness**, *n.* propinquitas.
neat, *adj.* nitidus. *Adv.* nitide. **neatness**, *n.* nitor.
nebula, *n.* nebula. **nebulous**, *adj.* nebulosus.
necessaries, *n.* quae ad victum cultumque pertinent. **necessary**, *adj.* necessarius. *it is* —, opus est, necesse est. *Adv.* necessario. **necessitate**, *v.tr. by* cogěre. **necessity**, *n.* necessitas ; *see* WANT.
neck, *n.* collum, cervix ; *pl.* cervices.
necklace, *n.* torques.
nectar, *n.* nectar.
need, *n.* necessitas. *v.tr.* alqā re egēre ; *to want*, desiderare. **needful**, *adj.* necessarius. **needless**, *adj. see* UN-NECESSARY. **needy**, *egens.* **neediness**, *n.* egestas, inopia.
needle, *n.* acus. **needlework**, *n.* opus acu factum.
nefarious, *adj.* nefarius. *Adv.* nefarie.
neglect, *v.tr.* neglegere, omittěre. **negligence**, *n.* neglegentia. **neglectful**, **negligent**, *adj.* neglegens.
negotiate, *v.tr.* agěre ; *to* — *a peace*, agěre de pace. **negotiation**, *n.* actio (*e.g.* de pace), pactio (*treaty*), condiciones, colloquium. **negotiator**, *n.* legatus.

negro, *n.* Aethiops, Afer. **negress**, *n.* femina Aethiops, Afra.
neigh, *v.intr.* hinnire. **neighing**, *n.* hinnitus.
neighbour, *n.* vicinus, finitimus. **neighbouring**, *adj.* vicinus, propinquus, proximus. **neighbourhood**, *n.* vicinitas, propinquitas ; *neighbours*, vicini. **neighbourly**, *adj.* ut decet vicinum.
neither, *pron.* neuter. *conj.* neither . . . *nor*, nec . . . nec, neque . . . neque, neve (neu) . . . neve (neu).
nephew, *n.* filius fratris, filius sororis.
ne plus ultra, *n.* quod optimum est.
nereid, *n.* Nereis.
nerve, *n.* nervus (sinew), *fig. see* VIGOUR. **nervous**, *adj.* nervosus, *of style* ; *see* WEAK ; *frightened*, timidus. *Adv.* *vigorously*, nervose ; *timide.* **nervousness**, *n. strength* (*in speech*, *etc.*), nervi; *see* FEAR.
nest, *n.* nidus. **nestling**, *n.* pullus.
net, *n.* rete, reticulum ; *a* — *for birds*, plaga. *v.tr.* reti capěre.
nettle, *n.* urtica. **nettled**, *adj.* iratus.
neuter, *adj.* neuter. **neutral**, *adj.* medius; *to be* —, medius esse, neutram partem sequi. **neutrality**, *n.* neutrius partis studium. **neutralize**, *v.tr. see* COUNTERBALANCE.
never, *adv.* numquam. **nevertheless**, *adv.* nihilominus (at)tamen.
new, *adj.* novus, recens (*unaccustomed*), insolitus ; *is there anything* — *?* num quidnam novi ? **new-born**, *adj.* recens natus ; catuli recentes (*puppies*). **new-comer**, *n.* advena. **new-fangled**, *adj.* mirus, novus. **new-fashioned**, *adj.* novus. **newly**, *adv.* nuper, modo (*lately*). **newness**, *n.* novitas. **news**, *n.* alqd novi ; *what* — *?* quid novi ? **newspaper**, *n.* acta publica, -orum.
newt, *n.* lacertus, lacerta (lizard).
next, *adj.* proximus ; *in the* — *year*, proximo anno. *Adv.* deinceps, deinde. *Prep. see* NEAR.
nibble, *v.intr.* admordēre, gustare (*to taste*).
nice, *adj.* suavis, dulcis ; *fastidious*, delicatus ; *of judgment, etc.*, subtilis. *Adv.* suaviter, subtiliter. **niceness**, **nicety**, *n.* suavitas ; fastidium ; subtilitas; *to a* —, ad unguem.
niche, *n.* aedicula (*for statues*).
nick, *n. in the* — *of time*, in (ipso) tempore.
nickname, *n.* nomen. *v.tr.* nomen per ludibrium dare.
niece, *n.* fratris filia, sororis filia.
niggardly, *adj. see* MISERLY. **niggardliness**, *n. see* MISERLINESS.
night, *n.* nox ; *by* —, nocte, noctu. **nightingale**, *n.* luscinia. **nightly**, *adj.* nocturnus.
nimble, *adj.* mobilis; *see* SWIFT.
nine, *adj.* novem ; — *times*, novie(n)s. **nineteen**, *adj.* undeviginti. **nineteenth**,

adj. undevicesimus. **ninety,** *adj.* nonaginta. **ninth,** *adj.* nonus.

no, *adv.* minime ; *one says yes, the other* —, hic ait, ille negat; *adj.* nullus, non ullus ; *in* — *wise,* nullo modo. **nobody,** *n.* nemo, nullus (*in genit. and abl. sing.*) ; *and* — nec quisquam **nowhere,** *adv.* nusquam.

noble, *adj. by birth,* nobilis ; *morally,* magnanimus, honestus. *Adv.* — *born,* nobili loco natus. *n. the nobles,* optimates, nobiles. **nobility,** *n. by birth,* nobilitas ; *moral* —, animus ingenuus.

nocturnal, *adj.* nocturnus.

nod, *v.intr.* nutare. *n.* nutus.

noise, *n.* strepitus, fremitus, sonitus, tumultus ; *to make a* —, strepēre. *v.tr. see* PUBLISH. **noiseless,** *adj.* quietus, tacitus. *Adv.* quiete, tacite, silentio. **noiselessness,** *n.* silentium. **noisy,** *adj.* strepens, tumultuosus. *Adv.* cum strepitu.

noisome, *adj.* foedus, teter.

nomadic, *adj.* vagus.

nomenclature, *n.* nomen.

nominal, *adj. and adv. opp. to real, really,* nomine, verbo.

nominate, *v.tr.* nominare, creare. **nomination,** *n.* nominatio. **nominative,** *n.* casus nominativus. **nominee,** *n. use* nominatus.

nonentity, *n.* nihil. **nonsense,** *n.* ineptiae. *Interj.* nugas ! gerrae ! **nonsensical,** *adj. see* FOOLISH.

none, *adj.* nullus, nemo.

nook, *n. see* ANGLE, CORNER.

noon, *n.* meridies.

noose, *n.* laqueus.

nor, *conj.* neque; *see* NEITHER.

normal, *adj. see* REGULAR.

north, *or* **northern,** *or* **northerly,** *adj.* septentrionalis. *n.* septentrio, *or pl.* septentriones. **north-east,** *adj.* inter septentriones et orientem spectans ; *the* — *wind,* Aquilo. **north pole,** *n.* axis (septentrionalis) **northwards,** *adv.* (ad) septentrionem versus.

nose, *n.* nasus, nares, -ium.

nostrils, *n.* nares, -ium, *f.*

not, *adv.* non, haud, haudquaquam ; *in double prohibitions,* neve (neu) . . . neve (neu); *after verbs of fearing,* ut; — *by any means,* nullo modo, nihil ; — *even,* ne . . . quidem; *but* —, non vero, non autem; *to say* —, *by* negare; — *pleasant,* iniucundus, ingratus.

notable, *adj. see* REMARKABLE.

notary, *n.* scriba (publicus).

notch, *v.tr.* incidĕre.

note, *n.* nota, signum ; *letter,* epistula (epistola), *v.tr. by* scribĕre; *see* NOTICE. **notes,** *n. pl.,* dictata, -orum (*of the student*) **note-book,** *n.* adversaria, commentarii, pugillares. **noted,** *adj. see* FAMOUS. **noteworthy, notable,** *adj. see*

REMARKABLE. **notice,** *n.* observatio, animadversio; *to take* —, animadvertĕre. *v.tr.* animadvertĕre. **noticeable,** *adj. see* REMARKABLE. **notify,** *v.tr.* alqm alcis rei certiorem facĕre. **notification,** *n.* denuntiatio.

nothing, *n.* nihil, nulla res, — *by no kind,* nihil tale; — *but,* nihil nisi, nihil aliud quam.

notice, *n.,* **notify,** *v.tr., see under* NOTE.

notion, *n. see* IDEA.

notorious, *adj.* notus, infamis, manifestus, *or by superl.* (*e.g. a* — *evil-doer*), homo sceleratissimus). **notoriety,** *n.* infamia.

notwithstanding, *adv.* tamen.

nought, *n. see* NOTHING.

noun, *n.* nomen.

nourish, *v.tr.* nutrire. **nourishment,** *n.* alimentum.

novel, *adj.* novus. *n.* fabula. **novelist,** *n.* qui fabulas componit. **novelty,** *n. as quality,* novitas; *new thing,* res nova.

November, *n.* November (mensis).

novice, *n.* tiro.

now, *adv.* nunc; iam; hoc tempore. **nowadays,** *adv.* hodie.

nowhere, *adv.* nusquam.

nude, *adj.* **nudity,** *n., see* NAKED.

nudge, *v.tr.* alci latus fodicare.

nuisance, *n. by* molestus.

null, *adj. to declare anything* — *and void,* rescindĕre ; *fig. by* nihil valēre. **nullify,** *v.tr.* ad irritum redigĕre.

numb, *adj.* torpens; *to be* —, torpēre. *v.tr.* alqm torpore afficĕre. **numbness,** *n.* torpor.

number, *n.* numerus ; *many,* copia, *or by* multi. *v.tr.* numerare. **numbering,** *n.* — *of the people,* census. **numberless,** *adj.* innumerus. **numerically,** *adv.* numero. **numerous,** *adj.* creber, frequens. *Adv.* magno numero.

nuptial, *adj.* nuptialis. **nuptials,** *n.* nuptiae.

nurse, *n.* nutrix ; *a* — *by* quae alqm curat. *v.tr.* nutrire, gestare (*to carry*), fovēre ; *in sickness,* curare. **nursing,** *n.* alumnus.

nut, *n.* nux. **nutshell,** *n.* putamen. **nutriment, nutrition,** *n. see* FOOD.

nymph, *n.* nympha, Dryas, Naias.

O

o ! **oh** ! *interj.* o ! proh ! heu ! **ohe** ! — *no,* minime vero.

oak, *n.* quercus, *of* —, **oaken,** quernus.

oakum, *n.* stuppa ; *made of* —, stuppeus.

oar, *n.* remus.

oath, *n.* iusiurandum, sacramentum (*military*) ; *to take an* — iusiurandum dare, sacramentum dicĕre ; *to swear allegiance,* in verba alcis iurare.

oats, *n.* avēna.

obdurate, *adj.* durus, pertinax.

obedient, *adj.* obediens. *Adv.* obedienter. obedience, *n.* obedientia, obtemperatio. obey, *v.tr.* parēre, obtemperare.

obeisance, *n. see* BOW.

obelisk, *n.* obeliscus.

obese, *adj. see* FAT.

object, *n.* res ; *to be an — of care to anyone,* alci esse curae (*dat.*) ; *— of desire,* desiderium ; *purpose,* finis, id quod cupio ; propositum ; *with what — ?* quo consilio ? *to have an —,* consilium sequi. *v.tr.* contra dicĕre, respondēre. objection, *n.* quod contra dicitur, excusatio ; *without the least —,* sine morā ; *see* HINDRANCE. objectionable, *adj.* malus. objector, *n.* qui contra dicit.

oblation, *n. see* SACRIFICE.

oblige, *v.tr.* obligare, obstringĕre ; cogĕre. obligation, *n.* officium, debitum ; *see* DUTY. obliging, *adj.* comis, facilis. *Adv.* comiter, facile. obligingness, *n.* facilitas.

oblique, *adj.* obliquus ; *— narrative,* oratio obliqua. *Adv.* ex obliquo.

obliterate, *v.tr.* delēre.

oblivion, *n.* oblivio. oblivious, *adj.* immemor.

oblong, *adj.* oblongus.

obloquy, *n.* opprobrium, convicium.

obnoxious, *adj.* noxius.

obol, *n.* obolus.

obscene, *adj.* obscenus. *Adv.* obscene.

obscure, *adj. see* DARK ; *fig.* obscurus, caecus. *Adv.* obscure, ambigue. *v.tr.* obscurare. obscurity, *n.* obscuritas.

obsequies, *n. see* FUNERAL.

obsequious, *adj. and adv. by* alci adulari. obsequiousness, *n.* adulatio.

observe, *v.tr.* (ob)servare, animadvertĕre (*to attend to*), contemplari ; *to — a custom* (con)servare. observance, *n.* mos, ritus. observant, *adj. see* ATTENTIVE. observation, *n.* observatio ; *remark,* dictum. observer, *n.* spectator.

obsolete, *adj.* obsoletus.

obstacle, *n.* impedimentum.

obstinate, *adj.* pertinax. *Adv.* pertinaciter. obstinacy, *n.* pertinacia.

obstreperous, *adj.* tumultuosus.

obstruct, *v.tr.* obstruĕre, obstare ; *see* HINDER. obstruction, *n.* impedimentum. obstructive, *adj.* quod impedimento est.

obtain, *v.tr.* potiri, adipisci. *v.intr., see* PREVAIL. obtaining, *n.* adeptio, impetratio.

obtrude, *v.tr. see* INTRUDE.

obtuse, *adj.* hebes. obtuseness, *n. see* DULNESS.

obviate, *v.tr.* obviam ire; occurrĕre.

obvious, *adj.* apertus, manifestus. *Adv.* manifeste.

occasion, *n. see* TIME, OPPORTUNITY ; *cause,* caus(s)a, auctor. *v.tr.* auctor esse alcis rei, movēre ; *see* CAUSE. occasionally, *adv.* raro, aliquando.

occident, *n. see* WEST.

occult, *adj.* occultus.

occupy, *v.tr.* habēre, tenēre ; *to take,* occupare, expugnare. occupancy, *n.* possessio. occupation, *n.* (*of a place*) occupatio, expugnatio ; (*in business*) negotium.

occur, *v.intr. render by* in mentem mihi alqd venit ; *in books,* reperiri, legi ; *to happen,* fieri, evenire. occurrence, *n.* res, eventum.

ocean, *n.* oceanus.

October, *n.* (mensis) October.

octogenarian, *n.* octoginta annos natus.

ocular, *adj. to give — evidence,* ante oculos proponĕre. oculist, *n.* medicus qui oculis medetur.

odd, *adj. uneven,* impar (*e.g. number*) ; *see* EXTRAORDINARY.

ode, *n.* carmen.

odious, *adj.* odiosus, invisus, offensus, *to be — to,* alci esse odio. *Adv.* odiose, invidiose. odiousness, *n.* odium. odium, *n.* invidia.

odour, *n.* odor.

Odyssey, *n.* Odyssēa.

of, *prep., by the genitive ; by an adjective (e.g. a basin — marble,* labrum marmoreum); ex; (*about*) de.

off, *adv. away from* ab, de, ex; *to go —,* decedĕre ; *to get —,* evadĕre ; *to carry —,* auferre ; *to be far —,* longe abesse.

offend, *v.tr.* offendĕre, laedĕre, violare; *to be —ed,* aegre *or* moleste ferre.

offence, *n.* offensio, ira ; *to take —,* irasci ; *to give —,* laedĕre ; *fault,* culpa. offender, *n.* reus (*accused*) ; *see* CRIMINAL. offensive, *adj.* odiosus, putidus. *Adv.* putide, *or by adj.* offensiveness, *n. by adj.*

offer, *v.tr.* offerre, porrigĕre, praebēre, praestare (*to afford*) ; *to — hospitality to anyone,* alqm invitare hospitio. *v.intr. to present itself,* offerri, dari. offering, *n. see* SACRIFICE.

office, *n.* munus, officium, provincia, magistratus. officer, *n. military,* praefectus militum. official, *adj. — report,* lit(t)erae publicae. *Adv.* publice. officiate, *v.intr. e.g. to — instead of another,* alcis officio fungi. officious, *adj.* molestus. *Adv.* moleste. officiousness, *n.* studium.

offscourings, *n.* purgamenta, -orum.

offspring, *n.* progenies.

oft, often, *adv.* saepe ; *very —,* saepissime.

ogle, *v.tr.* oculis limis intueri.

oil, *n.* oleum, olivum *(olive* —). *v.tr.* oleo ungĕre.

ointment, *n.* unguentum.

old, *adj.* vetus, antiquus ; —*er,* prior, superior ; *an* — *soldier,* veteranus miles ; *an* — *man,* senex ; *an* — *woman,* anus, old aged in sentence. **old-fashioned** *adj.* obsoletus, antiquus.

olden, *adj.* priscus. **older,** *comp.* maior *(eldest),* maximus natu.

olfactory, *adj.* quod ad odorem pertinet.

oligarchy, *n.* paucorum dominatio.

olive, *n.* oliva ; — -*tree,* olea. *Adj.* oleaginius.

Olympiad, *n.* Olympias. **Olympic,** *adj.* Olympicus ; *the* — *games,* Olympia, -orum.

omen, *n.* omen, portentum. **ominous,** *adj.* ominosus. *Adv.* ominose.

omit, *v.tr.* omittĕre. **omission,** *n.* intermissio: *leaving out,* praetermissio.

omnipotent, *adj. see* ALMIGHTY. **omnipresent,** *adj.* ubique praesens. **omniscient,** *adj.* qui omnia videt et audit. **omniscience,** *n. by adj.*

on, *prep. of place,* in *with ablat.,* ex *(e.g.* pendĕre ex arbore) ; a *or* ab *(e.g.* — *the side,* a parte) ; *time, without, a preposition (e.g.* quarto die); *adv.,* porro.

onward ! *interj.* perge, pergite.

one, *adj.* unus ; *a certain* —, quidam ; *some* —, aliquis ; *in negative sentences, any* —, quisquam ; *no* —, nemo ; altero pede claudus, *lame in* — *foot ;* — *after the other,* alius post alium ; singuli, *by* — ; *the* — . . . *other,* alter . . . alter, hic . . . ill ; timent inter se, *they fear* — *another ; it is all* — *to me,* mea nihil interest. **once,** *adv.* — *more,* iterum, de novo ; *more than* —, semel atque iterum ; *all at* —, repente, subito; *of time,* aliquando, quondam, olim (— *upon a time) ; if* — si quando. **one-eyed,** *adj.* luscus. **oneself,** *pron.* ipse.

onion, *n.* caepa (caepe)

only, *adj.* solus. *Adv.* solum, tantum ; *not* . . . *but also,* non tantum . . . , sed etiam.

onset, onslaught, *n.* incursio.

onward, *adv. see* ON.

onyx, *n.* onyx.

ooze, *v.intr.* manare, emanare *(also fig.).* **oozy,** *adj.* limosus.

opaque, *adj.* haud pellucidus.

open, *adj.* (ad)apertus, patens, (pro)patulus *(lying* —) ; hians *(wide* —, *yawning)* ; fores patentes *(wide* —) ; *the* — *sea,* altum ; *to be,* stand — *patēre ; manifest,* apertus ; *candid,* candidus. *Adv.* candide, palam. *v.tr.* aperire, patefacĕre, reserare *(to unbolt);* reclūdĕre *(to unlock) ;* (ex)pandĕre, revolvĕre *(to unroll, e.g. a book) ; to* —

a vein, venam secare ; *to begin,* exordiri. *v.intr.* se aperire, se pandĕre ; *to* — *again (of wounds),* recrudescĕre. **opening,** *n. an act,* apertio ; *aperture,* apertura *(in architecture),* foramen, os ; *beginning,* initium, exordium.

operate, *v.intr. see* ACT ; *to* — *upon,* render *by* secare alqm. **operation,** *n.* res gesta, negotium ; *in surgery, see* OPERATE.

opinion, *n.* sententia, iudicium; *a false* —, opinio falsa.

opponent, *n.* adversarius; *in speeches of an advocate,* iste.

opportune, *adj.* opportunus. *Adv.* opportune. **opportuneness,** *n.* opportunitas. **opportunity,** *n.* occasio ; facultas, copia.

oppose, *v.tr.* obicĕre, repugnare, resistĕre opponer, *n. see* OPPONENT. **opposite,** *adj.* adversus, obiectus. **opposition,** *n. see* RESISTANCE.

oppress, *v.tr.* premĕre. **oppression,** *n.* vexatio ; *see* TYRANNY. **oppressive,** *adj.* molestus, gravis. *Adv.* moleste, graviter.

opprobrium, *n.* (op)probrium. **opprobrious,** *adj.* probrosus.

optative, *adj., the* — *mood,* modus optativus.

optical, *adj. by* oculus *(e.g.* nervus oculorum).

option, *n.* optio, optio et potestas, arbitrium.

opulent, *adj.* opulentus. **opulence,** *n.* opulentia.

or, *conj.* aut, vel, ve *(enclit.) ;* sive, seu ; *in negative sentences,* neque ; — *at least,* aut certe, vel certe ; *either* . . . —, aut, vel . . . vel, sive . . . sive ; "— —" *in double questions, see* WHETHER.

oracle, *n.* oraculum, sors ; responsum ; *to give an* —, oraculum dare.

oral, *adj. praesens ; to have — communication,* coram sermonem cum alqo habēre.

oration, *n.* oratio, contio. **orator,** *n.* orator. **oratorical,** *adj.* oratorius. **oratory,** *n.* doctrina dicendi, ratio dicendi, rhetorice.

orb, *n.* globus, orbis. **orbed,** *adj.* in orbem circumactus. **orbit,** *n.* orbis, circulus.

orchard, *n.* pomarium.

orchid, *n.* orchis.

ordain, *v.tr. see* DECREE, APPOINT. **ordinance,** *n. see* DECREE.

ordeal, *n.* periculum; *see* TROUBLE.

order, *n.* ordo; *to set in* —, disponĕre; *to march in* —, compositi procedĕre; *in* —, ordine; *out of* —, extra ordinem; *division, class, genus ; rank,* ordo ; *fraternity,* collegium ; *command,* iussum, mandatum, senatus consultum; *in business.* mandatum. "*In* — *to*" *by*

ut *or* qui *with subj., etc.* *v.tr. to arrange*, componĕre, disponĕre; *to command*, iubēre, imperare. **orderly**, *adj.* compositus.
ordinal, *adj.*, — *number*, numerus ordinalis. **ordinance**, *n. see* DECREE.
ordinary, *adj.* usitatus, communis. **ordinarily**, *adv.* fere, plerumque.
ore, *n.* aes.
organ, *n. the* — *of speech*, lingua. **organic**, *adj.* (*e.g.* — *bodies*, animantia). **organize**, *v.tr.* ordinare. **organization**, *n.* temperatio ; — *of the state*, reipublicae forma. **organism**, *n.* compages (*e.g.* corporis), natura.
orgies, *n.* bacchanalia -ium ; *see* REVELRY.
Orient, *n.*, **Oriental**, *adj. see* EAST, EASTERN.
origin, *n.* orīgo, fons. **original**, *adj.* primus, principalis ; *new*, novus. *Adv.* initio, principio ; *n.* exemplum. **originality**, *n. gen. by* ORIGINAL. **originate**, *v.tr. see* CREATE. *v.intr. to* — (ex)oriri. **orginator**, *n.* auctor.
ornament, *n.* decus, ornatus. *v.tr.* (ex)ornare, decorare. **ornamental**, *adj.*, *render by verbs.* **ornate**, *adj.* (per)ornatus. *Adv.* ornate.
orphan, *n.* orbus. *fem.* orba. *Adj.* parentibus orbatus.
oscillate, *v.intr.* agitari ; *fig. see* HESITATE. **oscillation**, *n.* agitatio ; dubitatio.
osier, *n.* vimen. *Adj.* vimineus.
ossify, *v.tr.* in os mutare. *v.intr.* in os mutari.
ostensible, *adj.* simulatus. *Adv.* simulate. **ostentation**, *n.* ostentatio. **ostentatious**, *adj.* gloriosus. *Adv.* gloriose.
ostler, *n.* agaso.
ostracism, *n.* testarum suffragia, -orum ; *expulsion, by* expelli.
ostrich, *n.* struthiocamēlus.
other, *adj.* alius, alter (*of two*) ; —*s*, alii ; *the* —*s*, ceteri, reliqui. **otherwise**, *adv.* aliter.
ought, *v.aux.* debēre, *or by gerund or gerundive, or by* oportet.
ounce, *n.* uncia; *half-* —, semuncia ; *two* —*s*, sextans ; *three* —*s*, triens ; *four* —*s*, quadrans; *five* —*s*, quincunx; *six* —*s*, semis; *seven* —*s*, septunx ; *eight* —*s*. bes; *nine* —*s*, dodrans; *ten* —*s*, dextans; *eleven* —*s*, deunx; *twelve* —*s*, as.
our, *pron. adj.* noster; — *people*, nostri; *for* — *part*, per nos. **ourselves**, *pron. see* WE, SELF.
out, *adv.* extrinsecus; *to be* —, foris esse; *to go* —, exire foras; *to work* —, perficĕre ; *to breathe* —, exspirare ; *a fire breaks* —, incendium oritur ; *to spread* —, (ex)pandĕre. (*of*), *prep.*, *e or* ex (ex urbe, e vitā); extra (—*side of*); (*cause*), e, ex, a, ab *also* propter *and*

prae (*e.g.* — *of fear*, prae metu), *or by the ablative*, metu coactus; *to be* — *of one's mind*, non apud se esse.
outbid, *v.tr.* licitatione vincĕre.
outbreak, *n.* eruptio, initium, seditio (*sedition*).
outcast, *n.* exsul, extorris.
outcry, *n.* clamor; acclamatio.
outdo, *v.tr.* superare, vincĕre.
outer, *adj.* exterus, externus.
outflank, *v.tr.* circumire.
outlandish, *adj.* peregrinus, barbarus.
outlast, *v.tr.* diutius durare.
outlaw, *n.* proscriptus, ex(s)ul. *v.tr.* proscribĕre, aquā et igni interdicĕre. **outlawry**, *n.* proscriptio.
outlay, *n.* sumptus.
outlet, *n.* exitus, egressus; os (*of rivers*).
outline, *n.* —*s of a face*, lineamenta ; adumbratio (*sketch*). *v.tr.* describĕre, adumbrare.
outlive, *v.tr.* alci superesse.
outlook, *n. to have an* — *on*, ad alqd spectare; *fig.* spes.
outlying, *adj.* longinquus.
outnumber, *v.tr.* numero superare.
outpost, *n.* statio (*of troops*), propugnaculum.
outrage, *n.* iniuria. *v.tr.* alci affarre iniuriam. **outrageous**, *adj.* immanis, indignus. *Adv.* indigne, immoderate.
outright, *adv.* prorsus, omnino.
outrun, *v.tr.* cursu superare.
outset, *n.* initium.
outside, *adj.* externus; *as a noun, the* —, externa, -orum, superficies (*surface*); species. *Adv.* extra, foris.
outspoken, *adj. see* FRANK.
outspread, *adj.* passus.
outstanding, *adj. of debt, by* aes alienum.
outstrip, *v.tr.* cursu superare ; *fig. see* EXCEL.
outvote, *v.tr.* alqm suffragiis vincĕre.
outward, *adj.* exterus, externus; — *show* species. *Adv.* extra.
outweigh, *v.tr.* vincĕre.
outwit, *v.tr.* circumvenire.
outworks, *n.* munimenta (exteriora).
ovation, *n.* ovatio; *fig. to receive an* —, magnis clamoribus excipi.
oven, *n.* furnus.
over, *adv.* super, supra ; *to be* — (*remaining*), superesse, *prep.* super, supra *with accus.*
overawe, *v.tr.* terrēre.
overbalance, *v.tr.* praeponderare.
overbear, *v.tr.* vincĕre, superare. **overbearing**, *adj.* superbus.
overboard, *adj. to throw anything* —, alcis rei iacturam facĕre.
overboiled, *adj.* (*or part.*) nimis coctus.
overbold, *adj.* audax.
overburdened, *adj.* nimio onere oppressus.
overcast, *adj.* nubilus (*of the sky*).

overcharge, v.tr. nimio vendĕre.
overcome, v.tr. (de)vincĕre.
overdraw, v.tr. to — an account, aes alienum contrahĕre (to incur debt).
overdress, v.tr. nimis splendide se ornare.
overdue, adj. pecunia quam alqs iam solvĕre debuit.
overeat, v. reflex, heluari.
overfill, v.tr. supra modum implĕre.
overflow, n. inundatio fluminis. v.tr. inundare. v.intr. effundi; fig. abundare.
overgrow, v.intr. to be —n with foliage, frondibus obsitus esse.
overhang, v.intr. imminĕre, impendĕre.
overhasty, adj. praeproperus. Adv. praepropere.
overhaul, v.tr. *** EXAMINE.
overhead, adv. supra, desuper.
overhear, v.tr. excipĕre.
overheat, v.tr. alqd nimis cal(e)facĕre; to — oneself, by sudare.
overjoyed, adj. laetitiâ affectus.
overland, adj. terrâ (opp. mari).
overlap, v.tr. alci rei imminĕre.
overlay, v.tr. with gold, inaurare.
overload, v.tr. nimis onerare. overloaded, adj. nimis oneratus.
overlook, v.tr. observare, custodire, praeesse ; prospicĕre ; see PARDON ; to neglect, negligĕre ; to pass by, praetermittĕre. overlooker, n. custos, curator.
overmuch, adj. nimius. Adv. nimis, nimium.
overnight, adv. vesperi.
overpower, v.tr. vincĕre, debellare. overpowering, adj. see OVERWHELMING.
overreach, v.tr. circumscribĕre.
overrule, v.tr. (de)vincĕre.
overrun, v.tr. (per)vagari ; to be — with (of plants), alqâ re obsitus esse.
overscrupulous, adj. diligentior etc.
overseer, n. custos, (pro)curator.
oversight, n. error, erratum ; — of a business, curatio, procuratio, cura.
oversleep, v.intr. diutius dormire.
overspread, v.tr. obducĕre.
overt, adj. apertus, manifestus.
overtake, v.tr. consequi ; to surprise, opprimĕre. overtaken, adj. praeventus.
overtax, v.tr. iniquis oneribus premĕre.
overthrow, v.tr. deicĕre ; diruĕre ; opprimĕre. n. clades, strages.
overture, n. to make —s, condiciones proponĕre.
overturn, v.tr. subvertĕre.
overweening, adj. superbus.
overwhelm, v.tr. opprimĕre. overwhelmed, part., — with grief, dolore oppressus. overwhelming, adj. gravissimus.
overwork, v.intr. and reflex. nimis laborare.
overwrought, adj. or part. laboribus confectus (worn by labours).

overzealous, adj. nimis studiosus.
owe, v.tr. debēre ; it was owing to you, per te stetit quominus. owing, adj. see DUE.
owl, n. ulula, noctua, strix; like an —, noctuïnus (e.g. oculi).
own, adj. proprius; generally by meus, tuus, suus, etc., or by ipsius ; peculiaris, privatus, privus ; my, your — people, servants, mei, tui, etc. v.tr. see ACKNOWLEDGE ; see POSSESS. owner, n. possessor, dominus. ownership, n. possessio, auctoritas, — by long use, usucapio.
ox, n. bos ; young —, iuvencus ; a driver of —en, bubulcus. oxherd, n. armentarius.
oyster, n. ostrea. oyster-shell, n. testa.

P

pabulum, n. pabulum.
pace, n. gradus, passus ; gressus ; to keep — with, gradus aequare ; at a slow —, tarde, lente. v.intr. gradi, ambulare, spatiari (to walk about). v.tr. passibus metiri.
pacific, adj. by pacis. pacification, n. pacificatio, pax. pacificator, n. pacificator, pacis auctor. pacify, v.tr. placare; sedare.
pack, v.tr. for a march, sarcinas colligĕre, vasa colligĕre ; stipare (to — closely). n. bundle, fasciculus, sarcina.
pack-ass, n. asinus clitellarius. packhorse, n. equus clitellarius. packsaddle, n. clitellae. package, n. sarcina, fasciculus.
pact, n. pactio, pactum.
paddle, n. remus. v.intr. navem remo impellĕre.
page, n. puer ex aulâ.
page, n. of a book, pagina.
pageant, n. spectaculum, pompa. pageantry, n. see above.
pagoda, n. templum or aedes.
pail, n. situla (sitülus).
pain, n. dolor, maestitia, desiderium ; violent —, cruciatus. v.tr. alqm cruciare or dolore afficĕre. v.intr. dolēre. painful, adj. vehemens, gravis, acerbus. Adv. graviter, acerbe, magno cum dolore.
painless, adj. sine dolore. Adv. by adj. pains, n. toil, opera, labor, negotium, studium ; with great —, magno labore; to take —, operam dare. painstaking, adj. operosus.
paint, v.tr. pingĕre ; to — the face, fucare. n. pigmentum, color, fucus (cosmetic). paint-brush, n. penicillus.
painter, n. pictor. painting, n. pictura, ars (pingendi).

pair, *n.* par, iugum (*of oxen*) ; bini (*two at a time*). *v.tr.* (con)iungĕre. *v.intr.* coniungi.

palace, *n.* domus regia, *or simply* regia.

palate, *n.* palatum ; *a fine* —, subtile palatum. **palatable,** *adj.* iucundus, dulcis.

palaver, *n.* nugae.

pale, *adj.* pallidus ; *to be* —, pallēre ; *of colours, by* sub (*e.g.* subflavus, — *yellow*). *v.intr.* pallescĕre. **paleness,** *n.* pallor.

pale, paling, *n.* palus, sudes (*a stake*).

palfrey, *n.* equus *or* caballus.

palimpsest, *n.* palimpsestus.

palisade, *n.* vallum.

pall, *n.* pallium.

pall, *v.intr.* taedet.

palladium, *n.* palladium.

pallet, *n.* lectulus.

palliate, *v.tr.* excusare, extenuare. **palliation,** *n.* use verb (*e.g. the* — *of his fault,* culpam excusavit).

pallid, *adj. see* PALE.

palm, *n.* palma ; *adorned with* —, palmatus. *v.tr. to* — *off upon anyone,* alqd alci supponĕre. **palmer,** *n. see* PILGRIM. **palmy,** *adj.* florens, optimus.

palpable, *adj.* quod sentire possumus ; *fig.* manifestus (*manifest*), evidens. *Adv.* manifesto, evidenter.

palpitate, *v intr.* palpitare.

paltry, *adj.* vilis.

pamper, *v.tr.* nimis indulgēre.

pamphlet, *n.* libellus. **pamphleteer,** *n.* libellorum scriptor.

pan, *n.* sartago, patina, patella. **pancake,** *n.* placenta.

panacea, *n. lit.* panchrestum medicamentum.

pander, *n.* leno. *v.intr. to* — *to* ; *see* FLATTER.

panegyric, *n.* laudatio ; laus, laudes. **panegyrist,** *n.* laudator ; praedicator (*in public*).

panel, *n.* abacus ; *panelled ceiling* lacunar.

pang, *n.* dolor.

panic, *n.* pavor, terr

pannier, *n.* clitellæ. i

panoply, *n. see* ARMOUR.

panorama, *n. see* PROSPECT.

pant, *v.intr. to* — *for breath,* aegre ducĕre spiritum, anhelare. **panting,** *n.* anhelitus.

pantaloon, *n. perhaps* sannio, scurra, *m.*

pantheism, *n.* ratio eorum qui deum in universā rerum naturā situm esse putant. **pantheist,** *n.* qui deum, *etc.*, putat; *see above.*

panther, *n.* panthēra, pardus.

pantomime, *n.* mimus, pantomīmus.

pantry, *n.* cella penaria.

paper, *n.* charta, † papyrus, *f.*; *papers,*
scripta, -orum, tabellae ; *public* —*s,* tabulae publicae; *newspaper,* acta (diurna), -orum.

papyrus, *n.* papyrus (papyrum).

par, *n. by* aequalis.

parable, *n.* similitudo. **parabolical,** *adj.* per similitudinem.

parade, *n. military,* decursus ; *show,* apparatus. *v.intr.* (*of troops*), decurrĕre. *v.tr.* ostentare.

Paradise, *n.* (*after death*), sedes beatorum.

paradox, *n.* paradoxum.

paragon, *n.* specimen.

paragraph, *n.* caput.

parallel, *adj. fig.* (con)similis.

paralyse, *v.tr.* pede (manu, *etc.*) captus esse (*to be* —*d*).

paramount, *adj.* summus, maximus *; see* SUPERIOR.

paramour, *n. see* LOVER.

parapet, *n.* pluteus, lorica (*milit. term*).

paraphernalia, *n.* apparatus.

paraphrase, *n.* circumlocutio, paraphrasis.

parasite, *n.* parasitus ; *a plant,* planta parasitica.

parasol, *n.* umbella, umbraculum.

parboiled, *adj.* semicoctus.

parcel, *n.* fascis. *v.tr.* partiri, distribuĕre.

parch, *v.tr.* (ex)siccare, (ex)urĕre. *v.intr.* (ex)siccari. **parched,** *adj.* aridus.

parchment, *n.* membrana.

pardon, *v.tr.* ignoscĕre ; *to* — *a debt,* pecuniam creditam remittĕre. *n.* venia, remissio; *to ask* —, remissionem petĕre.

pare, *v.tr.* (de)secare, circumsecare.

parent, *n.* parens, genitor. **parentage,** *n.* stirps, genus. **parental,** *adj., by the genit.* — *love,* parentum amor. *Adv.* parentum more. **parentless,** *adj.* orbatus (parentibus).

parenthesis, *n.* interpositio, interclusio.

parity, *n. see* EQUALITY.

park, *n.* vivarium (*preserve*) ; saeptum ; horti; viridarium.

parley, *v.intr.* colloqui; (*military*), *to* —, legatos de condicionibus mittĕre. *n.* colloquium, sermo.

parliament, *n.* senatus ; *act of* —, senatus consultum ; *house of* —, curia ; *member of* —, senator. **parliamentary,** *adj.* senatorius, quod ad senatum pertinet.

parody, *n.* Greek παρωδια.

parole, *n.* (*military*) fides (data).

paroxysm, *n.* febris accessio; *fig.* vis *or* impetus, *or by* part. (*e.g.* irā impulsus).

parricide, *n.* parricīda ; *the act,* parricidium.

parrot, *n.* psittacus.

parry, *v.tr. and intr. to* — *a thrust or stroke,* ictum vitare, cavēre, repellĕre defendĕre (*to ward off*)

parsimonious, adj. parcus, **tenax,** malignus. Adv. parce, maligne. **parsimony,** n. parsimonia.

parsley, n. apium.

part, n. pars, membrum, locus; lowest, highest — by infimus, summus; in two, three —s, etc., bipartito, tripartito, etc.; the greater —, aliquantum; the one —, the other —, pars ... pars, alii (-ae, -a) ... alii (-ae, -a); I for my —, ego quidem, equidem; to divide into —s, in partes dividĕre; to have a — in anything, alcis rei particeps esse; partly, per partes; to take one's —, defendĕre; in these —s, hāc regione, hic v.tr. dividĕre, partiri. v.intr. discedĕre.

parting, n. discessus. **partly,** adv. partim, ex parte.

partake, v.tr., to — of, particeps esse alcis rei. **partaker,** n. socius.

parthenon, n. Parthenon.

partial, adj. alterius partis studiosus; iniquus (unfair). Adv. cupide, inique, ex (alqâ) parte. **partiality,** n. studium, gratia.

participate, v.intr. and tr., by particeps alcis rei, consors, socius alcis rei. **participation,** n. in anything, societas alcis rei. **participator,** n. socius.

participle, n. participium.

particle, n. particula, frustum (of food).

particoloured, adj. versicolor, varius.

particular, adj. separatus; peculiar to anyone, proprius; praecipuus; peculiaris; singularis; exacting, diligens, accuratus; a — friend; see INTIMATE. **particulars,** n., to go into —, singula sequi. **particularity,** n. diligentia. **particularize,** v.tr. per nomina citare. **particularly,** adv. sedulo, studiose, diligenter; praesertim.

partisan, n. homo alcis studiosus, fautor. **partisanship,** n. studium, favor.

partition, n. see DIVISION, SEPARATION; in a house, paries.

partner, n. socius; in marriage, coniu(n)x. **partnership,** n. societas.

partridge, n. perdix.

party, n. pars, or pl. partes, factio (polit.); to belong to a —, partes sequi; — leader, caput factionis; — spirit, studium; a large —, multitudo; a card —, lusus; **party-wall,** n. paries.

parvenu, n. novus homo.

pasha, n. satrapes, -ae and -is, m.

pass, v.intr. transire, transgredi, transcendĕre or superare (to — through, over, e.g. a mountain); to — through the gate, portā exire, introire; of time, praeterire; time —es quickly, tempus fugit; perferri (of a law); to come to —, accidĕre; (as I —ed along, in —ing, in transitu; to — by, praeterire; to let none — by, go past, neminem praetermittĕre. v.tr. to go beyond,

transgredi, transire; of time, degĕre, consumĕre; to — the night, pernoctare; to — accounts, rationes ratas habĕre; to — sentence, sententiam dicĕre or ferre (by votes); to — a law, decernĕre (of the Senate); legem esse iubĕre (of the people). — on, v.intr. pergĕre. — over, v.tr. praeterire (silentio), relinquĕre. n. aditus, angustiae (narrow —), fauces, -ium, saltus. **passable,** adj. pervius, tritus, or transitu facilis; tolerable, mediocris. Adv. mediocriter. **passage,** n. transitus, transvectio (of goods); transgressus, traiectus; — across a river, transitus or transvectio fluminis; to grant a — to anyone, dare alci iter per agros urbesque; way, road, iter, via, aditus, -ūs; — of a book, locus, caput; bird of —, avis advena. **passenger,** n. viator (on foot), vector (on horseback, by carriage, ship). **passing,** n. in commerce, permutatio, venditio.

password, n. tessera. **past,** adj. and n., praeteritus, prior, superior; the —, praeterita, -orum; in the — night, nocte priore or superiore. Adv. praeter. As prep. praeter, trans. **pastime,** n. ludus, oblectamentum.

passion, n. suffering, perpessio; (longing), cupiditas; libido (sensual); anger, ira, iracundia; fondness for, alcis rei studium; to conquer —, cupidates coërcēre. **passionate,** adj. cupidus, incitatus, impotens (e.g. irae); ardens, cerebrosus. Adv. cupide, studiose, ardenter. **passionateness,** n. animi ardor, furor. **passionless,** adj. cupiditatis expers. **passive,** adj. to remain —, quiescēre; alqd patienter ferre. Adv. aequo animo, patienter. **passiveness,** n. patientia.

pastoral, adj. pastoralis; agrestis; — poem, carmen bucolicum.

pastry, n. crustum.

pasture, n. ager pascuus. v.tr. pascĕre. v.intr. pabulari, pasci.

pat, n. plaga lĕvis. Adv. in tempore opportuno.

patch, n. pannus. v.tr. (re)sarcire. **patchwork,** n. cento.

patent, adj. manifestus, apertus. n. letter —, edictum.

paternal, adj. paternus, patrius.

path, n. via, semita, trames, callis. **pathless,** adj. invius.

pathetic, adj. flebilis, tristis. Adv. flebiliter, maeste. **pathos,** n. maestitia, tristitia.

patience, n. patientia, tolerantia, (e.g. tolerantia doloris), perseverantia, aequus animus; to have — with anyone, alqm patienter ferre; — ! i.e. wait ! exspecta ! mane ! **patient,** adj. patiens, tolerans; to be —, ex(s)pectare, manēre, quiescēre. Adv. patienter, aequo animo. n. aeger (sick person).

patois, n. sermo rusticus.
patrician, adj. and n. patricius ; the —s, patricii.
patrimony, n. patrimonium.
patriot, n. patriae amans, civis bonus; to be a —, amare patriam. **patriotic,** adj. patriae amans. Adv. patriae caus(s)ā. **patriotism,** n. patriae amor, pietas.
patrol, v.intr. circumire stationes, or vigilias, or urbem.
patron, n. protector, patrŏnus, fautor.
patronage, n. patrocinium, clientela.
patroness, n. patrona.
patter, v.intr. crepare. n. crepitus.
pattern, n. exemplum.
paucity, n. paucitas, or by adj. pauci.
paunch, n. abdōmen, venter.
pauper, n. see POOR.
pause, n. mora, respiratio, distinctio (in music), intervallum (interval), inter-missio. v.intr. moram facĕre, inter-sistĕre; intermittĕre.
pave, v.tr. lapide (con)sternĕre; munire (to make a road). **pavement,** n. pavimentum, via strata (paved road). **paving,** n. stratura. **paving-stone,** n. saxum quadratum.
pavilion, n. see TENT.
paw, n. pes, ungula. v.tr. (solum, etc.) pedibus ferire.
pawn, v.tr. alqd pignori dare.
pawn, n. at chess, latrunculus, latro.
pay, v.tr. (per)solvĕre, pendĕre, numerato solvĕre (ready money) ; to — a penalty, poenas dare or solvĕre ; to atone for, luĕre. v.intr. fructum ferre. n. merces, (wages), stipendium (of a soldier), quaestus (gain). **payable,** adj. sol-vendus. **pay-day,** n. dies quo merces solvenda est. **paymaster,** n. in the army, tribunus aerarius. **payment,** n. solutio, repraesentatio (ready-money).
pea, n. pisum, cicer.
peace, n. pax, otium (leisure), concordia, in —, in pace: to treat for —, agĕre de pacis condicionibus; to make —, facĕre pacem ; to keep or preserve —, pacis fidem servare. interj. tace, tacete! Pax ! **peaceable,** adj. placidus, concors. Adv. placide, concorditer. **peaceful,** adj. tranquillus. Adv. tranquille. **peaceful-ness,** n., **peacemaker,** n. see PEACE. **peace-offering,** n. piaculum.
peacock, n. pavo.
peak, n. by summus or extremus; point, apex.
peal, n. sonitus; — of laughter, cachin-nus ; — of thunder tonitrus. v.intr. sonare.
pear, n. pirum. **pear-tree,** n. pirus, f.
pearl, n. margarita.
peasant, n. agricola, m., agricultor, rusticus, agrestis. **peasantry,** n. agrestes.
pease, n. see PEA.

pebble, n. calculus, lapillus.
peccadillo, n. culpa, delictum. **peccant,** adj. peccans.
peck, n. perhaps modius. v.tr. rostro caedĕre.
peculation, n. peculatus; to commit —, pecuniam avertĕre.
peculiar, adj. proprius, meus, tuus, suus, peculiaris, privatus, singularis; it is — to every man, cuiusvis hominis est ; singular, mirus, novus. Adv. praesertim, maxime. **peculiarity,** n. proprietas, natura.
pecuniary, adj. pecuniarius.
pedagogue, n. paedagogus (the slave who accompanied a child to school) ; magister.
pedant, n. homo ineptus; homo putidus.
pedantic, adj. ineptus, putidus. Adv. inepte, putide. **pedantry,** n. ineptiae.
pedestal, n. of a column, etc., basis.
pedestrian, n. pedes. Adj. pedester.
pedigree, n. stemma.
pedlar, n. institor.
peel, n. cutis, corium. v.tr. cutem, etc. detrahĕre. v.intr. cutem (de)ponĕre.
peep, v.intr. prospicĕre ; to — at, oculis percurrĕre. n. a(d)spectus.
peep, v.intr. of chickens, pipare.
peer, n. equal, par ; noble, unus e patriciis. **peerage,** n. to raise to the —, ad amplissimum gradum producĕre. **peerless,** adj. unicus. Adv. unice.
peer, v.intr. (per)scrutare.
peevish, adj. morosus, difficilis. Adv. morose, iracunde. **peevishness,** n. morositas, iracundia.
pelf, n. lucrum.
pelisse, n. pallium.
pell-mell, adv. promiscue, confuse, passim.
pellucid, adj. see TRANSPARENT.
pelt, v.tr. lapides in alqm conicĕre. **pelting,** adj. (of rain) maximus.
pen, n. calamus, stilus (of metal) ; fold, saeptum. v.tr. scribĕre ; to fold, saeptis includĕre. **penmanship,** n. ars bene scribendi.
penalty, n. poena, damnum, multa.
penance, n. satisfactio, piaculum.
penitence, n. paenitentia. **penitent,** adj. paenitens. **penitentiary,** n. car-cer.
pencil, n. o painter, penicillus ; for writing, stilus.
pending adj. in law ; the matter is still —, adhuc sub iudice lis est. prep. per with accus. (during), dum (until).
pendulous, adj. pendulus.
penetrable, adj. pervius. **penetrate,** v.tr. and intr. penetrare ; penetrare per locum ; pervadĕre locum ; (to be heard), ad aures pervadĕre, translucĕre (of light) ; the cry —s into the camp,

clamor in castra perfertur ; to — into
a country, procedere ; se insinuare (by
stealth). penetrating, adj. of cold,
etc., penetralis, acutus ; fig. sagax,
callidus. penetration, n. acumen,
sagacitas.

peninsula, n paeninsula.

penny, n. as, nummus (sestertius) ;
to pay to the last —, ad assem solvere.

pension, n. annua (pl.). v.tr. annua, etc.,
alci praebēre. pensioner, n. cui annua
praebentur.

pensive, adj. in cogitatione (or cogita-
tionibus) defixus. Adv. use adj. pen-
siveness, n. cogitatio, tristitia.

pentameter, n. (versus) pentameter.

penthouse, n. as militi. term, vinea.

penurious, adj. parcus. Adv. parce ac
tenuiter. penuriousness, n. parsimonia. penury, n. inopia, egestas.

people, n. vulgus, -i, n. plebs (the
common —) ; the —, homines ; the
young —, adolescentuli ; towns—, oppidani, cives (citizens) ; before the —,
palam ; with adjs., e.g. many —,
multi ; good —, boni ; my, your, etc.,
—, mei, tui ; in the name of the —,
publice ; populus (forming a State) ;
gens, a — of the same race. or
coloniam or colonos deducěre, or locum
incolis frequentare ; fig. complēre (to
fill). populace, n. plebs (commons),
vulgus (mob). popular, adj. the —
party, popularis ; favourite, populo
gratus ; to be —, gratiā plurimum
posse, Adv. populariter. popularity,
n. gratia, populi favor. populate,
v.tr. frequentare ; with settlers, coloniam
deducěre. population, n. civium or
incolarum numerus, cives, incolae.
populous, adj. frequens, celeber. popu-
lousness, n. celebritas hominum or
civium frequentia.

pepper, n. piper.

per, prep. = by ; per annum, a year.

peradventure, adv. forte, fortasse,
forsitan.

perambulate, v.tr. iter facěre per locum,
peragrare, percurrěre, circumire, pervagari.

perceivable, adj. quod sentiri potest.
perceive, v.tr. sentire, audire, vidēre;
cerněre ; notare ; fig. animadvertěre;
cognoscěre ; observare, intellegěre. per-
ceptibility, n. by perceptible, adj.
insignis, manifestus. Adv. manifeste.

perception, n. by percipěre.

perch, n. (pole) pertica. v.intr. insidēre;
insidēre (to remain on).

perch, n. a fish, perca.

perchance, adv. see PERADVENTURE.

percolate, v.intr. permanare.

percussion, n. ictus, pulsus.

perdition, n. exitium.

peremptory, adj. confidens arrogans ;

to give — orders, arroganter praecipěre.
Adv. confidenter, arroganter.

perennial, adj. perennis. Adv. by adj.
or perpetuo.

perfect, adj. plenus, integer, absolutus,
perfectus. Adv. plene, absolute, perfecte, or by summo, "omnia" dent —
right, rectissime). v.tr. excolěre (e.g.
orationem), conficěre, perficěre. n. praeteritum perfectum (gram.). perfection,
n. integritas, absolutio, perfectio ; to
bring to —, absolvěre or perficěre.

perfidious, adj. perfidus, perfidiosus.
Adv. perfide, perfidiose. perfidy, n.
perfidia.

perforate, v.tr. terebrare, perforare.

perforce, adv. vi, per vim, necessario,
or by invitus.

perform, v.tr. (per)agěre, gerěre, (per)-
fungi, administrare, exsequi ; conficěre;
to — a part, partes agěre ; to — sacred
rites, sacra facěre. performance, n.
actio, administratio, confectio, opus,
functio ; the thing performed, negotium, officium ; on the stage, fabula
(e.g. during the —, dum fabula agitur).
performer, n. actor, auctor, or by PER-
FORM; artis musicae peritus.

perfume, n. odor, unguentum. v.tr.
odoribus perfundēre. perfumer, n.
myropola, unguentarius.

perfunctory, adj. neglegens.

perhaps, adv. fortasse, forsitan ; unless
—, nisi forte, nisi si.

peril, n. see DANGER. perilous, adj.
see DANGEROUS.

period, n. tempus or tempora, tempestas,
aetas, spatium temporis. periodical,
adj. sollemnis (sol(l)enn-). Adv. certis
temporibus.

peripatetic, adj. peripateticus ; the —s,
Peripatetici.

perish, v.intr. perire, caděre, occiděre,
occidi, interfici ; more — from hunger
than by the sword, plures fame quam
ferrum absumpsit. perishable, adj.
quod corrumpi potest, fragilis, caducus,
brevis. perishableness, n. fragilitas,
brevitas.

peristyle, n. peristyl(i)um.

perjure, v.tr. falsum iurare, periurare.
perjured, adj. periurus. perjury, n.
falsum iusiurandum, periurium.

permanency, n. perpetuitas, stabilitas. permanent, adj. by permaněro,
or by perpetuus, stabilis. Adv. perpetuo.

permissible, adj. licitus, concessus ; to
be —, licēre. permission, n. concessio;
potestas, copia ; licentia ; to have the
—, mihi licet ; with your —, pace
tuā ; without anyone's —, iniussu
alcis. permissive, adj. by verbs.
permit, v.tr. siněre, conceděre, per-
mittěre potestatem facěre, veniam
dare.

permutation, n. (per)mutatio.

pernicious, adj. perniciosus, exitiosus, exitialis. Adv. perniciose. perniciousness, n. vis nocendi; who does not see the — of this thing? quis non intellegit hanc rem nocēre?

peroration, n. peroratio, conclusio.

perpendicular, adj. directus (ad perpendiculum).

perpetrate, v.tr. committěre or in se admittěre. perpetration, n. by verb. perpetrator, n. of a crime, auctor facinoris; qui scelus commisit.

perpetual, adj. perpetuus. Adv. perpetuo. perpetuate, v.tr. perpetuum reddēre, continuare. perpetuation, n. by verb. perpetuity, n. perpetuitas.

perplex, v.tr. of persons, mentem perturbare. perplexing, adj. difficilis, anceps, dubius. perplexity, n. dubi tatio; see DOUBT.

persecute, v.tr. insectari, vexare. persecution, n. insectatio, vexatio. persecutor, n. vexator, insectator.

perseverance, n. perseverantia, constantia, assiduitas, pertinacia, pervicacia; patientia. persevere, v.intr. perseverare, constare, perstare, consistěre, (per)manēre; pergěre. persevering, adj. perseverans, constans, assiduus, tenax, pertinax. Adv. perseveranter, constanter, pertinaciter.

persist, v.intr. see PERSEVERE.

person, n. homo; caput; in his, etc., own —, ipse, praesens, coram; body, corpus, facies; — represented on the stage, persona; gram. persona. personage, n. great man, homo nobilis. personality, n. (bona) sua. personate, v.tr. alcis partes agěre. personify, v.tr. humanā specie indurěre.

perspicacious, adj. perspicax, sagax, acutus, acer. perspicacity, n. perspicacitas, ingenium acutum.

perspiration, n. sudor. perspire, v.intr. sudare.

persuade, v.tr. persuadēre; adducěre. persuasion, n. persuasio. persuasive, adj. persuasiveness, n. with verb (e.g. a — speech, oratio ad persuadendum accommodata).

pert, adj. procax. Adv. procaciter. pertness, n. procacitas.

pertain, v.intr. pertinēre ad, alcis iuris esse (to be his of right); what —s to this, quod pertinet ad hoc.

pertinacious, adj. pertinax. Adv. pertinaciter. pertinacity, n. pertinacia.

perturbation, n. perturbatio; see DISTURBANCE.

perusal, n. lectio, perlectio. peruse, v.tr. perlegěre, pervolutare.

pervade, v.tr. permanare; to — the mind, in animum penetrare.

perverse, adj. perversus, pravus. Adv. fig. perverse. perverseness, n. perversitas. perversion, n. corruptio, depravatio. pervert, v.tr. corrumpěre.

pest, n. see PESTILENCE; fig. pestis. pester, v.tr. see ANNOY.

pestilence, n. pestilentia, lues. pestilential, adj. pestilens, foedus.

pestle, n. pilum, pistillum.

pet, n. deliciae, amores, -um; see FAVOURITE. v.tr. fovēre.

petition, n. see PRAYER, REQUEST; formal —, petitio; to grant a —, alci petenti satisfacěre. v.tr. petěre alqd ab alqo, rogare; implorare. petitioner, n. qui supplicat.

petrify, v.tr. in lapidem mutare; fig. obstupefacěre; to be petrified (with astonishment, etc.), obstupescěre.

pettifogger, n. causidicus. petty, adj. see PALTRY.

petulance, n. petulantia. petulant, adj. petulans.

phantom, n. somnium; they are mere —s, et falsa et inania sunt; see GHOST.

Pharisee, n. fig. see HYPOCRITE.

pharmacy, n. medicina.

phase, n. status, condicio or ratio (the thing has passed into a new —, res nova fit).

pheasant, n. (avis) Phasiana; Phasianus (Fas-).

phenomenon, n. prodigium, portentum; res mira.

phial, n. see BOTTLE.

philanthropy, n. humanitas. philanthropist, n., philanthropical, adj. humanus. Adv. humane.

Philippic, n. (oratio) Philippica; fig. oratio in alqm habita.

philologist, n. grammaticus, philologus. philology, n. grammatica (or grammatice). philological, adj. grammaticus.

philosopher, n. philosophus; the true —, sapiens. philosophy, n. philosophia. philosophical, adj. by the genit., philosophiae, philosophorum; = wise, sapiens. Adv. philosophorum more, sapienter. philosophize, v.intr. philosophari (lit.), disputare (to expound).

philtre, n. philtrum.

phlegm, n. pituita; dullness, tarditas ingenii; patientia, lentitudo. phlegmatic, adj. tardus, lentus. Adv. patienter, lente.

phoenix, n. phoenix.

phrase, n. locutio. phraseology, n. locutio, dicendi genus, oratio.

physic, n. see MEDICINE. physical, adj. natural, by the genit. naturae, or corporis. Adv. naturā. physician, n. see DOCTOR. physics, n. physica, -orum. physiognomy, n. lineamenta, -orum, n. os vultusque, facies.

pick, v.tr and intr. rostro tunděre (of

birds) ; *to* — *a bone*, rodĕre ; *to gather*, carpĕre ; *to* — *up*, colligĕre, tollĕre. *n.* —*axe*, dolābra ; *a* —*pocket*, fur. **picked**, *adj.* delectus (*of troops*), eximius.

picket, *see* PICQUET.

pickle, *n.* salsura ... *fish*, pisces muriā condire.

picquet, *n.* statio.

pictorial, *adj. and adv.* tabulis ornatus.

picture, *n.* pictura, tabula (picta) ; *likeness*, imago (picta). *v.tr. to* — *in the mind*, animo fingĕre ; *in words*, depingĕre. **picturesque**, *adj.* amoenus ; *see* BEAUTIFUL.

pie, *n. see* PASTRY.

piece, *n.* pars, fragmentum, segmen, frustum, truncus, crusta ; *of cloth*, pannus ; *aliquantum* (*e.g. of land*, agri) ; *a very large* —, multum *with genit.* ; *a* — *of money*, nummus ; *made out of one* —, *or into one* —, solidus ; *fabula* (*a theatrical* —), cantus (*of music*) ; *in* —*s*, —*meal*, minutatim. *v.tr.* consuĕre ; *see* PATCH.

pied, *adj.* maculosus.

pier, *n.* pila (pontis) ; moles, moles lapidum (*mole*).

pierce, *v.tr. to* — *through*, transfigĕre. **piercing**, *adj.* acer, acutus.

piety, *n.* pietas erga Deum, religio, sanctitas. **pious**, *adj.* pius erga Deum, religiosus, sanctus. *Adv.* pie, sancte.

pig, *n.* porcus, sus. **piggish**, *adj.* suillus, porcinus. **pigheaded**, *adj. see* OBSTINATE.

pigeon, *n.* columba, palumbes ; — *house*, columbarium ; turris.

pigment, *n. see* PAINT.

pigmy, *n. see* DWARF.

pike, *n.* hasta.

pile, *n.* strues, accervus ; rogus (*funeral* —, *also* — *of wood*) ; (*for building on*), sublica ; *a bridge built on* —*s*, pons sublicius. *v.tr.* (co)acervare, cumulare ; *to* — *up*, insŭro struem, exstruĕre (*e.g. rogum*).

pilfer, *v.tr. and intr.* ; *see* STEAL.

pilgrim, *n.* viator, *or* qui in loca sacra migrat ; —*'s staff*, baculum. **pilgrimage**, *n.* iter.

pill, *n.* pilula ; *he swallowed the* —, haec concoxit.

pillage, *n.* rapina, depopulatio. *v.tr.* populari, spoliare. *v.intr.* praedari. **pillager**, *n.* praedator, populator.

pillar, *n.* columen (*fig. e.g.* columen reipublicae), pila, columna. **pillared**, *adj.* columnatus.

pillory, *n. fig.* alqm cruciare ; *see* TORMENT.

pillow, *n.* pulvinus. *v.tr.* (suf)fulcire.

pilot, *n.* gubernator. *v.tr.* gubernare.

pimple, *n.* pustula. **pimpled, pimply**, *adj.* pustulosus.

pin, *n.* acus. *v.tr.* acu (af)figĕre.

pincushion, *n.* thēca (= *case*).

pincers, *n. pl.* forceps. **pinch**, *v.tr. fig. to* —, urĕre (*of a shoe, frost, etc.*); *of poverty*, urgĕre. **pinching**, *adj. of poverty, etc., by* extremus, summus, etc.

pine, *n.* pīnus, *f.*

pine, *v.intr.* tabescĕre, confici ; *to* — *for anything*, alqd desiderare. **pining**, *n.* tabes.

pinion, *n. of a bird*, penna (pinna) ; *fetter*, compes. *v.tr.* (re)vincire.

pink, *adj.* puniceus.

pinnacle, *n.* fastigium (*lit. and fig.*).

pint, *n. perhaps*, sextarius ; *half a* — hemina ; *quarter of a* —, quartarius.

pioneer, *n.* qui primus alqd facit.

pious, *adj.* pius, sanctus.

pip, *v.intr.* pipire.

pip, *n. of fruit*, semen, granum, acinus.

pipe, *n. for water, etc.*, tubus ; *musical*, fistula, tibia. *v.intr.* fistulā canĕre *or* cantare. **pipe-clay**, *n.* creta fig(u)lina.

piper, *n.* tibicen.

pipkin, *n.* olla.

piquant, *adj.* acutus, salsus ; facetus. *Adv.* acute, salse. **piquancy**, *n.* sal, vis. **pique**, *n.* simultas. *v.tr. see* IRRITATE; *to* — *oneself*, gloriari.

piracy, *n.* latrocinium maris. **pirate**, *n.* praedo (maritimus), pīrāta. **piratical**, *adj.* piraticus.

pit, *n.* puteus, fovea, scrobis, fossa ; *in the theatre*, cavea (cavea ima *for the nobility*, cavea media *and* summa *more nearly* = *pit*). **pit against**, *v.tr.* alqm alci opponĕre. **pit-a-pat**, *adv. to go* —, palpitare. **pitfall**, *n.* fovea.

pitch, *n.* pix ; *of* —, *as black as* —, piceus ; — *pine*, picea ; — *dark*, (tenebris) obductus. **pitchy**, *adj.* picatus.

pitch, *n.* degree, gradus, *or by* summus, extremus, *or* ultimus *with n.* (*i.e. to the highest* — *of madness, and* summam amentiam) ; *in music*, sonus, vox ; *a high* —, vox acuta ; *low* —, vox gravis. *v.tr. to* — *a tent*, tabernaculum ponĕre ; *to throw*, iacĕre. *v.intr. to* — *upon*, incidĕre. **pitchfork**, *n.* furca.

pitcher, *n. see* JAR.

piteous, pitiable, *adj.* miser, miserabilis. *Adv.* misĕre, miserabiliter. **pitiful**, *adj. full of pity*, clemens, misericors; *see* PITEOUS ; *mean*, abiectus, vilis. *Adv.* clementer, abiecte. **pitifulness**, *n.* clementia ; *by adj. or* humilitas.

pitiless, *adj.* durus. *Adv.* crudeliter, saeve. **pitilessness**, *n.* crudelitas, saevitia. **pity**, *n.* misericordia. *v.tr.* misĕrēri, me miseret.

pittance, *n.* mercedula, pecunia exigus.

pivot, *n. fig. see* HINGE.

placable, *adj.* placabilis. **placability,** *n.* placabilitas.

placard, *n.* libellus. *v.tr.* libellum proponere.

place, *n.* locus, campus (*open* —), regio ; *at this* —, his, hoc loco; *from which* —, unde ; *from every* —, undique ; *at different* —*s,* passim ; *situation, office, munus* ; *in* — *of,* loco alcis ; *in the first* —, primo, primum ; *in the next* —, deinceps. *v.tr.* ponere, statuere, constituere ; *to* — *in different spots,* disponere; *in line of battle,* instruere; — *before,* proponere ; *to* — *round,* circumdare.

placid, *adj.* placidus.

plagiarism, *n.* furtum.

plague, *n.* pestis, pestilentia ; *fig.* malum ; *the* — *take you !* in malam crucem ! *v.tr.* vexare, sol(l)icitare, cruciare; *with requests,* precibus fatigare.

plain, *adj.* smooth, aequus, planus ; *manifest,* apertus, manifestus ; *unadorned,* simplex, inornatus, incomptus ; *distinctus* ; *see* UGLY. *Adv.* clare, manifeste ; simpliciter, inornate, distincte ; sincere. *n.* planities, aequus et planus locus, campus, aequor (*also surface of the sea*). *Adj.* **plainness,** *n.* clearness, perspicuitas ; simplicitas (*of dress, etc.*) ; *see* FRANKNESS ; UGLINESS.

plaint, *n.* *see* COMPLAINT. **plaintiff,** *n.* accusator, qui (*or* quae) petit ; *to appear as the principal* —, suo nomine accusare. **plaintive,** *adj.* miserabilis. *Adv.* miserabiliter. **plaintiveness,** *n.* by *adj.*

plait, *n.* sinus, ruga ; *of hair,* gradus. *v.tr. see* FOLD ; *the hair,* comam in gradus formare.

plan, *n. a sketch,* forma, descriptio ; *of a building,* aedificandi descriptio ; *in idea,* consilium, propositum, ratio. *v.tr.* consilium inire.

plane, *n. geometrical,* forma plana ; *tool,* runcina.

plane, *n. a tree,* platanus, *f.*

planet, *n.* stella errans.

plank, *n.* tabula, axis ; *to nail* —*s,* coaxare (coass-). *v.tr.* coaxare. **planking,** *n.* coaxatio, *or pl. of* PLANK.

plant, *n.* herba, planta. *v.tr.* serere, (de)ponere ; *a colony,* coloniam deducere. **plantation,** *n.* arbustum, quercetum, locus arboribus consitus. **planter,** *n.* sator, qui serit. **planting,** *n.* satio, satus.

plash, *n.* murmur, fremitus. *v.tr.* murmurare, fremere.

plaster, *n.* gypsum, tectorium ; *in medicine,* emplastrum. *v.tr.* gypsare, gypso illinere. **plasterer,** *n.* tector.

plate, *n.* bractea, lam(i)na (*of metal*) ; *at table,* patella ; *collectively,* vasa (-orum) argentea. *v.tr. to* — *with silver,* argento inducere.

platform, *n.* suggestus, -ūs.

Platonic, *adj.* Platonicus, Academicus ; (*the* — *philosophy,* academia). **Platonist,** *n. the* —*s,* academici.

plaudit, *n.* plausus.

plausible, *adj. probable,* veri similis, probabilis ; *in bad sense,* speciosus. *Adv.* veri similiter ; speciose, per speciem. **plausibility,** *n.* verisimilitudo; species.

play, *v.intr. and tr. to* — *an instrument,* canere, †modulari, psallere, *with ablat. of the instrument played* ; *to* — *amuse oneself,* ludere ; *to* — *at dice,* tesseris *or* talis ludere, alea *or* aleam ludere ; *to act,* agere partes. *n. amusement,* ludus ; lusus (*playing*), lusio (*the act*) ; *spectaculum,* fabula (*theatrical*); **player,** *n.* (*musical*), fidicen, *on a stringed instrument* ; *fem.* citharista, *m.*, citharoedus ; cornicen (*horn or cornet*), tibicen (*a piper*), tubicen (*trumpeter*) ; *for amusement,* lusor ; *see* GAMBLER ; — *on the stage,* actor. **playfellow, playmate,** *n.* aequalis. **playful,** *adj.* lascivus, iocosus. *Adv.* iocose. **playfulness,** *n.* lascivia. **playwriter, playwright,** *n.* qui fabulas scribit.

plea, *n. defendant's* —, defensio, oratio pro se ; *to make a* — *in court,* caus(s)am dicere ; *excuse,* excusatio. **plead,** *v.intr. in law,* cau(s)sam agere, versari in foro (*to be a pleader*) ; *in gen.* alqd excusare. **pleader,** *n.* orator, causidicus.

pleasant, *or* **pleasing,** *adj.* acceptus, gratus, iucundus, dulcis, urbanus (*polite*), lepidus ; — *conversation,* sermo venustus et urbanus ; *places,* loca amoena. *Adv.* iucunde, dulce, lepide, amoene. **pleasantry,** *n.* facetiae, iocus. **please,** *v.intr.* placere, delectare, gratus esse ; *it* —*s,* placet (*of a decree of the senate*) ; *if you* —, vis (si vis) ; *to be* —*d,* gaudere. **pleasing,** *adj. see* PLEASANT. **pleasure,** *n.* voluptas ; *will,* arbitrium ; delectatio, oblectamentum (*object of* —) ; *according to* — ex arbitrio eius (*or* suo).

plebeian, *n. the* —*s,* plebeii, plebs. *Adj.* plebeius.

pledge, *n.* pignus, arrhabo. *v.tr.* (op)pignerare ; *to* — *your word,* fidem obligare.

Pleiades, *n.* Pleiades.

plenipotentiary, *n.* legatus.

plenitude, *n. see* FULLNESS.

plenteous, plentiful, *adj.* uber, copiosus. *Adv.* abundanter, copiose. **plenty,** *n.* copia, abundantia ; — *of anything,* satis *with genit.*

pliant, pliable, *adj.* lentus, flexibilis ; *fig.* mobilis, mollis. **pliancy, pliability,** *n.* lentitia ; inconstantia, mollitia.

plight, *n. see* STATE. *v.tr. see* PLEDGE.

plod, *v.intr.* tardius progredi ; *to toil,*

contendĕre et laborare. **plodding**, adj.
esse industriā singulari.

plot, plat, n. of ground, agellus, area.

plot, n. coniuratio ; to form a —
conspirare, coniurare ; in dramatic
writings, argumentum fabulae. v.tr.
and intr. see above. **plotter**, n. see
[illegible]

plough, n. aratrum ; —man, arator ;
—share, vomer ; — handle, stiva. v.tr.
arare, aratro subigĕre.

pluck, v.tr. vellĕre ; to — flowers, flores
carpĕre ; to — up, evellĕre, eruĕre ; to
— up courage, animum recipĕre. n.
courage, virtus.

plum, n. prunum. **plum-tree**, n. prunus.

plumage, n. plumae, pennae. **plume**,
n. pluma, penna. v. reflex to — oneself
on, iactare. **plumy**, adj. plumis
obductus.

plummet, plumb-line, n. linea, perpendiculum.

plump, adj. pinguis.

plunder, v.tr. praedari, exspoliare,
nudare, depopulari (to lay waste). n.
praeda, rapina ; to live by —, rapto
vivĕre. **plunderer**, n. spoliator, populator.

plunge, v.tr. to — into, mergĕre in alqd ;
demergĕre or submergĕre. v.intr. to —
into, (im)mergĕre, submergĕre ; fig. se
mergĕre in alqd.

plural, adj. numerus pluralis.

ply, v.tr. exercēre.

poacher, n. fur.

pocket, n. sacculus, crumēna ; sinus,
fold (in sense of —, poet.). v.tr.
auferre. **pocket-book**, n. pugillares,
-ium. **pocket-handkerchief**, n. su-
darium.

pod, n. siliqua.

poem, n. carmen, pŏēma. **poet**, n.
pŏēta, scriptor, †vates (inspired —).
poetaster, n. pŏēta malus. **poetical**,
adj. pŏēticus. Adv. pŏētice. **poetry**,
n. pŏētice or pŏētica.

poignant, adj. acer.

point, n. acumen, cuspis, spiculum,
fastigium, vertex ; of land, promontorium ; locus (spot), punctum temporis
(minute) ; I am on the — of, etc.,
in eo est ut, etc. ; res (subject), caput
(main —), cardo (main — in dispute), de quo agitur (the — in dispute) ; not to the —, nihil ad rem.
v.tr. (prae)acuĕre ; with the finger, digito monstrare. **point-blank**, adj. directus ; to give a — refusal, alqd prorsus
negare. Adv. plane, omnino. **pointed**,
adj. (prae)acutus ; fig. salsus ; ad alqd
appositus. Adv. salse, apposite.

pointer, n. dog, canis (venaticus).

pointless, adj. see BLUNT ; fig. insulsus, ineptus.

poise, v.tr. librare.

poison, n. venēnum, virus. v.tr. veneno
imbuĕre ; fig. to — the minds, animos
inficĕre malis libidinibus. **poisoned**,
adj. venenatus (e.g. an arrow), veneno
necatus (killed by poison). **poisoner**, n.
veneficus. **poisoning**, n. veneficium.
poisonous, adj. venenatus.

poke, n.tr. [illegible], ignem excitare. v.intr. to —
about, perscrutari.

pole, n. long rod, contus ; of the earth,
axis, cardo. **polar**, adj. septentrionalis
(northern). **poleaxe**, n. see AXE.

polecat, n. feles.

polemics, n. disputationes.

policy, n. ratio rei publicae gerendae, disciplina reipublicae ; fig. prudentia,
consilium. **politic**, adj. prudens, sagax.
political, adj. civilis ; publicus ; a —
discussion, sermo de republica habitus ;
— science, ratio civilis. **politics**, n.
respublica (e.g. ad rem publicam accedĕre,
to take up —). **polity**, n. respublica.

polish, v.tr. (ex)polire. n. nitor, candor;
fig. (his writings lack —, scriptis eius
lima deest) ; see POLITENESS. **polished**,
adj. past part. of POLISH ; see
POLITE.

polite, adj. urbanus, comis. Adv.
urbane, comiter. **politeness**, n.
urbanitas, comitas.

poll, n. see HEAD ; **polling-booth**, n.
saeptum.

pollard, n. arbor (am)putata.

pollute, v.tr. polluĕre. **pollution**, n.
pollutio.

poltroon, n. see COWARD.

polygamy, n. plures uxores habēre.

polytheist, n. qui multos deos colit.

pomatum, n. capillare.

pomegranate, n. malum granātum or
Punicum.

pomp, n. apparatus. **pompous**, adj.
magnificus, gloriosus ; of style, inflatus,
tumidus. Adv. magnifice, gloriose.
pompousness, pomposity, n. magnificentia, arrogantia.

pond, n. stagnum, piscina (fish —).

ponder, v.tr. and intr. ponderare, secum reputare. **ponderous**, adj. see
WEIGHTY.

poniard, n. see DAGGER.

pontiff, n. pontifex.

pony, n. mannus, or equus parvus.

poodle, n. canis.

pool, n. lacuna.

poop, n. puppis.

poor, adj. in kind or nature, malus,
vilis, mediocris, deterior, peior ; —
living, tenuis victus ; — speech, oratio
ieiuna ; barren, sterilis macer ; not
rich, pauper, egens, inops ; the
—, pauperes, capite censi; pitiable,
miser, infelix ; — fellow ! me (te)
miserum ! n. poorly, adv. mediocriter,
misere. **poverty**, n. paupertas, egestas,
inopia.

pop, *n.* crepitus. *v.intr.* crepare *to — out*, evadĕre. ex(s)ilire.

poplar, *n.* pōpulus, *f.* ; *of the —*, pōpuleus.

poppy, *n.* papāver, -ĕris, *n.*

popular, *adj.* in vulgus gratus. populate, *v.tr. see* PEOPLE.

porch, *n.* vestibulum.

pore, *n.* foramen. porous, *adj.* rarus.

pore, *v.tr. to — over*, totum se abdĕre in alqd.

pork, *n.* (caro) suilla. porker, *n.* porcus.

porridge, *n.* puls.

port, *n.* portus.

portable, *adj.* quod portari potest.

portcullis, *n.* cataracta.

portend, *v.intr.* portendĕre, praenuntiare.

portent, *n.* portentum, omen. portentous, *adj.* portentosus. *Adv.* monstr(u)ose.

porter, *n.* ianitor ; *see* GATE-KEEPER ; *carrier*, baiŭlus.

portfolio, *n.* scrinium.

porthole, *n.* fenestra.

portico, *n.* porticus, -ūs, *f.*

portion, *n.* pars, portio.

portrait, *n.* imago (picta). portray, *v.tr.* depingĕre.

position, *n.* collocatio, status ; situs, positus ; *fig.* status, locus ; res, fortuna.

positive, *adj.* certain, certus ; *a — statement*, affirmatio ; *— degree*, positivus (gradus). *Adv.* affirmate, certo ; *to assert positively*, affirmare. positiveness, *n.* certainty (*e.g.* alqd certum habēre).

possess, *v.tr.* possidēre, tenēre, alqā re praeditus (*gifted with*) ; est mihi liber (*I — a book*) ; Hortensius erat tantā memoriā ut, *etc.* (*Hortensius — such a memory, that, etc.*) ; *not to —*, carēre re. possession, *n.* possessio ; *a taking —*, occupatio ; bona, -orum. possessive, *adj.* possessivus (casus). possessor, *n.* dominus.

possible, *adj.* quod esse, fieri *or* effici potest ; *it is — that, etc.*, fieri potest ut, etc. ; *as quick as —*, quam celerrime. *Adv.* fieri potest ut, etc. possibility, *n.* condicio, facultas *or* copia faciendi ; *they deny the — of anything*, alqd fieri posse negant.

post, *n.* postis ; palus, cippus (*esp. gravestone*) ; *military station*, locus, statio, praesidium ; *of letters, to send through the —*, per tabellarios mittĕre. *v.tr.* *of letters, etc. see above* ; *of troops*, (dis)ponĕre, (col)locare ; *a notice, etc.*, proponĕre. postage, *n.* vecturae pretium ; *to pay the —*, pro vecturā solvere. postern, *n.* postica. post-haste, *adv.* summā celeritate *or* quam celerrime. postman, *n.* tabellarius. postscript, *n.* alqd epistulae additum.

posterior, *adj.* posterior.

posterity, *n.* posteritas, posteri.

posthumous, *adj.* post patrem mortuum natus.

postpone, *v.tr.* differre, proferre.

postulate, *n.* sumptio.

posture, *n.* status, habitus, gestus.

pot, *n.* olla ; *a small —*, ollula. pot-herb, *n.* olus, *n.* pothouse, *n.* caupona. potsherd, *n.* testa.

potent, *adj. see* POWERFUL.

potentate, *n.* rex, tyrannus.

potential, *adj. see* POSSIBLE.

potion, *n.* potio.

potter, *n.* figulus ; *a —'s work*, opus figlinum, opera fictilia, *n. pl.* ; *workshop*, figlina. pottery, *n. the art*, ars figularis ; *things made* ; *see* POTTER.

pouch, *n.* sacculus, saccus.

pounce, *v.intr. to — upon* ; *see* SEIZE.

pound, *n.* libra, (libra) pondo (*in weight*) ; *of moneys, use* argentum *or* pecunia ; *for stray animals*, saeptum publicum. *v.tr.* (con)tundĕre.

pour, *v.tr.* fundĕre ; *to — into*, infundĕre in alqd. *v.intr. of rain*, (ef)fundi ; *fig. to — forth*, (ef)fundi, *or* se (ef)fundĕre. pouring, *adj.* effusus (*of rain*).

poverty, *n. see* POOR.

powder, *n.* pulvis. *v.tr. to reduce to —*, in pulverem conterĕre.

power, *n.* potentia *or* vires, -ium ; *external*, potestas, ius ; (*of doing anything*), copiae, facultates ; *in my —*, in meā potestate ; imperium (*military*) ; *unlimited —*, summum imperium. powerful, *adj.* validus ; *in influence, etc.*, potens, valens, gravis. *Adv.* graviter, valde (*very —*). powerless, *adj.* invalidus, impotens. powerlessness, *n.* infirmitas.

practicable, *adj.* quod fieri potest, facilis. practicability, *n.* facultas, potestas. practical, *adj.* — *knowledge*, usus. *Adv.* (ex) usu. practice, *n.* usus, usus rerum (*exercise and experience*) ; exercitatio ; *of a physician*, medicinae usus. practise, *v.tr.* exercēre.

practitioner, *n.* medicus.

praetor, *n.* praetor. praetorian, *adj.* praetorius, praetorianus. praetorship, *n.* praetura.

prairie, *n.* campus.

praise, *v.tr.* laudare. *n.* laus ; laudatio (*oration*). praiseworthy, *adj.* laudabilis, laude dignus. *Adv.* laudabiliter.

prance, *v.intr.* ex(s)ultare (*of a horse*).

prank, *n. to play —s, perhaps* lascivire.

prate, prattle, *v. see* CHATTER.

pray, *v.intr. and tr.* precari, preces facĕre, supplicare, orare ; *to — for*, petĕre ; *to entreat for*, petĕre, implorare. prayer, *n.* supplicatio, preces. prayerful, *adj.* prayerfully, *adv.* supplex. praying, *n.* preces, -um, supplicatio.

preach, *v.tr. and intr.* orationem habēre.

preamble, n. exordium.

precarious, adj. incertus. Adv. parum or non certo.

precaution, n. cautio, or by verb, praecavēre.

precede, v.tr. antecedēre. precedence, n. to have the —, alci antecedēre ; to let anyone have the —, alci cedēre.

preceding, adj. praecedens ; prior, superior ; immediately before, proximus. precedent, n. see EXAMPLE.

precept, n. praeceptum.

preceptor, n. magister.

precincts, n. ambitus.

precious, adj. egregius, pulcherrimus ; — stones, gemmae.

precipice, n. locus praeceps.

precipitate, v.tr. praecipitare, delēre ; inferri or se inferre in alqd (to rush into). Adj. praeceps. Adv. temere.

precipitancy, precipitation, n. temeritas. precipitous, adj. praeceps, praeruptus.

precise, adj. (de)finitus, accuratus, subtilis. Adv. subtiliter; by ipse (e.g. ipso in tempore, precisely at the right time).

preclude, v.tr. see HINDER, EXCLUDE.

precocious, adj. praecox ; see PREMATURE.

preconceived, adj. praeiudicatus. preconception, n. sententia praeiudicata.

preconcerted, adj. ex composito (factus, etc.).

precursor, n. praecursor, praenuntius.

predatory, adj. praedatorius.

predecessor, n. in office, decessor ; he is my —, succedo ei.

predestine, v.tr. praedestinare.

predetermine, v.tr. praefinire.

predicament, n. difficultas.

predicate, n. attributio, attributum. v.tr. de alqa re praedicare, dicēre.

predict, v.tr. praedicēre. prediction, n. praedictio.

predilection, n. see AFFECTION.

predispose, v.tr. praeparare. predisposed, adj. proclivis ad alqd. predisposition, n. animi ad alqd proclivitas, studium.

predominance, n. potentia ; plures. predominate, v.intr. dominari ; plures esse. predominating, adj. see CHIEF.

pre-eminence, n. praestantia. pre-eminent, adj. praestans, insignis. Adv. praecipue.

pre-exist, v.intr. antea exstare or esse.

preface, n. prooemium. v.tr. praefari ; prooemium scribēre. prefatory, adj. to make a few — remarks, pauca praefari.

prefect, n. praefectus. prefecture, n. praefectura.

prefer, v.tr. praeponēre, anteferre, malle; see PROMOTE. preferable, adj. praeoptandus, or by compar. of adj. Adv.

potius. preference, n. by verb PREFER.

preferment, n. by honos (office).

prefix, v.tr. anteponēre.

pregnant, adj. praegnans ; of events, maximi momenti.

prejudge, v.tr. prius indicare quam sciat.

prejudice, n. to have a — against any one, male de alqo opinari. v.tr. alienare ab alqo ; to become —d against anyone, ab alqo alienari. prejudicial, adj. see INJURIOUS.

preliminary, adj. see PREFATORY.

prelude, n. prooemium ; fig. prolusio.

premature, adj. praematurus, immaturus. Adv. praemature.

premeditate, v.tr. praemeditari ; —d act, quod ex consulto fit. premeditation, n. praemeditatio.

premise, v.tr. praefari. premises, n. aedificium (or in pl.), domus.

premisses, n. concessa, -orum.

premium, n. praemium.

premonition, n. monitum. premonitory, adj. quod praemonet.

preoccupy, v. praeoccupare ; to be —ted, totus alci rei deditus esse. preoccupation, n. animus alci rei deditus.

preparation, n. praeparatio ; for a war, apparatus belli ; to make — for a war, bellum (ap)parare. preparatory, adj. quod parat. prepare, v.tr. (ap)parare, instruēre ; to — oneself for, se parare ; ante meditari (a lesson, etc.), commentari (e.g. a plan, a sermon).

prepossess, v.tr. capēre, permulcēre (to win over) ; animum conciliare. prepossessing, adj. see AGREEABLE. prepossession, n. sententia praeiudicata.

prerogative, n. quod alci proprium est.

presage, v.tr. portendēre, praesagire. n. praesagium.

prescient, adj. sagax.

prescribe, v.tr. praescribēre. prescription, n. custom, usus ; medical, medicamenti praescriptio.

presence, n. praesentia ; in anyone's —, coram ; (when addressing anyone), dicēre apud alqm ; — of mind, perhaps animus ad omnia paratus. present, adj. qui nunc est, qui hodie est; the — state of things, hic rerum status; haec tempora, = the — time ; at —, in praesenti ; for the —, in praesens ; tense, praesens tempus ; to be —, adesse. Adv. mox, statim. v.tr. to — arms, telum erigere honoris caus(s)a. n. see GIFT.

presentiment, n. see FOREBODE.

preserve, v.tr. sustinēre, sustentare; servare, conservare, tueri ; to conserve, condire. n. fructus conditus. preserver, n. (con)servator, salutis auctor. preservation, n. salus, incolumitas.

preside, v.intr. praesidēre ; praeesse.

presidency, n. praefectura or (e.g. the Indian Presidencies), provincia. pre-

sident, *n.* praeses, princeps, caput ; qui praeest.

press, *n. machine,* prelum, torcular (*for wine, etc.*). *v.tr.* prelo premĕre ; *to squeeze,* premĕre ; *to urge,* urgĕre, premĕre ; *his creditors —ed him,* ei instabant creditores. *v.intr. to — forward,* contendĕre. **pressing,** *adj.* maximi momenti, gravis. **pressure,** *n.* pressio, impetus, nisus ; *fig. under — of danger,* pericula coactus.

prestige, *n.* nomen, gloria, fama.

presume, *v.intr.* sibi arrogare, sumĕre ut ; putare. **presumption,** *n.* arrogantia ; *conjecture,* coniectura. **presumptive,** *adj.* quod ex coniectura cognitum est. *Adv.* ex coniectura. **presumptuous,** *adj.* arrogans. *Adv.* arroganter. **presumptuousness,** *n. see* PRESUMPTION.

pretence, *n.* simulatio, species ; *without —,* sine fuco ac fallaciis. **pretend,** *v.tr. and intr.* simulare. **pretended,** *adj.* simulatus, fictus. **pretender,** *n.* simulator ; qui regnum sibi arrogat. **pretension,** *n.* postulatio ; *just —,* ius ; *display,* ostentatio.

preterite, *n.* praeteritum (tempus).

preternatural, *adj. and adv.* quod praeter naturam fit.

pretext, *n.* (caus(s)a, simulatio ; *under the — of,* per caus(s)am, nomine alcis rei.

pretty, *adj.* bellus, pulcher, formosus, venustus. *Adv.* belle, pulchre, venuste.

prevail, *v.intr.* esse, obtinĕre, adducĕre alqm ut (*to persuade*), multum pollēre (*to have much force*) ; *— with anyone,* apud alqm ; *— over,* superare ; *a —ing opinion,* opinio vulgata. **prevalent,** *adj.* (per)vulgatus, communis.

prevaricate, *v.intr.* tergiversari. **prevarication,** *n.* tergiversatio.

prevent, *v.tr.* prohibēre, impedire. **prevention,** *n. by verb.* **preventive,** *adj.* quod impedit *or* obstat.

previous, *adj. see* PRECEDING.

prey, *n.* praeda ; *beast of —,* fera. *v.intr.* praedari ; *to — upon,* (bestiam) venari ; *fig.* animum, *etc.,* consumĕre.

price, *n.* pretium ; annona (*— of corn*) ; *to fix the —,* pretium facĕre ; *at a high, low, —* magni, parvi, *etc.* ; *what is the —?* quanti hoc vendis ? quanti hoc constat ? (*what does that cost ?*) ; *to raise the —,* pretium augĕre. *v.tr.* pretium alci constituĕre. **priceless,** *adj.* inaestimabilis.

prick, *v.tr.* pungĕre, stimulare, mordēre ; *to — up one's ears,* aures erigĕre. *n.* punctus, *or by verb.* **prickle,** *n.* aculeus, spina. **prickly,** *adj.* aculeatus, spinosus.

pride, *n.* superbia, insolentia, arrogantia, fastidium.

priest, *n.* sacerdos, antistes (*both also = priestess*), flamen (*e.g.* flamen Dialis ;

high *—,* pontifex maximus. **priestess,** *n. see* PRIEST. **priestly,** *adj. by genit.* sacerdotis *or* sacerdotum.

primal, primeval, *adj. see* ANCIENT.

primary, *adj.* primus, principalis. *Adv.* primo (*at first*), praecipue (*chiefly*).

prime, *adj.* primus, first ; *excellent,* optimus. *n. the best,* flos ; *— of life,* aetas vigens.

primitive, *adj.* priscus, antiquus.

primogeniture, *n.* aetatis privilegium.

prince, *n.* iuvenis regii generis, filius principis ; *king,* rex. **princess,** *n.* mulier regii generis ; filia regis.

principal, *adj.* primus, princeps, praecipuus. *Adv.* maxime, praecipue, praesertim. *n. of a school,* magister ; *capital,* caput, pecuniae.

principle, *n.* principium ; ratio ; *of conduct,* dogma ; consilium, praeceptum, institutum ; *the highest moral —,* summum bonum ; *a man of firm —,* homo constans, homo gravis ; *from —,* ratione ; *to remain true to one's —,* sibi constare.

prior, *adj.* prior. *n.* antistes, *or* magister.

prison, *n.* custodia, carcer, vincula, -orum. *n.* ; *to cast into —,* in vincula mittĕre, conicĕre. **prisoner,** *n.* captus, -a (*in war*), captivus ; *by the police,* comprehensus.

pristine, *adj.* pristinus, priscus (*ancient*).

prithee ! *interj.* quaeso, tandem, cedo.

privacy, *n.* solitudo. **private,** *adj.* privatus, proprius (*opp. communis*), domesticus ; *affairs,* res privata. *Adv.* clam, secreto, occulte, privatim (*in a private capacity*). *n. in the army,* miles. **privateer,** navis (praedatoria). **privation,** *n.* egestas, paupertas.

privilege, *n.* privilegium, beneficium, commodum ; *exemption,* immunitas, gratia. **privileged,** *adj. exempt from,* immunis.

privy, *adj. see* PRIVATE. **privy-purse,** *n.* fiscus.

prize, *n.* praemium, palma. *v.tr.* magni aestimare. **prize-fighter,** *n.* pugil.

pro and con, in utramque partem.

probable, *adj.* probabilis, veri similis. *Adv.* probabiliter, verisimiliter. **probability,** *n.* probabilitas, verisimilitudo.

probe, *v.tr. see* EXAMINE.

probity, *n.* probitas.

problem, *n.* quaestio. **problematical,** *adj.* dubius, incertus.

proboscis, *n.* manus, *f.* (*of an elephant*).

proceed, *v.intr.* progredi ; *to come from,* oriri ; *to act,* agĕre, facĕre ; *to — against,* litem alci intendĕre. **proceeding,** *n. in law ; legal —,* actio ; *to commence —s,* actionem alci intendĕre ; *transactions,* acta, -orum. **proceeds,** *n.* reditus, fructus.

process, *n.* ratio, actio (*at law*).

procession, *n.* pompa ; *to hold a* —, pompam ducere.

proclaim, *v.tr.* declarare, edicĕre (*a law, etc.*), promulgare (*to make known*) ; proponĕre (*to placard*) ; praedicĕre (*through the herald*) ; pronuntiare (*to announce*). proclamation, *n.* pronuntiatio, declaratio ; edictum ; libellus (*a written* —).

proconsul, *n.* pro consule. proconsular, *adj.* proconsularis.

procrastination, *n. see* DELAY.

procure, *v.tr.* (com)parare. afferre, acquirĕre, expedire. procurator, *n.* procurator. procuring, *n.* comparatio.

prodigal, *adj. see* EXTRAVAGANT. pro-digality, *n.* effusio (*us act*), sumptus profusi (*luxury*).

prodigious, *adj.* ingens. prodigy, *n.* res mirabilis, miraculum.

produce, *v.tr.* *bring forward*, proferre ; edĕre (*publish*) ; (pro)creare ; gignĕre, parĕre ; (ef)fundĕre (*of the earth*), facĕre (*by skill*). *n.* fructus. product, *n. see* PRODUCTION. production, *n.* opus ; *of art*, opera et artificia. productive, *adj.* fertilis. productiveness, *n. see* FERTILITY.

proem, *n.* prooemium.

profane, *v.tr.* violare, polluĕre. *Adj.* profanus, impius. *Adv.* impie. pro-fanation, profaneness, profanity, *n.* impietas.

profess, *v.tr.* profitĕri ; persequi (*e.g.* Academiam) ; *pretend*, se alqd esse simulare. professed, *adj.* manifestus, apertus. *Adv.* per speciem. profession, *n.* declaration, *by* se alqd (esse) profitĕri ; verbo (*opp.* re(verā)) ; *employment*, munus. professor, *n.* qui alqd docet.

proffer, *v.tr.* promittĕre ; *see* OFFER.

proficiency, *n. by* scientia, facilitas. proficient, *adj.* doctus, sciens alcis rei.

profit, *n.* lucrum, fructus, *v.intr.* alci (rei) prodesse ; *to progress*, proficĕre ; *to gain*, fructum ferre. profitable, *adj.* quaestuosus, fructuosus, utilis. *Adv.* utiliter. profitless, *adj.* inutilis, irritus. *Adv.* frustra, incassum.

profligacy, *n.* animus perditus, flagitium. profligate, *n.* homo flagitiosus ; homo perditus. *Adj.* perditus, sceleratus. *Adv.* perdite, turpiter.

profound, *adj.* altus, profundus. *Adv.* penitus, prorsus. profundity, *n.* altitudo.

profuse, *adj. see* LAVISH.

progenitor, *n.* parens.

progeny, *n.* progenies.

prognosticate, *v.tr. see* FORETELL.

progress, *n.* *journey*, iter ; *advance*, progressus ; *to make little* —, parum proficĕre. *v.intr.* progedi. progres-sion, *n.* progressus. progressive, *adj.* qui progreditur. *Adv.* gradatim.

prohibit, *v.tr.* vetare. prohibition, *n.* interdictum. prohibitive, prohibitory, *adj.* qui, quae, quod vetat.

project, *n.* consilium, propositum. *v.intr.* prominĕre, exstare. projectile, *n.* (telum) missile. projection, *n. by verb.*

proletariat, *n.* proletarii.

prolific, *adj. see* FRUITFUL.

prolix, *adj.* longus, verbosus. prolixity, *by adj.* PROLIX.

prologue, *n.* prologus.

prolong, *v.tr.* prorogare, producĕre, continuare, trahĕre, prolatare (*e.g.* comitia). prolongation, *n.* productio, prolatio (*e.g.* diei). prolonged, *adj.* longus.

promenade, *n.* ambulatio.

prominence, *n.* eminentia ; *fig. of rank etc.* fama, gloria *or by* praestare. pro-minent, *adj. and adv. by* prominĕre, exstare, praestare.

promiscuous, *adj.* promiscuus. *Adv.* promiscue.

promise, *v.tr.* promittĕre, pollicĕri, (de)spondĕre (*formally*). *v.intr. to be likely*, veri simile esse. *n.* promissio, fides, promissum. promising, *adj.* (*e.g. a* — *pupil*, puer industrius). pro-missory, *adj.* — *note*, chirographum.

promontory, *n.* promontorium, *a small* —, lingua.

promote, *v.tr.* augĕre, alci favēre, alci consulĕre ; servire alcis commodis (*to anyone's interest*) ; *to* — *in office*, anyone, tollĕre, augĕre, (ex)ornare ; promovēre ad munus. promoter, *n.* auctor, adiutor, fautor. promotion, *n.* — *of our welfare*, amplificatio nostrarum rerum ; — *to a higher office*, dignitatis accessio.

prompt, *adj.* promptus. *Adv.* cito. *v.tr.* subicĕre, prompter, *n.* qui subicit. promptitude, promptness, *n.* celeritas

promulgate, *v.tr.* promulgare. promul-gation, *n.* promulgatio.

prone, *adj.* fusl, pronus ; *tending to* pronus.

prong, *n.* dens, -tis.

pronoun, *n.* pronomen (*gram.*).

pronounce, *v.tr.* enuntiare, exprimĕre, dicĕre ; *formally*, efferre verbis ; *a sentence, an opinion*, sententiam dicĕre, pronuntiare. pronunciation, *n.* appel-latio ; pronuntiatio.

proof, *n.* probatio ; ignum, docu-mentum ; *to give* — argumenta *or* rationes afferre. prove, *v.tr.* significare, probare ; *to* — *by one's actions*, prae-stare ; *to* — *oneself as, etc.*, se praebēre ; demonstrare (*to show*). *v.intr. to turn out*, fieri, evadĕre. proven, *p.part. e.g. not* —, non liquet.

prop, *n.* adminiculum. *fig.* praesidium, *v.tr.* fulcire ; alci adesse.

propagate, *v.tr.* propagare ; *to produce,* gignĕre. **propagation**, *n.* propagatio ; *of a report, etc.,* rumorem serĕre.

propel, *v.tr.* propellĕre.

propensity, *n.* animus proclivis ad alqd.

proper, *adj.* proprius ; *becoming,* decōrus ; *suitable,* idoneus. *Adv.* proprie, vere. **property**, *n.* patrimonium, possessiones (*landed* —), bona, -orum, fortunae; census; *by* res (*sing.* or *plur.*). **proprietary**, *adj. by* proprius. **proprietor**, *n.* dominus. **proprietorship**, *n.* possessio.

prophecy, *n. the act,* praedictio ; *that which is prophesied,* praedictum. **prophesy**, *v.tr.* praedicĕre, canĕre, augurari. *v.intr.* futura praedicĕre. **prophet**, *n.* vates. **prophetess**, *n.* vates. **prophetic**, *adj.* praesagiens, vaticinus. *Adv.* divinitus (*inspired*).

propinquity, *n.* propinquitas, affinitas (*by marriage*).

propitious, *adj.* propitius, aequus, secundus. *Adv. by adj.* **propitiousness**, *n. by adj.* propitiate, *v.tr. see* CONCILIATE. **propitiation**, *n.* placatio (*e.g.* deorum). **propitiatory**, *adj. by verb.*

proportion, *n.* proportio, commensus ; *symmetria;* ratio; *an arithmetical* —, ratio arithmetica ; *in* — *to,* pro *with abl. v.tr.* alqd dirigĕre ad alqam rem. **proportional, proportionate**, *adj.* pro *with abl.*

proposal, *n.* condicio ; — *of a law,* legislatio, rogatio ; *suggestion, plan,* consilium ; *to make a* —, condicionem proponĕre. **propose**, *v.tr.* proponĕre; *to* — *a law,* legem ferre or rogare. **proposer**, *n. of a law,* (legis)lator, *in gen.* auctor. **proposition**, *n. see* PROPOSAL; propositum.

propriety, *n.* decōrum.

prorogue, *v.tr.* prorogare. **prorogation**, *n.* prorogatio.

proscribe, *v.tr.* proscribĕre. **proscription**, *n.* proscriptio.

prose, *n.* prosa (oratio), oratio soluta. **prosaic**, *adj.* ieiunus, frigidus.

prosecute, *v.tr. to carry out,* gerĕre, perficĕre ; *to bring an action against,* accusare, postulare. **prosecution**, *n. use verb* ; accusatio. **prosecutor**, *n.* accusator.

proselyte, *n.* discipulus. **proselytize**, *v.tr.* alqm discipulum facĕre.

prospect, *n. view,* prospectus, conspectus; *to have a* —, spectare ad locum ; *hope,* spes ; *some* —, specula. **prospective**, *adj.* futurus. *Adv.* in futurum.

prosper, *v.intr.* crescĕre, provenire, bonā fortunā uti. **prosperity**, *n.* res secundae; *general* —, salus communis. **prosperous**, *adj.* secundus, fortunatus. *Adv.* secunde, fortunate.

prostitute, *n.* meretrix.

prostrate, *v.tr.* (pro)sternĕre ; *to* — *oneself before anyone,* ad pedes alcis procumbĕre. *Adj. by part. of verb.* **prostration**, *n. by the verb.*

protect, *v.tr.* tuĕri, defendĕre, munire, custodire, alci praesidio esse. **protection**, *n.* praesidium, defensio, clientēla (*of a patron and client*) ; *to take under* —, in fidem recipĕre. **protective**, *adj. use verb.* **protector**, *n.* defensor, propugnator.

protest, *v.intr.* asseverare, affirmare, adiurare (*upon oath*) ; *by the gods,* (ab)testari deos ; *to* — *against,* intercedĕre, intercessionem facĕre (*esp. of a magistrate*). *n.* interpellatio (*interruption of a speaker*), intercessio.

prototype, *n.* exemplum.

protract, *v.tr.* producĕre.

protrude, *v.tr.* protrudĕre. *v.intr.* prominĕre.

protuberance, *n.* tuber. **protuberant**, *adj.* eminens.

proud, *adj.* superbus, fastidiosus. *Adv.* superbe.

prove, *v.tr. see* PROOF.

provender, *n.* pabulum.

proverb, *n.* proverbium; *according to the* —, ut aiunt. **proverbial**, *adj.* quod in proverbium venit. *Adv.* ut est in proverbio.

provide, *v.tr.* instruĕre, ornare, (com)parare, praebēre. *v.intr.* iubēre, edicĕre (*of an edict*) ; *he is* — *d for,* habet unde vivat. **provided**, *conj.* — *that,* dum(modo) *with subj.* **providence**, *n.* forethought, providentia; *divine* —, deus or dei (di(i)). **provident**, *adj.* providus, diligens. *Adv.* diligenter, *or by adj.* **providentially**, *adv.* dis faventibus, divinitus. **provision**, *v.tr. to* — *a town,* oppidum rebus necessariis instruĕre ; *stipulation,* condicio. **provisional**, *adj. by* ad or in tempus. **provisions**, *n.* cibus, cibaria, -orum, commeatus, frumentum.

province, *n. duty,* provincia, officium ; *district,* regio, provincia. **provincial**, *adj.* provincialis ; — (*manners*), *etc.* inurbanus.

proviso, *n.* condicio.

provocation, *n.* **provocative**, *adj. by* PROVOKE.

provoke, *v.tr.* (com)movēre ; *to make angry,* alci stomachum movēre. **provoking**, *adj.* molestus. *Adv.* moleste.

prow, *n.* prora.

prowess, *n.* virtus.

prowl, *v.intr.* vagari ; *for plunder,* praedari.

proximity, *n. see* NEARNESS.

proxy, *n.* procurator ; *by* —, per procuratorem.

prude, *n.* mulier putida (*affected*).

prudence, *n.* prudentia, diligentia.

prudent, *adj.* prudens, diligens. *Adv.* prudenter, diligenter.

prune, *v.tr. trees*, arbores (am)putare, tondēre (*e.g. hedges*) ; *fig.* resecare. **pruner**, *n. of trees*, putator. **pruning-hook**, *n.* falx.

pry, *v.tr. and intr.* investigare.

psalm, *n.* psalmus (*Eccl.*). **psaltery**, *n.* psalterium.

pshaw ! *interj.* phui !

public, *adj.* quod coram omnibus fit, publicus ; *concerning the State, etc.*, publicus, forensis ; *at the — expense*, sumptu publico ; *— opinion*, vulgi opinio ; *— -house*, caupona. *Adv.* palam, coram omnibus, in publico, foris. *n. the —*, homines, vulgus, -i, lectores (*the readers*). **publican**, *n.* publicanus ; *innkeeper*, caupo. **publication**, *n.* editio libri ; *the book*, liber. **publicity**, *n. e.g. of proceedings*, consilia coram omnibus inita ; *to shun —*, fugēre homines. **publish**, *v.tr.* edēre. **publisher**, *n. of a book*, qui librum edendum curat.

pudding, *n.* placenta — *cake*).

puddle, *n. see* POOL.

puerile, *adj.* puerilis.

puff, *v.tr.* inflare ; *to be —ed up*, tumescēre. *v.intr.* flare, spirare ; *to pant*, anhelare. **puffy**, *adj.* inflatus.

pugilism, *n.* pugilatus. **pugilist**, *n.* pugil.

pull, *v.tr. to tweak*, vellēre ; *drag*, trahēre ; *— out*, eripēre. *n.* tractus.

pullet, *n.* pullus gallinaceus

pulley, *n.* trochlea.

pulmonary, *adj.* quod ad pulmones pertinet.

pulp, *n.* caro (*of fruit*).

pulpit, *n.* suggestus.

pulsate, *v.intr.* palpitare, moveri. **pulsation**, *n.* palpitatio, motus. **pulse**, *n. use* venae.

pulse, *n. vegetable*, legumen

pulverize, *v.tr.* in pulverem redigēre ; *fig.* porcellōro.

pumice, *n.* pumex

pump, *n.* antlia. *v.intr.* antliā exhaurire ; *to — a ship*, sentinam exhaurire.

pun, *n.* facetiae.

punch, *n. drill*, terebra ; *see* BLOW. *v.tr.* terebrare ; tundēre.

punctilio, *n. perhaps*, diligentia, fastidium **punctilious**, *adj.* diligens, accuratus. *Adv.* diligenter, accurate. **punctiliousness**, *n.* sol(l)icitudo, diligentia.

punctual, *adj.* diligens, ad tempus. *Adv.* diligenter, ad tempus. **punctuality**, *n.* diligentia (*care*); fides. **punctuate**, *v.tr.* interpungēre. **punctuation**, *n.* interpunctio ; *— mark*, interpunctum.

puncture, *n.* punctum. *v.tr.* pungēre.

pungent, *adj.* acer, mordax. *Adv.* acriter.

punish, *v.tr.* punire, poenā afficēre ; *to — any violation of one's rights*, violata iura exsequi ; *to be — ed*, puniri, *also* poenas dare. **punishable**, *adj.* poenā dignus. **punisher**, *n.* vindex, ultor. **punishment**, *n.* animadversio ; *the — itself*, poena, multa, supplicium (*cruel —*); *capital —*, poena capitis.

puny, *adj.* pusillus (*e.g. animus*); *a — fellow*, homuncio.

pupil, *n.* pupula, pupilla ; *at a school, etc.*, alumnus, discipulus.

puppy, *n.* catellus.

purchase, *v.tr.* (co)emēre. *n. act*, emptio ; *thing bought*, merx, quod emptum est. **purchasable**, *adj.* venalis. **purchaser**, *n.* emptor.

pure, *adj.* purus, integer, castus, insons (*innocent*), incorruptus ; (*not mixed*) *— water*, aqua pura ; *fig.* purus, sincerus. *Adv.* pure, integre, caste ; *entirely*, plane. **purity**, *n.* castitas ; *— of a language*, sermo purus ; munditia verborum (*free from foul language*); innocentia. **purify**, *v.tr.* expurgare, purificare ; lustrare. **purification**, *n.* purgatio, lustratio.

purgation, *n.* purgatio, lustratio. **purge**, *v.tr.* purgare.

purl, *v.intr.* murmurare, sonare.

purloin, *v.tr.* avertēre.

purple, *n.* purpura, ostrum, conchylium, color purpureus.

purport, *v.tr. see* MEAN.

purpose, *n.* propositum, consilium, voluntas, *or by* velle ; *on —*, consulto, de industriā ; *to what —*, quo consilio ; *to no —*, *without —*, nullo consilio, temere ; *to the —*, ad rem. *Adv.* consulto. *v.tr.* statuēre. **purposeless**, *adj.* inanis, irritus, inutilis.

purse, *n.* marsupium, sacculus. **purse-proud**, *adj.* pecuniā superbus.

pursuant, *prep. — to*, ex lege, ex decreto.

pursue, *v.tr.* persequi, sensectari **pursuit**, *n.* insectatio, studium, cupiditas.

push, *v.tr.* pellēre, trudēre ; *forward*, propellēre ; *back*, repellēre ; *down*, depellēre. *v.intr. to — on*, contendēre, instare. *n.* (im)pulsus, impetus. **pushing**, *adj.* acer.

pusillanimous, *adj.* timidus, abiectus. *Adv.* timide, abiecte. **pusillanimity**, *n.* timiditas, animus timidus, animi demissio.

put, *v.tr. in gen.*, ponēre ; *to — away*, abdēre ; *to — upon*, imponēre ; *to — before*, proponēre *to — on one side*, reponēre ; *to — down*, deponēre ; *to — forward*, producēre (*e.g. a candidate*); *to — off*, differre ; *to — on*, induēre, *a dress* ; *to — out*, sicēre, expellēre, ex(s)tinguĕre (*to quench*) ; to — to *fiight*, fugare ; to be — to *flight*, fugĕre.

putative, *adj.* falsus *or* qui dicitur esse.

putrefaction, *n. by verb* PUTREFY.

putrefy, *v.tr.* putrefacĕre. *v.intr.* putrescĕre. **putrid,** *adj.* putridus.

putty, *n.* gluten.

puzzle, *n. a difficulty,* nodus. *v.tr.* impedire, *v.intr.* in angustiis esse. **puzzling,** *adj.* difficilis, ambiguus.

Pygmy. *n.* pygmaeus ; *dwarf,* nanus.

pyramid, *n.* pyramis.

pyre, *n.* rogus.

Q

quack, *n. of a duck, by verb* ; *v.intr.* tetrinnire.

quadrennial, *adj.* quat(t)uor annorum.

quadrille, *n.* saltatio.

quadruped, *n.* quadrupes.

quadruple, *adj.* quadruplex.

quaff, *v.tr. see* DRINK.

quag(mire), *n.* palus. **quaggy,** *adj.* paluster.

quail, *n.* coturnix.

quail, *v.intr.* animo deficĕre.

quaint, *adj.* lepidus (*pretty*) ; insolitus, novus. *Adv.* novo *or* insolito, mire.

quake, *v.intr.* tremĕre. **quaker,** *n.* unus ex iis qui se amicos appellant.

qualify, *v.tr.* instruĕre ; *to — oneself,* se praeparare ; *to modify,* deminuĕre. **qualification,** *n.* ius, potestas. **qualified,** *adj.* idoneus, dignus.

quality, *n.* proprium, natura, genus, ratio, vis, qualitas ; *it is one — of a good orator, etc.,* est boni oratoris, etc. ; *of what —,* qualis ; *of such a —,* talis ; *a noble —,* virtus ; *kind, sort,* nota (*e.g. wine of good —,* vinum bonae notae).

qualm, *n.* defectio (*faintness*), fastidium (*loathing*) ; *fig.* (*I have a — of conscience,* mens mihi angitur).

quantity, *n.* numerus, copia, aliquot ; *a great —,* magnus numerus, acervus, nubes (*e.g.* pulveris) ; vis, pondus ; *in prosody,* ᵉmensura.

quarrel, *n.* iurgium, rixa, altercatio. *v.intr.* rixari, altercari. **quarrelsome,** *adj.* rixis deditus.

quarry, *n.* lapicidinae. *v.tr.* excidĕre.

quarry, *n. = game,* praeda.

quart, *n.* (*as a measure*) duo sextarii.

quartan, *n.* febris quartana.

quarter, *n.* quarta pars (*late*) ; *every — of a year,* tertio quoque mense; *district,* vicus. *v.tr.* quadrifariam dividĕre ; *troops,* milites per hospitia disponĕre. **quarter-deck,** *n.* puppis. **quartering,** *n.* milites per hospitia dispositi.

quarterly, *adj. and adv.* trimestris ; tertio quoque mense. **quarters,** *n.pl.* habitatio, tectum, hospitium ; *of troops,* castra, -orum ; *to be in winter —,* in hibernis esse ; *close —,* cominus ; *to come to close —,* manum conserĕre.

quash, *v.tr.* — *an indictment, etc.,* rescindĕre.

quaver, *v.intr. see* VIBRATE.

quay, *n.* margo, crepido.

queen, *n.* regina ; — *bee,* rex apium. **queenly,** *adj.* regius.

queer, *adj.* novus, insolitus.

quell, *v.tr.* opprimĕre ; *see* CONQUER.

quench, *v.tr.* sedare, ex(s)tinguĕre.

querulous, *adj.* queribundus, querulus.

query, *v.intr., n. see* QUESTION.

quest, *n. see* SEEK.

question, *n.* interrogatio ; (inter)rogatum ; res, caus(s)a ; *to ask a —,* interrogare ; *the — arises,* quaeritur ; *now the — is,* nunc id agitur. *v.tr.* (inter)rogare. **questionable,** *adj.* dubius.

quibble, *n.* cavillatio. *v.intr.* cavillari. **quibbler,** *n.* cavillator. **quibbling,** *adj.* captiosus.

quick, *adj.* acer, alacer ; *see* SHARP. *Adv.* cito, celeriter. *n. to cut to the —,* ad vivum resecare (*lit.*), mordĕre (*fig.*).

quicken, *v.tr.* animare ; accendĕre.

quicklime, *n.* calx viva. **quickness,** *n.* velocitas ; ingenii alacritas. **quicksand,** *n.* syrtis. **quick-sighted,** *adj.* perspicax. **quick-sightedness,** *n.* perspicacitas. **quicksilver,** *n.* argentum vivum. **quick-tempered,** *adj.* iracundus. **quick-witted,** *adj.* alcer.

quiescent, *adj. by* quiescĕre.

quiet, *adj.* tranquillus, otiosus. *Adv.* silentio ; tranquille, otiose. *n.* tranquillitas, otium. *v.tr.* tranquillare. **quietness,** *n. see* QUIET.

quill, *n.* penna ; spina ; plectrum.

quilt, *n.* stragulum.

quinquennial, *adj.* quinquennalis.

quintessence, *n.* flos, floris, *m.*

quip, *n.* facetiae.

quire, *n.* chartae scapus (= 20 *sheets*).

quit, *v.tr. see* LEAVE.

quite, *adv.* prorsus, omnino; satis.

quits, *adv. we are —,* iam sumus pares.

quiver, *n.* pharetra. *v.intr.* tremĕre.

qui vive, *n. on the —,* alacer.

quoit, *n.* discus.

quote, *v.tr.* afferre.

quoth, *v.intr.* inquit, ait.

quotidian, *adj.* cot(t)idianus.

R

rabbit, *n.* cuniculus.

rabble, *n.* faex populi, turba.

rabid, *adj.* rabidus. *Adv.* rabide.

race, n. genus ; gens. **raciness**, n. suous. **racy**, adj. salsus.
race, n. cursus, certamen. v.intr. certare. **race-course**, n. curriculum, circus.
racehorse, n. equus. **racer**, n. on foot, cursor.
rack, n. tormentum. v.tr. fig. torquēre.
racket, n. strepitus.
radiance, n. fulgor, nitor. **radiant**, adj. nitidus, fulgens ; laetus. Adv. nitide, feliciter. **radiate**, v.intr. radiare.
radical, adj. and n. insitus ; innatus ; in politics, novarum rerum cupidus. Adv. radicitus, omnino.
radish, n. radix.
radius, n. radius.
raffle, n. alea.
raft, n. ratis.
rafter, n. tignum transversarium.
rag, n. pannus. **ragamuffin**, n. homo pannosus. **ragged**, adj. (of men) pannosus.
rage, n. furor, iracundia. v.intr. furēre, saevire. **raging**, adj. see VIOLENT.
rail, n. cancelli (pl.) ; on a railway, ferrum. v.tr. to — off, saeptis claudēre. **railing**, n. clathri. **railway**, n. via ferro strata.
rail, v.intr. to — at, alqm conviciis consectari. **raillery**, n. iocus, cavillatio.
raiment, n. vestis, vestimentum.
rain, n. pluvia, imber; **rainbow**, caelestis arcus. v.impers. it —s, pluit. **rainy**, adj. pluvius.
raise, v.tr. (at)tollēre ; erigēre (e.g. malum) ; the price, etc., by offerre ; salary, augēre ; in condition, augēre ; the voice, by tollēre ; to — a siege, oppugnatione desistēre.
rake, n. pecten, rastrum ; fig. homo perditus. v.tr. radēre (ground). **rakish**, adj. dissolutus.
rally, v.tr. troops, aciem restituēre ; to banter, irridēre. v.intr. of troops, se colligēre ; se reficēre, convalescēre (from illness).
ram, n. aries (sheep and battering —) v.tr. trudere, fistucare.
ramble, v.intr. errare, vagari. n. ambulatio ; to go for a —, ire ambulatum. **rambler**, n. homo vagus. **rambling**, adj. vagus.
rampant, adj. ferox, superbus ; to be —, superbire; in heraldry, erectus.
rampart, n. vallum, agger; fig. praesidium.
rancid, adj. rancidus.
rancour, n. odium (occultum). **rancorous**, adj. malignus, invidus, inimicus. Adv. maligne, inimice.
random, adj. at —, temere.
range, v.tr. see RANK ; see ROAM. n. ordo, series, montes continui, teli iactus.
rank, n. of troops, ordo ; in their —, ordinati ; degree, ordo, gradus honoris ; in civil life, locus, dignitas. v.tr. ordinare, disponēre, ascribere; see CONSIDER. v.intr. to — with, eodem loco esse cum alqo.
rank, adj. of plants, luxuriosus ; of smell, foetidus.
rankle, v.intr. mordere, pungēre.
ransack, v.tr. exhaurire, spoliare ; scrutari.
ransom, n. pretium, redemptio. v.tr. redimēre (pecuniā).
rant, v.tr. declamare.
rap, v.intr. pulsare. n. pulsatio.
rapacious, adj. rapax. **rapacity**, n. cupiditas.
rapid, adj. rapidus. Adv. rapide. n. gurges. **rapidity**, n. see SPEED.
rapier, n. perhaps pugio.
rapture, n. summa voluptas. **rapturous**, adj. beatus.
rare, adj. rarus, inusitatus. Adv. raro. **rarefy**, v.tr. extenuare. **rarity**, n. raritas, res rara.
rascal, n. homo sceleratus. **rascality**, n. scelus. **rascally**, adj. sceleratus.
rase, v.tr. solo aequare.
rash, adj. praeceps, inconsultus. Adv. inconsulte, temere. **rashness**, n. temeritas.
rasp, v.tr. radēre.
rat, n. mus.
rate, n. at the —, pro modo, pro ; — of interest, usura ; tax, vectigal ; at any —, certe. v.tr. aestimare.
rather, adv. potius ; immo potius ; I would —, by malo.
ratification, n. sanctio, or by **ratify**, v.tr. a treaty, sancire pactum.
ration, n. cibus diuturnus.
rational, adj. ratione praeditus. **rationality**, n. ratio.
rattle, v.intr. crepare. v.tr. to — the chains, vincula movēre. n. crepitus ; plaything, † crepitaculum. **rattlesnake**, n. serpens.
ravage, v.tr. vastare, populari. n. vastatio, populatio.
rave, v.intr. furēre.
raven, n. corvus.
ravening, adj. rapax. **ravenous**, adj. cibi avidus. Adv. voraciter.
ravine, n. fauces, -ium, saltus.
raving, adj. see RAVE, MAD.
ravish, v.tr. stuprare ; to charm, oblectare. **ravisher**, n. raptor. **ravishing**, adj. dulcis.
raw, adj. crudus; incultus.
ray, n. radius; of hope, specula.
razor, n. culter tonsorius.
reach, v.tr. and intr. see EXTEND ; to touch, attingēre ; to arrive at, pervenire ad ; to — the harbour, portum capēre. n. within —, quod manu prehendi potest.
react, v.tr. to — upon, afficēre.

read, *v.tr. and intr.* legĕre, recitare *(aloud);*
well —, satis lit(t)eratus. **reader,** *n.*
lector, recitator *(aloud).* **reading,** *n.*
lectio, recitatio *(aloud).*
ready, *adj.* instructus, paratus, promptus,
expeditus ; *part. fut. act.* (*e.g.* mori-
turus, periturus) ; *to be* —, ad manum
esse ; *to get* —, parare ; *finished,* perfectus ; — *money,* pecunia praesens ;
obliging, facilis. *Adv.* prompte, libenter ; *easily,* facile. **readiness,** *n. to*
be in —, paratus esse ; animus paratus,
facilitas.
real, *adj.* verus, sincērus, germanus
(*genuine*) ; *in law, a* — *estate,* fundus.
Adv. truly, profecto ; *ironically,* scilicet,
in question, itane vero ? **reality,** *n.*
res verae, verum, veritas ; *in* —, re, re
verā. **realize,** *v.tr.* efficĕre, perficĕre ;
intellegĕre (animo).
realm, *n.* civitas, regnum.
reanimate, *v.tr.* mortuo vitam reddĕre ;
fig. to — *anyone's hope,* ad novam spem
excitare.
reap, *v.tr.* (de)metĕre ; *fig.* fructum
capĕre. **reaper,** *n.* messor. **reaping-
hook,** *n.* falx.
reappear, *v.intr.* redire.
rear, *n.* agmen novissimum ; *to form*
the —, agmen claudĕre.
rear, *v.tr. see* RAISE ; *of plants, etc.,*
alĕre ; *of children,* educare. *v.intr. of*
horses, ex(s)ultare.
reason, *n.* = *cause,* principium, initium,
causa ; *to state a* —, rationem afferre ;
for this —, *that, etc.,* propterea (quod),
quod, quare ; *there is no* — *why, etc.,*
non est cur ; ratio, mens (*understanding*) ; *moderation,* aequitas, moderatio ;
in —, ex aequo. *v.intr.* ratiocinari,
disputare. **reasonable,** *adj.* moderate,
aequus, iustus, modicus ; *to buy at a*
— *cost,* bene emĕre. *Adv.* rationi convenienter, iure. **reasonableness,** *n.*
ratio ; moderatio. **reasoner,** *n.* dis-
putator. **reasoning,** *n.* ratiocinatio.
argumentatio.
reassemble, *v.tr.* recolligĕre. *v.intr.*
convenire.
reassert, *v.tr.* iterare, confirmare.
reassume, *v.tr.* recipĕre.
reassure, *v.tr.* confirmare.
rebel, *v.intr.* seditionem movēre, deficĕre
ab. *n.* homo seditiosus. **rebellion,** *n.*
seditio. **rebellious,** *adj.* seditiosus,
novarum rerum cupidus. *Adv.* seditiose.
rebound, *v.intr.* repercuti.
rebuff, *v.tr.* repellĕre ; *see* REFUSAL.
rebuild, *v.tr.* de integro aedificare, restituĕre.
rebuke, *v.tr.* reprehendĕre. (verbis)
castigare. *n.* reprehensio. **rebuker,** *n.*
reprehensor.
rebut, *v.tr.* redarguĕre.
recall, *v.tr.* revocare, retractare ; me-

moriam revocare. *n.* revocatio *or by*
verbs, receptus (*of troops*).
recant, *v.tr.* retractare. **recantation,**
n. use verb.
recapitulate, *v.tr.* enumerare, referre.
recapitulation, *n.* enumeratio.
recapture, *v.tr.* recipĕre. *n. by verb.*
recede, *v.intr.* recedĕre, retro cedĕre.
receipt, *n.* acceptio, *or by* accipĕre (*e.g.*
pecuniā acceptā). **receive,** *v.tr.* accipĕre ; *to* — *a person,* salutare (*to*
greet). **receiver,** *n.* qui accipit, re-
ceptor (*of thieves*). **receptacle,** *n.*
receptaculum, armarium (*for clothes*).
reception, *n.* acceptio, *or by verbs* ;
receptio, hospitium. **receptive,** *adj.*
aptus ad discendum. **receptiveness,**
n. receptivity, *n.* docilitas. **recipient,**
n. qui accipit.
recent, *adj.* recens ac novus. *Adv.* nuper.
receptacle, *see under* RECEIVE.
recess, *n.* recessus ; *holidays,* feriae.
recipe, *n.* praeceptum.
reciprocal, *adj.* mutuus. *Adv.* mutuo,
invicem. **reciprocate,** *v.tr.* inter se
dare.
recital, *n.* narratio. **recite,** *v.tr.* recitare ; dicĕre, (e)narrare. **recitation,**
n. lectio, recitatio. **receiver,** *n.* recitator.
reckless, *adj.* neglegens, imprudens.
Adv. neglegenter, temere, imprudenter.
recklessness, *n.* temeritas.
reckon, *v.tr.* computare ; *see* CONSIDER.
reckoning, *n.* ratio ; *to form a* —,
aestimare rem ; *by my* —, meā opinione.
reclaim, *v.tr.* repetĕre, recipĕre, vindicare ; *fig.* revocare ad virtutem.
recline, *v.tr.* reclinare. *v.intr.* iacēre.
(ac)cubare (*at table*). **reclining,** *adj.*
(re)supinus (*on the back*).
recluse, *n.* homo solitarius.
recognize, *v.tr.* a(d)gnoscĕre, acknow-
ledge, cognoscĕre, (com)probare (*approve*). **recognizance,** *n. to enter*
into —*s,* vadimonium facĕre.
recoil, *v.intr.* repercuti, resilire ; *to* —
at, refugĕre.
recollect, *v.tr.* (com)meminisse, re-
cordari, haud immemor esse alcis rei ;
I cannot — *it,* memoriā alqd excessit.
recollection, *n.* memoria, recordatio
(*the act*) ; *to bring to one's* —, in
memoriam revocare.
recommence, *v.tr.* de integro instaurare,
(red)integrare, iterare. *v.intr.* renasci.
or by pass. of verbs above.
recommend, *v.tr.* commendare ; *to* —
oneself, gratus esse. **recommendation,**
n. commendatio, laudatio ; *letter of* —,
lit(t)erae commendaticius ; *to give a*
letter of —, commendare per lit(t)eras.
recompense, *n.* merces, munus. *v.tr.*
remunerari.
reconcile, *v.tr.* placare, expiare (*e.g.*
numen, manes) ; reconciliare ; *to* —
oneself, reconciliari ; *to make con-*

gruous, accommodare. **reconcilable,** *adj.* placabilis. **reconciler,** *n.* conciliator. **reconciliation,** *n.* conciliatio.

recondite, *adj.* reconditus.

reconnoitre, *v.tr.* cognoscĕre, explorare.

reconsider, *v.tr.* denuo considerare.

record, *v.tr.* referre in tabulas, libellum, *etc. n.* lit(t)erae, tabulae, monumentum. **records,** *pl.* annales, -ium, fasti (*calendar*), tabulae (publicae). **record office,** *n.* tabularium.

recount, *v.tr.* referre, narrare ; *see* RELATE.

recourse, *n. to have — to,* perfugĕre ad ; *in bad sense,* ad alqd descendĕre.

recover, *v.tr.* recipĕre. *v.intr.* convalescĕre ; *so or* animum colligĕre. **recoverable,** *adj.* quod restitui or reparari, *etc.,* potest. **recovery,** *n.* recuperatio ; valetudo confirmata ; *in law,* evictio.

recreant, *n. see* COWARD.

recreate, *v.tr.* renovare, animum relaxare. **recreation,** *n.* requies, animi relaxatio.

recrimination, *n.* accusatio mutua.

recruit, *v.tr. and intr. one's strength,* se *or* vires recreare ; *the army,* milites conscribĕre, delectum habēre. *n.* novus miles, tiro. **recruiting,** *n.* delectus.

rectify, *v.tr.* corrigĕre, emendare.

rectilinear, *adj.* (di)rectus.

rectitude, *n.* integritas, honestas.

recumbent, *adj.* (re)supinus.

red, *adj.* ruber ; rubicundus ; *— hair,* capillus rufus *or* rutilus ; *the — sea,* Sinus Arabicus. **redden,** *v.tr.* † rubefacĕre. *v.intr.* (e)rubescĕre. **red-hot,** *adj.* candens, fervens. **redness,** *n.* rubor.

redeem, *v.tr.* redimĕre, liberare. **redeemer,** *n.* liberator. **redemption,** *n.* redemptio, liberatio.

redolent, *adj.* alqd redolens.

redouble, *v.tr.* reduplicare.

redound, *v.intr.* redundare ; *it —s to my credit,* est mihi honori. **redundant,** *adj.* redundans.

redress, *v.tr. to — a wrong,* iniuriam sarcire. *n.* remedium, *or by verb.*

reduce, *v.tr. — to order,* in integrum reducĕre ; *to poverty,* redigĕre ; *pretium* (im)minuĕre. **reduction,** *n. by verbs.*

re-echo, *v.intr.* resonare.

reed, *n.* arundo, calamus. **reedy,** *adj.* arundineus.

reef, *n.* scopuli, saxa ; *of a sail,* velum. *v.tr.* vela subducĕre.

reek, *v.intr.* fumare.

reel, *n.* glomus (*ball*) *dance,* saltatio. *v.intr.* vacillare.

re-elect, *v.tr.* reficĕre.

re-establish, *v.tr.* restituĕre. **re-establisher,** *n.* restitutor. **re-establishment,** *n.* restitutio.

refer, *v.tr.* delegare ad alqm ; *fig.* referre. *v.intr. to anything,* spectare ad alqd. **referee,** *n.* arbiter. **reference,** *n. by verbs ; to have — to, with — to, etc.,* by quod attinet ad, *or by de with abl.*

refill, *v.tr.* replēre.

refine, *v.tr.* liquore (vinum), purgare ; *fig.* (ex)polire. **refined,** *adj.* (ex)politus, urbans ; *a — palate,* palatum subtile. **refinement,** *n. of manners, etc.,* urbanitas ; *of language, etc.,* subtilitas.

reflect, *v.tr.* repercutĕre. *v.intr. to — on,* considerare ; secum meditari ; **reflection,** *n. of rays, etc.,* repercussus ; *image,* imago ; *thought,* cogitatio ; *as quality,* mens ; *blame,* reprehensio.

reform, *v.tr. to make anew, renovare ; to amend,* emendare. *v.intr.* se corrigĕre. *n.* correctio ; *of manners,* morum mutatio. **reformation,** *n. see* REFORM. **reformatory,** *n.* carcer.

refraction, *n.* refractio radiorum. **refractory,** *adj.* contumax. **refractoriness,** *n.* contumacia.

refrain, *v.tr.* (se) abstinēre ; *to — from tears,* lacrimas tenēre.

refresh, *v.tr.* recreare, reficĕre ; *to — oneself,* animum integrare. **refreshing,** *adj.* reficiens, dulcis. **refreshment,** *n.* id quod corpus reficit, laxamentum (*for the mind*); *—s,* cibus.

refrigerate, *v.tr.* refrigerare.

refuge, *n.* refugium, secessus ; *to seek a — at a place,* fugĕre ad locum ; *to have a —,* receptum habēre. **refugee,** *n.* fugitivus, exul, extorris, profugus.

refulgent, *adj. see* BRIGHT.

refund, *v.tr.* reddĕre, (dis)solvĕre (*e.g. a debt, nomen).*

refuse, *v.tr.* recusare, (de)negare, repudiare. *n.* purgamen(tum), faex, quisquiliae. **refusal,** *n.* recusatio, repulsa (*rejection of a candidate*).

refute, *v.tr.* refellĕre, revincĕre, confutare, diluĕre (*crimen*), **refutation,** *n.* confutatio.

regain, *v.tr.* recipĕre, recuperare.

regal, *adj. see* ROYAL.

regale, *v.tr. see* ENTERTAIN ; *to — oneself, see* FEAST.

regalia, *n.* insignia regia (*pl.*).

regard, *v.tr.* animadvertĕre, observare, intueri (in) alqd, respicĕre, spectare ; *as —s so-and-so,* by pertinēre ad, *etc.; not to —,* neglegĕre ; *to care for,* colĕre, magni aestimare. *n.* respectus, cura ; *with — to, see* REFERENCE ; *esteem,* studium, amor, pietas ; *kind —s* (etiam atque etiam) vale (valete). **regardful,** *adj. see* ATTENTIVE. **regardless,** *adj.* neglegens. *Adv.* neglegenter.

regatta, *n. see* RACE.

regency, *n.* regni administratio, interregnum. **regent,** *n.* interrex.

regicide, *n.* regis caedes ; *to commit —*

13

regem interficĕre ; *the murderer*, regis interfector.

regiment, *n.* legio, turma equitum (*of cavalry*).

region, *n.* regio, tractus, plaga (*of the sky*), loca, *pl.*

register, *n.* liber, tabulae, album ; *to enter in a* —, in album referre. *v.tr.* in acta publi a referre, in tabulas referre.

registrar, qui in acta publica refert.

regret, *n.* (com)miseratio, dolor, desiderium (*longing*), paenitentia. *v.tr.* dolēre, aegre or moleste ferre, lugēre (*to mourn*) ; *to repent*, paenitet ; *to feel the loss of*, desiderare.

regular, *adj.* ordinatus, aequalis et congruens ; omnibus partibus absolutus et perfectus ; aequabilis, constans ; certus, rectus ; — *troops*, milites legionarii ; *legitimate*, *ordinary*, iustus, legitimus ; *the* — *consuls*, consules ordinarii ; — *income*, status reditus. *Adv.* ordine, constanter, recte, ordinate, composite, iuste. **regularity**, *n.* ordo, constantia, aequabilitas. **regulate**, *v.tr.* ordinare, componĕre, dirigĕre ; *see* ARRANGE. **regulation**, *n.* ratio, ordo, mos, lex ; *order*, iussum, praeceptum ; —*s*, instituta et leges.

reign, *v.intr.* regnare, imperium tenēre, imperare ; *n.* regnum, dominatio, principatus, imperium ; *in the* — *of*, regnante or rege alqo.

reimburse, *v.tr. see* INDEMNIFY, REFUND.

rein, *n.* habena, frenum, lorum, *pl.* frena or freni ; *to pull the* —*s*, habenas adducĕre ; *to loosen the* —*s*, frenos dare. *v.tr.* frenare ; *to* — *in*, habenas adducĕre.

reindeer, *n.* reno.

reinforce, *v.tr.* amplificare, augēre ; *to* — *an army*, auxiliis confirmare. **reinforcement**, *n.* supplementum, novae copiae, auxilium, subsidium.

reins, *n.* renes, -um, *m.*

reinstate, *v.tr.* in (regnum, *etc.*), reducĕre, or *by* restituĕre.

reinvigorate, *v.tr. see* REFRESH.

reiterate, *v.tr. see* REPEAT.

reject, *v.tr.* reicĕre, improbare, reprobare, repudiare, spernĕre, contemnĕre ; *to* — *prayers*, preces aversari. **rejection**, *n.* reiectio, improbatio, repudiatio, repulsa (*of a candidate*).

rejoice, *v.intr.* gaudēre, laetari, gestire ; *see* GLAD. *v.tr.* (ex)hilarare, hilarem facĕre, laetificare ; laetitiā afficĕre. **rejoicing**, *n.* voluptas, gaudium, laetitia.

rejoin, *v.intr. see* RETURN ; *see* ANSWER.

relapse, *v.intr.* recidĕre (in graviorem morbum) ; relabi. *n. use verb.*

relate, *v.tr.* (e)narrare, dicĕre, referre, tradĕre (*to hand down*) ; *to pertain to*, attingĕre ad. **related**, *adj.* propinquus, cognatus, affinis (*by marriage*), consan-

guineus. **relation**, *n.* ratio, coniunctio; *in* — *to*, quod ad alqm attinet ; *relative*, propinquus ; *see* NARRATION. **relationship**, *n.* propinquitas, consanguinitas ; *fig.* coniunctio. **relative**, *adj.* quod in comparatione positum est ; — *to*, de. *Adv.* comparate. *n. see* RELATION ; relativum (*gram.*).

relax, *v.tr.* (re)laxare ; *in attention*, animum relaxare ; *in anything*, desistĕre (*e.g.* incepto). **relaxation**, *n.* solutio, animi remissio, oblectamentum. **relaxing**, *adj.* gravis.

relay, *n.* equi per viam dispositi.

release, *v.tr.* dimittĕre, libertatem alci dare, manu mittĕre (*a slave*), exauctorare (*soldiers*), liberare (*from obligation*). *n.* liberatio, remissio (*e.g.* poenae).

relent, *v.intr.* mitescĕre, placari. **relentless**, *adj.* immisericors, crudelis. *Adj.* crudeliter. **relentlessness**, *n.* saevitia, crudelitas.

relevant, *adj.* quod ad rem est.

reliance, *n. see* RELY.

relics, *n.* reliquiae. **relict**, *n.* vidua.

relief, *n. fig.* sublevatio, levamen(tum), remedium, auxilium, subsidium (*of soldiers*) ; *in painting*, asperitas.

relieve, *v.tr.* exonerare, levare, laxare ; *to* — *a sentinel*, revocare ; *of soldiers*, succedĕre (*with dat.*).

religion, *n.* religio, pietas erga Deum, sacra, -orum ; *a man without* —, homo neglegens deorum. **religious**, *adj.* pius erga Deum, religiosus ; — *observances*, caerimoniae. *Adv.* pie, religiose.

relinquish, *v.tr.* relinquĕre.

relish, *n. a* — *for*, gustatus. *v.tr. see* ENJOY.

reluctance, *n. with* —, coactus or invitus. **reluctant**, *adj.* invitus, coactus.

rely, *v.intr.* (con)fidĕre, niti ; —*ing upon*, fretus. **reliance**, *n.* fides, fiducia.

remain, *v.intr.* (per)manēre, durare, stare ; *to* — *faithful to your promise*, promissis stare ; *to* — *in the camp*, castris se tenēre ; superesse (*to survive*, *to be left over*). **remainder**, *n.* residuum, quod restat. **remaining**, *adj.* reliquus. **remains**, *n. pl.* reliqua or reliquiae ; quod superest ; *dead body*, cadaver, cineres, -um (*ashes*).

remand, *v.tr.* remittĕre ; *in law*, comperendinare reum. *n.* comperendinatio.

remark, *v.tr. see* PERCEIVE ; dicĕre. *n.* dictum. **remarkable**, *adj.* notabilis, mirus, insignis. *Adv.* mire, insigniter (*remarkably beautiful*, pulcherrimus).

remedy, *n.* medicina, remedium. **remedial**, *adj.* salutaris.

remember, *v.tr.* meminisse, haud immemor esse ; *I don't* — *it*, memoriā excidit. **remembrance**, *n.* memoria, recordatio.

remind, *v.tr.* (ad)monēre. **reminiscence**, *n. see* REMEMBRANCE.

remit, *v.tr.* mittĕre ; *punishment,* poenam remittĕre. **remiss,** *adj. see* NEGLIGENT. **remittance,** *n. by* pecunia.

remnant, *n. see* REMAINDER.

remonstrance, *n.* (ad)monitio. **remonstrate,** *v.tr.* (ad)monere.

remorse, n. peccati dolor. **remorseless,** *see* PITILESS.

remote, *adj.* remotus. *Adv.* remote, procul. **remoteness,** *n.* longinquitas.

remove, *v.tr.* amovēre, avehēre ; tollĕre, auferre. *v.intr.* se (a)movēre ; abire, discedĕre ; (e)migrare (ex) loco. **removal,** *n.* deportatio ; migratio.

remunerate, *v.tr.* (com)pensare. **remuneration,** *n.* remuneratio, compensatio ; *for a —,* pretio.

rend, *v.tr.* (di)scindĕre, divellĕre. **rending,** *n.* discidium. **rent,** *n. tear, use verb.*

render, *v.tr.* reddĕre, referre (*e.g.* gratias, *thanks*), dare, praestare, *to — an account,* rationem referre ; *to make,* facĕre, reddĕre, *or by verbs, e.g.* augēre (*to — greater*). **render up,** *v.tr. see* SURRENDER.

rendezvous, *n.* locus ad conveniendum.

renegade, *n. deserter,* transfuga.

renew, *v.tr.* (re)novare ; reficĕre, redintegrare. **renewable,** *adj.* qui renovari potest. **renewal,** *n.* renovatio ; *of a war,* rebellio.

renounce, *v.tr.* renuntiare, se abdicare (*e.g.* magistratu) ; *to — an opinion,* sententiā decedĕre. **renunciation,** *n.* cessio.

renovate, *v.tr. see* RENEW.

renown, *n.* fama, gloria, laus. **renowned,** *adj.* clarus, illustris.

rent, *n.* merces. *v.tr. to let out,* locare ; *to hire,* conducĕre.

reopen, *v.tr.* iterum recludĕre. *v.intr. of wounds,* recrudescĕre (*also fig.*).

repair, *v.tr.* reficĕre, restituĕre. **repairs,** *pl. use verb.*

repair, *v.intr. se conferre or redpĕre [?]*

reparation, *n. see* SATISFACTION.

repartee, *n. see* WIT.

repast, *n. see* MEAL.

repay, *v.tr.* reddĕre, solvĕre ; *fig.* compensare. **repayment,** *n.* solutio, *or by verb.*

repeal, *v.tr.* rescindĕre, tollĕre, abolēre, abrogare. *n.* abrogatio.

repeat, *v.tr.* repetĕre, iterare, redintegrare, retractare. **repeated,** *adj.* repetitus, iteratus. *Adv.* saepenumero, etiam atque etiam. **repetition,** *n.* iteratio, redintegratio.

repel, *v.tr.* repellĕre, fugare ; *to — an accusation,* culpam a se amovēre.

repent, *v.intr.* mores suos mutare. *v.tr. I —,* paenitet me alcis rei. **repentance,** *n.* paenitentia. **repentant,** *adj.* paenitens.

---

repetition, *n. see* REPEAT.

repine, *v.intr. to — at,* (con)queri alqd. **repining,** *n.* maeror, querela.

replace, *v.tr.* reponĕre, substituĕre.

replenish, *v.tr.* implēre, complēre, replēre. **repletion,** *n.* satietas.

reply, *v.tr.* respondēre. *n.* responsum. rescribĕre. *n.* responsum.

report, *v.tr.* nuntiare, renuntiare ; *per lit(t)eras significare ; memoriae tradĕre ; it is —ed,* dicitur. *n.* relatio, narratio, renuntiatio ; *rumour,* fama ; *noise,* fragor. **reporter,** *n.* nuntius, notarius (*shorthand writer*).

repose, *v.tr.* reponĕre. *v.intr.* quiescĕre. *n.* quies. **repository,** *n.* receptaculum.

reprehend, *v.tr.* reprehendĕre. **reprehensible,** *adj.* culpā dignus.

represent, *v.tr.* repraesentare, exprimĕre, (ef)fingĕre, pingĕre ; indicare ; *a drama,* fabulam dare ; *to — one's country,* gerĕre personam civitatis. **representation,** *n. the act, by the verb ; see* LIKENESS, PICTURE ; *of a play,* actio ; *verbal,* explicatio. **representative,** *n.* vicarius (*substitute*), procurator ; legatus.

repress, *v.tr.* opprimĕre.

reprieve, *v.tr. by* differre, proferre, prolatare (*to delay*). *n. by* mora.

reprimand, *v.tr.* reprehendĕre. *n.* reprehensio.

reprisal, *n. to make — s,* par pari referre.

reproach, *n.* animadversio ; probrum. *v.tr.* convicium facĕre, maledicĕre. **reproachful,** *adj.* contumeliosus, *or by verb.* *Adv.* contumeliose, *or by verb.*

reprobate, *adj.* perditus, profligatus. *n.* homo perditus, *etc.*

reproduce, *v.tr.* denuo ferre ; reficĕre. **reproduction,** *n.,* **reproductive,** *adj. by verb.*

reproof, *n.* reprehensio. **reprove,** *v.tr.* reprehendĕre. **reprover,** *n.* reprehensor, castigator.

reptile, *n. by* serpens.

republic, *n.* respublica. **republican,** *adj. gen.* reipublicae. *n.* reipublicae liberae studiosus.

republish, *v.tr.* librum denuo edĕre.

repudiate, *v.tr. see* REJECT. **repudiation,** *n. of a son,* abdicatio filii ; *divortium (of a wife) ; see* REJECTION.

repugnant, *adj.* repugnans, diversus, alienus, odiosus. **repugnance,** *n.* repugnantia rerum, odium ; *to feel —,* abhorrēre.

repulse, *v.tr.* repellĕre, reicĕre. *n. by the verbs ; of a candidate,* repulsa. **repulsive,** *adj.* odiosus.

repurchase, *v.tr.* redimĕre.

reputable, *adj. see* RESPECTABLE.

reputation, *n. merely* fama existimatio, gloria, laus ; *bad —,* infamia. **repute,** *n. to be in good —,* bene audire. **reputed,** *adj.* qui dicitur.

13*

request, *n.* preces, -um, supplicium ; *at your* —, te petente, te auctore; *at my* —, rogatu meo ; *what is your* —*?* quid petis ? *v.tr.* precari, orare, rogare, petĕre, supplicare; *to invite*, vocare.

require, *v.tr.* poscĕre, desiderare, egĕre, imperare (*to command*) ; *to be* —*d*, opus esse ; *if circumstances* —, si res postulat. **requirement**, *n.* postulatio, *or by verbs.* **requisite**, *adj.* necessarius ; *to be* —, opus esse. *n.* necessitas, usus, res necessaria. **requisition**, *n.* petitio, quod imperatur.

requite, *v.tr.* reddĕre, compensare.

rescind, *v.tr.* rescindĕre, abrogare.

rescript, *n.* sententia, decretum, rescriptum.

rescue, *v.tr.* liberare, servare, ab alqā re eripĕre. *n.* liberatio, *or by* (con)servare.

research, *n.* eruditio, investigatio.

resemblance, *n.* similitudo. **resemble**, *v.tr.* similis esse.

resent, *v.tr.* aegre *or* moleste ferre. **resentful**, *adj.* iracundus. *Adv.* iracunde. **resentment**, *n.* iracundia.

reservation, *n.* condicio ; *with this* —, *that*, *etc.*, hac condicione. **reserve**, *v.tr.* retinēre, excipĕre (*to except*), reponĕre (*to store up*). *n.* copia ; *troops*, subsidia, -orum ; *fig.* recondĕre ; *in manners*, taciturnitas, cautio ; *without* —, aperte, sincere. **reserved**, *adj.* taciturnus, cautus. **reservoir**, *n.* lacus, castellum, cisterna.

reside, *v.intr.* habitare, sedem habēre. **residence**, *n.* habitatio; domus. **resident**, *n. by verbs.*

residue, *n.* quod reliquum est. **residuary**, *adj.* — *legatee*, heres.

resign, *v.tr. an office*, deponĕre, abdicare se magistratu; *to be* —*ed*, aequo animo ferre. **resignation**, *n.* abdicatio ; *morally*, animus submissus.

resin, *n.* resīna. **resinous**, *adj.* resinosus.

resist, *v.tr.* resistĕre, repugnare. **resistance**, *n.* pugna, certamen. **resistless**, *adj. and adv.* cui nullo modo resisti potest.

resolute, *adj.* fortis, firmus, constans. *Adv.* fortiter, constanter. **resoluteness**, *n. see* RESOLUTION. **resolution**, *n.* constantia ; *purpose*, sententia, consilium ; *plebiscitum*. **resolve**, *v.intr.* decernĕre, constituĕre.

resonant, *adj.* resonans.

resort, *v.intr.* locum celebrare, frequentare ; *to* — *to extremes*, ad extrema decurrĕre. *n.* conveniendi locus.

resound, *v.intr.* resonare.

resource, *n.* auxilium. **resources**, *n.* facultates, opes, *pl.*, pecunia.

respect, *v.tr.* verēri ; colĕre. *n.* observantia, reverentia; *in every* —, omnino. **respectable**, *adj.* honestus. *Adv.* honeste, bene. **respectability**, *n.* honestas. **respecting**, *adj.* de *with abl.* **respec-**

tive, *adj. and adv.* proprius, suus, *etc.*, *or by* quisque.

respire, *v.intr.* respirare. **respiration**, *n.* respiratio, spiritus.

respite, *n. and v.tr. see* REPRIEVE

resplendent, *adj.* splendidus.

respond, *v.intr.*, **response**, *n. see* ANSWER. **respondent**, *n.* reus (*in a criminal trial*), is unde petitur (*in a civil*). **responsible**, *adj.* obligatus ; *to be* —, alqd praestare (*to guarantee for*). **responsibility**, *n.* use obligatus. **responsive**, *adj.* apertus.

rest, *n.* tranquillitas, otium. *v.intr.* (con)quiescĕre ; *to* — *upon*, alqā re (in)niti. *v.tr.* ponĕre. **restive**, *adj.* contumax. **restless**, *adj.* inquietus, turbidus. *Adv.* use *adj.* **restlessness**, *n.* inquies, sollicitudo.

rest, *n. remainder*, quod restat, reliquum. **restoration**, *n.* refectio, *or by verb.* **restorative**, *adj. and n.* medicina. **restore**, *v.tr.* reficĕre, reducĕre, reddĕre (*to give back*); *to health*, sanare.

restrain, *v.tr.* reprehendĕre, tenēre, retinēre, cohibēre, reprimĕre. **restraint**, *n.* moderatio, temperatio; frenum.

restrict, *v.tr.* coercēre, circumscribĕre. **restriction**, *n. see* RESTRAINT. **restrictive**, *n.* qui coercet.

result, *v.intr.* oriri, fieri, evenire. *n.* exitus, eventus ; *to lead to a* —, exitum habēre; *general* —, summa.

resume, *v.tr. see* RECOMMENCE.

resuscitate, *v.tr.* ab inferis excitare : reficĕre.

retail, *v.tr.* divendĕre, distrahĕre. **retail dealer**, *n.* propōla.

retain, *v.tr.* tenēre, (con)servare. **retainer**, *n.* cliens, unus e suis ; *fee*. arr(h)a(bo).

retake, *v.tr.* recipĕre; *to* — *from*, alqd alci auferre.

retaliate, *v.tr.* par pari referre.

retard, *v.tr.* (re)morari, (re)tardare, detinēre, proferre.

retch, *v.intr.* nauseare.

retire, *v.intr.* recedĕre (*with* a, *etc.*), decedĕre de, se removēre, se referre (*to go back*), se recipĕre. **retired**, *adj.* remotus, solitarius. **retirement**, *n.* solitudo, vita otiosa. **retiring**, *adj. see* MODEST.

retort, *v.* regerĕre alqd alci. *n.* relatio; *see* REPLY.

retrace, *v.tr.* repetĕre; *one's footsteps*, pedem referre.

retreat, *n.* reditus, receptus (*of soldiers*, *etc.*), fuga ; *see* REFUGE. *v.intr.* se recipĕre, pedem referre (*in fighting*), copias reducĕre.

retrench, *v.tr.* sumptus minuĕre.

retribution, *n.* poena. **retributive**, *adj.* pro poena.

retrieve, *v.tr. see* RECOVER. **retriever**, *n.* canis.

retrograde, *v.intr.* in peius mutari. *Adj.* peior, deterior ; *a — movement*, *use* retro. retrogression, *n.* regressus.

retrospect, *n.* (praeteritorum) memoria. retrospective, *adj.* qui alqd respicit. *Adv.* by retro.

return, *v.intr.* reverti, redire. *v.tr.* reddĕre. *n.* reditus, regressus ; *giving back, by verb ; see* PROFIT. returned, *adj.* redux.

reunite, *v.tr.* iterum coniungĕre ; *fig.* reconciliare. reunion, *n.* reconciliatio.

reveal, *v.tr.* patefacĕre, aperire (in medium), divulgare.

revel, *v.intr.* comis(s)ari. *n. and* revelry, *n.* comis(s)atio. reveller, *n.* comis(s)ator.

revenge, *n.* ultio, vindicatio. *v.tr.* ulcisci, vindicare. revengeful, *adj.* ultionis cupidus, iratus. *Adv.* irato animo.

revenue, *n.* vectigal, reditus.

reverberate, *v.intr. see* RESOUND. reverberation, *n.* repercussus.

reverence, *n.* veneratio, verecundia ; *religious —,* pietas erga Deum ; *to make a —,* alqm salutare. revere, *v.tr.* colĕre, verĕri. reverend, *adj.* reverendus. reverent, *adj.* verecundus, pius. *Adv.* verecunde, pie.

reverie, *n.* cogitatio.

reverse, *v.tr.* invertĕre, (com)mutare. *n. change,* (com)mutatio, vicissitudo, *pl.* vices ; *contrary,* contrarium ; *defeat,* clades ; *hind part,* pars aversa. reversible, *adj.* qui facile inverti potest. reversion, *n. legal,* hereditas. revert, *v. intr.* redire.

review, *v.tr.* inspicĕre, recensēre ; lustrare (*with religious rites*). *n.* conspectus, *or by verbs ; of troops,* recensio, lustratio.

revile, *v.tr.* conviciari, alci maledicĕre. reviler, *n.* conviciator, maledicus. reviling, *n.* maledictio, convicium.

revise, *v.tr. see* CORRECT. revision, *n.* lima, emendatio.

revisit, *v.tr.* revisĕre.

revive, *v.intr.* ad vitam redire, renasci (*fig. of things*). *v.tr.* vitam alci reddĕre; reficĕre.

revoke, *v.tr.* abrogare, rescindĕre. revocable, *adj.* qui (quae, quod) facile mutari potest. revocation, *n.* abrogatio.

revolt, *v.intr.* seditionem movēre, desciscēre ab alqo, deficĕre. *n.* seditio, defectio. revolting, *adj.* taeter, turpis.

revolution, *n. turning,* conversio, an fractus, (solis) ; *political —,* novae res. revolutionary, *adj. lit.* seditiosus, novarum rerum studiosus ; *fig.* novissimus. revolutionist, *n.* (homo) novarum rerum cupidus. revolutionize, *v.tr.* commutare.

revolve, *v.intr. se* (re)volvĕre, circumverti. *v.tr.* alqd animo volvĕre.

revulsion, *n.* (com)mutatio.

reward, *v.tr.* praemium dare, munerari. *n.* remuneratio, praemium.

rewrite, *v.tr.* iterum scribĕre.

rhetoric, *n.* rhetorica *or* rhetorice.

rheumatism, *n.* cruciatus *or* dolor.

rhinoceros, *n.* rhinoceros.

rhythm, *n.* numerus *or pl.* numeri, modus. rhythmical, *adj.* numerosus. *Adv.* numerose.

rib, *n.* costa ; *of a ship,* statumen.

ribald, *adj.* obscenus.

riband, ribbon, *n.* redimiculum, vitta.

rich, *adj.* dives, locuples, opulentus, opimus (*abundant*), lautus (*luxurious*) ; ferax (*yielding*). *Adv.* copiose, abundanter, laute. riches, *n.* divitiae, opes, copiae (*all pl.*). richness, *n.* copia, ubertas (*of soil, etc.*).

rid, get rid of, *v.tr.* deponĕre, dimittĕre ; *to have got — of,* solutum. riddance, *n. good —,* abi (abite).

riddle, *n.* aenigma, ambages. riddled, *adj. e.g. —* with wounds, graviter vulneratus.

ride, *v.intr.* equitare, equo vehi ; *to — at anchor,* in ancoris consistĕre. rider, *n.* eques. riding, *n.* equitatio.

ridge, *n.* iugum.

ridicule, *n. see* MOCKERY. *v.tr.* deridēre ; *see* MOCK. ridiculous, *adj.* ridiculus, ridendus. *Adv.* (per)ridicule.

rife, *adj. to be —,* fertur, fama percrebeait.

rifle, *v.tr. see* PLUNDER.

rift, *n.* rima.

rig, *v.tr.* armare. rigging, *n.* armamenta, -orum.

right, *adj. not left,* dexter ; *— hand,* dextra ; *morally —,* aequus, rectus, iustus ; *it is —,* fas est ; *it is not — of you to, etc.,* non recte fecisti quod, etc. ; *correct,* rectus, verus ; *at the — time,* in tempore, opportune, ad tempus ; *you are —,* res ita est ut dixisti. *Adv.* recte, iuste, merito, bene. *n.* ius, potestas; *ius (divino iure) ; by —s,* iure, merito. righteous, *adj.* bonus, aequus, iustus. *Adv.* bene, iuste. righteousness, *n.* probitas. rightful, *adj.* legitimus, iustus, debitus. *Adv.* lege, legitime, iuste.

rigid, *adj.* rigidus, rigens, immobilis, severus. *Adv.* rigide, severe. rigidity, *n.* rigor. rigorous, *adj. see* RIGID. rigour, *n.* rigor, severitas.

rill, *n.* rivus.

rim, *n.* labrum ; ora (*of a shield, etc.*).

rime, *n.* pruina.

rind, *n.* cortex, liber.

ring, *n.* circulus, orbis, an(n)ulus ; inaures, -ium, *f.* (*ear- —s*) ; *circle, fig.* corona. *v.tr. and intr.* tinnire ; *of bells,* sonare (*intr.*) ; *to resound,* resonare ; *to surround,* circumdare. ringing, *adj.* canorus. *n.* sonus. ringleader, *n.* auctor, dux; *fig.* fax. ringlet, *n.* cirrus.

rinse, *v.tr.* eluěre, perlněre; lavare.

riot, *n.* seditio, motus, tumultus, vis repentina ; rixa (*brawling*). *v.intr.* seditionem (tumultum, *etc.*) concitare ; tumultuari. rioter, *n.* (homo) seditiosus, turbulentus, *etc.* riotous, *adj.* seditiosus, turbulentus ; — *living,* luxuria. *Adv.* turbulente, seditiose.

rip, *v.tr.* scinděre, divellěre.

ripe, *adj.* maturus, tempestivus ; *a — old age,* senectus ; *— judgment,* indicium. ripen, *v.tr.* maturare. *v.intr.* maturari, maturescěre. ripeness, *n.* maturitas.

ripple, *v.intr.* perhaps leni murmure defluěre, susurrare. *n. perhaps* unda.

rise, *v.intr.* (ex)surgěre, consurgěre, assurgěre ; expergisci (*to awake*) ; *of the sun, etc.,* (ex)oriri ; *of the wind,* consurgěre ; *to increase,* crescěre ; *to — in the air,* (in) sublime ferri ; *to — from beneath,* emergěre ; *of thoughts,* subire mentem ; *to — in dignity, etc.,* ad honores ascenděre ; *to — again,* resurgěre. *n. and* rising, *n.* (ex)ortus, a(d)scensus (*of a hill*) ; *origin,* ortus, caus(s)a, origo ; *to give — to ; see* CAUSE ; *— in price,* annona carior (*of corn*), *in gen. use verb; see* REBELLION. rising, *adj. of ground* (collis).

risibility, *n. by* ridēre.

risk, *n.* periculum, discrimen. *v.tr.* in discrimen vocare.

rite, *n. by* ritus.

rival, *n.* aemulus, rivalis (*a lover*), competitor (*political*). *Adj.* aemulans cum alqo. *v.tr.* contenděre cum alqo, aemulari. rivalry, *n.* aemulatio.

river, *n.* fluvius, flumen. *Adj.* fluvialis. river-god, *n.* numen fluminis.

rivet, *v.tr.* clav(ul)o figěre. *n.* clavus (*nail*).

road, *n.* via, iter ; *on the —,* in *or* ex itinere. roads, *n.* roadstead, statio.

roam, *v.intr.* palari, vagari. roaming, *adj.* vagus.

roar, *v.intr.* mugire, freměre, vociferari (*of men*) : mugitus, vociferatio.

roast, *v.tr.* torrēre. *Adj.* assus ; — *meat,* assum ; — *beef,* assum bubulum.

rob, *v.tr.* rapěre, latrocinari, despoliare. robber, *n.* praedo, latro, fur. robbery, *n.* rapina, spoliatio (*the act*).

robe, *n.* vestis, stola, palla, trabea (*robe of state*). *v.tr.* vestire.

robust, *adj.* robustus.

rock, *n.* saxum, rupes, scopulus, cautes. rocky, *adj.* scopulosus, saxeus (*made of rock*).

rock, *v.tr.* movēre, quatěre. *v.intr.* movēre.

rod, *n.* virga, ferula, decempěda (*in land-surveying*).

roe, *n. of fish,* ova, -orum, *pl.*

roe, *n.* caprea. roebuck, *n.* capreolus, caprea.

rogation, *n.* rogatio.

rogue, *n.* (homo) perfidus, sceleratus. roguery, *n.* fraus, dolus. roguish, *adj.* perfidus ; *saucy,* lascivus. *Adv.* perfide, lascive.

roll, *v.tr.* volvěre, devolvěre (*down*), versare (*over and over*). *v.intr.* volutari, volvi ; *tears — down his cheeks,* lacrimae per genas manant. *n.* orbis, cylindrus ; volumen (*of paper*). roller, *n.* cylindrus, phalangae (*put under ships*). roll-call, *to answer to the —,* ad nomina respondēre.

romance, *n.* fabula. *v.intr.* fabulari. romantic, *adj.* fictus, amoenus (*of a place*). *Adv.* ut in fabulis fit.

roof, *n.* tectum, culmen. *v.tr.* *to —,* tecto tegěre. roofless, *adj.* homeless, sine tecto.

room, *n.* locus, spatium, *e.g. to make —,* locum dare; *apartment,* conclave, cubiculum. roomy, *adj.* spatiosus.

roost, *v.intr.* stabulari.

root, *n.* radix ; *by the —s,* radicitus ; *fig.* caus(s)a (*cause*). *v.intr.* radicari, inveterascěre (*both fig.*). *v.tr.* *to — up,* evellěre. rooted, *adj.* inveteratus.

rope, *n.* restis, funis.

rose, *n.* rosa. rosy, *adj.* roseus.

rosemary, *n.* ros marinus.

rosin, *n.* resina.

rostrum, *n.* rostra, -orum.

rot, *v.intr.* putrescěre. *n.* tabes. rotten, *adj.* putridus.

rotate, *v.intr.* se volvěre, volvi. rotation, *n. in —,* ordine.

rotundity, *n.* figura rotunda, rotunditas.

rouge, *n.* fucus. *v.intr.* fucare.

rough, *adj.* asper, hirsutus, turbidus ; horridus (*e.g.* verba), raucus (*hoarse*) ; *of character,* inhumanus. *Adv.* aspere, inhumane. roughen, *v.tr.* (ex)asperare.

roughness, *n.* asperitas, duritia ; *of manners,* inurbanitas.

round, *adj.* rotundus, globosus. *v.tr.* rotundare, curvare ; *fig.* polire, concluděre. *n. see* CIRCLE ; *in fighting,* certamen ; *in music,* cantus. *Adv. and prep.* circa, circum. roundabout, *adj. and adv.* devius ; *a — way,* ambages. rounded, *adj.* teres, rotundus. roundly, *adv.* plane, prorsus.

rouse, *v.tr.* excitare.

rout, *v.tr. the enemy,* hostes dissipare. *n. see* MOB, DEFEAT.

route, *n. see* WAY, JOURNEY.

routine, *n.* usus, ordo.

rove, *v.intr. see* RAMBLE. rover, *n.* qui errat, *etc.*; pirata.

row, *n.* ordo, series ; — *of seats,* sedilia prima, secunda, *etc.* ; *in a —,* (ex) ordine.

row, *n. see* QUARREL, NOISE.

row, *v.intr.* remigare: *to — with all one's*

might, remis contendĕre. *v.tr.* remis propellĕre.

royal, *adj.* regius, *or by gen.* regis. *Adv.* regaliter, regio more. **royalty**, *n.* regia potestas.

rub, *v.tr.* terĕre, atterĕre (*against*), fricare (*e.g. a floor*), permulcēre (*stroke*); *to — out*, delēre.

rubbish, *n. see* REFUSE ; nugae, gerrae.

rubble, *n.* rudus.

rudder, *n.* gubernaculum, clavus.

ruddy, *adj.* rubicundus. **ruddiness**, *n.* color rubicundus.

rude, *adj.* rudis (*inexperienced*) ; — *verses*, versus incompositi; *unmannerly*, inurbanus, insolens. *Adv.* incomposite, inurbane, insolenter. **rudeness**, *n.* inurbanitas, insolentia.

rudiments, *n. pl.* rudimenta. **rudimentary**, *adj.* inchoatus.

rue, *n.* ruta.

rue, *v.tr. see* REPENT. **rueful**, *adj. see* SORROWFUL.

ruffian, *n.* latro, sicarius. **ruffianly**, *adj.* nefarius, sceleratus.

ruffle, *v.tr.* agitare; *to be —d*, inhorrescēre; *fig. see* IRRITATE.

rug, *n.* stragulum. **rugged**, *adj. see* ROUGH.

ruin, *n. —s*, ruinae ; ruina, exitium ; *that was to —*, hoc ei exitio fuit. *v.tr.* pessumdare, perdĕre, confícĕre. **ruinous**, *adj. see* PERNICIOUS ; (*of expense*), maximus.

rule, *v.tr. and intr.* regĕre ; regnare, reipublicae praeesse ; *to — passions*, temperare. *n.* lex, praeceptum ; norma. **ruler**, *n.* rector, qui alci rei praeest; *for drawing*, regula.

rumble, *v.intr.* mugire, murmurare.

ruminate, *v.intr.* ruminare *or* ruminari.

rumour, *n.* rumor, fama. *v.tr. it is —ed*, fertur.

run, *v.intr.* (de)currĕre, aufugĕre (*away*), cursare, trepidare (*to — about*) ; *to — against anyone*, incurrĕre in alqm ; *to — over, through*, percurrĕre. *n.* cursus. **runaway**, *n.* fugitivus. **runner**, *n.* cursor. **running**, *adj. — water*, aqua viva.

rupture, *n.* fractura ; *fig.* discordia. *v.tr.* frangĕre.

rural, *adj.* rusticus, agrestis.

rush, *n.* iuncus, s(c)irpus ; *made of —*, iunceus; *full of —es*, iuncosus.

rush, *v.intr. see* RUN.

russet, *adj.* fuscus (*dusky*).

rust, *n.* robigo, ferrugo (*of iron*). *v.intr.* robiginem trahĕre; *fig.* corrumpi. **rusty**, *adj.* robiginosus.

rustic, *adj.* rusticus.

rustle, *v.intr.* crepare; (*of leaves*), perhaps † susurrare. *n.* crepitus, sonus.

rut, *n.* orbita.

S

sable, *adj.* niger, ater.

sabre, *n.* acinaces, -is.

sacerdotal, *adj.* quod ad sacerdotes pertinet.

sack, *n.* saccus. *v.tr. see* PLUNDER.

sackcloth, *n.* cilicium ; *in — and ashes*, sordidatus.

sacred, *adj.* sacer, sanctus. *Adv.* sancte. **sacredness**, *n.* sanctitas.

sacrifice, *n.* sacrificium, sacra, -orum, *n.*, hostia (*the victim*) ; *— loss*, damnum. *v.tr.* sacrificare, hostiam immolare; *fig.* dedĕre. **sacrificial**, *adj. by genit. of* sacrificium.

sacrilege, *n.* sacrilegium. **sacrilegious**, *adj.* sacrilegus.

sad, *adj.* maestus, tristis ; *causing sadness*, gravis, acerbus *Adv.* maeste, tristiter. **sadden**, *v.tr.* dolore, *etc.*, afficĕre. **sadness**, *n.* maestitia, tristitia.

saddle, *n.* ephippium. *v.tr.* equum sternĕre.

safe, *adj.* tutus, incolumis. *Adv.* tuto, tute. **safe-conduct**, *n.* fides (publica). **safeguard**, *n.* propugnaculum. **safety**, *n.* salus, incolumitas ; *in —*, tutus, *etc.*

saffron, *n.* crocus. *Adj.* croceus.

sagacious, *adj.* sagax, prudens. *Adv.* sagaciter, prudenter. **sagacity**, *n.* sagacitas, prudentia.

sage, *adj. see* WISE. *n.* sapiens.

sail, *n.* velum ; *to set —*, vela dare ; *to furl —*, vela subducĕre. *v.intr.* navigare; *to — over, transvehi* ; *to — past*, praetervehi. **sailing**, *n.* navigatio. **sailor**, *n.* nauta, *m.*

saint, *n.* (vir) sanctus, (femina) sancta.

sake, *n. for the — of*, ob, propter, per (*with accus.*), pro (*with abl.*), caus(s)ā *or* gratiā (*with genit.*).

salaam, *n. by* corpus humi prosternĕre.

salad, *n.* acetaria, -orum.

salamander, *n.* salamandra.

salary, *n.* merces.

sale, *n.* venditio, hasta (*auction*) ; *to offer for —*, venum dare. **salesman**, *n.* venditor.

salient, *adj. see* PRINCIPAL.

saline, *adj.* salsus.

sallow, *adj.* pallidus.

sally, *v.tr.* erumpĕre. *n.* eruptio.

salt, *n.* sal. *Adj.* salsus. *v.tr.* sale condire. **salt-cellar**, *n.* salinum. **salt-mine, salt-pit, salt-works**, *n.* salinae.

salubrious, *adj.* saluber, *or* salubris. *Adv.* salubriter. **salubriousness**, *n.* salubritas. **salutary**, *adj.* salutaris ; *see* USEFUL.

salute, *v.tr.* salutare ; *in letters*, alc multam *or* plurimam salutem dicĕre. *n. see* KISS. **salutation**, *n.* salutatio.

salvation, *n.* salus.

salve, *n.* unguentum ; *for the eyes*, collyrium.

same, *adj.* Idem, eadem, idem ; — *as*, followed by et, ac, qui (quae, quod), etc., *it is the* — *to me*, meâ nihil interest ; *in the* — *way*, eodem modo ; *at the* — *time*, eodem tempore ; *to the* — *place*, eodem.

sample, *n.* exemplum.

sanctify, *v.tr.* (con)secrare. **sanction**, *n.* confirmatio, auctoritas ; *with, without the* — *of*, iussu, iniussu alcis. *v.tr.* sancire. **sanctity**, *n.* sanctitas. **sanctuary**, *n.* templum, penetralia, -ium, asylum (*refuge*).

sand, *n.* arēna, saburra. **sand-bank**, *n.* syrtis. **sand-glass**, *n.* clepsydra. **sandstone**, *n.* tofus. **sandy**, *adj.* arenosus.

sandal, *n.* solea ; *wearing* —*s*, soleatus.

sane, *adj.* sanus, mentis compos ; *not to be* —, mente captus esse.

sanguinary, *adj.* cruentus, † sanguineus. **sanguine**, *adj.*, *see* HOPEFUL.

sap, *n.* sucus. *v.tr. to undermine*, cuniculos agĕre ; *fig.* corrumpĕre, haurire. **sapless**, *adj.* suco carens. **sapling**, *n.* arbor novella. **sapper**, *n.* qui cuniculos agit.

sapient, *adj.* sapiens ; *to be* —, sapĕre.

sarcasm, *n.* dictum aculeatum. **sarcastic**, *adj.* acerbus. *Adv.* acerbe.

sarcophagus, *n.* sarcophagus.

sardonyx, *n.* sardonyx.

sash, *n.* cingulum.

satchel, *n.* pera, sacculus, loculus.

satellite, *n.* satelles, -itis.

satiate, *v.tr.* (ex)satiare ; *to* — *oneself with food*, cibo satiari. **satiety**, *n.* satietas.

satire, *n.* satira (satura), carmen probrosum. **satirical**, *adj.* acerbus. *Adv.* acerbe. **satirist**, *n.* satirarum scriptor. **satirize**, *v.tr.* perstringĕre, mordēre.

satisfaction, *n.* satisfactio, voluptas, poena. **satisfactory**, *adj.* idoneus ; gratus ; *see* EXCELLENT. *Adv.* bene, ex sententia. **satisfy**, *v.tr.* satisfacĕre, placēre.

satrap, *n.* satrapes, -ae *and* -is, *m.*

saturate, *v.tr.* saturare.

Saturnalia, *n.* Saturnalia, -ium, *n.*

satyr, *n.* satyrus.

sauce, *n.* ius, condimentum.

saucer, *n.* patella.

saucy, *adj.* petulans, procax. *Adv.* petulanter, procaciter. **sauciness**, *n.* impudentia, procacitas.

saunter, *v.intr.* ambulare, morari ; *to* — *about*, vagari.

sausage, *n.* tomaculum.

savage, *adj.* ferus, incultus, saevus. *Adv.* ferociter. **savageness**, *n.* ferocitas.

save, *v.tr. preserve*, (con)servare ; *to deliver*, liberare ; *to* — *money* com-

pendium facĕre ; *to* — *labour*, laborem diminuĕre. *prep. see* EXCEPT. **saving**, *adj.* parcus, frugi (*indecl.*). **saviour**, *n.* (con)servator, liberator.

savour, *n.* sapor. *v.tr.* sapĕre. **savoury**, *adj.* conditus, suavis.

saw, *n.* = *saying*, dictum, proverbium.

saw, *n.* serra. *v.tr.* serrâ (dis)secare. **sawdust**, *n.* scob(i)s. **sawed**, *adj.* serratus.

say, *v.tr.* dicĕre, (e)loqui ; *to* — *that not*, negare ; *I* — *yes*, aio ; *I* — *no*, nego ; inquit, ait (—*s he*). **saying**, *n.* verbum, proverbium.

scabbard, *n.* vagina.

scaffold, *n.* machina.

scald, *v.tr.* urĕre.

scale, *n. of a fish*, squama ; *pair of* —*s*, libra. **scaly**, *adj.* squamosus.

scale, *n. gradation*, gradus. *v.tr.* a(d)scendĕre. **scaling-ladder**, *n.* scalae.

scalp, *n.* cutis capitis.

scamp, *n. see* KNAVE. **scamper**, *v.intr. see* HURRY.

scan, *v.tr.* inspicĕre, contemplari ; pedibus versum metiri.

scandal, *n. see* DISGRACE ; *see* SLANDER. **scandalize**, *v.tr. see* SHOCK. **scandalous**, *adj.* turpis.

scant, **scanty**, *adj.* exiguus, parvis. *Adv.* exigue. **scantiness**, *n.* exiguitas.

scar, *n.* cicatrix.

scarce, *adj.* rarus. *Adv.* vix. **scarcity**, *n.* raritas, inopia.

scare, *v.tr.* terrēre.

scarf, *n.* fascia, mitella.

scarlet, *adj.* coccineus. *n.* coccum. **scarlet fever**, *n.* febris.

scathe, *v.tr. of words*, mordēre. **scatheless**, *adj.* incolumis.

scatter, *v.tr.* spargĕre ; dissipare, fundĕre (*of an army*). *v.intr.* diffugĕre.

scene, *n.* scaena. **scenery**, *n. of a theatre*, apparatus ; *prospect*, locus (*or pl.* loca).

scent, *n., an odour*, odor ; *perfume*, unguentum. *v.tr.* olfacĕre ; odoribus perfundĕre. **scent-bottle**, *n.* arcula. **scented**, *adj.* odoratus.

sceptical, *adj.*, **sceptic**, *n.* qui dubitat.

sceptre, *n.* sceptrum.

schedule, *n.* libellus.

scheme, *n.* consilium, ratio ; *to form a* —, rationem inire.

school, *n.* schola, ludus lit(t)erarum ; *disciples*, schola, secta ; *teaching*, disciplina. *v.tr.* docēre. **schoolfellow**, *n.* condiscipulus. **schoolmaster**, *n.* magister. **school-mistress**, *n.* magistra. **scholar**, *n.* discipulus, alumnus. **scholarly**, *adj.* eruditus. **scholarship**, *n.* lit(t)erae, doctrina.

science, *n.* scientia, ars, doctrina, disciplina ; *the* — *of music, grammar, etc.*, musica, grammatica, -orum.

scientific, adj. doctrinā eruditus, doctus. Adv. erudite.

scimitar, n. acinăces.

scintillation, n. scintilla (spark). scintillate, v.intr. scintillare.

scion, n. progenies.

scoff, n. ludibrium. v.tr. ludibrio habēre ; to be —ed at, ludibrio esse. scoffer, n. irrisor. scoffing, n. ludificatio.

scold, v.tr. obiurgare, increpare. n. obiurgator; of a woman, iurgiis addicta. scolding, n. obiurgatio, convicium.

scoop, n. see LADLE. v.tr. (ex)cavare.

scope, n. purpose, propositum, consilium; space, spatium; liberty, copia, potestas.

scorch, v.tr. torrēre. v.intr. torrēri.

scorched, adj. torridus. scorching, adj. torridus.

score, n. account, ratio, nomen ; on the — of friendship, amicitiae nomine ; to pay a —, pecuniam solvěre; number, viginti. v.tr. notare, signare (to mark).

scorn, n. contemptus, fastidium. v.tr. contemnēre. scorner, n. contemptor. scornful, adj. fastidiosus ; see PROUD. Adv. fastidiose.

scorpion, n. scorpio.

scot, n. — free, immunia, inultus.

scoundrel, n. homo nefarius, nequam.

scour, v.tr. (de)tergēre, (ex)purgare ; to — the land, percurrēre.

scourge, n. whip, flagellum ; plague, pestis. v.tr. virgis caedēre. scourging, n. by verb.

scout, n. explorator, speculator.

scowl, v.intr. frontem contrahēre.

scramble, v.tr. to — up, manibus pedibusque a(d)scendēre.

scrap, n. frustum, fragmentum; the —s, frusta.

scrape, n. angustiae, difficultas. v.tr. radēre ; to — off, abradēre ; to — together, congerēre. scraper, n. flesh —, strigil.

scratch, v.tr. scabĕre, radĕre ; to — out, delēre.

scrawl, n. v.tr. see WRITE.

scream, n. clamor, ululatus ; of an infant, vagitus. v.intr. clamare, ululare, vagire.

screech, v.intr. ululare ; — owl, ulula. screeching, n. ululatus.

screen, n. umbraculum; fig. praesidium. v.tr. defendēre.

screw, n. clavus (nail). v.tr. clavis adigĕre.

scribe, n. scriba, m. librarius.

scrofula, n. struma. scrofulous, adj. strumosus.

scroll, n. volumen.

scrub, v.tr. (de)fricare, (de)tergere.

scruple, n. (a weight), scrupulum ; dubitatio, religio. v.intr. to — to, dubitare with infin. ; religione ac metu

teneri. scrupulous, adj. religiosus, accuratus, diligens. Adv. religiose, accurate, diligenter, or by superl. (e.g. — clean, mundissimus).

scrutiny, n. scrutatio. scrutineer, n. scrutator. scrutinize, v.tr. scrutari.

scuffle, n. rixa.

scull, v.intr. remigare. sculler, n. remex.

scullery, n. culina (= kitchen).

sculpture, n. ars fingendi, sculptura ; work carved, opus, signum. v.tr. scalpēre, sculpēre. sculptor, n. sculptor.

scum, n. spuma; fig. faex.

scurf, n. porrigo.

scurrilous, adj. contumeliosus, scurrilis. Adv. contumeliose. scurrility, n. contumelia.

scurvy, n. adj. ignobilis.

scutcheon, n. insigne (or in pl.).

scuttle, n. cista (box).

scythe, n. falx.

sea, n. mare, oceanus, pelagus ; the high —, altum ; — -weed, alga. Adj. marinus, maritimus.

seal, n. signum. v.tr. (con)signare ; —ing-wax, cera.

seal, n. (an animal), phoca.

seam, n. sutura.

sear, v.tr. (ad)urĕre.

search, n. investigatio. v.tr. investigare ; (— for) quaerēre, (ex)petēre.

season, n. tempus, tempestas. v.tr. condire. seasonable, adj. tempestivus, opportunus. Adv. tempestive, opportune. seasoning, n. condimentum.

seat, n. sella, cathedra (chair) ; — at the theatre, etc., subsellia. v.tr. (or set), ponēre, collocare ; to — yourself, considēre. v. intr. to be seated, or to sit, sedēre.

secede, v.intr. abire, decedēre ; sententiam mutare. seceder, n. transfuga. secession, n. secessio.

seclude, v.tr. secludēre, removēre. secluded, adj. remotus; see LONELY. seclusion, n. solitudo.

second, adj. secundus, alter. Adv. secunde, deinde. in a fight, qui alci adest; momentum (temporis). v.tr. alci adesse, auxilio esse. secondary, adj. inferior. seconder, n. suasor (e.g. legis). second-rate, adj. inferior.

secrecy, n. silentium; to keep anything in —, rem occultam habēre.

secret, adj. arcanus (of plans, etc.), occultus ; furtive, furtivus. Adv. clam, furtim. n. res occulta, arcana, -orum.

secrete, v.tr. see HIDE.

secretary, n. scriba, m.

sect, n. secta, schola.

section, n. pars, portio.

secure, adj. careless, securus (i.e. sine curā), incautus; safe, tutus. Adv. secure, tuto. v.tr. tutum reddĕre ; confirmare. security, n. salus, incolu-

mitas ;   *pledge*, pignus ;   vadimonium
(*bail*).
sedan, *n.* lectīca.
sedate, *adj.* sedatus, gravis.   *Adv.*
sedate, graviter. **sedateness**, *n.* gravitas. **sedative**, *n.* sedatio (*e.g.* animi) ;
medicina quae dolorem compescit.
sedentary, *adj.* sedentarius.
sedge, *n.* ulva. **sedgy**, *adj.* ulvis
obductus.
sediment, *n.* faex, sedimentum.
sedition, *n.* seditio. **seditious**, *adj.*
seditiosus.   *Adv.* seditiose.
seduce, *v.tr.* corrumpĕre. **seducer**, *n.*
corruptor, *or by verb.* **seduction**, *n.*
stuprum ;   charm, lepos. **seductive**,
adj. pleasant, amoenus; qui corrumpit,
etc.
sedulous, *adj.* sedulus, diligens, accuratus.   *Adv.* sedulo, diligenter, accurate.
sedulity, *n.* diligentia.
see, *v.tr. and intr.* vidēre, cernĕre ;   *to
understand*, intellegĕre ;   *to — to*, alci
rei consulĕre (*or* ut, ne).   **seer**, *n.* vates.
seed, *n.* semen; *fig.* semen, stirps. **seed-
plot**, *n.* seminarium. **seed-time**, *n.*
sementis. **seedling**, *n.* arbor novella.
seek, *v.tr.* quaerĕre, petĕre, indagare ;
to — to do, studēre. **seeker**, *n.*
indagator, investigator. **seeking**, *n.*
indagatio, investigatio.
seem, *v.intr.* vidēri ;   *to — good, fit*,
videri (*impers.*)   **seeming**, *adj.* fictus,
speciosus.   *Adv.* in speciem, ut videtur.
seemly, *adj.* decōrus;   *not —*, indecorus;
it is —, decet ;   *it is not —* dedecet,
non decet.
seethe, *v.tr.* coquĕre.
segment, *n.* segmentum.
segregate, *v.tr.* segregare, removēre.
seize, *v.tr.* (ap)prehendĕre, corripĕre ;
occupare ; to be —d by illness, morbo
affici ;   *with fear*, timore percelli.
seizure, *n.* raptus.
seldom, *adv.* raro.
select, *v.tr.* legĕre, eligĕre, deligĕre.
adj. delectus. **selection**, *n.* delectus ;
number chosen, res selectae ;   *— of
passages*, ecloga.
self, *pron.* se, ipse ;   *I my—*, egomet
(*so* tute, ipsemet) ;   *of him—*, suämet
sponte ;   *we ourselves*, nos ipsi ;   *he
is beside him—*, mente est captus ;
— -deceit, error ;   *— -love*, amor sui ;
— -seeking, cupiditas. **selfish**, *adj.*
(*and adv.*) suarum rerum cupidus.
selfishness, *n.* cupiditas mea (tua, *etc.*),
avaritia. **self-willed**, *adj.* pertinax.
sell, *v.tr.* vendĕre, venditare; *to be sold*,
vendi, vēnire. **seller**, *n.* venditor,
mercator, propōla. **selling**, *n.* venditio.
semblance, *n.* species, imago.
semicircle, *n.* hemicyclium.
senate, *n.* senatus. **senate-house** *n.*
curia. **senator**, *n.* senator. **senatorial**,
adj. senatorius.

send, *v.tr.* mittĕre: *to — across*, transmittĕre ;   *away*, dimittĕre ;   *to — back*,
remittĕre ;   *to — for*, arcessĕre ;   *to —
out*, emittĕre ;   *to — forward*, praemit-
tĕre.
senior, *adj.* prior, maior (natu);   *to be
—*, alci aetate antecedĕre.
sensation, *n.* sensus (*of pain*, dolor ;   *—
of joy*, gaudium) ;   *excitement, perhaps*
(animi) commotio ;   *to make a —*,
admirationem movēre. **sensational**, *adj.*
mirificus, admirabilis.   *Adv.* mirifice,
admirabiliter. **sense**, *n.* sensus ; iudicium, sapientia; *meaning (of a word)*,
vis, significatio ;   *— of sight*, sensus
videndi ;   *the — s*, sensus ;   *— of taste*,
gustatus ;   *— of hearing*, auditus ;   *—
of smell*, odoratus ; **senseless**, *adj.*
sensu carens; rationis expers. **sensible**,
adj. sapiens, prudens.   *Adv.* sapienter.
sensitive, *adj. perhaps* acer, sol(l)icitus,
tener. **sensual**, *adj.* libidinosus.   *Adv.*
libidinose. **sensuality**, *n.* libido.
sentence, *n.* sententia ;   iudicium.
v.tr. condemnare. **sententious**, *adj.*
sententiosus.   *Adv.* sententiose.
sentiment, *n.* opinion, sententia ; *feeling*,
sensus. **sentimental**, *adj.* mollis.
sentinel *or* **sentry**, *n.* vigil, statio.
separable, *adj.* separabilis. **separate**,
v.tr. separare, dividĕre.   *Adj. and adv.*
separatus, *etc.*, *or by* suus, separatim.
separation, *n.* separatio, disiunctio.
September, *n.* (mensis) September.
septennial, *adj.* qui (quae, quod) septimo
quoque anno fit.
sepulchre, *n.* sepulc(h)rum. **sepulchral**,
adj. sepulc(h)ralis.
sequel, *n.* quod sequitur, exitus.   se-
quence, *n.* ordo, series.
serene, *adj. see* TRANQUIL.
serf, *n.* servus. **serfdom**, *n.* servitus.
serge, *n.* pannus.
serious, *adj.* gravis, tristis;   *important*,
magni momenti.   *Adv.* graviter, triste.
seriousness, *n.* gravitas, severitas.
serpent, *n.* serpens.
serried, *adj.* densus, confertus.
serve, *v.tr.* servire alci ;   ministrare :
to — meat, inferre cibos ;   *as a soldier*,
merēri. **servant**, *n.* servus, ancilla,
minister, puer. **service**, *n.* opera,
servitium, ministerium. **serviceable**,
adj. utilis, aptus. **servile**, *adj.* servilis ;   *fig. see* LOW, MEAN. **servility**,
n. adulatio. **servitude**, *n.* servitudo,
servitus.
session, *n.* — *of Parliament*, senatus.
set, *v.tr.* (im)ponĕre, statuĕre, sistĕre ;
to — in order, parare ;   *to — over*,
praeficĕre.   *v.intr. of the sun, etc.*,
occidĕre. **setting**, *n.* occasus, (*e.g.*
solis).
settle, *v.tr.* constituĕre;   dirimĕre (*e.g.*
bellum) ;   *to — a debt, etc.*, solvĕre.

v.intr. considĕre, so collocare. **settlement,** *n.* pactum, foedus ; colonia (*colony*). **settler,** *n.* advena, colonus.

seven, *adj.* septem, septeni (*each*) ; — *times,* septie(n)s. **seventh,** *adj.* septimus. **seventhly,** *adv.* septimum. **seventeen,** *adj.* septemdecim. **seventeenth,** *adj.* septimus decimus. **seventy,** *adj.* septuaginta. **seventieth,** *adj.* septuagesimus.

sever, *v.tr.* dividĕre, disiungĕre.

several, *adj.* nonnulli, plures. *Adv.* use *distributive numerals, also* quisque.

severe, *adj.* severus, acerbus, gravis. *Adv.* severe, acerbe, graviter. **severity,** *n.* severitas, gravitas.

sew, *v.tr.* suĕre.

sewer, *n.* cloaca.

sex, *n.* sexus.

shabby, *adj.* sordidus ; *fig. see* MEAN. **shabbiness,** *n. use adj.*; sordes, -ium (*of conduct*).

shackles, *n.* vincula ; — *for the feet,* pedicae ; *for the hands,* manicae. **shackle,** *v.tr.* vinculis colligare ; *fig.* impedimento esse.

shade, *n.* umbra ; *ghosts,* † umbrae, manes, *pl. v.tr.* † umbrare; *see* DARKEN. **shady,** *adj.* umbrosus, opacus. **shadow,** *n.* umbra. **shadowy,** *adj.* inanis, vanus.

shaft, *n.* arrow. sagitta ; *handle,* hastile; *of a carriage,* temo (*pole*), *or by* lora (*reins*) ; *of a mine, etc.,* puteus.

shake, *v.tr.* quatĕre ; *to — hands,* iungĕre dextras ; *to — off,* excutĕre. *v.intr.* algitari, tremĕre. **shaking,** *n.* quassatio (*act.*), tremor (*pass.*).

shallow, *adj.* tenuis ; *full of —s,* vadosus; *fig.* parum subtilis. *n.* vadum.

sham, *n.* fallacia, dolus; *without —,* sine fuco ac fallaciis.

shambles, *n.* laniena.

shame, *n.* modesty, pudor, verecundia; pudicitia ; *to have lost the sense of —,* pudorem posuisse ; *moral turpitude,* turpitudo, ignominia ; dedecus ; — *!* o indignum facinus! *v.tr.* pudore, etc., alqm afficĕre. **shamefaced,** *adj. see* MODEST. **shameful,** *adj.* turpis, foedus, flagitiosus. *Adv.* turpiter, foede, flagitiose. **shamefulness,** *n.* turpitudo, ignominia. **shameless,** *adj.* impudens. *Adv.* impudenter. **shamelessness,** *n.* impudentia.

shank, *n.* crus, tibia.

shape, *n.* forma, figura. *v.tr.* (con)formare, fingĕre. **shapeless,** *adj.* informis, deformis. **shapely,** *adj.* formosus.

share, *n.* pars, portio, sors ; *of a plough,* vomer. *v.tr.* partiri ; sortiri, dare. **sharer,** *n.* particeps, socius.

shark, *n.* pristis.

sharp, *adj.* acutus; *fig.* acer, acerbus ; *there is — fighting,* acriter pugnatur ; *mental,* acutus, subtilis; *words,* mordax, severus ; — *-witted,* sagax. *Adv.*

acute, acriter, sagaciter, subtiliter. **sharpen,** *v.tr.* (ex)acuĕre. **sharper,** *n.* fraudator. **sharpness,** *n. by adj.* acutus ; *fig.* severitas ; — *of intellect,* acumen, ingenium acutum.

shatter, *v.tr.* frangĕre ; *fig.* frangĕre, quassare.

shave, *v.tr.* (ab)radĕre, barbam tondĕre. **shavings,** *n.* assulae.

shawl, *n. see* MANTLE.

she, illa, ista, haec, ea.

sheaf, *n.* manipulus, fascis.

shear, *v.tr.* tondĕre. **shearer,** *n.* qui tondet. **shearing.** *n.* tonsura. **shears,** *n.* forfices.

sheath, *n.* vagina. **sheathe,** *v.tr.* in vaginam recondĕre.

shed, *n.* tugurium; *military,* vinea.

shed, *v.tr.* (dif)fundĕre, profundĕre ; *to — tears,* lacrimare. **shedding,** *n.* effusio, profusio; — *of tears,* fletus; — *of leaves, by* decidere.

sheep, *n.* ovis. **sheep-fold,** *n.* ovile. **sheepish,** *adj.* insulsus.

sheer, *adj. see* STEEP; merus; — *folly,* mera *or* maxima stultitia.

sheet, *n.* lodix (*blanket*); *of paper,* scheda, charta ; *of lead,* (plumbi) lamina; *of a sail,* pes. **sheet-anchor,** *n.* ancora. **sheet-lightning,** *n.* fulgur.

shelf, *n.* pluteus, pegma.

shell, *n.* testa, concha (*of fish*), cortex (*of fruit, etc.*). **shell-fish,** *n.* concha.

shelter, *n.* teg(i)men ; *protection,* perfugium, asylum, defensio. *v.tr.* tegĕre, defendĕre ; tutari, protegĕre tuĕri.

shelving, *adj.* declivis.

shepherd, *n.* pastor.

shew, *v.tr.* ostendĕre; *to explain,* demonstrare.

shield, *n.* scutum, ancile (*sacred —*). *v.tr.* defendĕre.

shift, *n.* resource, consilium, ratio, via; *a dishonest —,* ambages, dolus. *v.tr. to change,* (per)mutare. **shifty,** *adj. see* CUNNING.

shin, *n.* tibia ; crus, cruris, *n.*

shine, *v.intr.* fulgĕre, nitĕre.

ship, *n.* navis, navis longa (*a — of war*); biremis (*having two banks of oars, so* triremis, *etc.*) ; — *wreck,* naufragium. *v.tr.* in navem imponĕre.

shirt, *n.* subucula.

shiver, *v.tr.* frangĕre. *v.intr.* tremĕre, algĕre.

shoal, *n.* vadum, vada, *pl.*

shock, *n.* impetus; *fig.* offensio. *v.tr.* offendĕre, commovĕre. **shocking,** *adj.* odiosus ; *a — life,* vita turpis. *Adv.* pessime.

shoe, *n.* calceus, solea (*sandal*); *horse —,* solea ferrea. *v.tr. to — a horse,* affigĕre soleas ferreas. **shoemaker,** *n.* sutor.

shoot, *n.* virga. *v.intr. to — out, as*

ears of corn, (spicas) emittĕre. *v.tr.*
iacēre; (e)mittĕre; *to — at*, telis petĕre.
shooting-star, *n. see* METEOR.
shop, *n.* taberna, officina (*work—*). *v.intr.*
emĕre. **shopkeeper**, *n.* tabernarius.
shore, *n.* litus, ora. *v.tr.* fulcire.
short, *adj.* brevis, concisus ; *— of
stature*, humilis ; *(in a speech) to be*
—, ne plura. **short-sighted**, *adj.*
myops ; *fig.* imprudens. **shorten**,
v.tr. contrahere, praecidĕre. **shorthand**, *n.* notae. **shortly**, *adv.* paucis
verbis, breviter. **shortness**, *adj.*
brevitas.
shot, *n. to fire a —*, telum emittĕre.
shoulder, *n.* humerus. *v.tr.* tollĕre.
shout, *n.* clamor. *v.tr.* (con)clamare.
shove, *v.tr.* trudĕre. *n.* impulsus.
show, *n.* spectaculum, ludi ; ostentatio
(*display*). *v.tr.* ostentare ; *to — off*,
se ostentare. **showy**, *adj.* splendidus.
shower, *n.* imber. *v.tr.* effundĕre.
showery, *adj.* pluvialis.
shred, *n.* frustum.
shrew, *n.* mulier iurgiis dedita. **shrewd**,
adj. prudens, sagax. *Adv.* sagaciter,
prudenter. **shrewdness**, *n.* prudentia,
sol(l)ertia. **shrewish**, *adj. see* QUAR-
RELSOME.
shriek, *n.* ululatus. *v.intr.* ululare.
v.tr. clamare.
shrill, *adj.* acutus, argutus. *Adv.* acute,
argute.
shrine, *n.* aedicula, delubrum.
shrink, *v.intr.* se contrahĕre ; *through
fear*, pedem referre; *from duty*, abhorrēre, recedĕre. **shrinking**, *n.* contractio;
see FEAR.
shrivel, *v.intr.* (cor)rugari, contrahi.
shroud, *v.tr.* velare, mortuum vestimento
induĕre.
shrub, *n.* frutex. **shrubbery**, *n.* arbustum.
shrug, *v.tr. the shoulders*, humeros
movēre.
shudder, *n.* horror, tremor. *v.intr.*
horrēre, tremĕre ; *to — greatly*, per-
horrescĕre.
shuffle, *v.tr. mix*, (com)miscēre. *v.intr.*
tergiversari (*of conduct*), claudicare
(*to limp*). **shuffler**, *n.* homo fallax.
shuffling, *n.* fraus, dolus.
shun, *v.tr.* (de)fugĕre, vitare. **shunning**,
n. fuga, vitatio.
shut, *v.tr.* claudĕre, operire; *the eyes*,
oculos operire; *the hand*, manum comprimĕre ; *to — in*, includĕre ; *to
— out*, excludĕre. **shutter**, *n.* foriculae,
valvae.
shuttle, *n.* radius (textorius).
shy, *adj.* timidus, verecundus. *v.tr.
of a horse*, terrēri. *Adv.* timide,
verecunde. **shyness**, *n.* timor, pudor.
sibilant, *adj.* sibilans.
sibyl, *n.* sibylla. **sibylline**, *adj.* sibyl-
linus.

sick, *adj.* aeger; *to rise from a — bed*,
assurgĕre ex morbo; *to feel —*, nauseare;
to be —, vomĕre; *fig. by impers.* taedet.
sickly, *adj.* morbosus. **sickness**, *n.*
morbus, aegrotatio ; *epidemic*, pestilentia.
sickle, *n.* falx.
side, *n.* latus, pars (*party*) ; *on that
—*, iilinc, ultro; *on this — and on that*,
cicra ultroque ; *on all —s*, omnibus
partibus ; *on this —*, hinc ; *on both
—s*, utrimque. *v.intr. to — with*,
favēre, studēre, alcis studiosus esse.
sideboard, *n.* abacus. **sideways**, *adv.*
oblique, ab obliquo, ex obliquo.
sidereal, *adj. by genit.* siderum.
siege, *n.* oppugnatio, obsidio.
sieve, *n.* cribrum. **sift**, *v.tr.* cribrare;
fig. investigare.
sigh, *n*, suspirium. *v.intr.* suspiria
ducĕre, suspirare. **sighing**, *n.* sus-
piratus.
sight, *n.* visus, videndi facultas, conspectus ; (*view*), a(d)spectus ; *— of the
eye*, oculi acies ; *at first —*, primo
a(d)spectu ; spectaculum (*a show*) ;
in —, in conspectu ; *to take out of —*,
oculis subducĕre ; *to catch — of*, conspicĕre. *v.tr.* conspicĕre.
sign, *n.* signum, indicium, vestigium
(*footmark*), insigne (*badge*), nutus
(*nod*) ; *a good —*, omen faustum ; *a
bad —*, omen sinistrum. *v.tr. to —
a document*, (con)signare, (nomen)
subscribĕre, *as witnesses*, scribendo
adesse. **signal**, *adj.* insignis, egregius.
Adv. insigniter, egregie. *n.* signum ;
to give the — for an attack, signum dare.
v.tr. see above SIGNAL. **signalize**,
v.tr. declarare (*to show*), alci or alci
rei decori esse (*to be an honour to*).
signature, *n.* subscriptio, nomen
subscriptum. **signet**, *n.* signum (*seal*).
significance, **signification**, *n.* significatio. **significant**, *adj. see* EXPRES-
SIVE. **signify**, *v.tr.* significare (*to
make signs*), valēre (*to be equivalent*),
velle (*to wish*).
silence, *n.* silentium, taciturnitas ;
to keep —, tacēre. **silent**, *adj.* tacitus,
silens ; *to be —*, silēre, tacēre ; *to be
— about*, celare. *Adv.* tacite, silentio.
silk, *n.* bombyx. **silkworm**, *n.* bombyx.
silken, *adj.* bombycinus.
sill, *n.* limen.
silly, *adj.* stultus, ineptus. *Adv.* stulte,
inepte. **silliness**, *n.* stultitia, ineptiae.
silt, *n.* limus. *v.tr.* limo opplēre.
silver, *n.* argentum. *Adj. and* **silvery**,
argentĕus ; *plated with —*, argentatus ;
— mine, argenti metalla, -orum.
similar, *adj.* similis. *Adv.* similiter.
similarity, *n.* similitudo. **simile**, *n.*
similitudo. **similitude**, *n.* similitudo.
simper. *v.intr.* subridēre, stulte ridēre.
simple, *adj.* simplex ; *silly*, stolidus ;

sheer, merus. *Adv.* simpliciter ; *see*
ONLY. **simpleton**, *n.* homo stultus.
simplicity, *n.* simplicitas, innocentia.
simplify, *v.tr.* explicare.
simulate, *v.tr.* simulare. **simulation**,
n. simulatio.
simultaneous, *adj.* quòd eodem tempore
fit. *Adv.* eodem tempore, simul.
sin, *n.* peccatum, flagitium. *v.intr.*
peccare. **sinful**, *adj.* impius, flagitiosus.
sinless, *adj.* integer, sanctus. **sinner**,
n. qui peccavit.
since, *adv. long* —, iamdudum. *Prep.*
by e, ex, a, ab, post ; *a long time* —,
iamdiu ; — *childhood*, a puero. *Conj.*
of time, cum ; *of cause*, cum with *subj.*
sincere, *adj.* sincerus ; probus, verus.
Adv. sincere, simpliciter ; *yours sin-*
cerely, vale (valete). **sincerity**, *n.* simplicitas, fides.
sinew, *n.* nervus. **sinewy**, *adj.* nervosus.
sing, *v.tr. and intr.* canĕre, cantare.
singer, *n.* cantator, cantatrix. **singing**,
n. cantus.
singe, *v.tr.* adurĕre.
single, *adj.* unus, unicus ; *unmarried*
man, caelebs. *Adv.* singillatim. *v.tr.*
to — *out*, eligĕre. **singular**, *adj.*
singularis ; eximius ; *strange*, mirabilis. *Adv.* singulariter, eximie, mirabiliter. **singularity**, *n.* insolentia, *or*
use adj.
sinister, *adj.* sinister.
sink, *v.tr.* (sub)mergĕre. *v.intr.* (con)-
sidĕre, submergi ; *to* — *into sleep*,
somno opprimi ; *to be sunk in debt*,
aere alieno obrui. *n.* sentina.
sip, *v.tr.* degustare. *n. use verb.*
sir, *n.* dominus ; *in addresses.* vir
optime.
sire, *n.* pater, genitor.
siren, *n.* siren.
sirocco, *n.* auster.
sister, *n.* soror, germana.
sit, *v.intr.* sedĕre, considĕre (*to* —
down) ; *at table*, accumbĕre. **sitting**,
n. sessio, sessus.
site, *n.* situs. **situate**, *adj.* positus ,
to be — *near*, adiacēre. **situation**, *n.*
position, situs ; *office*, munus.
six, *adj.* sex, seni (— *each*) ; — *times*,
sexie(n)s. **sixth**, *adj.* sextus. **six-**
teen, *adj.* sedecim. **sixteenth**, *adj.*
sextus decimus. **sixty**, *adj.* sexaginta.
sixtieth, *adj.* sexagesimus.
size, *n.* mensura, amplitudo ; *glue*,
gluten.
skein, *n.* filorum glomus.
skeleton, *n.* ossa, -ium.
sketch, *n.* adumbratio. *v.tr.* describĕre,
adumbrare.
skewer, *n.* vera (*spit*).
skiff, *n.* scapha.
skill, *n.* peritia. **skilful**, *adj.* peritus
rei, prudens. *Adv.* perite, prudenter.
skim, *n.* spuma. *v.tr.* despumare ; *to*

read quickly, percurrĕre. *v.intr.* volare
(*to fly*).
skin, *n.* cutis, pellis. *v.tr.* pelle exuĕre.
skin-deep, *adj.* levis.
skip, *n.* saltus. *v.intr.* salire. *v.tr. to*
pass over, praeterire.
skipper, *n.* navis magister.
skirmish, *n.* praelium leve. **skirmisher**,
n. veles.
skirt, *v.tr. to* — *the shore*, legĕre oram.
skittish, *adj.* lascivus ; *to be* —
lascivire. *Adv.* lascive.
skulk, *v.intr.* latēre.
sky, *n.* caelum ; *under the open* — ;
sub divo. **skylark**, *n.* alauda.
slack, *adj.* laxus, piger ; — *in duty*,
neglegens. **slacken**, *v.tr.* laxare ; *to*
— *work*, opus remittĕre. *Adv.* lente,
neglegenter. **slackness**, *n.* neglegentia.
slake, *v.tr.* sitim sedare.
slander, *n.* calumnia. *v.tr.* calumniari.
slanderer, *n.* obtrectator. **slandering**,
n. obtrectatio. **slanderous**, *adj.* famosus.
Adv. per calumniam.
slant, *adj.* obliquus. *Adv.* oblique.
slap, *n.* alapa.
slash, *n.* vulnus, ictus. *v.tr.* caedĕre.
slate, *n.* tabula ; *for a roof*, tegula.
v.tr. tegulis consternĕre.
slattern, *n.* mulier sordida.
slaughter, *n.* caedes, clades. *v.tr.*
caedĕre, mactare (*a victim*). **slaughter-**
house, *n.* lanièna. **slaughterer**, *n.*
lanius.
slave, *n.* servus, ancilla (*female* —).
slave-dealer, *n.* venalicius. **slave-**
labour, *n.* opus servile. **slave-**
market, *n.* forum. **slavery**, *n.*
servitus. **slave-trade**, *n.* venditio servorum. **slave-war** *or* -**rising**, *n.*
bellum servile. **slavish**, *adj.* servilis.
Adv. serviliter.
slay, *v.tr.* interficĕre. **slayer** *n.* interfector.
sleek, *adj.* levis, nitidus ; *to be* —
nitēre.
sleep, *n.* somnus ; *to fall in* —, dormi-
tare. *v.intr.* dormire. **sleepless**, *adj.*
insomnis. **sleeplessness**, *n.* vigilantia.
sleepy, *adj.* somno gravis.
sleet, *n.* nix grandine mixta.
sleeve, *n.* manica ; *to laugh in one's* —,
furtim ridēre.
slender, — *adj.* tenuis, gracilis. *Adv.*
tenuiter (*poorly*). **slenderness**, *n.* tenuitas, gracilitas.
slice, *n.* (panis) frustum. *v.tr.* secare.
slide, *v.intr.* labi. *n.* lapsus.
slight, *adj.* levis, gracilis. *v.tr.* contemnĕre.
slim, *adj.* exilis. **slimness**, *n.* exilitas.
slime, *n.* limus. **slimy**, *adj.* limosus.
sling, *n.* funda ; *for the arm*, fascia.
v.tr. mittĕre.
slink, *v.intr. to* — *away*, sese subducĕre.
slip, *n.* lapsus ; *fig.* culpa ; *of a plant*,

14

surculus. *v.intr.* labi. **slipper**, *n.* creplda. **slippery**, *adj.* lubricus.

slit, *n.* fissura, scissura. *v.tr.* scindĕre.

slope, *n.* declivitas (*downwards*), acclivitas (*upwards*). *v.intr.* vergĕre. **sloping**, *adj.* declivis, acclivis.

sloth, *n.* ignavia. **slothful**, *adj.* ignavus. *Adv.* ignave.

slough, *n.* palus.

sloven, *n.* homo sordidus. **slovenliness**, *n.* sordes, neglegentia.

slow, *adj.* lentus. *Adv.* lente, paul(l)atim. **slowness**, *n.* tarditas.

slug, *n.* limax. **sluggard**, *n.* homo ignavus. **sluggish**, *adj.* segnis. *Adv.* segniter. **sluggishness**, *n.* ignavia.

sluice, *n.* emissarium.

slumber, *n. and v. see* SLEEP.

slur, *n.* dedecus. *v.tr.* *to — over*, extenuare.

sly, *adj.* subdolus. *Adv.* subdole. **slyness**, *n.* dolus.

smack, *n. a taste*, sapor. *v.intr. to — of*, sapĕre.

smack, *n. a blow*, alapa. *v.tr.* alapam alci ducĕre.

small, *adj.* parvus ; *a — soul*, animus pusillus ; *as — as*, *how — l* quantulus. **smallness**, *n.* parvitas.

smallpox, *n.* pestilentia.

smart, *n.* dolor, cruciatus. *v.intr.* dolĕre. *Adj.* acer ; *witty*, salsus ; *in dress*, nitidus. **smartness**, *n.* sal ; *in dress, use adj.*

smear, *v.tr.* (il)linĕre.

smell, *n.* odoratus (*the sense*) ; odor ; *to have a bad —*, male olĕre. *v.intr. to — of*, (re)dolĕre alqd ; *to —*, olfacĕre.

smelt, *v.tr.* fundĕre.

smile, *n.* risus ; *with a —*, subridens. *v.intr.* (sub)ridĕre.

smite, *v.tr.* ferire, percutĕre.

smith, *n.* faber ferrarius (*a blacksmith*). **smithy**, *n.* officina ferraria.

smoke, *n.* fumus. *v.intr.* fumare. **smoky**, *adj.* fumosus.

smooth, *adj.* lēvis, teres ; blandus ; tranquillus ; *temper*, aequus. *Adv. gen. by adj.* ; blande ; tranquille ; *temper*, aequo animo. *v.tr.* lēvare, limare (*with file*) ; tranquillare. **smoothness**, *n.* lēvitas, tranquillitas, aequanimitas.

smother, *v.tr.* suffocare.

smouldering, *adj.* fumans.

smuggle, *v.tr.* merces portorio non soluto importare. **smuggler**, *n.* qui merces vetitas importat.

smut, *n.* fuligo. **smutty**, *n.* fumosus.

snail, *n.* cochlea. **snail's-shell**, *n.* cochleae testa.

snake, *n.* anguis, serpens. **snaky**, *adj.* † vipereus.

snap, *v.intr.* crepare ; frangi. *v.tr.* frangĕre ; *to — the fingers*, digitis concrepare ; *to — at*, lit. *and fig.*

petĕre, arripĕre. *n.* crepitus. **snappish**, *adj.* morosus, mordax. *Adv.* morose.

snare, *n.* laqueus, plaga, insidiae. *-arum.* *v.tr.* illaqueare.

snarl, *v.intr.* fremĕre.

snatch, *v.tr. and intr.* rapĕre ; *to — at*, captare.

sneak, *v.intr.* irrepĕre ; *to — away*, furtim se subducĕre. *n.* homo abiectus.

sneer, *n.* derisus. *v.tr.* deridĕre.

sneeze, *v.intr.* sternuĕre. **sneezing**, *n.* sternutamentum.

snip, *v.tr.* circumcidĕre, amputare.

snore, *v.intr.* stertĕre.

snort, *n.* fremitus.

snout, *n.* rostrum.

snow, *n.* nix ; *—flake*, nix ; *— -storm*, nives. *v.tr.* ning(u)ĕre ; *it —s*, ningit. **snowy**, *adj.* nivosus ; *— -white*, niveus.

snub, *v.tr.* *n.* *see* REBUKE. **snubnosed**, *adj.* simus.

snuff, *n. of a candle*, fungus ; *— -box*, pyxis.

so, *adv.* sic, ita, hunc in modum, hoc modo, tam . . . quam ; *— then*, itaque ; *see* THEREFORE ; *— that*, ut ; *— much*, tantum, tantopere, adeo ; *not — much*, minus ; *— great . . . as*, tantum . . . quantum ; *— many . . . as*, tot . . . quot ; *— few*, tam pauci ; *— quickly*, tam celeriter ; *— far from*, tantum abest ut . . . non ; *— often*, totie(n)s . . . quotie(n)s.

soak, *v.intr.* macerare ; *to — up*, bibĕre ; *to — through*, permanare. **soaking**, *adj. of rain*, effusus.

soap, *n.* sapo.

soar, *v.intr.* se tollĕre, subvolare (*of birds, etc.*).

sob, *n.* singultus. *v.intr.* singultire.

sober, *adj.* sobrius, temperans, moderatus ; sevērus. *Adv.* sobrie, moderate, sevēre. **sobriety**, **soberness**, *n.* sobrietas, moderatio, sevēritas.

sociable, *adj.* comis, affabilis. **social**, *adj.* sociabilis, facilis. **society**, *n.* societas, sodalitas, factio (*party*), collegium (*corporation*) ; *in general*, societas humana ; *assemblage*, conventus, circulus (*a club*) ; *to avoid —*, homines fugĕre.

sock, *n.* soccus.

Socratic, *adj.* Socraticus.

sod, *n.* caespes ; *green —*, caespes vivus.

soda, *n.* nitrum.

sodden, *adj.* madidus.

sofa, *n.* lectulus.

soft, *adj.* mollis, effēminatus. *Adv.* molliter, effeminate. **soften**, *v.tr.* (e)mollire, mitigare. *v.intr.* molliri, mollescĕre. **softness**, *n.* mollitia.

soil, *n.* solum ; *good —*, solum pingue ; *poor —*, solum exile. *v.tr.* polluĕre, maculare.

sojourn, *v.intr.* commorari. *n.* commoratio. **sojourner,** *n.* hospes, advena.

solace, *n.* solatio (*the act*), levamen- (tum) *v.tr.* alqm (con)solari.

solar, *adj.* solaris, *or by genit.* solis.

solder, *n.* ferrumen.

soldier, *n.* miles ; *foot* —, pedes ; *horse* —, eques. **soldierly,** *adj.* militaris. **soldiery,** *n.* milites *or* miles.

sole, *adj.* solus, unus. *Adv.* solum, tantum. **solitary,** *adj.* solus, desertus. **solitude,** *n.* solitudo.

sole, *n. of the foot* (pedis) planta, solum ; *of a shoe,* solum.

sole, *n.* = *fish,* solea.

solemn, *adj.* sanctus, religiosus. *Adv.* sancte. **solemnize,** *v.tr.* celebrare. **solemnization,** *n.* celebratio. **solemnity,** *n.* sol(l)emne ; reverentia. *See* SERIOUS-NESS.

solicit, *v.tr.* sol(l)icitare, orare alqm alqd. **solicitation,** *n.* preces, -um. **solicitous,** *adj.* sol(l)icitus. *Adv.* sol(l)-icite. **solicitude,** *n.* sol(l)icitudo, *to be an object of* —, curae esse alci.

solid, *adj.* solidus, stabilis. *Adv.* solide, stabiliter. **solidity,** *n.* soliditas.

solitary, *adj. see under* SOLE.

solstice, *n.* solstitium (*summer* —), bruma (*winter* —) ; *relating to the* —, solstitialis, brumalis.

solve, *v.tr.* (dis)solvere. **soluble,** *adj.* quod dissolvi potest; *fig.* quod explanari potest. **solution,** *n. act* (dis)solutio ; *explanation,* explicatio.

some, *adj.* aliquis (*in plu.*) quis (*after* si), aliquot (*e.g.* aliquot hominum) ; — . . . *others,* alii . . . alii ; —*one,* aliquis ; *one or other,* nescio quis **somehow,** *adv.* nescio quomodo. **something,** *n.* aliquid. nonnihil. **sometimes,** *adv.* interdum. **somewhat,** *n.* aliquantu-(lu)m. **somewhere,** *adv.* alicubi.

somniferous, *adj.* † somnifer.

somnolent, *adj. see* SLEEPY.

son, *n.* filius, † natus ; *a* — -*in-law,* gener.

song, *n.* cantus, carmen. **songster,** *n.* cantor.

sonorous, *adj.* sonorus. *Adv.* sonore.

soon, *adv.* cito ; brevi tempore, mox ; *very* —, extemplo ; *as* — *as,* simul ac. **sooner,** *adv. rather,* potius ; *I had* —*er,* mallem.

soot, *n.* fuligo. **sooty,** *adj.* fuligine oblitus.

sooth, *n. in* —, vere, certe. **soothsayer,** *n.* (h)aruspex. **soothsaying,** *n.* augurium.

soothe, *v.tr.* placare, sedare. **soothing,** *adj. by part. or by* blandus. *Adv.* blande.

sop, *n.* frustum. *v.tr.* macerare.

sophism, *n.* sophisma. **sophist,** *n.* sophista. **sophistical,** *adj.* captiosus. *Adv.* captiose. **sophistry,** *n.* artes.

soporific, *adj.* † soporifer, † soporus.

sorcerer, *n.* veneficus. **sorceress,** *n.* saga. **sorcery,** *n.* ars magica.

sordid, *adj.* sordidus, abiectus. *Adv.* sordide. **sordidness,** *n.* sordes.

sore, *n.* ulcus ; *fig.* molestia. *Adj. distressing,* gravis, acerbus; *fig. to be* — *about anything,* alqa graviter ferre. *Adv.* moleste.

sorrow, *n.* dolor, tristitia, desiderium (*longing*), luctus (*mourning*). *v.intr.* dolere, maerere, dolore affici, desiderare.

sorrowful, *adj.* tristis, maestus, molestia affectus; *to be* —, dolere.

sort, *n.* mos, modus, genus; *of what* — ? qualis ? *of this* —, huiuscemodi ; *of that* —, eiusmodi ; *he is not the* — *of man to,* non is est qui *with subj.* *v.tr.* (in genera) digerere.

sortie, *n.* eruptio ; *to make a* — erumpere.

sot, *n. by* homo ebriosus.

soul, *n.* anima, animus, spiritus, mens.

sound, *adj.* sanus, salvus, incolumis, sospes, integer, robustus ; *to be* — *in health,* bene valere ; *of sleep,* altus. *Adv.* salve, robuste, alte. **soundness,** *n.* bona valetudo, salus ; *of argument,* gravitas.

sound, *n.* sonus, vox, clamor (*din*). *v.tr.* sonare ; *to* — *a trumpet,* tubam inflare ; *to* — *a retreat,* receptui canere. *v.intr.* sonare, canere (*of trumpets*).

sound, *n.* = *strait,* fretum.

sour, *adj.* acidus (*sharp*), acerbus. *Adv.* acerbe, morose. **sourness,** *n.* acerbitas; morositas (*fig.*).

source, *n.* fons, caput.

south, *n.* meridies, plaga meridiana ; auster (*the* — *wind*) ; — *west wind,* africus. **southern,** *adj.* meridianus, australis. **southwards,** *adv.* in *or* ad meridiem.

sovereign, *adj.* sui iuris ; *remedy,* remedium efficacissimum. *n.* rex, dominus, tyrannus. **sovereignty,** *n.* imperium, dominatio, regnum.

sow, *n.* sus.

sow, *v.tr.* serere. **sower,** *n.* sator. **sowing,** *n.* satio, satus.

space, *n.* spatium, locus. **spacious,** *adj.* amplus. **spaciousness,** *n.* amplitudo.

spade, *n.* pala.

span, *n.* palmus ; — *of life,* exigua vitae brevitas. *v.tr.* iungere (*e.g.* flumen ponte).

spangle, *n.* bractea. *v.tr.* (bracteis) distinguere.

spar, *n.* trabs.

spar, *v.intr.* pugnis certare.

spare, *v.tr.* alci *or* alci rei parcere.

spark, *n.* scintilla ; *of hope,* specula. **sparkle,** *v.intr.* fulgere, nitere. **sparkling,** *n.* nitor.

sparrow, *n.* passer, -eris, *m.*

spatter, *v.tr.* a(d)spergĕre.

spawn, *n.* piscium ova, -orum.

speak, *v.intr.* fari, loqui, dicĕre ; *to —
Greek,* Graece loqui ; *to make a speech,*
orationem habēre ; *to — together,*
colloqui. speaker, *n.* orator, qui dicit.

speaking, *n.* locutio, sermo. speech,
n. oratio ; contio (*before a popular
assembly*). speechless, *adj. see* DUMB.

spear, *n.* hasta. *v.tr.* hastā transfīgĕre.

special, *adj.* praecipuus, proprius,
peculiaris. specially, *adv.* praecipue,
imprimis, maxime, *or by superl.*

species, *n.* genus. specific, *adj.* proprius ; — *charges, etc.,* singuli. *n.
see* REMEDY.

specify, *v.tr.* si(n)gillatim enumerare.
specification, *n.* enumeratio.

specimen, *n.* exemplum.

specious, *adj.* speciosus.

speck, *n.* macula. speckle, *v.tr.* (com)-
maculare. speckled, *adj.* maculis distinctus.

spectacle, *n.* spectaculum.

spectator, *n.* spectator.

spectre, *n. see* GHOST.

speculate, *v.intr.* cogitare. speculation,
n. cogitatio ; *scientific —,* rerum contemplatio ; *in business,* negotium.

speech, *n. see* SPEAK.

speed, *n.* celeritas. *v.tr.* fortunare,
secundare. speedy, *adj.* celer. speedily,
adv. cito, celeriter.

spell, *n.* carmen. spell-bound, *adj.*
stupefactus.

spend, *v.tr.* consumĕre, impendĕre ; *to —
time,* tempus agĕre. spendthrift, *n.*
nepos.

spew, *v.tr.* (e)vomĕre.

sphere, *n.* sphaera, globus ; *fig.* munus.
spherical, *adj.* globosus.

sphinx, *n.* sphinx.

spice, *n.* condimentum. spicy, *adj. fig.*
salsus.

spider, *n.* aranea. spider's web, *n.*
aranea.

spike, *n.* clavus (*nail*), cuspis (*head of a
weapon*).

spikenard, *n.* nardus.

spill, *v.tr.* effundĕre.

spin, *v.tr.* nēre, texĕre telam ; versare
(*to turn*). *v.intr.* circumagi. spinner, *n.*
qui stamina net. spindle, *n.* fusus.

spine, *n.* spina.

spinster, *n.* innupta, virgo.

spiral, *adj.* tortuosus (*of a line*).

spire, *n.* turris.

spirit, *n.* spiritus ; *soul,* animus ; — *of
the age,* horum temporum mores, -um ;
to understand the — of a writer, mentem scriptoris assequi ; *the —s of
the departed,* manes, -ium. spirited,
adj. animosus, fortis. spiritless, *adj.*
ignavus, fractus. spiritual, *adj. by
the gen.* animi *or* ingenii.

spit, *n.* veru.

spit, *v.intr.* (ex)spuĕre.

spite, *n.* malevolentia. *v.tr. see* ANNOY.
spiteful, *adj.* malignus. *Adv.* maligne.

splash, *v.tr.* a(d)spergĕre.

spleen, *n. fig.* odium. splenetic, *adj.*
malevolus.

splendid, *adj.* splendidus, (prae) clarus.
Adv. splendide, (prae)clare. splendour,
n. splendor; apparatus (*pomp*).

splint, *n.* ferulae. splinter, *n.* ligni
fragmentum.

split, *n.* scissura. *v.tr.* scindĕre. *v.intr.*
(dif)findi.

spoil, *n.* praeda, spolia. *v.tr.* spoliare
(*plunder*), corrumpĕre. spoiler, *n.*
spoliator. spoiling, spoliation, *n.*
spoliatio.

spoke, *n.* (*of a wheel*), radius.

sponge, *n.* spongia. *v.tr.* abstergĕre.

sponsor, *n.* sponsor.

spontaneous, *adj.* libens. *Adv.* ultro.
spontaneousness, spontaneity, *n. by*
arbitrium.

spoon, *n.* cochlear.

sport, *n.* ludus ; *hunting,* venatio ;
mockery, ludibrium. *v.intr.* ludĕre ; *to
frolic, frisk,* lascivire. sportive, *adj.*
lascivus, iocosus. *Adv.* lascive, iocose.

sportiveness, *n.* lascivia, iocus.

sportsman, *n.* venator.

spot, *n.* macula, nota ; *place,* locus.
v.tr. notare, maculare. spotless, *adj.*
sine maculis, purus. *Adv.* sine maculis,
pure. spotted, *adj.* maculosus.

spouse, *n.* co(n)iunx.

spout, *n.* os ; *pipe,* fistula. *v.intr.*
erumpĕre, exsilire.

sprawl, *v.intr.* humi prostratus iacēre.

spray, *n.* spuma (*foam*).

spread, *v.tr.* (ex)pandĕre, explicare,
extendĕre, sternĕre, (di)vulgare. *v.intr.*
patēre, extendi, (di)vulgari (*fig.*).

sprig, *n.* surculus, virgula.

sprightliness, *n.* alacritas ; facetiae.
sprightly, *adj.* alacer, facetus.

spring, *n.* origo, fons, caus(s)a ; *of the
year,* ver. *v.intr.* salire ; *down,* desilire ;
forward, prosilire ; *from,* (ex)oriri ; *to
— up,* crescĕre (*grow*) ; surgĕre. *v.tr.
to — a leak,* rimas agĕre ; *to — a mine,*
cuniculum igni explodĕre. spring tide,
n. aestus maximus.

sprinkle, *v.tr.* spargĕre, a(d)spergĕre.

sprite, *n.* faunus, nympha.

sprout, *n.* surculus. *v.intr.* germinare.

spruce, *adj.* comptus, ornatus. *Adv.*
compte, ornate.

spur, *n.* calcar. *v.tr.* equo calcaria
subdĕre.

spurious, *adj.* adulterinus, falsus.

spurn, *v.tr.* fastidire, repudiare.

spy, *n.* explorator. *v.intr.* explorare.

squabble, *n.* rixa, altercatio. *v.intr.*
rixari

squadron, *n.* equitum turma, ala ; — *of
ships,* classis.

squalid, *adj.* sordidus.

squall, *n.* subita tempestas ; *crying,* vāgitus. *v.intr.* vagire.

squalor, squalidity, squalidness, *n.* sordes, squalor. *Adj.* sordidus, squalidus.

squander, *v.tr.* perdere, dissipare.

squanderer, *n.* nepos.

square, *adj.* quadratus. *n.* quadratum, *n. v.tr.* quadrare.

squash, *v.tr. see* CRUSH.

squat, *v.intr.* subsidĕre.

squeak, *n.* stridor. *v.intr.* stridēre.

squeamish, *adj.* fastidiosus. **squeamishness,** *n.* fastidium.

squeeze, *n.* compressio. *v.tr.* premĕre ; *to — out,* exprimĕre.

squint, *v.intr.* limis oculis esse, limis spectare.

squirrel, *n.* sciūrus.

stab, *n.* ictus, vulnus. *v.tr.* (con)fodĕre. **stabber,** *n.* sicarius.

stable, *adj.* stabilis ; *fig.* constans. *n.* stabulum. *v.tr.* stabulare. **stability,** *n.* stabilitas, constantia.

stack, *n.* acervus. *v.tr.* cumulare.

staff, *n.* baculum, scipio, fustis ; *augur's —,* lituus ; *shepherd's —,* pedum ; *herald's —,* caduceus ; *— of officers,* legati et praefecti et tribuni militum ; *any other —,* socii, ministri.

stag, *n.* cervus.

stage, *n.* proscaenium, scaena (*to go upon the —,* in scaenam prodire) ; *degree,* gradus ; *of a journey,* iter. **stage-coach,** *n.* vehiculum publicum.

stagger, *v.intr.* titubare, incertis ire pedibus. *v.tr.* animum percutĕre.

stagnant, *adj.* (*pond*) stagnum.

stain, *n.* macula, decoloratio (*the act*) ; nota (*mark*) ; *fig.* dedecus. *v.tr. see* DYE, DIRTY ; *fig.* maculare, foedare. **stainless,** *adj.* purus.

stair, *n.* gradus ; *—case,* scalae.

stake, *n.* palus ; *at gambling,* pignus. *v.tr.* (de)ponĕre.

stale, *adj.* vetus ; *to become —,* obsolescĕre.

stalk, *n.* caulis, culmus (*green stalk*). *v.intr.* (magnifice) incedĕre.

stall, *n.* stabulum ; *little shop,* taberna. *v.tr.* stabulare.

stammer, *v.intr.* balbutire.

stamp, *n.* signum, imago (impressa) ; *persons of that —,* eiusmodi homines ; *of the foot,* (pedis) supplosio. *v.intr.* pedibus calcare. *v.tr. under foot,* conculcare ; *to mark,* signare.

stanch, *v.tr. see* STAUNCH.

stand, *n. to come to a —,* subsistĕre ; *to take a —,* locum capĕre. *v.intr.* stare, consistĕre ; *to — still,* quiescĕre ; *to — by anyone,* alci adesse ; *to — for an office,* munus petĕre ; *to — up,* surgĕre. *v.tr. see* ENDURE. **standing,** *adj. — water,* aqua stagnans *— army,* milites.

standstill, *n. to be at a —,* haerēre.

standard, *n.* vexillum; aquila; *measure,* regula. **standard-bearer,** *n.* vexillarius, signifer, aquilifer.

staple, *n. see* PYYUL.

star, *n.* astrum, sidus, stella. **stargazer,** *n.* astrologus. **starry,** *adj.* stellifer, astris distinctus et ornatus.

starboard, *adj. and n.* latus navis dextrum.

stare, *n.* obtutus, -ūs. *v.intr.* intueri, stupēre (*with astonishment*).

stark, *adj.* rigens.

starling, *n.* sturnus.

start, *n.* saltus ; *by fits and —s,* haud uno tenore ; *setting out,* profectio. *v.intr.* trepidare ; *to set out,* proficisci.

startle, *v.tr.* terrēre. *Adj.* **startling,** mirificus.

starve, *v.tr.* fame consumĕre. *v.intr.* fame consumi.

state, *n.* condicio, res, fortuna ; *a city,* civitas, respublica ; *grandeur,* apparatus. *v.tr.* affirmare. **stately,** *adj.* erectus, nobilis ; *of banquets, etc.,* lautus. **stateliness,** *n. use adj.* **statesman,** *n.* vir reipublicae peritus. **statesmanship,** *n.* ars reipublicae regendae **station,** *n. see* POSITION, RANK. *v.tr. see* PLACE, SET. **stationary,** *adj.* stativus (*stativa castra*), fixus.

statue, *n.* statua, imago.

stature, *n.* statura.

statute, *n.* lex.

staunch, *adj.* bonus ; *a — friend,* amicus, fidelis. *v.tr.* sanguinem sistĕre.

stay, *v.tr. to prop,* fulcire ; *to stop,* cohibēre. *v.intr.* commorari, manēre.

stead, *n. in — of,* pro, loco.

steady, steadfast, *adj.* firmus, constans, fidelis. *Adv.* firme, constanter, fideliter. **steadiness, steadfastness,** *n.* firmitas, constantia.

steak, *n.* offula.

steal, *v.tr.* furari, avertĕre **stealth,** *n. by —,* furtim, clam. **stealth(i)y,** *adj.* furtivus, clandestinus. *Adv.* furtim, clam.

steam, *n.* vapor, nidor. *v.tr.* vaporare. **steamboat,** *n.* navis vi vaporis impulsa.

steed, *n.* equus.

steel, *n.* chalybs; *sword,* ferrum. *v.tr. see* HARDEN.

steep, *adj.* praeceps, arduus. *n.* locus praeceps. *v.tr.* imbuĕre. **steepness,** *n. use adj.*

steeple, *n.* turris.

steer, *v.tr.* gubernare, regĕre. **steering,** *n.* gubernatio. **steersman,** *n.* gubernator, rector (*fig.*).

steer, *n.* iuvencus.

stem, *n.* arboris stirps *or* truncus (*of a tree*), calamus (*of a plant*) ; *race,* stirps, genus. *v.tr.* cohibēre, reprimĕre ; *to — the sedition,* seditionem sedare.

step, *n.* gradus, passus ; *to keep —
with,* alcis gradus aequare ; *— by —,*
gradatim. *v.intr.* gradi ; *forwards,*
progredi; *over,* transire. stepbrother,
n. filius vitrici, filius novercae. stepdaughter, *n.* privigna. stepfather,
n. vitricus. stepmother, *n.* noverca.
stepsister, *n.* filia vitrici *or* novercae.
stepson, *n.* privignus.

stereotyped, *adj.* tritus.

sterile, *adj.* sterilis. sterility, *n.*
sterilitas.

sterling, *adj.* verus, bonus.

stern, *adj.* severus. *Adv.* severe. sternness, *n.* severitas.

stern, *n.* puppis (*poop*).

steward, *n.* dispensator, villicus *or* vilicus (*of the farm*). stewardship, *n.* procuratio, administratio.

stick, *n.* baculum, virga, fustis. *v.intr.*
haerēre, cohaerēre ; *fig.* haesitare,
dubitare. *v.tr.* (af)figēre (*to — to*).

sticky, *adj.* lentus, tenax.

stiff, *adj.* rigidus ; *to be —,* rigēre. *Adv.*
rigide. stiffen, *v.tr.* rigidum facēre.
stiffness, *n.* rigor, rigiditas.

stifle, *v.tr.* suffocare ; *fig.* opprimēre.
ex(s)tinguēre.

stigma, *n.* nota.

stile, *n.* claustra, -orum (*barrier*).

still, *adj.* tranquillus, tacitus, silens,
immotus (*motionless*) ; *— night,* nox
tacita ; *be —,* taceas, quaeso ! quiesce !
v.tr. sedare, reprimēre. *Adv.* adhuc,
etiam ; *see* NEVERTHELESS. stilling,
n. sedatio. stillness, *n.* silentium,
quies ; tranquillitas.

stilted, *adj. see* INFLATED.

stimulate, *v.tr.* stimulare, excitare.
stimulus, *n.* stimulus, incitamentum.

sting, *n.* aculeus ; *the wound,* ictus.
v.tr. pungēre. stinging, *adj.* mordens,
acerbus.

stingy, *adj.* parcus, malignus. *Adv.*
parce, maligne. stinginess, *n.* parsimonia, malignitas.

stink, *n. and v.intr. see* SMELL.

stint, *n.* inopia. *v.tr.* parce dare ;
privare.

stipend, *n. see* SALARY. stipendiary,
adj. mercenarius.

stipulate, *v.intr.* parcisci. stipulation,
n. pactum, condicio.

stir, *n.* motus, tumultus. *v.tr.* (com)-
movēre. *v.intr.* moveri, progredi.

stitch, *v.tr.* (con)suēre.

stock, *n.* (arboris) truncus ; *—s for ship-
building,* navalia, -ium ; *the —s, by*
pedicae (*fetters*) ; *family,* gens, stirps ;
quantity, magna copia. *v.tr.* instruēre.
Adj. see COMMONPLACE, TRITE. *Adv.
— -still,* immotus.

stockade, *n.* vallum.

stoic, *adj. and n.* stoicus. stoical,
stoically, *adj. and adv.* stoice, stoico

ut aiunt more. stoicism, *n.* ratio
stoicorum.

stomach, *n.* stomachus.

stone, *n.* lapis, saxum ; *of fruit,* nucleus ; *precious —,* gemma. *v.tr.* lapides in alqm conicēre. stony, *adj.*
lapideus (*of stone*), saxosus. stony-
hearted, *adj.* durus.

stool, *n.* scabellum.

stoop, *v.intr.* se inclinare. stooping,
n. corporis inclinatio. *Adj.* pronus.

stop, *v.intr.* (con)sistēre, morari ; *to
cease,* cessare. *v.tr.* sistēre ; impedire ;
to block up, viam interclūdēre. *n.*
impedimentum ; (*in printing*) interpunctum ; *without —,* sine morā.
stoppage, *n.* impedimentum.

store, *n.* copia ; *— of provisions,* commeatus ; *— -house,* apothēca, horreum.
v.tr. condēre.

stork, *n.* ciconia.

storm, *n.* tempestas. *v.tr.* expugnare. *v.intr.* furēre. storming, *n.*
expugnatio. stormy, *adj.* turbidus ;
fig. tumultuosus. *Adv.* turbide. irate.

story, *n.* narratio, fabula ; *falsehood,*
mendacium ; (*of a building*) tabulatio,
tabulatum.

stout, *adj.* crassus, validus. *Adv.*
fortiter, acriter.

stove, *n.* focus, caminus.

stow, *v.tr. see* STORE.

straggle, *v.intr.* vagari.

straight, *adj.* (di)rectus, erectus. *Adv.
—way,* statim. straighten, *v.tr.* corri-
gēre. straightforward, *adj.* simplex.

strain, *n.* contentio ; *see* TUNE ; *in this
—,* ita, sic. *v.tr.* contendēre (in *or* ad) ;
see FILTER.

strait, *adj.* angustus. *n.* fretum ; *poverty,*
res angustae. straiten, *v.tr.* in angustias adducēre; impedire.

strand, *n.* litus, ripa. *v.tr.* in litus
eici.

strange, *adj. foreign,* peregrinus, barbarus ; *unusual,* insolitus ; *not belonging
to one,* alienus. *Adv.* mirabiliter.
strangeness, *n.* novitas. stranger, *n.*
hospes, advena.

strangle, *v.tr.* gulam laqueo frangēre.

strap, *n.* lorum. *v.tr.* loris (con)-
stringēre (*to bandage*).

stratagem, *n.* dolus, insidiae. strategic,
adj. quod ad prudentem ducem pertinet.
strategist, *n.* dux peritus. strategy,
n. ars belli gerendi.

straw, *n.* stramentum. strawberry, *n.*
fragum.

stray, *v.intr.* (ab)errare.

streak, *n.* linea. *v.tr.* lineis distinguēre.

stream, *n.* flumen ; *down —,* flumine
secundo ; *up —,* flumine adverso. *v.intr.*
fluēre.

streamer, *n.* vexillum, signum.

street, *n.* via, vicus.

strength, *n.* vis (*or pl.* vires). strengthen, v.tr. firmare. v.intr. by pass. corroborari, etc.; see INCREASE. **strengthened**, adj. confirmatus. **strengthening**, n. confirmatio.

strenuous, adj. strenuus. Adv. strenue, acriter. **strenuousness**, n. (g)navitas, studium.

stress, n. momentum, vis; with —, cum vi, graviter; of weather, tempestas.

stretch, v.tr. (ex)tendĕre; to — forth, porrigĕre. v.intr. see REACH. n. at a —, uno tenore. **stretcher**, n. see LITTER.

strew, v.tr. sternĕre, spargĕre.

strict, adj. accurate, accuratus, diligens; severus. Adv. truly, re verâ, reapse; accurate; severe. **strictness**, n. accuratio, severitas. **stricture**, n. animadversio.

stride, n. ingens gradus. v.intr. ingentes gradus ferre.

strife, n. certamen, altercatio, rixa. **strive**, v.intr. (e)niti, contendĕre, conari; to — against, resistĕre. **striving**, n. see EFFORT; — after, appetitio.

strike, v.tr. ferire, pulsare, verberare (lash), caedĕre; to be struck, vapulare; (as a clock) sonare; lightning —s, de caelo tangitur alqd; to be struck blind, captus esse oculis; a bargain, pacisci; against, in alqd incurrĕre; (of a ship) saxis illidi. **striking**, adj. see REMARKABLE.

string, n. filum, funiculus; a bow —, nervus; musical, nervus, fides, -ium. v.tr. to — an instrument, nervos aptare; to — together, see BIND. **stringent**, adj. see SEVERE.

strip, v.tr. spoliare, nudare, exuĕre; of wealth, opibus spoliare. n. pars; — of paper, scidula chartae.

stripe, n. see STREAK; STROKE.

stripling, n. adulescens.

stroke, n. verber; see LINE; of lightning, fulmen; of fortune, etc., eventus; master- —, summa ars. v.tr. permulcēre.

stroll, n. ambulatio. v.intr. ambulare.

strong, adj. validus, firmus, fortis; to be — (in influence), pollēre; — wind, ventus vehemens; of arguments, gravis; — position, locus munitus. Adv. valide, firmiter, fortiter.

structure, n. aedificium, aedes, opus. structura; — of a sentence, forma.

struggle, n. luctatio. v.intr. luctari.

strut, v. intr. superbe incedĕre.

stubble, n. stipulae.

stubborn, adj. pertinax. Adv. pertinaciter. **stubbornness**, n. pertinacia.

stud, n. bulla; horses, equi. v.tr. alqâ re distinguĕre.

study, n. studium, meditatio; room for —, conclave. v.tr. alci rei studēre. **student**, n. alcis rei studiosus. stu-

dious, adj. lit(t)erarum studiosus. Adv. summo studio.

stuff, n. materia, materies; baggage, impedimenta, -orum; household —, supellex; kitchen —, culinaria; — gown, etc., textile; excubitorum, nugas! v.tr. refercire, replēre. **stuffing**, n. fartum (food), tomentum (of cushions).

stumble, v.intr. offendĕre. **stumbling**, n. offensio.

stump, n. caudex, truncus.

stun, v.tr. fig. stupefacĕre. **stunned**, adj. fig. stupefactus.

stupefy, v.tr. stupefacĕre; to be stupefied, torpescĕre, stupēre. **stupefaction**, n. stupor.

stupendous, adj. ingens, immanis.

stupid, adj. stupidus, stolidus. Adv. stupide, stolide. **stupidity**, n. stupiditas. stupor, n. stupor, torpor.

sturdy, adj. see STRONG.

sturgeon, n. acipenser.

stutter, v.intr. balbutire;

sty, n. hara.

style, n. genus, habitus, mos. v.tr. appellare. **stylish**, adj. elegans. Adv. eleganter. **stylishness**, n. elegantia.

suave, adj. urbanus. **suavity**, n. urbanitas.

subdivide, v.tr. iterum dividĕre. **subdivision**, n. pars.

subdue, v.tr. in imperium redigĕre, domare.

subject, v.tr. subicĕre. n. civis; in grammar, subiectum; matter discussed, etc., res. Adj. imperio subiectus, parens. **subjection**, n. servitus. **subjective**, adj. e.g. viewed —ly in myself, meo quidem iudicio.

subjoin, v.tr. subiungĕre.

subjugate, v.tr. domare.

subjunctive, adj. — mood, modus subiunctivus or coniunctivus.

sublime, adj. sublimis. Adv. sublime, excelse. **sublimity**, n. sublimitas.

submarine, adj. quod sub mari (positum) est.

submerge, v.tr. submergĕre. **submersion**, n. use verb.

submit, v.tr. submittĕre; cedĕre. **submission**, n. animus submissus (as state). **submissive**, adj. see OBEDIENT.

subordinate, adj. inferior. **subordination**, n. obsequium, disciplina; alqd alci rei posthabēre.

suborn, v.tr. subornare.

subscribe, v.tr. subscribĕre; to agree to, assentiri. **subscriber**, n. subscriptor (one who signs).

subsequent, adj. (sub)sequens. Adv. postea.

subserve, v.tr. auxilio esse alci, subservire. **subservience**, n. obtemperatio.

subside, v.intr. considĕre.

subsidy, n. vectigal.

subsist, *v.intr.* to — on, vesci. **subsistence,** *n.* victus.

substance, *n.* corpus, res ; *property,* res, bona, -orum. **substantial,** *adj.* gravis, magni momenti ; — *victory,* aliquid victoriae. *Adv.* magnā ex parte. **substantiate,** *v.tr.* see PROVE. **substantive,** *n.* nomen.

substitute, *n.* vicarius. *v.tr.* sufficĕre *(of a magistrate).* **substitution,** *n.* use verb.

subterfuge, *n.* tergiversatio.

subterranean, *adj.* subterraneus.

subtle, *adj.* subtilis ; acutus. *Adv.* tīliter, acute. **subtlety,** *n. of intellect, etc.,* acumen ; *cunning,* calliditas. **subtleties,** *n.* argutiae.

subtract, *v.tr.* deducĕre. **subtraction,** *n. by* deducĕre.

suburban, *adj.* suburbanus.

subvert, *v.tr.* subvertĕre.

succeed, *v.intr.* alci succedĕre ; *to have success,* bene evenire. **success,** *n.* res secundae. **successful,** *adj.* felix. *Adv.* feliciter, prospere. **succession,** *n.* successio *(in office, etc.)* ; *order,* series ; *in* —, ex ordine. **successive,** *adj.* continuus. *Adv.* (ex) ordine. **successor,** *n.* successor.

succinct, *adj.* brevis. *Adv.* breviter.

succour, *n.* auxilium. *v.tr.* succurrĕre.

succumb, *v.intr.* succumbĕre.

such, *adj. pron.* talis.

suck, *v.tr.* sugĕre. **sucker,** *n.* surculus.

suckle, *v.tr.* mammam alci dare. **suckling,** *n.* (infans) lactens.

sudden, *adj.* subitus, inopinatus. *Adv.* subito, ex tempore.

sue, *v.tr.* in ius vocare *(at law)* ; *to — for an office,* ambire magistratum ; *to entreat,* sol(l)icitare; *to — for payment,* nomina exigĕre.

suet, *n.* sebum.

suffer, *v.tr.* pati, tolerare ; *to permit,* permittĕre, sinĕre ; *to — shipwreck,* naufragium facĕre ; *to — pain, etc.,* dolorem accipĕre. *v.intr.* dolorem ferre, dolore affici, poenas dare *(as punishment),* aegrotare *(to be ill).* **sufferance,** *n.* patientia. **sufferer,** *n.* aeger, qui patitur. **suffering,** *n.* dolor, res adversae.

suffice, *v.intr.* sufficĕre ; satis esse. **sufficient,** *adj.* satis. **sufficiency,** *n.* quod satis est.

suffocate, *v.tr.* suffocare.

suffrage, *n.* suffragium.

suffuse, *v.tr.* suffundĕre.

sugar, *n.* — -*plums,* cup(p)edia, -orum.

suggest, *v.tr.* monēre, subicĕre. **suggestion,** *n.* admonitio, consilium. **suggestive,** *adj.* qui alqd repraesentat ; *see* SUGGEST.

suicide, *n. to commit* —, sibi mortem consciscĕre.

suit, *n.* actio, lis, caus(s)a ; *clothes,* pestis; *petition,* rogatio. *v.tr by* decet,

convenit, *impers.* **suitable,** *adj.* idoneus, aptus ; *of time,* opportunus. **suitableness,** *n.* congruentia, opportunitas. *Adv.* congruenter, apte, opportune.

suite, *n.* comitatus; *of rooms,* conclavia, -ium.

suitor, *n. see* LOVER.

sulky, sullen, *adj.* morosus. *Adv.* morose. **sulkiness, sullenness,** *n.* morositas.

sully, *v.tr.* maculare, inquinare.

sulphur, *n.* sulfur ; *dipped in* —, sulfuratus.

sultry, *adj.* aestuosus. **sultriness,** *n.* aestus.

sum, *n.* summa ; *of money,* pecunia. *v.tr.* computare, *to — up,* breviter repetĕre. **summary,** *n. see* EPITOME. *Adj.* brevis ; *hasty,* inconsideratus. *Adv.* breviter, inconsiderate.

summer, *adj. and n.* aestas ; *at the beginning of* —, aestate ineunte ; *at the end of* —, aestate extremā ; *— -house, see* ARBOUR.

summit, *n.* cacumen, vertex, *also by* summus ; *fig.* fastigium, *or by* summus.

summon, *v.tr.* appellare, citare ; (ad) vocare, arcessĕre ; *to — up courage,* animum colligĕre. **summons,** *n. by verb or in abl.,* accitu *(at the — of).*

sumptuary, *adj.* sumptuarius. **sumptuous,** *adj.* sumptuosus. *Adv.* sumptuose. **sumptuousness,** *n.* (magnus) apparatus.

sun, *n.* sōl ; *the rising* —, sol oriens ; *setting* —, sol occidens. **sunbeam,** *n.* radius solis. **sunburnt,** *adj.* adustus. **sundial,** *n.* solarium. **sunrise, sunset,** *n.* ortus, occasus solis. **sunshine,** *n.* sōl.

sunny, *adj.* apricus; *fig.* felix.

sunder, *v.tr.* separare, disiungĕre.

sundry, *adj.* diversi, plures, nonnulli.

sup, *v.tr.* cenare.

superable, *adj.* superabilis.

superabound, *v.intr.* superesse.

superannuated, *adj.* ob senectutem muneribus exsolutus.

superb, *adj.* magnificus, lautus.

supercilious, *adj.* superbus, fastidiosus. **superciliousness,** *n.* superbia.

superficial, *adj.* exterior, externus ; lēvis. *Adv.* lēviter. **superficiality,** *n.* lēvitas.

superfine, *adj.* tenuissimus.

superfluous, *adj. to be* —, superesse. **superfluity,** *n.* quod supervacaneum est.

superhuman, *adj. a — task,* opus quod ultra hominis vires est.

superintend, *v.tr.* praeesse alci. **superintendence,** *n.* administratio. **superintendent,** *n.* qui rebus praeest.

superior, *adj.* superior, melior. **superiority,** *n.* prior locus.

superlative, *adj.* superlativus *(gram.),* optimus.

supernal, *adj.* caelestis.

supernatural, *adj.* caelestis ; *to happen*

by — agency, dīvīnĭtus fieri. Adv. dīvīnĭtus.

supernumerary, adj. of soldiers, a(d)-scrīptivus.

superscribe, v.tr. inscrĭbĕre in alqā re. superscription, n. inscriptio.

supersede, v.tr. alci succedĕre.

superstition, n. superstitio. superstitious, adj. superstĭtiosus. Adv. super-stitiose.

supervene, v.intr. see FOLLOW.

supervise, v.tr. (pro)curare. supervision, n. (pro)curatio.

supine, n. supīnum (gram.). Adj. supīnus (on the back); neglegens. Adv. neglegenter. supineness, n. neglegentia.

supper, n. cena.

supplant, v.tr. in alterius locum irrepĕre.

supple, adj. mollis.

supplement, n. supplementum (of troops).

suppliant, adj. and n. supplex. supplicate, v.tr. supplicare. supplication, n. supplicatio (formal), obsecratio.

supply, v.tr. suppeditare. n. subsidium; copia; of provision, commeatus.

support, v.tr. sustinēre; to keep, etc., alĕre; to help, alci adesse; favēre. n. see PROP; maintenance, victus; auxilium. supporter, n. adiutor; at an election, suffragator.

suppose, v.tr. putare; opinari. supposing that, conj. fac ita esse. supposition, n. coniectura. supposititious, adj. subditus.

suppress, v.tr. supprimĕre; sedition, restinguĕre. suppression, n. use verb.

supreme, adj. supremus, summus. supremacy, n. imperium, dominatio. Adv. maxime.

sure, adj. certus; it is —, constat. Adv. certe, profecto. surety, n. vas; sponsor (person).

surface, n. superficies, or by summus with noun.

surfeit, n. salietas. v.tr. to — oneself, se ingurgitare; fig. satiāre.

surge, n. fluctus, -um. v.intr. fluctuare.

surly, adj. morosus. Adv. morose. surliness, n. morositas.

surmise, n. coniectura. v.tr. suspicari.

surmount, v.tr. superare. surmountable, adj. (ex)superabilis.

surname, n. cognomen.

surpass, v.tr. praestare.

surplus, n. quod superest.

surprise, n. (ad)miratio; a sudden attack, subita incursio. v.tr. de proviso excipĕre; surprising, adj. see WONDERFUL.

surrender, v.tr. dare, tradĕre; intr. in deditionem venire. n. deditio; traditio.

surreptitious, adj. furtivus. Adv. furtim, clam.

surround, v.tr. circumdăre; circumvenire, circumvallare.

survey, v.tr. spectare, considerare, intuēri, oculis perlustrare, perspicĕre; contemplari animo; fig. to measure land, agrum metiri. n. contemplatio, conspectus. surveyor, n. (of land) decempedator, metator.

survive, v.intr. superstes esse. survival, n. use verb. survivor, n. superstes.

susceptible, adj. capax (e.g. capax amicitiae), obnoxius; mollis. susceptibility, n. use adj.

suspect, v.tr. suspicari. suspicion, n. suspicio. suspicious, adj. suspiciosus. Adv. suspiciose, with suspicion; or adj.

suspend, v.tr. suspendĕre; interrupt, delay, differre; from office, loco (sub)-movēre. suspense, n. dubitatio; to be in —, in dubio esse. suspension, n. dilatio (delay); — of hostilities, indutiae.

sustain, v.tr. sustinēre. sustenance, n. alimentum, victus.

sutler, n. lixa.

swaddle, v.tr. fasciis involvĕre. swaddling-bands, n. fasciae.

swagger, v.intr. gloriari, se iactare.

swallow, n. hirundo.

swallow, v.tr. sorbēre; (de)vorare.

swamp, n. palus; —s, palustria, -ium. v.tr. (de)mergĕre, immergĕre. swampy, adj. paluster, and palustris.

swan, n. cygnus.

swarm, n. conventus, frequentia, — of bees, examen. v.intr. confluĕre; to — as bees, examinare.

swarthy, adj. fuscus, adustus.

sway, n. imperium, dominatio. v.tr. regĕre, imperare.

swear, v.tr. and intr. iurare, iusiurandum dare; to — falsely, periurare. swearing, n. exsecrationes, maledicta, -orum.

sweat, n. sudor. v.intr. and tr. sudare.

sweep, v.tr. verrĕre; v.intr. to — along, percurrĕre. sweepings, n. quisquiliae.

sweet, adj. dulcis, iucundus. Adv. dulce, iucunde; to taste, dulci esse sapore. sweeten, v.tr. dulcem reddĕre, dulcedo, iucunditas. sweetheart, n. deliciae. sweetness, n. dulcedo, iucunditas.

swell, v.intr. (in)tumescĕre, crescĕre; to be swollen, tumēre. v.tr. inflare, tumefacĕre; to — the sails, vela tendĕre. swelling, n. tumor, tuber.

swerve, v.intr. declinare de or a.

swift, adj. citus, velox, celer, pernix. Adv. cito, celeriter, perniciter. swiftness, n. celeritas, pernicitas.

swim, v.intr. nare, natare; to — over, tranare. swimmer, n. natator, nandi peritus. swimming, n. natatio, ars natandi.

swindle, v.tr. fraudare. swindler, n. fraudator. swindling, n. fraudatio.

swine, n. sus, porcus; — -herd, subulcus, suarius.

swing, *v.tr.* agitare, vibrare, iactare. *v.intr.* agitari, vibrari, iactari.

switch, *n.* virga. vimen.

swoon, *v.intr. and n. see* FAINT.

swoop, *n.* impetus. *v.intr. to — upon*, impetum in alqd facĕre.

sword, *n.* gladius, ensis (*in poetry*).

sycophant, *n.* delator, adulator. **sycophancy**, *n.* adulatio.

sylvan, *adj.* silvester.

symbol, *n.* symbolum, signum.

symmetry, *n.* symmetria, proportio ; — *in style*, concinnitas. **symmetrical**, *adj.* par, similis. *Adv.* pariter, similiter.

sympathy, *n.* consensus. **sympathetic**, *adj. and adv.* dolore *or* laetitiā alcis affectus. **sympathize**, *v.intr.* eadem sentire; miscerĕre.

symptom, *n.* signum, indicium.

syndicate, *n.* societas.

synonymous, *adj.* idem significans.

synopsis, *n. see* EPITOME.

system, *n.* ratio, disciplina. **systematic**, *adj.* ordinatus. *Adv.* ordinate, composite.

T

tabby, *adj.* maculosus.

table, *n.* mensa ; *at —*, apud mensam ; *fare*, cena, victus ; *a good —*, lauta cena ; *— of laws*, legum tabula. **table-land**, *n.* planities magna et edita. **tablet**, *n.* tabula, tabella.

tacit, *adj.* tacitus. *Adv.* tacite. **taciturn**, *adj.* taciturnus. **taciturnity**, *n.* taciturnitas.

tack, *n.* clavulus ; *plan*, consilium. *v.tr. see* NAIL ; *sew together*, consuĕre. *v.intr.* navem flectĕre. **tackle**, *n.* instrumenta. **tackling**, *n.* armamenta, -orum, *n.*

tact, *n.* ars. **tactics**, *n. pl.* res militaris. **tactician**, *n.* rei militaris perītus.

tail, *n.* cauda.

tailor, *n.* sartor.

taint, *v.tr.* corrumpĕre. *v.intr.* corrumpi, vitiari. *n.* contagio. **tainted**, *adj.* vitiatus.

take, *v.tr.* sumĕre, capĕre, accipĕre ; *to — anyone in custody*, alqm comprehendĕre ; *to — back again*, reducĕre ; *—n as a whole*, omnino ; *to — in good part*, in bonam partem accipĕre ; *to — it ill, amiss*, aegre ferre ; *to — away*, auferre ; *to — off*, detrahĕre ; *to — oneself off*, clam se subducĕre ; *fig. to select*, excerpĕre ex ; *to — up*, tollĕre. *v.intr. to — to books*, lit(t)eris studĕre. **taking**, *n.* expugnatio (*of a city*).

tale, *n.* narratio, historia, fabula, fabella (*short story*). **tale-bearer**, *n.* delator (*informer*). **tell**, *v.tr.* (e)narrare, referre (*report*), dicĕre ; posteris tradĕre, *to*

hand down. *v.intr. to have effect.* valēre ; *a telling speech*, oratio gravis.

teller, *n.* narrator, auctor rerum gestarum ; *one who numbers*, qui numerat.

talent, *n.* talentum ; *gift*, ingenium, indoles ; virtus (*cleverness*), facultas (*capability*). **talented**, *adj. a very — man*, homo eximii ingenii.

talk, *v.intr.* loqui ; *together*, colloqui inter se ; *to — over, see* DISCUSS. *n. familiar*, sermo, colloquium; *foolish —*, ineptiae. **talkative**, *adj.* loquax. *Adv.* loquaciter. **talkativeness**, *n.* loquacitas.

talker, *n.* (homo) loquax.

tall, *adj.* procērus ; *a — man*, homo magni corporis. **tallness**, *n.* procēritas. *or by adjs.*

tallow, *n.* sebum.

talon, *n.* unguis.

tambourine, *n.* tympanum.

tame, *adj.* cicur, mansuetus, mitis ; *to grow —*, mansuescĕre ; *fig.* demissus ; *of language, etc.*, ieiunus, frigidus. *Adv.* demisse, abiecte, frigide. *v.tr.* mansuefacĕre, domare ; frenare, coĕrcēre, delenire. **tameness**, *n. by adjs. and verbs.* **tamer**, *n.* domitor, *fem.* domitrix. **taming**, *n.* domitus.

tamper, *v.intr. see* MEDDLE.

tan, *v.tr. to — skins*, subigĕre, conficĕre ; (*of the sun*), colorare.

tangible, *adj.* tactilis, quod manu tenēre possumus.

tangle, *n.* nexus, nodus.

tantalize, *v.tr. see* TEASE.

tantamount, *adj. see* SAME.

tap, *v.intr.* lēviter ferire.

tap, *n.* ictus.

taper, *n.* cereus.

tapestry, *n.* tapete.

tar, *n.* pix.

tardy, *adj.* tardus, lentus. *Adv.* lente. **tardiness**, *n.* tarditas.

target, *n.* scopos.

tarnish, *v.tr.* inquinare. *v.intr.* inquinari.

tarry, *v.intr.* cunctari, morari.

tart, *n.* scriblita, crustulum.

tart, *adj.* acerbus. *Adv.* acerbe. **tartness**, *n.* acerbitas.

task, *n.* pensum, opus.

taste, *v.tr.* gustare. *v.intr.* sapere ; *pleasant*, iucunde sapere. *n.* sapor ; *subjectively*, elegantia (*refined —*), iudicium. **tasteful**, *adj.* elegans, venustus. *Adv.* eleganter. **tasteless**, *adj.* sine sapore; *fig.* inelegans. *Adv.* ineleganter. **tastelessness**, *n.* cui nullus sapor est ; *fig.* insulsitas.

tatter, *n.* pannus. **tattered**, *adj.* pannosus.

tattle, *v.tr.* garrire. **tattler**, *n.* homo garrulus.

tattoo, *v.tr.* notis compungĕre.

taunt, *v.tr.* conviciari. *n.* convicium.

taunting, adj. contumēliosus. Adv. contumēliose.

tavern, n. caupona. **tavern-keeper,** n. caupo.

tawdry, adj. speciosior quam decet.

tax, n. vectigal, tributum. v.tr. tributum or vectigal imponĕre. **taxable,** adj. vectigalis. **tax-gatherer,** n. vectigalium exactor.

teach, v.tr. (e)docēre. **teachable,** adj. docilis. **teachableness,** n. docilitas. **teacher,** n. doctor, magister. **teaching,** n. doctrina, disciplina.

team, n. iugum.

tear, n. lacrima, flētus (weeping). **tearful,** adj. lacrimans. Adv. flebiliter, multis cum lacrimis. **tearless,** adj. siccus (e.g. eyes), sine lacrimis.

tear, v.tr. (di)scindere, (di)lacerare, vellĕre, divellĕre ; to be torn by passion, etc., distrahi ; to — down, rescindĕre ; to — open, resignare (a letter).

tease, v.tr. fatigare, vexare.

technical, adj. a — term, artis vocabulum.

tedious, adj. longus, molestus, lentus ; not to be —, ne longus sim. Adv. moleste, lente. **tediousness,** n. molestia, taedium.

teem, v.intr. turgēre (to swell) ; to begin to —, turgescĕre ; plenus esse. **teeming,** adj. see FRUITFUL.

tell, v.tr. see under TALE.

temerity, n. temeritas.

temper, v.tr. temperare ; miscēre. n. ingenium, natura, animus ; anger, iracundia ; to be in a —, irasci. **temperament,** n. temperatio ; see DISPOSITION. **temperance,** n. continentia, temperantia, moderatio. **temperate,** adj. temperans, continens, moderatus, sobrius ; of climate, temperatus. Adv. temperanter, continenter, frugaliter. **temperateness,** n. temperantia. **temperature,** n. by caelum ; mild —, temperatio, temperies. **tempered,** adj. good- —, mitis ; ill- —, morosus.

tempest, n. tempestas, procella. **tempestuous,** adj. turbidus, turbulentus, violentus, vehemens. Adv. turbulente, violenter, vehementer. **tempestuousness,** n. violentia ; of manners, vehementia.

temple, n. aedes sacra, templum, delubrum.

temples, n. (of the head) tempora, -um.

temporal, adj. externus, humanus ; — affairs, res externae ; opposed to "spiritual," profanus.

temporary, adj. by ad tempus. **temporarily,** adv. ad tempus.

tempt, v.tr. (at)tentare, so(l)licitare, pellicĕre, inducĕre. **temptation,** n. tentatio, so(l)licitatio, illecebrae (allure-

ments) ; to lead into —, in discrimen adducĕre. **tempter,** n. tentator.

ten, adj. decem ; deni (— each, — at once) ; containing —, denarius ; — o'clock, hora quarta ; — times, decie(n)s.

tenable, adj. docimus.

tenacious, adj. tenam. Adv. tenaciter. **tenaciousness, tenacity,** n. tenacitas.

tenant, n. conductor, incola, habitator. **tend,** v.tr. curare, colĕre.

tend, v.intr. tendĕre. **tendency,** n. inclinatio, studium. **tender,** v.tr. see OFFER.

tender, adj. tener ; misericors. Adv molliter ; indulgenter. **tenderness,** n. teneritas; amor.

tendon, n. nervus.

tendril, n. clavicula (o a vine), viticula. **tenement,** n. see HOUSE.

tenet, n. praeceptum ; the —s, disciplina.

tenor, n. tenor, sententia (meaning).

tense, n. tempus.

tension, n. intentio.

tent, n. tabernaculum ; general's — praetorium.

tenterhooks, n. to be on —, ex(s)pectatione angi.

tenure, n. possessio or possidēre.

tepid, adj. tepidus; to be —, tepēre; to make —, tepefacĕre. Adv. tepide.

term, n. limited time, dies, e.g. to fix a —, diem statuĕre; Gram., see WORD; to be on good —s with anyone, alcis familiaritate uti. **terminate,** v.intr. finiri, terminari. **termination,** n. finis.

terrace, n. ambulatio.

terrestrial, adj. ad terram pertinens, terrestris.

terrible, adj. terribilis, atrox, immanis, dirus. Adv. atrociter, foede. **terrific,** adj. see TERRIBLE. **terrify,** v.tr. alqm (per)terrēre. **terror,** n. terror ; metus.

territory, n. ager, regio.

terse, adj. e.g. style, by pressus, brevis. Adv. presse, breviter. **terseness,** n. brevitas.

tertian, n. (febris) tertiana.

tessellated, adj. tessellatus.

test, n. see TRIAL. v.tr. tentare, experiri.

testament, n. testamentum (will). **testator,** n. testator. **testatrix,** n. testatrix. **testify,** v.tr. testari. **testimonial,** n see CERTIFICATE. **testimony,** n. testimonium.

testy, adj. morosus.

tether, v.tr. and n. see BIND.

tetrarch, n. tetrarcha, m.

text, n. verba, -orum.

textile, adj. textilis.

than, conj. quam ; or by the ablat.

thank, v.tr. gratias alci agĕre ; heartily, maximas gratias agĕre ; thank you, or no, — you ! benigne (dicis) ! **thankful,** adj. gratus. Adv. grato animo.

thankfulness, *n.* animus gratus. thankless, *adj.* ingratus. *Adv.* ingrate.

thanks, *n.* gratiae ; *to return* — *for,* gratias agĕre (quod) ; — *God !* est dis gratia ! thanksgiving, *n.* supplicatio.

thankworthy, *adj.* gratiā dignus. gratus.

that, *demonstr. pron.* ille, illa, illud, iste, ista, istud ; alter (*the other of two*) ; *such a one, etc.,* is, ea, id ; *at* — *time,* id temporis. *rel. pron.* qui, quae, quod. *conj.* quod ut; *acc. and infin.*

thatch, *n.* stramentum. thatched, *adj.* — *house,* casa stramento tecta.

thaw, *v.tr.* (dis)solvĕre. *v.intr.* (dis)solvi. *n. use verb.*

the, — *more, etc.,* . . . — *more, etc.,* quo . . . eo. quanto . . . tanto.

theatre, *n.* theatrum. theatrical, *adj.* scaenicus. *Adv.* more histrionum.

theft, *n.* furtum. thief, *n.* fur. thieve, *v.intr. see* STEAL. thievish, *adj.* furax.

their, *poss. pron.* suus (*referring to the subject*), eorum, illorum. theirs, *poss. pron.* suus or illorum.

them, *pers. pron.* eos, illos, ipsos ; *to them,* eis.

theme, *n.* propositum, argumentum.

then, *adv.* tunc, tum.

thence, *adv.* illinc. thenceforth, *adv.* inde.

theory, *n.* ratio, doctrina, ars, praecepta, -orum. theoretical, *adj.* — *knowledge,* ratio. *Adv.* ratione.

there, *adv.* ibi ; *to be* —, adesse ; *thither,* illuc. thereabouts, *adv.* prope (*near*), fere (*nearly*). thereafter, thereupon, *adv.* deinde, statim.

therefore, *adv.* igitur, itaque. therein, *adv.* in eo, in eis (iis), *etc.*

they, *pers. pron.* ii, illi.

thick, *adj.* crassus, spissus (*of darkness, etc.*). *Adv.* dense, spisse. thicken, *v.tr.* densare. *v.intr.* densari, spissari, concrescĕre, *to* curdle. thicket, *n.* dumētum. thickness, *n.* crassitudo. spissitas.

thief, *n. see* THEFT.

thigh, *n.* femur.

thin, *adj.* tenuis, macer, dilutus (*e.g. wine*). *v.tr.* attenuare. *Adv.* tenuiter, graciliter, rare. thinness, *n.* tenuitas, gracilitas, raritas, macies.

thine, *pron.* tuus.

thing, *n.* res, negotium ; —*s,* res ; *by adj. n.pl.* (*e.g. wonderful* —*s,* mira).

think, *v.intr. and tr.* cogitare, intellegĕre ; — *about,* de alqa re cogitare ; *to suppose,* putare, censēre, credĕre ; *to judge,* iudicare, sentire. thought, *n.* cogitatio, cogitatum, mens, sententia (*opinion*), animus (*mind*), consilium. thoughtful, *adj.* in cogitatione defixus, sapiens. *Adv.* sapienter, prudenter. thoughtless, *adj.* neglegens, imprudens, temerarius (*rash*). *Adv.* neglegenter, temere. thoughtlessness, *n.* neglegentia.

third, *adj. see* THREE.

thirst, *n.* sitis. *v.intr.* sitire; *fig. to* — *after,* sitire alqd. thirsty, *adj.* sitiens. *Adv.* sitienter (*fig.*).

thirteen, *adj.* tredecim ; — *times,* tredecie(n)s. thirteenth, *adj.* tertius decimus. thirty, *adj.* triginta ; — *each,* triceni ; — *times,* tricie(n)s. thirtieth, *adj.* trigesimus.

this, *dem. pron.* hic, haec, hoc (*or* qui, quae, quod *at the beginning of a new sentence*) ; *on* — *side,* cis, citra ; *what is on* — *side,* citerior.

thistle, *n.* carduus.

thither, *adv.* eo, in eum locum ; *hither and* —, huc et (atque) illuc.

thong, *n.* lorum.

thorn, *n.* spina, sentis, vepres (— *bush*) ; dumetum. thorny, *adj.* spinosus (*lit., fig.*); arduus.

thorough, *adj. see* COMPLETE. *Adv.* omnino, plane. thoroughbred, *adj.* generosus.

thoroughfare, *n. by* transitus, via, *or by* transire.

thou, *pers. pron.* tu, tute (*emphatic*).

though, *conj. see* ALTHOUGH.

thought, *n. see under* THINK.

thousand, *adj.* mille ; mil(l)ia, -ium, *pl. of* mille ; *a* — *times,* mil(l)ie(n)s. thousandth, *adj.* mil(l)esimus.

thrash, *v.tr. to* — *corn,* frumentum deterēre. thrashing, *n.* tritura. thrashing-floor, *n.* area. thrashing-machine, *n.* tribulum.

thread, *n. lit.* filum, linum. threadbare, *adj* obsolētus ; tritus (*of topics, etc.*).

threat, *n.* denuntiatio. threaten, *v.tr.* minas iacĕre ; denuntiare ; *it* —*s to, etc.,* in eo est ut, *etc., or with part. fut. act.* ; *to be at hand* (im)minēre, instare. threatening, *adj.* minax, imminens (*e.g. war, danger*), praesens. *Adv.* mināciter.

three, *adj.* tres, tria ; — *hundred,* trecenti. threefold, triple, *adj.* triplex. thrice, *adj.* ter. third, *adj.* tertius. *Adv.* tertio. *n.* tertia pars ; *heir to a* — heres ex triente ; *two* —*s,* bes.

threshold, *n.* limen.

thrift, *n.* frugalitas. thrifty, *adj.* frugi, parcus. *Adv.* parce.

thrill, *v.tr.* commovēre. *v.intr.* — *with joy, etc.,* ex(s)ultare. thrilling, *adj.* mirus, horrendus.

thrive, *v.intr. by* crescĕre; vigēre, florēre.

throat, *n.* iugulum, guttur.

throb, *v.intr.* palpitare.

throne, *n.* solium, sedes, imperium (*fig.*).

throng, *n.* frequentia. *v.tr.* frequentare.

throstle, *n.* turdus.

throttle, *v.tr.* animam intercludĕre.

through, *prep.* per *with accus.* throughout, *prep. see* THROUGH ; *adv. see* ENTIRELY.

throw, *v.tr.* iacĕre, mittĕre, conicĕre.

n. iactus, missus. **thrower,** *n.* iaculator.

thrust, *v.tr. see* PUSH. *n.* ictus, plaga.

thumb, *n.* pollex.

thump, *n. see* BLOW. *v.tr. see* BEAT.

thunder, *n.* (coni)tonitrus, tonitru (*in*)tonare

thunderbolt, *n.* fulmen. **thunder-struck,** *adj.* obstupefactus.

thus, *adv.* ita, sic.

thwart, *v.tr. see* HINDER. *n.* transtrum.

thy, *pron.* tuus.

thyme, *n.* thymum.

ticket, *n.* tessera.

tickle, *v.tr* titillare.

tide, *n.* aestus (maritimus).

tidings, *n.* nuntius alcis rei.

tidy, *adj.* nitidus.

tie, *v.tr.* to — *a knot,* nodum facĕre ; *see* BIND.

tier, *n.* ordo, -inis.

tiger, *n.* tigris.

tight, *n.* strictus, a(d)strictus (*fitting* —), angustus ; — *rope,* funis contentus. **tighten,** *v.tr.* stringĕre, contendĕre. *Adv. and* **tightness,** *n. use adj.*

tile, *n.* tegula, tessera (*for paving*).

till, *prep.* ad, usque ad ; — *to-morrow,* in crastinum. *conj.* dum, donec, quoad ; *not* —, non prius quam.

till, *v.tr.* arare, colĕre. **tillage,** *n.* cultus, cultura. **tiller,** *n.* arator, agricola.

till, *n. money* —, arca. **tiller,** *n.* clavus.

tilt, *v.tr.* invertĕre.

timber, *n.* materia or materies.

time, *n.* tempus, dies, spatium, aetas, tempestas (*season*), saeculum (*a long* —, *a generation*), otium (*leisure*) ; *in our* —, nostrā memoriā ; *at the right* tempore ; *in ancient* —s, antiquitus ; *from the* — *when,* ex quo (tempore) ; *in good* —, *mature ; in the mean* —, interea, interim. **timely,** *adj.* maturus (*of fruits, etc.*), opportunus. *Adv.* mature, opportune. **time-server,** *n.* adulator.

timid, *adj.* timidus, verecundus (*bashful*), ignavus (*cowardly*). *Adv.* timide, verecunde. **timidity,** *n.* pavor. **timorous,** *adj. see* TIMID.

tin, *n.* plumbum album.

tinge, *v.tr.* imbuĕre, inficĕre.

tinder, *n.* fomes, -itis, *m.*

tingle, *v.intr.* tinnire.

tinkle, *v.intr.* tinnire, tinnire. **tinkling,** *n.* † tinnitus.

tinsel, *n. lit.* bractea (*metal leaf*) ; *fig.* species.

tip, *n.* cacumen, summa. *v.tr.* (prae)-acuĕre (*sharpen*), praefigĕre ; — *over,* invertere. **tiptoe,** *n.* in digitos erecti ; *fig.* (ex)spectatione, *etc.*) intentus.

tipsy, *adj.* temulentus. *Adv.* temulenter, *or by adj.*

tire, *v.tr.* (de)fatigare. *v.intr.* (de)-fatigari. **tired,** *adj.* defessus. **tiresome,** *adj.* molestus, lentus (*slow*).

tiring, *adj.* quod (de)fatigat, *or by* laboriosus.

tiro, *n.* tiro ; rudis et tiro.

tit-bit, *n.* cup(p)edia, -orum.

tithe, *n.* decuma. *v.tr.* decumas imponĕre

title, *n.* titulus, inscriptio (*in a book*), nomen ; *to give a book a* —, inscribĕre librum. **tilted,** *adj. by birth, etc.,* nobilis. **titular,** *adj. by nomine, opp. to* re.

to, *prep.* ad, in (*into*) ; *with names of towns and small islands* accus. *without* ad ; — *this or that place,* huc or illuc ; — *the temple of Vestae, Jupiter,* ad Vestae, Iovis ; — *the country,* — *home,* rus, domum ; *it properly the sign of the Latin dative* (mihi dedit librum, *he gave a book* — *me*) ; *in order to,* ut (or ne) *with subj.* ; ad diem solvĕre, *to pay* — *the day ;* — *a man,* ad unum. **to-day,** *n.* hodiernus dies. *Adv.* hodie. **to-morrow,** *n,* crastinus dies. *Adv.* cras.

toad, *n.* bufo ; — *stool,* fungus. **toady,** *n. and v.tr. see* FLATTER.

toast, *v.tr.* torrēre ; *drink health,* salutem alci propinare. *n.* panis tostus.

toe, *n.* (pedis) digitus.

together, *adv.* unā (cum), simul ; *all* —, cuncti.

toil, *n.* magnus labor. *v.intr. see* WORK. **toilsome,** *adj.* laboriosus. *Adv.* laboriose.

toilet, *n. to make one's* —, se vestire.

token, *n.* signum.

tolerable, *adj.* tolerabilis ; *middling,* modicus. *Adv.* mediocriter. **tolerate,** *v.tr.* tolerare, aequo animo ferre ; *to allow,* pati. **tolerance,** *n.* indulgentia.

toll, *n.* vectigal.

toll, *v.intr. and tr. by* sonare.

tomb, *n.* sepulc(h)rum. **tombstone,** *n.* lapis.

tome, *n.* liber.

tone, *n.* sonus, vox.

tongs, *n., the* — , forceps.

tongue, *n.* lingua.

too, *adv.* etiam, quoque, praeterea ; — *much,* nimium.

tool, *n. collective,* instrumentum.

tooth, *n.* dens ; — *ache,* dolor dentium.

top, *n.* summus *with noun* (*e.g.* summus mons) ; *a child's* —, turbo. *Adj.* summus (*highest*).

topic, *n.* argumentum.

topsy-turvy, *adv. to turn* —, omnia turbare et miscere.

torch, *n.* fax, taeda.

torment, *v.tr.* (ex)cruciare, torquĕre, vexare. *n.* cruciatus, tormentum. **tormentor,** *n. see* TORTURER ; vexator (*fig.*)

tornado, *n.* turbo.

torpedo, *n.* torpēdo (*the fish*).

torpid, *adj.* torpens (*lit. and fig.*).

torpor, *n.* torpor.

torrent, *n.* torrens ; — *of words,* flumen verborum.

torrid, *adj.* torridus.

tortoise, *n.* testudo.

torture, *n.* tormenta, -orum, *n.* cruciatus. *v.tr.* (ex)torquēre, (ex)cruciāre. **torturer**, *n.* tortor, carnifex.

toss, *v.tr.* iactare. *n.* iactus.

total, *adj.* totus, omnis. *Adv.* omnīno. *n.* summa. **totality**, *n.* summa *or by adj.* TOTAL.

totter, *v.intr.* labare.

touch, *v.tr.* tangĕre ; *fig.* alqm dolore, *etc.,* afficĕre. *n.* tactio, tactus. **touching**, *prep.* de. **touchy**, *adj.* iracundus.

tough, *adj.* lentus. **toughness**, *n.* lentitia.

tour, *n. iter.* **tourist**, *n. see* TRAVELLER.

tow, *n.* stuppa.

tow, *v.tr.* trahĕre.

toward, *prep.* ad, in, versus (*always after its noun*) *with accus.* ; adversus ; *to go —* anyone, obviam ire alci ; *inclinations, etc.,* — *a person,* erga ; *genit.* (caritas patriae, *love — one's native land*) ; ad meridiem, — *midday ;* sub vesperum, — *evening.*

towel, *n.* mantēle (mantile).

tower, *n.* turris ; *fig.* arx *or* praesidium. *v.intr.* exstare ; *to — over,* alci loco imminēre.

town, *n.* urbs, oppidum, municipium ; *—'s-people,* oppidani ; *— hall,* curia. *Adj.* urbanus.

toy, *n. trifles,* nugae.

trace, *n.* vestigium, indicium (*sign*), significatio (*indication*). *v.tr. to draw,* delineare, adumbrare ; *to follow by footsteps,* persequi, indagare. **tracer**, *n.* investigator, indagator. **tracing**, *n.* investigatio, indagatio. **track**, *n. see* PATH : TRACE. *v.tr* vestigia persequi.

tract, *n.* spatium, tractus ; *treatise,* libellus. **tractable**, *adj.* docilis, facilis. *Adv.* obedienter. **tractableness**, *n.* obedientia, facilitas.

trade, *n. see* COMMERCE ; mercatura ; ars, artificium. *v.tr.* mercaturam facĕre, mercari, negotiari. **tradesman**, **trader**, *n.* caupo; *see* MERCHANT.

tradition, *n.* traditio, memoria. **traditional**, **traditionary**, *adj.* posteris traditus.

traffic, *n.* commercium.

tragedy, *n.* tragoedia ; *fig.* casus. **tragedian**, *n.* actor, tragoedus, tragicus actor. **tragic**, *adj.* tragicus ; *fig.* tristis, atrox. *Adv.* tragice, miserabiliter, atrociter.

tain, *v.tr. educate,* (e)docēre, instituĕre ; *soldiers,* exercēre. *n. of a gown,* syrma (*gown with a train*) *or by* quod verrit terram; *procession,* pompa ; *series,* ordo, series. **trainer**, *n. of horses,* equorum domitor; *of athletes,* magister. **training**, *n.* disciplina, exercitatio.

trait, *n.* linea.

traitor, *n.* proditor, maiestatis reus. **traitorous**, *adj. see* TREACHEROUS.

tramp, *v.intr. see* WALK. *n.* iter.

trample, *v.tr. and intr.* (pedibus) (con)-culcare; *fig.* opprimĕre.

trance, *n.* secessus mentis et animi a corpore.

tranquil, *adj.* tranquillus. **tranquillity**, *n.* tranquillitas. **tranquillize**, *v.tr.* tranquillare.

transact, *v.tr. business,* rem gerĕre, transigĕre. **transaction**, *n.* res, negotium.

transcend, *v.tr.* praestare, excellĕre. **transcendent**, *adj.* praestans, eximius.

transcribe, *v.tr.* transcribĕre. **transcript**, *n.* exemplum.

transfer, *v.tr.* tra(ns)ducĕre, transportare, transferre in; *to make over,* (con)cedĕre. *n.* translatio, mancipium (*of property*). **transference**, *n.* tra(ns)latio.

transfigure, *v.tr.* (com)mutare.

transfix, *v.tr.* (con)fodĕre.

transform, *v.tr.* (com)mutare.

transfuse, *v.tr.* transfundĕre.

transgress, *v.tr.* violare. *v.intr.* alqd contra leges facĕre. **transgression**, *violatio,* peccatum. **transgressor**, *n.* violator.

transient, *adj.* brevis, fugax. **transit**, *n* transitus. **transition**, *n.* transitus.

transitive, *adj. verb.* verbum transitivum.

translate, *v.tr.* (con)vertĕre, reddĕre. **translator**, *n.* interpres.

translucent, *adj.* pellucidus.

transmit, *v tr.* mittĕre. **transmission**, *n.* missio, *or by verb.*

transmute, *v.tr. see* CHANGE.

transparent, *adj.* pellucidus: manifestus; *to be —,* pellucēre. *Adv.* manifeste. **transparency**, *n.* perspicuitas.

transpire, *v.intr.* exhalari ; emanare, percrebrescĕre.

transplant, *v.tr.* transferre.

transport, *v.tr.* transferre ; *fig. to be — ed,* gaudēre. *n.* navis oneraria.

transpose, *v.tr.* transmutare.

transverse, *adj.* transversus. *Adv.* transverse.

trap, *n.* muscipulum (*mouse- —*) ; *see* SNARE. *v.tr.* irretire. **trappings**, *n.* ornatus.

trash, *n.* quisquiliae ; nugae. **trashy**, *adj. see* WORTHLESS.

travail, *v.tr.* parturire.

travel, *v.tr.* iter facĕre. *n.* iter. **traveller**, *n.* viator, vector.

traverse, *v.tr.* pervagari.

tray, *n.* ferculum.

treacherous, *adj.* perfidus. *Adv.* perfidiose. **treachery**, *n.* perfidia.

tread, *v.intr.* ingredi. *v.tr. to — upon,* calca e. *n.* (in)gressus.

treason, *n. to commit —,* maiestatem minuĕre.

treasure, n. gaza, divitiae. v.tr. condĕre.
treasure-house, n. thesaurus. **treasurer,** n. praefectus aerarii. **treasury,** 2. aerarium.
treat, v.tr. curare ; disputare (discuss) ;
to behave towards anyone, to — anti ;
to — as an enemy, (in) hostium numero habĕre. v.intr. to — with, agere cum alqo. *to — delectatio, spectaculum.* **treatise,** n. disputatio, liber, libellus. **treatment,** n. tractatio, curatio ; kind —, humanitas ; cruel —, saevitia. **treaty,** n. pactum (contract), foedus ; according to the —, ex pacto ; to break a —, foedus violare.
treble, adj. see TRIPLE ; voice, vox acuta. v.tr. triplex facĕre.
tree, n. arbor.
tremble, v.intr. tremĕre, vacillare, horrēre ; to cause to —, tremefacĕre.
trembling, adj. tremens, tremulus. n. tremor ; without —, intrepide.
tremendous, adj. terribilis ; ingens, immanis. Adv. magnopere, maxime.
tremulous, adj. see TREMBLING.
trench, n. fossa. v.tr. fossam facĕre.
trencher, n. see PLATE.
trespass, v.intr. fines tramire; fig., see TRANSGRESS. **trespasser,** n. fig. violator.
tress, n. comae (= hair).
trial, n. tentatio, experimentum, conatus, (attempt) ; in law, iudicium : put on his —, accusare. **try,** v.tr. tentare, experiri, conari ; in law, to — a case, iudicare. **trying,** adj. gravis, molestus.
triangle, n. triangulum. **triangular,** adj. triangulus, triquetrus.
tribe, n. tribus ; gens, populus ; by tribes, tributim.
tribulation, n. miseria, res miserae.
tribunal, n. tribunal (platform) ; iudicium.
tribune, n. tribunus militum, tribunus plebis (of the people). **tribuneship,** n. tribunicia potestas.
tribute, n. tributum, vectigal. **tributary,** adj. vectigalis, tributarius. n. — of a river, (e.g. a — of the Rhone, flumen quod in Rhodanum influit).
trick, n. dolus, fraus, ars, artificium; all manner of —s, astutiae. v.tr. see DECEIVE. **trickery,** n. fallacia.
trickle, v.intr. manare, stillare.
trident, n. tridens.
trifle, n. res parva, res parvi momenti : —s, nugae ; to buy for a —, vili emĕre. v.intr. lascivire, nugari, alqd negligĕre.
trifler, n. nugator. **trifling,** adj. lēvis, parvus. n. lascivia, ineptiae.
trim, adj. see NEAT. v.tr. to — the hair, recidĕre ; arbores (am-)putare ; to — the sails, vela pandĕre. v.intr. in politics, consilia mutare. **trimming,** n. ornatus.
trio, n. tres, tria.

trip, v.intr. offendĕre ; to — along, celeriter ire. v.tr. supplantare alqm.
tripartite, adj. tripartitus (triper-).
tripe, n. omāsum.
triple, adj. triplex.
trinod n trjnus.
trireme, n. (navis) triremis.
trite, adj. communis, notus.
triumph, n. triumphus ; fig. victoria, ex(s)ultatio. v.intr. triumphare , fig. ex(s)ultare. **triumphal,** adj. triumphalis. **triumphant,** victor (fem. victrix); elatus.
triumvir, n. triumvir. **triumvirate,** n. triumviratus.
trivial, adj. by lēvis, parvus.
trochee, n. trochaeus.
troop, n. caterva, grex ; —s, copiae.
trooper, n. eques.
trophy, n. tropaeum.
tropic, n. the —s, regiones torridae.
troth, n. fides ; to plight —, fidem alci dare.
troubadour, n. citharoedus.
trouble, v.tr. agitare ; perturbare, vexare; fatigare. n. perturbatio, labor, molestia, incommodum ; to take — over anything, alci rei operam dare ; with great —, vix ; without —, sine negotio. **troubler,** n. turbator, or by verb. **troublesome,** adj. molestus, gravis, laboriosus, difficilis.
trough, n. alveus.
truce, n. indutiae.
truckle, v.intr. alci assentari.
trudge, v.intr. see WALK.
true, adv. vērus ; sincērus, fidēlis ; in answers, — ! certe. Adv. vere, sincere, sane. **true-born, true-bred,** adj. verus et sincerus. **true-hearted,** adj. fidēlis. **true-heartedness,** n. fidēlitas. **truth,** n. vēritas ; to speak —, verum : in —, vero. **truthful,** adj. verus, verax. **truthfulness,** n. vēritas.
trump up, v. r. fingĕre.
trumpery, n. see TRASH.
trumpet, n. tuba, cornu ; to sound the — for retreat, receptui canĕre v.tr. fig. bucinator esse alcis rei, praedicare. **trumpeter,** n. bucinator.
truncheon, n. scipio; fustis.
trunk, n. of a tree, truncus ; of the body, truncus, corpus ; chest, arca ; of an elephant, manus.
trust, n. fiducia, fides ; in oneself, fidentia ; thing —ed, quod creditum est. v.intr. (con)fidĕre, credĕre ; not to —, diffidĕre. v.tr. (con)credĕre, committĕre. **trustee,** n. custos, procurator. **trustworthiness,** n. fides. **trustworthy,** adj. constans, fidēlis.
tub, n. dolium, labrum.
tube, n. tubus.
tuck, v.tr. to — up a garment, succingĕre.
tuft, n. e.g. of hair, crinis (or pl crines)

of feathers, crista. **tufted,** *adj.*
cristatus.

tug, *v.tr.* trahĕre. *n.* navis quae aliam
navem trahit.

tuition, *n. see* INSTRUCTION.

tumble, *v.intr.* se volutare. *v.tr.* omnio
perturbare.

tumid, *adj.* timidus, inflatus.

tumour, *n.* tumor, tuber.

tumult, *n.* timultus, strepitus ; motus.
tumultuous, *adj.* turbulentus. *Adv.*
turbulente.

tumulus, *n.* tumulus.

tun, *n.* dolium.

tune, *n.* cantus, carmen ; *to be in* —,
concentum servare ; *out of* —, absonus.
tuneful, *adj.* canōrus, musicus.

tunic, *n.* tunica.

tunnel, *n.* cuniculus. *v.tr.* cuniculum
facĕre.

turban, *n.* mitra.

turbid, *adj.* turbidus.

turbot, *n.* rhombus.

turbulence, *n.* tumultus. **turbulent,**
adj., turbulentus.

tureen, *n.* patina.

turf, *n.* caespes.

turgid, *adj.* tumidus.

turmoil, *n.* turba.

turn, *v.tr. to* — *a wheel, etc.* (con)tor-
quĕre, circumagĕre; vertĕre (*e.g.* navem),
versare, flectĕre, retorquĕre (*back*) ; *to*
— *the mind to,* alqd animadvertĕre ; *to*
— *a coat,* vestem reficĕre ; *to* — *away,*
dimittĕre. *v.intr.* se (con)vertĕre, (con)-
verti ; *from side to side,* se versare ; *to*
— *away,* se avertĕre ; *to* — *back,*
redire ; *to* — *out well (of a thing),* bene
evenire ; *of leaves,* colorem mutari. *n.*
things take a bad —, res male vertit ;
it is your —, nunc tuae sunt partes.
turn against, *v.tr.* alqm alienare.
v.intr. alienari. **turn over,** *v.tr. a*
book, librum evolvĕre ; *to* — *a new leaf.*
mores emendare. **turnkey,** *n.* ianitor
carceris.

turnip, *n.* rapum.

turpitude, *n.* turpitudo.

turret, *n.* turricula.

turtle, *n.* testudo ; — *-dove,* turtur.

tusk, *n.* dens.

tutelage, *n.* tutēla. **tutor,** *n.* magister,
praeceptor.

twang, *v.intr.* sonare. *n.* sonus.

tweak, *v.tr.* vellĕre, vellicare.

twelve, *adj.* duodecim, duodeni —
each). **twelfth,** *adj.* duodecimus.
twelvemonth, *n.* annus.

twenty, *adj.* viginti, viceni (— *each*).
twentieth, *adj.* vicēsimus.

twig, *n.* virgo, surculus.

twilight, *n.* crepusculum.

twin, *n. and adj.* geminus.

twine, *v.tr.* flectĕre. *v.intr.* implecti. *n.*
linum.

twinge, *v.tr.* urĕre. *n.* dolor.

twinkle, *v.intr.* † coruscare, fulgĕre.
twinkling, *n.* fulgor ; *in the* — *of an*
eye, temporis puncto.

twirl, *v.tr.* versare.

twist, *v.tr.* (in)torquĕre. *v.intr.* se torquĕre.

twit, *v.tr.* alqd alci obicĕre.

two, *adj.* duo, bini (— *each*) ; —*fdd,*
duplex. **twice,** *adv.* bis.

type, *n.* exemplum ; *symbol,* figura.
typify, *v.tr. see* REPRESENT.

tyrant, *n.* tyrannus crudēlis. **tyrannical,**
adj. crudēlis. *Adv.* tyrannice. **tyrannize,**
v.tr. vexare. **tyranny,** *n.* tyrannis,
dominatio.

tyro, *n. see* TIRO.

U

ubiquitous, *adj.* omnibus locis praesens.

udder, *n.* uber, -ēris, *n.*

ugly, *adj.* dēfornis, foedus. *Adv.* dē-
formiter, foede. **ugliness,** *n.* dēformitas,
foeditas.

ulcer, *n.* ulcus. **ulcerate,** *v.intr.* suppurare.

ulterior, *adj.* ulterior.

ultimate, *adj.* extrēmus, ultimus. *Adv.*
ad extrēmum.

umbrage, *n. see* OFFENCE. **umbrageous,**
adj. see SHADY.

umpire, *n.* arbiter.

un-, *prefix ; by the prefix* in, *or by* non,
or by sine.

unabashed, *adj.* constans ; impudens.

unabated, *adj.* integer (— *whole*).

unable, *adj.* non posse, nequire.

unacceptable, *adj.* ingratus.

unaccompanied, *adj.* solus, sine comi-
tatu.

unaccomplished, *adj.* imperfectus.

unaccustomed, *adj.* insuetus, insolitus,
inexpertus.

unacquainted, *adj.* (alcis rei) ignarus,
imperitus, inscius.

unadorned, *adj.* inornatus, incomptus,
simplex.

unadulterated, *adj.* sincērus, integer,
incorruptus.

unadvisable, *adj.* inutilis, temerarius.

unadvised, *adj.* imprudens, inconsultus. *Adv.* imprudenter, inconsulte.

unaffected, *adj.* simplex, candidus,
inaffectatus ; *not moved,* immotus ;
to remain —, *etc.,* non affici. *Adv.*
simpliciter, sine fuco ac fallaciis.

unaffrighted, *adj.* interritus.

unaided, *adj.* sine auxilio.

unalienable, *adj.* qui alienari non potest.

unalleviated, *adj.* non mītigatus.

unalloyed, *adj.* purus (*lit.*), sincērus
(*fig.*).

unaltered, *adj.* immutatus, integer.

unambitious, *adj.* modestus, *or* qui honores non petit.

unamiable, *adj.* difficilis.

unanimity, *n.* consensio, concordia.

unanimous, *adj.* concors, unanimus. *Adv.* una voce, una mente.

unanswerable, *adj.* qui refelli non potest.

unanswered, *adj.* to leave —, non respondere.

unappalled, *adj.* interritus.

unappeased, *adj.* non satiatus.

unapproachable, *adj. of places,* invius ; *of persons,* ad quem aditus difficilis est.

unarmed, *adj.* inermis, nudus.

unasked, *adj.* (sua) sponte, ultro.

unassuming, *adj.* modestus.

unattainable, *adj.* quod attingi non potest.

unattempted, *adj. to leave nothing —,* omnia experiri.

unattended, *adj.* sine comitibus.

unauthentic, *adj.* incertus (*e.g.* rumor).

unauthorized, *adj.* illicitus ; *to be — (to do a thing),* faciendi alqd ius non habere.

unavailable, *adj.* inutilis. **unavailing,** *adj.* irritus, vanus.

unavenged, *adj.* inultus.

unavoidable, *adj.* quod evitari non potest.

unavowed, *adj. see* SECRET.

unaware, *adj.* inscius, nescius.

unaware, unawares, *adv.* inopinatus, inopinans, improvisus, subitus, praeter opinionem, improviso.

unawed, *adj.* interritus.

unbar, *v.tr.* reserare.

unbearable, *adj. see* INTOLERABLE.

unbeaten, *adj. e.g.* path, non tritus.

unbecoming, *adj. see* INDECOROUS.

unbeliever, *n.* qui non credit. **unbelieving,** *adj.* incredulus.

unbend, *v.tr.* remittere ; (re)laxare.

unbewailed, *adj.* † infletus.

unbiased, *adj.* simplex.

unbidden, *adj.* invocatus.

unbind, *v.tr.* (dis)solvere, laxare.

unblemished, *adj.* purus, integer.

unborn, *adj.* nondum natus.

unborrowed, *adj. see* ORIGINAL.

unbosom, *v.tr.* se alci patefacere.

unbought, *adj.* non emptus.

unbound, *adj. of hair,* passus.

unbounded, *adj.* infinitus ; *fig. see* IMMODERATE.

unbribed, *adj.* incorruptus.

unbridled, *adj.* effrenatus.

unbroken, *adj.* integer ; *of horses,* indomitus.

unbrotherly, *adj.* parum fraternus.

unbuckle, *v.tr.* solvere.

unburden, *v.tr.* exonerare.

unburied, *adj.* inhumatus.

unburnt, *adj.* crudus (*of bricks*).

uncalled, *adj.* invocatus.

uncared, *adj.* — *for,* neglectus.

unceasing, *adj.* perpetuus, assiduus.

unceremonious, *adj.* simplex, parum comis. *Adv.* simpliciter, inurbane.

uncertain, *adj.* incertus, dubius, anceps ; *to be —,* dubitare. *Adv.* incerte. **uncertainty,** *n. use* UNCERTAIN.

unchain, *v.tr.* vincula solvere.

unchangeable, *adj.* constans. *Adv.* constanter. **unchangeableness,** *n.* constantia. **unchanged,** *adj.* stabilis.

uncharitable, *adj.* inhumanus. *Adv.* inhumane. **uncharitableness,** *n.* inhumanitas.

unchaste, *adj.* impurus, libidinosus.

unchecked, *adj.* liber.

uncivil, *adj. see* IMPOLITE. **uncivilized,** *adj.* rudis, barbarus.

unclasp, *v.tr.* refibulare.

uncle, *n.* patruus, avunculus.

unclean, *adj. see* DIRTY, UNCHASTE.

unclouded, *adj.* serenus (*lit.* and *fig.*).

uncoil, *v.tr.* evolvere.

uncoined, *adj.* infectus.

uncoloured, *adj.* purus : *fig.* sine fuco ac fallaciis.

uncombed, *adj.* horridus, in com(p)tus.

uncomfortable, *adj.* molestus, incommodus. *Adv.* incommode.

uncommanded, *adj.* iniussus, sponte (sua).

uncommissioned, *adj. an — officer,* succenturio.

uncommon, *adj.* rarus, singularis. *Adv.* raro.

uncommunicative, *adj. see* SILENT.

uncomplaining, *adj.* patiens.

uncompleted, *adj.* imperfectus.

unconcerned, *adj.* securus ; *to be — about,* neglegere.

unconditional, *adj.* simplex, absolutus, purus. *Adv.* simpliciter, absolute.

uncongenial, *adj. see* UNPLEASANT.

unconnected, *adj. see* SEPARATE.

unconquerable, *adj. see* INVINCIBLE.

unconquered, *adj.* invictus.

unconscious, *adj.* sensu carens ; *ignorant,* ignarus.

unconsecrated, *adj.* non consecratus, profanus.

unconsidered, *adj.* neglectus ; *to leave nothing —,* omnia diligenter circumspicere.

unconstitutional, *adj.* quod contra legem fit.

unconstrained, *adj.* liber.

uncontaminated, *adj.* in(con)taminatus.

uncontrollable, *adj.* impotens, effrenatus. **uncontrolled,** *adj.* liber.

uncooked, *adj.* crudus, incoctus.

uncorrupt, *adj.* incorruptus.

uncourteous, *adj.* inurbanus.

uncouth, *adj.* incultus, rusticus. **uncouthness,** *n.* inhumanitas.

uncover, *v.tr.* detegere, aperire; *the head,* caput aperire.

uncultivated, *adj. of soil,* incultus, vastus; *fig.* rudis.

uncurbed, *adj. see* UNBRIDLED.

uncut, *adj* intonsus, integer (*whole*).

undamaged, *adj.* inviolatus, integer.

undaunted, *adj.* intrepidus.

undecided, *adj.* nondum diiudicatus, incertus, anceps.

undefended, *adj.* indefensus, nudus.

undefiled, *adj. see* UNBLEMISHED.

undefined, *adj.* infinitus.

undeniable, *adj.* evidens. *Adv.* certo, sine dubio.

under, *prep. expressing rest,* sub *with* ablat. *; with verbs of motion,* sub *with* accus.; *adv. and prep.* subter, infra ; — the shade, in umbra ; — the leadership of Hannibal, ablat. abs. Hannibale duce ; — seven years old, nondum septem annos natus ; — these circumstances, quae cum ita sint ; — sail, passis velis ; to be — age, haud sui iuris esse.

underdone, *adj.* semicoctus.

under-garment, *n.* tunica.

undergo, *v.tr.* alqd subire, pati ; to — punishment, poenas dare *or* pendere.

underground, *adj. see* SUBTERRANEOUS.

undergrowth, *n.* virgulta, -orum.

underhand, *adj.* occultus, furtivus, clandestinus.

undermine, *v.tr.* (cuniculis) subruere ; labefacere.

undermost, *adj.* infimus.

underneath, *adv.* subter, infra.

underrate, *v.tr.* minoris aestimare.

undersell, *v.tr.* minoris (quam ceteri) vendere.

undersigned, *adj.* the —, qui nomen subscripsit.

understand, *v.tr.* accipere, intellegere ; to — Latin, Latine scire. **understanding,** *n.* mens.

undertake, *v.tr.* incipere, suscipere.

undertaker, *n. of funerals,* libitinarius.

undertaking, *n.* inceptum, opus.

undervalue, *v.tr.* parvi aestimare, contemnere.

underwood, *n.* virgulta, -orum.

undeserved, *adj.* immeritus, indignus. *Adv.* immerito. **undeserving,** *adj.* immerens.

undesigned, *adj.* fortuitus. *Adv.* casu, imprudenter. **undesigning,** *adj.* simplex.

undesirable, *adj. see* WORTHLESS.

undetected, *adj.* secretus.

undeveloped, *adj.* immaturus.

undigested, *adj. of food,* crudus; *of plans, etc.,* imperfectus.

undiminished, *adj.* integer.

undiscerning, *adj.* hebes.

undisciplined, *adj.* inexercitatus, rudis.

undisguised, *adj.* sincerus. *Adv.* sincere.

undisturbed, *adj.* otiosus ; to leave anyone —, alqm non vexare.

undivided, *adj.* indivisus, communis.

undo, *v.tr.* a knot, etc., (dis)solvere,

expedire ; see RUIN. **undone.** *adj.* infectus; ruined, perditus.

undoubted, *adj.* non dubius, certus *Adv.* sine dubio.

undress, *v.tr.* exuere alqm veste, nudare. *v.intr.* (de)ponere vestem. **undressed,** *adj.* non vestitus, nudus.

undue, *adj.* immodicus. *Adv.* nimis, nimium.

undutiful, *adj.* impius.

unearthly, *adj.* non mortalis.

uneasy, *adj.* so(l)licitus ; to be —, angi. **uneasiness,** *n.* (animi) perturbatio ; to feel —, perturbari. *Adv.* moleste, aegre.

unedifying, *adj.* frigidus, insulsus (of a discourse, etc.).

uneducated, *adj.* indoctus.

unembarrassed, *adj.* liber.

unemployed, *adj.* negotiis vacuus (free from business), otiosus.

unencumbered, *adj.* liber.

unenlightened, *adj.* indoctus.

unenterprising, *adj.* iners, socors.

unequal, *adj.* inaequalis, impar, dispar, dissimilis, dissonus (of sounds), iniquus (of a battle, etc.). *Adv.* inaequaliter, impariter, inique. **unequalled,** *adj.* summus.

unerring, *adj.* certus.

uneven, *adj.* iniquus, asper ; an — number, numerus impar. **unevenness,** *n.* iniquitas, asperitas.

unexamined, *adj.* inexploratus.

unexampled, *adj.* singularis, inauditus.

unexercised, *adj.* inexercitatus.

unexhausted, *adj. untired,* integer ; inexhaustus.

unexpected, *adj.* inopinatus, improvisus. *Adv.* (ex)improviso.

unexplored, *adj.* inexploratus.

unfading, *adj. e.g.* — laurels, gloria immortalis.

unfailing, *adj.* perpetuus, certus.

unfair, *adj.* iniquus, iniustus, immeritus. *Adv.* inique, iniuste. **unfairness,** *n.* iniquitas.

unfaithful, *adj.* infidelis, perfidiosus ; to be —, fidem fallere. *Adv.* infideliter. **unfaithfulness,** *n.* infidelitas, perfidia.

unfamiliar, *adj.* novus.

unfasten, *v.tr.* (re)solvere, (re)laxare, refigere.

unfathomable, *adj.* immensus, infinitus.

unfavourable, *adj.* iniquus, malignus, adversus, aversus, inopportunus (not suitable) ; of omens, infaustus ; — circumstances, res adversae. *Adv.* inique, maligne, male. **unfavourableness,** *n.* iniquitas, *or by adj.*

unfeathered, *adj.* implumis.

unfeeling, *adj.* durus, ferreus, inhumanus. *Adv.* inhumane, crudeliter.

unfeigned, *adj.* verus, sincerus. *Adv.* vere, sincere.

unfilial, *adj.* impius. *Adv.* impie.

unfit, *adj.* inutilis. **unfitness,** *n.* inutilitas.

unfix, *v.tr.* refigĕre. **unfixed,** *adj.* mobilis.

unfledged, *adj.* implumis.

unfold, *v.tr.* explicare.

unforeseen, *adj.* improvisus.

unforgiving, *adj.* implacabilis.

unforgotten, *adj.* *use* immortali memoriā retinēre.

unformed, *adj.* informis, nondum perfectus.

unfortified, *adj.* immunitus.

unfortunate, *adj.* *see* UNLUCKY.

unfounded, *adj.* vanus, fictus.

unfrequented, *adj.* desertus.

unfriendly, inimicus. **unfriendliness,** *n.* inimicitia.

unfruitful, *adj.* sterilis. **unfruitfulness,** *n.* sterilitas.

unfulfilled, *adj.* irritus, fallax.

unfurl, *v.tr. to — the sails,* vela pandĕre.

unfurnished, *adj. house,* domus nuda atque inanis.

ungainly, *adj.* inhabilis.

ungenerous, *adj.* illiberalis. *Adv.* illiberaliter.

ungentle, *adj.* asper. **ungentlemanlike, ungentlemanly,** *adj.* incultus, indecōrus.

ungird, *v.tr.* discingĕre.

ungodly, *adj.* *see* IMPIOUS.

ungovernable, *adj.* effrēnatus, ferox, impotens. *Adv.* effrēnate, impotenter.

ungoverned, *adj.* *see* UNBRIDLED.

ungraceful, *adj.* invenustus. **ungracious,** *adj.* iniquus, iratus. *Adv.* iniquo animo.

ungrateful, *adj.* ingratus.

ungrounded, *adj.* vanus, irritus.

ungrudging, *adj.* *see* LIBERAL.

unguarded, *adj.* sine custōdiā, indefensus ; *imprudent,* imprudens. *Adv.* imprudenter, temere.

unguent, *n.* unguentum.

unhallowed, *adj.* profanus.

unhappy, *adj.* infelix, miser ; *position,* res adversae. *Adv.* infeliciter, misere. **unhappiness,** *n.* miseria.

unharmed, *adj.* inviolatus, salvus.

unharness, *v.tr.* disiungĕre.

unhealthy, *adj.* infirmus, aeger ; *see* UNWHOLESOME.

unheard, *adj.* inauditus.

unheeded, *adj.* neglectus.

unheroic, *adj.* ignavus.

unhesitating, *adj.* strenuus. *Adv.* strenue.

unhewn, *adj.* rudis.

unhindered, *adj.* non impeditus, liber.

unhinge, *v.tr. fig. with the mind —d,* mente captus.

unhistorical, *adj.* commenticius, fictus.

unholy, *adj.* profanus ; *see* IMPIOUS.

unhonoured, *adj.* inhonoratus.

unhook, *v.tr.* refigĕre ; refibulare.

unhoped for, *adj.* inspĕratus ; praeter opīnionem.

unhurt, *adj.* integer, incolumis, incorruptus.

uniform, *adj.* unius generis, constans, aequabilis. *Adv.* constanter, aequabiliter. **uniformity,** *n.* aequabilitas, constantia.

unimpaired, *adj.* integer.

unimpeachable, *adj.* *see* TRUSTWORTHY.

unimportant, *adj.* lĕvis, nullius momenti.

uninformed, *adj.* indoctus.

uninhabited, *adj.* desertus.

uninitiated, *adj.* profanus ; *fig.* alcis rei expers.

uninjured, *adj.* incolumis, integer.

uninspired, *adj. of a speech,* iciunus, frigidus.

uninstructed, *adj.* indoctus.

unintelligible, *adj.* obscurus. *Adv.* obscure.

unintentional, *adj.* insciens. *Adv.* forte ; *I did it unintentionally,* insciens feci.

uninteresting, *adj.* ieiunus, frigidus.

unintermitting, *adj.* continuus.

uninterred, *adj.* inhumatus.

uninterrupted, *adj.* continuus, assiduus. *Adv.* continenter, uno tenore.

uninvestigated, *adj.* inexploratus.

uninvited, *adj.* invocatus.

union, *n.* *see under* UNITE.

unique, *adj.* unicus, singularis.

unison, *n. (in music)* concordia vocum.

unite, *v.tr.* (con)iungĕre, (con)sociare (*as companions*), miscēre. *v.intr.* se (con)iungĕre ; miscēri (*of two rivers, etc.*). **union,** *n.* (con)iunctio, consociatio ; *united body,* societas. **unity,** *n.* *see* AGREEMENT.

universal, *adj.* universus. *Adv.* in universum : — *beloved,* ab omnibus dilectus. **universe,** *n.* rerum natura.

unjust, *adj.* iniustus, iniquus. *Adv.* iniuste, inique. **unjustifiable,** *adj.* iniquissimus ; *see* INEXCUSABLE. *Adv.* iniquissimo modo.

unkept, *adj.* neglectus.

unkind, *adj.* inhumanus. *Adv.* inhumane. **unkindness,** *n.* inhumanitas.

unknowing, *adj.* inscius. **unknown,** *adj.* ignotus, incognitus, ignobilis (*of obscure birth*) ; *a person — to me,* nescio quis.

unlamented, *adj.* non deploratus.

unlawful, *adj.* qui contra leges est. *Adv.* contra legem.

unlearn, *v.tr.* dediscĕre. **unlearned,** *adj.* indoctus. *Adv.* indocte.

unless, *conj.* nisi ; si non.

unlettered, *adj.* *see* UNLEARNED.

unlike, *adj.* dissimilis. **unlikely,** *adj.* *see* IMPROBABLE.

unlimited, *adj.* infinitus.

unload, *v.tr.* exonerare, levare.

unlock, *v.tr.* recludĕre, reserare.

unlooked for, *adj.* inex(s)pectatus

unloose, *v.tr.* solvĕre (*a ship,* *etc.*) liberare.

unlucky, *adj.* infelix (*of omens*).

unmade, *adj.* non factus ; *of a bed,* non stratus.

unman, *v.tr.* enervare. **unmanned,** *adj.* perculsus.

unmanageable, *adj.* *see* UNGOVERNABLE.

unmanly, *adj.* viro indignus, mollis.

unmannerly, *adj.* rusticus, inurbanus.

unmarried, *adj.* caelebs; innupta.

unmask, *v.tr.* detegĕre.

unmatched, *adj.* unicus; egregius.

unmeaning, *adj.* inanis.

unmentioned, *adj. to leave* —, omittĕre.

unmerciful, *adj.* immitis, inhumanus.

unmindful, *adj.* immemor.

unmingled, unmixed, *adj.* merus, *fig.* simplex.

unmistakable, *adj.* *see* CLEAR, CERTAIN.

unmoor, *v.tr.* solvĕre.

unmoved, *adj.* immotus.

unnatural, *adj.* praeter naturam; impius, inhumanus. *Adv.* contra naturam.

unnavigable, *adj.* innavigabilis.

unnecessary, unneedful, *adj.* quod non opus est, vanus. *Adv.* praeter rem.

unnerve, *v.tr.* *see* UNMAN.

unnoticed, *adj.* *to leave* —, praetermittĕre.

unobserved, *adj.* *see* UNNOTICED.

unoccupied, *adj.* *see* UNEMPLOYED, UNINHABITED.

unoffending, *adj.* innocens.

unopened, *adj.* non apertus ; *of a letter,* lit(t)erae non resignatae.

unostentatious, *adj.* *see* MODEST.

unpack, *v.tr.* *see* UNLOAD.

unpaid, *adj.* non solutus.

unpalatable, *adj.* amarus.

unparalleled, *adj.* unicus, singularis.

unpardonable, *adj.* inexpiabilis.

unpatriotic, *adj.* patriae immemor.

unperceived, *adj.* *see* UNNOTICED.

unphilosophical, *adj.* philosophiae expers.

unpitying, *adj.* *see* UNMERCIFUL.

unpleasant, *adj.* molestus, ingratus. *Adv.* moleste, ingrate. **unpleasantness,** *n.* incommodum, molestia.

unpolished, *adj.* impolītus (*lit. and* *fig.*).

unpolluted, *adj.* impollutus, castus.

unpopular, *adj.* invidiosus ; *to become* —, in invidiam venire **unpopularity,** *n.* invidia.

unpractised, *adj.* inexercitatus.

unprecedented, *adj.* novus, inaudītus.

unprejudiced, *adj.* integer ac liber.

unpremeditated, *adj.* (verba, *etc.*) sine consilio dicta.

unprepared, *adj.* imparatus.

unprepossessing, *adj.* *see* DISAGREEABLE.

unpretending, *adj.* *see* MODEST.

unprincipled, *adj.* improbus, perditus.

unproductive, *adj.* *see* BARREN, USELESS.

unprofitable, *adj.* *see* UNPRODUCTIVE.

unpropitious, *adj.* *see* UNFAVOURABLE.

unprotected, *adj.* indefensus, nudus.

unprovided, *adj.* inops.

unprovoked, *adj.* non lacessitus, ultro

unpublished, *adj.* nondum editus.

unpunished, *adj.* impunītus, inultus.

unpurchased, *adj.* non emptus.

unquestionable, *adj.* non dubius, certus. *Adv.* sine dubio.

unravel, *v.tr.* retexĕre; *fig.* explicare.

unread, *adj.* non lectus.

unreasonable, *adj.* *it is* —, iniquum est. *Adv.* inique.

unreconciled, *adj.* non placatus.

unrefined, *adj.* crudus ; *fig. see* RUDE.

unrelenting, *adj.* *see* CRUEL.

unremitting, *adj.* continuus (*e.g.* labor).

unrepentant, *adj.* quem non poenitet alcis rei.

unresented, *adj.* inultus, impunītus.

unreserved, *adj.* liber; ; *see* FRANK.

unrest, *n.* inquies, -ētis.

unrestrained, *adj.* effrenatus.

unrevenged, *adj.* inultus.

unrewarded, *adj.* sine praemio.

unriddle, *v.tr.* solvĕre, explicare.

unrighteous, *adj.* improbus. *Adv.* improbe. **unrighteousness,** *n.* improbitas.

unripe, *adj.* immaturus. **unripeness,** *n.* immaturitas.

unrivalled, *adj.* eximius, praestans.

unrobe, *v.tr.* *see* UNDRESS.

unroof, *v.tr.* *see* UNCOVER.

unruffled, *adj.* *see* TRANQUIL.

unruly, *adj.* *see* UNGOVERNABLE.

unsafe, *adj.* intutus; *see* DANGEROUS.

unsaid, *adj.* indictus.

unsatisfactory, *adj.* non idoneus, malus. *Adv.* minus bene.

unseal, *v.tr.* resignare.

unseasonable, *adj.* intempestivus, importunus, immaturus. *Adv.* intempestive, importune.

unseemly, *adj.* *see* INDECOROUS.

unseen, *adj.* invisus.

unserviceable, *adj.* inutilis.

unsettle, *v.tr.* turbare; perturbare. **unsettled,** — *weather,* caelum varians : (*moral*), inconstans, incertus.

unshackled, *adj.* liber.

unshaved, *adj.* intonsus.

unsheathe, *v.tr.* gladium e vaginā educĕre.

unship, *v.tr.* exponĕre.

unshod, *adj.* pedibus nudis.

unshorn, *adj.* intonsus.

unshrinking, *adj.* intrepidus.

unsightly, *adj.* *see* UGLY.

unskilful, unskilled, *adj.* imperitus, rudis. *Adv.* inepte, imperite. **unskilfulness,** *n.* imperitia.

unsolicited, *adj.* *see* VOLUNTARY.

unsophisticated, *adj.* simplex.
unsorted, *adj.* incompositus.
unsound, *adj.* (*timber*) cariosus ; puter ; *see* UNHEALTHY ; INSANE ; *of opinions,* futilis
unsown, *adj.* non satus.
unsparing, *adj. see* LIBERAL.
unspeakable, *adj.* infandus.
unspoiled, *adj.* incorruptus, integer.
unstable, unsteady, *adj.* mobilis, inconstans. **unsteadiness,** *n.* inconstantia.
unstained, *adj. see* PURE.
unstring, *v.tr.* a bow, † arcum retendĕre.
unstrung, *adj.* *of the nerves, etc.,* fractus.
unstudied, *adj.* (*of style*) simplex.
unsubdued, *adj.* indomitus.
unsuccessful, *adj.* irritus, infelix. *Adv.* infeliciter.
unsuitable, unsuited, *adj.* by alienus ab; incommodus. *Adv.* incommode.
unsuspected, *adj.* non suspectus. **unsuspicious,** *adj.* simplex, candidus. *Adv.* simpliciter, candide.
untainted, *adj.* incorruptus, non infectus.
untamed, *adj.* indomitus.
untasted, *adj.* ingustatus.
untaught, *adj.* indoctus.
unteachable, *adj.* indocilis.
unthankful, *adj. see* UNGRATEFUL.
unthinking, *adj. see* THOUGHTLESS.
untie, *v.tr.* (dis)solvĕre, laxare.
until, *conj.* dum, donec, quoad.
untilled, *adj.* inaratus.
untimely, *adj. see* UNSEASONABLE.
untinged, *adj.* purus.
untiring, *adj. see* INDEFATIGABLE.
unto, *prep. see* TO.
untold, *adj.* non dictus ; *see* COUNTLESS.
untouched, *adj.* by intactus.
untoward, *adj. see* UNFAVOURABLE.
untried, *adj.* inexpertus.
untrodden, *adj.* e.g. path, via non trita.
untroubled, *adj.* tranquillus, placidus
untrue, *adj.* falsus. *Adv.* falso, ficte.
untruth, *n.* mendacium.
unturned, *adj.* to leave no stone —, omnibus modis aggredi.
untwine, untwist, *v.tr.* (re)solvĕre.
unused, *adj. see* UNACCUSTOMED ; novus. **unusual,** *adj.* insolitus.
unutterable, *adj.* infandus.
unvanquished, *adj.* invictus.
unvaried, unvarying, *adj. see* UNCHANGED.
unvarnished, *adj. fig.* simplex, sine fuco ac fallaciis.
unversed, *adj.* nexpertus, tiro ac rudis.
unviolated, *adj.* inviolatus.
unwalled, *adj.* sine muris.
unwarlike, *adj.* imbellis.
unwary, *adj.* imprudens. *Adv.* imprudenter. **unwariness,** *n.* imprudentia.

unwashed, *adj.* illotus.
unwavering, *adj. see* FIRM.
unwearied, *adj.* indefessus, integer.
unweave, *v.tr.* retexĕre.
unwelcome, *adj.* ingratus.
unwell, *adj.* see ILL.
unwholesome, *adj.* insalubris, gravis.
unwieldy, *adj.* inhabilis, vasti corporis.
unwilling, *adj.* invitus. *Adv.* by alqo invito. **unwillingness,** *n. see* RELUCTANCE.
unwind, *v.tr.* retexĕre.
unwise, *adj.* stultus. *Adv.* stulte.
unwitting, *adj. and adv.* inscius.
unwonted, *adj. see* UNUSUAL.
unworthy, *adj.* indignus. **unworthiness,** *n.* indignitas.
unwounded, *adj.* sine vulnere, integer.
unwrap, *v.tr.* evolvĕre; explicare.
unwrinkle, *v.tr.* erugare.
unwritten, *adj.* still —, non scriptus.
unwrought, *adj.* rudis.
unyielding, *adj. see* INFLEXIBLE.
unyoke, *v.tr.* disiungĕre.
up, *adv.* sursum ; — *the river,* adverso flumine ; — *the hill,* in adversum montem ; *to go* —, a(d)scendĕre ; — *to,* tenus with abl. (*always after the case*).
upwards, *adv.* sursum ; sublime ; *see* MORE.
upbraid, *v.tr.* reprehendĕre. **upbraiding,** *n.* obiurgatio.
uphill, *adv.* adverso colle, adversus collem. *Adj* arduus; *difficilis.*
uphold, *v.tr.* sustinēro.
upland, *adj.* editus.
upon, *prep.* super *with accus.* ; in *with accus. or ablat.* ; — *this condition,* eā condicione.
upper, *adj.* superus, superior. **uppermost,** *adj.* summus.
upright, *adj.* (di)rectus, erectus ; (*moral*) probus. *Adv.* recte, *or adj.* ; probe, honeste. **uprightness,** *n.* probitas.
uproar, *n. see* NOISE.
upset, *v.tr.* evertĕre *v.tr.* evertĕre.
upshot, *n.* exitus, eventus.
upsidedown, *adj.* to turn —, omnia turbare et miscēre.
upstart, *n.* novus homo.
urbanity, *n.* urbanitas.
urge, *v.tr.* impellĕre, stimulare ; (ad)hortari ; ab alqo petĕre, ut *or* ne. **urgent,** *adj.* gravis, magni momenti. *Adv.* vehementer, magnopere. **urgency,** *n.* necessitas.
urn, *n.* urna.
usage, *n.* mos, consuetudo. **use,** *n.* usus ; *to make* — *of,* uti ; *to come into* —, in usum venire ; *to be of great* —, magno usui esse. *v.tr.* uti ; adhibēre. **useful,** *adj.* utilis, idoneus ; *to be* —, usui esse. *Adv.* utiliter. **usefulness,** *n.* utilitas, usus. **useless,** *adj.* inutilis irritus. *Adv.* frustra.

usher, *v.tr.* introducĕre ; — *in, fig. see* BEGIN.

usual, *adj.* solitus, sol(l)emnis, tritus (*commonplace*), vulgaris ; *it is* —, solet ; *more than* —, plus solito. *Adv.* fere, plerumque.

usufruct, *n.* usus et frustus.

usurp, *v.tr.* (as)sumĕre, occupare. **usurper,** *n.* qui regnum occupat.

usury, *n.* fenerari. **usurer,** *n.* fenerator. **usurious,** *adj.* avarus. **usury,** *n.* usura, feneratio, fenus.

utensil, *n.* vas ; *in farming,* instrumentum ; —*s,* utensilia, -ium : supellex (*furniture*).

utility, *n. see* USEFULNESS.

utmost, *adj.* extremus, summus.

utter, uttermost, *adj.* totus ; *see* EXTREME. *Adv.* penitus, funditus, omnino.

utter, *v.tr.* to — *a sound,* sonitum edĕre, emittĕre. **utterance,** *n.* dictum ; *see* PRONUNCIATION.

V

vacancy, *n.* vacuum, inanitas ; *of office, by* vacuus. **vacant,** *adj.* vacuus. **vacate,** *v.tr.* vacuefacĕre ; *an office,* se abdicare. **vacation,** *n.* feriae. **vacuity, vacuum,** *n. see* VACANCY.

vacillate, *v.intr.* vacillare. **vacillating,** *adj.* dubius. **vacillation,** *n.* dubium.

vagabond, vagrant, *adj.* vagus. *n.* grassator ; scelestus. **vagary,** *n.* nugae ; *see* WHIM.

vague, *adj.* incertus, anceps. *Adv.* incerte, ambigue. **vagueness,** *n.* dubitatio.

vain, *adj. worthless,* inanis ; *fruitless,* irritus ; *to labour in* —, operam perdĕre ; *proud,* superbus, gloriosus. *Adv.* **in vain,** frustra, nequi(c)quam ; *proudly,* gloriose, superbe. **vainglorious,** *adj.* gloriosus. **vanity,** *n. emptiness,* inanitas ; *pride,* ambitio, ostentatio.

vale, *n. see* VALLEY.

valiant, valorous, *adj.* fortis, animosus, acer. *Adv.* fortiter, acriter. **valour,** *n.* fortitudo, virtus.

valid, *adj.* gravis, bonus, ratus ; *to be* —, valēre. **validity,** *n.* gravitas (*of a witness, etc.*), fides.

valley, *n.* (con)vallis.

value, *v.tr.* aestimare, ducĕre, habēre. *n.* aestimatio, pretium, virtus (*inner worth*). **valuable,** *adj.* magni pretii. **valuation,** *n.* aestimatio. **valuer** *n,* cui alqd aestimat. **valueless,** *see* WORTHLESS.

van, *n. o an army,* primum agmen.

van, *n. : ! e* CART, WAGON.

vanish, *v.intr.* (e)vanescĕre.

vanity, *n. see under* VAIN.

vanquish, *v.tr.* (de)vincĕre, superare. **vanquisher,** *n.* victor.

vapid, *adj.* vapidus (*of wine*) ; *fig. see* INSIPID.

vapour, *n.* vapor, nebula.

variable, *adj. see* CHANGEABLE. **variableness,** *n. see* CHANGE. **variance,** *n.* discordia. **variation,** *n.* varietas ; *see* CHANGE. **variegated,** *adj.* varius. **variegate,** *v.tr.* variare. **variety,** *n.* varietas, diversitas. **various,** *adj.* varius, diversus. *Adv.* varie, diverse. **vary,** *v.tr.* variare. *v.intr.* variare, com) mutari.

varlet, *n. see* SERVANT, ROGUE.

vase, *n.* vas, vasis, *n. see* JAR.

vassal, *n.* cliens. **vassalage,** *n.* clientela.

vast, *adj.* vastus, immanis. *Adv.* magnopere, valde. **vastness,** *n.* magnitudo.

vat, *n.* cupa, dolium.

vault, *n. arched roof,* camera, fornix ; *see* ARCH ; —*ed chamber,* fornix. *v.tr.* confornicare ; *leap,* salire.

vaunt, *v.intr.* and *n. see* BOAST.

veal, *n.* (caro) vitulina.

veer, *v.intr.* se vertĕre, verti.

vegetables, *n.* olus *or pl.* olera, -um, *n.* ; — *market,* forum olitorium. **vegetate,** *v.intr. fig.* hebescĕre. **vegetation,** *n.* herbae, plantae.

vehemence, *n.* vis, impetus, ardor. **vehement,** *adj.* vehemens, gravis, acer. *Adv.* vehementer, valde, acriter.

vehicle, *n. see* CARRIAGE, WAGON.

veil, *n.* rica, flammeolum (*bridal* —) *v.tr.* velare, tegĕre.

vein, *n.* vena.

vellum, *n.* membrana.

velocity, *n.* velocitas.

venal, *adj.* venalis, nummarius.

vend, *v.tr.* vendĕre. **vendor,** *n.* venditor.

venerable, *adj.* venerabilis. **venerate,** *v.tr.* colĕre, observare, venerari. **veneration,** *n.* cultus, veneratio.

vengeance, *n.* ultio.

venial, *adj.* venia dignus.

venison, *n.* (caro) ferina.

venom, *n.* venenum. **venomous,** *adj.* venenatus.

vent, *n.* spiramentum, foramen ; *by* effundĕre. *v.tr. to* — *one's passion,* iram effundĕre.

ventilate, *v.tr.* ventilare ; *fig.* in medium proferre. **ventilation,** *n. use verb.*

venture, *n.* experimentum, periculum, alea (*hazard*), facinus (*bold act*) ; *at a* —, temere, forte. *v.intr. and tr.* periclitari, audēre : conari (*to attempt*). **venturesome, venturous,** *adj.* audax. *Adv.* audaciter. **venturousness,** *n.* audacia.

veracious, *adj.* verus. **veracity,** *n.* veritas.

veranda, *n.* subdialia, -ium, *or* porticus.

verb, *n.* verbum. **verbal,** *adj. by* verbum *or* vox. *Adv. by* praesens, *or* ipse *or* coram. **verbatim,** *adv.* ad verbum. **verbose,** *adj.* verbosus. **verboseness, verbosity,** *n.* copia verborum, *or by* copiose dicĕre.

verdant, *adj.* viridis. **verdure,** *n.* viriditas.

verdict, *n. in law,* responsum, arbitrium, iudicium; *to pronounce a* —, decernĕre. **verdigris,** *n.* aerugo.

verge, *n. brink,* margo, ora ; *fig. (e.g. on the* — *of danger,* imminente periculo. **verger,** *n.* apparitor.

verge, *v.intr. to* — *upon,* attingĕre.

verification, *n.* confirmatio. **verify,** *v.tr.* comprobare. **verily,** *adv.* profecto, sane. **verity,** *n. see* TRUTH.

verisimilitude, *n.* verisimilitudo. **veri table,** *adj.* verus.

vermilion, *n.* minium. *Adj.* miniatus.

vernacular, *adj.* sermo patrius, lingua nostra.

versatile, *adj.* versatilis ; *of genius,* varius et multiplex. **versatility,** *n.* facilitas, mobilitas.

verse, *n.* versus. **versify,** *v.tr.* carmina facĕre.

versed, *adj.* exercitatus, peritus.

vertex, *n.* vertex, *or by* summus. **vertical,** *adj.* (di)rectus: perpendiculum. *Adv.* recte, ad perpendiculum.

vertigo, *n.* vertigo.

very, *adj. see* TRUE, REAL. *Adv.* satis *with adjs. and advs., (e.g.* non satis se tutum in Argis videbat) ; vehementer, *with* dolĕre, gaudĕre, *etc.; by a superl.*

vesper, *n. evening star,* Hesperus, Vesper.

vessel, *n.* vas, vasis (*pl.* vasa, -orum, *n.*); *blood* —, arteriae, venae; *ship,* navis.

vest, *n.* tunica. *v.tr.* vestire **vested,** *adj. e.g. rights, by* ius, iuris, *n.* **vesture,** *n. see* GARMENT.

vestal, *n.* Vestalis (virgo).

vestibule, *n.* vestibulum.

vestige, *n.* vestigium.

vetch, *n.* vicia.

veteran, *adj. and n.* veteranus.

vetro, *n.* intercessio *(of the tribunes). v.tr.* rogationi intercedĕre *(of the tribunes); see* FORBID.

vex, *v.tr.* vexare, commovĕre ; *to be* —*ed at,* aegre ferre; *I am* —*ed at,* me piget alcis rei. **vexation,** *n.* molestia ; *full of* —, indignabundus. **vexatious,** *adj.* molestus. *Adv.* moleste, graviter.

viands, *n.* cibus.

vibrate, *v.intr.* vibrare ; *of sound,* tinnire. **vibration,** *n.* motus.

vicarious, *adj. and adv.* alcis loco.

vice *(prefix) by* pro *or* sub *(e.g.* subpraefectus, proconsul).

vice, *n.* turpitudo, vitia, -iorum. **vicious,**

adj. turpis, flagitiosus, sceleratus. *Adv.* turpiter, flagitiose. **viciousness,** *n. see* VICE.

vicissitude, *n.* vicissitudo, vicissitudines.

victim, *n.* hostia. **victimize,** *v.tr. see* CHEAT.

victor, *n.* victor. **victorious,** *adj.* victor, victrix. *Adv. by adj.* **victory,** *n.* victoria; *to gain* —, vincĕre.

victuals, *n.* cibus, alimenta, -orum. **victual,** *v.tr.* rem frumentariam comparare.

vie, *v.intr.* aemulari.

view, *v.tr. see* LOOK, SEE. *n.* prospectus, conspectus ; *to be in* —, in conspectu esse; *point of* —, ratio.

vigil, *n. see* WATCH. **vigilance,** *n.* vigilantia. **vigilant,** *adj.* vigilans, diligens. *Adv.* vigilanter, diligenter.

vigour, *n.* vis (*pl.* vires), robur, **vigorous,** *adj.* validus, impiger, acer. *Adv.* fortiter, acriter.

vile, *adj.* turpis, foedus. *Adv.* turpiter, foede. **vileness,** *n.* turpitudo.

villa, *n.* villa.

village, *n.* pagus, vicus. **villager,** *n.* paganus.

villain, *n.* homo sceleratus. **villainous,** *adj.* flagitiosus. **villainy,** *n. see* WICKEDNESS; *as act,* scelus, facinus.

vindicate, *v.tr. a right,* ius tenĕre, retinĕre ; *one's character,* sibi constare. **vindication,** *n.* defensio. **vindictive,** *adj.* ulciscendi cupidus.

vine, *n.* vitis. *Adj.* vinearius, *or by genit. of* vitis ; — *dresser,* vinitor ; —*yard,* vinea. **vinegar,** *n.* acetum.

vintage, *n.* vindemia ; *to gather the* , vindemiare uvas *or* vinum.

violate, *v.tr.* violare. **violable,** *adj.* † violabilis. **violation,** *n.* violatio.

violence, *n.* vis, ardor, aestus *(of a fever, etc.).* **violator,** *n.* violator. **violent,** *adj.* acer, vehemens, gravis *(of illness, weather, etc.).* *Adv.* acriter, graviter.

violet, *n.* viŏla; *bed of* —*s,* violarium.

viper, *n.* vipera, aspis.

virgin, *n.* virgo.

virile, *adj. (e.g. age)* virilis. **virility,** *n.* virilitas.

virtue, *n.* virtus, honestas ; *by* — *of,* per *with accus. or* ex *with ablat.*

virtual, *adj. and adv.* re non verbo. **virtuous,** *adj.* virtute praeditus, probus, castus.

virulence, *n.* vis, gravitas *(e.g. morbi)* ; *fig.* acerbitas. **virulent,** *adj.* gravis ; *fig.* acerbus. *Adv.* graviter, acerbe.

visage, *n. see* FACE.

viscera, *n.* viscera, -um.

viscid, *adj.* † tenax, glutinosus.

visible, *adj.* quod cerni potest, apertus, manifestus. *Adv.* manifesto. **vision,** *n.* visus, a(d)spectus, sensus videndi ;

species, simulacrum. **visionary**, *adj.* inanis; *of character,* fanaticus.

visit, *n.* salutatio *(of friends and clients in the morning). v.tr.* alqm (in)visĕre. adire. salutare, salutatum venire. **visitation**, *n. punishment,* poena. **visitor**, *n.* salutator, hospes.

visor, *n.* buccula *(cheek-piece).*

vista, *n.* prospectus.

vital, *adj.* vitalis ; *important,* maximi momenti. *Adv.* maximi momenti. **vitality**, *n.* animus.

vitiate, *v.tr.* corrumpĕre. **vitiation**, *n.* corruptio.

vitreous, *adj.* vitreus.

vituperate, *v.tr. see* SCOLD. **vituperation**, *n.* reprehensio. **vituperative**, *adj. see* ABUSIVE.

vivacious, *adj.* vividus. **vivacity**, *n.* vigor. **vivid**, *adj.* vividus; *see* LIVELY.

vixen, *n.* vulpes; *quarrelsome woman,* mulier iurgiosa.

vocabulary, *n.* index verborum.

vocal, *adj.* vocalis; *— music,* cantus.

vocation, *n.* officium, munus.

vocative, *n.* casus vocativus.

vociferate, *v.intr.* vociferari. **vociferation**, *n.* vociferatio. **vociferous**, *adj. and adv.* magno (cum) clamore.

vogue, *n. to be in —,* moris esse.

voice, *n.* vox. *v.tr. see* UTTER.

void, *adj. see* EMPTY *n.* inanitas, vacuum.

volatile, *adj. fig.* lĕvis, mobilis. **volatility**, *n. fig.* lĕvitas; mobilitas.

volcano, *n.* mons flammas eructans.

volition, *n.* voluntas.

volley, *n.* tormenta (-orum) emissa.

voluble, *adj. see* FLUENT.

volume, *n.* liber, volumen *(roll of parchment)* **voluminous**, *adj. by* multus.

voluntary, *adj.* volens, *or by* sponte (meâ, *etc.). Adv.* (meâ, *etc.*) voluntate; ultro. **volunteer**, *v.intr. of soldiers.* nomen dare.

voluptuous, *adj.* libidinosus. **voluptuousness**, *n.* voluptas, *(pl.)* libidines.

vomit, *v.tr. and intr.* (e)vomĕre.

voracious, *adj.* edax, cibi avidus. *Adv.* avide *(lit. or fig.).* **voracity**, *n.* cibi aviditas, voracitas.

vortex, *n.* vertex, turbo.

votary, *n.* (con)secratus, studiosus.

vote, *n.* sententia, suffragium. *v.intr.* sententiam ferre, suffragium ferre, censere. **voter**, *n.* suffragator, qui suffragium fert. **voting-tablet**, *n.* tabella.

votive, *adj.* votivus *(e.g.* ludi).

vouch, *v.tr* testari, affirmare. *v.intr.* spondēre.

vouchsafe, *v.intr.* concedĕre.

vow, *n.* votum. *v.tr.* (de)vovēre.

vowel, *n.* lit(t)era vocalis.

voyage, *n.* navigatio, cursus. *v.intr.* navigare.

vulgar, *adj.* vulgaris, plebeius; *see* RUDE. **vulgarity**, *n. see* RUDENESS.

vulnerable, *adj.* qui (quae, quod vulnerari potest.

vulture, *n.* vultur.

W

wade, *v.intr.* flumen vado transire.

waft, *v.tr.* ferre, portare.

wag, *v.tr.* movēre. *n.* homo iocosus. **waggish**, *adj.* iocosus.

wage, *v.tr.* bellum gerĕre. **wager**, *n.* sponsio. **wages**, *n.* merces, stipendium.

wagon, *n.* plaustrum. **wagoner**, *n.* plaustri ductor.

wagtail, *n.* motacilla.

waif, *n.* inops, egens.

wail, *v.intr.* plangĕre. *n.* planctus.

wain, *n.* plaustrum.

wainscot, *n.* paries, -ĕtis, *m. (partition).*

waist, *n.* corpus medium. **waistcoat**, *n.* subucula.

wait, *v.intr.* manēre ; *to — for,* ex-(s)pectare; *to — on,* ministrare.

waiter, *n.* minister, puer. **waiting**, *n. delay* ; mora, commoratio ; *at table,* ministerium. **waitress**, **waiting-maid**, *n.* ancilla.

waive, *v.tr.* concedĕre.

wake, *v.tr.* excitare. *v.intr.* excitari. *etc.* **wakeful**, *adj.* vigil. **wakefulness**, *n.* insomnia, vigilia.

walk, *v.intr.* ire, ingredi, cedĕre ; spatiari *(for exercise)* ; *to — (opp. to ride, etc.),* pedibus ire. *n. the act of —ing,* (de)ambulatio ; *manner,* ingressus. **walker**, *n.* qui (de)ambulat, ambulator. **walking**, *n. see* WALK.

wall, *n.* murus, moenia, -ium ; paries *(party-). v.tr.* muro cingĕre, munire.

wallet, *n.* pera, saccus, mantica.

wallow, *v.intr. — in the mire,* in luto volutari.

walnut, *n.* iuglans; *— tree,* iuglans.

wan, *adj.* pallidus.

wand, *n.* virga.

wander, *v.intr.* vagari, errare; *to — over,* pervagari ; *to — in mind,* delirare. **wanderer**, *n.* erro, peregrinator. **wandering**, *adj.* vagus ; *fig.* neglegens *(inattentive),* delirus *(crazy).*

wane, *v.intr.* decrescĕre *(moon, day, etc.),* senescĕre.

want, penuria, inopia, egestas, desiderium defectio ; *to be in — of anything,* alqâ re carēre, egēre. *v.intr.* deesse, abesse, deficĕre, desiderari. *v.tr. to require,* egēre, opus est, desiderare, requirĕre. **wanting**, *adj. by* deesse.

wanton, *adj. e.g. boys,* lascivus ; protervus : dissolutus. *Adv.* ultro *(without provocation),* lascive, petulanter.

v.intr. lascivire. **wantonness**, *n.* lascivia, petulantia.

war, *n.* bellum ; *civil*, intestinum, civile. *v.intr.* bellum gerĕre. **war-cry**, *n.* clamor. **warfare**, *n. see* WAR. **war-horse**, *n.* equus. **warlike**, *adj.* militaris, bellicosus, ferox. **warrior**, *n.* miles.

warble, *v.tr.* cancĕre. **warbling**, *n.* cantus.

ward (*off*), *v.tr. in fencing*, ictum vitare ; cavēre ; arcēre, deprecari (*by entreaties*). *n. carcer* (*prison*) ; *a minor*, pupillus. **warden, warder**, *n.* custos. **wardrobe**, *n.* vestiarium, vestimenta, -orum (*garments*). **wardship**, *n.* tutela.

ware, *n.* merx. **warehouse**, *n.* horreum, cella. *v.tr.* condĕre.

warm, *adj.* calidus ; *luke*— —, tepidus ; *to be* —, calēre. *v.tr.* calefacĕre, fovēre. **warmth**, *n.* calor; fervor.

warn, *v.tr.* (prae)monēre *or* admonēre. **warning**, *n.* (ad)monitio (*the act*), monitus, (ad)monitum, exemplum (*example*).

warp, *n.* (*in manufacture*) stamen. *v.intr.* (*of wood, etc.*) pandare, pandari. *v.tr. fig.* torquēre.

warrant, *v.tr.* confirmare ; *see* PROMISE, UNDERTAKE. *n.* auctoritas. **warranty**, *n.* satisdatio.

warrior, *n. see under* WAR.

wary, *adj.* cautus.

wash, *v.tr.* lavare, abluēre. *v.intr.* lavari.

wasp, *n.* vespa.

waste, *v.tr.* vastare, (de)populari; consumĕre (*of disease, etc.*); *to squander*, perdĕre. *v.intr. e.g. the body*, (con)tabescĕre. *n.* loca deserta ; *of expenditure*, sumptus profusi ; *loss*, iactura, damnum. *Adj.* desertus et incultus. **wasteful**, *adj.* profusus. *Adv.* profuse. **wastefulness**, *n.* profusio.

watch, *n.* excubiae, vigiliae ; *a* —*man*, **vigil** ; *of time*, vigilia. *v.intr.* (per)vigilare. *v.tr.* tuēri, spectare ; *to guard*, custodire ; *to* — *for*, ex(s)pectare. **watch-fire**, *n.* ignis. **watchful**, *adj.* vigilans. *Adv.* vigilanter **watchfulness**, *n.* vigilantia. **watchman**, *n.* vigil. **watch-tower**, *n.* specula. **watchword**, *n.* tessera, signum.

water, *n.* aqua ; *fresh* —, aqua dulcis ; *to fetch* —, aquam petĕre, aquari ; —*bearer*, aquarius, aquator ; —*bottle*, ampulla ; —*clock*, clepsydra. *Adj.* aquatilis, aquarius. *v.tr.* irrigare. **watering**, *n.* —*place* (*i.e. mineral springs*) aquae; *of seaside*, (*e.g.* oppidum maritimum) ; —*pot*, hydria, urceus. **water-snake**, *n.* hydrus. **waterworks**, *n.* aquaeductus (*an aqueduct*). **watery**, *adj.* aquatilis, aquosus (*abounding in water*).

wattle, *n. hurdle*, crates ; *of a cock*, palea. *v.tr.* contexĕre.

wave, *n.* unda, fluctus. *v.tr.* agitare, iactare. *v.intr.* undare, agitari.

waver, *v.intr.* fluctuare, dubitare. **waverer**, *n.* (homo) inconstans, **wavering**, *n.* inconstantia, dubitatio.

wax, *n.* cera. **waxen**, *adj.* cereus.

wax, *v.intr.* crescĕre.

way, *n.* via, iter, aditus, cursus ; *ratio* (*plan or manner*), mos (*custom*), consilium (*plan*) ; *a short* —, compendiaria (*usually fig.*), *two* —*s*, bivium ; *three*, trivium ; *four*, quadrivium ; — *there is none*, avia, -orum ; *by* —*s*, iter dovium ; *out of the* —, remotus ; *on the* —, ex itinere , —*s and means*, opes, -um, ratio ; *by the* —, ut hoc dicam ; *to get under* — (*of a ship*), (ancoram) solvĕre, tollĕre. **wayfarer**, *n.* viator. **waylay**, *v.tr.* alci insidiari *or* insidias facĕre. **wayside**, *n. and adj.* ad viam. **wayward**, *adj. see* WILFUL.

we, *pron.* nos.

weak, *adj.* tenuis, lēvis, imbecillus, debilis, invalidus, confectus (*worn out*). **weakly**, *adv.* tenuiter, infirme. **weaken**, *v.tr.* debilitare, infirmare ; (*to lessen*), frangĕre, labefactare. **weakness**, *n.* tenuitas, exilitas (*e.g. in dicendo*), debilitas, lēvitas (*of arguments, etc.*), vitium (*fault*).

weal, *n. the public* —, salus publica, respublica.

weal, *n. mark on the body*, vibex.

wealth, *n.* res secundae, divitiae, opes, -um. **wealthy**, *adj.* locuples, opulentus.

weapon, *n.* arma, -orum, telum.

wear, *v.tr.* gerĕre, indutus esse alqā re ; *to* — *the toga*, togatus esse ; *to* — *away*, terĕre ; *see* CONSUME. *v.intr.* usu delēri ; *to* — *off*, evanescĕre. *n.* usus. **wearing**, *n.* usus ; — *apparel*, vestimentum. **worn**, *adj.* usu detritus; — *out* (*hackneyed*), contritus, obsoletus ; (*tired out*), fessus ; *with wounds, etc.*, vulneribus, *etc.*, confectus.

weary, *adj.* fessus ; *disgusted with*, by taedet. *v.tr.* (de)fatigare ; — *with*, obtundĕre. *v.intr. by* taedet. **weariness**, *n.* lassitudo ; *fig.* taedium. **wearisome**, *adj.* longus, laboriosus.

weasel, *n.* mustela.

weather, *n.* caelum, tempestas. *v.tr. lit.* alqm locum circumvehi ; *fig.* superare ; — *a storm*, vim tempestatis perferre.

weave, *v.tr.* (con)texĕre. **weaver**, *n.* textor. **web**, *n.* textum, tela.

wed, *v.tr. see* MARRY. **wedlock**, **wedding**, *n. see* MARRIAGE.

wedge, *n.* cuneus ; — *shaped*, cuneatus.

week, *n.* septem dies. **weekdays**, *n.* dies negotiosi.

weep, *v.intr. and tr.* lacrimare, vagire (*of little children*). weeping, *m.* fletus ; vagitus.

weigh, *v.tr.* (ex)pendĕre, *lit. and fig. ; — down,* opprimĕre (*lit. and fig.*). *v.intr. to — heavily,* magni ponderis esse. weight, *n.* pondus ; momentum (*lit. and fig.*). weighty, *adj.* gravis (*lit. and fig.*). *Adv.* graviter.

weir, *n.* moles.

welcome, *adj.* acceptus, gratus. *n.* salutatio. *v.tr.* salutare. *Interj.* salve (*pl.* salvete). welfare, *n.* salus, felicitas. well, *adv.* bene, recte ; *very —,* optime ; *exclamation,* esto ! *Adj.* salvus, integer; *to be —,* valēre. well-affected, *adj.* benevolus. well-being, *n.* salus. well-born, *adj.* nobilis. well-bred, *adj.* urbanus. well-disposed, *adj. see* WELL-AFFECTED. well-educated, well-informed, *adj.* doctus, eruditus. well-fed, *adj.* pinguis. well-known, *adj.* omnibus notus. well-meaning, *adj.* benevolus, amicus. well-spent, *adj. e.g. life,* vita bene acta.

weld, *v.tr.* (con)ferruminare.

well, *n.* puteus. *v.intr. — up,* scatēre.

west, *n.* occidens, occasus (solis). *Adj. — wind,* Zephyrus. westward, *adj.* ad occasum. western, *adj.* occidentalis.

wet, *adj.* humidus, madidus. *v.tr.* madefacĕre. wetness, *n.* humor.

wether, *n.* vervex, -ēcis, *m.*

whale, *n.* balaena.

wharf, *n.* navale, crepĭdo.

what, *pron. interrog.* quid ? *that which,* (id) quod. whatever, *pron.* quicunque, quisquis.

wheat, *n.* triticum; *wheaten,* triticeus.

wheedle, *v.tr. and intr.* illicĕre ; blandiri (*with dat.*).

wheel, *n.* rota. *v.tr.* push forward, propellĕre. *v.intr.* signa convertĕre (*of soldiers*).

wheeze, *v.intr.* anhelare.

whelp, *n.* catulus.

when, *adv. and conj.* cum, quo tempore, ubi, quando, ut; *interrogative,* quando ? quo tempore ? whence, *adv. interrog.,* unde ? whenever, whensoever, *conj.* quandocunque, quotie(n)s.

where, *adv. and conj. interrogative,* ubi ? *as relative,* ubi, quā. whereas, *adv.* quoniam, cum. whereby, *adv.* ex quo. wherefore, *adv.* quamobrem ; *interrog.* cur ? wherein, *adv.* in quo, in quibus, ubi. wherever, *adv.* ubicunque, quacunque (*at any place*). whereof, *adv.* cuius, quorum. whereon, *adv.* quo facto. whereto, *adv.* quem ad finem.

wherry, *n.* cymba, linter.

whet, *v.tr.* (ex)acuĕre. whetstone, *n.* cos.

whether, *conj.* ne, num, utrum an ; sive—sive (seu—seu).

whey, *n.* serum.

which, *pron. see* WHO.

whiff, *n.* halitus (*breath*).

while, *n. a little —,* pau(l)lulum (*temporis*) ; *for a short —,* pau(l)lisper ; *a little — after,* paul(l)o post. (whilst) *conj.* dum, donec, *or by* inter *with gerund. v.tr. to — away the time,* tempus fallĕre.

whim, *n.* libido. whimsical, *adj.* difficilis. lĕvis (*fickle*).

whimper, whine, *v.intr.* vagire. whimpering, *n.* whining, *n.* vagitus.

whinny, *v.intr.* hinnire.

whip, *n.* scutica, flagellum. *v.tr.* verberare.

whirl, *v.tr.* (con)torquēre. whirlpool, *n.* vorago, gurges. whirlwind, *n.* turbo.

whirr, *v.tr.* stridēre (stridĕre). *n.* stridor.

whiskers, *n. by* genae pilosae.

whisper, *v.intr.* susurrare. *v.tr.* insusurrare in aures. *n.* susurrus.

whist, *n.* alea (*dice*). *interj.* st ! tace, tacete.

whistle, *v.intr. and tr.* sibilare; *of the wind,* stridēre. *n.* sibilus. whistler, *n.* qui sibilat, tibicen (*on the pipe*).

whit, *n., not a —,* minime.

white, *adj.* albus, candidus, canus (*hoary*), niveus. *n.* album, candor. white-haired, *adj.* albis capillis. white lead, *n.* cerussa. whiten, *v.tr.* dealbare. *v.intr.* albescĕre, canescĕre. whiteness, *n.* candor. whitewash, *v.tr.* dealbare.

whither, *adv., as interrog.,* quo ? *antecedent,* quo.

whiz, *v.intr.* stridēre. *n.* stridor. whizzing, *adj.* stridens. *n.* stridor.

who, *rel. pron.* qui, quae, quod. *Interrog. pron.* quis, quae, quid ? whoever, *n.* quicunque.

whole, *adj.* integer (*uninjured*), totus, omnis. *n. the —,* totum, tota res, summa. wholly, *adv.* omnino, funditus. wholesale, *n.* mercatura magna. wholesome. *adj.* salutaris, utilis. wholesomeness, *n.* salubritas.

whoop, *n.* clamor.

whose, *adj. rel. and interrog. pron.* cuius.

why, *adv. as interrog.* cur ? quare ? *Conj.* cur.

wicked, *adj.* impius, sceleratus, perditus, malus. *Adv.* impie, scelerate, perdite, male. wickedness, *n.* impietas, scelus, facinus, turpitudo.

wicker, *adj.* vimineus ; *— work,* crates.

wide, *adj.* latus. *Adv.* late. widen, *v.tr.* amplificare. *v.intr.* patescĕre (*e.g. a plain*). width, *n.* amplitudo, latitudo.

widow, *n.* vidua. widowed, *adj.* viduus. widower, *n.* viduus.

wield, *v.tr.* tractare.

wife, *n.* coniu(n)x, uxor.

wild, *adj.* ferus, agrestis, incultus, saevus, *a — beast,* fera. *Adv.* ferociter, saeve. **wilderness,** *n.* loca deserta, -orum, solitudo. **wildness,** *n.* ferocia.

wile, *n.* ars, dolus. **wily,** *adj.* astutus.

wilful, *adj.* contumax, pertinax. *Adv.* contumaciter. **wilfulness,** *n.* contumacia.

will, *n.* voluntas ; *testament,* testamentum. *v.tr.* velle. **willing,** *adj.* libens, paratus. *Adv.* libenter. **willingness,** *n.* voluntas.

willow, *n.* salix.

wily, *adj. see* WILE.

win, *v.tr. see* GET, GAIN. *v.intr.* vincĕre. **winner,** *n.* victor.

winning, *adj.* suavis, comis.

wind, *n.* ventus. **windmill,** *n.* mola venti. **windpipe,** *n.* aspera arteria. **windward,** *adj.* ad ventum conversus. **windy,** *adj.* ventosus.

wind, *v.tr.* torquĕre, glomerare ; — *up,* trochleā tollĕre. *v.intr.* se sinuare. **winding,** *adj.* tortuosus. *n.* flexus, **windlass,** *n.* ergata.

window, *n.* fenestra.

wine, *n.* vinum ; *sour —,* vappa. **wine-cellar,** *n.* apotheca. **wine-merchant,** *n.* vinarius.

wing, *n.* ala ; — *of an army,* cornu, ala ; — *of a door,* foris ; *folding-doors,* valvae. *v.tr.* volare. **winged,** *adj.* † aliger.

wink, *n.* nictus. *v.intr.* nictare ; *to — at, fig.* indulgēre alci, con(n)ivēre in alqā re.

winnow, *v.tr.* corn. frumentum evannēre. **winnowing fan,** *n.* vannus, *f.*

winter, *n.* hiem(p)s. *Adj.* hiemalis, hibernus, *or genit. of* hiem(p)s ; — *quarters,* hiberna, -orum. *v.intr.* hiemare.

wipe, *v.tr.* detergēre ; — *out (fig.),* abolēro.

wire, *n.* filum or filum ferreum.

wise, *adj.* sapiens, prudens ; *to be —,* sapĕre. *n. in no ,* nullo modo. *Adv.* sapienter. **wisdom,** *n.* sapientia, prudentia.

wish, *v.tr. and intr.* velle, cupĕre ; *if you — it,* si vis ; *I don't — it,* nolo ; *to — for,* cupĕre. *n.* optatio, desiderium ; *votum (prayer) ; according to my —,* ex sententiā.

wistful, wistfully, wistfulness, *adj.* (*e.g. his face bore a — expression,* ille desiderium vultu expressit).

wit, *n.* (ingenii) acumen, facetiae, sal, -is ; *to —,* nempe, scilicet. **witless,** *adj. see* FOOLISH. **witticism,** *n. see* WIT. **witty,** *adj.* facetus, salsus. *Adv.* facete.

witch, *n.* venefica, saga. **witchcraft,** *n.* veneficium, magice.

with *prep.* cum, una cum ; *by means*

of, per ; in a hostile sense, cum, contra, adversus.

withal, *adv.* simul.

withdraw, *v.tr.* avertĕre, removēre, detrahĕre, au ferre ; *of troops,* revocare. *n intr* se recipĕre ab, *etc.,* se removēre ab, *etc.*

wither, *v.tr.* torrēre ; *fig.* perdĕre. *v.intr.* (ex)arescĕre. **withered,** *adj.* marcidus ; rugosus (*wrinkled*).

withhold, *v.tr.* retinēre.

within, *prep.* intra, inter, in *with abl. Adv.* intus.

without, *prep.* extra, sine. *Adv.* extra, foris (*out of doors*).

withstand, *v.tr.* resistĕre.

witness, *n.* testis ; spectator (*onlooker*). *v.tr. and intr.* testari ; *behold,* vidēre.

wizard, *n.* magus, veneficus.

woad, *n.* vitrum.

woe, *n.* dolor. *Interj.* vae! **woeful,** *adj. see* SAD.

wolf, *n.* lupus ; *of the —,* lupinus. **wolfish,** *adj.* saevus.

woman, *n.* femina, mulier. **womanish,** *adj.* muliebris, mollis. **womanly,** *adj.* muliebris.

womb, *n.* alvus, uterus.

wonder, *n.* (ad)miratio ; *see* ASTONISHMENT ; *a wonderful thing,* res mira, portentum, miraculum. *v.intr.* (ad)mirari. **wonderful,** *adj.* mirus, (ad)mirabilis. *Adv.* mire, (ad)mirabiliter.

wont, *n.* usus, mos, consuetudo. *Adj. to be —,* solēre.

woo, *v.tr.* amare, in matrimonium petĕre.

wood, *n.* lignum, *or pl.* ligna materia, silva (*forest*). **wooden,** *adj.* ligneus. **wood-cutter,** *n.* qui ligna caedit. **wood-nymph,** *n.* (Hama)dryas. **woodpecker,** *n.* picus. **wood-pigeon,** *n.* palumbes. **wooded, woody,** *adj.* silvestris.

woof, *n.* subtemen, trama.

wool, *n.* lana. **woollen, woolly,** *adj.* laneus.

word, *n.* vocabulum ; verbum ; *upon my —,* meā fide. *v.tr. see* EXPRESS. **wordy,** *adj.* verbosus.

work, *n.* opus, pensum, liber (*literary —*) ; *toil,* opera, labor (*with an effort*). *v.intr. to — at,* (e)laborare in alqa re, operam dare alci rei. **work-basket,** *n.* quasillum (quasillus). **working,** *adj. — day,* dies negotiosus. **workman,** *n.* agri cultor (*in the field*) ; operarius ; operae (*pl.*) ; faber. **workmanship,** *n.* ars, opus. **workshop,** *n.* officina, fabrica.

world, *n.* mundus ; *the globe,* orbis (terrarum), terrae ; *what in the — ?* quid tandem ? *mankind,* omnes ; *the ancient —,* antiquitas, veteres, -um.

worm, *n.* vermis, tinea (*in wood and*

books). **worm-eaten,** *adj.* cariosus ; to be —, vermiculari.

worn, *part. and adj. ; see* WEAR.

worry, *v.tr.* (di)laniare (*tear, of dogs, etc.*); *fig.* vexare.

worse, *adj.* peior. *Adv.* peius. **worst,** *adj.* pessimus. *Adv.* pessime. *v.tr.* vincěre.

worship, *n.* veneratio ; *divine* —, Dei (deorum) cultus ; *to attend* —, sacris adesse. *v.tr.* colěre. **worshipper,** *n.* cultor.

worsted, *n.* lana (*wool*). *Adj.* laneus.

worth, *n. value,* aestimatio, pretium ; *moral* —, virtus. *Adj. see* WORTHY ; *it is* — *while,* operae pretium est, *with infin.; to be* —, valěre. **worthy,** *adj.* dignus *with abl. Adv.* digne. **worthiness,** *n.* dignitas, honestas. **worthless,** *adj.* vilis, inutilis ; *morally,* perditus. **worthlessness,** *n.* vilitas, *or by adj.*

wound, *n.* vulnus, cicatrix (*scar*). *v.tr.* vulnerare. **wounded,** *adj.* vulneratus, saucius; *fig.* dolore affectus.

wrangle, *v.intr. see* QUARREL.

wrap, *v.tr.* involvěre, velare. **wrapper,** *n.* tegumentum.

wrath, *n.* ira, iracundia. **wrathful,** *adj.* iratus, iracundus. *Adv.* irate, iracunde.

wreak, *v.tr. see* REVENGE.

wreath, *n.* corona, sertum. **wreathe,** *v.tr.* nectěre.

wreck, *n.* naufragium. *v.tr.* frangěre navem in scopulos ; *to be* —*ed,* naufragium facěre. **wrecked,** *adj.* naufragus.

wrench, *v.tr. see* TEAR, PULL.

wrest, *v.tr.* eripěre, extorquěre ; *fig.* perverse interpretari.

wrestle, *v.intr.* luctari. **wrestler,** *n.* luctator, athleta, *m.* **wrestling,** *n.* luctatio.

wretch, *n.* homo improbus ; *poor* —, homo miserrimus. **wretched,** *adj.* miserabilis, miser, tristis ; *malus,* nequam (*worthless*). *Adv.* misere, nequiter. **wretchedness,** *n.* miseria.

wriggle, *v.intr.* se torquěre.

wring, *v.tr.* — *the neck,* gulam frangěre ; — *clothes,* aquam expriměre linteis.

wrinkle, *n.* ruga. *v.tr.* rugare ; — *the forehead,* frontem contrahěre. **wrinkled,** *adj.* rugosus.

wrist, *n.* prima palmae pars.

writ, *n.* scriptum; *in law,* lit(t)erae.

write, *v.tr.* scriběre. **writer,** *n.* qui lit(t)eras facit; scriba, scriptor (*author*). **writing,** *n. the act of,* scriptio ; *the thing written,* scriptum ; *art of* —, ars scribendi. **writing-case,** *n.* scrinium. **writing-desk,** *n.* mensa. **writing-paper,** *n.* charta. **writing-tablet,** *n.* cera, tabula.

writhe, *v.intr.* torquěri.

wrong, *adj.* falsus ; *morally* —, pravus ;

n. an unjust act, iniuria. *v.tr.* iniuriā alqm afficěre. **wrongdoer,** *n. see* WICKED. **wrongly,** *adv.* male, nequiter, turpiter. **wrongful,** *adj.* **wrongfully,** *adv. see* WRONG AND UNJUST.

wroth, *adj.* irae plenus.

wrought, *adj.* factus, confectus.

wry, *adj.* distortus *or* perversus (*e.g.* oculi).

Y

yard, *n. by* tres pedes longus.

yard, *n.* area, *open place in a ship,* antenna.

yawn, *v.intr.* oscitare ; *to open wide,* scindi, hiare ; *n.* oscitatio ; *opening,* hiatus.

ye, *pron.* vos.

yea, *adv. see* YES.

year, *n.* annus ; *last* —, anno superiore ; *at the end of the* —, extremo anno ; *every other* —, alternis annis ; *each* —, quotannis ; *a period of two* —*s,* biennium. **yearly,** (*or annual*), *adj.* annuus, anniversarius. *Adv.* quotannis.

yearn, *v.tr. to* — *for,* alqd desiderare. **yearning,** *n.* desiderium.

yell, *v.intr. see* SCREAM.

yellow, *adj.* flavus, fulvus. † croceus (*of saffron colour*) ; *to be* —, flavěre. **yellow-haired,** *adj.* flavus. **yellowish,** *adj.* subflavus.

yelp, *v.intr.* gannire. **yelping,** *n.* gannitus.

yes, *adv.* ita, ita est, sic est, recte, certe, vere, etiam, sane. *I say* —, aio.

yesterday, *adv.* heri.

yet, *conj.* (at)tamen, sed, at. *Adv.* etiam ; *not* —, nondum.

yew, *n.* — *tree,* taxus. *Adj.* taxicus.

yield, *v.tr. see* PRODUCE ; SURRENDER. *v.intr. to a request,* precibus ceděre. **yielding,** *adj.* facilis, indulgens.

yoke, *n.* iugum. *v.tr.* coniungěre. **yokefellow,** *n.* socius, coniu(n)x (*in marriage*).

yolk, *n.* (*of an egg*) ovi luteum, vitellus.

yonder, *adj.* ille, iste. *Adv.* illic.

yore, *adv.* olim, quondam.

you, *pron. see* THOU ; *pl.* vos. **your,** *adj.* tuus ; *in the pl.* vester. **yourself, yourselves,** *pron. reflex.* tu ipse, vos ipsi.

young, *adj.* parvus ; — *person,* adulescens ; iuvenis ; filius (*son*) ; *the* — *people, see* YOUTH ; *of animals,* novellus ; *a* — *horse, a foal,* pullus equinus ; *of trees, etc.,* novellus ; *a* — *vine,* vitis novella. *n.* (*collective*), partus ; *to bring forth* —, fetus eděre. **younger,** *adj.* iunior, (natu) minor. **youngest,** *adj.* (natu) minimus.

youth, *n. abstract* pueritia, aetas

puerilis, iuventus ; *in* — puer *or*
adulescens (*when a boy, a* —) *from* —,
a puero ; *young people,* iuventus ;
young man, iuvenis. **youthful,** *adj.*
see YOUNG. *Adv.* puerorum ritu.

Z

zeal, *n.* studium, industria ; ardor.
zealous. *adj.* studiosus (*with genit.*),

acer. *Adv.* studiose, acriter.
zenith, *n. in the* —, supra verticem.
zephyr, *n.* Zephyrus, Favonius.
zero, *n. by* nihil ; *to be at* — (*fig.*), nihil
valēre.
████, ██ ██ ██████ ; ██, ██████.
zigzag, *n. paths,* anfractus viarum.
zodiac, *n.* orbis signifer ; *sign of* —
sidus.
zone, *n. see* GIRDLE ; *in geog.* † zona
caeli regio.
zoology, *n.* animantium descriptio.

A FEW GEOGRAPHICAL NAMES

WITH CLASSICAL OR LATER LATIN EQUIVALENTS

AFRICA, Africa ; African, *adj.* Africus ;
    subst. Afer.
Aix, Aquae Sextiae.
Alsace, Alsatia.
Amiens, Ambianum, Samarobriva.
Arras, Atrebatum.
Artois, Artesia.
Asia, Asia ; Asiatic, *adj.* Asiaticus,
    Asianus.
Atlantic Ocean, Oceanus Atlanticus.
Austria, Austria.
Auvergne, Arvernia.

BLACK SEA, Pontus Euxinus.
Bristol, Venta Silurum.
Burgundy, Burgundia.

CADIZ, Gades.
Calais, Caletum.
Cambridge, Cantabrigia.
Canterbury, Cantuaria, Durovernum.
Carinthia, Carinthia.
Carthagena, Carthago Nova.
Caspian Sea. Mare Caspium.
Castile, Castilia.
Cologne, Colonia Agrippina.
Constance, Constantia.
Constantinople, Byzantium, Constanti-
    nopolis.
Cordova, Corduba.
Corfu, Corcyra.
Cyprus, Cyprus.

DALMATIA, Dalmatia ; *adj.* Dalmaticus.
Damascus, Damascus ; *adj.* Damasce-
    nus.
Danube, R., Ister, Danubius (Danu-
    vius).
Don, R., Tanais.

EBRO, R., Iberus.
Edinburgh, Edinum.
Elba, Ilva, Aethalia.
England, Anglia ; English, *adj.* Anglus,
    Anglicus.

FIESOLE, Faesulae.
Florence, Florentia.
France, Gallia.
Frejus, Forum Iulii.
Friesland, Frisia.

GARONNE, R., Garumna.
Geneva, Geneva, Genava.
Geneva, Lake of, Lacus Lemannus.
Germany, Germania.
Glasgow, Glasgua.
Gloucester, Claudia Castra.
Greece, Graecia.
Guadalquivir, Baetis.
Guienne, Aquitania.

HOLLAND, Hollandia, Batavia.

INDIA, India.
Ireland, Hibernia.
Istria, Histria.
Italy, Italia.

JERICHO, Hiericho.
Jerusalem, Hierosolyma.

KENT, Cantium.

LINCOLN, Lindum Colonia.
Lombardy, Longobardia.
London, Londinium.
Lyons, Lugdunum.

MAAS, R., Mosa.
Malta, Melita.
Man, Isle of, Mona.
Manchester, Mancunium.
Marne, R., Matrŏna.
Marseilles, Massilia.
Mediterranean Sea, Mare Internum.
    Mare Mediterraneum, Mare Nostrum,
    Mare Magnum.

Messina, Messana.
Meuse, R., Mosa.
Milan, Mediolanum.
Modena, Mutina.
Morea, Peloponnesus.
Moselle, R., Mosella.
Munich, Monacum.
Munster, Monasterium.

NAPLES, Neapolis, Parthenope.
Netherlands, Belgica.
Newcastle, Novum Castrum.
North Sea, Oceanus Septentrionalis.
Northumberland, Northumbria.
Norway, Norvegia.
Norwich, Norvicum.

ORKNEY ISLANDS, Orcades.
Oxford, Oxonia.

PADUA, Patavium.
Palatinate, Palatinatus.
Palermo, Panormus.
Paris, Lutetia.
Po, R., Padus.
Poland, Polonia.
Portugal, Lusitania.
Prague, Praga.
Provence, Provincia.
Prussia, Borussia, Prussia.

RED SEA, Sinus Arabicus.
Rheims, Remi.
Rhine, R., Rhenus.
Rhone, R., Rhodanus.
Rochester, Durobrivae.
Rome, Roma.
Russia, Russia.

SALISBURY, Sarisberia, Oarium.
Saone, R., Araris.
Sardinia, Sardinia.
Savoy, Sabaudia.
Scheldt, R., Scaldis.
Scilly Isles, Silures, Cassiterides.
Scotland, Scotia, Caledonia.
Seine, R., Sequana.
Shrewsbury, Salopia.
Sicily, Sicilia.
Sorrento, Sorrentum.
Spain, Hispania.
Switzerland, Helvetia.

TARANTO, Tarentum.
Tarragona, Tarraco.
Thames R., Tamesis, or Tamesa.
Tiber, R., Tiberis.
Tivoli, Tibur.
Trier, Augusta Trevirorum.
Turin, Augusta Taurinorum.
Tuscany, Etruria.

VENICE, Venetiae.
Verona, Verona.
Vienna, Vindobona.
Vistula, R., Vistula.

WARSAW, Varsovia.
Wight, Isle of, Vectis.
Winchester, Venta Belgarum.
Worcester, Vigornia.

YORK, Eboracum.

ZANTE, Zacynthus.
Zurich, Turicum, Tigurium.

GLOSSARY

OF

A FEW COMMON ENGLISH NAMES

WITH CLASSICAL OR LATER LATIN EQUIVALENTS

ALBERT, Albertus.
Alexander, Alexander.
Anna }
Anne } Anna.
Antony, Antonius.
Augustine, Augustinus.

BENEDICT, Benedictus.
Bernard, Bernardus.

CECILIA, Caecilia.
Charles, Carolus.
Claude, Claudius.
Clement, Clemens.
Constance, Constantia.
Cyprian, Cyprianus.
Cyril, Cyrillus.

EDMUND, Edmundus.
Edward, Eduardus.
Ellen }
Eleanor } Helena.
Elinor }
Emily, Aemilia.

FELIX, Felix.
Florence, Florentia.
Francis }
Frank } Franciscus.
Frederic, Fredericus.

GEORGE, Georgius.
Gregory, Gregorius.

HELEN, Helena.
Henry, Henricus.
Hilary, Hilarius.
Horace, Horatius.

JAMES, Iacobus.
John, Iohannes.
Joseph, Iosephu
Julia, Iulia.
Julian, Iulianus.
Justin, Iustinus.

LAWRENCE, Laurentius.
Lewis, Ludovicus.
Lucy, Lucia.

MARGARET, Margarita.
Mark, Marcus.
Mary, Maria.

PAUL, Paulus.
Peter, Petrus.
Philip, Philippus.

RALPH, Radulfus.
Richard, Ricardus.
Robert, Robertus.

STEPHEN, Stephanus.

THOMAS, Thomas.
Timothy, Timotheus.

VALENTINE, Valentinus.
Vincent, Vincentius.

WALTER, Gualterus.
William, Gulielmus.